THE MILITARY BALANCE 2017

published by

for

The International Institute for Strategic Studies
ARUNDEL HOUSE | 13–15 ARUNDEL STREET | TEMPLE PLACE | LONDON | WC2R 3DX | UK

THE **MILITARY BALANCE** 2017

The International Institute for Strategic Studies
ARUNDEL HOUSE | 13–15 ARUNDEL STREET | TEMPLE PLACE | LONDON | WC2R 3DX | UK

DIRECTOR-GENERAL AND CHIEF EXECUTIVE **Dr John Chipman**
DIRECTOR FOR DEFENCE AND MILITARY ANALYSIS **Dr Bastian Giegerich**
EDITOR **James Hackett**
ASSOCIATE EDITOR **Nicholas Payne**

MILITARY AEROSPACE **Douglas Barrie**
LAND WARFARE **Brigadier (Retd) Benjamin Barry**
MILITARY FORCES AND EQUIPMENT **Henry Boyd**
NAVAL FORCES AND MARITIME SECURITY **Nick Childs**
DEFENCE ECONOMICS **Lucie Béraud-Sudreau**
RESEARCH ANALYSTS **Joseph Dempsey, Monty d'Inverno, Ian Keddie, Amanda Lapo, Tom Waldwyn**

EDITORIAL **Alice Aveson, Melissa DeOrio, Teresa Herzenberg, Jill Lally, Chris Raggett, Gaynor Roberts, Nancy Turner, Carolyn West**
DESIGN, PRODUCTION, INFORMATION GRAPHICS **John Buck, Kelly Verity**
CARTOGRAPHY **John Buck, Kelly Verity**
RESEARCH SUPPORT **Anne Shannon Baxter, Mark Cazalet, Yvonni-Stefania Efstathiou, Harriet Ellis, Michael Tong**

This publication has been prepared by the Director-General and Chief Executive of the Institute and his Staff, who accept full responsibility for its contents. The views expressed herein do not, and indeed cannot, represent a consensus of views among the worldwide membership of the Institute as a whole.

FIRST PUBLISHED February 2017

© The International Institute for Strategic Studies 2017
All rights reserved. No part of this publication may be reproduced, stored, transmitted, or disseminated, in any form, or by any means, without prior written permission from Taylor & Francis, to whom all requests to reproduce copyright material should be directed, in writing.

ISBN 978-1-85743-900-7
ISSN 0459-7222

Cover images: FRONT: *Rafale* aircraft (JEAN-PIERRE MULLER/AFP/Getty Images), *Musudan* missile (KCNA/AFP/Getty Images), USS *Zumwalt* (U.S. Navy photo/Released), *Leopard* 2 tank (SHAPE NATO); BACK: Iraqi special forces (THOMAS COEX/AFP/Getty Images), China's *Cloud Shadow* UAV (Alan Warnes).

The Military Balance (ISSN 0459-7222) is published annually by Routledge Journals, an imprint of Taylor & Francis, 4 Park Square, Milton Park, Abingdon, Oxfordshire OX14 4RN, UK.

A subscription to the institution print edition, ISSN 0459-7222, includes free access for any number of concurrent users across a local area network to the online edition, ISSN 1479-9022.

All subscriptions are payable in advance and all rates include postage. Journals are sent by air to the USA, Canada, Mexico, India, Japan and Australasia. Subscriptions are entered on an annual basis, i.e. January to December. Payment may be made by sterling cheque, dollar cheque, international money order, National Giro, or credit card (Amex, Visa, Mastercard).

Please send subscription orders to: USA/Canada: Taylor & Francis Inc., Journals Department, 530 Walnut Street, Suite 850, Philadelphia, PA 19106, USA. UK/Europe/Rest of World: Routledge Journals, T&F Customer Services, T&F Informa UK Ltd., Sheepen Place, Colchester, Essex, CO3 3LP, UK.

Contents

Indexes of Tables, Figures and Maps 4
Editor's Introduction 5

Part One **Capabilities, Trends and Economics**

Chapter 1 **Defence and military analysis** 7
   The changing defence-industrial landscape 7; Special-operations forces 11; Twenty-first-century challenges to twentieth-century deterrence 15

Chapter 2 **Comparative defence statistics** 19
   Selected European aerospace defence consolidation, 1990–2016 21; Key defence statistics 22; Battlefield missiles and rockets: Russian and US equipment capabilities 24; Attack helicopter operators and fleets, 1997–2016 25; Anti-submarine warfare: fixed-wing-aircraft fleets 26

Chapter 3 **North America** 27
   United States: defence policy and economics 27;   Armed forces data section 42;
   Canada: defence policy 40;   Selected arms procurements and deliveries 61

Chapter 4 **Europe** 63
   Regional defence policy and economics 63;   UK: defence policy and economics 82;
   Nordic and Baltic security 75;   Armed forces data section 90;
   France: defence policy and economics 77;   Selected arms procurements and deliveries 176

Chapter 5 **Russia and Eurasia** 183
   Russia: defence policy and economics 183;   Armed forces data section 199;
   Ukraine: defence policy 196;   Selected arms procurements and deliveries 234

Chapter 6 **Asia** 237
   Regional defence policy and economics 237;   Vietnam: defence policy and economics 264;
   Australia: defence policy 249;   Armed forces data section 269;
   China: defence policy and economics 251;   Selected arms procurements and deliveries 341
   Japan: defence policy 262;

Chapter 7 **Middle East and North Africa** 351
   Regional defence policy and economics 351;   Armed forces data section 368;
   Saudi Arabia: defence policy and economics 362;   Selected arms procurements and deliveries 414

Chapter 8 **Latin America and the Caribbean** 417
   Regional defence policy and economics 417;   Colombia: defence policy 429;
   Argentina: defence policy and economics 423;   Armed forces data section 431;
   Brazil: defence policy 428;   Selected arms procurements and deliveries 476

Chapter 9 **Sub-Saharan Africa** 479
   Regional defence policy and economics 479;   Armed forces data section 495;
   Eritrea: defence policy and economics 490;   Selected arms procurements and deliveries 547

Chapter 10 **Country comparisons and defence data** 549
   Selected training activity 2016 550;   Select unmanned maritime systems in service 561;
   International comparisons of defence   Military ISR satellites: operational totals 562;
   expenditure and military personnel 553;   Precision-guided munitions, 1991–2011 562;
   Global distribution of main battle tanks, 2016 560; Selected non-state armed groups:
   Principal surface combatants and patrol ships 561;   observed forces and equipment holdings 563

Part Two **Reference**

Explanatory Notes 565
   Principal land definitions 569; Principal naval definitions 570; Principal aviation definitions 571

List of abbreviations for data sections 573

Index of country/territory abbreviations 575

Index of countries and territories 576

Index of TABLES

1. US National Defense Budget Function and other selected budgets 1996, 2007–17 37
2. Selected arms procurements and deliveries, North America 61
3. Selected arms procurements and deliveries, Europe 176
4. Russia: new-build naval vessels armed with the 3M14 *Kalibr* (SS-N-30)/3M54 (SS-N-27 *Sizzler*) cruise missile 190
5. Russian defence expenditure as % of GDP 191
6. Russian procurement of new weapons in 2011–15 and goals of the State Armament Programme to 2020 (approximate) 195
7. Ukraine: increased exercise frequency 198
8. Selected arms procurements and deliveries, Russia and Eurasia 234
9. North Korea: ballistic-missile test launches in 2016 243
10. China: new Central Military Commission structure 253
11. China: PLA's new theatre commands 254
12. Selected arms procurements and deliveries, Asia 341
13. Selected arms procurements and deliveries, Middle East and North Africa 414
14. Selected arms procurements and deliveries, Latin America and the Caribbean 476
15. South Africa's defence budget by service 489
16. Selected arms procurements and deliveries, Sub-Saharan Africa ... 547
17. Selected training activity 2016 550
18. International comparisons of defence expenditure and military personnel 553
19. Principal surface combatants and patrol ships over 9,500 tonnes full-load displacement 561
20. Select unmanned maritime systems in service, by weight 561
21. Military ISR satellites: operational totals 562
22. List of abbreviations for data sections 573
23. Index of country/territory abbreviations 575
24. Index of countries and territories 576

Index of FIGURES

North America
1. *Gerald R. Ford*-class aircraft carrier 34
2. US Navy carriers: maintenance and availability 36
3. US defence expenditure as % of GDP 37
4. DoD Base Budget Authority and OCO funding, FY1978–FY2021 38
5. Total US armed-forces-equipment procurement funding (including OCO), FY2001–FY2017 40

Europe
6. NATO's enhanced forward presence, as of Oct 2016 66
7. NATO's eastern flank – selected capability reductions, 1993–2016 67
8. Europe defence spending by country and sub-region 2016 72
9. Europe: selected ongoing or completed procurement priorities in 2016 73
10. Europe regional defence expenditure as % of GDP 74
11. *Ajax*: the British Army's new armoured reconnaissance vehicles ... 85
12. UK planned equipment-support spending 2016–25 88

Russia and Eurasia
13. Generating Russia's battalion tactical groups 184
14. Estimated Russian defence expenditure as % of GDP 192
15. Russia's Almaz Antey S-400 (SA-21 *Growler*) air-defence system ... 194
16. Ukrainian defence budget, 2010–17 196

Asia
17. Asia defence spending by country and sub-region 247
18. Asia regional defence expenditure as % of GDP 247
19. Asia: selected ongoing or completed procurement priorities in 2016 248
20. Australia: ten-year division of investment stream to FY2025–26 (%) 250
21. China: People's Liberation Army reorganisation 256

Middle East and North Africa
22. Estimated Middle East and North Africa defence expenditure 2016: sub-regional breakdown 358
24. Middle East and North Africa: selected ongoing or completed procurement priorities in 2016 359
23. Middle East and North Africa regional defence expenditure as % of GDP 359

Latin America and the Caribbean
25. Latin America and the Caribbean defence spending by country & sub-region 421
26. Latin America and the Caribbean regional defence expenditure as % of GDP 422
27. Latin America and the Caribbean: selected ongoing or completed procurement priorities in 2016 423
28. Argentina's defence budgets, 2015–17 427

Sub-Saharan Africa
29. African Standby Force: regional standby forces 482
30. Sub-Saharan Africa regional defence expenditure as % of GDP ... 487
31. Defence spending in sub-Saharan Africa by sub-region, 2010–16 (current US billion dollars) 489
32. Sub-Saharan Africa: selected ongoing or completed procurement priorities in 2016 490

Country comparisons
33. Global distribution of main battle tanks, 2016 560
34. Precision-guided munitions: increasing use by Western forces, 1991–2011 562

Index of MAPS

1. Europe regional defence spending 71
2. Kaliningrad: Russia's potential missile capability 185
3. Russia: operational strategic commands 188
4. Russia and Eurasia regional defence spending 192
5. US military dispositions in the Western Pacific 238
6. Asia regional defence spending 246
7. China: People's Liberation Army theatre commands 255
8. Vietnam: military regions, air and naval bases 267
9. Middle East and North Africa regional defence spending 358
10. Latin America and the Caribbean regional defence spending 420
11. Argentina's main military bases and key defence-industrial sites 424
12. Support to the campaign against Boko Haram in northeast Nigeria and the Lake Chad region, Jan 2015–Aug 2016 481
13. Sub-Saharan Africa regional defence spending 488
14. Eritrean armed forces: military zones and basing 492

Editor's Introduction
Challenges to defence cooperation

Amid a sense of surprise and, in many quarters, shock at the result of the US presidential election and the UK's referendum to leave the EU, there was one constant in 2016 – that the global security environment remained as unremittingly bleak as before. Perhaps the only bright spot of note was the peace accord in Colombia.

Many current security challenges have endured for years; most are transnational in impact. These may include real or perceived threats from non-state actors or newly assertive states to access to the global commons; they may stem from the proliferation of defence technology or military know-how, or the use of cyber power by state and non-state actors; they also include climate change and natural disasters and may derive from the increasing pace of technological and social change. Within this context, newly assertive states – particularly Russia but also including China and, recently, some Gulf states – continue to flex, and in some cases use their military muscle. This not only raises the risk of heightened international tension but also of possible military confrontation.

Wars in Syria and Yemen, hugely damaging to these countries' populations, infrastructure and futures, grind on remorselessly. In Yemen, Gulf states remain confronted by formidable adversaries with still-potent capabilities. Conflict continues on Europe's doorstep, with Ukraine's east still witnessing daily combat. Russia's military activity has prompted modest hikes in NATO defence budgets and, for the Alliance's larger states, a renewed focus on conventional-combat capabilities and deterrence. In the Asia-Pacific region, North Korea conducted two nuclear tests and further, more complex missile tests in 2016.

In Asia, the dominant theme in defence policymaking is developing greater capacity for conventional warfare. Many military budgets continue to rise, with average real-terms growth of 5.8% during 2014–16. These increases have fuelled military-modernisation programmes designed to recapitalise ageing inventories and respond to the growing capabilities of potential adversaries. Advanced weapons systems are also becoming more widespread, ranging from anti-ship missiles to modern air- and coastal-defence systems. The traditional dominance of Western states in naval fleet size and tonnage is being eroded, and more nations in the Asia-Pacific are introducing vessels of 9,500 tonnes or larger. China has also been strengthening its capacity to project military power into the Western Pacific and Indian Ocean. Island-building activities continue in the South China Sea, but the most extensive and far-reaching change has been the overhaul to the PLA's organisational structure, followed by the transition from seven 'military regions' to five 'theatre commands'.

For Russia, the overt display of its military capability continues to be a key objective of its operations in Syria. As before, it still uses Syria as a test-bed for its military systems. In 2016, its continued employment of precise weapons was notable. The Kh-101 cruise missile was observed being launched for the first time from the Tu-95 strategic bomber. Economic problems have led Moscow to delay or postpone some of its military procurements. Shipbuilding plans may have slowed, but Russia's ambition to equip an increasing number of naval platforms – including a new icebreaker – with power-projection capabilities such as the *Kalibr* cruise missile is important. Notwithstanding the concerns of NATO's eastern member states, Russia's most significant troop movements have related to strengthening its military presence on the border with Ukraine – presumably to deter Kiev from attempting to impose a military solution in its east.

A key lesson for Russia from the use of force in both Ukraine and Syria is that these actions have brought Moscow back to the diplomatic top table. For Moscow, this underscored the utility of military force as a coercive tool. The messaging apparent in its employment of military power, meanwhile, met its narrative of a once-again powerful state able to deploy capabilities previously only held by the West. One concern for the international community lies in how this attitude towards the use of force may be perceived by other states, and whether it may embolden them to deploy military force. There is also a risk for the West in terms of whether its responses are sufficiently firm or united.

Russia's various military activities sustained a sense of heightened insecurity across Europe during 2016. Successful Islamist terrorist attacks on the continent were further reminders of vulnerability to instability originating in Europe's southern and southeastern margins. The flow of refugees and other migrants into Europe only slowed in 2016. Pressure on receiving countries to settle and integrate those arrivals remained high, while some European nations' military forces continued to deploy to tackle illegal migration and rescue those at risk. These missions, on some of Europe's borders and in the Mediterranean Sea, and the refugee crisis, further energised the rhetoric of nationalist politicians in Europe.

The renaissance of populist politics in the West, and the rise of 'insurgent' political movements harnessing economic and political discontent, have rocked political orthodoxies and challenge cooperative approaches to security and military policy. Donald Trump's victory in the US presidential election was the biggest challenge to prevailing political attitudes, although a similar populist and rhetoric-heavy platform had upset received wisdom earlier in the year in the UK (with the 'Brexit' referendum), while the populist Rodrigo Duterte was elected president of the Philippines in May after an equally rhetoric-heavy campaign. In 2017, other politicians will face an increased challenge from political groups and movements that have in some cases questioned the benefits from and desirability of closer international cooperation. Indeed, the risk is that cooperative approaches to security and military policy may be imperilled both by emerging policy prescriptions and the rhetoric employed during election campaigns. Even if this tone is subsequently moderated, it can erode the consistency and clarity of political-military messaging that is important for credible and effective deterrence. The precise effect of this rhetoric remains unclear. For example, after his election Donald Trump stressed the importance of NATO, rather than – as he did during the campaign – focusing on some allies' failure to meet the aim to spend 2% of GDP on defence. However, lingering uncertainties could erode Alliance cohesion, not least by introducing doubts over future US commitment to NATO's Article 5 guarantee; they may also embolden potential adversaries and damage strategic stability.

These worries might, however, improve European states' focus on defence, including on spending. However, even if Europe spends more, it needs to spend more smartly: boosting R&D and equipment spending rather than on personnel and pensions, and driving industrial collaboration, would be more useful than simply aiming to meet targets. They may also finally propel closer bilateral cooperation between European states, and multilateral cooperation between the EU and NATO, where there is a chance now for more tangible progress. Brexit has been followed by a growing momentum among other EU members to improve defence cooperation among themselves, and between the EU and NATO. Even post-Brexit, of course, the UK will still be able to play a part in EU-level security structures, if it negotiates an agreement. London might be interested in maintaining access to EU-wide collaborative science and technology developments, not least in light of the European Commission's plan, as part of the November 2016 European Defence Action Plan (EDAP), to boost defence procurement and, notably, establish a European Defence Fund for defence technology and equipment R&D.

Coordination and cooperation can drive financial efficiencies, and can also have tangible security benefits. Cohesive responses to Russia's challenge are currently the preference for the West, including the EU and NATO. Sanctions have become an effective vehicle by which this cooperation delivers real effect. International cooperation after Russia's illegal annexation of Crimea in 2014 led to a range of sanctions on Moscow, and these are biting. This, and other sanctions regimes involved strenuous international negotiation and concerted political traction. Above all, they required patience, and cooperation between states, against a backdrop of understanding that there was common benefit from such cooperation.

Indeed, with security challenges increasingly global in cause and effect, in a world interconnected by the movement of people, trade and technology and facing common environmental challenges including from climate change and natural disasters, isolation from the effects of global-security challenges is impossible. The responses required to address current and future security challenges most effectively are similarly complex; they are very often best conceived and executed with partners. Doing so cleverly can better distribute the financial, material and political resources necessary to tackle these tasks comprehensively. This has long been NATO's approach. Years of close military cooperation have led to real military benefits. NATO-enabled cooperation has helped Western air forces to deploy and operate together rapidly, generating more effect than if they were to deploy independently. NATO has invoked its Article 5 collective-defence pledge only once, to assist the US after the terrorist attacks of 9/11. While much cooperation now still relates to the ongoing counter-terror struggle (as in Syria and Iraq), NATO also embarked on a significant plan to boost its forward presence in Eastern Europe in order to reassure nervous allies and insert a more credible deterrent to Russia, once it became clear that the old plan to rapidly reinforce allies faced a challenge from Russia's capabilities in the region. Western states, and NATO, also realise that they need to sharpen focus on the potential for conventional combat with technologically advanced adversaries. There are now questions about whether European troop reductions went too far, and more debates about whether to reintroduce conscription.

Globally, military modernisation drives continue, with advanced capabilities more widespread. In the West there has been renewed focus on how to use advanced capability developments and adaptability and innovation to maintain military-technological advantage. The EU's EDAP is one way of trying to stimulate better results in this area: Europe's defence R&D has long been fragmented with only minimal coordination and collaboration. But these initiatives will be mirrored elsewhere. China, for instance, is carefully watching the US Third Offset Strategy. This drive for asymmetric technology-advantage risks becoming increasingly costly for Western states; as a result, defence establishments are keen to leverage capabilities and broader lessons developed in the civilian sector.

Despite a widespread political reaction against some of the social and economic ramifications of globalisation, the interrelation between rapid environmental and societal changes, coupled with the acceleration in economic interrelationships and technology development, means that there may be in future more, and more complex, security threats, not fewer. In combination, they mean that the world will continue to 'shrink' and as such it is more important to avoid retreat into military and defence-industrial nationalism.

It should not be necessary to list the benefits of economic, political and military cooperation. Tackling issues at source before they become crises; helping to build resilience in unstable areas; and developing local economies and security capacities all take patient collaboration. Meanwhile, greater cooperation boosts confidence and transparency between allies and potential adversaries, and can improve capability development and operations. These, in turn, can show the practical benefits of a cohesive political approach. Although NATO, for instance, has faced institutional challenges before – such as France's decision to leave the Alliance's integrated command structures in 1966 – the internal and external challenges to cohesion and cooperation are perhaps now as great as, if not greater than, at any time in the recent past.

Chapter One
The changing defence-industrial landscape

In 2016 there was renewed impetus for defence industries in many nations to engage in mergers and acquisitions, as well as divestments. This resulted from a combination of market uncertainty, budgetary constraints and procurement considerations, and was apparent despite a worsening security environment for many nations. Although the scale of overall defence expenditure remains significant, defence markets remain a challenge for industry, not least as firms attempt to grapple with volatile political and economic environments, which all require careful insight and measured strategies: in today's defence marketplace there are no one-size-fits-all answers.

2016 developments

In the United States, while United Technologies Corporation (UTC) rebuffed an acquisition attempt by Honeywell International in February 2016, this venture was indicative of mergers and acquisitions (M&A) activity in the broader defence marketplace. In Europe, for instance, there was notable activity in the air- and land-systems sectors. Airbus announced in March 2016 that it had agreed the sale of its defence-electronics business to private-equity firm KKR for US$1.2 billion, although European electronics specialist Thales and land-systems company Rheinmetall had also been interested in acquiring this business. Divesting itself of its defence-electronics arm was part of the restructuring plan for Airbus's Defence and Space business, which was made public in September 2014. Although Airbus's departure from the defence-electronics market was not on the same level as UTC's sale, in 2015, of its Sikorsky military-helicopter business, both episodes showed that companies are critically examining their defence and aerospace portfolios.

In December 2015, two of Europe's land-systems prime contractors, France's Nexter and Germany's Krauss-Maffei Wegmann, began to operate jointly under the banner of KNDS (KMW + Nexter Defence Systems). KNDS is a 50/50 joint holding company that, if it is successful, is intended to provide the basis for even further integration. Meanwhile, Finmeccanica – headquartered in Italy – changed its name to Leonardo in April 2016. The company continued to restructure throughout the year, at the same time shedding some non-defence and aerospace business.

Russia, China and India have also had concerns over their defence-industrial base, although their efforts have largely focused on attempting to improve efficiency. Efforts to recapitalise Russia's ageing defence-industrial infrastructure in the air, land and maritime sectors have shown limited and varying degrees of progress against a backdrop of increasing pressure on spending. India's policy goal of growing its national production capacity has resulted in continuing efforts to increase private-sector involvement in what has long been a bastion of state-owned industry. China, meanwhile, has also been trying to improve the performance and efficiency of its defence sector; this effort has led to the emergence of some privately owned firms.

If anything, recent M&A activity serves as a reminder of the dynamic nature of the defence-industrial landscape. For democratic governments, it is a landscape that they can influence, but not fully direct. State-procurement choices offer one means of shaping the sector, although policymakers will often go to considerable lengths to stress that equipment selections have been or will be made on performance and price, and without consideration of broader industrial or political factors. Autocratic states, on the other hand, enjoy a greater degree of control in their ability to shape the sector, although this brings its own problems, not least of all the risk of overt political interference in the defence industry.

US procurement competition

In October 2015, Northrop Grumman emerged as the victor among the big three US defence-aerospace manufacturers when it was selected as prime contractor for the US Air Force's (USAF's) Long-Range Strike Bomber (LRS-B). The competition had pitted Northrop Grumman against a Boeing–Lockheed Martin team. The three main US defence-aerospace primes – Boeing, Lockheed Martin and Northrop Grumman – are also competing, this time independent of one another, to be the prime contractor for the air force's T-X advanced jet trainer project, to replace the

T-38 *Talon*. For the T-X project, Boeing is teamed with Sweden's Saab while Lockheed Martin is partnering with Korean Aerospace Industries. A request for proposals was expected to be released by the end of 2016 and the air force should have selected the prime contractor by 2017 or early 2018.

In July 2016, what was formerly known as the US Navy's Unmanned Carrier Launched Airborne Surveillance and Strike System (UCLASS) and subsequently the Carrier Based Airborne Refuelling System, was renamed the MQ-25A *Stingray*. The programme requirements have been revised again and the initial variant will now be an uninhabited air-to-air tanker. It is envisaged that deliveries will begin in the early 2020s. The outcome of the LRS-B, the T-X and the *Stingray* programmes could prompt further industrial realignment, depending on which companies win or lose.

Sikorsky and the rotary-wing sector

Sikorsky is one of the three largest helicopter manufacturers in the US; the others are Boeing Defense and Bell Helicopter (owned by Textron). The two largest US rotary-wing programmes by value, the CH-53K *King Stallion* heavy-lift helicopter and the *Black Hawk* family, are both Sikorsky products. Indeed, in 2015 Sikorsky had a US$49bn order backlog, mainly from the Pentagon, and according to its own figures had a 65% share of the Department of Defense's (DoD's) 'programs of record' (funded programmes). In 2016 the DoD also funded the purchase of a further 70 UH-60M *Black Hawk* utility and 24 HH-60M *Pave Hawk* medical-evacuation helicopters. Furthermore, Sikorsky was selected in 2014 as contractor for the US$1.3bn Turkish Utility Helicopter, based on the *Black Hawk*; the US$3.2bn US Presidential Helicopter (using the S-92); and the US$8bn US Air Force's Combat Rescue Helicopter.

The UH-60 *Black Hawk* has been an extraordinary success story for Sikorsky. The design emerged in 1976 as the winner in a 'fly-off' against the Boeing YUH-61 and was selected to meet the US Army's Utility Tactical Transport Aircraft System requirement. The selection effectively took Boeing out of the medium-utility-helicopter sector for at least four decades, and assured Sikorsky a dominant position in the addressable export market.

However, the US Army and the Pentagon are now considering the *Black Hawk*'s eventual replacement, as part of the Future Vertical Lift (FVL) family of air vehicles, the first of which will begin to be fielded in the 2030s. The rewards for the winning firm (or firms) could be considerable, assuming that the programme comes to fruition. The US Army's record on rotary-wing procurement is variable: the army cancelled the RAH-66 *Comanche* scout-attack helicopter in 2004; ten years later it cancelled the Armed Reconnaissance Helicopter programme, itself a less expensive successor to the RAH-66 requirement.

Sikorsky – in a joint bid with Boeing – had been in one of the two teams selected in August 2014 for the Joint Multi-role Technology Demonstrator, a precursor to the FVL programme and valued at some US$500 million. The other team comprised Bell Helicopter. The FVL project will likely lead to three platforms: a light vehicle intended for the reconnaissance role; a medium-lift air system to succeed the *Black Hawk*; and a heavy platform to replace the CH-47 *Chinook*. The medium-lift requirement appears likely to be the first vehicle to emerge, even though the US Army's multi-role *Kiowa Warrior* helicopter, which was withdrawn from service in mid-2016, has no direct replacement planned before the advent of the FVL programme.

For all that, the decision to sell Sikorsky reflects the challenges faced by private-sector companies operating in the defence-aerospace arena. The range of mature products in Sikorsky's portfolio, coupled with the prospect of a long-term US fleet-recapitalisation programme, is likely to have influenced UTC's considerations over whether to retain Sikorsky, notwithstanding the potential value of these deals. Concerns over defence funding levels in the US – as well as a flat international defence market – will also have featured in UTC's thinking. Indeed, challenging market conditions were indicated in mid-2015 by Sikorsky's plan to reduce its workforce by 1,400 (from a total of 15,200).

Industrial landscaping

Boeing, Airbus, Textron and private-equity company Blackstone had all been suggested during 2015 as potential suitors for Sikorsky. A tie-up with Bell or Boeing would have created the largest Western helicopter company. Combining Sikorsky with Airbus's rotary-wing business would have created an even larger firm. Anti-trust issues, however, would have posed a risk to some of these merger or acquisition options. The acquisition of Sikorsky by Lockheed Martin was approved by US regulatory authorities in September 2015, effectively sustaining the number of US rotary-wing primes at three.

Nonetheless, large, landscape-defining mergers have been approved by the Pentagon and Department of Justice in the past. In 1996, Boeing and McDonnell Douglas announced their intention to merge. The merger, in 1997, was part of a cycle of consolidation resulting from the post-Cold War downturn in US defence spending. The US defence industry responded to the changing market environment and then-defense secretary Les Aspin's caution in 1993 (delivered at a Pentagon dinner since known as 'The Last Supper') that industrial consolidation was not just desirable but also inevitable. However, while the number of US defence and aerospace primes has reduced considerably since the end of the Cold War, Europe has found it far harder to re-scale its defence industries in order to address problems of overcapacity and duplication.

European outlook

Cognisant of the significance of the defence-aerospace industrial revolution under way in the US and the implications of reduced European defence spending, in the late 1990s Berlin, London and Paris encouraged a similar process. Their December 1997 Trilateral declaration noted 'the urgent need to restructure the aerospace and defence electronics industries. This should embrace civil and military activities in the field of aerospace and should lead to European integration based on a balanced partnership … we welcome the fact that a number of European companies including Daimler-Benz Aerospace, Aérospatiale and British Aerospace have already demonstrated their intention to regroup their activities.'

Unsurprisingly, it has proven more challenging to consolidate transnationally than domestically. Local politics and national industrial drivers have thwarted merger ambitions on more than one occasion. The most notable example is the 2013 failure of the proposed merger of BAE Systems and EADS, itself an echo of the proposed 1997 tie-up between British Aerospace and Daimler Benz Aerospace (DASA). The earlier attempt was thwarted by GEC's decision to sell its defence business, with this concern bought soon after by British Aerospace, which had postponed the plan to merge with DASA. In 2013, while the British and French governments accepted the rationale for the merger and supported it, the German government blocked the deal due to concerns over the possible impact on EADS's Germany-based military-business units. Leaving aside the political hurdles, the underlying rationale for continuing restructuring and consolidation remains valid across all of Europe's defence-industrial domains. However, progress remains patchy: there has been partial pan-European consolidation in the air-systems and guided-weapons sectors, for example EADS (known from 2014 as Airbus) and missile manufacturer MBDA Systems, but naval- and land-systems companies continue to be structured around primarily national entities.

This is not to say that there cannot be closer cooperation. Nexter and KMW, two of Europe's main land-systems manufacturers, began to try to more closely align their businesses from mid-2014, indicating an interest in jointly developing a successor to the *Leclerc* and *Leopard* 2 main battle tanks. In June 2014 the companies signed a memorandum of understanding intended to pave the way for the 50/50 'strategic alliance' that was agreed in December 2015 and led to the creation of the joint holding company KNDS, under which the two companies will market their products. However, this is not yet a merger. Both companies retain their identities and continue to market similar products. Joint-platform developments will be central to future integration, notably those designed to meet the French and German armies' requirement for a future main battle tank. Export successes will also be crucial, but the German government has blocked the sale of the KMW *Leopard* 2 to Saudi Arabia since 2011. Paris wants Berlin to accept a more relaxed approach to some foreign weapons sales.

Re-emerging and new competitors

Russia's defence industry has also been restructuring, with core capabilities increasingly brought together in large, state-owned companies. Nonetheless, the defence industry continues to struggle to produce new equipment at the rate stipulated in recent state armament programmes (SAPs). Indeed, funding pressure grew as the government finalised the 2018–25 SAP against a backdrop of worsening economic conditions.

Russia's United Aircraft Corporation (UAC) was established as a state-owned joint-stock company in 2006. UAC has since brought together design bureaus including Sukhoi, Yakovlev, MiG, Tupolev and Ilyushin, along with the numerous manufacturing plants associated with each of these design houses. However, the departure of Mikhail Pogosyan as UAC president at the beginning of 2015 was significant as it reflected growing interest in the defence sector by major conglomerate Rostec. Rostec is a diversified holding company with a considerable number of defence manufacturers within its portfolio.

Pogosyan's replacement – Yury Slyusar, a former deputy industry and trade minister – is reportedly close to Rostec head Viktor Chemezov. Slyusar's appointment was viewed by these same analysts as one that suited the Rostec CEO; Chemesov had reportedly been looking to strengthen the concern's position in defence aerospace.

The government pursued a similar approach to consolidation in the naval domain when it established the United Shipbuilding Corporation in 2007. This grouped together 58 companies involved in surface-ship and submarine manufacture. Fulfilling state-armament ambitions in this domain has, however, proved an even greater challenge than in the air sector. Latterly, the Russian defence industry has also needed to fill the component and sub-systems gaps left by the collapse of defence relations with Ukraine. In the naval sector this included the provision of gas-turbine engines, while affected areas in the air domain included missile components and turbofan engines for cruise missiles.

China has also been trying to improve its defence-industrial performance as part of the overall development of the country's military capacity. In 2013, the main defence-regulatory body, the State Administration for Science, Technology and Industry for National Defence (SASTIND), permitted defence firms to issue equities on their military-asset holdings for the first time; this was part of a move to use capital markets to generate funding for weapons research, development and acquisition. In mid-2015 the government established the 'Strategic Committee of Science, Technology and Industry Development for National Defense', a think-tank tasked with looking at ways of improving defence-industry performance. In August 2016, the government created the Aero Engine Corp. of China, consolidating the aerospace-propulsion-business units of other state-owned aerospace and defence firms. Military-turbofan-engine development and manufacture has proved an area of persistent weakness for China's aerospace industry. Based loosely on a Soviet defence-industrial model, China's defence industry remains inefficient by Western standards. As China looks to further develop its presence in the export market with more capable systems, the demands made upon the defence industry to ensure the adequate availability of logistics and support for its export customers will increase, requiring a more responsive industrial sector. However, logistics and through-life support have proved a vulnerability for China in the past.

Both Russia and China have sought limited foreign tie-ups for their defence industries, although the extent of these has been adversely affected by the global political environment and other concerns. The two nations are also developing bilateral cooperation, for example the late 2014 agreement between Rostec and China's AVIC to pursue 'strategic cooperation', followed by a 2015 framework agreement between Russian Helicopters and China's AVIC to jointly develop a 'prospective heavy helicopter'.

Overall, the global defence-industrial sector remains in a state of flux, with continuing – if patchy – consolidation in the West. Budgetary pressures will continue to force companies to look at non-organic ways of producing growth, for instance by acquiring competitors or purchasing companies in complementary areas of the defence market and attempting to identify new geographical markets. In more extreme cases, a firm might seek to exit the market altogether, or at least sell off parts of its non-core defence business.

Russia and China face similar challenges in attempting to improve the effectiveness of their respective industries, though from considerably different economic positions. In Europe, even when consolidation has occurred – for example, in the aerospace sector – challenges remain. A key example is how, or even whether, to sustain in the medium term the ability to design and manufacture high-end, crewed combat aircraft and how ambitious any programme would be. In the US, the Pentagon wants to maintain the capacity for US industry to compete at the national industrial level for combat-aircraft requirements, although the challenge of sustaining three military-aircraft primes can only increase. Industry thinking will also be affected by the trajectory of DoD defence spending, whether it enjoys single-figure growth or remains flat. Expenditure issues will also influence Russia's defence sector, with further consolidation likely in order to try to reduce inefficiency. India, meanwhile, will continue to attempt to encourage private-sector companies to enter the defence realm. Even China may have to more carefully consider its defence spending should its economic growth prove more modest than in the past; this could prompt greater interest in rationalising its sprawling defence sector.

Special-operations forces

Amid an increasingly fluid and challenging contemporary security environment, there is increased demand worldwide for military forces skilled in operating below the threshold of large-scale armed conflict. As United States Army General Joseph Votel said in August 2014, US Special Operations Command (USSOCOM) has entered the 'golden age for special operations'.

US special-operations forces (SOF) are currently operating in more than 130 countries and are essential to war-fighting efforts in Afghanistan, Iraq and Syria, as well as sustained counter-terrorism missions in Africa and Asia. The multinational SOF command in Afghanistan has included SOF from large NATO nations as well as contingents from diverse smaller nations such as Albania, Hungary, Latvia and the United Arab Emirates. Meanwhile, the United Kingdom's SOF have operated not only in Afghanistan, but also in Iraq, Libya, Sierra Leone and Syria whilst, after departing Afghanistan, French SOF have been active in Libya, Mali and Syria. Russian SOF have been central to operations in Chechnya, Georgia, South Ossetia, eastern Ukraine and Crimea. Sophisticated Russian campaigns to seize Crimea and enter eastern Ukraine were led by the 'little green men' from Spetsnaz and elite airborne and naval infantry units.

In the Middle East, Jordanian, Saudi Arabian and UAE SOF are waging a sustained campaign alongside proxy forces and a small conventional force in Yemen. Jordanian Special Operations Command is modelled on the much larger USSOCOM and runs a regional SOF training hub. Since waging a proxy war against the UK and US in Iraq until 2010, Iran has continued to use the Islamic Revolutionary Guard Corps' Quds Force to sustain its influence over Shia militias and the Iraqi government, wage a campaign against the Islamic State, otherwise known as ISIS or ISIL, in Iraq and sustain the beleaguered Syrian Army through direct combat-advisory support as well as support delivered through its Lebanese proxy force, Hizbullah.

SOF comprise a strategic capability for many nations and a niche capability for others. There are other conceptions too: in some states, special forces are little more than elite infantry, while others have been nurtured as regime-protection forces; others still fall outside the command of defence ministries. Since the terrorist attacks on the US on 11 September 2001, SOF have become an indispensable component of Western military campaigns and efforts, short of large-scale armed conflict, to protect national security. Nations outside the West, meanwhile, have examined the ways in which this capability has been used, and can be expected to integrate relevant lessons into future force planning. Indeed, understanding the capabilities and limitations of special forces will be critical for all states in developing future forces and employing them successfully.

Special operations and special-operations forces

Special operations encompass the use of small units in direct or indirect military actions to achieve strategic effect. Direct action has traditionally meant 'surgical' strikes or raids against key nodes in enemy networks, including facilities and individuals. Indirect military action focuses on enabling proxies to conduct unconventional warfare, such as to destabilise a regime or stiffen internal defence against insurgents, guerrillas or organised-crime networks.

SOF utilise specialised personnel, equipment, education, training and tactics that combine to generate capabilities beyond those of conventional military forces. In 1987, the US Congressional Research Service identified 'five truths' about special forces that remain relevant today: humans are more important than hardware; quality is better than quantity; special-operations forces cannot be mass-produced; competent special-operations forces cannot be created after emergencies occur; and most special operations require non-SOF assistance. Specialised selection and training is required to prepare SOF to conduct high-risk operations in territory, airspace or waters controlled by the enemy. Moreover, operating with local forces in complex environments requires not only knowledge, but also cultural sensitivity and interpersonal skills.

These capabilities, beyond those of conventional military forces, are necessary to accomplish sensitive missions that often require SOF to operate primarily through proxies, accomplish objectives clandestinely and avert not only mission failure, but also political embarrassment.

Missions and capabilities

SOF missions and capabilities vary from nation to nation. Missions often entail efforts short of war to deter adversaries, build effective security forces in partner nations and enhance regional security through cooperation against common threats. Through the relationships developed during training and advisory missions, as well as sustained deployments in particular regions, SOF can help their civilian and military commanders understand emerging security threats within the context of local political, social, economic, geographic and ideological dynamics – dynamics that US SOF doctrine aggregates under the 'human aspects of military operations'. In what some have labelled 'grey zone' competitions short of war, SOF efforts may include propaganda and disinformation, organised-crime activities or ambiguous paramilitary operations meant to destabilise a country. SOF may also counter those unconventional-warfare activities in the conduct of special reconnaissance to expose and counter adversary behaviour. As part of larger efforts to counter an adversary's irregular or limited warfare, USSOCOM's Special Operations Forces Operating Concept, issued in February 2016, emphasises SOF's ability to 'influence actors relevant to the problem' through efforts that 'range from Military Information Support Operations to precise and discreet application of SOF's robust strike capability'.

Some SOF, such as US Joint Special Operations Command and the UK's Special Air Service, have become particularly adept at protracted 'manhunting' of senior terrorist leaders. Two prominent examples of this capability include the airstrike in 2006 that killed the leader of al-Qaeda in Iraq, Abu Musab al-Zarqawi, and the raid into Pakistan that killed Osama bin Laden in 2011. Special operations might also include unconventional warfare to destabilise a regime or foreign internal defence to stabilise a friendly regime. However, not all special-operations missions, such as hostage rescues, are part of broader special-warfare campaigns. Indeed, in some countries these types of missions may instead be the preserve of highly trained police units.

Special warfare is attractive because it provides an intermediate option between the large-scale commitment of conventional forces and long-range strikes. Depending on the scenario, a small special-operations force can have significant effect, for example US special operations in El Salvador in the 1980s, which comprised less than 100 advisers. Other examples include the ongoing efforts of small French, Italian, UK and US SOF contingents in Libya.

Advanced intelligence collection and analysis can magnify a small force's effects, as can the use of other enabling capabilities, such as manned and remotely piloted aircraft. Foreign SOF accompanying local forces can bring those enabling capabilities to bear at their partner's behest. Operating 'by, with, and through' partner forces can help to minimise perceptions of undue foreign interference that might offend cultural sensibilities or undercut the legitimacy of those partners. SOF, therefore, hold the promise of imposing high costs on enemies with relatively small-scale efforts that are less invasive and more palatable not only abroad, but also to populations at home. Smaller-scale efforts are also easier than large-scale conventional efforts for Western nations to sustain fiscally and politically. Examples include the decades-long US SOF support for Colombian and Philippine defence forces' counter-insurgency campaigns.

Special operations can also complement a larger conventional military effort. SOF can supplement conventional-force operations with special reconnaissance, raids against high-value targets and combat-advisory missions with local partners. In large-scale conventional campaigns, SOF might conduct unconventional warfare to disrupt a state's anti-access/area-denial capabilities and allow conventional forces to have freedom of action. And due to the proliferation of mobile intermediate- and long-range ballistic-missile launchers, SOF may be the only forces capable of operating deep in enemy territory to sabotage or destroy long-range precision weapons or weapons of mass destruction. Coalition experiences in Afghanistan and Iraq highlighted the value of SOF integration with conventional-force efforts. But unclear command relationships and inadequate campaign plans frustrated effective SOF–conventional-force integration in Iraq until 2007 and in Afghanistan until 2010. Late in both wars, revised campaign plans integrated the efforts of SOF with conventional forces and oriented them toward achieving sustainable outcomes. The lesson was that, without effective integration into a holistic campaign plan, SOF risk detracting from, rather than contributing to, policy goals.

SOF limitations

Effective integration into broader campaigns requires an understanding of special forces' limitations as well as capabilities. There are limits to what might be achieved through proxies or partners, and SOF are almost always reliant on some degree of support from conventional forces. Even US SOF, which possess robust aviation, intelligence and logistical support, need to be augmented by conventional forces in order to conduct sustained operations of significant scale, such as those ongoing in Afghanistan, Iraq and Syria. Local partners can prove unreliable not only due to a lack of human capital, training or institutional capacity, but also because their interests might prove incongruent with those of the nation employing SOF. As the US Special Operations Forces Operating Concept observes, 'the application of SOF capabilities alone will not achieve policy objectives'. For example, the inability of SOF and their proxies to secure terrain and consolidate military gains politically has proven to be the most consequential limitation of the protracted SOF-led campaign against ISIS.

Other limitations include the global proliferation of information technologies that often expose covert activity. Moreover, the covert nature of SOF campaigns may prove politically unacceptable in democratic nations that value transparency and oversight of military operations. If SOF or their proxies engage in behaviour such as extrajudicial killings or criminality, exposure of that behaviour is likely to undermine not only the war effort locally, but also the willingness of the nation employing SOF to sustain the effort.

Employing and building SOF

In addition to remaining aware of SOF capabilities and limitations, special operations must put politics and policy goals at the centre of the effort. SOF efforts must be part of integrated campaigns designed to achieve those goals. For example, enabling partners will often require more than training, to include convincing those partners that necessary reforms are in their interest. Successful security-sector reform requires the integration of SOF efforts with institutional capacity-building and, in internal defence missions, a clear connection to policing and the rule of law. Efforts to build professionalism, respect for human rights and anti-corruption safeguards often prove more important than the development of tactical capabilities in partner military organisations. For nations employing SOF, patience may be as important as integration into a broader strategy. There are no short-term SOF-based solutions to long-term problems, especially those involving capable enemies or complex political and social dynamics.

Just as nations should integrate SOF efforts into broader campaigns, a nation's SOF capabilities should fit into the broader defence portfolio and strategy. The discrete nature of many of the tasks SOF are called on to perform requires not only specialised selection and training, but also culturally sensitive personnel with a high level of interpersonal skills. Appreciation of this human dimension in forming special-operations forces is not new. Indeed, as US and other SOF expanded after 2001, SOF commanders prioritised the maintenance of demanding selection and training processes. What is new is the joint, high-technology-enabled SOF that have been developed by Australia, Canada, the UK and the US, among others. Advanced intelligence, surveillance and reconnaissance capabilities, tied to precision strike and the ability to conduct raids enabled by manned and unmanned aircraft, provide those forces with extended operational reach – especially against enemies that do not possess sophisticated air-defence or electronic-warfare capabilities.

Perhaps the most important lesson in building SOF is the value of joint integration, as was the case in *Operation Eagle Claw*, the failed US attempt in April 1980 to rescue hostages from Tehran. The principal cause of failure was the ad hoc formation of a team drawn hastily from across the services. By the end of the year, the US Department of Defense formed Joint Special Operations Command. USSOCOM was established seven years later.

USSOCOM itself is a joint command (in addition to the regional combatant commands, Cyber Command and Strategic Command) and resembles a fifth US armed service. The Army provides 'green berets', the elite Delta Force, the Ranger Regiment and a regiment of helicopters; the US Navy provides SEALs and Marine SOF enabled by small boats and underwater systems; and the US Air Force provides a range of transport aircraft, long-range helicopters and gunships. Some other SOF follow this model, such as Australia, Canada and the UK. Since 2001, US and other SOF operations have emphasised not only joint integration within SOF, but also the integration of SOF efforts with national intelligence agencies, law enforcement and conventional forces.

Developing future SOF capabilities

Not all SOF organisations are small. While SOF in Australia, Canada and the UK number about 2,000–3,000 personnel each, USSOCOM is over 63,000 strong, and China's relatively new People's Liberation Army

SOF are estimated at 85,000. Russian SOF are about 15,000 strong. Although the size of SOF, their composition and their mission profiles vary widely, many SOF organisations will require new capabilities to cope with new technologies, increased urbanisation, the proliferation of destructive weapons and enemy countermeasures that increase SOF vulnerabilities. Those countermeasures are not only technical – such as air defence, electronic warfare and cyber warfare – but also tactical and operational, such as the use of sophisticated propaganda, alliances with organised-crime networks and intermingling with civilian populations. In many ways, these are also challenges for ground forces more broadly, but SOF will require more rapid, mobile and adaptable capabilities.

SOF will require new technologies to keep pace with increasingly capable and elusive enemies. These include advanced sensors and robotic and autonomy-enabled systems. To overcome countermeasures to those capabilities, SOF will need robust and redundant communications links that can operate whilst degraded. Technologies that provide uninterrupted communications in congested and contested environments, such as dense urban areas and subterranean facilities, will be particularly valuable for forces that have domestic or overseas responsibilities for countering terrorism or weapons of mass destruction. Commercial technologies that are readily available to state and non-state actors will require new tools within SOF intelligence architectures, such as social-media skimming and advanced decryption. At the same time, 'big data' analytical tools that help fuse and impose order on data collected across land, maritime, aerospace, cyberspace and electromagnetic domains will prove valuable in directing reconnaissance and targeting against networked enemy organisations.

While many SOF innovations will occur in the realms of intelligence, information and cyberspace, improvements in the physical realm will be necessary as well. Lighter machine guns and equipment will provide greater dismounted mobility in the near term, while biomedical technologies and other technologies such as exoskeletons promise future capabilities that increase special operators' endurance and military prowess. SOF will continue to rely heavily on manned and remotely piloted aircraft, but will also need to improve stealth and protection to operate them against capable enemies. Also, they will continue to require transportable, highly mobile vehicles, which, along with more powerful ground-weapon systems, will grow in importance, especially when the aerospace domain is contested. For large-scale operations or sustained special-warfare campaigns, SOF (or those supporting them) will need the capability to conduct micro-logistical resupply operations across macro distances.

Increasing the speed of innovation is certain to grow in importance. USSOCOM's SOFWERX, an organisation designed to foster collaboration with industry, may serve as a model for others. Working with industry is of increasing importance because of the pace of change in dual-use technologies developed primarily for the commercial sector. Furthermore, commercial technologies can help small special-operations forces control costs by compensating for their inability to achieve the economies of scale associated with larger conventional forces, for which ministries would buy in large quantities.

Meanwhile, because hostile nation-states as well as terrorist, insurgent and criminal organisations often employ sophisticated strategies that include propaganda, disinformation, political subversion and criminality, SOF must develop new competencies that extend beyond physical battlegrounds. Those will depend more on people than technology. Identifying the right people through recruitment, selection and assessment, and then developing individual and team proficiency, will continue to distinguish the best SOF organisations. Therefore, investments in education, language skills and tough, realistic training will likely remain more important than incorporating cutting-edge technologies.

The greatest risk associated with SOF may be the tendency to regard their capabilities as simple, low-cost solutions to complex problems. At the tactical level, even the most elite small units can be overcome by less sophisticated enemies that possess advantages in numbers or firepower. At the strategic level, special operations that are disconnected from broader efforts might confuse activity with progress and exacerbate rather than ameliorate problems. Indeed, the greatest opportunity to achieve positive outcomes from special operations lies in integrated campaigns that combine SOF capabilities with operations by conventional forces and other elements of national and multinational power to address the root causes of threats rather than their symptoms.

Twenty-first-century challenges to twentieth-century deterrence

The concept of deterrence is as old as conflict itself. In terms of the military dynamics between states, however, it was not a dominant factor in determining strategy until the advent of nuclear weapons and the emergence of the language and doctrines of nuclear deterrence. For the half-century after the atomic bombs detonated over Hiroshima and Nagasaki, nuclear deterrence was pre-eminent, driven primarily by the Cold War ideological and military stand-off between the Soviet Union and the United States and their respective alliances. Since the end of the Cold War, other threats that were previously suppressed by the reach and power of US–Soviet influence – and this nuclear dominance – have been joined by challenges from emerging threats and novel technologies as well as more sophisticated and capable high-end conventional capabilities. All these now combine to require a far more complex tapestry of interrelated, nuanced and flexible deterrence concepts than was previously the case.

Changing strategic environment

Multiple potential adversaries may pose strategic threats to Western interests. Each has distinct values, political systems, ideologies and strategic cultures, with a wide range of risk-taking propensity, but the threats they pose are not yet fully understood. Any deterrence strategy must be flexible in its ability to evolve and meaningful in relation to these potential challenges, although those responsible for considering and executing deterrence strategies are not necessarily those analysing and countering these novel and changing threats.

As the threat picture has broadened there has been increasing divergence in the stakes that states perceive in the outcomes of crises or conflicts. This divergence has undoubtedly undermined the credibility of some deterrent statements, particularly if deterrence messaging has not kept pace. Meanwhile, the proliferation of asymmetric capability (however it is characterised, including hybrid or ambiguous operations) and capabilities in other 'weapons of mass destruction', and cyber and space has expanded the potential scope of deterrence, further complicating the development of any deterrence strategy. This complexity increases as a crisis expands into operations and conflict, meaning that in many non-nuclear scenarios, deterring escalation may be more important than deterring the initial aggression.

This should not be taken as indicating that these new and novel challenges lessen the importance of nuclear deterrence; but they do demand that nuclear deterrence is not conducted in a vacuum. The current cycle of delivery-system and warhead-modernisation programmes, particularly in China, Russia, the United Kingdom and the US, will in the next decade focus attention on the nuclear dimension. In addition, the changing emphasis on the role of nuclear weapons in nuclear-weapons states' security doctrines (the US and the UK trying to reduce, and Russia's doctrine increasingly highlighting the importance of these weapons) adds a further layer of complexity. This in turn has led NATO and Russia to generate very different perspectives on the employment of nuclear weapons under conceivable scenarios; this raises the risk of miscommunication and misunderstanding. The Warsaw Summit communiqué in July 2016 included the harshest assessment of Russia's increased threat to the Alliance in decades: 'Russia's aggressive actions, including provocative military activities in the periphery of NATO territory and its demonstrated willingness to attain political goals by the threat and use of force, are a source of regional instability, fundamentally challenge the Alliance, have damaged Euro-Atlantic security, and threaten our long-standing goal of a Europe whole, free, and at peace.' There was no change from previous summit communiqués, however, in relation to the nuclear dimension.

Some of these novel and emerging challenges have the potential to influence or even risk triggering activity in the nuclear area – particularly given the challenges of managing escalation. Therefore, a far more sophisticated understanding of the interrelationships between these challenges, as well as their risks and perhaps even opportunities, is required to develop meaningful cross-domain deterrence strategies that will underpin and improve strategic stability well into the first half of this century.

Whatever the need for deterrence in other domains and against other challenges, and the absolute necessity of understanding cross-domain relationships, the effects of getting it wrong in the nuclear domain are likely to remain the worst. The nuclear domain is therefore likely to remain the benchmark of strategic stability against which to judge activities in other areas.

Development of deterrence theory

To understand the effects of each of these challenges it is necessary to examine the process by which a deterrence strategy is developed, how this is evolving and how it needs further to change. Traditional deterrence relies upon several key components, which were at their simplest in the purely nuclear domain: an identifiable and discrete adversary who can deliver an identifiable event, which you seek to deter by means of an event delivering equal or greater harm against it; a means of communicating resolve and deterrent intent to that adversary; and a reliable means of avoiding misinterpretation of rhetoric and action.

Deterrence activities seek to influence emphatically the calculus and decisions of an adversary and as such they are about influencing adversary perceptions. Once a state has structured its activities such that no third party will misunderstand them, what the target adversary believes or thinks is all that matters. Adversary perceptions are a function of three variables. The first is who the adversary is: their identity, values, fears and aspirations, their goals and objectives, strategy and doctrine, and capabilities. The second concerns the decision over which influence, and deterrence, is desired: for example, whether they would use nuclear weapons. The third relates to the circumstances in which the decision is being made.

Tailored deterrence strategies are particularly challenging when seeking to deter an adversary whose cultural outlook, language and set of values is very different. Indeed, deterrence activities must be dynamic and reactive, because adversary perceptions will shift over time. There is no 'one size fits all' approach. Deterrence is therefore adversary-, objective- and time-specific and plans must seek to deter 'X' from doing 'Y' under 'Z' conditions. This has become considerably more difficult as a result of the growth in the range and nature of the threats and challenges that deterrence planning is now being asked to accommodate.

The rise of significant non-state threats, less discrete and immediately attributable capabilities (including biological, cyber and information/influence capabilities) and deliberately asymmetric doctrine and operations at the state level all combine to skew and complicate the relative comfort of balanced nuclear deterrence.

In attempting to deter adversaries, the most problematic targets for nations or alliances are non-state actors. Their values, objectives and means differ from those of state actors, while they might not possess the physical dependencies that make states more susceptible to deterrence messaging and influence. Apart from the straightforward challenge of determining exactly who these groups are, their lack of identifiable structure brings greater uncertainty over how their decision-makers perceive the costs, benefits and consequences of restraint regarding the actions to be deterred; there is undoubtedly here a significant asymmetry in the stakes that either side may perceive. These actors also differ markedly in their susceptibility to efforts to credibly threaten to impose costs on their behaviours. In contrast to traditional state actors, deterrence of non-state actors is frustrated by an almost total lack of well-established means of communication between them and the state wishing to deter them. They are also the most threatening to the social fabric of those they oppose and they are probably the least threatened by traditional high-end military deterrence.

Emerging challenges

Several key changes to the global environment have already made deterrence more challenging; they will likely make it more so. The first is how the world communicates across borders and ideologies. The second is the significant divergence in awareness and comprehension of nuclear policy and capability between liberal Western states and their potential adversaries – made more important by the differing importance in strategy noted above. And the third is the pursuit of offensive cyber capabilities and long-range precision conventional capabilities by some nuclear-armed states. The latter capabilities, as well as bringing their own deterrence dilemma, bring further risk and uncertainty to the nuclear-deterrence calculus.

The recent profound changes in the means and protocols of social and government communications make it more problematic to maintain the necessary and clear communications between the state decision-makers responsible for managing escalation and deterrence in crises. This is particularly the case where liberal Western states have sophisticated and articulate opposition groups whose messaging is often more agile and available than that of the government. No Western nuclear-weapon state has yet had to face such a crisis in the 'Twittersphere' – although the influence that social media can have on political debate is starting to be understood – and these states have little concept of how a coherent message from government would be maintained and adjusted to sustain a deterrence message nor how that would be reliably communicated to the right decision-maker in the adversary state at the right time in the crucible of modern media.

The part-deliberate and part-accidental blurring of the edges and the gap between nuclear-weapon use and precision conventional and novel weapons poses a further challenge to strategic stability. This blurring disappeared from doctrine after the early days of the atomic age, but the most recent publicly available doctrine in Russia and the US has resurrected concepts of a seamless spectrum of deterrence and conflict in which high-end conventional and low-end nuclear abut each other or even overlap. There is growing rhetoric, led by Russia, over the possible use of non-strategic nuclear weapons to control escalation at the high end of a conventional conflict. Their doctrine has the objective of 'cauterising' the conflict to prevent both continuing conventional but also any further nuclear escalation. The likely success of this doctrine is unproven and has been frequently and compellingly challenged.

Increasingly there is a concerning return in official Russian and US doctrine to linear models of deterrence that mask the emerging set of complex interrelationships. US open-source presentations refer to the 'spectrum of deterrence' as if conflicts with complex components will follow a 'game plan' of escalation that is both relatively predictable and manageable with mutually recognised moments of 'pause', with 'off ramps' where de-escalatory pressure will have the desired effect. While clearly these presentations simplify complex analysis for illustrative briefing, there is a risk that the multifaceted nature of the layers of action and deterrence that exist throughout crises and conflict will not be fully considered by teams using similar shorthand representations regularly.

The reliance of modern society on the digital storage and sharing of information, seamlessly and continuously and regardless of national borders, has brought unsettling warnings about national and international vulnerability to cyber attack. In recent years, some analysts have sought to equate the potential effects of the most significant cyber attack with that of a nuclear detonation, either to make the case that offensive cyber capability could be deployed in lieu of a nuclear deterrent, or to give a role for nuclear weapons in deterring high-effect cyber warfare. This search for equivalence to 'understood' deterrence norms is understandable, but creates its own challenges. Although some states might have advanced capabilities in this regard (such as the US), a cyber attack that might have a major negative effect on the structure of a society is in general terms not always immediately attributable. Amid a complex and chaotic crisis, determining who had mounted a cyber attack to the level required for a devastating response by another weapon would be intensely problematic, and this significantly erodes the credibility of 'equivalent' deterrence in this context. The 2013 US Defense Science Board report into cyber resilience examined this in detail, but in determining that 'attribution can be accomplished for attacks that would reach the level of really harming the country, because attacks of that scale require planning and multiple attack vectors – which usually leave clues' may have been more optimistic than it should have been in this regard.

At the same time, these new capabilities raise risks to the unspoken protocols that led some adversary strategic communications and warning capabilities to become effective no-go areas. The US and the Soviet Union, and latterly China and the other P5 members, were careful to not take actions that would affect elements of the others' strategic warning, detection and nuclear command-and-control systems, to ensure that the risk of misinterpretation was as low as possible in peacetime and in crisis. The rise in offensive cyber capabilities, almost certainly controlled in a different government area, and with the potential for action by non-state actors, risks inadvertent interference with this 'protocol' – the danger is that, in time of crisis, 'what can we do?' may be insufficiently constrained by 'what should we do?'. In addition, precision long-range and high-speed conventional munitions, threatening significant elements of the adversary's critical security infrastructure, risk precipitating a nuclear response.

Deterrence planning in the twenty-first century

Any assessment of adversary perceptions is plagued with uncertainty. As such, deterrence analysis and planning must characterise and seek to reduce these gaps in knowledge and take them into account in subsequent strategies and plans in order to manage uncertainty. Historically, as decisions to act in Iraq in 2003 showed, the interface between those that gather and analyse intelligence and the decision-makers has not handled this area with sufficient candour. Analyses of campaign failures in the recent past have invariably pointed to this very human flaw as contributing to failure.

At the higher end of deterrence, where the effects of getting these judgements wrong could be catastrophic, structures and processes should be designed explicitly to reduce this possibility, and the strategies themselves must consider risks associated with making the wrong judgements. Moreover, in the complex tapestry of modern deterrence there is a need to understand the potential and uncertain regional and global effects deterrent actions have on actors beyond the adversary itself, including allies. These uncertainties demand the application of resources and measured analysis; assumptions would fatally undermine a credible strategy.

Effective deterrence activities will involve all elements of national power as well as those of allies, and planning must embrace collaboration across governments and between international partners. Consequently, what is required to 'wage deterrence' today is more complex and more coordinated than Western democracies could manage until now. Deterrence must be campaign-based, with an ability to influence the perceptions of multiple adversaries in a dynamic environment. This will only be achieved by campaigns that are coherent collaborations of individual strategies that are, in turn, adversary-specific, based on sophisticated understanding of each adversary and hedged against uncertainties that may exist in this analysis. They must integrate activity from the whole of government in analysis, strategy development, planning and execution, and understanding and achieving the integration of hard and soft power.

To work effectively, these strategies must be continuous and proactive through peacetime, crisis and conflict. They must have a strategic goal of preventing crisis, not just responding to it, and understanding that the adversary calculus will shift profoundly across each of these phases. These days, maintaining a 'general deterrence' approach risks the failure of deterrence as a result of misunderstanding the adversary's decision-making calculus. What is most important is that, having agreed necessary outcomes for the deterrence campaign, this runs constantly and not just in crisis. There are several reasons why this is crucial to success. The scope of potential deterrence activities in relative peacetime is far broader than in crisis or actual conflict. Some deterrent activities require repetition to become effective, or take more time to have the desired effect than is available in time of crisis. In addition, the peacetime environment – where time is less of a factor and the fog is hopefully thinner – is simply more conducive to credible and clear communication. In crisis or conflict, the adversary decision-makers may be incapable of receiving messages because of actions taken by either side. The understanding one side has of the other's decision-making process may change as a crisis escalates, resulting in some elements of government playing a reduced role or being removed from the process altogether. This may render previous lines of communication ineffective at the moment of greatest need.

Implications

Achieving success in deterrence is difficult and, as has been examined above, is becoming more challenging, but its importance to strategic stability remains clear. There are no simple answers to this complex range of deterrence demands. There are, however, several key themes that emerge:

While it is tempting to fall back on current nuclear deterrence to deter large-scale cyber warfare and other 'weapons of mass destruction' even further than the current declaratory statements, there is significant risk that these would not be credible responses and therefore would be unlikely to, by themselves, deter.

Except for nuclear-weapon use, the control of escalation, across the domains and between domains, may be more important than the prevention of the initial conflict. Traditional deterrence activities may not support both.

More modern challenges, particularly non-state actors and offensive cyber, demand the 'whole of government' coherent approach to deterrence that has so far been heavy on rhetoric but light on delivery in the West.

A thorough analysis is required of the effects that other domains have upon each other and on nuclear deterrence in particular, to ensure that activities in one domain have no unintended negative consequences upon another.

Nuclear-deterrence strategies must become more dynamic and capable of adaption to a more multipolar challenge.

The communication of deterrence is insufficiently understood or practised, particularly across multiple domains to multiple adversaries in peacetime and crisis, including exploitation of the advantages of modern media (and suppression of the disadvantages), to optimise the credibility and understanding of the message, particularly at critical crisis points. Without good communications, credibility is reduced and deterrent effect may be negated. Without credibility and communications, these expensive capabilities risk irrelevance when most required.

Chapter Two
Comparative defence statistics

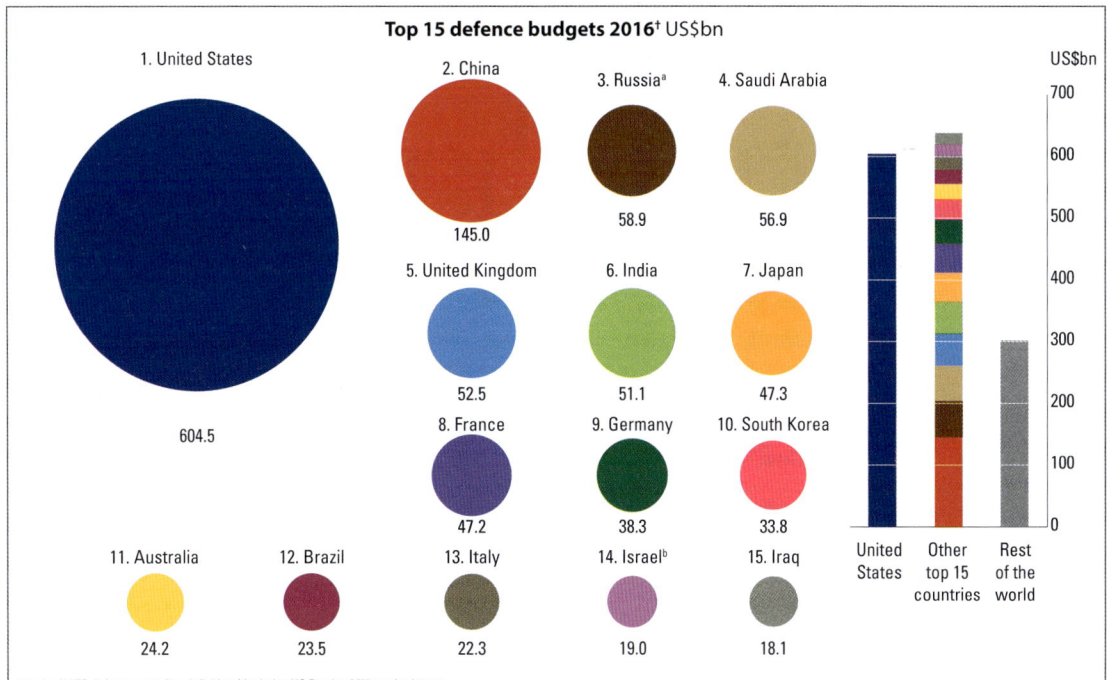

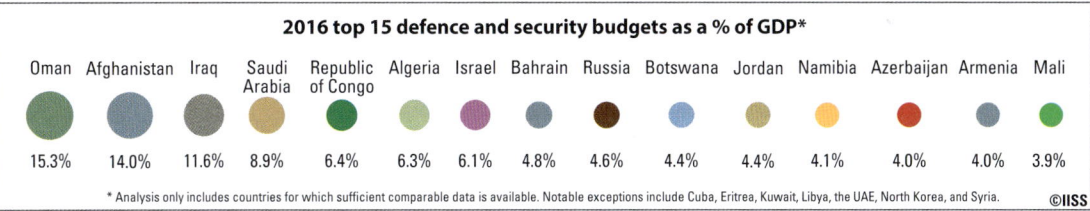

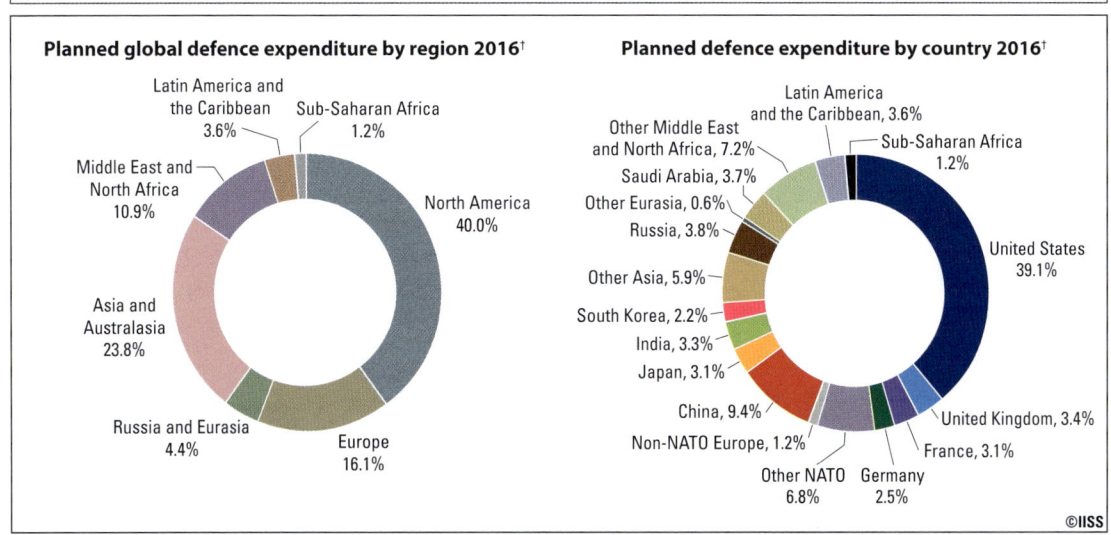

† At current prices and exchange rates

20 THE MILITARY BALANCE 2017

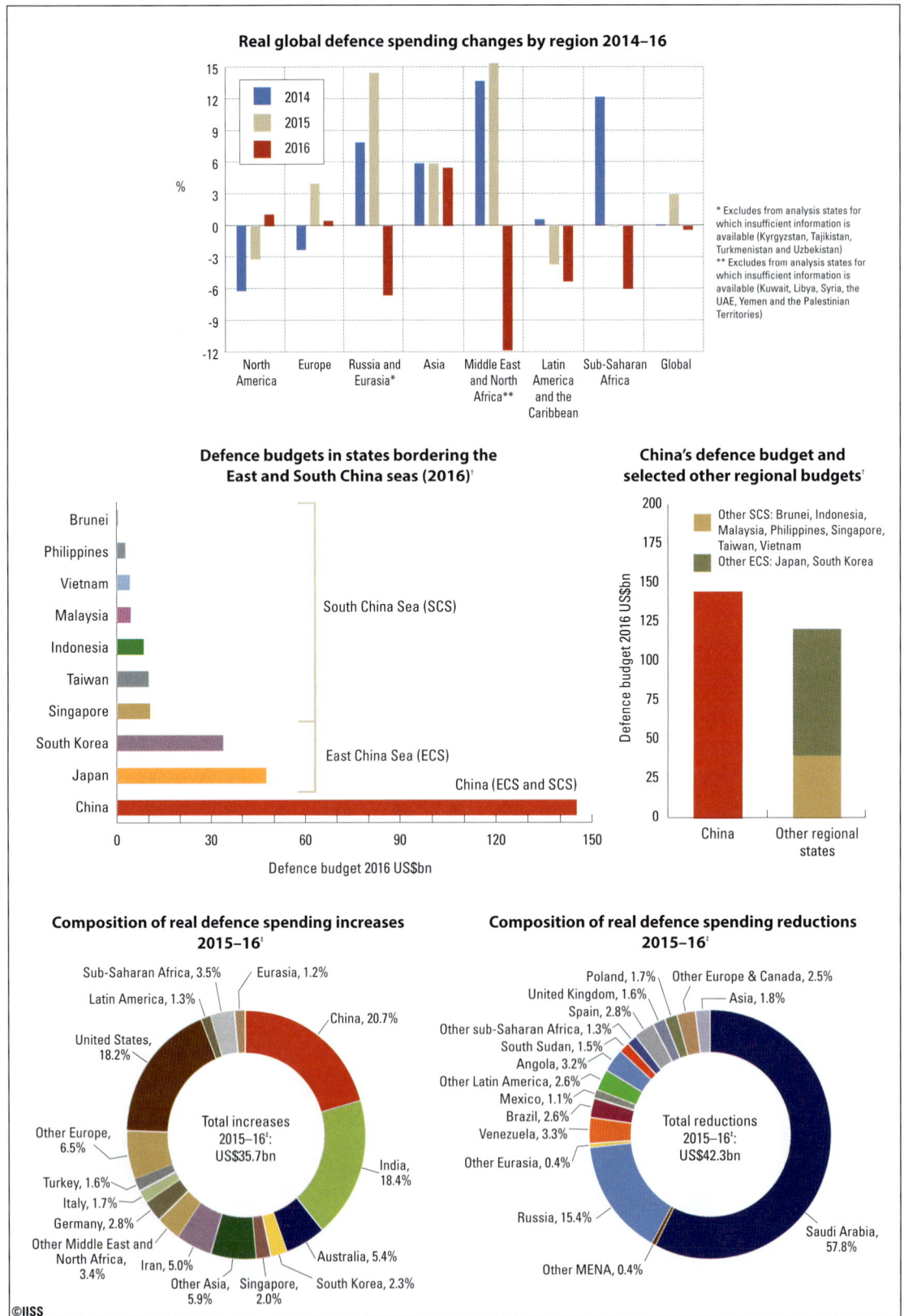

Selected European aerospace defence consolidation, 1990–2016

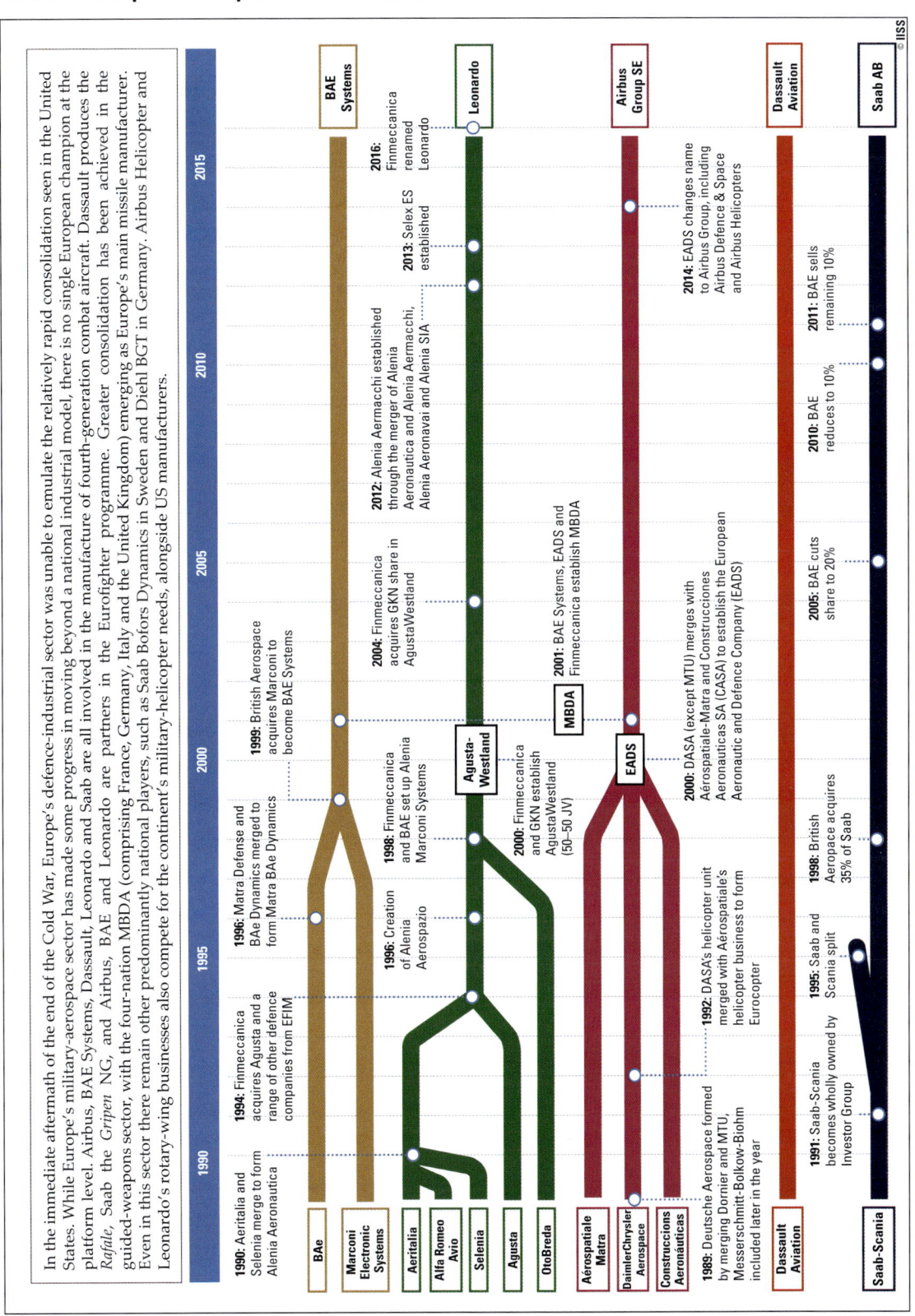

Key defence statistics

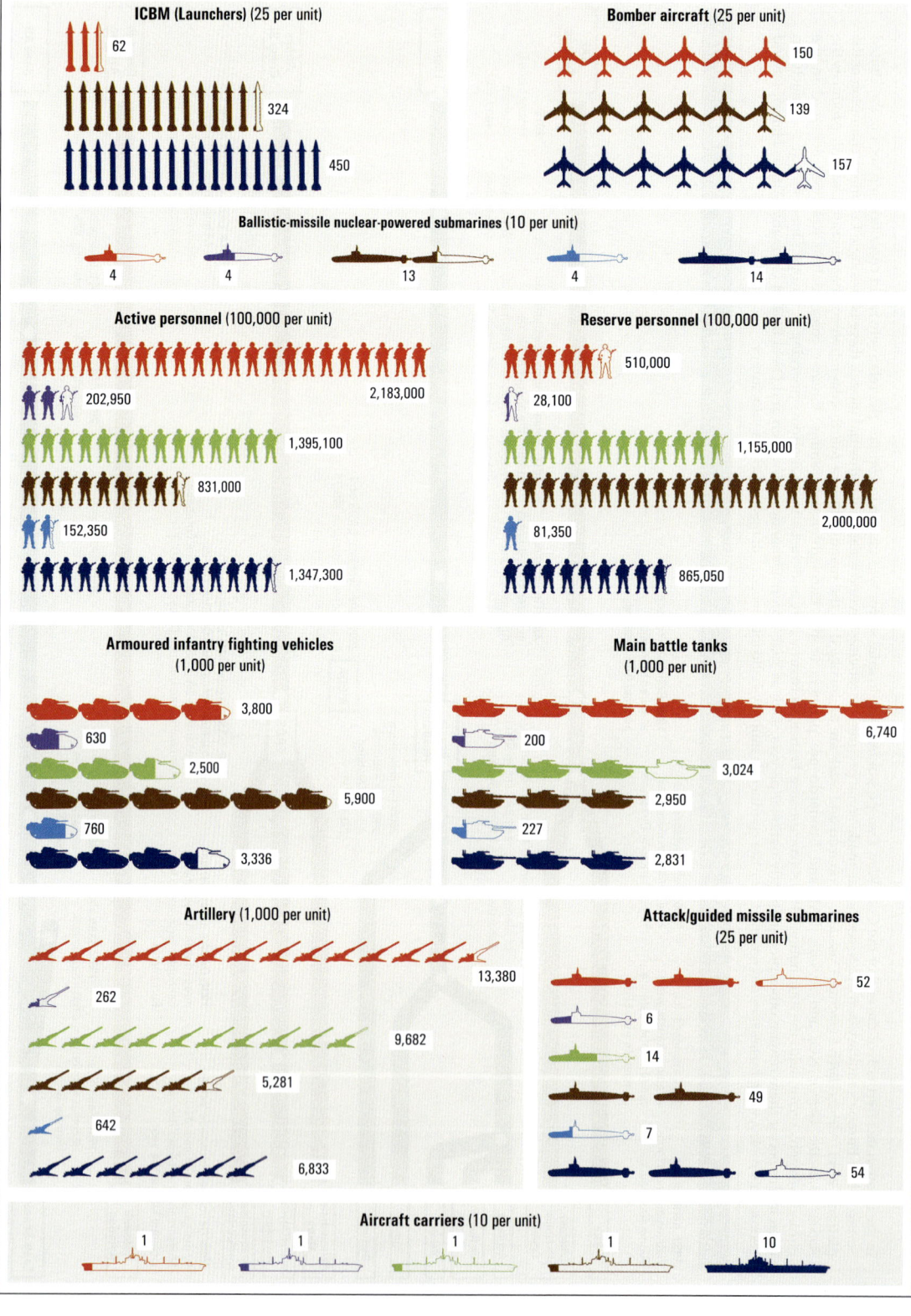

Comparative defence statistics

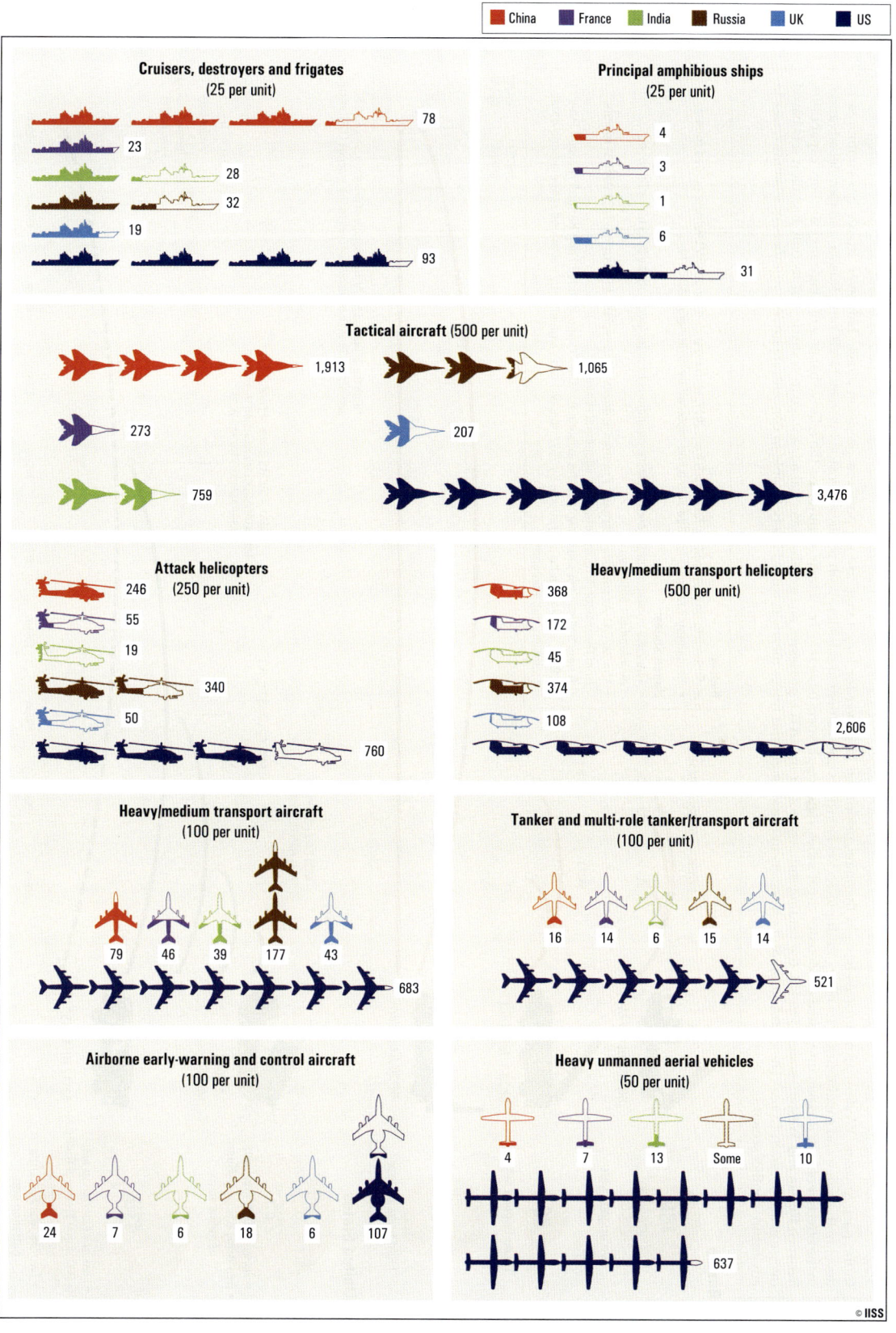

Battlefield missiles and rockets: Russian and US equipment capabilities

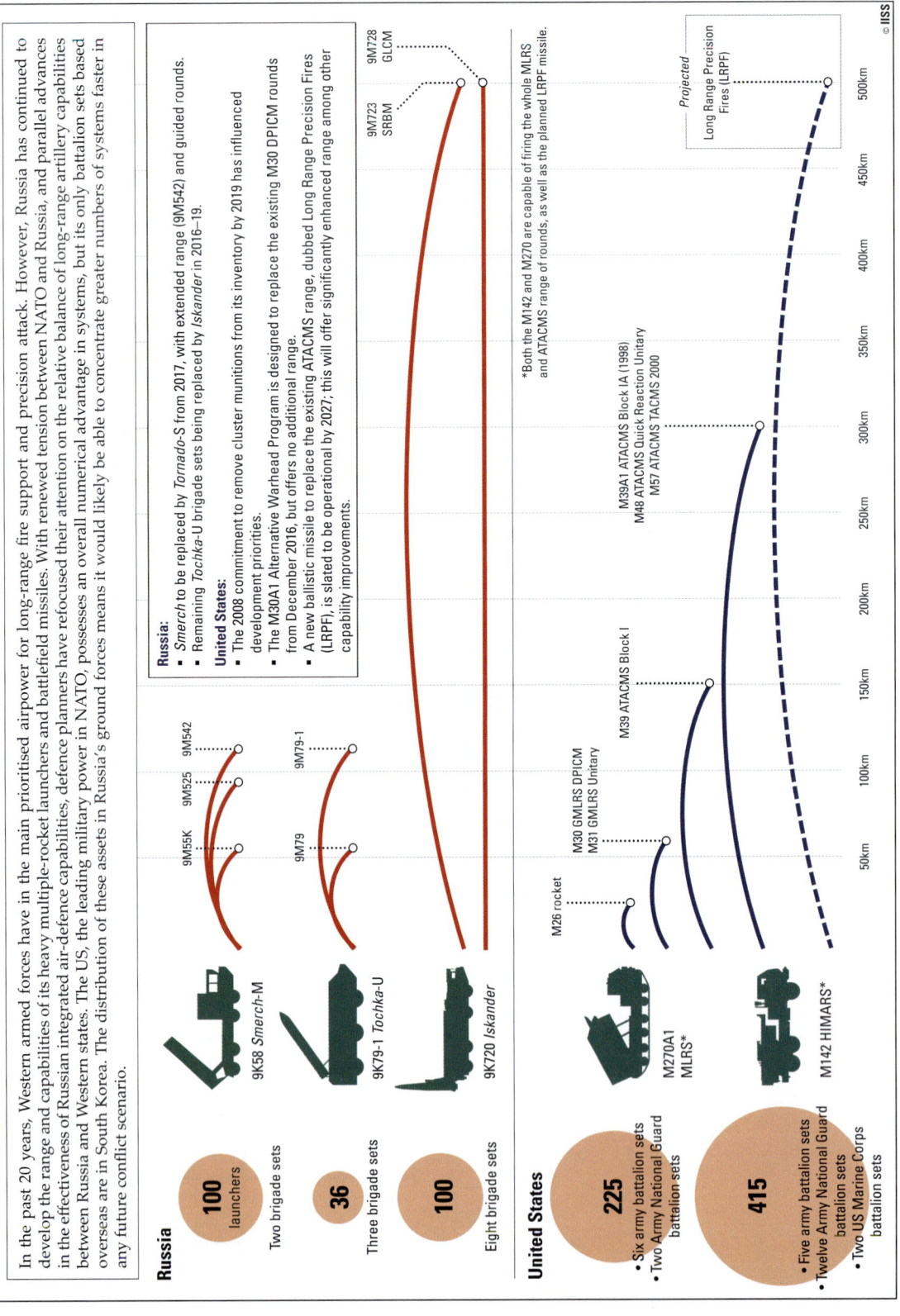

Comparative defence statistics

Attack helicopter operators and fleets, 1997–2016

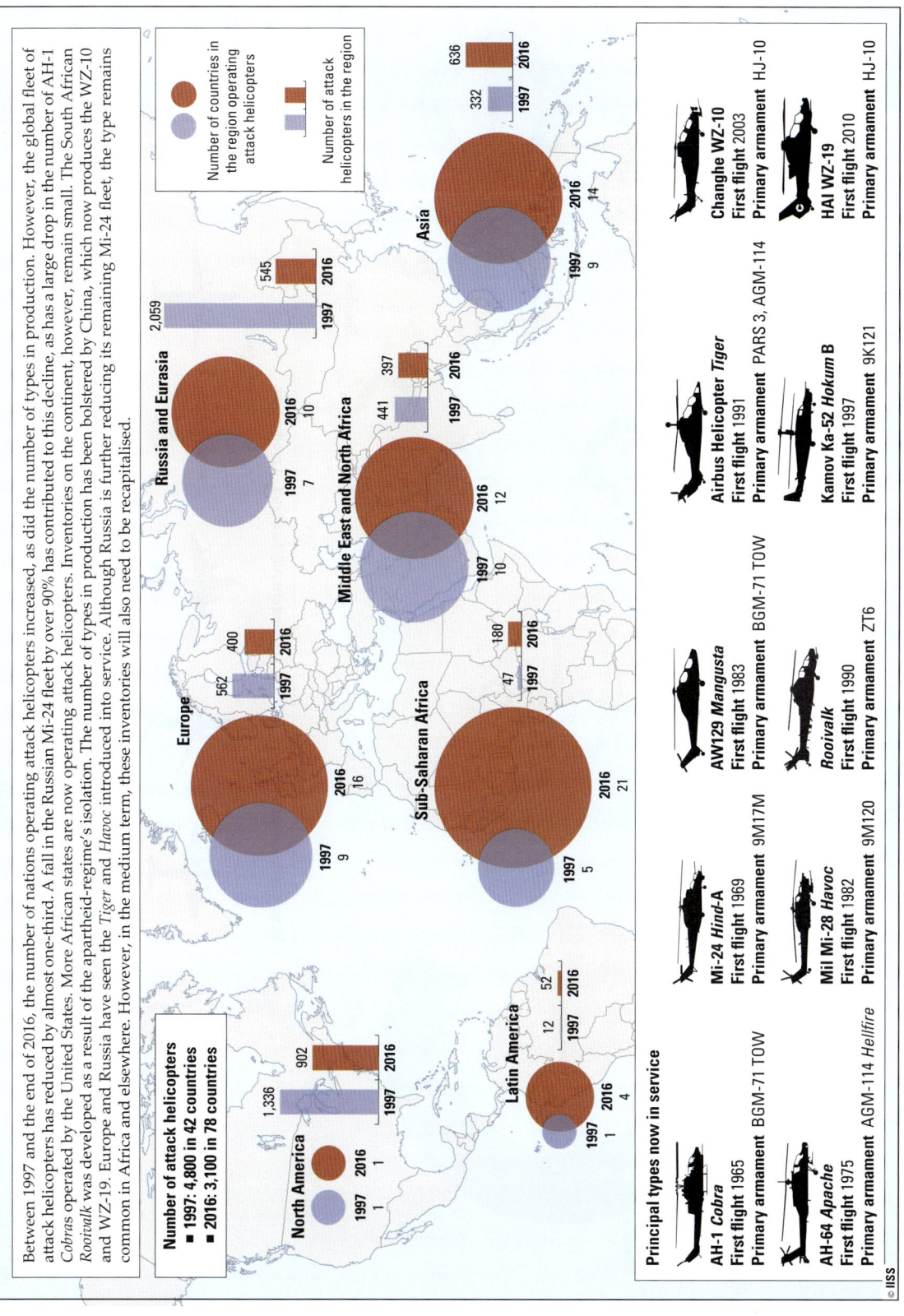

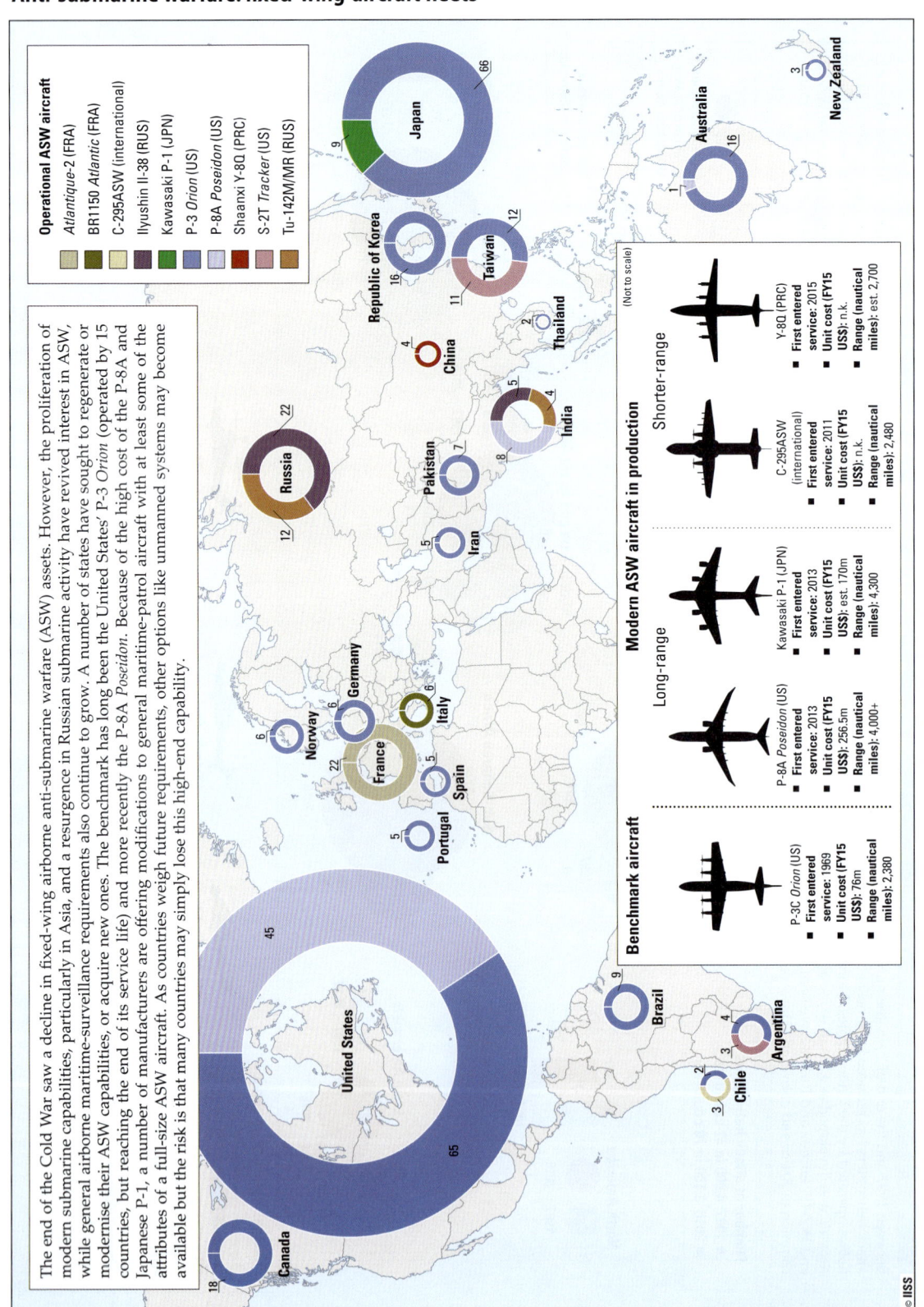

Chapter Three
North America

UNITED STATES

After one of the most contentious elections in US history, Donald Trump was due to take the oath of office as the 45th president of the United States on 20 January 2017. The 2016 presidential campaign showed that, on both the left and the right in American politics, there are more and more citizens who question America's role in the world. This may place the nature and duration of some military deployments under greater scrutiny, and prompt a call for more innovative approaches to burden-sharing; these already exist in relation to funding: there are many cases of significant host-nation financial support for US overseas deployments. Trump's election indicates that there is, in time, likely to be significant discontinuity with the security policies of the Obama administration. Policy proposals were at the end of 2016 still vague, and it was possible that some of his national-security appointments would be relatively unfamiliar with the workings of the Department of Defense (DoD) and the armed forces. Nonetheless, if the past is any guide, it will take months to confirm cabinet officers and to craft and implement any significant changes in direction. The DoD will be largely under the stewardship of military officers and career civil servants until the president has his team in place. Therefore, much of what had been planned in FY2016 will likely carry over into FY2017.

Return of great-power competition

In late 2016, General Martin Dempsey, the former chairman of the Joint Chiefs of Staff, gave the next administration some recommendations on the US armed forces. In an interview in the September/October issue of *Foreign Affairs*, Dempsey noted that 'it's the most dangerous period in my lifetime … we've got lots of things cropping up at the same time. We have multiple challenges competing for finite resources – and grotesque uncertainty with regard to the military budget.' Earlier in 2016, Secretary of Defense Ashton Carter, in his 2017 Defense Posture Statement, entitled 'Taking the Long View, Investing for the Future', described challenges from 'great power competition from a resurgent Russia and a rising China, regional threats from North Korea and Iran, and the enduring need to counter terrorism'.

In response to both an increasingly capable and assertive China, as well as Russian military operations in Europe and the Middle East, in 2016 the DoD became increasingly vocal about the potential implications of such great-power competition. The Pentagon's civilian leadership, as well as the uniformed leadership of the armed forces, expressed the need to redress long-standing shortfalls in modernisation and training aimed at deterring aggression by great-power competitors, and countering the advanced capabilities that they possess and sell to others. According to the 2017 posture statement, for the DoD 'this means we must have – and be seen to have – the ability to impose unacceptable costs on an advanced aggressor that will either dissuade them from taking provocative action, or make them deeply regret it if they do'. The statement continued: 'Russia and China are our most stressing competitors, as they've both developed and are continuing to advance military systems that threaten our advantages in specific areas, and in some cases, they're developing weapons and ways of war that seek to achieve their objectives in ways they hope would preempt a response by the United States'. For the armed forces, these challenges mean that they have to be able to fight full-spectrum combat against high-end adversaries while at the same time engaging in low-intensity enduring operations that utilise skills hard-won over the past 15 years.

There are persistent threats from non-state actors, particularly the Islamic State, also known as ISIS or ISIL, and this is recognised as an enduring challenge for the DoD and other agencies. At the same time, the DoD continues to emphasise the need to plan for conflict with regional powers such as North Korea and Iran. Pyongyang continues to defy predictions of instability and collapse, and ended 2016 with military capabilities more advanced than those it had at the beginning of the year. North Korea's nuclear and missile tests foreshadow a time when Kim Jong-un's regime could have the capability to strike the US and its allies with nuclear-capable ballistic missiles launched from land or sea. Whereas Iran has pledged to freeze its nuclear programme in accordance with the Joint Comprehensive Plan of Action (JCPOA), many are concerned that Tehran will use part of the infusion of cash that it received after acceding to the JCPOA to fund its armed forces and its proxies in the region and elsewhere (although the embargo on the sale of many conventional weapons to Iran is to remain in force for five years after the 18 October 2015 adoption of the JCPOA).

All this is taking place within the context of uncertain funding that has dogged the US defence establishment in recent years. The Budget Control Act of 2011 is still law, and only delayed sequestration by two years. Carter noted that, unless sequestration is addressed, the Pentagon 'will face $100 billion in cuts from 2018 to 2021, which would introduce unacceptable risks'. The year 2016 also saw the Obama administration's 'rebalance' towards the Asia-Pacific continue, although this was not without challenges. Whereas ties with Australia, Japan and South Korea remain strong, the election of Rodrigo Duterte as president of the Philippines resulted in a setback in US–Philippine relations. Duterte's public statements about Obama and call for the withdrawal of US advisers from the Philippines represented a sharp downturn in a relationship that had grown closer under Duterte's predecessor. For instance, at a joint press conference with Carter and then Philippine defence minister Voltaire Gazmin in April, the sides announced new military cooperation based on the US–Philippines Enhanced Defense Cooperation Agreement and the US-proposed Maritime Security Initiative. As part of these measures, US aircraft began flying out of Clark Air Base soon after, with A-10s flying over Scarborough Shoal in the South China Sea. At the time of writing, US officials were still trying to determine the full policy implications of Manila's statements. During 2016, there was also a renewed emphasis on Europe in Washington's defence strategy. In response to the concerns of its Central and Eastern European members, NATO decided at its Warsaw Summit, held on 8–9 July, to rotationally deploy four battalions in Estonia, Latvia, Lithuania and Poland, beginning in 2017. The US is to be the lead nation in the battalion deploying to Poland. US forces in Europe are much reduced in number from those stationed there during the Cold War (see *The Military Balance 2017* wall chart) but in the last two years the US has been devoting greater attention to Europe, not just through these rotational deployments and increased exercise activity, but also through the quadrupling of funding for the Pentagon's European Reassurance Initiative and the development of ballistic-missile-defence architecture in Europe.

In November 2015, Carter announced the Force of the Future initiative, designed to maintain the DoD's competitive edge. Key components include strengthening family benefits, improving the officer-promotion system and attracting top civilian talent. Importantly, modifications to the current 'up-or-out' promotion system, which limits the number of times an officer can be passed over for promotion before they are required to leave the service, will require changes to the Defense Officer Personnel Management Act (DOPMA). There has been opposition inside the Pentagon to changing the military-personnel system, but the most vocal critic has been Senator John McCain, chairman of the Senate Armed Services Committee, who stated that the Force of the Future initiative was 'an outrageous waste of official time and resources', signalling that changes to DOPMA are by no means certain. Carter defended the proposals, saying in a press conference that they were necessary for future force effectiveness and that the DoD had to make investments in future technology and personnel, while at the same time meeting its current global commitments.

Other initiatives include recommending changes to military retirement and proposals to alter the provisions of the 30-year-old Goldwater–Nichols Act. Goldwater–Nichols streamlined the US military chain of command and altered the role of combatant commanders to try to better integrate the services' military capability. The DoD has also gone further than dispensing with the 'don't ask, don't tell' policy of preventing lesbian, gay or bisexual troops from serving openly in the military, and is preparing a transition plan to enable transgender individuals to serve. Furthermore, women are now allowed to serve in any position in the armed forces. Captain Kristen Griest, one of the first two women to graduate from the army's Ranger School, transferred from the military police to become the army's first female infantry officer. Both the army and the marine corps are planning to bring women into armour and infantry posts, although the number of volunteers was reported to be low. This is a significant cultural change but the US military has a long track record of successfully diversifying the force. DoD and service leaders have stated that standards will not change.

Third Offset Strategy

The return of great-power competition, with nations like China and Russia armed with anti-access/area-denial (A2/AD) capabilities, has the potential to challenge the United States' ability to project military power. This has been highlighted in the European context as a problem for NATO states more broadly, as Russia deploys additional capabilities in its Western Military District that could in theory complicate any Alliance plans to rapidly reinforce its Eastern allies. China too is developing and deploying more advanced military capabilities that could – if employed – call into question unrestricted US access to parts of the Asia-Pacific in times of crisis. The concern will be that these developments might ultimately cast doubt on Washington's security guarantees to allies and others. Moreover, responding to Chinese and Russian military modernisation, and deployments resulting from the concerns of allies, is imposing considerable costs on the US. Many US defence-modernisation programmes were in train before Russia's recent military extroversion or China's growing assertiveness in the Asia-Pacific, but these security dynamics have in some respects given more focus to the process. Again, the challenge for US forces is one of scale. To conduct full-spectrum operations on a global scale means maintaining capabilities and skills that are useful in low-intensity environments and in tackling the threats seen in Iraq or Afghanistan; it also means developing cutting-edge military systems that can dominate the battlespace in a contest with a peer competitor. This, of course, comes at great cost, and simply resetting the US armed forces on their return from the past 15 years of complex operations is expensive enough.

Therefore, there is a requirement for innovative and adaptive thinking, and ways of working, both inside defence structures and with the civilian sector. Staying one step ahead does not simply mean focusing on new and bespoke equipment. It also means thinking cleverly about combinations of new and old capabilities, sometimes drawn from outside traditional defence establishments or industries – such as civilian-sector developments in small-scale unmanned-aerial-vehicle (UAV) technology. It also means revisiting elements of legacy technologies that would enable continued operations against a peer competitor capable of, for instance, degrading the electromagnetic spectrum. In general terms, retaining a technical and operational edge is not seen by the US as a purely quantitative contest. As Assistant Secretary of Defense Stephen Welby said in April 2016, 'the US must seek asymmetric advantages – particularly those that take advantage of US strengths in military and commercial technological innovation.'

In response to these challenges, the DoD has launched its Third Offset Strategy in an effort to regain advantage and force competitors to respond to US developments. A number of new organisations have been established to formulate and implement the strategy, including the Strategic Capabilities Office, which seeks to develop and field high-leverage capabilities in the near term, and the Defense Innovation Unit Experimental (DIUx), which seeks to build relationships with, and harvest innovations from, the commercial-technology sector. DIUx now has three offices. The first was set up in Silicon Valley in 2015, and other offices followed in Boston and Austin in 2016 following its 'reboot' as DIUx 2.0. The initiative has its critics, with some questioning the effectiveness of DIUx in light of the DoD's acquisition processes, unless these become quicker. Meanwhile, DIUx Managing Partner Raj Shah has said that the contracting process DIUx is now using, the Commercial Systems Opening (CSO), is open to all DoD groups, and that under the CSO 'the average time for awarding a contract is 53 days'. In the second quarter of FY2016, the DoD reported that DIUx had awarded '12 agreements for a total of $36 million'. In addition, the department's civilian and military leadership has emphasised the need to re-energise war-gaming, modelling and simulation as ways to explore new concepts and technologies.

The Third Offset Strategy is also beginning to influence the defence budget. The DoD's FY2017 budget request included US$3.6bn earmarked for Third Offset programmes and a total of US$18bn spread over the next five years. This included US$3bn to counter A2/AD threats, US$500m for guided munitions, US$3bn for undersea warfare, US$3bn for human–machine collaboration and teaming, US$1.7bn for cyber and electronic warfare, and US$500m for expanding war-gaming and operational-concept tests and demonstrations.

Readiness issues

The DoD faces readiness issues caused by budget cuts, reduced armed forces, continued deployments to combat zones in Afghanistan and Iraq, counter-terrorism operations, and ongoing operations to reassure allies, partners and friends, particularly given increased military activity by Russia and China.

The March 2016 posture statements of the service secretaries and chiefs reflect deep concerns about readiness. For example, Acting Army Secretary Patrick Murphy and Army Chief of Staff General Mark Milley said, in their testimony before the Senate, that, 'unfortunately, less than one-third of Army forces are at acceptable readiness levels to conduct sustained ground combat in a full spectrum environment against a highly lethal hybrid threat or near-peer adversary'. Secretary of the Air Force Deborah James and then-air force chief of staff General Mark Welsh struck a similar chord. In their Senate testimony of March 2016, they said that 'while our Airmen remain heavily engaged around the world, the average age of our aircraft is at an all-time high, and the size of our force and state of our full-spectrum readiness are at or near all-time lows. Non-stop combat since Operation DESERT STORM has placed a substantial burden on our Airmen and their families while straining the readiness of our personnel and the systems they operate.' However, Chief of Naval Operations Admiral John Richardson's succinct appraisal perhaps best sums up the readiness gaps among all the services: 'the challenges are increasing and funding is decreasing.'

The reality of renewed global competition with near-peer adversaries with significant capabilities calls into question defence-industrial capacity. General Dempsey, when discussing advanced weapons systems such as the F-35, expressed his concerns beyond platform costs: 'many of these systems are designed to be two or three or four times more capable than their predecessors … and we have reason to believe that it will actually be true. On the other hand, if we don't find a way to make sure that we have an industrial base capable of replenishing losses … That's a great concern of mine.'

Modernisation challenges

One looming set of force-modernisation decisions that the new administration will have to face concerns the US nuclear force, the vast majority of which dates to the late Cold War. Modernisation of all three legs of the US nuclear triad is planned, although questions remain over the funding of such large-ticket items. The *Columbia*-class nuclear-powered ballistic-missile submarine (SSBN, formerly the SSBN-X) is scheduled to begin construction in 2021 and enter service in 2031, a half-century after its predecessor, the *Ohio* class, first entered service. The air force's B-21 low-observable bomber (formerly the Long-Range Strike Bomber), which is to be produced by Northrop Grumman, is projected to have the capability to carry out both conventional and nuclear missions. The commander of US Air Force Global Strike Command expects that the air force will order a minimum of 100 B-21 bombers, with an initial operating capability expected by 2030. Less developed is the replacement for the ageing intercontinental-ballistic-missile force, the Ground-Based Strategic Deterrent, which is meant to deliver a land-based missile that can serve the US until 2075.

Army

For over a decade, the US Army adapted to the demands of the Afghan and Iraqi theatres by largely focusing training and equipping efforts on counter-insurgency and counter-terrorism imperatives. In addition to ongoing rotations to Afghanistan and the Middle East to counter the Taliban and ISIS, the army supports other worldwide commitments. Army Chief of Staff General Milley noted in his February 2016 testimony before Congress that 'the Army has approximately 190,000 Soldiers deployed to 140 countries'. This means that just more than 40% of the US Army is committed to global operations, with this constituting 60% of the total demands arising from the combatant commands.

Given the changing international environment, particularly Russia's activities in Ukraine and Syria, Milley's stated top priority is readiness for 'sustained ground combat in a full spectrum environment against a highly lethal hybrid threat or near-peer adversary'. The challenge for the army and the broader armed forces is how to conduct expeditionary operations against adversaries with sophisticated A2/AD capabilities while having only minimal forward presence. The results of war games conducted by several think tanks, which found that Russia could present a fait accompli in Baltic states in very short order, were particularly sobering for the army. Milley's assessment is that, after 15 years of continuous counter-insurgency and counter-terrorism combat operations, coupled with ongoing end-strength cuts – the army is currently on a path to having 980,000 troops (450,000 regular; 335,000 National Guard; 195,000 reserve) – and budget reductions, less than one-third of the army is ready for mid- and high-end adversaries. Consequently, the army is refocusing training on decisive operations and retooling its combat-training centres (CTCs) to that end, with 19 CTC rotations scheduled in FY2016 and FY2017. Milley is also working to increase National Guard training days and to increase their CTC rotations from two to four.

However, the focus on near-term readiness comes at a cost. The army is reducing its modernisation spending and the remainder is largely focused on five major areas: aviation (the upgrade of existing helicopters, better protection and the Future Vertical Lift programme); networking (to enable operations in a contested cyber- and electronic-warfare environment, and merging cyber and electronic warfare into a cyber directorate on the Army Staff); integrated air and missile defence; combat vehicles (upgrades of current vehicles, including efforts to provide active protection, and a Combat Vehicle Modernization Strategy); and preparing for emerging threats (long-range precision 'fires' to attack distant targets). The army's FY2017 budget request to support these priorities is US$125.1bn (US$1.4bn less than the enacted FY2016 budget). Of that total, nearly 60% is for the compensation of soldiers and army civilians, leaving 22% for readiness and 18% for modernisation.

Under the National Defense Authorization Act for FY2015, Congress mandated a National Commission on the Future of the Army. The commission was tasked with examining 'the structure of the Army and policy assumptions related to the size and force mixture of the Army in order to make an assessment of the size and force structure of the Army's active and reserve components'. It conducted its deliberations within the constraints of sizing the army against the president's FY2016 budget, and published its report in January 2016. The commission found that an army of 980,000 is a 'minimally sufficient' force, and is likely insufficient for addressing rapidly emerging threats. Other key commission recommendations (the report had 63) included: stopping further army end-strength cuts; putting an armoured brigade combat team (BCT) in Europe and a combat-aviation brigade (CAB) in South Korea; keeping 24 *Apache* battalions in the army, with four in the National Guard; disbanding two infantry BCTs to provide personnel for other, more pressing demands; and using more multi-component active/reserve units.

Milley has publicly stated that he is supportive of the commission's recommendations, depending on resource availability in the FY2017 budget. He has also worked to mend fences with the National Guard, after 2016 saw the end of what amounted to a three-year-long protest by the National Guard over its structure, particularly the army's Aviation Restructuring Initiative. This initiative had planned to move all AH-64 *Apache* helicopters into the active army.

The army's goal, under current budget constraints, is to establish in FY2017 a force of 30 active BCTs and 11 CABs, along with 28 National Guard BCTs and eight CABs. Furthermore, the DoD has committed to maintaining three BCTs – one *Stryker*, one airborne and one armoured (currently rotational) – in Europe as part of its planned US$3.4bn European Reassurance Initiative.

Finally, the US Army Training and Doctrine Command (TRADOC) followed the chief of staff's lead and reorientated much of its conceptual work on war against hybrid and state threats. Its 2016 *Unified Quest* war game focused on fighting a near-peer adversary in Europe in 2030, expeditionary operations in the Middle East, deterrence in the Asia-Pacific and complex challenges to the homeland. TRADOC's 'Joint Operating Environment 2035' document, published in July 2016, depicts a world of 'contested norms and persistent disorder', caused particularly by China, Russia and other 'revisionist' states. To deter and win in this future, TRADOC is developing a multi-domain battle concept to show how land forces can provide concepts and capabilities to defeat highly capable peer enemies across the land, air, maritime, space and cyber domains.

As such, 2017 may well be the year that the army returns to its focus on high-end adversaries – much as it did with the 'Air–Land Battle' concept in the early 1980s, after the Vietnam War, when it almost exclusively focused on achieving victory against a numerically superior adversary as part of a NATO force. However, the army will have to balance how it prepares for peer adversaries with likely operations against lower-end opponents, while supporting humanitarian and peacekeeping contingencies.

US Marine Corps

The Marine Corps faces similar challenges to other US armed services: the demands of constant operations coupled with the need to reset after 15 years of land-focused stability and counter-insurgency activity, and also to prepare the force to flexibly adapt to future contingencies amid an uncertain security environment. In his March 2016 posture statement before the Senate, the marines' commandant, General Robert Neller, noted five focus areas for the corps: personnel quality, skills and retention; readiness, which has been affected by 'the fiscal reductions and instability of the past few years' (in aviation, for instance, 'aviation units are currently unable to meet our training and mission requirements, primarily due to Ready Basic Aircraft shortfalls'); training, simulation and experimentation, such as re-emphasising operations in a degraded command, control, communications, computing and intelligence environment, and improved war-gaming facilities; integration with the naval and joint force; and modernisation and technology. He continued: 'you can also expect the Marine Corps to continue to pursue technologies that enhance our warfighting capabilities such as unmanned aerial systems (UAS) and robotics, artificial intelligence, 3-D printing, and autonomous technologies that provide tactical and operational advantage'. Finally, at a meeting of the Marine Corps Association in May, Neller made clear the type of adversary on which these efforts will focus: 'I think our enemy is going to be different, I think it's going to be a near-peer enemy.'

Ground-vehicle modernisation remains a priority, with key programmes including the amphibious combat vehicle (ACV) and 'survivability upgrades' to the amphibious assault vehicle and the joint light tactical vehicle. In November 2015, the marines awarded two contracts to BAE Systems and SAIC to build a total of 13 prototype vehicles for the ACV programme, which is designed to eventually provide a replacement for the marines' ageing AAV-7s. The selected ACV, which is due to be an eight-wheeled highly mobile platform, is scheduled for an initial operating capability in 2020. According to the marines, it will 'provide protection akin to the Mine-Resistant Ambush Protected vehicles with landward maneuverability and mobility that is superior to that of the AAV. The ACV will also be outfitted with a precision weapons station, which will provide significant enhanced lethality, and will have a robust swim capability, allowing it to operate within the littorals.' During the transition period, the AAV-7 is being upgraded. According to the marines, this process will ensure that the AAV-7 remains a viable platform until 2035.

In September 2016, the Marine Corps released its new operating concept, 'How an Expeditionary Force Operates in the 21st Century'. The document describes how the service will 'design, develop, and field' a future force to deal with often technologically advanced opponents. There is a focus on the combined-arms-manoeuvre approach of the Marine Air-Ground Task Force (MAGTF) and the corps' expeditionary character, utilising information warfare and networking across all domains. The concept also cites a return to the force's maritime roots, including a 'renewed focus on naval integration', as well as integration with special forces. The marines are experimenting with new training disciplines and adaptation challenges, as seen during the mid-2016 MAGTF *Integrated Exercise 16*, which took place in California in July. It is part of the marines' Sea Dragon 2025 plan, designed to generate innovation in training, equipment and force employment, among other elements. The exercise saw a marine battalion execute a complex five-day exercise integrating unmanned and robotic systems against an adaptable enemy that used 'commercially available and military technologies' and that employed 'advanced hybrid military tactics'.

US Air Force

The United States Air Force (USAF) remains the best-resourced and -equipped air force in the world. However, this does not exempt it from problems. Combat aircraft and tanker fleets are ageing, budgets remain under pressure and a pilot shortfall is likely to only get worse, at least in the short term.

Having succeeded in shepherding a strategic platform, the B-21 dual-capable bomber, through the down-select process in late 2015, the service is now attempting to do the same for the T-X programme to replace the T-38 *Talon* in the lead-in fighter-trainer role. A draft request for proposals was issued to industry in July 2016. The air force could pick a competition winner in the third quarter of 2017, with a requirement for up to 350 of the selected type. Initial operational capability for the T-X is scheduled for 2024.

Training has again come under the spotlight as the air force grapples with a shortfall in tactical-aircraft pilots. A concerted recruitment effort by US airlines would likely begin with a trawl through USAF flight crew, and the aircrew demographics of US commercial carriers suggest this is a clear possibility. The air force is presently 700 pilots short of its full complement, and some projections indicate this will rise over the next two to three years to around 1,000. In attempting to avoid the worst effects of this shortage, aircrew on ground postings are taking multiple jobs in order to try to manage the demand on an already under-strength resource. However, with this increased workload for ground postings, coupled with the continuing high tempo of operations, any airline recruitment drive would pose an additional challenge for USAF pilot numbers.

There has also been continuing pressure on USAF UAV aircrew, with the air force pursuing a 'get well plan' in an attempt to address this. It has raised the retention bonus from US$25,000 to US$35,000 per year for UAV pilots who have reached the end of their active-duty commitment but are willing to remain in the service.

Meanwhile, the air force declared an initial operational capability for its first squadron of F-35A combat aircraft in August 2016. However, the F-35 is the better part of a decade late in entering the inventory, and at a slower production rate than needed, leaving the USAF looking to extend the lives of some of its present combat-aircraft types, including the F-15C *Eagle* and the F-16C *Fighting Falcon*.

The KC-46A *Pegasus* tanker aircraft was cleared for production by the DoD in August 2016, after the aircraft met the so-called 'Milestone C' target. The air force aims to buy 179 of the aircraft in order to replace the KC-135; the first 18 aircraft are expected to be delivered by January 2018.

Alongside a T-X decision in 2017, the USAF is also looking to make progress on its Long-Range Standoff (LRSO) requirement for a replacement to the AGM-86 air-launched cruise missile. Two risk-reduction contracts may be awarded before the end of the year, with a single manufacturer likely to be selected in 2022. The air force wants to introduce the LRSO weapon into service by 2030.

US Navy

In 2016 the US Navy continued to face questions over its ability to sustain its commitments and over the affordability and suitability of its long-term shipbuilding programme. With the backdrop of an evolving strategic environment – and the prospect that this would drive demands, such as that for an increased forward naval presence in and around Europe – the US Navy was in 2016 conducting a new Force Structure Assessment. This could lead to a further adjustment to its headline goal of a fleet of 308 ships. One particular area of focus was thought to be the long-term planning requirement for 48 nuclear-powered attack submarines.

As part of this process, the US Navy was also continuing work on an alternative-carrier study, looking at potential options other than 100,000-tonne nuclear-powered super-carriers. However, there is little expectation that the study will advocate significant change. It was in part a response to ongoing concerns over the cost increases and delays with the new *Ford*-class carriers. Delivery of the first ship, the USS *Gerald R. Ford*, was further delayed until 2017 (see pp. 34–5).

Significantly, the first of the navy's revolutionary 15,000-tonne DDG-1000 destroyers, the USS *Zumwalt*, was delivered in May 2016 and commissioned on 15 October. Originally, over 30 ships were envisaged for this class, but numbers are now down to three. Although costly, the ships and their main guns, which utilise railgun technology, are intended to give the navy a tailored capability for land-attack. Meanwhile, there remains congressional resistance to the navy's proposal to extend the life of its ageing 22-strong *Ticonderoga*-class cruisers by putting half of the ships into maintenance, and updating and reactivating them as the remaining operational ships reach retirement.

The troubled Littoral Combat Ship (LCS)/frigate programme also faced further upheaval. More vessels joined the fleet in 2016, but Secretary of Defense Carter capped total programme numbers at 40 rather than 52. In addition, he called for the navy to select one of the two current LCS designs to be developed as an uprated frigate version that would be used to complete the programme – a process begun by his predecessor, Chuck Hagel. That selection is scheduled for 2018 or 2019. But, in June 2016, the US Government Accountability Office raised new doubts about whether the US Navy's upgraded LCS/frigate plan would produce significant additional capability or survivability.

Efforts to revive offensive-missile capability throughout the surface fleet progressed during the year. In March 2016, there was a test of the anti-ship capability of the SM-6 air-defence missile; then, in July, there was a ship-launched demonstration of the Long-Range Anti-Ship Missile currently under development. In August, it was announced that the USS *Coronado* would be the first LCS to be equipped with the *Harpoon* anti-ship missile, following a test-firing from the ship during the RIMPAC multinational exercise.

The US Navy conducted three freedom-of-navigation operations in the South China Sea in the run-up to the UN Permanent Court of Arbitration's judgement in August. There were also a number of high-profile carrier deployments, including the first dual-carrier exercise in about two years, which took place in the Philippine Sea in June.

Figure 1 *Gerald R. Ford*-class aircraft carrier

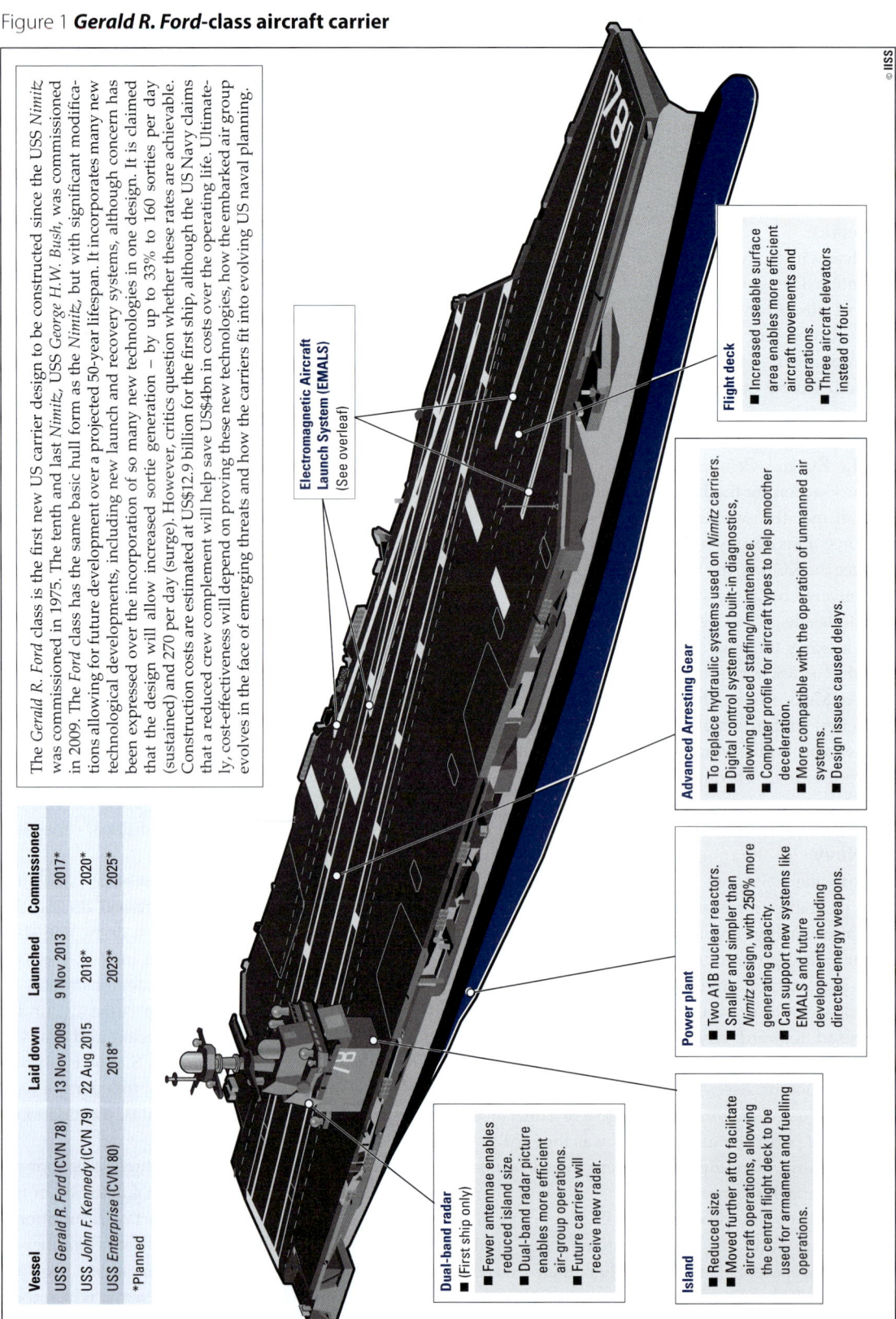

The *Gerald R. Ford* class is the first new US carrier design to be constructed since the USS *Nimitz* was commissioned in 1975. The tenth and last *Nimitz*, USS *George H.W. Bush*, was commissioned in 2009. The *Ford* class has the same basic hull form as the *Nimitz*, but with significant modifications allowing for future development over a projected 50-year lifespan. It incorporates many new technological developments, including new launch and recovery systems, although concern has been expressed over the incorporation of so many new technologies in one design. It is claimed that the design will allow increased sortie generation – by up to 33% to 160 sorties per day (sustained) and 270 per day (surge). However, critics question whether these rates are achievable. Construction costs are estimated at US$12.9 billion for the first ship, although the US Navy claims that a reduced crew complement will help save US$4bn in costs over the operating life. Ultimately, cost-effectiveness will depend on proving these new technologies, how the embarked air group evolves in the face of emerging threats and how the carriers fit into evolving US naval planning.

Vessel	Laid down	Launched	Commissioned
USS *Gerald R. Ford* (CVN 78)	13 Nov 2009	9 Nov 2013	2017*
USS *John F. Kennedy* (CVN 79)	22 Aug 2015	2018*	2020*
USS *Enterprise* (CVN 80)	2018*	2023*	2025*

*Planned

Electromagnetic Aircraft Launch System (EMALS)
(See overleaf)

Flight deck
- Increased useable surface area enables more efficient aircraft movements and operations.
- Three aircraft elevators instead of four.

Advanced Arresting Gear
- To replace hydraulic systems used on *Nimitz* carriers.
- Digital control system and built-in diagnostics, allowing reduced staffing/maintenance.
- Computer profile for aircraft types to help smoother deceleration.
- More compatible with the operation of unmanned air systems.
- Design issues caused delays.

Power plant
- Two A1B nuclear reactors.
- Smaller and simpler than *Nimitz* design, with 250% more generating capacity.
- Can support new systems like EMALS and future developments including directed-energy weapons.

Dual-band radar
- (First ship only)
- Fewer antennae enables reduced island size.
- Dual-band radar picture enables more efficient air-group operations.
- Future carriers will receive new radar.

Island
- Reduced size.
- Moved further aft to facilitate aircraft operations, allowing the central flight deck to be used for armament and fuelling operations.

© IISS

Figure 1 *Gerald R. Ford*-class aircraft carrier

Current *Nimitz* carrier air wing

Aircraft type	Composition	Numbers
Fighter/ground attack	• 1 or 2 sqns of F/A-18C • 2 or 3 sqns of F/A-18E/F	44 4 or 5
Electronic warfare	1 sqn of either 4 EA-6B or 5 EA-18G	4
Airborne early-warning and control	1 sqn of E-2C	4
Multi-role helicopter	1 sqn of MH-60S	8
Anti-submarine-warfare helicopter	1 sqn of MH-60R	11
	Total	71 or 72

Possible carrier air wing for 2025

Aircraft type	Composition	Numbers
Fighter/ground attack	• 2 sqns of F-35C • 1 sqn of F/A-18E • 1 sqn of F/A-18F	20 12 12
Electronic warfare	1 sqn of EA-18G	5
Airborne early-warning and control	1 sqn of E-2D	5
Tanker & ISR UAV	1 sqn of MQ-25A *Stingray*	6
Multi-role & anti-submarine-warfare helicopter	MH-60R/S or replacement	19*
	Total	79

*Includes helicopters operated off other vessels in the carrier battle group
Sources: US Navy, CNAS

Future embarked air component

E-2D *Hawkeye*
- Improved radar, networking and battle-management capabilities.
- Possible future ballistic-missile-defence capability.

F-35C *Lightning* II Joint Strike Fighter
- Fifth-generation combat aircraft.

MQ-25A *Stingray*
- Unmanned in-flight refuelling aircraft and surveillance platform.
- Planned to relieve workload on F/A-18 fleet.
- Potential future development of surveillance and strike roles.

Electromagnetic Aircraft Launch System (EMALS)

EMALS represents a significant change in carrier-launch technology, with an electrical system replacing the steam catapult. This is intended to provide a range of improvements in:

Power
- Designed to provide 29% more overall power than the standard US Navy steam catapult (total of 122 MJ).
- Power delivery can be calibrated more effectively, so catering for a wider range of aircraft characteristics, crucially including UAVs.
- Smoother acceleration, reducing airframe wear and tear.

Size
- Reduced volume and weight in comparison to the steam catapult. At a weight of 486 tonnes, mostly on the top-side of the vessel, this machinery has the potential to affect ship handling in heavy seas.

Maintenance
- Along with the new arresting gear, this is part of a move towards fully electric ship-wide power delivery and distribution. Reducing the requirement for steam generation should simplify overall maintenance.
- EMALS has a modular design, intended to ease maintenance.
- However, during tests, problems with isolating electric currents in EMALS components has complicated maintenance. Until solved, this could prove to be a greater maintenance challenge, on operations, than the steam-catapult system.
- The USN's new railguns use similar power systems. Tests on these show that constant use produces large amounts of thermal energy, which is potentially damaging. This has implications for EMALS, such as extra cooling requirements.

Figure 2 US Navy carriers: maintenance and availability

The US Navy's carrier fleet is under considerable strain. The fleet is supposed to be 11 strong – a number mandated by Congress. However, a supposedly temporary reduction to ten hulls, following the retirement of USS *Enterprise*, has been prolonged by delays in the delivery of the new USS *Gerald R. Ford*. A major factor in carrier availability and operational planning is the schedule of refuelling and complex overhauls, essentially mid-life modernisations, which last approximately three years. But the high tempo of recent operations has reduced readiness and increased wear and tear on the force. Together with budget and shipyard cuts, this has meant that some of the regular maintenance schedules have been extended. For the Pentagon, this has compounded operational-planning problems as deployments have had to be adjusted and in some cases extended, and is creating periodic carrier-deployment gaps, such as in the Gulf in late 2015. Initiatives like the Optimised Fleet Response Plan are designed to reduce the duration of deployments, increase their predictability and rebuild readiness. But such efforts are themselves under strain due to continuing high operational demand.

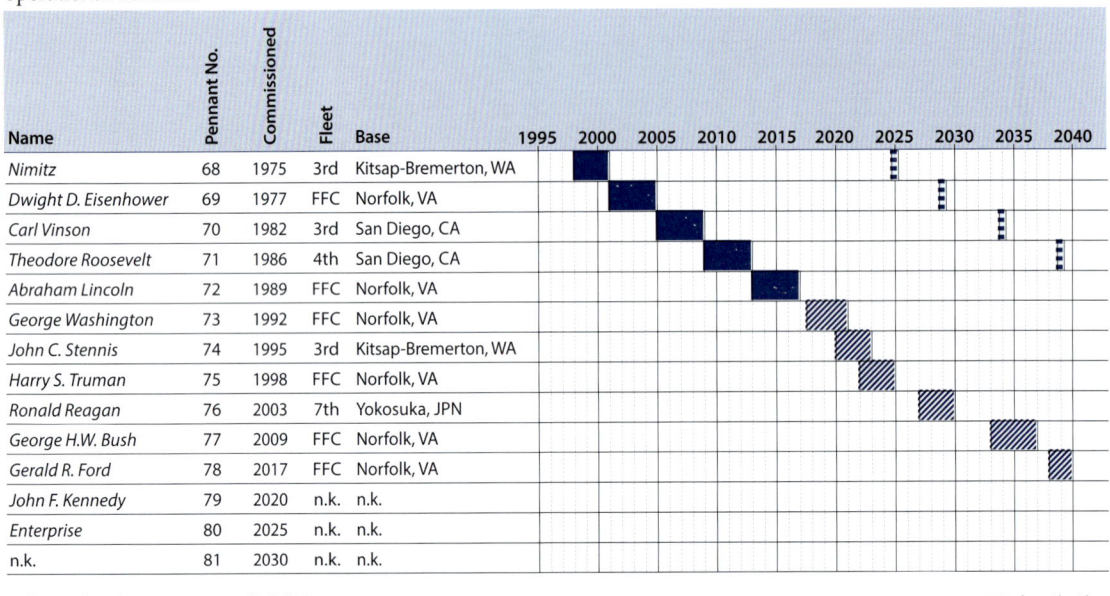

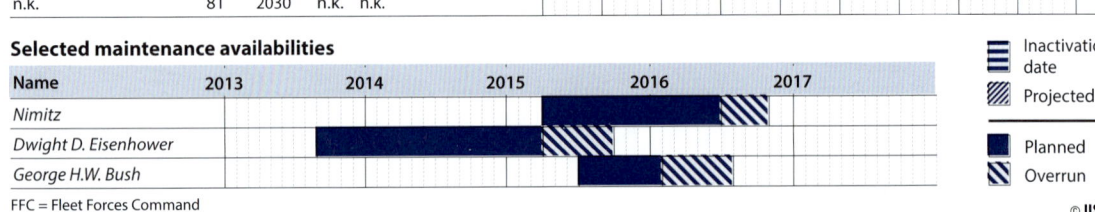

FFC = Fleet Forces Command
Sources: Huntington Ingalls Industries, US Navy, Defense News

Unusually, the US Navy also briefly undertook concurrent operations with two carriers in the Mediterranean for the first time in several years. These included strikes from the USS *Harry S. Truman* against ISIS targets in Syria. Despite this well-publicised surge in carrier activity (following a widely noted gap in the carrier presence in the Persian Gulf in late 2015), the US Navy still faced a challenge in stabilising and sustaining its carrier deployments (see above).

US Coast Guard

As with the coastguards of other countries, there has been a renewed focus on the prospects of the US Coast Guard taking further maritime-security responsibilities, despite significant budget pressures on its major recapitalisation programme. Amid concerns that this modernisation plan will not fully meet future demands, in 2016 Congress provided funds for a ninth *Legend*-class National Security Cutter, although this was not sought by the coast guard. A tenth cutter could be added by Congress in FY2017. However, there is equal concern about the impact of this order on funding for the rest of the programme. In September 2016, Florida's Eastern Shipbuilding won the US$110m contract to complete detailed design work and start the construction phase of a new class of smaller offshore-patrol cutters, with the first planned to be delivered in FY2021. The contract could eventually cover up to nine vessels, at a total cost of US$2.38bn. With an increased focus on the lack of modern US capabilities to operate in the Arctic, particularly when compared to Russia, the coast guard is also seeking significant funding from 2017 for a new polar icebreaker, construction of which would start in 2020, at a total estimated cost of US$1bn.

DEFENCE ECONOMICS

FY2017 Defense Budget Request

The president's FY2017 budget for the DoD requested a total of US$590.5bn: US$523.9bn for the base discretionary budget, US$7.8bn in mandatory spending and an additional US$58.8bn in discretionary supplemental funding for the Overseas Contingency Operations (OCO) fund, for war-related spending. The total FY2017 request includes US$148bn for the army, US$166.9bn for the air force (which by tradition includes the DoD's classified spending), US$164.9bn for the navy and US$103bn for defence-wide spending.

The US$112.1bn requested for procurement for FY2017 is US$8.9bn less than was enacted for FY2016 in real terms – a 7.4% decrease. Procurement spending has been crowded out by faster-growing military-personnel and operations and maintenance (O&M) costs, as well as decisions to reduce procurement spending in order to comply with the Budget Control Act of 2011 caps. Between FY2001 and FY2017, O&M spending rose at a rate of 2.73% annually, making it the fastest-growing share of defence spending. Overall, people – including uniformed and civilian personnel – account for nearly half of the total defence budget.

The FY2017 OCO request includes US$41.7bn for *Operation Freedom's Sentinel* in Afghanistan and US$7.5bn for *Operation Inherent Resolve* in Iraq. This would support 3,550 troops on the ground in the region, principally for training and partnering with

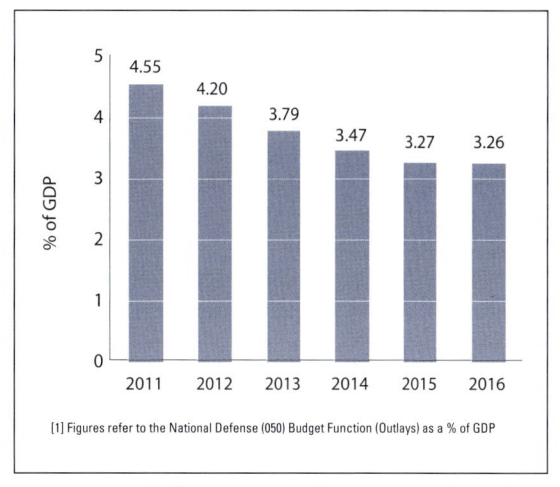

Figure 3 **US defence expenditure** as % of GDP[1]

[1] Figures refer to the National Defense (050) Budget Function (Outlays) as a % of GDP

Table 1 **US National Defense Budget Function and other selected budgets 1996, 2007–17**

(US$bn)	National Defense Budget Function		Department of Defense		Atomic Energy Defense Activities	Department of Homeland Security	Department of Veterans Affairs	Total Federal Government Outlays	Total Federal Budget Surplus/ Deficit
FY	BA	Outlay	BA	Outlay	BA	BA	BA		
1996	266.2	265.7	254.5	253.2	11.7	n.a.	38.7	1,560	-107
2007	625.8	551.3	603.0	528.6	17.2	39.7	79.5	2,729	-161
2008	696.2	616.1	674.7	594.7	16.6	50.6	88.4	2,983	-459
2009	697.6	661.0	667.6	636.8	23.0	46.0	96.9	3,518	-1,413
2010	721.2	693.5	695.6	666.7	18.2	45.4	124.3	3,457	-1,294
2011	717.0	705.6	691.5	678.1	18.5	41.6	122.8	3,603	-1,300
2012	681.4	677.9	655.4	650.9	18.3	45.9	124.0	3,537	-1,087
2013	610.2	633.4	585.2	607.8	17.5	61.9	135.9	3,455	-680
2014	622.3	603.5	595.7	577.9	18.4	44.1	165.7	3,506	-485
2015	598.4	589.6	570.9	562.5	19.0	45.3	160.5	3,668.3	-438.4
2016 est	615.4	604.5	587.1	576.3	20.0	46.9	163.9	3,951.3	-615.8
2017 est	619.5	617.0	590.6	586.8	20.5	47.0	178.7	4,147.2	-503.5

Notes
FY = Fiscal Year (1 October–30 September)
[1] The National Defense Budget Function subsumes funding for the DoD, the Department of Energy Atomic Energy Defense Activities and some smaller support agencies (including Federal Emergency Management and Selective Service System). It does not include funding for International Security Assistance (under International Affairs), the Veterans Administration, the US Coast Guard (Department of Homeland Security), nor for the National Aeronautics and Space Administration (NASA). Funding for civil projects administered by the DoD is excluded from the figures cited here.
[2] Early in each calendar year, the US government presents its defence budget to Congress for the next fiscal year, which begins on 1 October. The government also presents its Future Years Defense Program (FYDP), which covers the next fiscal year plus the following five. Until approved by Congress, the budget is called the Budget Request; after approval, it becomes the Budget Authority (BA).

Iraqi security forces in the fight against ISIS, and would provide US$600m and US$250m to train and equip Iraqi forces and Syrian rebel groups respectively. At US$3.4bn, the FY2017 request for the European Reassurance Initiative is a fourfold increase over the funds appropriated for FY2016. It would fund US$1.9bn of enhanced pre-positioning in Eastern Europe, principally army equipment sets; double funding for an increased US military presence to US$1.05bn; and increase funding for improved infrastructure, exercises and training. Meanwhile, US$5.2bn of the OCO request is allocated to base-budget needs. A senior DoD official recently acknowledged that there is about US$30bn in base-budget costs currently funded through the OCO account. While the DoD has not specifically enumerated these costs, they support the military's regional presence in the Middle East.

After adjusting for inflation, the US$582.7bn of discretionary funding requested for the DoD for FY2017 is US$8bn, or 1.35%, lower than the FY2016 enacted appropriations. Significantly, the total FY2017 DoD request of US$590bn is 25% lower than the FY2010 peak of US$784bn, at the height of the wars in Iraq and Afghanistan, but about 12% above average spending under the Reagan administration. At US$58.8bn, the FY2017 OCO request is about 10% of the total defence budget, down from a height of 28% in FY2007 and FY2008. Although less in absolute dollars, the drawdown in defence spending between FY2010 and FY2015 has been faster than any since the end of the Korean War, at a compound annual growth rate of -5.5%. Even as total defence spending reached historical highs in real terms over the past 15 years, it reached historical lows as a percentage of GDP.

The Future Years Defense Program (FYDP) projection of the base defence budget calls for spending to rise by about US$23bn in FY2018, before largely holding steady at that level to the end of FY2026. However, US defence and non-defence federal spending will be constrained to the end of FY2021 by caps imposed by the Budget Control Act of 2011. This bill was enacted to reduce government spending after a failure to reach legislative agreement about overall federal spending on discretionary and entitlement programmes, driven by concerns about deficit spending and federal debt. The bill imposed equal but separate ceilings on defence and non-defence discretionary spending from FY2013 to FY2021. It is enforced by an automatic 'sequester' if the amounts allocated to defence or non-defence programmes by Congress exceed that fiscal year's cap. In a sequester, funding for all defence and non-defence programmes is reduced evenly to bring spending back below the appropriate spending-cap level. The Budget Control Act of 2011 led to sharp initial decreases in both defence and non-defence spending, but has been amended for every fiscal year since FY2013 to allow for modest increases in the caps.

The DoD has consistently proposed short- and long-term budget plans that would require more funding than allowed under the Budget Control Act caps. Over the remaining four years of the current Budget Control Act caps (FY2018–FY2021), the FY2017 projection of the base defence-budget-funding needs is US$105.3bn greater than the budget

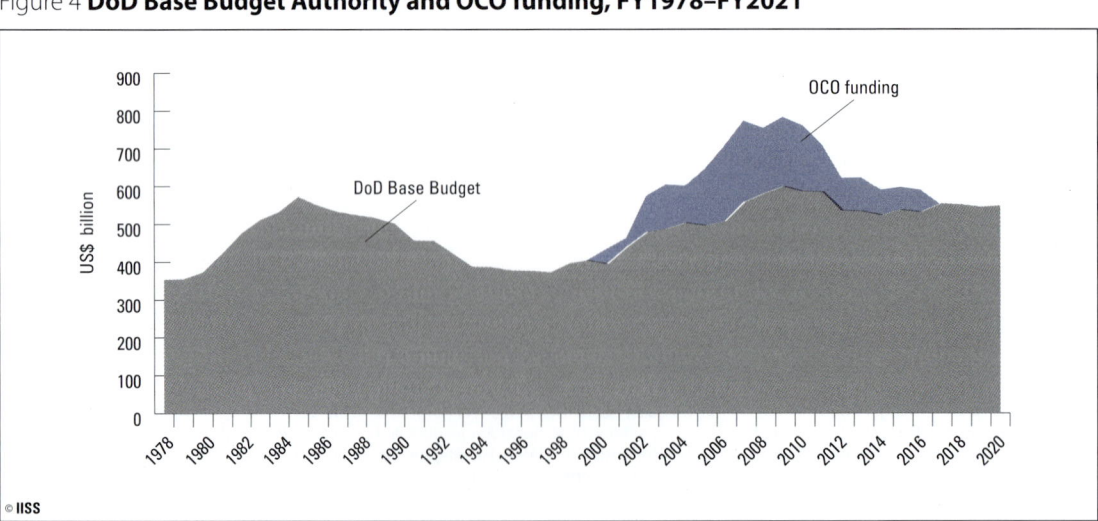

Figure 4 **DoD Base Budget Authority and OCO funding, FY1978–FY2021**

caps in constant FY2017 dollars – an indication that the DoD's plans do not match current budgetary limitations. Including the US$30bn in OCO funding that the DoD relies on to meet base-budget needs, the actual gap rises to between US$50bn and US$60bn annually – about 10% of the total defence budget.

Budget turmoil continues

However, the FY2017 base discretionary-budget request of US$523.9bn for defence is consistent with the caps on defence and non-defence discretionary spending established by the Budget Control Act, as amended most recently by the Bipartisan Budget Act of 2015. This two-year agreement raised the caps for base-budget defence and non-defence spending by US$25bn each for FY2016 and by US$15bn each for FY2017. It also set US$58.8bn as the targeted level for OCO spending in FY2017.

The Bipartisan Budget Act of 2015, the result of a budget deal reached in October 2015, was intended to provide much-needed stability for the DoD for FY2016 and FY2017, and to avert the turbulence that would be caused by beginning FY2017 under a continuing resolution. However, the lack of an appropriations bill in Congress before the beginning of the FY2016 fiscal year on 1 October 2015 forced the DoD to enter FY2016 under three 'continuing resolutions', spanning 1 October–11 December, 11–16 December, and 16–22 December 2015. A continuing resolution extends the appropriations level of the prior fiscal year for a specified amount of time, with a slight adjustment for inflation, allowing the government to continue spending money and avoiding a government shutdown. But utilising the prior year's funding levels for programmes precludes starting new ones or shifting funding between programmes or appropriation types. New projects are prohibited and those that have large increases in requested funding from the prior year are effectively on hold until Congress passes an appropriations bill. As has become the norm in recent years, these short-term continuations of the FY2015 appropriations levels allowed the government to continue functioning until the passage of the FY2016 consolidated appropriations bill on 18 December 2015. The routine use of continuing resolutions in lieu of timely appropriations bills has forced the Pentagon to effectively compress the fiscal year into three quarters.

As foreshadowed by the December 2015 budget fight, the two-year deal broke down entirely early in the FY2017 budgeting process. The fundamental differences between and among Republicans and Democrats in Congress over the appropriate balance between defence and non-defence spending, the level of OCO funding and appropriate military force structure remain unresolved.

Although both are controlled by Republicans, the House of Representatives and the Senate have taken different approaches. The House defence-policy bill directs US$18bn of the total US$58.8bn OCO funding to the base budget, principally for additional procurement funding towards items on the DoD's unfunded priority lists. It also terminates the authorisation for OCO funding on 1 April 2017, in an effort to force (or allow) an incoming administration to request additional money to support war-funding needs. Similarly, the House defence-appropriations bill redirects US$16bn from the OCO to the base budget. The Senate defence-authorisation and -appropriations bills fund the OCO at the requested US$58.8bn without redirecting OCO funding to base-budget spending. However, Senate Democrats have blocked the defence-appropriations bill, citing concerns that Senate Republicans would fund defence at the negotiated higher levels, while funding non-defence government spending – including homeland security, foreign affairs, healthcare, education and other priorities – without the US$15bn increase for FY2017 agreed in the budget deal. These budget debates, and disagreements between the administration and Congress about military reform, force-structure mandates, military-base realignment and closures, reorganisation of some of the DoD bureaucracy, and Guantanamo detainees, led the White House to threaten to veto the bills.

President Barack Obama's July 2016 announcement that 8,400, rather than 5,500, US troops will remain in Afghanistan until early 2017 led to increased pressure from Republicans for additional OCO funding. In late September 2016, Secretary Carter announced plans for the DoD to ask for an estimated US$3bn–6bn after the elections. The recent public acknowledgement that the DoD has relied on about US$30bn in OCO funding for long-term forward-presence and readiness requirements also undermines the administration's arguments against the 'budget gimmick' of adding additional funding to OCO to support base-budget requirements – the central disagreement with Republicans in the FY2017 fight over the defence-appropriations and -policy bills. This revelation could also alienate congressional Democrats, who may feel that the administration has been short-changing domestic-spending priorities while protecting the

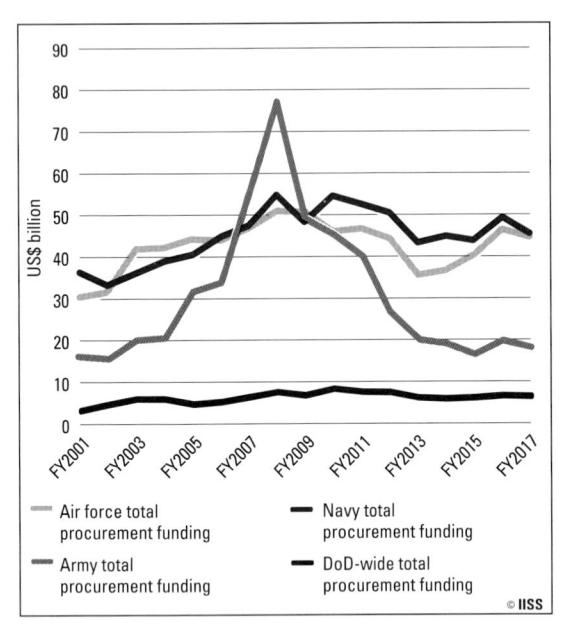

Figure 5 **Total US armed-forces-equipment procurement funding (including OCO), FY2001–FY2017**

Pentagon's funding, violating the stated principle of even relief from the budget caps.

A bright spot came on 29 September 2016 with the smooth passage of a continuing resolution that allowed FY2016 funding levels to continue until 9 December 2016, and that avoided a deeply politicised government shutdown immediately before the elections. The conclusion of this year's budget impasse was contingent on the results of the 8 November elections. Although president-elect Donald Trump was expected to favour higher levels of defence spending, his precise policy position remained unclear at the time of writing. Due to the divisive politics around defence spending and the lack of incentive to compromise during the so-called 'lame-duck' session before the change in government, there was little prospect of a budget deal by 9 December 2016, likely forcing a series of continuing resolutions into January 2017.

Planning for the future

Within the Pentagon, there are strong debates about the right balance between high-end capabilities suitable for conflict with a peer or near-peer adversary, and increased capacity for global presence, with greater numbers of less capable but perhaps more affordable systems. Innovation is a focus across all services and within the DoD, as evidenced by the department's Third Offset Strategy. This focuses on high-end, next-generation technologies and capabilities in priority areas such as surface strike, countering the anti-access challenge, submarine and other undersea capabilities, human–machine teaming, and cyber and electronic warfare.

With large, high-priority procurement programmes already under way, including those for the F-35, the *Virginia*-class attack submarine, the *Ford*-class carrier, the *Arleigh Burke*-class destroyer, the B-21 bomber and the KC-46 tanker, the navy and the air force are well positioned to be the budgetary beneficiaries of a focus on higher-end capabilities. Army leaders are aggressively pushing for greater funding, with Army Chief of Staff General Milley arguing that the current budget is insufficient to fully fund present-day readiness, the army's end-strength target (450,000 regular troops) and the modernisation of army equipment. Beyond FY2021, the Pentagon faces a 'bow wave' of procurement spending, rising from the FY2017 request of US$173bn to an estimated peak of US$191bn by FY2023, as concurrent acquisition programmes enter full-rate production.

With personnel costs accounting for nearly half of the Pentagon's budget, personnel reforms could save substantial money over the long term. After creating a hybrid pension and defined-contribution retirement-savings plan for new service members in the FY2016 bills, Congress's appetite for further reforms is low. The military-healthcare system is ripe for reform, but Congress has made only slight adjustments to co-payments made by military retirees in the past few years. In the FY2017 bills, the House and the Senate continued recent efforts at defence-acquisition reform using sharply divergent approaches, with the former promoting rapid prototyping, agility and open architectures, and the latter major acquisition bureaucracy changes.

CANADA

In April 2016, the Liberal government under Prime Minister Justin Trudeau's administration launched a new Defence Policy Review, due to report in early 2017, on the premise that a thoroughgoing assessment of post-Afghanistan defence and security needs had yet to be undertaken. The last major review was the 2008 Canada First Defence Strategy of the previous Conservative administration.

Statements from the new government suggested that the review could see a reorientation of defence needs and a change to the ways in which the Canadian armed forces are employed in the future, with less emphasis on expeditionary combat missions. Air and maritime requirements seemed set to take priority at the likely expense of land forces. A public-consultation process on the review took place between April and July 2016.

However, this left a number of major procurement programmes – both long-standing and, in several cases, long-delayed – facing further uncertainty. Since the 1990s, governments of both parties have been accused of failing to provide sufficient defence funding at key periods. In March 2016, the federal budget included a new delay in some C$3.7 billion (US$2.8bn) of defence-procurement funding until 2020 or later. There has also been sustained public criticism of the length of time it has taken to develop some programmes. The net result has been the emergence of capability gaps (particularly in maritime-logistics support) and questions over whether and when they will be filled.

The change of administration has thrown into even sharper focus the fate of the controversial plan to purchase 65 F-35 Joint Strike Fighters. In opposition, the Liberal Party expressed support for a combat aircraft that emphasised North American air defence rather than a stealthy first-strike capability. The government announced in late 2016 a new competition to replace Canada's CF-18 *Hornet* fighters and an interim buy of *Super Hornet*s.

In May 2016, the government announced modifications to the National Shipbuilding Procurement Strategy in order to produce a sustainable industrial plan for the recapitalisation of naval and coastguard platforms. It promised improved oversight and transparency for programmes. This came amid official acknowledgement that the total bill for the 15-ship Canadian Surface Combatant (CSC) plan could be significantly higher than the C$26.2bn (US$19.9bn) budgeted.

The navy has been particularly hard-hit by enduring procurement problems, with significant reductions in capability, notably in air defence and afloat support. Following the withdrawal of both of the navy's elderly replenishment vessels, HMCS *Protecteur* and HMCS *Preserver*, it has had to rely on agreements first with the Chilean and then the Spanish navies for afloat support, plus the modification of a commercial vessel as an interim solution from 2017 until the first *Queenston*-class Joint Support Ship becomes available in 2021.

The CSC project, designed to replace the navy's *Iroquois*-class destroyers and *Halifax*-class frigates, now looks likely to be essentially an off-the-shelf rather than bespoke design, albeit with distinct variants to account for the differing roles of the destroyers and frigates being replaced. Among the other main planks of the maritime re-equipment programme, the first of the much-delayed *Harry DeWolf*-class Arctic/offshore-patrol ships is now in-build, with the second due to begin construction in the latter half of 2016. The navy is also seeking to upgrade and extend the lives of its *Victoria*-class submarines until their replacements can be introduced in the mid-2030s.

By the end of February 2016, the new administration had enacted its election pledge to cease Canadian airstrikes against Islamic State, also known as ISIS or ISIL, targets in Iraq and Syria. By then, Canadian CF-18 *Hornet*s had carried out some 1,378 sorties in support of US-led coalition operations. However, the deployment of one CC-150T *Polaris* air-to-air refuelling aircraft and up to two CP-140 *Aurora* surveillance aircraft was maintained. Furthermore, in what was described as a 'refocusing' of the Canadian coalition effort, Canada tripled the size of its train, advise and assist mission with the Iraqi security forces. The total number of personnel committed to what Canada terms Operation Impact rose from approximately 650 to about 830, supported by three CH-146 *Griffon* tactical transport helicopters. Canadian armed forces medical personnel were also attached to an Australian-led medical facility at Taji, in Iraq.

Although Canada continues to fare poorly when it comes to the NATO defence-spending target, spending under 1% of GDP, to underscore its commitment to the Alliance, Canada confirmed at the 2016 Warsaw Summit that it would be one of four framework nations to lead a NATO battlegroup as part of the enhanced Alliance forward presence in Europe. Canada will provide a core of 450 personnel to the battlegroup in Latvia. It also reaffirmed the commitment of a frigate to NATO maritime operations and an air task force of up to six CF-18 *Hornet*s, although when and where these will deploy had not been confirmed (aircraft have in the past deployed to Iceland and for the Baltic Air Policing mission in Lithuania). Canada has also deployed some 220 troops on rotation to Poland. Meanwhile, it has maintained around 200 personnel in Ukraine for support activities as part of Western capacity-building efforts with the Ukrainian armed forces.

Canada CAN

Canadian Dollar $		2015	2016	2017
GDP	C$	1.98tr	2.02tr	
	US$	1.55tr	1.53tr	
per capita	US$	43,280	42,319	
Growth	%	1.1	1.2	
Inflation	%	1.1	1.6	
Def bdgt	C$	17.7bn	17.3	
	US$	13.8bn	13.2bn	
US$1= C$		1.28	1.32	

Population 35,362,905

Age	0 – 14	15 – 19	20 – 24	25 – 29	30 – 64	65 plus
Male	7.9%	2.9%	3.4%	3.4%	23.9%	8.1%
Female	7.5%	2.7%	3.2%	3.3%	23.6%	10.1%

Capabilities

The Liberal government has sought to emphasise commitments to NATO and North American defence, and also its enhanced support and training role in the coalition against ISIS following Canada's withdrawal from combat air operations. Throughout much of 2016, the new administration was engaged in a major defence-policy review which was likely to refocus key aspects of policy, arguing that there had been significant changes to the strategic context in which the Canadian armed forces operated. The 2016 federal budget included further deferments in procurement spending beyond those announced by the previous administration. Officials argued that the industrial base could not support the planned procurement in the time frame previously planned. But there have been persistent criticisms that the resources available have failed to match procurement plans and recapitalisation needs. Spending cuts in recent years have particularly affected the procurement schedules of major programmes, sustainment, readiness and the maintenance of forces, with the navy especially affected by the gap in afloat-tanker support. The announcement of streamlined procurement using an adapted off-the-shelf design for the future surface combatant will have implications for industrial capability. The government in late 2016 announced a new competition to replace Canada's CF-18 fighters, with an interim buy of 18 *Super Hornet*s until the replacement arrives. The new government had, in its election material, raised the likelihood that Canada would finally abandon its participation in the F-35 Joint Strike Fighter programme, and seek alternative options. Canada retains training staff in Iraq, and announced an expanded presence in Europe. Ottawa's status as a framework nation for one of four new NATO multinational battlegroups includes a commitment to deploy and sustain a battalion and a headquarters. Canada is also sustaining a forward frigate deployment to NATO maritime forces in Europe. (See pp. 40–1.)

ACTIVE 63,000 (Army 34,800 Navy 8,300 Air Force 19,900) **Paramilitary 4,500**

RESERVE 30,000 (Army 23,450 Navy 4,600 Air 1,950)

ORGANISATIONS BY SERVICE

Space
EQUIPMENT BY TYPE
SATELLITES • SPACE SURVEILLANCE 1 *Sapphire*

Army 34,800
FORCES BY ROLE
MANOEUVRE
Mechanised
1 (1st) mech bde gp (1 armd regt, 2 mech inf bn, 1 lt inf bn, 1 arty regt, 1 cbt engr regt, 1 log bn)
2 (2nd & 5th) mech bde gp (1 armd recce regt, 2 mech inf bn, 1 lt inf bn, 1 arty regt, 1 cbt engr regt, 1 log bn)
COMBAT SUPPORT
1 engr regt
3 MP pl
AIR DEFENCE
1 SAM regt
EQUIPMENT BY TYPE
ARMOURED FIGHTING VEHICLES
MBT 82: 42 *Leopard* 2A4 (trg role); 20 *Leopard* 2A4M (being upgraded); 20 *Leopard* 2A6M; (61 *Leopard* 1C2 in store)
RECCE ε160 LAV-25 *Coyote*
APC 1,155
  APC (T) 332: 64 Bv-206; 235 M113; 33 M577 (CP)
  APC (W) 810: 545 LAV-III *Kodiak* (incl 33 RWS); ε90 LAV 6.0; 175 LAV *Bison* (incl 10 EW, 32 amb, 32 repair, 64 recovery)
AUV 13: 7 *Cougar*; 6 TAPV
ENGINEERING & MAINTENANCE VEHICLES
AEV 8: 5 *Buffalo*; 3 *Leopard* 2 AEV
ARV 13: 2 BPz-3 *Büffel*; 11 *Leopard* 2 ARV
ANTI-TANK/ANTI-INFRASTRUCTURE
RCL 84mm 1,075 *Carl Gustav*
ARTILLERY 287
TOWED 163 **105mm** 126: 98 C3 (M101); 28 LG1 MkII; **155mm** 37 M777
MOR 124: **81mm** 100; **SP 81mm** 24 LAV *Bison*
UNMANNED AERIAL VEHICLES • ISR • Light *Skylark*
AIR DEFENCE • SAM • Point-defence *Starburst*

Reserve Organisations 23,450

Canadian Rangers 5,000 Reservists
Provide a limited military presence in Canada's northern, coastal and isolated areas. Sovereignty, public-safety and surveillance roles
FORCES BY ROLE
MANOEUVRE
Other
5 (patrol) ranger gp (187 patrols)

Army Reserves 18,450 Reservists
Most units have only coy-sized establishments
FORCES BY ROLE
COMMAND
10 bde gp HQ

MANOEUVRE
Reconnaissance
18 recce regt (sqn)
Light
51 inf regt (coy)
COMBAT SUPPORT
16 fd arty regt (bty)
3 indep fd arty bty
10 cbt engr regt (coy)
1 EW regt (sqn)
4 int coy
10 sigs regt (coy)
COMBAT SERVICE SUPPORT
10 log bn (coy)
3 MP coy

Royal Canadian Navy 8,300; 4,600 reserve (12,900 total)
EQUIPMENT BY TYPE
SUBMARINES • SSK 4:
 4 *Victoria* (ex-UK *Upholder*) with 6 single 533mm TT with Mk48 *Sea Arrow* HWT (3 currently operational)
PRINCIPAL SURFACE COMBATANTS 13
 DESTROYERS • DDHM 1 mod *Iroquois* with 1 Mk41 29-cell VLS with SM-2MR SAM, 2 triple 324mm ASTT with Mk46 LWT, 1 *Phalanx* CIWS, 1 76mm gun (capacity 2 SH-3 (CH-124) *Sea King* ASW hel)
 FRIGATES • FFGHM 12 *Halifax* with 2 quad lnchr with RGM-84 Block II *Harpoon* AShM, 2 octuple Mk48 VLS with RIM-7P *Sea Sparrow* SAM/RIM-162 ESSM SAM, 2 twin 324mm ASTT with Mk46 LWT, 1 *Phalanx* CIWS, 1 57mm gun (capacity 1 SH-3 (CH-124) *Sea King* ASW hel) (rolling modernisation programme until 2017)
**MINE WARFARE • MINE COUNTERMEASURES •
MCO** 12 *Kingston*
LOGISTICS AND SUPPORT 10
 AGOR 1 *Quest*
 AX 9: **AXL** 8 *Orca*; **AXS** 1 *Oriole*

Reserves 4,600 reservists
24 units tasked with crewing 10 of the 12 MCOs, harbour defence & naval control of shipping

Royal Canadian Air Force (RCAF) 19,900
FORCES BY ROLE
FIGHTER/GROUND ATTACK
 4 sqn with F/A-18A/B *Hornet* (CF-18AM/BM)
ANTI-SUBMARINE WARFARE
 2 sqn with SH-3 *Sea King* (CH-124)
MARITIME PATROL
 2 sqn with P-3 *Orion* (CP-140 *Aurora*)
SEARCH & RESCUE/TRANSPORT
 4 sqn with AW101 *Merlin* (CH-149 *Cormorant*); C-130E/H/H-30/J-30 (CC-130) *Hercules*
 1 sqn with DHC-5 (CC-115) *Buffalo*
TANKER/TRANSPORT
 1 sqn with A310/A310 MRTT (CC-150/CC-150T)
 1 sqn with KC-130H
TRANSPORT
 1 sqn with C-17A (CC-177) *Globemaster*
 1 sqn with CL-600 (CC-144B)
 1 (utl) sqn with DHC-6 (CC-138) *Twin Otter*
TRAINING
 1 sqn with F/A-18A/B *Hornet* (CF-18AM/BM)
 1 sqn with P-3 *Orion* (CP-140 *Aurora*)
 1 sqn with SH-3 *Sea King* (CH-124)
TRANSPORT HELICOPTER
 5 sqn with Bell 412 (CH-146 *Griffon*)
 3 (cbt spt) sqn with Bell 412 (CH-146 *Griffon*)
 1 (Spec Ops) sqn with Bell 412 (CH-146 *Griffon* – OPCON Canadian Special Operations Command)
 1 sqn with CH-47F (CH-147F) *Chinook*
EQUIPMENT BY TYPE
AIRCRAFT 95 combat capable
 FGA 77: 59 F/A-18A (CF-18AM) *Hornet*; 18 F/A-18B (CF-18BM) *Hornet*
 ASW 18 P-3 *Orion* (CP-140M *Aurora*)
 TKR/TPT 7: 2 A310 MRTT (CC-150T); 5 KC-130H
 TPT 59: **Heavy** 5 C-17A (CC-177) *Globemaster*; **Medium** 35: 10 C-130E (CC-130) *Hercules*; 6 C-130H (CC-130) *Hercules*; 2 C-130H-30 (CC-130) *Hercules*; 17 C-130J-30 (CC-130) *Hercules*; **Light** 10: 6 DHC-5 (CC-115) *Buffalo*; 4 DHC-6 (CC-138) *Twin Otter*; **PAX** 9: 3 A310 (CC-150 *Polaris*); 6 CL-600 (CC-144B/C)
 TRG 4 DHC-8 (CT-142)
HELICOPTERS
 ASW 35 26 SH-3 (CH-124) *Sea King*; 9 CH-148 *Cyclone*
 MRH 68 Bell 412 (CH-146 *Griffon*)
 TPT 29: **Heavy** 15 CH-47F (CH-147F) *Chinook*; **Medium** 14 AW101 *Merlin* (CH-149 *Cormorant*)
RADARS 53
 AD RADAR • NORTH WARNING SYSTEM 47: 11 AN/FPS-117 (range 200nm); 36 AN/FPS-124 (range 80nm)
 STRATEGIC 6: 4 Coastal; 2 Transportable
AIR-LAUNCHED MISSILES
 ASM AGM-65 *Maverick*
 AAM • IR AIM-9L *Sidewinder*; **SARH** AIM-7M *Sparrow*
 ARH AIM-120C AMRAAM
BOMBS
 Laser-guided: GBU-10/GBU-12/GBU-16 *Paveway* II; GBU-24 *Paveway* III

NATO Flight Training Canada
EQUIPMENT BY TYPE
AIRCRAFT
 TRG 45: 26 T-6A *Texan* II (CT-156 *Harvard* II); 19 *Hawk* 115 (CT-155) (advanced wpns/tactics trg)

Contracted Flying Services – Southport
EQUIPMENT BY TYPE
AIRCRAFT
 TPT • Light 7 Beech C90B *King Air*
 TRG 11 G-120A
HELICOPTERS
 MRH 9 Bell 412 (CH-146)
 TPT • Light 7 Bell 206 *Jet Ranger* (CH-139)

Canadian Special Operations Forces Command 1,500
FORCES BY ROLE
SPECIAL FORCES
 1 SF regt (Canadian Special Operations Regiment)
 1 SF unit (JTF 2)

COMBAT SERVICE SUPPORT
1 CBRN unit (Canadian Joint Incidence Response Unit – CJIRU)
TRANSPORT HELICOPTER
1 (Spec Ops) sqn, with Bell 412 (CH-146 *Griffon* – from the RCAF)
EQUIPMENT BY TYPE
NBC VEHICLES 4 LAV *Bison* NBC
HELICOPTERS • MRH 10 Bell 412 (CH-146 *Griffon*)

Canadian Forces Joint Operational Support Group
FORCES BY ROLE
COMBAT SUPPORT
1 engr spt coy
1 (close protection) MP coy
1 (joint) sigs regt
COMBAT SERVICE SUPPORT
1 (spt) log unit
1 (movement) log unit

Paramilitary 4,500

Canadian Coast Guard 4,500
Incl Department of Fisheries and Oceans; all platforms are designated as non-combatant
EQUIPMENT BY TYPE
PATROL AND COASTAL COMBATANTS 64
 PSOH 1 *Leonard J Cowley*
 PSO 1 *Sir Wilfred Grenfell* (with hel landing platform)
 PCO 13: 2 *Cape Roger*; 1 *Gordon Reid*; 9 *Hero*; 1 *Tanu*
 PCC 1 *Harp*
 PB 48: 1 *Post*; 1 *Quebecois*; 1 *Vakta*; 10 Type-300A; 36 Type-300B; 1 *S. Dudka*; 1 *Simmonds* (on loan from RCMP)
AMPHIBIOUS • LANDING CRAFT • UCAC 4 Type-400
LOGISTICS AND SUPPORT 44
 ABU 7
 AG 5
 AGB 15
 AGOR 9 (coastal and offshore fishery vessels)
 AGOS 8
HELICOPTERS • TPT 37: **Medium** 1 S-61; **Light** 36: 3 Bell 206L *Long Ranger*; 4 Bell 212; 15 Bell 429; 14 Bo-105

Royal Canadian Mounted Police
In addition to the below, the RCMP also operates more than 370 small boats under 10 tonnes
EQUIPMENT BY TYPE
PATROL AND COASTAL COMBATANTS • PB 3: 1 *Inkster*; 2 *Nadon*

Cyber
Canada published its Cyber Security Strategy in October 2010 and published an Action Plan regarding implementation of the strategy in 2013. The Canadian Forces Network Operation Centre is the 'national operational cyber defence unit' permanently assigned to support Canadian forces' operations, but future force-development issues relating to military cyber come under the office of the Director General Cyber, of Brigadier-General rank, which also incorporates the Canadian Forces Cyber Task Force, a body that among other tasks examines future cyber capabilities. The armed forces' Information Management Group (IMG) is responsible for electronic warfare and network defence. The Canadian Force Information Operations Group, under the IMG, commands the Canadian Forces Information Operations Group Headquarters; the Canadian Forces Electronic Warfare Centre; the Canadian Forces Network Operation Centre, which is the 'national operational cyber defence unit' permanently assigned to support Canadian Forces operations; the Canadian Forces Signals Intelligence Operations Centre; the Canadian Forces Station Leitrim; and 764 Communications Squadron.

DEPLOYMENT

ALBANIA
OSCE • Albania 1

BOSNIA-HERZEGOVINA
OSCE • Bosnia and Herzegovina 1

CYPRUS
UN • UNFICYP (*Operation Snowgoose*) 1

DEMOCRATIC REPUBLIC OF THE CONGO
UN • MONUSCO (*Operation Crocodile*) 9

EGYPT
MFO (*Operation Calumet*) 70

GERMANY
NATO (ACO) 287

HAITI
UN • MINUSTAH (*Operation Hamlet*) 4

IRAQ
Operation Impact 207; 3 Bell 412 (CH-146 *Griffon*) hel

KUWAIT
Operation Impact 2 P-3 Orion (CP-140M); 1 A310 MRTT (C-150T)

MEDITERRANEAN SEA
NATO • SNMG 2: 1 FFGHM

MIDDLE EAST
UN • UNTSO (*Operation Jade*) 4 obs

POLAND
NATO • *Operation Reassurance* 220; 1 inf coy(+)

SERBIA
NATO • KFOR *Joint Enterprise* (*Operation Kobold*) 5
OSCE • Kosovo 6

SOUTH SUDAN
UN • UNMISS (*Operation Soprano*) 5; 5 obs

UKRAINE
Operation Unifier 200
OSCE • Ukraine 21

UNITED STATES
US CENTCOM (*Operation Foundation*) 17
US NORTHCOM/NORAD/NATO (ACT) 300

FOREIGN FORCES

United Kingdom 250; 2 trg unit; 1 hel flt with SA341 *Gazelle*
United States 150

United States US

United States Dollar $		2015	2016	2017
GDP	US$	18.0tr	18.6tr	
per capita	US$	56,084	57,294	
Growth	%	2.6	1.6	
Inflation	%	0.1	1.2	
Def bdgt [a]	US$	590bn	604bn	617bn

[a] National Defense Budget Function (50) Outlays. Includes DoD funding, as well as funds for nuclear-weapons-related activities undertaken by the Department of Energy. Excludes some military retirement and healthcare costs

Population   323,995,528

Age	0 – 14	15 – 19	20 – 24	25 – 29	30 – 64	65 plus
Male	9.6%	3.3%	3.6%	3.6%	22.4%	6.8%
Female	9.2%	3.2%	3.4%	3.5%	23.0%	8.5%

Capabilities

The US remains the world's most capable military power. Its forces are well trained and uniquely designed for power projection and intervention on a global scale across the full spectrum of operations. It is actively developing its defensive and offensive cyber capabilities and retains a nuclear triad with a substantial arsenal of warheads. The Pentagon continues to develop the plans for its 'rebalance' to the Asia-Pacific, but remains concerned with continuing global instability in the form of transnational, hybrid and regional insurgencies; China's military modernisation; increasing Russian assertiveness; and the Islamic State in Iraq and Syria. The armed forces are preoccupied with retaining and institutionalising capabilities and skills learnt in the Iraq and Afghan theatres while also dealing with budget cuts, force downsizing and the modernisation of much-used equipment. There are particular concerns about the readiness of naval and ground forces, and how to surge capability if required. The US Army was refocusing its attention on addressing readiness, boosting training and focusing on high-end adversaries, although there has been reduced spending on some modernisation initiatives. The US Marines unveiled a new operating concept, describing how the future force would tackle adversaries including technically advanced opponents. In contrast with recent practice, the Pentagon decided that it would classify its new National Military Strategy, and it would address how to deal more effectively with adversarial competition short of armed conflict that is increasingly inter-regional. Major modernisation initiatives are under way in the US strategic nuclear forces. In the face of mounting concern that the US military technological edge is being eroded, there is increased focus on innovative approaches to retain that advantage. Pentagon budget proposals included a new focus on advanced weaponry and reinforcement in Europe, to counter emerging threat systems and also to retain US military advantage; meanwhile, investments continued in the Pentagon's 'Third Offset' strategy. (See pp. 27–40.)

ACTIVE 1,347,300 (Army 475,350 Navy 327,750 Air Force 316,950 US Marine Corps 184,250 US Coast Guard 43,000)

CIVILIAN 14,850 (US Special Operations Command 6,550 US Coast Guard 8,300)

RESERVE 865,050 (Army 542,550 Navy 100,750 Air Force 174,650 Marine Corps Reserve 38,950 US Coast Guard 8,150)

ORGANISATIONS BY SERVICE

US Strategic Command

HQ at Offutt AFB (NE). Five missions: US nuclear deterrent; missile defence; global strike; info ops; ISR

US Navy
EQUIPMENT BY TYPE
SUBMARINES • STRATEGIC • SSBN 14 *Ohio* SSBN with up to 24 UGM-133A *Trident* D-5 nuclear SLBM, 4 single 533mm TT with Mk48 *Sea Arrow* HWT

US Air Force • Global Strike Command
FORCES BY ROLE
MISSILE
  9 sqn with LGM-30G *Minuteman* III
BOMBER
  6 sqn (incl 1 AFRC) with B-52H *Stratofortress* (+1 AFRC sqn personnel only)
  2 sqn with B-2A *Spirit* (+1 ANG sqn personnel only)
EQUIPMENT BY TYPE
SURFACE-TO-SURFACE MISSILE LAUNCHERS
  ICBM • Nuclear 450 LGM-30G *Minuteman* III (capacity 1–3 MIRV Mk12/Mk12A per missile)
  BBR 90: 20 B-2A *Spirit*; 70 B-52H *Stratofortress*
AIR-LAUNCHED MISSILES
  ALCM • Nuclear AGM-86B

Strategic Defenses – Early Warning

North American Aerospace Defense Command (NORAD) – a combined US–CAN org
EQUIPMENT BY TYPE
RADAR
  NORTH WARNING SYSTEM 50: 14 AN/FPS-117 (range 200nm); 36 AN/FPS-124 (range 80nm)
  SOLID STATE PHASED ARRAY RADAR SYSTEM (SSPARS) 5: 2 AN/FPS-123 Early Warning Radar located at Cape Cod AFS (MA) and Clear AFS (AK); 3 AN/FPS-132 Upgraded Early Warning Radar located at Beale AFB (CA), Thule (GL) and Fylingdales Moor (UK)

SPACETRACK SYSTEM 10: 1 AN/FPS-85 Spacetrack Radar at Eglin AFB (FL); 6 contributing radars at Cavalier AFS (ND), Clear (AK), Thule (GL), Fylingdales Moor (UK), Beale AFB (CA) and Cape Cod (MA); 3 Spacetrack Optical Trackers located at Socorro (NM), Maui (HI), Diego Garcia (BIOT)
PERIMETER ACQUISITION RADAR ATTACK CHARACTERISATION SYSTEM (PARCS) 1 AN/FPQ-16 at Cavalier AFS (ND)
DETECTION AND TRACKING RADARS 5 located at Kwajalein Atoll, Ascension Island, Australia, Kaena Point (HI), MIT Lincoln Laboratory (MA)
GROUND BASED ELECTRO OPTICAL DEEP SPACE SURVEILLANCE SYSTEM (GEODSS) Socorro (NM), Maui (HI), Diego Garcia (BIOT)
STRATEGIC DEFENCES – MISSILE DEFENCES
SEA-BASED: *Aegis* engagement cruisers and destroyers
LAND-BASED: 26 ground-based interceptors at Fort Greely (AK); 4 ground-based interceptors at Vandenburg AFB (CA)

Space
EQUIPMENT BY TYPE
SATELLITES 127
COMMUNICATIONS 39: 3 AEHF; 6 DSCS-III; 2 *Milstar*-I; 3 *Milstar*-II; 5 MUOS; 1 PAN-1 (P360); 6 SDS-III; 6 UFO; 7 WGS SV2
NAVIGATION/POSITIONING/TIMING 31: 12 NAVSTAR Block IIF; 19 NAVSTAR Block IIR/IIRM
METEOROLOGY/OCEANOGRAPHY 6 DMSP-5
ISR 14: 4 FIA *Radar*; 5 *Evolved Enhanced/Improved Crystal* (visible and infrared imagery); 2 *Lacrosse* (*Onyx* radar imaging satellite); 1 ORS-1; 1 *TacSat*-4; 1 *TacSat*-6
ELINT/SIGINT 26: 2 *Mentor* (advanced *Orion*); 3 Advanced *Mentor*; 4 *Mercury*; 1 NRO L-67; 1 *Trumpet*; 3 Improved *Trumpet*; 12 SBWASS (Space Based Wide Area Surveillance System; Naval Ocean Surveillance System)
SPACE SURVEILLANCE 5: 4 GSSAP; 1 SBSS (Space Based Surveillance System)
EARLY WARNING 6: 4 DSP; 2 SBIRS *Geo*-1

US Army 475,350
FORCES BY ROLE
Sqn are generally bn sized and tp are generally coy sized
COMMAND
3 (I, III & XVIII AB) corps HQ
1 (2nd) inf div HQ
SPECIAL FORCES
(see USSOCOM)
MANOEUVRE
Armoured
1 (1st) armd div (2 (2nd & 3rd ABCT) armd bde (1 armd recce sqn, 3 armd bn, 1 SP arty bn, 1 cbt engr bn, 1 CSS bn); 1 (1st SBCT) mech bde (1 armd recce sqn, 3 mech inf bn, 1 arty bn, 1 cbt engr bn, 1 CSS bn); 1 MRL bde HQ; 1 log bde; 1 (hy cbt avn) hel bde)
1 (1st) cav div (3 (1st–3rd ABCT) armd bde (1 armd recce sqn, 3 armd bn, 1 SP arty bn, 1 cbt engr bn, 1 CSS bn); 1 MRL bde (1 MRL bn); 1 log bde; 1 (hy cbt avn) hel bde)
1 (1st) inf div (2 (1st & 2nd ABCT) armd bde (1 armd recce sqn, 3 armd bn, 1 SP arty bn, 1 cbt engr bn, 1 CSS bn); 1 log bde; 1 (cbt avn) hel bde)
Mechanised
1 (3rd) inf div (1 (1st ABCT) armd bde (1 armd recce sqn, 3 armd bn, 1 SP arty bn, 1 cbt engr bn, 1 CSS bn); 1 (2nd IBCT) lt inf bde; (1 recce sqn, 3 inf bn, 1 arty bn, 1 cbt engr bn, 1 CSS bn); 1 lt inf bn; 1 MRL bde HQ; 1 log bde; 1 (cbt avn) hel bde)
1 (4th) inf div (1 (3rd ABCT) armd bde (1 armd recce sqn, 3 armd bn, 1 SP arty bn, 1 cbt engr bn, 1 CSS bn); 1 (1st SBCT) mech bde (1 armd recce sqn, 3 mech inf bn, 1 arty bn, 1 cbt engr bn, 1 CSS bn); 1 (2nd IBCT) lt inf bde (1 recce sqn, 3 inf bn, 1 arty bn, 1 cbt engr bn, 1 CSS bn); 1 MRL bde HQ; 1 log bde; 1 (hy cbt avn) hel bde)
1 (7th) inf div (2 (1st & 2nd SBCT, 2nd ID) mech bde (1 armd recce sqn, 3 mech inf bn, 1 arty bn, 1 cbt engr bn, 1 CSS bn))
1 (1st SBCT, 25th ID) mech bde (1 armd recce sqn, 3 mech inf bn, 1 arty bn, 1 cbt engr bn, 1 CSS bn)
2 (2nd & 3rd CR) mech bde (1 armd recce sqn, 3 mech sqn, 1 arty sqn, 1 cbt engr sqn, 1 CSS sqn)
Light
1 (10th Mtn) inf div (3 (1st–3rd IBCT) lt inf bde (1 recce sqn, 3 inf bn, 1 arty bn, 1 cbt engr bn, 1 CSS bn); 1 log bde; 1 (cbt avn) hel bde)
1 (25th) inf div (2 (2 & 3rd IBCT) inf bde (1 recce sqn, 2 inf bn, 1 arty bn, 1 cbt engr bn, 1 CSS bn); 1 log bde; 1 (cbt avn) hel bde)
Air Manoeuvre
1 (82nd) AB div (3 (1st–3rd AB BCT) AB bde (1 recce bn, 3 para bn, 1 arty bn, 1 cbt engr bn, 1 CSS bn); 1 (cbt avn) hel bde; 1 log bde)
1 (101st) air aslt div (3 (1st–3rd AB BCT) AB bde (1 recce bn, 3 para bn, 1 arty bn, 1 cbt engr bn, 1 CSS bn); 1 (cbt avn) hel bde; 1 log bde)
1 (173rd AB BCT) AB bde (1 recce bn, 2 para bn, 1 arty bn, 1 cbt engr bn, 1 CSS bn)
1 (4th AB BCT, 25th ID) AB bde (1 recce bn, 2 para bn, 1 arty bn, 1 cbt engr bn, 1 CSS bn)
Other
1 (11th ACR) trg armd cav regt (OPFOR) (2 armd cav sqn, 1 CSS bn)
COMBAT SUPPORT
3 MRL bde (2 MRL bn)
1 MRL bde (4 MRL bn)
4 engr bde
2 EOD gp (2 EOD bn)
10 int bde
2 int gp
4 MP bde
1 NBC bde
3 (strat) sigs bde
4 (tac) sigs bde
COMBAT SERVICE SUPPORT
2 log bde
3 med bde
1 tpt bde
HELICOPTER
2 (cbt avn) hel bde
1 (cbt avn) hel bde HQ

AIR DEFENCE
5 SAM bde

Reserve Organisations

Army National Guard 343,700 reservists
Normally dual funded by DoD and states. Civil-emergency responses can be mobilised by state governors. Federal government can mobilise ARNG for major domestic emergencies and for overseas operations

FORCES BY ROLE
COMMAND
  8 div HQ
SPECIAL FORCES
  (see USSOCOM)
MANOEUVRE
  Reconnaissance
  1 armd recce sqn
  Armoured
  2 (ABCT) armd bde (1 armd recce sqn, 3 armd bn, 1 SP arty bn, 1 cbt engr bn, 1 CSS bn)
  2 (ABCT) armd bde (1 armd recce sqn, 2 armd bn, 1 SP arty bn, 1 cbt engr bn, 1 CSS bn)
  1 (ABCT) armd bde (1 armd recce sqn, 3 armd bn, 1 SP arty bn, 1 cbt spt bn, 1 CSS bn)
  1 (ABCT) armd bde (1 armd recce sqn, 2 armd bn, 1 SP arty bn, 1 cbt spt bn, 1 CSS bn)
  1 armd bn
  Mechanised
  1 (SBCT) mech bde (1 armd recce sqn, 3 mech inf bn, 1 arty bn, 1 cbt engr bn, 1 CSS bn)
  1 (SBCT) mech bde (1 armd recce sqn, 3 mech inf bn, 1 arty bn, 1 engr coy, 1 int coy, 1 sigs coy, 1 CSS bn)
  Light
  2 (IBCT) lt inf bde (1 recce sqn, 3 inf bn, 1 arty bn, 1 cbt engr bn, 1 CSS bn)
  10 (IBCT) lt inf bde (1 recce sqn, 2 inf bn, 1 arty bn, 1 cbt engr bn, 1 CSS bn)
  8 (IBCT) lt inf bde (1 recce sqn, 2 inf bn, 1 arty bn, 1 cbt spt bn, 1 CSS bn)
  10 lt inf bn
  Air Manoeuvre
  1 AB bn
COMBAT SUPPORT
  8 arty bde
  1 SP arty bn
  8 engr bde
  1 EOD regt
  3 int bde
  3 MP bde
  1 NBC bde
  2 (tac) sigs bde
  17 (Mnv Enh) cbt spt bde
COMBAT SERVICE SUPPORT
  10 log bde
  17 (regional) log spt gp
HELICOPTER
  8 (cbt avn) hel bde
  5 (theatre avn) hel bde
AIR DEFENCE
  3 SAM bde

Army Reserve 198,850 reservists
Reserve under full command of US Army. Does not have state-emergency liability of Army National Guard

FORCES BY ROLE
SPECIAL FORCES
  (see USSOCOM)
COMBAT SUPPORT
  4 engr bde
  4 MP bde
  2 NBC bde
  2 sigs bde
  3 (Mnv Enh) cbt spt bde
COMBAT SERVICE SUPPORT
  9 log bde
  11 med bde
HELICOPTER
  1 (theatre avn) hel bde

Army Stand-by Reserve 700 reservists
Trained individuals for mobilisation

EQUIPMENT BY TYPE
ARMOURED FIGHTING VEHICLES
  MBT 2,384: 775 M1A1 SA *Abrams*; 1,609 M1A2 SEPv2 *Abrams*; (ε3,500 more M1 *Abrams* in store)
  ASLT 134 M1128 *Stryker* MGS
  RECCE 1,745: ε1,200 M3A2/A3 *Bradley*; 545 M1127 *Stryker* RV; (ε800 more M3 *Bradley* in store)
  IFV 2,834: ε2,500 M2A2/A3 *Bradley*; 334 M7A3/SA BFIST (OP); (ε2,000 more M2 *Bradley* in store)
  APC 10,746
    APC (T) ε5,000 M113A2/A3 (ε8,000 more in store)
    APC (W) 2,812: 1,972 M1126 *Stryker* ICV; 348 M1130 *Stryker* CV (CP); 188 M1131 *Stryker* FSV (OP); 304 M1133 *Stryker* MEV (Amb)
    PPV 2,934: 2,633 *MaxxPro Dash*; 301 *MaxxPro* LWB (Amb)
    AUV 9,016: 2,900 M1117 ASV; 465 M1200 *Armored Knight* (OP); 5,651 M-ATV
ENGINEERING & MAINTENANCE VEHICLES
  AEV 425+: 7+ M1 ABV; 250 M9 ACE; 168 M1132 *Stryker* ESV
  ARV 1,090+: 360 M88A1; 730 M88A2 (ε1,000 more M88A1 in store); some M578
  VLB 60: 20 REBS; 40 *Wolverine* HAB
  MW *Aardvark* JSFU Mk4; 3+ *Hydrema* 910 MCV-2; M58/M59 MICLIC; M139; *Rhino*
NBC VEHICLES 234 M1135 *Stryker* NBCRV
ANTI-TANK/ANTI-INFRASTRUCTURE • MSL
  SP 1,133: 133 M1134 *Stryker* ATGM; ε1,000 M1167 HMMWV TOW
  MANPATS FGM-148 *Javelin*
ARTILLERY 5,312
  SP 155mm 963: 950 M109A6; 13 M109A7 (ε500 more M109A6 in store)
  TOWED 1,242: **105mm** 821 M119A2/3; **155mm** 421 M777A1/A2
  MRL 227mm 600: 375 M142 HIMARS; 225 M270A1 MLRS
  MOR 2,507: **81mm** 990 M252; **120mm** 1,076 M120/M1064A3; **SP 120mm** 441 M1129 *Stryker* MC

SURFACE-TO-SURFACE MISSILE LAUNCHERS
SRBM • Conventional MGM-140A/B ATACMS; MGM-168 ATACMS (All launched from M270A1 MLRS or M142 HIMARS MRLs)
RADAR • LAND 209+: 98 AN/TPQ-36 *Firefinder* (arty); 56 AN/TPQ-37 *Firefinder* (arty); 55 AN/TPQ-53 (arty); AN/MLQ-40 *Prophet*; AN/MLQ-44 *Prophet Enhanced*
AMPHIBIOUS 116
PRINCIPAL AMPHIBIOUS SHIPS 8
LSL 8 *Frank Besson* (capacity 15 *Abrams* MBT)
LANDING CRAFT 108
LCU 35 LCU-2000
LCM 73 LCM-8 (capacity either 1 MBT or 200 troops)
AIRCRAFT
ISR 19: 14 RC-12X *Guardrail*; 5 RC-12 *Guardrail* (trg)
ELINT 8: 5 EO-5C ARL-M (COMINT/ELINT); 2 EO-5B ARL-C (COMINT); 1 TO-5C (trg)
TPT 156: **Light** 152: 113 Beech A200 *King Air* (C-12 *Huron*); 28 Cessna 560 *Citation* (UC-35A/B/C); 11 SA-227 *Metro* (C-26B/E); **PAX** 4: 1 Gulfstream IV (C-20F); 3 Gulfstream V (C-37A)
TRG 4 T-6D *Texan* II
HELICOPTERS
ATK 596: 450 AH-64D *Apache*; 146 AH-64E *Apache*
MRH 60 OH-58D *Kiowa Warrior*
ISR 44 OH-58A *Kiowa*
SAR 227: 19 HH-60L *Black Hawk*; 208 HH-60M *Black Hawk* (medevac)
TPT 2,956: **Heavy** 435: 75 CH-47D *Chinook*; 360 CH-47F *Chinook*; **Medium** 1,872: 450 UH-60A *Black Hawk*; 850 UH-60L *Black Hawk*; 572 UH-60M *Black Hawk*; **Light** 427: 362 UH-72A *Lakota*; 65 UH-1H/V *Iroquois*
TRG 153 TH-67 *Creek*
UNMANNED AERIAL VEHICLES 341
CISR • Heavy 105 MQ-1C *Gray Eagle*
ISR • Medium 236 RQ-7B *Shadow*
AIR DEFENCE • SAM 1,103+
Long-range 400 MIM-104D/E *Patriot* PAC-2 GEM/GEM-T
Short-range NASAMS
Point-defence 703+: FIM-92 *Stinger*; 703 M1097 *Avenger*
MISSILE DEFENCE 120
Long-range 40 THAAD
Medium-range 80 MIM-104F *Patriot* PAC-3/PAC-3 MSE
AIR-LAUNCHED MISSILES
ASM AGM-114 *Hellfire*

US Navy 327,750

Comprises 2 Fleet Areas, Atlantic and Pacific. 5 Fleets: 3rd – Pacific; 4th – Caribbean, Central and South America; 5th – Indian Ocean, Persian Gulf, Red Sea; 6th – Mediterranean; 7th – W. Pacific; plus Military Sealift Command (MSC); Naval Reserve Force (NRF). For Naval Special Warfare Command, see US Special Operations Command

EQUIPMENT BY TYPE
SUBMARINES 68
STRATEGIC • SSBN 14 *Ohio* opcon US STRATCOM with up to 24 UGM-133A *Trident* D-5 nuclear SLBM, 4 single 533mm TT with Mk48 *Sea Arrow* HWT
TACTICAL 54

SSGN 46:
4 *Ohio* (mod) with total of 154 *Tomahawk* LACM, 4 single 533mm TT with Mk48 *Sea Arrow* HWT
7 *Los Angeles* with 1 12-cell VLS with *Tomahawk* LACM; 4 single 533mm TT with Mk48 *Sea Arrow* HWT
22 *Los Angeles* (Imp) with 1 12-cell VLS with *Tomahawk* LACM, 4 single 533mm TT with Mk48 *Sea Arrow* HWT
10 *Virginia* Flight I/II with 1 12-cell VLS with *Tomahawk* LACM, 4 single 533mm TT with Mk48 ADCAP mod 6 HWT
3 *Virginia* Flight III with 2 6-cell VLS with *Tomahawk* LACM, 4 single 533mm TT with Mk48 ADCAP mod 6 HWT
SSN 8:
5 *Los Angeles* with 4 single 533mm TT with Mk48 *Sea Arrow* HWT
3 *Seawolf* with 8 single 660mm TT with up to 45 *Tomahawk* LACM/Mk48 *Sea Arrow* HWT
PRINCIPAL SURFACE COMBATANTS 103
AIRCRAFT CARRIERS • CVN 10 *Nimitz* with 2–3 octuple Mk29 lnchr with RIM-7M/P *Sea Sparrow* SAM, 2 Mk49 GMLS with RIM-116 SAM, 2 *Phalanx* Mk15 CIWS (typical capacity 55 F/A-18 *Hornet* FGA ac; 4 EA-18G *Growler* EW ac; 4 E-2C/D *Hawkeye* AEW ac; 6 H-60 *Seahawk* hel)
CRUISERS • CGHM 23:
22 *Ticonderoga* with *Aegis* Baseline 5/6/8/9 C2, 2 quad lnchr with RGM-84 *Harpoon* AShM, 2 61-cell Mk41 VLS with SM-2ER SAM/SM-3 SAM/SM-6/*Tomahawk* LACM, 2 triple 324mm ASTT with Mk46 LWT, 2 *Phalanx* Block 1B CIWS, 2 127mm guns (capacity 2 SH-60B *Seahawk* ASW hel)
1 *Zumwalt* with 20 4-cell Mk57 VLS with RIM-162 ESSM SAM/SM-2ER SAM/ASROC ASW/*Tomahawk* LACM, 2 155mm guns (capacity 2 MH-60R *Seahawk* ASW hel or 1 MH-60R *Seahawk* ASW hel and 3 *Fire Scout* UAV)
DESTROYERS 62
DDGHM 34 *Arleigh Burke* Flight IIA with *Aegis* Baseline 6/7 C2, 1 29-cell Mk41 VLS with ASROC ASW/SM-2ER SAM/SM-3 SAM/SM-6 SAM/*Tomahawk* LACM, 1 61-cell Mk41 VLS with ASROC ASW/SM-2ER SAM/SM-3 SAM/SM-6 SAM/*Tomahawk* LACM, 2 triple 324mm ASTT with Mk46 LWT, 2 *Phalanx* Block 1B CIWS, 1 127mm gun (capacity 2 SH-60B *Seahawk* ASW hel)
DDGM 28 *Arleigh Burke* Flight I/II with *Aegis* Baseline 5/9 C2, 2 quad lnchr with RGM-84 *Harpoon* AShM, 1 32-cell Mk41 VLS with ASROC ASW/SM-2ER SAM/SM-3 SAM/SM-6 SAM/*Tomahawk* LACM, 1 64-cell Mk41 VLS with ASROC ASW/SM-2 ER SAM/*Tomahawk* LACM, 2 Mk49 GMLS with RIM-116 RAM SAM, 2 triple 324mm ASTT with Mk46 LWT, 2 *Phalanx* Block 1B CIWS, 1 127mm gun, 1 hel landing platform
FRIGATES • FFHM 8:
4 *Freedom* with 1 21-cell Mk49 lnchr with RIM-116 SAM, 1 57mm gun (capacity 2 MH-60R/S *Seahawk* hel or 1 MH-60 with 3 MQ-8 *Fire Scout* UAV)
4 *Independence* with 1 11-cell SeaRAM lnchr with

RIM-116 SAM, 1 57mm gun (capacity 1 MH-60R/S *Seahawk* hel and 3 MQ-8 *Fire Scout* UAV)

PATROL AND COASTAL COMBATANTS 57
  PCFG 10 *Cyclone* with 1 quad Mk 208 lnchr with BGM-176B *Griffin B* SSM
  PCF 3 *Cyclone*
  PBF 2 Mk VI
  PBR 42

MINE WARFARE • MINE COUNTERMEASURES 11
  MCO 11 *Avenger* with 1 SLQ-48 MCM system; 1 SQQ-32(V)3 Sonar (mine hunting)

COMMAND SHIPS • LCC 2 *Blue Ridge* with 2 *Phalanx* Mk15 CIWS (capacity 3 LCPL; 2 LCVP; 700 troops; 1 med hel) (of which 1 vessel partially crewed by Military Sealift Command personnel)

AMPHIBIOUS
  PRINCIPAL AMPHIBIOUS SHIPS 31
    LHA 1 *America* with 2 octuple Mk29 GMLS with RIM-162D ESSM SAM; 2 Mk49 GMLS with RIM-116 RAM SAM, 2 *Phalanx* Mk15 CIWS (capacity 6 F-35B *Lightning* II FGA ac; 12 MV-22B *Osprey* tpt ac; 4 CH-53E *Sea Stallion* hel; 7 AH-1Z *Viper*/UH-1Y *Iroquois* hel; 2 MH-60 hel)
    LHD 8 *Wasp* with 2 octuple Mk29 GMLS with RIM-7M/RIM-7P *Sea Sparrow* SAM, 2 Mk49 GMLS with RIM-116 RAM SAM, 2 *Phalanx* Mk15 CIWS (capacity: 6 AV-8B *Harrier* II FGA; 4 CH-53E *Sea Stallion* hel; 6 MV-22B *Osprey* tpt ac; 4 AH-1W/Z hel; 3 UH-1Y hel; 3 LCAC(L); 60 tanks; 1,687 troops)
    LPD 10 *San Antonio* with 2 21-cell Mk49 GMLS with RIM-116 SAM (capacity 2 CH-53E *Sea Stallion* hel or 2 MV-22 *Osprey*; 2 LCAC(L); 14 AAAV; 720 troops)
    LSD 12:
      4 *Harpers Ferry* with 2 Mk 49 GMLS with RIM-116 SAM, 2 *Phalanx* Mk15 CIWS, 1 hel landing platform (capacity 2 LCAC(L); 40 tanks; 500 troops)
      8 *Whidbey Island* with 2 Mk49 GMLS with RIM-116 SAM, 2 *Phalanx* Mk15 CIWS, 1 hel landing platform (capacity 4 LCAC(L); 40 tanks; 500 troops)
  LANDING CRAFT 245
    LCU 32 LCU-1600 (capacity either 2 M1 *Abrams* MBT or 350 troops)
    LCP 108: 75 LCPL; 33 Utility Boat
    LCM 25: 10 LCM-6; 15 LCM-8
    LCAC 80 LCAC(L) (capacity either 1 MBT or 60 troops (undergoing upgrade programme))

LOGISTICS AND SUPPORT 22
  AFDL 1 *Dynamic*
  AGE 4: 1 MARSS; 1 *Sea Fighter*; 1 *Sea Jet*; 1 *Stiletto* (all for testing)
  AGOR 5 (all leased out): 1 *Ocean*; 3 *Thomas G Thompson*; 1 *Kilo Moana*
  APB 3
  ARD 3
  AX 1 *Prevail*
  AXS 1 *Constitution*
  SSA 2 (for testing)
  SSAN 1 (for propulsion plant training)
  UUV 1 *Cutthroat* (for testing)

Naval Reserve Forces 100,750

Selected Reserve 58,000

Individual Ready Reserve 42,750

Naval Inactive Fleet

Under a minimum of 60–90 days notice for reactivation; still on naval vessel register

EQUIPMENT BY TYPE
PRINCIPAL SURFACE COMBATANTS 1
  AIRCRAFT CARRIERS • CV 1 *Kitty Hawk*
AMPHIBIOUS 12
  2 **LHA**
  5 **LPD**
  5 **AK**
LOGISTICS AND SUPPORT 2
  AOE 1
  ATF 1 *Mohawk*

Military Sealift Command (MSC)

Combat Logistics Force
EQUIPMENT BY TYPE
LOGISTICS AND SUPPORT 30
  AO 15 *Henry J. Kaiser*
  AOE 3 *Supply*
  AKEH 12 *Lewis and Clark*

Prepositioning
EQUIPMENT BY TYPE
LOGISTICS AND SUPPORT 25
  AG 2: 1 *V Adm K.R. Wheeler*; 1 *Fast Tempo*
  AK 4: 2 *LTC John U.D. Page*; 1 *Maj. Bernard F. Fisher*; 1 *CPT David I. Lyon*
  AKEH 2 *Lewis and Clark*
  AKR 10: 2 *Bob Hope*; 1 *Stockham*; 7 *Watson*
  AKRH 5 *2nd Lt John P. Bobo*
  ESD 2 *Montford Point*

Sealift
(At a minimum of 4 days' readiness)
EQUIPMENT BY TYPE
LOGISTICS AND SUPPORT 26
  AOT 6 (long-term chartered, of which 1 *Empire State*; 1 *Galveston*; 1 *Lawrence H. Gianella*; 1 *Maersk Peary*; 1 *SLNC Pax*; 1 *SLNC Goodwill*)
  AK 5: 3 *Sgt Matej Kocak*; 2 (long-term chartered, of which 1 *TransAtlantic*; 1 *Sea Eagle*)
  AKR 12: 5 *Bob Hope*; 2 *Gordon*; 2 *Shughart*; 1 *1st Lt Harry L Martin*; 1 *LCpl Roy M Wheat*; 1 *Watson*
  AP 3: 2 *Guam*; 1 *Westpac Express*

Special Mission
EQUIPMENT BY TYPE
LOGISTICS AND SUPPORT 24
  AGM 3: 1 *Howard O. Lorenzen*; 1 *Invincible* (commercial operator); 1 Sea-based X-band Radar
  AGOS 5: 1 *Impeccable* (commercial operator); 4 *Victorious*
  AGS 7: 6 *Pathfinder*; 1 *Waters*

AS 9 (long-term chartered, of which 1 *C-Champion*, 1 *C-Commando*, 1 *Malama*, 1 *Dolores Chouest*, 1 *Dominator*, 4 *Arrowhead*)

Service and Command Support
EQUIPMENT BY TYPE
LOGISTICS AND SUPPORT 22
  ARS 4 *Safeguard*
  AFSB 1 *Ponce* (modified *Austin*-class LPD) with 1 AN/SEQ-3 LaWS laser
  AH 2 *Mercy*, with 1 hel landing platform
  ARC 1 *Zeus*
  AS 2 *Emory S Land*
  ATF 4 *Powhatan*
  EPF 7 *Spearhead*
  ESD 1 *Lewis B Puller*

US Maritime Administration (MARAD)

National Defense Reserve Fleet
EQUIPMENT BY TYPE
LOGISTICS AND SUPPORT 34
  ACS 2 *Keystone State*
  AG 3
  AGOS 3
  AGS 3
  AK 15: 5; 10 (breakbulk)
  AOT 4
  AP 4

Ready Reserve Force
Ships at readiness up to a maximum of 30 days
EQUIPMENT BY TYPE
LOGISTICS AND SUPPORT 46
  ACS 6 *Keystone State*
  AK 4: 2 *Wright* (breakbulk); 2 *Cape May* (heavy lift)
  AKR 35: 1 *Adm W.M. Callaghan*; 8 *Algol*; 26 *Cape Island*
  AOT 1 *Petersburg*

Augmentation Force
COMBAT SERVICE SUPPORT
  1 (active) log bn (Navy Cargo Handling)
  6 (reserve) log bn (Navy Cargo Handling)

Naval Aviation 98,600
10 air wg. Average air wing comprises 8 sqns: 4 with F/A-18; 1 with MH-60R; 1 with EA-18G; 1 with E-2C/D; 1 with MH-60S

FORCES BY ROLE
FIGHTER/GROUND ATTACK
  5 sqn with F/A-18C *Hornet*
  19 sqn with F/A-18E *Super Hornet*
  11 sqn with F/A-18F *Super Hornet*
ANTI-SUBMARINE WARFARE
  11 sqn with MH-60R *Seahawk*
  1 ASW/CSAR sqn with HH-60H *Seahawk*
  3 ASW/ISR sqn with MH-60R *Seahawk*; MQ-8B *Fire Scout*
ELINT
  1 sqn with EP-3E *Aries* II
ELINT/ELECTRONIC WARFARE
  13 sqn with EA-18G *Growler*
MARITIME PATROL
  5 sqn with P-3C *Orion*
  6 sqn with P-8A *Poseidon*
  1 sqn (forming) with P-8A *Poseidon*
AIRBORNE EARLY WARNING & CONTROL
  7 sqn with E-2C *Hawkeye*
  3 sqn with E-2D *Hawkeye*
COMMAND & CONTROL
  2 sqn with E-6B *Mercury*
MINE COUNTERMEASURES
  2 sqn with MH-53E *Sea Dragon*
TRANSPORT
  2 sqn with C-2A *Greyhound*
TRAINING
  1 (FRS) sqn with EA-18G *Growler*
  1 (FRS) sqn with C-2A *Greyhound*; E-2C/D *Hawkeye*; TE-2C *Hawkeye*
  1 sqn with E-6B *Mercury*
  2 (FRS) sqn with F/A-18A/A+/B/C/D *Hornet*; F/A-18E/F *Super Hornet*
  1 (FRS) sqn with F-35C *Lightning* II
  1 (FRS) sqn with MH-53 *Sea Dragon*
  2 (FRS) sqn with MH-60S *Knight Hawk*; HH-60H *Seahawk*
  1 (FRS) sqn with MH-60R *Seahawk*
  1 (FRS) sqn with MH-60R *Seahawk*
  1 sqn with P-3C *Orion*
  1 (FRS) sqn with P-3C *Orion*; P-8A *Poseidon*
  6 sqn with T-6A/B *Texan* II
  1 sqn with T-44A/C *Pegasus*
  5 sqn with T-45A/C *Goshawk*
  1 sqn with TC-12B *Huron*
  3 hel sqn with TH-57B/C *Sea Ranger*
  1 (FRS) UAV sqn with MQ-8B *Fire Scout*; MQ-8C *Fire Scout*
TRANSPORT HELICOPTER
  14 sqn with MH-60S *Knight Hawk*
  1 tpt hel/ISR sqn with MH-60S *Knight Hawk*; MQ-8B *Fire Scout*
ISR UAV
  1 sqn with MQ-4C *Triton* (personnel only)

EQUIPMENT BY TYPE
AIRCRAFT 1,036 combat capable
  FGA 810: 19 F-35C *Lightning* II; 10 F/A-18A/A+ *Hornet*; 9 F/A-18B *Hornet*; 170 F/A-18C *Hornet*; 41 F/A-18D *Hornet*; 290 F/A-18E *Super Hornet*; 271 F/A-18F *Super Hornet*
  ASW 110: 65 P-3C *Orion*; 45 P-8A *Poseidon*
  EW 117 EA-18G *Growler**
  ELINT 9 EP-3E *Aries* II
  AEW&C 76: 51 E-2C *Hawkeye*; 25 E-2D *Hawkeye*
  C2 16 E-6B *Mercury*
  TPT • Light 68: 4 Beech A200 *King Air* (C-12C *Huron*); 20 Beech A200 *King Air* (UC-12F/M *Huron*); 35 C-2A *Greyhound*; 2 DHC-2 *Beaver* (U-6A); 7 SA-227-BC *Metro* III (C-26D)
  TRG 609: 44 T-6A *Texan* II; 232 T-6B *Texan* II; 7 T-38C *Talon*; 55 T-44A/C *Pegasus*; 74 T-45A *Goshawk*; 170 T-45C *Goshawk*; 25 TC-12B *Huron*; 2 TE-2C *Hawkeye*

HELICOPTERS
ASW 225 MH-60R *Seahawk*
MRH 271 MH-60S *Knight Hawk* (Multi Mission Support)
MCM 28 MH-53E *Sea Dragon*
ISR 3 OH-58C *Kiowa*
CSAR 11 HH-60H *Seahawk*
TPT 13: **Heavy** 2 CH-53E *Sea Stallion*; **Medium** 3 UH-60L *Black Hawk*; **Light** 8: 5 UH-72A *Lakota*; 2 UH-1N *Iroquois*; 1 UH-1Y *Venom*
TRG 119: 43 TH-57B *Sea Ranger*; 76 TH-57C *Sea Ranger*
UNMANNED AERIAL VEHICLES • ISR 90
Heavy 40: 20 MQ-8B *Fire Scout*; 16 MQ-8C *Fire Scout*; 4 RQ-4A *Global Hawk* (under evaluation and trials)
Medium 35 RQ-2B *Pioneer*
Light 15 RQ-21A *Blackjack*
AIR-LAUNCHED MISSILES
AAM • IR AIM-9 *Sidewinder*; **IIR** AIM-9X *Sidewinder* II; **SARH** AIM-7 *Sparrow*; **ARH** AIM-120C-5/C-7/D AMRAAM
ASM AGM-65F *Maverick*; AGM-114B/K/M *Hellfire*; AGM-154A/C JSOW
AShM AGM-84D *Harpoon*; AGM-119A *Penguin* 3
ARM AGM-88B/C/E HARM
ALCM • Conventional AGM-84E/H/K SLAM/SLAM-ER
BOMBS
Laser-guided: GBU-10/12/16 *Paveway* II; GBU-24 *Paveway* III
INS/GPS guided: GBU-31/32/38 JDAM; Enhanced *Paveway* II; GBU-54 Laser JDAM

Naval Aviation Reserve
FORCES BY ROLE
FIGHTER/GROUND ATTACK
1 sqn with F/A-18A+ *Hornet*
ANTI-SUBMARINE WARFARE
1 sqn with MH-60R *Seahawk*
ELECTRONIC WARFARE
1 sqn with EA-18G *Growler*
MARITIME PATROL
2 sqn with P-3C *Orion*
TRANSPORT
5 log spt sqn with B-737-700 (C-40A *Clipper*)
2 log spt sqn with Gulfstream III/IV (C-20D/G); Gulfstream V/G550 (C-37A/C-37B)
5 sqn with C-130T *Hercules*
TRAINING
2 (aggressor) sqn with F-5F/N *Tiger* II
1 (aggressor) sqn with F/A-18A+ *Hornet*
TRANSPORT HELICOPTER
2 sqn with HH-60H *Seahawk*
EQUIPMENT BY TYPE
AIRCRAFT 78 combat capable
FTR 32: 2 F-5F *Tiger* II; 30 F-5N *Tiger* II
FGA 29 F/A-18A+ *Hornet*
ASW 12 P-3C *Orion*
EW 5 EA-18G *Growler**
TPT 47: **Medium** 24 C-130T *Hercules*; **PAX** 23: 15 B-737-700 (C-40A *Clipper*); 1 Gulfstream III (C-20D); 3 Gulfstream IV (C-20G); 1 Gulfstream V (C-37A); 3 Gulfstream G550 (C-37B)

HELICOPTERS
ASW 7 MH-60R *Seahawk*
MCM 7 MH-53E *Sea Dragon*
CSAR 16 HH-60H *Seahawk*

US Marine Corps 184,250
3 Marine Expeditionary Forces (MEF), 3 Marine Expeditionary Brigades (MEB), 7 Marine Expeditionary Units (MEU) drawn from 3 div. An MEU usually consists of a battalion landing team (1 SF coy, 1 lt armd recce coy, 1 recce pl, 1 armd pl, 1 amph aslt pl, 1 inf bn, 1 arty bty, 1 cbt engr pl), an aviation combat element (1 medium-lift sqn with attached atk hel, FGA ac and AD assets) and a composite log bn, with a combined total of about 2,200 personnel. Composition varies with mission requirements
FORCES BY ROLE
SPECIAL FORCES
(see USSOCOM)
MANOEUVRE
Reconnaissance
3 (MEF) recce coy
Amphibious
1 (1st) mne div (2 armd recce bn, 1 recce bn, 1 tk bn, 2 mne regt (4 mne bn), 1 mne regt (3 mne bn), 1 amph aslt bn, 1 arty regt (3 arty bn, 1 MRL bn), 1 cbt engr bn, 1 EW bn, 1 int bn, 1 sigs bn)
1 (2nd) mne div (1 armd recce bn, 1 recce bn, 1 tk bn, 3 mne regt (3 mne bn), 1 amph aslt bn, 1 arty regt (2 arty bn), 1 cbt engr bn, 1 EW bn, 1 int bn, 1 sigs bn)
1 (3rd) mne div (1 recce bn, 1 inf regt (3 inf bn), 1 arty regt (2 arty bn), 1 cbt spt bn (1 armd recce coy, 1 amph aslt coy, 1 cbt engr coy), 1 EW bn, 1 int bn, 1 sigs bn)
COMBAT SERVICE SUPPORT
3 log gp
EQUIPMENT BY TYPE
ARMOURED FIGHTING VEHICLES
MBT 447 M1A1 *Abrams*
IFV 502 LAV-25
APC • APC (W) 207 LAV variants (66 CP; 127 log; 14 EW)
AAV 1,311 AAV-7A1 (all roles)
AUV 2,429: 1,725 *Cougar*; 704 M-ATV
ENGINEERING & MAINTENANCE VEHICLES
AEV 38 *Buffalo*; 42 M1 ABV
ARV 185: 60 AAVRA1; 45 LAV-R; 80 M88A1/2
VLB 6 Joint Aslt Bridge
ANTI-TANK/ANTI-INFRASTRUCTURE • MSL
SP 106 LAV-AT
MANPATS FGM-148 *Javelin*; FGM-172B SRAW-MPV; TOW
ARTILLERY 1,521
TOWED 832: **105mm**: 331 M101A1; **155mm** 501 M777A2
MRL 227mm 40 M142 HIMARS
MOR 649: **81mm** 535 M252; **SP 81mm** 65 LAV-M; **120mm** 49 EFSS
RADAR • LAND 23 AN/TPQ-36 *Firefinder* (arty)
UNMANNED AERIAL VEHCILES
ISR • Light 100 BQM-147 *Exdrone*
AIR DEFENCE • SAM • Point-defence FIM-92 *Stinger*

Marine Corps Aviation 34,700
3 active Marine Aircraft Wings (MAW) and 1 MCR MAW
Flying hours 365 hrs/yr on tpt ac; 248 hrs/yr on ac; 277 hrs/yr on hel

FORCES BY ROLE
FIGHTER
  1 sqn with F/A-18A++ *Hornet*
  6 sqn with F/A-18C *Hornet*
  4 sqn with F/A-18D *Hornet*
FIGHTER/GROUND ATTACK
  5 sqn with AV-8B *Harrier* II
  2 sqn with F-35B *Lightning* II
ELECTRONIC WARFARE
  3 sqn with EA-6B *Prowler*
COMBAT SEARCH & RESCUE/TRANSPORT
  1 sqn with Beech A200/B200 *King Air* (UC-12F/M *Huron*); Beech 350 *King Air* (UC-12W *Huron*); Cessna 560 *Citation Ultra/Encore* (UC-35C/D); DC-9 *Skytrain* (C-9B *Nightingale*); Gulfstream IV (C-20G); HH-1N *Iroquois*
TANKER
  3 sqn with KC-130J *Hercules*
TRANSPORT
  14 sqn with MV-22B *Osprey*
  2 sqn (forming) with MV-22B *Osprey*
TRAINING
  1 sqn with AV-8B *Harrier* II; TAV-8B *Harrier*
  1 sqn with F/A-18B/C/D *Hornet*
  1 sqn with F-35B *Lightning* II
  1 sqn with MV-22B *Osprey*
  1 hel sqn with AH-1W *Cobra*; AH-1Z *Viper*; HH-1N *Iroquois*; UH-1Y *Venom*
  1 hel sqn with CH-53E *Sea Stallion*
ATTACK HELICOPTER
  5 sqn with AH-1W *Cobra*; UH-1Y *Venom*
  3 sqn with AH-1Z *Viper*; UH-1Y *Venom*
TRANSPORT HELICOPTER
  8 sqn with CH-53E *Sea Stallion*
  1 (VIP) sqn with MV-22B *Osprey*; VH-3D *Sea King*; VH-60N *Presidential Hawk*
ISR UAV
  3 sqn with RQ-7B *Shadow*; RQ-21A *Blackjack*
AIR DEFENCE
  2 bn with M1097 *Avenger*; FIM-92 *Stinger* (can provide additional heavy-calibre support weapons)

EQUIPMENT BY TYPE
AIRCRAFT 462 combat capable
  FGA 435: 48 F-35B *Lightning* II; 6 F-35C *Lightning* II; 45 F/A-18A++ *Hornet*; 7 F/A-18B *Hornet*; 107 F/A-18C *Hornet*; 92 F/A-18D *Hornet*; 114 AV-8B *Harrier* II; 16 TAV-8B *Harrier*
  EW 27 EA-6B *Prowler**
  TKR 45 KC-130J *Hercules*
  TPT 20: **Light** 17: 5 Beech A200/B200 *King Air* (UC-12F/M *Huron*); 5 Beech 350 *King Air* (C-12W *Huron*); 7 Cessna 560 *Citation Ultra/Encore* (UC-35C/D); **PAX** 3: 2 DC-9 *Skytrain* (C-9B *Nightingale*); 1 Gulfstream IV (C-20G)
  TRG 3 T-34C *Turbo Mentor*
TILTROTOR • TPT 268 MV-22B *Osprey*
HELICOPTERS
  ATK 148: 96 AH-1W *Cobra*; 52 AH-1Z *Viper*
  SAR 4 HH-1N *Iroquois*
  TPT 267: **Heavy** 139 CH-53E *Sea Stallion*; **Medium** 19: 8 VH-60N *Presidential Hawk* (VIP tpt); 11 VH-3D *Sea King* (VIP tpt); **Light** 109 UH-1Y *Venom*
UNMANNED AERIAL VEHICLES
  ISR 56: **Medium** 31 RQ-7B *Shadow*; **Light** RQ-21A *Blackjack*
AIR DEFENCE
  SAM • Point-defence FIM-92 *Stinger*; M1097 *Avenger*
AIR-LAUNCHED MISSILES
  AAM • IR AIM-9M *Sidewinder*; **IIR** AIM-9X *Sidewinder* II; **SARH** AIM-7P *Sparrow*; **ARH** AIM-120C AMRAAM
  ASM AGM-65E/F IR *Maverick*; AGM-114 *Hellfire*; AGM-176 *Griffin*; AGM-154A/C JSOW
  AShM AGM-84D *Harpoon*
  ARM AGM-88 HARM
  LACM AGM-84E/H/K SLAM/SLAM-ER
BOMBS
  Laser-guided GBU-10/12/16 *Paveway* II
  INS/GPS guided GBU-31 JDAM

Reserve Organisations

Marine Corps Reserve 38,950
FORCES BY ROLE
MANOEUVRE
  Reconnaissance
  2 MEF recce coy
  Amphibious
  1 (4th) mne div (1 armd recce bn, 1 recce bn, 2 mne regt (3 mne bn), 1 amph aslt bn, 1 arty regt (2 arty bn, 1 MRL bn), 1 cbt engr bn, 1 int bn, 1 sigs bn)
COMBAT SERVICE SUPPORT
  1 log gp

Marine Corps Aviation Reserve 11,600 reservists
FORCES BY ROLE
FIGHTER
  1 sqn with F/A-18A++ *Hornet*
TANKER
  2 sqn with KC-130J/T *Hercules*
TRANSPORT
  2 sqn with MV-22B *Osprey*
TRAINING
  1 sqn with F-5F/N *Tiger* II
ATTACK HELICOPTER
  1 sqn with AH-1W *Cobra*; UH-1Y *Venom*
TRANSPORT HELICOPTER
  1 sqn with CH-53E *Sea Stallion*
ISR UAV
  1 sqn with RQ-7B *Shadow*

EQUIPMENT BY TYPE
AIRCRAFT 23 combat capable
  FTR 12: 1 F-5F *Tiger* II; 11 F-5N *Tiger* II
  FGA 11 F/A-18A++ *Hornet*
  TKR 19: 5 KC-130J *Hercules*; 14 KC-130T *Hercules*
  TPT • Light 7: 2 Beech 350 *King Air* (UC-12W *Huron*); 5 Cessna 560 *Citation Ultra/Encore* (UC-35C/D)

TILTROTOR • TPT 12 MV-22B *Osprey*
HELICOPTERS
ATK 16 AH-1W *Cobra*
TPT 28: **Heavy** 6 CH-53E *Sea Stallion*; **Light** 22 UH-1Y *Venom*
UNMANNED AERIAL VEHICLES
ISR • **Medium** 8 RQ-7B *Shadow*

Marine Stand-by Reserve 700 reservists
Trained individuals available for mobilisation

US Coast Guard 40,000 (military) 8,300 (civilian)

9 districts (4 Pacific, 5 Atlantic)
EQUIPMENT BY TYPE
PATROL AND COASTAL COMBATANTS 165
PSOH 24: 1 *Alex Haley*; 13 *Famous*; 5 *Hamilton*; 5 *Legend*
PCO 31: 14 *Reliance* (with 1 hel landing platform); 17 *Sentinel* (Damen 4708)
PCC 37 *Island*
PBI 73 *Marine Protector*
LOGISTICS AND SUPPORT 79
ABU 52: 16 *Juniper*; 4 WLI; 14 *Keeper*; 18 WLR
AG 13: 1 *Cosmos*; 4 *Pamlico*; 8 *Anvil*
AGB 13: 9 *Bay*; 1 *Mackinaw*; 1 *Healy*; 2 *Polar* (of which one in reserve)
AXS 1 *Eagle*

US Coast Guard Aviation
EQUIPMENT BY TYPE
AIRCRAFT
SAR 20: 11 HC-130H *Hercules*; 9 HC-130J *Hercules*
TPT 24: **Medium** 4 C-27J *Spartan*; **Light** 18 CN-235-200 (HC-144A – MP role); **PAX** 2 Gulfstream V (C-37A)
HELICOPTERS
SAR 154: 52 MH-60T *Jayhawk*; 102 AS366G1 (MH-65C/D) *Dauphin* II

US Air Force (USAF) 316,950

Flying hours Ftr 160, bbr 260, tkr 300, airlift 340

Almost the entire USAF (plus active force ANG and AFR) is divided into 10 Aerospace Expeditionary Forces (AEF), each on call for 120 days every 20 months. At least 2 of the 10 AEFs are on call at any one time, each with 10,000–15,000 personnel, 90 multi-role ftr and bbr ac, 31 intra-theatre refuelling aircraft and 13 aircraft for ISR and EW missions

Global Strike Command (GSC)
2 active air forces (8th & 20th); 8 wg
FORCES BY ROLE
SURFACE-TO-SURFACE MISSILE
9 ICBM sqn with LGM-30G *Minuteman* III
BOMBER
4 sqn with B-1B *Lancer*
2 sqn with B-2A *Spirit*
5 sqn (incl 1 trg) with B-52H *Stratofortress*
COMMAND & CONTROL
1 sqn with E-4B

TRANSPORT HELICOPTER
3 sqn with UH-1N *Iroquois*

Air Combat Command (ACC)
2 active air forces (9th & 12th); 12 wg. ACC numbered air forces provide the air component to CENTCOM, SOUTHCOM and NORTHCOM
FORCES BY ROLE
FIGHTER
3 sqn with F-22A *Raptor*
FIGHTER/GROUND ATTACK
4 sqn with F-15E *Strike Eagle*
5 sqn with F-16C/D *Fighting Falcon* (+6 sqn personnel only)
1 sqn with F-35A *Lightning* II
GROUND ATTACK
3 sqn with A-10C *Thunderbolt* II (+1 sqn personnel only)
ELECTRONIC WARFARE
1 sqn with EA-18G *Growler* (personnel only – USN aircraft)
2 sqn with EC-130H *Compass Call*
ISR
2 sqn with E-8C J-STARS (personnel only)
5 sqn with OC-135/RC-135/WC-135
2 sqn with U-2S
AIRBORNE EARLY WARNING & CONTROL
5 sqn with E-3B/C/G *Sentry*
COMBAT SEARCH & RESCUE
2 sqn with HC-130J *Combat King* II
2 sqn with HH-60G *Pave Hawk*
TRAINING
1 sqn with A-10C *Thunderbolt* II
1 sqn with E-3B/C *Sentry*
2 sqn with F-15E *Strike Eagle*
1 sqn with F-22A *Raptor*
1 sqn with RQ-4A *Global Hawk*; TU-2S
2 UAV sqn with MQ-1B *Predator*
3 UAV sqn with MQ-9A *Reaper*
COMBAT/ISR UAV
4 sqn with MQ-1B *Predator*
1 sqn with MQ-1B *Predator*/MQ-9A *Reaper*
2 sqn with MQ-9A *Reaper*
1 sqn with RQ-170 *Sentinel*
ISR UAV
2 sqn with EQ-4B/RQ-4B *Global Hawk*

Pacific Air Forces (PACAF)
Provides the air component of PACOM, and commands air units based in Alaska, Hawaii, Japan and South Korea. 3 active air forces (5th, 7th, & 11th); 8 wg
FORCES BY ROLE
FIGHTER
2 sqn with F-15C/D *Eagle*
2 sqn with F-22A *Raptor* (+1 sqn personnel only)
FIGHTER/GROUND ATTACK
5 sqn with F-16C/D *Fighting Falcon*
GROUND ATTACK
1 sqn with A-10C *Thunderbolt* II
AIRBORNE EARLY WARNING & CONTROL
2 sqn with E-3B/C *Sentry*

COMBAT SEARCH & RESCUE
  1 sqn with HH-60G *Pave Hawk*
TANKER
  1 sqn with KC-135R (+1 sqn personnel only)
TRANSPORT
  1 sqn with B-737-200 (C-40B); Gulfstream V (C-37A)
  2 sqn with C-17A *Globemaster*
  1 sqn with C-130H *Hercules*
  1 sqn with Beech 1900C (C-12J); UH-1N *Huey*
TRAINING
  1 (aggressor) sqn with F-16C/D *Fighting Falcon*

United States Air Forces Europe (USAFE)

Provides the air component to both EUCOM and AFRICOM. 1 active air force (3rd); 5 wg

FORCES BY ROLE
FIGHTER
  1 sqn with F-15C/D *Eagle*
FIGHTER/GROUND ATTACK
  2 sqn with F-15E *Strike Eagle*
  3 sqn with F-16C/D *Fighting Falcon*
COMBAT SEARCH & RESCUE
  1 sqn with HH-60G *Pave Hawk*
TANKER
  1 sqn with KC-135R *Stratotanker*
TRANSPORT
  1 sqn with C-130J-30 *Hercules*
  2 sqn with Gulfstream III/IV (C-20B/H); Gulfstream V (C-37A); Learjet 35A (C-21A)

Air Mobility Command (AMC)

Provides strategic and tactical airlift, air-to-air refuelling and aeromedical evacuation. 1 active air force (18th); 12 wg and 1 gp

FORCES BY ROLE
TANKER
  4 sqn with KC-10A *Extender*
  9 sqn with KC-135R/T *Stratotanker* (+2 sqn with personnel only)
TRANSPORT
  1 VIP sqn with B-737-200 (C-40B); B-757-200 (C-32A)
  1 VIP sqn with Gulfstream III/IV (C-20B/H)
  1 VIP sqn with VC-25 *Air Force One*
  2 sqn with C-5M *Super Galaxy*
  9 sqn with C-17A *Globemaster* III
  1 sqn with C-130H *Hercules* (+1 sqn personnel only)
  5 sqn with C-130J-30 *Hercules* (+1 sqn personnel only)
  1 sqn with Gulfstream V (C-37A)
  2 sqn with Learjet 35A (C-21A)

Air Education and Training Command

1 active air force (2nd), 10 active air wg and 1 gp

FORCES BY ROLE
TRAINING
  1 sqn with C-17A *Globemaster* III
  1 sqn with C-130J-30 *Hercules*
  4 sqn with F-16C/D *Fighting Falcon*
  4 sqn with F-35A *Lightning* II
  1 sqn with KC-46A *Pegasus* (forming)
  1 sqn with KC-135R *Stratotanker*
  5 (flying trg) sqn with T-1A *Jayhawk*
  10 (flying trg) sqn with T-6A *Texan* II
  10 (flying trg) sqn with T-38C *Talon*
  1 UAV sqn with MQ-1B *Predator*

EQUIPMENT BY TYPE
SURFACE-TO-SURFACE MISSILE LAUNCHERS
  ICBM • Nuclear 450 LGM-30G *Minuteman* III (capacity 1–3 MIRV Mk12/Mk12A per missile)
AIRCRAFT 1,430 combat capable
  BBR 139: 61 B-1B *Lancer*; 20 B-2A *Spirit*; 58 B-52H *Stratofortress*
  FTR 265: 96 F-15C *Eagle*; 10 F-15D *Eagle*; 159 F-22A *Raptor*
  FGA 883: 211 F-15E *Strike Eagle*; 456 F-16C *Fighting Falcon*; 114 F-16D *Fighting Falcon*; 102 F-35A *Lightning* II
  ATK 143 A-10C *Thunderbolt* II
  EW 14 EC-130H *Compass Call*
  ISR 41: 2 E-9A; 4 E-11A; 2 OC-135B *Open Skies*; 27 U-2S; 4 TU-2S; 2 WC-135 *Constant Phoenix*
  ELINT 22: 8 RC-135V *Rivet Joint*; 9 RC-135W *Rivet Joint*; 3 RC-135S *Cobra Ball*; 2 RC-135U *Combat Sent*
  AEW&C 31: 18 E-3B *Sentry*; 6 E-3C *Sentry*; 7 E-3G *Sentry*
  C2 4 E-4B
  TKR 156: 126 KC-135R *Stratotanker*; 30 KC-135T *Stratotanker*
  TKR/TPT 59 KC-10A *Extender*
  CSAR 15 HC-130J *Combat King* II
  TPT 350: **Heavy** 205: 35 C-5M *Super Galaxy*; 170 C-17A *Globemaster* III; **Medium** 98: 13 C-130H *Hercules*; 85 C-130J/J-30 *Hercules*; **Light** 21: 4 Beech 1900C (C-12J); 17 Learjet 35A (C-21A); **PAX** 26: 4 B-737-700 (C-40B); 4 B-757-200 (C-32A); 5 Gulfstream III (C-20B); 2 Gulfstream IV (C-20H); 12 Gulfstream V (C-37A); 2 VC-25A *Air Force One*
  TRG 1,129: 178 T-1A *Jayhawk*; 445 T-6A *Texan* II; 506 T-38A/C *Talon*
HELICOPTERS
  CSAR 75 HH-60G *Pave Hawk*
  TPT • Light 62 UH-1N *Huey*
UNMANNED AERIAL VEHICLES 352
  CISR • Heavy 308: 110 MQ-1B *Predator*; 198 MQ-9A *Reaper*
  ISR • Heavy 44: 3 EQ-4B; 31 RQ-4B *Global Hawk*; ε10 RQ-170 *Sentinel*
AIR DEFENCE • SAM • Point-defence FIM-92 *Stinger*
AIR-LAUNCHED MISSILES
  AAM • IR AIM-9 *Sidewinder*; **IIR** AIM-9X *Sidewinder* II; **SARH** AIM-7M *Sparrow*; **ARH** AIM-120C/D AMRAAM
  ASM AGM-65D/G *Maverick*; AGM-130A; AGM-176 *Griffin*
  ALCM • Nuclear AGM-86B (ALCM); **Conventional** AGM-86C (CALCM); AGM-86D (penetrator); AGM-158 JASSM; AGM-158B JASSM-ER
  ARM AGM-88A/B HARM
  EW MALD/MALD-J
BOMBS
  Laser-guided GBU 10/12/16 *Paveway* II, GBU-24 *Paveway* III
  INS/GPS guided GBU 31/32/38 JDAM; GBU-54 Laser JDAM; GBU-15 (with BLU-109 penetrating warhead or Mk84); GBU-39B Small Diameter Bomb (250lb); GBU-43B MOAB; GBU-57A/B MOP; Enhanced *Paveway* III

Reserve Organisations

Air National Guard 105,350 reservists
FORCES BY ROLE
BOMBER
1 sqn with B-2A *Spirit* (personnel only)
FIGHTER
5 sqn with F-15C/D *Eagle*
1 sqn with F-22A *Raptor* (+1 sqn personnel only)
FIGHTER/GROUND ATTACK
11 sqn with F-16C/D *Fighting Falcon*
GROUND ATTACK
4 sqn with A-10C *Thunderbolt* II
ISR
1 sqn with E-8C J-STARS
COMBAT SEARCH & RESCUE
2 sqn with HC-130P/N *Combat King*
1 sqn with MC-130P *Combat Shadow*
3 sqn with HH-60G *Pave Hawk*
TANKER
17 sqn with KC-135R *Stratotanker* (+1 sqn personnel only)
3 sqn with KC-135T *Stratotanker*
TRANSPORT
1 sqn with B-737-700 (C-40C)
4 sqn with C-17A *Globemaster* (+2 sqn personnel only)
14 sqn with C-130H *Hercules* (+1 sqn personnel only)
1 sqn with C-130H/LC-130H *Hercules*
2 sqn with C-130J-30 *Hercules*
1 sqn with Learjet 35A (C-21A)
1 sqn with WC-130H *Hercules*
TRAINING
1 sqn with C-130H *Hercules*
1 sqn with F-15C/D *Eagle*
4 sqn with F-16C/D *Fighting Falcon*
COMBAT/ISR UAV
4 sqn with MQ-1B *Predator*
2 sqn with MQ-9A *Reaper* (+4 sqn personnel only)

EQUIPMENT BY TYPE
AIRCRAFT 475 combat capable
FTR 157: 127 F-15C *Eagle*; 10 F-15D *Eagle*; 20 F-22A *Raptor*
FGA 356: 311 F-16C *Fighting Falcon*; 45 F-16D *Fighting Falcon*
ATK 86 A-10C *Thunderbolt* II
ISR 16 E-8C J-STARS
ELINT 11 RC-26B *Metroliner*
CSAR 9: 6 HC-130N *Combat King*; 3 HC-130P *Combat King*
TKR 172: 148 KC-135R *Stratotanker*; 24 KC-135T *Stratotanker*
TPT 220: **Heavy** 34 C-17A *Globemaster* III; **Medium** 174: 132 C-130H *Hercules*; 20 C-130J/J-30 *Hercules*; 10 LC-130H *Hercules*; 4 MC-130P *Combat Shadow*; 8 WC-130H *Hercules*; **Light** 2 Learjet 35A (C-21A); **PAX** 5: 3 B-737-700 (C-40C); 2 B-757-200 (C-32A)
HELICOPTERS • **CSAR** 18 HH-60G *Pave Hawk*
UNMANNED AERIAL VEHICLES • **CISR** • **Heavy** 70: 35 MQ-1B *Predator*; 35 MQ-9A *Reaper*

Air Force Reserve Command 69,300 reservists
FORCES BY ROLE
BOMBER
1 sqn with B-52H *Stratofortress* (personnel only)
FIGHTER
2 sqn with F-22A *Raptor* (personnel only)
FIGHTER/GROUND ATTACK
2 sqn with F-16C/D *Fighting Falcon* (+2 sqn personnel only)
GROUND ATTACK
1 sqn with A-10C *Thunderbolt* II (+2 sqn personnel only)
ISR
1 (Weather Recce) sqn with WC-130J *Hercules*
AIRBORNE EARLY WARNING & CONTROL
1 sqn with E-3B/C *Sentry* (personnel only)
COMBAT SEARCH & RESCUE
1 sqn with HC-130P/N *Combat King*
2 sqn with HH-60G *Pave Hawk*
TANKER
4 sqn with KC-10A *Extender* (personnel only)
6 sqn with KC-135R *Stratotanker* (+2 sqn personnel only)
TRANSPORT
1 (VIP) sqn with B-737-700 (C-40C)
1 sqn with C-5A *Galaxy*
1 sqn with C-5B *Galaxy* (+1 sqn personnel only)
1 sqn with C-5M *Super Galaxy* (personnel only)
2 sqn with C-17A *Globemaster* (+9 sqn personnel only)
8 sqn with C-130H *Hercules*
1 sqn with C-130J-30 *Hercules*
1 (Aerial Spray) sqn with C-130H *Hercules*
TRAINING
1 (aggressor) sqn with A-10C *Thunderbolt* II; F-15C/E *Eagle*; F-16 *Fighting Falcon*; F-22A *Raptor* (personnel only)
1 sqn with A-10C *Thuinderbolt* II
1 sqn with B-52H *Stratofortress*
1 sqn with C-5M *Super Galaxy*
1 sqn with F-16C/D *Fighting Falcon*
5 (flying training) sqn with T-1A *Jayhawk*; T-6A *Texan* II; T-38C *Talon* (personnel only)
COMBAT/ISR UAV
2 sqn with MQ-1B *Predator*/MQ-9A *Reaper* (personnel only)
ISR UAV
1 sqn with RQ-4B *Global Hawk* (personnel only)

EQUIPMENT BY TYPE
AIRCRAFT 97 combat capable
BBR 18 B-52H *Stratofortress*
FGA 53: 49 F-16C *Fighting Falcon*; 4 F-16D *Fighting Falcon*
ATK 55 A-10C *Thunderbolt* II
ISR 10 WC-130J *Hercules* (Weather Recce)
CSAR 8 HC-130P/N *Combat King*
TKR 70 KC-135R *Stratotanker*
TPT 100: **Heavy** 30: 5 C-5A *Galaxy*; 3 C-5B *Galaxy*; 4 C-5M *Super Galaxy*; 18 C-17A *Globemaster* III; **Medium** 66: 56 C-130H *Hercules*; 10 C-130J-30 *Hercules*; **PAX** 4 B-737-700 (C-40C)
HELICOPTERS • **CSAR** 16 HH-60G *Pave Hawk*

Civil Reserve Air Fleet

Commercial ac numbers fluctuate
AIRCRAFT • **TPT** 517 international (391 long-range and 126 short-range); 36 national

Air Force Stand-by Reserve 16,858 reservists

Trained individuals for mobilisation

US Special Operations Command (USSOCOM) 63,150; 6,550 (civilian)

Commands all active, reserve and National Guard Special Operations Forces (SOF) of all services based in CONUS

Joint Special Operations Command

Reported to comprise elite US SOF, including Special Forces Operations Detachment Delta ('Delta Force'), SEAL Team 6 and integral USAF support

US Army Special Operations Command 34,100

FORCES BY ROLE
SPECIAL FORCES
  5 SF gp (4 SF bn, 1 spt bn)
  1 ranger regt (3 ranger bn; 1 cbt spt bn)
COMBAT SUPPORT
  1 civil affairs bde (5 civil affairs bn)
  1 psyops gp (3 psyops bn)
  1 psyops gp (4 psyops bn)
COMBAT SERVICE SUPPORT
  1 (sustainment) log bde (1 sigs bn)
HELICOPTER
  1 (160th SOAR) hel regt (4 hel bn)

EQUIPMENT BY TYPE
ARMOURED FIGHTING VEHICLES
  APC • **APC (W)** 12 *Pandur*
  AUV 640 M-ATV
HELICOPTERS
  MRH 50 AH-6M/MH-6M *Little Bird*
  TPT 130: **Heavy** 68 MH-47G *Chinook*; **Medium** 62 MH-60K/L/M *Black Hawk*
UAV
  CISR • **Heavy** 12 MQ-1C *Gray Eagle*
  ISR • **Light** 29: 15 XPV-1 *Tern*; 14 XPV-2 *Mako*
  TPT • **Heavy** 28 CQ-10 *Snowgoose*

Reserve Organisations

Army National Guard
FORCES BY ROLE
SPECIAL FORCES
  2 SF gp (3 SF bn)

Army Reserve
FORCES BY ROLE
COMBAT SUPPORT
  2 psyops gp
  4 civil affairs comd HQ
  8 civil affairs bde HQ
  32 civil affairs bn (coy)

US Navy Special Warfare Command 9,850

FORCES BY ROLE
SPECIAL FORCES
  8 SEAL team (total: 48 SF pl)
  2 SEAL Delivery Vehicle team

Reserve Organisations

Naval Reserve Force
FORCES BY ROLE
SPECIAL FORCES
  8 SEAL det
  10 Naval Special Warfare det
  2 Special Boat sqn
  2 Special Boat unit
  1 SEAL Delivery Vehicle det

US Marine Special Operations Command (MARSOC) 3,000

FORCES BY ROLE
SPECIAL FORCES
  1 SF regt (3 SF bn)
COMBAT SUPPORT
  1 int bn
COMBAT SERVICE SUPPORT
  1 spt gp

Air Force Special Operations Command (AFSOC) 16,200

FORCES BY ROLE
GROUND ATTACK
  1 sqn with AC-130U *Spectre*
  2 sqn with AC-130W *Stinger* II
TRANSPORT
  3 sqn with CV-22B *Osprey*
  1 sqn with DHC-8; Do-328 (C-146A)
  2 sqn with MC-130H *Combat Talon*
  3 sqn with MC-130J *Commando* II
  3 sqn with PC-12 (U-28A)
TRAINING
  1 sqn with M-28 *Skytruck* (C-145A)
  1 sqn with CV-22A/B *Osprey*
  1 sqn with HC-130J *Combat King* II; MC-130J *Commando* II
  1 sqn with Bell 205 (TH-1H *Iroquois*)
  1 sqn with HH-60G *Pave Hawk*; UH-1N *Huey*
COMBAT/ISR UAV
  2 sqn with MQ-9 *Reaper*

EQUIPMENT BY TYPE
AIRCRAFT 27 combat capable
  ATK 27: 2 AC-130J *Ghostrider*; 13 AC-130U *Spectre*; 12 AC-130W *Stinger* II
  CSAR 3 HC-130J *Combat King* II
  TPT 93: **Medium** 49: 14 MC-130H *Combat Talon* II; 35 MC-130J *Commando* II; **Light** 49: 9 Do-328 (C-146A); 4 M-28 *Skytruck* (C-145A); 36 PC-12 (U-28A)
TILT-ROTOR 49 CV-22A/B *Osprey*
HELICOPTERS
  CSAR 3 HH-60G *Pave Hawk*
  TPT • **Light** 34: 24 Bell 205 (TH-1H *Iroquois*); 10 UH-1N *Huey*

UNMANNED AERIAL VEHICLES • CISR • Heavy 30
MQ-9 *Reaper*

Reserve Organisations

Air National Guard
FORCES BY ROLE
ELECTRONIC WARFARE
1 sqn with C-130J *Hercules*/EC-130J *Commando Solo*
ISR
1 sqn with Beech 350ER *King Air* (MC-12W *Liberty*)
TRANSPORT
1 flt with B-737-200 (C-32B)
EQUIPMENT BY TYPE
AIRCRAFT
EW 3 EC-130J *Commando Solo*
ISR 13 Beech 350ER *King Air* (MC-12W *Liberty*)
TPT 5: **Medium** 3 C-130J *Hercules*; **PAX** 2 B-757-200 (C-32B)

Air Force Reserve
FORCES BY ROLE
TRAINING
1 sqn with AC-130U *Spectre* (personnel only)
1 sqn with M-28 *Skytruck* (C-145A) (personnel only)
COMBAT/ISR UAV
1 sqn with MQ-9 *Reaper* (personnel only)

Cyber

US Cyber Command
Cyber Mission Force (13 national mission teams; 68 cyber protection teams; 27 combat mission teams; 25 support teams)

US Army Cyber Command (ARCYBER)
4 signals commands; 1 information operations command; 1 intelligence and security command; 9 signals brigades; 1 military intelligence brigade; 1 cyber protection brigade; 1 reserve cyber operations group

US Fleet Cyber Command (10th Fleet)
2 information operations task forces (3 task groups); 2 network operations and defence task forces (5 task groups); 5 fleet and theatre operations task forces (9 task groups); 1 cryptologic operations task force (10 task groups); 1 cyber warfare development task force

Marine Forces Cyberspace Command (MARFORCYBER)
1 cyberspace warfare group; 13 cyber mission force teams; 2 combat mission teams; 1 network operations security centre

Air Forces Cyber (24th Air Force)
2 cyberspace wings; 1 combat communications wing; 4 cyberspace operations groups; 1 cyberspace engineering installation group; 2 combat communications groups; 1 operations centre

960th Cyberspace Operations Group
Air Force Reserve Command formation. Administratively part of 10th Air Force. Commands 1 network warfare squadron; 1 combat operations squadron; 3 network operations squadrons; 4 combat communications squadrons

The Department of Defense (DoD) Cyber Strategy, released in 2015, named cyber as the primary strategic threat to the US, 'placing it above terrorism' for the first time since 9/11. The US has well-developed cyber capabilities, and there are military cyber elements within each service branch, under US Cyber Command (itself under US Strategic Command), co-located with the National Security Agency (NSA). The NSA director also heads Cyber Command, although it has been reported that the Pentagon might recommend creating two separate forces. Cyber Command requested a budget of US$505m for FY2017, representing an 8.4% increase on the previous year. It plans a Cyber Mission Force (CMF) of 133 teams, to reach full operating capability in 2018. In late September 2016, the CMF reached initial operating capability. All the armed services have their own cyber components, both US-based and deployable. The US Air Force plans to merge offensive and defensive cyber operations into a full-spectrum cyber capability called the Cyber Operations Squadron by 2026. The Air Force Academy's new cyber specialisation graduated its first three cadets in mid-2016. The Marine Corps created a new cyber unit, the Cyberspace Warfare Group, in March 2016. This group is responsible for supporting cyberspace mission teams and for carrying out defensive and offensive operations in support of the marines and cyber command. High-level DoD cyber exercises include the defence-focused *Cyber Flag* and *Cyber Guard* series, which involve broader actors from across government and includes critical-national-infrastructure scenarios. In October 2012, then-president Barack Obama signed Presidential Policy Directive 20 (PPD-20), the purpose of which was to establish clear standards for US federal agencies in confronting threats in cyberspace. This document was made public in the Snowden leaks. It is notable for the distinction it draws between defensive and offensive cyber operations. According to PPD-20, the US 'shall identify potential targets of national importance where [offensive cyber-effects operations] can offer a favorable balance of effectiveness and risk as compared with other instruments of national power, establish and maintain [offensive cyber-effects operations] capabilities integrated as appropriate with other US offensive capabilities, and execute those capabilities in a manner consistent with the provisions of this directive'. PPD-20 states that presidential approval is required for any cyber operations with 'significant consequences'. DARPA's Plan X programme has been funding research on cyber warfare since 2013. US$460m has recently been awarded to various private contractors, who will assist Cyber Command in developing and supplying cyber weapons in cooperation with US intelligence agencies and providing technical support to Cyber Command in planning, organising and coordinating defensive and offensive military activities.

DEPLOYMENT

AFGHANISTAN
NATO • *Operation Resolute Support* 7,006; 1 div HQ; 1 div HQ (fwd); 1 mech bde HQ; 1 lt inf bde HQ; 1 armd recce sqn, 2 mech bn; 2 inf bn; 1 cbt avn bde
US Central Command • *Operation Freedom's Sentinel* 1,400
   EQUIPMENT BY TYPE
   RC-12X *Guardrail*; EC-130H *Compass Call*; C-130 *Hercules*; AH-64 *Apache*; OH-58 *Kiowa*; CH-47 *Chinook*; UH-60 *Black Hawk*; HH-60 *Pave Hawk*; RQ-7B *Shadow*; MQ-1 *Predator*; MQ-9 *Reaper*

ALBANIA
OSCE • Albania 1

ARABIAN SEA
US Central Command • Navy • 5th Fleet: 1 SSGN; 1 SSN; 1 CGHM; 3 DDGHM; 1 DDGM; 1 LSD
Combined Maritime Forces • TF 53: 1 AE; 2 AKE; 1 AOH; 3 AO

ARUBA
US Southern Command • 1 Forward Operating Location

ASCENSION ISLAND
US Strategic Command • 1 detection and tracking radar at Ascension Auxiliary Air Field

ATLANTIC OCEAN
US Northern Command • US Navy: 6 SSBN; 22 SSGN; 4 CVN; 8 CGHM; 11 DDGHM; 9 DDGM; 3 PCF; 3 LHD; 3 LPD; 5 LSD

AUSTRALIA
US Pacific Command • 1,250; 1 SEWS at Pine Gap; 1 comms facility at Pine Gap; 1 SIGINT stn at Pine Gap
US Strategic Command • 1 detection and tracking radar at Naval Communication Station Harold E Holt

BAHRAIN
US Central Command • 5,000; 1 HQ (5th Fleet); 2 AD bty with MIM-104E/F *Patriot* PAC-2/3

BELGIUM
US European Command • 900

BOSNIA-HERZEGOVINA
OSCE • Bosnia and Herzegovina 5

BRITISH INDIAN OCEAN TERRITORY
US Strategic Command • 300; 1 Spacetrack Optical Tracker at Diego Garcia; 1 ground-based electro optical deep space surveillance system (*GEODSS*) at Diego Garcia
US Pacific Command • 1 MPS sqn (MPS-2 with equipment for one MEB) at Diego Garcia with 5 logistics and support ships; 1 naval air base at Diego Garcia, 1 support facility at Diego Garcia

CAMEROON
US Africa Command • 300

CANADA
US Northern Command • 150

CENTRAL AFRICAN REPUBLIC
UN • MINUSCA 6

COLOMBIA
US Southern Command • 50

CUBA
US Southern Command • 950 (JTF-GTMO) at Guantánamo Bay

CURACAO
US Southern Command • 1 Forward Operating Location

DEMOCRATIC REPUBLIC OF THE CONGO
UN • MONUSCO 3

DJIBOUTI
US Africa Command • 3,150; 1 tpt sqn with C-130H/J-30 *Hercules*; 1 spec ops sqn with MC-130H/J; PC-12 (U-28A); 1 CSAR sqn with HH-60G *Pave Hawk*; 1 naval air base

EGYPT
MFO 410; elm 1 ARNG inf bn; 1 ARNG spt bn

EL SALVADOR
US Southern Command • 1 Forward Operating Location (Military, DEA, USCG and Customs personnel)

GERMANY
US Africa Command • 1 HQ at Stuttgart
US European Command • 36,850; 1 Combined Service HQ (EUCOM) at Stuttgart–Vaihingen
   US Army 22,000
   FORCES BY ROLE
   1 HQ (US Army Europe (USAREUR)) at Heidelberg; 1 SF gp; 1 mech bde; 1 recce bn; 1 arty bn; 1 (cbt avn) hel bde HQ; 1 int bde; 1 MP bde; 1 sigs bde; 1 spt bde; 1 (APS) armd bde eqpt set
   EQUIPMENT BY TYPE
   M1 *Abrams*; M2/M3 *Bradley*; *Stryker*, M109; M777; AH-64 *Apache*; CH-47 *Chinook*; UH-60 *Black Hawk*
   US Navy 950
   USAF 12,650
   FORCES BY ROLE
   1 HQ (US Air Force Europe (USAFE)) at Ramstein AB; 1 HQ (3rd Air Force) at Ramstein AB; 1 ftr wg at Spangdahlem AB with 1 ftr sqn with 24 F-16C/D *Fighting Falcon*; 1 tpt wg at Ramstein AB with 16 C-130J-30 *Hercules*; 2 Gulfstream (C-20H); 9 Learjet (C-21A); 1 C-40B
   USMC 1,200

GREECE
US European Command • 370; 1 naval base at Makri; 1 naval base at Soudha Bay; 1 air base at Iraklion

GREENLAND (DNK)
US Strategic Command • 170; 1 AN/FPS-132 Upgraded Early Warning Radar and 1 Spacetrack Radar at Thule

GUAM
US Pacific Command • 5,150; 4 SSGN; 1 MPS sqn (MPS-3 with equipment for one MEB) with 4 Logistics and Support vessels; 1 tpt hel sqn with MH-60S; 1 AD bty with THAAD; 1 air base; 1 naval base

HAITI
UN • MINUSTAH 4

HONDURAS
US Southern Command • 410; 1 avn bn with CH-47F *Chinook*; UH-60 *Black Hawk*

IRAQ
US Central Command • *Operation Inherent Resolve* 5,262; 1 air aslt div HQ; 1 mne coy; 1 SP arty bty with 4 M109A6; 1 fd arty bty with 4 M777A2; 1 MRL bty with 4 M142 HIMARS; 1 atk hel sqn with AH-64D *Apache*

ISRAEL
US Strategic Command • 1 AN/TPY-2 X-band radar at Mount Keren

ITALY
US European Command • 12,550
US Army 4.550; 1 AB IBCT(-)
US Navy 3,950; 1 HQ (US Navy Europe (USNAVEUR)) at Naples; 1 HQ (6th Fleet) at Gaeta; 1 MP sqn with 4 P-8A *Poseidon* at Sigonella
USAF 3,700; 1 ftr wg with 2 ftr sqn with 21 F-16C/D *Fighting Falcon* at Aviano
USMC 300

JAPAN
US Pacific Command • 47,050
US Army 2,900 1 SF gp; 1 avn bn; 1 SAM regt
US Navy 12,000; 1 HQ (7th Fleet) at Yokosuka; 1 base at Sasebo; 1 base at Yokosuka
EQUIPMENT BY TYPE
1 CVN; 3 CGHM; 2 DDGHM; 6 DDGM; 1 LCC; 4 MCO; 1 LHD; 1 LPD; 2 LSD
USAF 11,450
FORCES BY ROLE
1 HQ (5th Air Force) at Okinawa – Kadena AB; 1 ftr wg at Misawa AB with (2 ftr sqn with 22 F-16C/D *Fighting Falcon*); 1 wg at Okinawa – Kadena AB with (2 ftr sqn with 27 F-15C/D *Eagle*; 1 tkr sqn with 15 KC-135R *Stratotanker*; 1 AEW&C sqn with 2 E-3B/C *Sentry*; 1 CSAR sqn with 10 HH-60G *Pave Hawk*); 1 tpt wg at Yokota AB with 10 C-130H *Hercules*; 3 Beech 1900C (C-12J); 1 Spec Ops gp at Okinawa – Kadena AB with (1 sqn with 5 MC-130H *Combat Talon*; 1 sqn with 5 MC-130J *Commando* II); 1 ISR sqn with RC-135 *Rivet Joint*
USMC 20,700
FORCES BY ROLE
1 mne div (3rd); 1 ftr sqn with 12 F/A-18D *Hornet*; 1 tkr sqn with 12 KC-130J *Hercules*; 2 tpt sqn with 12 MV-22B *Osprey*
US Strategic Command • 1 AN/TPY-2 X-band radar at Shariki; 1 AN/TPY-2 X-Band radar at Kyogamisaki

JORDAN
US Central Command • *Operation Inherent Resolve* 2,000: 1 FGA sqn with 12 F-16C *Fighting Falcon*; 1 AD bty with MIM-104E/F *Patriot* PAC-2/3; 6 MQ-1 *Predator*; 2 MQ-9 *Reaper*

KOREA, REPUBLIC OF
US Pacific Command • 28,500
US Army 19,200
FORCES BY ROLE
1 HQ (8th Army) at Seoul; 1 div HQ (2nd Inf) located at Tongduchon; 1 armd bde; 1 (cbt avn) hel bde; 1 ISR hel bn; 1 arty bde; 1 AD bde
EQUIPMENT BY TYPE
M1 *Abrams*; M2/M3 *Bradley*; M109; M270 MLRS; AH-64 *Apache*; OH-58D *Kiowa Warrior*; CH-47 *Chinook*; UH-60 *Black Hawk*; MIM-104 *Patriot*/FIM-92A *Avenger*; 1 (APS) armd bde eqpt set
US Navy 250
USAF 8,800
FORCES BY ROLE
1 (AF) HQ (7th Air Force) at Osan AB; 1 ftr wg at Osan AB with (1 ftr sqn with 20 F-16C/D *Fighting Falcon*; 1 atk sqn with 24 A-10C *Thunderbolt* II); 1 ftr wg at Kunsan AB with (2 ftr sqn with 20 F-16C/D *Fighting Falcon*); 1 ISR sqn at Osan AB with U-2S
USMC 250

KUWAIT
US Central Command • 13,000; 1 armd bde; 1 ARNG (cbt avn) hel bde; 1 spt bde; 4 AD bty with MIM-104E/F *Patriot* PAC-2/3; 1 (APS) armd bde set; 1 (APS) inf bde set

LIBERIA
UN • UNMIL 5; 3 obs

MALI
UN • MINUSMA 10

MARSHALL ISLANDS
US Strategic Command • 1 detection and tracking radar at Kwajalein Atoll

MEDITERRANEAN SEA
US European Command • US Navy • 6th Fleet: 4 DDGM; 1 LHD; 1 LPD; 1 LCC

MIDDLE EAST
UN • UNTSO 2 obs

MOLDOVA
OSCE • Moldova 3

NETHERLANDS
US European Command • 380

NIGER
US Africa Command • 250

NORWAY
US European Command • 1 (APS) SP 155mm arty bn set

PACIFIC OCEAN
US Pacific Command • US Navy • 3rd Fleet: 8 SSBN; 20 SSGN; 7 SSN; 4 CVN; 9 CGHM; 18 DDGHM; 7 DDGM; 8 FFHM; 3 MCO; 3 LHD; 1 LHA; 5 LPD; 4 LSD

PERSIAN GULF
US Central Command • Navy • 5th Fleet: 1 CVN; 2 CGHM; 1 DDGM; 10 PCFG; 6 (Coast Guard) PCC
Combined Maritime Forces • CTF-152: 4 MCO; 1 AFSB

PHILIPPINES
US Pacific Command • 75

PORTUGAL
US European Command • 220; 1 spt facility at Lajes

QATAR
US Central Command • 8,000: 1 bbr sqn with 6 B-52H *Stratofortress*; 1 ISR sqn with 4 RC-135 *Rivet Joint*; 1 ISR sqn with 4 E-8C JSTARS; 1 tkr sqn with 24 KC-135R/T *Stratotanker*; 1 tpt sqn with 4 C-17A *Globemaster*; 4 C-130H/J-30 *Hercules*; 2 AD bty with MIM-104E/F *Patriot* PAC-2/3
US Strategic Command • 1 AN/TPY-2 X-band radar

ROMANIA
US European Command • 550

SAUDI ARABIA
US Central Command • 400

SERBIA
NATO • KFOR • *Joint Enterprise* 635; elm 1 ARNG inf bde HQ; 1 inf bn
OSCE • Kosovo 4

SINGAPORE
US Pacific Command • 180; 1 log spt sqn; 1 spt facility

SOUTH SUDAN
UN • UNMISS 6

SPAIN
US European Command • 2,950; 1 air base at Morón; 1 naval base at Rota

THAILAND
US Pacific Command • 300

TURKEY
US European Command • 2,700; 1 atk sqn with 12 A-10C *Thunderbolt* II; 1 tkr sqn with 14 KC-135; 1 CISR UAV sqn with MQ-1B *Predator* UAV; 1 ELINT flt with EP-3E *Aries* II; 1 air base at Incirlik; 1 support facility at Ankara; 1 support facility at Izmir
US Strategic Command • 1 AN/TPY-2 X-band radar at Kürecik

UKRAINE
310 (trg mission)
OSCE • Ukraine 73

UNITED ARAB EMIRATES
US Central Command • 5,000: 1 ftr sqn with 6 F-22A *Raptor*; 1 FGA sqn with 12 F-15E *Strike Eagle*; 1 ISR sqn with 4 U-2; 1 AEW&C sqn with 4 E-3 *Sentry*; 1 tkr sqn with 12 KC-10A; 1 ISR UAV sqn with RQ-4 *Global Hawk*; 2 AD bty with MIM-104E/F *Patriot* PAC-2/3

UNITED KINGDOM
US European Command • 8,700
FORCES BY ROLE
1 ftr wg at RAF Lakenheath with 1 ftr sqn with 24 F-15C/D *Eagle*, 2 ftr sqn with 23 F-15E *Strike Eagle*; 1 ISR sqn at RAF Mildenhall with OC-135/RC-135; 1 tkr wg at RAF Mildenhall with 15 KC-135R/T *Stratotanker*; 1 CSAR sqn with 8 HH-60G *Pave Hawk*; 1 Spec Ops gp at RAF Mildenhall with (1 sqn with 8 CV-22B *Osprey*; 1 sqn with 8 MC-130J *Commando* II)
US Strategic Command • 1 AN/FPS-132 Upgraded Early Warning Radar and 1 Spacetrack Radar at Fylingdales Moor

FOREIGN FORCES
Canada 17 USCENTCOM; 303 NORTHCOM (NORAD)
Germany Air Force: trg units with 40 T-38 *Talon*; 69 T-6A *Texan* II; 24 *Tornado* IDS; • Missile trg at Fort Bliss (TX)
Netherlands 1 hel trg sqn with AH-64D *Apache*; CH-47D *Chinook*
Singapore Air Force: trg units with F-16C/D; 12 F-15SG; AH-64D *Apache*; 6+ CH-47D *Chinook* hel
United Kingdom 660

Table 2 **Selected arms procurements and deliveries, North America**

Designation	Type	Quantity (Current)	Contract Value	Prime Nationality	Prime Contractor	Order Date	First Delivery Due	Notes
Canada (CAN)								
TAPV (*Commando* Mod)	Recce & AUV	193 & 307	C$603m (US$603.8m)	US	Textron (Textron Systems Canada)	2012	2016	Tactical Armoured Patrol Vehicle. Option for 100 more. Delays pushed back beginning of deliveries to Aug 2016
Harry DeWolf class	PSOH	8	C$2.5bn (US$2.4bn)	CAN	Irving Shipyard	2013	2018	For navy. Arctic Offshore Patrol Ship project. Based on NOR Coast Guard *Svalbard* class. Keel laid on first of class Sep 2016
CH-148 *Cyclone*	Med tpt hel	28	C$2bn (US$1.5bn)	US	Lockheed Martin (Sikorsky)	2004	2025	Programme has suffered from delays. Original contract signed 2004 and amended contract signed early 2014. Full operating capability now delayed until 2025
United States (US)								
JLTV	AUV	1,145	US$923.1m	US	Oshkosh Corporation	2015	2016	Plan to order 49,099 vehicles. Currently 1,021 budgeted for army and 124 for USMC. Legal challenge to contract award in 2015 has delayed initial operating capability until late 2019 for army and 2020 for USMC. First vehicles delivered for testing in Oct 2016
Virginia class	SSGN	24	US$67.4bn	US	General Dynamics (Electric Boat)/ Huntingdon Ingalls Industries (Newport News Shipbuilding)	1998	2004	Thirteenth of class and third Flight III boat commissioned late 2016
Gerald R. Ford class	CVN	2	US$21.5bn	US	Huntingdon Ingalls Industries (Newport News Shipbuilding)	2008	2017	Second of class keel laid in late 2015. First of class was expected to commission end of 2016 but problems in trials have delayed this
Zumwalt class	CGHM	3	US$12.4bn	US	General Dynamics (Bath Iron Works (BIW))	2008	2015	DDG-1000; first of class commissioned Oct 2016
Arleigh Burke class	DDGHM	74	US$79.5bn	US	General Dynamics (BIW)/ Huntingdon Ingalls Industries (Ingalls Shipbuilding)	1985	1991	Sixty-fourth of class launched Dec 2015. Sixty-third of class in sea trials late 2016
Freedom class *Independence* class	FFHM FFHM	12 12	US$12.2bn	US/AUS/ US/ITA	General Dynamics/ Austal (Austal USA)/Lockheed Martin/Fincantieri (Marinette Marine)	2004	2008	Littoral Combat Ship programme. Original plan cut from 52 to 40 vessels. Eighth vessel commissioned Oct 2016. Small Surface Combatant to be selected in FY2018, based on one of two LCS designs
America class	LHA	2	US$7bn	US	Huntingdon Ingalls Industries (Ingalls Shipbuilding)	2007	2014	First vessel commissioned Oct 2014. Third vessel planned; will be an LHD
San Antonio class	LPD	12	US$20.4bn	US	Northrop Grumman (Avondale Shipyard)/ Huntingdon Ingalls Industries (Ingalls Shipbuilding)	1996	2002	Tenth of class commissioned Oct 2016

Table 2 **Selected arms procurements and deliveries, North America**

Designation	Type	Quantity (Current)	Contract Value	Prime Nationality	Prime Contractor	Order Date	First Delivery Due	Notes
B-21 *Raider* (LRS-B)	Bbr ac	See notes	US$1.6bn	US	Northrop Grumman	2015	n.k.	Contract for design phase estimated at US$21.4bn. Includes options for first 21 aircraft from total planned fleet of 100. Average procurement cost of each aircraft cannot be greater than US$550m
F-35A *Lightning II*	FGA ac	178	US$29.7bn	US	Lockheed Martin	2007	2011	CTOL variant. Programme of record for 1,763 aircraft. Initial operating capability declared Aug 2016
F-35B *Lightning II*	FGA ac	42	US$8.6bn	US	Lockheed Martin	2008	2011	STOVL variant. Programme of record for 311 aircraft
F-35C *Lightning II*	FGA ac	65	US$14.4bn	US	Lockheed Martin	2010	2012	CV variant. Programme of record for 369 aircraft
FA-18E/F *Super Hornet*	FGA ac	568	US$43.9bn	US	Boeing	2003	2009	FY2017 would fund an additional two aircraft
P-8A *Poseidon*	ASW ac	79	US$17bn	US	Boeing	2011	2012	FY2017 would fund an additional 11 aircraft
EA-18G *Growler*	EW ac	160	US$12.9bn	US	Boeing	2003	2009	Deliveries expected to be completed by end of 2018
KC-46A *Pegasus*	Tkr ac	19	US$3.9bn	US	Boeing	2011	2015	First two production aircraft in test. FY2017 would fund an additional 15
C-130J-30 *Hercules*	Med tpt ac	117	US$9.2bn	US	Lockheed Martin	1995	1999	Deliveries ongoing. FY2017 would fund additional three
CV-22 *Osprey*	Tilt-rotor ac	51	US$4.3bn	US	Textron (Bell)/ Boeing	2002	2006	For USAF
MV-22 *Osprey*	Tilt-rotor ac	320	US$27.3bn	US	Textron (Bell)/ Boeing	1997	1999	For USMC; FY2017 would fund an additional 16
AH-1Z *Viper*	Atk hel	108	US$3.6bn	US	Textron (Bell)	2010	2013	New build
AH-64E *Apache*	Atk hel	252	US$5.7bn	US	Boeing	2010	2011	Seventeen new build and 235 remanufactured helicopters. FY2017 would fund an additional 52 remanufactured
CH-47F/MH-47G *Chinook*	Hvy tpt hel	321	US$9.1bn	US	Boeing	2000	2004	Remanufactured helicopters. FY2017 would fund an additional 22 remanufactured
UH-60M/HH-60M *Black Hawk*	Med tpt hel	873	US$15bn	US	Lockheed Martin (Sikorsky)	2004	2006	Deliveries ongoing. FY2017 would fund an additional 36 helicopters
EC145 (UH-72A *Lakota*)	Lt tpt hel	425	US$2.7bn	Int'l	Airbus Group (Airbus Group Inc)	2006	2006	For army
MH-60R *Seahawk*	ASW hel	278	US$11.3bn	US	Lockheed Martin (Sikorsky)	2000	2006	Deliveries expected to be completed by end of 2018
MQ-1C *Gray Eagle*	UAV (ISR Hvy)	167	US$2.8bn	US	General Atomics/ ASI	2010	2011	For army
MQ-4C *Triton*	UAV (ISR Hvy)	4	US$687.3m	US	Northrop Grumman	2016	2017	FY2017 would fund an additional two UAVs
MQ-8C *Fire Scout*	UAV (ISR Hvy)	50	US$968m	US	Northrop Grumman	2012	2013	FY2017 would fund one additional UAV
MQ-9 *Reaper*	UAV (CISR Hvy)	323	US$5.7bn	US	General Atomics	2001	2002	Deliveries ongoing. FY2017 would fund an additional 24 UAVs
RQ-4A/B *Global Hawk*	UAV (ISR Hvy)	55	US$4.4bn	US	Northrop Grumman	1995	1997	Deliveries ongoing
Terminal High-Altitude Area Defense (THAAD)	SAM	42	US$3.6bn	US	Lockheed Martin	2010	2012	Final launcher due to be delivered Dec 2016

Chapter Four
Europe

Crises and instability: more of the same

A heightened sense of insecurity prevailed across Europe during 2016. Successful Islamist terrorist attacks in Belgium, France, Germany and Turkey highlighted the continent's vulnerability to instability and violence originating on its southern and southeastern margins. Meanwhile, although the flow of refugees and other migrants into Europe slowed in 2016, pressure on receiving countries to settle and integrate those arrivals remained high, and on occasion caused local tensions. This continuing crisis meant that some European states sustained largely maritime deployments designed to assist those in danger and deter the activities of human traffickers.

At the same time, there was no measurable improvement in relations with Russia. Moscow's continued military modernisation and strategic extroversion was again demonstrated by the intervention in Syria, direct support for armed separatists in eastern Ukraine and significant military deployments in Crimea and on Ukraine's borders. Armed conflict persisted in Europe, with fighting between Ukrainian government and separatist forces intensifying in mid-year. There was also continuing concern over Moscow's capabilities in the area of information and influence operations.

Government ministries and military headquarters across the continent began to accept that these simultaneous security challenges were likely to endure, and that emerging crises needed to be confronted quickly and in a joined-up fashion. Indeed, this was reflected in defence documentation issued in 2015–16 by a number of states, including Finland, Germany, Italy, Norway and the United Kingdom. Nonetheless, while European countries' threat perceptions may increasingly reflect similar concerns, there was little overall alignment in responses.

Added to this challenging external picture was the uncertainty and political distraction created by the UK's decision to leave the European Union. The precise terms of this 'Brexit', which was unlikely to come into force before 2019, remained unclear, but the referendum took political bandwidth away from looming security challenges. The effect on the UK's important, if numerically modest, contributions to EU military operations was also uncertain. And, to the south, an attempted military coup on 15 July imperilled democracy in key NATO member Turkey. This triggered a far-reaching crackdown within the armed forces and across government (see pp. 68–9).

Spending and personnel

As noted in *The Military Balance 2016*, concern over the deteriorating security environment, coupled with a slight improvement in regional economic activity, has allowed for a modest increase in defence spending. NATO estimated on 4 July that 2016 would bring a 3% increase in real defence spending among its European members (and Canada). NATO Secretary-General Jens Stoltenberg, encouraged by those estimates, even suggested at the margins of the NATO Summit in Warsaw, held on 8–9 July, that defence expenditure had 'turned a corner'. The increase in absolute spending was evident, and this trend is likely to continue over coming years, judging by financial-planning documents published by European governments. However, even though NATO member states agreed in 2014 to spend 2% of their GDP on defence by 2024, meeting this target still seemed elusive when rising GDP across the continent was taken into account.

A second indicator of military strength, reduced since 1989 and now re-examined, was the size of European armed forces. According to *Military Balance* data, active personnel totals across key NATO European members France, Germany, Italy and the UK fell from around 1.3 million in 1996 to around 716,000 in 2016. While it was expected that there would be reductions after the Cold War, and personnel numbers have been progressively lowered by defence reviews and funding cuts, some experts are now asking whether these reductions have gone too far.

Indeed, with just over 176,000 active personnel as of June 2016, Germany's Bundeswehr fell to its smallest size since its inception in 1955, and was still struggling to fill all posts with qualified personnel. The German defence white paper published on 13 July (see p. 64) advises that this overall strength might have to increase in light of the security environment, suggesting the Bundeswehr might open up to non-German EU citizens – an unprecedented move in Germany – because of demographic pressure and competition for talent from other sectors. Meanwhile, France announced plans to increase the size of its military reserve forces to a total of 40,000 from the current level of just under 30,000. In addition, at the end of July, French President François Hollande confirmed that a National Guard focused on homeland-security tasks would be created by combining existing reserve forces, including police and gendarmerie. In April, Poland confirmed that it intended to establish a Territorial Defence Force with a plan for 53,000 personnel by the end of 2019, and first units standing up in 2017. These reservists would perform tasks related to infrastructure protection; some units would be equipped with portable air-defence systems and light anti-tank guided weapons.

New white paper defines Germany's security and defence agenda

On 13 July 2016, the German cabinet approved a new white paper on 'German Security Policy and the Future of the Bundeswehr' after a wide-ranging national and international consultation process that continued throughout 2015. As Germany does not have a national-security strategy, the *Weissbuch* provides high-level political guidance for security policy, as well as for the tasks and missions of the German armed forces. The document centres on the overall assessment that Germany has become a more significant actor in international security. It promises that Germany will accept greater responsibility for international peace and security and assume leadership roles, including in defence.

The 2016 white paper (which replaces the 2006 edition) points to an elevated risk of inter-state armed conflict – partly driven by the aggressive behaviour and ambitions of emerging powers – as well as a multitude of other transnational security challenges. Russia, in particular, is mentioned as being interested in strategic rivalry and as constituting a challenge for European security. Given this adjusted threat assessment, the white paper emphasises territorial and collective defence within NATO. While this is not explicitly prioritised above other Bundeswehr missions, the analysis in the white paper leads to the conclusion that a German contribution to deterrence has to include the ability to engage in high-intensity combined-arms combat. Given that future threats are likely to materialise in geographically contained areas and with little warning, the armed forces have to improve their readiness and rapid-response capability. Staying true to its character as a high-level strategy document, the white paper does not translate this assessment into a specific level of military ambition or detailed force goals. It is therefore likely that German force planners will require either new *Verteidigungspolitische Richtlinien* (defence-policy guidelines) or a new *Konzeption der Bundeswehr* (Bundeswehr concept) – lower-level strategy documents, whose current versions date back to 2011 and 2013 respectively.

To deal with the increasing demands being placed on it, the Bundeswehr will require increased funding and reliable access to high-quality personnel. The defence budget is showing a modest upward trajectory, which is likely to last until at least 2020 – the present horizon for cabinet-approved financial planning. Meanwhile, Germany is considering opening up its armed forces to non-German EU citizens to help address personnel challenges and competition for suitable talent from other sectors. In addition, the government decided to abandon a fixed upper ceiling for active personnel strength and replace it with a so-called 'breathing' body of personnel – in other words, a flexible personnel strength, dependent on demand.

The white paper states that multinational cooperation and integration with other European armed forces are core Bundeswehr principles. Within NATO, Germany will pursue these approaches through the 'framework nations' concept. Berlin was the principal sponsor of this concept and sees it as an important means for multinational capability development. The white paper also declared that improved harmonisation of force-planning processes among European NATO members was a policy goal. In the EU, Germany will seek to activate hitherto dormant features of the Lisbon Treaty, such as permanent structured cooperation on defence, which would enable a group of EU member states to pursue cooperation in this area. Furthermore, Germany has declared it will support the creation of a permanent civil–military operational headquarters within the Brussels-based security and defence structures. In the aftermath of the United Kingdom's decision to leave the EU, opposition to such moves is likely to be more muted. But the most far-reaching ideas concerning Europe relate to defence-industrial matters. The white paper promotes standardised capability requirements for multinational programmes, which would in practice require an early design freeze and production arrangements based on industrial excellence rather than percentages of off-take (dividing production shares on the basis of the proportion of overall production that a customer buys); it also argues for harmonised arms-export policies among EU members. The result would be a Europeanisation of regional defence industry, with the potential to improve efficiency and also trigger consolidation.

Germany steps up its cyber defence

Germany has boosted its cyber-defence capabilities by implementing far-reaching reforms to its cyber-security structures. A new Directorate-General Cyber/IT (CIT) was created within the Federal Ministry of Defence on 1 October 2016, with two divisions for Cyber/IT Governance and IT-Services/Information Security. The director-general of this body serves as Chief Information Officer and point of contact for other federal ministries and agencies. The directorate-general's tasks include advancing technical cyber/IT capabilities, and guiding cyber policies. Furthermore, a new 'Cyber and Information Space Command' (KdoCIR) is due to be operational in April 2017 as the sixth military branch within the German armed forces, reflecting the military importance of cyberspace for Germany. All of the Bundeswehr's current and newly created cyber and IT capabilities will be pooled in the new branch. It is planned to be about 13,500 strong, comprising both military and civilian personnel, and will be led by a Chief of Staff for Cyber and Information Space (InspCIR). The overall aim of these reforms is to assign current capabilities to defined responsibilities; protect Bundeswehr and national cyber and IT infrastructure; and improve capabilities in order to better respond to cyber attacks.

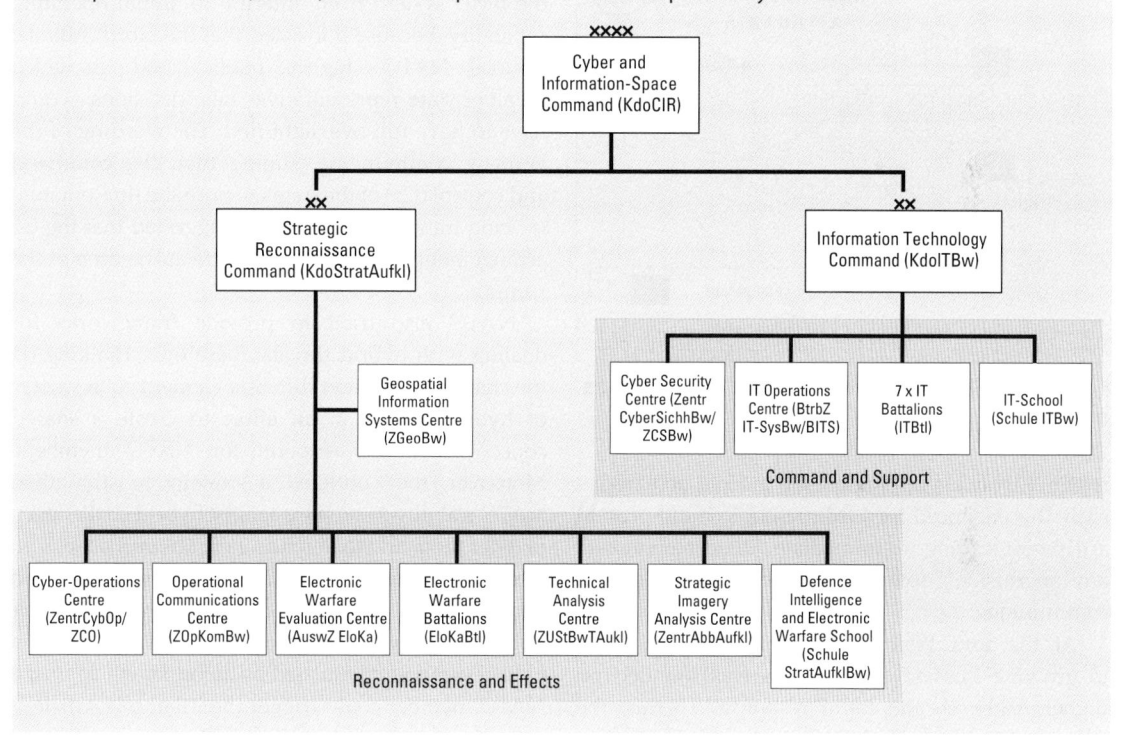

NATO's Warsaw Summit

At the Warsaw Summit, NATO governments declared that the major objectives of the Alliance's 2014 Readiness Action Plan (RAP) had been achieved. On the margins of the meeting, Stoltenberg declared that NATO had 'delivered the biggest reinforcement of … collective defence in a generation'. Core elements included the tripling of the NATO Response Force (NRF) from roughly 13,000 to more than 40,000 personnel and the creation of the Very High Readiness Joint Task Force, a 5,000-strong formation, itself part of the NRF. A new element in NATO's approach, formalised at the Warsaw Summit, was the so-called 'enhanced forward presence' – the deployment of one multinational battlegroup each to Estonia, Latvia, Lithuania and Poland by 2017. The UK, Canada, Germany and the US will be the respective framework nations for these battalion-sized formations, providing the core capabilities and enablers to be augmented by other allies. The precise capability mix was left to the framework nations to determine in coordination with the host nation. While the deployment was supposed to be sustainable on a rotational basis, and involve combat-ready forces, by August 2016 the precise composition of these units remained unclear, as did detail on the rotational

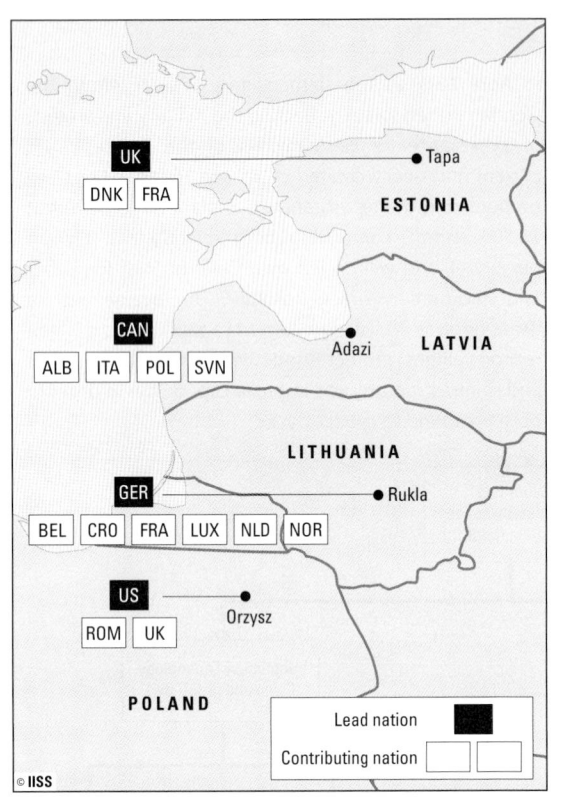

Figure 6 **NATO's enhanced forward presence, as of Oct 2016**

roster. Involving approximately 1,000–1,200 troops each, this enhanced forward presence would present a tripwire leading to 'immediate Allied response to any aggression', according to the Warsaw Summit communiqué.

At the 2014 Wales Summit, NATO's response to growing Russian assertiveness was founded on higher readiness and rapid response. To this, the Warsaw Summit added the priority of developing heavy conventional forces. This was largely driven by the assessment that Russian forces had capabilities that could achieve temporary conventional superiority in geographically limited spaces, such as the Baltic region, and could also then deny or at least severely constrain NATO's ability to introduce reinforcements. This, of course, is seen as undermining the credibility of NATO deterrence. Having introduced capabilities including air defence, coastal defence and electronic warfare, as well as ballistic missiles, in Kaliningrad and Crimea, and later also in Syria, Russia presented a credible anti-access/area-denial (A2/AD) challenge. Penetrating these A2/AD screens required heavier forces than the 2014 RAP had envisioned for the NATO tripwire, should it be activated, to allow for both rapid response and credible reinforcement.

Overall, NATO deterrence is based on a mix of nuclear, conventional and missile-defence capabilities. At the Warsaw Summit, NATO declared that its ballistic-missile-defence (BMD) system had reached initial operating capability. This system includes US *Aegis*-equipped destroyers forward deployed to Spain, an early-warning radar in Turkey and a BMD site in Romania. Another BMD site, due to be completed in 2018, is under development in Poland. France had reportedly refused to change the status of the BMD system from 'interim' to 'initial operating capability' because it insisted that the North Atlantic Council, NATO's highest political body in which member-state representatives take decisions, would have to have full oversight first. The wording of the Warsaw communiqué, stating that 'the command and control (C2) of the Aegis Ashore site [in Romania] is being transferred to NATO' suggested that the C2 arrangement was not yet complete at the time of the summit.

NATO also tried to provide frameworks for dealing with hybrid threats: these offer thinking on the characteristics and different elements of a variety of hybrid threats in an effort to create a shared conceptual reference point for NATO members. Moreover, they outlined a strategy to strengthen NATO's ability to prepare against hybrid challengers, to deter them and to defend against hybrid attacks. In this context, possible hybrid scenarios were reviewed and potential Alliance assistance to a member under hybrid attack was discussed. NATO clarified that a hybrid campaign launched by an opponent against a NATO member could trigger the Alliance's Article V collective-defence commitment. This move was likely inspired by a desire to strengthen NATO's ability to exert control over escalation dynamics in a hybrid-attack situation. Earlier, at a June defence-ministerial meeting, NATO established guidelines and requirements to strengthen national resilience and civil preparedness, stressing that the first line of defence against hybrid attacks would always rest with the member state in question.

Despite a strategic partnership between NATO and the EU, established in 2002, collaboration had long been hampered by an unresolved political dispute centred on the EU's decision to grant membership to Cyprus in 2004; this led Turkey to effectively block meaningful exchange. As a result, collaboration was

Figure 7 NATO's eastern flank – selected capability reductions, 1993–2016

Since 1993, there have been significant reductions in the military holdings of East European states; these nations subsequently joined NATO. The Baltic states have increased personnel, but continue to lack tanks and combat aircraft. However, these reductions will have been made in tandem with efforts to improve capabilities by replacing legacy systems with smaller numbers of more modern, capable platforms. There has also been a wider trend in force reductions across NATO members, and in Russia's military forces. Nevertheless, the scale of this overall reduction in Eastern Europe is indicative of the recent shift towards smaller expeditionary forces in these countries – a posture subject to renewed scrutiny in light of concerns over territorial defence following Russia's actions in Ukraine.

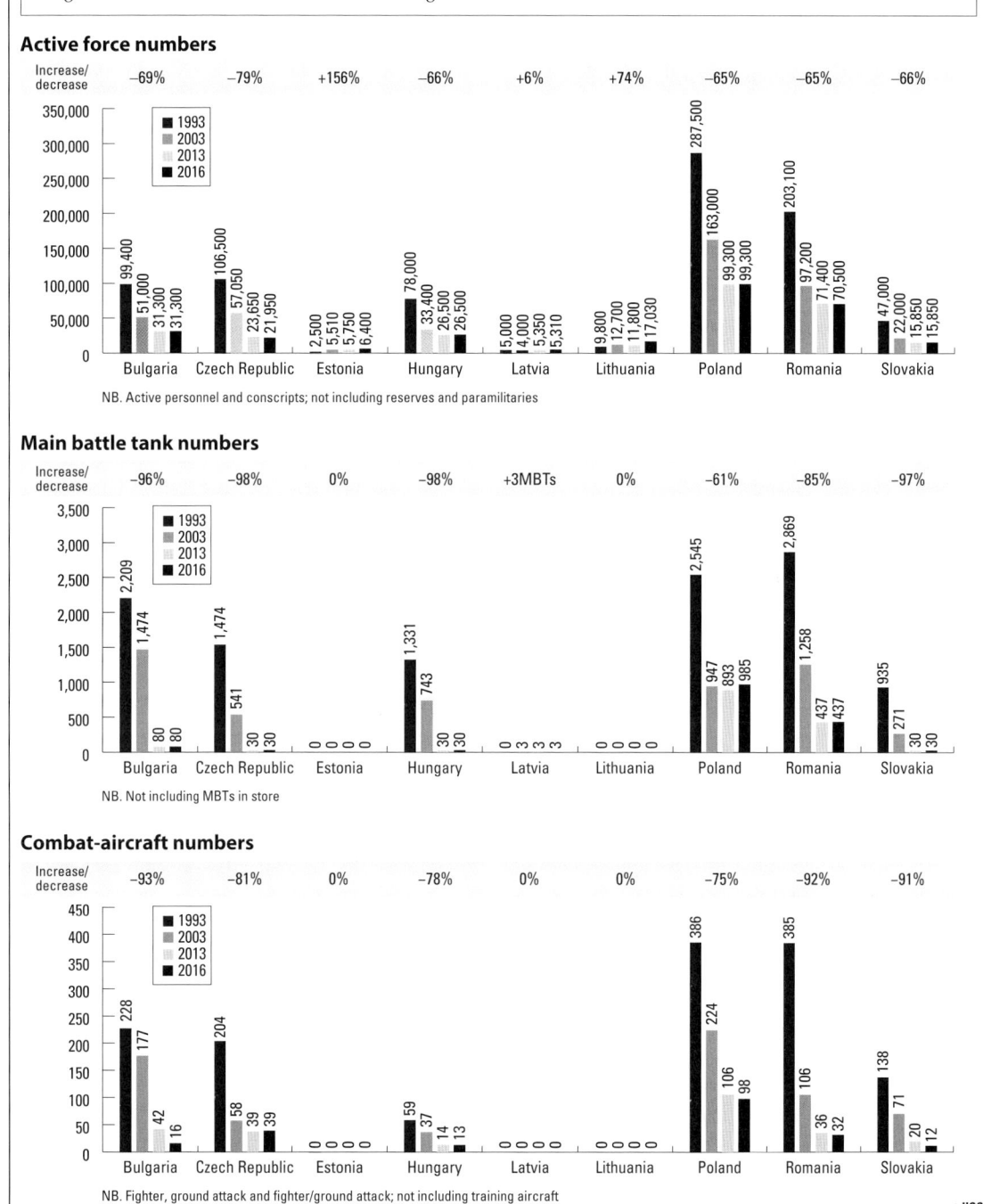

Active force numbers

Country	Increase/decrease	1993	2003	2013	2016
Bulgaria	−69%	99,400	51,000	31,300	31,300
Czech Republic	−79%	106,500	57,050	23,650	21,950
Estonia	+156%	2,500	5,510	5,750	6,400
Hungary	−66%	78,000	33,400	26,500	26,500
Latvia	+6%	5,000	14,000	5,350	5,310
Lithuania	+74%	9,800	12,700	11,800	17,030
Poland	−65%	287,500	163,000	99,300	99,300
Romania	−65%	203,100	97,200	71,400	70,500
Slovakia	−66%	47,000	22,000	15,850	15,850

NB. Active personnel and conscripts; not including reserves and paramilitaries

Main battle tank numbers

Country	Increase/decrease	1993	2003	2013	2016
Bulgaria	−96%	2,209	1,474	80	80
Czech Republic	−98%	1,474	541	30	30
Estonia	0%	0	0	0	0
Hungary	−98%	1,331	743	30	30
Latvia	+3MBTs	0	3	3	3
Lithuania	0%	0	0	0	0
Poland	−61%	2,545	947	893	985
Romania	−85%	2,869	1,258	437	437
Slovakia	−97%	935	271	30	30

NB. Not including MBTs in store

Combat-aircraft numbers

Country	Increase/decrease	1993	2003	2013	2016
Bulgaria	−93%	228	177	42	16
Czech Republic	−81%	204	58	39	39
Estonia	0%	0	0	0	0
Hungary	−78%	59	37	14	13
Latvia	0%	0	0	0	0
Lithuania	0%	0	0	0	0
Poland	−75%	386	224	106	98
Romania	−92%	385	106	36	32
Slovakia	−91%	138	71	20	12

NB. Fighter, ground attack and fighter/ground attack; not including training aircraft

© IISS

built informally, often driven more by personal relationships than institutional dynamics. At the 2016 Warsaw Summit, the president of the European Council, the president of the European Commission and the NATO secretary-general signed a new joint declaration designed to instil 'new impetus and new substance' in cooperation. With members of both organisations perceiving similar security challenges, and in recognition of the complementary capacities the two frameworks could provide (for example, to address hybrid threats and risks), this development was overdue. Areas highlighted in the 2016 declaration include early warning, intelligence sharing, strategic communications, cyber security and coordinated exercises. Fittingly, NATO announced at the Warsaw Summit that it would overhaul its intelligence structures, marked by the establishment of a new joint intelligence and security division overseen by an assistant secretary-general. This body is tasked with enhancing the efficiency with which intelligence provided by allies is used for NATO operational planning and decision-making, as well as increasing the capacity within NATO to provide information on Russia and threats emanating from the southern flank.

EU defence debate at a turning point

An unintended consequence of the UK's decision to leave the EU was that it prompted several leaders to identify defence as an area that could demonstrate progress on European cooperation and even integration. Hollande suggested on 14 July that Europeans should consider conducting more external military operations together, and indicated he hoped Germany would be a key partner in this endeavour. In August, Paolo Gentiloni and Roberta Pinotti, the Italian foreign and defence ministers respectively, suggested in *Le Monde* that the EU's founding members should set up a multinational force with a common budget in order to show that European cooperation delivers

Turkey – fallout from the coup attempt

The failed coup attempt of 15 July 2016 led to a major shake-up of the Turkish Armed Forces (TAF). This is likely to have long-term repercussions for the military's domestic and international role, including in NATO, as well as Turkey's broader relations with its Western allies.

Although many of the details of the coup attempt remain unclear – including how it was planned and the identities of its ringleaders – President Recep Tayyip Erdogan and the ruling Justice and Development Party have blamed the followers of the 75-year-old former Islamic preacher Fethullah Gülen, who has been living in exile in the United States since 1999.

In the two months after the coup attempt, nearly 40,000 people were detained and over 80,000 state employees were suspended on suspicion of having links to Gülen. The latter included a large number of serving military personnel. By September 2016, the number of serving officers in the three armed services had fallen by 10% to 30,000. The largest decline was in the upper echelons of the military: in October 2016, the total number of generals and admirals in the services stood at 201, down 38% from the previous total of 358.

It was expected that some newly vacant positions, including in the highest ranks, would be filled by appointments. However, the government made it clear that the purges would be followed both by the reform and downsizing of the TAF, and by the allocation of more heavy weaponry to the Turkish National Police (TNP) to enable it to fulfil some of the tasks traditionally undertaken by the military. These reforms are likely to accelerate the observed change in emphasis in the war against the Kurdistan Workers' Party (PKK) in southeast Turkey, where elements of the TNP have been increasingly taking on roles previously performed by the TAF.

In the immediate aftermath of the coup attempt, the government announced plans to radically restructure the TAF. These included a change to the chain of command whereby the three services would now report to the Ministry of National Defense rather than the Turkish General Staff (TGS). This would have reduced the TGS to a coordinating rather than a command role. However, when the reforms were announced in late July 2016, they left the three services under the TGS, although they introduced major changes in other areas.

Prior to July, the Gendarmerie – which is responsible for law enforcement in rural areas – was theoretically under the TGS but temporarily placed under the Ministry of the Interior in times of peace. In practice, the Gendarmerie was effectively a branch of the TAF. Its officers were drawn from the military high schools that supplied officers to the Turkish Land Forces and the Gendarmerie was always commanded by a serving four-star general on secondment from the land forces. Since the reforms of July 2016, the Gendarmerie has been fully detached from the TGS and integrated into the Ministry of the Interior in a manner similar to the TNP.

security for European citizens. German Chancellor Angela Merkel, meeting with Hollande and Italian Prime Minister Matteo Renzi on 22 August, said 'we feel that faced with Islamist terrorism and in light of the civil war in Syria, that we need to do more for our internal and external security', pointing to intelligence sharing and defence cooperation in particular. On 12 September, German Minister of Defence Ursula von der Leyen and her French counterpart Jean-Yves Le Drian published a joint food-for-thought paper presenting ideas for 'comprehensive, realistic and credible defence in the European Union'. This bilateral initiative calls for a permanent EU headquarters to run military and civilian EU operations, a European medical command to pool and share resources, and, following the example of the European Air Transport Command, the development of a European transport and logistics hub. To a certain degree, these arguments and initiatives are driven by the need to show that there is life in the European project after Brexit.

However, the impetus provided by France, Germany and Italy coincided with long-running efforts within Brussels-based institutions to instil a new sense of purpose in the flagging EU Common Security and Defence Policy (CSDP).

The EU Global Strategy for Foreign and Security Policy (EUGS) was presented to EU heads of state and government on 28 June 2016 by Federica Mogherini, the EU high representative for foreign affairs and security policy, and vice-president of the European Commission. The document, entitled 'Shared Vision, Common Action: A Stronger Europe', replaces the ambitious language of its 2003 predecessor with a more measured call for 'principled pragmatism' as the guideline for the EU's external engagement. Within this framework, the strategy defines its five priorities as the security of European citizens, resilience, integrated conflict management, cooperative regional order and progress on global governance.

In addition, the July reforms abolished both the four-year military high schools (traditionally the main source of future officers) and the military academies, which trained cadets. Members of the officer corps will now be drawn from civilian high schools. The government also lifted the ban on graduates of Islamic high schools (known as *Imam Hatip Lisesi*, with around 1m students currently enrolled) becoming members of the officer corps. The military academies have been replaced by a National Defense University, which will be overseen by the Ministry of National Education. Similarly, all of the military hospitals, which were previously run by the TGS, are now administered by the Ministry of Health.

As well as disrupting chains of command, the failed coup attempt has severely damaged both the morale and the cohesion of the officer corps. It was prepared in such secrecy that it came as much as a shock to most of the Turkish armed forces as it did to the rest of the country. That said, there is also a general belief that the officer corps still retains some members who were originally planning to participate in the coup but changed their minds once they realised that it would fail. The purges have been heavy-handed and often seemingly arbitrary, as they have targeted officers who opposed the attempted putsch. As a result, many remaining officers are reported to now be both fearful for their futures and suspicious that their colleagues might be closet putschists.

In the longer term, the July reforms are likely to have a profound impact on the ethos of the Turkish officer corps. Although there is evidence to suggest that the TAF had been infiltrated by a small number of Gülen sympathisers, overall the officer corps had prided itself on its staunch commitment to the secular principles espoused by Mustafa Kemal Atatürk, who founded the modern Turkish Republic in 1923. Experts now consider the possibility that the Turkish officer corps could in time become more religiously conservative and look less to the West as a model, particularly given the lifting of the ban on *Imam Hatip Lisesi* graduates, while the abolition of the Turkish Armed Forces' distinct status may increase the chance of the force becoming politicised.

At the political level, the failed coup has already exacerbated existing strains in Turkey's relations with its NATO allies, particularly the US. Although the evidence pointed to it being a purely Turkish affair, many Turks – including some in government – were convinced that the US was in some way involved in the failed coup attempt. This belief has been reinforced by Washington's continuing refusal to extradite Gülen and his leading followers to Turkey – citing the absence of any evidence that proves their involvement – to face trial for instigating the revolt. The resulting tensions are likely to overshadow Ankara's relations with its Western allies for the foreseeable future. Although Turkey is unlikely to adopt an actively confrontational position, these tensions might restrict the scope for Turkish cooperation with other NATO members in areas where it could significantly benefit the Alliance, including in Syria and in the Black Sea.

The EUGS suggests that defence cooperation among EU members has the potential to improve 'interoperability, effectiveness, efficiency and trust: it increases the output of defence spending'. The strategy makes the case for harmonised defence-planning cycles among EU member states and suggests that defence cooperation must become the default mode in Europe. It does not, however, advance an outright integrationist agenda. The strategy introduces notions of deterrence, full-spectrum defence and the protection of the Union into the EU vocabulary but, while it did not elaborate on precisely what these terms meant in an EU context, they have the potential to significantly expand the security and defence role currently defined in the CSDP. Fleshing out the detail would presumably fall to the sectoral sub-strategies that the EUGS seeks to initiate.

The Netherlands – holding the presidency of the Council of the EU in the first half of 2016 – had pushed hard for an EU defence white paper. In bodies such as the EU Military Staff and the European External Action Service, and in the European Commission, there was a willingness to engage in the follow-on work needed for such a document, and some of the groundwork had already been done before the EUGS presentation. On 14 September, EC President Jean-Claude Juncker delivered his 2016 State of the Union address before the members of the European Parliament. In his speech, Juncker hinted at an accelerated schedule for the creation of a European Border and Coast Guard, and suggested it was time to set up a permanent civil–military EU headquarters to run EU operations, to set up a European fund to support research and innovation in defence, and to activate permanent structured cooperation among member states, as foreseen in the Lisbon Treaty. However, by September, there remained no explicit mandate from EU member states to translate the foreign- and security-policy priorities defined in the EUGS into a military level of ambition that would provide guidance for capability development in the form of force requirements, and also outline the steps that would help harmonise defence-planning assumptions across EU member states. Member states were, it seemed, waiting for Mogherini to spur them into action.

DEFENCE ECONOMICS

Macroeconomics

At a projected rate of 1.7%, growth across the euro area was sluggish in 2016 and remained vulnerable to economic and political risk. Europe's slow recovery was reflected in the euro area's low inflation (0.3% in 2016). However, this occurred in the context of favourable economic conditions for Europe in 2015–16. Energy prices remained low, while the European Central Bank (ECB) continued its accommodating monetary policy. Private consumption was sustained by job creation – the labour market continued to improve in 2016 – and lower oil prices, as well as low consumer inflation rates. The ECB's monetary policy eased loan conditions for households and firms, which contributed to economic recovery. Additionally, eurozone government deficits were expected to decrease from 2.1% of GDP to 1.9% in 2016, which, according to the ECB forecast in September, would likely allow for increased government spending.

However, Europe's economic recovery remained vulnerable to a number of risks, not least the uncertainty over the course, and effect, of the United Kingdom's exit from the EU. In the immediate aftermath of the June 2016 referendum's surprise result, there was volatility in financial markets and a 10% drop in the value of sterling. In the long run, the referendum result generated uncertainty for the European and broader global economy. The IMF's 2016 growth forecast for the UK was revised down from 1.9% to 1.8% (-0.1 percentage points) and for 2017 from 2.2% to 1.1% (-1.1%). For the eurozone, Brexit could – according to the European Commission – reduce GDP growth by 0.1 percentage points in 2016 and 0.2–0.4 percentage points in 2017.

Other negative factors threatened the prospects for European growth. The Organisation for Economic Co-operation and Development (OECD) highlighted in June the risk of a low-growth trap for the world economy: low growth expectations leading to lower trade, investment and wages, which in turn negatively affect growth. Furthermore, Europe continued to face broader uncertainties relating to the security situation on its periphery and the nature, and cohesiveness, of reactions to these challenges from European capitals. Governments were preoccupied by continued conflict in Ukraine and, in mid-year, the attempted coup in Turkey. In Western Europe, a number of votes due between late 2016 and mid-2017 also contributed to the uncertainty, including a constitutional referendum in Italy in December 2016, after which the prime minister resigned, the French presidential election in May 2017 and Germany's federal elections in autumn 2017. Overall, the economic uncer-

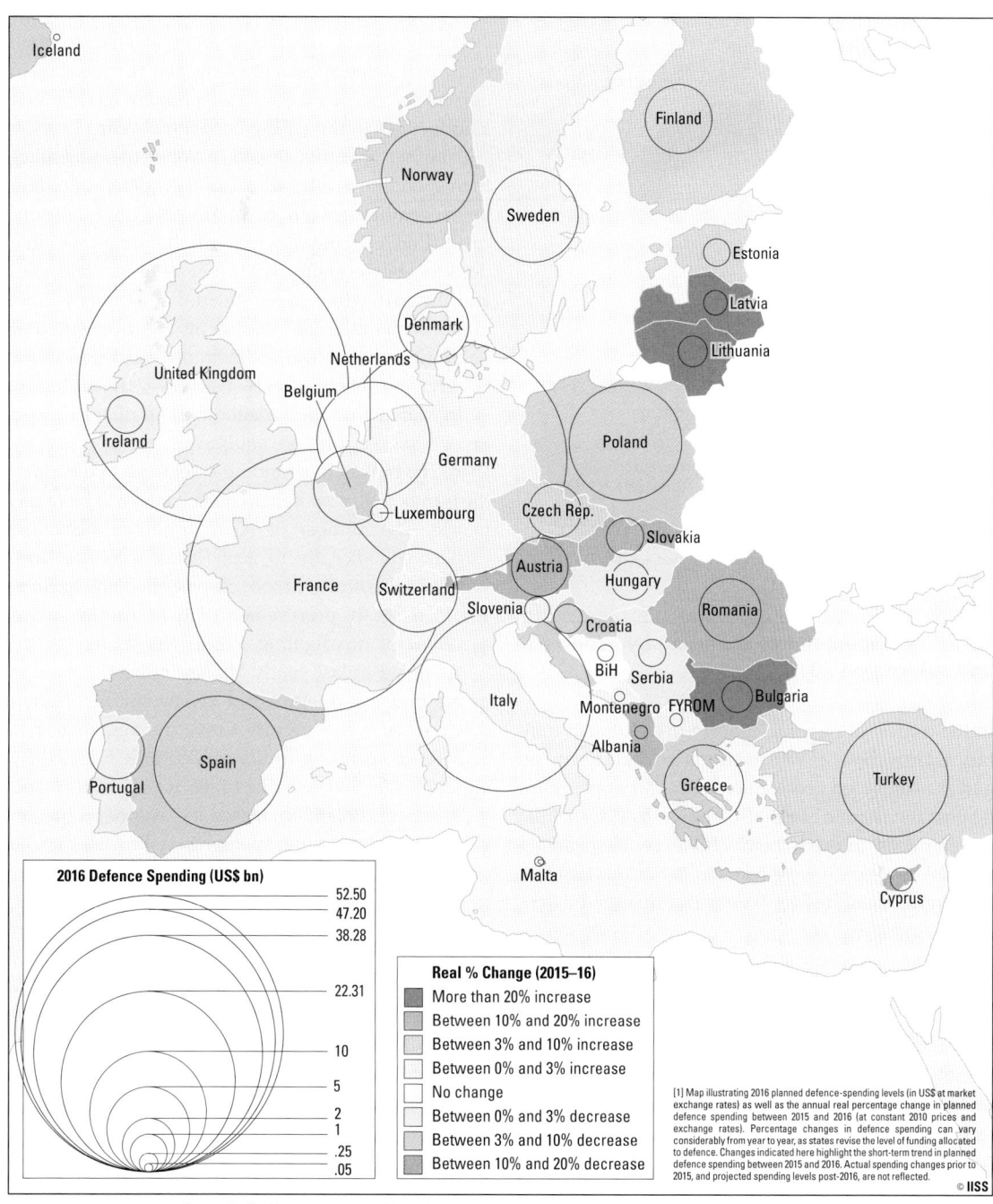

Map 1 Europe regional defence spending[1]

Sub-regional groupings referred to in defence economics text: Central Europe (Austria, Czech Republic, Germany, Hungary, Poland, Slovakia and Switzerland), Northern Europe (Denmark, Estonia, Finland, Latvia, Lithuania, Norway and Sweden), Southern Europe (Cyprus, Greece, Italy, Malta, Portugal and Spain), Southeastern Europe (Bulgaria, Romania and Turkey), the Balkans (Albania, Bosnia-Herzegovina, Croatia, FYROM, Montenegro, Serbia and Slovenia) and Western Europe (Belgium, France, Iceland, Ireland, Luxembourg, the Netherlands and the United Kingdom).

tainty might lead some European states to limit their defence ambitions in light of still-limited fiscal space in coming years – although, with the 2016 spending trend still on the up, much depends on national threat perceptions.

Defence spending and procurement

Across Europe, defence spending increased between 2015 and 2016 (by 0.47% in real terms, when measured using constant 2010 US dollars), having increased by 3.96% between 2014 and 2015 by the same measure.

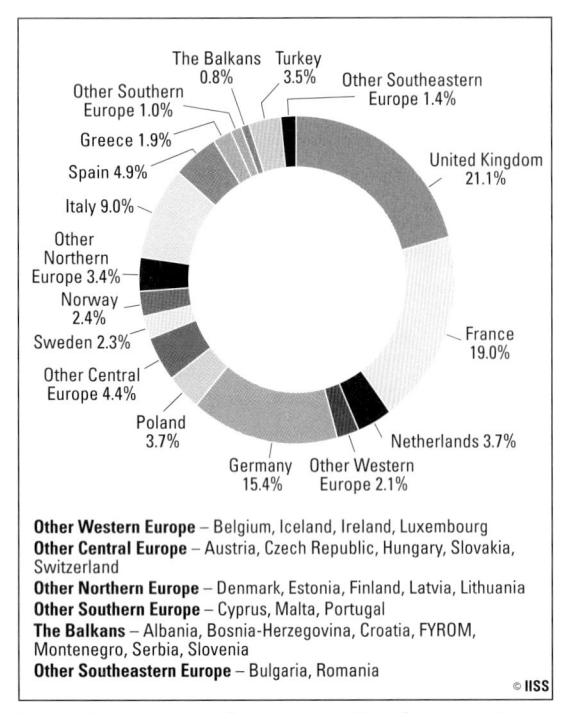

Figure 8 Europe defence spending by country and sub-region 2016

Other Western Europe – Belgium, Iceland, Ireland, Luxembourg
Other Central Europe – Austria, Czech Republic, Hungary, Slovakia, Switzerland
Other Northern Europe – Denmark, Estonia, Finland, Latvia, Lithuania
Other Southern Europe – Cyprus, Malta, Portugal
The Balkans – Albania, Bosnia-Herzegovina, Croatia, FYROM, Montenegro, Serbia, Slovenia
Other Southeastern Europe – Bulgaria, Romania

Shares: United Kingdom 21.1%; France 19.0%; Germany 15.4%; Italy 9.0%; Spain 4.9%; Other Central Europe 4.4%; Poland 3.7%; Netherlands 3.7%; Turkey 3.5%; Other Northern Europe 3.4%; Norway 2.4%; Sweden 2.3%; Other Western Europe 2.1%; Greece 1.9%; Other Southeastern Europe 1.4%; Other Southern Europe 1.0%; The Balkans 0.8%.

© IISS

In the context of ongoing concern over Russian military assertiveness, as well as efforts to tackle terrorism and the continued prosecution of military operations against the Islamic State, also known as ISIS or ISIL, commitments to reach the NATO target to spend 2% of GDP on defence were restated in various capitals, although annual budget trajectories diverged across Europe's sub-regions.

Central European states increased their defence budgets by a combined total of 1.9% (in current US dollars) in 2016. In Germany, a balanced budget in 2015 and 1.7% economic growth in 2016 (the eurozone average) combined with assessments of a changed security environment and Germany's security role as assessed in the July 2016 white paper (see textbox, p. 64) such that current government planning projected an increased defence budget from 2016 to 2020. The defence budget was €34.3 billion (US$38.3bn) in 2016 and was set to increase to €36.6bn (US$41.3bn) in 2017. The budget increase will be primarily used to expand personnel numbers (by 14,300 service personnel and 4,400 civilians over seven years) and to modernise equipment.

In 2014, Germany signed the Wales declaration at that year's NATO Summit. This committed NATO allies to aim to move towards a guideline of 2% of GDP spent on defence by 2024. However, given Germany's GDP, meeting this target would entail, in 2020, a defence budget of €69.8bn (US$80.2bn) in current prices. (The German government has planned a budget of €39.2bn (US$45bn) for that year.)

Another objective agreed in Wales was that allies then spending less than 20% of their defence budget on new equipment and related research and development (R&D) should aim to reach that target within a decade. For Germany, this is a more immediate goal, and the 2016 white paper stated that Germany must 'in particular increase investments in armaments and equipment so that over the medium term we meet the twenty per cent mark set by NATO'.

In March 2016, Berlin announced a plan to spend €130bn (US$145bn) on equipment procurement by 2030. The bulk of this funding is set to go to the army: the number of *Leopard* main battle tanks will be raised to 328. The number of *Boxer* armoured personnel carriers will increase to 402; *Fennek* reconnaissance vehicles 248; and PzH 2000 self-propelled howitzers to 101. Plans for the procurement of up to 192 *Marder* and 342 *Puma* infantry fighting vehicles were also reported.

As noted in last year's *Military Balance*, Poland is in the midst of a significant defence-modernisation drive. In 2016 the country drove the aggregate rise in defence spending in Central Europe. Enabled by a growth rate that was due to reach 3.1% in 2016 and 3.4% in 2017, Poland increased its defence budget by 4.2% in 2016 (excluding spending on the final tranche of F-16 combat-aircraft deliveries in 2015) and plans to do so again by 4.7% in 2017 (in US dollars). But, at 1.9% of GDP in 2016 and 2017, this fell just short of the NATO 2% of GDP target. Meanwhile, the Law and Justice government that took office after the 2015 elections sought to revise the previous government's 'Technical Modernisation Plan' for Poland's armed forces. The principal requirements for the country's defence-modernisation programme remain in place. They include the *Wisla* medium-range air-defence programme, the *Narew* short-range air-defence programme, attack helicopters, submarines and unmanned aerial vehicles (UAVs). However, the precise details of the procurement plan are unclear, and a revised document was expected by the end of 2016. In common with other Eastern European states, Poland was also re-examining the question of personnel levels: a new 'Territorial Defence Force', comprising around 45,000 personnel, was announced in 2016. Although this will incur extra infrastructure, salary and training costs, it is not a conscript force.

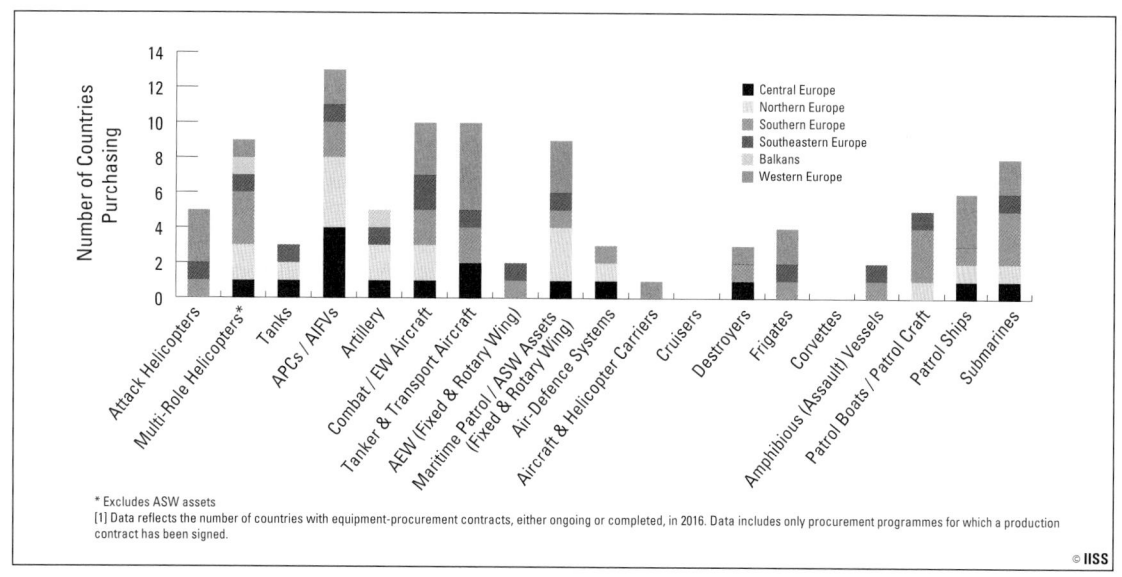

Figure 9 **Europe: selected ongoing or completed procurement priorities in 2016**[1]

* Excludes ASW assets
[1] Data reflects the number of countries with equipment-procurement contracts, either ongoing or completed, in 2016. Data includes only procurement programmes for which a production contract has been signed.

A report issued in September 2016 suggested that conscription could return in Sweden from 2018 (Stockholm transitioned to an all-volunteer force in 2010). Should conscription return, this will likely mean extra costs. Sweden has increased its defence spending (by 1.8% between 2015 and 2016 in US dollars), driven by changing threat perceptions and the resulting renewed attention on defence capability. Indeed, in total, Northern Europe increased its defence spending in 2016 (by 4.3% in current US dollars). The rise was particularly apparent in the Baltic states. Although the overall sums are relatively modest when compared with their larger European partners, they are striking in terms of the recent trajectory of defence funding in these countries. Estonia increased its defence spending by 7.8%, to account for 2.2% of its GDP, in 2016. Procurement priorities include UAVs, anti-armour systems, personal weapons and munitions. In 2016, Latvia and Lithuania increased their defence spending by 45.2% and 36.2% respectively. For Vilnius, part of this budget increase will be used to fund conscription, which Lithuania decided to reinstate in 2015; it has been reported that Latvia is also considering a return to conscription, although at the time of writing there had been no policy announcement on the matter. Norway extended conscription to women in 2015 and announced in 2016 a reorganisation of its defence forces, with efficiency savings set to fund new procurement. This will be supported by a 2.6% increase in defence spending between 2015 and 2016.

Southern European defence budgets declined slightly, by 0.1% between 2015 and 2016 (in current US dollars). Although Southern European countries face similar security challenges to other European states, including terrorism and human-trafficking networks in the Mediterranean, their prioritisation of threats can be different. At the same time, their slow recovery from years of austerity – and other pressing draws on the public purse – limits their capacity to increase defence spending. For instance, Greece decreased its defence budget by 2% in 2016 (in current US dollars). Italy remains in a difficult economic position, as growth was lower than expected (0.8% in 2016, according to the IMF), which limited the government's fiscal space and prevented the reduction of Italy's indebtedness (133.2% of GDP). Consequently, the Italian government plans to cut its total budget in 2017. Although in 2016 Italian defence expenditure increased by 3.8% to €20bn (US$22.3bn) in US dollars – up from €19.4bn (US$21.5bn) in 2015 – this figure is nonetheless a reduction compared to 2013 (€20.7bn, or US$27.5bn) and 2014 (€20.3bn, or US$27bn). Furthermore, Italy's latest three-year budget programme (*Documento Programmatico Pluriennale per la Difesa per il Triennio 2016–2018*) details plans to reduce allocations further to €19.3bn (US$21.8bn) in 2017 and €19.2bn (US$21.8bn) in 2018. Overall, in 2015 and 2016, Italy spent 1.2% of its GDP on defence; Italy's white paper published in April 2015 did not make any commitments with regard to the 2% NATO target.

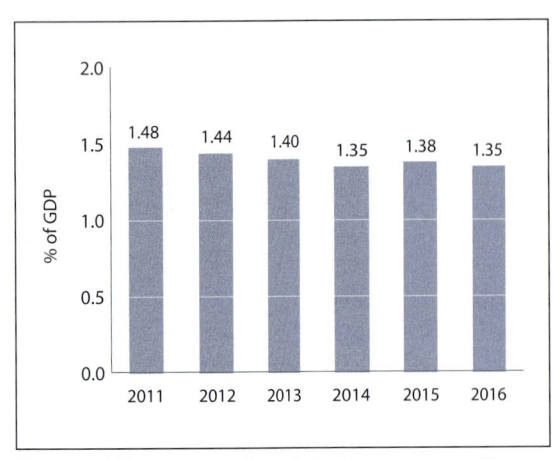

Figure 10 **Europe regional defence expenditure** as % of GDP

Year	% of GDP
2011	1.48
2012	1.44
2013	1.40
2014	1.35
2015	1.38
2016	1.35

In contrast with the trends in Central and Northern Europe, defence spending in Western Europe decreased by 4.3% in 2016 when compared to 2015 (in current US dollars). This downward trend was largely driven by the UK. Although in nominal terms the UK budget increased by 0.3%, from £38.2bn to £38.3bn (including costs of operations and MoD income), this was a fall of 10.1% in current US dollars from US$58.4bn to US$52.5bn. The 2015 Strategic Defence and Security Review (SDSR) planned that £178bn (US$244bn) would be spent on equipment and equipment support before 2025, but this figure might need revision if post-Brexit growth is lower than was expected at the time of the SDSR's publication. Furthermore, the fall of the pound could raise the cost of the UK's procurement plans (see pp. 87–8).

The French defence budget rose by 1.2% in 2016 (in US dollars). As such, this was an increase compared to the 2013 *Loi de Programmation Militaire* (Military Programming Law), which originally planned for a constant budget between 2013 and 2019. Following the terrorist attacks of 2015–16, an increasing number of political leaders called for additional defence spending to reach the NATO target of 2%. Besides increased funding for counter-terrorism, France also increased expenditure for operations *Barkhane* (in the Sahel) and *Chammal* (in Iraq and Syria). The requirements of these ongoing operations helped prompt the decision to buy four additional C-130J transport aircraft and additional MQ-9 *Reaper* UAVs from the US.

Also hit by terrorist attacks in March 2016, Belgium released in June its 'Strategic Vision' for 2030. This document pledges to raise Belgium's defence spending from 0.9% of GDP in 2016 to 1.3% in 2030.

Defence industry and exports

Despite the stable trend in regional defence spending, European defence companies' total revenue fell. As well as governments spending defence funds on areas other than equipment, this could perhaps be explained by the difference in the release of industry sales data (2015) and government budget data (2016), and by exchange-rate variations. Overall, the total revenue for the *Defense News* global top 100 defence companies fell from US$385.66bn in 2014 to US$356.68bn in 2015. European firms' revenue followed this downward trend, from US$101.73bn in 2014 to US$95.43bn in 2015. Among the 29 European defence firms included in the top 100, only four saw their sales increase: Cobham, Dassault Aviation, Turkish Aerospace Industries and RUAG. Dassault's defence revenue increased by 41.63% in 2015, and the company went up from 58th place to 43rd. These results were largely driven by the Egyptian and Qatari orders for the *Rafale* combat aircraft. Another contract with India for 36 *Rafale*s was signed in September 2016, after France was selected for exclusive negotiations in 2012.

KNDS, the holding company created as a first step towards the merger of France's Nexter and Germany's KMW, made its first appearance in the top 100. Although the agreement between the two firms seemed to herald a new era of Europe-wide defence-industry restructuring, no other major transnational consolidation occurred in 2016. Meanwhile, Europe's naval sector has been identified as a possible area for restructuring; notable firms include Saab/Kockums in Sweden, TKMS in Germany, DCNS in France, Navantia in Spain and Fincantieri in Italy. However, experience suggests that multilateral defence cooperation can remain difficult even when countries have similar security concerns: an example is the long-running joint Norway–Sweden project for the *Archer* artillery system. In 2016, Sweden announced that it would eventually buy 24 of these weapons that were originally destined for Norway, for a total of SEK450m (US$53m).

An indication of the difficulties in pursuing multilateral cooperation in Europe comes from the 2016 evaluation of the 'defence package' directives adopted by the EU in 2009 to support a more integrated defence market. Seven years after their adoption, the directives failed to produce any effect on the

European defence trade and industrial base. Directive 2009/81/EC aimed to enable more open competition in defence procurement, obliging member states to publish tenders and limit the use of Article 346 of the Treaty on the Functioning of the European Union.

Among its provisions, Article 346 states that '(a) No Member State shall be obliged to supply information the disclosure of which it considers contrary to the essential interests of its security; (b) Any Member State may take such measures as it considers necessary for the protection of the essential interests of its security which are connected with the production of or trade in arms, munitions and war material; such measures shall not adversely affect the conditions of competition in the internal market regarding products which are not intended for specifically military purposes'.

This article has been used by states to select domestic companies and, despite Directive/81/EC, the publication of tenders and contracts remains variable. The second part of the 'package', Directive 2009/43/EC, is aimed at facilitating arms transfers across EU member states by harmonising licences and certifying companies. However, the contents of licences and product lists are too diverse for firms to make effective use of them.

Nevertheless, in the aftermath of the Brexit vote, there were renewed calls for greater defence-industrial cooperation in Europe. In September 2016, Germany, France and the European Commission proposed the inclusion of a defence R&D programme in the EU budget for 2021–27. France and Germany proposed setting aside €90m (US$101m) between 2017 and 2019 for that purpose. The types of programmes that could be funded this way include those for UAVs or cyber defence. While taking small steps towards increasing more effective cooperation, this policy builds on previous announcements; the EC had already declared that it wanted to include defence R&D funding in its 2021–27 budget.

In recent years, the main export destination for European military equipment has been the Middle East and North Africa. In 2014 (the year with the latest data available), countries in these regions accounted for 33.41% of EU export licences (in financial terms, this amounted to €32.9bn (US$43.7bn) out of a total of €98.4bn (US$130.8bn) of approved licences). This flow of arms exports to the Middle East was a focus of a second conference of the states party to the Arms Trade Treaty, held during 22–26 August 2016. In the year before the conference, non-governmental organisations had campaigned against weapons exports to Saudi Arabia due to its role in the war in Yemen, with Amnesty International, for instance, arguing that such sales were a violation of the treaty. The European Parliament adopted a non-binding resolution in February 2016 to demand an embargo on the sale of arms to Saudi Arabia. Following this decision, the Dutch parliament adopted in March a bill enacting a presumption of denial of export licences to Saudi Arabia, and the Spanish congress adopted in April a motion to deny export licences to states party to the conflict in Yemen. Britain was also under pressure to halt weapons sales to Saudi Arabia, with two parliamentary committees stating that they should be suspended; a judicial review regarding the legality of the sales was under way late in the year. Other European states have expressed caution over sales to Middle Eastern countries. Sweden said in March 2015 that it would not renew a ten-year-old memorandum of understanding on military cooperation with Saudi Arabia, although the government said at the same time that: 'commercial agreements regarding the export of defense products to the Kingdom of Saudi Arabia will not be affected by the decision not to renew the Memorandum of Understanding.' Although German Minister for Economic Affairs and Energy Sigmar Gabriel indicated in 2013 that Germany would implement stricter controls on arms exports to the Middle East, Germany continues to licence such sales to Middle Eastern countries.

NORDIC AND BALTIC SECURITY

Russia's renewed flexing of its military power has sharpened focus on security challenges in Scandinavia and the Baltic Sea region, after two decades in which few security analysts and policymakers considered these areas to be of real strategic significance. International attention on Afghanistan and Iraq, as well as global challenges such as terrorism, allowed decision-makers in the region to take what, especially in Sweden, became known as a 'strategic time-out'. This led to a substantial 'peace dividend' of reductions in defence budgets and military capabilities – particularly in Denmark, Norway and Sweden – and a lengthy period of reflection on the purpose of the region's armed forces. The outcome was that defence thinking and military capabilities in most Nordic countries, with the exception of Finland, shifted away from a focus on territorial defence to the development of expeditionary forces capable of tackling security threats in developing countries.

Today, the security situation has been transformed in Scandinavia and the Baltic Sea region. Russian military modernisation and Moscow's overt exercise of its military and security capabilities, not only in terms of its actions in Ukraine and Syria but also fears of its broader information and influence capabilities (and the potential for these to be deployed below the threshold that could prompt an armed response) has led to the emergence of a common threat perception among regional states. For the first time in 25 years, war in the Baltic Sea region is not only considered a possibility but is also increasingly studied in war games and military exercises, which have been taking place in the region at a higher frequency than at any time since the collapse of the Soviet Union in 1991.

Institutional alignment

For Nordic states, however, this convergence of threat perceptions is taking place within a context of diverse institutional affiliations, and where each country has been pursuing distinct defence policies. This legacy has the potential to affect their ability to act together militarily.

Although the five Nordic states are often regarded as culturally, politically and societally similar, their security policies and institutional affiliations differ. **Iceland** is a member of NATO but not of the EU and, although it has no defence forces of its own, it has a bilateral defence treaty with the United States. **Norway** is a member of NATO but not of the EU, although it has taken part in EU missions. Oslo has a relatively small but capable defence force closely linked to the United Kingdom and the US, especially in the maritime domain. **Denmark** is a member of both NATO and the EU, but has an opt-out on the euro and the EU's fledgling defence dimension, although Copenhagen has also taken part in EU missions. Denmark's military has transformed into a force optimised for multinational operations abroad. **Sweden**, meanwhile, is a member of the EU but not of the eurozone, and it too has taken part in EU missions. It is not a NATO member. A painstaking reform process started in 2009, intended to reduce establishment strength and transition to a professional force. Conscription was suspended in 2010, but concern over a deteriorating strategic environment has recently led Sweden to re-invest in defence. **Finland** is a member of the EU, has taken part in EU missions and has adopted the euro. Like Sweden, it is not a NATO member. Alone among the Nordic states, Finland has retained its traditional concept of large armed forces comprising a relatively compact, conscript-based military, with a significant reserve that could be mobilised in wartime.

In contrast to these different approaches to defence and security integration, regional neighbours Estonia, Latvia, Lithuania, Poland and Germany are all members of NATO and the EU, take part in both organisations' military and security missions, and have all adopted the euro.

Therefore, contemporary Nordic defence cooperation can be seen as an attempt to overcome the diversity of Nordic security and military policies. In 2009 regional states established Nordic Defence Cooperation (NORDEFCO), placing an institutional framework around the modest cooperation on defence materiel and related issues that had previously proceeded in an ad hoc fashion. The primary driver for this cooperation was, and remains, the prospect of financial savings, such as making better use of shrinking defence budgets through common equipment procurements. At the launch of NORDEFCO, it was publicly stated that the framework was not intended to replace existing, or build new, military alliances. Nonetheless, it was widely seen as a way of bringing the Nordic countries closer together militarily, despite their different affiliations with NATO and the EU. In 2011 the Baltic states were invited by the then-Swedish chairmanship to join some of the NORDEFCO cooperation areas, and in 2012 they were for the first time invited to participate in a meeting of the NORDEFCO military-coordination committee. There are many areas of potential cooperation: cyber security is an obvious area of common interest, while in 2016 it was reported that NORDEFCO would produce a study on the possibility of including the Baltic states in its initiative to develop a secure communications system for its members. As such, NORDEFCO has contributed to an increased level of intra-regional defence cooperation that goes beyond its original Nordic focus.

Given the different institutional memberships held by the Nordic countries, the developments of the last two to three years – especially Russia's annexation of Crimea – have had significant consequences. Norway is increasing its defence investments and restated the importance of NATO in its June 2016 'Long-Term Defence Plan'. NATO and the transatlantic community, the document said, remained 'the cornerstone of Norwegian security and defence policy'. Denmark, too, stressed NATO's importance in advance of the 2016 Warsaw Summit and, like Norway, has earmarked personnel for NATO's enhanced forward presence in Poland, Estonia, Latvia and Lithuania. Sweden and Finland, on the other hand, may be militarily non-aligned but maintain close cooperation on a bilateral level, as well as with a number of NATO member states. However, the two states differ in terms of how they deal with the Russian challenge and the issue of how close their ties with NATO should become.

Finland and Sweden: future directions

In **Finland**, official policy has for years included a so-called 'NATO option' – an explicit possibility of applying for membership should international circumstances warrant it. However, few Finnish politicians actively advocate NATO membership and public opinion is against it. Although Finland's June 2016 'Government Report on Finnish Foreign and Security Policy' said 'the presence and action of NATO brings security to the region' and the document argued it was 'important to Finland that NATO continue its Open Doors policy', analysts observe that in recent years there has been some return to Cold War-era visions around non-alignment and attempts to 'build bridges' between the West and Russia. This was exemplified by reciprocal presidential visits between Helsinki and Moscow in 2016. Finland's president, Sauli Niinistö, has also noted that Finland cannot provide 'security guarantees' to the Baltic states.

Meanwhile, Finland makes substantial efforts in its bilateral defence-related partnerships with Sweden and the US, but the non-binding character of these relationships – in contrast to those of a mutual-defence alliance such as NATO – is always underlined in Finnish discourse. Indeed, while Finland talks of 'deepened' Finland–NATO cooperation, Helsinki is clear that 'partnership cooperation neither includes any Article V based security guarantees nor obligations'. Non-alignment, conscription and a pragmatic attitude towards Russia remain the pillars of Finnish defence policy.

In **Sweden**, current policy explicitly excludes any possibility of applying for NATO membership. However, four out of the eight parties in parliament – the entire centre-right opposition – openly advocate membership, and public opinion has changed markedly: around 35% of Swedes are now reportedly in favour of membership, whilst around 35% are against and the rest undecided. This is a clear shift from only a few years ago, and can likely be attributed both to perceived Russian aggression and a realisation that Sweden's armed forces now have only a limited ability to defend the entire country without external help.

The Swedish government has voiced strong criticism of Russian actions in Ukraine and elsewhere, while Swedish public opinion is also reportedly sceptical about Russia's policies. Simultaneously, the government has implemented a Host Nation Support Agreement with NATO (in 2014); signed defence-related memorandums of understanding with Denmark, the UK and the US (all NATO countries); and based its security policy on a unilateral 'declaration of solidarity' with EU and Nordic countries. None of these initiatives, however, amounts to military alignment or any form of security guarantee.

Adhering to a broad parliamentary agreement reached in 2015, the Swedish defence budget will increase slightly and the country's military posture has been reinforced by some concrete steps, such as the reintroduction of a military contingent on the strategically significant island of Gotland, which was essentially demilitarised more than ten years ago.

The Nordic states' security environment has changed a great deal in recent years. There is now a common threat perception, but institutional variance and ad hoc solutions mean that both NATO and the Nordic countries might find it difficult to act together in the event of a military conflict in the region. For NATO and the US, though, Finnish and perhaps especially Swedish territory would seem of obvious importance for any major military operation in the Baltic Sea region; this could lead to increased demands for closer defence integration between NATO, the US and the Nordic states, regardless of the Nordic states' institutional affiliations.

FRANCE

French military forces remain heavily engaged both abroad and at home. Since January 2015, multiple successful terror attacks across France (in Paris, Saint-Quentin-Fallavier, Magnanville, Nice and Saint-Etienne-du-Rouvray) and numerous unsuccessful attempts have absorbed significant resources from France's defence and security forces. Terrorism has proved to be an enduring challenge, and is seen as the most immediate threat to national security. The attacks varied in scale and sophistication, but all appeared to have been inspired, sponsored and, in some cases, even logistically supported by the Islamic

State, also known as ISIS or ISIL. Nonetheless, as noted in *The Military Balance 2016*, far from reducing its overseas commitments, France has done more. In his speech before parliament a few days after the November 2015 attacks, President François Hollande declared that 'France is at war' and announced greater involvement in the operations against ISIS in Iraq and Syria.

National resilience remains high in the face of those attacks. At the organisational level, security forces and first responders were effective even when faced with complex coordinated attacks such as those of November 2015. However, there was some criticism of the lack of coordination among, and resources for, the intelligence services, when it emerged that several terrorists involved in the attacks had previously been identified and placed under surveillance. At the political level, the national unity demonstrated after the *Charlie Hebdo* attack in January 2015 has decreased. With attacks continuing and the 2017 elections approaching (the presidential elections will take place in May and the National Assembly elections in June), some government policies proved controversial. These included the proposal to give constitutional status to the law to strip convicted terrorists with dual citizenship of their French nationality; in the end, this was not submitted to congress. Meanwhile, although French society also demonstrated its resilience, there are indications that the Islamist terrorist threat might have a domestic political impact. Following the July 2016 attack in Nice, some opinion polls showed that the struggle against terrorism might become a key consideration driving voter preferences during the 2017 elections.

As the government anticipates that there will be a long-term need for personnel to participate in homeland-security missions, it plans to increase the defence ministry's operational reserve forces from 28,700 to 40,000 by 2018. Hollande announced in July 2016 a plan to create a National Guard – an 84,000-strong force drawing from reserves of the armed forces, the police and the gendarmerie. The National Guard should be able to provide 5,000–8,000 personnel on call-up, although the plan remains controversial, particularly in terms of its funding.

While terrorism, and in particular combating ISIS, is France's priority in terms of security policy, Paris continues to aspire to retain armed forces capable of full-spectrum combat. This is illustrated by Hollande's speech on nuclear deterrence in Istres in February 2015 and the French commitment to NATO, reflected in its continuing involvement in the Baltic Air Policing mission, alongside permanent missions (air defence and nuclear deterrence) and foreign operations. In his speech, Hollande warned against the risk of future strategic surprises, including the possibility of a major state-based threat to France, and the continuing need for a nuclear deterrent with both a naval and an air component. This stance in support of nuclear deterrence has also been supported by major contenders for the 2017 election. As such, despite the current emphasis on counter-terrorism operations, all branches of the French armed forces remain committed to full-spectrum challenges.

Operations

Operational activity remains continuous and high-tempo. Chief of Defense Staff General Pierre de Villiers has described the French armed forces as being at 'full throttle', given the 30,000 troops deployed within and outside France's borders. These deployments have been driven by the domestic terror threat, and led the authorities to mobilise 13,000 troops – including 10,000 from the army – for homeland-security duties as part of *Operation Sentinelle*; 11,000 are deployed on standing tasks overseas and under 7,000 are deployed overseas on operations. The *Sentinelle* mission has become the French forces' largest operational commitment. Although domestic deployments were supposed to gradually decrease, they were maintained in light of the November 2015 and July 2016 attacks. To reduce the strain on personnel numbers, parliament voted in July 2015 for new funds to recruit 11,000 more troops by the end of 2016. However, there has been debate over the tasks open to these troops: the current legal framework does not allow soldiers to conduct intelligence tasks, make arrests or engage in kinetic counter-terrorism operations on French soil. This leaves the military with relatively mundane patrolling and guard duties. In August 2016, the government announced that it might re-frame the operation: there should no longer be any static guard tasks and the number of soldiers deployed will be reduced to 7,000 – with 3,000 more on alert and readily deployable.

Overseas, France's 'war on terrorism' continues. About 1,000 personnel are deployed in the Middle East on operations in support of the coalition against ISIS. *Operation Chammal* involves 12 *Rafale* combat aircraft as well as *Atlantique* 2 and E-3F aircraft for intelligence, surveillance and reconnaissance (ISR) and airborne early-warning and control tasks, as well as a KC-135 tanker. For four weeks in September, they were temporarily reinforced by the *Charles de Gaulle* aircraft carrier – its last deployment before an 18-month-long refit – and its 24 *Rafale* M aircraft, as well as supporting naval vessels. These included three French frigates and one French *Rubis*-class nuclear-powered attack submarine (SSN), as well as the American *Arleigh Burke*-class destroyer USS *Ross* and the German frigate *Augsburg*. Since the start of the operation, French forces have undertaken over 4,000 sorties and 850 airstrikes. A land component has been conducting training missions with Iraqi regular and special forces in Baghdad and Erbil. After the Nice attacks, Paris also dispatched to Iraq an artillery contingent consisting of four CAESAR 155mm guns and their crews; these conducted fire-support missions in support of Iraqi forces, notably during the battle for Mosul.

However, for all the focus on tackling ISIS in the Middle East, France's principal military deployment remains *Opération Barkhane* in the Sahel (Chad, Burkina Faso, Mali, Mauritania and Niger). *Barkhane* consists of about 3,500 troops organised around two battlegroups based in Gao, in Mali, and N'Djamena, in Chad, with a network of forward-operating bases and combat outposts. Although *Barkhane* is structured as a mobile force, equipped with 17 helicopters and 400 armoured and transport vehicles, the theatre of operations – at around five million square kilometres – means that the mission remains stretched. At the time of writing, the air component comprised four combat aircraft (*Mirage* 2000C/D), between six and ten strategic- and tactical-lift aircraft and five unmanned aerial vehicles (UAVs) (including three MQ-9 *Reaper*s) for ISR missions. *Barkhane* also has a key enabling role in supporting local forces in their fight against terrorist groups. However, with regional security showing little sign of improvement, Paris is now envisioning an even wider role for the operation, potentially aiming to check Boko Haram's activities around Lake Chad and addressing threats emanating from Libya, the southern region of which provides sanctuary for various jihadist movements.

Libya is a growing concern for France. Although Paris has made it clear that it would not intervene without a formal request from the Libyan government, there have been reports of French special operations in the country. Meanwhile, the French Navy has been operating along the Libyan coast as part of the EU-led *Operation Sophia*, aimed at enforcing the UN arms embargo there and controlling illegal immigration across the Mediterranean.

This high operational tempo has significantly increased the stress on equipment. The attrition rate for helicopter engines is ten times higher in recent operations than in normal (training) use, while 17% of land vehicles are considered unserviceable on their return from operations. Although availability rates are still high on operations (70–90%, depending on the equipment), this figure tends to drop in training periods to between 40% and 70%.

To keep up with this operational pace, France has had to reduce other commitments, such as to NATO's military presence in Eastern Europe, as well as to other operations deemed to be of lower priority, including *Opération Sangaris* in the Central African Republic. This mission was brought to a close in November, although 250 troops will remain as a reserve force. Operations *Corymbe* in the Gulf of Guinea and *Atalanta* in the Indian Ocean are still engaged on anti-piracy missions, with a *Mistral*-class amphibious-assault platform deployed on *Corymbe*. Standing 'presence' missions continue in Côte d'Ivoire, Djibouti, Gabon, Senegal and the United Arab Emirates, with up to 3,800 French personnel conducting long-term military-assistance and -training tasks there.

France also remains engaged in Europe, and with European partners. In August 2016, France again became the lead nation in the Baltic Air Policing mission – and would remain so until the end of the year – flying four *Mirage* 2000-5 combat aircraft out of the Lithuanian air base at Siauliai. France has committed a company-sized unit to NATO's enhanced forward presence in the Baltic states and Poland. Unlike Canada, Germany, the United Kingdom and the United States, it did not become a lead nation, which would have required the deployment of a battalion-sized battlegroup. Meanwhile, six years after the signing of the Lancaster House treaties, Anglo-French defence cooperation also continues to develop. London and Paris agreed in March 2016 to continue making progress on the 'Future Combat Air System' project, confirming that they would 'prepare for the full-scale development of unmanned combat air system (UCAS) operational demonstrators by 2025'. Meanwhile, both sides reported that exercise *Griffin Strike*, conducted in April 2016, successfully validated the Combined Joint Expeditionary Force concept.

After the United Kingdom's 23 June vote to leave the EU, President Hollande re-emphasised defence cooperation at a European level. He has since then argued in favour of a more 'protective EU', not strictly focused on security and defence, with a call for stronger cooperation in counter-terrorism and on overseas operations, where France hopes to see greater commitment from other EU members. At the EU's September 2016 Bratislava Summit, France and Germany pushed for new (and old) initiatives, including: strengthening EU border controls by creating a dedicated force; making better use of EU battlegroups; making it easier to fund EU operations abroad; pursuing common research and development projects; pooling support, logistics or intelligence assets between members; and establishing an EU military headquarters.

Major military reforms and programmes
Army
On 28 May 2015, the French Army officially unveiled a plan to change its organisational structure, 'Au Contact', in order to produce a flexible force capable of tackling contemporary threats. With the army having mainly focused on expeditionary roles, Au Contact is also intended to produce a force able to better balance the army's role, and visibility, in security tasks – particularly at home. A new command for French territory (*Commandement Terre pour le Territoire National*, or COM TN) was established in June 2016 to prepare for and enable deployments on national soil. The army has been divided into 13 commands to bolster functional coherence, with key capabilities – such as special forces and army aviation (including a new aviation brigade); intelligence, information and communication systems; and logistics – reinforced and consolidated into new dedicated commands.

Force Scorpion – an operational force composed of two newly recreated divisions (the 1st in Besançon and the 3rd in Marseille) – is a key pillar of this structure. 'Divisions' disappeared from the French Army in the late 1990s; they are now returning to the French order of battle. These two new divisions comprise six combined-arms brigades: two armoured, two medium and two light (airborne and mountain). The overall aim of this process is to prepare these units for the equipment due to arrive as part of the army's *Scorpion* programme, which is intended to improve the equipment held by combined-arms tactical groups (*Groupement Tactique Interarmees*, or GTIA), the French Army's principle unit of operation. The army expects to deploy abroad its first *Scorpion* battlegroup by 2021. The first phase of this includes the delivery by 2020 of 780 *Griffon* multi-role armoured personal carriers, in different variants; the *Griffon* has been developed by a consortium including Nexter, Renault Trucks Defense and Thales. It also includes the delivery, within the same time frame, of 110 6x6 *Jaguar* armoured reconnaissance vehicles, designed to replace the AMX-10RC, ERC-90 *Sagaie* and VAB HOT. The transformation programme also includes an upgrade to the 200 *Leclerc* main battle tanks valued at around €330m (US$366m), with this work undertaken by Nexter.

One of the major tactical innovations of the programme will be the introduction of a new information system (SICS), designed to create a more coherent communications and information-sharing architecture. In this vein, the army is also improving its UAV capabilities. Sagem won the Tactical Drone System (SDT) programme competition to provide a medium-altitude long-endurance UAV capability and is due to deliver 14 *Patroller* UAVs and four ground-control stations at an estimated cost of €300m (US$335m). According to Sagem, by 2018 the *Patroller* will take over from the *Sperwer* UAV currently in service with the 61st Artillery Regiment.

Navy
The French Navy is implementing the Horizon Marine 2025 plan. Released in December 2014, this set out the navy's ambition to remain a full-spectrum force while meeting the operational requirements of deterrence, forward presence and intervention. Built by France's DCNS, the first new *Barracuda*-class SSN, *Suffren*, is due to undergo sea trials in mid-2017 and should be delivered to the navy by 2018. *Suffren* is the first of a series of six SSNs to replace the current *Rubis* class. The ships are expected to be commissioned between 2018 and 2028 at a rate of one every two years, with the total programme cost estimated at €8.5 billion (US$9.5bn). The navy's other major build is the FREMM (multi-mission frigate) programme. Eight ships are due in this class – a second-generation stealth frigate – and three have been delivered. The most recent, *Languedoc*, reached its home port of Toulon in March 2016. It is equipped with the new land-attack cruise missile (*Missile de Croisière Naval*), which will also equip the *Barracuda*-class submarines.

Air force
In line with the priorities outlined in its 2013 strategic plan, the air force continues to modernise, with particular emphasis on the ability to provide a flexible air contribution to foreign operations, either autonomously or in coalition, and requiring not only

modern combat aircraft but renewed tanker, airlift and ISR capabilities. A key programme is that to replace France's C-135FR tankers. The first Airbus A330 Multi-Role Tanker Transport was ordered in 2014, followed by an additional eight in December 2015. The last three aircraft should be ordered in 2018, with the first two due for delivery before 2019. The C-135FRs have been in service for more than 50 years, and age is a challenge across a number of fleets, including fixed-wing training aircraft. Procurement of the Airbus A-400M *Atlas* aircraft remains slow, with technical problems continuing to delay deliveries, as well as operational use. The ninth aircraft procured, and the first possessing real tactical capability (self-defence against man-portable air-defence systems, air-dropping paratroopers and landings on austere runways), was delivered to the French Air Force in June 2016. Because of these delays, and the A-400M's inability to refuel helicopters, the defence ministry ordered four Lockheed Martin C-130Js in January 2016 for an estimated €493m (US$550m). Two of these are C-130Js and two are KC-130Js, the latter with the capability to refuel helicopters in-flight. With Germany also planning to buy between four and six C-130s, Paris and Berlin announced in October 2016 their intention to pool these new assets in order to reduce costs and increase readiness.

Renewal of the nuclear deterrent is also in train. Studies have begun on the replacement of the ASMP-A nuclear cruise missile. This work on a successor system – dubbed the ASN4G – is believed to explore hypersonics or advanced stealth in order to ensure that the future Strategic Air Forces (which, from 2018, will be composed of two *Rafale* squadrons) will remain credible against defended airspace. At sea, the first batch of M51.2 submarine-launched ballistic missiles was to be fielded on a *Le Triomphant*-class nuclear-powered ballistic-missile submarine (SSBN) in 2016. This missile is equipped with new warheads (dubbed *Tête Nucléaire Océanique*), designed to replace the TN75 warhead deployed on the M51. Although the research and development process for the next SSBN class continues, President Hollande said at Istres that this submarine would have roughly the same dimensions as the current class. The new boats should be operational by the mid-2030s.

DEFENCE ECONOMICS

Defence spending has continued to follow the upward trend that began in 2015, reflecting not only increased domestic threat levels, but also the high level of operational activity of France's armed forces at home and abroad. In accordance with the *Loi de Programmation Militaire* (Military Programming Law, or LPM), updated and voted through in summer 2015, France should spend €32bn (US$36bn) on defence in 2016 (pensions excluded). The revised LPM plans for increases in defence spending until 2019. Indeed, the rise in terrorist attacks led Hollande to announce, in Versailles, that security considerations would be given precedence over the Stability and Growth Pact, which urges EU member states to limit their public deficits. The terrorist attacks of 13 November 2015 led the government to add about €100m (US$111m) to the 2016 defence budget, mostly to replenish ammunition stocks following operations in Iraq and Syria, but also to support *Operation Sentinelle* (the homeland-security deployment) and the development of reserve forces, as well as investments in intelligence capabilities. At the same time, the 2016 budget for the Ministry of the Interior was increased by €350m (US$391m), while the Ministry of Justice budget rose by €250m (US$279m). The increases were designed to allow these institutions to strengthen personnel resources in the face of the terrorist threat.

The budget request for 2017 increases defence spending by €600m (US$670m), in addition to what was planned for 2017 by the revised LPM. If implemented, this should bring the 2017 defence budget to €32.7bn (US$36.5bn) instead of €32.26bn (US$36bn), excluding pensions. According to the revised LPM, this upward trend in defence spending – the first since the early 2000s – should continue and accelerate until 2019, by which time it should reach €34bn (US$38bn) excluding pensions.

With security and defence issues at the forefront of the political agenda, presidential candidates for the 2017 elections have outlined increasingly ambitious spending plans. For example, the major contenders for the centre-right and right-wing parties' primary election – who included former prime ministers Alain Juppé and François Fillon, as well as Bruno Le Maire – have stated that they intend to go beyond the planned boost to defence, vowing to increase spending from the 2016 level of 1.78% of GDP (NATO definition) to 2% by 2025–27, and to start drafting a new LPM as of 2017.

Major exports and industrial landscape
France's defence industry was buoyed by booming export sales in 2015, which reached €16.9bn

(US$18.8bn) in orders – more than twice the amount in 2013 (€6.9bn, or US$9.2bn) or 2014 (€8.2bn, or US$10.9bn). Approximately 80% of these exports have gone to the Middle East. The aerospace sector accounted for more than €14bn (US$15.5bn) of the orders, followed by €1.5bn (US$1.7bn) for the naval industry, while land industries' share amounted to €400m (US$444m), or 5% of France's total defence exports.

In the aerospace sector, long-awaited Dassault *Rafale* sales generated the most attention. Egypt signed the first *Rafale* deal in February 2015, setting out the transfer of 24 jets for €5.2bn (US$5.8bn), while in late 2016 negotiations were still under way for the purchase of 12 more. Qatar signed a contract in December 2015 for 24 *Rafales* at €6.3bn (US$7bn), with an option for 12 more. Deliveries to Egypt began in 2016, and those to Qatar were scheduled to begin in 2018. Following Indian Prime Minister Narendra Modi's announcement in April 2015 that he wished to purchase 36 *Rafales*, long negotiations over the sale concluded in 2016 with a deal worth some €8bn (US$9bn) finally signed on 23 September. Meanwhile, the United Arab Emirates expressed interest in acquiring 60 *Rafales*, although no agreement is likely to be reached before 2017 or 2018.

Dassault's success is driving the rest of the French aerospace sector, with the order books of Thales and MBDA growing because of demand for *Rafale*-related components and ammunition. The latter two firms are also negotiating with Turkey over the sale of an air-defence system, believed by analysts to be worth around €3–4bn (US$3.3–4.5bn). Airbus Group signed a €1.1bn (US$1.2bn) contract with Kuwait for 30 *Caracal* helicopters, with deliveries beginning in August 2018. However, the company has been waiting for over two years for Qatar to confirm a pending agreement on 22 NH90 helicopters. Also, after a change of government in Poland, negotiations over the sale of 50 *Caracal* helicopters were delayed by issues related to offset measures, before Warsaw announced in early October 2016 that the talks had failed.

France's shipbuilding sector was more buoyant during 2016, following the announcement in April that DCNS was the 'preferred international partner' for Australia's future submarine programme. The deal for 12 *Shortfin Barracuda* Block 1A submarines is worth an estimated €34.5bn (US$38.5bn). While DCNS was also hopeful of a deal with the Royal Norwegian Navy for between four and six submarines, to be decided by the end of 2016, there have also been setbacks: Qatar chose Italy's Fincantieri over DCNS for a €5bn (US$6bn) contract for four corvettes and three other vessels. The *Mistral* vessels built as part of the contract with Russia were eventually sold to Egypt (the contract having been cancelled by the French government in the wake of Russia's actions in Ukraine). Meanwhile, a year after selling a FREMM-class destroyer to Egypt, DCNS's construction of a *Gowind*-2500 frigate for Egypt continued; the remaining three vessels of this class are to be built in Egypt.

The most significant recent development in the land sector remains Nexter's alliance with German firm Krauss-Maffei Wegmann to form KNDS; the alliance was finalised in December 2015 (see p. 9). Meanwhile, Paris managed to safeguard the €3bn (US$4bn) deal it had signed in 2014 with Riyadh to finance equipment deliveries to Lebanon (including 250 armoured vehicles, 7 *Cougar* helicopters and 24 CAESAR 155mm artillery systems). Saudi Arabia withdrew from the deal in February 2016, but it was later agreed that the equipment would go to the Saudi armed forces instead of the Lebanese military.

UNITED KINGDOM

Since the publication of the October 2015 Strategic Defence and Security Review (SDSR), the United Kingdom's Ministry of Defence (MoD) and armed forces have begun implementing the changes required to meet the review's increased military ambition (see *The Military Balance 2016*, pp. 72–4). There have also been modest increases in UK forces deployed to Eastern Europe and on other operations overseas. At the same time, there are indications that reversing the previous 'hollowing out' of the UK's conventional combat capability cannot be taken for granted, despite its aspiration to play a leading role in NATO.

Operations and deployments

In the wake of the 2015–16 terrorist attacks in Belgium and France, around 10,000 British troops were placed at high readiness to rapidly assist UK police forces in responding to a major terrorist attack; this was the armed forces' largest peacetime commitment. A modest increase to the 450 troops committed to NATO's *Operation Resolute Support* in Afghanistan was announced in July. UK training teams, advisers and experts were also deployed to countries including

Mali, Nigeria, Pakistan, Saudi Arabia, Tunisia and Ukraine, as well as other enduring engagements – such to as the British Peace Support Team (East Africa). Meanwhile, the Royal Navy continued to assist *Operation Sophia*, the European Union mission designed to counter migrant- and weapons-smuggling networks in the Mediterranean, among other tasks.

The year 2016 also saw the UK increase its contribution to UN peacekeeping operations. This is in line with the ambition of the 2015 SDSR to double the number of military personnel contributed by the UK to these operations. In early September, Secretary of State for Defence Michael Fallon led an international defence-ministerial conference to strengthen peacekeeping so as to better tackle contemporary security challenges. At the time of the event, Fallon announced a strengthened contribution to the UN mission in South Sudan. Lead elements deployed in June, and it is envisaged that a battalion-level force of 450 engineers, infantry personnel and medics will eventually be in-country. In May, the first contingent of an additional 70 troops arrived to reinforce the UK's contribution to the UN mission in Somalia. Figures released by the UN in August listed a total of 337 UK personnel deployed on UN missions.

With Parliament's approval that airstrikes could be extended from Iraq to Syria, *Operation Shader*, the UK element of the US-led campaign against the Islamic State, also known as ISIS or ISIL, became the UK's largest overseas mission, involving well over 1,000 personnel and equipment, including *Typhoon* FGR4 and *Tornado* GR4 combat aircraft, as well as MQ-9 *Reaper* unmanned aerial vehicles (UAVs). The UK continued to state that its contribution to the campaign was second only to that of the United States. There were also reports of UK special forces working with the moderate opposition in Syria and with government forces in Libya.

International activity

A major pillar of the 2015 SDSR was making the UK armed forces increasingly 'international by design', with defence engagement becoming a properly funded military task. This was illustrated by the October 2015 ceremony to break ground at the new British naval base at Mina Salman in Bahrain. This permanent facility was announced a year earlier at the 2014 IISS Manama Dialogue, giving the UK, according to then-foreign secretary Philip Hammond, 'the capability to send more and bigger

British Army regional alignment

To enhance the effectiveness of defence engagement, some British Army brigades have been aligned to regions of the world that are a high priority for UK defence strategy. The brigades have become the default organisation through which army exercises and land-force capability-building takes place in these regions.

- 4th Infantry Brigade — Northern Africa
- 7th Infantry Brigade — Western Africa
- 8th Engineer Brigade — South Asia
- 11th Infantry Brigade — Southeast Asia
- 42nd Infantry Brigade — Eastern Africa
- 51st Infantry Brigade — Gulf region
- 102nd Logistic Brigade — Southern Africa
- 160th Infantry Brigade — Europe and Central Asia

ships and to sustain them and their crews in permanent facilities'.

Deployment of *Typhoon* combat aircraft to NATO's Baltic Air Policing mission continued in 2016, as did small maritime and land exercise-related deployments to Poland and the Baltic region. As well as increasing UK commitments to NATO's standing maritime groups, it was announced that a UK battalion would be assigned – on a rotational basis – to NATO's enhanced forward presence in Eastern Europe. The UK would deploy to Estonia in May 2017 a 'fully combat capable' armoured battalion comprising – according to the defence secretary – 800 troops, *Warrior* armoured fighting vehicles, tactical UAVs and a troop of *Challenger* 2 main battle tanks, joined by rotational troops from Denmark and France. A UK company would also deploy to Poland. At the time of writing, the deployment timeline was unclear.

16 Air Assault Brigade joined US airborne forces participating in the Polish exercise *Anakonda* and subsequently trained with French airborne forces in Germany. The Army also prepared for its leadership of the multinational brigade contribution to NATO's Very High Readiness Joint Task Force in 2017. A British armoured infantry brigade headquarters and two of its battlegroups – with contingents from Denmark, Estonia, Latvia, Norway, Poland, Romania and Spain, as well as a wide variety of supporting logistic troops – exercised in this role in Canada, Germany and the UK.

In April 2016, the Anglo-French Combined Joint Expeditionary Force was tested in the exercise *Griffin*

Strike, which saw the deployment of combined land, maritime and air component headquarters, and a total of 3,500 UK and 2,000 French personnel, with five ships and ten aircraft from each country. Meanwhile, March saw around 1,500 UK Army combat-support and logistics troops travel to Jordan for exercise *Shamal Storm 2016*. This validation exercise for troops comprising the UK's Vanguard Enabling Group was, according to the MoD, designed to test the logistic support group's ability to deploy globally and so support the movement of the Army's deployable forces.

The UK also continued to stress its commitment to lead the multinational Joint Expeditionary Force (JEF), which includes Denmark, Estonia, Latvia, Lithuania, the Netherlands and Norway. According to a November 2015 memorandum of understanding, the JEF is 'a UK framework for a rapidly deployable force capable of conducting the full spectrum of operations'. With full operational capability planned for 2018, exercise *Joint Venture 2016* in July saw the UK test its new two-star UK Standing Joint Force Headquarters along with its JEF partners.

Implementation of SDSR 2015

There was evidence in 2016 not only of investment in modernisation, but also of the services having to live with financial constraints to their ambitions. Much of the new money from SDSR 2015 is being spent up front on counter-terrorism, special-forces and cyber capabilities. For example, a Joint Cyber and Electromagnetic Activities Group was formed to 'ensure new cyber effects are properly integrated with other military activities'. But many of the other conventional-capability enhancements are being delivered from the turn of this decade onwards.

Army
The Army began to rebuild its ability to field a full division of three combat brigades. It also developed its plans to field new 'specialist infantry battalions' optimised for defence engagement, as well as two new 'strike brigades', equivalent to US *Stryker* Brigade Combat Teams. Procurement of wheeled armoured personnel carriers to equip these formations was accelerated. It is expected that the contract will be for an 'off-the-shelf' vehicle, with the first projected for test in 2017. Meanwhile, a £7 million (US$10m) contract was awarded in July to QinetiQ to evaluate active protection systems for armoured vehicles. The off-the-shelf replacement of the current fleet of AH-64D *Apache* attack helicopters with 50 new AH-64Es (the type in service with the US Army) was announced the same month. The first of the new 'E' variants is projected to enter UK service in 2022.

Royal Navy
The plan to replace the Royal Navy (RN) *Vanguard*-class nuclear-powered ballistic-missile submarines with 'Successor' boats was endorsed by a parliamentary vote in July, whilst the third *Astute*-class nuclear-powered attack submarine, HMS *Artful*, was officially commissioned. The MoD acknowledged in early 2016 that reliability problems with the integrated electrical propulsion system on the Type-45 destroyers will require a major re-engineering package. As the defence secretary stated in a March 2016 letter to Parliament's defence committee, 'the performance and design of the Power and Propulsion System is simply not able to deliver the resilience and reliability required'. The effort to remedy these issues, *Project Napier*, started in 2014 and has two key elements – an Equipment Improvement Plan and Power Improvement Plan – that together are intended to 'update the T45 Power and Propulsion System to deliver long term availability improvements and operational benefits'. The Type-45 will be a key element of the fleet defence for the UK's new aircraft carriers. The first of class, HMS *Queen Elizabeth*, was set for initial sea trials in the first quarter of 2017. In November 2016 the MoD announced that, 'subject to final contract negotiations', the first steel would be cut for the new Type-26 vessel in summer 2017.

Personnel, equipment and budgetary pressures continued to affect the navy in 2016. A destroyer and a frigate have, in effect, been laid up in extended readiness. The forward repair ship RFA *Diligence* has been put up for sale early. It was also confirmed that the SDSR ambition to maintain 'up to six' ocean-patrol vessels has been pegged at five.

Royal Air Force
With the planned withdrawal of *Tornado* GR4 combat aircraft in 2019, work continued to integrate the *Brimstone* 2 short-range missile and the *Storm Shadow* land-attack cruise missile with the *Typhoon*. Meanwhile, the *Brimstone* 2 missile entered operational service on the *Tornado*.

Contracts were signed in 2016 for three *Zephyr* and 20 *Protector* UAVs, and for nine P-8 *Poseidon* maritime-patrol aircraft (MPA). *Protector* is an extended-range version of the General Atomics *Reaper* intended to have the capability to operate in non-military

Figure 11 **Ajax: the British Army's new armoured reconnaissance vehicles**

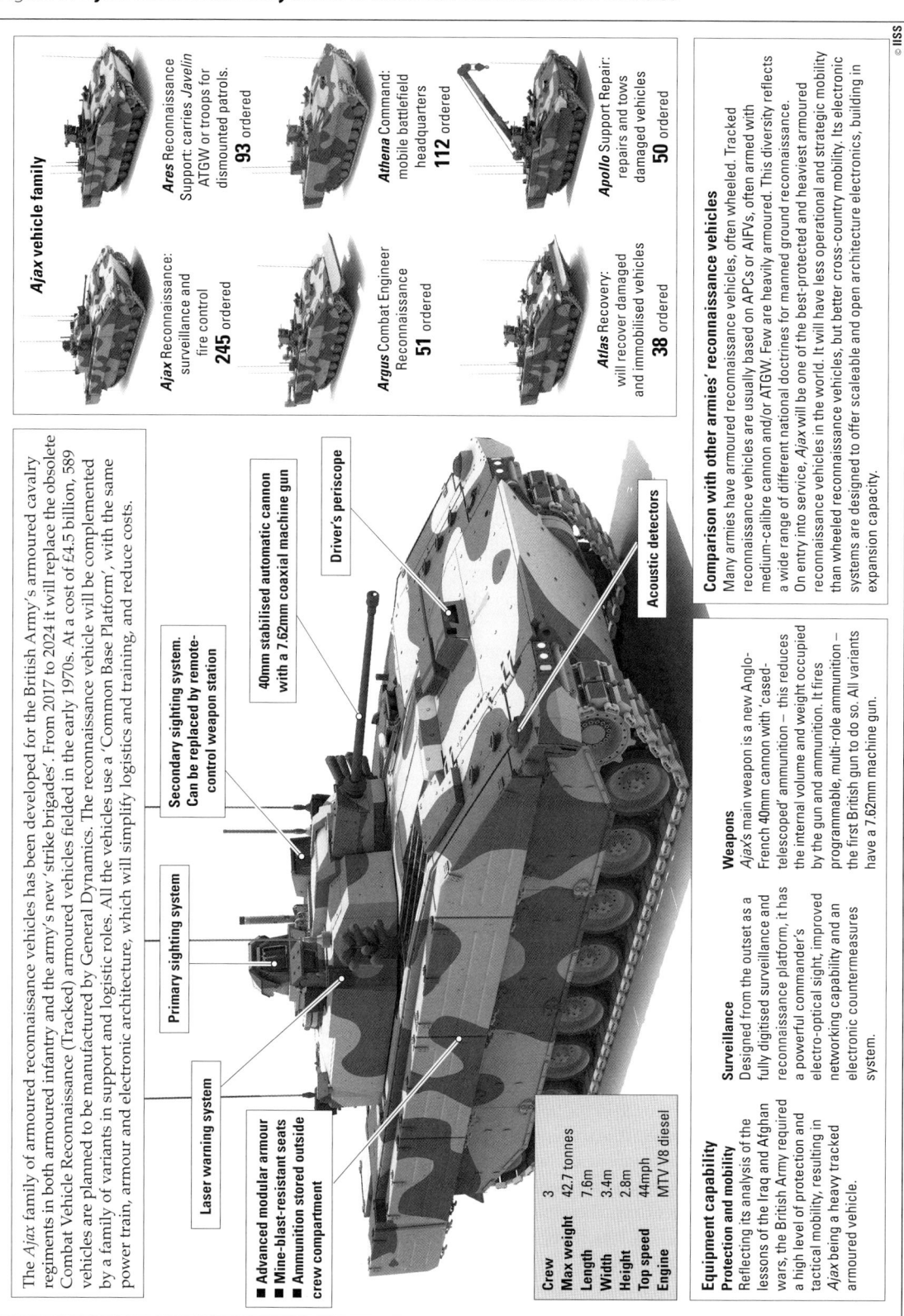

The *Ajax* family of armoured reconnaissance vehicles has been developed for the British Army's armoured cavalry regiments in both armoured infantry and the army's new 'strike brigades'. From 2017 to 2024 it will replace the obsolete Combat Vehicle Reconnaissance (Tracked) armoured vehicles fielded in the early 1970s. At a cost of £4.5 billion, 589 vehicles are planned to be manufactured by General Dynamics. The reconnaissance vehicle will be complemented by a family of variants in support and logistic roles. All the vehicles use a 'Common Base Platform', with the same power train, armour and electronic architecture, which will simplify logistics and training, and reduce costs.

Ajax vehicle family

Ajax Reconnaissance: surveillance and fire control
245 ordered

Ares Reconnaissance Support: carries *Javelin* ATGW or troops for dismounted patrols.
93 ordered

Argus Combat Engineer Reconnaissance
51 ordered

Athena Command: mobile battlefield headquarters
112 ordered

Atlas Recovery: will recover damaged and immobilised vehicles
38 ordered

Apollo Support Repair: repairs and tows damaged vehicles
50 ordered

Equipment capability
Protection and mobility
Reflecting its analysis of the lessons of the Iraq and Afghan wars, the British Army required a high level of protection and tactical mobility, resulting in *Ajax* being a heavy tracked armoured vehicle.

- Advanced modular armour
- Mine-blast-resistant seats
- Ammunition stored outside crew compartment

Crew	3
Max weight	42.7 tonnes
Length	7.6m
Width	3.4m
Height	2.8m
Top speed	44mph
Engine	MTV V8 diesel

Surveillance
Designed from the outset as a fully digitised surveillance and reconnaissance platform, it has a powerful commander's electro-optical sight, improved networking capability and an electronic countermeasures system.

Weapons
Ajax's main weapon is a new Anglo-French 40mm cannon with 'cased-telescoped' ammunition — this reduces the internal volume and weight occupied by the gun and ammunition. It fires programmable, multi-role ammunition — the first British gun to do so. All variants have a 7.62mm machine gun.

Comparison with other armies' reconnaissance vehicles
Many armies have armoured reconnaissance vehicles, often wheeled. Tracked reconnaissance vehicles are usually based on APCs or AIFVs, often armed with medium-calibre cannon and/or ATGW. Few are heavily armoured. This diversity reflects a wide range of different national doctrines for manned ground reconnaissance. On entry into service, *Ajax* will be one of the best-protected and heaviest armoured reconnaissance vehicles in the world. It will have less operational and strategic mobility than wheeled reconnaissance vehicles, but better cross-country mobility. Its electronic systems are designed to offer scaleable and open architecture electronics, building in expansion capacity.

Labels on vehicle:
- Laser warning system
- Primary sighting system
- Secondary sighting system. Can be replaced by remote-control weapon station
- 40mm stabilised automatic cannon with a 7.62mm coaxial machine gun
- Driver's periscope
- Acoustic detectors

© IISS

airspace. The P-8 is expected to enter service by 2020. Although the Royal Air Force (RAF) lost its MPA capability with the retirement of *Nimrod* in 2010, the RAF had retained experience in MPA missions through the *Seedcorn* project, which allowed British aircrews to fly with their Australian, Canadian, New Zealand and US MPA counterparts.

The last of 14 A330 *Voyager* tanker/transport aircraft was handed over to the RAF in July, while the ninth of a planned 22 A400M transport aircraft was also delivered that month. Although the A400M continues to be hampered by gearbox issues, manufacturer Airbus claims these will be resolved in mid-2017. RAF and RN helicopters were withdrawn from the UK search-and-rescue role in 2016. The mission transferred to the coastguard, with replacement helicopters operated by a private contractor.

Capability challenges
An army report analysing Russian tactics and capabilities used in eastern Ukraine, leaked in August, identified a number of weaknesses in UK land capability. It included the assessment that the UK's artillery – like that of other NATO armies – is outnumbered, outranged and outgunned by Russian artillery.

Another leaked report, by the outgoing commander of Joint Forces Command, General Richard Barrons, painted a convincing picture of forces with insufficient logistics, resilience and networked capability to adequately counter Russian forces. For example, not only would UK forces struggle to overcome Russian anti-access/area-denial capability, they also have insufficient air defence. Although the 2015 SDSR had stated that there was 'no immediate direct military threat to the UK mainland', there were, Barrons assessed, sufficient Russian military and cyber threats to the UK to justify rebuilding a military homeland-defence capability.

These assessments and personnel challenges (see textbox) showed that, whilst the 2015 SDSR and subsequent initiatives re-emphasised the UK military contribution to NATO deterrence, rebuilding British forces' conventional combat capability to a level sufficiently balanced and robust to meet their NATO roles will require both funds and time. In the meantime, UK forces would remain vulnerable to Russian forces and other 'near peer' adversaries.

Meanwhile, a Defence Innovation Initiative was announced by the MoD in September 2016 in order to try and maintain future military advantage. Similar in purpose to the US Third Offset Strategy, it aims to make the MoD, the armed forces and their suppliers more effective by exploiting emerging technology from both the military and civilian sectors. A ten-year,

Personnel

Although armed-forces recruitment increased in 2016, overall personnel strength continued to decline. In June 2016, the armed forces had a shortfall in trained personnel of more than 4%. Significant shortages of key specialist skills threatened the operational effectiveness of the Royal Air Force (RAF) and the Royal Navy (RN) and reduced the likelihood of achieving the modest growth of both services authorised by the 2015 Strategic Defence and Security Review. The risk appeared greatest in RN specialists, with considerable under-manning of sailors in engineering (10%), submarine engineering (7%), logistics (5%) and medical (9%) branches.

Annual pay increases remained limited to 1%, during a period when average wage growth in the United Kingdom has been twice that. Growth in the UK economy and employment were probably also significant 'pull' factors in leading key personnel to leave for the civilian sector. So too was the poor condition of a significant proportion of service-family accommodation. Reports by both the Armed Forces' Pay Review Body and the UK National Audit Office showed a significant increase in already high levels of dissatisfaction with accommodation, and an 80% increase in complaints on the topic. The Armed Forces' Pay Review Body also found that morale was declining and that 'high levels of gapping over a sustained period along with high voluntary and total outflows placed some operational capability and branch structures at risk'.

Taken together, these factors indicate a sustained problem in retaining older, more experienced service personnel, including those in high demand in RAF and RN specialist roles. Any downturn in the UK economy could boost recruiting and retention, but these efforts would in turn be jeopardised by any subsequent reductions in defence spending.

Meanwhile, it was announced in July that the remaining restrictions on the employment of women in land-combat units would be removed, opening to women roles in some units of the Royal Armoured Corps (RAC) from November 2016 – to be reviewed after six months, and then expanded to other RAC units. Roles in the infantry, the RAF Regiment and the Royal Marines will be opened to women by the end of 2018.

UK–EU defence relations after Brexit

The surprise June 2016 referendum vote in favour of leaving the European Union ('Brexit') has significant implications for the EU's security and defence policy and its military operations. Overall, the United Kingdom's withdrawal will weaken the EU's military capability. It will leave France as the only large EU country with full-spectrum war-fighting forces deployable at range, as well as the political and military culture to both engage in combat and lead demanding expeditionary operations.

Although no negotiations had started at the time of writing, there is a possibility that the UK will now also at some point withdraw from both the EU Military Staff and the European Defence Agency (EDA) unless the parties can reach agreements similar to the administrative arrangements signed with some non-EU states allowing them to participate in EDA activities. Further negotiations will be needed on the future of the UK's contributions to EU military and security operations, such as the mission in Bosnia, *Operation Althea*, and the EU counter-piracy mission, *Operation Atalanta*, for which the UK provides the operational headquarters.

Public statements by the UK defence secretary clearly indicated that the UK aspires to increase military activity with Europe, NATO and globally. Secretary of State for Defence Michael Fallon stated that 'leaving the European Union means we will be working harder to commit more to NATO and our key allies ... Britain is not stepping back. On the contrary, we're stepping up. We remain committed to European security and we are not turning our back on Europe or the world.' These sentiments may have influenced recent decisions to increase UK troop numbers in Afghanistan, Iraq and South Sudan. Alongside continued Anglo-French military cooperation and the UK-led Joint Expeditionary Force initiatives, there is also likely to be greater UK–Germany military cooperation.

Provided that the UK defence budget continues to grow as planned, it should be possible for London to increase both defence engagement and operational activity in Europe and beyond. But if economic shocks resulting from Brexit depress the UK economy and therefore GDP, the sustainability of these ambitions and the planned growth in UK defence capabilities will be in doubt.

£800m (US$1.1 billion) innovation fund is intended to encourage the development of new capabilities and approaches, especially disruptive technologies. A laser demonstrator was one key project selected in 2016 by this innovation fund, and a £30m (US$41m) deal was announced with MBDA UK to build a prototype by 2019. Early work has covered miniature UAVs that mimic insect flight, new airborne jammers and quantum-technology sensors. The initiative has top-level support and has been welcomed by the UK defence industry, especially small- and medium-sized companies, but it is too early to predict its impact on UK military capability or on the defence industry.

DEFENCE ECONOMICS

Macroeconomics

The result of the UK's 23 June 2016 referendum on membership of the EU has generated uncertainty about the UK's future economic health, as well as the direction of its economic policy. The IMF and the Organisation for Economic Co-operation and Development (OECD) projected in September 2016 that Brexit would have only a limited short-term impact on the UK's 2016 growth, largely thanks to good economic results at the start of the year and the measures taken by the Bank of England after the vote. However, these institutions' forecasts for coming years predict that the UK economy will slow. As a result, and because of uncertainty over the upcoming UK–EU negotiations, IMF growth predictions for 2017 were revised downwards from 2.2% to 1.1%. Based on this assessment, Brexit could cost the UK economy up to one percentage point of growth in 2017. Some British institutions released similar assessments, with the British Chambers of Commerce projecting 1% growth in 2017 instead of 2.3%. Should these negative economic forecasts come to pass, and the broader UK economy contract, it is likely that Brexit will have a negative effect on the defence budget.

Defence spending and procurement

Although the government committed in the SDSR to annually increase defence spending to FY2020/21 by 0.5% per year in real terms, economic uncertainty following the 23 June vote has made this trajectory less certain. In 2016, the defence budget, including the cost of operations and MoD income, was estimated at £38.3bn (US$52.5bn), a nominal increase of 0.3% compared to the £38.2bn (US$58.4bn) budget in 2015. This, however, came with a focus on procurement: the MoD announced that more than £178bn (US$244bn) would be spent on equipment and equip-

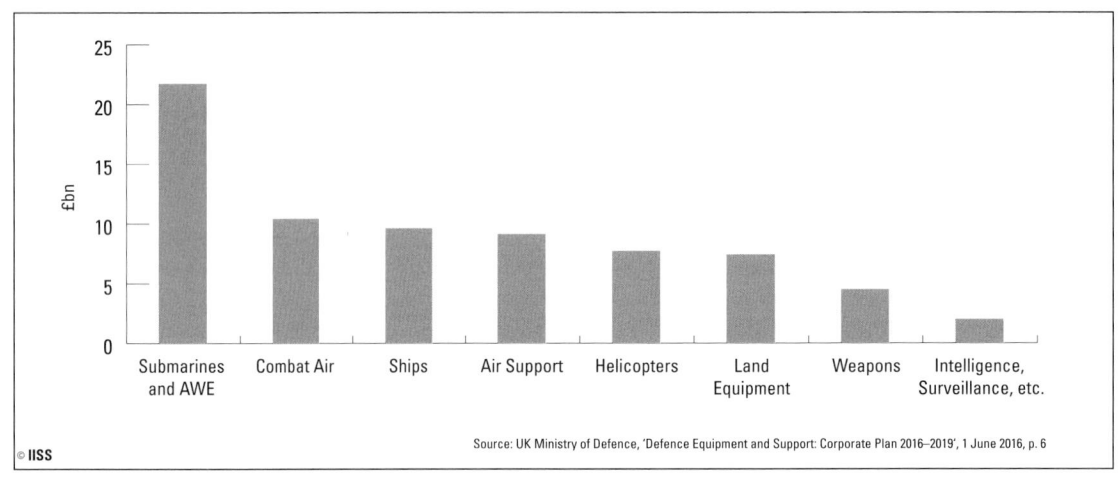

Figure 12 **UK planned equipment-support spending 2016–25**

ment support between 2016 and 2026. Part of this funding is to come from the ministry's efficiency savings and from outsourcing.

Future submarines and the atomic-weapons establishment are projected to receive the bulk of the £178bn (together £21.7bn, or US$29.8bn), followed by combat aircraft (£10.4bn, or US$14.3bn) and naval vessels (£9.6bn, or US$13.2bn) (see above). More broadly, key procurement plans over the next decade involve Lockheed Martin's F-35 combat aircraft, Boeing's P-8 maritime-patrol aircraft, *Protector* UAVs and a reduced number of Type-26 Global Combat Ships. In addition, an F-35 squadron will be brought into service faster than previously planned, while procurements (including of the new *Ajax* armoured vehicle) will also be required to equip the army's new Strike Brigades.

Yet the uncertain consequences of the Brexit vote could disrupt the MoD's spending plans in two ways. Firstly, the 2015 SDSR and the Spending Review were based on GDP growth estimates of 2.4% in 2016 and 2.5% in 2017. Should actual growth be lower than projected in 2015, constraints on government finances might mean that the spending plans laid down in the SDSR will need to be modified. The UK plans to increase its core MoD budget in 2017 and 2018 and meet its objective to reach the NATO target to spend 2% of GDP on defence. However, if GDP is lower than expected, then the defence budget would decrease in real terms as a result. Secondly, the post-Brexit slide in the value of the pound against the dollar (by 10% as of September 2016) could also – if this remains at low levels – affect the MoD budget. The UK imports or plans to import a number of major weapons platforms from the United States (including *Protector* UAVs, *Apache* helicopters, P-8 maritime-patrol aircraft and F-35 combat aircraft). The fall in the pound could increase the cost of these imports. Overall, these scenarios mean that the MoD's spending power could well be more constrained than originally envisioned in the 2015 SDSR and the Spending Review.

UK defence industry and exports

However, Brexit should have little impact on the UK's defence industry. Indeed, the fall in value of the pound could prove beneficial for British firms' export contracts. According to the latest data available, British defence manufacturers won defence export orders worth £7.7bn (US$11.8bn) in 2015, down from £8.5bn (US$14bn) in 2014. The UK's largest defence-export markets in 2015 were the Middle East (63%), North America (16%) and Asia (13%). Key contracts in the Middle East in 2015 included Saudi Arabia's purchase of 22 *Hawk* advanced jet trainers in December 2015, doubling the original Saudi *Hawk* order in 2012. Weapons exports to North America mainly consisted of F-35 components, while the bulk of the UK's Asia-Pacific exports in 2015 comprised orders of Thales's *Starstreak* air-defence missile systems from Malaysia and Thailand.

The UK defence industry continued to have export success in 2016. This was particularly reflected in the order book of BAE Systems, the UK's largest defence company. Key export contracts included £136m (US$187m) to refurbish 262 Swedish Army CV90 armoured vehicles via BAE's Swedish subsidiary, BAE Systems Hägglunds, and £111m (US$152) for BAE's US subsidiary to produce new Assault Amphibious Vehicles for Japan. Kuwait's order with Italy's Leonardo for 28 *Typhoon* combat aircraft meant that BAE in the UK was due to perform work on the contract with an estimated value of £1bn, or US$1.4bn. A contract was signed with the Royal Australian Navy to refine the design of the Type-26 Global Combat Ship to meet Australian requirements (the UK government has also committed to the type). Meanwhile, in the second half of 2016, BAE was awarded a contract by the Brazilian Army to upgrade its M109A5 howitzers and another by the US Navy to upgrade Mk45 naval guns. At the time of writing, BAE Systems was awaiting news on whether Saudi Arabia would order a further tranche of *Typhoon* combat aircraft – possibly up to 48. These export successes are supported by government export-promotion activities. Such initiatives have been strengthened in recent years, as symbolised by the launch of the Defence Growth Partnership (DGP) in 2014. A core aim of the DGP was to improve cooperation between industry and government when bidding for international defence contracts, promoting a 'Team UK' approach in order to increase exports. The DGP led to the incorporation of defence-industry staff in the UK Trade & Investment Defence & Security Organisation, the government body charged with assisting defence industries in their export efforts. In July 2106, the UK Parliament's Committees on Arms Export Controls launched an inquiry to examine the government's role in arms-export support and to evaluate the DGP. The DGP also included efforts to boost defence innovation, with the creation of the Defence Solutions Centre in 2015 and the launch of 'innovation challenges'. In this regard, the MoD's announcement in 2016 of the creation of a Defence Innovation Initiative can be seen as the latest segment in the UK government's desire to boost domestic innovation in terms of capability design, production and development, as well as in harnessing lessons relating to technology and innovation, and ways of working, observed in the private sector.

Albania ALB

Albanian Lek		2015	2016	2017
GDP	lek	1.44tr	1.50tr	
	US$	11.4bn	12.1bn	
per capita	US$	3,946	4,210	
Growth	%	2.8	3.4	
Inflation	%	1.9	1.1	
Def exp [a]	lek	16.7bn		
	US$	132		
Def bdgt [b]	lek	12.7bn	14.2bn	14.9bn
	US$	101m	115m	120m
FMA (US)	US$	2.4m	2.4m	2.4m
US$1=lek		125.93	123.85	

[a] NATO definition
[b] Excludes military pensions

Population 3,038,594

Ethnic groups: Albanian 82.6% Greek 0.9% Romani 0.3% Macedonian 0.2% Other or unspecified 15.7%

Age	0–14	15–19	20–24	25–29	30–64	65 plus
Male	9.7%	4.4%	5.0%	4.7%	20.3%	5.4%
Female	8.7%	4.1%	4.7%	4.8%	22.3%	6.1%

Capabilities

Albania's armed forces are limited to internal-security and disaster-relief tasks, and small-scale peacekeeping or training deployments. International engagement is increasingly important and several initiatives are under way to increase interoperability with foreign forces. NATO Secretary-General Jens Stoltenberg made his first visit to Albania at the end of 2015 to reaffirm the important role NATO plays in collective defence for the country. During a visit to the Pentagon in late 2014, Albania's defence minister highlighted a need for equipment modernisation to NATO standards. The small air brigade operates only helicopters, and the naval element has only littoral capabilities. Significant procurement of new equipment has been limited to two helicopters and some armoured vehicles for the military police. In 2016, Albania hosted British forces for the fifth consecutive year of exercise *Albanian Lion*. Albanian cooperation with other NATO allies included multilateral exercises, combined CBRN training in the US and training with the Turkish Armed Forces. Albanian forces have consistently been involved in NATO operations, and in 2016 doubled the number of personnel deployed to Afghanistan.

ACTIVE 8,000 (Land Force 3,000 Naval Force 650 Air Force 550 Other 3,800) **Paramilitary 500**

ORGANISATIONS BY SERVICE

Land Force 3,000
FORCES BY ROLE
SPECIAL FORCES
  1 SF bn
  1 cdo bn
MANOEUVRE
Light
  3 lt inf bn
COMBAT SUPPORT
  1 mor bty
  1 NBC coy
EQUIPMENT BY TYPE
ARTILLERY • MOR 93: **82mm** 81; **120mm** 12

Naval Force 650
EQUIPMENT BY TYPE
PATROL AND COASTAL COMBATANTS • PBF 5
Archangel

Coast Guard
EQUIPMENT BY TYPE
PATROL AND COASTAL COMBATANTS 22
  PB 9: 4 *Iluria* (Damen Stan 4207); 3 Mk3 *Sea Spectre*; 2 (other)
  PBR 13: 4 Type-227; 1 Type-246; 1 Type-303; 7 Type-2010

Air Force 550
Flying hours at least 10–15 hrs/yr
EQUIPMENT BY TYPE
HELICOPTERS
  TPT 26: **Medium** 4 AS532AL *Cougar*; **Light** 22: 1 AW109; 5 Bell 205 (AB-205); 7 Bell 206C (AB-206C); 8 Bo-105; 1 H145

Regional Support Brigade 700
FORCES BY ROLE
COMBAT SUPPORT
  1 cbt spt bde (1 engr bn, 1 (rescue) engr bn, 1 CIMIC det)

Military Police
FORCES BY ROLE
COMBAT SUPPORT
  1 MP bn
EQUIPMENT BY TYPE
ARMOURED FIGHTING VEHICLES
  AUV IVECO LMV

Logistics Brigade 1,200
FORCES BY ROLE
COMBAT SERVICE SUPPORT
  1 log bde (1 tpt bn, 2 log bn)

DEPLOYMENT

Legal provisions for foreign deployment:
Constitution: Codified constitution (1998)
Decision on deployment of troops abroad: By the parliament upon proposal by the president (Art. 171 II)

AFGHANISTAN
NATO • *Operation Resolute Support* 43

BOSNIA-HERZEGOVINA
EU • EUFOR • *Operation Althea* 1

MALI
EU • EUTM Mali 3

SERBIA
NATO • KFOR 12
OSCE • Kosovo 3

UKRAINE
OSCE • Ukraine 3

FOREIGN FORCES

Armenia OSCE 1
Austria OSCE 2
Bosnia-Herzegovina OSCE 1
Canada OSCE 1
Germany OSCE 1
Hungary OSCE 1
Ireland OSCE 1
Italy OSCE 1
Macedonia (FYROM) OSCE 1
Moldova OSCE 1
Montenegro OSCE 2
Serbia OSCE 1
United Kingdom OSCE 2
United States OSCE 1

Austria AUT

Euro €		2015	2016	2017
GDP	€	337bn	347bn	
	US$	374bn	387bn	
per capita	US$	43,414	44,561	
Growth	%	0.9	1.4	
Inflation	%	0.8	0.9	
Def bdgt [a]	€	1.84bn	2.07bn	2.32bn
	US$	2.05bn	2.31bn	
US$1=€		0.90	0.90	

[a] Includes military pensions and spending on DG Sports

Population 8,711,770

Age	0–14	15–19	20–24	25–29	30–64	65 plus
Male	7.2%	2.6%	3.2%	3.3%	24.4%	8.3%
Female	6.8%	2.5%	3.0%	3.2%	24.6%	10.8%

Capabilities

Defence-policy objectives are based on the 2013 National Security Strategy. They include the provision of military capability to maintain Austria's sovereignty; territorial integrity; military assistance to the civil authorities; and participation in crisis-management missions abroad. Austria's level of ambition for crisis-response operations is to be able to deploy and sustain a minimum (on average) of 1,100 military personnel and up to 100 experts in theatre. In February 2016, Austria completed a review of its armed-forces-reform programme (ÖBH 2018). The programme was initially designed in 2014 to maintain capability in an environment of budget cuts. The review showed that, compared to 2004, core capability indicators had dropped significantly: flight hours were down by 24%, personnel was down 16% and armoured vehicles by 60%. But the number of soldiers Austria deployed to international missions remained the same, therefore increasing strain on the force. The review pointed to a security environment where migration flows, international terrorism and continuing international military-crisis-management operations threatened to overwhelm the capacity of the Bundesheer. The initial plan called for a reduction in materiel and personnel, and changes were under way. However, the review of ÖBH 2018 argued that personnel cuts had to stop and that investment should be directed toward better training and more exercises, command and control, ISR, individual soldier equipment and mobility. The government has agreed to provide additional spending of around €1.2bn between 2016 and 2020. A new defence plan (Landesverteidigung 21.1-LV21.1) includes structural changes to the defence ministry as well as at the operational and tactical command-and-control level. Austria has taken on the lead-nation role for the Mountain Training Initiative in the EU pooling-and-sharing framework and has begun to coordinate more closely with the NATO Mountain Warfare Centre of Excellence in Slovenia. The Austrian government has authorised the deployment of up to 2,200 troops to assist the civilian authorities in border-control tasks in light of increasing migration flows reaching Austria via the Balkans. Plans to increase this number to more than 6,000 were proposed by the defence minister. The costs of these domestic-security tasks are largely covered by the general government budget. Procurement priorities for 2017 include AB-212 helicopter mid-life upgrades, improved airspace surveillance, ongoing land-vehicle procurements, including the continued installation of electrically operated remote weapons stations and the testing of new reconnaissance systems.

ACTIVE 21,350 (Land Forces 11,600 Air 2,700 Support 7,050)

Conscript liability 6 months recruit trg, 30 days reservist refresher trg for volunteers; 120–150 days additional for officers, NCOs and specialists. Authorised maximum wartime strength of 55,000

RESERVE 146,000 (Joint structured 25,200; Joint unstructured 120,800)

Some 7,000 reservists a year undergo refresher trg in tranches

ORGANISATIONS BY SERVICE

Land Forces 11,850
FORCES BY ROLE
MANOEUVRE
  Mechanised
    1 (3rd) bde (1 recce/SP arty bn, 1 armd bn, 1 mech inf bn, 1 inf bn, 1 cbt engr bn, 1 CBRN defence coy, 1 spt bn)

1 (4th) bde (1 recce/SP arty bn, 1 armd bn, 1 mech inf bn, 1 inf bn, 1 CBRN defence coy, 1 spt bn)

Light
1 (6th) bde (3 inf bn, 1 cbt engr bn, 1 CBRN defence coy, 1 spt bn)
1 (7th) bde (1 recce/arty bn, 3 inf bn, 1 cbt engr bn, 1 CBRN defence coy, 1 spt bn)

EQUIPMENT BY TYPE
ARMOURED FIGHTING VEHICLES
 MBT 40 *Leopard* 2A4
 AIFV 112 *Ulan*
 APC • APC (W) 78 *Pandur*
 AUV 61: 23 *Dingo* 2; 38 IVECO LMV
ENGINEERING & MAINTENANCE VEHICLES
 ARV 26: 20 4KH7FA-SB; 6 M88A1
 MW 6 AID2000 *Trailer*
NBC VEHICLES 12 *Dingo* 2 AC NBC
ANTI-TANK/ANTI-INFRASTRUCTURE
 MSL • MANPATS *Bill* 2 (PAL 2000)
ARTILLERY 120
 SP 155mm 30 M109A5ÖE
 MOR 120mm 90 sGrW 86 (10 more in store)

Air Force 2,700

The Air Force is part of Joint Forces Comd and consists of 2 bde; Air Support Comd and Airspace Surveillance Comd

Flying hours 160 hrs/yr on hel/tpt ac; 110 hrs/yr on ftr

FORCES BY ROLE
FIGHTER
 2 sqn with *Typhoon*
ISR
 1 sqn with PC-6B *Turbo Porter*
TRANSPORT
 1 sqn with C-130K *Hercules*
TRAINING
 1 trg sqn with Saab 105Oe*
 1 trg sqn with PC-7 *Turbo Trainer*
TRANSPORT HELICOPTER
 2 sqn with Bell 212 (AB-212)
 1 sqn with OH-58B *Kiowa*
 1 sqn with S-70A *Black Hawk*
 2 sqn with SA316/SA319 *Alouette* III
AIR DEFENCE
 2 bn
 1 radar bn

EQUIPMENT BY TYPE
AIRCRAFT 33 combat capable
 FTR 15 Eurofighter *Typhoon* Tranche 1
 TPT 11: **Medium** 3 C-130K *Hercules*; **Light** 8 PC-6B *Turbo Porter*
 TRG 30: 12 PC-7 *Turbo Trainer*; 18 Saab 105Oe*
HELICOPTERS
 MRH 24 SA316/SA319 *Alouette* III
 ISR 10 OH-58B *Kiowa*
 TPT 32: **Medium** 9 S-70A *Black Hawk*; **Light** 23 Bell 212 (AB-212)
AIR DEFENCE
 SAM • **Point-defence** *Mistral*
 GUNS 35mm 24 Z-FlAK system (6 more in store)
AIR-LAUNCHED MISSILES • **AAM** • **IIR** IRIS-T

Special Operations Forces
FORCES BY ROLE
SPECIAL FORCES
 2 SF gp
 1 SF gp (reserve)

Support 7,050

Support forces comprise Joint Services Support Command and several agencies, academies and schools

Cyber

The Austrian Cyber Security Strategy was approved in March 2013. A Cyber Security Steering Group to coordinate on a government level has been established. An Austrian Cyber Security Law, based on EU NIS directive, is planned by 2017. Operational-coordination structures are in train, including the Cyber Defence Centre/CDC (MoD), the Cyber Security Centre/CSC (Ministry of the Interior) and the Computer Security Incident Response Capability/CSIRC (Chancellery). FOC is planned for 2017. The defence ministry's primary goal is to ensure national defence in cyberspace as well as securing defence-ministry and armed-forces ICT. This led to the Military Cyber Emergency Readiness Team (milCERT), which is now at full operational capability, rising situational awareness and developing capabilities for Computer Network Operations (CNO) within the CDC (currently at IOC).

DEPLOYMENT

Legal provisions for foreign deployment:
Constitution: incl 'Federal Constitutional Law' (1/1930)
Specific legislation: 'Bundesverfassungsgesetz über Kooperation und Solidarität bei der Entsendung von Einheiten und Einzelpersonen in das Ausland' (KSE-BVG, 1997)
Decision on deployment of troops abroad: By government on authorisation of the National Council's Main Committee; simplified procedure for humanitarian and rescue tasks (Art. 23j of the 'Federal Constitutional Law'; § 2 of the KSE-BVG)

AFGHANISTAN
NATO • *Operation Resolute Support* 10

ALBANIA
OSCE • Albania 2

BOSNIA-HERZEGOVINA
EU • EUFOR • *Operation Althea* 313; 1 inf bn HQ; 1 inf coy

CENTRAL AFRICAN REPUBLIC
EU • EUTM RCA 3

CYPRUS
UN • UNFICYP 4

LEBANON
UN • UNIFIL 183; 1 log coy

MALI
EU • EUTM Mali 8
UN • MINUSMA 8

MIDDLE EAST
UN • UNTSO 4 obs
SERBIA
NATO • KFOR 465; 2 mech inf coy
OSCE • Kosovo 1
UKRAINE
OSCE • Ukraine 19
WESTERN SAHARA
UN • MINURSO 5 obs

Belgium BEL

Euro €		2015	2016	2017
GDP	€	409bn	421bn	
	US$	454bn	470bn	
per capita	US$	40,529	41,491	
Growth	%	1.4	1.4	
Inflation	%	0.6	2.1	
Def exp [a]	€	3.80bn		
	US$	4.22bn		
Def bdgt [b]	€	3.61bn	3.49bn	3.48bn
	US$	4.01bn	3.90bn	
US$1=€		0.90	0.90	

[a] NATO definition
[b] Includes military pensions

Population   11,409,077

Age	0–14	15–19	20–24	25–29	30–64	65 plus
Male	8.8%	2.8%	3.0%	3.2%	23.4%	8.0%
Female	8.3%	2.7%	2.9%	3.2%	23.2%	10.4%

Capabilities

In July 2016, the Belgian government published its strategic vision for defence, indicating the general direction for Belgian defence policy until 2030. Brussels intends first of all to stabilise Belgium's defence effort and then to provide for growth after 2020. The plan envisages a reduced personnel component of around 25,000. However, a large number of impending service retirements means that a gradual increase in recruitment is planned after 2017 as part of the overall move towards this number. The government is also keen to ensure that this reduction does not compromise operational capability, and so is investing in short-term requirements related to aircraft readiness, personal equipment and land-forces vehicles. Overall policy priorities remain unchanged, with defence policy based on multilateral solidarity with NATO, the EU and the UN; attacks in 2016 have again highlighted the threat from terrorism and have impelled closer counter-terror cooperation with France. Belgium is working with the Netherlands to consider the replacement of both countries' *Karel Doorman* (M)-class frigates. As part of the defence plan, the government envisages launching five investment projects in the short term: fighter aircraft, frigates, mine countermeasures, UAVs and land-combat vehicles. This includes plans for new light reconnaissance vehicles and upgrades to *Pandur* armoured personnel carriers. The navy has benefited from the acquisition of two new patrol and coastal combatants, while the air force is due to receive F-16 aircraft updates and ASRAAM, as well as the long-awaited A400M. Belgium continues to pursue high readiness levels and deployable niche capabilities. Large numbers of Belgian troops were deployed for domestic-security operations following terrorist attacks in 2016, although Belgium maintains overseas deployments on EU and UN missions, as well as in the Middle East on missions targeting ISIS.

ACTIVE 29,600 (Army 10,750 Navy 1,550 Air 5,650 Medical Service 1,300 Joint Service 10,350)

RESERVE 6,750
1,200 assigned to units and headquarters in peacetime; others on ORBAT but only assigned in time of crisis

ORGANISATIONS BY SERVICE

Land Component 10,750
FORCES BY ROLE
SPECIAL FORCES
  1 SF gp
MANOEUVRE
  Reconnaissance
  1 ISR bn (2 ISR coy, 1 surv coy)
  Mechanised
  1 (med) bde (4 mech bn)
  Light
  1 (lt) bde (1 cdo bn, 1 lt inf bn, 1 para bn)
COMBAT SUPPORT
  1 arty bn (1 arty bty, 1 mor bty, 1 AD bty)
  2 engr bn (1 cbt engr coy, 1 lt engr coy, 1 construction coy)
  1 EOD unit
  1 CBRN coy
  1 MP coy
  3 CIS sigs gp
COMBAT SERVICE SUPPORT
  3 log bn
EQUIPMENT BY TYPE
ARMOURED FIGHTING VEHICLES
  IFV 37: 19 *Piranha* III-C DF30; 18 *Piranha* III-C DF90
  APC • APC (W) 118: 40 *Pandur*; 64 *Piranha* III-C (CP); 14 *Piranha* III-PC
  AUV 645: 208 *Dingo* 2 (inc 52 CP); 437 IVECO LMV
ENGINEERING & MAINTENANCE VEHICLES
  AEV 8 *Piranha* III-C
  ARV 12: 3 *Pandur*; 9 *Piranha* III-C
  VLB 4 *Leguan*
ARTILLERY 105
  TOWED 105mm 14 LG1 MkII
  MOR 91: **81mm** 39; **120mm** 52
AIR DEFENCE • SAM • Point-defence *Mistral*

Naval Component 1,550

EQUIPMENT BY TYPE
PRINCIPAL SURFACE COMBATANTS 2
  FRIGATES • **FFGHM** 2 *Leopold* I (ex-NLD *Karel Doorman*) with 2 quad lnchr with *Harpoon* AShM, 1 16-cell Mk48 VLS with RIM-7P *Sea Sparrow* SAM, 4 single Mk32 324mm ASTT with Mk46 LWT, 1 *Goalkeeper* CIWS, 1 76mm gun (capacity 1 med hel)
PATROL AND COASTAL COMBATANTS
  PCC 2 *Castor*
MINE WARFARE • MINE COUNTERMEASURES
  MHC 6 *Flower* (*Tripartite*)
LOGISTICS AND SUPPORT 3
  AGFH 1 *Godetia* (log spt/comd) (capacity 1 *Alouette* III)
  AGOR 1 *Belgica*
  AXS 1 *Zenobe Gramme*

Naval Aviation

(part of the Air Component)
EQUIPMENT BY TYPE
HELICOPTERS
  ASW 4 NH90 NFH
  MRH 3 SA316B *Alouette* III

Air Component 5,650

Flying hours 165 hrs/yr on cbt ac. 300 hrs/yr on tpt ac. 150 hrs/yr on hel; 250 hrs/yr on ERJ

FORCES BY ROLE
FIGHTER/GROUND ATTACK/ISR
  4 sqn with F-16AM/BM *Fighting Falcon*
SEARCH & RESCUE
  1 sqn with *Sea King* Mk48
TRANSPORT
  1 sqn with A330; ERJ-135 LR; ERJ-145 LR; *Falcon* 20 (VIP); *Falcon* 900B
  1 sqn with C-130H *Hercules*
TRAINING
  1 OCU sqn with F-16AM/BM *Fighting Falcon*
  1 sqn with SF-260D/M
  1 BEL/FRA unit with *Alpha Jet**
  1 OCU unit with AW109
TRANSPORT HELICOPTER
  2 sqn with AW109 (ISR)
ISR UAV
  1 sqn with RQ-5A *Hunter* (B-*Hunter*)
EQUIPMENT BY TYPE
AIRCRAFT 88 combat capable
  FTR 59: 49 F-16AM *Fighting Falcon*; 10 F-16BM *Fighting Falcon*
  TPT 19: **Medium** 11 C-130H *Hercules*; **Light** 4: 2 ERJ-135 LR; 2 ERJ-145 LR; **PAX** 4: 1 A321; 2 *Falcon* 20 (VIP); 1 *Falcon* 900B
  TRG 61: 29 *Alpha Jet**; 9 SF-260D; 23 SF-260M
HELICOPTERS
  ASW 4 NH90 NFH opcon Navy
  MRH 3 SA316B *Alouette* III opcon Navy
  SAR 3 *Sea King* Mk48 (to be replaced by NH90 NFH)
  TPT 24: **Medium** 4 NH90 TTH; **Light** 20 AW109 (ISR)

UNMANNED AERIAL VEHICLES
  ISR • Heavy 12 RQ-5A *Hunter* (B-*Hunter*) (1 more in store)
AIR-LAUNCHED MISSILES
  AAM • IR AIM-9M *Sidewinder*; **ARH** AIM-120B AMRAAM
BOMBS
  Laser-guided: GBU-10/GBU-12 *Paveway* II; GBU-24 *Paveway* III
  INS/GPS guided: GBU-31 JDAM; GBU-38 JDAM; GBU-54 Laser JDAM (dual-mode)

Cyber

A national Cyber Security Strategy was released in 2012. The defence ministry released a Cyber Security Strategy for Defence in 2014, outlining three pillars of its cyber-security capability: Cyber Defence, Cyber Intelligence and Cyber Counter-Offensive. It stated that defence 'has to have a minimum response capability by end of 2014', an 'initial operating capacity' by the end of 2016 and a 'full operational capacity' by 2020. In mid-2015, recruitment was opened for additional cyber specialists within the defence ministry.

DEPLOYMENT

Legal provisions for foreign deployment:
Constitution: Codified constitution (1831)
Specific legislation: 'Loi relatif à la mise en oeuvre des forces armées, à la mise en condition, ainsi qu'aux périodes et positions dans lesquelles le militaire peut se trouver' (1994)
Decision on deployment of troops abroad: By the government (Federal Council of Ministers) and the minister of defence (1994 law, Art. 88, 106, 167 of constitution)

AFGHANISTAN
NATO • *Operation Resolute Support* 62

CENTRAL AFRICAN REPUBLIC
EU • EUTM RCA 9

DEMOCRATIC REPUBLIC OF THE CONGO
UN • MONUSCO 1; 1 obs
Land Component 52 (trg)

FRANCE
NATO • Air Component 28 *Alpha Jet* located at Cazaux/Tours

IRAQ
Operation Valiant Phoenix 16

JORDAN
Operation Desert Falcon 106; 6 F-16AM *Fighting Falcon*

LEBANON
UN • UNIFIL 1

MALI
EU • EUTM Mali 125
UN • MINUSMA 7

MIDDLE EAST
UN • UNTSO 2 obs

NORTH SEA
NATO • SNMG 1: 1 FFGHM
NATO • SNMCMG 1: 1 MHC

UKRAINE
OSCE • Ukraine 4

FOREIGN FORCES
United States US European Command: 900

Bosnia-Herzegovina BIH

Convertible Mark		2015	2016	2017
GDP	mark	28.2bn	29.0bn	
	US$	16.0bn	16.5bn	
per capita	US$	4,140	4,289	
Growth	%	3.2	3.0	
Inflation	%	-1.0	-0.7	
Def bdgt [a]	mark	335m	334m	
	US$	190m	191m	
FMA (US)	US$	4m	4m	4m
US$1=mark		1.76	1.75	

[a] Includes military pensions

Population 3,861,912

Ethnic groups: Bosniac 50.1% Serb 30.7% Croat 15.4% Other or unspecified 3.7%

Age	0–14	15–19	20–24	25–29	30–64	65 plus
Male	6.9%	3.0%	3.1%	3.7%	26.4%	5.5%
Female	6.5%	2.9%	2.9%	3.6%	26.9%	8.5%

Capabilities

Bosnia's armed forces comprise troops from all three formerly warring ex-Yugoslavian entities. The country's 2005 Defence Law noted a path to NATO membership. Talks between neighbouring states have been held to discuss the possibility of a joint Balkan force, able to respond to natural disasters or humanitarian-relief needs. Bosnia's invitation to join NATO's membership action plan is still pending due to an unresolved defence-property issue, including defence-ministry barracks and buildings, which has delayed progress on the membership issue for over five years. The US has donated demining equipment through the Humanitarian Mine Action programme as part of a continued effort to rid the country of landmines and unexploded ordnance. A joint EU, NATO and Bosnian training exercise was completed in 2016, fulfilling the first of two exercises agreed in 2015. Exercise *Quick Response* is planned to be repeated in 2017. Bosnian troops also take part in peacekeeping missions.

ACTIVE 10,500 (Armed Forces 10,500)

ORGANISATIONS BY SERVICE

Armed Forces 10,500
1 ops comd; 1 spt comd

FORCES BY ROLE
MANOEUVRE
Light
  3 inf bde (1 recce coy, 3 inf bn, 1 arty bn)
COMBAT SUPPORT
  1 cbt spt bde (1 tk bn, 1 engr bn, 1 EOD bn, 1 int bn, 1 MP bn, 1 CBRN coy, 1 sigs bn)
COMBAT SERVICE SUPPORT
  1 log comd (5 log bn)
EQUIPMENT BY TYPE
ARMOURED FIGHTING VEHICLES
  MBT 45 M60A3
  APC • APC (T) 20 M113A2
ENGINEERING & MAINTENANCE VEHICLES
  VLB MTU
  MW *Bozena*
ANTI-TANK/ANTI-INFRASTRUCTURE • MSL
  SP 60: 8 9P122 *Malyutka*; 9 9P133 *Malyutka*; 32 BOV-1; 11 M-92
  MANPATS 9K11 *Malyutka* (AT-3 *Sagger*); 9K111 *Fagot* (AT-4 *Spigot*); 9K115 *Metis* (AT-7 *Saxhorn*); HJ-8; *Milan*
ARTILLERY 224
  TOWED 122mm 100 D-30
  MRL 122mm 24 APRA-40
  MOR 120mm 100 M-75

Air Force and Air Defence Brigade 800
FORCES BY ROLE
HELICOPTER
  1 sqn with Bell 205; Mi-8MTV *Hip*; Mi-17 *Hip* H
  1 sqn with Mi-8 *Hip*; SA342H/L *Gazelle* (HN-42/45M)
AIR DEFENCE
  1 AD bn
EQUIPMENT BY TYPE
AIRCRAFT
  FGA (7 J-22 *Orao* in store)
  ATK (6 J-1 (J-21) *Jastreb*; 3 TJ-1(NJ-21) *Jastreb* all in store)
  ISR (2 RJ-1 (IJ-21) *Jastreb** in store)
  TRG (1 G-4 *Super Galeb* (N-62)* in store)
HELICOPTERS
  MRH 13: 4 Mi-8MTV *Hip*; 1 Mi-17 *Hip* H; 1 SA-341H *Gazelle* (HN-42); 7 SA-342L *Gazelle* (HN-45M)
  TPT 21: **Medium** 8 Mi-8 *Hip* **Light** 13 Bell 205 (UH-1H *Iroquois*)
  TRG 1 Mi-34 *Hermit*
AIR DEFENCE
  SAM
    Short-range 20 2K12 *Kub* (SA-6 *Gainful*)
    Point-defence 7+: 6 9K31 *Strela*-1 (SA-9 *Gaskin*); 9K34 *Strela*-3 (SA-14 *Gremlin*); 1 9K35M3 *Strela*-10M3 (SA-13 *Gopher*); 9K310 (SA-16 *Gimlet*)
  GUNS 764
    SP 169: **20mm** 9 BOV-3 SPAAG; **30mm** 154: 38 M53; 116 M-53/59; **57mm** 6 ZSU-57-2
    TOWED 595: **20mm** 468: 32 M55A2, 4 M38, 1 M55 A2B1, 293 M55A3/A4, 138 M75; **23mm** 38: 29 ZU-23, 9 GSh-23; **30mm** 33 M-53; **37mm** 7 Type-55; **40mm** 49: 31 L60, 16 L70, 2 M-12

DEPLOYMENT

Legal provisions for foreign deployment:
Constitution: Codified constitution within Dayton Peace Agreement (1995)
Specific legislation: 'Law on participation of military, police, state and other employees in peacekeeping operations and other activities conducted abroad'
Decision on deployment of troops abroad: By the members of the Presidency (2003 'Defence Law' Art. 9, 13)

AFGHANISTAN
NATO • *Operation Resolute Support* 55

ALBANIA
OSCE • Albania 1

DEMOCRATIC REPUBLIC OF THE CONGO
UN • MONUSCO 5 obs

MALI
UN • MINUSMA 2

SERBIA
OSCE • Kosovo 9

UKRAINE
OSCE • Ukraine 32

FOREIGN FORCES

Part of EUFOR – *Operation Althea* unless otherwise stated.
Albania 1
Austria 313; 1 inf bn HQ; 1 inf coy
Bulgaria 10 • OSCE 1
Canada OSCE 1
Chile 15
Czech Republic 2
Finland 6
Germany OSCE 3
Greece 1
Hungary 47
Ireland 7 • OSCE 4
Italy 4 • OSCE 5
Macedonia (FYORM) 3
Netherlands 3 • OSCE 1
Poland 38
Romania 39
Russia OSCE 2
Serbia OSCE 1
Slovakia 40 • OSCE 1
Slovenia 16
Spain 2 • OSCE 2
Switzerland 20
Turkey 234; 1 inf coy
United Kingdom 4; • OSCE 2
United States OSCE 5

Bulgaria BLG

Bulgarian Lev L		2015	2016	2017
GDP	L	86.4bn	88.3bn	
	US$	49.0bn	50.4bn	
per capita	US$	6,843	7,091	
Growth	%	3.0	3.0	
Inflation	%	-1.1	-1.6	
Def exp [a]	L	1.1bn		
	US$	633m		
Def bdgt [b]	L	989m	1.19bn	1.17bn
	US$	560m	678m	
FMA (US)	US$	5m	5m	5m
US$1=L		1.76	1.75	

[a] NATO definition
[b] Excludes military pensions

Population 7,144,653

Age	0–14	15–19	20–24	25–29	30–64	65 plus
Male	7.5%	2.4%	2.7%	3.5%	25.1%	7.7%
Female	7.0%	2.2%	2.5%	3.2%	25.0%	11.3%

Capabilities

Despite long-term plans for reform, the armed forces still rely heavily on Soviet-era equipment, although this was addressed by the 2015 publication of the Bulgarian Armed Forces 2020 development programme. All the forces will undergo some degree of reorganisation as part of this plan and major upgrades have been approved for a number of key equipment types. In 2016, the defence ministry stated it has budgeted for the procurement of two new patrol vessels, which are due in service by 2022. There are as-yet-unapproved plans for 16 new or second-hand multi-role combat aircraft, with first-tranche deliveries expected between 2018 and 2020. In the interim, Bulgaria's MiG-29 fleet will be further life-extended. Training with neighbours and NATO partners continues, highlighting the importance of the Alliance to Bulgaria's security. In late 2015, a NATO Force Integration Unit was established in Sofia as part of the plan to boost NATO states' military presence in Europe's east as part of a 'tailored forward presence'. In 2016, Bulgarian and US troops participated in exercise *Platinum Lynx* in Romania and the country also hosted US land forces in a number of exercises to increase interoperability and combat-readiness. In the wake of Europe's migrant crisis, parliament voted in 2016 to allow the use of Bulgarian troops with police authority to support security on the border with Turkey.

ACTIVE 31,300 (Army 16,300 Navy 3,450 Air 6,700 Central Staff 4,850) **Paramilitary 16,000**

RESERVE 3,000 (Joint 3,000)

ORGANISATIONS BY SERVICE

Army 16,300
Forces are being reduced in number

FORCES BY ROLE
SPECIAL FORCES
1 spec ops bde (1 SF bn, 1 para bn, 1 mtn inf bn)
MANOEUVRE
  Reconnaissance
  1 recce bn
  Mechanised
  2 mech bde (4 mech inf bn, 1 SP arty bn, 1 cbt engr bn, 1 log bn, 1 SAM bn)
COMBAT SUPPORT
1 arty regt (1 fd arty bn, 1 MRL bn)
1 engr regt (1 cbt engr bn, 1 ptn br bn, 1 engr spt bn)
1 NBC bn
COMBAT SERVICE SUPPORT
1 log regt

EQUIPMENT BY TYPE
ARMOURED FIGHTING VEHICLES
  MBT 80 T-72
  IFV 160: 90 BMP-1; 70 BMP-23
  APC 120
    APC (T) 100 MT-LB
    APC (W) 20 BTR-60
  AUV 7 M1117 ASV
ENGINEERING & MAINTENANCE VEHICLES
  AEV MT-LB
  ARV T-54/T-55; MTP-1; MT-LB
  VLB BLG67; TMM
NBC VEHICLES *Maritza* NBC
ANTI-TANK/ANTI-INFRASTRUCTURE
  MSL
    SP 24 9P148 *Konkurs* (AT-5 *Spandrel*)
    MANPATS 9K111 *Fagot* (AT-4 *Spigot*); 9K111-1 *Konkurs* (AT-5 *Spandrel*); (9K11 *Malyutka* (AT-3 *Sagger*) in store)
  GUNS 126: **85mm** (150 D-44 in store); **100mm** 126 MT-12
ARTILLERY 311
  SP 122mm 48 2S1
  TOWED 152mm 24 D-20
  MRL 122mm 24 BM-21
  MOR 120mm 215 2S11 SP *Tundzha*
RADARS • LAND GS-13 *Long Eye* (veh); SNAR-1 *Long Trough* (arty); SNAR-10 *Big Fred* (veh, arty); SNAR-2/-6 *Pork Trough* (arty); *Small Fred/Small Yawn* (veh, arty)
AIR DEFENCE
  SAM • Point-defence 9K32 *Strela* (SA-7 *Grail*)‡; 24 9K33 *Osa* (SA-8 *Gecko*)
  GUNS 400
    SP 23mm ZSU-23-4
    TOWED 23mm ZU-23; **57mm** S-60; **100mm** KS-19

Navy 3,450
EQUIPMENT BY TYPE
PRINCIPAL SURFACE COMBATANTS • FRIGATES • 4
  FFM 3 *Drazki* (ex-BEL *Wielingen*) with 1 octuple Mk29 GMLS with RIM-7P *Sea Sparrow* SAM, 2 single 533mm ASTT with L5 HWT, 1 sextuple 375mm MLE 54 Creusot-Loire A/S mor, 1 100mm gun (Fitted for but not with 2 twin lnchr with MM-38 *Exocet* AShM)
  FF 1 *Smeli* (ex-FSU *Koni*) with 2 RBU 6000 *Smerch* 2 A/S mor, 2 twin 76mm guns

PATROL AND COASTAL COMBATANTS 3
  PCFG 1 *Mulnaya*† (ex-FSU *Tarantul* II) with 2 twin lnchr with P-15M *Termit*-M (SS-N-2C *Styx*) AShM, 2 AK630M CIWS, 1 76mm gun
  PCT 2 *Reshitelni* (ex-FSU *Pauk* I) with 4 single 406mm TT, 2 RBU 1200 A/S mor, 1 76mm gun
MINE COUNTERMEASURES 6
  MHC 1 *Tsibar* (*Tripartite* – ex-BEL *Flower*)
  MSC 3 *Briz* (ex-FSU *Sonya*)
  MSI 2 *Olya* (ex-FSU)
AMPHIBIOUS 1
  LCU 1 *Vydra*
LOGISTICS AND SUPPORT 8: 2 **AGS**; 2 **AOL**; 1 **ARS**; 2 **ATF**; 1 **AX**

Naval Aviation
EQUIPMENT BY TYPE
HELICOPTERS • ASW 3 AS565MB *Panther*

Air Force 6,700
Flying hours   30–40 hrs/yr

FORCES BY ROLE
FIGHTER/ISR
  1 sqn with MiG-29A/UB *Fulcrum*
TRANSPORT
  1 sqn with An-30 *Clank*; C-27J *Spartan*; L-410UVP-E; PC-12M
TRAINING
  1 sqn with L-39ZA *Albatros**
  1 sqn with PC-9M
ATTACK HELICOPTER
  1 sqn with Mi-24D/V *Hind* D/E
TRANSPORT HELICOPTER
  1 sqn with AS532AL *Cougar*; Bell 206 *Jet Ranger*; Mi-17 *Hip* H

EQUIPMENT BY TYPE
AIRCRAFT 22 combat capable
  FTR 16: 12 MiG-29A *Fulcrum*; 4 MiG-29UB *Fulcrum* (Some MiG-21bis *Fishbed*/MiG-21UM *Mongol* B in store)
  ISR 1 An-30 *Clank*
  TPT 7: **Medium** 3 C-27J *Spartan*; **Light** 4: 1 An-2T *Colt*; 2 L-410UVP-E; 1 PC-12M
  TRG 12: 6 L-39ZA *Albatros**; 6 PC-9M (basic)
HELICOPTERS
  ATK 6 Mi-24D/V *Hind* D/E
  MRH 6 Mi-17 *Hip* H
  TPT 18: **Medium** 12 AS532AL *Cougar*; **Light** 6 Bell 206 *Jet Ranger*
UNMANNED AERIAL VEHICLES • EW *Yastreb*-2S
AIR DEFENCE
  SAM
    Long-range S-200 (SA-5 *Gammon*); S-300 (SA-10 *Grumble*)
    Medium-range S-75 *Dvina* (SA-2 *Guideline*)
    Short-range S-125 *Pechora* (SA-3 *Goa*); 2K12 *Kub* (SA-6 *Gainful*)
AIR-LAUNCHED MISSILES
  AAM • IR R-3 (AA-2 *Atoll*)‡ R-73 (AA-11 *Archer*) **SARH** R-27R (AA-10 *Alamo* A)
  ASM Kh-29 (AS-14 *Kedge*); Kh-25 (AS-10 *Karen*)

Paramilitary 16,000

Border Guards 12,000
Ministry of Interior
FORCES BY ROLE
MANOEUVRE
 Other
  12 paramilitary regt
EQUIPMENT BY TYPE
PATROL AND COASTAL COMBATANTS 26
 PB 18: 1 *Obzor* (NLD Damen Stan Patrol 4207); 9 *Grif* (FSU *Zhuk*); 3 *Nesebar* (ex-GER *Neustadt*); 5 *Burgas* (GER Lurssen 21)
 PBF 8 *Emine* (EST Baltic 130)

Security Police 4,000

DEPLOYMENT

Legal provisions for foreign deployment:
Constitution: Codified constitution (1991)
Decision on deployment of troops abroad: By the president upon request from the Council of Ministers and upon approval by the National Assembly (Art. 84 XI)

AFGHANISTAN
NATO • *Operation Resolute Support* 110

ARMENIA/AZERBAIJAN
OSCE • Minsk Conference 1

BOSNIA-HERZEGOVINA
EU • EUFOR • *Operation Althea* 10
OSCE • Bosnia and Herzegovina 1

LIBERIA
UN • UNMIL 1 obs

MALI
EU • EUTM Mali 5

SERBIA
NATO • KFOR 12

UKRAINE
OSCE • Ukraine 32

Croatia CRO

Croatian Kuna k		2015	2016	2017
GDP	k	334bn	341bn	
	US$	48.9bn	49.9bn	
per capita	US$	11,573	11,858	
Growth	%	1.6	1.9	
Inflation	%	-0.5	-1.0	
Def exp [a]	k	4.59bn		
	US$	669m		
Def bdgt	k	4.39bn	4.02bn	4.08bn
	US$	642m	588m	
FMA (US)	US$	2.5m	2.5m	1m
US$1=k		6.84	6.84	

[a] NATO definition

Population 4,313,707
Ethnic groups: Croatian 90.4% Serbian 4.3% Bosniac 0.7% Italian 0.4% Hungarian 0.3% Other or unspecified 3.9%

Age	0–14	15–19	20–24	25–29	30–64	65 plus
Male	7.3%	2.9%	3.0%	3.2%	24.4%	7.4%
Female	6.9%	2.7%	2.8%	3.1%	24.9%	11.4%

Capabilities

Croatia joined NATO in 2009 having reformed its armed forces to create a small professional force, with a focus on international peacekeeping duties. However, challenging economic conditions have further delayed reforms, including the replacement of an ageing Soviet-era equipment inventory. There are several overdue equipment improvements required to sustain the country's military capabilities. Croatia continues to work towards the long-term goals laid out in its 2005 defence review and the associated 2006–15 long-term-development plan, as well as the National Security Strategy, Defence Strategy and Military Strategy. Several key equipment acquisitions have been made via the US Excess Defense Articles programme; Croatia is reportedly acquiring *Kiowa Warrior* helicopters through this process. Further investment in replacements for legacy equipment will be required in the near term, with the replacement of the MiG-21 aircraft fleet viewed as one of the country's most important procurement goals. Five inshore-patrol vessels are to be delivered to the naval coastguard service in 2017 as part of a wider naval-modernisation plan. Despite some challenges to the domestic defence industry, exports of defence equipment, including small arms, have risen over the last few years. Croatia regularly takes part in NATO exercises.

ACTIVE 15,550 (Army 11,250 Navy 1,300 Air 1,250 Joint 1,850) **Paramilitary 3,000**
Conscript liability Voluntary conscription, 8 weeks

ORGANISATIONS BY SERVICE

Joint 1,850 (General Staff)

FORCES BY ROLE
SPECIAL FORCES
1 SF bn

Army 11,250
FORCES BY ROLE
MANOEUVRE
  Armoured
  1 armd bde (1 tk bn, 1 armd bn, 2 armd inf bn, 1 SP arty bn, 1 ADA bn, 1 cbt engr bn)
  Light
  1 mot inf bde (2 mech inf bn, 2 mot inf bn, 1 fd arty bn, 1 ADA bn, 1 cbt engr bn)
  Other
  1 inf trg regt
COMBAT SUPPORT
1 arty/MRL regt
1 AT regt
1 engr regt
1 int bn
1 MP regt
1 NBC bn
1 sigs regt
COMBAT SERVICE SUPPORT
1 log regt
AIR DEFENCE
1 ADA regt
EQUIPMENT BY TYPE
ARMOURED FIGHTING VEHICLES
  MBT 75 M-84
  IFV 102 M-80
  APC 194
    APC (T) 15 BTR-50
    APC (W) 142: 1 BOV-VP; 23 LOV OP; 118 *Patria* AMV
  PPV 37 *Maxxpro*
  AUV 151+: 4 *Cougar* HE; IVECO LMV; 147 M-ATV
ENGINEERING & MAINTENANCE VEHICLES
  ARV M84A1; WZT-3
  VLB 3 MT-55A
  MW *Bozena*; 1 *Rhino*
ANTI-TANK/ANTI-INFRASTRUCTURE • MSL
  SP 28 POLO BOV 83
  MANPATS 9K11 *Malyutka* (AT-3 *Sagger*); 9K111 *Fagot* (AT-4 *Spigot*); 9K111-1 *Konkurs* (AT-5 *Spandrel*); 9K115 *Metis* (AT-7 *Saxhorn*); *Milan* (reported)
ARTILLERY 221
  SP 14: **122mm** 8 2S1; **155mm** 6 PzH 2000
  TOWED 64: **122mm** 27 D-30; **130mm** 19 M-46H1; **155mm** 18 M1H1
  MRL 39: **122mm** 37: 6 M91 *Vulkan*; 31 BM-21 *Grad*; **128mm** 2 LOV RAK M91 R24
  MOR 104: **82mm** 29 LMB M96; **120mm** 75: 70 M-75; 5 UBM 52
AIR DEFENCE
  SAM • Point 9 *Strijela*-10 CRO
  GUNS 96
    SP 20mm 39 BOV-3 SP
    TOWED 20mm 57 M55A4

Navy 1,300
Navy HQ at Split

EQUIPMENT BY TYPE
PATROL AND COASTAL COMBATANTS 5
  PCFG 1 *Končar* with 2 twin lnchr with RBS-15B Mk I AShM, 1 AK630 CIWS, 1 57mm gun
  PCG 4:
    2 *Kralj* with 4 single lnchr with RBS-15B Mk I AShM, 1 AK630 CIWS, 1 57mm gun (with minelaying capability)
    2 *Vukovar* (ex-FIN *Helsinki*) with 4 single lnchr with RBS-15B Mk I AShM, 1 57mm gun
MINE WARFARE • MINE COUNTERMEASURES •
MHI 1 *Korcula*
AMPHIBIOUS
  LCT 2 *Cetina* (with minelaying capability)
  LCVP 3: 2 Type-21; 1 Type-22
LOGISTICS AND SUPPORT • AKL 1
COASTAL DEFENCE • AShM 3 RBS-15K

Marines
FORCES BY ROLE
MANOEUVRE
  Amphibious
  2 indep mne coy

Coast Guard
FORCES BY ROLE
Two divisions, headquartered in Split (1st div) and Pula (2nd div)

EQUIPMENT BY TYPE
PATROL AND COASTAL COMBATANTS • PB 4 *Mirna*
LOGISTICS AND SUPPORT •
  AKL 1 PT-71
  AX 2

Air Force and Air Defence 1,250
Flying hours 50 hrs/yr

FORCES BY ROLE
FIGHTER/GROUND ATTACK
  1 (mixed) sqn with MiG-21bis/UMD *Fishbed*
TRANSPORT
  1 sqn with An-32 *Cline*
TRAINING
  1 sqn with PC-9M; Z-242L
  1 hel sqn with Bell 206B *Jet Ranger* II
TRANSPORT HELICOPTER
  2 sqn with Mi-8MTV *Hip* H; Mi-8T *Hip* C; Mi-171Sh
EQUIPMENT BY TYPE
AIRCRAFT 9 combat capable
  FGA 9: 5 MiG-21bis *Fishbed*; 4 MiG-21UMD *Fishbed*
  TPT • Light 2 An-32 *Cline*
  TRG 25: 20 PC-9M; 5 Z-242L
HELICOPTERS
  MRH 16: 11 Mi-8MTV *Hip* H; 5 OH-58D *Kiowa Warrior*
  TPT 21: **Medium** 13: 3 Mi-8T *Hip* C; 10 Mi-171Sh; **Light** 8 Bell 206B *Jet Ranger* II
UNMANNED AERIAL VEHICLES
  ISR • Medium *Hermes* 450
AIR DEFENCE • SAM
  Long-range S-300 (SA-10 *Grumble*)

Point-defence 9K31 *Strela*-1 (SA-9 *Gaskin*); 9K34 *Strela*-3 (SA-14 *Gremlin*); 9K310 *Igla*-1 (SA-16 *Gimlet*)
RADAR • AIR 11: 5 FPS-117; 3 S-600; 3 PRV-11
AIR-LAUNCHED MISSILES • AAM • IR R-3S (AA-2 *Atoll*)‡; R-60 (AA-8 *Aphid*)

Special Forces Command
FORCES BY ROLE
SPECIAL FORCES
  2 SF gp
EQUIPMENT BY TYPE
ARMOURED FIGHTING VEHICLES
  APC • PPV 5 *Maxxpro*
  AUV 15 M-ATV

Paramilitary 3,000
Police 3,000 armed

DEPLOYMENT
Legal provisions for foreign deployment:
Constitution: Codified constitution (2004)
Decision on deployment of troops abroad: By the parliament (Art. 7 II); simplified procedure for humanitarian aid and military exercises

AFGHANISTAN
NATO • *Operation Resolute Support* 105

INDIA/PAKISTAN
UN • UNMOGIP 9 obs

LEBANON
UN • UNIFIL 1

SERBIA
NATO • KFOR 26
OSCE • Kosovo 1

UKRAINE
OSCE • Ukraine 11

WESTERN SAHARA
UN • MINURSO 7 obs

Cyprus CYP

Euro €		2015	2016	2017
GDP	€	17.4bn	17.9bn	
	US$	19.3bn	19.9bn	
per capita	US$	22,822	23,425	
Growth	%	1.5	2.8	
Inflation	%	-1.5	-1.0	
Def bdgt	€	275m	319m	319m
	US$	305m	356m	
US$1=€		0.90	0.90	

Population 1,205,575

Age	0–14	15–19	20–24	25–29	30–64	65 plus
Male	8.0%	3.2%	4.6%	4.8%	25.3%	5.1%
Female	7.6%	2.8%	3.8%	3.9%	24.2%	6.7%

Capabilities
The country's national guard is predominantly a land force supplemented by small air and maritime units. It is intended to act as a deterrent to any possible Turkish incursion, and to provide enough opposition until military support can be provided by its primary ally, Greece. The air wing has a small number of rotary- and fixed-wing utility platforms, including attack helicopters, while the maritime wing is essentially a coastal-defence and constabulary force. Cyprus exercised with several international partners in 2016, including Austria, Israel, the UK and the US. Compulsory service in the national-guard service was reformed in 2016, reducing the length of service to 14 months. The reforms also included approval to hire 3,000 professional soldiers, to serve initially for 12 months. According to the defence minister, this move is the first step towards creating a professional army. Expeditionary deployments have been limited, with some officers joining UN and EU missions.

ACTIVE 12,000 (National Guard 12,000)
Paramilitary 750
Conscript liability 14 months

RESERVE 50,000 (National Guard 50,000)
Reserve service to age 50 (officers dependent on rank; military doctors to age 60)

ORGANISATIONS BY SERVICE

National Guard 1,300 regular; 10,700 conscript (total 12,000)
FORCES BY ROLE
SPECIAL FORCES
  1 comd (regt) (1 SF bn)
MANOEUVRE
  Armoured
  1 lt armd bde (2 armd bn, 1 armd inf bn)
  Mechanised
  1 (1st) mech inf div (1 armd recce bn, 2 mech inf bn)
  1 (2nd) mech inf div (1 armd recce bn, 2 armd bn, 2 mech inf bn)
  Light
  3 (4th, 7th & 8th) lt inf bde (2 lt inf regt)
COMBAT SUPPORT
  1 arty comd (8 arty bn)
COMBAT SERVICE SUPPORT
  1 (3rd) spt bde
EQUIPMENT BY TYPE
ARMOURED FIGHTING VEHICLES
  MBT 134: 82 T-80U; 52 AMX-30B2
  RECCE 67 EE-9 *Cascavel*
  IFV 43 BMP-3
  APC 294
    APC (T) 168 *Leonidas*
    APC (W) 126 VAB (incl variants)
ENGINEERING & MAINTENANCE VEHICLES
  ARV 3: AMX-30D; 1 BREM-1
ANTI-TANK/ANTI-INFRASTRUCTURE
  MSL
    SP 33: 15 EE-3 *Jararaca* with *Milan*; 18 VAB with HOT

MANPATS *Milan*
RCL **106mm** 144 M40A1
GUNS • TOWED **100mm** 20 M-1944
ARTILLERY 432
SP **155mm** 24: 12 Mk F3; 12 *Zuzana*
TOWED 84: **105mm** 72 M-56; **155mm** 12 TR-F-1
MRL 22: **122mm** 4 BM-21; **128mm** 18 M-63 *Plamen*
MOR 302: **81mm** 170 E-44; (70+ M1/M9 in store); **107mm** 20 M2/M30; **120mm** 112 RT61
AIR DEFENCE
SAM
Short 18: 12 *Aspide*; 6 9K322 *Tor* (SA-15 *Gauntlet*)
Point *Mistral*
GUNS • TOWED 60: **20mm** 36 M-55; **35mm** 24 GDF-003 (with *Skyguard*)

Maritime Wing
FORCES BY ROLE
COMBAT SUPPORT
1 (coastal defence) AShM bty with MM-40 *Exocet* AShM
EQUIPMENT BY TYPE
PATROL AND COASTAL COMBATANTS 4
PBF 4: 2 Rodman 55; 2 *Vittoria*
COASTAL DEFENCE • AShM 3 MM-40 *Exocet*

Air Wing
EQUIPMENT BY TYPE
AIRCRAFT
TPT • Light 1 BN-2B *Islander*
TRG 1 PC-9
HELICOPTERS
ATK 11 Mi-35P *Hind*
MRH 7: 3 AW139 (SAR); 4 SA342L1 *Gazelle* (with HOT for anti-armour role)
TPT • Light 2 Bell 206L3 *Long Ranger*

Paramilitary 750+

Armed Police 500+
FORCES BY ROLE
MANOEUVRE
Other
1 (rapid-reaction) paramilitary unit
EQUIPMENT BY TYPE
ARMOURED FIGHTING VEHICLES
APC • APC (W) 2 VAB VTT
HELICOPTERS • MRH 4: 2 AW139; 2 Bell 412SP

Maritime Police 250
EQUIPMENT BY TYPE
PATROL AND COASTAL COMBATANTS 10
PBF 5: 2 *Poseidon*; 1 *Shaldag*; 2 *Vittoria*
PB 5 SAB-12

DEPLOYMENT
Legal provisions for foreign deployment:
Constitution: Codified constitution (1960)
Decision on deployment of troops abroad: By parliament, but president has the right of final veto (Art. 50)

LEBANON
UN • UNIFIL 2

FOREIGN FORCES
Argentina UNFICYP 362; 2 inf coy; 1 hel flt
Austria UNFICYP 4
Brazil UNFICYP 3
Canada UNFICYP 1
Chile UNFICYP 14
Greece Army: 950; ε200 (officers/NCO seconded to Greek-Cypriot National Guard)
Hungary UNFICYP 77; 1 inf pl
Paraguay UNFICYP 14
Serbia UNFICYP 47; elm 1 inf coy
Slovakia UNFICYP 159; elm 1 inf coy; 1 engr pl
Ukraine UNFICYP 2
United Kingdom 2,270; 2 inf bn; 1 hel sqn with 4 Bell 412 *Twin Huey* • Operation Shader 650: 1 FGA sqn with 6 *Tornado* GR4; 6 *Typhoon* FGR4; 1 *Sentinel* R1; 1 E-3D *Sentry*; 1 A330 MRTT *Voyager* KC3; 2 C-130J *Hercules* • UNFICYP 275: 1 inf coy

TERRITORY WHERE THE GOVERNMENT DOES NOT EXERCISE EFFECTIVE CONTROL

Data here represents the de facto situation on the northern section of the island. This does not imply international recognition as a sovereign state.

Capabilities

ACTIVE 3,500 (Army 3,500) **Paramilitary 150**
Conscript liability 24 months

RESERVE 26,000 (first line 11,000 second line 10,000 third line 5,000)
Reserve liability to age 50

ORGANISATIONS BY SERVICE

Army ε3,500
FORCES BY ROLE
MANOEUVRE
Light
7 inf bn
EQUIPMENT BY TYPE
ANTI-TANK/ANTI-INFRASTRUCTURE
MSL • MANPATS *Milan*
RCL • **106mm** 36
ARTILLERY • MOR • **120mm** 73

Paramilitary

Armed Police ε150
FORCES BY ROLE
SPECIAL FORCES
1 (police) SF unit

Coast Guard
PATROL AND COASTAL COMBATANTS 6
  PCC 5: 2 SG45/SG46; 1 *Rauf Denktash*; 2 US Mk 5
  PB 1

FOREIGN FORCES
TURKEY
Army ε43,000
  FORCES BY ROLE
  1 corps HQ, 1 armd bde, 2 mech inf div, 1 avn comd
  EQUIPMENT BY TYPE
  ARMOURED FIGHTING VEHICLES
    MBT 348: 8 M48A2 (trg); 340 M48A5T1/2
    APC • APC (T) 627: 361 AAPC (incl variants); 266 M113 (incl variants)
  ANTI-TANK/ANTI-INFRASTRUCTURE
    MSL • MANPATS Milan; TOW
    RCL 106mm 192 M40A1
  ARTILLERY 648
    SP 155mm 90 M44T
    TOWED 102: **105mm** 72 M101A1; **155mm** 18 M114A2; **203mm** 12 M115
    MRL 122mm 6 T-122
    MOR 450: **81mm** 175; **107mm** 148 M30; **120mm** 127 HY-12
  PATROL AND COASTAL COMBATANTS 1 PB
  AIRCRAFT • TPT • Light 3 Cessna 185 (U-17)
  HELICOPTERS • TPT 4 Medium 1 AS532UL *Cougar* **Light** 3 Bell 205 (UH-1H *Iroquois*)
  AIR DEFENCE • GUNS • TOWED 20mm Rh 202; **35mm** 16 GDF-003; **40mm** 48 M1

Czech Republic CZE

Czech Koruna Kc		2015	2016	2017
GDP	Kc	4.56tr	4.69tr	
	US$	185bn	194bn	
per capita	US$	17,570	18,326	
Growth	%	4.5	2.5	
Inflation	%	0.3	0.6	
Def exp [a]	Kc	47.3bn		
	US$	1.92bn		
Def bdgt [b]	Kc	43.8bn	47.8bn	52.5bn
	US$	1.78bn	1.97bn	
FMA (US)	US$	1m	1m	
US$1=Kc		24.60	24.24	

[a] NATO definition
[b] Includes military pensions

Population   10,660,932

Age	0–14	15–19	20–24	25–29	30–64	65 plus
Male	7.7%	2.3%	2.8%	3.4%	25.2%	7.7%
Female	7.3%	2.1%	2.7%	3.2%	24.6%	10.8%

Capabilities

Published in 2015, the Czech national-security strategy confirms that NATO is central to the country's security and asserts that stability and security in Europe have deteriorated. Overall, while a direct military attack was deemed unlikely, aggression against NATO or EU member states could not be ruled out. The strategy indicates that growing importance is attached to the armed forces. According to the Concept of the Czech Armed Forces 2025, adopted in December 2015, armed-forces restructuring will proceed in two phases, with recruitment and the procurement of new equipment being the focus up to 2020 and investment in the modernisation of existing equipment and defence infrastructure the focus between 2020 and 2025. Defence spending is set to rise, while long-term defence-planning guidelines for 2030, also published in 2015, support an increase in the active personnel number to 27,000. The 2016 defence budget saw a modest spending boost, although the principal increases seemed to be for operations and maintenance and personnel costs, including salaries (not pensions). The Czech Republic is trying to use additional defence spending to replace legacy equipment in order to both modernise the armed forces and reduce dependence on Russia for spare parts and services. The Czech fleet of BMP-2 infantry fighting vehicles was singled out by the ministry of defence as posing a readiness challenge and driving up maintenance costs; the army has been using these since 1984. Recruitment is also a core priority for the defence ministry. Some units are severely understrength, achieving just 60% of their nominal strength. The government adopted an Active Reserve Law in 2016. This aims to incentivise greater engagement in the reserves, which is planned to grow in size.

ACTIVE 21,950 (Army 12,750, Air 6,800, Other 2,400) **Paramilitary 3,100**

ORGANISATIONS BY SERVICE

Army 12,200
FORCES BY ROLE
MANOEUVRE
  Reconnaissance
  1 ISR/EW regt (1 recce bn, 1 EW bn)
  Armoured
  1 (7th) mech bde (1 tk bn, 2 armd inf bn, 1 mot inf bn)
  Mechanised
  1 (4th) rapid reaction bde (2 mech inf bn, 1 mot inf bn, 1 AB bn)
COMBAT SUPPORT
  1 (13th) arty regt (2 arty bn)
  1 engr regt (3 engr bn, 1 EOD bn)
  1 CBRN regt (2 CBRN bn)
COMBAT SERVICE SUPPORT
  1 log regt (2 log bn, 1 maint bn)

Active Reserve
FORCES BY ROLE
COMMAND
  14 (territorial defence) comd

MANOEUVRE
Armoured
1 armd coy
Light
14 inf coy (1 per territorial comd) (3 inf pl, 1 cbt spt pl, 1 log pl)
EQUIPMENT BY TYPE
ARMOURED FIGHTING VEHICLES
MBT 30 T-72M4CZ; (93 T-72 in store)
RECCE (34 BPzV *Svatava* in store)
IFV 222: 120 BMP-2; 102 *Pandur* II (inc variants); (98 BMP-1; 65 BMP-2 all in store)
APC
APC (T) (17 OT-90 in store)
APC (W) (3 OT-64 in store)
AUV 21 *Dingo* 2; IVECO LMV
ENGINEERING & MAINTENANCE VEHICLES
ARV 10 VPV-ARV (12 more in store)
VLB 3 MT-55A (3 more in store)
MW UOS-155 *Belarty*
ANTI-TANK/ANTI-INFRASTRUCTURE
MSL • MANPATS 9K111-1 *Konkurs* (AT-5 *Spandrel*); *Spike*-LR
ARTILLERY 96
SP 152mm 48 M-77 *Dana*; (38 more in store)
MOR 120mm 48: 40 M-1982; 8 SPM-85; (45 M-1982 in store)
RADAR • LAND 3 ARTHUR

Air Force 6,800

Principal task is to secure Czech airspace. This mission is fulfilled within NATO Integrated Extended Air Defence System (NATINADS) and, if necessary, by means of the Czech national reinforced air-defence system. The air force also provides CAS for army SAR, and performs a tpt role

Flying hours 120 hrs/yr cbt ac; 150 for tpt ac

FORCES BY ROLE
FIGHTER/GROUND ATTACK
1 sqn with *Gripen* C/D
1 sqn with L-159 ALCA/L-159T
TRANSPORT
2 sqn with A319CJ; C-295M; CL-601 *Challenger*; L-410 *Turbolet*; Yak-40 *Codling*
TRAINING
1 sqn with L-39ZA *Albatros**
ATTACK HELICOPTER
1 sqn with Mi-24/Mi-35 *Hind*
TRANSPORT HELICOPTER
1 sqn with Mi-17 *Hip* H; Mi-171Sh
1 sqn with Mi-8 *Hip*; Mi-17 *Hip* H; PZL W-3A *Sokol*
AIR DEFENCE
1 (25th) SAM regt (2 AD gp)
EQUIPMENT BY TYPE
AIRCRAFT 48 combat capable
FGA 14: 12 *Gripen* C (JAS 39C); 2 *Gripen* D (JAS 39D)
ATK 25: 20 L-159 ALCA; 5 L-159T
TPT 15: **Light** 12: 4 C-295M; 6 L-410 *Turbolet*; 2 Yak-40 *Codling*; **PAX** 3: 2 A319CJ; 1 CL-601 *Challenger*
TRG 9 L-39ZA *Albatros**

HELICOPTERS
ATK 17: 7 Mi-24 *Hind* D; 10 Mi-35 *Hind* E
MRH 5 Mi-17 *Hip* H
TPT • **Medium** 30: 4 Mi-8 *Hip*; 16 Mi-171Sh; 10 PZL W3A *Sokol*
AIR DEFENCE • SAM
Point-defence 9K35 *Strela*-10 (SA-13 *Gopher*); 9K32 *Strela*-2‡ (SA-7 *Grail*) (available for trg RBS-70 gunners); RBS-70
AIR-LAUNCHED MISSILES
AAM • IR AIM-9M *Sidewinder*; ARH AIM-120C-5 AMRAAM
BOMBS
Laser-guided: GBU *Paveway*

Other Forces

FORCES BY ROLE
SPECIAL FORCES
1 SF gp
MANOEUVRE
Other
1 (presidential) gd bde (2 bn)
1 (honour guard) gd bn (2 coy)
COMBAT SUPPORT
1 int gp
1 (central) MP comd
3 (regional) MP comd
1 (protection service) MP comd

Paramilitary 3,100

Border Guards 3,000

Internal Security Forces 100

Cyber

In 2011 the National Security Authority was established as the country's leading cyber-security body. The National Cyber Security Centre and Government CERT (as part of the NSA) and the Cyber Security Council were established on the basis of this. A New Law on Cyber Security entered into force in January 2015. Moreover, a new edition of the National Cyber Security Strategy and the Action Plan for 2015 to 2020 were published. The National Cyber Security Strategy states that the country will look 'to increase national capacities for active cyber defence and cyber attack countermeasures'. The defence ministry develops its own cyber-defence capabilities according to specific tasks based on NATO or EU documents and the requirements of the National Action Plan. The defence-ministry security director also leads on cyber security.

DEPLOYMENT

Legal provisions for foreign deployment:
Constitution: Codified constitution (1992), Art. 39, 43
Decision on deployment of troops abroad: External deployments require approval by parliament. As an exception, such as in urgent cases, the government can decide on such a deployment for up to 60 days with the aim of fulfilling international treaty obligations concerning collective defence

AFGHANISTAN
NATO • *Operation Resolute Support* 214
UN • UNAMA 2 obs

ARMENIA/AZERBAIJAN
OSCE • Minsk Conference 1

BOSNIA-HERZEGOVINA
EU • EUFOR • *Operation Althea* 2

CENTRAL AFRICAN REPUBLIC
UN • MINUSCA 3 obs

DEMOCRATIC REPUBLIC OF THE CONGO
UN • MONUSCO 3 obs

EGYPT
MFO 18; 1 C-295M

ICELAND
NATO • Iceland Air Policing: 5 *Gripen* C

IRAQ
Operation Inherent Resolve 31

MALI
EU • EUTM Mali 39
UN • MINUSMA 25

SERBIA
NATO • KFOR 12
OSCE • Kosovo 2
UN • UNMIK 2 obs

SYRIA/ISRAEL
UN • UNDOF 3

UKRAINE
OSCE • Ukraine 17

Denmark DNK

Danish Krone kr		2015	2016	2017
GDP	kr	1.99tr	2.02tr	
	US$	295bn	303bn	
per capita	US$	52,139	53,243	
Growth	%	1.0	1.0	
Inflation	%	0.5	0.4	
Def exp [a]	kr	22.6bn		
	US$	3.36bn		
Def bdgt [b]	kr	23.7bn	23.7bn	24.1bn
	US$	3.52bn	3.55bn	
US$1=kr		6.73	6.67	

[a] NATO definition
[b] Includes military pensions

Population 5,593,785

Age	0–14	15–19	20–24	25–29	30–64	65 plus
Male	8.5%	3.3%	3.4%	3.1%	22.5%	8.5%
Female	8.1%	3.1%	3.3%	3.1%	22.7%	10.5%

Capabilities

Danish military capabilities remain compact but effective despite pressures on spending and deployments. The 2013–17 defence agreement is based on a broad political settlement from 2012. A new defence agreement will be negotiated before the end of 2017, setting out spending requirements and the future direction of the Danish armed forces, to be implemented post-2018. There has been some discussion over whether Denmark could reintroduce or update high-end capabilities to improve its full-spectrum capabilities, such as anti-submarine warfare; intelligence, surveillance and reconnaissance; and ground-based air defence. Improved Danish ties to NATO, NORDEFCO and other regional neighbours mark an increasing trend among many of the Baltic states. Denmark has contributed to the NATO Baltic Air Policing mission. Denmark and Sweden signed an agreement in early 2015 for further cooperation in air and naval operations in the region. A wider defence agreement, aimed at deterring Russia, was signed in April 2015 between Denmark, Finland, Iceland, Norway and Sweden. Procurement of the F-35A Joint Strike Fighter as a replacement for the country's ageing F-16AM/BM fleet was confirmed in June 2016, with airframe numbers reduced to 27 for cost reasons. The defence department will be aware of the possible impact that programme costs could have on other capability areas. Industrial support from Terma, Denmark's largest defence company, was important to the decision, as many key F-35 components and composites are produced by the firm. The ageing *Lynx* helicopter fleet operating on Danish naval vessels is being replaced by the MH-60R *Seahawk*. In early 2016, Denmark reaffirmed its commitment to operations against the Islamic State with the planned additional deployment of special-operations personnel, F-16s and a C-130J transport aircraft to Iraq for airstrikes and the training/support of Iraqi and Kurdish forces. In 2016, Denmark increased the number of support personnel taking part in NATO's Afghanistan training mission.

ACTIVE 16,600 (Army 8,400 Navy 2,100 Air 2,900 Joint 3,200)
Conscript liability 4–12 months, most voluntary

RESERVES 45,700 (Army 34,300 Navy 5,300 Air Force 4,750 Service Corps 1,350)

ORGANISATIONS BY SERVICE

Army 8,400

Div and bde HQ are responsible for trg only; if necessary, can be transformed into operational formations

FORCES BY ROLE
COMMAND
 1 div HQ
 2 bde HQ
MANOEUVRE
 Reconnaissance
 1 recce bn
 1 ISR bn

Armoured
  1 tk bn
Mechanised
  5 mech inf bn
COMBAT SUPPORT
  1 SP arty bn
  1 cbt engr bn
  1 construction bn
  1 EOD bn
  1 MP bn
  1 sigs regt (1 sigs bn, 1 EW coy)
COMBAT SERVICE SUPPORT
  1 log regt (1 spt bn, 1 log bn, 1 maint bn, 1 med bn)
EQUIPMENT BY TYPE
ARMOURED FIGHTING VEHICLES
  MBT 34 Leopard 2A4/5
  IFV 44 CV9030 Mk II
  APC 314
    APC (T) 235 M113 (incl variants); (196 more in store awaiting disposal)
    APC (W) 79 Piranha III (incl variants)
  AUV 84 Eagle IV
ENGINEERING & MAINTENANCE VEHICLES
  ARV 10 Bergepanzer 2
  VLB 6 Biber
  MW 14 910-MCV-2
ANTI-TANK/ANTI-INFRASTRUCTURE
  MSL • MANPATS TOW
  RCL 84mm 186 Carl Gustav
ARTILLERY 24
  SP 155mm 12 M109
  MOR • TOWED 120mm 12 Soltam K6B1
RADAR • LAND ARTHUR
AIR DEFENCE • SAM • Point-defence FIM-92 Stinger

Navy 2,100
EQUIPMENT BY TYPE
PRINCIPAL SURFACE COMBATANTS 3
  DESTROYERS • DDGHM 3 Iver Huitfeldt with 4 quad lnchr with RGM-84 Harpoon Block II AShM, 1 32-cell Mk41 VLS with RIM-162 ESSM SAM, 2 12-cell Mk56 VLS with RIM-162 SAM, 2 twin 324mm TT with MU90 LWT, 2 76mm guns (capacity 1 med hel)
PATROL AND COASTAL COMBATANTS 13
  PSOH 4 Thetis 1 76mm gun (capacity 1 Super Lynx Mk90B)
  PSO 2 Knud Rasmussen with 1 76mm gun, 1 hel landing platform
  PCC 7: 1 Agdlek; 6 Diana
MINE WARFARE • MINE COUNTERMEASURES 6
  MCI 4 MSF MK-I
  MSD 2 Holm
LOGISTICS AND SUPPORT 13
  ABU 2 (primarily used for MARPOL duties)
  AE 1 Sleipner
  AG 2 Absalon (flexible support ships) with 4 quad lnchr with RGM-84 Block 2 Harpoon 2 AShM, 3 12-cell Mk 56 VLS with RIM-162B Sea Sparrow SAM, 2 twin 324mm TT with MU90 LWT, 2 Millenium CIWS, 1 127mm gun (capacity 2 AW101 Merlin; 2 LCP, 7 MBT or 40 vehicles; 130 troops)
  AGS 2 Holm
  AKL 2 Seatruck
  AXL 2 Holm
  AXS 2 Svanen

Air Force 2,900
Flying hours 165 hrs/yr

Tactical Air Command
FORCES BY ROLE
FIGHTER/GROUND ATTACK
  2 sqn with F-16AM/BM Fighting Falcon
ANTI-SUBMARINE WARFARE
  1 sqn with Super Lynx Mk90B
SEARCH & RESCUE/TRANSPORT HELICOPTER
  1 sqn with AW101 Merlin
  1 sqn with AS550 Fennec (ISR)
TRANSPORT
  1 sqn with C-130J-30 Hercules; CL-604 Challenger (MP/VIP)
TRAINING
  1 unit with MFI-17 Supporter (T-17)
EQUIPMENT BY TYPE
AIRCRAFT 44 combat capable
  FTR 44: 34 F-16AM Fighting Falcon; 10 F-16BM Fighting Falcon (30 operational)
  TPT 8: **Medium** 4 C-130J-30 Hercules; **PAX** 4 CL-604 Challenger (MP/VIP)
  TRG 27 MFI-17 Supporter (T-17)
HELICOPTERS
  ASW 9: 6 Super Lynx Mk90B; 3 MH-60R Seahawk
  MRH 8 AS550 Fennec (ISR) (4 more non-operational)
  TPT • Medium 13 AW101 Merlin (8 SAR; 5 Tpt)
AIR-LAUNCHED MISSILES
  AAM • IR AIM-9L Sidewinder; **IIR** AIM-9X Sidewinder II; **ARH** AIM-120 AMRAAM
  ASM AGM-65 Maverick
BOMBS
  Laser-guided EGBU-12/GBU-24 Paveway II/III
  INS/GPS guided GBU-31 JDAM

Control and Air Defence Group
1 Control and Reporting Centre, 1 Mobile Control and Reporting Centre. 4 Radar sites

Special Operations Command
FORCES BY ROLE
SPECIAL FORCES
  1 SF unit
  1 diving unit

Reserves

Home Guard (Army) 34,300 reservists (to age 50)
FORCES BY ROLE
MANOEUVRE
  Light
    2 regt cbt gp (3 mot inf bn, 1 arty bn)
    5 (local) def region (up to 2 mot inf bn)

Home Guard (Navy) 4,500 reservists (to age 50)
EQUIPMENT BY TYPE
PATROL AND COASTAL COMBATANTS 30
PB 30: 17 MHV800; 1 MHV850; 12 MHV900

Home Guard (Air Force) 4,750 reservists (to age 50)

Home Guard (Service Corps) 1,350 reservists

Cyber

A National Strategy for Cyber and Information Security was released in December 2014. A Centre for Cyber Security was established in 2012 within the defence-intelligence service. The Danish Defence Agreement 2013–17 noted funding allocations directed to 'provide a capacity that can execute defensive and offensive military operations in cyberspace'. Denmark has developed a cyber-defence capability for static networks, and is developing a cyber-defence capability to support deployable networks. After legal frameworks are in place, it is reported that Denmark intends to develop 'cyber-offensive and exploitation capability'.

DEPLOYMENT

Legal provisions for foreign deployment:
Constitution: Codified constitution (1849)
Decision on deployment of troops abroad: On approval by the parliament (Art. 19 II)

AFGHANISTAN
NATO • Operation Resolute Support 90

IRAQ
Operation Inherent Resolve 220

MALI
UN • MINUSMA 47

MEDITERRANEAN SEA
NATO • SNMG 2: 1 AG

MIDDLE EAST
UN • UNTSO 10 obs

MOLDOVA
OSCE • Moldova 1

SERBIA
NATO • KFOR 35

SOUTH SUDAN
UN • UNMISS 12; 2 obs

TURKEY
Operation Inherent Resolve 110; 7 F-16AM *Fighting Falcon*

UKRAINE
OSCE • Ukraine 13

Estonia EST

Euro €		2015	2016	2017
GDP	€	20.5bn	21.0bn	
	US$	22.7bn	23.5bn	
per capita	US$	17,288	17,896	
Growth	%	1.1	1.5	
Inflation	%	0.1	0.5	
Def Exp [a]	€	423m		
	US$	469m		
Def bdgt [b]	€	421m	451m	477m
	US$	467m	503m	
FMA (US)	US$	1.5m	2m	1.6m
US$1=€		0.90	0.90	

[a] NATO definition
[b] Includes military pensions

Population 1,258,545

Ethnic groups: Estonian 70% Russian 25% Ukranian 1.7% Belarussian 1% Other or unspecified 2.3%

Age	0–14	15–19	20–24	25–29	30–64	65 plus
Male	8.2%	2.2%	2.6%	3.8%	23.2%	6.6%
Female	7.9%	2.1%	2.4%	3.5%	24.6%	12.9%

Capabilities

There has been an increased focus on national defence in Estonia since conflict began in eastern Ukraine in 2014. An additional air base was provided by the country in 2014 for NATO's ongoing Baltic Air Policing mission, while Estonian officials have complained about Russian incursions in their airspace; the air-policing mission will likely be increasingly important to Estonian security. Conscription was reintroduced in 2015, and the defence minister announced in 2016 that women would, from 2018, be able to serve in all units in which conscripts are trained. Defence spending increased in 2016, reflecting the assessment among those European nations bordering Russia that their security requires more attention. Following the NATO Warsaw Summit in 2016, it was announced that a multinational battlegroup would be deployed on a rotational basis to Estonia. Infrastructure investment will further increase the country's NATO integration, and a number of barracks were completed in 2016 in preparation for the first rotational deployments as part of NATO's enhanced forward presence. Estonia continues to develop its cyber capabilities. Since 2011 it has been developing a cyber range (a virtual environment for cyber training) and in 2014 NATO decided to establish a cyber range, based in Estonia's facility. There was further investment in this capability by NATO in 2016. Estonia is also a member of the UK-led multinational Joint Expeditionary Force. The annual exercise *Spring Storm* took place in Estonia in early 2016. Estonian special-forces troops have deployed to Ukraine in order to train Ukrainian special-forces teams as part of a US-led training initiative.

ACTIVE 6,400 (Army 5,700 Navy 400 Air 300)
Defence League 15,800

Conscript liability 8 months, officers and some specialists 11 months (Conscripts cannot be deployed)

RESERVE 12,000 (Joint 12,000)

ORGANISATIONS BY SERVICE

Army 2,600; 3,100 conscript (total 5,700)
4 def region. All units except one inf bn are reserve based
FORCES BY ROLE
MANOEUVRE
  Light
    1 (1st) bde (1 recce coy, 3 inf bn, 1 arty bn, 1 AD bn, 1 cbt engr bn, 1 spt bn)
    1 (2nd) inf bde (1 inf bn, 1 spt bn)
COMBAT SUPPORT
  1 sigs bn
COMBAT SERVICE SUPPORT
  1 log bn

Defence League 15,800
15 Districts
EQUIPMENT BY TYPE
ARMOURED FIGHTING VEHICLES
  IFV 12 CV9035
  APC 158
    APC (W) 151: 56 XA-180 *Sisu*; 80 XA-188 *Sisu*; 15 BTR-80
    PPV 7 *Mamba*
ANTI-TANK/ANTI-INFRASTRUCTURE
  MSL • MANPATS FGM-148 *Javelin*; Milan; IMI MAPATS
  RCL 160+; **106mm**: 30 M40A1; **84mm** *Carl Gustav*; **90mm** 130 PV-1110
ARTILLERY 376
  TOWED 66: **122mm** 42 D-30 (H 63); **155mm** 24 FH-70
  MOR 310: **81mm** 131: 41 B455; 10 NM 95; 80 M252; **120mm** 179: 14 2B11; 165 M/41D
AIR DEFENCE • SAM • Point-defence *Mistral*

Navy 300; 100 conscript (total 400)
EQUIPMENT BY TYPE
MINE WARFARE • **MINE COUNTERMEASURES** 4
  MCCS 1 *Tasuja* (ex-DNK *Lindormen*)
  MHC 3 *Admiral Cowan* (ex-UK *Sandown*)
LOGISTICS AND SUPPORT 1
  ABU 1 *Ristna* (ex-FIN *Rihtniemi*)

Air Force 300
Flying hours 120 hrs/yr

FORCES BY ROLE
TRANSPORT
  1 sqn with An-2 *Colt*
TRANSPORT HELICOPTER
  1 sqn with R-44 *Raven* II
EQUIPMENT BY TYPE
AIRCRAFT • **TPT** • **Light** 2 An-2 *Colt*
HELICOPTERS • **TPT** • **Light** 4 R-44 *Raven* II

Special Operations Forces
FORCES BY ROLE
SPECIAL FORCES
  1 spec ops bn

Paramilitary

Border Guard
The Estonian Border Guard is subordinate to the Ministry of the Interior. Air support is provided by the Estonian Border Guard Aviation Corps
EQUIPMENT BY TYPE
PATROL AND COASTAL COMBATANTS 22
  PCO 1 *Kindral Kurvits*
  PCC 1 *Kou* (FIN *Silma*)
  PB 9: 1 *Maru* (FIN *Viima*); 8 (other)
  PBR 11
AMPHIBIOUS • **LANDING CRAFT** • **LCU** 2
LOGISTICS & SUPPORT • **AGF** 1 *Balsam*
AIRCRAFT • **TPT** • **Light** 2 L-410
HELICOPTERS • **MRH** 3 AW139

Cyber
Estonia substantially developed its cyber-security infrastructure after it came under cyber attack in 2007. It adopted a national Cyber Security Strategy in 2008 and in 2009 added a Cyber Security Council to the Security Committee of the Government of the Republic, which supports strategic-level inter-agency cooperation. Tallinn hosts the NATO Cooperative Cyber Security Centre of Excellence (CCDCOE), and the NATO *Locked Shields* cyber exercise takes place annually in Estonia, as has the Cyber Coalition exercise since 2013. A Cyber Security Strategy for 2014–17 advocates greater integration of capability, saying that specialists from the armed forces and the Estonian Defence League will be integral in developing military cyber-defence capabilities. The recently adopted Estonian Defence League Act explicitly integrates its Cyber Defence Unit into the national defence system.

DEPLOYMENT

Legal provisions for foreign deployment:
Constitution: Codified constitution (1992)
Decision on deployment of troops abroad: By parliament (Art. 128). Also, International Military Cooperation Act stipulates conditions for deployment abroad. For collective-defence purposes, ratification of the North Atlantic Treaty is considered a parliamentary decision that would allow cabinet to deploy troops. The president, chairman of the parliament and chairman of the parliament's State Defence Commission shall be immediately informed of such a decision. For other international operations, a separate parliamentary decision is necessary: the Ministry of Defence prepares a draft legal act and coordinates this with the Ministry of Foreign Affairs and the Ministry of Justice. It also asks the opinion of the chief of defence. The draft is then proposed to the cabinet for approval and submission for parliamentary consideration

AFGHANISTAN
NATO • *Operation Resolute Support* 6

IRAQ
Operation Inherent Resolve 10

LEBANON
UN • UNIFIL 50

MALI
EU • EUTM Mali 10
UN • MINUSMA 10

MIDDLE EAST
UN • UNTSO 6 obs

MOLDOVA
OSCE • Moldova 1

NORTH SEA
NATO • SNMCMG 1: 1 MHC

SERBIA
NATO • KFOR 2

UKRAINE
OSCE • Ukraine 7

FOREIGN FORCES

Germany NATO Baltic Air Policing 4 Eurofighter *Typhoon*

Finland FIN

Euro €		2015	2016	2017
GDP	€	209bn	214bn	
	US$	232bn	239bn	
per capita	US$	42,414	43,492	
Growth	%	0.2	0.9	
Inflation	%	-0.2	0.4	
Def bdgt [a]	€	2.77bn	2.94bn	2.86bn
	US$	3.07bn	3.28bn	
US$1=€		0.90	0.90	

[a] Excludes military pensions

Population 5,498,211

Age	0–14	15–19	20–24	25–29	30–64	65 plus
Male	8.4%	2.8%	3.1%	3.2%	22.7%	9.0%
Female	8.0%	2.7%	3.0%	3.0%	22.3%	11.7%

Capabilities

Finland's armed forces are primarily focused on territorial defence, although the conflict in eastern Ukraine has re-sharpened focus on defence matters, as have incursions into Baltic states' airspace by Russian aircraft. A new defence white paper was due to be published by 2017, as was the ministry of defence's new strategic plan, STRATPLAN 2035. The previous strategic plan focused on a future joint operational concept and joint capability development. Finland's principal multilateral defence relationships include the EU, NATO, NORDEFCO and the Northern Group, as well as bilateral cooperation, in particular with the United States and Sweden. At the NATO Wales Summit in 2014, Finland joined the Enhanced Opportunities Partners programme. In February 2016, the government stated that it was preparing legislation to allow the Finnish Armed Forces (FAF) to act in support of the EU and partner nations abroad. A long period of decline in the defence budget was reversed in 2016 with a 6.8% increase. The air force launched in October 2015 the HX Fighter Program to replace Finland's F/A-18s with multi-role combat aircraft; the F/A-18s are planned to be out of service by 2025 and the replacement is due to be selected by the early 2020s. It is not possible to replace the capability of the Hornet fleet within current budget parameters. The government suggested that budget cuts may result in fewer aircraft than originally planned, with unmanned systems suggested as possible solutions to any capability gaps. A letter of intent was signed with Finland's Rauma Marine Constructions in September 2016 for the navy's Squadron 2020 programme, which is planned to replace the navy's four patrol boats and two minelayers with corvette-sized vessels capable of operating in ice conditions. Construction is scheduled to begin in 2019. Other development programmes include cyber capabilities, self-propelled artillery, surface-to-surface missiles and anti-tank capabilities. Finland contributed special forces and a navy vessel to NATO's BALTOPS exercise in June 2016. The US Army trained with Finnish counterparts as part of *Arrow 16* in May, while the same month saw the US deploy F-15s to Finland as part of operation *Atlantic Resolve*. Reservist refresher training was increased in 2015 and the creation of a rapid-reaction element with a border-security focus was announced.

ACTIVE 22,200 (Army 16,000 Navy 3,500 Air 2,700)
Paramilitary 2,700

Conscript liability 6–9–12 months (12 months for officers, NCOs and soldiers with special duties). Conscript service was reduced by 15 days in early 2013

RESERVE 230,000 (Army 150,000 Navy 20,000 Air 26,000) **Paramilitary 11,500**

25,000 reservists a year do refresher training: total obligation 40 days (75 for NCOs, 100 for officers) between conscript service and age 50 (NCOs and officers to age 60)

ORGANISATIONS BY SERVICE

Army 5,000; 11,000 conscript (total 16,000)
FORCES BY ROLE
Finland's army maintains a mobilisation strength of about 285,000. In support of this requirement, two conscription cycles, each for about 15,000 conscripts, take place each year. After conscript training, reservist commitment is to the age of 60. Reservists are usually assigned to units within their local geographical area. All service appointments or deployments outside Finnish borders are voluntary for all members of the armed services. All brigades are reserve based

Reserve Organisations 60,000 in manoeuvre forces and 225,000 in territorial forces

FORCES BY ROLE
SPECIAL FORCES
  1 SF bn
MANOEUVRE
  Armoured
  2 armd BG (regt)
  Mechanised
  2 (Karelia & Pori Jaeger) mech bde
  Light
  3 (Jaeger) bde
  6 lt inf bde
COMBAT SUPPORT
  1 arty bde
  1 AD regt
  7 engr regt
  3 sigs bn
COMBAT SERVICE SUPPORT
  Some log unit
HELICOPTER
  1 hel bn

EQUIPMENT BY TYPE
ARMOURED FIGHTING VEHICLES
  MBT 120: 100 *Leopard* 2A4; 20 *Leopard* 2A6
  IFV 196: 94 BMP-2; 102 CV90
  APC 613
    APC (T) 142: 40 MT-LBu; 102 MT-LBV
    APC (W) 471: 260 XA-180/185 *Sisu*; 101 XA-202 *Sisu* (CP); 48 XA-203 *Sisu*; 62 AMV (XA-360)
ENGINEERING & MAINTENANCE VEHICLES
  AEV 6 *Leopard* 2R CEV
  ARV 27: 15 MTP-LB; 12 VT-55A
  VLB 27: 12 BLG-60M2; 6 *Leopard* 2S; 9 SISU *Leguan*
  MW *Aardvark* Mk 2; KMT T-55; RA-140 DS
ANTI-TANK/ANTI-INFRASTRUCTURE
  MSL • MANPATS *Spike*-MR; *Spike*-LR
ARTILLERY 647
  SP 122mm 36 2S1 *Gvozdika* (PsH 74)
  TOWED 324: **122mm** 234 D-30 (H 63); **130mm** 36 M-46 (K 54); **155mm** 54 K 83/GH-52 (K 98)
  MRL 227mm 22 M270 MLRS
  MOR 120mm 265: 261 Krh/92; 4 XA-361 AMOS
HELICOPTERS
  MRH 7: 5 Hughes 500D; 2 Hughes 500E
  TPT • Medium 20 NH90 TTH
UNMANNED AERIAL VEHICLES
  ISR • Medium 11 ADS-95 *Ranger*
AIR DEFENCE
  SAM
    Short-range 44: 20 *Crotale* NG (ITO 90); 24 NASAMS II FIN (ITO 12)
    Point-defence 16+: 16 ASRAD (ITO 05); FIM-92 *Stinger* (ITO 15); RBS 70 (ITO 05/05M)
  GUNS 400+: **23mm** ItK 95/ZU-23-2 (ItK 61); **35mm** some

Navy 1,600; 1,900 conscript (total 3,500)

FORCES BY ROLE
Naval Command HQ located at Turku; with two subordinate Naval Commands (Gulf of Finland and Archipelago Sea); 1 Naval bde; 3 spt elm (Naval Materiel Cmd, Naval Academy, Naval Research Institute)

EQUIPMENT BY TYPE
PATROL AND COASTAL COMBATANTS 18
  PCG 4 *Hamina* with 4 RBS-15 (15SFE) AShM, 1 octuple VLS with *Umkhonto* SAM, 1 57mm gun
  PBF 10 *Jehu* (U-700) (capacity 24 troops)
  PBG 4 *Rauma* with 6 RBS-15SF3 (15SF) AShM
MINE WARFARE 15
  MINE COUNTERMEASURES 10
    MCC 3 *Katanpää* (expected FOC 2017)
    MSI 7: 4 *Kiiski*; 3 *Kuha*
  MINELAYERS • ML 5:
    2 *Hameenmaa* with 1 octuple VLS with *Umkhonto* SAM, 2 RBU 1200 A/S mor, up to 100–120 mines, 1 57mm gun
    3 *Pansio* with 50 mines
AMPHIBIOUS • LANDING CRAFT 51
  LCU 1 *Kampela*
  LCP 50
LOGISTICS AND SUPPORT 7
  AG 3: 1 *Louhi*; 2 *Hylje*
  AX 4: 3 *Fabian Wrede*; 1 *Lokki*

Coastal Defence

FORCES BY ROLE
MANOEUVRE
  Amphibious
  1 mne bde
COMBAT SUPPORT
  1 cbt spt bde (1 AShM bty)

EQUIPMENT BY TYPE
COASTAL DEFENCE
  AShM 4 RBS-15K AShM
  ARTY • 130mm 30 K-53tk (static)
ANTI-TANK/ANTI-INFRASTRUCTURE
  MSL • MANPATS *Spike* (used in AShM role)

Air Force 1,950; 750 conscript (total 2,700)

3 Air Comds: Satakunta (West), Karelia (East), Lapland (North)

Flying hours 90–140 hrs/yr

FORCES BY ROLE
FIGHTER/GROUND ATTACK
  3 sqn with F/A-18C/D *Hornet*
ISR
  1 (survey) sqn with Learjet 35A
TRANSPORT
  1 flt with C-295M
  4 (liaison) flt with PC-12NG
TRAINING
  1 sqn with *Hawk* Mk50/51A/66* (air defence and ground attack trg)
  1 unit with L-70 *Vinka*

EQUIPMENT BY TYPE
AIRCRAFT 107 combat capable
  FGA 62: 55 F/A-18C *Hornet*; 7 F/A-18D *Hornet*
  MP 1 F-27-400M
  ELINT 1 C-295M

TPT • **Light** 10: 2 C-295M; 3 Learjet 35A (survey; ECM trg; tgt-tow); 5 PC-12NG
TRG 73: 29 *Hawk* Mk50/51A*; 16 *Hawk* Mk66*; 28 L-70 *Vinka*
AIR-LAUNCHED MISSILES • AAM • IR AIM-9 *Sidewinder*; **IIR** AIM-9X *Sidewinder*; **ARH** AIM-120 AMRAAM

Paramilitary

Border Guard 2,700
Ministry of Interior. 4 Border Guard Districts and 2 Coast Guard Districts
FORCES BY ROLE
MARITIME PATROL
    1 sqn with Do-228 (maritime surv); AS332 *Super Puma*; Bell 412 (AB-412) *Twin Huey*; Bell 412EP (AB-412EP) *Twin Huey*;AW119KE *Koala*
EQUIPMENT BY TYPE
PATROL AND COASTAL COMBATANTS 52
    PCO 1 *Turva*
    PCC 3: 2 *Tursas*; 1 *Merikarhu*
    PB 48
AMPHIBIOUS • LANDING CRAFT • UCAC 6
AIRCRAFT • TPT • Light 2 Do-228
HELICOPTERS
    MRH 5: 3 Bell 412 (AB-412) *Twin Huey*; 2 Bell 412EP (AB-412EP) *Twin Huey*
    TPT 9: **Medium** 5 AS332 *Super Puma*; **Light** 4 AW119KE *Koala*

Reserve 11,500 reservists on mobilisation

Cyber
Finland published a national cyber-security strategy in 2013 and published an implementation programme for this in 2014. In accordance with the strategy, the Finnish Defence Forces will create a comprehensive cyber-defence capacity for their statutory tasks; the strategy continues that 'a military cyber-defence capacity encompasses intelligence as well as cyber-attack and cyber-defence capabilities'. Full operational capability is planned by 2020, and the cyber division is organised under the defence forces' C5 Agency.

DEPLOYMENT
Legal provisions for foreign deployment:
Specific legislation: 'Act on Military Crisis Management (211/2006)'
Decision on deployment of troops abroad: The President of the Republic upon proposal by the Council of State (Act on Military Crisis Management (211/2006), paragraph 2). Before making the proposal the Council of State must consult the parliament (Act on Military Crisis Management (211/2006), paragraph 3)

AFGHANISTAN
NATO • *Operation Resolute Support* 30

BOSNIA-HERZEGOVINA
EU • EUFOR • *Operation Althea* 6

INDIA/PAKISTAN
UN • UNMOGIP 6 obs

IRAQ
Operation Inherent Resolve 100

LEBANON
UN • UNIFIL 308; elm 1 mech inf bn

MALI
EU • EUTM Mali 7
UN • MINUSMA 5

MIDDLE EAST
UN • UNTSO 17 obs

SERBIA
NATO • KFOR 20
OSCE • Kosovo 1

SYRIA/ISRAEL
UN • UNDOF 2

UGANDA
EU • EUTM Somalia 7

UKRAINE
OSCE • Ukraine 23

France FRA

Euro €		2015	2016	2017
GDP	€	2.18tr	2.23tr	
	US$	2.42tr	2.49tr	
per capita	US$	37,653	38,537	
Growth	%	1.3	1.3	
Inflation	%	0.1	0.3	
Def exp [a]	€	39.2bn		
	US$	43.5bn		
Def bdgt [b]	€	42.0bn	42.3bn	43.2bn
	US$	46.6bn	47.2bn	
US$1=€		0.90	0.90	

[a] NATO definition
[b] Includes pensions

Population   66,836,154

Age	0–14	15–19	20–24	25–29	30–64	65 plus
Male	9.5%	3.1%	3.0%	3.1%	22.1%	8.2%
Female	9.1%	2.9%	2.8%	3.0%	22.4%	10.9%

Capabilities

France continues to play a leading military role in the UN, NATO and the EU, and maintains a full-spectrum war-fighting capability. The continuous deployment of large numbers of troops to support domestic counter-terrorism operations following high-profile terror attacks in the country in 2015 and 2016, as well as an increased operational tempo abroad across multiple theatres, has driven Paris to reverse the trend of defence-budget cuts and personnel contractions. This high tempo has also increased the stress on equipment. There is a plan to increase the defence ministry's operational reserve forces, while the president announced in 2016 a plan to create a National Guard, drawing from the reserves of the armed forces, the police and gendarmerie. The army and navy continued to implement their Au Contract and Horizon Maritime 2025 plans respectively. The country has a well-developed defence industry, with the majority of defence procurement undertaken domestically. Recently merged Nexter and Germany's Krauss-Maffei Wegmann have begun to develop a new main battle tank for the French and German armies. French defence sales are robustly supported by its government; a notable success came when DCNS was selected as the preferred contractor for Australia's submarine requirement. France participated in exercise *Griffin Strike* with the UK in April, which culminated in the formal validation of the Combined Joint Expeditionary Force. In March 2016, it was announced that the military reserve across all three services was to be expanded by 12,000 personnel, to a total of 40,000 by 2018, with a corresponding increase in funding. This includes money that will be earmarked for further equipment purchases, including nuclear submarines, *Tiger* and NH90 helicopters, unspecified special-forces and cyber equipment, and offshore-patrol vessels. An order of four C-130s, to make up for temporary gaps in A400M capabilities, will introduce an additional tactical-airlift capability upon delivery. France's continued deployments abroad have demonstrated its ability to support expeditionary forces independently, however the focus on domestic security has led to reductions in training and limited the capability to deploy additional troops overseas. Exercise deployments in Eastern Europe were increased in line with NATO's reassurance initiatives and in August 2016 France took command of NATO's Baltic Air Policing mission. Paris has continued to commit forces to Djibouti and the EU anti-piracy operation in the Indian Ocean, while deploying aircraft and training personnel in the US-led campaign against the Islamic State in Iraq and Syria. (See pp. 77–82.)

ACTIVE 202,950 (Army 109,450 Navy 35,400 Air 42,050, Other Staffs 16,050) Paramilitary 103,400

RESERVE 28,100 (Army 15,750 Navy 4,650 Air 4,250 Other Staffs 3,450) Paramilitary 40,000

ORGANISATIONS BY SERVICE

Strategic Nuclear Forces

Navy 2,200
EQUIPMENT BY TYPE
SUBMARINES • STRATEGIC • SSBN 4
  1 *Le Triomphant* with 16 M45 SLBM with 6 TN-75 nuclear warheads, 4 single 533mm TT with F17 Mod 2 HWT/SM-39 *Exocet* AShM (in refit until 2018/19)
  3 *Le Triomphant* with 16 M51 SLBM with 6 TN-75 nuclear warheads, 4 single 533mm TT with F17 Mod 2 HWT/SM-39 *Exocet* AShM
AIRCRAFT • FGA 20 *Rafale* M F3 with ASMP-A msl

Air Force 1,800
Air Strategic Forces Command
FORCES BY ROLE
STRIKE
  1 sqn with *Mirage* 2000N with ASMP/ASMP-A msl
  1 sqn with *Rafale* B with ASMP/ASMP-A msl
TANKER
  1 sqn with C-135FR; KC-135 *Stratotanker*
EQUIPMENT BY TYPE
AIRCRAFT 43 combat capable
  FGA 43: 23 *Mirage* 2000N; 20 *Rafale* B
  TKR/TPT 11 C-135FR
  TKR 3 KC-135 *Stratotanker*

Paramilitary

Gendarmerie 40

Space
EQUIPMENT BY TYPE
SATELLITES 9
  COMMUNICATIONS 3: 2 *Syracuse*-3 (designed to integrate with UK *Skynet* & ITA *Sicral*); 1 *Athena-Fidus* (also used by ITA)
  ISR 4: 2 *Helios* (2A/2B); 2 *Pleiades*
  EARLY WARNING 2 *Spirale*

Army 109,450
Regt and BG normally bn size
FORCES BY ROLE
COMMAND
  1 corps HQ (CRR-FR)
  2 div HQ
MANOEUVRE
Reconnaissance
  1 recce regt
Armoured
  1 (2nd) armd bde (2 tk regt, 3 armd inf regt, 1 SP arty regt, 1 engr regt)
  1 (7th) armd bde (1 tk regt, 1 armd BG, 3 armd inf regt, 1 SP arty regt, 1 engr regt)
  1 armd BG (UAE)
Mechanised
  1 (6th) lt armd bde (2 armd cav regt, 1 armd inf regt, 1 mech inf regt, 1 mech inf regt(-), 1 SP arty regt, 1 engr regt)
  1 (FRA/GER) mech bde (1 armd cav regt, 1 mech inf regt)
  1 mech regt (Djibouti)
Light
  1 (27th) mtn bde (1 armd cav regt, 3 mech inf regt, 1 arty regt, 1 engr regt)
  3 inf regt (French Guiana & French West Indies)
  1 inf regt (New Caledonia)
  1 inf bn (Côte d'Ivoire)
  1 inf coy (Mayotte)
Air Manoeuvre
  1 (11th) AB bde (1 armd cav regt, 4 para regt, 1 arty regt, 1 engr regt, 1 spt regt)
  1 AB regt (La Réunion)
  1 AB bn (Gabon)

Amphibious
1 (9th) amph bde (2 armd cav regt, 1 armd inf regt, 2 mech inf regt, 1 SP arty regt, 1 engr regt)
Other
4 SMA regt (French Guiana, French West Indies & Indian Ocean)
3 SMA coy (French Polynesia, Indian Ocean & New Caledonia)
COMBAT SUPPORT
1 MRL regt
2 engr regt
2 EW regt
1 int bn
1 CBRN regt
5 sigs regt
COMBAT SERVICE SUPPORT
5 tpt regt
1 log regt
1 med regt
3 trg regt
HELICOPTER
1 (4th) hel bde (3 hel regt)
ISR UAV
1 UAV regt
AIR DEFENCE
1 SAM regt

Special Operation Forces 2,200
FORCES BY ROLE
SPECIAL FORCES
2 SF regt
HELICOPTER
1 hel regt

Reserves 15,750 reservists
Reservists form 79 UIR (Reserve Intervention Units) of about 75 to 152 troops, for 'Proterre' – combined land projection forces bn, and 23 USR (Reserve Specialised Units) of about 160 troops, in specialised regt
EQUIPMENT BY TYPE
ARMOURED FIGHTING VEHICLES
  MBT 200 *Leclerc*
  ASLT 248 AMX-10RC
  RECCE 1,556: 90 ERC-90F4 *Sagaie*; 1,466 VBL
  IFV 630: 520 VBCI VCI; 110 VBCI VCP (CP)
  APC 2,313
    APC (T) 53 BvS-10
    APC (W) 2,260: 2,200 VAB; 60 VAB VOA (OP)
  AUV 14 *Aravis*
ENGINEERING & MAINTENANCE VEHICLES
  AEV 54 AMX-30EBG
  ARV 48+: 30 AMX-30D; 18 *Leclerc* DNG; VAB-EHC
  VLB 67: 39 EFA; 18 PTA; 10 SPRAT
  MW 24+: AMX-30B/B2; 4 *Buffalo*; 20 *Minotaur*
NBC VEHICLES 40 VAB NRBC
ANTI-TANK/ANTI-INFRASTRUCTURE • MSL
  SP 325: 30 VAB HOT; 110 VAB *Milan*; 185 VAB *Eryx*
  MANPATS FGM-148 *Javelin*; *Milan*
ARTILLERY 262+
  SP 155mm 109: 32 AU-F-1; 77 CAESAR
  TOWED 155mm 12 TR-F-1
  MRL 227mm 13 M270 MLRS
  MOR 128+: **81mm** LLR 81mm; **120mm** 128 RT-F-1
RADAR • LAND 66: 10 *Cobra*; 56 RASIT/RATAC
AIRCRAFT • TPT • Light 13: 5 PC-6B *Turbo Porter*; 5 TBM-700; 3 TBM-700B
HELICOPTERS
  ATK 55: 39 *Tiger* HAP; 16 *Tiger* HAD
  MRH 129: 18 AS555UN *Fennec*; 111 SA341F/342M *Gazelle* (all variants)
  TPT 164: **Heavy** 8 H225M *Caracal* (CSAR); **Medium** 121: 26 AS532UL *Cougar*; 18 NH90 TTH; 77 SA330 *Puma*; **Light** 35 H120 *Colibri* (leased)
UNMANNED AERIAL VEHICLES
  ISR • Medium 24 SDTI (*Sperwer*)
AIR DEFENCE • SAM • Point-defence *Mistral*

Navy 35,400
EQUIPMENT BY TYPE
SUBMARINES 10
  STRATEGIC • SSBN 4:
    1 *Le Triomphant* opcon Strategic Nuclear Forces with 16 M45 SLBM with 6 TN-75 nuclear warheads, 4 single 533mm TT with F17 Mod 2 HWT/SM-39 *Exocet* AShM (currently undergoing modernisation programme to install M51 SLBM; expected completion 2018/19)
    3 *Le Triomphant* opcon Strategic Nuclear Forces with 16 M51 SLBM with 6 TN-75 nuclear warheads, 4 single 533mm TT with F17 Mod 2 HWT/SM-39 *Exocet* AShM
  TACTICAL • SSN 6:
    6 *Rubis* with 4 single 533mm TT with F-17 HWT/SM-39 *Exocet* AShM
PRINCIPAL SURFACE COMBATANTS 24
  AIRCRAFT CARRIERS 1
    CVN 1 *Charles de Gaulle* with 4 octuple VLS with *Aster* 15 SAM, 2 sextuple *Sadral* lnchr with *Mistral* SAM (capacity 35–40 *Super Etendard/Rafale* M/E-2C *Hawkeye/AS365 Dauphin*)
  DESTROYERS • DDGHM 12:
    2 *Cassard* with 2 quad lnchr with MM-40 *Exocet* Block 2 AShM, 1 Mk13 GMLS with SM-1MR SAM, 2 sextuple *Sadral* lnchr with *Mistral* SAM, 2 single 533mm ASTT with L5 HWT, 1 100mm gun (capacity 1 AS565SA *Panther* ASW hel)
    2 *Forbin* with 2 quad lnchr with MM-40 *Exocet* Block 3 AShM, 1 48-cell VLS with *Aster* 15/*Aster* 30 SAM, 2 twin 324mm ASTT with MU90, 2 76mm gun (capacity 1 NH90 TTH hel)
    2 *Georges Leygues* with 2 quad lnchr with MM-40 *Exocet* AShM, 1 octuple lnchr with *Crotale* SAM, , 2 sextuple *Sadral* lnchr with *Mistral* SAM, 2 single 533mm ASTT with L5 HWT, 1 100mm gun (capacity 2 *Lynx* hel)
    3 *Georges Leygues* (mod) with 2 quad lnchr with MM-40 *Exocet* AShM, 1 octuple lnchr with *Crotale* SAM, 2 twin *Simbad* lnchr with *Mistral* SAM, 2 single 324mm ASTT with MU90 LWT, 1 100mm gun (capacity 2 *Lynx* hel)
    3 *Aquitaine* with 2 octuple *Sylver* A70 VLS with MdCN (SCALP Naval) LACM, 2 quad lnchr with MM-40 *Exocet* Block 3 AShM, 2 octuple *Sylver* A43 VLS with

Aster 15 SAM, 2 twin B515 324mm ASTT with MU90 LWT, 1 76mm gun (capacity 1 NH90 NFH hel)
FRIGATES • FFGHM 11:
6 *Floreal* with 2 single lnchr with MM-38 *Exocet* AShM, 1 twin *Simbad* lnchr with *Mistral* SAM, 1 100mm gun (capacity 1 AS565SA *Panther* hel)
5 *La Fayette* with 2 quad lnchr with MM-40 *Exocet* Block 3 AShM, 1 octuple lnchr with *Crotale* SAM, (space for fitting 2 octuple VLS lnchr for *Aster* 15/30), 1 100mm gun (capacity 1 AS565SA *Panther*/SA321 *Super Frelon* hel)
PATROL AND COASTAL COMBATANTS 22
FSM 9 *D'Estienne d'Orves* with 1 twin *Simbad* lnchr with *Mistral* SAM, 4 single ASTT, 1 100mm gun
PSO 2 *d'Entrecasteaux* with 1 hel landing platform
PCC 7: 4 *L'Audacieuse* (all deployed in the Pacific or Caribbean); 3 *Flamant*
PCO 4: 1 *Lapérouse*; 1 *Le Malin*; 1 *Fulmar*; 1 *L'Adroit* (*Gowind*)
MINE WARFARE • MINE COUNTERMEASURES 18
MCD 4 *Vulcain*
MHC 3 *Antarès*
MHO 11 *Éridan*
AMPHIBIOUS
PRINCIPAL AMPHIBIOUS SHIPS 3
LHD 3 *Mistral* with 2 twin *Simbad* lnchr with *Mistral* SAM, (capacity up to 16 NH90/SA330 *Puma*/AS532 *Cougar*/*Tiger* hel; 2 LCAC or 4 LCM; 13 MBTs; 50 AFVs; 450 troops)
LANDING SHIPS • LST 1 *Batral* (capacity 12 trucks; 140 troops)
LANDING CRAFT 40
LCT 4 EDA-R
LCM 11 CTM
LCVP 25
LOGISTICS AND SUPPORT 35
ABU 1 *Telenn Mor*
AFS 1 *Revi*
AG 3 *Chamois*
AGE 1 *Corraline*; 1 *Lapérouse* (used as trials ships for mines and divers)
AGI 1 *Dupuy de Lome*
AGM 1 *Monge*
AGOR 2: 1 *Pourquoi pas?* (used 150 days per year by Ministry of Defence; operated by Ministry of Research and Education otherwise); 1 *Beautemps-beaupré*
AGS 3 *Lapérouse*
AORH 3 *Durance* with 1-3 twin *Simbad* lnchr with *Mistral* SAM (capacity 1 SA319 *Alouette* III/AS365 *Dauphin*/*Lynx*)
ATF 2 *Malabar*
AXL 12: 8 *Léopard*; 2 *Glycine*; 2 *Engageante*
AXS 4: 2 *La Belle Poule*; 2 other

Naval Aviation 6,500

Flying hours 180–220 hrs/yr on strike/FGA ac

FORCES BY ROLE
STRIKE/FIGHTER/GROUND ATTACK
2 sqn with *Rafale* M F3
1 sqn (forming) with Rafale M F3
ANTI-SURFACE WARFARE
1 sqn with AS565SA *Panther*
ANTI-SUBMARINE WARFARE
2 sqn (forming) with NH90 NFH
1 sqn with *Lynx* Mk4
MARITIME PATROL
2 sqn with *Atlantique* 2
1 sqn with *Falcon* 20H *Gardian*
1 sqn with *Falcon* 50MI
AIRBORNE EARLY WARNING & CONTROL
1 sqn with E-2C *Hawkeye*
SEARCH & RESCUE
1 sqn with AS365N/F *Dauphin* 2
TRAINING
1 sqn with EMB 121 *Xingu*
1 unit with SA319B *Alouette* III
1 unit with *Falcon* 10MER
1 unit with CAP 10M
EQUIPMENT BY TYPE
AIRCRAFT 54 combat capable
FGA 42 *Rafale* M F3
ASW 12 *Atlantique* 2 (10 more in store)
AEW&C 3 E-2C *Hawkeye*
SAR 4 *Falcon* 50MS
TPT 26: **Light** 11 EMB-121 *Xingu*; **PAX** 15: 6 *Falcon* 10MER; 5 *Falcon* 20H *Gardian*; 4 *Falcon* 50MI
TRG 7 CAP 10M
HELICOPTERS
ASW 34: 18 *Lynx* Mk4; 16 NH90 NFH
MRH 47: 9 AS365N/F/SP *Dauphin* 2; 2 AS365N3; 16 AS565SA *Panther*; 20 SA319B *Alouette* III
AIR-LAUNCHED MISSILES
AAM • IR R-550 *Magic* 2; **IIR** *Mica* IR; **ARH** *Mica* RF
ASM AASM; AS-30L
AShM AM-39 *Exocet*
LACM ASMP-A
BOMBS
Laser-guided: GBU-12 *Paveway* II

Marines 2,000

Commando Units 550
FORCES BY ROLE
MANOEUVRE
Reconnaissance
1 recce gp
Amphibious
2 aslt gp 1 atk swimmer gp
1 raiding gp
COMBAT SUPPORT
1 cbt spt gp
COMBAT SERVICE SUPPORT
1 spt gp

Fusiliers-Marin 1,450
FORCES BY ROLE
MANOEUVRE
Other
2 sy gp
7 sy coy

Reserves 4,650 reservists

Air Force 42,050

Flying hours 180 hrs/yr

FORCES BY ROLE
STRIKE
   1 sqn with *Mirage* 2000N with ASMP/ASMP-A msl
   1 sqn with *Rafale* B with ASMP/ASMP-A msl
SPACE
   1 (satellite obs) sqn
FIGHTER
   1 sqn with *Mirage* 2000-5
   1 sqn with *Mirage* 2000B/C
FIGHTER/GROUND ATTACK
   3 sqn with *Mirage* 2000D
   1 (composite) sqn with *Mirage* 2000-5/D (Djibouti)
   2 sqn with *Rafale* B/C
   1 sqn with *Rafale* B/C (UAE)
ELECTRONIC WARFARE
   1 flt with C-160G *Gabriel* (ESM)
AIRBORNE EARLY WARNING & CONTROL
   1 (Surveillance & Control) sqn with E-3F *Sentry*
SEARCH & RESCUE/TRANSPORT
   4 sqn with C-160R *Transall*; CN-235M; SA330 *Puma*; AS555 *Fennec* (Djibouti, French Guiana, Gabon, Indian Ocean & New Caledonia)
TANKER
   1 sqn with C-135FR; KC-135 *Stratotanker*
TANKER/TRANSPORT
   2 sqn with C-160R *Transall*
TRANSPORT
   1 sqn with A310-300; A330; A340-200 (on lease)
   1 sqn with A400M
   2 sqn with C-130H/H-30 *Hercules*; C-160R *Transall*
   2 sqn with CN-235M
   1 sqn with EMB-121
   1 sqn with *Falcon* 7X (VIP); *Falcon* 900 (VIP); *Falcon* 2000
   3 flt with TBM-700A
   1 (mixed) gp with AS532 *Cougar*; C-160 *Transall*; DHC-6-300 *Twin Otter*
TRAINING
   1 OCU sqn with *Mirage* 2000D
   1 OCU sqn with *Rafale* B/C F3
   1 OCU sqn with SA330 *Puma*; AS555 *Fennec*
   1 OCU unit with C-160 *Transall*
   1 (aggressor) sqn with *Alpha Jet**
   4 sqn with *Alpha Jet**
   3 sqn with Grob G120A-F; TB-30 *Epsilon*
   1 OEU with *Mirage* 2000, *Rafale*, *Alpha Jet**
TRANSPORT HELICOPTER
   2 sqn with AS555 *Fennec*
   2 sqn with AS332C/L *Super Puma*; SA330 *Puma*; H225M *Caracal*
ISR UAV
   1 sqn with *Harfang*; MQ-9A *Reaper*
AIR DEFENCE
   3 sqn with *Crotale* NG; SAMP/T
   1 sqn with SAMP/T

EQUIPMENT BY TYPE
SATELLITES *see* Space
AIRCRAFT 297 combat capable
   FTR 41: 35 *Mirage* 2000-5/2000C; 6 *Mirage* 2000B
   FGA 190: 67 *Mirage* 2000D; 23 *Mirage* 2000N; 52 *Rafale* B; 48 *Rafale* C
   ELINT 2 C-160G *Gabriel* (ESM)
   AEW&C 4 E-3F *Sentry*
   TKR 3 KC-135 *Stratotanker*
   TKR/TPT 11 C-135FR
   TPT 128: **Heavy** 9 A400M; **Medium** 37: 5 C-130H *Hercules*; 9 C-130H-30 *Hercules*; 23 C-160R *Transall*; **Light** 70: 19 CN-235M-100; 8 CN-235M-300; 5 DHC-6-300 *Twin Otter*; 23 EMB-121 *Xingu*; 15 TBM-700; **PAX** 12: 3 A310-300; 1 A330; 2 A340-200 (on lease); 2 *Falcon* 7X; 2 *Falcon* 900 (VIP); 2 *Falcon* 2000
   TRG 107: 64 *Alpha Jet**; 18 Grob G120A-F; 25 TB-30 *Epsilon* (incl many in storage)
HELICOPTERS
   MRH 37 AS555 *Fennec*
   TPT 43: **Heavy** 11 H225M *Caracal*; **Medium** 32: 3 AS332C *Super Puma*; 4 AS332L *Super Puma*; 3 AS532UL *Cougar* (tpt/VIP); 22 SA330B *Puma*
UNMANNED AERIAL VEHICLES
   ISR • Heavy 7: 4 *Harfang*; 3 MQ-9A *Reaper*
AIR DEFENCE
   SAM
      Long-range 9 SAMP/T
      Short-range 12 *Crotale* NG
   GUNS 20mm Cerbere 76T2
AIR-LAUNCHED MISSILES
   AAM • IR R-550 *Magic* 2; **IIR** Mica IR; **SARH** Super 530D; **ARH** Mica RF
   ASM AASM; AS-30L; *Apache*
   LACM ASMP-A; SCALP EG
BOMBS
   Laser-guided: GBU-12 *Paveway* II

Security and Intervention Brigade

FORCES BY ROLE
SPECIAL FORCES
   3 SF gp
MANOEUVRE
   Other
   24 protection units
   30 (fire fighting and rescue) unit

Reserves 4,250 reservists

Paramilitary 103,400

Gendarmerie 103,400; 40,000 reservists

EQUIPMENT BY TYPE
ARMOURED FIGHTING VEHICLES
   ASLT 28 VBC-90
   APC • APC (W) 153 VXB-170 (VBRG-170)
ARTILLERY • MOR 81mm some
PATROL AND COASTAL COMBATANTS 39
   PB 39: 4 *Géranium*; 1 *Glaive*; 2 VSC 14; 24 VSCM; 8 EBSLP
HELICOPTERS • TPT • Light 60: 25 AS350BA *Ecureuil*; 20 H135; 15 H145

Customs (Direction Générale des Douanes et Droits Indirects)

EQUIPMENT BY TYPE
PATROL AND COASTAL COMBATANTS 30
    PCO 2: 1 *Jacques Oudart Fourmentin*; 1 *Kermovan*
    PB 28: 7 *Plascoa* 2100; 7 *Haize Hegoa*; 2 *Avel Gwalarn*; 1 *Rafale*; 1 *Arafenua*; 1 *Vent d'Amont*; 1 *La Rance*; 8 others

Coast Guard (Direction des Affaires Maritimes)

EQUIPMENT BY TYPE
PATROL AND COASTAL COMBATANTS 25
    PCO 1 *Themis*
    PCC 1 *Iris*
    PB 23: 4 *Callisto*; 19 others
LOGISTICS AND SUPPORT • AG 7

Cyber

The French Network and Information Security Agency (ANSSI) was established in 2009 to conduct surveillance on sensitive government networks and respond to cyber attacks. The 2008 French Defence White Paper placed emphasis on cyber threats, calling for programmes in offensive and defensive cyber-war capabilities. In July 2011, the defence ministry produced a classified Joint Cyber Defence Concept. The French Ministry of Defence is in charge of the defence of its networks and information systems. The head of the Cyber Defence Cell also serves as the head of the French cyber operational command. France's cyber operational command is responsible for coordinating cyber-defence efforts within the MoD as well as planning and commanding cyber operations within the Planning and Operations centre, located within the Joint Staff. Both the army and air force have electronic-warfare units (EW). Information Command (COM INT) was established in mid-2016 and is subordinate to Land Forces Command. It consists of the 44th and 54th Signals Regiments and the 785th EW Company. The Air Force has one EW squadron. The Analysis Centre for Defensive Cyber Operations in the MoD (CALID) is charged with responding to cyber attacks and cooperates with other nations' military CERTs.

DEPLOYMENT

Legal provisions for foreign deployment:
Constitution: Codified constitution (1958)
Specific legislation: 'Order of 7 January 1959'
Decision on deployment of troops abroad: De jure: by the minister of defence, under authority of the PM and on agreement in council of ministers ('Order of 7 January 1959', Art. 16, Art. 20-1 of constitution)

BURKINA FASO
Operation Barkhane 220; 1 SF gp

CENTRAL AFRICAN REPUBLIC
Operation Sangaris 350; 1 mech coy(+); 1 AS555UN *Fennec*
EU • EUTM RCA 80
UN • MINUSCA 9

CHAD
Operation Barkhane 1,250; 1 mech inf BG; 1 air unit with 1 C-130H *Hercules*; 1 C-160 *Transall*; 1 hel det with 4 *Tiger*; 2 SA330 *Puma*

CÔTE D'IVOIRE
900; 1 (Marine) inf bn
UN • UNOCI 5

DEMOCRATIC REPUBLIC OF THE CONGO
UN • MONUSCO 2

DJIBOUTI
1,450; 1 (Marine) combined arms regt with (2 recce sqn, 2 inf coy, 1 arty bty, 1 engr coy); 1 hel det with 2 SA330 *Puma*; 1 SA342 *Gazelle*; 1 LCM; 1 FGA sqn with 4 *Mirage* 2000-5/D; 1 SAR/tpt sqn with 1 C-160 *Transall*; 2 SA330 *Puma*

EGYPT
MFO 1

FRENCH GUIANA
2,100; 1 (Foreign Legion) inf regt; 1 (Marine) inf regt; 1 SMA regt; 2 PCC; 1 tpt sqn with 3 CN-235M; 5 SA330 *Puma*; 4 AS555 *Fennec*; 3 gendarmerie coy; 1 AS350BA *Ecureuil*

FRENCH POLYNESIA
900: (incl Centre d'Expérimentation du Pacifique); 1 SMA coy; 1 naval HQ at Papeete; 1 FFGHM; 1 PSO; 1 PCO; 1 AFS; 3 *Falcon* 200 *Gardian*; 1 SAR/tpt sqn with 2 CN-235M

FRENCH WEST INDIES
1,000; 1 (Marine) inf regt; 2 SMA regt; 2 FFGHM; 1 LST; 1 naval base at Fort de France (Martinique); 4 gendarmerie coy; 2 AS350BA *Ecureuil*

GABON
350; 1 AB bn

GERMANY
2,000 (incl elm Eurocorps and FRA/GER bde); 1 (FRA/GER) mech bde (1 armd cav regt, 1 mech inf regt)

GULF OF ADEN & INDIAN OCEAN
EU • *Operation Atalanta* 1 FFGHM

GULF OF GUINEA
Operation Corymbe 1 LHD

INDIAN OCEAN
1,600 (incl La Réunion and TAAF); 1 (Marine) para regt; 1 (Foreign Legion) inf coy; 1 SMA regt ; 1 SMA coy; 2 FFGHM; 1 PCO; 1 LCM; 1 naval HQ at Port-des-Galets (La Réunion); 1 naval base at Dzaoudzi (Mayotte); 1 SAR/tpt sqn with 2 CN-235M; 5 gendarmerie coy; 1 SA319 *Alouette* III

IRAQ
Operation Chammal 550; 1 SP arty bty with 4 CAESAR

JORDAN
Operation Chammal 6 *Rafale* F3; 1 *Atlantique* 2

LEBANON
UN • UNIFIL 779; 1 mech BG; VBL; VBCI; VAB; *Mistral*

LITHUANIA
NATO • Baltic Air Policing 4 *Mirage* 2000-5

MALI
Operation Barkhane 1,680; 1 mech inf BG; 1 log bn; 1 hel unit with 3 NH90 TTH; 4 SA330 *Puma*; 4 SA342 *Gazelle*
EU • EUTM Mali 13
UN • MINUSMA 26

MEDITERRANEAN SEA
Operation Chammal 1 SSN; 1 CVN; 3 DDGHM; 1 AORH
EU • EU NAVFOR MED: 1 *Atlantique* 2

MIDDLE EAST
UN • UNTSO 1 obs

NEW CALEDONIA
1,450; 1 (Marine) mech inf regt; 1 SMA coy; 6 ERC-90F1 *Lynx*; 1 FFGHM; 1 PSO; 2 PCC; 1 base with 2 *Falcon* 200 *Gardian* at Nouméa; 1 tpt unit with 2 CN-235 MPA; 3 SA330 *Puma*; 4 gendarmerie coy; 2 AS350BA *Ecureuil*

NIGER
Operation Barkhane 350; 1 FGA det with 4 *Mirage* 2000D; 1 tkr/tpt det with 1 C-135FR; 1 C-160 *Transall*; 1 UAV det with 2 *Harfang*; 3 MQ-9A *Reaper*

SENEGAL
350; 1 *Falcon* 50MI

SERBIA
NATO • KFOR 2
OSCE • Kosovo 1

UGANDA
EU • EUTM Somalia 1

UKRAINE
OSCE • Ukraine 19

UNITED ARAB EMIRATES
650: 1 armd BG (1 tk coy, 1 arty bty); *Leclerc*; CAESAR; 1 FGA sqn with 8 *Rafale* F3; 1 C-135FR

WESTERN SAHARA
UN • MINURSO 7 obs

FOREIGN FORCES
Belgium 28 *Alpha Jet* trg ac located at Cazaux/Tours
Germany 400 (GER elm Eurocorps)
Singapore 200; 1 trg sqn with 12 M-346 *Master*

Germany GER

Euro €		2015	2016	2017
GDP	€	3.03tr	3.13tr	
	US$	3.37tr	3.49tr	
per capita	US$	40,952	42,326	
Growth	%	1.5	1.7	
Inflation	%	0.1	0.4	
Def exp [a]	€	35.9bn		
	US$	39.8bn		
Def bdgt [b]	€	33.0bn	34.3bn	36.6bn
	US$	36.6bn	38.3bn	
US$1=€		0.90	0.90	

[a] NATO definition
[b] Includes military pensions

Population 80,722,792

Age	0–14	15–19	20–24	25–29	30–64	65 plus
Male	6.6%	2.5%	2.7%	3.2%	24.6%	9.6%
Female	6.2%	2.4%	2.6%	3.1%	24.3%	12.2%

Capabilities

Germany published a white paper on security policy and the future of the armed forces in July 2016. The document commits Germany to a leadership role in European defence and emphasises the importance of NATO and the need for Germany's armed forces to be able to contribute to collective-defence tasks. Compared to previous strategy documents, the white paper acknowledges the return of interstate armed conflict and describes Russia as a challenge to European security rather than a partner. Germany is in the process of establishing a Cyber Command, which was due to achieve initial operating capability in April 2017. The initial aim is to centralise responsibility for cyber, information technology, military intelligence and electronic warfare, geographic information services and some communications tasks in one command. In this process, Germany is expected to strengthen its capacity for Computer Network Operations. Current government budget planning foresees a modest annual growth in the defence budget from 2016 out to 2020. Budget parameters are reviewed annually by the cabinet and rolling five-year budget plans are agreed on that basis. Available additional funding is likely to mostly benefit the army. Once agreed goals are implemented, for example to increase equipment levels for operational units from 70% to 100%, additional modernisation steps would require yet more funding. Defence Minister Ursula von der Leyen has also announced the objective of increasing active force numbers. Given that the Bundeswehr is already struggling with recruitment and retention after conscription was suspended in 2011, the ministry is due to recommend recruitment goals with a seven-year time horizon and a shift towards a more flexible approach to generating the authorised personnel strength. The German armed forces are struggling to improve their readiness levels in light of increasing demands on NATO's eastern flank. As several reports to parliament have outlined, the budget cuts of previous years have led to a shortage of spare parts and maintenance problems. (See pp. 64–5.)

ACTIVE 176,800 (Army 59,300 Navy 16,300 Air 28,200 Joint Support Service 41,400 Joint Medical Service 19,700 Other 11,900) Paramilitary 500

Conscript liability Voluntary conscription only. Voluntary conscripts can serve up to 23 months

RESERVE 27,600 (Army 6,300 Navy 1,100 Air 3,400 Joint Support Service 12,250 Joint Medical Service 3,100 Other 1,450)

ORGANISATIONS BY SERVICE

Space
EQUIPMENT BY TYPE
SATELLITES 7
  COMMUNICATIONS 2 COMSATBw (1 & 2)
  ISR 5 SAR-*Lupe*

Army 59,300
FORCES BY ROLE
COMMAND
  elm 2 (1 GNC & MNC NE) corps HQ
MANOEUVRE
  Armoured
  1 (1st) armd div (1 (9th) armd bde (1 armd recce bn, 1 tk bn, 2 armd inf bn, 1 lt inf bn, 1 cbt engr bn, 1 spt bn); 1 (21st) armd bde (1 armd recce bn, 1 tk bn, 1 armd inf bn, 1 mech inf bn, 1 cbt engr bn, 1 spt bn); 1 (41st) mech inf bde (1 armd recce bn, 2 armd inf bn, 1 lt inf bn, 1 cbt engr bn, 1 sigs bn, 1 spt bn); 1 SP arty bn; 1 sigs bn)
  1 (10th) armd div (1 (12th) armd bde (1 armd recce bn, 1 tk bn, 2 armd inf bn, 1 cbt engr bn, 1 spt bn); 1 (37th) mech inf bde (1 armd recce bn, 1 tk bn, 1 armd inf bn, 1 mech inf bn, 1 engr bn, 1 spt bn); 1 (23rd) mtn inf bde (1 recce bn, 3 mtn inf bn, 1 cbt engr bn, 1 spt bn); 1 SP arty bn; 1 SP arty trg bn; 1 sy bn)
  1 tk bn (for NLD 43rd Bde)
  Light
  2 lt inf bn (GER/FRA bde)
  Air Manoeuvre
  1 (rapid reaction) AB div (1 SOF bde (2 SOF bn); 1 AB bde (2 recce coy, 2 para regt, 2 cbt engr coy); 1 atk hel regt; 2 tpt hel regt; 1 sigs coy)
COMBAT SUPPORT
  1 arty bn (GER/FRA bde)
  1 cbt engr coy (GER/FRA bde)
COMBAT SERVICE SUPPORT
  1 spt bn (GER/FRA bde)
EQUIPMENT BY TYPE
ARMOURED FIGHTING VEHICLES
  MBT 306: 286 *Leopard* 2A6; 20 *Leopard* 2A7
  RECCE 191: 166 *Fennek* (incl 14 engr recce, 14 fires spt); 25 *Wiesel* (16 recce; 9 engr)
  IFV 565: 390 *Marder* 1A2/A3/A4/A5; 88 *Puma*; 87 *Wiesel* 1 Mk20 (with 20mm gun)
  APC 1,256

  APC (T) 453: 194 Bv-206D/S; 259 M113 (inc variants)
  APC (W) 803: 272 *Boxer* (inc variants); 531 TPz-1 *Fuchs* (inc variants)
  AUV 848: 316 *Dingo* 2; 495 *Eagle* IV; 176 *Eagle* V
ENGINEERING & MAINTENANCE VEHICLES
  AEV 42 *Dachs*
  ARV 97: 56 ARV *Leopard* 1; 41 BPz-3 *Büffel*
  VLB 47: 22 *Biber*; 25 M3
  MW 15 *Keiler*
NBC VEHICLES 8 TPz-1 *Fuchs* NBC
ANTI-TANK/ANTI-INFRASTRUCTURE • MSL
  SP 64 *Wiesel* with TOW
  MANPATS *Milan*
ARTILLERY 223
  SP 155mm 99 PzH 2000
  MRL 227mm 38 M270 MLRS
  MOR 120mm 86 *Tampella*
RADARS • LAND 82: 9 *Cobra*; 61 RASIT (veh, arty); 12 RATAC (veh, arty)
HELICOPTERS
  ATK 42 *Tiger*
  MRH/ISR 49 Bo-105M/P1/P1A1 (with HOT)
  TPT 103: **Medium** 48 NH90; **Light** 55: 39 Bell 205 (UH-1D *Iroquois*); 14 H135; 2 H145M
UNMANNED AERIAL VEHCIELS
  ISR 128: **Medium** 43 KZO; **Light** 85 LUNA

Navy 16,300
EQUIPMENT BY TYPE
SUBMARINES • TACTICAL • SSK 6:
  6 Type-212A with 6 single 533mm TT with 12 A4 *Seehecht* DM2 HWT
PRINCIPAL SURFACE COMBATANTS 15
  DESTROYERS • DDGHM 7:
    4 *Brandenburg* with 2 twin lnchr with MM-38 *Exocet* AShM, 1 16-cell Mk41 VLS with RIM-7M/P, 2 Mk49 GMLS with RIM-116 RAM SAM, 2 twin 324mm ASTT with Mk46 LWT, 1 76mm gun (capacity 2 *Sea Lynx* Mk88A hel)
    3 *Sachsen* with 2 quad Mk141 lnchr with RGM-84F *Harpoon* AShM, 1 32-cell Mk41 VLS with SM-2MR/RIM-162B ESSM SAM, 2 21-cell Mk49 GMLS with RIM-116 RAM SAM, 2 triple Mk32 324mm ASTT with MU90 LWT, 1 76mm gun (capacity; 2 *Sea Lynx* Mk88A hel)
  FRIGATES 8
    FFGHM 3 *Bremen* with 2 quad Mk141 lnchr with RGM-84A/C *Harpoon* AShM, 1 octuple Mk29 GMLS with RIM-7M/P *Sea Sparrow* SAM, 2 Mk49 GMLS with RIM-116 RAM SAM, 2 twin 324mm ASTT with Mk46 LWT, 1 76mm gun (capacity 2 *Sea Lynx* Mk88A hel)
    FFGM 5 *Braunschweig* (K130) with 2 twin lnchr with RBS-15 AShM, 2 Mk49 GMLS each with RIM-116 RAM SAM, 1 76mm gun, 1 hel landing platform
MINE WARFARE • MINE COUNTERMEASURES 33
  MHO 12: 10 *Frankenthal* (2 used as diving support); 2 *Kulmbach*
  MSO 2 *Ensdorf*
  MSD 18 *Seehund*

AMPHIBIOUS 2
  LCU 2 Type-520
LOGISTICS AND SUPPORT 26
  AFSH 3 *Berlin* (Type-702) (capacity 2 *Sea King* Mk41 hel; 2 RAMs)
  AG 5: 2 *Schwedeneck* (Type-748); 3 *Stollergrund* (Type-745)
  AGI 3 *Oste* (Type-423)
  AGOR 1 *Planet* (Type-751)
  AO 2 *Walchensee* (Type-703)
  AOR 6 *Elbe* (Type-404) with 1 hel landing platform (2 specified for PFM support; 1 specified for SSK support; 3 specified for MHC/MSC support)
  AOT 2 *Spessart* (Type-704)
  APB 3: 1 *Knurrhahn*; 2 *Ohre*
  AXS 1 *Gorch Fock*

Naval Aviation 2,000
EQUIPMENT BY TYPE
AIRCRAFT 8 combat capable
  ASW 8 AP-3C *Orion*
  TPT • Light 2 Do-228 (pollution control)
HELICOPTERS
  ASW 22 *Lynx* Mk88A with *Sea Skua*
  SAR 21 *Sea King* Mk41
AIR-LAUNCHED MISSILES • AShM *Sea Skua*

Naval Special Forces Command
FORCES BY ROLE
SPECIAL FORCES
  1 SF coy

Sea Battalion
FORCES BY ROLE
MANOEUVRE
  Amphibious
    1 mne bn

Air Force 28,200
Flying hours   140 hrs/yr (plus 40 hrs high-fidelity simulator)

FORCES BY ROLE
FIGHTER
  2 wg (2 sqn with Eurofighter *Typhoon*)
FIGHTER/GROUND ATTACK
  1 wg (2 sqn with *Tornado* IDS)
  1 wg (2 sqn with Eurofighter *Typhoon*)
ISR
  1 wg (1 ISR sqn with *Tornado* ECR/IDS; 1 UAV sqn (ISAF only) with *Heron*)
TANKER/TRANSPORT
  1 (special air mission) wg (3 sqn with A310 MRTT; A319; A340; AS532U2 *Cougar* II; *Global* 5000)
TRANSPORT
  2 wg (total: 3 sqn with C-160D *Transall*)
  1 wg (1 sqn (forming) with A400M *Atlas*)
TRAINING
  1 sqn located at Holloman AFB (US) with *Tornado* IDS
  1 unit (ENJJPT) located at Sheppard AFB (US) with T-6 *Texan* II; T-38A
  1 hel unit located at Fassberg
TRANSPORT HELICOPTER
  1 tpt hel wg (3 sqn with CH-53G/GA/GE/GS *Stallion*; 1 sqn with H145M)
AIR DEFENCE
  1 wg (3 SAM gp) with MIM-104C/F *Patriot* PAC-2/3
  1 AD gp with ASRAD *Ozelot*; C-RAM *Mantis*
  1 AD trg unit located at Fort Bliss (US) with ASRAD *Ozelot*; C-RAM *Mantis*; *Patriot*
  3 (tac air ctrl) radar gp

Air Force Regiment
FORCES BY ROLE
MANOEUVRE
  Other
    1 sy regt
EQUIPMENT BY TYPE
AIRCRAFT 209 combat capable
  FTR 121 Eurofighter *Typhoon*
  ATK 68 *Tornado* IDS
  ATK/EW 20 *Tornado* ECR*
  TKR/TPT 4 A310 MRTT
  TPT 54: **Heavy** 5 A400M; **Medium** 40 C-160D *Transall*; **PAX** 9: 1 A310; 2 A340 (VIP); 2 A319; 4 *Global* 5000
  TRG 109: 69 T-6A *Texan* II, 40 T-38A
HELICOPTERS
  MRH 15 H145M
  TPT 74: **Heavy** 71 CH-53G/GA/GS/GE *Stallion*; **Medium** 3 AS532U2 *Cougar* II (VIP)
UNMANNED AERIAL VEHICLES • ISR • Heavy *Heron*
AIR DEFENCE
  SAM
    Long-range 30 MIM-104C/F *Patriot* PAC-2/PAC-3
    Point-defence 10 ASRAD *Ozelot* (with FIM-92 *Stinger*)
  GUNS 35mm 12 C-RAM *Mantis*
AIR-LAUNCHED MISSILES
  AAM • IR AIM-9L/Li *Sidewinder*; **IIR** IRIS-T; **ARH** AIM-120A/B AMRAAM
  LACM *Taurus* KEPD 350
  ARM AGM-88B HARM
BOMBS
  Laser-guided GBU-24 *Paveway* III, GBU-54 JDAM

Joint Support Service 41,400
FORCES BY ROLE
COMBAT SUPPORT
  4 EW bn
  3 MP regt
  2 NBC bn
  6 sigs bn
COMBAT SERVICE SUPPORT
  6 log bn
  1 spt regt

Joint Medical Services 19,700
FORCES BY ROLE
COMBAT SERVICE SUPPORT
  3 med regt

Paramilitary

Coast Guard 500
EQUIPMENT BY TYPE
PATROL AND COASTAL COMBATANTS 12
PCO 6: 3 *Bad Bramstedt*; 1 *Bredstedt*; 2 *Sassnitz*
PB 6: 5 *Prignitz*; 1 *Rettin*

Cyber

Germany issued a Cyber Security Strategy in February 2011. The National Cyber Security Council, an inter-ministerial body at state-secretary level, analyses cyber-related issues. A National Cyber Response Centre was set up at the Federal Office for Information Security on 1 April 2011. In 2016 Germany boosted its cyber capabilities by implementing far-reaching reforms. A new Directorate-General Cyber/IT (CIT) was created within the Federal Ministry of Defence, with two divisions for Cyber/IT Governance and IT-Services/Information Security. The Director-General serves as Chief Information Officer and point of contact for other federal ministries and agencies. The Directorate-General's tasks include advancing technical cyber/IT capabilities, and guiding cyber policies. Furthermore, a new 'Cyber and Information Space Command (KdoCIR)' will become operational in April 2017 as the sixth military branch within the German armed forces. All of the Bundeswehr's current and newly created cyber and IT capabilities will be pooled in the new branch. It will be about 13,500 strong, comprising both military and civilian personnel, and will be led by a Chief of Staff for Cyber and Information Space (InspCIR). The overall aim of these reforms is to assign current capabilities to defined responsibilities, protect Bundeswehr and national cyber and IT infrastructure, and improve capabilities in order to better respond to cyber attacks.

DEPLOYMENT

Legal provisions for foreign deployment:
Constitution: Codified constitution ('Basic Law', 1949)
Specific legislation: 'Parlamentsbeteiligungsgesetz' (2005)
Decision on deployment of troops abroad: a) By parliament: prior consent for anticipated military involvement; simplified consent procedure for deployments of limited intensity or extension; subsequent consent admitted in cases requiring immediate action or deployments aimed at rescuing persons from danger, provided parliamentary discussion would have endangered life; b) by government: preparation, planning and humanitarian aid and assistance provided by the armed forces where weapons are carried for self-defence, provided it is not expected that military personnel will be involved in armed engagements; other deployments short of an involvement or anticipated involvement in armed engagements

AFGHANISTAN
NATO • *Operation Resolute Support* 965; 1 bde HQ; *Heron* UAV
UN • UNAMA 1 obs

ALBANIA
OSCE • Albania 1

BOSNIA-HERZEGOVINA
OSCE • Bosnia and Herzegovina 3

DJIBOUTI
EU • *Operation Atalanta* 1 AP-3C *Orion*

ESTONIA
NATO • Baltic Air Policing 4 Eurofighter *Typhoon*

FRANCE
400 (incl GER elm Eurocorps)

IRAQ
123 (trg spt)

LEBANON
UN • UNIFIL 126; 1 FFGM

MALI
EU • EUTM Mali 131
UN • MINUSMA 249; 2 obs

MEDITERRANEAN SEA
EU • EU NAVFOR MED: 1 DDGHM; 1 AOR
NATO • SNMCMG 2: 1 MHO
Operation Inherent Resolve 1 FFGHM

MOLDOVA
OSCE • Moldova 2

NORTH SEA
NATO • SNMG 1: 1 FFGM
NATO • SNMCMG 1: 1 AOR

POLAND
67 (GER elm MNC-NE)

SERBIA
NATO • KFOR 699
OSCE • Kosovo 3

SOUTH SUDAN
UN • UNMISS 5; 11 obs

SUDAN
UN • UNAMID 8

TURKEY
Operation Inherent Resolve 200; 6 *Tornado* ECR; 1 A310 MRTT

UGANDA
EU • EUTM Somalia 11

UKRAINE
OSCE • Ukraine 40

UNITED STATES
Trg units with 40 T-38 *Talon*; 69 T-6A *Texan* II at Goodyear AFB (AZ)/Sheppard AFB (TX); 1 trg sqn with 14 *Tornado* IDS at Holloman AFB (NM); NAS Pensacola (FL); Fort Rucker (AL); Missile trg at Fort Bliss (TX)

WESTERN SAHARA
UN • MINURSO 3 obs

FOREIGN FORCES

Canada NATO 226

France 2,000; 1 (FRA/GER) mech bde (1 armd cav regt, 1 mech inf regt)
United Kingdom 4,400; 1 armd bde(-) (1 tk regt, 1 armd inf bn, 1 SP arty regt, 1 cbt engr regt, 1 maint regt, 1 med regt)
United States
US Africa Command: **Army**; 1 HQ at Stuttgart
US European Command: 36,850; 1 combined service HQ (EUCOM) at Stuttgart-Vaihingen
  Army 22,000; 1 HQ (US Army Europe (USAREUR) at Heidelberg; 1 SF gp; 1 mech bde; 1 armd recce bn; 1 arty bn; 1 (cbt avn) hel bde HQ; 1 int bde; 1 MP bde; 1 sigs bde; 1 spt bde; 1 (APS) armd bde eqpt set; M1 *Abrams*; M2/M3 *Bradley*; *Stryker*; M109; M119A2; M777; AH-64 *Apache*; CH-47 *Chinook*; UH-60 *Black Hawk*
  Navy 950
  USAF 12,650; 1 HQ (US Airforce Europe (USAFE)) at Ramstein AB; 1 HQ (3rd Air Force) at Ramstein AB; 1 ftr wg at Spangdahlem AB with 1 ftr sqn with 24 F-16CJ *Fighting Falcon*; 1 airlift wg at Ramstein AB with 16 C-130J-30 *Hercules*; 2 C-20 *Gulfstream*; 9 C-21 *Learjet*; 1 C-40B
  USMC 1,200

Greece GRC

Euro €		2015	2016	2017
GDP	€	176bn	175bn	
	US$	195bn	196bn	
per capita	US$	17,989	18,078	
Growth	%	-0.2	0.1	
Inflation	%	-1.1	-0.1	
Def exp [a]	€	4.19bn		
	US$	4.65bn		
Def bdgt [b]	€	4.27bn	4.16bn	4.02bn
	US$	4.73bn	4.64bn	
US$1=€		0.90	0.90	

[a] NATO definition
[b] Includes military pensions

Population 10,773,253

Age	0-14	15-19	20-24	25-29	30-64	65 plus
Male	7.2%	2.4%	2.5%	2.7%	24.9%	9.1%
Female	6.8%	2.3%	2.4%	2.8%	25.3%	11.6%

Capabilities

Greece's armed forces have traditionally been well funded, given territorial-defence tasks and a requirement to support Cyprus. Spending as a proportion of GDP is second only to the US within NATO, in spite of several years of challenging fiscal circumstances. The general staff is aiming to produce more flexible, agile and mobile forces at the tactical and operational levels. The past year has seen growing ties with Israel, including joint training, as well as continued tension with Turkey over airspace violations. The effects of the financial crisis have hampered the procurement of new equipment and there were cuts to military salaries, as well as reductions in training and exercises. The country's stored P-3B *Orion*s are being modernised and upgraded, adding to Greece's capability for maritime patrol and anti-submarine warfare. Work began in July 2016. Other priorities include the acquisition of more Type-214 submarines, upgrades to the *Posideon*-class submarines and the procurement of FREMM frigates. Development of the national defence industry in order to preserve local maintenance capabilities and equipment readiness is a priority. Greece trains widely with NATO allies and other partners.

ACTIVE 142,950 (Army 93,500 Navy 15,600 Air 20,750 Joint 11,600) **Paramilitary 4,000**
Conscript liability Up to 9 months in all services

RESERVE 220,500 (Army 181,500 Navy 5,000 Air 34,000)

ORGANISATIONS BY SERVICE

Army 48,500; 45,000 conscripts (total 93,500)
Units are manned at 3 different levels – Cat A 85% fully ready, Cat B 60% ready in 24 hours, Cat C 20% ready in 48 hours (requiring reserve mobilisation). 3 military regions

FORCES BY ROLE
COMMAND
  2 corps HQ (incl NDC-GR)
  1 armd div HQ
  3 mech inf div HQ
  1 inf div HQ
SPECIAL FORCES
  1 SF comd
  1 cdo/para bde
MANOEUVRE
  Reconnaissance
  4 recce bn
  Armoured
  4 armd bde (2 armd bn, 1 mech inf bn, 1 SP arty bn)
  Mechanised
  9 mech inf bde (1 armd bn, 2 mech bn, 1 SP arty bn)
  Light
  1 inf div
  3 inf bde (1 armd bn, 3 inf regt, 1 arty regt)
  Air Manoeuvre
  1 air mob bde
  1 air aslt bde
  Amphibious
  1 mne bde
COMBAT SUPPORT
  1 arty regt (1 arty bn, 2 MRL bn)
  3 AD bn (2 with I-*Hawk*, 1 with *Tor* M1)
  3 engr regt
  2 engr bn
  1 EW regt
  10 sigs bn
COMBAT SERVICE SUPPORT
  1 log corps HQ
  1 log div (3 log bde)

HELICOPTER
1 hel bde (1 hel regt with (2 atk hel bn), 2 tpt hel bn, 4 hel bn)

EQUIPMENT BY TYPE
ARMOURED FIGHTING VEHICLES
MBT 1,341: 170 *Leopard* 2A6HEL; 183 *Leopard* 2A4; 513 *Leopard* 1A4/5; 100 M60A1/A3; 375 M48A5
RECCE 229 VBL
IFV 398 BMP-1
APC 2,562
 APC (T) 2,551: 86 *Leonidas* Mk1/2; 2,252 M113A1/A2; 213 M577 (CP)
 PPV 11 *Maxxpro*
ENGINEERING & MAINTENANCE VEHICLES
ARV 261: 12 *Büffel*; 43 *Leopard 1*; 94 M88A1; 112 M578
VLB 12+: 12 *Leopard 1*; *Leguan*
MW *Giant Viper*
ANTI-TANK/ANTI-INFRASTRUCTURE
MSL
 SP 600: 196 HMMWV with 9K135 *Kornet*-E (AT-14 *Spriggan*); 42 HMMWV with *Milan*; 362 M901
 MANPATS 9K111 *Fagot* (AT-4 *Spigot*); *Milan*; TOW
RCL 84mm *Carl Gustav*; 90mm EM-67; SP 106mm 581 M40A1
ARTILLERY 3,607
SP 587: 155mm 442: 418 M109A1B/A2/A3GEA1/A5; 24 PzH 2000; 203mm 145 M110A2
TOWED 553: 105mm 347: 329 M101; 18 M-56; 155mm 206 M114
MRL 147: 122mm 111 RM-70; 227mm 36 M270 MLRS
MOR 2,320: 81mm 1,700; 107mm 620 M30 (incl 231 SP)
SURFACE-TO-SURFACE MISSILE LAUNCHERS
SRBM • Conventional MGM-140A ATACMS (launched from M270 MLRS)
RADAR • LAND 76: 3 ARTHUR, 5 AN/TPQ-36 *Firefinder* (arty, mor); 8 AN/TPQ-37(V)3; 40 BOR-A; 20 MARGOT
AIRCRAFT • TPT • Light 18: 1 Beech 200 *King Air* (C-12C) 2 Beech 200 *King Air* (C-12R/AP *Huron*); 15 Cessna 185 (U-17A/B)
HELICOPTERS
ATK 28: 19 AH-64A *Apache*; 9 AH-64D *Apache*
TPT 136: Heavy 18: 12 CH-47D *Chinook*; 6 CH-47SD *Chinook*; Medium 11 NH90 TTH; Light 107: 93 Bell 205 (UH-1H *Iroquois*); 14 Bell 206 (AB-206) *Jet Ranger*
UNMANNED AERIAL VEHICLES
ISR • Medium 4 *Sperwer*
AIR DEFENCE
SAM 614
 Medium-range 42 MIM-23B I-*Hawk*
 Short-range 21 9K331 *Tor*-M1 (SA-15 *Gauntlet*)
 Point-range 92+: 38 9K33 *Osa*-M (SA-8B *Gecko*); 54 ASRAD HMMWV; FIM-92 *Stinger*
GUNS • TOWED 727: 20mm 204 Rh 202; 23mm 523 ZU-23-2

National Guard 33,000 reservists
Internal security role
FORCES BY ROLE
MANOEUVRE
Light
1 inf div

Air Manoeuvre
1 para regt
COMBAT SUPPORT
8 arty bn
4 AD bn
COMBAT SUPPORT
1 hel bn

Navy 14,150; 1,450 conscript; (total 15,600)
EQUIPMENT BY TYPE
SUBMARINES • TACTICAL • SSK 11:
 3 *Poseidon* (GER Type-209/1200) with 8 single 533mm TT with SUT HWT
 1 *Poseidon* (GER Type-209/1200) (modernised with AIP technology) with 8 single 533mm TT with SUT HWT
 3 *Glavkos* (GER Type-209/1100) with 8 single 533mm TT with UGM-84C *Harpoon* AShM/SUT HWT
 4 *Papanikolis* (GER Type-214) with 8 single 533mm TT with UGM-84C *Harpoon* AShM/SUT HWT
PRINCIPAL SURFACE COMBATANTS 13
 FRIGATES • FFGHM 13:
 4 *Elli* Batch I (ex-NLD *Kortenaer* Batch 2) with 2 quad Mk141 lnchr with RGM-84A/C *Harpoon* AShM, 1 octuple Mk29 GMLS with RIM-7M/P *Sea Sparrow* SAM, 2 twin 324mm ASTT with Mk46 LWT, 1 *Phalanx* CIWS, 1 76mm gun (capacity 2 Bell 212 (AB-212) hel or 1 S-70B *Seahawk* hel)
 2 *Elli* Batch II (ex-NLD *Kortenaer* Batch 2) with 2 quad Mk141 lnchr with RGM-84A/C *Harpoon* AShM, 1 octuple Mk29 GMLS with RIM-7M/P *Sea Sparrow* SAM, 2 twin 324mm ASTT with Mk46 LWT, 1 *Phalanx* CIWS, 2 76mm gun (capacity 2 Bell 212 (AB-212) hel or 1 S-70B *Seahawk* hel)
 3 *Elli* Batch III (ex-NLD *Kortenaer* Batch 2) with 2 quad Mk141 lnchr with RGM-84A/C *Harpoon* AShM, 1 octuple Mk29 lnchr with RIM-7M/P *Sea Sparrow* SAM, 2 twin 324mm ASTT with Mk46 LWT, 1 *Phalanx* CIWS, 1 76mm gun (capacity 2 Bell 212 (AB-212) hel)
 4 *Hydra* (GER MEKO 200) with 2 quad lnchr with RGM-84G *Harpoon* AShM, 1 16-cell Mk48 Mod 5 VLS with RIM-162 ESSM SAM, 2 triple 324mm ASTT each with Mk46 LWT, 2 *Phalanx* CIWS, 1 127mm gun (capacity 1 S-70B *Seahawk* ASW hel)
PATROL AND COASTAL COMBATANTS 33
 CORVETTES • FSGM 5 *Roussen* (*Super Vita*) with 2 quad lnchr with MM-40 *Exocet* Block 2 AShM, 1 21-cell Mk49 GMLS with RIM-116 RAM SAM, 1 76mm gun (3 additional vessels in build)
PCFG 12:
 2 *Kavaloudis* (FRA *La Combattante* IIIB) with 6 single lnchr with RB 12 *Penguin* AShM, 2 single 533mm TT with SST-4 HWT, 2 76mm gun
 3 *Kavaloudis* (FRA *La Combattante* IIIB) with 2 twin lnchr with RGM-84C *Harpoon* AShM, 2 single 533mm TT with SST-4 HWT, 2 76mm gun
 3 *Laskos* (FRA *La Combattante* III) with 4 MM-38 *Exocet* AShM, 2 single 533mm TT with SST-4 HWT, 2 76mm gun

1 *Laskos* (FRA *La Combattante* III) with 2 twin lnchr with RGM-84C *Harpoon* AShM, 2 single 533mm TT with SST-4 HWT, 2 76mm gun

1 *Votsis* (ex-GER *Tiger*) with 2 twin Mk-141 lnchr with RGM-84C *Harpoon* AShM, 1 76mm gun

2 *Votsis* (ex-GER *Tiger*) with 2 twin MM-38 *Exocet* AShM, 1 76mm gun

PCO 8:
2 *Armatolos* (DNK *Osprey*) with 1 76mm gun
2 *Kasos* with 1 76mm gun
4 *Machitis* with 1 76mm gun

PB 8: 4 *Andromeda* (NOR *Nasty*); 2 *Stamou*; 2 *Tolmi*

MINE COUNTERMEASURES 4
MHO 4: 2 *Evropi* (ex-UK *Hunt*); 2 *Evniki* (ex-US *Osprey*)

AMPHIBIOUS
LANDING SHIPS • LST 5:
5 *Chios* (capacity 4 LCVP; 300 troops) with 1 76mm gun, 1 hel landing platform

LANDING CRAFT 14
LCU 4
LCA 7
LCAC 3 *Kefallinia* (*Zubr*) with 2 AK630 CIWS, (capacity either 3 MBT or 10 APC (T); 230 troops)

LOGISTICS AND SUPPORT 49
ABU 2
AG 2 *Pandora*
AGOR 1 *Naftilos*
AGS 2: 1 *Stravon*; 1 *Pytheas*
AOR 2 *Axios* (ex-GER *Luneburg*)
AORH 1 *Prometheus* (ITA *Etna*) with 1 *Phalanx* CIWS
AOT 4 *Ouranos*
AWT 6 *Kerkini*
AXS 5

Coastal Defence

EQUIPMENT BY TYPE
COASTAL DEFENCE • AShM 4 MM-40 *Exocet*

Naval Aviation

FORCES BY ROLE
ANTI-SUBMARINE WARFARE
1 div with S-70B *Seahawk*; Bell 212 (AB-212) ASW

EQUIPMENT BY TYPE
AIRCRAFT • ASW (5 P-3B *Orion* in store undergoing modernisation)
HELICOPTERS
ASW 18: 7 Bell 212 (AB-212) ASW; 11 S-70B *Seahawk*
AIR-LAUNCHED MISSILES
ASM AGM-114 *Hellfire*
AShM AGM-119 *Penguin*

Air Force 18,650; 2,100 conscripts (total 20,750)

Tactical Air Force
FORCES BY ROLE
FIGHTER/GROUND ATTACK
2 sqn with F-4E *Phantom* II
3 sqn with F-16CG/DG Block 30/50 *Fighting Falcon*
3 sqn with F-16CG/DG Block 52+ *Fighting Falcon*
2 sqn with F-16C/D Block 52+ ADV *Fighting Falcon*
1 sqn with *Mirage* 2000-5EG/BG Mk2
1 sqn with *Mirage* 2000EG/BG
ISR
1 sqn with RF-4E *Phantom* II
AIRBORNE EARLY WARNING
1 sqn with EMB-145H *Erieye*

EQUIPMENT BY TYPE
AIRCRAFT 239 combat capable
FGA 232: 34 F-4E *Phantom* II; 69 F-16CG/DG Block 30/50 *Fighting Falcon*; 55 F-16CG/DG Block 52+; 30 F-16 C/D Block 52+ ADV *Fighting Falcon*; 20 *Mirage* 2000-5EG Mk2; 5 *Mirage* 2000-5BG Mk2; 17 *Mirage* 2000EG; 2 *Mirage* 2000BG
ISR 7 RF-4E *Phantom* II*
AEW 4 EMB-145AEW (EMB-145H) *Erieye*
AIR-LAUNCHED MISSILES
AAM • IR AIM-9L/P *Sidewinder*; R-550 *Magic* 2 **IIR** IRIS-T; *Mica* IR; **ARH** AIM-120B/C AMRAAM; *Mica* RF
ASM AGM-65A/B/G *Maverick*; AGM-154C JSOW
LACM SCALP EG
AShM AM-39 *Exocet*
ARM AGM-88 HARM
BOMBS
Electro-optical guided: GBU-8B HOBOS
Laser-guided: GBU-10/12/16 *Paveway* II; GBU-24 *Paveway* III
INS/GPS-guided GBU-31 JDAM

Air Defence

FORCES BY ROLE
AIR DEFENCE
6 sqn/bty with MIM-104A/B/D *Patriot*/*Patriot* PAC-1 SOJC/*Patriot* PAC-2 GEM
2 sqn/bty with S-300PMU-1 (SA-10C *Grumble*)
12 bty with *Skyguard*/RIM-7 *Sparrow*/guns; *Crotale* NG/GR; *Tor*-M1 (SA-15 *Gauntlet*)

EQUIPMENT BY TYPE
AIR DEFENCE
SAM
Long-range 48: 36 MIM-104A/B/D *Patriot*/*Patriot* PAC-1 SOJC/PAC-2 GEM; 12 S-300PMU-1 (SA-10C *Grumble*)
Short-range 13+: 9 *Crotale* NG/GR; 4 9K331 *Tor*-M1 (SA-15 *Gauntlet*); some *Skyguard*/*Sparrow*
GUNS 35+ 35mm

Air Support Command

FORCES BY ROLE
SEARCH & RESCUE/TRANSPORT HELICOPTER
1 sqn with AS332C *Super Puma* (SAR/CSAR)
1 sqn with AW109; Bell 205A (AB-205A) (SAR); Bell 212 (AB-212 - VIP, tpt)
TRANSPORT
1 sqn with C-27J *Spartan*
1 sqn with C-130B/H *Hercules*
1 sqn with EMB-135BJ *Legacy*; ERJ-135LR; Gulfstream V

EQUIPMENT BY TYPE
AIRCRAFT
TPT 26: **Medium** 23: 8 C-27J *Spartan*; 5 C-130B *Hercules*;

10 C-130H *Hercules*; **Light** 2: 1 EMB-135BJ *Legacy*; 1 ERJ-135LR; **PAX** 1 Gulfstream V
HELICOPTERS
TPT 31: **Medium** 12 AS332C *Super Puma*; **Light** 19: 12 Bell 205A (AB-205A) (SAR); 4 Bell 212 (AB-212) (VIP, Tpt); 3 AW109

Air Training Command
FORCES BY ROLE
TRAINING
2 sqn with T-2C/E *Buckeye*
2 sqn with T-6A/B *Texan* II
1 sqn with T-41D
EQUIPMENT BY TYPE
AIRCRAFT • TRG 93: 30 T-2C/E *Buckeye*; 20 T-6A *Texan* II; 25 T-6B *Texan* II; 18 T-41D

Paramilitary

Coast Guard and Customs 4,000
EQUIPMENT BY TYPE
PATROL AND COASTAL COMBATANTS 124:
   PCC 3
   PCO 1 *Gavdos* (Damen 5009)
   PBF 54
   PB 66
LOGISTICS AND SUPPORT • YPC 4
AIRCRAFT • TPT • Light 4: 2 Cessna 172RG *Cutlass*; 2 TB-20 *Trinidad*
HELICOPTERS
SAR: 3 AS365N3

Cyber
A new Joint Cyber Command in the Hellenic National Defence General Staff was established in 2014, replacing the existing Cyber Defence Directorate. The National Policy on Cyber Defence is under development and expected to be complete by the end of 2016.

DEPLOYMENT
Legal provisions for foreign deployment:
Constitution: Codified constitution (1975/1986/2001)
Specific legislation: 'Law 2295/95' (1995)
Decision on deployment of troops abroad: By the Government Council on Foreign Affairs and Defence

AFGHANISTAN
NATO • *Operation Resolute Support* 4

BOSNIA-HERZEGOVINA
EU • EUFOR • *Operation Althea* 1

CYPRUS
Army 950 (ELDYK army); ε200 (officers/NCO seconded to Greek-Cypriot National Guard) (total 1,150);
1 mech bde (1 armd bn, 2 mech inf bn, 1 arty bn); 61 M48A5 MOLF MBT; 80 *Leonidas* APC; 12 M114 arty; 6 M110A2 arty

LEBANON
UN • UNIFIL 46; 1 PCFG

MALI
EU • EUTM Mali 2

MEDITERRANEAN SEA
NATO • SNMG 2: 1 FFGHM; 1 FSGM; 1 PCO
NATO • SNMCMG 2: 1 AOR

SERBIA
NATO • KFOR 112; 1 inf coy
OSCE • Kosovo 3

UKRAINE
OSCE • Ukraine 21

FOREIGN FORCES
United States US European Command: 370; 1 naval base at Makri; 1 naval base at Soudha Bay; 1 air base at Iraklion

Hungary HUN

Hungarian Forint f		2015	2016	2017
GDP	f	33.7tr	35.1tr	
	US$	121bn	117bn	
per capita	US$	12,240	11,903	
Growth	%	2.9	2.0	
Inflation	%	-0.1	0.4	
Def exp [a]	f	316bn		
	US$	1.1bn		
Def bdgt [b]	f	299bn	299bn	
	US$	1.07bn	996m	
US$1=f		279.45	299.90	

[a] NATO definition
[b] Excludes military pensions

Population 9,874,784

Age	0–14	15–19	20–24	25–29	30–64	65 plus
Male	7.6%	2.7%	3.1%	3.2%	24.0%	7.0%
Female	7.2%	2.5%	2.9%	3.1%	25.0%	11.6%

Capabilities
Territorial defence and the ability to participate in NATO and other international operations are central tenets of the 2012 National Military Strategy. This included the medium-term aim of having forces capable of taking part in high-intensity operations. The air force operates the *Gripen* combat aircraft under lease, and Hungary also hosts the multinational C-17 strategic-airlift unit. Elements of its land-systems inventory remain centred on ageing Soviet-era equipment, and replacement schedules appear to be slipping. Hungary coordinates policy with the Czech Republic, Poland and Slovakia in the so-called Visegrád 4 (V4) format, including on defence. The V4 EU Battlegroup was on standby in the first half of 2016 and is scheduled to be on standby again in the second half of 2019. Key acquisition plans include vehicle modernisation, EOD and CBRN capability development and air-defence modernisation. In October 2015, NATO agreed to set up a NATO Force Integration Unit, a small headquarters,

in Hungary. Given that Hungary has also been directly affected by increasing migration pressure, its armed forces have been involved in internal border-control operations, assisting national police forces.

ACTIVE 26,500 (Army 10,300 Air 5,900 Joint 10,300) Paramilitary 12,000

RESERVE 44,000 (Army 35,200 Air 8,800)

ORGANISATIONS BY SERVICE

Hungary's armed forces have reorganised into a joint force.

Land Component 10,300 (incl riverine element)

FORCES BY ROLE
SPECIAL FORCES
1 SF bn
MANOEUVRE
Mechanised
1 (5th) mech inf bde (1 armd recce bn; 3 mech inf bn, 1 cbt engr coy, 1 sigs coy, 1 log bn)
1 (25th) mech inf bde (1 tk bn; 1 mech inf bn, 1 AB bn, 1 arty bn, 1 AT bn, 1 log bn)
COMBAT SUPPORT
1 engr regt
1 EOD/rvn regt
1 CBRN bn
1 sigs regt
COMBAT SERVICE SUPPORT
1 log regt
EQUIPMENT BY TYPE
ARMOURED FIGHTING VEHICLES
MBT 30 T-72
IFV 120 BTR-80A
APC • APC (W) 260 BTR-80
ENGINEERING & MAINTENANCE VEHICLES
AEV BAT-2
ARV BMP-1 VPV; T-54/T-55; VT-55A
VLB BLG-60; MTU; TMM
NBC VEHICLES 24+: 24 K90 CBRN Recce; PSZH-IV CBRN Recce
ANTI-TANK/ANTI-INFRASTRUCTURE
MSL • MANPATS 9K111 *Fagot* (AT-4 *Spigot*); 9K111-1 *Konkurs* (AT-5 *Spandrel*)
ARTILLERY 69
TOWED 152mm 18 D-20
MOR 51: **82mm** 50; **120mm** 1 M-43
PATROL AND COASTAL COMBATANTS • PBR 2
MINE COUNTERMEASURES • MSR 4 *Nestin*

Air Component 5,900

Flying hours   50 hrs/yr

FORCES BY ROLE
FIGHTER/GROUND ATTACK
1 sqn with *Gripen* C/D
TRANSPORT
1 sqn with An-26 *Curl*
TRAINING
1 sqn with Yak-52
ATTACK HELICOPTER
1 sqn with Mi-24 *Hind*
TRANSPORT HELICOPTER
1 sqn with Mi-8 *Hip*; Mi-17 *Hip* H
AIR DEFENCE
1 SAM regt (9 bty with *Mistral*; 3 bty with 2K12 *Kub* (SA-6 *Gainful*))
1 radar regt
EQUIPMENT BY TYPE
AIRCRAFT 13 combat capable
FGA 13: 12 *Gripen* C; 1 *Gripen* D
TPT • Light 4 An-26 *Curl*
TRG 8 Yak-52
HELICOPTERS
ATK 11: 3 Mi-24D *Hind* D; 6 Mi-24V *Hind* E; 2 Mi-24P *Hind* F
MRH 7 Mi-17 *Hip* H
TPT • Medium 13 Mi-8 *Hip*
AIR DEFENCE
SAM • Point-defence 16 2K12 *Kub* (SA-6 *Gainful*); *Mistral*
RADAR 29: 3 RAT-31DL; 6 P-18; 6 SZT-68UM; 14 P-37
AIR-LAUNCHED MISSILES
AAM • IR AIM-9 *Sidewinder*; R-73 (AA-11 *Archer*) **SARH** R-27 (AA-10 *Alamo* A); **ARH** AIM-120C AMRAAM
ASM AGM-65 *Maverick*; 3M11 *Falanga* (AT-2 *Swatter*); 9K114 *Shturm*-V (AT-6 *Spiral*)
BOMBS • Laser-guided *Paveway* II

Paramilitary 12,000

Border Guards 12,000 (to reduce)

Ministry of Interior
FORCES BY ROLE
MANOEUVRE
Other
1 (Budapest) paramilitary district (7 rapid reaction coy)
11 (regt/district) paramilitary regt
EQUIPMENT BY TYPE
ARMOURED FIGHTING VEHICLES
APC • APC (W) 68 BTR-80

Cyber

The National Cyber Security Strategy, coordinating cyber security at the governmental level, is led by the prime minister's office. There is also a National Cyber Defence Forum and a Hungarian Cyber Defence Management Authority within the National Security Authority. In 2013, the defence ministry developed a Military Cyber Defence concept. A Computer Incident Response Capability (MilCIRC) and Military Computer Emergency Response Team (MilCERT) have also been established.

DEPLOYMENT

Legal provisions for foreign deployment:
Legislation: Fundamental Law (2011)
Decision on deployment of troops abroad: Government decides on cross-border troop movements or employment, in the case of NATO (Paragraph 2). For operations not based on NATO or EU decisions, the Fundamental Law gives

parliament the prerogative to decide on the employment of Hungarian armed forces or foreign forces in, or from, Hungarian territory

AFGHANISTAN
NATO • *Operation Resolute Support* 90

BOSNIA-HERZEGOVINA
EU • *Operation Althea* 47

CENTRAL AFRICAN REPUBLIC
UN • MINUSCA 2; 2 obs

CYPRUS
UN • UNFICYP 77; 1 inf pl

IRAQ
Operation Inherent Resolve 139

LEBANON
UN • UNIFIL 4

MALI
EU • EUTM Mali 3

SERBIA
NATO • KFOR 366; 1 inf coy (KTM)
OSCE • Kosovo 3

UGANDA
EU • EUTM Somalia 4

UKRAINE
OSCE • Ukraine 30

WESTERN SAHARA
UN • MINURSO 7 obs

Iceland ISL

Icelandic Krona Kr			2015	2016	2017
GDP		Kr	2.21tr	2.40tr	
		US$	16.7bn	19.4bn	
per capita		US$	50,277	57,889	
Growth		%	4.0	4.9	
Inflation		%	1.6	1.7	
Sy Bdgt [a]		Kr	3.97bn	3.81bn	
		US$	30m	31m	
US$1=Kr			131.92	123.20	

[a] Coast Guard budget

Population 335,878

Age	0–14	15–19	20–24	25–29	30–64	65 plus
Male	10.4%	3.3%	3.6%	3.7%	22.5%	6.6%
Female	10.0%	3.3%	3.5%	3.5%	22.1%	7.5%

Capabilities

Iceland is a NATO member but maintains only a coastguard service and no armed forces. Iceland hosts NATO and regional partners for the Icelandic Air Policing mission, exercises, transits and naval task groups. Significant increases in Russian air and naval activities in the Atlantic and close to NATO airspace have led to complaints from Iceland that aircraft could threaten civil flights. The US Navy was reportedly seeking funds in 2017 to upgrade facilities at Keflavik air base. The base closed in 2006 but the US plans to refurbish the facilities in order to enable operations by P-8 *Poseidon* aircraft from the strategically important site. It was reported that US officials proposed the re-establishment of regular patrols from the base, although on a rotational basis.

ACTIVE NIL Paramilitary 250

ORGANISATIONS BY SERVICE

Paramilitary

Iceland Coast Guard 250
EQUIPMENT BY TYPE
PATROL AND COASTAL COMBATANTS 3
  PSOH: 2 *Aegir*
  PSO 1 *Thor*
LOGISTICS AND SUPPORT • AGS 1 *Baldur*
AIRCRAFT • TPT • Light 1 DHC-8-300 (MP)
HELICOPTERS
  TPT • Medium 2 AS332L1 *Super Puma*

FOREIGN FORCES

Czech Republic Iceland Air Policing: 5 *Gripen* C (Aircraft and personnel from various NATO members on a rotating basis)

Ireland IRL

Euro €			2015	2016	2017
GDP		€	256bn	276bn	
		US$	284bn	308bn	
per capita		US$	61,206	65,871	
Growth		%	26.3	4.9	
Inflation		%	-0.0	0.3	
Def bdgt [a]		€	899m	898m	921m
		US$	997m	1.00bn	
US$1=€			0.90	0.90	

[a] Includes military pensions and capital expenditure

Population 4,952,473

Age	0–14	15–19	20–24	25–29	30–64	65 plus
Male	11.0%	3.1%	2.9%	3.2%	23.9%	5.9%
Female	10.5%	3.0%	2.8%	3.2%	23.6%	6.9%

Capabilities

The armed forces' core missions remain defending the state against armed aggression, although the 2015 white paper broadened the scope of the national-security risk assessment beyond traditional military and paramilitary threats. The new assessment lists as priority threats inter- and intra-state conflict, cyber attacks, terrorism, emergencies and natural disasters as well as espionage and transnational organised crime. After the white paper, Dublin identified 88 projects to be completed over a ten-year period. Key priorities after 2017 include a mid-life upgrade for the army's *Piranha* armoured personnel carriers and the replacement of the air corps' Cessnas with three larger utility aircraft equipped for ISR tasks. These aircraft will primarily operate in the ISR and special-operations-forces roles, while also being capable of MEDEVAC and logistics support. Ireland is developing a cyber capability and a National Cyber Security Centre has been established. A small number of defence-force personnel are attached to the CSIRT-IE team, and the principal focus of the defence forces will remain network security. The army maintains substantial EOD capabilities. Ireland continues to contribute to multinational peacekeeping operations in the Golan Heights and Lebanon, and has deployed an offshore-patrol vessel to the EU *Operation Sophia* mission in the Mediterranean.

ACTIVE 9,100 (Army 7,300 Navy 1,100 Air 700)

RESERVE 2,630 (Army 2,400 Navy 200 Air 30)

ORGANISATIONS BY SERVICE

Army 7,300
FORCES BY ROLE
SPECIAL FORCES
  1 ranger coy
MANOEUVRE
  Reconnaissance
  1 armd recce sqn
  Mechanised
  1 mech inf coy
  Light
  1 inf bde (1 cav recce sqn, 4 inf bn, 1 arty regt (3 fd arty bty, 1 AD bty), 1 fd engr coy, 1 sigs coy, 1 MP coy, 1 tpt coy)
  1 inf bde (1 cav recce sqn, 3 inf bn, 1 arty regt (3 fd arty bty, 1 AD bty), 1 fd engr coy, 1 sigs coy, 1 MP coy, 1 tpt coy)
EQUIPMENT BY TYPE
ARMOURED FIGHTING VEHICLES
  APC 107
    APC (W) 80: 56 *Piranha* III; 24 *Piranha* IIIH
    PPV 27 RG-32M
ANTI-TANK/ANTI-INFRASTURCTURE
  MSL • MANPATS FGM-148 *Javelin*
  RCL 84mm *Carl Gustav*
ARTILLERY 298
  TOWED 23: **105mm** 23: 17 L118 Light Gun; 6 L119 Light Gun
  MOR 275: **81mm** 180; **120mm** 95
AIR DEFENCE
  SAM • Point-defence RBS-70
  GUNS • TOWED **40mm** 32 L/70 each with 8 *Flycatcher*

Reserves 2,400 reservists
FORCES BY ROLE
MANOEUVRE
  Reconnaissance
  1 (integrated) armd recce sqn
  2 (integrated) cav sqn
  Mechanised
  1 (integrated) mech inf coy
  Light
  14 (integrated) inf coy
COMBAT SUPPORT
  4 (integrated) arty bty
  2 engr gp
  2 MP coy
COMBAT SERVICE SUPPORT
  2 med det
  2 tpt coy

Naval Service 1,100
EQUIPMENT BY TYPE
PATROL AND COASTAL COMBATANTS 9
  PSOH 1 *Eithne* with 1 57mm gun
  PSO 5: 2 *Roisin* with 1 76mm gun; 3 *Samuel Beckett* with 1 76mm gun
  PCO 2 *Orla* (ex-UK *Peacock*) with 1 76mm gun
LOGISTICS AND SUPPORT 2
  AXS 2

Air Corps 700
2 ops wg; 2 spt wg; 1 trg wg; 1 comms and info sqn
EQUIPMENT BY TYPE
AIRCRAFT
  MP 2 CN-235 MPA
  TPT • **Light** 6: 5 Cessna FR-172H; 1 Learjet 45 (VIP)
  TRG 7 PC-9M
HELICOPTERS:
  MRH 6 AW139
  TPT • **Light** 2 H135 (incl trg/medevac)

Cyber
The Department of Communications, Energy and Natural Resources has lead responsibilities relating to cyber security, and established a National Cyber Security Centre (NCSC) to assist in identifying and protecting Ireland from cyber attacks. The department has produced a Cyber Security Strategy 2015–17, which says that 'the Defence Forces maintains a capability in the area of cyber security for the purpose of protecting its own networks and users'.

DEPLOYMENT
Legal provisions for foreign deployment:
Constitution: Codified constitution (1937)
Specific legislation: 'Defence (Amendment) Act' 2006
Decision on deployment of troops abroad: Requires a) the authorisation of the operation by the UNSC or UNGA; b) the approval of the Irish government; and c) the approval of parliament, in accordance with Irish law. There is no requirement for parliamentary approval for dispatch as part of an international force where that force is unarmed or where the contingent does not exceed twelve members. Government approval is necessary for the deployment of Irish personnel for training, participation in exercises abroad; monitoring, observation, advisory or reconnaissance missions; and humanitarian operations in response to actual or potential disasters or emergencies

ALBANIA
OSCE • Albania 1

BOSNIA-HERZEGOVINA
EU • EUFOR • *Operation Althea* 7
OSCE • Bosnia and Herzegovina 4

CÔTE D'IVOIRE
UN • UNOCI 2 obs

DEMOCRATIC REPUBLIC OF THE CONGO
UN • MONUSCO 3

LEBANON
UN • UNIFIL 218; elm 1 mech inf bn

MALI
EU • EUTM Mali 10

MIDDLE EAST
UN • UNTSO 11 obs

SERBIA
NATO • KFOR 12
OSCE • Kosovo 3

SYRIA/ISRAEL
UN • UNDOF 136; 1 inf coy

UKRAINE
OSCE • Ukraine 14

WESTERN SAHARA
UN • MINURSO 3 obs

Italy ITA

Euro €		2015	2016	2017
GDP	€	1.64tr	1.66tr	
	US$	1.82tr	1.85tr	
per capita	US$	29,867	30,294	
Growth	%	0.8	0.8	
Inflation	%	0.1	-0.1	
Def exp [a]	€	17.6bn		
	US$	19.6bn		
Def bdgt [b]	€	19.4bn	20.0bn	19.3bn
	US$	21.5bn	22.3bn	
US$1=€		0.90	0.90	

[a] NATO definition
[b] Includes military pensions

Population 62,007,540

Age	0–14	15–19	20–24	25–29	30–64	65 plus
Male	7.0%	2.4%	2.5%	2.7%	24.5%	9.2%
Female	6.7%	2.3%	2.5%	2.7%	25.3%	12.2%

Capabilities

Italy's White Paper on International Security and Defence, published in April 2015, called for a review of the armed forces' organisations, personnel and command structure and equipment. Related plans were expected to be published in a strategic defence review by the end of 2016. The 2015 white paper's planned changes include reducing bureaucratic and upper-echelon personnel in favour of joint solutions between the services. Continued spending reductions looked set to continue in the short term. Cuts in defence spending have had negative effects on equipment maintenance and training. The expected retirement of much of the naval fleet over the next ten years has triggered a long-term replacement plan, and in 2015 the navy received a funding boost to this end. In December 2015, the Italian Air Force took delivery of its first F-35A combat aircraft. But the planned acquisition of a new SIGINT aircraft was put on hold, leaving the air force with a capability gap. Italy has an advanced defence industry: Leonardo is headquartered there, and the country hosts Europe's F-35 assembly facility, the only facility of its type outside of the US, which also acts as the central European hub for maintenance of the aircraft. Italy produces many of its armoured vehicles domestically and is currently in the process of upgrading its *Centauro*s with a new 120mm gun and upgraded armour, as well as purchasing a family of vehicles based on the *Freccia* infantry fighting vehicle. Italy continues to support NATO operations in Afghanistan, maintaining a training and advisory presence in Herat, and Italian forces have supported operations against the Islamic State in Iraq. Maritime deployments have been aimed at countering terrorism and human trafficking, as well as search and rescue in the Mediterranean. Italy is the lead nation in the EUNAVFOR–MED force, which is headquartered in Rome. The country also takes part in NATO exercises and air-policing missions.

ACTIVE 174,500 (Army 102,200 Navy 30,400 Air 41,900) **Paramilitary 182,350**

RESERVES 18,300 (Army 13,400 Navy 4,900)

ORGANISATIONS BY SERVICE

Space
EQUIPMENT BY TYPE
SATELLITES 8
  COMMUNICATIONS 4: 1 *Athena-Fidus* (also used by FRA); 3 *Sicral*
  ISR 4 *Cosmo* (*Skymed*)

Army 102,200
Regt are bn sized
FORCES BY ROLE
COMMAND
  1 (NRDC-ITA) corps HQ (1 spt bde, 1 sigs regt, 1 spt regt)
MANOEUVRE
  Mechanised
  1 (*Friuli*) div (1 (*Ariete*) armd bde (1 cav regt, 2 tk regt, 1 mech inf regt, 1 SP arty regt, 1 cbt engr regt, 1 log regt); 1 (*Pozzuolo del Friuli*) cav bde (1 cav regt, 1 air mob regt, 1 amph regt, 1 arty regt, 1 cbt engr regt, 1 log regt, 2 avn regt)
  1 (*Acqui*) div (1 (*Pinerolo*) mech bde (3 mech inf regt, 1 SP arty regt, 1 cbt engr regt); 1 (*Granatieri*) mech bde

(1 cav regt, 1 mech inf regt); 1 (*Garibaldi Bersaglieri*) mech bde (1 cav regt, 1 tk regt, 2 mech inf regt, 1 SP arty regt, 1 cbt engr regt); 1 (*Aosta*) mech bde (1 cav regt, 3 mech inf regt, 1 SP arty regt, 1 cbt engr regt); 1 (*Sassari*) lt mech bde (3 mech inf regt, 1 cbt engr regt))

Mountain
1 (*Tridentina*) mtn div (2 mtn bde (1 cav regt, 3 mtn inf regt, 1 arty regt, 1 mtn cbt engr regt, 1 spt bn, 1 log regt))

Air Manoeuvre
1 (*Folgore*) AB bde (1 cav regt, 3 para regt, 1 arty regt, 1 cbt engr regt, 1 log regt)

COMBAT SUPPORT
1 arty comd (3 arty regt, 1 NBC regt)
1 AD comd (2 SAM regt, 1 ADA regt)
1 engr comd (2 engr regt, 1 ptn br regt, 1 CIMIC regt)
1 EW/sigs comd (1 EW/ISR bde (1 EW regt, 1 int regt, 1 STA regt); 1 sigs bde with (7 sigs regt))

COMBAT SERVICE SUPPORT
1 log comd (2 log regt, 1 med unit)

HELICOPTER
1 hel bde (3 hel regt)

EQUIPMENT BY TYPE
ARMOURED FIGHTING VEHICLES
 MBT 160 C1 *Ariete*
 ASLT 259 B1 *Centauro*
 IFV 355: 200 VCC-80 *Dardo*; 155 VBM 8×8 *Freccia*
 APC 890
  APC (T) 361: 246 Bv-206; 115 M113 (incl variants)
  APC (W) 529 *Puma*
 AUV 10 *Cougar*; IVECO LMV
 AAV 16: 14 AAVP-7; 1 AAVC-7; 1 AAVR-7
ENGINEERING & MAINTENANCE VEHICLES
 AEV 40 *Leopard* 1; M113
 ARV 137 *Leopard* 1
 VLB 64 *Biber*
 MW 9: 6 *Buffalo*; 3 *Miniflail*
NBC VEHICLES 14 VAB NRBC
ANTI-TANK/ANTI-INFRASTRUCTURE
 MSL • MANPATS *Spike*; *Milan*
 RCL 80mm *Folgore*
ARTILLERY 971
 SP 155mm 192: 124 M109L; 68 PzH 2000
 TOWED 155mm 163 FH-70
 MRL 227mm 21 MLRS
 MOR 595: **81mm** 270: 212 Brandt; 58 Expal **120mm** 325: 183 Brandt; 142 RT-61 (RT-F1)
AIRCRAFT • TPT • Light 6: 3 Do-228 (ACTL-1); 3 P-180 *Avanti*
HELICOPTERS
 ATK 43 AW129CBT *Mangusta*
 MRH 15 Bell 412 (AB-412) *Twin Huey*
 TPT 131: **Heavy** 19: 13 CH-47C *Chinook*; 6 CH-47F *Chinook*; **Medium** 31 NH90 TTH; **Light** 81: 6 AW109; 34 Bell 205 (AB-205); 26 Bell 206 *Jet Ranger* (AB-206); 15 Bell 212 (AB-212)
AIR DEFENCE
 SAM
  Long-range 16 SAMP/T
  Short-range 32 *Skyguard*/*Aspide*
  Point-range FIM-92 *Stinger*
 GUNS • SP 25mm 64 SIDAM

Navy 30,400
EQUIPMENT BY TYPE
SUBMARINES • TACTICAL • SSK 7:
 4 *Pelosi* (imp *Sauro*, 3rd and 4th series) with 6 single 533mm TT with Type-A-184 HWT
 3 *Salvatore Todaro* (Type-U212A) with 6 single 533mm TT with Type-A-184 HWT/DM2A4 HWT
PRINCIPAL SURFACE COMBATANTS 19
 AIRCRAFT CARRIERS • CVS 2:
  1 *Cavour* with 4 octuple VLS with *Aster* 15 SAM, 2 76mm guns (capacity mixed air group of 20 AV-8B *Harrier* II; AW101 *Merlin*; NH90; Bell 212)
  1 *G. Garibaldi* with 2 octuple *Albatros* lnchr with *Aspide* SAM, 2 triple 324mm ASTT with Mk46 LWT (capacity mixed air group of 18 AV-8B *Harrier* II; AW101 *Merlin*; NH90; Bell 212)
 DESTROYERS • DDGHM 9:
  2 *Andrea Doria* with 2 quad lnchr with *Otomat* Mk2A AShM, 1 48-cell VLS with *Aster* 15/*Aster* 30 SAM, 2 single 324mm ASTT with MU90 LWT, 3 76mm guns (capacity 1 AW101 *Merlin*/NH90 hel)
  2 *Luigi Durand de la Penne* (ex-*Animoso*) with 2 quad lnchr with *Otomat* Mk 2A AShM/*Milas* A/S, 1 Mk13 GMLS with SM-1MR SAM, 1 octuple *Albatros* lnchr with *Aspide* SAM, 2 triple 324mm ASTT with Mk46 LWT, 1 127mm gun, 3 76mm guns (capacity 1 NH90 or 2 Bell 212 (AB-212) hel)
  1 *Bergamini* (GP) with 2 quad lnchr with *Otomat* Mk2A AShM, 1 16-cell VLS with *Aster* 15/*Aster* 30 SAM, 2 triple 324mm ASTT with MU90 LWT, 1 127mm gun, 1 76mm gun (capacity 2 AW101/NH90 hel)
  4 *Bergamini* (ASW) with 2 quad lnchr with *Otomat* Mk2A AShM, 1 16-cell VLS with *Aster* 15/*Aster* 30 SAM, 2 triple 324mm ASTT with MU90 LWT, 2 76mm gun (capacity 2 AW101/NH90 hel)
 FRIGATES • FFGHM 8:
  2 *Artigliere* with 8 single lnchr with *Otomat* Mk 2 AShM, 1 octuple *Albatros* lnchr with *Aspide* SAM, 1 127mm gun, (capacity 1 Bell 212 (AB-212) hel)
  6 *Maestrale* with 4 single lnchr with *Otomat* Mk2 AShM, 1 octuple *Albatros* lnchr with *Aspide* SAM, 2 triple 324mm ASTT with Mk46 LWT, 1 127mm gun (capacity 1 NH90 or 2 Bell 212 (AB-212) hel)
PATROL AND COASTAL COMBATANTS 18
 CORVETTES 4
  FSM 4 *Minerva* with 1 octuple *Albatros* lnchr with *Aspide* SAM, 1 76mm gun
 PSOH 6:
  4 *Comandante Cigala Fuligosi* with 1 76mm gun (capacity 1 Bell 212 (AB-212)/NH90 hel)
  2 *Comandante Cigala Fuligosi* (capacity 1 Bell 212 (AB-212) or NH90 hel)
 PCO 4 *Cassiopea* with 1 76mm gun (capacity 1 Bell 212 (AB-212) hel)
 PB 4 *Esploratore*
MINE WARFARE • MINE COUNTERMEASURES 10
 MHO 10: 8 *Gaeta*; 2 *Lerici*

AMPHIBIOUS
  PRINCIPAL AMPHIBIOUS SHIPS 3
    LHD 2:
      2 *San Giorgio* with 1 76mm gun (capacity 3-4 AW101/ NH90/Bell 212; 3 LCM 2 LCVP; 30 trucks; 36 APC (T); 350 troops)
    LPD 1:
      1 *San Giusto* with 1 76mm gun (capacity 2 AW101 Merlin/ NH90/Bell 212; 3 LCM 2 LCVP; 30 trucks; 36 APC (T); 350 troops)
  LANDING CRAFT 24: 15 **LCVP**; 9 **LCM**
LOGISTICS AND SUPPORT 62
  ABU 5 *Ponza*
  AFD 9
  AGE 2: 1 *Vincenzo Martellota*; 1 *Raffaele Rosseti*
  AGI 1 *Elettra*
  AGOR 1 *Leonardo* (coastal)
  AGS 3: 1 *Ammiraglio Magnaghi* with 1 hel landing platform; 2 *Aretusa* (coastal)
  AKSL 6 *Gorgona*
  AORH 3: 1 *Etna* with 1 76mm gun (capacity 1 AW101/ NH90/Bell 212 hel); 2 *Stromboli* with 1 76mm gun (capacity 1 AW101/NH90 hel)
  AOT 7 *Depoli*
  ARSH 1 *Anteo* (capacity 1 Bell 212 (AB-212) hel)
  ATS 6 *Ciclope*
  AWT 7: 1 *Bormida*; 2 *Simeto*; 4 *Panarea*
  AXL 3 *Aragosta*
  AXS 8: 1 *Amerigo Vespucci*; 1 *Palinuro*; 1 *Italia*; 5 *Caroly*

Naval Aviation 2,200

FORCES BY ROLE
FIGHTER/GROUND ATTACK
  1 sqn with AV-8B *Harrier* II; TAV-8B *Harrier* II
ANTI-SUBMARINE WARFARE/TRANSPORT
  5 sqn with AW101 ASW *Merlin*; Bell 212 ASW (AB-212AS); Bell 212 (AB-212); NH90 NFH
MARITIME PATROL
  1 flt with P-180
AIRBORNE EARLY WANRING & CONTROL
  1 flt with AW101 AEW *Merlin*
EQUIPMENT BY TYPE
AIRCRAFT 16 combat capable
  FGA 16: 14 AV-8B *Harrier* II; 2 TAV-8B *Harrier* II
  MP 3 P-180
HELICOPTERS
  ASW 39: 10 AW101 ASW *Merlin*; 12 Bell 212 ASW; 17 NH90 NFH
  AEW 4 AW101 AEW *Merlin*
  TPT 14: **Medium** 8 AW101 *Merlin*; **Light** 6 Bell 212 (AB-212)
AIR-LAUNCHED MISSILES
  AAM • **IR** AIM-9L *Sidewinder*; **ARH** AIM-120 AMRAAM
  ASM AGM-65 *Maverick*
  AShM *Marte* Mk 2/S

Marines 3,000

FORCES BY ROLE
MANOEUVRE
  Amphibious
    1 mne regt (1 SF coy, 1 mne bn, 1 cbt spt bn, 1 log bn)
    1 (boarding) mne regt (2 mne bn)
    1 landing craft gp
  Other
    1 sy regt (3 sy bn)
EQUIPMENT BY TYPE
ARMOURED FIGHTING VEHICLES
  APC (T) 24 VCC-1
  AAV 19: 15 AAVP-7; 3 AAVC-7; 1 AAVR-7
ENGINEERING & MAINTENANCE VEHICLES
  ARV 1 AAV-7RAI
ANTI-TANK/ANTI-INFRASTRUCTURE
  MSL• MANPATS *Milan*; *Spike*
ARTILLERY
  MOR 23: **81mm** 13 Brandt; **120mm** 10 Brandt
AIR DEFENCE • **SAM** • **Point-defence** FIM-92 *Stinger*

Air Force 41,900

FORCES BY ROLE
FIGHTER
  4 sqn with Eurofighter *Typhoon*
FIGHTER/GROUND ATTACK
  1 sqn with AMX *Ghibli*
  1 (SEAD/EW) sqn with Tornado ECR
  2 sqn with Tornado IDS
FIGHTER/GROUND ATTACK/ISR
  1 sqn with AMX *Ghibli*
MARITIME PATROL
  1 sqn (opcon Navy) with BR1150 *Atlantic*
TANKER/TRANSPORT
  1 sqn with KC-767A
COMBAT SEARCH & RESCUE
  1 sqn with AB-212 ICO
SEARCH & RESCUE
  1 wg with AW139 (HH-139A); Bell 212 (HH-212); HH-3F *Pelican*
TRANSPORT
  2 (VIP) sqn with A319CJ; AW139 (VH-139A); *Falcon* 50; *Falcon* 900 *Easy*; *Falcon* 900EX; SH-3D *Sea King*
  2 sqn with C-130J/C-130J-30/KC-130J *Hercules*
  1 sqn with C-27J *Spartan*
  1 (calibration) sqn with P-180 *Avanti*
TRAINING
  1 OCU sqn with Eurofighter *Typhoon*
  1 sqn with MB-339PAN (aerobatic team)
  1 sqn with MD-500D/E (NH-500D/E)
  1 OCU sqn with Tornado
  1 OCU sqn with AMX-T *Ghibli*
  1 sqn with MB-339A
  1 sqn with MB-339CD*
  1 sqn with SF-260EA, 3 P2006T (T-2006A)
ISR UAV
  1 sqn with MQ-9A *Reaper*; RQ-1B *Predator*
AIR DEFENCE
  2 bty with *Spada*
EQUIPMENT BY TYPE
AIRCRAFT 252 combat capable
  FTR 82 Eurofighter *Typhoon*
  FGA 74: 63 AMX *Ghibli*; 8 AMX-T *Ghibli*; 3 F-35A *Lightning* II (in test)
  ATK 53 Tornado IDS

ATK/EW 15 *Tornado* ECR*
ASW 6 BR1150 *Atlantic*
SIGINT 1 AML Gulfstream III
TKR/TPT 6: 4 KC-767A; 2 KC-130J *Hercules*
TPT 66: **Medium** 31: 9 C-130J *Hercules*; 10 C-130J-30 *Hercules*; 12 C-27J *Spartan*; **Light** 25: 15 P-180 *Avanti*; 10 S-208 (liaison); **PAX** 11: 1 A340-541; 3 A319CJ; 2 *Falcon* 50 (VIP); 2 *Falcon* 900 *Easy*; 3 *Falcon* 900EX (VIP)
TRG 103: 3 M-346; 21 MB-339A; 28 MB-339CD*; 21 MB-339PAN (aerobatics); 30 SF-260EA
HELICOPTERS
MRH 58: 10 AW139 (HH-139A/VH-139A); 2 MD-500D (NH-500D); 46 MD-500E (NH-500E)
CSAR 4 AW101 (HH-101A)
SAR 12 HH-3F *Pelican*
TPT 31: **Medium** 2 SH-3D *Sea King* (liaison/VIP); **Light** 29 Bell 212 (HH-212)/AB-212 ICO
UNMANNED AERIAL VEHICLES • ISR • **Heavy** 14: 9 MQ-9A *Reaper*; 5 RQ-1B *Predator*
AIR DEFENCE • SAM • **Short** SPADA
AIR-LAUNCHED MISSILES
AAM • IR AIM-9L *Sidewinder*; IIR IRIS-T; ARH AIM-120 AMRAAM
ARM AGM-88 HARM
LACM SCALP EG/*Storm Shadow*
BOMBS
Laser-guided/GPS: Enhanced *Paveway* II; Enhanced *Paveway* III

Joint Special Forces Command (COFS)

Army
FORCES BY ROLE
SPECIAL FORCES
 1 SF regt (9th *Assalto paracadutisti*)
 1 STA regt
 1 ranger regt (4th *Alpini paracadutisti*)
COMBAT SUPPORT
 1 psyops regt
TRANSPORT HELICOPTER
 1 spec ops hel regt

Navy (COMSUBIN)
FORCES BY ROLE
SPECIAL FORCES
 1 SF gp (GOI)
 1 diving gp (GOS)

Air Force
FORCES BY ROLE
SPECIAL FORCES
 1 wg (sqn) (17th *Stormo Incursori*)

Paramilitary

Carabinieri
FORCES BY ROLE
SPECIAL FORCES
 1 spec ops gp (GIS)

Paramilitary 182,350

Carabinieri 103,750
The Carabinieri are organisationally under the MoD. They are a separate service in the Italian Armed Forces as well as a police force with judicial competence

Mobile and Specialised Branch
FORCES BY ROLE
MANOEUVRE
 Other
  1 (mobile) paramilitary div (1 bde (1st) with (1 horsed cav regt, 11 mobile bn); 1 bde (2nd) with (1 (1st) AB regt, 2 (7th & 13th) mobile regt))
HELICOPTER
 1 hel gp
EQUIPMENT BY TYPE
ARMOURED FIGHTING VEHICLES
 APC • APC (T) 3 VCC-2
PATROL AND COASTAL COMBATANTS • PB 69
AIRCRAFT • TPT • **Light:** 1 P-180 *Avanti*
HELICOPTERS
 MRH 24 Bell 412 (AB-412)
 TPT • **Light** 19 AW109

Customs 68,100
(Servizio Navale Guardia Di Finanza)
EQUIPMENT BY TYPE
PATROL AND COASTAL COMBATANTS 179
 PCF 1 *Antonio Zara*
 PBF 146: 19 *Bigliani*; 24 *Corrubia*; 9 *Mazzei*; 62 V-2000; 32 V-5000/V-6000
 PB 32: 24 *Buratti*; 8 *Meatini*
LOGISTICS AND SUPPORT • AX 1 *Giorgio Cini*

Coast Guard 10,500
(Guardia Costiera – Capitanerie Di Porto)
EQUIPMENT BY TYPE
PATROL AND COASTAL COMBATANTS 332
 PCO 3: 2 *Dattilo*; 1 *Gregoretti*
 PCC 32: 3 *Diciotti*; 1 *Saettia*; 22 200-class; 6 400-class
 PB 297: 21 300-class; 3 454-class; 72 500-class; 12 600-class; 47 700-class; 94 800-class; 48 2000-class
AIRCRAFT • MP 6: 3 ATR-42 MP *Surveyor*, 1 P-180GC; 2 PL-166-DL3
HELICOPTERS • MRH 11: 7 AW139; 4 Bell 412SP (AB-412SP *Griffin*)

Cyber
Overall responsibility for cyber security rests with the presidency of the Council of Ministers and the Inter-Ministerial Situation and Planning Group, which includes, among others, representatives from the defence, interior and foreign-affairs ministries. A Joint Integrated Concept on Computer Network Operations was approved in 2009 and, in 2014, a Joint Interagency Concept on Cyberwarfare. The National Strategic Framework for Cyberspace Security, released in 2013, says that the defence ministry 'plans, executes and sustains Computer Network Operations (CNO) in the cyber domain in order to prevent, localize

and defend (actively and in-depth), oppose and neutralise all threats and/or hostile actions in the cyber domain'.

DEPLOYMENT

Legal provisions for foreign deployment:
Constitution: Codified constitution (1949)
Decision on deployment of troops abroad: By the government upon approval by the parliament

AFGHANISTAN
NATO • *Operation Resolute Support* 827; 1 mech inf bde HQ; 1 mech inf regt(-); 1 avn bn(-); AW129 *Mangusta*; CH-47; NH90

ALBANIA
OSCE • Albania 1

BOSNIA-HERZEGOVINA
EU • EUFOR • *Operation Althea* 5
OSCE • Bosnia and Herzegovina 4

EGYPT
MFO 78; 3 PB

GULF OF ADEN & INDIAN OCEAN
EU • *Operation Atalanta* 1 DDGHM

IRAQ
Operation Inherent Resolve 1,120; 1 inf regt; 1 hel sqn with 4 AW129 *Mangusta*; 4 NH90

KUWAIT
Operation Inherent Resolve 4 AMX; 2 MQ-9A *Reaper*; 1 KC-767A

LEBANON
UN • UNIFIL 1,112; 1 cav bde HQ; 1 cav BG; 1 hel bn; 1 engr coy; 1 sigs coy

LIBYA
UN • UNSMIL 300; 1 inf coy; 1 log unit; 1 fd hospital

MALI
EU • EUTM Mali 10
UN • MINUSMA 1

MEDITERRANEAN SEA
EU • EU NAVFOR MED: 1 CVS
NATO • SNMG 2: 1 FFGHM
NATO • SNMCMG 2: 1 MHO

SERBIA
NATO • KFOR 542; 1 inf BG HQ; 1 Carabinieri unit
OSCE • Kosovo 14

TURKEY
NATO • *Operation Active Fence*: 1 SAM bty with SAMP/T

UGANDA
EU • EUTM Somalia 112

UKRAINE
OSCE • Ukraine 25

FOREIGN FORCES

United States US European Command: 12,550
Army 4,550; 1 AB IBCT(-)
Navy 3,950; 1 HQ (US Navy Europe (USNAVEUR)) at Naples; 1 HQ (6th Fleet) at Gaeta; 1 ASW Sqn with 4 P-8A *Poseidon* at Sigonella
USAF 3,700; 1 ftr wg with 2 ftr sqn with 21 F-16C/D *Fighting Falcon* at Aviano
USMC 300

Latvia LVA

Euro €		2015	2016	2017
GDP	€	24.3bn	25.0bn	
	US$	27.0bn	27.9bn	
per capita	US$	13,573	14,141	
Growth	%	2.7	2.5	
Inflation	%	0.2	0.2	
Def exp [a]	€	254m		
	US$	281m		
Def bdgt [b]	€	255m	368m	449m
	US$	283m	411m	
FMA (US)	US$	1.5m	2m	
US$1= €		0.90	0.90	

[a] NATO definition
[b] Includes military pensions

Population   1,965,686

Ethnic groups: Latvian 62% Russian 27% Belarussian 3% Polish 2.2%

Age	0–14	15–19	20–24	25–29	30–64	65 plus
Male	7.7%	2.2%	2.9%	3.8%	23.1%	6.3%
Female	7.3%	2.1%	2.7%	3.7%	25.2%	13.0%

Capabilities

In common with other Baltic states, Latvia has been concerned by rising tensions over the conflict in eastern Ukraine. Latvia's armed forces are largely structured around ground troops, focused on NATO standardisation and supporting NATO deployments and partnering with neighbours. A new national-defence concept was proposed in June 2016. Investment in armoured vehicles has delivered new capabilities to the Latvian Army in the shape of 123 second-hand British tracked armoured vehicles; deliveries of these began in 2015. Latvia has also purchased anti-tank weapons and logistics vehicles as part of a wider investment in the army. Latvia has pledged to increase the defence budget to meet the NATO spending target of 2% of GDP on defence. An order for long-range surveillance radars will upgrade Latvia's air-defence capability as part of a wider plan to modernise forces. NATO's Force Integration Unit was activated in Latvia in September 2015, and Latvia will host one of the rotational battlegroups (led by Canada) as part of NATO's Enhanced Forward Presence. Latvia took part in multiple exercises during 2016, including *Anakonda 16* in Poland.

ACTIVE 5,310 (Army 1,250 Navy 550 Air 310 Joint Staff 2,600 National Guard 600)
RESERVE 7,850 (National Guard 7,850)

ORGANISATIONS BY SERVICE

Joint 2,600
FORCES BY ROLE
SPECIAL FORCES
  1 SF unit
COMBAT SUPPORT
  1 MP bn

Army 1,250
FORCES BY ROLE
MANOEUVRE
  Light
    1 inf bde (2 inf bn, 1 cbt spt bn HQ, 1 CSS bn HQ)

National Guard 600; 7,850 part-time (8,450 total)
FORCES BY ROLE
MANOEUVRE
  Light
    11 inf bn
COMBAT SUPPORT
  1 arty bn
  1 AD bn
  1 engr bn
  1 NBC bn
COMBAT SERVICE SUPPORT
  3 spt bn
EQUIPMENT BY TYPE
ARMOURED FIGHTING VEHICLES
  MBT 3 T-55 (trg)
  RECCE 9+ FV107 *Scimitar*
  AUV 8+: 6+ FV103 *Spartan*; 2+ FV105 *Sultan* (CP)
ANTI-TANK/ANTI-INFRASTRUCTURE
  MANPATS *Spike*-LR
  RCL **84mm** *Carl Gustav*; **90mm** 130 Pvpj 1110
ARTILLERY 76
  TOWED **100mm** 23 K-53
  MOR 53: **81mm** 28 L16; **120mm** 25 M120

Navy 550 (incl Coast Guard)
Naval Forces Flotilla separated into an MCM squadron and a patrol-boat squadron. LVA, EST and LTU have set up a joint naval unit, BALTRON, with bases at Liepaja, Riga, Ventspils (LVA), Tallinn (EST), Klaipeda (LTU). Each nation contributes 1–2 MCMVs
EQUIPMENT BY TYPE
PATROL AND COASTAL COMBATANTS 5
  PB 5 *Skrunda* (GER *Swath*)
MINE WARFARE • MINE COUNTERMEASURES 6
  MHO 5 *Imanta* (ex-NLD *Alkmaar/Tripartite*)
  MCCS 1 *Vidar* (ex-NOR)
LOGISTICS AND SUPPORT 1
  AXL 1 *Varonis* (comd and spt ship, ex-NLD)

Coast Guard
Under command of the Latvian Naval Forces
EQUIPMENT BY TYPE
PATROL AND COASTAL COMBATANTS
  PB 6: 1 *Astra*; 5 KBV 236 (ex-SWE)

Air Force 310
Main tasks are airspace control and defence, maritime and land SAR and air transportation.
FORCES BY ROLE
TRANSPORT
  1 (mixed) tpt sqn with An-2 *Colt*; Mi-17 *Hip* H; PZL Mi-2 *Hoplite*
AIR DEFENCE
  1 AD bn
  1 radar sqn (radar/air ctrl)
AIRCRAFT • TPT • Light 4 An-2 *Colt*
HELICOPTERS
  MRH 4 Mi-17 *Hip* H
  TPT • Light 2 PZL Mi-2 *Hoplite*
AIR DEFENCE
  SAM • Point-defence RBS-70
  GUNS • TOWED **40mm** 24 L/70

Paramilitary

State Border Guard
EQUIPMENT BY TYPE
PATROL AND COASTAL COMBATANTS
  PB 3: 1 *Valpas* (ex-FIN); 1 *Lokki* (ex-FIN); 1 *Randa*

Cyber
The Cyber Security Strategy of Latvia was published in 2014. Latvia established military CERT unit in early 2016. The unit cooperates closely with the national CERT, participates in international exercises and increases cyber-defence capabilities. A Cyber Defence Unit has been operational in the National Guard since 2014. Its main role is to ensure the formation of reserve cyber-defence capabilities, which could be used both for civil and military tasks.

DEPLOYMENT

Legal provisions for foreign deployment:
Constitution: Codified constitution (1922)
Specific legislation: 'Law on Participation of the National Armed Forces of Latvia in International Operations' (1995) (Annex of 21 Jan 2009 allows Latvian armed forces to take part in quick-response units formed by NATO/EU)
Decision on deployment of troops abroad: a) By parliament (Section 5 I of the 1995 'Law on Participation', in combination with Art. 73 of constitution); b) by cabinet, for rescue or humanitarian operations (Section 5 II of the 1995 law) or military exercises in non-NATO states (Section 9 of the 1995 law); c) by defence minister for rescue and humanitarian-aid operations in NATO/EU states. Latvian units can be transferred under the control of an international organisation or another country to

conduct international operations for a limited time frame only in compliance with and under conditions defined by a parliamentary decree

AFGHANISTAN
NATO • *Operation Resolute Support* 18

IRAQ
Operation Inherent Resolve 6

MALI
EU • EUTM Mali 7
UN • MINUSMA 1

NORTH SEA
NATO • SNMCMG 1: 1 MHO

UKRAINE
OSCE • Ukraine 7

Lithuania LTU

Euro €		2015	2016	2017
GDP	€	37.1bn	38.3bn	
	US$	41.2bn	42.8bn	
per capita	US$	14,180	14,899	
Growth	%	1.6	2.6	
Inflation	%	-0.7	0.5	
Def exp [a]	€	425m		
	US$	471m		
Def bdgt [b]	€	425m	575m	725m
	US$	471m	642m	
FMA (US)	US$	1.5m	2m	1.5m
US$1=€		0.90	0.90	

[a] NATO definition
[b] Includes military pensions

Population 2,854,235

Ethnic groups: Lithuanian 84.2% Polish 6.6%, Russian 5.8%, Belarussian 1.2%

Age	0–14	15–19	20–24	25–29	30–64	65 plus
Male	7.7%	2.8%	3.2%	3.5%	22.4%	6.6%
Female	7.3%	2.6%	2.9%	3.3%	24.9%	12.9%

Capabilities

Lithuania's armed forces are primarily designed for limited territorial defence and cooperation with NATO partners. As with the other small Baltic states, Lithuania has expressed concern over events in eastern Ukraine since early 2014. Reassurance from NATO has taken the form of bolstered air-policing deployments to the region. A new Armed Defence Concept was approved by the State Defence Council in April 2015. It was agreed to reform the structure of the land forces, with changes to the mechanised infantry brigade and the establishment of a new motorised infantry brigade. In March 2014, the Lithuanian parliament signed an Agreement on Foreign, Security and Defence Policy for 2014–20, committing to spend 2% of GDP on defence by 2020. The country's defence budget was boosted by more than 35% in 2016, with further increases expected in order to modernise and bolster defence capability. Additional spending and a number of recent procurements will give the army more capability. Lithuania and Latvia reached an agreement in July 2015 to jointly pursue a new air-defence system. The reintroduction of conscription was made permanent by the country's State Defence Council in March 2016. Vilnius has also authorised the implementation of a rapid-reaction force to tackle potential hybrid scenarios. Training increased in 2016, including in urban-combat scenarios, while the country's armed forces took part in regional exercises, including BALTOPS 16 and *Saber Strike 16*.

ACTIVE 17,030 (Army 11,050 Navy 680 Air 1,100 Other 4,200) **Paramilitary 11,300**
Conscript liability 9 months (voluntary)

RESERVE 6,700 (Army 6,700)

ORGANISATIONS BY SERVICE

Army 6,200; 4,850 active reserves (total 11,050)
FORCES BY ROLE
MANOEUVRE
  Mechanised
    1 (1st) mech bde (1 recce coy, 4 mech inf bn, 1 arty bn)
  Light
    1 (2nd) mot inf bde (2 mot inf bn)
COMBAT SUPPORT
  1 engr bn
COMBAT SERVICE SUPPORT
  1 trg regt
EQUIPMENT BY TYPE
ARMOURED FIGHTING VEHICLES
  APC • APC (T) 234 M113A1
ENGINEERING & MAINTENANCE VEHICLES
  AEV 8 MT-LB
  ARV 4 M113
ANTI-TANK/ANTI-INFRASTRUCTURE
  MSL
    SP 10 M1025A2 HMMWV with FGM-148 *Javelin*
    MANPATS FGM-148 *Javelin*
  RCL 84mm *Carl Gustav*
ARTILLERY 50
  SP 2 PzH 2000
  TOWED 105mm 18 M101
  MOR 120mm 30: 5 2B11; 10 M/41D; 15 M113 with Tampella
AIR DEFENCE • SAM • Point-defence GROM

Reserves

National Defence Voluntary Forces 4,850 active reservists
FORCES BY ROLE
MANOEUVRE
  Other
    6 (territorial) def unit

Navy 680

LVA, EST and LTU established a joint naval unit, BALTRON, with bases at Liepaja, Riga, Ventpils (LVA), Tallinn (EST), Klaipeda (LTU)

EQUIPMENT BY TYPE
PATROL AND COASTAL COMBATANTS 4
   PCC 3 *Zematis* (ex-DNK *Flyvefisken*) with 1 76mm gun
   PB 1 *Selis* (ex-NOR *Storm*) with 1 76mm gun
MINE WARFARE • MINE COUNTERMEASURES 4
   MHC 3: 1 *Sūduvis* (ex-GER *Lindau*); 2 *Skulvis* (ex-UK *Hunt*)
   MCCS 1 *Jotvingis* (ex-NOR *Vidar*)
LOGISTICS AND SUPPORT • AAR 1 *Šakiai*

Air Force 1,100

Flying hours 120 hrs/yr

FORCES BY ROLE
AIR DEFENCE
   1 AD bn
EQUIPMENT BY TYPE
AIRCRAFT
   TPT 5: **Medium** 3 C-27J *Spartan*; **Light** 2 L-410 *Turbolet*
   TRG 1 L-39ZA *Albatros*
HELICOPTERS
   MRH 3 AS365M3 *Dauphin* (SAR)
   TPT • **Medium** 3 Mi-8 *Hip* (tpt/SAR)
AIR DEFENCE • SAM • Point-defence FIM-92 *Stinger*; RBS-70

Special Operation Force

FORCES BY ROLE
SPECIAL FORCES
   1 SF gp (1 CT unit; 1 Jaeger bn, 1 cbt diver unit)

Logistics Support Command 1,400

FORCES BY ROLE
COMBAT SERVICE SUPPORT
   1 log bn

Training and Doctrine Command 900

FORCES BY ROLE
COMBAT SERVICE SUPPORT
   1 trg regt

Other Units 1,900

FORCES BY ROLE
COMBAT SUPPORT
   1 MP bn

Paramilitary 11,300

Riflemen Union 7,800

State Border Guard Service 3,500

Ministry of Interior

EQUIPMENT BY TYPE
PATROL AND COASTAL COMBATANTS • PB 3: 1 *Lokki* (ex-FIN); 1 KBV 041 (ex-SWE); 1 KBV 101 (ex-SWE)

AMPHIBIOUS • LANDING CRAFT • UCAC 2 *Christina* (*Griffon* 2000)
AIRCRAFT • TPT • Light 1 Cessna 172RG
HELICOPTERS • TPT • Light 5: 1 BK-117 (SAR); 2 H120 *Colibri*; 2 H135

Cyber

Parliament adopted a law on cyber security in December 2014. This sets the basic rules and principles for governing cyber security on a national level and identifies responsible institutions and their areas of responsibility. The Ministry of Defence (MoD) is in charge of formulating national cyber security policy. To support this new function, the MoD established the Cyber Security and Information Technology Department. To support other national entities (focusing on state information resources, and critical-information infrastructure owners) in their cyber-security activities, the National Cyber Security Centre (NCSC) was established under the MoD. NCSC has a number of responsibilities and rights including: monitoring not only military but also other institutions' networks; performing penetration testing of critical-information systems or government networks; tasking national entities to improve their cyber-security measures; and disconnecting infected systems for 48 hours from the internet or national networks without a court order.

DEPLOYMENT

Legal provisions for foreign deployment:
Constitution: Codified constitution (1992)
Decision on deployment of troops abroad: By parliament (Art. 67, 138, 142). According to legislation, the defence minister has the authority to establish the exact amount or size of contingent to be deployed, and the duration of the deployment, not exceeding the limits set out by the parliament

AFGHANISTAN
NATO • *Operation Resolute Support* 21

MALI
EU • EUTM Mali 3

NORTH SEA
NATO • SNMCMG 1: 1 MHC

SERBIA
NATO • KFOR 1

UKRAINE
OSCE • Ukraine 2
JMTG-U 16

FOREIGN FORCES

France NATO Baltic Air Policing 4 *Mirage* 2000-5

Luxembourg LUX

Euro €		2015	2016	2017
GDP	€	52.1bn	54.6bn	
	US$	57.8bn	61.0bn	
per capita	US$	102,717	105,829	
Growth	%	4.8	3.5	
Inflation	%	0.1	0.2	
Def exp [a]	€	225m		
	US$	249m		
Def bdgt	€	193m	197m	
	US$	214m	220m	
US$1=€		0.90	0.90	

[a] NATO definition

Population 582,291

Age	0–14	15–19	20–24	25–29	30–64	65 plus
Male	8.7%	3.0%	3.3%	3.6%	25.1%	6.6%
Female	8.2%	2.9%	3.1%	3.5%	23.9%	8.3%

Capabilities

Luxembourg maintains limited military capabilities in order to participate in European collective security and crisis management. It is part of the European Multi-Role Tanker Transport Fleet programme, having ordered one A330 MRTT. Delivery of an A400M medium strategic-transport aircraft is expected in 2018–19. Personnel are embedded within European headquarters and take part in the EU training mission in Mali. Luxembourg contributes a contractor-operated *Merlin* IIIC maritime-patrol aircraft to the EU counter-human-trafficking operation in the Mediterranean. Following an April 2015 agreement, the Belgian and Dutch air forces are responsible for policing Luxembourg's airspace.

ACTIVE 900 (Army 900) Paramilitary 600

ORGANISATIONS BY SERVICE

Army 900
FORCES BY ROLE
MANOEUVRE
 Reconnaissance
  2 recce coy (1 to Eurocorps/BEL div, 1 to NATO pool of deployable forces)
EQUIPMENT BY TYPE
ARMOURED FIGHTING VEHICLES
 AUV 48 *Dingo* 2
ANTI-TANK/ANTI-INFRASTRUCTURE
 MSL • MANPATS TOW
ARTILLERY • MOR 81mm 6

Paramilitary 600

Gendarmerie 600

DEPLOYMENT

Legal provisions for foreign deployment:
Constitution: Codified constitution (1868)
Specific legislation: 'Loi du 27 juillet 1992 relatif à la participation du Grand-Duché de Luxembourg à des opérations pour le maintien de la paix (OMP) dans le cadre d'organisations internationales'
Decision on deployment of troops abroad: By government after formal consultation of relevant parliamentary committees and the Council of State (Art. 1–2 of the 1992 law)

AFGHANISTAN
NATO • *Operation Resolute Support* 1

MALI
EU • EUTM Mali 2

SERBIA
NATO • KFOR 23

UKRAINE
OSCE • Ukraine 2

Macedonia, Former Yugoslav Republic FYROM

Macedonian Denar d		2015	2016	2017
GDP	d	560bn	579bn	
	US$	10.1bn	10.5bn	
per capita	US$	4,871	5,060	
Growth	%	3.7	2.2	
Inflation	%	-0.2	0.1	
Def bdgt	d	5.65bn	5.90bn	
	US$	102m	107m	
FMA (US)	US$	4m	3.6m	3.6m
US$1=d		55.52	55.16	

Population 2,100,025

Ethnic groups: Macedonian 64.2%; Albanian 25.2%; Turk 3.9%; Romani 2.7%; Serb 1.8%; Bosniac 0.9%

Age	0–14	15–19	20–24	25–29	30–64	65 plus
Male	8.9%	3.4%	3.6%	3.8%	24.4%	5.6%
Female	8.3%	3.2%	3.4%	3.6%	24.1%	7.5%

Capabilities

Macedonia maintains a small joint force focused on the army, with a modest maritime and air wing. The country continues to aspire to NATO and EU membership, and joined the NATO Membership Action Plan in 1999. However, this aspiration is hindered by a number of factors including an impasse with Greece over the state's name and a shrinking defence budget. The country's 2014–23 modernisation plan is intended to reform the armed forces and update their equipment to NATO standards. Exercises have taken place with US and Polish forces, and there is close cooperation with the Czech armed forces on information exchange and military education. Macedonia has been chosen to host SEEBRIG headquarters from 2020 to 2026, and already hosts the Balkan Medical Task Force Headquarters. SEEBRIG is a brigade-size formation established by seven participating nations, agreed in 1998 as part of the Agreement on The Multinational Peace Force SouthEastern Europe. The use of the army to assist with border security in 2016 highlighted issues including low pay, overdue wages and poor conditions.

ACTIVE 8,000 (Army 8,000) Paramilitary 7,600

RESERVE 4,850

ORGANISATIONS BY SERVICE

Army 8,000
FORCES BY ROLE
SPECIAL FORCES
1 SF regt (1 SF bn, 1 Ranger bn)
MANOEUVRE
Mechanised
1 mech inf bde (1 tk bn, 4 mech inf bn, 1 arty bn, 1 engr bn, 1 NBC coy)
COMBAT SUPPORT
1 MP bn
1 sigs bn
COMBAT SERVICE SUPPORT
1 log bde (3 log bn)

Reserves
FORCES BY ROLE
  MANOEUVRE Light
  1 inf bde
EQUIPMENT BY TYPE
ARMOURED FIGHTING VEHICLES
  MBT 31 T-72A
  RECCE 10 BRDM-2
  IFV 11: 10 BMP-2; 1 BMP-2K (CP)
  APC 200
    APC (T) 47: 9 *Leonidas*; 28 M113; 10 MT-LB
    APC (W) 153: 57 BTR-70; 12 BTR-80; 84 TM-170 *Hermelin*
ANTI-TANK/ANTI-INFRASTRUCTURE
  MSL • MANPATS *Milan*
  RCL 57mm; 82mm M60A
ARTILLERY 126
  TOWED 70: 105mm 14 M-56; 122mm 56 M-30 M-1938
  MRL 17: 122mm 6 BM-21; 128mm 11
  MOR 39: 120mm 39

Marine Wing
EQUIPMENT BY TYPE
PATROL AND COASTAL COMBATANTS • PB 2
Botica

Aviation Brigade
FORCES BY ROLE
TRAINING
  1 flt with Z-242; Bell 205 (UH-1H *Iroquois*)

ATTACK HELICOPTER
1 sqn with Mi-24K *Hind* G2; Mi-24V *Hind* E
TRANSPORT HELICOPTER
1 sqn with Mi-8MTV *Hip*; Mi-17 *Hip* H
AIR DEFENCE
1 AD bn
EQUIPMENT BY TYPE
AIRCRAFT
  TPT • Light 1 An-2 *Colt*
  TRG 5 Z-242
HELICOPTERS
  ATK 4 Mi-24V *Hind* E (10: 2 Mi-24K *Hind* G2; 8 Mi-24V *Hind* E in store)
  MRH 6: 4 Mi-8MTV *Hip*; 2 Mi-17 *Hip* H
  TPT • Light 2 Bell 205 (UH-1H *Iroquois*)
AIR DEFENCE
  SAM • Point-defence 8 9K35 *Strela*-10 (SA-13 *Gopher*); 9K310 *Igla*-1 (SA-16 *Gimlet*)
  GUNS 40mm 36 L20

Paramilitary

Police 7,600 (some 5,000 armed)
incl 2 SF units
EQUIPMENT BY TYPE
ARMOURED FIGHTING VEHICLES
  APC
    APC (T) M113
    APC (W) BTR-80; TM-170 *Heimlin*
  AUV *Ze'ev*
HELICOPTERS
  MRH 1 Bell 412EP *Twin Huey*
  TPT • Light 2: 1 Bell 206B (AB-206B) *Jet Ranger* II; 1 Bell 212 (AB-212)

DEPLOYMENT

Legal provisions for foreign deployment of armed forces:
Constitution: Codified constitution (1991)
Specific legislation: 'Defence Law' (2005)
Decision on deployment of troops abroad: a) by the government if deployment is for humanitarian missions or military exercises; b) by the parliament if for peacekeeping operations ('Defence Law', Art. 41)

AFGHANISTAN
NATO • *Operation Resolute Support* 39

ALBANIA
OSCE • Albania 1

BOSNIA-HERZEGOVINA
EU • EUFOR • *Operation Althea* 3

LEBANON
UN • UNIFIL 1

SERBIA
OSCE • Kosovo 16

UKRAINE
OSCE • Ukraine 23

Malta MLT

Euro €		2015	2016	2017
GDP	€	8.79bn	9.37bn	
	US$	9.75bn	10.5bn	
per capita	US$	22,713	24,298	
Growth	%	6.2	4.1	
Inflation	%	1.2	1.2	
Def bdgt [a]	€	50m	52m	61m
	US$	56m	58m	
US$1= €		0.90	0.90	

[a] Excludes military pensions

Population 415,196

Age	0–14	15–19	20–24	25–29	30–64	65 plus
Male	7.7%	2.9%	3.2%	3.5%	24.0%	8.6%
Female	7.3%	2.7%	3.0%	3.3%	23.3%	10.5%

Capabilities

The armed forces consist of a limited number of army personnel supported by small naval and air units. Malta's defence-spending growth has been modest, however some modernisation measures are being funded by the European Internal Security Fund, including the acquisition of a new offshore-patrol vessel and new EOD equipment. In addition, Malta has also earmarked €2.5m for new equipment, including another light aircraft. Malta has begun work on a new military training school at the Pembroke army base. The country participates in various European training missions as well as the EUNAVFOR–MED mission in the Mediterranean. The government has announced a modest increase in personnel and intends to increase reservist numbers. Budget allocations for personnel increased between 2015 and 2016 and, while equipment funding was reduced over the same period, the armed forces plan to continue strengthening air- and maritime-surveillance capabilities with the stated aim of protecting Malta's and the EU's borders.

ACTIVE 1,950 (Armed Forces 1,950)

RESERVE 180 (Emergency Volunteer Reserve Force 120 Individual Reserve 60)

ORGANISATIONS BY SERVICE

Armed Forces of Malta 1,950
FORCES BY ROLE
SPECIAL FORCES
  1 SF unit
MANOEUVRE
  Light
  1 (1st) inf regt (3 inf coy, 1 cbt spt coy)
COMBAT SUPPORT
  1 (3rd) cbt spt regt (1 cbt engr sqn, 1 EOD sqn, 1 maint sqn)
COMBAT SERVICE SUPPORT
  1 (4th) CSS regt (1 CIS coy, 1 sy coy)

Maritime Squadron
Organised into 5 divisions: offshore patrol; inshore patrol; rapid deployment and training; marine engineering; and logistics
EQUIPMENT BY TYPE
PATROL AND COASTAL COMBATANTS 8
  PCO 1 *Emer*
  PCC 1 *Diciotti*
  PB 6: 4 Austal 21m; 2 *Marine Protector*
LOGISTICS AND SUPPORT 2
  AAR 2 *Cantieri Vittoria*

Air Wing
1 base party. 1 flt ops div; 1 maint div; 1 integrated log div; 1 rescue section
EQUIPMENT BY TYPE
AIRCRAFT
  TPT • **Light** 4: 2 Beech 200 *King Air* (maritime patrol); 2 BN-2B *Islander*
  TRG 3 *Bulldog* T MK1
HELICOPTERS
  MRH 6: 3 AW139 (SAR); 3 SA316B *Alouette* III

DEPLOYMENT

Legal provisions for foreign deployment:
Constitution: Codified constitution (1964)
Decision on deployment of troops abroad: The government decides on a case-by-case basis on the deployment of Maltese military personnel abroad (Malta Armed Forces Act, Chapter 220 of the Laws of Malta)

Montenegro MNE

Euro €		2015	2016	2017
GDP	€	3.60bn	3.81bn	
	US$	3.99bn	4.24bn	
per capita	US$	6,409	6,809	
Growth	%	3.2	5.1	
Inflation	%	1.6	0.5	
Def bdgt [a]	€	60m	62m	66m
	US$	67m	69m	
FMA (US)	US$	1.2m	1m	1m
US$1=€		0.90	0.90	

[a] Includes military pensions

Population 644,578

Ethnic groups: Montenegrin 45%; Serb 28.7%; Bosniac 8.6%; Albanian 4.9%; Croat 1%

Age	0–14	15–19	20–24	25–29	30–64	65 plus
Male	7.4%	2.0%	2.5%	3.8%	28.2%	5.9%
Female	7.7%	2.6%	2.8%	3.4%	24.8%	8.9%

Capabilities

Montenegro's armed forces are small and primarily organised around the army, with few air and naval assets. The force is supported by a significant paramilitary organisation. Capability remains focused on internal security and limited support to international peacekeeping. Montenegro joined the NATO accession protocol in May 2016, officially becoming a NATO 'invitee'. The country can now participate in the Alliance's meetings as an observer, an important step towards full membership. Reform and professionalisation of the armed forces has been slow, with only a small part of the defence budget spent on modernisation. The country intends to replace its ageing Soviet-era equipment with modern US or European equipment. Procurement priorities include light and medium helicopters and light armoured vehicles. The country's defence industry has sold large numbers of surplus small arms and anti-tank weapons abroad. Montenegro has furthered ties with future NATO partners and neighbours, including Croatia, Germany, Serbia, Slovenia and the US, through extensive exercises. In 2016, the country took part in the US-led *Immediate Response* command-post exercise. Montenegrin forces have deployed to Afghanistan with NATO, affording them valuable experience.

ACTIVE 1,950 (Army 875 Navy 350 Air Force 225 Other 500) **Paramilitary 10,100**

ORGANISATIONS BY SERVICE

Army 875
FORCES BY ROLE
MANOEUVRE
  Reconnaissance
  1 recce coy
  Light
  1 mot inf bn
COMBAT SUPPORT
  1 MP coy
EQUIPMENT BY TYPE
ARMOURED FIGHTING VEHICLES
  APC • **APC (W)** 8 BOV-VP M-86
ANTI-TANK/ANTI-INFRASTRUCTURE
  SP 9 BOV-1
  MSL • **MANPATS** 9K111 *Fagot* (AT-4 *Spigot*); 9K111-1 *Konkurs* (AT-5 *Spandrel*)
ARTILLERY 149
  TOWED 122mm 12 D-30
  MRL 128mm 18 M-63/M-94 *Plamen*
  MOR 105: **82mm** 73; **120mm** 32

Navy 350
1 Naval Cmd HQ with 4 operational naval units (patrol boat; coastal surveillance; maritime detachment; and SAR) with additional sigs, log and trg units with a separate Coast Guard element. Some listed units are in the process of decommissioning
EQUIPMENT BY TYPE
PATROL AND COASTAL COMBATANTS 5
  PSO 1 *Kotor* with 1 twin 76mm gun (1 further vessel in reserve)
  PCFG 2 *Rade Končar*† (of which 1 in refit) with 2 single lnchr with P-15 *Termit* (SS-N-2B *Styx*) AShM (missiles disarmed)
  PB 2 *Mirna* (Type-140) (Police units)
LOGISTICS AND SUPPORT 3
  AXS 1 *Jadran*†

Air Force 225
Golubovci (Podgorica) air base under army command
FORCES BY ROLE
TRAINING
  1 (mixed) sqn with G-4 *Super Galeb*; Utva-75 (none operational)
TRANSPORT HELICOPTER
  1 sqn with SA341/SA342L *Gazelle*
EQUIPMENT BY TYPE
AIRCRAFT • **TRG** (4 G-4 *Super Galeb* non-operational; 4 Utva-75 non-operational)
HELICOPTERS
  MRH 13 SA341/SA342L (HN-45M) *Gazelle*

Paramilitary ε10,100

Montenegrin Ministry of Interior Personnel ε6,000

Special Police Units ε4,100

DEPLOYMENT
Legal provisions for foreign deployment:
Constitution: Constitution (2007)
Decision on deployment of troops abroad: The Assembly, on the proposal of the Council for Defence and Security, decides on the use of Montenegrin armed forces in international forces (Article 82, item 8).

AFGHANISTAN
NATO • *Operation Resolute Support* 14
ALBANIA
OSCE • Albania 2
MALI
EU • EUTM Mali 1
SERBIA
OSCE • Kosovo 1
UKRAINE
OSCE • Ukraine 2

Multinational Organisations

Capabilities

The following represent shared capabilities held by contributors collectively rather than as part of national inventories.

ORGANISATIONS BY SERVICE

NATO AEW&C Force
Based at Geilenkirchen (GER). 12 original participating countries (BEL, CAN, DNK, GER, GRC, ITA, NLD, NOR,

PRT, TUR, USA) have been subsequently joined by 5 more (CZE, ESP, HUN, POL, ROM).

FORCES BY ROLE
AIRBORNE EARLY WARNING & CONTROL
1 sqn with B-757 (trg); E-3A *Sentry* (NATO standard)
EQUIPMENT BY TYPE
AIRCRAFT
AEW&C 16 E-3A *Sentry* (NATO standard)
TPT • PAX 1 B-757 (trg)

Strategic Airlift Capability

Heavy Airlift Wing based at Papa air base (HUN). 12 participating countries (BLG, EST, FIN, HUN, LTU, NLD, NOR, POL, ROM, SVN, SWE, USA).

EQUIPMENT BY TYPE
AIRCRAFT • TPT • Heavy 3 C-17A *Globemaster*

Strategic Airlift Interim Solution

Intended to provide strategic-airlift capacity pending the delivery of A400M aircraft by leasing An-124s. 14 participating countries (BEL, CZE, FIN, FRA, GER, GRC, HUN, LUX, NOR, POL, SVK, SVN, SWE, UK)

EQUIPMENT BY TYPE
AIRCRAFT • TPT • Heavy 2 An-124-100 (4 more available on 6–9 days' notice)

Netherlands NLD

Euro €		2015	2016	2017
GDP	€	677bn	690bn	
	US$	751bn	770bn	
per capita	US$	44,323	45,210	
Growth	%	2.0	1.7	
Inflation	%	0.2	0.1	
Def exp [a]	€	8.00bn		
	US$	8.87bn		
Def bdgt [b]	€	8.00bn	8.23bn	8.69bn
	US$	8.88bn	9.19bn	
US$1=€		0.90	0.90	

[a] NATO definition
[b] Includes military pensions

Population 17,016,967

Age	0–14	15–19	20–24	25–29	30–64	65 plus
Male	8.5%	3.0%	3.1%	3.2%	23.3%	8.3%
Female	8.1%	2.9%	3.0%	3.2%	23.3%	10.1%

Capabilities

Despite the limited size of its forces, the Netherlands makes significant contributions to NATO and EU military operations. They have become more integrated with their NATO allies, particularly Belgium and Germany, and there is an air-policing agreement with Belgium and Luxembourg. The army is increasingly incorporated in Bundeswehr training and its 43rd mechanised and 11th airmobile brigades are integrated into host German divisions as part of a rapid-reaction force. Defence-budget cuts have been arrested and increased allocations will allow for the consolidation of rapid-reaction and expeditionary capabilities. The Netherlands is part of the MRTT project and will buy two A330 tankers with Luxembourg. The Dutch defence ministry stated that 'These will be NATO property and will be stationed at Eindhoven Air Base for pooling and sharing'. There is a small defence industry. DutchAero, a subsidiary of KMWE, agreed with Pratt and Whitney in January 2016 to manufacture engine components for the F-35, while the country also collaborated with Germany on the *Fennek* and *Boxer* armoured vehicles. Dutch forces are well trained and fully professional, and personnel levels appear adequate for their operational roles. The army continues to replace tracked armoured vehicles with lighter wheeled platforms. The Netherlands received its first two F-35A combat aircraft in May; eight are to be received by 2019. The air force is focusing on upgrading and expanding its CH-47 helicopter fleet. In late 2015, the Dutch government opted for a life-extension programme for its *Patriot* air-defence system. The Netherlands has participated in EU missions to combat piracy and human trafficking in Somalia and the Mediterranean. The country has extended its training mission in Iraq until the end of 2017 and the navy is scheduled to train Libyan coastguard personnel. The joint Defence Cyber Command was due to become operational by December 2016.

ACTIVE 35,410 (Army 18,860 Navy 8,500 Air 8,050)
Military Constabulary 5,900

RESERVE 4,500 (Army 4,000 Navy 80 Air 420)
Military Constabulary 160
Reserve liability to age 35 for soldiers/sailors, 40 for NCOs, 45 for officers

ORGANISATIONS BY SERVICE

Army 18,860
FORCES BY ROLE
COMMAND
 elm 1 (1 GNC) corps HQ
SPECIAL FORCES
 4 SF coy
MANOEUVRE Reconnaissance
 1 ISR bn (2 armd recce sqn, 1 EW coy, 2 int sqn, 1 UAV bty)
Mechanised
 1 (43rd) mech bde (1 armd recce sqn, 2 armd inf bn, 1 engr bn, 1 maint coy, 1 med coy)
 1 (13th) lt mech bde (1 recce sqn, 2 lt mech inf bn, 1 engr bn, 1 maint coy, 1 med coy)
Air Manoeuvre
 1 (11th) air mob bde (3 air mob inf bn, 1 engr coy, 1 med coy, 1 supply coy, 1 maint coy)
COMBAT SUPPORT
 1 SP arty bn (3 SP arty bty)
 1 AD comd (1 AD sqn; 1 AD bty)
 1 CIMIC bn
 1 engr bn
 2 EOD coy 1 (CIS) sigs bn 1 CBRN coy

COMBAT SERVICE SUPPORT
1 med bn
5 fd hospital
3 maint coy
2 tpt bn

Reserves 2,700 reservists
National Command
Cadre bde and corps tps completed by call-up of reservists (incl Territorial Comd)
FORCES BY ROLE
MANOEUVRE
  Light
  3 inf bn (could be mobilised for territorial def)
EQUIPMENT BY TYPE
ARMOURED FIGHTING VEHICLES
  RECCE 196 *Fennek*
  IFV 192 CV9035N
  APC • APC (W) 103 *Boxer* (8 driver trg; 52 amb; 35 CP; 8 log)
  AUV 76 *Bushmaster* IMV
ENGINEERING & MAINTENANCE VEHICLES
  AEV 35: 25 *Boxer*; 10 *Kodiak*
  ARV 25 BPz-3 *Büffel*
  VLB 13 *Leopard* 1
  MW *Bozena*
NBC VEHICLES 6 TPz-1 *Fuchs* NBC
ANTI-TANK/ANTI-INFRASTRUCTURE • MSL
  SP 40 *Fennek* MRAT
  MANPATS *Spike*-MR (*Gil*)
ARTILLERY 119:
  SP 155mm 18 PzH 2000
  MOR 101: **81mm** 83 L16/M1; **120mm** 18 Brandt
RADAR • LAND 6+: 6 AN/TPQ-36 *Firefinder* (arty, mor); WALS; 10 *Squire*
AIR DEFENCE • SAM
  Long-range 20 MIM-104D/F *Patriot* PAC-2 GEM/PAC-3 (TMD Capable)
  Short-range 6 NASAMS II
  Point-defence 18+: FIM-92 *Stinger*; 18 *Fennek* with FIM-92 *Stinger*

Navy 8,500 (incl Marines)
EQUIPMENT BY TYPE
SUBMARINES • TACTICAL • SSK 4:
  4 *Walrus* with 4 single 533mm TT with Mk48 *Sea Arrow* HWT
PRINCIPAL SURFACE COMBATANTS 6
  DESTROYERS • DDGHM 4:
    3 *De Zeven Provinciën* with 2 quad Mk141 lnchr with RGM-84F *Harpoon* AShM, 1 40-cell Mk41 VLS with SM-2MR/ESSM SAM, 2 twin 324mm ASTT with Mk46 LWT, 1 *Goalkeeper* CIWS, 1 127mm gun, (capacity 1 NH90 hel)
    1 *Zeven Provinciën* with 2 quad Mk141 lnchr with RGM-84F *Harpoon* AShM, 1 40-cell Mk41 VLS with SM-2MR/ESSM SAM, 2 twin 324mm ASTT with Mk46 LWT, 2 *Goalkeeper* CIWS, 1 127mm gun, (capacity 1 NH90 hel)
  FRIGATES • FFGHM 2:
    2 *Karel Doorman* with 2 quad Mk141 lnchr with RGM-84A/C *Harpoon* AShM, 1 16-cell Mk48 VLS with RIM-7P *Sea Sparrow* SAM, 2 twin 324mm ASTT with Mk46 LWT, 1 *Goalkeeper* CIWS, 1 76mm gun, (capacity 1 NH90 hel)
PATROL AND COASTAL COMBATANTS
  PSOH 4 *Holland* with 1 76mm gun (capacity 1 NH90 hel)
MINE WARFARE • MINE COUNTERMEASURES
  MHO 6 *Alkmaar* (*Tripartite*)
AMPHIBIOUS
  PRINCIPAL AMPHIBIOUS SHIPS • LPD 2:
    1 *Rotterdam* with 2 *Goalkeeper* CIWS, (capacity 6 NH90/AS532 *Cougar* hel; either 6 LCVP or 2 LCU and 3 LCVP; either 170 APC or 33 MBT; 538 troops)
    1 *Johan de Witt* with 2 *Goalkeeper* CIWS, (capacity 6 NH90 hel or 4 AS532 *Cougar* hel; either 6 LCVP or 2 LCU and 3 LCVP; either 170 APC or 33 MBT; 700 troops)
  LANDING CRAFT 17
    LCU 5 Mk9
    LCVP 12 Mk5
LOGISTICS AND SUPPORT 8
  AFSH 1 *Karel Doorman* with 2 *Goalkeeper* CIWS, (capacity 6 NH90/AS532 *Cougar* or 2 CH-47F *Chinook* hel; 2 LCVP) (in refit following engine damage, return to service expected Jan 2017)
  AGS 2 *Snellius*
  AK 1 *Pelikaan*
  AOT 1 *Patria*
  AS 1 *Mercuur*
  AXL 1 *Van Kingsbergen*
  AXS 1 *Urania*

Marines 2,650
FORCES BY ROLE
SPECIAL FORCES
  1 SF gp (1 SF sqn, 1 CT sqn)
MANOEUVRE
  Amphibious
  2 mne bn
  1 amph aslt gp
COMBAT SERVICE SUPPORT
  1 spt gp (coy)
EQUIPMENT BY TYPE
ARMOURED FIGHTING VEHICLES
  APC • APC (T) 160: 87 Bv-206D; 73 BvS-10 *Viking*
ENGINEERING & MAINTENANCE VEHICLES
  ARV 4 BvS-10; 4 *Leopard* 1
  MED 4 BvS-10
ANTI-TANK/ANTI-INFRASTRUCTURE
  MSL • MANPATS *Spike*-MR (*Gil*)
ARTILLERY • MOR 81mm 12 L16/M1
AIR DEFENCE • SAM • Point-defence FIM-92 *Stinger*

Air Force 8,050
Flying hours 180 hrs/yr

FORCES BY ROLE
FIGHTER/GROUND ATTACK
  3 sqn with F-16AM/BM *Fighting Falcon*
ANTI-SUBMARINE WARFARE/SEARCH & RESCUE
  1 sqn with NH90 NFH

TANKER/TRANSPORT
1 sqn with C-130H/H-30 *Hercules*
1 sqn with KDC-10; Gulfstream IV
TRAINING
1 OEU sqn with F-35A *Lightning* II
1 sqn with PC-7 *Turbo Trainer*
1 hel sqn with AH-64D *Apache*; CH-47D *Chinook* (based at Fort Hood, TX)
ATTACK HELICOPTER
1 sqn with AH-64D *Apache*
TRANSPORT HELICOPTER
1 sqn with AS532U2 *Cougar* II
1 sqn with CH-47D/F *Chinook*
EQUIPMENT BY TYPE
AIRCRAFT 63 combat capable
FTR 61 F-16AM/BM *Fighting Falcon*
FGA 2 F-35A *Lightning* II (in test)
TKR 2 KDC-10
TPT 5: **Medium** 4: 2 C-130H *Hercules*; 2 C-130H-30 *Hercules*; **PAX** 1 Gulfstream IV
TRG 13 PC-7 *Turbo Trainer*
HELICOPTERS
ATK 28 AH-64D *Apache*
ASW 12 NH90 NFH
TPT 25: **Heavy** 25: 11 CH-47D *Chinook*; 6 CH-47F *Chinook*; **Medium** 8 AS532U2 *Cougar* II, 8 NH90 TTH
AIR-LAUNCHED MISSILES
AAM • IR AIM-9L/M/N *Sidewinder*; ARH AIM-120B AMRAAM
ASM AGM-114K *Hellfire*; AGM-65D/G *Maverick*
BOMBS
Laser-guided GBU-10/GBU-12 *Paveway* II; GBU-24 *Paveway* III (all supported by LANTIRN)

Paramilitary

Royal Military Constabulary 5,900

Subordinate to the Ministry of Defence, but performs most of its work under the authority of other ministries
FORCES BY ROLE
MANOEUVRE
  Other
    5 paramilitary district (total: 28 paramilitary unit)
EQUIPMENT BY TYPE
ARMOURED FIGHTING VEHICLES
  APC • APC (W) 24 YPR-KMar

Cyber

The Defence Cyber Strategy was updated in early 2015. A Defence Cyber Command (DCC) was launched in September 2014 within the army, but comprising personnel from all the armed services. The DCC will be responsible for the cyber security of the defence organisation and its partners. According to the defence ministry, 'the armed forces can attack, manipulate and disable the digital systems of opponents. Potential opponents might be other states, terrorist or other organisations, or hackers.' A Defence Cyber Doctrine is being developed and it was planned that a Joint Defence Cyber Command would be operational by December 2016.

DEPLOYMENT

Legal provisions for foreign deployment:
Constitution: Codified constitution (1815)
Decision on deployment of troops abroad: By the government (Art. 97). Deployment is a cabinet decision. Parliament is involved in decisions on armed forces' deployment to maintain or promote the international legal order, including the provision of humanitarian aid in armed conflicts, as described in Article 100

AFGHANISTAN
NATO • *Operation Resolute Support* 120

BOSNIA-HERZEGOVINA
EU • EUFOR • *Operation Althea* 3
OSCE • Bosnia and Herzegovina 1

GULF OF ADEN & INDIAN OCEAN
EU • *Operation Atalanta* 1 DDGHM

IRAQ
Operation Inherent Resolve 130

JORDAN
Operation Inherent Resolve 35

MALI
EU • EUTM Mali 1
UN • MINUSMA 315; 1 SF coy; 1 atk hel sqn; 1 hel sqn; 1 int coy

MEDITERRANEAN SEA
NATO • SNMG 2: 1 DDGHM

MIDDLE EAST
UN • UNTSO 11 obs

NORTH SEA
NATO • SNMCMG 1: 1 MHO

SERBIA
NATO • KFOR 5

SOUTH SUDAN
UN • UNMISS 7

SYRIA/ISRAEL
UN • UNDOF 2

UGANDA
EU • EUTM Somalia 7

UKRAINE
OSCE • Ukraine 11

UNITED STATES
1 hel trg sqn with AH-64D *Apache*; CH-47D *Chinook* based at Fort Hood (TX)

FOREIGN FORCES

United Kingdom Air Force 90
United States US European Command: 380

Norway NOR

Norwegian Kroner kr		2015	2016	2017
GDP	kr	3.13tr	3.18tr	
	US$	388bn	376bn	
per capita	US$	74,598	71,497	
Growth	%	1.6	0.8	
Inflation	%	2.2	3.2	
Def exp [a]	kr	46.9bn		
	US$	5.82bn		
Def bdgt [b]	kr	46.9bn	50.4bn	50.9bn
	US$	5.82bn	5.97bn	
US$1=kr		8.06	8.44	

[a] NATO definition
[b] Includes military pensions

Population   5,265,158

Age	0–14	15–19	20–24	25–29	30–64	65 plus
Male	9.2%	3.2%	3.4%	3.6%	23.4%	7.6%
Female	8.8%	3.0%	3.2%	3.4%	22.2%	9.0%

Capabilities

Norway sustains small but well-equipped and highly trained armed forces. Territorial defence is at the heart of Oslo's security policy. Around a third of the country's troops are conscripts at any one time. Norway's continuing focus on the High North has been brought into sharper focus as a result of the more challenging relationship with Russia. In June 2016, Norway published its Long Term Defence Plan, which stated that further adjustments to the armed forces were needed to address evolving security challenges at home and abroad, including in intelligence and surveillance as well as combat power. 'Years of underfunding, combined with a high operational tempo', the document said, 'have created shortfalls in training, maintenance and upgrades'. The government intends to increase defence budgets and prioritise operational activity and readiness in order to effectively respond to threats as part of NATO. The plan was agreed by parliament in November. Equipment recapitalisation is ongoing, reflecting defence expenditures that will largely be directed towards new procurements, including F-35A Joint Strike Fighters, armoured fighting vehicles (CV90 variants), helicopters (NH90s), a support ship and missiles. Parliament also voted in November in favour of the government's proposal to replace submarines and maritime-patrol aircraft, and to boost the air-defence capability. US marines were integrated with Norwegian forces for a live-fire exercise ahead of the large NATO exercise *Cold Response 2016* in central Norway. In January 2015, Norwegian conscription became gender neutral. Around one-third of conscripts in 2016's intake were female, with expectations that this will rise. Around 10,000 conscripts are needed each year from a pool of about 60,000; the inclusion of women is likely to make this competition for places harder and increase the calibre of service personnel. A new Ranger Company is planned for northern Norway, focusing on the border with Russia.

Norwegian F-16s deployed to Iceland to lead NATO's air-policing mission to the country for a month in June 2016. A US Marine Corps contingent will deploy to Vaernes, on a rotational basis, from January 2017.

ACTIVE 24,950 (Army 9,950 Navy 4,350 Air 2,618 Central Support 6,150 Home Guard 600)
Conscript liability 18 months maximum. Conscripts first serve 12 months from 19–21, and then up to 4–5 refresher training periods until age 35, 44, 55 or 60 depending on rank and function. Active numbers include conscripts on initial service. Conscription extended to women in 2015

RESERVE 45,590 (Army 270 Navy 320 Home Guard 45,000)
Readiness varies from a few hours to several days

ORGANISATIONS BY SERVICE

Army 4,950; 5,000 conscript (total 9,950)

The mechanised brigade – Brigade North – trains new personnel of all categories and provides units for international operations. At any time around one-third of the brigade will be trained and ready to conduct operations. The brigade includes one high-readiness armoured battalion (Telemark Battalion) with combat support and combat service support units on high readiness

FORCES BY ROLE
MANOEUVRE
  Reconnaissance
  1 (GSV) bn (1 (border) recce coy, 1 spt coy, 1 trg coy)
  Armoured
  1 armd inf bde (1 ISR bn, 2 armd bn, 1 lt inf bn, 1 arty bn, 1 engr bn, 1 MP coy, 1 CIS bn, 1 spt bn, 1 med bn)
  Light
  1 lt inf bn (His Majesty The King's Guards)

EQUIPMENT BY TYPE
ARMOURED FIGHTING VEHICLES
  MBT 52 *Leopard* 2A4
  IFV 116 CV9030N
  APC 390
    APC (T) 315 M113 (incl variants)
    APC (W) 75 XA-186 *Sisu*/XA-200 *Sisu*
  AUV 20+: 20 *Dingo* 2; IVECO LMV
ENGINEERING & MAINTENANCE VEHICLES
  AEV 22 *Alvis*
  ARV 9+: 3 M88A1; M578; 6 *Leopard* 1
  VLB 35: 26 *Leguan*; 9 *Leopard* 1
  MW 9 910 MCV-2
NBC VEHICLES TPz-1 *Fuchs* NBC
ANTI-TANK/ANTI-INFRASTRUCTURE
  MANPATS FGM-148 *Javelin*
  RCL 84mm *Carl Gustav*
ARTILLERY 204
  SP 155mm 18 M109A3GN
  MOR 186: 81mm 150 L16; SP 81mm 12 M125A2; SP 107mm 24 M106A1
RADAR • LAND 12 ARTHUR

Navy 2,350; 2,000 conscripts (total 4,350)

Joint Command – Norwegian National Joint Headquarters. The Royal Norwegian Navy is organised into four elements under the command of the chief of staff of the Navy: the naval units 'Kysteskadren', the schools 'Sjoforsvarets Skoler', the naval bases and the coastguard 'Kystvakten'

FORCES BY ROLE
MANOEUVRE
 Reconnaissance
 1 ISR coy (Coastal Rangers)
COMBAT SUPPORT
 1 EOD pl

EQUIPMENT BY TYPE
SUBMARINES • TACTICAL • SSK 6 *Ula* with 8 single 533mm TT with A3 *Seal* DM2 HWT
PRINCIPAL SURFACE COMBATANTS 5
 DESTROYERS • DDGHM 5 *Fridtjof Nansen* with *Aegis* C2 (mod), 2 quad lnchr with NSM AShM, 1 8-cell Mk41 VLS with ESSM SAM, 2 twin 324mm ASTT with *Sting Ray* LWT, 1 76mm gun, (capacity 1 NH90 hel)
PATROL AND COASTAL COMBATANTS 23:
 PSO 1 *Harstad*
 PCFG 6 *Skjold* with 8 single lnchr with NSM AShM, 1 76mm gun
 PBF 16 S90N (capacity 20 troops)
MINE WARFARE • MINE COUNTERMEASURES 6:
 MSC 3 *Alta* with 1 twin *Simbad* lnchr with *Mistral* SAM
 MHC 3 *Oksoy* with 1 twin *Simbad* lnchr with *Mistral* SAM
LOGISTICS AND SUPPORT 6
 AGI 1 *Marjata* with 1 hel landing platform
 AGS 1 *HU Sverdrup II*
 ATS 1 *Valkyrien*
 AX 2 *Kvarven*
 AXL 1 *Reine*

Coast Guard

EQUIPMENT BY TYPE
PATROL AND COASTAL COMBATANTS 14
 PSOH 3 *Nordkapp* with 1 57mm gun
 PSO 4: 3 *Barentshav*; 1 *Svalbard* with 1 57mm gun, 1 hel landing platform
 PCC 5 *Nornen*
 PCO 7: 1 *Aalesund*; 1 *Reine*

Air Force 2,618 ; 1,000 conscript (total 3,618)

Joint Command – Norwegian National HQ
Flying hours 180 hrs/yr

FORCES BY ROLE
FIGHTER/GROUND ATTACK
 2 sqn with F-16AM/BM *Fighting Falcon*
MARITIME PATROL
 1 sqn with P-3C *Orion*; P-3N *Orion* (pilot trg)
ELECTRONIC WARFARE
 1 sqn with *Falcon* 20C (EW, Flight Inspection Service)
SEARCH & RESCUE
 1 sqn with *Sea King* Mk43B
TRANSPORT
 1 sqn with C-130J-30 *Hercules*
TRAINING
 1 sqn with MFI-15 *Safari*
TRANSPORT HELICOPTER
 2 sqn with Bell 412SP *Twin Huey*
 1 sqn with NH90 (forming)
AIR DEFENCE
 1 bn with NASAMS II

EQUIPMENT BY TYPE
AIRCRAFT 63 combat capable
 FTR 57: 47 F-16AM *Fighting Falcon*; 10 F-16BM *Fighting Falcon*
 ASW 6: 4 P-3C *Orion*; 2 P-3N *Orion* (pilot trg)
 EW 3 *Falcon* 20C
 TPT • Medium 4 C-130J-30 *Hercules*
 TRG 16 MFI-15 *Safari*
HELICOPTERS
 ASW 6 NH90 NFH
 SAR 12 *Sea King* Mk43B
 MRH 18: 6 Bell 412HP; 12 Bell 412SP
AIR DEFENCE
 SAM • Short-range NASAMS II
AIR-LAUNCHED MISSILES
 AAM • IR AIM-9L *Sidewinder*; IIR AIM-9X *Sidewinder* II; IRIS-T; ARH AIM-120B AMRAAM
BOMBS
 Laser-guided EGBU-12 *Paveway* II
 INS/GPS guided JDAM

Special Operations Command (NORSOCOM)

FORCES BY ROLE
SPECIAL FORCES
 1 (armed forces) SF comd (2 SF gp)
 1 (navy) SF comd (1 SF gp)

Central Support, Administration and Command 5,550; 600 conscripts (total 6,150)

Central Support, Administration and Command includes military personnel in all joint elements and they are responsible for logistics and CIS in support of all forces in Norway and abroad

Home Guard 600 (45,000 reserves)

The Home Guard is a separate organisation, but closely cooperates with all services. The Home Guard can be mobilised on very short notice for local security operations

Land Home Guard 41,150 with reserves

11 Home Guard Districts with mobile Rapid Reaction Forces (3,000 troops in total) as well as reinforcements and follow-on forces (38,150 troops in total)

Naval Home Guard 1,900 with reserves

Consisting of Rapid Reaction Forces (500 troops), and 17 'Naval Home Guard Areas'. A number of civilian vessels can be requisitioned as required

EQUIPMENT BY TYPE
PATROL AND COASTAL COMBATANTS • PB 11: 4 *Harek*; 2 *Gyda*; 5 *Alusafe* 1290

Air Home Guard 1,450 with reserves
Provides force protection and security detachments for air bases

Cyber
The defence ministry is responsible for defending military networks and national coordination in armed conflict. The 2012 Cyber Security Strategy for Norway contained cross-governmental guidelines for cyber defence. Norwegian Armed Forces Cyber Defence supports the armed forces with establishing, operating and protecting networks. It is responsible for defending military networks against cyber attack. It also supports the Norwegian Armed Forces at home and abroad with the establishment, operation, development and protection of communications systems, and is responsible for defending military networks against cyber attacks as well as developing Network Based Defence.

DEPLOYMENT
Legal provisions for foreign deployment: Constitution: Codified constitution (1814)
Decision on deployment of troops abroad: By royal prerogative exercised by the government (Art. 25, 26)

AFGHANISTAN
NATO • *Operation Resolute Support* 50

EGYPT
MFO 3

IRAQ
Operation Inherent Resolve 120

JORDAN
Operation Inherent Resolve 60

MALI
UN • MINUSMA 71; 1 avn sqn

MIDDLE EAST
UN • UNTSO 13 obs

NORTH SEA
NATO • SNMG 1: 1 DDGHM
NATO • SNMCMG 1: 1 MHC

SERBIA
NATO • KFOR 2

SOUTH SUDAN
UN • UNMISS 10; 5 obs

UKRAINE
OSCE • Ukraine 13

FOREIGN FORCES
United States US European Command: 1 (APS) 155mm SP Arty bn eqpt set

Poland POL

Polish Zloty z		2015	2016	2017
GDP	z	1.79tr	1.85tr	
	US$	475bn	467bn	
per capita	US$	12,492	12,309	
Growth	%	3.7	3.1	
Inflation	%	-0.9	-0.6	
Def exp [a]	z	39.9bn		
	US$	10.6bn		
Def bdgt [b]	z	38.2bn	35.9bn	37.4bn
	US$	10.1bn	9.08bn	
FMA (US)	US$	9m	6m	3.5m
US$1=z		3.77	3.96	

[a] NATO definition
[b] Includes military pensions

Population 38,523,261

Age	0–14	15–19	20–24	25–29	30–64	65 plus
Male	7.6%	2.6%	3.1%	3.6%	25.2%	6.4%
Female	7.1%	2.4%	3.0%	3.4%	25.7%	10.0%

Capabilities
Territorial defence and NATO membership are two central pillars of Poland's defence policy. The change of government following parliamentary elections in October 2015 led to a review of Polish defence priorities and a Strategic Defence Review was expected to focus on the threat posed by an assertive Russia and the growing A2/AD capacity highlighted by the development in Russian military capabilities. A new Technical Modernization Programme (TMP), covering 2017–26, was expected in late 2016. It was likely that the new TMP would significantly revise previous capability priorities, which would have a knock-on effect for contracts and acquisition programmes. The government is considering command-structure reforms and it seems likely that Poland will reinstate the service commands abolished in 2014. Warsaw continues plans to strengthen its domestic defence-industrial base. Technology transfer and international partnering are seen as mechanisms to develop domestic industry, most of which is now consolidated in the government-owned holding company Polska Grupa Zbrojeniowa (PGZ). The government declared PGZ as its preferred partner and cancelled some smaller acquisition projects that only had privately owned bidders. The government has also announced plans to raise defence spending to 2.2% of GDP by 2020. Warsaw also established a fund to bolster the defence-modernisation ambitions of neighbours – the so-called Regional Security Assistance Programme – which will facilitate loans for armaments programmes and also serve to strengthen the position of Polish defence firms in regional markets. The fund is aimed at Poland's Visegrád 4 partners, as well as Bulgaria, Romania and the Baltic states. In 2016, Poland announced that it would set up a 53,000-strong territorial-defence force organised in 17 light infantry brigades. While some of these units would be

tasked with critical-infrastructure protection, others would be trained in unconventional-warfare tactics. The first brigades were due to stand up in 2017, with the full force established by 2019.

ACTIVE 99,300 (Army 48,200 Navy 7,700 Air Force 16,600 Special Forces 3,000 Joint 23,800) Paramilitary 73,400

ORGANISATIONS BY SERVICE

Army 48,200
FORCES BY ROLE
COMMAND
  elm 1 (MNC NE) corps HQ
MANOEUVRE
  Reconnaissance
  3 recce regt
  Armoured
  1 (11th) armd cav div (2 armd bde, 1 mech bde, 1 arty regt)
  Mechanised
  1 (12th) div (2 mech bde, 1 (coastal) mech bde, 1 arty regt)
  1 (16th) div (2 armd bde, 2 mech bde, 1 arty regt)
  1 (21st) mech bde (1 armd bn, 3 mech bn, 1 arty bn, 1 AD bn, 1 engr bn)
  Air Manoeuvre
  1 (6th) air aslt bde (3 air aslt bn)
  1 (25th) air cav bde (3 air cav bn, 2 tpt hel bn, 1 (casevac) med unit)
COMBAT SUPPORT
  2 engr regt
  1 ptn br regt
  2 chem regt
HELICOPTER
  1 (1st) hel bde (2 atk hel sqn with Mi-24D/V *Hind* D/E, 1 CSAR sqn with Mi-24V *Hind* E; PZL W-3PL *Gluszec*; 2 ISR hel sqn with Mi-2URP; 2 hel sqn with Mi-2)
AIR DEFENCE
  3 AD regt
EQUIPMENT BY TYPE
ARMOURED FIGHTING VEHICLES
  MBT 985: 142 *Leopard* 2A4; 105 *Leopard* 2A5; 233 PT-91 *Twardy*; 505 T-72/T-72M1D/T-72M1
  RECCE 366: 237 BRDM-2; 37 BWR; 92 WD R-5
  IFV 1,968: 1,268 BMP-1; 700 *Rosomak*
  APC • PPV 30 *Maxxpro*
  AUV 85: 40 *Cougar* (on loan from US); 45 M-ATV
ENGINEERING & MAINTENANCE VEHICLES
  AEV IWT; MT-LB
  ARV 65+: 10 *Leopard* 1; 15 MT-LB; TRI; WPT-TOPAS; 40 WZT-3
  VLB 52: 4 *Biber*; 48 BLG67M2
  MW 18: 14 *Bozena*; 4 *Kalina* SUM
ANTI-TANK/ANTI-INFRASTRUCTURE
  MSL • MANPATS 9K11 *Malyutka* (AT-3 *Sagger*); 9K111 *Fagot* (AT-4 *Spigot*); *Spike*-LR
ARTILLERY 769
  SP 405: **122mm** 292 2S1 *Gvozdika*; **152mm** 111 M-77 *Dana*; **155mm** 2 *Krab*

  MRL 122mm 180: 75 BM-21; 30 RM-70; 75 WR-40 *Langusta*
  MOR 184: **98mm** 89 M-98; **120mm** 95 M120
RADAR • LAND 3 LIWIEC (veh, arty)
HELICOPTERS
  ATK 28 Mi-24D/V *Hind* D/E
  MRH 64: 7 Mi-8MT *Hip*; 3 Mi-17 *Hip* H; 1 Mi-17AE *Hip* (aeromedical); 5 Mi-17-1V *Hip*; 16 PZL Mi-2URP *Hoplite*; 24 PZL W-3W/WA *Sokol*; 8 PZL W-3PL *Gluszec* (CSAR)
  TPT 34: **Medium** 9: 7 Mi-8T *Hip*; 2 PZL W-3AE *Sokol* (aeromedical); **Light** 25 PZL Mi-2 *Hoplite*
AIR DEFENCE
  SAM
    Short-range 20 2K12 *Kub* (SA-6 *Gainful*)
    Point-defence 64+: 9K32 *Strela*-2‡ (SA-7 *Grail*); 64 9K33 *Osa*-AK (SA-8 *Gecko*); GROM
  GUNS 352
    SP 23mm 28: 8 ZSU-23-4; 20 ZSU-23-4MP *Biala*
    TOWED 23mm 324; 252 ZU-23-2; 72 ZUR-23-2KG/PG

Navy 7,700
EQUIPMENT BY TYPE
SUBMARINES • TACTICAL 5
  SSK 5:
    4 *Sokol* (ex-NOR Type-207) with 8 single 533mm TT
    1 *Orzel* (ex-FSU *Kilo*) with 6 single 533mm TT each with T-53/T-65 HWT
PRINCIPAL SURFACE COMBATANTS 2
  FRIGATES • FFGHM 2 *Pulaski* (ex-US *Oliver Hazard Perry*) with 1 Mk13 GMLS with RGM-84D/F *Harpoon* AShM/SM-1MR SAM, 2 triple 324mm ASTT with MU90 LWT, 1 *Phalanx* Block 1B CIWS, 1 76mm gun (capacity 2 SH-2G *Super Seasprite* ASW hel) (1 vessel used as training ship)
PATROL AND COASTAL COMBATANTS 4
  CORVETTES • FSM 1 *Kaszub* with 2 quad lnchr with 9K32 *Strela*-2 (SA-N-5 *Grail*) SAM, 2 twin 533mm ASTT with SET-53 HWT, 2 RBU 6000 *Smerch* 2 A/S mor, 1 76mm gun
  PCFGM 3:
    3 *Orkan* (ex-GDR *Sassnitz*) with 1 quad lnchr with RBS-15 Mk3 AShM, 1 quad lnchr (manual aiming) with *Strela*-2 (SA-N-5 *Grail*) SAM, 1 AK630 CIWS, 1 76mm gun
MINE WARFARE • MINE COUNTERMEASURES 20
  MCCS 1 *Kontradmirał Xawery Czernicki*
  MHO 3 *Krogulec*
  MSI 17: 1 *Gopło*; 12 *Gardno*; 4 *Mamry*
AMPHIBIOUS 8
  LANDING SHIPS • LSM 5 *Lublin* (capacity 9 tanks; 135 troops)
  LANDING CRAFT • LCU 3 *Deba* (capacity 50 troops)
LOGISTICS AND SUPPORT 21
  AGI 2 *Moma*
  AGS 9: 2 *Heweliusz*; 4 *Wildcat* 40; 3 (coastal)
  AORL 1 *Baltyk*
  AOL 1 *Moskit*
  ARS 4: 2 *Piast*; 2 *Zbyszko*
  ATF 2
  AX 1 *Wodnik* with 1 twin AK230 CIWS
  AXS 1 *Iskra*

COASTAL DEFENCE • AShM MM-40 *Exocet*
AIR DEFENCE • SAM
  Short-range *Crotale* NG/GR

Naval Aviation 1,300

FORCES BY ROLE
ANTI SUBMARINE WARFARE/SEARCH & RESCUE
  1 sqn with Mi-14PL *Haze* A; Mi-14PL/R *Haze* C
  1 sqn with PZL W-3RM *Anakonda*; SH-2G *Super Seasprite*
MARITIME PATROL
  1 sqn with An-28RM; An-28E
TRANSPORT
  1 sqn with An-28TD; M-28B TD *Bryza*
  1 sqn with An-28TD; M-28B; Mi-17 *Hip* H; PZL Mi-2 *Hoplite*; PZL W-3T; 1 PZL W-3A
EQUIPMENT BY TYPE
AIRCRAFT
  MP 10: 8 An-28RM *Bryza*; 2 An-28E *Bryza*
  TPT • Light 4: 2 An-28TD *Bryza*; 2 M-28B TD *Bryza*
HELICOPTERS ASW 11: 7 Mi-14PL *Haze*; 4 SH-2G *Super Seasprite*
  MRH 1 Mi-17 *Hip* H
  SAR 8: 2 Mi-14PL/R *Haze* C; 4 PZL W-3RM *Anakonda*; 2 PZL W-3WA RM *Anakonda*
  TPT • Light 7: 4 PZL Mi-2 *Hoplite*; 1 PZL W-3A; 2 PZL-W-3T

Air Force 16,600

Flying hours 160–200 hrs/yr

FORCES BY ROLE
FIGHTER
  2 sqn with MiG-29A/UB *Fulcrum*
FIGHTER/GROUND ATTACK
  3 sqn with F-16C/D Block 52+ *Fighting Falcon*
FIGHTER/GROUND ATTACK/ISR
  2 sqn with Su-22M-4 *Fitter*
SEARCH AND RESCUE
  1 sqn with Mi-2; PZL W-3 *Sokol*
TRANSPORT
  1 sqn with C-130E; PZL M-28 *Bryza*
  1 sqn with C-295M; PZL M-28 *Bryza*
TRAINING
  1 sqn with PZL-130 *Orlik*
  1 sqn with TS-11 *Iskra*
  1 hel sqn with SW-4 *Puszczyk*
TRANSPORT HELICOPTER
  1 (Spec Ops) sqn with Mi-17 *Hip* H
  1 (VIP) sqn with Mi-8; W-3WA *Sokol*
AIR DEFENCE
  1 bde with S-125 *Neva* SC (SA-3 *Goa*); S-200C *Vega* (SA-5 *Gammon*)

EQUIPMENT BY TYPE
AIRCRAFT 98 combat capable
  FTR 32: 26 MiG-29A *Fulcrum*; 6 MiG-29UB *Fulcrum*
  FGA 66: 36 F-16C Block 52+ *Fighting Falcon*; 12 F-16D Block 52+ *Fighting Falcon*; 12 Su-22M-4 *Fitter*; 6 Su-22UM3K *Fitter*
  TPT 44: Medium 5 C-130E *Hercules*; Light 39: 16 C-295M; 23 M-28 *Bryza* TD
  TRG 62: 2 M-346; 28 PZL-130 *Orlik*; 32 TS-11 *Iskra*
HELICOPTERS
  MRH 8 Mi-17 *Hip* H
  TPT 70: Medium 30: 9 Mi-8 *Hip*; 11 PZL W-3 *Sokol*; 10 PZL W-3WA *Sokol* (VIP); Light 40: 16 PZL Mi-2 *Hoplite*; 24 SW-4 *Puszczyk* (trg)
AIR DEFENCE • SAM
  Long-range 1 S-200C *Vega* (SA-5 *Gammon*)
  Short-range 17 S-125 *Neva* SC (SA-3 *Goa*)
AIR-LAUNCHED MISSILES
  AAM • IR R-60 (AA-8 *Aphid*); R-73 (AA-11 *Archer*); AIM-9 *Sidewinder*; R-27T (AA-10B *Alamo*); ARH AIM-120C AMRAAM
  ASM AGM-65J/G *Maverick*; Kh-25 (AS-10 *Karen*); Kh-29 (AS-14 *Kedge*)

Special Forces 3,000

FORCES BY ROLE
SPECIAL FORCES
  3 SF units (GROM, FORMOZA & cdo)
COMBAT SUPPORT/
  1 cbt spt unit (AGAT)
COMBAT SERVICE SUPPORT
  1 spt unit (NIL)

Paramilitary 73,400

Border Guards 14,300
Ministry of Interior

Maritime Border Guard 3,700
EQUIPMENT BY TYPE
PATROL AND COASTAL COMBATANTS 18
  PCC 2 *Kaper*
  PBF 6: 2 *Straznik*; 4 IC16M
  PB 10: 2 *Wisloka*; 2 *Baltic* 24; 1 Project MI-6
  AMPHIBIOUS • LANDING CRAFT • UCAC 2 *Griffon* 2000TDX

Prevention Units (Police) 59,100
Anti-terrorist Operations Bureau n.k.
Ministry of Interior

Cyber

In January 2015, the National Security Bureau issued a Cyber Security Doctrine. The document discussed national security in the cyber dimension, describing it as a strategic objective. The national cyber environment was also diagnosed, as were internal and external threats, risks and opportunities. The doctrine stipulates the most significant tasks needed in order to build national cyber-security capability. It was reported that the document noted the need to pursue 'active cyberdefence, including offensive actions in cyberspace, and maintaining readiness for cyberwar'.

DEPLOYMENT

Legal provisions for foreign deployment:
Constitution: Codified constitution (1997); Act on Principles of Use or External Deployment of the Polish Armed Forces (17/12/1998)

Decision on deployment of troops abroad:
a) By president on request of prime minister in cases of direct threat (Art. 136);
b) In general, specified by ratified international agreement or statute (both must be passed by parliament, Art. 117)

AFGHANISTAN
NATO • *Operation Resolute Support* 180
UN • UNAMA 1 obs

ARMENIA/AZERBAIJAN
OSCE • Minsk Conference 1

BOSNIA-HERZEGOVINA
EU • EUFOR • *Operation Althea* 38

CENTRAL AFRICAN REPUBLIC
EU • EUTM RCA 2

CÔTE D'IVOIRE
UN • UNOCI 1 obs

DEMOCRATIC REPUBLIC OF THE CONGO
UN • MONUSCO 2 obs

IRAQ
Operation Inherent Resolve 60

KUWAIT
Operation Inherent Resolve 4 F-16C *Fighting Falcon*

SERBIA
NATO • KFOR 253; 1 inf coy
OSCE • Kosovo 1
UN • UNMIK 1 obs

SOUTH SUDAN
UN • UNMISS 1 obs

UKRAINE
OSCE • Ukraine 38

FOREIGN FORCES

Canada *Operation Reassurance* 220; 1 inf coy(+)
Germany 67 (elm MNC-NE corps HQ)

Portugal PRT

Euro €		2015	2016	2017
GDP	€	179bn	184bn	
	US$	199bn	206bn	
per capita	US$	19,117	19,759	
Growth	%	1.5	1.0	
Inflation	%	0.5	0.7	
Def exp [a]	€	2.38bn		
	US$	2.64bn		
Def bdgt	€	1.96bn	1.95bn	1.97bn
	US$	2.17bn	2.18bn	
US$1=€		0.90	0.90	

[a] NATO definition

Population 10,833,816

Age	0–14	15–19	20–24	25–29	30–64	65 plus
Male	8.1%	3.0%	3.0%	3.2%	23.7%	7.8%
Female	7.4%	2.7%	2.7%	2.8%	24.3%	11.3%

Capabilities

Principal roles for Portugal's armed forces include NATO, EU and UN operations, homeland defence and maritime security. Following April 2013's Defesa 2020 document, Portugal adopted a military-planning law for 2015–26, setting key milestones for platform-acquisition and -modernisation programmes. The plan envisages a reduction in army strength and the recalibration of the forces into 'immediate reaction forces' (FRI), 'permanent forces for the defence of national sovereignty' (FPAS) and modular forces (FMD). Investment plans support Portugal's ambition to field rapid-reaction and maritime-surveillance capabilities for territorial defence and multinational operations. In 2016, Lisbon reduced personnel numbers and made a significant cut to its operations and maintenance budget. Portugal sold 12 of its F-16 combat aircraft to Romania in 2016, as well as a training, logistics, support and update package. Land capabilities have been boosted by additional *Pandur* II armoured fighting vehicles and the army plans to upgrade its *Leopard* 2A6 tanks, electronic-warfare capacity and air defence (the latter from 2022). The navy plans to modernise its frigates and submarines and to acquire patrol vessels and a logistic-support vessel. The air force intends to modernise its remaining F-16s and its P-3C *Orion* maritime-patrol aircraft, and continue the acquisition of precision-guided munitions. The country's commitment to NATO collective defence was demonstrated by its lead role in the Baltic Air Policing mission in 2016.

ACTIVE 29,600 (Army 15,400 Navy 8,050 Air 6,150)
Paramilitary 44,000

RESERVE 211,950 (Army 210,000 Navy 1,250, Air Force 700)
Reserve obligation to age 35

ORGANISATIONS BY SERVICE

Army 17,800
5 territorial comd (2 mil region, 1 mil district, 2 mil zone)
FORCES BY ROLE
SPECIAL FORCES
  1 SF bn
MANOEUVRE
  Reconnaissance
    1 ISR bn
  Mechanised
    1 mech bde (1 cav tp, 1 tk regt, 2 mech inf bn, 1 arty bn, 1 AD bty, 1 engr coy, 1 sigs coy, 1 spt bn)
    1 (intervention) bde (1 cav tp, 1 recce regt, 2 mech inf bn, 1 arty bn, 1 AD bty, 1 engr coy, 1 sigs coy, 1 spt bn)
  Air Manoeuvre
    1 (rapid reaction) bde (1 cav tp, 1 cdo bn, 2 para bn, 1 arty bn, 1 AD bty, 1 engr coy, 1 sigs coy, 1 spt bn)
  Other
    1 (Azores) inf gp (2 inf bn, 1 AD bty)
    1 (Madeira) inf gp (1 inf bn, 1 AD bty)
COMBAT SUPPORT
  1 STA bty
  1 engr bn
  1 EOD unit
  1 ptn br coy
  1 EW coy
  2 MP coy
  1 CBRN coy
  1 psyops unit
  1 CIMIC coy (joint)
  1 sigs bn
COMBAT SERVICE SUPPORT
  1 construction coy
  1 maint coy
  1 log coy
  1 tpt coy
  1 med unit
AIR DEFENCE
  1 AD bn

Reserves 210,000
FORCES BY ROLE
MANOEUVRE
  Light
    3 (territorial) def bde (on mobilisation)
EQUIPMENT BY TYPE
ARMOURED FIGHTING VEHICLES
  MBT 58: 37 *Leopard* 2A6; 21 M60A3 TTS
  RECCE 47: 14 V-150 *Chaimite*; 33 VBL
  IFV 22 *Pandur* II MK 30mm
  APC 416
    APC (T) 252: 170 M113A1; 32 M113A2; 50 M577A2 (CP)
    APC (W) 164: 20 V-200 *Chaimite*; 144 *Pandur* II (all variants)
ENGINEERING & MAINTENANCE VEHICLES
  AEV M728
  ARV 13: 6 M88A1, 7 *Pandur*
  VLB M48

ANTI-TANK/ANTI-INFRASTRUCTURE
  MSL
    SP 20: 16 M113 with TOW; 4 M901 with TOW
    MANPATS *Milan*; TOW
  RCL 236: **84mm** 162 *Carl Gustav*; **90mm** 29 M67; **106mm** 45 M40A1
ARTILLERY 319
  SP 155mm 23: 6 M109A2; 17 M109A5
  TOWED 55: **105mm** 31: 18 L119 Light Gun; 8 M101A1; 5 Model 56 pack howitzer; **155mm** 24 M114A1
  MOR 241: **81mm** 143; **SP 81mm** 15: 3 M125A1; 12 M125A2; **107mm** 11 M30; **SP 107mm** 18: 3 M106A1; 15 M106A2; **120mm** 54 Tampella
AIR DEFENCE
  SAM • Point-defence 29+: 5 M48A2 *Chaparral*; 24 M48A3 *Chaparral*; FIM-92 *Stinger*
  GUNS • TOWED 20mm 26 Rh 202

Navy 8,050 (incl 1,250 Marines)
EQUIPMENT BY TYPE
SUBMARINES • TACTICAL • SSK 2 *Tridente* (GER Type-214) with 8 533mm TT with *Black Shark* HWT
PRINCIPAL SURFACE COMBATANTS 5
  FRIGATES • FFGHM 5:
    2 *Bartolomeu Dias* (ex-NLD *Karel Doorman*) with 2 quad Mk141 lnchr with RGM-84C *Harpoon* AShM, 1 16-cell Mk48 VLS with RIM-7M *Sea Sparrow* SAM, 2 Mk32 twin 324mm ASTT with Mk46 LWT, 1 *Goalkeeper* CIWS, 1 76mm gun (capacity: 1 *Lynx* Mk95 (*Super Lynx*) hel)
    3 *Vasco Da Gama* with 2 quad Mk141 lnchr with RGM-84C *Harpoon* AShM, 1 octuple Mk 29 GMLS with RIM-7M *Sea Sparrow* SAM, 2 Mk32 triple 324mm ASTT with Mk46 LWT, 1 *Phalanx* Block 1B CIWS, 1 100mm gun (capacity 2 *Lynx* Mk95 (*Super Lynx*) hel)
PATROL AND COASTAL COMBATANTS 23
  CORVETTES • FS 5:
    3 *Baptista de Andrade* with 1 100mm gun, 1 hel landing platform
    2 *Joao Coutinho* with 1 twin 76mm gun, 1 hel landing platform
  PSO 2 *Viana do Castelo* with 1 hel landing platform
  PCC 4: 3 *Cacine*; 1 *Tejo* (ex-DNK *Flyvisken*)
  PBR 12: 2 *Albatroz*; 5 *Argos*; 4 *Centauro*; 1 *Rio Minho*
LOGISTICS AND SUPPORT 11
  AGS 4: 2 *D Carlos* I (ex-US *Stalwart*); 2 *Andromeda*
  AORL 1 *Bérrio* (ex-UK *Rover*) with 1 hel landing platform (for medium hel)
  AXS 6: 1 *Sagres*; 1 *Creoula*; 1 *Polar*; 2 *Belatrix*; 1 *Zarco*

Marines 1,250
FORCES BY ROLE
SPECIAL FORCES
  1 SF det
MANOEUVRE
  Light
    2 lt inf bn
COMBAT SUPPORT
  1 mor coy
  1 MP det

EQUIPMENT BY TYPE
ARTILLERY • MOR 120mm 30

Naval Aviation
EQUIPMENT BY TYPE
HELICOPTERS • ASW 5 *Lynx* Mk95 (*Super Lynx*)

Air Force 6,150
Flying hours 180 hrs/yr on F-16 *Fighting Falcon*

FORCES BY ROLE
FIGHTER/GROUND ATTACK
  2 sqn with F-16AM/BM *Fighting Falcon*
MARITIME PATROL
  1 sqn with P-3C *Orion*
ISR/TRANSPORT
  1 sqn with C-295M
COMBAT SEARCH & RESCUE
  1 sqn with with AW101 *Merlin*
TRANSPORT
  1 sqn with C-130H/C-130H-30 *Hercules*
  1 sqn with *Falcon* 50
TRAINING
  1 sqn with *Alpha Jet**
  1 sqn with SA316 *Alouette* III
  1 sqn with TB-30 *Epsilon*

EQUIPMENT BY TYPE
AIRCRAFT 41 combat capable
  FTR 30: 26 F-16AM *Fighting Falcon*; 4 F-16BM *Fighting Falcon*
  ASW 5 P-3C *Orion*
  ISR: 7: 5 C-295M (maritime surveillance), 2 C-295M (photo recce)
  TPT 13: **Medium** 5: 2 C-130H *Hercules*; 3 C-130H-30 *Hercules* (tpt/SAR); **Light** 5 C-295M; **PAX** 3 *Falcon* 50 (tpt/VIP)
  TRG 22: 6 *Alpha Jet**; 16 TB-30 *Epsilon*
HELICOPTERS
  MRH 6 SA316 *Alouette* III (trg, utl)
  TPT • **Medium** 12 AW101 *Merlin* (6 SAR, 4 CSAR, 2 fishery protection)
AIR-LAUNCHED MISSILES
  AAM • IR AIM-9L/I *Sidewinder*; ARH AIM-120 AMRAAM
  ASM AGM-65A *Maverick*
  AShM AGM-84A *Harpoon*
BOMBS
  Laser-guided/GPS GBU-49 *Enhanced Paveway* II
  INS/GPS guided GBU-31 JDAM

Paramilitary 44,000

National Republican Guard 22,400
EQUIPMENT BY TYPE
PATROL AND COASTAL COMBATANTS 32
  PBF 12
  PB 20
HELICOPTERS • MRH 7 SA315 *Lama*

Public Security Police 21,600

Cyber
A Cyberdefence Centre is being established, under the command of the Portuguese CHOD.

DEPLOYMENT
Legal provisions for foreign deployment:
Constitution: Codified constitution (1976) (revised in 2005)
Decision on deployment of troops abroad: By government

AFGHANISTAN
NATO • *Operation Resolute Support* 10
UN • UNAMA 1 obs

CENTRAL AFRICAN REPUBLIC
EU • EUTM RCA 11

IRAQ
Operation Inherent Resolve 32

MALI
EU • EUTM Mali 12
UN • MINUSMA 2

NORTH SEA
NATO • SNMG 1: 1 FFGHM

SERBIA
NATO • KFOR 185; 1 AB coy (KTM)

UGANDA
EU • EUTM Somalia 4

UKRAINE
OSCE • Ukraine 5

FOREIGN FORCES
United States US European Command: 220; 1 spt facility at Lajes

Romania ROM

New Lei		2015	2016	2017
GDP	lei	713bn	753bn	
	US$	178bn	187bn	
per capita	US$	8,956	9,439	
Growth	%	3.8	5.0	
Inflation	%	-0.6	-1.5	
Def exp [a]	lei	10.3bn		
	US$	2.58bn		
Def bdgt [b]	lei	9.94bn	11.2bn	10.6bn
	US$	2.48bn	2.78bn	
FMA (US)	US$	5.4m	5.4m	4.4m
US$1=lei		4.01	4.04	

[a] NATO definition
[b] Includes military pensions

Population   21,599,736

Age	0–14	15–19	20–24	25–29	30–64	65 plus
Male	7.4%	2.7%	2.8%	3.8%	25.4%	6.5%
Female	7.0%	2.6%	2.7%	3.7%	25.8%	9.6%

Capabilities

Romania's armed forces are structured around territorial defence and support to NATO, and have contributed to missions in Afghanistan and Iraq during the last decade. A new military strategy was approved in May 2016, covering a period of four years, including equipment procurement and the force structure to 2026. NATO sees Romania as strategically important; the *Aegis* Ashore ballistic-missile-defence system is based at US Naval Support Facility Deveselu, becoming formally operational in May 2016. Force modernisation is a priority, with ageing Soviet-era equipment seen as a limiting factor for the country's military capability. The financing of ongoing projects, as well as meeting critical procurement requirements, were key components of the 2016 defence budget; the long-term plan to meet the NATO defence-spending goal of 2% of GDP was articulated. The first six of 12 refurbished Portuguese F-16 combat aircraft were delivered to Romania in September 2016 as part of a long-overdue plan to replace the country's ageing MiG-21 fleet. Other requirements include intelligence, surveillance and reconnaissance capabilities, self-propelled artillery, and integrated short-range and very-short-range air-defence systems. Romania is also a member of the Strategic Airlift Capability C-17 unit. Romanian forces continue to be involved in a range of international exercises, training with NATO partners in the Black Sea as part of the *Sea Shield 16* exercise. Bucharest also deployed troops to Poland for the *Anakonda 16* exercise and hosted US forces for *Saber Guardian 16*. The additional recruitment of some 2,000 personnel on four-year contracts (to be activated in 2017) was made a priority. Romania has called for a permanent NATO deployment to the Black Sea as a counter to Russian activity in the region.

ACTIVE 70,500 (Army 39,600 Navy 6,600 Air 10,300 Joint 14,000) **Paramilitary 79,900**

RESERVE 50,000 (Joint 50,000)

ORGANISATIONS BY SERVICE

Army 39,600

Readiness is reported as 70–90% for NATO-designated forces (1 div HQ, 1 mech bde, 1 inf bde & 1 mtn inf bde) and 40–70% for other forces

FORCES BY ROLE
COMMAND
  2 div HQ (2nd & 4th)
  elm 1 div HQ (MND-SE)
SPECIAL FORCES
  1 SF bde (2 SF bn, 1 para bn, 1 log bn)
MANOEUVRE
  Reconnaissance
  3 recce bn
  Mechanised
  5 mech bde (1 tk bn, 2 mech inf bn, 1 arty bn, 1 AD bn, 1 log bn)
  Light
  1 inf bde (2 inf bn, 1 arty bn, 1 AD bn, 1 log bn)
  1 inf bde (2 inf bn, 1 mtn inf bn, 1 arty bn, 1 AD bn, 1 log bn)
  Mountain
  2 mtn inf bde (3 mtn inf bn, 1 arty bn, 1 AD bn, 1 log bn)
COMBAT SUPPORT
  1 arty bde (3 MRL bn, 1 log bn)
  3 arty regt
  1 engr bde (1 engr bn, 2 ptn br bn, 1 log bn)
  3 engr bn
  3 sigs bn
  1 CIMIC bn
  1 MP bn
  3 CBRN bn
COMBAT SERVICE SUPPORT
  3 spt bn
AIR DEFENCE
  3 AD regt

EQUIPMENT BY TYPE
ARMOURED FIGHTING VEHICLES
  MBT 437: 250 T-55; 42 TR-580; 91 TR-85; 54 TR-85 M1
  IFV 124: 23 MLI-84; 101 MLI-84 JDER
  APC 1,247
    APC (T) 75 MLVM
    APC (W) 607: 69 B33 TAB *Zimbru*; 31 *Piranha* III; 367 TAB-71; 140 TAB-77
    TYPE VARIANTS 505 APC
    PPV 60 *Maxxpro*
  AUV 362 TABC-79
ENGINEERING & MAINTENANCE VEHICLES
  ARV 3 BPz-2
ANTI-TANK/ANTI-INFRASTRUCTURE
  MSL • SP 134: 12 9P122 *Malyutka* (AT-3 *Sagger*); 74 9P133 *Malyutka* (AT-3 *Sagger*); 48 9P148 *Konkurs* (AT-5 *Spandrel*)
  GUNS
    SP 23 SU-100
    TOWED 100mm 209 M-1977
ARTILLERY 899
  SP 122mm 24: 6 2S1; 18 Model 89
  TOWED 422: **122mm** 72 (M-30) M-1938 (A-19); **152mm** 350: 247 M-1981; 103 M-1985
  MRL 122mm 187: 133 APR-40; 54 LAROM
  MOR 120mm 266 M-1982
RADARS • LAND 8 SNAR-10 *Big Fred*
AIR DEFENCE • GUNS 66
  SP 35mm 42 *Gepard*
  TOWED • 35mm 24 GDF-203

Navy 6,600

EQUIPMENT BY TYPE
PRINCIPAL SURFACE COMBATANTS 3
  DESTROYERS 3
    DDGH 1 *Marasesti* with 4 twin lnchr with P-15M *Termit*-M (SS-N-2C *Styx*) AShM, 2 triple 533mm ASTT with RUS 53–65 ASW, 2 RBU 6000 *Smerch* 2 A/S mor, 2 twin 76mm guns (capacity 2 SA-316 (IAR-316) *Alouette* III hel)
    DDH 2 *Regele Ferdinand* (ex-UK Type-22), with 2 triple 324mm TT, 1 76mm gun (capacity 1 SA330 (IAR-330) *Puma*)

PATROL AND COASTAL COMBATANTS 25
  CORVETTES 4
    FSH 2 *Tetal* II with 2 twin 533mm ASTT, 2 RBU 6000 *Smerch* 2 A/S mor, 2 AK630 CIWS, 1 76mm gun (capacity 1 SA316 (IAR-316) *Alouette* III hel)
    FS 2 *Tetal* I with 2 twin 533mm ASTT with RUS 53-65 ASW, 2 RBU 2500 *Smerch* 1 A/S mor, 2 twin 76mm guns
  PCFG 3 *Zborul* with 2 twin lnchr with P-15M *Termit-M* (SS-N-2C *Styx*) AShM, 2 AK630 CIWS, 1 76mm gun
  PCFT 3 *Naluca* with 4 single 533mm ASTT
  PCR 8:
    5 *Brutar* II with 2 BM-21 MRL, 1 100mm gun
    3 *Kogalniceanu* with 2 BM-21 MRL, 2 100mm guns
  PBR 6 VD 141 (ex-MSI now used for river patrol)
MINE WARFARE 11
  MINE COUNTERMEASURES 10
    MSO 4 *Musca* with 2 RBU 1200 A/S mor, 2 AK230 CIWS
    MSI 6 VD141 (used for river MCM)
  MINELAYERS • ML 1 *Corsar* with up to 100 mines, 2 RBU 1200 A/S mor, 1 57mm gun
LOGISTICS AND SUPPORT 8
  AE 2 *Constanta* with 2 RBU 1200 A/S mor, 2 twin 57mm guns
  AGOR 1 *Corsar*
  AGS 2: 1 *Emil Racovita*; 1 *Catuneanu*
  AOL 1 *Tulcea*
  ATF 1 *Grozavu*
  AXS 1 *Mircea*

Naval Infantry
FORCES BY ROLE
MANOEUVRE
  Light
    1 naval inf bn
EQUIPMENT BY TYPE
ARMOURED FIGHTING VEHICLES
  AUV 14: 11 ABC-79M; 3 TABC-79M

Air Force 10,300
Flying hours 120 hrs/yr

FORCES BY ROLE
FIGHTER
  2 sqn with MiG-21 *Lancer* C
FIGHTER GROUND ATTACK
  1 sqn (forming) with with F-16AM/BM *Fighting Falcon*
GROUND ATTACK
  1 sqn with IAR-99 *Soim*
TRANSPORT
  1 sqn with An-30 *Clank*; C-27J *Spartan*
  1 sqn with C-130B/H *Hercules*
TRAINING
  1 sqn with IAR-99 *Soim**
  1 sqn with SA316B *Alouette* III (IAR-316B); Yak-52 (Iak-52)
TRANSPORT HELICOPTER
  2 (multi-role) sqn with IAR-330 SOCAT *Puma*
  3 sqn with SA330 *Puma* (IAR-330)

AIR DEFENCE
  1 AD bde
COMBAT SERVICE SUPPORT
  1 engr spt regt
EQUIPMENT BY TYPE
AIRCRAFT 53 combat capable
  FTR 6: 5 F-16AM *Fighting Falcon*; 1 F-16BM *Fighting Falcon*
  FGA 26: 6 MiG-21 *Lancer* B; 20 MiG-21 *Lancer* C
  ISR 2 An-30 *Clank*
  TPT • Medium 12: 7 C-27J *Spartan*; 4 C-130B *Hercules*; 1 C-130H *Hercules*
  TRG 33: 10 IAR-99*; 11 IAR-99C *Soim**; 12 Yak-52 (Iak-52)
HELICOPTERS
  MRH 30: 22 IAR-330 SOCAT *Puma*; 8 SA316B *Alouette* III (IAR-316B)
  TPT • Medium 36: 21 SA330L *Puma* (IAR-330L); 15 SA330M *Puma* (IAR-330M)
  AIR DEFENCE • SAM • Medium-range 14: 6 S-75M3 *Volkhov* (SA-2 *Guideline*); 8 MIM-23 *Hawk* PIP III
AIR-LAUNCHED MISSILES
  AAM • IR AIM-9M *Sidewinder*; R-73 (AA-11 *Archer*); R-550 *Magic* 2; *Python* 3 **ARH** AIM-120C AMRAAM
  ASM *Spike*-ER
BOMBS
  Laser-guided GBU-12 *Paveway*
  INS/GPS guided GBU-38 JDAM

Paramilitary 79,900

Border Guards 22,900 (incl conscripts)
Ministry of Interior
EQUIPMENT BY TYPE
PATROL AND COASTAL COMBATANTS 14
  PCO 1 *Stefan cel Mare* (Damen OPV 900)
  PBF 1 *Bigliani*
  PB 12: 4 *Neustadt*; 3 *Mai*; 5 SNR-17

Gendarmerie ε57,000
Ministry of Interior

Cyber
In 2013, Romania adopted its first Cyber Security Strategy, which defines the conceptual framework, aim, objectives, priorities and courses of action for providing cyber security at the national level. A military CERT (CERTMIL) exists within the Ministry of National Defence, having responsibility for cyber-incident management in the defence realm.

DEPLOYMENT

Legal provisions for foreign deployment:
Constitution: Codified constitution (1991)
Decision on deployment of troops abroad: a) By parliament (Art. 62); or b) by president upon parliamentary approval (Art. 92)

AFGHANISTAN
NATO • Operation Resolute Support 624
UN • UNAMA 2 obs

BOSNIA-HERZEGOVINA
EU • EUFOR • *Operation Althea* 39

CENTRAL AFRICAN REPUBLIC
EU • EUTM RCA 2

CÔTE D'IVOIRE
UN • UNOCI 3 obs

DEMOCRATIC REPUBLIC OF THE CONGO
UN • MONUSCO 22 obs

IRAQ
Operation Inherent Resolve 50

MALI
EU • EUTM Mali 1
UN • MINUSMA 1

SERBIA
NATO • KFOR 55
OSCE • Kosovo 1
UN • UNMIK 1 obs

SOUTH SUDAN
UN • UNMISS 2; 5 obs

UGANDA
EU • EUTM Somalia 1

UKRAINE
OSCE • Ukraine 55

FOREIGN FORCES

United States US European Command: 550

Serbia SER

Serbian Dinar d		2015	2016	2017
GDP	d	3.97tr	4.15tr	
	US$	36.5bn	37.8bn	
per capita	US$	5,120	5,294	
Growth	%	0.7	2.5	
Inflation	%	1.4	1.3	
Def bdgt	d	56.0bn	55.8bn	
	US$	515m	507m	
FMA (US)	US$	1.8m	1.8m	1.8m
US$1=d		108.81	109.96	

Population 7,143,921

Ethnic groups: Serbian 83.3% Hungarian 3.353 % Romani 2.05% Bosniac 2.02% Croatian 0.8%

Age	0–14	15–19	20–24	25–29	30–64	65 plus
Male	7.5%	2.8%	3.1%	3.3%	24.6%	7.4%
Female	7.1%	2.6%	2.9%	3.1%	25.0%	10.6%

Capabilities

Serbia's armed forces are undergoing a restructuring process to enable improved ties with NATO; however, the country has EU membership as its objective. In 2015 the country agreed a NATO Individual Partnership Action Plan to enable greater cooperation with the Alliance. Serbia's forces have reduced in size over the last decade but remain capable of territorial defence, internal security and limited support to peacekeeping missions. Long-term moves towards acquiring Western equipment appear to have reversed in favour of acquiring Russian hardware. A commission for military–technical cooperation between Russia and Serbia was reportedly expected to meet at the start of 2017, where air-defence systems and combat aircraft were due to be top of the list for Belgrade. The prime minister has indicated Serbia's interest in purchasing a small number of Russian MiG-29 fighters. Russia delivered two new Mi-17V-5 helicopters in July 2016 and further deals could be on the table. However, Serbia hosted only two high-profile exercises with Russia in 2016, taking part in more training activities overall with NATO countries. Serbia also participates in UN peacekeeping operations.

ACTIVE 28,150 (Army 13,250 Air Force and Air Defence 5,100 Training Command 3,000 Guards 1,600 Other MoD 5,200)
Conscript liability 6 months (voluntary)

RESERVE 50,150

ORGANISATIONS BY SERVICE

Army 13,250
FORCES BY ROLE
SPECIAL FORCES
1 SF bde (1 CT bn, 1 cdo bn, 1 para bn, 1 log bn)
MANOEUVRE
Mechanised
1 (1st) bde (1 tk bn, 2 mech inf bn, 1 inf bn, 1 SP arty bn, 1 MRL bn, 1 AD bn, 1 engr bn, 1 log bn)
3 (2nd, 3rd & 4th) bde (1 tk bn, 2 mech inf bn, 2 inf bn, 1 SP arty bn, 1 MRL bn, 1 AD bn, 1 engr bn, 1 log bn)
COMBAT SUPPORT
1 (mixed) arty bde (4 arty bn, 1 MRL bn, 1 spt bn)
2 ptn bridging bn
1 NBC bn
1 sigs bn
2 MP bn

Reserve Organisations
FORCES BY ROLE
MANOEUVRE
Light
8 (territorial) inf bde
EQUIPMENT BY TYPE
ARMOURED FIGHTING VEHICLES
MBT 212: 199 M-84; 13 T-72
RECCE 46 BRDM-2
IFV 323 M-80
APC • APC (W) 39 BOV-VP M-86
ENGINEERING & MAINTENANCE VEHICLES
AEV IWT
ARV M84A1; T-54/T-55
VLB MT-55; TMM

ANTI-TANK/ANTI-INFRASTRUCTURE
  MSL
    SP 48 BOV-1 (M-83) with 9K11 *Malyutka* (AT-3 *Sagger*)
    MANPATS 9K11 *Malyutka* (AT-3 *Sagger*); 9K111 *Fagot* (AT-4 *Spigot*)
    RCL 90mm 6 M-79
ARTILLERY 515
  SP 122mm 67 2S1 *Gvozdika*
  TOWED 204: **122mm** 78 D-30; **130mm** 18 M-46; **152mm** 36 M-84 NORA-A; **155mm** 72: 66 M114 (M1); 6 M-65
  MRL 81: **128mm** 78: 18 M-63 *Plamen*; 60 M-77 *Organj*; **262mm** 3 M-87 *Orkan*
  MOR 163: **82mm** 106 M-69; **120mm** 57 M-74/M-75
AIR DEFENCE
  SAM
    Short-range 77 2K12 *Kub* (SA-6 *Gainful*);
    Point-defence 17+: 12 9K31M *Strela*-1M (SA-9 *Gaskin*); 5 9K35M *Strela*-10M; 9K32M *Strela*-2M (SA-7 *Grail*)‡; *Šilo* (SA-16 *Gimlet*)
  GUNS • TOWED 40mm 36 Bofors L70

River Flotilla

The Serbian-Montenegrin navy was transferred to Montenegro upon independence in 2006, but the Danube flotilla remained in Serbian control. The flotilla is subordinate to the Land Forces

EQUIPMENT BY TYPE
PATROL AND COASTAL COMBATANTS 5
  PBR 5: 3 Type-20; 2 others
MINE WARFARE • MINE COUNTERMEASURES 4
  MSI 4 *Nestin* with 1 quad lnchr with *Strela* 2M (SA-N-5 *Grail*) SAM
AMPHIBOUS • LANDING CRAFT • LCU 5 Type-22
LOGISTICS AND SUPPORT 2
  AGF 1 *Kozara*
  AOL 1

Air Force and Air Defence 5,100

Flying hours: Ftr – 40 hrs/yr
FORCES BY ROLE
FIGHTER
  1 sqn with MiG-21bis *Fishbed*; MiG-29 *Fulcrum*
FIGHTER/GROUND ATTACK
  1 sqn with G-4 *Super Galeb**; J-22 *Orao*
ISR
  2 flt with IJ-22 *Orao* 1*; MiG-21R *Fishbed* H*
TRANSPORT
  1 sqn with An-2; An-26; Do-28; Yak-40 (Jak-40); 1 PA-34 *Seneca* V
TRAINING
  1 sqn with G-4 *Super Galeb** (adv trg/light atk); SA341/342 *Gazelle*; Utva-75 (basic trg)
ATTACK HELICOPTER
  1 sqn with SA341H/342L *Gazelle*; (HN-42/45); Mi-24 *Hind*
TRANSPORT HELICOPTER
  2 sqn with Mi-8 *Hip*; Mi-17 *Hip* H; Mi-17V-5 *Hip*
AIR DEFENCE
  1 bde (5 bn (2 msl, 3 SP msl) with S-125 *Neva* (SA-3 *Goa*); 2K12 *Kub* (SA-6 *Gainful*); 9K32 *Strela*-2 (SA-7 *Grail*); 9K310 *Igla*-1 (SA-16 *Gimlet*))
  2 radar bn (for early warning and reporting)
COMBAT SUPPORT
  1 sigs bn
COMBAT SERVICE SUPPORT
  1 maint bn
EQUIPMENT BY TYPE
AIRCRAFT 60 combat capable
  FTR 7+ : 2+ MiG-21bis *Fishbed*; 2+ MiG-21UM *Mongol* B; 2 MiG-29 *Fulcrum*; 1 MiG-29UB *Fulcrum*
  FGA 17 J-22 *Orao* 1
  ISR 12: 10 IJ-22R *Orao* 1*; 2 MiG-21R *Fishbed* H*
  TPT • **Light** 10: 1 An-2 *Colt*; 4 An-26 *Curl*; 2 Do-28 *Skyservant*; 2 Yak-40 (Jak-40); 1 PA-34 *Seneca* V
  TRG 45: 24 G-4 *Super Galeb**; 11 Utva-75; 10 *Lasta* 95
HELICOPTERS
  ATK 2 Mi-24 *Hind*
  MRH 52: 1 Mi-17 *Hip* H; 2 Mi-17V-5 *Hip*; 2 SA341H *Gazelle* (HI-42); 34 SA341H *Gazelle* (HN-42)/SA342L *Gazelle* (HN-45); 13 SA341H *Gazelle* (HO-42)/SA342L1 *Gazelle* (HO-45)
  TPT • **Medium** 8 Mi-8T *Hip* (HT-40)
AIR DEFENCE
  SAM
    Short-range 15: 6 S-125 *Pechora* (SA-3 *Goa*); 9 2K12 *Kub* (SA-6 *Gainful*)
    Point-defence 9K32 *Strela*-2 (SA-7 *Grail*)‡; 9K310 *Igla*-1 (SA-16 *Gimlet*)
  GUNS • TOWED 40mm 24 Bofors L-70
AIR-LAUNCHED MISSILES
  AAM • IR R-60 (AA-8 *Aphid*)
  ASM AGM-65 *Maverick*; A-77 *Thunder*

Guards 1,600

FORCES BY ROLE
MANOEUVRE
  Other
    1 (ceremonial) gd bde (1 gd bn, 1 MP bn, 1 spt bn)

DEPLOYMENT

Legal provisions for foreign deployment:
Constitution: Codified constitution (2006)
Decision on deployment of troops abroad: By parliament (Art. 140)

ALBANIA
OSCE • Albania 1

BOSNIA-HERZEGOVINA
OSCE • Bosnia and Herzegovina 1

CENTRAL AFRICAN REPUBLIC
EU • EUTM RCA 4
UN • MINUSCA 70; 2 obs; 1 med coy

CÔTE D'IVOIRE
UN • UNOCI 1 obs

CYPRUS
UN • UNFICYP 47; 1 inf pl

DEMOCRATIC REPUBLIC OF THE CONGO
UN • MONUSCO 8

LEBANON
UN • UNIFIL 177; 1 mech inf coy

LIBERIA
UN • UNMIL 1 obs

MALI
EU • EUTM Mali 3

MIDDLE EAST
UN • UNTSO 1 obs

UGANDA
EU • EUTM Somalia 6

UKRAINE
OSCE • Ukraine 13

TERRITORY WHERE THE GOVERNMENT DOES NOT EXERCISE EFFECTIVE CONTROL

Data here represents the de facto situation in Kosovo. This does not imply international recognition as a sovereign state. In February 2008, Kosovo declared itself independent. Serbia remains opposed to this, and while Kosovo has not been admitted to the United Nations, a number of states have recognised Kosovo's self-declared status.

Kosovo Security Force 2,500; reserves 800

The Kosovo Security Force was formed in January 2009 as a non-military organisation with responsibility for crisis response, civil protection and EOD. The force is armed with small arms and light vehicles only. A July 2010 law created a reserve force. It is undergoing a professionalisation process.

FOREIGN FORCES

All under Kosovo Force (KFOR) command unless otherwise specified
Albania 12 • OSCE 3
Armenia 35
Austria 465; 2 mech inf coy • OSCE 1
Bosnia-Herzegovina OSCE 9
Bulgaria 12
Canada 5 • OSCE 6
Croatia 26 • OSCE 1
Czech Republic 12 • OSCE 2 • UNMIK 2 obs
Denmark 35
Estonia 2
Finland 20 • OSCE 1
France 2 • OSCE 1
Georgia OSCE 1
Germany 699 • OSCE 3
Greece 112; 1 inf coy • OSCE 3
Hungary 366; 1 inf coy (KTM) • OSCE 3
Ireland 12 • OSCE 3
Italy 542; 1 inf BG HQ; 1 Carabinieri unit • OSCE 14
Kyrgyzstan OSCE 3
Lithuania 1
Luxembourg 23

Macedonia (FYROM) OSCE 16
Moldova 41 • UNMIK 1 obs
Montenegro OSCE 1
Netherlands 5
Norway 2
Poland 253; 1 inf coy • OSCE 1 • UNMIK 1 obs
Portugal 185; 1 AB coy (KTM)
Romania 55 • OSCE 1 • UNMIK 1 obs
Slovakia OSCE 1
Slovenia 253; 1 mot inf coy; 1 MP unit; 1 hel unit
Spain OSCE 2
Sweden 3 • OSCE 4
Switzerland 222; 1 inf coy • OSCE 1
Tajikistan OSCE 1
Turkey 395; 1 inf coy • OSCE 2 • UNMIK 1 obs
Ukraine 40 • OSCE 1 • UNMIK 2 obs
United Kingdom 1 • OSCE 12
United States 635; elm 1 ARNG inf bde HQ; 1 inf bn • OSCE 4

Slovakia SVK

Euro €		2015	2016	2017
GDP	€	78.1bn	80.8bn	
	US$	86.6bn	90.3bn	
per capita	US$	15,979	16,648	
Growth	%	3.6	3.4	
Inflation	%	-0.3	-0.2	
Def exp [a]	€	889m		
	US$	986m		
Def bdgt	€	797m	881m	
	US$	884m	983m	
US$1=€		0.90	0.90	

[a] NATO definition

Population 5,445,802

Age	0–14	15–19	20–24	25–29	30–64	65 plus
Male	7.8%	2.6%	3.2%	3.7%	25.5%	5.7%
Female	7.4%	2.5%	3.0%	3.6%	25.9%	9.1%

Capabilities

Slovakia released a new defence white paper in September 2016, setting out its security priorities and a plan to increase defence capabilities. Faced with an ageing air-force inventory based on Soviet-era equipment, Bratislava is planning to replace its small fighter and rotary-wing transport fleets in the latter half of this decade. Financial constraints will make an outright replacement of the fighter fleet unlikely; Slovakia has begun negotiations with Sweden regarding a lease arrangement for *Gripen* E aircraft. Such a move would provide the air force with a Western fighter and enhance interoperability with EU and NATO partners. There are also ambitions to replace land equipment and improve the overall technology level in the armed forces. Slovakia was set to take delivery of *Black Hawk* helicopters from 2016 to replace its multi-role

Mi-17s under a foreign-military-sale agreement with the US. In 2015, the country secured a Polish-government-sponsored loan to finance the purchase of Rosomak 8x8 vehicles; however, by November 2016 it was uncertain whether the deal would proceed. Slovakia has a small defence-industrial base, which conducts some repair and maintenance contracts for local and foreign customers, for example the Trenčín aircraft-repair plant (which operates under the defence ministry) in 2016 secured a contract to overhaul three Afghan Mi-17s. In October 2015, NATO agreed to set up a NATO Force Integration Unit, a small headquarters, in Slovakia, which activated in September 2016. Slovak officials have indicated that it is becoming increasingly difficult to maintain a healthy balance between spending on training and exercises and modernisation programmes. Slovakia announced in August 2016 that it was starting an Active Reserves pilot project after amending the law on conscription, to help address shortfalls in specialist capacities, such as engineering. A volunteer military-training programme continues, with the first graduates completing the 12-week training cycle at the end of September 2016.

ACTIVE 15,850 (Army 6,250 Air 3,950 Central Staff 2,550 Support and Training 3,100)
Conscript liability 6 months

ORGANISATIONS BY SERVICE

Central Staff 2,550
FORCES BY ROLE
SPECIAL FORCES
  1 (5th) spec ops bn

Army 6,250
FORCES BY ROLE
MANOEUVRE
  Armoured
    1 (2nd) armd bde (1 recce bn, 1 tk bn, 1 armd inf bn, 1 mot inf bn, 1 mixed SP arty bn)
  Mechanised
    1 (1st) mech bde (3 armd inf bn, 1 MRL bn, 1 engr bn, 1 NBC bn)
COMBAT SUPPORT
  1 MP bn
COMBAT SERVICE SUPPORT
  1 spt bde (2 log bn, 1 maint bn, 1 spt bn)
EQUIPMENT BY TYPE
ARMOURED FIGHTING VEHICLES
  MBT 30 T-72M
  IFV 239: 148 BMP-1; 91 BMP-2
  APC 101+
    APC (T) 72 OT-90
    APC (W) 22: 7 OT-64; 15 *Tatrapan* (6×6)
    PPV 7+ RG-32M
  AUV IVECO LMV
ENGINEERING & MAINTENANCE VEHICLES
  ARV MT-55; VT-55A; VT-72B; WPT-TOPAS
  VLB AM-50; MT-55A
  MW *Bozena*; UOS-155 *Belarty*

ANTI-TANK/ANTI-INFRASTRUCTURE
  SP 9S428 with *Malyutka* (AT-3 *Sagger*) on BMP-1; 9P135 *Fagot* (AT-4 *Spigot*) on BMP-2; 9P148 *Konkurs* (AT-5 *Spandrel*) on BRDM-2
  MANPATS 9K11 *Malyutka* (AT-3 *Sagger*); 9K111-1 *Konkurs* (AT-5 *Spandrel*)
ARTILLERY 68
  SP 19: **152mm** 3 M-77 *Dana*; **155mm** 16 M-2000 *Zuzana*
  TOWED **122mm** 19 D-30
  MRL 30: **122mm** 4 RM-70; **122/227mm** 26 RM-70/85 MODULAR
RADAR • LAND SNAR-10 *Big Fred* (veh, arty)
AIR DEFENCE • SAM
  Point-defence 48+: 48 9K35 *Strela*-10 (SA-13 *Gopher*); 9K32 *Strela*-2 (SA-7 *Grail*); 9K310 *Igla*-1 (SA-16 *Gimlet*)

Air Force 3,950

Flying hours 90 hrs/yr for MiG-29 pilots (NATO Integrated AD System); 90 hrs/yr for Mi-8/17 crews (reserved for EU & NATO)

FORCES BY ROLE
FIGHTER
  1 sqn with MiG-29AS/UBS *Fulcrum*
TRANSPORT
  1 flt with An-26 *Curl*
  1 flt with L-410FG/T/UVP *Turbolet*
TRANSPORT HELICOPTER
  1 sqn with Mi-8 *Hip*; Mi-17 *Hip* H
  1 sqn with PZL MI-2 *Hoplite*
TRAINING
  1 sqn with L-39CM/ZA/ZAM *Albatros*
AIR DEFENCE
  1 bde with 2K12 *Kub* (SA-6 *Gainful*); 9K32 *Strela*-2 (SA-7 *Grail*); S-300 (SA-10 *Grumble*)
EQUIPMENT BY TYPE
AIRCRAFT 23 combat capable
  FTR 12: 10 MiG-29AS *Fulcrum*; 2 MiG-29UBS *Fulcrum*;
  TPT • **Light** 9: 1 An-26 *Curl*; 2 L-410FG *Turbolet*; 2 L-410T *Turbolet*; 4 L-410UVP *Turbolet*
  TRG 13: 6 L-39CM *Albatros**; 5 L-39ZA *Albatros**; 2 L-39ZAM *Albatros**
HELICOPTERS
  ATK (15: 5 Mi-24D *Hind* D; 10 Mi-24V *Hind* E all in store)
  MRH 13 Mi-17 *Hip* H
  TPT 7: **Medium** 1 Mi-8 *Hip*; **Light** 6 PZL MI-2 *Hoplite*
AIR DEFENCE • SAM
  Long-range S-300PS (SA-10B *Grumble*)
  Short-range 2K12 *Kub* (SA-6 *Gainful*)
  Point-defence 9K32 *Strela*-2 (SA-7 *Grail*)‡
AIR-LAUNCHED MISSILES
  AAM • **IR** R-60 (AA-8 *Aphid*); R-73 (AA-11 *Archer*)
  SARH R-27R (AA-10A *Alamo*)
  ASM S5K/S5KO (57mm rockets); S8KP/S8KOM (80mm rockets)

DEPLOYMENT

Legal provisions for foreign deployment:
Constitution: Codified constitution (1992)

Decision on deployment of troops abroad: By the parliament (Art. 86)

AFGHANISTAN
NATO • *Operation Resolute Support* 40

BOSNIA-HERZEGOVINA
EU • EUFOR • *Operation Althea* 40
OSCE • Bosnia and Herzegovina 1

CYPRUS
UN • UNFICYP 159; elm 1 inf coy; 1 engr pl

MALI
EU • EUTM Mali 2

MIDDLE EAST
UN • UNTSO 2 obs

SERBIA
OSCE • Kosovo 1

UKRAINE
OSCE • Ukraine 9

Slovenia SVN

Euro €		2015	2016	2017
GDP	€	38.6bn	39.5bn	
	US$	42.8bn	44.1bn	
per capita	US$	20,747	21,370	
Growth	%	2.3	2.3	
Inflation	%	-0.5	-0.3	
Def exp [a]	€	361m		
	US$	401m		
Def bdgt [b]	€	400m	403m	420m
	US$	444m	450m	
US$1=€		0.90	0.90	

[a] NATO definition
[b] Includes military pensions

Population 1,978,029

Ethnic groups: Slovenian 83% Serbian 2% Croatian 1.8% Bosniac 1% Other or unspecified 12.2%

Age	0–14	15–19	20–24	25–29	30–64	65 plus
Male	6.9%	2.3%	2.6%	3.1%	26.0%	7.7%
Female	6.5%	2.2%	2.5%	3.0%	26.0%	11.2%

Capabilities

Territorial defence and the ability to take part in peace-support operations are central to Slovenia's defence strategy. The defence ministry was undertaking a Strategic Defence Review as of the end of 2016, which will form the basis for further reviews of Slovenia's strategic and operational documentation, such as (respectively) the Resolution on the General Long-Term Programme for the Development and Equipping of the Slovenian Armed Forces and the Medium-Term Defence Programme. The current focus of its medium-term defence programme 2016–20 is to stop defence capability eroding further. Development of the armed forces is constrained by the limited amount of available funding. Slovenia has launched several invitations to tender in order to sell off obsolete equipment, such as M-55S and BVP M-80A armoured vehicles, in an effort to raise funds for defence modernisation. Recruitment and retention is believed to face challenges from the civilian sector, which it was reported would be addressed with improved salaries and allowances. Slovenia acts as the framework nation for the NATO Mountain Warfare Centre of Excellence. Its small air wing is not equipped to provide air policing; Italy and Hungary currently partner in providing this capability. The country has contributed regularly to NATO and EU operations.

ACTIVE 7,250 (Army 7,250) **Paramilitary 5,950**

RESERVE 1,500 (Army 1,500) **Paramilitary 260**

ORGANISATIONS BY SERVICE

Army 7,250
FORCES BY ROLE
Regt are bn sized
SPECIAL FORCES
1 SF unit (1 spec ops coy, 1 CSS coy)
MANOEUVRE
Mechanised
1 (1st) mech inf bde (1 mech inf regt, 1 mtn inf regt, 1 cbt spt bn (1 ISR coy, 1 arty bty, 1 engr coy, 1 MP coy, 1 CBRN coy, 1 sigs coy, 1 SAM bty))
1 (72nd) mech inf bde (2 mech inf regt, 1 cbt spt bn (1 ISR coy, 1 arty bty, 1 engr coy, 1 MP coy, 1 CBRN coy, 1 sigs coy, 1 SAM bty))
COMBAT SUPPORT
1 EW coy
COMBAT SERVICE SUPPORT
1 log bde (1 log regt, (1 tk coy) 1 maint regt, 1 med regt)

Reserves
FORCES BY ROLE
MANOEUVRE
Mountain
2 inf regt (territorial – 1 allocated to each inf bde)
EQUIPMENT BY TYPE
ARMOURED FIGHTING VEHICLES
MBT 14 M-84 (trg role); (32 more in store)
RECCE 10 *Cobra* CBRN
APC • APC (W) 115: 85 *Pandur* 6×6 (*Valuk*); 30 *Patria* 8×8 (*Svarun*)
ENGINEERING & MAINTENANCE VEHICLES
ARV VT-55A
VLB MTU
ANTI-TANK/ANTI-INFRASTRUCTURE
MSL • MANPATS *Spike* MR/LR
ARTILLERY 68
TOWED • 155mm 18 TN-90
MOR 120mm 50 MN-9/M-74
AIR DEFENCE • SAM • Point-defence 9K338 *Igla*-S (SA-24 *Grinch*)

Army Maritime Element 130
FORCES BY ROLE
SPECIAL FORCES
　1 SF unit
EQUIPMENT BY TYPE
PATROL AND COASTAL COMBATANTS 2
　PBF 1 *Super Dvora* MkII
　PCC 1 *Triglav* III (RUS *Svetlyak*)

Air Element 610
FORCES BY ROLE
TRANSPORT
　1 sqn with *Falcon* 2000EX; L-410 *Turbolet*; PC-6B *Turbo Porter*;
TRAINING
　1 unit with Bell 206 *Jet Ranger* (AB-206); PC-9M*; Z-143L; Z-242L
TRANSPORT HELICOPTER
　1 sqn with AS532AL *Cougar*; Bell 412 *Twin Huey*
COMBAT SERVICE SUPPORT
　1 maint sqn
EQUIPMENT BY TYPE
AIRCRAFT 9 combat capable
　TPT 4: **Light** 3: 1 L-410 *Turbolet*; 2 PC-6B *Turbo Porter*
　PAX 1 *Falcon* 2000EX
　TRG 19: 9 PC-9M*; 2 Z-143L; 8 Z-242L
HELICOPTERS
　MRH 8: 5 Bell 412EP *Twin Huey*; 2 Bell 412HP *Twin Huey*; 1 Bell 412SP *Twin Huey* (some armed)
　TPT 8: **Medium** 4 AS532AL *Cougar*; **Light** 4 Bell 206 *Jet Ranger* (AB-206)

Paramilitary 5,950

Police 5,950; 260 reservists
Ministry of Interior (civilian; limited elements could be prequalified to cooperate in military defence with the armed forces during state of emergency or war)
PATROL AND COASTAL COMBATANTS • PBF 1 *Ladse*
HELICOPTERS
　MRH 1 Bell 412 *Twin Huey*,
　TPT • Light 5: 1 AW109; 2 Bell 206 (AB-206) *Jet Ranger*; 1 Bell 212 (AB-212); 1 H135

Cyber
A National Cyber Security Strategy was endorsed in February 2016 by the government

DEPLOYMENT
Legal provisions for foreign deployment:
Constitution: Codified constitution (1991)
Decision on deployment of troops abroad: By government (Art. 84 of Defence Act)

AFGHANISTAN
NATO • *Operation Resolute Support* 7

BOSNIA-HERZEGOVINA
EU • EUFOR • *Operation Althea* 16

IRAQ
Operation Inherent Resolve 6

LEBANON
UN • UNIFIL 15

MALI
EU • EUTM Mali 5

MEDITERRANEAN SEA
EU • EU NAVFOR MED: 1 PCC

MIDDLE EAST
UN • UNTSO 3 obs

SERBIA
NATO • KFOR 253; 1 mot inf coy; 1 MP unit; 1 hel unit

UKRAINE
OSCE • Ukraine 2

Spain ESP

Euro €		2015	2016	2017
GDP	€	1.08tr	1.12tr	
	US$	1.20tr	1.25tr	
per capita	US$	25,843	27,012	
Growth	%	3.2	3.1	
Inflation	%	-0.5	-0.3	
Def exp [a]	€	10.0bn		
	US$	11.1bn		
Def bdgt [b]	€	11.8bn	10.9bn	
	US$	13.1bn	12.2bn	
US$1=€		0.90	0.90	

[a] NATO definition
[b] Includes military pensions

Population　48,563,476

Age	0–14	15–19	20–24	25–29	30–64	65 plus
Male	7.9%	2.4%	2.5%	2.9%	26.0%	7.6%
Female	7.5%	2.3%	2.3%	2.7%	25.6%	10.2%

Capabilities

The Spanish Army conducted a comprehensive force-structure review in 2016. Nine brigades and the mountain command were reorganised into eight multipurpose brigades optimised for deployable operations, with a greater emphasis on mechanised formations and more special-operations forces. The Joint Special Operations Command, established in 2014 to coordinate the three services' special-operations forces, was expected to reach full operational capability in 2016. Following years of financial pressure, Spain's defence budget has seen a modest increase, although in 2016 only the navy's budget increased; those of the army and air force declined. The procurement budget increased slightly. The country has indigenous maritime, aerospace and armoured-vehicle industries. Work on the new S-80 submarine programme is being undertaken by state-owned Navantia. Spain has announced that it will participate in funding the

European MALE 2020 unmanned-aerial-vehicle (UAV) project, although in February 2016 Spain signed a contract for four MQ-9 Block 5 MALE UAVs. Upgrade plans for the navy include five new F-110 frigates, offshore-patrol vessels, SH-60F helicopters and vehicles for the marines. Spain's equipment and logistic-support capability appears to be sufficient to meet its national commitments and contribution to NATO operations and exercises. Spain has deployed a *Patriot* air-defence battery and radar to Turkey, hosted large-scale amphibious exercises and contributed a battalion-sized contingent to *Operation Resolute Support*. It was the Framework Nation for the NATO Very High Readiness Joint Task Force in 2016 and the NATO Rapid Deployable Corps (Spain) was the land component command of the enhanced NATO Response Force in 2016. Spain led the Baltic Air Policing mission in 2016. It retains a small contingent in Afghanistan as part of the NATO HQ.

ACTIVE 123,200 (Army 70,400 Navy 21,200 Air 20,400 Joint 11,200) **Paramilitary 76,750**

RESERVE 8,200 (Army 2,450 Navy 2,750 Air 2,300 Other 700)

ORGANISATIONS BY SERVICE

Space
EQUIPMENT BY TYPE
SATELLITES • COMMUNICATIONS 2: 1 *Spainsat*; 1 *Xtar-Eur*

Army 70,400
The Land Forces High Readiness HQ Spain provides one NATO Rapid Deployment Corps HQ (NRDC-ESP).
FORCES BY ROLE
COMMAND
 1 corps HQ (CGTAD/NRDC-ESP) (1 int regt, 1 MP bn)
 2 div HQ
SPECIAL FORCES
 1 comd (4 spec ops bn, 1 int coy, 1 sigs coy, 1 log bn)
MANOEUVRE
 Reconnaissance
 1 armd cav regt (2 armd recce bn)
 Mechanised
 3 (10th, 11th & 12th) mech bde (1 armd regt (1 armd recce bn, 1 tk bn), 1 mech inf regt (1 armd inf bn, 1 mech inf bn), 1 lt inf bn, 1 SP arty bn, 1 AT coy, 1 AD coy, 1 engr bn, 1 int coy, 1 NBC coy, 1 sigs coy, 1 log bn)
 1 (1st) mech bde (1 armd regt (1 armd recce bn, 1 tk bn), 1 mech inf regt (1 armd inf bn, 1 mech inf bn), 1 mtn inf bn, 1 SP arty bn, 1 AT coy, 1 AD coy, 1 engr bn, 1 int coy, 1 NBC coy, 1 sigs coy, 1 log bn)
 2 (2nd/La Legion & 7th) lt mech bde (1 armd recce bn, 1 mech inf regt (2 mech inf bn), 1 lt inf bn, 1 fd arty bn, 1 AT coy, 1 AD coy, 1 engr bn, 1 int coy, 1 NBC coy, 1 sigs coy, 1 log bn)
 Air Manoeuvre
 1 (6th) bde (1 recce bn, 3 para bn, 1 fd arty bn, 1 AT coy, 1 AD coy, 1 engr bn, 1 int coy, 1 NBC coy, 1 sigs coy, 1 log bn)

 Other
 1 (Canary Islands) comd (1 lt inf bde (3 lt inf regt, 1 fd arty regt, 1 AT coy, 1 engr bn, 1 int coy, 1 NBC coy, 1 sigs coy, 1 log bn); 1 spt hel bn; 1 AD regt)
 1 (Balearic Islands) comd (1 inf regt)
 2 (Ceuta and Melilla) comd (1 recce regt, 2 inf regt, 1 arty regt, 1 engr bn, 1 sigs coy, 1 log bn)
COMBAT SUPPORT
 1 arty comd (1 arty regt; 1 MRL regt; 1 coastal arty regt)
 1 engr comd (2 engr regt, 1 bridging regt)
 1 EW/sigs bde (1 EW regt, 3 sigs regt)
 1 EW regt
 1 NBC regt
 1 railway regt
 1 sigs regt
 1 CIMIC bn
COMBAT SERVICE SUPPORT
 1 log bde (5 log regt)
 1 med bde (1 log unit, 2 med regt, 1 fd hospital unit)
HELICOPTER
 1 hel comd (1 atk hel bn, 2 spt hel bn, 1 tpt hel bn, 1 sigs bn, 1 log unit (1 spt coy, 1 supply coy))
AIR DEFENCE
 1 AD comd (3 SAM regt, 1 sigs unit)
EQUIPMENT BY TYPE
ARMOURED FIGHTING VEHICLES
 MBT 331: 108 *Leopard* 2A4; 223 *Leopard* 2A5E
 RECCE 271: 84 B1 *Centauro*; 187 VEC-M1
 IFV 150 *Pizarro* (incl 21 comd)
 APC 875
  APC (T) 453 M113 (incl variants)
  APC (W) 312 BMR-600/BMR-600M1
  PPV 110 RG-31
 AUV IVECO LMV
ENGINEERING & MAINTENANCE VEHICLES
 AEV 26 CZ-10/25E
 ARV 38: 16 *Leopard* REC; 1 AMX-30; 5 BMR REC; 4 *Centauro* REC; 12 M113
 VLB 16: 1 M47; 15 M60
ANTI-TANK/ANTI-INFRASTRUCTURE
 MSL • MANPATS *Spike*-LR; TOW
ARTILLERY 1,557
 SP 155mm 96 M109A5
 TOWED 281: **105mm** 217: 56 L118 Light Gun; 161 Model 56 pack howitzer; **155mm** 64 SBT 155/52 SIAC
 MOR 1,180: **81mm** 777; **120mm** 403
RADAR • LAND 6: 4 ARTHUR; 2 AN/TPQ-36 *Firefinder*
COASTAL DEFENCE • ARTY 155mm 19 SBT 155/52 APU SBT V07
HELICOPTERS
 ATK 10: 6 *Tiger* HAP-E; 4 *Tiger* HAD-E
 MRH 17 Bo-105 HOT
 TPT 82: **Heavy** 17 CH-47D *Chinook* (HT-17D); **Medium** 38: 16 AS332B *Super Puma* (HU-21); 12 AS532UL *Cougar*; 6 AS532AL *Cougar*; 4 NH90 TTH; **Light** 27: 6 Bell-205 (HU-10B *Iroquois*); 5 Bell 212 (HU.18); 16 H135 (HE.26/HU.26)
UAV • ISR • Medium 6: 2 *Searcher* MkII-J (PASI); 4 *Searcher* MkIII (PASI)
AIR DEFENCE
 SAM
  Long-range 18 MIM-104C *Patriot* PAC-2

Medium-range 42 MIM-23B I-*Hawk* Phase III
Short-range 21: 8 NASAMS; 13 *Skyguard/Aspide*
Point-defence *Mistral*
GUNS • TOWED 35mm 91 GDF-005/GDF-007

Navy 21,200 (incl Naval Aviation and Marines)
EQUIPMENT BY TYPE
SUBMARINES • TACTICAL • SSK 3:
3 *Galerna* with 4 single 533mm TT with F17 Mod 2/L5 HWT
PRINCIPAL SURFACE COMBATANTS 11
DESTROYERS • DDGHM 5:
5 *Alvaro de Bazan* with *Aegis* Baseline 5 C2, 2 quad Mk141 lnchr with RGM-84F *Harpoon* AShM, 1 48-cell Mk41 VLS with SM-2MR/RIM-162B *Sea Sparrow* SAM, 2 twin 324mm ASTT with Mk46 LWT, 1 127mm gun (capacity 1 SH-60B *Seahawk* ASW hel)
FRIGATES • FFGHM 6:
6 *Santa Maria* with 1 Mk13 GMLS with RGM-84C *Harpoon* AShM/SM-1MR SAM, 2 Mk32 triple 324mm ASTT with Mk46 LWT, 1 *Meroka* mod 2 CIWS, 1 76mm gun (capacity 2 SH-60B *Seahawk* ASW hel)
AMPHIBIOUS
PRINCIPAL AMPHIBIOUS SHIPS 3:
LHD 1 *Juan Carlos* I (capacity 18 hel or 10 AV-8B FGA ac; 4 LCM-1E; 42 APC; 39 MBT; 900 troops)
LPD 2 *Galicia* (capacity 6 Bell 212 or 4 SH-3D *Sea King* hel; 4 LCM or 2 LCM & 8 AAV; 130 APC or 33 MBT; 540 troops)
LANDING CRAFT 14
LCM 14 LCM 1E
LOGISTICS AND SUPPORT 2
AORH 2: 1 *Patino* (capacity 3 Bell 212 or 2 SH-3D *Sea King* hel); 1 *Cantabria* (capacity 3 Bell 212 or 2 SH-3D *Sea King* hel)

Maritime Action Force
EQUIPMENT BY TYPE
PATROL AND COASTAL COMBATANTS 23
PSOH 4 *Meteoro* (*Buques de Accion Maritima*) with 1 76mm gun
PSO 7:
3 *Alboran* each with 1 hel landing platform
4 *Descubierta* with 1 76mm gun
PCO 4 *Serviola* with 1 76mm gun
PCC 3 *Anaga* with 1 76mm gun
PB 4: 2 P-101; 2 *Toralla*
PBR 1 *Cabo Fradera*
MINE WARFARE • MINE COUNTERMEASURES 6
MHO 6 *Segura*
LOGISTICS AND SUPPORT 29
AGI 1 *Alerta*
AGOR 1 (with ice-strengthened hull, for polar research duties in Antarctica)
AGS 3: 2 *Malaspina*; 1 *Castor*
AK 2: 1 *Martin Posadillo* with 1 hel landing platform; 1 *El Camino Español*
AP 1 *Contramaestre Casado* with 1 hel landing platform
ASR 1 *Neptuno*
ATF 4: 1 *Mar Caribe*; 1 *Mahon*; 1 *La Grana*, 1 *Las Palmas*
AXL 8: 4 *Contramaestre*; 4 *Guardiamarina*
AXS 8

Naval Aviation 800
Flying hours 150 hrs/yr on AV-8B *Harrier* II FGA ac; 200 hrs/yr on hel
FORCES BY ROLE
FIGHTER/GROUND ATTACK
1 sqn with AV-8B *Harrier* II Plus
ANTI-SUBMARINE WARFARE
1 sqn with SH-60B *Seahawk*
TRANSPORT
1 (liaison) sqn with Cessna 550 *Citation* II; Cessna 650 *Citation* VII
TRAINING
1 sqn with Hughes 500MD8
1 flt with TAV-8B *Harrier*
TRANSPORT HELICOPTER
1 sqn with Bell 212 (HU-18)
1 sqn with SH-3D *Sea King*
EQUIPMENT BY TYPE
AIRCRAFT 13 combat capable
FGA 13: 8 AV-8B *Harrier* II Plus; 4 AV-8B *Harrier* II (upgraded to II Plus standard); 1 TAV-8B *Harrier* (on lease from USMC)
TPT • Light 4: 3 Cessna 550 *Citation* II; 1 Cessna 650 *Citation* VII
HELICOPTERS
ASW 19: 7 SH-3D *Sea King* (tpt); 12 SH-60B *Seahawk*
MRH 9 Hughes 500MD
TPT • Light 7 Bell 212 (HA-18)
AIR-LAUNCHED MISSILES
AAM • IR AIM-9L *Sidewinder*; **ARH** AIM-120 AMRAAM
ASM AGM-65G *Maverick*
AShM AGM-119 *Penguin*

Marines 5,800
FORCES BY ROLE
SPECIAL FORCES
1 spec ops bn
MANOEUVRE
Amphibious
1 mne bde (1 recce unit, 1 mech inf bn, 2 inf bn, 1 arty bn, 1 log bn)
Other
1 sy bde (5 mne garrison gp)
EQUIPMENT BY TYPE
ARMOURED FIGHTING VEHICLES
MBT 16 M60A3TTS
APC • APC (W) 34: 32 *Piranha* IIIC; 1 *Piranha* IIIC (amb); 1 *Piranha* IIIC EW (EW)
AAV 18: 16 AAV-7A1/AAVP-7A1; 2 AAVC-7A1
ENGINEERING & MAINTENANCE VEHICLES
AEV 4 *Piranha* IIIC
ARV 2: 1 AAVR-7A1; 1 *Piranha* IIIC
ARTILLERY 18
SP 155mm 6 M109A2
TOWED 105mm 12 Model 56 pack howitzer

ANTI-TANK/ANTI-INFRASTRUCTURE
MSL • MANPATS Spike-LR; TOW-2
AIR DEFENCE • SAM • Point-defence Mistral

Air Force 20,400

The Spanish Air Force is organised in 3 commands – General Air Command, Combat Air Command and Canary Islands Air Command

Flying hours 120 hrs/yr on hel/tpt ac; 180 hrs/yr on FGA/ftr

FORCES BY ROLE
FIGHTER
  2 sqn with Eurofighter *Typhoon*
FIGHTER/GROUND ATTACK
  5 sqn with F/A-18A/B MLU *Hornet* (EF-18A/B MLU)
MARITIME PATROL
  1 sqn with P-3A/M *Orion*
ISR
  1 sqn with Beech C90 *King Air*
  1 sqn with Cessna 550 *Citation* V; CN-235 (TR-19A)
ELECTRONIC WARFARE
  1 sqn with C-212 *Aviocar*; *Falcon* 20D/E
SEARCH & RESCUE
  1 sqn with AS332B/B1 *Super Puma*; CN-235 VIGMA
  1 sqn with AS332B *Super Puma*; CN-235 VIGMA
  1 sqn with C-212 *Aviocar*; CN-235 VIGMA; SA330J/L *Puma* (AS330)
TANKER/TRANSPORT
  1 sqn with KC-130H *Hercules*
TRANSPORT
  1 VIP sqn with A310; *Falcon* 900
  1 sqn with C-130H/H-30 *Hercules*
  1 sqn with C-212 *Aviocar*
  2 sqn with C-295
  1 sqn with CN-235
TRAINING
  1 OCU sqn with Eurofighter *Typhoon*
  1 OCU sqn with F/A-18A/B (EF-18A/B MLU) *Hornet*
  1 sqn with Beech F33C *Bonanza*
  2 sqn with C-101 *Aviojet*
  1 sqn with C-212 *Aviocar*
  1 sqn with T-35 *Pillan* (E-26)
  2 (LIFT) sqn with F-5B *Freedom Fighter*
  1 hel sqn with H120 *Colibri*
  1 hel sqn with S-76C
TRANSPORT HELICOPTER
  1 sqn with AS332M1 *Super Puma*; AS532UL *Cougar* (VIP)
EQUIPMENT BY TYPE
AIRCRAFT 169 combat capable
  FTR 78: 59 Eurofighter *Typhoon*; 19 F-5B *Freedom Fighter*
  FGA 86: 20 F/A-18A *Hornet* (EF-18A); 54 EF-18A MLU; 12 EF-18B MLU
  ASW 5: 2 P-3A *Orion*; 3 P-3M *Orion*
  MP 8 CN-235 VIGMA
  ISR 2 CN-235 (TR-19A)
  EW 5: 1 C-212 *Aviocar* (TM.12D); 2 *Falcon* 20D; 2 *Falcon* 20E
  TKR 5 KC-130H *Hercules*
  TPT 75: **Heavy** 1 A400M; **Medium** 7: 6 C-130H *Hercules*; 1 C-130H-30 *Hercules*; **Light** 59: 3 Beech C90 *King Air*; 22 Beech F33C *Bonanza*; 10 C-212 *Aviocar* (incl 9 trg); 13 C-295; 8 CN-235; 3 Cessna 550 *Citation* V (ISR); **PAX** 8: 2 A310; 1 B-707; 5 *Falcon* 900 (VIP)
  TRG 102: 65 C-101 *Aviojet*; 37 T-35 *Pillan* (E-26)
HELICOPTERS
  TPT 43: **Medium** 21: 9 AS332B/B1 *Super Puma*; 4 AS332M1 *Super Puma*; 2 AS532UL *Cougar* (VIP); 4 SA330J *Puma* (AS330); 2 SA330L *Puma* (AS330); **Light** 22: 14 H120 *Colibri*; 8 S-76C
AIR DEFENCE • SAM
  Short-range Skyguard/Aspide
  Point-defence Mistral
AIR-LAUNCHED MISSILES
  AAM • IR AIM-9L/JULI *Sidewinder*; IIR IRIS-T; SARH AIM-7P *Sparrow*; ARH AIM-120B/C AMRAAM
  ARM AGM-88B HARM
  ASM AGM-65G *Maverick*
  AShM AGM-84D *Harpoon*
  LACM Taurus KEPD 350
BOMBS
  Laser-guided: GBU-10/12/16 *Paveway* II; GBU-24 *Paveway* III; EGBU-16 *Paveway* II; BPG-2000

Emergencies Military Unit (UME)

FORCES BY ROLE
COMMAND
  1 div HQ
MANOEUVRE
  Other
  5 Emergency Intervention bn
  1 Emergency Support and Intervention regt
COMBAT SUPPORT
  1 sigs bn
HELICOPTER
  1 hel bn opcon Army

Paramilitary 76,750

Guardia Civil 75,500

17 regions, 54 Rural Comds
FORCES BY ROLE
SPECIAL FORCES
  8 (rural) gp
MANOEUVRE
  Other
  15 (traffic) sy gp
  1 (Special) sy bn
EQUIPMENT BY TYPE
AIRCRAFT • TPT • Light 2 CN-235-300
HELICOPTERS
  MRH 20: 2 AS653N3 *Dauphin*; 18 Bo-105ATH
  TPT • Light 21: 8 BK-117; 13 H135

Guardia Civil Del Mar 1,250

EQUIPMENT BY TYPE
PATROL AND COASTAL COMBATANTS 72
  PSO 1 with 1 hel landing platform
  PCC 2
  PBF 34
  PB 29

Cyber
A Joint Cyber Command was set up in 2013. In 2014, short/medium-term goals included achieving FOC on 'CNDefense, CNExploitation, and CNAttack'. Spain's intelligence CERT (CCN–CERT) coordinates CERT activities.

DEPLOYMENT
Legal provisions for foreign deployment:
Constitution: Codified constitution (1978)
Specific legislation: 'Ley Orgánica de la Defensa Nacional' (2005)
Decision on deployment of troops abroad: a) By the government (Art. 6 of the 'Defence Law'); b) parliamentary approval is required for military operations 'which are not directly related to the defence of Spain or national interests' (Art. 17 of the 'Defence Law')

AFGHANISTAN
NATO • *Operation Resolute Support* 7

BOSNIA-HERZEGOVINA
EU • EUFOR • *Operation Althea* 2
OSCE • Bosnia and Herzegovina 2

CENTRAL AFRICAN REPUBLIC
EU • EUTM RCA 22

DJIBOUTI
EU • *Operation Atalanta* 1 P-3M Orion

GULF OF ADEN & INDIAN OCEAN
EU • *Operation Atalanta* 1 FFGHM; 1 PSOH

IRAQ
Operation Inherent Resolve 300

LEBANON
UN • UNIFIL 609; 1 armd inf bde HQ; 1 mech inf BG

MALI
EU • EUTM Mali 107

MEDITERRANEAN SEA
EU • EU NAVFOR MED: 1 FFGHM; 1 CN-235

NORTH SEA
NATO • SNMG 1: 1 DDGHM

SERBIA
OSCE • Kosovo 2

TURKEY
NATO • *Operation Active Fence* 1 SAM bty with MIM-104C Patriot PAC-2

UGANDA
EU • EUTM Somalia 17

UKRAINE
OSCE • Ukraine 17

FOREIGN FORCES
United States US European Command: 2,100; 1 air base at Morón; 1 naval base at Rota

Sweden SWE

Swedish Krona Skr		2015	2016	2017
GDP	Skr	4.16tr	4.36tr	
	US$	493bn	517bn	
per capita	US$	50,050	51,604	
Growth	%	4.2	3.6	
Inflation	%	0.7	1.1	
Def bdgt [a]	Skr	48.3bn	49.1bn	50.3bn
	US$	5.72bn	5.83bn	
US$1=Skr		8.43	8.43	

[a] Excludes military pensions and peacekeeping expenditure

Population   9,880,604

Age	0–14	15–19	20–24	25–29	30–64	65 plus
Male	8.9%	2.7%	3.3%	3.6%	22.2%	9.3%
Female	8.3%	2.5%	3.1%	3.5%	21.7%	10.9%

Capabilities

Sweden's armed forces remain configured for territorial defence, and the equipment and capabilities of all three services reflect this task. In June 2015, a defence bill for 2016–20 was adopted, which set out the aims of strengthening operational capabilities and deepening multilateral and bilateral defence relationships. Increased cooperation with neighbours and NATO has been a prevalent theme for the last few years. Sweden signed a statement of intent with the US in June 2016, which it sees as important for regional security. A Programme of Defence Cooperation was signed with the UK in the same month. In light of Russia's annexation of Crimea in 2014, national defence became a topic of debate, and this has increased since the escalation in Russian military activity in the Baltic region. Anxiety over Swedish preparedness has led to greater cooperation with NATO and NORDEFCO partners, as well as further deliberation over Swedish membership of the Alliance. Future capabilities will depend on the delivery of key procurements, including *Gripen* JAS-39E combat aircraft and Type-A26 submarines. In response to security concerns, the government announced an increase in planned defence spending, with funds being spent on naval modernisation and permanently redeploying troops to the strategically important island of Gotland – a battlegroup deployment is planned by the end of 2018. There has been a marked increase in training and cooperation with NATO countries and local partners, such as Finland. In 2016, Sweden participated in international exercises, including BALTOPs, *Saber Strike*, *Cold Response* and *Arrow 16*, while a cross-border air-defence exercise saw Swedish and US Air Force aircraft deploy to Finland. The armed forces have struggled to recruit enough personnel and in 2016 it was reported that a return to conscription was being considered. The chief of the armed forces stated that the change in the post-Cold War landscape will require a downgrading of international missions in order to prioritise domestic readiness.

ACTIVE 29,750 (Army 6,850 Navy 2,100 Air 2,700 Other 18,100) **Paramilitary 750 Voluntary Auxiliary Organisations 21,200**

ORGANISATIONS BY SERVICE

Army 6,850

The army has been transformed to provide brigade-sized task forces depending on the operational requirement

FORCES BY ROLE
COMMAND
　2 bde HQ
MANOEUVRE
　Reconnaissance
　1 recce bn
　Armoured
　3 armd coy
　Mechanised
　5 mech bn
　Light
　1 mot inf bn
　1 lt inf bn
　Air Manoeuvre
　1 AB bn
　Other
　1 sy bn
COMBAT SUPPORT
　2 arty bn
　2 engr bn
　2 MP coy
　1 CBRN coy
COMBAT SERVICE SUPPORT
　1 tpt coy
AIR DEFENCE
　2 AD bn

Reserves

FORCES BY ROLE
MANOEUVRE
　Other
　40 Home Guard bn
EQUIPMENT BY TYPE
ARMOURED FIGHTING VEHICLES
　MBT 129: 9 *Leopard* 2A4 (Strv-121); 120 *Leopard* 2A5 (Strv 122)
　IFV 354 CV9040 (Strf 9040)
　APC 1,106
　　APC (T) 431: 281 Pbv 302; 150 BvS10 MkII
　　APC (W) 315: 34 XA-180 *Sisu* (Patgb 180); 20 XA-202 *Sisu* (Patgb 202); 148 XA-203 *Sisu* (Patgb 203); 113 Patria AMV (XA-360/Patgb 360)
　　PPV 360 RG-32M
ENGINEERING & MAINTENANCE VEHICLES
　AEV 6 *Kodiak*
　ARV 40: 14 Bgbv 120; 26 CV90
　MW *Aardvark* Mk2; 33 Area Clearing System
ANTI-TANK/ANTI-INFRASTRUCTURE
　MSL • MANPATS RB-55
　RCL 84mm *Carl Gustav*
ARTILLERY 304
　SP 155mm 8 *Archer*
　MOR 296; **81mm** 212 M/86; **120mm** 84 M/41D
RADAR • LAND ARTHUR (arty)
AIR DEFENCE
　SAM
　　Medium-range MIM-23B *Hawk* (RBS-97)
　　Point-defence RBS-70
　GUNS • SP 40mm 30 Strv 90LV

Navy 1,250; 850 Amphibious (total 2,100)

EQUIPMENT BY TYPE
SUBMARINE • TACTICAL • SSK 5:
　3 *Gotland* (AIP fitted) with 2 single 400mm TT with Tp432/Tp 451, 4 single 533mm TT with Tp613/Tp62
　2 *Sodermanland* (AIP fitted) with 6 single 533mm TT with Tp432/Tp451/Tp613/Tp62
PATROL AND COASTAL COMBATANTS 147
　CORVETTES • FSG 5 *Visby* with 8 RBS-15 AShM, 4 single 400mm ASTT with Tp45 LWT, 1 57mm gun, 1 hel landing platform
　PCGT 4:
　　2 *Göteborg* with 4 twin lnchr with RBS-15 Mk2 AShM, 4 single 400mm ASTT with Tp431 LWT, 4 Saab 601 A/S mor, 1 57mm gun
　　2 *Stockholm* with 4 twin lnchr with RBS-15 Mk2 AShM, 4 Saab 601 mortars, 4 single 400mm ASTT with Tp431 LWT, 1 57mm gun
　PBF 129 Combat Boat 90E/H/HS (capacity 20 troops)
　PBR 9 *Tapper*
MINE WARFARE • MINE COUNTERMEASURES 10
　MCC 5 *Koster*
　MCD 2 *Spårö* (*Styrsö* Mod)
　MSD 3: 2 *Sam*; 1 *Sokaren*
AMPHIBIOUS • LANDING CRAFT 11
　LCVP 8 *Trossbat*
　LCAC 3 *Griffon* 8100TD
LOGISTICS AND SUPPORT 18
　AG 2: 1 *Carlskrona* with 2 57mm gun, 1 hel landing platform (former ML); 1 *Trosso* (spt ship for corvettes and patrol vessels but can also be used as HQ ship)
　AGF 3 Combatboat 450
　AGI 1 *Orion*
　AGS 2 (Government Maritime Forces)
　AK 1 *Loke*
　ARS 2: 1 *Belos* III; 1 *Furusund* (former ML)
　AX 5 *Altair*
　AXS 2: 1 *Falken*; 1 *Gladan*

Amphibious 850

FORCES BY ROLE
MANOEUVRE
　Amphibious
　1 amph bn
EQUIPMENT BY TYPE
　ARTILLERY • MOR 81mm 12 M/86
　COASTAL DEFENCE • AShM 8 RBS-17 *Hellfire*

Air Force 2,700

Flying hours　100–150 hrs/yr

FORCES BY ROLE
FIGHTER/GROUND ATTACK/ISR
  6 sqn with JAS 39C/D *Gripen*
TRANSPORT/ISR/AEW&C
  1 sqn with C-130H *Hercules* (Tp-84); KC-130H *Hercules* (Tp-84); Gulfstream IV SRA-4 (S-102B); S-100B/D *Argus*
TRAINING
  1 unit with Sk-60
AIR DEFENCE
  1 (fighter control and air surv) bn
EQUIPMENT BY TYPE
AIRCRAFT 97 combat capable
  FGA 97 JAS 39C/D *Gripen*
  ELINT 2 Gulfstream IV SRA-4 (S-102B)
  AEW&C 3: 1 S-100B *Argus*; 2 S-100D *Argus*
  TKR 1 KC-130H *Hercules* (Tp-84)
  TPT 8: **Medium** 5 C-130H *Hercules* (Tp-84); **Light** 2 Saab 340 (OS-100A/Tp-100C); **PAX** 1 Gulfstream 550 (Tp-102D)
  TRG 67 Sk-60W
UNMANNED AERIAL VEHICLES
  ISR • **Medium** 8 RQ-7 *Shadow* (AUV 3 *Örnen*)
AIR-LAUNCHED MISSILES
  ASM AGM-65 *Maverick* (RB-75)
  AShM RB-15F
  AAM • **IR** AIM-9L *Sidewinder* (RB-74); **IIR** IRIS-T (RB-98); **ARH** AIM-120B AMRAAM (RB-99); *Meteor* (entering service)
BOMBS
  Laser-Guided GBU-12 *Paveway* II
  INS/GPS guided GBU-39 Small Diameter Bomb

Armed Forces Hel Wing
FORCES BY ROLE
TRANSPORT HELICOPTER
  3 sqn with AW109 (Hkp 15A); AW109M (Hkp-15B); NH90 (Hkp-14) (SAR/ASW); UH-60M *Black Hawk* (Hkp-16)
EQUIPMENT BY TYPE
HELICOPTERS
  ASW 1 NH90 ASW
  TPT 48: **Medium** 28: 15 UH-60M *Black Hawk* (Hkp-16); 13 NH90 TTH (Hkp-14); **Light** 20: 12 AW109 (Hkp-15A); 8 AW109M (Hkp-15B)

Special Forces
FORCES BY ROLE
SPECIAL FORCES
  1 spec ops gp
COMBAT SUPPORT
  1 cbt spt gp

Other 18,100
Includes staff, logistics and intelligence personnel
FORCES BY ROLE
COMBAT SUPPORT
  1 EW bn
  1 psyops unit

COMBAT SERVICE SUPPORT
  2 log bn
  1 maint bn
  4 med coy
  1 tpt coy

Paramilitary 750

Coast Guard 750
EQUIPMENT BY TYPE
PATROL AND COASTAL COMBATANTS 25
  PSO 3 *Poseidon* (Damen Multipurpose Vessel 8116)
  PCO 1 KBV-181 (fishery protection)
  PCC 6: 2 KBV-201; 4 *Sipe*
  PB 15: 10 KBV-301; 5 KBV-312
  AMPHIBIOUS • **LANDING CRAFT** • **UCAC** 2: 1 *Griffon* 2000TDX (KBV-592); 1 *Griffon* 2450TD

Air Arm
EQUIPMENT BY TYPE
  AIRCRAFT • **TPT** • **Light** 3 DHC-8Q-300

Cyber
Sweden has a national CERT, is involved in informal CERT communities and is a member of the European Government CERTs group (EGC). A national cyber-security strategy has also been adopted. Four ministries have a cyber remit: defence, foreign affairs, justice, and enterprise and industry. The Swedish Civil Contingencies Agency (AMS), which reports to the defence ministry, is in charge of supporting and coordinating security nationwide. According to the 2015 defence bill, 'cyber defence capabilities are an important part of the Swedish Defence. Vital systems must be protected from attack. This also requires the ability to carry out active operations in the cyber domain.'

DEPLOYMENT
Legal provisions for foreign deployment:
Constitution: Constitution consists of four fundamental laws; the most important is 'The Instrument of Government' (1974)
Decision on deployment of troops abroad: By the government upon parliamentary approval (Ch. 10, Art. 9)

AFGHANISTAN
NATO • *Operation Resolute Support* 23

ARMENIA/AZERBAIJAN
OSCE • Minsk Conference 1

DEMOCRATIC REPUBLIC OF THE CONGO
UN • MONUSCO 2 obs

INDIA/PAKISTAN
UN • UNMOGIP 5 obs

IRAQ
Operation Inherent Resolve 35

KOREA, REPUBLIC OF
NNSC • 5 obs

MALI
EU • EUTM Mali 9
UN • MINUSMA 209; 1 int coy

MIDDLE EAST
UN • UNTSO 7 obs

MOLDOVA
OSCE • Moldova 3

SERBIA
NATO • KFOR 3
OSCE • Kosovo 4

SOUTH SUDAN
UN • UNMISS 2 obs

UGANDA
EU • EUTM Somalia 4

UKRAINE
OSCE • Ukraine 23

Switzerland CHE

Swiss Franc fr		2015	2016	2017
GDP	fr	639bn	647bn	
	US$	664bn	662bn	
per capita	US$	80,603	79,578	
Growth	%	0.8	1.0	
Inflation	%	-1.1	-0.4	
Def bdgt [a]	fr	4.59bn	4.61bn	4.67bn
	US$	4.77bn	4.72bn	
US$1=fr		0.96	0.98	

[a] Includes military pensions

Population 8,179,294

Age	0–14	15–19	20–24	25–29	30–64	65 plus
Male	7.8%	2.7%	2.9%	3.2%	24.7%	7.9%
Female	7.3%	2.6%	2.8%	3.2%	24.6%	10.1%

Capabilities

Overwhelmingly conscript-based, the armed forces are geared for territorial defence and limited participation in international peace-support operations. The Swiss government has begun to reduce its armed forces – the goal is a total strength after mobilisation of 100,000 troops drawn from a pool of 140,000. This reflects the assessment that in the militia-based system not all personnel would realistically be available for active service in times of conflict. However, the smaller force is supposed to benefit from additional equipment. This armed-forces-development plan, approved in March 2016, emphasises improvements in readiness, training and equipment. Implementation of this plan is due to take place in 2018–21. The approach to readiness is changing to a more flexible model in which different units would be called up for active service gradually on different timelines. Plans to replace the ageing F-5 *Tiger* II aircraft with the *Gripen* were scrapped after a national referendum rejected the proposal in May 2014. With Switzerland's air-policing capabilities diminished, the government intends to relaunch its attempt to procure a new combat aircraft. This time, the effort will be expanded to include the replacement of the Swiss F/A-18 *Hornet* fighter jets, which are expected to reach the end of their life cycle around 2025. This revision reflects the government's assessment that delivery is unlikely to begin before 2025. Meanwhile, service-life extension for these platforms is due to be discussed in parliament in 2017. Upgrades are also planned to AS532 and AS332 helicopters, while a range of ground-mobility assets, including bridging, is due to be addressed before 2020.

ACTIVE 20,950 (Joint 20,950)

Conscript liability Recruit trg of 18, 21 or 25 weeks (depending on military branch) at age 19–20, followed by 7, 6 or 5 refresher trg courses (3 weeks each) over a 10-year period between ages 20–30

RESERVE 144,270 (Army 93,100 Air 22,870 Armed Forces Logistic Organisation 13,700 Command Support Organisation 14,600)

Civil Defence 74,000 (55,000 Reserve)

ORGANISATIONS BY SERVICE

Joint 3,350 active; 17,600 conscript (20,950 total)

Land Forces (Army) 93,100 on mobilisation

4 Territorial Regions. With the exception of military security all units are non-active

FORCES BY ROLE
COMMAND
4 regional comd (2 engr bn, 1 sigs bn)
MANOEUVRE
  Armoured
  1 (1st) bde (1 recce bn, 2 armd bn, 2 armd inf bn, 1 sp arty bn, 2 engr bn, 1 sigs bn)
  1 (11th) bde (1 recce bn, 2 armd bn, 2 armd inf bn, 1 inf bn, 2 SP arty bn, 1 engr bn, 1 sigs bn)
  Light
  1 (2nd) inf bde (1 recce bn, 4 inf bn, 2 SP arty bn, 1 engr bn, 1 sigs bn)
  1 (5th) inf bde (1 recce bn, 3 inf bn, 2 SP arty bn, 1 engr bn, 1 sigs bn)
  1 (7th) reserve inf bde (3 recce bn, 3 inf bn, 2 mtn inf bn, 1 sigs bn)
  1 (9th) mtn inf bde (5 mtn inf bn, 1 SP Arty bn, 1 sigs bn)
  1 (12th) mtn inf bde (2 inf bn, 3 mtn inf bn, 1 (fortress) arty bn, 1 sigs bn)
  1 (10th) reserve mtn inf bde (1 recce bn, 2 armd bn, 3 inf bn, 2 mtn inf bn, 2 SP arty bn, 2 sigs bn)
  Other
  1 sy bde
COMBAT SERVICE SUPPORT
  1 armd/arty trg unit
  1 inf trg unit
  1 engr rescue trg unit
  1 log trg unit

EQUIPMENT BY TYPE
ARMOURED FIGHTING VEHICLES
  MBT 134 *Leopard 2* (Pz-87 *Leo*)
  IFV 186: 154 CV9030; 32 CV9030 CP
  APC 914
    APC (T) 238 M113A2 (incl variants)
    APC (W) 676: 346 *Piranha* II; 330 *Piranha* I/II/IIIC (CP)
  AUV 441 *Eagle* II
ENGINEERING & MAINTENANCE VEHICLES
  AEV 12 *Kodiak*
  ARV 25 *Büffel*
  MW 46: 26 Area Clearing System; 20 M113A2
NBC VEHICLES 12 *Piranha* IIIC CBRN
ANTI-TANK/ANTI-INFRASTRUCTURE
  MSL • SP 106 *Piranha* I TOW-2
ARTILLERY 433
  SP 155mm 133 M109
  MOR • 81mm 300 Mw-72
PATROL AND COASTAL COMBATANTS • PBR 11 *Aquarius*
AIR DEFENCE • SAM • Point-defence FIM-92 *Stinger*

Air Force 22,870 (incl air defence units and military airfield guard units)

Flying hours   200–250 hrs/yr

FORCES BY ROLE
FIGHTER
  3 sqn with F-5E/F *Tiger* II
  3 sqn with F/A-18C/D *Hornet*
TRANSPORT
  1 sqn with Beech 350 *King Air*; DHC-6 *Twin Otter*; PC-6 *Turbo Porter*; PC-12
  1 VIP Flt with Beech 1900D; Cessna 560XL *Citation*; *Falcon* 900EX
TRAINING
  1 sqn with PC-7CH *Turbo Trainer*; PC-21
  1 sqn with PC-9 (tgt towing)
  1 OCU Sqn with F-5E/F *Tiger* II
TRANSPORT HELICOPTER
  6 sqn with AS332M *Super Puma*; AS532UL *Cougar*; H135M
ISR UAV
  1 sqn with ADS 95 *Ranger*
EQUIPMENT BY TYPE
AIRCRAFT 86 combat capable
  FTR 54: 42 F-5E *Tiger* II; 12 F-5F *Tiger* II
  FGA 31: 25 F/A-18C *Hornet*; 6 F/A-18D *Hornet*
  TPT 22: **Light** 21: 1 Beech 350 *King Air*; 1 Beech 1900D; 1 Cessna 560XL *Citation*; 1 DHC-6 *Twin Otter*; 15 PC-6 *Turbo Porter*; 1 PC-6 (owned by armasuisse, civil registration); 1 PC-12 (owned by armasuisse, civil registration); **PAX** 1 *Falcon* 900EX
  TRG 44: 28 PC-7CH *Turbo Trainer*; 8 PC-9; 8 PC-21
HELICOPTERS
  MRH 20 H135M
  TPT • **Medium** 25: 14 AS332M *Super Puma*; 11 AS532UL *Cougar*
UNMANNED AERIAL VEHICLES
  ISR • **Medium** 16 ADS 95 *Ranger* (4 systems)

AIR-LAUNCHED MISSILES • AAM • IR AIM-9P *Sidewinder*; **IIR** AIM-9X *Sidewinder* II; **ARH** AIM-120B AMRAAM

Ground Based Air Defence (GBAD)

GBAD assets can be used to form AD clusters to be deployed independently as task forces within Swiss territory.

EQUIPMENT BY TYPE
AIR DEFENCE
  SAM • **Point** *Rapier*; FIM-92 *Stinger*
  GUNS 35mm Some
  RADARS • AD RADARS *Skyguard*

Armed Forces Logistic Organisation 13,700 on mobilisation

FORCES BY ROLE
COMBAT SERVICE SUPPORT
  1 log bde

Command Support Organisation 14,600 on mobilisation

FORCES BY ROLE
COMBAT SERVICE SUPPORT
  1 spt bde

Civil Defence 74,000 (55,000 Reserve)

(not part of armed forces)

Cyber

Five major Swiss government organisations maintain an overview of elements of cyber threats and responses: the Federal Intelligence Service; the Military Intelligence Service; the Command Support Organisation; Information Security and Facility Protection; and the Federal Office for Civil Protection. A National Cyber Defence Strategy was published in 2012. As cyber protection is decentralised, the Federal Department of Finance is in charge of implementing the strategy until 2017.

DEPLOYMENT

Legal provisions for foreign deployment:
Constitution: Codified constitution (1999)
Decision on deployment of troops abroad:
Peace promotion (66, 66a, 66b Swiss Mil Law): UN.OSCE mandate. Decision by govt; if over 100 tps deployed or op over 3 weeks Fed Assembly must agree first, except in emergency
Support service abroad (69, 60 Swiss Mil Law): Decision by govt; if over 2,000 tps or op over 3 weeks Fed Assembly must agree in next official session

BOSNIA-HERZEGOVINA
EU • EUFOR • *Operation Althea* 20

DEMOCRATIC REPUBLIC OF THE CONGO
UN • MONUSCO 3

INDIA/PAKISTAN
UN • UNMOGIP 3 obs

KOREA, REPUBLIC OF
NNSC • 5 officers

MALI
UN • MINUSMA 8

MIDDLE EAST
UN • UNTSO 15 obs

SERBIA
NATO • KFOR 222 (military volunteers); 1 inf coy
OSCE • Kosovo 1

SOUTH SUDAN
UN • UNMISS 2

UKRAINE
OSCE • Ukraine 16

WESTERN SAHARA
UN • MINURSO 1 obs

Turkey TUR

New Turkish Lira L		2015	2016	2017
GDP	L	1.95tr	2.20tr	
	US$	718bn	736bn	
per capita	US$	9,186	9,317	
Growth	%	4.0	3.3	
Inflation	%	7.7	8.4	
Def exp [a]	L	32.7bn		
	US$	12.0bn		
Def bdgt [b]	L	22.8bn	26.2bn	28.8bn
	US$	8.38bn	8.76bn	
US$1=L		2.72	2.99	

[a] NATO definition
[b] Includes funding for Undersecretariat of Defence Industries. Excludes military procurement allocations

Population 80,274,604

Age	0–14	15–19	20–24	25–29	30–64	65 plus
Male	12.8%	4.2%	4.0%	4.0%	22.0%	3.2%
Female	12.3%	4.0%	3.9%	3.9%	21.6%	4.1%

Capabilities

Turkey has capable armed forces intended to meet national-defence requirements and NATO obligations, and aims to provide a highly mobile force able to fight across the spectrum of conflict. The air force is well equipped and well trained. There is also an ambitious equipment-procurement plan in place. However, there have been delays to some strategically important projects, including a military satellite. A failed military-coup attempt in July 2016 led to the dismissal of large numbers of officers and a shake-up of force structures, with implications for the country's domestic and international role. The regional threat posed by conflict in Syria and by the Islamic State in 2016 placed the Turkish armed forces on high alert on the border. In August, Turkish land forces entered Syria under *Operation Euphrates Shield*, while the air force has conducted airstrikes against the Islamic State. Action against both internal and external Kurdish elements in Iraq and Syria has also taken place. The armed forces participate in multinational exercises with NATO partners, and NATO retains significant facilities in Turkey, most notably at Incirlik Air Base. (See pp. 68–9.)

ACTIVE 355,200 (Army 260,200 Navy 45,600 Air 50,000) **Paramilitary 156,800**
Conscript liability 15 months. Active figure reducing

RESERVE 378,700 (Army 258,700 Navy 55,000 Air 65,000)
Reserve service to age of 41 for all services

ORGANISATIONS BY SERVICE

Space
EQUIPMENT BY TYPE
SATELLITES • ISR 1 *Gokturk-2*

Army ε260,200 (including conscripts)
FORCES BY ROLE
COMMAND
  4 army HQ
  9 corps HQ
SPECIAL FORCES
  4 cdo bde
  1 mtn cdo bde
  1 cdo regt
MANOEUVRE
  Armoured
  1 (52nd) armd div (2 armd bde, 1 mech bde)
  7 armd bde
  Mechanised
  2 (28th & 29th) mech div
  14 mech inf bde
  Light
  1 (23rd) mot inf div (3 mot inf regt)
  11 mot inf bde
COMBAT SUPPORT
  2 arty bde
  1 trg arty bde
  6 arty regt
  2 engr regt
AVIATION
  4 avn regt
  4 avn bn
EQUIPMENT BY TYPE
ARMOURED FIGHTING VEHICLES
  MBT 2,492: 325 *Leopard* 2A4; 170 *Leopard* 1A4; 227 *Leopard* 1A3; 250 M60A1; 500 M60A3; 170 M60T; 850 M48A5 T1/T2 (2,000 more in store)
  RECCE ε250 *Akrep*
  IFV 650 ACV AIFV
  APC 4,013
    APC (T) 3,643: 830 ACV AAPC; 2,813 M113/M113A1/M113A2
    APC (W) 70+ *Cobra*
  PPV 300+ *Kirpi*

ENGINEERING & MAINTENANCE VEHICLES
  AEV 12+: 12 M48; M113A2T2
  ARV 150: 12 *Leopard* 1; 105 M48T5; 33 M88A1
  VLB 52 Mobile Floating Assault Bridge
  MW *Tamkar*
ANTI-TANK/ANTI-INFRASTRUCTURE
  MSL 1,363
    SP 365 ACV TOW
    MANPATS 9K135 *Kornet*-E (AT-14 *Spriggan*); *Cobra*; *Eryx*; *Milan*
  RCL 3,869: **57mm** 923 M18; **75mm** 617; **106mm** 2,329 M40A1
  ARTILLERY 7,795+
    SP 1,076: **105mm** 391: 26 M108T; 365 M52T; **155mm** 430: ε150 M44T1; ε280 T-155 *Firtina* (K9 *Thunder*); **175mm** 36 M107; **203mm** 219 M110A2
    TOWED 760+: **105mm** 75+ M101A1; **155mm** 523: 517 M114A1/M114A2; 6 *Panter*; **203mm** 162 M115
    MRL 146+: **107mm** 48; **122mm** ε36 T-122; **227mm** 12 M270 MLRS; **302mm** 50+ TR-300 *Kasirga* (WS-1)
    MOR 5,813+
      SP 1,443+: **81mm**; **107mm** 1,264 M106; **120mm** 179
      TOWED 4,370: **81mm** 3,792; **120mm** 578
SURFACE-TO-SURFACE MISSILE LAUNCHERS
  SRBM • **Conventional** MGM-140A ATACMS (launched from M270 MLRS)
RADAR • **LAND** AN/TPQ-36 *Firefinder*; 2 *Cobra*
AIRCRAFT
  ISR 5 Beech 350 *King Air*
  TPT • **Light** 8: 5 Beech 200 *King Air*; 3 Cessna 421
  TRG 49: 45 Cessna T182; 4 T-42A *Cochise*
HELICOPTERS
  ATK 49: 18 AH-1P *Cobra*; 12 AH-1S *Cobra*; 5 AH-1W *Cobra*; 4 TAH-1P *Cobra*; 9 T129A; 7 T129B
  MRH 28 Hughes 300C
  TPT 221+: **Heavy** 3 CH-47F *Chinook*; **Medium** 78+: 30 AS532UL *Cougar*; 48+ S-70A *Black Hawk*; **Light** 141: 12 Bell 204B (AB-204B); ε45 Bell 205 (UH-1H *Iroquois*); 64 Bell 205A (AB-205A); 20 Bell 206 *Jet Ranger*
UNMANNED AERIAL VEHICLES
  ISR • **Heavy** *Falcon* 600/*Firebee*; **Medium** CL-89; *Gnat*; **Light** *Harpy*
AIR DEFENCE
  SAM • **Point-defence** 148+: 70 *Altigan* PMADS octuple *Stinger* lnchr, 78 *Zipkin* PMADS quad *Stinger* lnchr; FIM-43 *Redeye* (being withdrawn); FIM-92 *Stinger*
  GUNS 1,664
    SP 40mm 262 M42A1
    TOWED 1,402: **20mm** 439 GAI-D01; **35mm** 120 GDF-001/GDF-003; **40mm** 843: 803 L/60/L/70; 40 T-1

Navy ε45,000 (including conscripts)

EQUIPMENT BY TYPE
SUBMARINES • TACTICAL • SSK 13:
  5 *Atilay* (GER Type-209/1200) with 8 single 533mm ASTT with SST-4 HWT
  8 *Preveze/Gür* (GER Type-209/1400) with 8 single 533mm ASTT with UGM-84 *Harpoon* AShM/*Tigerfish* Mk2 HWT

PRINCIPAL SURFACE COMBATANTS 18
  FRIGATES • FFGHM 18:
    2 *Barbaros* (mod GER MEKO 200 F244 & F245) with 2 quad Mk141 lnchr with RGM-84C *Harpoon* AShM, 1 octuple Mk29 lnchr with *Aspide* SAM, 2 Mk32 triple 324mm ASTT with Mk46 LWT, 3 *Sea Zenith* CIWS, 1 127mm gun (capacity 1 Bell 212 (AB-212) hel)
    2 *Barbaros* (mod GER MEKO 200 F246 & F247) with 2 quad Mk141 lnchr with RGM-84C *Harpoon* AShM, 1 8-cell Mk41 VLS with *Aspide* SAM, 2 Mk32 triple 324mm ASTT with Mk46 LWT, 3 *Sea Zenith* CIWS, 1 127mm gun (capacity 1 Bell 212 (AB-212) hel)
    3 *Gabya* (ex-US *Oliver Hazard Perry* class) with 1 Mk13 GMLS with RGM-84C *Harpoon* AShM/SM-1MR SAM, 1 8-cell Mk41 VLS with RIM-162 SAM, 2 Mk32 triple 324mm ASTT with Mk46 LWT, 1 *Phalanx* Block 1B CIWS, 1 76mm gun (capacity 1 S-70B *Seahawk* ASW hel)
    5 *Gabya* (ex-US *Oliver Hazard Perry* class) with 1 Mk13 GMLS with RGM-84C *Harpoon* AShM/SM-1MR SAM, 2 Mk32 triple 324mm ASTT with Mk46 LWT, 1 *Phalanx* Block 1B CIWS, 1 76mm gun (capacity 1 S-70B *Seahawk* ASW hel)
    4 *Yavuz* (GER MEKO 200TN) with 2 quad Mk141 lnchr with RGM-84C *Harpoon* AShM, 1 octuple Mk29 GMLS with *Aspide* SAM, 2 Mk32 triple 324mm ASTT with Mk46 LWT, 3 *Sea Zenith* CIWS, 1 127mm gun (capacity 1 Bell 212 (AB-212) hel)
    2 *Ada* with 2 quad lnchr with RCM-84C *Harpoon* AShM, 1 Mk49 21-cell lnchr with RIM-116 SAM, 2 Mk32 twin 324mm ASTT with Mk46 LWT, 1 76mm gun (capacity 1 S-70B *Seahawk* hel)
PATROL AND COASTAL COMBATANTS 53:
  CORVETTES • FSGM 6:
    6 *Burak* (ex-FRA *d'Estienne d'Orves*) with 2 single lnchr with MM-38 *Exocet* AShM, 4 single 324mm ASTT with Mk46 LWT, 1 Mk54 A/S mor, 1 100mm gun
  PCFG 19:
    4 *Dogan* (GER Lurssen-57) with 2 quad lnchr with RGM-84A/C *Harpoon* AShM, 1 76mm gun
    9 *Kilic* with 2 quad Mk 141 lnchr with RGM-84C *Harpoon* AShM, 1 76mm gun
    4 *Rüzgar* (GER Lurssen-57) with 2 quad lnchr with RGM-84A/C *Harpoon* AShM, 1 76mm gun
    2 *Yildiz* with 2 quad lnchr with RGM-84A/C *Harpoon* AShM, 1 76mm gun
  PCC 15 *Tuzla*
  PBFG 2 *Kartal* (GER *Jaguar*) with 4 single lnchr with RB 12 *Penguin* AShM, 2 single 533mm TT
MINE WARFARE • MINE COUNTERMEASURES 15:
  MHO 11: 5 *Engin* (FRA *Circe*); 6 *Aydin*
  MSC 4 *Seydi* (US *Adjutant*)
AMPHIBIOUS
  LANDING SHIPS • LST 4:
    1 *Ertugrul* (ex-US *Terrebonne Parish*) with 3 76mm guns, (capacity 18 tanks; 400 troops) (with 1 hel landing platform)
    1 *Osman Gazi* with 1 *Phalanx* CIWS, (capacity 4 LCVP; 17 tanks; 980 troops) (with 1 hel landing platform)
    2 *Sarucabey* with 1 *Phalanx* CIWS (capacity 11 tanks; 600 troops) (with 1 hel landing platform)

LANDING CRAFT 30
    LCT 21: 2 C-120/130; 11 C-140; 8 C-151
    LCM 9: 1 C-310; 8 C-320
LOGISTICS AND SUPPORT 35
    ABU 2: 1 AG5; 1 AG6 with 1 76mm gun
    AGS 2: 1 *Cesme* (ex-US *Silas Bent*); 1 *Cubuklu*
    AORH 2 *Akar* with 1 twin 76mm gun, 1 *Phalanx* CIWS, 1 hel landing platform
    AOT 2 *Burak*
    AOL 1 *Gurcan*
    AP 1 *Iskenderun*
    ARS 2: 1 *Isin*; 1 *Kemer*
    ASR 1 *Akin*
    ATF 9: 1 *Akbas*; 1 *Degirmendere*; 1 *Gazal*; 1 *Inebolu*; 5 *Onder*
    AWT 3 *Sogut*
    AXL 8
    AX 2 *Pasa* (ex-GER *Rhein*)

Marines 3,000
FORCES BY ROLE
MANOEUVRE
    Amphibious
    1 mne bde (3 mne bn; 1 arty bn)

Naval Aviation
FORCES BY ROLE
ANTI-SUBMARINE WARFARE
    2 sqn with Bell 212 ASW (AB-212 ASW); S-70B *Seahawk*
    1 sqn with ATR-72-600; CN-235M-100; TB-20 *Trinidad*
EQUIPMENT BY TYPE
AIRCRAFT
    MP 6 CN-235M-100
    TPT • **Light** 7: 2 ATR-72-600; 5 TB-20 *Trinidad*
HELICOPTERS
    ASW 29: 11 Bell 212 ASW (AB-212 ASW); 18 S-70B *Seahawk*

Air Force ε50,000
2 tac air forces (divided between east and west)
Flying hours 180 hrs/yr

FORCES BY ROLE
FIGHTER/GROUND ATTACK
    1 sqn with F-4E *Phantom* 2020
    8 sqn with F-16C/D *Fighting Falcon*
ISR
    1 sqn with F-16C/D *Fighting Falcon*
    1 unit with *King Air* 350
AIRBORNE EARLY WARNING & CONTROL
    1 sqn (forming) with B-737 AEW&C
EW
    1 unit with CN-235M EW
SEARCH & RESCUE
    1 sqn with AS532AL/UL *Cougar*
TANKER
    1 sqn with KC-135R *Stratotanker*
TRANSPORT
    1 sqn with A400M; C-160D *Transall*
    1 sqn with C-130B/E/H *Hercules*
    1 (VIP) sqn with Cessna 550 *Citation* II (UC-35); Cessna 650 *Citation* VII; CN-235M; Gulfstream 550
    3 sqn with CN-235M
    10 (liaison) flt with Bell 205 (UH-1H *Iroquois*); CN-235M
TRAINING
    1 sqn with F-16C/D *Fighting Falcon*
    1 sqn with F-5A/B *Freedom Fighter*; NF-5A/B *Freedom Fighter*
    1 sqn with SF-260D
    1 sqn with KT-1T
    1 sqn with T-38A/M *Talon*
    1 sqn with T-41D *Mescalero*
AIR DEFENCE
    4 sqn with MIM-14 *Nike Hercules*
    2 sqn with *Rapier*
    8 (firing) unit with MIM-23 *Hawk*
MANOEUVRE
    Air Manoeuvre
    1 AB bde

EQUIPMENT BY TYPE
AIRCRAFT 364 combat capable
    FTR 53: 18 F-5A *Freedom Fighter*; 8 F-5B *Freedom Fighter*; 17 NF-5A *Freedom Fighter*; 10 NF-5B *Freedom Fighter* (48 F-5s being upgraded as LIFT)
    FGA 280: 20 F-4E *Phantom* 2020; 27 F-16C *Fighting Falcon* Block 30; 162 F-16C *Fighting Falcon* Block 50; 14 F-16C *Fighting Falcon* Block 50+; 8 F-16D Block 30 *Fighting Falcon*; 33 F-16D *Fighting Falcon* Block 50; 16 F-16D *Fighting Falcon* Block 50+
    ISR 5 Beech 350 *King Air*
    EW 2+ CN-235M EW
    AEW&C 4 B-737 AEW&C
    TKR 7 KC-135R *Stratotanker*
    TPT 89: **Heavy** 3 A400M; **Medium** 35: 6 C-130B *Hercules*; 12 C-130E *Hercules*; 1 C-130H *Hercules*; 16 C-160D *Transall*; **Light** 50: 2 Cessna 550 *Citation* II (UC-35 - VIP); 2 Cessna 650 *Citation* VII; 46 CN-235M; **PAX** 1 Gulfstream 550
    TRG 172: 34 SF-260D; 70 T-38A/M *Talon*; 28 T-41D *Mescalero*; 40 KT-1T
HELICOPTERS
    TPT 40: **Medium** 20: 6 AS532AL *Cougar* (CSAR); 14 AS532UL *Cougar* (SAR); **Light** 20 Bell 205 (UH-1H *Iroquois*)
UNMANNED AERIAL VEHICLES • **ISR** 27: **Heavy** 9 *Heron*; **Medium** 18 *Gnat* 750
AIR DEFENCE
    SAM
        Long-range MIM-14 *Nike Hercules*
        Medium-range MIM-23 *Hawk*
        Point-defence *Rapier*
AIR-LAUNCHED MISSILES
    AAM • **IR** AIM-9S *Sidewinder*; *Shafrir* 2(‡); **IIR** AIM-9X *Sidewinder* II; **SARH** AIM-7E *Sparrow*; **ARH** AIM-120A/B AMRAAM
    ARM AGM-88A HARM
    ASM AGM-65A/G *Maverick*; AGM-154A JSOW; AGM-154C JSOW; *Popeye* I
BOMBS
    Electro-optical guided GBU-8B HOBOS (GBU-15)
    Laser-guided *Paveway* I; *Paveway* II

Paramilitary 156,800

Gendarmerie 152,100
Ministry of Interior; Ministry of Defence in war
FORCES BY ROLE
SPECIAL FORCES
1 cdo bde
MANOEUVRE
Other
1 (border) paramilitary div
2 paramilitary bde
EQUIPMENT BY TYPE
ARMOURED FIGHTING VEHICLES
RECCE *Akrep*
APC • **APC (W)** 560: 535 BTR-60/BTR-80; 25 *Condor*
AIRCRAFT
ISR Some O-1E *Bird Dog*
TPT • **Light** 2 Do-28D
HELICOPTERS
MRH 19 Mi-17 *Hip* H
TPT 36: **Medium** 13 S-70A *Black Hawk*; **Light** 23: 8 Bell 204B (AB-204B); 6 Bell 205A (AB-205A); 8 Bell 206A (AB-206A) *Jet Ranger*; 1 Bell 212 (AB-212)

Coast Guard 4,700
EQUIPMENT BY TYPE
PATROL AND COASTAL COMBATANTS 102
PSOH 4 *Dost* with 1 76mm gun
PBF 60
PB 38
AIRCRAFT • **MP** 3 CN-235 MPA
HELICOPTERS • **MRH** 8 Bell 412EP (AB-412EP – SAR)

DEPLOYMENT
Legal provisions for foreign deployment:
Constitution: Codified constitution (1985)
Decision on deployment of troops abroad: a) In general, by parliament (Art. 92); b) in cases of sudden aggression and if parliament is unable to convene, by president (Art. 92, 104b)

AFGHANISTAN
NATO • *Operation Resolute Support* 523; 1 mot inf bn(-)

ARABIAN SEA & GULF OF ADEN
Combined Maritime Forces • CTF-151: 1 FFGHM

BOSNIA-HERZEGOVINA
EU • EUFOR • *Operation Althea* 234; 1 inf coy

CYPRUS (NORTHERN)
ε43,000; 1 army corps HQ; 1 armd bde; 2 mech inf div; 1 avn comd; 8 M48A2 (trg;) 340 M48A5T1/T2; 361 AAPC (incl variants); 266 M113 (incl variants); 72 M101A1; 18 M114A2; 12 M115; 90 M44T; 6 T-122; 175 81mm mor; 148 M30; 127 HY-12; 66 *Milan*; 48 TOW; 192 M40A1; Rh 202; 16 GDF-003; 48 M1; 3 Cessna 185 (U-17); 1 AS532UL *Cougar*; 3 UH-1H *Iroquois*; 1 PB

IRAQ
Army: 2,000; 1 armd BG

LEBANON
UN • UNIFIL 50; 1 PCFG

MEDITERRANEAN SEA
NATO • SNMG 2: 1 FSGM
NATO • SNMCMG 2: 1 MHO

QATAR
Army: 150 (trg team)

SERBIA
NATO • KFOR 395; 1 inf coy
OSCE • Kosovo 2
UN • UNMIK 1 obs

SOMALIA
UN • UNSOM 1 obs

SYRIA
Operation Euphrates Shield 350; 1 SF coy; 1 armd coy(+); 1 arty unit

UKRAINE
OSCE • Ukraine 14

FOREIGN FORCES
Denmark *Inherent Resolve* 110; 7 F-16AM *Fighting Falcon*
Germany *Inherent Resolve* 200; 6 *Tornado* ECR; 1 A310 MRTT
Italy *Active Fence*: 1 bty with SAMP/T
Saudi Arabia *Inherent Resolve* 6 F-15S *Eagle*
Spain *Active Fence*: 1 bty with MIM-104C *Patriot* PAC-2
United States US European Command: 2,700; 1 atk sqn with 12 A-10C *Thunderbolt* II; 1 tkr sqn with 14 KC-135; 1 CISR sqn with MQ-1B *Predator* UAV; 1 ELINT flt with EP-3E *Aries* II; 1 spt facility at Izmir; 1 spt facility at Ankara; 1 air base at Incirlik • US Strategic Command: 1 AN/TPY-2 X-band radar at Kürecik

United Kingdom UK

British Pound £		2015	2016	2017
GDP	£	1.87tr	1.93tr	
	US$	2.86tr	2.65tr	
per capita	US$	43,902	40,412	
Growth	%	2.2	1.8	
Inflation	%	0.1	0.7	
Def exp [a]	£	39.0bn		
	US$	59.6bn		
Def bdgt [b]	£	38.2bn	ε38.3bn	
	US$	58.4bn	ε52.5bn	
US$1=£		0.65	0.73	

[a] NATO definition
[b] Includes total departmental expenditure limits; costs of military operations; and external income earned by the MoD

Population 64,430,428

Age	0–14	15–19	20–24	25–29	30–64	65 plus
Male	8.9%	2.9%	3.3%	3.6%	23.0%	8.0%
Female	8.5%	2.8%	3.2%	3.4%	22.5%	9.9%

Capabilities

The UK is one of the few European countries with the capability for expeditionary combat operations. Its current top policy priorities are contributing to the US-led campaign against the Islamic State and being on standby to assist the police and security services to counter domestic terrorism. It is making a major contribution to NATO's Readiness Action Plan, but it will be some time before British forces have been modernised sufficiently for the UK to have a credible full-spectrum combat capability against a peer competitor such as Russia. All three services and Joint Forces Command have begun action to implement the capability outcomes of the 2015 Strategic Defence and Security Review (SDSR). The UK retains an expeditionary logistic capability sufficient to meet its policy requirements; however, peacetime logistic support within the UK is highly dependent on contractors. The country has a significant defence industry but does not have the ability to meet all of its defence-industry and logistic requirements. Recruitment increased in 2016 but overall personnel strength continued to decline; in June 2016 the forces were more than 4% short of trained personnel. However, the removal of remaining restrictions on the employment of women in land combat units was announced, opening – incrementally – roles in the infantry, armoured corps, RAF Regiment and Royal Marines. The UK is investing in special-forces, counter-terrorist and cyber capabilities. The army has also begun to rebuild its ability to field a full division of three combat brigades, and started to better define the SDSR initiatives to form new 'strike brigades'. The new aircraft carrier, HMS *Queen Elizabeth*, was set for initial sea trials in the first quarter of 2017. The UK plans to increase the size of the forces it can deploy overseas and the speed with which they can deploy, but the limiting factor is likely to be personnel numbers, as opposed to equipment availability. The UK has invested considerable resources in both strategic airlift and sealift. Current lift capacity is sufficient to deploy and sustain niche, small- and medium-scale contingents, but a large-scale deployment would require additional civilian air and sea assets. During 2016, the army trained and prepared for leadership of the NATO Very High Readiness Joint Task Force in 2017. The UK also continues to have an active programme of collective training exercises. (See pp. 82–9.)

ACTIVE 152,350 (Army 86,700 Navy 32,350 Air 33,300)

RESERVE 81,350 (Regular Reserve 44,200 (Army 29,900, Navy 6,900, Air 7,400); Volunteer Reserve 35,350 (Army 29,300, Navy 3,450, Air 2,600); Sponsored Reserve 2,000)
Includes both trained and those currently under training within the Regular Forces, excluding university cadet units.

ORGANISATIONS BY SERVICE

Strategic Forces 1,000

Royal Navy
EQUIPMENT BY TYPE
SUBMARINES • STRATEGIC • SSBN 4:
  4 *Vanguard* with 1 16-cell VLS with UGM-133A *Trident* II D-5 nuclear SLBM, 4 533mm TT with *Spearfish* HWT (each boat will not deploy with more than 40 warheads, but each missile could carry up to 12 MIRV; some *Trident* D-5 capable of being configured for sub-strategic role)
MSL • SLBM • Nuclear 48 UGM-133A *Trident* II D-5 (fewer than 160 declared operational warheads)

Royal Air Force
EQUIPMENT BY TYPE
RADAR • STRATEGIC 1 Ballistic Missile Early Warning System (BMEWS) at Fylingdales Moor

Space
EQUIPMENT BY TYPE
SATELLITES • COMMUNICATIONS 8: 1 NATO-4B; 3 *Skynet*-4; 4 *Skynet*-5

Army 83,900; 2,800 Gurkhas (total 86,700)

Regt normally bn size
FORCES BY ROLE
COMMAND
  1 (ARRC) corps HQ
MANOEUVRE
  Armoured
  1 (3rd) armd div (3 armd inf bde (1 armd recce regt, 1 tk regt, 2 armd inf bn, 1 mech inf bn); 1 log bde (6 log regt; 4 maint regt; 3 med regt))
  Light
  1 (1st) lt inf div (1 (4th) inf bde (1 recce regt, 1 lt mech inf bn; 1 lt inf bn); 1 (7th) inf bde (1 recce regt, 2 lt

mech inf bn; 2 lt inf bn); 1 (11th) inf bde (1 lt mech inf bn; 1 lt inf bn; 1 (Gurkha) lt inf bn); 2 (38th & 42nd) inf bde (2 lt inf bn); 1 (51st) inf bde (1 recce regt; 2 lt mech inf bn; 1 lt inf bn); 1 (160th) inf bde (1 lt inf bn); 1 log bde (3 log regt; 2 maint bn; 2 med regt))
2 lt inf bn (London)
1 (Gurkha) lt inf bn (Brunei)
Air Manoeuvre
1 (16th) air aslt bde (1 recce pl, 2 para bn, 1 fd arty regt, 1 cbt engr regt, 1 MP coy, 1 log regt, 1 med regt)
COMBAT SUPPORT
1 arty bde (3 SP arty regt, 2 fd arty regt)
2 AD regt
1 engr bde (5 cbt engr regt, 2 EOD regt, 1 engr regt, 1 (air spt) engr regt, 1 log regt)
1 (geographic) engr regt
1 ISR bde (1 STA regt, 1 EW regt, 3 int bn, 2 ISR UAV regt)
1 MP bde (3 MP bn)
1 sigs bde (7 sigs regt)
1 sigs bde (2 sigs regt; 1 (ARRC) sigs bn)
1 (77th) cbt spt bde (6 cbt spt/spt gp (incl psyops, media ops & civil affairs))
COMBAT SERVICE SUPPORT
1 log bde (2 log regt)
1 med bde (3 fd hospital)

Reserves

Army Reserve 29,300 reservists

The Army Reserve (AR) generates individuals, sub-units and some full units. The majority of units are subordinate to regular formation headquarters and paired with one or more regular units

FORCES BY ROLE
MANOEUVRE
  Reconnaissance
  3 recce regt
  Armoured
  1 armd regt
  Light
  13 lt inf bn
  Air Manoeuvre
  1 para bn
COMBAT SUPPORT
  2 arty regt
  1 STA regt
  1 MRL regt
  5 engr regt
  3 engr sqn
  3 EOD sqn
  4 int bn
  4 sigs regt
COMBAT SERVICE SUPPORT
  11 log regt
  6 maint regt
  3 med regt
  10 fd hospital
ISR UAV
  1 ISR UAV regt
AIR DEFENCE
  1 AD regt

EQUIPMENT BY TYPE
ARMOURED FIGHTING VEHICLES
  MBT 227 *Challenger* 2
  RECCE 638: 197 *Jackal*; 110 *Jackal* 2; 130 *Jackal* 2A; 201 FV107 *Scimitar*
  IFV 623: 466 FV510 *Warrior*; 88 FV511 *Warrior* (CP); 51 FV514 *Warrior* (OP); 18 FV515 *Warrior* (CP)
  APC 1,301
    APC (T) 880 *Bulldog* Mk3
    PPV 421 *Mastiff* (6×6)
  AUV 1,237: 398 *Foxhound*; 275 FV103 *Spartan* (incl variants); 396 *Panther* CLV; 168 *Ridgback*
ENGINEERING & MAINTENANCE VEHICLES
  AEV 98: 66 *Terrier*; 32 *Trojan*
  ARV 261: 80 *Challenger* ARRV; 35 FV106 *Samson*; 105 FV512 *Warrior*; 41 FV513 *Warrior*
  MW 64 *Aardvark*
  VLB 60: 27 M3; 33 *Titan*
NBC VEHICLES 8 TPz-1 *Fuchs* NBC
ANTI-TANK/ANTI-INFRASTRUCTURE • MSL
  SP *Exactor* (*Spike* NLOS)
  MANPATS FGM-148 *Javelin*
ARTILLERY 592
  SP 155mm 89 AS90
  TOWED 105mm 108 L118 Light Gun
  MRL 227mm 35 M270B1 MLRS
  MOR 81mm 360 L16A1
RADAR • LAND 150: 6 *Giraffe* AMB; 5 *Mamba*; 139 MSTAR
AMPHIBIOUS • LCU 3 Ramped Craft Logistic
UNMANNED AERIAL VEHICLES • ISR • Medium 8 *Watchkeeper* (21+ more in store)
AIR DEFENCE • SAM
  Point-defence 74: 60 FV4333 *Stormer* with *Starstreak*; 14 *Rapier* FSC; *Starstreak* (LML)

Joint Helicopter Command

Tri-service joint organisation including Royal Navy, Army and RAF units

Army

FORCES BY ROLE
ISR
  1 regt (1 sqn with BN-2 *Defender/Islander*; 1 sqn with SA341B *Gazelle* AH1)
ATTACK HELICOPTER
  1 regt (2 sqn with AH-64D *Apache*; 1 trg sqn with AH-64D *Apache*)
  1 regt (2 sqn with AH-64D *Apache*)
HELICOPTER
  1 regt (1 sqn with AW159 *Wildcat* AH1)
  1 (spec ops) sqn with *Lynx* AH9A
  1 (spec ops) sqn with AS365N3; SA341B *Gazelle* AH1
  1 flt with Bell 212 (Brunei)
  1 flt with SA341B *Gazelle* AH1 (Canada)
TRAINING
  1 hel regt (1 sqn with AH-64D *Apache*; 1 sqn with AS350B *Ecureuil*; 1 sqn with Bell 212; *Lynx* AH9A; SA341B *Gazelle* AH1)
COMBAT SERVICE SUPPORT
  1 maint regt

Army Reserve
FORCES BY ROLE
HELICOPTER
1 hel regt (4 sqn personnel only)

Royal Navy
FORCES BY ROLE
ATTACK HELICOPTER
1 lt sqn with AW159 *Wildcat* AH1
TRANSPORT HELICOPTER
2 sqn with AW101 *Merlin* HC3/3A/3i

Royal Air Force
FORCES BY ROLE
TRANSPORT HELICOPTER
3 sqn with CH-47D/SD/F *Chinook* HC3/4/4A/6
2 sqn with SA330 *Puma* HC2
TRAINING
1 OCU sqn with CH-47D/SD/F *Chinook* HC3/4/4A/6; SA330 *Puma* HC2
EQUIPMENT BY TYPE
AIRCRAFT • TPT • Light 13: 9 BN-2T-4S *Defender*; 4 BN-2 *Islander* AL1
HELICOPTERS
ATK 50 AH-64D *Apache*
MRH 94: 5 AS365N3; 34 AW159 *Wildcat* AH1; 21 *Lynx* AH9A; 34 SA341B *Gazelle* AH1
TPT 125: **Heavy** 60: 38 CH-47D *Chinook* HC4/4A; 8 CH-47SD *Chinook* HC3; 14 CH-47F *Chinook* HC6; **Medium** 48: 25 AW101 *Merlin* HC3/3A/3i; 23 SA330 *Puma* HC2; **Light** 17: 9 AS350B *Ecureuil*; 8 Bell 212

Royal Navy 32,350
EQUIPMENT BY TYPE
SUBMARINES 11
STRATEGIC • SSBN 4:
4 *Vanguard*, opcon Strategic Forces with 1 16-cell VLS with UGM-133A *Trident* II D-5 nuclear SLBM, 4 single 533mm TT with *Spearfish* HWT (each boat will not deploy with more than 40 warheads, but each missile could carry up to 12 MIRV; some *Trident* D-5 capable of being configured for sub-strategic role)
TACTICAL • SSN 7:
4 *Trafalgar* with 5 single 533mm TT with *Tomahawk* LACM/*Spearfish* HWT
3 *Astute* with 6 single 533mm TT with *Tomahawk* LACM/*Spearfish* HWT
PRINCIPAL SURFACE COMBATANTS 19
DESTROYERS 6
DDGHM 3 *Daring* (Type-45) with 2 quad lnchr with RGM-84C *Harpoon*, 1 48-cell VLS with *Sea Viper* SAM, 2 *Phalanx* Block 1B CIWS, 1 114mm gun (capacity 1 *Lynx*/AW101 *Merlin* hel)
DDHM 3 *Daring* (Type-45) with 1 48-cell VLS with *Sea Viper* SAM, 2 *Phalanx* Block 1B CIWS, 1 114mm gun (capacity 1 *Lynx*/AW101 *Merlin* hel)
FRIGATES • FFGHM 13:
11 *Norfolk* (Type-23) with 2 quad Mk141 lnchr with RGM-84C *Harpoon* AShM, 1 32-cell VLS with *Sea Wolf* SAM, 2 twin 324mm ASTT with *Sting Ray* LWT, 1 114mm gun (capacity either 2 *Lynx* or 1 AW101 *Merlin* hel)
2 *Norfolk* (Type-23) with 2 quad Mk141 lnchr with RGM-84C *Harpoon* AShM, 1 32-cell VLS with *Sea Ceptor* SAM, 2 twin 324mm ASTT with *Sting Ray* LWT, 1 114mm gun (capacity either 2 *Lynx* or 1 AW101 *Merlin* hel)
PATROL AND COASTAL COMBATANTS 22
PSO 4: 3 *River*; 1 *River* (mod) with 1 hel landing platform
PBI 18: 16 *Archer* (trg); 2 *Scimitar*
MINE WARFARE • MINE COUNTERMEASURES 16
MCO 8 *Hunt* (incl 4 mod *Hunt*)
MHC 8 *Sandown* (1 decommissioned and used in trg role)
AMPHIBIOUS
PRINCIPAL AMPHIBIOUS SHIPS 3
LPD 2 *Albion* with 2 *Goalkeeper* CIWS (capacity 2 med hel; 4 LCU or 2 LCAC; 4 LCVP; 6 MBT; 300 troops) (1 at extended readiness)
LPH 1 *Ocean* with 3 *Phalanx* Block 1B CIWS (capacity 18 hel; 4 LCVP; 800 troops)
LOGISTICS AND SUPPORT 4
AGB 1 *Protector* with 1 hel landing platform
AGS 3: 1 *Scott*; 2 *Echo* (all with 1 hel landing platform)

Royal Fleet Auxiliary
Support and miscellaneous vessels are mostly manned and maintained by the Royal Fleet Auxiliary (RFA), a civilian fleet owned by the UK MoD, which has approximately 1,900 personnel with type comd under CINCFLEET
AMPHIBIOUS • PRINCIPAL AMPHIBIOUS SHIPS 3
LSD 3 *Bay* (capacity 4 LCU; 2 LCVP; 24 CR2 *Challenger* 2 MBT; 350 troops)
LOGISTICS AND SUPPORT 12
AORH 3: 2 *Wave*; 1 *Fort Victoria* with 2 *Phalanx* CIWS
AORL 2 *Rover* with 1 hel landing platform
AFSH 2 *Fort Rosalie*
AG 1 *Argus* (aviation trg ship with secondary role as primarily casualty-receiving ship)
AKR 4 *Point* (not RFA manned)

Naval Aviation (Fleet Air Arm) 5,000
FORCES BY ROLE
ANTI-SUBMARINE WARFARE
3 sqn with AW101 ASW *Merlin* HM2
1 sqn with AW159 *Wildcat* HMA2; *Lynx* HMA8
AIRBORNE EARLY WARNING
1 sqn with *Sea King* AEW7
TRAINING
1 sqn with Beech 350ER *King Air*
1 sqn with G-115 (op under contract)
1 sqn with *Hawk* T1
1 OCU sqn with AW101 ASW *Merlin* HM2
1 OCU sqn with AW159 *Wildcat* HMA2
EQUIPMENT BY TYPE
AIRCRAFT 12 combat capable
TPT • Light 4 Beech 350ER *King Air* (*Avenger*)
TRG 17: 5 G-115 (op under contract); 12 *Hawk* T1*
HELICOPTERS
ASW 68: 28 AW159 *Wildcat* HMA2; 10 *Lynx* HMA8; 30 AW101 ASW *Merlin* HM2

AEW 8 *Sea King* AEW7
AIR-LAUNCHED MISSILES • AShM *Sea Skua*

Royal Marines 6,800

FORCES BY ROLE
MANOEUVRE
  Amphibious
  1 (3rd Cdo) mne bde (3 mne bn; 1 amph aslt sqn; 1 (army) arty regt; 1 (army) engr regt; 1 ISR gp (1 EW sqn; 1 cbt spt sqn; 1 sigs sqn; 1 log sqn), 1 log regt)
  3 landing craft sqn opcon Royal Navy
  Other
  1 (Fleet Protection) sy gp
EQUIPMENT BY TYPE
ARMOURED FIGHTING VEHICLES
  APC (T) 99 BvS-10 Mk2 *Viking*
ANTI-TANK/ANTI-INFRASTUCTURE
  MSL • MANPATS FGM-148 *Javelin*
ARTILLERY 50
  TOWED 105mm 18 L118 Light Gun
  MOR 81mm 32 L16A1
RADAR • **LAND** 4 MAMBA (*Arthur*)
PATROL AND COASTAL COMBATANTS • **PB** 2 *Island*
AMPHIBIOUS • **LANDING CRAFT** 33
  LCU 10 LCU Mk10 (capacity 4 *Viking* APC or 120 troops)
  LCVP 19: 3 LCVP Mk5A (capacity 35 troops) (planned OSD Dec 2016); 16 LCVP Mk5B (capacity 35 troops)
  UCAC 4 *Griffon* 2400TD
AIR DEFENCE • **SAM** • **Point-defence** *Starstreak*

Royal Air Force 33,300

Flying hours 210 hrs/yr on fast jets; 290 on tpt ac; 240 on hels

FORCES BY ROLE
FIGHTER
  2 sqn with *Typhoon* FGR4/T3
FIGHTER/GROUND ATTACK
  3 sqn with *Typhoon* FGR4/T3
  1 Sqn with F-35B *Lightning* II (forming)
GROUND ATTACK
  3 sqn with *Tornado* GR4/4A
ISR
  1 sqn with *Sentinel* R1
  1 sqn with *Shadow* R1
ELINT
  1 sqn with RC-135W *Rivet Joint*
AIRBORNE EARLY WARNING & CONTROL
  1 sqn with E-3D *Sentry*
SEARCH & RESCUE
  1 sqn with Bell 412EP *Griffin* HAR-2
TANKER/TRANSPORT
  2 sqn with A330 MRTT *Voyager* KC2/3
TRANSPORT
  1 (comms) sqn with AW109E/SP; BAe-146; BN-2A *Islander* CC2
  1 sqn with A400M *Atlas*
  1 sqn with C-17A *Globemaster*
  3 sqn with C-130J/J-30 *Hercules*

TRAINING
  1 OCU sqn with *Tornado*
  1 OCU sqn with *Typhoon*
  1 OEU sqn with *Typhoon, Tornado*
  1 OEU with F-35B *Lightning* II
  1 OCU sqn with E-3D *Sentry; Sentinel* R1
  1 OEU sqn with E-3D *Sentry; Sentinel* R1
  1 sqn with Beech 200 *King Air*
  1 sqn with EMB-312 *Tucano* T1
  2 sqn with *Hawk* T1/1A/1W
  1 sqn with *Hawk* T2
  3 sqn with *Tutor*
COMBAT/ISR UAV
  2 sqn with MQ-9A *Reaper*
EQUIPMENT BY TYPE
AIRCRAFT 267 combat capable
  FGA 142: 4 F-35B *Lightning* II (in test); 138 *Typhoon* FGR4/T3
  ATK 65 *Tornado* GR4/GR4A
  ISR 11: 5 *Sentinel* R1; 6 *Shadow* R1
  ELINT 2 RC-135W *Rivet Joint*
  AEW&C 6 E-3D *Sentry*
  TKR/TPT 14 A330 MRTT *Voyager* KC2/3
  TPT 57: **Heavy** 19: 11 A400M *Atlas*; 8 C-17A *Globemaster*; **Medium** 24: 10 C-130J *Hercules*; 14 C-130J-30 *Hercules*; **Light** 10: 5 Beech 200 *King Air* (on lease); 2 Beech 200GT *King Air* (on lease); 3 BN-2A *Islander* CC2; **PAX** 4 BAe-146 CC2/C3
  TRG 200: 39 EMB-312 *Tucano* T1 (42 more in store); 101 G-115E *Tutor*; 28 *Hawk* T2*; 32 *Hawk* T1/1A/1W* (ε46 more in store)
HELICOPTERS
  MRH 5: 1 AW139; 4 Bell 412EP *Griffin* HAR-2
  TPT • **Light** 3: 2 AW109E; 1 AW109SP
UNMANNED AERIAL VEHICLES • **CISR** • **Heavy** 10 MQ-9A *Reaper*
AIR-LAUNCHED MISSILES
  AAM • IR AIM-9L/L(I) *Sidewinder;* IIR ASRAAM; ARH AIM-120C-5 AMRAAM
  ASM AGM-114 *Hellfire;* Brimstone; Dual-Mode Brimstone; Brimstone II
  ALCM Storm Shadow
BOMBS
  Laser/GPS-guided GBU-10 *Paveway* II; GBU-24 *Paveway* III; Enhanced *Paveway* II/III; *Paveway* IV

Royal Air Force Regiment

FORCES BY ROLE
MANOEUVRE
  Other
  6 sy sqn
COMBAT SUPPORT
  2 CBRN sqn

Tri-Service Defence Helicopter School

FORCES BY ROLE
TRAINING
  1 hel sqn with Bell 412EP *Griffin* HT1
  2 hel sqn with AS350B *Ecureuil*
EQUIPMENT BY TYPE
HELICOPTERS
  MRH 10 Bell 412EP *Griffin* HT1
  TPT • **Light** 27: 25 AS350B *Ecureuil*; 2 AW109E

Volunteer Reserve Air Forces
(Royal Auxiliary Air Force/RAF Reserve)
MANOEUVRE
  Other
    5 sy sqn
COMBAT SUPPORT
  2 int sqn
COMBAT SERVICE SUPPORT
  1 med sqn
  1 (air movements) sqn
  1 (HQ augmentation) sqn
  1 (C-130 Reserve Aircrew) flt

UK Special Forces
Includes Royal Navy, Army and RAF units
FORCES BY ROLE
SPECIAL FORCES
  1 (SAS) SF regt
  1 (SBS) SF regt
  1 (Special Reconnaissance) SF regt
  1 SF BG (based on 1 para bn)
AVIATION
  1 wg (includes assets drawn from 3 Army hel sqn, 1 RAF tpt sqn and 1 RAF hel sqn)
COMBAT SUPPORT
  1 sigs regt

Reserve
FORCES BY ROLE
SPECIAL FORCES
  2 (SAS) SF regt

Cyber

Joint Forces Cyber Group
2 Joint Cyber Units and a Joint Cyber Reserve

The Office of Cyber Security & Information Assurance (OSCIA) works with the Cyber Security Operations Centre (CSOC) and ministries and agencies to implement cyber-security programmes. CSOC is hosted by GCHQ. A Cyber Security Strategy was published in November 2011. The Defence Cyber Operations Group was set up in 2011 to place 'cyber at the heart of defence operations, doctrine and training'. This group was transferred to Joint Forces Command on this formation's establishment in April 2012. A Joint Forces Cyber Group was set up in 2013, including a Joint Cyber Reserve, providing support to two Joint Cyber Units and other information-assurance units across the defence establishment. Increased concern about the potential of information operations in and through the cyber domain was central to the 2015 creation of 77 Bde. The 2015 SDSR designated cyber a tier-one risk, and stated that the UK would respond to a cyber attack in the same way as it would an equivalent conventional attack, and outlined a £1.9 billion investment over the next five years in protecting the UK from cyber attacks and developing sovereign capabilities in cyberspace. A new National Cyber Security Strategy is expected in late 2016. It has been announced that as part of this the government will over the next five years more than double the funds allocated to cyber in the 2011–16 strategy. A new CSOC under the MoD will replace the existing CSOC, which is presently under GCHQ. A new National Cyber Centre, coming under GCHQ and expected to open in October 2016, will play a leading role in the forthcoming strategy, working closely with the new CSOC. CSOC was also due to open in late 2016, directed at defending MoD networks.

DEPLOYMENT
Legal provisions for foreign deployment:
Constitution: Uncodified constitution which includes constitutional statutes, case law, international treaties and unwritten conventions
Decision on deployment of troops abroad: By the government

AFGHANISTAN
NATO • *Operation Resolute Support* 450; 1 inf bn(-)

ALBANIA
OSCE • Albania 2

ARABIAN SEA & GULF OF ADEN
1 DDGHM; 1 LPH; 1 LSD; 1 AORH

ARMENIA/AZERBAIJAN
OSCE • Minsk Conference 1

ASCENSION ISLAND
20

ATLANTIC (NORTH)/CARIBBEAN
1 AORH

ATLANTIC (SOUTH)
1 FFGHM

BAHRAIN
80; 1 BAe-146

BELIZE
17

BOSNIA-HERZEGOVINA
EU • EUFOR • *Operation Althea* 4
OSCE • Bosnia and Herzegovina 2

BRITISH INDIAN OCEAN TERRITORY
40; 1 Navy/Marine det

BRUNEI
2,000; 1 (Gurkha) lt inf bn; 1 jungle trg centre; 1 hel flt with 3 Bell 212

CANADA
250; 2 trg units; 1 hel flt with SA341 *Gazelle* AH1

CYPRUS
2,270; 2 inf bn; 1 SAR sqn with 4 Bell 412 *Twin Huey*; 1 radar (on det)
Operation Shader 650: 1 FGA sqn with 6 *Tornado* GR4; 6 *Typhoon* FGR4; 1 *Sentinel* R1; 1 E-3D *Sentry*; 1 A330 MRTT *Voyager* KC3; 2 C-130J *Hercules*
UN • UNFICYP 275; 1 inf coy

DEMOCRATIC REPUBLIC OF THE CONGO
UN • MONUSCO 5

EGYPT
MFO 2

FALKLAND ISLANDS
1,010: 1 inf coy(+); 1 AD det with *Rapier*; 1 PSO; 1 ftr flt with 4 *Typhoon* FGR4; 1 tkr/tpt flt with C-130J *Hercules*

GERMANY
4,400; 1 armd inf bde(-) (1 tk regt, 1 armd inf bn, 1 SP arty regt, 1 cbt engr regt, 1 maint regt, 1 med regt)

GIBRALTAR
560 (incl Royal Gibraltar regt); 2 PB

IRAQ
Operation Shader 550

KENYA
260 (trg team)

KUWAIT
40 (trg team)
Operation Shader MQ-9A *Reaper*

MALI
EU • EUTM Mali 30
UN • MINUSMA 2

MEDITERRANEAN SEA
EU • EU NAVFOR MED: 1 LSD; 1 AGS
NATO • SNMG 2: 1 MCO

MOLDOVA
OSCE • Moldova 2

NEPAL
60 (Gurkha trg org)

NETHERLANDS
120

NIGERIA
30 (trg team)

NORTH SEA
NATO • SNMCMG 1: 1 MHC

OMAN
70

PERSIAN GULF
Operation Kipion 2 MCO; 2 MHC; 1 LSD

QATAR
Operation Shader 1 RC-135W *Rivet Joint*

SERBIA
NATO • KFOR 1
OSCE • Kosovo 12

SIERRA LEONE
10

SOMALIA
UN • UNSOM 41; 3 obs

SOUTH SUDAN
UN • UNMISS 9

UGANDA
EU • EUTM Somalia 4

UKRAINE
OSCE • Ukraine 29
Operation Orbital 100 (trg team)

UNITED ARAB EMIRATES
1 tpt flt with C-17A *Globemaster*; C-130J *Hercules*; A330 MRTT *Voyager*

UNITED STATES
660

FOREIGN FORCES

United States
US European Command: 8,700; 1 ftr wg at RAF Lakenheath with (1 ftr sqn with 24 F-15C/D *Eagle*, 2 ftr sqn with 23 F-15E *Strike Eagle*); 1 ISR sqn at RAF Mildenhall with OC-135/RC-135; 1 tkr wg at RAF Mildenhall with 15 KC-135R/T *Stratotanker*; 1 CSAR sqn at RAF Lakenheath with 8 HH-60G *Pave Hawk*: 1 Spec Ops gp at RAF Mildenhall with (1 sqn with 8 CV-22B *Osprey*; 1 sqn with 8 MC-130J *Commando II* • US Strategic Command: 1 AN/FPS-132 Upgraded Early Warning Radar and 1 *Spacetrack* radar at Fylingdales Moor

Table 3 Selected arms procurements and deliveries, Europe

Designation	Type	Quantity (Current)	Contract Value	Prime Nationality	Prime Contractor	Order Date	First Delivery Due	Notes
Belgium (BEL)								
A400M *Atlas*	Hvy tpt ac	7	n.k.	Int'l	Airbus Group (Airbus Defence & Space)	2003	2018	Delivery expected 2018/19
Croatia (CRO)								
PzH 2000	Arty (SP 155mm)	12	€41m (US$49.5m)	GER	Government surplus	n.k.	2015	Deliveries to be complete by end of 2016
OH-58D *Kiowa Warrior*	MRH hel	16	US$34.8m	US	Government surplus	2016	2016	Ex-US Army surplus. First five delivered Jul 2016
Denmark (DNK)								
Piranha 5	APC (W)	209	DKK4.5bn (US$663.2m)	US (CHE)	General Dynamics (General Dynamics European Land Systems – MOWAG)	2015	2018	First training vehicles to be delivered 2018. Serial deliveries to begin 2019. All to be delivered by 2023
MH-60R *Seahawk*	ASW hel	9	DKK4bn (US$686m)	US	Lockheed Martin (Sikorsky)	2012	2015	To replace *Lynx*. First three entered service May 2016
Estonia (EST)								
CV9035	IFV	44	€113m (US$150.2m)	NLD	Government surplus	2014	2016	First batch delivered Oct 2016
Finland (FIN)								
Leopard 2A6	MBT	100	n.k.	NLD	Government surplus	2014	2015	Deliveries ongoing
AGM-158 JASSM	Msl (Tactical LACM)	n.k.	n.k.	US	Lockheed Martin	2015	n.k.	Deliveries to be complete by 2019
France (FRA)								
Griffon	APC (W)	780	n.k.	FRA	GME	2014	2018	For phase one of the *Scorpion* programme. To replace AMX10RC, ERC *Sagaie* and VAB HOT. Programme of record for 1,722 vehicles
Jaguar	Recce	110	n.k.	FRA	GME	2014	2020	For phase one of the *Scorpion* programme. To replace VAB. Programme of record for 248 vehicles
MMP	MANPATS	400	€631.4m (US$700.6m)	Int'l	MBDA	2014	2017	To replace *Milan*. Series production began 2016; deliveries to begin 2017
Suffren class	SSN	6	€7.9bn (US$9.2bn)	FRA	DCNS	2006	2017	*Barracuda* programme. One SSN to be delivered every two years until 2027. First planned to enter service 2017
Aquitaine class	DDGHM	8	See notes	FRA	DCNS	2002	2012	FREMM programme. FRA now to get eight ships instead of 11. Programme cost amounted to €9.7bn (US$10.8bn) as of end of 2015. Fourth ship for FRA began sea trials Sep 2016

Table 3 **Selected arms procurements and deliveries, Europe**

Designation	Type	Quantity (Current)	Contract Value	Prime Nationality	Prime Contractor	Order Date	First Delivery Due	Notes
Frégates de Taille Intermédiaire	FFGHM	5	n.k.	FRA	DCNS	2015	2023	To replace *La Fayette* class
MdCN	LACM	150	See notes	Int'l	MBDA	2007	2015	Original contract value €910m (US$1.2bn) for 250 missiles. Initial operating capability with *Suffren*-class SSN in 2018
Rafale F3	FGA ac	180	See notes	FRA	Dassault	1984	2006	Programme cost amounted to €46.6bn (US$51.7bn) by end of 2015. Deliveries ongoing
KC-130J	Tkr ac	2	n.k.	US	Lockheed Martin	2016	2019	–
A330 MRTT	Tkr/Tpt ac	12	€3.6bn (US$4.8bn)	Int'l	Airbus Group (Airbus Defence & Space)	2014	2018	–
A400M *Atlas*	Hvy tpt ac	50	See notes	Int'l	Airbus Group (Airbus Defence & Space)	2003	2013	FRA programme cost amounted to €9.2bn (US$10.2bn) by end of 2015. Tenth aircraft delivered Jul 2016
C-130J *Hercules*	Med tpt ac	2	n.k.	US	Lockheed Martin	2016	2017	–
Tiger	Atk hel	80	See notes	Int'l	Airbus Group (Airbus Helicopters)	1999	2005	Forty HAP, 40 HAD variant. Programme cost amounted to €6.4bn (US$7.1bn) by end of 2015. All HAP delivered. HAD variant deliveries ongoing
NH90 NFH	ASW hel	27	n.k.	FRA/GER/ITA/NLD	NHIndustries	2000	2010	For navy; deliveries ongoing
NH90 TTH	Med tpt hel	75	n.k.	FRA/GER/ITA/NLD	NHIndustries	2007	2012	For army; deliveries ongoing
MQ-9 *Reaper*	UAV (ISR Hvy)	6	n.k.	US	General Atomics	2014	2016	Second and third orders
Meteor	Msl (AAM)	200	n.k.	Int'l	MBDA	2011	2018	For integration with *Rafale* F3-R
CERES System	Satellite (SIGINT)	3	n.k.	Int'l/FRA	Airbus Group (Airbus Defence & Space)/Thales (Thales Alenia Space)	2015	2020	–
COMSAT NG	Satellite (Comms)	2	n.k.	Int'l/FRA	Airbus Group (Airbus Defence & Space)/Thales (Thales Alenia Space)	2015	2021	To replace *Syracuse* III X-band satellites
Germany (GER)								
Puma	IFV	350	n.k.	GER	PSM	2007	2015	To replace *Marder* 1A3/A4/A5 IFVs. Order reduced from 450. Deliveries ongoing
Boxer (8x8)	APC (W)	131	ε€476m (εUS$528m)	GER/NLD	ARTEC	2015	2017	Second order
Baden-Württemberg class	DDGHM	4	€2.6bn (US$3.6bn)	GER	TKMS	2007	2016	First planned to commission end of 2016. Final delivery due late 2018
Eurofighter Typhoon	FGA ac	143	n.k.	GER/ITA/ESP/UK	Eurofighter (Airbus Defence & Space)	1998	2003	Deliveries ongoing
A400M *Atlas*	Hvy tpt ac	53	n.k.	Int'l	Airbus Group (Airbus Defence & Space)	2003	2014	Fifth aircraft delivered Sep 2016

Table 3 **Selected arms procurements and deliveries, Europe**

Designation	Type	Quantity (Current)	Contract Value	Prime Nationality	Prime Contractor	Order Date	First Delivery Due	Notes
Tiger (UHT variant)	Atk hel	68	See notes	Int'l	Airbus Group (Airbus Helicopters)	1984	2005	Parliament approved reduced deal for 68 *Tiger*, 18 NH90 *Sea Lion* and 82 NH90 TTH for €8.46bn (US$9.4bn). Deliveries ongoing
NH90 *Sea Lion*	ASW hel	18	See notes	FRA/GER/ITA/NLD	NHIndustries	2013	2017	Parliament approved reduced deal for 68 *Tiger*, 18 NH90 *Sea Lion* and 82 NH90 TTH for €8.46bn (US$9.4bn)
NH90 TTH	Med tpt hel	82	See notes	FRA/GER/ITA/NLD	NHIndustries	2000	2007	Parliament approved reduced deal for 68 *Tiger*, 18 NH90 *Sea Lion* and 82 NH90 TTH for €8.46bn (US$9.4bn). Fifty for army; 32 for air force. Deliveries ongoing
Meteor	Msl (AAM)	n.k.	n.k.	Int'l	MBDA	2013	n.k.	For integration with Eurofighter *Typhoon*
Greece (GRC)								
CH-47D *Chinook*	Hvy tpt hel	10	n.k.	US	Government surplus	n.k.	2016	Ex-US Army surplus. First three delivered Nov 2016
NH90 TTH	Med tpt hel	20	€657m (US$620.5m)	FRA/GER/ITA/NLD	NHIndustries	2003	2011	Sixteen tactical-transport variants and four special-operations variants. Delivery began Jun 2011. Deliveries ongoing
Ireland (IRL)								
Samuel Beckett class	PSO	4	n.k.	UK	Babcock Marine	2010	2014	Second of class commissioned Sep 2015. Third of class floated out Mar 2016. Fourth vessel ordered Jun 2016
Italy (ITA)								
Salvatore Todaro class (Type-212A)	SSK	2	€915m (US$1.45bn)	ITA	Fincantieri	2008	2015	Second batch; option exercised from 1996 contract. With AIP. First hull of order, third of class, delivered Jul 2016
Bergamini class	DDGHM	10	n.k.	ITA	Orizzonte Sistemi Navali	2002	2013	Sixth of class launched Dec 2015. Ninth and tenth vessels ordered 2015
Pattugliatori Polivalenti d'Altura	FFGHM	7	See notes	ITA	Fincantieri/Leonardo	2015	2021	Seven frigates and a logistics support ship for €4.3bn (US$4.8bn). Option for three more frigates
New amphibious assault ship	LHD	1	€1.1bn (US$1.22m)	ITA	Fincantieri/Leonardo	2015	2022	To replace *Giuseppe Garibaldi* CVS
Logistics Support Ship	AFS	1	See notes	ITA	Fincantieri/Leonardo	2015	2019	Seven frigates and a logistics support ship for €4.3bn (US$4.8bn). Keel laid Jul 2016
Eurofighter *Typhoon*	FGA ac	96	n.k.	GER/ITA/ESP/UK	Eurofighter (Leonardo)	1998	2004	Programme of record for 121 aircraft. Eighty-second delivered Jun 2016
F-35A *Lightning II*	FGA ac	8	n.k.	US (ITA)	Lockheed Martin (Leonardo)	2013	2015	Programme of record for 60 F-35A and 30 F-35B. First three aircraft at Luke Air Force Base for training
Gulfstream G550 CAEW	AEW&C ac	2	US$750m	ISR	IAI	2012	2015	First aircraft being outfitted for ISR prior to delivery
ATR-72MP	MP ac	4	n.k.	ITA	Leonardo	2009	n.k.	To be fitted with long-range surveillance suite

Table 3 **Selected arms procurements and deliveries, Europe**

Designation	Type	Quantity (Current)	Contract Value	Prime Nationality	Prime Contractor	Order Date	First Delivery Due	Notes
NH90 NFH/TTH	ASW/Med tpt hel	116	n.k.	FRA/GER/ITA/NLD	NHIndustries	2000	2007	Sixty TTH for army; 46 NFH and 10 TTH for navy. Deliveries ongoing
CH-47F *Chinook*	Hvy tpt hel	16	€900m (US$1.23bn)	US	Boeing	2009	2014	Deliveries ongoing
HH-101A *Caesar* (AW101)	CSAR hel	12	n.k.	ITA	Leonardo	n.k.	2015	First four helicopters entered service Feb 2016
Piaggio P.1HH *Hammerhead*	UAV	6	n.k.	ITA	Piaggio Aerospace	2015	2016	–
Meteor	Msl (AAM)	n.k.	n.k.	Int'l	MBDA	n.k.	n.k.	For integration with *Typhoon*

Latvia (LVA)

Designation	Type	Quantity (Current)	Contract Value	Prime Nationality	Prime Contractor	Order Date	First Delivery Due	Notes
CVR(T) Family	AFV	123	€48m (US$67.5m)	UK	Government surplus	2014	2015	Total to include five variants. Deliveries ongoing

Lithuania (LTU)

Designation	Type	Quantity (Current)	Contract Value	Prime Nationality	Prime Contractor	Order Date	First Delivery Due	Notes
Vilkas (*Boxer*)	IFV	88	ε€58.3m (εUS$435.4m)	GER/NLD	ARTEC	2016	2017	IFV variants with 30mm gun and anti-tank missile
PzH 2000	Arty (SP 155mm)	21	€58.3m (US$64.7m)	GER	Government surplus	2015	2016	Order includes other vehicles. First vehicles delivered Jun 2016

Luxembourg (LUX)

Designation	Type	Quantity (Current)	Contract Value	Prime Nationality	Prime Contractor	Order Date	First Delivery Due	Notes
A400M *Atlas*	Hvy tpt ac	1	n.k.	Int'l	Airbus Group (Airbus Defence & Space)	2003	2018	–

NATO

Designation	Type	Quantity (Current)	Contract Value	Prime Nationality	Prime Contractor	Order Date	First Delivery Due	Notes
RQ-4 *Global Hawk* Block 40	ISR UAV	5	€1.3bn (US$1.7bn)	US	Northrop Grumman	2012	2016	Part of NATO's Alliance Ground Surveillance programme. First flight Dec 2015. First delivery expected by end of 2016. Initial operating capability expected 2017/18

Netherlands (NLD)

Designation	Type	Quantity (Current)	Contract Value	Prime Nationality	Prime Contractor	Order Date	First Delivery Due	Notes
Boxer (8x8)	APC (W)	200	€595m (US$747m)	GER/NLD	ARTEC	2006	2013	To replace YPR 765. Deliveries ongoing
F-35A *Lightning* II	FGA ac	4	n.k.	US	Lockheed Martin	2013	2014	Programme of record for 37 aircraft. Two test aircraft delivered
A330 MRTT	Tkr/Tpt ac	2	n.k.	Int'l	Airbus Group (Airbus Defence & Space)	2016	2020	Will be used by NATO
CH-47F *Chinook*	Hvy tpt hel	14	n.k.	US	Boeing	2015	2019	–

Norway (NOR)

Designation	Type	Quantity (Current)	Contract Value	Prime Nationality	Prime Contractor	Order Date	First Delivery Due	Notes
CV90	IFV/IFV upgrade	144	GB£500m (US$750m)	UK (SWE)	BAE Systems (BAE Systems Hägglunds)	2012	2015	Forty-one new build CV90s and 103 existing CV9030s to be upgraded. Two pre-series upgraded CV9030s in trials. Deliveries ongoing
F-35A *Lightning* II	FGA ac	4	n.k.	US	Lockheed Martin	2012	2015	Programme of record for 52 aircraft. First four at Luke Air Force Base for training

Table 3 **Selected arms procurements and deliveries, Europe**

Designation	Type	Quantity (Current)	Contract Value	Prime Nationality	Prime Contractor	Order Date	First Delivery Due	Notes
NH90 NFH/TTH	ASW/Med tpt hel	14	n.k.	FRA/GER/ITA/NLD	NHIndustries	2001	2013	Deliveries ongoing; six NHF and eight TTH
Poland (POL)								
Rosomak	IFV	997	US$2.2bn	FIN/POL	Patria/PGZ (Rosomak)	2003	2004	Includes 2013 follow-on order for 307 vehicles
Krab	Arty (SP 155mm)	120	εUS$1.58bn	POL/ROK	HSW/Hanwha Techwin	2014	2016	First contract signed in 2014 for 24 ROK K-9 chassis and licenced production rights. First chassis delivered Apr 2016; 96 POL licence-built Krab ordered Nov 2016
RAK-a	Arty (Mor SP 120mm)	64	PLN968.3m (US$244.01m)	POL	PGZ (HSW)	2016	2017	Order also includes delivery of 32 command vehicles
Naval Strike Missile (NSM)	AShM	6	NOK1.3bn (US$206.3m)	NOR	Kongsberg	2014	n.k.	Order for second squadron of NSMs
Romania (ROM)								
F-16AM/BM Fighting Falcon	FGA ac	12	ε€628m (εUS$834.1m)	PRT	Government surplus	2013	2016	Nine ex-PRT F-16 mid-life updates and three ex-USAF aircraft upgraded to mid-life-update status by PRT. First batch of six delivered Sep 2016
Slovakia (SVK)								
Scipio (Rosomak)	IFV	30	n.k.	POL	PGZ (Rosomak)	2015	n.k.	Programme of record for 100 vehicles. Contract status unclear
UH-60M Black Hawk	Tpt hel	4	US$170.1m	US	Lockheed Martin (Sikorsky)	2015	n.k.	–
Spain (ESP)								
Pizarro	IFV	212	€707m (US$747m)	US (ESP)	General Dynamics (General Dynamics European Land Systems – SBS)	2003	2016	Second order. Five variants. First batch of this order delivered Jan 2016
Isaac Peral class (S-80A)	SSK	4	n.k.	ESP	Navantia	2003	2017	Delivery further delayed by redesign. Problems with build of first of class halted work on other three boats
Eurofighter Typhoon	FGA ac	74	n.k.	GER/ITA/ESP/UK	Eurofighter (Airbus Defence & Space)	1998	2003	Deliveries since 2012 have gone into storage
A400M Atlas	Hvy tpt ac	27	n.k.	Int'l	Airbus Group (Airbus Defence & Space)	2003	2016	First delivery now scheduled for 2018. Current plans envisage an operational fleet of only 14 aircraft. First ESP aircraft delivered Nov 2016
Tiger (HAP/HAD)	Atk hel	24	ε€1.35bn (εUS$1.5bn)	Int'l	Airbus Group (Airbus Helicopters)	2003	2007	Six HAP-E delivered 2007/08. HAD-E variant deliveries ongoing
HT-29 Caimán (NH90 TTH)	Med tpt hel	22	n.k.	FRA/GER/ITA/NLD	NHIndustries	2007	2012	Order reduced to 22 helicopters. Deliveries ongoing
MQ-9 Blk 5 Reaper	UAV (ISR Hvy)	4	n.k.	US	General Atomics	2016	n.k.	–

Table 3 **Selected arms procurements and deliveries, Europe**

Designation	Type	Quantity (Current)	Contract Value	Prime Nationality	Prime Contractor	Order Date	First Delivery Due	Notes
Meteor	Msl (AAM)	n.k.	n.k.	Int'l	MBDA	n.k.	n.k.	For integration with Eurofighter Typhoon
Sweden (SWE)								
FH-77 BW L52 Archer 6x6	Arty (SP 155mm)	24	n.k.	UK	BAE Systems (BAE Land & Armaments)	2010	2013	Four pre-production vehicles delivered Sep 2013; series production deliveries ongoing since 2015
Type-A26	SSK	2	SEK7.6bn (US$901m)	SWE	Saab	2015	2022	Steel cut for first of class Sep 2015
JAS Gripen E/F	FGA ac	60	US$2.5bn	SWE	Saab	2013	2018	–
NH90 NFH/TTH	ASW/ Med tpt hel	18	n.k.	FRA/GER/ITA/NLD	NHIndustries	2001	2007	Thirteen tpt/SAR and five ASW variants. Option for seven further helicopters
Meteor	Msl (AAM)	n.k.	n.k.	Int'l	MBDA	n.k.	n.k.	Missile entered service Jul 2016
Turkey (TUR)								
Altay	MBT	4	US$500m	TUR	Otokar	2007	2014	Development and production of four prototypes. Plans to order up to 250 more after testing
Firtina 155mm/52-cal	Arty (SP 155mm)	350	n.k.	ROK	Samsung Techwin	2001	2003	ROK Techwin K9 Thunder. Built under licence in TUR. Deliveries ongoing
Kirpi	PPV	468	n.k.	TUR	BMC	2009	2010	Delivery resumed after 2011 suspension
Type-214	SSK	6	€1.96bn (US$2.9bn)	GER	MFI/TKMS (HDW)	2011	n.k.	To be built at Gölcük Shipyard. Steel cut for first of class Oct 2015
Ada class	FFGHM	4	n.k.	TUR	Istanbul Naval Shipyard/RMK Marine	1996	2011	Contract retendered and third and fourth vessels to be built at Istanbul Naval Shipyard. Third of class launched Jun 2016
Anadolu class	LHD	1	n.k.	TUR/ESP	SEDEF/Navantia	2015	2021	Based on ESP Juan Carlos I class. To be built in TUR with Navantia's assistance. First of class laid down Apr 2016
F-35A Lightning II	FGA ac	2	n.k.	US	Lockheed Martin	2015	n.k.	Programme of record for 100 aircraft. Two ordered in Low-rate Initial Production 7
A400M Atlas	Hvy tpt ac	10	n.k.	Int'l	Airbus Group (Airbus Defence & Space)	2003	2014	Third aircraft delivered Dec 2015
T-129B	Atk hel	50	US$3bn	TUR/ITA	TAI/Aselsan/Leonardo	2007	2015	Option on further 41. Seventh helicopter delivered Oct 2016
CH-47F Chinook	Hvy tpt hel	6+	n.k.	US	Boeing	2011	2014	Original aim to acquire 14 for US$1.2bn, but order cut to six: five for army and one for Special Forces Command. Additional unknown amount ordered in 2015
T-70 (S-70i)	Med tpt hel	109	US$3.5bn	US/TUR	Lockheed Martin (Sikorsky/PZL Mielec)/TAI	2014	2021	Turkish Utility Helicopter programme. First prototype rolled out Jun 2016
Gokturk-1	Satellite	1	€270m (US$380m)	ITA/FRA	Telespazio/Thales	2009	n.k.	Launch delayed

Table 3 **Selected arms procurements and deliveries, Europe**

Designation	Type	Quantity (Current)	Contract Value	Prime Nationality	Prime Contractor	Order Date	First Delivery Due	Notes
United Kingdom (UK)								
Ajax	Recce	589	GB£3.5bn (US$5.765bn)	US (UK)	General Dynamics (General Dynamics UK)	2014	2017	245 Ajax armed recconnaissance vehicles and 344 other vehicles in five variants. To replace CVR(T) fleet
Dreadnought class	SSBN	4	See notes	UK	BAE Systems	See notes	2028	Several design and construction contracts made since 2012 totalling over GB£4bn (US$5.4bn). Construction of related equipment has begun. To replace Vanguard class
Astute class	SSN	7	n.k.	UK	BAE Systems	1994	2010	Third of class commissioned Mar 2016
Queen Elizabeth class	CV	2	εGB£6.2bn (εUS$9.7bn)	UK	BAE Systems	2007	2017	Both vessels now to be brought into service. First of class to begin sea trials in 2017
Tide class	AOT	4	GB£452m (US$597m)	ROK	DSME	2012	2016	MARS programme. First of class has suffered delays and is now in sea trials. All vessels planned to be in service by 2018
Eurofighter Typhoon	FGA ac	160	n.k.	GER/ITA/ESP/UK	Eurofighter GmbH (BAE Systems)	1998	2004	Deliveries ongoing
F-35B Lightning II	FGA ac	8	n.k.	US	Lockheed Martin	2008	2012	Programme of record for 138 aircraft. All delivered aircraft in test in US. Low-rate Initial Production 9 planned to include six aircraft for UK
P-8A Poseidon	ASW ac	9	εGB£3bn (εUS$3.2bn)	US	Boeing	2016	2019	–
RC-135 Rivet Joint	ELINT ac	3	εGB£700m (US$1bn)	US	Boeing	2010	2013	Second aircraft delivered Sep 2015
A400M Atlas	Hvy tpt ac	22	n.k.	Int'l	Airbus Group (Airbus Defence & Space)	2003	2014	Eleventh aircraft delivered Oct 2016
AH-64E Apache Guardian	Atk hel	50	US$2.3bn	US	Boeing	2016	2020	In-service date expected to be in 2022
Meteor	Msl (AAM)	n.k.	n.k.	Int'l	MBDA	n.k.	2018	For integration with Eurofighter Typhoon

Chapter Five
Russia and Eurasia

RUSSIA

Russia's deployment of military force to Syria in September 2015 significantly bolstered the position of Syria's leader, Bashar al-Assad, at a time when Assad's hold on power was looking increasingly tenuous. With this mission now more than one year old, it allows further examination of Russia's modernising armed forces and the capabilities of its weapons systems.

More broadly, on the defence-policy level, the Syria operation has reinforced the view that not only is Russia willing and able to deploy its armed forces, but also that it is prepared to use military force in situations when it perceives itself to be suffering – or to be at risk of suffering – geopolitical losses. As such, Russia's employment of military force in Syria, in and on the border with Ukraine, and also perhaps its military activities in Europe, can be seen as an attempt by Moscow to use military power as a coercive tool in order to further its political objectives. However, the military lever is not used in isolation; rather, it is just one policy component and is deployed alongside a range of other tools, including information and influence operations.

In Ukraine, the direct application of Russian military power resulted in the rapid seizure of Crimea. When Moscow perceived that its interests were threatened by Ukrainian military advances, military pressure was once more applied – for instance at Zelenopillya and Ilovaisk in 2014 and Debaltseve in 2015. Moscow's deployment of force was intended to coerce Kiev in relation to the negotiating process as much as it was to tactically assist its proxies on the ground in Ukraine. Similarly, as noted by one IISS expert, Russia's intervention in Syria can be seen as 'part of the international bargaining process over the civil war that began in 2011'. In addition, the 'brinkmanship in relation to NATO' could be perceived as being 'linked to the efforts Russia has been undertaking for many years to push back against increased military activity – particularly US military activity – along its borders'.

However, Russia's flexing of military muscle has impelled NATO's eastern member states towards closer integration with the Alliance; it has also spurred NATO to move more military equipment into these countries to reassure them. Russia's long-standing concern about the eastward movement of NATO and Eastern European states' integration into the Alliance is evident in its defence documentation and continued protests against the deployment of NATO's ballistic-missile-defence infrastructure in Eastern Europe. This concern is also demonstrated by Moscow's military activities in Europe, including increased activity within and close to Russia's borders, as well as its messaging – for example acknowledging that *Iskander* ballistic missiles are now stationed in Russia's Kaliningrad enclave (previously, these systems had only been temporarily moved into Kaliningrad on exercises).

Russia's latest National Security Strategy, released in December 2015, contained familiar themes and, in light of post-2014 tensions, displayed more continuity than discontinuity. The language was at times stark: 'The further expansion of the [NATO] alliance, and the location of its military infrastructure closer to Russian borders pose a threat to national security.' Opportunities for stability were retreating, the document stated, due to the siting in Europe, Asia and the Middle East of 'components of the US missile defense system, practical implementation of the "global strike" concept, and the deployment of strategic conventional precision-guided weapons systems and also the deployment of weapons in space'.

In November 2015, President Vladimir Putin signed a new State Defence Plan for 2016–20. This document remains classified, but reportedly places emphasis on Russia's strategic nuclear forces, and gives details of forces allocated to the Western Military District. Clues about Moscow's military priorities were also found in the president's December 2015 report to the Defence Ministry Board. Firstly, he said, although the defence plan had just been issued, a rapidly changing global environment meant that the defence ministry and other departments had to be ready, if necessary, to submit modifications. Secondly, modernisation and re-equipping of the armed forces should continue, although there was 'no excess funding, and everything that has been planned must be implemented according to the deadlines indicated in our plans and within the framework of the budgetary funding allocated earlier'. Thirdly, nuclear and space forces should be strengthened. Fourthly, training should be improved, and during snap inspections 'particular attention should be given to transporting troops over long distances' and 'creating groups in threatened areas' as well as 'air defence through a practical rise in aviation, with manoeuvres using anti-aircraft missile and radio engineering components'. Finally, military cooperation with allies should be improved.

A post-New Look era

Russia's most recent defence-modernisation drive was launched in late 2008 under then-defence minister Anatoly Serdyukov. Dubbed the *Novy Oblik* (New Look), it was designed to redress some of the deficiencies evident in the August 2008 war with Georgia and to restructure and rearm Russia's armed forces, moving away from the mass-mobilisation model towards formations held at permanent readiness. Since then, not only is there a new defence minister in post (Sergei Shoigu, who was appointed in 2011), but the original plans for the armed forces have altered. New structures were adopted, tested and – when found wanting – adjusted. An ambitious plan for the air force that would have meant a move towards large air bases housing mixed air groups, with a set of smaller satellite airfields, was tried and eventually shelved. The army, meanwhile, which had implemented a process of 'brigadisation' on its ground forces, found that the plan to move towards light, medium and heavy formations was unworkable. Indeed, this simple three-tier structure envisaged in the *Novy Oblik* is being left further behind. There were further structural changes in Russia's land forces in 2016. The number of divisions containing units with a traditional regimental structure increased and the number of brigades reduced, although the brigade tier will not be completely abandoned. Nonetheless, it is apparent that Shoigu has significantly moved beyond the *Novy Oblik*.

Meanwhile, the armed forces' construction activity mainly focused on the western border area in 2016. Infrastructure to provide bases for new military units associated with the redeployed 20th Combined-Arms Army (CAA) continued to be built. The 20th CAA is moving from Nizhny Novgorod (east of Moscow) to Voronezh and is intended to significantly strengthen Russia's presence on the border with Ukraine. Construction of barracks, hangars, training ranges and sports facilities, along with social infrastructure, is also under way along the border with Ukraine in order to accommodate troops on a long-term basis.

Figure 13 **Generating Russia's battalion tactical groups**

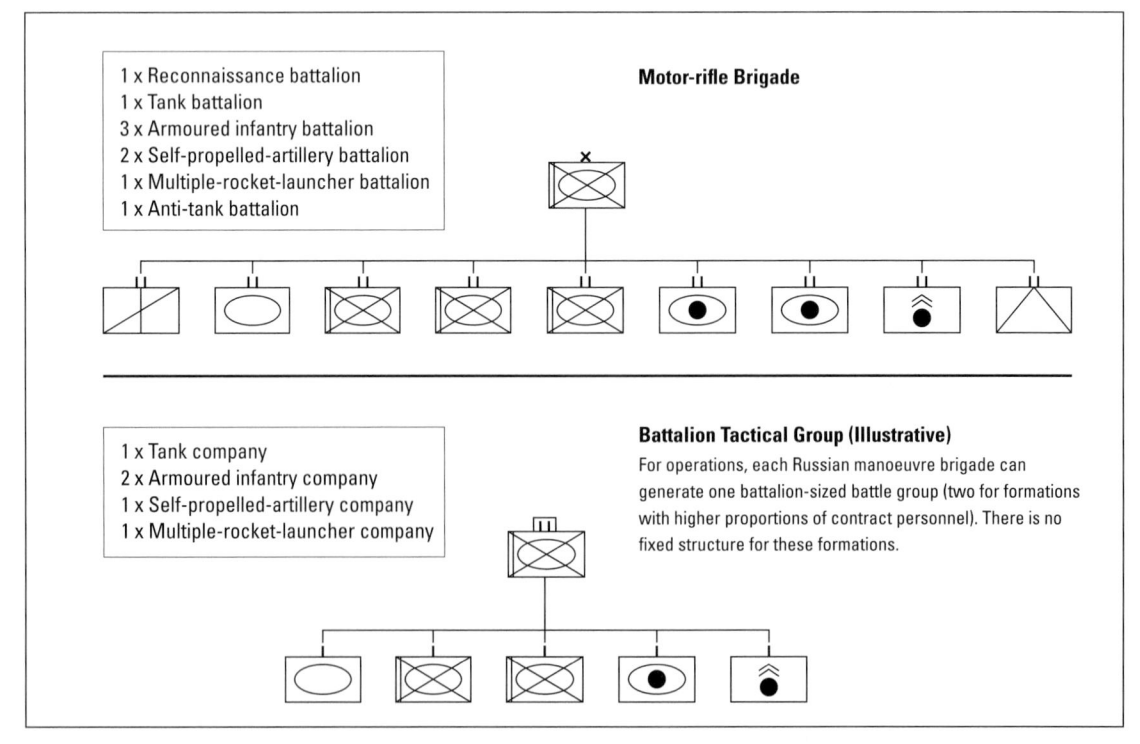

Motor-rifle Brigade

- 1 x Reconnaissance battalion
- 1 x Tank battalion
- 3 x Armoured infantry battalion
- 2 x Self-propelled-artillery battalion
- 1 x Multiple-rocket-launcher battalion
- 1 x Anti-tank battalion

Battalion Tactical Group (Illustrative)

For operations, each Russian manoeuvre brigade can generate one battalion-sized battle group (two for formations with higher proportions of contract personnel). There is no fixed structure for these formations.

- 1 x Tank company
- 2 x Armoured infantry company
- 1 x Self-propelled-artillery company
- 1 x Multiple-rocket-launcher company

The 20th CAA will be underpinned by new divisions being formed on the traditional regimental structure (three motor-rifle and one tank regiment for a motor-rifle division and three tank regiments and one motor-rifle regiment for a tank division), which are due to be deployed in 2017. This planned order of battle shows that the Russian command felt that the military structures in place near Ukraine in 2014 and 2015 were too ad hoc and that it is not ruling out the possibility of full-scale military conflict with Ukraine. It also perhaps indicates that 'divisional' and 'army' levels of command are useful for organising disparate formations (including brigades and battalion tactical groups) as well as more rapidly bringing to bear the capabilities normally held at these higher-level formations. At the present time, though, only the 3rd Motor-rifle Division seems destined for the 20th CAA; the other two divisions currently forming in the west are due to come under the command of the 1st Guards Tank Army and the 49th Army.

The question of names is also significant. The renewed importance attached to symbolism and historical continuity in the Russian armed forces is reflected in the titles and honorifics recently allocated to military units; this is also useful for messaging. The 1st Guards Tank Army, recreated in 2014 in the Western Military District, was one of the Soviet Union's most celebrated manoeuvre units of the Second World War, and was part of the Group of Soviet Forces in Germany during the Cold War. This army is stationed outside Moscow and includes divisions and brigades, reportedly including the Tamanskaya (2nd Guards) Motor-rifle Division and the Kantimarovskaya (4th Guards) Tank Division. These units were re-established in 2014 from one brigade each and were part of the 20th CAA until its relocation south.

Meanwhile, units now earmarked for posting to Russia's southwest include the 150th Motor-rifle Division, which is due to be based at Novocherkassk (historically, this was one of the units that captured

Map 2 Kaliningrad: Russia's potential missile capability

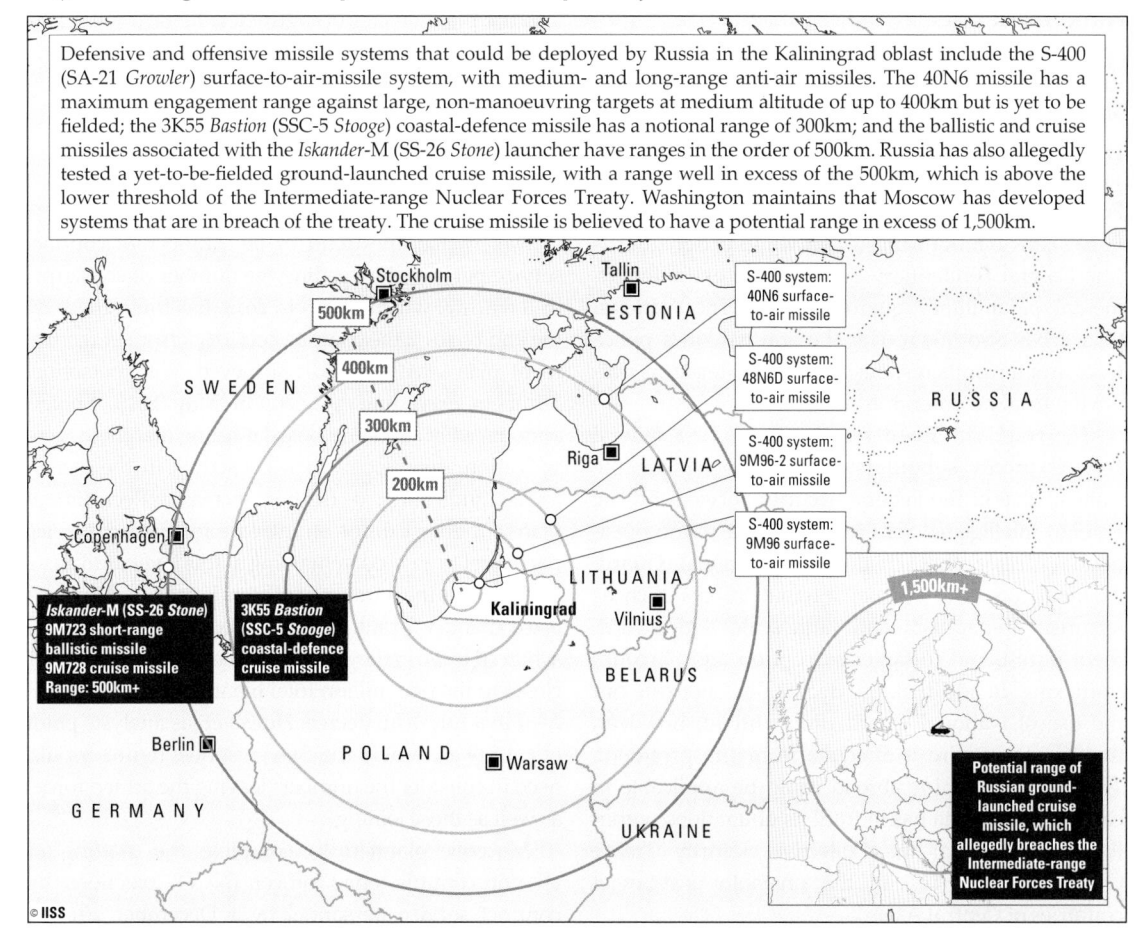

Defensive and offensive missile systems that could be deployed by Russia in the Kaliningrad oblast include the S-400 (SA-21 *Growler*) surface-to-air-missile system, with medium- and long-range anti-air missiles. The 40N6 missile has a maximum engagement range against large, non-manoeuvring targets at medium altitude of up to 400km but is yet to be fielded; the 3K55 *Bastion* (SSC-5 *Stooge*) coastal-defence missile has a notional range of 300km; and the ballistic and cruise missiles associated with the *Iskander*-M (SS-26 *Stone*) launcher have ranges in the order of 500km. Russia has also allegedly tested a yet-to-be-fielded ground-launched cruise missile, with a range well in excess of the 500km, which is above the lower threshold of the Intermediate-range Nuclear Forces Treaty. Washington maintains that Moscow has developed systems that are in breach of the treaty. The cruise missile is believed to have a potential range in excess of 1,500km.

Berlin in 1945) and will come under a new army to be created in Rostov oblast; the 3rd Motor-rifle Division in Boguchar (during the Cold War this unit was in East Germany); and the recreated 144th Motor-rifle Division at Yelnya, Smolensk (the 144th was stationed in Estonia during the Cold War).

Further north, the creation of an administrative structure for the 11th Army Corps in the Kaliningrad enclave reflects the increasing complexity introduced by the various military formations stationed there. The 11th Army Corps controls an integrated land grouping of brigades that is only marginally below the strength of a fully fledged combined-arms army. Previously, all of these brigades – including motor-rifle brigades and the single artillery brigade and missile brigade – were administered by the Baltic Fleet Staff, but that experiment proved unsuccessful. Although the 11th Army Corps is still operationally subordinated to the Baltic Fleet, its headquarters is manned by experienced officers from the ground forces, who are responsible for coordinating activity across this large grouping.

National Guard

Another significant change in the composition of Russia's armed forces was the formation of the National Guard in 2016. This organisation incorporates a number of existing structures: the Internal Troops, riot-police squads (including OMON, or Police Special Forces, and SOBR, or Rapid-Response Forces), the Interior Ministry air wing, prison guards (the Federal Penitentiary Service) and extra-departmental paramilitary guard services. The National Guard has also taken over the anti-narcotics police force and the units responsible for counter-arms trafficking from the Interior Ministry.

The National Guard has the status of a federal service directly subordinated to the president, the same as that of the Federal Security Service and the Foreign Intelligence Service. According to the presidential decree that created the National Guard, its main role is to combat internal threats such as terrorism, separatism and large-scale anti-government unrest, and to target corruption and narcotics trafficking. In addition, the decree does not rule out the use of National Guard units abroad; however, this would require a directive from the president. The ability to deploy abroad could be applicable in cases where Russia has to fulfil its obligations within the framework of the Collective Security Treaty Organisation (CSTO) in the unstable post-Soviet countries of Central Asia.

The strength of this new federal service was set at 340,000 military and civilian personnel. Like the Internal Troops, the National Guard will be equipped with light wheeled armoured vehicles, including the new Russian mine-resistant ambush-protected vehicle and a small number of BTR-82s, as well as mortars. In addition to law enforcement, counter-terrorism tasks and combating weapons and drugs trafficking, the National Guard is also tasked with territorial defence.

Personnel

In 2015, the two call-up campaigns netted 297,000 conscripts for the armed forces. The number of draft evaders, according to official figures, continues to decline and was fewer than 4,000 that year. This figure is consistent with the small number of draft-evasion cases that reach the courts – each year there are only 500–700 convictions. The 2016 spring call-up plan was set 3% higher, with a total for the year of just over 300,000, comprising about 155,000 for the spring draft and 152,000 for the autumn draft. This total is also the planned call-up figure for the next few years and should be achievable, despite Russia's still-slow emergence from the 'demographic trough' stemming from the collapse of the birth rate in the 1990s. By 2020, the number of young people reaching conscription age will start to grow, which is expected to ease Russia's personnel challenge.

Meanwhile, the trend of the number of contract service personnel exceeding the number of conscripts in the army, which began in 2014, has intensified. By the end of 2015, the contract-service-personnel recruitment plan was reportedly achieved, with personnel numbers exceeding 352,000. In May 2016, Shoigu announced at a military board meeting that there were 30% more contractors than conscripts in the armed forces, indicating a further increase. Recruitment plans for 2017 call for an increase in contract service personnel to 425,000, remaining at this level until 2020. By that time, the number of officers is projected to reach 220,000 and warrant officers 50,000. If these totals are achieved by 2017 they will bring the personnel number closer to the one million total mentioned by the president in a July 2016 decree. However, as analysts point out, a full account of the true personnel figures would need to consider the numbers leaving the armed forces as well as those joining.

Moscow planned to complete the staffing of all non-commissioned officer (NCO) positions by contract service personnel by 1 December 2016. It was estimated that by the summer 90% of NCO positions in the Western Military District were filled by contracted personnel. There is also a plan to staff all positions associated with the operation of complex weapons with contract service personnel. It is hoped that this move will address inherent deficiencies in the Russian army's mixed-manning principle (whereby contract and conscript personnel serve in the same units), which is intended to be maintained into the foreseeable future. It is very unlikely that conscription will end: it is useful as a social tool, and also creates pools of potential recruits for contract service and trained reservists.

Training

There were no apparent and significant changes in the intensity of major training exercises in 2015–16. The practice of 'snap' inspections continued with comparable frequency, including large-scale inspections involving entire military districts. The largest of these took place in August 2016, with three military districts – Southern, Western and Central –simultaneously put on alert, along with the Northern Fleet and the airborne troops. The aim of this inspection was to practise the concentration of forces in the south-western part of Russia for potential contingencies in the Caucasus and against Ukraine. However, even these exercises and inspections took place without any large-scale call-up of reservists, and involved only hundreds or low thousands of personnel.

In addition to affording combat-training benefits, snap inspections appear to be of increasing importance as a measure against corruption or deception. As a result of a snap inspection in the Baltic Fleet in June 2016, the fleet's commander, chief of staff and dozens of high-ranking officers were dismissed. The reason given for this action was that the inspection revealed shortcomings in combat training and that reporting by these units had distorted the true conditions, reportedly including poor management, a suspected collision involving one of the fleet's submarines, and substandard accommodation. While these dismissals no doubt shook up the Baltic Fleet, they would also have been intended as a message to others. For instance, while there has been a significant clampdown by Moscow on negative reporting about the armed forces, stories of corruption and substandard accommodation still emerge.

As reported by the defence ministry, the number of inter-service exercises in 2015 involving the army, aerospace forces, navy and airborne troops increased by 30% in comparison with 2014, while the number of joint exercises was up by 50%. This suggests increasing sophistication in routine combat training and an aim for greater realism at the operational level, despite Russia's operation in Syria being partially funded by monies allocated for combat training (which reportedly helped the defence ministry avoid going over budget in 2015).

Syria

Russia officially announced in March 2016 that the Syria operation had been completed, despite continuing operations both in the air and on the ground. The direct participation by Russian armed forces in ground combat decreased, but the aerial-bombing campaign continued uninterrupted, although with fewer aircraft taking part. The Syria deployment has demonstrated Russia's capability to maintain an expeditionary force for a protracted period of time, utilising pilots from front-line units. From the outside, the level of munitions resupply also seems to be adequate for the designated missions. In addition, Russia's Long-Range Aviation force has regularly delivered airstrikes flying from Russia and, on one occasion at least, Iran. Strikes with air-, sea- and submarine-launched cruise missiles also continued. Russia continues to use the operation as a test bed and showcase for its military equipment.

With the Syria mission continuing, Russia has yet to draw its final conclusions, but early lessons continue to emerge, for example the critical importance of unmanned aerial vehicles (UAVs) in modern warfare. Shoigu has stated that the number of UAVs in the armed forces needs to increase; this will no doubt also spur the ongoing development of armed Russian UAVs.

Other lessons for Russian forces include the need for tactical air controllers able to guide aircraft and weapons onto targets. This capability was refined by Western armed forces over the decade and a half of combat in Iraq and Afghanistan. Russia has met the requirement by using personnel from special-forces units, among others, and the role will likely be identified as a future training requirement. The campaign has also shown that Russian forces are adept at complex train-and-assist missions. Inserted into tenuous tactical situations, Russian advisers have contributed to the effective coordination of the actions of disparate military formations, including elements of the Syrian army and various militia groups, some of which are likely to have contained Iranian or

Iranian-backed components. Russian advisers have also contributed to the training of some remaining Assad formations.

Another lesson for the long term is the utility of retaining the conventionally armed Tu-22M3 *Backfire* bomber in Russia's Long-Range Aviation fleet. Although the Tu-160 *Blackjack* and the Tu-95MS *Bear* strategic bombers have also been involved in prosecuting attacks in Syria with air-launched cruise missiles, the Tu-22M3, using ordinary free-fall bombs, has proven more cost-effective and has accounted for the vast majority of such sorties. This will no doubt buttress the project to upgrade the aircraft to the Tu-22M3M standard and to extend its service life. The development of guided weapons for the Tu-22 has also intensified, including the Kh-32 long-range anti-ship missile.

Dropping free-fall bombs from a fast jet bomber will not be suitable for every future contingency, not least where low-yield or precision munitions are required in order to limit civilian casualties or minimise damage to infrastructure. As such, Russia's employment of more precise weapons, including KAB-500 satellite-guided bombs, is significant. By way of comparison, in the 2011 Libya air campaign, NATO air forces were reported to have only used precision-guided air-launched weapons; in this context, the Russian armed forces have some way to go.

The Syria operation has also called into question the need to retain the Su-25 *Frogfoot* ground-attack aircraft, even in its upgraded form. The air force's 12-strong Su-25SM squadron was withdrawn from Syria in March 2016, and at the time of writing it was unclear whether the type had returned. To avoid being hit by rebel air defences, these aircraft had to fly at an altitude where they were less effective than Su-24 *Fencer* and Su-34 *Fullback* fighter/ground-attack aircraft, although the addition of defensive-aid suites might mitigate such danger. The effectiveness of the Su-34, the main platform for the Russian air force's precision-guided weapons, has been officially rated as high, with further contracts expected in addition to the 100-plus aircraft that have been ordered.

Ukraine

In 2016, Russia decided to begin building permanent military infrastructure on the border with Ukraine, instead of maintaining its armed forces in field camps (see above). Within a short space of time, a number of military units of significant size will be positioned close to the Ukrainian border, including the relocated 20th CAA in Voronezh. Furthermore, the high level of operational and strategic mobility persistently rehearsed in exercises would allow new combat groups to be quickly formed on the border if necessary.

Similar exercise activity has been observed in relation to Crimea. Instead of deploying new units there,

Map 3 **Russia: operational strategic commands**

more exercises are now designed to practise the redeployment of additional units from Russia. After the situation on the border between the peninsula and Ukraine escalated in August 2016, several Russian motor-rifle and airborne battalions were temporarily deployed to Crimea by ferry and by air, with additional aircraft, including Su-34s and helicopters, flying in. Once the combined road and rail bridge across the Kerch Strait is complete in around 2020–21, Russia will be able to reinforce its forces in Crimea more rapidly. At the same time, Crimea's air defences are also being re-equipped. The formerly Ukrainian Feodosiya-based air-defence regiment received S-400 surface-to-air-missile systems in 2016.

However, further increases to the strength of the Russian forces in Crimea are being delayed because of funding problems. Instead of a planned new airborne-assault regiment on detachment to Crimea from the 7th Airborne Assault Division in Dzhankoy, only a separate battalion will be formed in 2017. This regiment is not due to be fully formed before 2019.

Meanwhile, the channels used to supply separatists in eastern Ukraine are still operational; the Ukrainian defence ministry asserted throughout 2016 that regular units from the Russian armed forces have been deployed in eastern Ukraine.

The Arctic

In northern Russia, Operational Strategic Command (OSK) North, based on the Northern Fleet, has yet to officially become Russia's fifth such body, despite its de facto status as an OSK in all but name.

Meanwhile, Russia's military Arctic-infrastructure developments have centred on three major island bases in the Novaya Zemlya archipelago and the islands of Kotelny and Alexandra Land. Novaya Zemlya contains the largest of these bases and is home to the Northern Fleet's newly created S-300 surface-to-air-missile regiment, which is the only major military unit in the islands. It protects the archipelago's military sites and the approaches to the Kola Peninsula and its main naval bases. The two other island bases have small, combined tactical groups of troops, several hundred strong, equipped with a small number of *Pantsir* short-range air-defence systems suitable only for point defence. Kotelny Island also has a battery of Rubezh SS-C-3 *Styx* anti-ship missiles.

The other new bases located along the northern coast are no more than small radar outposts with a few dozen troops to operate them. For Moscow, the main value of these bases is that they enable improved air and sea surveillance over the region.

Meanwhile, an Arctic motor-rifle brigade planned for the Yamal Peninsula had not begun to form by late 2016, and its creation is now in doubt. Nonetheless, Shoigu announced that Russia's Arctic military infrastructure was to be strengthened by re-forming a coastal-defence division in the Chukotka Peninsula, which borders Alaska, in 2018. It is not yet clear whether this will be a motor-rifle division, as was the case during the Soviet Union era, or a combined formation of missile, artillery and air-defence units.

New island-based military infrastructure should also serve to strengthen defences on Russia's Far Eastern coast, from Chukotka to maritime territory bordering China. Survey expeditions to the Kuril Islands of Matua and Paramushir to find sites for these bases took place in 2016. They will reinforce the 68th Army Corps, located in the Kuril Islands and Sakhalin. Additionally, the Pacific Fleet's 72nd Coastal Missile Brigade, located near Vladivostok, was re-equipped with the modern *Bastion*-P anti-ship-missile system, which will serve to enhance Russian capabilities in the region.

The Caucasus

The year 2016 was marked by further efforts by Russia to strengthen its military position in the Caucasus. At the end of 2015, Russia and Abkhazia signed a treaty to form a joint group of forces. In summer 2016 the treaty was presented to the Russian parliament for ratification and was due to be signed by the end of the year. Russia's 7th Military Base, which is located in the self-declared republic, will underpin the group of forces, while the Russian defence ministry will appoint the group's commander. Abkhazia plans to contribute two motor-rifle battalions, a special-forces detachment, an artillery group and an air group – virtually all of its combat-ready forces. The treaty is planned to last for ten years with the possibility of automatic extension by five-year periods.

Negotiations on a new agreement on Russian forces based in Armenia intensified after a brief military flare-up between Azerbaijan and Armenia over the disputed region of Nagorno-Karabakh in April 2016. A treaty signed in 2002 on the joint use of Russian and Armenian troops for defence reportedly could be superseded by a treaty on a more integrated joint grouping of troops subordinate to a united headquarters.

Ground forces

As noted in last year's *Military Balance*, Russia showcased its new-generation armoured vehicles at its 2015 Victory Day parade. Deliveries of prototype batches of these vehicles began later that year. This included T-14 *Armata* main battle tanks (MBTs) and T-15 heavy infantry fighting vehicles, which are based on the *Armata* chassis. Meanwhile, modifications to the T-72 MBT were, for a time, reduced. Whereas in 2013–14, 260–290 tanks a year were upgraded to T-72B3 standard, in 2015 that number fell to 170 (though it rebounded significantly in 2016). In addition, missile brigades continued to re-equip with the *Iskander* tactical ballistic missile at a rate of two brigades a year.

Following large-scale purchases over recent years, the number of UAVs in service reached 1,720 at the end of 2015. The vast majority of these are concentrated in the land forces and the airborne troops. The multi-role *Orlan-10* UAV remains the principal type, with 450 purchased in 2014–15 alone.

In 2016, flight testing began on prototypes of light-class (with a maximum take-off weight of 1.2 tonnes) and medium-class (with five tonnes take-off weight) armed UAVs designed for the aerospace forces. The development of these UAVs dates back to late 2011. The heaviest armed UAV (which is in the 20-tonne class) is still at the design stage, and analysts believe this may indicate a delay in progress.

Aerospace forces

In 2015, there was a slight fall in the number of fixed- and rotary-wing aircraft delivered to the aerospace forces; however, 97 new aircraft and 81 helicopters were still delivered that year.

In 2014, one of the Sukhoi T-50 future-combat-aircraft prototypes was damaged by fire. This was rebuilt in 2015 and another prototype made its maiden flight in April 2016 – six separate prototypes are now involved in the flight tests. Missile launches from the aircraft's internal carriage bays and external hard-points have begun. The contract to supply the air force with the first pre-production batch is expected to be signed in late 2017 and will include 12 aircraft to be delivered by 2020.

The first flight of the upgraded Tu-160M2 strategic bomber, after production restarted in 2015, is scheduled for 2020, and deliveries are scheduled to start in 2023. This will inevitably have a negative impact on the timetable for the development of the PAK–DA next-generation bomber, which was planned as a replacement for Russia's ageing strategic-bomber fleet.

Navy

While three modernised Project 955 *Borey*-class ballistic-missile submarines were handed over to the navy in 2013–14, the delivery of the follow-on five Project 955As has been delayed. The handover date for the first 955A has been tentatively pushed back from 2017 to 2018, with the rest scheduled to be completed between 2019 and 2021.

Surface-warship deliveries are also suffering delays. The *Poliment-Redut* air-defence system, intended to constitute the main defensive armament for future Russian warships from the corvette class up, is not operationally ready, which is proving to be a significant problem for the navy. Intensive trials of the first fully fledged version of the system – on board the Project 22350 destroyer *Admiral Gorshkov* – continued in 2016.

Table 4 **Russia: new-build naval vessels armed with the 3M14 *Kalibr* (SS-N-30)/3M54 (SS-N-27 *Sizzler*) cruise missile**

Class name	Project no.	Type	Quantity on order	Shipyard	Known fleet(s)	First-of-class entering service
Yasen	0885.0/0885.1	SSGN	6	Sevmash Shipyard	Northern	2013
Varshavyanka	636.3	SSK	12	Admiralty Shipyard	Black Sea & Pacific	2014
Lada	677	SSK	3	Admiralty Shipyard	Northern	2010
Admiral Gorshkov	22350	DDGHM	6	Severnaya Verf	Northern	2016
(Arctic Offshore Patrol Vessel)	23550	DDGH	2	Admiralty Shipyard	Northern	2020
Gremyashchiy	20385	FFGHM	2	Severnaya Verf	n.k.	2018
Admiral Grigorovich	11356M	FFGHM	6	Yantar Shipyard	Black Sea	2016
Vasily Bykov	22160	FFGM	6	Zelenodolsk Shipyard	Black Sea	2017
Grad Sviyazhsk (*Buyan*-M)	21631	FSGM	12	Zelenodolsk Shipyard	Caspian & Black Sea	2013
Karakurt	22800	PCG	7	Pella Shipyard	Northern	2017

While programmes to build major surface vessels have stalled, more attention is being paid to small missile ships armed with long-range cruise missiles. The ninth Project 21631 *Buyan*-M vessel was laid down in 2015; this type will be followed by 18 Project 22800 *Karakurt* small missile ships with similar armament. They have a displacement of 800 tonnes and reportedly better seafaring characteristics. A development that will be of interest to foreign defence analysts concerns the number of vessels – including missile boats and an icebreaker – that are now being produced with the capability to carry cruise missiles (see Table 4).

Russia's naval-aviation forces are receiving improved capabilities. Coastal-defence fighter regiments are beginning to upgrade to the Su-30SM. Twenty of these aircraft are due to be delivered to the navy by the end of 2018. In order to form the air wing for the aircraft carrier *Admiral Kuznetsov*, a second carrier-based aircraft regiment, armed with the multirole MiG-29KR/KUBR, was formed in the Northern Fleet. The old carrier-borne Su-33 *Flanker* D is in line for an upgrade, including new targeting and navigation systems, similar to those tested in Syria on the Su-24M2, which will enhance the Su-33's strike capabilities. During 2016, trial landings by the first prototypes of the Ka-52K maritime attack helicopter took place on the *Kuznetsov*. The Ka-52K was observed on the carrier's deck en route to Syria in late 2016; it was possible that the type would make its combat debut in the Middle East. Meanwhile, there is also a plan to develop a coaxial-rotor helicopter to replace the Ka-27 *Helix* anti-submarine-warfare helicopter.

Strategic forces

Upgrades to Russia's land- and sea-based strategic nuclear forces continue, with plans to update 40 missiles a year. In 2015, 21 *Yars* intercontinental ballistic missiles (ICBMs) were delivered to the Strategic Missile Troops, along with about ten *Bulava* submarine-launched ballistic missiles (SLBMs) and the same number of *Liner* (upgraded *Sineva*) SLBMs.

In August, a little later than planned, the first-stage engine for the new *Sarmat* heavy ICBM was test-fired. The missile's ejection tests were pushed back from the middle to the end of 2016 because of the delay. In these tests, the missile is cartridge-launched from the silo without then firing the main engine. Nevertheless, no changes have been announced to the plan for the missile to enter service in 2018.

Highly classified tests of the new A-235 *Nudol* missile-defence system have also been conducted. According to various estimates, four or five test launches have taken place since 2014, some of which were successful. The new system is characterised by its mobility (some analysts consider that it might comprise a two-tube firing unit), its ability to carry nuclear and non-nuclear payloads, and its kinetic intercept capability; it is believed that *Nudol* is intended to have the ability to hit targets in near space, including low-orbit satellites.

DEFENCE ECONOMICS

Defence spending

There was unprecedented growth in Russian defence spending in 2015, driven by a determination on the part of the country's political and military leaders that funding of the ambitious State Armament Programme (SAP) to 2020 would be maintained despite faltering economic performance. The proportion of military spending increased when measured against GDP, placing Russia in a small group of nations spending over 5% of GDP on defence. However, in an unrelated development, the Federal Service of State Statistics, Rosstat, was in the process of transferring to a new definition of GDP in 2015, in order to bring this more in line with international practices. This increased Russia's total nominal GDP in 2015 by approximately 9%; consequently the total share of all military-related spending declined from about 5.5% to just under 5%, whilst the official 'national defence' share published by Moscow declined to under 4% (see Table 5).

In preparing the 2016 budget, there was clearly awareness that this level of spending could not be sustained. In 2015, GDP declined by 3.7% and a contraction of -0.8% was forecast for 2016. In the event, a budget was adopted with spending on national

Table 5 **Russian defence expenditure** as % of GDP

	'National Defence'		Total military expenditure	
	Billion roubles	% GDP	Billion roubles	% GDP
2016[1]	3,160	3.69	3,972	4.64
2015	3,181	3.94	4,026	4.98
2014	2,479	3.18	3,222	4.13
2013	2,104	2.96	2,783	3.92
2012	1,813	2.71	2,505	3.74
2011	1,516	2.54	2,029	3.40
2010	1,277	2.57	1,760	3.54

[1] For comparability with earlier years, excluding a large sum allocated in the amended 2016 budget for the repayment of past defence-industry debts. GDP according to International Monetary Fund data. 2010–15: actual spending; 2016: federal budget for 2016.

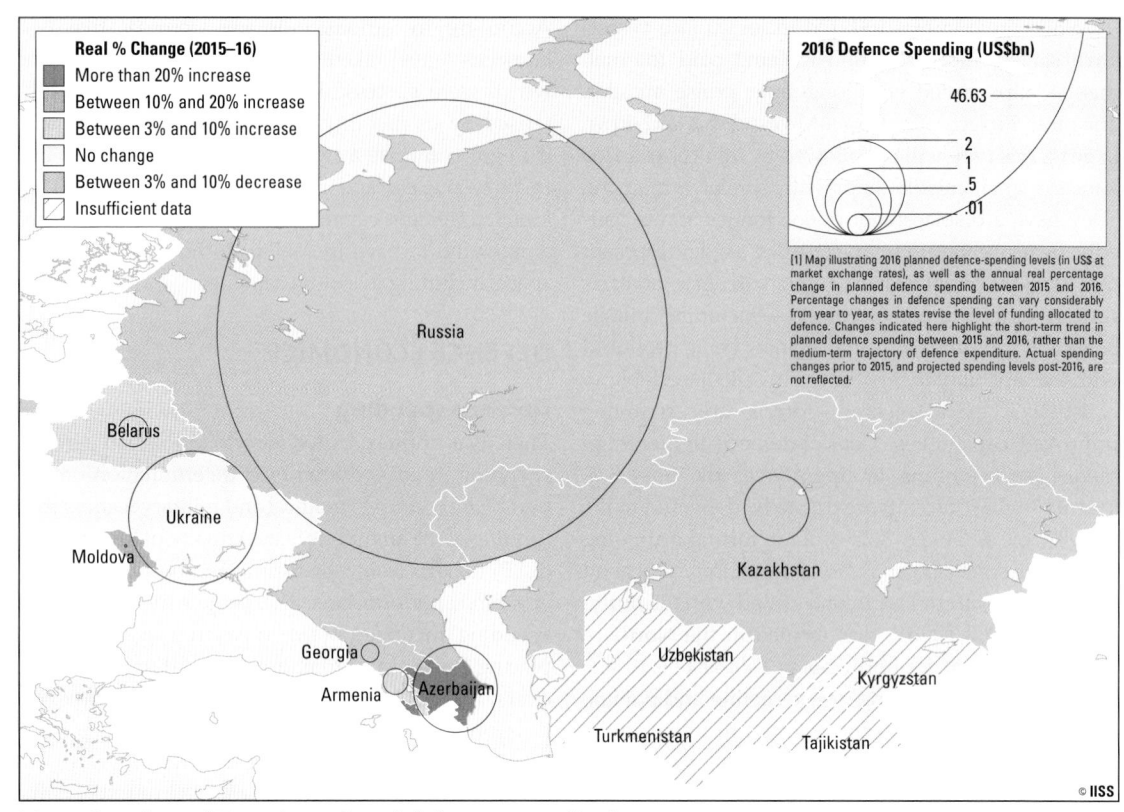

Map 4 **Russia and Eurasia regional defence spending**[1]

[1] Map illustrating 2016 planned defence-spending levels (in US$ at market exchange rates), as well as the annual real percentage change in planned defence spending between 2015 and 2016. Percentage changes in defence spending can vary considerably from year to year, as states revise the level of funding allocated to defence. Changes indicated here highlight the short-term trend in planned defence spending between 2015 and 2016, rather than the medium-term trajectory of defence expenditure. Actual spending changes prior to 2015, and projected spending levels post-2016, are not reflected.

defence decreasing slightly in nominal terms; this meant that national-defence allocations amounted to 3.7% of GDP and total military spending came to just over 4.6%. Spending on arms procurement under the SAP was held at the 2015 level by resorting to state-guaranteed credits to the tune of almost 210 billion roubles (US$3.4bn).

A feature of the 2016 defence budget was the formation of a large unexplained reserve fund, perhaps as large as US$2.1bn. This appears to have been created as a contingency fund to meet possible increased outlays arising from Russia's military activity in Syria. In the event, by late summer 2016, little if any of this fund had been spent. In late 2016, the Russian government also earmarked an additional 800bn roubles (US$11.9bn) for the defence ministry in relation to debt repayments. The government will be looking for savings in order to reduce a large budget deficit, and military spending may not escape intact. However, the unspent reserve fund might mean that cuts can be made with only modest impact on the activities of the defence ministry.

In 2017 Russia is reverting to a three-year federal budget. This system was abandoned for 2015 because of uncertain economic conditions. The draft budget for 2017–19 indicates that the 'national defence' budget will decline in 2017 compared to 2016 by 320bn roubles, which approximates to a decline of 14.5% in real terms (constant 2010 US dollars). In these circumstances, defence may face some reductions, though much will depend on Moscow's intentions for state defence procurement in the coming years.

Figure 14 **Estimated Russian defence expenditure** as % of GDP

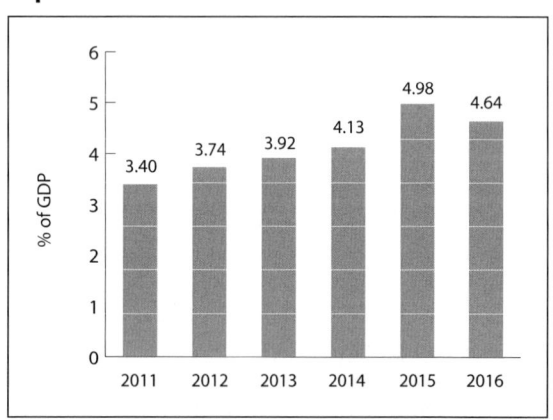

Year	% of GDP
2011	3.40
2012	3.74
2013	3.92
2014	4.13
2015	4.98
2016	4.64

State Armament Programme

Implementation of the ambitious SAP to 2020 continues. As shown in Table 6, success has varied between sectors. A major determinant has been the extent to which procurement has been based on systems that had already been developed by the start of the programme in 2011 – some of which have been upgraded – or on completely new systems still under development. While the new fifth-generation T-50 combat aircraft, designed to meet the PAK–FA requirement, is not yet in series production, test aircraft are being delivered and many other new fixed-wing aircraft and helicopters have also been delivered, some seeing action in Syria. However, the procurement rate of new helicopters has moderated as Russia strives to fully replace engines previously supplied by Ukraine, which was a major supplier of helicopter engines before 2014. Russia is now forced to fulfil this capacity domestically.

The strategic nuclear forces are receiving more than 20 *Yars* (RS-24, SS-27 Mod 2) ICBMs a year, whilst the new heavy, liquid-fuelled *Sarmat* (RS-28, SS-X-30) and the rail-based *Barguzin* are under development. The S-400 air-defence system, which has an enhanced radar and uses the 48N6 family of missiles (the 40N6 and 9M96 missiles have yet to be fielded), is being deployed as planned but the complementary S-500 system – intended for ballistic-missile defence – is yet to appear. The supply of new naval equipment has been more problematic. The programme to build *Borey*-A-class strategic submarines is behind schedule and there may still be problems with its *Bulava* ballistic missile. Perhaps partly to compensate for this, older *Delta*-IV-class submarines continue to be refitted in order to carry new *Sineva* (R-29RMU, SSN-23A *Skiff*) missiles, which have been upgraded to the *Lainer* (R-29RMU2.1). In addition, the production of new *Yasen*-class multi-role submarines has been much slower than envisaged and the target of seven delivered by 2020 will not be met. The construction rate of new surface ships has been slowed by the halt in delivery of power units from Ukraine and by Ukraine-related sanctions in the West. Both corvettes and frigates have been affected, and in compensation a programme has been launched to build a fleet of smaller project 22800 missile ships. However, construction of two *Tarantul*-V patrol boats that the navy began building in the 1990s has resumed.

Since 2011 the ground forces' new equipment has comprised upgrades to armoured vehicles and other systems, as well as modernised old equipment, and there have been few genuinely new weapons. Large-scale deployment of the new *Armata* platform (see *The Military Balance 2016*, p. 167), as well as *Kurganets*-25 and *Bumerang*, is still awaited, and although small initial batches are under delivery for testing, procurements for the ground forces before 2020 are likely to be modest. However, progress is being made in developing a range of UAVs and an increasing number are entering service. Russia's forces still lack an armed UAV, although systems are under development.

In early 2015 it became clear that the follow-on SAP, which continues to 2025, would be delayed. It was due to have started in 2016 but will now cover 2018–25. The delay appears to have arisen because of the troubled state of the economy and the need to implement a crash import-substitution campaign to counter the breakdown of deliveries from Ukraine and the impact of sanctions imposed by NATO and EU member states. The level of funding for the new armament programme is unresolved, with the finance ministry insisting on 12 trillion roubles (US$177.8bn) and the defence ministry on 24trn roubles (US$355.6bn). However, the available evidence – not least statements by Putin – indicates that the volume of new procurement may not be as large as that of the SAP to 2020; this was a once-and-for-all 'catching up' exercise after many years of almost no new procurement. According to the president, the highest level of spending on the state defence order will take place in 2017; after then it will gradually decline. Defence corporations are being urged to develop high technology civilian goods, and there is discussion of diversification and even conversion.

However, it is nonetheless likely that success in implementing the current programme to 2020 will be declared. The main performance indicator is the percentage of 'modern' armaments and other military hardware in the combat-ready equipment stocks. The definition of 'modern' has not been revealed but 'modernised' weaponry is known to be included in this category. The original target was for 30% of equipment holdings to be classified as 'modern' by the end of 2015, but officials have claimed a figure of 47%. At the present rate, the goal to achieve a modern-equipment level of 70% by 2020 will be close to fulfilment by the time the new SAP to 2025 begins. The faster implementation of these targets was probably achieved (from at least a formal statistical viewpoint) by an increased rate of procurement of modernised equipment as well as withdrawing old hardware faster than originally planned.

Figure 15 Russia's Almaz Antey S-400 (SA-21 *Growler*) air-defence system

The Almaz-Antey S-400 (SA-21 *Growler*) is replacing the S-300 (SA-10 *Grumble*/SA-20 *Gargoyle*) surface-to-air missile (SAM) as Russia's main medium-to-long-range relocatable air-defence system. Introduced into service in 2008–09, some 14 regiments have now been fielded. The S-400 offers layered air defence with the 40N6 and 48N6 families of missiles providing maximum engagement ranges of 400km and 200km respectively. Engagements at these ranges would most likely be limited to non-manoeuvring targets with significant radar signatures at medium or high altitudes. As well as using the 40N6 and 48N6 missile families, the S-400 can accommodate the shorter-range 9M96. This provides the system with engagement capability from 40km to 120km depending on the missile selected. The *Pantsir* (SA-22 *Greyhound*) point-defence gun-missile system is usually deployed with the S-400 in order to provide close-in air defence. The 9K38 *Igla* (SA-18 *Grouse*), 9K338 *Igla*-S (SA-24 *Grinch*) or 9K333 *Verba* man-portable SAM provides an inner layer for the engagement of any 'pop-up' targets such as attack helicopters that may have penetrated undetected.

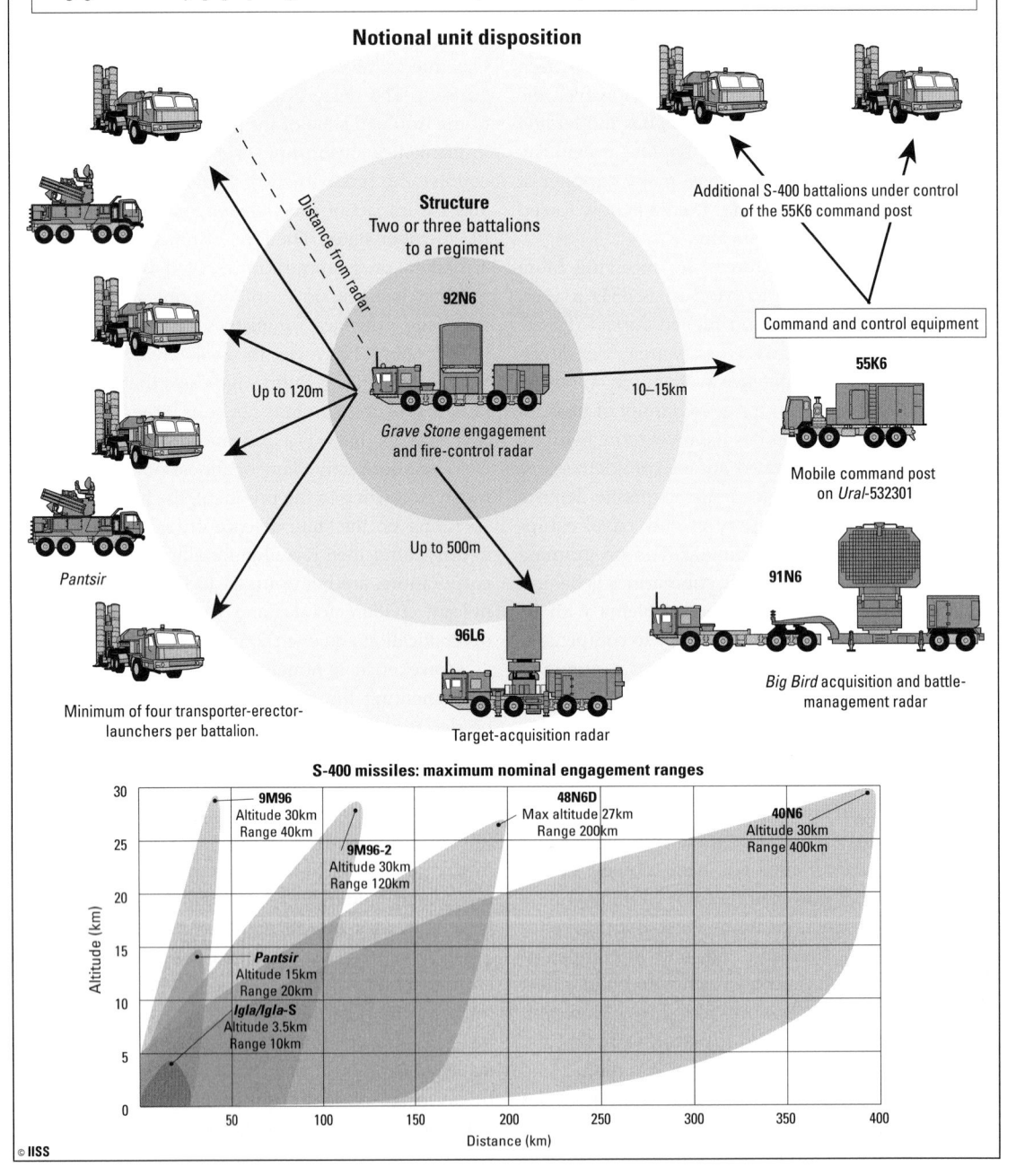

Notional unit disposition

Structure
Two or three battalions to a regiment

- 92N6 *Grave Stone* engagement and fire-control radar
- Up to 120m
- 10–15km
- Up to 500m
- 96L6 Target-acquisition radar
- *Pantsir*
- Minimum of four transporter-erector-launchers per battalion.
- Additional S-400 battalions under control of the 55K6 command post
- Command and control equipment
- 55K6 Mobile command post on *Ural*-532301
- 91N6 *Big Bird* acquisition and battle-management radar

S-400 missiles: maximum nominal engagement ranges

- **9M96**: Altitude 30km, Range 40km
- **9M96-2**: Altitude 30km, Range 120km
- **48N6D**: Max altitude 27km, Range 200km
- **40N6**: Altitude 30km, Range 400km
- **Pantsir**: Altitude 15km, Range 20km
- **Igla/Igla-S**: Altitude 3.5km, Range 10km

© IISS

Table 6 **Russian procurement of new weapons in 2011–15 and goals of the State Armament Programme to 2020 (approximate)**

Systems	Total 2011–15	Total to 2020
Intercontinental ballistic missiles	68	400+
Submarine-launched ballistic missiles	c.95	n.k.
Military satellites[a]	57	100+
Fixed-wing aircraft	342	c.850
Helicopters	516	1,150
Including combat	139	c.330
Unmanned aerial vehicles	c.600	4,000+
S-400 air-defence systems (divisions)	17	56
Strategic nuclear submarines	4	8
Multi-role nuclear submarines	1	7
Diesel-electric submarines	3	6–10
Large surface combat ships[b]	12	50
Tanks (new)	0	2,300+
Iskander missile systems[c]	6	10

[a] Total number, excluding failed launches [b] Mainly corvettes, frigates and small artillery ships [c] Brigades

Defence industry

In 2015, the Russian arms-procurement system reverted to systems that were in place before the reforms introduced by Serdyukov in 2008. Russia's specialised procurement organisation, the Federal Agency for the Delivery of Armament, Military and Special Equipment (Rosoboronpostavka), was disbanded, as was the independent monitoring body (Rosoboronzakaz). Arms acquisition for the defence ministry is now handled by its department for state procurement.

Meanwhile, the 2012 law on the state defence order was amended in summer 2015 in order to reinforce financial controls, so as to reduce the scale of illicit transfers of budget funding intended for procurement and research and development (R&D) to other purposes. There now exists an inter-agency control system involving the Federal Service for Financial Monitoring (Rosfinmonitoring), the Federal Anti-monopoly Service, the Central Bank and the defence ministry. All financial aspects of arms procurement are now handled through specially numbered, easily monitored accounts with nine authorised banks. In addition, a newly created information system allows real-time monitoring by the defence ministry and other agencies. When first introduced, this new system caused serious problems for Russia's defence industry, which lobbied successfully for some relaxation of it in the first half of 2016. Financial control was also strengthened by reducing the volume of credits allocated in advance: before 2015, the defence ministry had been making 100% advance payments to firms for state defence contracts, but this has been reduced to 80% in the case of some priority systems and 50% for others. There is little doubt that the ministry's power as a customer has been enhanced and opportunities cut for the unauthorised diversion of funding; it is also likely that cost reductions have been enforced. It is clear that Russia is gradually developing a more cost-effective procurement system.

With the implementation of the targeted federal programme 'Development of the defence-industrial complex', investment in the defence industry has increased and some new factories have been built, notably for the manufacture of air-defence systems by Almaz-Antey. In May 2016 this programme was incorporated into a new, classified state programme of the same title. It includes sub-programmes for import substitution, the development and production of strategic materials, and R&D for new production technologies. The total volume of funding up to 2020 is planned to be over 1trn roubles (around US$14bn).

With this improved funding, pay in the defence industry has significantly increased in recent years. This has made the recruitment of new personnel possible, leading to a reduction in the average age. Whereas only 20% of employees were under the age of 35 in 2009, by late 2015 the proportion was 30%. Productivity has also been increasing annually at a rapid rate, although this may be explained in part by price increases not fully taken into account in the price indices employed.

After almost two decades of meagre funding, Russia's defence industry has once again become a relatively modern and successful branch of the economy. During 2014 and 2015, military production is reported to have grown at an average rate of almost 20%, although the shipbuilding sector still lags behind. Correspondingly, the defence industry's political weight has been enhanced, facilitated by the energetic oversight of Deputy Prime Minister Dmitry Rogozin and the fact that Putin himself now chairs the Military-Industrial Commission and quite often officiates at its meetings. However, the Russian economy is not militarised to anything resembling the extent it was in Soviet times.

Arms exports

According to the Federal Service for Military-Technical Cooperation, in 2015 the total volume of armaments and military-services exports was

US$14.5bn, compared with US$15bn in 2014; this was the first decline for a number of years. However, according to the authoritative Centre for Analysis of World Arms Trade in Moscow, actual identified arms exports in current prices totalled US$13.9bn in 2015 compared with US$13.1bn in 2014. Moscow is hoping for increased export sales following the apparently successful use of Russian weaponry in Syria. There is now a willingness to export the latest equipment, such as the S-400 air-defence system, and the Su-35 combat aircraft, both of which are due to be sold to China.

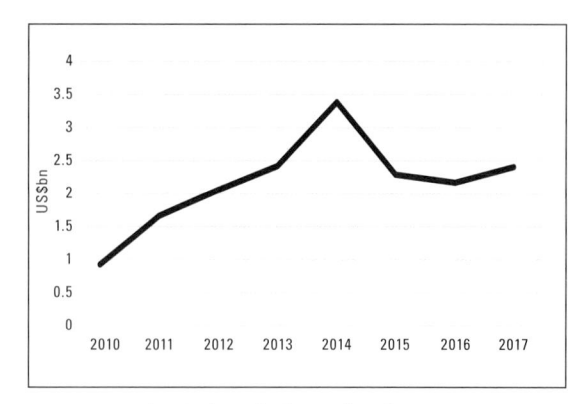

Figure 16 **Ukrainian defence budget, 2010–17**

UKRAINE

In 2014, Russia's occupation of Crimea and the outbreak of hostilities in the Donbas region soon afterwards shook Ukraine's military out of the lethargic state in which it had languished since the collapse of the Soviet Union. During these years, reduced investment in training, equipment availability and modernisation contributed to a lower level of military capability at the beginning of 2014. Although defence budgets modestly increased after 2010, legacy problems persisted, including the high proportion of funds allocated to personnel, which reduced available funding for investments. For example, in 2005 the Ukrainian defence ministry reported that personnel costs comprised 81.5% of the budget, with training and modernisation at 12% and weapons, equipment and infrastructure development at just 6.5%.

This legacy influenced the course of the fighting in 2014, and demonstrated that Kiev required time to improve the armed forces and its overall military capability. The gradual escalation of the conflict in the east gave Ukraine this time. As a result, Kiev has been able to stabilise the situation on the front line and also to begin reforming the army to better meet the demands of operating as a fighting force. Indeed, now the armed forces are principally considered an instrument of foreign and domestic policy, rather than an 'attribute of statehood'.

Military doctrine

A new edition of Ukraine's military doctrine was released in September 2015. The document reflects the significant changes in the country's security environment. Its preamble names Russia's military actions in Crimea and the Donbas region as the main threat to Ukraine's security and also the cause of the changes implemented in the new doctrine. The Russian Federation also features in the section on current military threats, listing various possible forms of aggression; it is the only country to appear in this category. Comprehensive reform of Ukraine's national-security system 'to a level suitable for membership of the European Union and NATO' is identified as a key task needed to help restore Ukrainian sovereignty in the east. According to the presidency this reform is designed to develop the armed forces to Western standards and achieve 'interoperability with NATO Forces'. A Strategic Defence Bulletin issued in June 2016 highlighted continuing problems for Ukraine's armed forces, including corruption, cyber vulnerabilities, flawed defence-planning procedures and the absence of an effective unified logistics system, among others. The bulletin was intended to act as a defence-planning document that will 'determine the main directions of Ukraine's Defence Policy and Development of Defence Forces by the end of 2020'.

Army structure

Since 2014, the main structural change to the Ukrainian armed forces has been the formation of new units. The ground forces have changed most fundamentally: four operational commands have been established (North, South, East and West), as well as two mechanised brigades, four motorised infantry brigades, one mountain-assault brigade and three artillery brigades. Several units have also been modified; for example, one of the multiple-rocket-launcher regiments has been fielded as a brigade, while a new brigade has been formed within the airborne troops.

The deployment of several new army brigades was a logical step in the continued integration into the regular army of the territorial-defence battalions. As noted in *The Military Balance 2016*, these battalions were at first separate from the army structure and subsequently attached to regular brigades. They were then integrated into the army as motorised infantry battalions. Some formed into groups of three as part of the motorised infantry brigades and the mountain brigade. The latter brigade incorporates two volunteer units, the Aydar and Donbas-Ukraine battalions (part of the Donbas-Ukraine Battalion moved from the National Guard to the armed forces). The remaining motorised infantry battalions became organic to the regular army brigades. Not as heavily armed as mechanised battalions, they were intended to take on secondary missions, such as homeland-security tasks. However, these units are likely to transform into normal mechanised battalions as they are supplied with more armoured vehicles and heavy infantry weapons deriving from the refit of old equipment that Kiev inherited from the Soviet Union.

The territorial-defence battalions were part of Ukraine's territorial-defence system; after they were integrated into the regular army, reserve rifle battalions took their place in this system. These battalions are intended to protect the territory of the administrative regions in which they are formed. However, based on the experience of the territorial battalions that formed in 2014, they could also be sent to the front line if the situation escalates.

Territorial-defence detachments, which are separate to the territorial-defence battalions and reserve rifle battalions, are far more numerous. These detachments can be established in every region should martial law be introduced, and are tasked with guarding important facilities. The core of these detachments comprises volunteer reservists, whilst other individuals subject to military service are also assigned. Given Ukraine's limited funding and the limited tasks assigned to the defence detachments, they are only issued with small-arms weapons. Consequently, many volunteers use their own money to buy legal firearms (including high-precision sniper rifles up to .50 calibre, which are allowed by Ukrainian law as hunting weapons), personal body armour, communications gear, personal equipment and transport. As a consequence, some of the territorial detachments are better armed, equipped and trained than soldiers in the regular army and can accomplish some of the missions assigned to light infantry.

Personnel and training

Since 2014, the personnel system has gone through several changes. At the outbreak of hostilities in the Donbas region, Ukraine's armed forces were almost wholly manned by contract service personnel. A process of downsizing over many years had also reduced total troop levels. However, this limited numerical strength – relative to what was required by the operational situation – led to the mobilisation of military reservists. Six waves of mobilisation took place during 2014–15, with personnel from the first wave starting their demobilisation with the arrival of the fourth tranche. Some 200,000 military reservists were mobilised in total.

However, the stabilisation of the situation on the front line, coupled with the unpopularity of mobilisation, meant that the seventh wave was repeatedly deferred. Instead, the authorities adopted a policy of increasing the number of contract service personnel. To that end, wages for contract troops increased significantly, from US$100 to US$300 per month – plus any additional payments for time spent in the combat zone. Given the general economic situation in Ukraine, a salary of this size will prove attractive to some.

As well as mobilisation waves, conscription was restored and its duration was increased from 12 to 18 months. Conscripts are not permitted to take part in combat operations in Donbas. However, following their discharge from conscript service into the reserve force, these reservists can be activated by another wave of mobilisation and sent to the front. In addition, soldiers demobilised from the first call-up waves were formed into a primary operational reserve and assigned to the units where they served; they have to return to these units when ordered.

There have also been significant changes to military training practices since early 2014. Conscripts and mobilised personnel now receive several months of basic training at training centres and/or their military units. The number of exercises has also increased significantly, including those undertaken by large-unit formations. In addition, some training is led by NATO and EU states' armed forces. Much of the training by foreign armed forces is conducted through the Joint Multinational Training Group–Ukraine, which integrates partner-nation training capacities (including from Canada, Estonia, Latvia, Lithuania, Poland, the United Kingdom and the United States) at the International Peacekeeping and Security Center in Yavoriv, Lviv. Foreign-training assistance is not new, and was conducted from the 1990s by states including the US under NATO's Partnership for Peace programme, which Ukraine joined in 1994. Foreign

Table 7 **Ukraine: increased exercise frequency**

Unit size	2013	2015
Brigade	0	14
Battalion	7	87
Company	33	261

assistance is also being provided to Ukraine with regard to the defence-reform process and doctrine modernisation.

The amount of training conducted within the Ukrainian armed forces has also changed (see Table 7). In the land forces and the airborne troops, for instance, training increased significantly between 2013 and 2015. This has bolstered the operational experience troops are receiving on the front line.

Tactical changes

After offensive operations by Ukraine in the Donbas region in summer 2014, the application of military force by Russia at Zelenopillya in Luhansk oblast and Ilovaisk in Donetsk oblast led the Ukrainian Army to switch to a positional-defence posture. Since autumn of that year, the tactics employed by Ukraine's forces have not changed significantly and are based on the control of 'strongpoints'.

Ukrainian tactics have evolved and consist of improving the fortification of positions, both directly on the line of contact and at the rear. Behind army lines in the Donbas region, around 300 platoon strongpoints have been constructed from reinforced concrete (including firing points and personnel shelters) in addition to earth-and-timber structures. Private construction companies were contracted to carry out the work at an average cost of US$100,000 per platoon strongpoint.

The construction of layered defences, along with improvements in the fortification of front-line strongpoints, have in large measure determined the stability of Ukraine's defensive line. Since spring 2015, pro-Russian forces in Donbas have been unable to mount a single successful large-scale offensive operation. Furthermore, Ukraine's focus on fortification has largely reduced the effectiveness of artillery employed by its opponents.

Inventory changes

Most of the armament that has augmented Ukrainian Army inventories has come from the repair and modernisation of Soviet-era weapons. This covers a wide range of equipment, from small arms to artillery, armoured vehicles and combat aircraft, and constitutes an essential resource for Ukraine to draw on in order to increase its combat power. While the nominal amount of equipment in service remains unchanged, repair and modernisation have served to increase the proportion that is combat-ready. For example, 30 armoured vehicles, 20 artillery systems and three fighter aircraft, all refitted, were delivered to the armed forces to coincide with the 25th anniversary of Ukraine's independence in August 2016.

Wheeled armoured vehicles (BTR-3 and BTR-4 armoured personnel carriers, and *Dozor*-B and *Cossack* armoured cars) and KrAZ motor vehicles account for the majority of the new indigenous military hardware delivered to the armed forces. Licensed assembly by KrAZ of Streit Group's *Cougar* and *Spartan* armoured vehicles is also taking place. Meanwhile, the Mayak 120mm M120-15 *Molot* mortar – which is a copy of the Soviet 2B11 mortar – stands out among the new models of artillery and is being delivered in quantity. Deliveries have also begun of the Ukrainian-designed *Stugna*-P anti-tank guided missile and main battle tank (MBT) guided missiles. According to official sources, in 2015 Ukraine's armed forces received 30 *Stugna*-P launchers with 507 missiles and 380 MBT missiles.

Meanwhile, military aid continues to arrive in Ukraine from abroad, primarily in the form of vehicles. Various modifications of the US HMMWV, as well as commercial pickup trucks and jeeps from different manufacturers, account for the bulk of vehicles being delivered as aid. Kiev bought 75 obsolescent AT105 *Saxon* wheeled armoured vehicles from the UK, which are reportedly performing well under Ukrainian service conditions. Counter-battery radars have been delivered by the US.

The switch to positional warfare, combined with restrictions on the use of heavy weapons in line with the Minsk accords, have led to a change in the Ukrainian Army's inventory. For example, the proportion of heavy machine guns has increased significantly. For instance, 1910/1930-model Maxim machine guns are being delivered to front-line troops in substantial numbers. According to official data, 35,000 of these were in storage in Ukraine in 2011. In addition, improvised machine-gun mounts taken from armoured vehicles previously scrapped or disabled in combat have become widespread, and are being fitted to 7.62mm PKT or 12.7mm DShK and NSVT machine guns. These mounts are made by small civilian companies, funded by volunteer donations.

Armenia ARM

Armenian Dram d		2015	2016	2017
GDP	d	5.03tr	5.21tr	
	US$	10.5bn	10.8bn	
per capita	US$	3,521	3,596	
Growth	%	3.0	3.2	
Inflation	%	3.7	-0.5	
Def bdgt [a]	d	199bn	207bn	
	US$	416m	428m	
FMA (US)	US$	1.7m	1.7m	1m
US$1=d		477.93	484.16	

[a] Includes imported military equipment, excludes military pensions

Population 3,051,250

Age	0–14	15–19	20–24	25–29	30–64	65 plus
Male	10.1%	3.2%	3.8%	4.6%	22.3%	4.4%
Female	8.9%	2.9%	3.7%	4.7%	24.9%	6.6%

Capabilities

The armed forces' main focus is territorial defence, given continuing tensions with neighbouring Azerbaijan over Nagorno-Karabakh. Armenia completed a Strategic Defence Review in May 2011. Conscription continues, but there is also a growing cohort of professional officers. Overall military doctrine remains influenced strongly by Russian thinking, but overseas deployments, including to Afghanistan, Kosovo and Lebanon, have enabled personnel to learn from international counterparts. The country aims to develop its peacekeeping contingent into one brigade operating to NATO standards, so that Armenia can deploy a self-sustaining battalion that is interoperable with NATO forces. Yerevan and NATO are also in talks over the reform of Armenian military education; a National Defense Research University opened in January 2016. Armenia is actively engaged in a NATO Individual Partnership Action Plan. Armenia is also a CSTO member. However, defence ties with Russia continue on a broad range of issues and in November 2016 Moscow approved the concept for a Joint Group of Forces with Armenia. It was reported that this would be commanded by the Armenian General Staff in peacetime. Equipment is mainly of Russian origin, and in July 2015 a US$200m loan from Moscow was ratified with the aim of purchasing modern Russian weapons between 2015 and 2017, including artillery systems. The country received 9K720 *Iskander*-E missiles with a 300km range from Russia in September 2016. Serviceability and maintenance of mainly ageing aircraft has been a problem for the air force. In June 2016, Armenia ratified a joint air-defence system with Russia, which was submitted to Russia's Duma in October.

ACTIVE 44,800 (Army 41,850 Air/AD Aviation Forces (Joint) 1,100 other Air Defence Forces 1,850) **Paramilitary 4,300**
Conscript liability 24 months

RESERVES
Some mobilisation reported, possibly 210,000 with military service within 15 years

ORGANISATIONS BY SERVICE

Army 22,900; 18,950 conscripts (total 41,850)
FORCES BY ROLE
SPECIAL FORCES
  1 SF bde
MANOEUVRE
  Mechanised
  1 (1st) corps (1 recce bn, 1 tk bn, 2 MR regt, 1 maint bn)
  1 (2nd) corps (1 recce bn, 1 tk bn, 2 MR regt, 1 lt inf regt, 1 arty bn)
  1 (3rd) corps (1 recce bn, 1 tk bn, 4 MR regt, 1 lt inf regt, 1 arty bn, 1 MRL bn, 1 sigs bn, 1 maint bn)
  1 (4th) corps (4 MR regt; 1 SP arty bn; 1 sigs bn)
  1 (5th) corps (with 2 fortified areas) (1 MR regt)
  Other
  1 indep MR trg bde
COMBAT SUPPORT
  1 arty bde
  1 MRL bde
  1 AT regt
  1 AD bde
  2 AD regt
  2 (radiotech) AD regt
  1 engr regt
EQUIPMENT BY TYPE
ARMOURED FIGHTING VEHICLES
  MBT 109: 3 T-54; 5 T-55; 101 T-72
  RECCE 12 BRM-1K (CP)
  IFV 86: 75 BMP-1; 6 BMP-1K (CP); 5 BMP-2
  APC • APC (W) 130: 8 BTR-60; 100 BTR-60 look-a-like; 18 BTR-70; 4 BTR-80
ENGINEERING & MAINTENANCE VEHICLES
  AEV MT-LB
  ARV BREhM-D; BREM-1
ANTI-TANK/ANTI-INFRASTRUCTURE
  MSL • SP 22: 9 9P148 *Konkurs* (AT-5 *Spandrel*); 13 9P149 *Shturm* (AT-6 *Spiral*)
ARTILLERY 232
  SP 38: **122mm** 10 2S1 *Gvozdika*; **152mm** 28 2S3 *Akatsiya*
  TOWED 131: **122mm** 69 D-30; **152mm** 62: 26 2A36 *Giatsint*-B; 2 D-1; 34 D-20
  MRL 51: **122mm** 47 BM-21 *Grad*; **273mm** 4 WM-80
  MOR 120mm 12 M120
SURFACE-TO-SURFACE MISSILE LAUNCHERS
  SRBM • Conventional 16: 8 9K72 *Elbrus* (SS-1C *Scud* B); 4 9K79 *Tochka* (SS-21 *Scarab*); 4 9K720 *Iskander*-E
RADAR • LAND 6 SNAR-10
UNMANNED AERIAL VEHICLES
  ISR • Light 15 *Krunk*
AIR DEFENCE
  SAM
    Medium-range 2K11 *Krug* (SA-4 *Ganef*); S-75 *Dvina* (SA-2 *Guideline*)
    Short-range 2K12 *Kub* (SA-6 *Gainful*); S-125 *Pechora* (SA-3 *Goa*)

Point-defence 9K33 *Osa* (SA-8 *Gecko*); 9K310 *Igla*-1 (SA-16 *Gimlet*); 9K38 *Igla* (SA-18 *Grouse*)
GUNS
  SP 23mm ZSU-23-4
  TOWED 23mm ZU-23-2

Air and Air Defence Aviation Forces 1,100
1 Air & AD Joint Command
FORCES BY ROLE
GROUND ATTACK
  1 sqn with Su-25/Su-25UBK *Frogfoot*
EQUIPMENT BY TYPE
AIRCRAFT 15 combat capable
  ATK 15: 13 Su-25 *Frogfoot*; 2 Su-25UBK *Frogfoot*
  TPT 3: **Heavy** 2 Il-76 *Candid*; **PAX** 1 A319CJ
  TRG 14: 4 L-39 *Albatros*; 10 Yak-52
HELICOPTERS
  ATK 7 Mi-24P *Hind*
  ISR 4: 2 Mi-24K *Hind*; 2 Mi-24R *Hind* (cbt spt)
  MRH 10 Mi-8MT (cbt spt)
  C2 2 Mi-9 *Hip G* (cbt spt)
  TPT • Light 7 PZL Mi-2 *Hoplite*
AIR DEFENCE • SAM • Long-range S-300 (SA-10 *Grumble*); S-300PM (SA-20 *Gargoyle*)

Paramilitary 4,300

Police
FORCES BY ROLE
MANOEUVRE
  Other
  4 paramilitary bn
EQUIPMENT BY TYPE
ARMOURED FIGHTING VEHICLES
  RECCE 5 BRM-1K (CP)
  IFV 50: 5 BMD-1; 44 BMP-1; 1 BMP-1K (CP)
  APC • APC (W) 24 BTR-60/BTR-70/BTR-152

Border Troops
Ministry of National Security
EQUIPMENT BY TYPE
ARMOURED FIGHTING VEHICLES
  RECCE 3 BRM-1K (CP)
  IFV 43: 5 BMD-1; 35 BMP-1
  APC • APC (W) 23: 5 BTR-60; 18 BTR-70

DEPLOYMENT
Legal provisions for foreign deployment:
Constitution: Codified constitution (1995, amended 2005)
Specific legislation: 'Law on Defence of the Republic of Armenia'
Decision on deployment of troops abroad: by the president, in accordance with 'Law on Defence of the Republic of Armenia' (Article 5 (2) (1)). Also, under Art. 55 (13) of constitution, president can call for use of armed forces (and National Assembly shall be convened) (Also Art. 81 (3) of constitution)

AFGHANISTAN
NATO • *Operation Resolute Support* 65

ALBANIA
OSCE • Albania 1

LEBANON
UN • UNIFIL 33

MALI
UN • MINUSMA 1

SERBIA
NATO • KFOR 35

UKRAINE
OSCE • Ukraine 2

FOREIGN FORCES
OSCE figures represent total Minsk Conference mission personnel in both Armenia and Azerbaijan
Bulgaria OSCE 1
Czech Republic OSCE 1
Poland OSCE 1
Russia 3,300: 1 mil base with (1 MR bde; 74 T-72; 80 BMP-1; 80 BMP-2; 12 2S1; 12 BM-21); 1 ftr sqn with 18 MiG-29 *Fulcrum*; 2 SAM bty with S-300V (SA-12 *Gladiator/Giant*); 1 SAM bty with 2K12 *Kub* (SA-6 *Gainful*)
Sweden OSCE 1
Ukraine OSCE 1
United Kingdom OSCE 1

Azerbaijan AZE

Azerbaijani New Manat m		2015	2016	2017
GDP	m	54.35bn	55.31bn	
	US$	54.05bn	35.69bn	
per capita	US$	5,739	3,759	
Growth	%	1.1	-2.4	
Inflation	%	4.0	10.2	
Def bdgt [a]	m	1.76bn	2.23bn	1.62bn
	US$	1.75bn	1.44bn	
FMA (US)	US$	1.7m	1.7m	1m
US$1=m		1.01	1.55	

[a] Official defence budget. Excludes a significant proportion of procurement outlays

Population 9,872,765

Age	0–14	15–19	20–24	25–29	30–64	65 plus
Male	12.2%	3.6%	4.6%	5.0%	21.6%	2.5%
Female	10.6%	3.2%	4.3%	4.8%	23.5%	4.0%

Capabilities

The principal focus for Azerbaijan's armed forces is territorial defence, in light of continuing tensions with neighbouring Armenia over Nagorno-Karabakh. Violence flared between the two states in April 2016. The armed forces rely on conscription, and readiness within the services varies between units. The air force also suffers from training and maintenance problems, and the armed forces cannot organically support external deployments.

While forces have yet to fully transition from a Soviet-era model, oil revenues have in the recent past allowed an increase in defence expenditure. These increases have enabled the acquisition of additional platform capabilities, such as TOS-1A multiple-rocket-launcher batteries and armoured fighting vehicles, as part of a US$1bn contract with Moscow. Baku's surveillance capability has been enhanced by the purchase of Israeli UAVs. Azerbaijan maintains a defence relationship with NATO and in 2016 the country was in the fourth cycle of its NATO Individual Partnership Action Plan. Baku maintains a close military relationship with Ankara. Peacekeeping deployments have included a small number of personnel in Afghanistan, with just under 100 troops in-country as of June 2016.

ACTIVE 66,950 (Army 56,850 Navy 2,200 Air 7,900)
Paramilitary 15,000
Conscript liability 18 months (12 for graduates)

RESERVE 300,000
Some mobilisation reported; 300,000 with military service within 15 years

ORGANISATIONS BY SERVICE

Army 56,850
FORCES BY ROLE
COMMAND
  5 corps HQ
MANOEUVRE
  Mechanised
  4 MR bde
  Light
  19 MR bde
  Other
  1 sy bde
COMBAT SUPPORT
  1 arty bde
  1 arty trg bde
  1 MRL bde
  1 AT bde
  1 engr bde
  1 sigs bde
COMBAT SERVICE SUPPORT
  1 log bde
EQUIPMENT BY TYPE
ARMOURED FIGHTING VEHICLES
  MBT 439: 95 T-55; 244 T-72; 100 T-90S
  RECCE 15 BRM-1
  IFV 191: 20 BMD-1; 43 BMP-1; 33 BMP-2; 88 BMP-3; 7 BTR-80A
  APC 568
    APC (T) 336 MT-LB
    APC (W) 142: 10 BTR-60; 132 BTR-70
    PPV 90: 45 *Marauder*; 45 *Matador*
ENGINEERING & MAINTENANCE VEHICLES
  AEV MT-LB
  MW *Bozena*

ANTI-TANK/ANTI-INFRASTRUCTURE
  MSL • MANPATS 9K11 *Malyutka* (AT-3 *Sagger*); 9K111 *Fagot* (AT-4 *Spigot*); 9K111-1 *Konkurs* (AT-5 *Spandrel*); 9K115 *Metis* (AT-7 *Saxhorn*); *Spike*-LR
ARTILLERY 554
  SP 87: **122mm** 46 2S1 *Gvozdika*; **152mm** 24: 6 2S3 *Akatsiya*; 18 2S19 *Msta-S*; **155mm** 5 ATMOS 2000; **203mm** 12 2S7 *Pion*
  TOWED 207: **122mm** 129 D-30; **130mm** 36 M-46; **152mm** 42: 18 2A36 *Giatsint-B*; 24 D-20
  GUN/MOR 120mm 36: 18 2S9 NONA-S; 18 2S31 *Vena*
  MRL 112+: **122mm** 52+: 43 BM-21 *Grad*; 9+ IMI *Lynx*; **128mm** 12 RAK-12; **220mm** 18 TOS-1A; **300mm** 30 9A52 *Smerch*
  MOR 120mm 112: 5 *Cardom*; 107 M-1938 (PM-38)
SURFACE-TO-SURFACE MISSILE LAUNCHERS
  SRBM • Conventional ε4 9M79 *Tochka* (SS-21 *Scarab*)
  RADAR • LAND SNAR-1 *Long Trough*/SNAR-2/-6 *Pork Trough* (arty); *Small Fred*/*Small Yawn*/SNAR-10 *Big Fred* (veh, arty); GS-13 *Long Eye* (veh)
UNMANNED AERIAL VEHICLES
  ISR • Medium 3 *Aerostar*
AIR DEFENCE • SAM
  Medium-range 2K11 *Krug* (SA-4 *Ganef*)
  Point-defence 9K33 *Osa* (SA-8 *Gecko*); 9K35 *Strela*-10 (SA-13 *Gopher*); 9K32 *Strela* (SA-7 *Grail*)‡; 9K34 *Strela*-3 (SA-14 *Gremlin*); 9K310 *Igla*-1 (SA-16 *Gimlet*); 9K338 *Igla*-S (SA-24 *Grinch*)

Navy 2,200
EQUIPMENT BY TYPE
PATROL AND COASTAL COMBATANTS 8
  CORVETTES • FS 1 *Kusar* (ex-FSU *Petya II*) with 2 RBU 6000 *Smerch* 2 A/S mor, 2 twin 76mm gun
  PSO 1 *Luga* (*Woodnik* 2 Class) (FSU Project 888; additional trg role)
  PCC 3: 2 *Petrushka* (FSU UK-3; additional trg role); 1 *Shelon* (ex-FSU Project 1388M)
  PB 3: 1 *Araz* (ex-TUR AB 25); 1 *Bryza* (ex-FSU Project 722); 1 *Poluchat* (ex-FSU Project 368)
MINE WARFARE • MINE COUNTERMEASURES 4
  MHC 4: 2 *Yevgenya* (FSU Project 1258); 2 *Yakhont* (FSU *Sonya*)
AMPHIBIOUS 6
  LSM 3: 1 *Polnochny A* (FSU Project 770) (capacity 6 MBT; 180 troops); 2 *Polnochny B* (FSU Project 771) (capacity 6 MBT; 180 troops)
  LCU 1 *Vydra*† (FSU) (capacity either 3 AMX-30 MBT or 200 troops)
  LCM 2 T-4 (FSU)
LOGISTICS AND SUPPORT • AGS 1 (FSU Project 10470)

Air Force and Air Defence 7,900
FORCES BY ROLE
FIGHTER
  1 sqn with MiG-29 *Fulcrum*
FIGHTER/GROUND ATTACK
  1 regt with Su-24 *Fencer*; Su-25 *Frogfoot*; Su-25UB *Frogfoot* B

TRANSPORT
1 sqn with An-12 *Cub*; Yak-40 *Codling*
ATTACK/TRANSPORT HELICOPTER
1 regt with Mi-8 *Hip*; Mi-24 *Hind*; PZL Mi-2 *Hoplite*
EQUIPMENT BY TYPE
AIRCRAFT 35 combat capable
  FTR 14 MiG-29 *Fulcrum*
  ATK 21: 2 Su-24 *Fencer*†; 16 Su-25 *Frogfoot*; 3 Su-25UB *Frogfoot* B
  TPT 4: Medium 1 An-12 *Cub*; **Light** 3 Yak-40 *Codling*
  TRG 12 L-39 *Albatros*
HELICOPTERS
  ATK 26 Mi-24 *Hind*
  MRH: 20+ Mi-17-IV *Hip*
  TPT 20: Medium 13 Mi-8 *Hip*; **Light** 7 PZL Mi-2 *Hoplite*
UAV • ISR • Medium 4 *Aerostar*
AIR DEFENCE • SAM
  Long S-200 *Vega* (SA-5 *Gammon*); S-300PM/PMU2 (SA-20 *Gargoyle*)
  Medium S-75 *Dvina* (SA-2 *Guideline*); 9K37M *Buk*-M1 (SA-11 *Gadfly*)
  Short S-125 *Neva* (SA-3 *Goa*)
AIR-LAUNCHED MISSILES • AAM • IR R-60 (AA-8 *Aphid*); R-73 (AA-11 *Archer*) **IR/SARH** R-27 (AA-10 *Alamo*)

Paramilitary ε15,000

State Border Service ε5,000
Ministry of Internal Affairs
EQUIPMENT BY TYPE
ARMOURED FIGHTING VEHICLES
  IFV 168 BMP-1/BMP-2
  APC • APC (W) 19 BTR-60/70/80
ARTILLERY • MRL 122mm 3 T-122
HELICOPTERS • ATK 24 Mi-35M *Hind*

Coast Guard
The Coast Guard was established in 2005 as part of the State Border Service.
EQUIPMENT BY TYPE
PATROL AND COASTAL COMBATANTS 17
  PCG 1 *Sa'ar* 62 with 1 8-cell lnchr with *Spike* NLOS SSM, 1 hel landing platform
  PBF 12: 1 *Osa* II (FSU Project 205); 6 *Shaldag* V; 2 *Silver Ships* 48ft; 3 *Stenka*
  PB 4: 2 *Baltic* 150; 1 *Point* (US); 1 *Grif* (FSU *Zhuk*)
LOGISTICS AND SUPPORT • ARS 1 *Iva* (FSU *Vikhr*)

Internal Troops 10,000+
Ministry of Internal Affairs
EQUIPMENT BY TYPE
ARMOURED FIGHTING VEHICLES
  APC • APC (W) 7 BTR-60/BTR-70/BTR-80

DEPLOYMENT
Legal provisions for foreign deployment:
Constitution: Codified constitution (1995)
Decision on deployment of troops abroad: By parliament upon proposal by president (Art. 109, No. 28)

AFGHANISTAN
NATO • *Operation Resolute Support* 94

UKRAINE
OSCE • Ukraine 1

FOREIGN FORCES
OSCE figures represent total Minsk Conference mission personnel in both Armenia and Azerbaijan
Bulgaria OSCE 1
Czech Republic OSCE 1
Poland OSCE 1
Sweden OSCE 1
Ukraine OSCE 1
United Kingdom OSCE 1

TERRITORY WHERE THE GOVERNMENT DOES NOT EXERCISE EFFECTIVE CONTROL

Data presented here represents an assessment of the de facto situation. Nagorno-Karabakh was part of Azerbaijan, but mostly populated by ethnic Armenians. In 1988, when inter-ethnic clashes between Armenians and Azeris erupted in Azerbaijan, the local authorities declared their intention to secede and join Armenia. Baku rejected this and armed conflict erupted. A ceasefire was brokered in 1994, since when Armenia has controlled most of Nagorno-Karabakh. While Armenia provides political, economic and military support to Nagorno-Karabakh, the region has declared itself independent – although this has not been recognised by any other state, including Armenia. Azerbaijan claims, and the rest of the international community generally regards, Nagorno-Karabakh and the occupied territories as part of Azerbaijan.

Nagorno-Karabakh
Available estimates vary with reference to military holdings in Nagorno-Karabakh. Main battle tanks are usually placed at around 200–300 in number, with similar numbers for other armoured combat vehicles and artillery pieces, and small numbers of helicopters. Overall personnel-strength estimates are between 18,000 and 20,000. Some of the equipment listed may belong to Armenian forces.

EQUIPMENT BY TYPE
ARMOURED FIGHTING VEHICLES
  MBT T-72
  RECCE BRDM-2
  IFV BMP-1; BMP-2
ANTI-TANK/ANTI-INFRASTRUCTURE
  MSL
    SP 9P148 *Konkurs* (AT-5 *Spandrel*); 9P149 *Shturm* (AT-6 *Spiral*)
    MANPATS 9K111-1 *Konkurs* (AT-5 *Spandrel*)
  RCL 73mm SPG-9
ARTILLERY 232
  SP 122mm 2S1 *Gvozdika*; **152mm** 2S3 *Akatsiya*
  TOWED 122mm D-30; **152mm** 2A36 *Giatsint*-B; D-20
  MRL 122mm BM-21 *Grad*; **273mm** WM-80

MOR 120mm M-74/M-75
SURFACE-TO-SURFACE MISSILE LAUNCHERS
   SRBM • Conventional 9K72 *Elbrus* (SS-1C *Scud* B)
HELICOPTERS
   ATK 5 Mi-24 *Hind*
   MRH 5 Mi-8MT *Hip*
AIR DEFENCE
   SAM
      Medium-range 2K11 *Krug* (SA-4 *Ganef*); S-75 *Dvina* (SA-2 *Guideline*)
      Short-range 2K12 *Kub* (SA-6 *Gainful*); S-125 *Pechora* (SA-3 *Goa*)
      Point-defence 9K33 *Osa* (SA-8 *Gecko*); 9K310 *Igla*-1 (SA-16 *Gimlet*); 9K38 *Igla* (SA-18 *Grouse*)
   GUNS
      SP 23mm ZSU-23-4
      TOWED 23mm ZU-23-2

Belarus BLR

Belarusian Ruble r		2015	2016	2017
GDP	r		870tr	953tr
	US$		54.6bn	48.1bn
per capita	US$		5,749	5,092
Growth	%		-3.9	-3
Inflation	%		13.5	12.7
Def bdgt	r		8.88tr	10.1tr
	US$		558m	509m
US$1=r			15,925.98	19,812.23
Population	9,570,376			

Age	0–14	15–19	20–24	25–29	30–64	65 plus
Male	8.0%	2.5%	3.0%	4.0%	24.2%	4.7%
Female	7.6%	2.3%	2.9%	3.9%	26.8%	10.0%

Capabilities

Maintaining territorial integrity is the fundamental task of the Belarusian armed forces. Russia is the country's principal defence partner, though relations have been strained in recent years and Minsk has also courted China and Ukraine. Although Russia would like to establish an air base in Belarus, there has been little real progress in this area, although Russia does deploy combat airpower to Baranovichi air base in Belarus. The training and equipment of territorial defence troops has improved, with the aim of operating them in cooperation with regular forces. Some years after discussions began, it was claimed in April that the joint air-defence system with Russia had been implemented; Minsk received a second-hand S-300PS (SA-10B *Grumble*) long-range SAM system from Russia at the beginning of 2016. Belarus also plans to replace its Soviet-era MiG-29 *Fulcrum* combat aircraft with Su-30SMs around the turn of the decade. A new military doctrine was approved in July 2016; this identified security challenges including from 'hybrid methods' as well as 'colour revolutions'. The defence authorities aim to have smaller, more mobile forces with improved counter-terrorism capabilities, driven by a need for increased capacity for territorial defence. Acquisition of the *Protivnik* air-defence radar from Russia and development of the *Polonez* multiple-launcher rocket system can be seen as part of this effort. Military pay remains low, with army captains reportedly earning only US$150 per month. There is debate among Belarusian commentators as to whether re-equipment and modernisation can be delivered given the state of the economy. Belarus has an indigenous defence industry, including vehicle and guided-weapons production, while the sector also undertakes upgrades for foreign customers. However, tensions with Russia have limited access to traditional Russian markets. In response, the defence industry has sought new markets to reduce dependence on Russia; boosting this sector was a focus of the military-doctrine document. Minsk aims to increase combat readiness, including through so-called readiness 'control checks'. Personnel reductions are being implemented as part of the country's revised defence policy. Most multinational training is carried out within the context of the CSTO.

ACTIVE 48,000 (Army 16,500 Air 15,000 Special Operations Forces 6,000 Joint 10,500) **Paramilitary 110,000**
Conscript liability 18 months (alternative service option)

RESERVE 289,500 (Joint 289,500 with mil service within last 5 years)

ORGANISATIONS BY SERVICE

Army 16,500
FORCES BY ROLE
COMMAND
   2 comd HQ (West & North West)
MANOEUVRE
   Mechanised
   2 mech bde
   2 mech bde(-)
COMBAT SUPPORT
   2 arty bde
   2 MRL regt
   2 engr regt
EQUIPMENT BY TYPE
ARMOURED FIGHTING VEHICLES
   MBT 515: 446 T-72; 69 T-80
   RECCE 136 BRM-1
   IFV 875 BMP-2
   APC • APC (T) 50 MT-LB
ENGINEERING & MAINTENANCE VEHICLES
   AEV MT-LB
   VLB MTU
ANTI-TANK/ANTI-INFRASTRUCTURE • MSL
   SP 236: 126 9P148 *Konkurs*; 110 9P149 *Shturm*
   MANPATS 9K111 *Fagot* (AT-4 *Spigot*); 9K111-1 *Konkurs* (AT-5 *Spandrel*); 9K115 *Metis* (AT-7 *Saxhorn*)
ARTILLERY 961
   SP 434: **122mm** 198 2S1 *Gvozdika*; **152mm** 236: 108 2S3 *Akatsiya*; 116 2S5; 12 2S19 *Msta*-S
   TOWED **152mm** 180: 48 2A36 *Giatsint*-B; 132 2A65 *Msta*-B
   GUN/MOR **120mm** 48 2S9 NONA-S

MRL 238: **122mm** 126 BM-21 *Grad*; **220mm** 72 9P140 *Uragan*; **300mm** 40: 36 9A52 *Smerch*; 4 *Polonez*
  MOR **120mm** 61 2S12
RADAR • LAND GS-13 *Long Eye*/SNAR-1 *Long Trough*/SNAR-2/-6 *Pork Trough* (arty); some *Small Fred/Small Yawn*/SNAR-10 *Big Fred* (veh, arty)

Air Force and Air Defence Forces 15,000

Flying hours 15 hrs/yr

FORCES BY ROLE
FIGHTER
  2 sqn with MiG-29S/UB *Fulcrum*
GROUND ATTACK
  2 sqn with Su-25K/UBK *Frogfoot* A/B
TRANSPORT
  1 base with An-12 *Cub*; An-24 *Coke*; An-26 *Curl*; Il-76 *Candid*; Tu-134 *Crusty*
TRAINING
  Some sqn with L-39 *Albatros*
ATTACK HELICOPTER
  Some sqn with Mi-24 *Hind*
TRANSPORT HELICOPTER
  Some (cbt spt) sqn with Mi-6 *Hook*; Mi-8 *Hip*; Mi-24K *Hind* G2; Mi-24R *Hind* G1; Mi-26 *Halo*
EQUIPMENT BY TYPE
AIRCRAFT 44 combat capable
  FTR 24 MiG-29S/UB *Fulcrum*
  FGA (21 Su-27/UB *Flanker* B/C non-operational/stored)
  ATK 12 Su-25K/UBK *Frogfoot* A/B
  TPT 11: **Heavy** 2 Il-76 *Candid* (+9 civ Il-76 available for mil use); **Medium** 3 An-12 *Cub*; **Light** 6: 1 An-24 *Coke*; 4 An-26 *Curl*; 1 Tu-134 *Crusty*
  TRG 8+: Some L-39 *Albatros*; 8 Yak-130 *Mitten**
HELICOPTERS
  ATK 4 Mi-24 *Hind*
  TPT 19: **Heavy** 5 Mi-26 *Halo*; **Medium** 14; 8 Mi-8 *Hip*; 6 Mi-8MTV-5 *Hip*
AIR-LAUNCHED MISSILES
  AAM • **IR** R-60 (AA-8 *Aphid*); R-73 (AA-11 *Archer*)
  SARH R-27R (AA-10 *Alamo* A)
  ASM Kh-25 (AS-10 *Karen*); Kh-29 (AS-14 *Kedge*)
  ARM Kh-58 (AS-11 *Kilter*)

Air Defence

AD data from Uzal Baranovichi EW radar

FORCES BY ROLE
AIR DEFENCE
  1 bde S-300PS (SA-10B *Grumble*)
  1 bde with S-300V(SA-12A *Gladiator*/SA-12B *Giant*)
  1 bde with 9K37 *Buk* (SA-11 *Gadfly*)
  1 bde with 9K37 *Buk* (SA-11 *Gadfly*); 9K332 *Tor*-M2E (SA-15 *Gauntlet*)
  2 bde with 9K33 *Osa* (SA-8 *Gecko*)
  3 regt with S-300PS (SA-10B *Grumble*)
EQUIPMENT BY TYPE
AIR DEFENCE • **SAM**
  Long-range S-300PS (SA-10B *Grumble*); S-300V (SA-12A *Gladiator*/SA-12B *Giant*)
  Medium-range 9K37 *Buk* (SA-11 *Gadfly*)
  Short-range 12 9K332 *Tor*-M2E (SA-15 *Gauntlet*)
  Point-defence 9K33 *Osa* (SA-8 *Gecko*); 9K35 *Strela*-10 (SA-13 *Gopher*)

Special Operations Command 6,000

FORCES BY ROLE
SPECIAL FORCES
  1 SF bde
MANOEUVRE
  Mechanised
  2 (mobile) mech bde
EQUIPMENT BY TYPE
ARMOURED FIGHTING VEHICLES
  APC • **APC (W)** 192: 39 BTR-70; 153 BTR-80
ARTILLERY • **TOWED 122mm** 48 D-30
ANTI-TANK/ANTI-INFRASTRUCTURE • **MSL**
  MANPATS 9K111 *Fagot* (AT-4 *Spigot*); 9K111-1 *Konkurs* (AT-5 *Spandrel*); 9K115 *Metis* (AT-7 *Saxhorn*)

Joint 10,500 (Centrally controlled units and MoD staff)

FORCES BY ROLE
SURFACE-TO-SURFACE MISSILE
  2 SRBM bde
COMBAT SUPPORT
  1 arty gp
  1 MRL bde
  2 engr bde
  1 EW unit
  1 NBC regt
  1 ptn bridging regt
  2 sigs bde
EQUIPMENT BY TYPE
ARMOURED FIGHTING VEHICLES
  APC • **APC (T)** 20 MT-LB
ARTILLERY 196
  SP 152mm 70 2S5 *Giatsint*-S
  TOWED 152mm 90 2A65 *Msta*-B
  300mm 36 9A52 *Smerch*
SURFACE-TO-SURFACE MISSILE LAUNCHERS
  SRBM • **Conventional** 96: 36 FROG/9M79 *Tochka* (SS-21 *Scarab*); 60 Scud

Paramilitary 110,000

State Border Troops 12,000
Ministry of Interior

Militia 87,000
Ministry of Interior

Internal Troops 11,000

DEPLOYMENT

LEBANON
UN • UNIFIL 5

UKRAINE
OSCE • Ukraine 7

Georgia GEO

Georgian Lari		2015	2016	2017
GDP	lari	31.7bn	33.8bn	
	US$	14.0bn	14.5bn	
per capita	US$	3,754	3,908	
Growth	%	2.8	3.4	
Inflation	%	4.0	2.6	
Def bdgt	lari	680m	670m	743m
	US$	300m	287m	317m
FMA (US)	US$	30m	20m	20m
US$1=lari		2.27	2.34	

Population 4,928,052

Age	0–14	15–19	20–24	25–29	30–64	65 plus
Male	9.4%	3.0%	3.6%	4.1%	21.5%	6.2%
Female	8.5%	2.6%	3.4%	4.0%	24.1%	9.6%

Capabilities

Georgia's main security preoccupations concern Russian military deployments and the breakaway regions of Abkhazia and South Ossetia, the former of which grew closer militarily to Russia over the past year by agreeing a joint group of forces. The armed forces continue to make efforts to address lessons from the conflict with Russia in 2008, which revealed significant shortcomings in key areas, including reservist organisation, and anti-armour and air-defence capabilities. The Israeli *Spyder*-SR system was subsequently acquired to bolster the country's air-defence capability and a battery of surface-to-air missiles was ordered in 2015. In mid-2016 it was announced that two air-force operational commands would be established. The US planned in 2015 to allocate US$20m to assist Georgia's armed forces via the European Reassurance Initiative. Further support is derived from the NATO–Georgia Substantial Package approved at the 2014 Wales Summit. As part of this, a NATO Joint Training and Evaluation Centre (JTEC) was inaugurated near Tbilisi in mid-2015. Rotational training of Georgian units at the JTEC began in May 2016. The country's Strategic Defence Review 2013–16 used a threat-based methodology to provide the main direction for future force development and force structure, called 'Objective Force 2016'. The 2014 Defence White Book identified priorities including improved professionalisation, mobility and combat readiness, and modernising defence planning and management, including intelligence and sustainment. Georgia abolished conscription in mid-2016 and from 1 November began enlisting contract-based personnel. The first entrant course was due to begin in March 2017, with a four-year term of service. Georgia deployed 850 personnel to NATO's *Resolute Support* mission in Afghanistan. The NATO assurance-measure exercise *Noble Partner 2016* involved Georgian, UK and US troops and was part of the country's training for its company-sized contribution to the NATO Response Force.

ACTIVE 20,650 (Army 17,750 Air 1,300 National Guard 1,600) **Paramilitary 5,400**

ORGANISATIONS BY SERVICE

Army 14,000; 3,750 conscript (total 17,750)

FORCES BY ROLE
SPECIAL FORCES
 1 SF bde
MANOEUVRE
 Light
 5 inf bde
 Amphibious
 2 mne bn (1 cadre)
COMBAT SUPPORT
 2 arty bde
 1 engr bde
 1 sigs bn
 1 SIGINT bn
 1 MP bn
COMBAT SERVICE SUPPORT
 1 med bn

EQUIPMENT BY TYPE
ARMOURED FIGHTING VEHICLES
 MBT 123: 23 T-55; 100 T-72
 RECCE 5: 1 BRM-1K; 4+ *Didgori*-2
 IFV 71: 25 BMP-1; 46 BMP-2
 APC 189+
  APC (T) 69+: 3+ *Lazika*; 66 MT-LB
  APC (W) 120+: 25 BTR-70; 19 BTR-80; 8+ *Didgori*-1; 3+ *Didgori*-3; 65 *Ejder*
 AUV 10 *Cougar*
ANTI-TANK/ANTI-INFRASTRUCTURE
 MSL • MANPATS 9K111 *Fagot* (AT-4 *Spigot*); 9K113 *Konkurs* (AT-5 *Spandrel*)
 GUNS • TOWED ε40: 85mm D-44; 100mm T-12
ARTILLERY 240
 SP 67: **122mm** 20 2S1 *Gvozdika*; **152mm** 46: 32 M-77 *Dana*; 13 2S3 *Akatsiya*; 1 2S19 *Msta*-S; **203mm** 1 2S7 *Pion*
 TOWED 71: **122mm** 58 D-30; **152mm** 13: 3 2A36 *Giatsint*-B; 10 2A65 *Msta*-B
 MRL **122mm** 37: 13 BM-21 *Grad*; 6 GradLAR; 18 RM-70
 MOR **120mm** 65: 14 2S12 *Sani*; 33 M-75; 18 M120
AIR DEFENCE • SAM
 Short-range *Spyder*-SR
 Point-defence *Grom*; 9K32 *Strela*-2 (SA-7 *Grail*)‡; 9K35 *Strela*-10 (SA-13 *Gopher*); 9K36 *Strela*-3 (SA-14 *Gremlin*); 9K310 *Igla*-1 (SA-16 *Gimlet*)

Air Force 1,300 (incl 300 conscript)

1 avn base, 1 hel air base

EQUIPMENT BY TYPE
AIRCRAFT 12 combat capable
 ATK 12: 3 Su-25 *Frogfoot*; 7 Su-25K *Frogfoot* A; 2 Su-25UB *Frogfoot* B
 TPT • **Light** 9: 6 An-2 *Colt*; 1 Tu-134A *Crusty* (VIP); 2 Yak-40 *Codling*
 TRG 9 L-29 *Delfin*
HELICOPTERS
 ATK 6 Mi-24 *Hind*
 TPT 29: **Medium** 17 Mi-8T *Hip*; **Light** 12 Bell 205 (UH-1H *Iroquois*)
UNMANNED AERIAL VEHICLES
 ISR • **Medium** 1+ *Hermes* 450

AIR DEFENCE • SAM
Medium 9K37 *Buk*-M1 (SA-11 *Gadfly*) (1-2 bn)
Point 8 9K33 *Osa* AK (SA-8B *Gecko*) (two bty); 9K33 *Osa* AKM (6-10 updated SAM systems)

National Guard 1,600 active reservists opcon
Army
FORCES BY ROLE
MANOEUVRE
  Light
    1 inf bde

Paramilitary 5,400

Border Police 5,400

Coast Guard
HQ at Poti. The Navy was merged with the Coast Guard in 2009 under the auspices of the Georgian Border Police, within the Ministry of the Interior

EQUIPMENT BY TYPE
PATROL AND COASTAL COMBATANTS 21
  PBF 6: 4 Ares 43m; 1 *Kaan 33*; 1 *Kaan 20*
  PB 15: 1 *Akhmeta*; 2 *Dauntless*; 2 *Dilos* (ex-GRC); 1 *Kutaisi* (ex-TUR AB 25); 2 *Point*; 7 *Zhuk* (3 ex-UKR) (up to 20 patrol launches also in service)
AMPHIBIOUS • LANDING CRAFT • LCU 1 *Vydra* (ex-BLG)

DEPLOYMENT

Legal provisions for foreign deployment of armed forces:
Constitution: Codified constitution (1995)
Decision on deployment of troops abroad: By the presidency upon parliamentary approval (Art. 100)

AFGHANISTAN
NATO • *Operation Resolute Support* 861; 1 lt inf bn
UN • UNAMA 3 obs

CENTRAL AFRICAN REPUBLIC
EU • EUTM RCA 5

MALI
EU • EUTM Mali 1

SERBIA
OSCE • Kosovo 1

UKRAINE
OSCE • Ukraine 11

TERRITORY WHERE THE GOVERNMENT DOES NOT EXERCISE EFFECTIVE CONTROL
Following the August 2008 war between Russia and Georgia, the areas of Abkhazia and South Ossetia declared themselves independent. Data presented here represents the de facto situation and does not imply international recognition as sovereign states.

FOREIGN FORCES
Russia 7,000; 1 mil base at Gudauta (Abkhazia) with (1 MR bde; 40 T-90A; 120 BTR-82A; 18 2S3; 12 2S12; 18 BM-21; some S-300 SAM; some atk hel); 1 mil base at Djava/Tskhinvali (S. Ossetia) with (1 MR bde; 40 T-72; 120 BMP-2; 36 2S3; 12 2S12)

Kazakhstan KAZ

Kazakhstani Tenge t		2015	2016	2017
GDP	t	40.9tr	45.2tr	
	US$	184bn	128bn	
per capita	US$	10,426	7,138	
Growth	%	1.2	-0.8	
Inflation	%	6.5	13.1	
Def bdgt	t	375bn	388bn	408bn
	US$	1.69bn	1.10bn	1.20bn
FMA (US)	US$	0.8m		
US$1=t		221.73	352.650	

Population 18,360,353

Ethnic groups: Kazakk 63.3%; Russian 23.7%; Uzbek 2.8%; Ukraninans 2.1%; Tatars 1.3%; German 1.1%; other or non-specified 5.7%

Age	0-14	15-19	20-24	25-29	30-64	65 plus
Male	12.7%	3.3%	4.2%	4.6%	20.4%	2.6%
Female	13.0%	3.2%	4.0%	4.6%	22.7%	4.8%

Capabilities

By regional standards, Kazakhstan's armed forces are both relatively sizeable and well equipped, following the acquisition of significant amounts of new and upgraded materiel in recent years. However, Kazakhstan's close defence relationship with Russia, reinforced through its membership of the CSTO and SCO, has been a key part of this recapitalisation process. Moscow operates a radar station at Balkash and, in 2015, provided the first five S-300PS surface-to-air-missile systems as part of a Joint Air-Defence Agreement. In the army, air-mobile units are held at the highest level of readiness, with other units at lower levels. Deployment remains concentrated in the country's eastern regions, with almost all combat formations based in either Almaty or East Kazakhstan. Airlift is being improved, with joint ventures and production envisaged with European companies for rotary-wing and medium-lift fixed-wing aircraft. However, airworthiness remains problematic. Kazakhstan took part in the *Steppe Eagle* exercise in June 2016. It also took part in the CSTO Collective Peacekeeping Forces exercise, *Unbreakable Brotherhood*, in August 2016.

ACTIVE 39,000 (Army 20,000 Navy 3,000 Air 12,000 MoD 4,000) **Paramilitary 31,500**
Conscript liability 12 months (due to be abolished)

ORGANISATIONS BY SERVICE

Army 20,000
4 regional comd: Astana, East, West and Southern
FORCES BY ROLE
MANOEUVRE
  Armoured
    1 tk bde
  Mechanised
    3 mech bde

Air Manoeuvre
4 air aslt bde
COMBAT SUPPORT
3 arty bde
1 SSM unit
3 cbt engr bde
EQUIPMENT BY TYPE
ARMOURED FIGHTING VEHICLES
  MBT 300 T-72BA
  RECCE 100: 40 BRDM-2; 60 BRM-1
  IFV 609: 500 BMP-2; 107 BTR-80A; 2 BTR-3E
  APC 359
    APC (T) 150 MT-LB
    APC (W) 207: 190 BTR-80; 17 Cobra
    PPV 2 Arlan
ENGINEERING & MAINTENANCE VEHICLES
  AEV MT-LB
ANTI-TANK/ANTI-INFRASTRUCTURE
  MSL
    SP 3+: 3 BMP-T; HMMWV with 9K111-1 Konkurs (AT-5 Spandrel); 9P149 Shturm (MT-LB with AT-6 Spiral)
    MANPATS 9K111 Fagot (AT-4 Spigot); 9K111-1 Konkurs (AT-5 Spandrel); 9K115 Metis (AT-7 Saxhorn)
  GUNS 100mm 68 MT-12/T-12
ARTILLERY 611
  SP 246: **122mm** 126: 120 2S1 Gvozdika; 6 Semser; **152mm** 120 2S3 Akatsiya
  TOWED 150: **122mm** 100 D-30; **152mm** 50 2A65 Msta-B; (**122mm** up to 300 D-30 in store)
  GUN/MOR 120mm 25 2S9 NONA-S
  MRL 127: **122mm** 100 BM-21 Grad; **220mm** 3 TOS-1A; **300mm** 24: 6 BM-30 Smerch; 18 IMI Lynx (with 50 msl); (**122mm** 100 BM-21 Grad; **220mm** 180 9P140 Uragan all in store)
  MOR 63 **SP 120mm** 18 Cardom; **120mm** 45 2B11 Sani/M120
SURFACE-TO-SURFACE MISSILE LAUNCHERS
  SRBM • Conventional 12 9K79 Tochka (SS-21 Scarab)

Navy 3,000
EQUIPMENT BY TYPE
PATROL AND COASTAL COMBATANTS 24
  PCG 3 Kazakhstan with 2 quad lnchr with 3M24 Uran (SS-N-25 Switchblade) AShM, 1 3M47 Ghibka lnchr with Igla (SA-N-10 Grouse) SAM
  PBF 5: 2 Saygak; 3 Sea Dolphin
  PB 16: 4 Almaty; 3 Archangel; 1 Dauntless; 4 Sardar; 1 Turk (AB 25); 2 Zhuk (of which 1 may be operational); 1 Other
LOGISTICS AND SUPPORT • AGS 1 Zhaik

Coastal Defence
FORCES BY ROLE
MANOEUVRE
  Mechanised
    1 naval inf bde
EQUIPMENT BY TYPE
ARMOURED FIGHTING VEHICLES
  IFV 70 BTR-82A

Air Force 12,000 (incl Air Defence)
Flying hours   100 hrs/yr
FORCES BY ROLE
FIGHTER
  1 sqn with MiG-29/MiG-29UB Fulcrum
  2 sqn with MiG-31B/MiG-31BM Foxhound
FIGHTER/GROUND ATTACK
  1 sqn with MiG-27 Flogger D; MiG-23UB Flogger C
  1 sqn with Su-27/Su-27UB Flanker
  1 sqn with Su-27/Su-30SM Flanker
GROUND ATTACK
  1 sqn with Su-25 Frogfoot
TRANSPORT
  1 unit with Tu-134 Crusty; Tu-154 Careless
  1 sqn with An-12 Cub, An-26 Curl, An-30 Clank, An-72 Coaler, C-295M
TRAINING
  1 sqn with L-39 Albatros
ATTACK HELICOPTER
  5 sqn with Mi-24V Hind
TRANSPORT HELICOPTER
  Some sqn with Bell 205 (UH-1H); H145; Mi-8 Hip; Mi-17V-5 Hip; Mi-171Sh Hip; Mi-26 Halo
AIR DEFENCE
  Some regt with S-75M Volkhov (SA-2 Guideline); S-125 Neva (SA-3 Goa); S-300/S-300PS (SA-10/10B Grumble); 2K11 Krug (SA-4 Ganef); S-200 Angara (SA-5 Gammon); 2K12 Kub (SA-6 Gainful)
EQUIPMENT BY TYPE
AIRCRAFT 103 combat capable
  FTR 46: 12 MiG-29 Fulcrum; 2 MiG-29UB Fulcrum; 32 MiG-31/MiG-31BM Foxhound
  FGA 43: 12 MiG-27 Flogger D; 2 MiG-23UB Flogger C; 21 Su-27 Flanker; 4 Su-27UB Flanker; 4 Su-30SM
  ATK 14: 12 Su-25 Frogfoot; 2 Su-25UB Frogfoot
  ISR 1 An-30 Clank
  TPT 19: **Medium** 2 An-12 Cub; **Light** 16: 6 An-26 Curl, 2 An-72 Coaler; 6 C-295; 2 Tu-134 Crusty; **PAX** 1 Tu-154 Careless
  TRG 17 L-39 Albatros
HELICOPTERS
  ATK 20 Mi-24V Hind (some upgraded)
  MRH 24: 20 Mi-17V-5 Hip; 4 Mi-171Sh Hip
  TPT 13: **Heavy** 4 Mi-26 Halo; **Light** 9: 3 Bell 205 (UH-1H); 6 H145
UNMANNED AERIAL VEHICLES
  ISR Heavy 2 Wing Loong
AIR DEFENCE • SAM
  Long-range S-200 Angara (SA-5 Gammon); S-300 (SA-10 Grumble); 40+ S-300PS (SA-10B Grumble)
  Medium-range 2K11 Krug (SA-4 Ganef); S-75M Volkhov (SA-2 Guideline)
  Short-range 2K12 Kub (SA-6 Gainful); S-125 Neva (SA-3 Goa)
  Point-defence 9K35 Strela-10 (SA-13 Gopher)
AIR-LAUNCHED MISSILES
  AAM • IR R-60 (AA-8 Aphid); R-73 (AA-11 Archer); **IR/SARH** R-27 (AA-10 Alamo); **SARH** R-33 (AA-9 Amos); **ARH** R-77 (AA-12 Adder – on MiG-31BM)
  ASM Kh-23 (AS-7 Kerry)‡; Kh-25 (AS-10 Karen); Kh-29 (AS-14 Kedge)

ARM Kh-27 (AS-12 *Kegler*); Kh-28 (AS-9 *Kyle*); Kh-58 (AS-11 *Kilter*)

Paramilitary 31,500

National Guard ε20,000
Ministry of Interior

State Security Service 2,500

Border Service ε9,000
Ministry of Interior
EQUIPMENT BY TYPE
AIRCRAFT • **Light** 4 An-26 *Curl*
HELICOPTERS • **TPT** • **Medium** 15: 1 Mi-171; 14 Mi-171Sh

DEPLOYMENT

CÔTE D'IVOIRE
UN • UNOCI 1 obs

WESTERN SAHARA
UN • MINURSO 3 obs

UKRAINE
OSCE • Ukraine 4

Kyrgyzstan KGZ

Kyrgyzstani Som s		2015	2016	2017
GDP	s	424bn	444bn	
	US$	6.65bn	5.79bn	
per capita	US$	1,113	956	
Growth	%	3.5	2.2	
Inflation	%	6.5	1.1	
Def bdgt	s	n.k.	n.k.	
	US$	n.k.	n.k.	
US$1=s		63.70	76.50	

Population   5,727,553

Ethnic groups: Kyrgyz 71.7%; Uzbek 14.3%; Russian 7.2%; Dungan 1.1%; Uygur 0.9%; other or unspecified 4.8%

Age	0–14	15–19	20–24	25–29	30–64	65 plus
Male	15.4%	4.2%	4.7%	4.8%	17.9%	2.0%
Female	14.7%	4.1%	4.5%	4.8%	19.8%	3.2%

Capabilities

Kyrgyzstan maintains one of the smaller armed forces in Central Asia, with ageing land equipment and limited air capabilities. The July 2013 military doctrine detailed plans to reform the armed forces, with enhanced command and control, effective military logistics and a modern air-defence system. To date there appears to have been little progress, and combat readiness remains low with large numbers of conscripts. Kyrgyzstan maintains a close strategic relationship with Russia and is a member of both the CSTO and the SCO. Moscow also maintains a number of military bases in the country, including a squadron of upgraded Su-25 ground-attack aircraft at Kant air base, which it has leased since 2003. It was reported that Kazakhstan will provide military technical assistance for the repair and modernisation of Kyrgystan's armoured vehicles. Kyrgystan hosted military drills as part of the SCO's *Peace Mission* exercise in September 2016.

ACTIVE 10,900 (Army 8,500 Air 2,400) **Paramilitary 9,500**
Conscript liability 18 months

ORGANISATIONS BY SERVICE

Army 8,500
FORCES BY ROLE
SPECIAL FORCES
  1 SF bde
MANOEUVRE
  Mechanised
  2 MR bde
  1 (mtn) MR bde
COMBAT SUPPORT
  1 arty bde
  1 AD bde
EQUIPMENT BY TYPE
ARMOURED FIGHTING VEHICLES
  MBT 150 T-72
  RECCE 30 BRDM-2
  IFV 320: 230 BMP-1; 90 BMP-2
  APC • **APC (W)** 55: 25 BTR-70; 20 BTR-70M; 10 BTR-80
ANTI-TANK/ANTI-INFRASTRUCTURE
  MSL • **MANPATS** 9K11 *Malyutka* (AT-3 *Sagger*); 9K111 *Fagot* (AT-4 *Spigot*); 9K111-1 *Konkurs* (AT-5 *Spandrel*)
  RCL 73mm SPG-9
  GUNS 100mm 36: 18 MT-12/T-12; 18 M-1944
ARTILLERY 228
  SP 122mm 18 2S1 *Gvozdika*
  TOWED 123: **122mm** 107: 72 D-30; 35 M-30 (M-1938); **152mm** 16 D-1
  GUN/MOR 120mm 12 2S9 NONA-S
  MRL 21: **122mm** 15 BM-21; **220mm** 6 9P140 *Uragan*
  MOR 120mm 54: 6 2S12; 48 M-120
AIR DEFENCE
  SAM • **Point** 9K32 *Strela*-2 (SA-7 *Grail*)‡
  GUNS 48
    SP 23mm 24 ZSU-23-4
    TOWED 57mm 24 S-60

Air Force 2,400
FORCES BY ROLE
FIGHTER
  1 regt with L-39 *Albatros**
TRANSPORT
  1 regt with An-2 *Colt*; An-26 *Curl*
ATTACK/TRANSPORT HELICOPTER
  1 regt with Mi-24 *Hind*; Mi-8 *Hip*
AIR DEFENCE
  Some regt with S-125 *Pechora* (SA-3 *Goa*); S-75 *Dvina* (SA-2 *Guideline*)

EQUIPMENT BY TYPE
AIRCRAFT 4 combat capable
  TPT • **Light** 6: 4 An-2 *Colt*; 2 An-26 *Curl*
  TRG 4 L-39 *Albatros**
HELICOPTERS
  ATK 2 Mi-24 *Hind*
  TPT • **Medium** 8 Mi-8 *Hip*
AIR DEFENCE • SAM
  Medium-range 2K11 *Krug* (SA-4 *Ganef*); S-75 *Dvina* (SA-2 *Guideline*)
  Short-range S-125 *Pechora* (SA-3 *Goa*)

Paramilitary 9,500

Border Guards 5,000 (KGZ conscript, RUS officers)

Internal Troops 3,500

National Guard 1,000

DEPLOYMENT

MOLDOVA
OSCE • Moldova 1

SERBIA
OSCE • Kosovo 3

SOUTH SUDAN
UN • UNMISS 2; 2 obs

SUDAN
UN • UNAMID 2 obs
UN • UNISFA 1 obs

UKRAINE
OSCE • Ukraine 16

FOREIGN FORCES

Russia ε500 Military Air Forces: 13 Su-25SM *Frogfoot*; 2 Mi-8 *Hip*

Moldova MDA

Moldovan Leu L		2015	2016	2017
GDP	L	122bn	133bn	
	US$	6.48bn	6.65bn	
per capita	US$	1,822	1,872	
Growth	%	-0.5	2	
Inflation	%	9.6	6.8	
Def bdgt	L	457m	581m	479m
	US$	24m	29m	
FMA (US)	US$	11m	13m	13m
US$1=L		18.87	19.96	
Population	3,510,485			

Age	0–14	15–19	20–24	25–29	30–64	65 plus
Male	9.0%	3.0%	3.7%	4.4%	23.6%	4.7%
Female	8.7%	2.8%	3.4%	4.2%	24.7%	7.5%

Capabilities

The primary role of the Moldovan armed forces is to maintain territorial integrity. The forces are constitutionally neutral. Chisinau has looked to continue to build relations with both Europe and NATO, and signed up to the NATO Defence Capacity Building Initiative in September 2014. The dispute over the separatist region of Transdniestr continues, with Russian forces still present there. There is concern over a 'hybrid' threat from Moscow. As of the third quarter of 2016, a draft National Defence Strategy was out for public comment; key aims include: 'providing proper financial support to the development of national defense system'; 'providing adequate human and material resources for the national defense system'; and 'ensuring the capacity of controlling and protecting the airspace'. Moldova deployed troops with KFOR and the services exercise with NATO states.

ACTIVE 5,150 (Army 3,250 Air 600 Logistic Support 1,300) **Paramilitary 2,400**
Conscript liability 12 months (3 months for university graduates)

RESERVE 58,000 (Joint 58,000)

ORGANISATIONS BY SERVICE

Army 1,300; 1,950 conscript (total 3,250)
FORCES BY ROLE
SPECIAL FORCES
  1 SF bn
MANOEUVRE
  Light
  3 mot inf bde
  1 lt inf bn
  Other
  1 gd bn
COMBAT SUPPORT
  1 arty bn
  1 engr bn
  1 NBC coy
  1 sigs bn
EQUIPMENT BY TYPE
ARMOURED FIGHTING VEHICLES
  APC 163
    APC (T) 69: 9 BTR-D; 60 MT-LB (variants)
    APC (W) 94: 13 BTR-80; 81 TAB-71
  ABCV 44 BMD-1
ANTI-TANK/ANTI-INFRASTRUCTURE
  MSL • **MANPATS** 9K111 *Fagot* (AT-4 *Spigot*); 9K111-1 *Konkurs* (AT-5 *Spandrel*)
  RCL **73mm** SPG-9
  GUNS **100mm** 37 MT-12
ARTILLERY 221
  TOWED 69: **122mm** 17 (M-30) M-1938; **152mm** 52: 21 2A36 *Giatsint*-B; 31 D-20
  GUN/MOR • **SP 120mm** 9 2S9 NONA-S
  MRL **220mm** 11 9P140 *Uragan*
  MOR 132: **82mm** 75 BM-37; **120mm** 57: 50 M-1989; 7 PM-38

RADAR • LAND 5: 2 ARK-1; 3 SNAR-10
AIR DEFENCE • GUNS • TOWED 39: 23mm 28 ZU-23; 57mm 11 S-60

Air Force 600 (incl 250 conscripts)
FORCES BY ROLE
TRANSPORT
   1 sqn with An-2 *Colt*; An-72 *Coaler*; Mi-8MTV-1/PS *Hip*; Yak-18
AIR DEFENCE
   1 regt with S-125 *Neva* (SA-3 *Goa*)
EQUIPMENT BY TYPE
AIRCRAFT
   TPT • Light 5: 2 An-2 *Colt*; 2 An-72 *Coaler*; 1 Yak-18
HELICOPTERS
   TPT • Medium 6: 2 Mi-8PS *Hip*; 4 Mi-8MTV-1 *Hip*
AIR DEFENCE • SAM • Short-range 3 S-125 *Neva* (SA-3 *Goa*)

Paramilitary 2,400
Ministry of Interior

OPON 900 (riot police)
Ministry of Interior

DEPLOYMENT
Legal provisions for foreign deployment:
Constitution: Codified constitution (1994)
Decision on deployment of troops abroad: By the parliament (Art. 66)

ALBANIA
OSCE • Albania 1

CENTRAL AFRICAN REPUBLIC
UN • MINUSCA 1; 2 obs

CÔTE D'IVOIRE
UN • UNOCI 1 obs

LIBERIA
UN • UNMIL 1 obs

SERBIA
NATO • KFOR 41
UN • UNMIK 1 obs

SOUTH SUDAN
UN • UNMISS 1; 3 obs

UKRAINE
OSCE • Ukraine 31

FOREIGN FORCES
Denmark OSCE 1
Estonia OSCE 1
Germany OSCE 2
Kyrgyzstan OSCE 1
Russia ε1,500 (including 441 peacekeepers) 7 Mi-24 *Hind*/Mi-8 *Hip*
Sweden OSCE 3
Ukraine 10 mil obs (Joint Peacekeeping Force)
United Kingdom OSCE 2
United States OSCE 3

Russia RUS

Russian Rouble r		2015	2016	2017
GDP	r	80.8tr	85.6tr	
	US$	1.33tr	1.27tr	
per capita	US$	9,243	8,838	
Growth	%	-3.7	-0.8	
Inflation	%	15.5	7.2	
Def exp [a]	r	4.03tr		
	US$	66.1bn		
Def bdgt	r	3.16tr	3.15tr	2.84tr
	US$	51.9bn	46.6bn	
US$1=r		60.94	67.49	

[a] Calculated to be comparable with the NATO definition of defence expenditure

Population 142,355,415

Ethnic groups: Tatar 3.71%; Armenian 0.8%; Bashkir 1.1%; Chechen 1%; Chuvash 1%

Age	0–14	15–19	20–24	25–29	30–64	65 plus
Male	8.7%	2.3%	2.7%	4.1%	24.2%	4.3%
Female	8.2%	2.2%	2.6%	4.0%	27.1%	9.6%

Capabilities

Russia's nuclear and conventional military capabilities continue to benefit from sustained government support, even in the face of Western sanctions and problems with the wider economy. The development and fielding of replacement strategic delivery systems continues, while deliveries of conventional weapon systems to the armed services are also being maintained, although some projects have been delayed or initial acquisition numbers reduced. Russian combat operations in Syria continued throughout the course of 2016, despite President Putin's claims in March 2016 that its main objectives since the start of the operation in September 2015 had been met. Although the number of combat aircraft deployed in-country was reduced, air attacks continued, including the use of air-, surface- and submarine-launched cruise missiles. The naval base at Tartus was also bolstered with the deployment of an S-300V4 (SA-23) long-range surface-to-air-missile system. The intervention is providing the Russian military with valuable operational experience with a range of new systems, at the same time as it tests its ability to support an expeditionary operation, and identifies capability gaps or capability shortfalls that need to be fully addressed. These include unmanned aerial vehicles and air-launched precision-guided weapons. Military support for Ukrainian separatists also continues to be provided. Russia's Western and Northern military districts were a renewed focus in 2016, with units being re-equipped with modern systems and readiness tests continuing. 'Snap exercises' were held across all the military regions in the year. One effect of the country's deteriorating economic situation has been the delay in concluding the next State Armament Programme; originally intended to have been started in 2016, this has now been pushed back to 2018. (See pp. 183–96.)

ACTIVE 831,000 (Army 270,000 Navy 150,000 Air 165,000 Strategic Rocket Force 50,000 Airborne 45,000 Special Operations Forces 1,000 Command and Support 150,000) Paramilitary 659,000
Conscript liability 12 months (conscripts now can opt for contract service immediately, which entails a 24-month contract)

RESERVE 2,000,000 (all arms)
Some 2,000,000 with service within last 5 years; reserve obligation to age 50

ORGANISATIONS BY SERVICE

Strategic Deterrent Forces ε80,000 (incl personnel assigned from the Navy and Aerospace Forces)

Navy
EQUIPMENT BY TYPE
SUBMARINES • STRATEGIC • SSBN 13:
  3 *Kalmar* (*Delta* III) with 16 R-29R *Volna* (SS-N-18 *Stingray*) nuclear SLBM
  6 *Delfin* (*Delta* IV) with 16 R-29RMU *Sineva* (SS-N-23 *Skiff*) nuclear SLBM (of which 1 in refit)
  1 *Akula* (*Typhoon*)† in reserve with capacity for 20 *Bulava* (SS-N-32) nuclear SLBM (trials/testing)
  3 *Borey* with 16 *Bulava* (SS-N-32) nuclear SLBM

Strategic Rocket Force Troops 50,000
3 Rocket Armies operating silo and mobile launchers organised in 12 divs. Regt normally with 10 silos (6 for RS-20/SS-18), or 9 mobile lnchr, and one control centre
FORCES BY ROLE
SURFACE-TO-SURFACE MISSILE
  10 ICBM regt with RS-12M *Topol* (SS-25 *Sickle*)
  8 ICBM regt with RS-12M2 *Topol*-M (SS-27 mod 1)
  3 ICBM regt with RS-18 (SS-19 *Stiletto*)
  9 ICBM regt with RS-20 (SS-18 *Satan*)
  6 ICBM regt with RS-24 *Yars* (SS-27 mod 2)
  8 ICBM regt (forming) with RS-24 *Yars* (SS-27 mod 2)
EQUIPMENT BY TYPE
SURFACE-TO-SURFACE MISSILE LAUNCHERS
  ICBM • Nuclear 324: ε90 RS-12M *Topol* (SS-25 *Sickle*) (mobile single warhead); 60 RS-12M2 *Topol*-M (SS-27 mod 1) silo-based (single warhead); 18 RS-12M2 *Topol*-M (SS-27 mod 1) road mobile (single warhead); 30 RS-18 (SS-19 *Stiletto*) (mostly mod 3, 6 MIRV per msl); 54 RS-20 (SS-18 *Satan*) (mostly mod 5, 10 MIRV per msl); 67 RS-24 *Yars* (SS-27 mod 2; ε3 MIRV per msl) road mobile; 5 RS-24 *Yars* (SS-27 mod 2; ε3 MIRV per msl) silo-based

Long-Range Aviation Command
FORCES BY ROLE
BOMBER
  1 sqn with Tu-160/Tu-160M1 *Blackjack*
  3 sqn with Tu-95MS/MS mod/MSM *Bear*
EQUIPMENT BY TYPE
AIRCRAFT
  BBR 76: 11 Tu-160 *Blackjack* with Kh-55/Kh-55SM (AS-15A/B *Kent*); 5 Tu-160M1 *Blackjack* with Kh-55/Kh-55SM (AS-15A/B *Kent*)/Kh-102 nuclear ALCM; 48 Tu-95MS/MS mod *Bear* H with Kh-55/Kh-55SM (AS-15A/B *Kent*)/Kh-102 nuclear ALCM; 12 Tu-95MSM *Bear* H with Kh-55/Kh-55SM (AS-15A/B *Kent*)/Kh-102 nuclear ALCM

Space Command
EQUIPMENT BY TYPE
SATELLITES 94
  COMMUNICATIONS 57: 2 *Garpun*; 13 *Gonets*-D/M (dual-use); 3 Mod *Globus* (*Raduga*-1M); 4 *Meridian*; 3 *Parus*; 3 *Raduga*; 21 *Rodnik* (*Strela*-3M); 8 *Strela*-3
  EARLY WARNING 1 *Tundra*
  NAVIGATION/POSITIONING/TIMING 26 GLONASS
  ISR 6: 2 *Bars*-M; 1 GEO-IK 2; 1 *Kondor*; 2 *Persona*
  ELINT/SIGINT 4: 3 *Liana* (*Lotos*-S); 1 *Tselina*-2
RADAR 12; Russia leases ground-based radar stations in Baranovichi (Belarus) and Balkhash (Kazakhstan). It also has radars on its own territory at Lekhtusi (St Petersburg); Armavir (Krasnodar); Olenegorsk (Murmansk); Mishelekvka (Irkuts); Kaliningrad; Pechora (Komi); Yeniseysk (Krasnoyarsk); Baranul (Altayskiy); Orsk (Orenburg) and Gorodets/Kovylkino (OTH)

Aerospace Defence Command
FORCES BY ROLE
AIR DEFENCE
  2 AD div HQ
  3 SAM regt with S-300PM/PM1 (SA-20 *Gargoyle*)
  6 SAM regt with S-400 (SA-21 *Growler*); 96K6 *Pantsir*-S1 (SA-22 *Greyhound*)
EQUIPMENT BY TYPE
AIR DEFENCE • SAM 186
  Long-range 150: 50 S-300PM (SA-20 *Gargoyle*); 100 S-400 (SA-21 *Growler*)
  Short-range 36 96K6 *Pantsir*-S1 (SA-22 *Greyhound*)
  MISSILE DEFENCE 68 53T6 (ABM-3 *Gazelle*); (32 51T6 (ABM-4 *Gorgon*) in store; probably destroyed)
  RADAR 1 ABM engagement system located at Sofrino (Moscow)

Army ε270,000 (incl conscripts)
4 military districts (West (HQ St Petersburg), Centre (HQ Yekaterinburg), South (HQ Rostov-on-Don) & East (HQ Khabarovsk), each with a unified Joint Strategic Command
FORCES BY ROLE
Formations marked as (-) are believed to have committed some or all of their personnel and equipment to newly forming divisions

COMMAND
11 army HQ
1 corps HQ
SPECIAL FORCES
7 (Spetsnaz) SF bde
MANOEUVRE
Reconnaissance
2 recce bde
Armoured
1 (4th) tk div (2 tk regt, 1 arty regt, 1 AD regt)
1 (90th) tk div (forming)
2 tk bde (1 armd recce bn; 3 tk bn; 1 MR bn; 1 arty bn; 1 MRL bn; 2 AD bn; 1 engr bn; 1 EW coy; 1 NBC coy)
2 tk bde(-)
3 (3rd, 144th & 150th) MR div (forming)
15 (BMP) MR bde (1 armd recce bn; 1 tk bn; 3 armd inf bn; 2 arty bn; 1 MRL bn; 1 AT bn; 2 AD bn; 1 engr bn; 1 EW coy; 1 NBC coy)
2 (BMP) MR bde(-)
Mechanised
1 (2nd) MR div (2 MR regt, 1 arty regt, 1 AD regt)
11 (BTR/MT-LB) MR bde (1 recce bn; 1 tk bn; 3 mech inf bn; 2 arty bn; 1 MRL bn; 1 AT bn; 2 AD bn; 1 engr bn; 1 EW coy; 1 NBC coy)
1 (BTR) MR bde(-)
2 MR bde (4–5 mech inf bn; 1 arty bn; 1 AD bn; 1 engr bn)
3 (lt/mtn) MR bde (1 recce bn; 2 mech inf bn; 1 arty bn)
1 (lt/mtn) MR bde(-)
1 (18th) MGA div (2 MGA regt; 1 arty regt; 1 tk bn; 2 AD bn)
SURFACE-TO-SURFACE MISSILE
8 SRBM/GLCM bde with 9K720 Iskander-M/K (SS-26 Stone/SS-C-7)
1 SRBM/GLCM bde with 9K720 Iskander-M/K (SS-26 Stone/SS-C-7) (forming)
1 SRBM bde with 9K79-1 Tochka-U (SS-21B Scarab)
COMBAT SUPPORT
8 arty bde
2 indep hy arty bn (2 more forming)
4 MRL bde
1 MRL regt
4 engr bde
1 MP bde
5 NBC bde
10 NBC regt
COMBAT SERVICE SUPPORT
10 log bde
AIR DEFENCE
13 AD bde
EQUIPMENT BY TYPE
ARMOURED FIGHTING VEHICLES
MBT 2,700: 1,100 T-72B/BA; 800 T-72B3; 450 T-80BV/U; 350 T-90/T-90A; (17,500 in store: 2,800 T-55; 2,500 T-62; 2,000 T-64A/B; 7,000 T-72/T-72A/B; 3,000 T-80B/BV/U; 200 T-90)
RECCE 1,700: 1,000 BRDM-2/2A; (1,000+ BRDM-2 in store); 700 BRM-1K (CP)
IFV 4,900: 500 BMP-1; 3,000 BMP-2; 500 BMP-3; 100 BTR-80A; 800 BTR-82A/AM; (8,500 in store: 7,000 BMP-1; 1,500 BMP-2)
APC 6,100+

APC (T) 3,500+: some BMO-T; 3,500 MT-LB; (2,000 MT-LB in store)
APC (W) 2,600: 800 BTR-60 (all variants); 200 BTR-70 (all variants); 1,500 BTR-80; 100+ BPM-97 Dozor; (4,000 BTR-60/70 in store)
AUV 100+: 100+ GAZ Tigr; some IVECO LMV
ENGINEERING & MAINTENANCE VEHICLES
AEV BAT-2; IMR; IMR-2; IRM; MT-LB
ARV BMP-1; BREM-1/64/K/L; BTR-50PK(B); M1977; MTP-LB; RM-G; T-54/55; VT-72A
VLB KMM; MT-55A; MTU; MTU-20; MTU-72; PMM-2
MW BMR-3M; GMX-3; MCV-2 (reported); MTK; MTK-2
ANTI-TANK/ANTI-INFRASTRUCTURE
MSL
SP BMP-T with 9K120 Ataka (AT-9 Spiral 2); 9P149 with 9K114 Shturm (AT-6 Spiral); 9P149M with 9K132 Shturm-SM (AT-9 Spiral-2); 9P157-2 with 9K123 Khrisantema (AT-15 Springer)
MANPATS 9K111M Fagot (AT-4 Spigot); 9K111-1 Konkurs (AT-5 Spandrel); 9K115 Metis (AT-7 Saxhorn); 9K115-1 Metis-M (AT-13 Saxhorn 2); 9K115-2 Metis-M1 (AT-13 Saxhorn 2); 9K135 Kornet (AT-14 Spriggan)
RCL 73mm SPG-9
GUNS • TOWED 100mm 526 MT-12; (**100mm** 2,000 T-12/MT-12 in store)
ARTILLERY 4,316+
SP 1,596: **122mm** 150 2S1 Gvozdika; **152mm** 1,386: 800 2S3 Akatsiya; 100 2S5 Giatsint-B; 450 2S19 Msta-S; 36 2S33 Msta-SM; **203mm** 60 2S7M Malka; (4,260 in store: **122mm** 2,000 2S1 Gvozdika; **152mm** 2,000: 1,000 2S3 Akatsiya; 850 2S5 Giatsint-S; 150 2S19 Msta-S; **203mm** 260 2S7 Pion)
TOWED 150: **152mm** 150 2A65 Msta-B; (12,415 in store: **122mm** 8,150: 4,400 D-30; 3,750 M-30 (M-1938); **130mm** 650 M-46; **152mm** 3,575: 1,100 2A36 Giatsint-B; 600 2A65 Msta-B; 1,075 D-20; 700 D-1 (M-1943); 100 M-1937 (ML-20); **203mm** 40 B-4M)
GUN/MOR 180+
SP 120mm 80+: 30 2S23 NONA-SVK; 50+ 2S34
TOWED 120mm 100 2B16 NONA-K
MRL 850+ **122mm** 550 BM-21 Grad/Tornado-G; **220mm** 200 9P140 Uragan; some TOS-1A; **300mm** 100 9A52 Smerch; (3,220 in store: **122mm** 2,420: 2,000 BM-21 Grad; 420 9P138; **132mm** 100 BM-13; **220mm** 700 9P140 Uragan)
MOR 1,540+: **82mm** 800+ 2B14; **120mm** 700 2S12 Sani; **240mm** 40 2S4 Tulpan; (2,590 in store: **120mm** 1,900: 1,000 2S12 Sani; 900 M-1938 (PM-38); **160mm** 300 M-160; **SP 240mm** 390 2S4 Tulpan)
SURFACE-TO-SURFACE MISSILE LAUNCHERS
SRBM 120:
Dual-capable 72 9K720 Iskander-M (SS-26 Stone)
Conventional 48 9K79-1 Tochka-U (SS-21B Scarab); (some Scud in store)
GLCM • Dual-capable Some Iskander-K (SS-C-7)
UNMANNED AERIAL VEHICLES
ISR • Heavy Tu-143 Reys; Tu-243 Reys/Tu-243 Reys D; Tu-300 Korshun **Light** BLA-07; Pchela-1; Pchela-2
AIR DEFENCE
SAM 1,520+
Long-range S-300V (SA-12 Gladiator/Giant); S-300V4 (SA-23)

Medium-range 350+ 9K317 *Buk*-M1-2/M2 (SA-11 *Gadfly*/SA-17 *Grizzly*)
Short-range 120+ 9K331/9K332 *Tor*-M/M1/M2/M2U (SA-15 *Gauntlet*)
Point-defence 1,050+: 250+ 2K22M *Tunguska* (SA-19 *Grison*); 400 9K33M3 *Osa-AKM* (SA-8B *Gecko*); 400 9K35M3 *Strela*-10 (SA-13 *Gopher*); 9K310 *Igla*-1 (SA-16 *Gimlet*); 9K34 *Strela*-3 (SA-14 *Gremlin*); 9K38 *Igla* (SA-18 *Grouse*); 9K333 *Verba*; 9K338 *Igla*-S (SA-24 *Grinch*)
GUNS
SP 23mm ZSU-23-4
TOWED 23mm ZU-23-2; **57mm** S-60

Reserves
Cadre formations
FORCES BY ROLE
MANOEUVRE
Mechanised
13 MR bde

Navy ε150,000 (incl conscripts)
4 major fleet organisations (Northern Fleet, Pacific Fleet, Baltic Fleet, Black Sea Fleet) and Caspian Sea Flotilla
EQUIPMENT BY TYPE
SUBMARINES 62
STRATEGIC • SSBN 13:
  3 *Kalmar* (*Delta* III) with 16 R-29R *Volna* (SS-N-18 *Stingray*) nuclear SLBM, 2 single 400mm TT, 4 single 533mm TT
  6 *Delfin* (*Delta* IV) with 16 R-29RMU *Sineva* (SS-N-23 *Skiff*) nuclear SLBM, 4 single 533mm TT (of which 1 in refit)
  1 *Akula* (*Typhoon*)† in reserve for training with capacity for 20 *Bulava* (SS-N-32) nuclear SLBM, 6 single 533mm TT
  3 *Borey* with 16 *Bulava* (SS-N-32) nuclear SLBM, 6 single 533mm TT
TACTICAL 49
  SSGN 9:
    8 *Antyey* (*Oscar* II) (of which 3 in refit) with 2 12-cell lnchr with 3M45 *Granit* (SS-N-19 *Shipwreck*) AShM, 2 single 650mm TT each with T-65 HWT, 4 single 553mm TT
    1 *Yasen* (*Graney*) with 1 octuple VLS with 3M54 (SS-N-27 *Sizzler*) AShM/3M55 *Onyx* (SS-N-26 *Strobile*) AShM/3M14 *Kalibr* (SS-N-30) dual-capable LACM; 8 single 533mm TT
  SSN 17:
    2 *Schuka*-B (*Akula* II) with 4 single 533mm TT fitted for 3M10 *Granat* (SS-N-21 *Sampson*) LACM (weapons in store), 4 single 650mm TT with T-65 HWT
    9 *Schuka*-B (*Akula* I) with 4 single 533mm TT fitted for 3M10 *Granat* (SS-N-21 *Sampson*) LACM (weapons in store), 4 single 650mm TT with T-65 HWT (of which 5 in refit)
    2 *Kondor* (*Sierra* II) with 4 single 533mm TT fitted for 3M10 *Granat* (SS-N-21 *Sampson*) LACM (weapons in store), 4 single 650mm TT with T-65 HWT
    1 *Barracuda* (*Sierra* I) (in reserve) with 4 single 533mm TT fitted for 3M10 *Granat* (SS-N-21 *Sampson*) LACM (weapons in store), RPK-2 (SS-N-15 *Starfish*) and T-53 HWT, 4 single 650mm TT with RPK-7 (SS-N-16 *Stallion*) AShM and T-65 HWT
    3 *Schuka* (*Victor* III) with 4 single 533mm TT fitted for 3M10 *Granat* (SS-N-21 *Sampson*) LACM (weapons in store), 2 single 650mm TT with T-65 HWT
  SSK 23:
    16 *Paltus* (*Kilo*) with 6 single 533mm TT with T-53 HWT
    6 *Varshavyanka* (*Kilo*) with 6 single 533mm TT with T-53 HWT/3M54 (SS-N-27 *Sizzler*) AShM/3M14 *Kalibr* (SS-N-30) dual-capable LACM
    1 *Lada* (AIP fitted) with 6 single 533mm TT
PRINCIPAL SURFACE COMBATANTS 33
  AIRCRAFT CARRIERS • CV 1 *Admiral Kuznetsov* with 1 12-cell VLS with 3M45 *Granit* (SS-N-19 *Shipwreck*) AShM, 4 sextuple VLS with 3K95 *Kindzhal* (SA-N-9 *Gauntlet*) SAM, 2 RBU-12000 *Udav* 1 A/S mor, 8 *Kortik* (CADS-N-1) CIWS with 3M311 (SA-N-11 *Grison*) SAM, 6 AK630 CIWS (capacity 18–24 Su-33 *Flanker* D Ftr ac; MiG-29KR FGA ac; 15 Ka-27 *Helix* ASW hel, 2 Ka-31R *Helix* AEW hel)
  CRUISERS 5
  CGHMN 2:
    2 *Orlan* (*Kirov*) with 10 twin VLS with 3M45 *Granit* (SS-N-19 *Shipwreck*) AShM, 2 twin lnchr with *Osa*-M (SA-N-4 *Gecko*) SAM, 12 octuple VLS with *Fort/Fort* M (SA-N-6 *Grumble*/SA-N-20 *Gargoyle*) SAM, 2 octuple VLS with 3K95 *Kindzhal* (SA-N-9 *Gauntlet*) SAM, 10 single 533mm ASTT, 1 RBU 12000 *Udav* 1 A/S mor, 2 RBU 1000 *Smerch* 3 A/S mor, 6 *Kortik* (CADS-N-1) CIWS with 3M311 (SA-N-11 *Grison*) SAM, 1 twin 130mm gun (capacity 3 Ka-27 *Helix* ASW hel) (of which 1 non-operational; undergoing extensive refit and expected to return to service in 2018)
  CGHM 3:
    3 *Atlant* (*Slava*) with 8 twin lnchr with *Vulkan* (SS-N-12 mod 2 *Sandbox*) AShM, 8 octuple VLS with *Fort/Fort* M (SA-N-6 *Grumble*/SA-N-20 *Gargoyle*) SAM, 2 single lnchr with *Osa*-M (SA-N-4 *Gecko*) SAM, 2 quintuple 533mm ASTT, 2 RBU 6000 *Smerch* 2 A/S mor, 6 AK650 CIWS, 1 twin 130mm gun (capacity 1 Ka-27 *Helix* ASW hel) (of which 1 currently non-operational; has been in refit since 2011)
  DESTROYERS 15
  DDGHM 14:
    5 *Sarych* (*Sovremenny*) (of which 2 in refit†) with 2 quad lnchr with 3M80 *Moskit* (SS-N-22 *Sunburn*) AShM, 2 twin lnchr with 3K90 *Uragan* (SA-N-7 *Gadfly*) SAM, 2 twin 533mm TT, 2 RBU 1000 *Smerch* 3 A/S mor, 4 AK630M CIWS, 2 twin 130mm guns (capacity 1 Ka-27 *Helix* ASW hel)
    8 *Fregat* (*Udaloy* I) with 2 quad lnchr with *Rastrub* (SS-N-14 *Silex*) AShM/ASW, 8 octuple VLS with 3K95 *Kindzhal* (SA-N-9 *Gauntlet*) SAM, 2 quad 533mm ASTT, 2 RBU 6000 *Smerch* 2 A/S mor, 4 AK630 CIWS, 2 100mm guns (capacity 2 Ka-27 *Helix* ASW hel)
    1 *Fregat* (*Udaloy* II) with 2 quad lnchr with 3M80 *Moskit* (SS-N-22 *Sunburn*) AShM, 8 octuple VLS

with 3K95 *Kindzhal* (SA-N-9 *Gauntlet*) SAM, 2 *Kortik* (CADS-N-1) CIWS with 3M311 (SA-N-11 *Grison*) SAM, 10 single 533mm ASTT, 2 RBU 6000 *Smerch* 2 A/S mor, 1 twin 130mm gun (capacity 2 Ka-27 *Helix* ASW hel)

DDGM 1:
1 *Komsomolets Ukrainy* (*Kashin* mod) with 2 quad lnchr with 3M24 *Uran* (SS-N-25 *Switchblade*) AShM, 2 twin lnchr with *Volnya* (SA-N-1 *Goa*) SAM, 5 single 533mm ASTT, 2 RBU 6000 *Smerch* 2 A/S mor, 1 twin 76mm gun

FRIGATES 12
FFGHM 8:
2 *Admiral Grigorovich* (*Krivak* IV) with 1 8-cell VLS with 3M54 (SS-N-27 *Sizzler*) AShM/3M55 *Oniks* (SS-N-26 *Strobile*)/3M14 *Kalibr* (SS-N-30) dual-capable LACM, 2 12-cell VLS with 9M317E *Shtil*-1 SAM, 2 twin 533mm TT, 1 RBU 6000 A/S mor, 2 AK630 CIWS, 1 100mm gun (capacity 1 Ka-27 *Helix* ASW hel)
2 *Jastreb* (*Neustrashimy*) with 2 quad lnchr with 3M24 *Uran* (SS-N-25 *Switchblade*) AShM, 4 octuple VLS with 3K95 *Kindzhal* (SA-N-9 *Gauntlet*) SAM, 6 single 533mm ASTT, 1 RBU 12000 *Udav* 1 A/S mor, 2 *Kortik* (CADS-N-1) CIWS with 3M311 (SA-N-11 *Grison*) SAM, 1 100mm gun (capacity 1 Ka-27 *Helix* ASW hel)
1 *Steregushchiy* (Project 20380) with 2 quad lnchr with 3M24 *Uran* (SS-N-25 *Switchblade*) AShM, 2 quad 324mm ASTT, 1 *Kortik* (CADS-N-1) CIWS with 3M311 (SA-N-11 *Grison*) SAM, 2 AK630 CIWS, 1 100mm gun (capacity 1 Ka-27 *Helix* ASW hel)
3 *Steregushchiy* (Project 20381) with 2 quad lnchr with 3M24 *Uran* (SS-N-25 *Switchblade*) AShM, 1 12-cell VLS with 3K96 *Redut* (SA-NX-28) SAM (in test), 2 quad 324mm ASTT, 1 *Kortik* (CADS-N-1) CIWS with 3M311 (SA-N-11 *Grison*) SAM, 2 AK630 CIWS, 1 100mm gun (capacity 1 Ka-27 *Helix* ASW hel)

FFGM 4:
1 *Gepard* with 2 quad lnchr with 3M24 *Uran* (SS-N-25 *Switchblade*) AShM, 1 twin lnchr with *Osa*-M (SA-N-4 *Gecko*) SAM, 2 AK630 CIWS, 1 76mm gun
1 *Gepard* with 1 8-cell VLS with 3M14 *Kalibr* (SS-N-30) dual capable LACM, 2 quad lnchr with 3M24 *Uran* (SS-N-25 *Switchblade*) AShM, 1 twin lnchr with *Osa*-M (SA-N-4 *Gecko*) SAM, 1 AK630 CIWS, 1 76mm gun
1 *Burevestnik* (*Krivak* I mod)† with 1 quad lnchr with *Rastrub* (SS-N-14 *Silex*) AShM/ASW, 1 twin lnchr with *Osa*-M (SA-N-4 *Gecko*) SAM, 2 533mm ASTT, 2 RBU 6000 *Smerch* 2 A/S mor, 2 twin 76mm guns
1 *Burevestnik* M (*Krivak* II) each with 1 quad lnchr with RPK-3 *Rastrub* (SS-N-14 *Silex*) AShM/ASW, 2 twin lnchr with 10 *Osa*-M (SA-N-4 *Gecko* SAM), 2 quad 533mm ASTT, 2 RBU 6000 *Smerch* 2 A/S mor, 2 100mm guns

PATROL AND COASTAL COMBATANTS 95
CORVETTES 48

FSGM 19
5 *Grad Sviyazhsk* (*Buyan*-M) with 1 octuple VLS with 3M54 (SS-N-27 *Sizzler*) AShM/3M14 *Kalibr* (SS-N-30) dual-capable LACM, 2 sextuple lnchr with 3M47 *Gibka* (SA-N-10 *Grouse*) SAM, 1 AK630-M2 CIWS, 1 100mm gun
2 *Sivuch* (*Dergach*) with 2 quad lnchr with 3M80 *Moskit* (SS-N-22 *Sunburn*) AShM, 1 twin lnchr with *Osa*-M (SA-N-4 *Gecko*) SAM, 2 AK630 CIWS, 1 76mm gun
12 *Ovod* (*Nanuchka* III) with 2 triple lnchr with P-120 *Malakhit* (SS-N-9 *Siren*) AShM, 1 twin lnchr with *Osa*-M (SA-N-4 *Gecko*) SAM, 1 AK630 CIWS, 1 76mm gun

FSM 29:
1 *Albatros* (*Grisha* III) with 1 twin lnchr with *Osa*-M (SA-N-4 *Gecko*) SAM, 2 twin 533mm ASTT, 2 RBU 6000 *Smerch* 2 A/S mor, 1 twin 57mm gun
19 *Albatros* (*Grisha* V) with 1 twin lnchr with Osa-M (SA-N-4 *Gecko*) SAM, 2 twin 533mm ASTT, 1 RBU 6000 *Smerch* 2 A/S mor, 1 76mm gun
3 *Astrakhan* (*Buyan*) with 1 sextuple lnchr with 3M47 *Gibka* (SA-N-10 *Grouse*) SAM, 1 A-215 *Grad*-M 122mm MRL, 2 AK630 CIWS, 1 100mm gun
6 *Parchim* II with 2 quad lnchr with *Strela*-2 (SA-N-5 *Grail*) SAM, 2 twin 533mm ASTT, 2 RBU 6000 *Smerch* 2 A/S mor, 1 AK630 CIWS, 1 76mm gun

PCFG 21:
3 *Molnya* (*Tarantul* II) with 2 twin lnchr with P-15M *Termit* (SS-N-2C/D *Styx*) AShM, 1 quad lnchr (manual aiming) with *Strela*-2 (SA-N-5 *Grail*) SAM, 2 AK630 CIWS, 1 76mm gun
18 *Molnya* (*Tarantul* III) with 2 twin lnchr with 3M80 *Moskit* (SS-N-22 *Sunburn*) AShM, 1 quad lnchr (manual aiming) with *Strela*-2 (SA-N-5 *Grail*) SAM, 2 AK630 CIWS, 1 76mm gun

PBM 12 *Grachonok* with 1 quad lnchr with 3M47 *Gibka* (SA-N-10 *Grouse*), (original design was as diving tender)
PBF 10: 8 *Raptor* (capacity 20 troops); 2 *Mangust*
PBR 4 *Shmel* with 1 76mm gun

MINE WARFARE • MINE COUNTERMEASURES 45
MHO 2 *Rubin* (*Gorya*) with 2 quad lnchr with *Strela*-2 (SA-N-5 *Grail*) SAM, 1 AK630 CIWS, 1 76mm gun
MSO 11: 10 *Akvamaren* (*Natya*); 1 *Agat* (*Natya* II) (all with 2 quad lnchr (manual aiming) with *Strela*-2 (SA-N-5 *Grail*) SAM, 2 RBU 1200 *Uragan* A/S mor, 2 twin AK230 CIWS
MSC 23: 21 *Yakhont* (*Sonya*) with 4 AK630 CIWS (some with 2 quad lnchr with *Strela*-2 (SA-N-5 *Grail*) SAM); 2 Project 1258 (*Yevgenya*)
MHI 9: 8 *Sapfir* (*Lida*) with 1 AK306 CIWS; 1 *Malakhit* (*Olya*)

AMPHIBIOUS
LANDING SHIPS • LST 19:
12 Project 775 (*Ropucha* I/II) with 2 twin 57mm guns (capacity either 10 MBT and 190 troops or 24 APC (T) and 170 troops)
3 Project 775M (*Ropucha* III) with 2 AK630 CIWS, 1 76mm gun (capacity either 10 MBT and 190 troops or 24 APC (T) and 170 troops)

4 *Tapir* (*Alligator*) with 2-3 twin lnchr with *Strela*-2 (SA-N-5 *Grail*) SAM, 2 twin 57mm guns (capacity 20 tanks; 300 troops)

LANDING CRAFT 28
  LCU 17:
    5 *Dyugon*
    12 Project 11770 (*Serna*) (capacity 100 troops)
  LCM 9 *Akula* (*Ondatra*) (capacity 1 MBT)
  LCAC 2 *Pomornik* (*Zubr*) with 2 AK630 CIWS (capacity 230 troops; either 3 MBT or 10 APC (T)

LOGISTICS AND SUPPORT ε269
  SSAN 7: 1 *Orenburg* (*Delta* III Stretch); 1 *Losharik*; 2 Project 1851 (*Paltus*); 3 *Kashalot* (*Uniform*)
  SSA 1 *Sarov*
  ABU 12: 8 *Kashtan*; 4 *Sura*
  AE 8: 6 *Muna*; 1 *Dubnyak*; 1 *Zvezdochka*
  AEM 3: 2 *Amga*; 1 *Lama*
  AG 1 *Potok*
  AGB 6: 2 *Dobrynya Mikitich*; 1 *Ilya Muromets*; 2 *Ivan Susanin*; 1 *Vladimir Kavraisky*
  AGE 1 *Tchusovoy*
  AGI 15: 2 *Alpinist*; 2 *Balzam*; 3 *Moma*; 7 *Vishnya*; 1 *Yuri Ivanov*
  AGM 1 *Marshal Nedelin*
  AGOR 8: 1 *Akademik Krylov*; 1 *Igor Belousov*; 1 *Seliger*; 2 *Sibiriyakov*; 2 *Vinograd*; 1 *Yantar*
  AGS 70: 8 *Biya*; 19 *Finik*; 7 *Kamenka*; 6 *Moma*; 9 *Onega*; 7 Project 19920/19920B; 2 *Vaygach*; 12 *Yug*
  AGSH 1 *Samara*
  AH 3 *Ob*†
  AK 3: 2 *Irgiz*; 1 *Pevek* with 1 AK306 CIWS
  AOL 11: 2 *Dubna*; 3 *Uda*; 6 *Altay* (mod)
  AOR 4 *Boris Chilikin*
  AORL 2: 1 *Kaliningradneft*; 1 *Olekma*
  AOS 2 *Luza*
  AR ε7 *Amur*
  ARC 4: 3 *Emba*; 1 Improved *Klasma*
  ARS 28: 1 *Kommuna*; 7 *Goryn*; 4 *Mikhail Rudnitsky*; 16 Project 23040
  AS 3 Project 2020 (*Malina*)
  ASR 1 *Elbrus*
  ATF 56: 1 *Alexander Piskunov*; 1 *Baklan*; ε3 *Katun*; 4 *Ingul*; 2 *Neftegaz*; 13 *Okhtensky*; 13 *Prometey*; 1 *Prut*; 4 *Sliva*; 14 *Sorum*
  AWT 1 *Manych*
  AXL 10: 8 *Petrushka*; 2 *Smolny* with 2 RBU 2500 A/S mor, 2 twin 76mm guns

Naval Aviation ε31,000
Flying hours 80+ hrs/yr

FORCES BY ROLE
FIGHTER
  1 sqn with MiG-31B/BS *Foxhound*
  1 sqn with Su-27/Su-27UB *Flanker*
  1 sqn with Su-33 *Flanker* D; Su-25UTG *Frogfoot*
FIGHTER/GROUND ATTACK
  1 regt with MiG-29KR/KUBR *Fulcrum*
  1 regt with MiG-31BM *Foxhound*; Su-24M/M2/MR *Fencer*

ANTI-SURFACE WARFARE/ISR
  1 regt with Su-24M/MR *Fencer*; Su-30SM
  1 sqn with Su-24M/MR *Fencer*
ANTI-SUBMARINE WARFARE
  3 sqn with Il-38/Il-38N *May**; Il-18D; Il-20RT *Coot* A; Il-22 *Coot* B
  8 sqn with Ka-27/Ka-29 *Helix*
  1 sqn with Mi-14 *Haze* A
  2 sqn with Tu-142MK/MZ/MR *Bear* F/J*
  1 unit with Ka-31R *Helix*
MARITIME PATROL/TRANSPORT
  1 sqn with An-26 *Curl*; Be-12 *Mail**; Mi-8 *Hip*
SEARCH & RESCUE/TRANSPORT
  1 sqn with An-12PS *Cub*; An-26 *Curl*; Tu-134
TRANSPORT
  1 sqn with An-12BK *Cub*; An-24RV *Coke*; An-26 *Curl*; An-72 *Coaler*; An-140
  2 sqn with An-26 *Curl*; Tu-134
TRAINING
  1 sqn with L-39 *Albatros*; Su-25UTG *Frogfoot*
  1 sqn with An-140; Tu-134; Tu-154, Il-38 *May*
ATTACK/TRANSPORT HELICOPTER
  1 sqn with Mi-24P *Hind*; Mi-8 *Hip*
TRANSPORT HELICOPTER
  1 sqn with Mi-8 *Hip*
AIR DEFENCE
  1 SAM regt with S-300PS (SA-10 *Grumble*)
  1 SAM regt with S-300PM (SA-20 *Gargoyle*)
  1 SAM regt with S-300PM (SA-20 *Gargoyle*); S-300PS (SA-10 *Grumble*)
  1 SAM regt with S-300PM (SA-20 *Gargoyle*); S-400 (SA-21 *Growler*)

EQUIPMENT BY TYPE
AIRCRAFT 205 combat capable
  FTR 68: 12 MiG-31B/BS *Foxhound*; 20 MiG-31BM *Foxhound*; 18 Su-33 *Flanker* D; 18 Su-27/Su-27UB *Flanker*
  FGA 32: 19 MiG-29KR *Fulcrum*; 4 MiG-29KUBR *Fulcrum*; 9 Su-30SM
  ATK 46: 41 Su-24M *Fencer*; 5 Su-25UTG *Frogfoot* (trg role)
  ASW 44: 12 Tu-142MK/MZ *Bear* F; 10 Tu-142MR *Bear* J (comms); 16 Il-38 *May*; 6 Il-38N *May*
  MP 4: 3 Be-12PS *Mail**; 1 Il-18D
  ISR 12 Su-24MR *Fencer* E*
  SAR 3 An-12PS *Cub*
  ELINT 4: 2 Il-20RT *Coot* A; 2 Il-22 *Coot* B
  TPT 48: **Medium** 2 An-12BK *Cub*; **Light** 44: 1 An-24RV *Coke*; 24 An-26 *Curl*; 6 An-72 *Coaler*; 3 An-140; 9 Tu-134; 1 Tu-134(UBL); **PAX** 2 Tu-154M *Careless*
  TRG 4 L-39 *Albatros*
HELICOPTERS
  ATK 8 Mi-24P *Hind*
  ASW 83: 63 Ka-27 *Helix*; 20 Mi-14 *Haze* A
  EW 8 Mi-8 *Hip* J
  AEW 2 Ka-31R *Helix*
  SAR 56: 16 Ka-27PS *Helix* D; 40 Mi-14PS *Haze* C
  TPT • Medium 36: 28 Ka-29 *Helix*; 4 Mi-8T *Hip*; 4 Mi-8MT *Hip*
AIR DEFENCE • SAM
  Long-range 106: 40 S-300PM (SA-20 *Gargoyle*); 50 S-300PS (SA-10B *Grumble*); 16 S-400 (SA-21 *Growler*)

AIR-LAUNCHED MISSILES
AAM • IR R-27T/ET (AA-10B/D *Alamo*); R-60 (AA-8 *Aphid*); R-73 (AA-11 *Archer*); SARH R-27R/ER (AA-10A/C *Alamo*); R-33 (AA-9A *Amos*)
ASM Kh-25 (AS-10 *Karen*); Kh-59 (AS-13 *Kingbolt*)
ARM Kh-25MP (AS-12 *Kegler*); Kh-58 (AS-11 *Kilter*)

Naval Infantry (Marines) ε35,000
FORCES BY ROLE
COMMAND
 1 corps HQ
SPECIAL FORCES
 1 (fleet) SF bde (1 para bn, 2–3 underwater bn, 1 spt unit)
 2 (fleet) SF bde (cadre) (1 para bn, 2–3 underwater bn, 1 spt unit)
MANOEUVRE
 Reconnaissance
 1 recce bde
 Mechanised
 3 MR bde
 1 MR regt
 6 indep naval inf bde
SURFACE-TO-SURFACE MISSILE
 1 SRBM bde with 9K79-1 *Tochka-U* (SS-21B *Scarab*)
COMBAT SUPPORT
 2 arty bde
AIR DEFENCE
 2 SAM regt with 9K33 *Osa* (SA-8 *Gecko*); *Strela*-1/*Strela*-10 (SA-9 *Gaskin*/SA-13 *Gopher*)
 2 SAM regt with S-400 (SA-21 *Growler*)
EQUIPMENT BY TYPE
ARMOURED FIGHTING VEHICLES
 MBT 250: 50 T-72B; 200 T-72B3
 IFV 1,000: 400 BMP-2; 600 BTR-82A
 APC 400
  APC (T) 300 MT-LB
  APC (W) 100 BTR-80
ANTI-TANK/ANTI-INFRASTRUCTURE
 MSL
  SP 60 9P148 with 9K111-1 *Konkurs* (AT-5 *Spandrel*); 9P149 with 9K114 *Shturm* (AT-6 *Spiral*); 9P157-2 with 9K123 *Khrisantema* (AT-15 *Springer*)
  MANPATS 9K111-1 *Konkurs* (AT-5 *Spandrel*); 9K135 *Kornet* (AT-14 *Spriggan*)
 GUNS 100mm T-12
ARTILLERY 365
 SP 163: 122mm 95 2S1 *Gvozdika*; 152mm 68: 50 2S3 *Akatsiya*; 18 2S19 *Msta-S*
 TOWED 152mm 100: 50 2A36 *Giatsint*-B; 50 2A65 *Msta-B*
 GUN/MOR 66
  SP 120mm 42: 12 2S23 NONA-SVK; 30 2S9 NONA-S
  TOWED 120mm 24 2B16 NONA-K
 MRL 122mm 36 BM-21 *Grad*
SURFACE-TO-SURFACE MISSILE LAUNCHERS
 SRBM • Conventional 12 9K79-1 *Tochka-U* (SS-21B *Scarab*)
AIR DEFENCE
 SAM
  Long-range 32 S-400 (SA-21 *Growler*)
  Point-defence 250+: 20 9K33 *Osa* (SA-8 *Gecko*); 50 9K31 *Strela*-1/9K35 *Strela*-10 (SA-9 *Gaskin*/SA-13 *Gopher*); 9K338 *Igla-S* (SA-24 *Grinch*)
 GUNS 23mm 60 ZSU-23-4

Coastal Missile and Artillery Troops 2,000
FORCES BY ROLE
COASTAL DEFENCE
 5 AShM bde
 1 AShM regt
EQUIPMENT BY TYPE
COASTAL DEFENCE
 ARTY • SP 130mm ε36 A-222 *Bereg*
 AShM 72+: 36 3K60 *Bal* (SS-C-6 *Sennight*); 36 3K55 *Bastion* (SS-C-5 *Stooge*); some 4K44 *Redut* (SS-C-1 *Sepal*); some 4K51 *Rubezh* (SS-C-3 *Styx*)

Aerospace Forces ε165,000 (incl conscripts)
Flying hours 60–100 hrs/yr (combat aircraft) 120+ (transport aircraft)

A joint CIS Unified Air Defence System covers RUS, ARM, BLR, KAZ, KGZ, TJK, TKM and UZB

FORCES BY ROLE
BOMBER
 4 sqn with Tu-22M3/MR *Backfire* C
 3 sqn with Tu-95MS/MS mod/MSM *Bear*
 1 sqn with Tu-160/Tu-160M1 *Blackjack*
FIGHTER
 1 sqn with MiG-29/MiG-29UB *Fulcrum* (Armenia)
 1 regt with MiG-29SMT/UBT *Fulcrum*
 1 regt with MiG-31BM *Foxhound*
 1 regt with MiG-31B/BS/BM *Foxhound*
 1 regt with MiG-31B/BS/BM *Foxhound*; Su-27/Su-27UB *Flanker*
 1 regt with Su-27/Su-27UB *Flanker*; Su-27SM *Flanker*; Su-35S *Flanker*
 1 regt with Su-27/Su-27UB *Flanker*
 1 regt with Su-30SM
FIGHTER/GROUND ATTACK
 1 regt with MiG-31BM *Foxhound*; Su-27SM *Flanker*; Su-30M2; Su-30SM; Su-35S *Flanker*
 1 regt with Su-35S *Flanker*; Su-30SM
 1 regt with Su-27SM *Flanker*; Su-27SM3 *Flanker*; Su-30M2
 1 regt with Su-25 *Frogfoot*; Su-30SM
GROUND ATTACK
 1 regt with Su-24M/M2 *Fencer*; Su-34 *Fullback*
 1 regt with Su-24M *Fencer*; Su-25SM *Frogfoot*
 2 sqn with Su-24M/M2 *Fencer*
 3 regt with Su-25SM/SM3 *Frogfoot*
 1 sqn with Su-25SM *Frogfoot* (Kyrgyzstan)
 2 regt with Su-34 *Fullback*
ELECTRONIC WARFARE
 1 sqn with Mi-8PPA *Hip*
ISR
 2 regt with Su-24MR *Fencer**
 2 sqn with Su-24MR *Fencer**
 1 flt with An-30 *Clank*
AIRBORNE EARLY WARNING & CONTROL
 1 sqn with A-50/A-50U *Mainstay*

TANKER
 1 sqn with Il-78/Il-78M *Midas*
TRANSPORT
 6 regt/sqn with An-12BK *Cub*; An-26 *Curl*; Tu-134 *Crusty*; Tu-154 *Careless*; Mi-8 *Hip*
 1 regt with An-124 *Condor*; Il-76MD *Candid*
 1 regt with An-12BK *Cub*; Il-76MD *Candid*
 1 sqn with An-22 *Cock*
 3 regt with Il-76MD *Candid*
ATTACK/TRANSPORT HELICOPTER
 1 bde with Ka-52A *Hokum* B; Mi-28N *Havoc* B; Mi-35 *Hind*; Mi-26 *Halo*; Mi-8MTV-5 *Hip*
 1 bde with Mi-28N *Havoc* B; Mi-35 *Hind*; Mi-26 *Halo*; Mi-8 *Hip*
 1 regt with Ka-52A *Hokum* B; Mi-28N *Havoc* B; Mi-35 *Hind*; Mi-8 *Hip*
 2 regt with Mi-28N *Havoc* B; Mi-35 *Hind*; Mi-8 *Hip*
 1 sqn with Mi-24P *Hind*; Mi-8 *Hip*
ATTACK HELICOPTER
 2 sqn with Ka-52A *Hokum* B
 2 sqn with Mi-24P *Hind*
 1 sqn with Mi-24P *Hind*; Mi-35 *Hind*
 1 sqn with Mi-28N *Havoc* B
TRANSPORT HELICOPTER
 9 sqn with Mi-8 *Hip*/Mi-26 *Halo*
AIR DEFENCE
 9 AD div HQ
 4 regt with 9K317 *Buk*-M1-2/M2 (SA-11 *Gadfly*/SA-17 *Grizzly*); S-300V (SA-12 *Gladiator*/*Giant*)
 7 regt with S-300PS (SA-10 *Grumble*)
 8 regt with S-300PM (SA-20 *Gargoyle*)
 5 regt with S-400 (SA-21 *Growler*); 96K6 *Pantsir*-S1 (SA-22 *Greyhound*)
EQUIPMENT BY TYPE
AIRCRAFT 1,046 combat capable
 BBR 139+: 62 Tu-22M3 *Backfire* C; 1+ Tu-22MR *Blackjack*; 48 Tu-95MS/MS mod *Bear*; 12 Tu-95MSM *Bear*; 11 Tu-160 *Blackjack*; 5 Tu-160M1 *Blackjack*
 FTR 210: 70 MiG-29/MiG-29UB *Fulcrum*; 20 MiG-31B/31BS *Foxhound*; 60 MiG-31BM *Foxhound*; 50 Su-27 *Flanker*; 10 Su-27UB *Flanker*
 FGA 323: 36 MiG-29SMT *Fulcrum*; 6 MiG-29UBT *Fulcrum*; 47 Su-27SM *Flanker*; 14 Su-27SM3 *Flanker*; 20 Su-30M2; 62 Su-30SM; 86 Su-34 *Fullback*; 52 Su-35S *Flanker*
 ATK 295: 100 Su-24M/M2 *Fencer*; 40 Su-25 *Frogfoot*; 140 Su-25SM/SM3 *Frogfoot*; 15 Su-25UB *Frogfoot*
 ISR 87: 4 An-30 *Clank*; 79 Su-24MR *Fencer**; 2 Tu-214ON; 2 Tu-214R
 EW 3 Il-22PP
 ELINT 32: 15 Il-20M *Coot* A; 5 Il-22 *Coot* B; 12 Il-22M *Coot* B
 AEW&C 18: 15 A-50 *Mainstay*; 3 A-50U *Mainstay*
 C2 8: 4 Il-80 *Maxdome*; 2 Il-82; 2 Tu-214SR
 TKR 15: 5 Il-78 *Midas*; 10 Il-78M *Midas*
 TPT 429: **Heavy** 111: 9 An-124 *Condor*; 2 An-22 *Cock*; 100 Il-76MD/MF *Candid*; **Medium** 65 An-12BK *Cub*; **Light** 235: 115 An-26 *Curl*; 25 An-72 *Coaler*; 5 An-140; 9 An-148-100E; 27 L-410; 54 Tu-134 *Crusty*; **PAX** 18 Tu-154 *Careless*
 TRG 231: 150 L-39 *Albatros*; 81 Yak-130 *Mitten*
HELICOPTERS
 ATK 340+: 90+ Ka-52A *Hokum* B; 100 Mi-24D/V/P *Hind*; 90+ Mi-28N *Havoc* B; 60+ Mi-35 *Hind*

 EW 27: 20 Mi-8PPA *Hip*; 7 Mi-8MTRP-1 *Hip*
 TPT 338: **Heavy** 32 Mi-26/Mi-26T *Halo*; **Medium** 306 Mi-8/Mi-8MT/Mi-8MTSh/Mi-8MTSh-VA/Mi-8MTV-5 *Hip*
 TRG 39: 19 Ka-226; 20 *Ansat*-U
UNMANNED AERIAL VEHICLES
 ISR • Medium *Forpost* (*Searcher* II)
AIR DEFENCE • SAM 508:
 Long-range 398: 120 S-300PM/PM1 (SA-20 *Gargoyle*); 170 S-300PS (SA-10B *Grumble*); 20 S-300V (SA-12 *Gladiator*/*Giant*); 88 S-400 (SA-21 *Growler*)
 Medium-range 80 9K317 *Buk*-M1-2/M2 (SA-11 *Gadfly*/SA-17 *Grizzly*)
 Short-range 30 96K6 *Pantsir*-S1/S2 (SA-22 *Greyhound*)
AIR-LAUNCHED MISSILES
 AAM • IR R-27T/ET (AA-10B/D *Alamo*); R-73 (AA-11 *Archer*); R-60T (AA-8 *Aphid*); **SARH** R-27R/ER (AA-10A/C *Alamo*); R-33/33S (AA-9 *Amos* A/B); **ARH** R-77-1 (AA-12B *Adder*); R-37M (AA-13 *Axehead*); **PRH** R-27P/EP (AA-10E/F *Alamo*)
 ARM Kh-25MP (AS-12 *Kegler*); Kh-31P/PM (AS-17A *Krypton*); Kh-58 (AS-11 *Kilter*)
 ASM Kh-25 (AS-10 *Karen*); Kh-29 (AS-14 *Kedge*); Kh-31A/AM (AS-17B *Krypton*); Kh-38; Kh-59/Kh-59M (AS-13 *Kingbolt*/AS-18 *Kazoo*)
 AShM Kh-22 (AS-4 *Kitchen*); Kh-32 (development being concluded)
 LACM
  Nuclear Kh-55/Kh-55SM (AS-15A/B *Kent*); Kh-102
  Conventional Kh-101; Kh-555
BOMBS
 Laser-guided KAB-500; KAB-1500L
 TV-guided KAB-500KR; KAB-1500KR; KAB-500OD; UPAB 1500
 INS/GLONASS-guided KAB-500S

Airborne Troops ε45,000
FORCES BY ROLE
SPECIAL FORCES
 1 (AB Recce) SF bde
MANOEUVRE
 Air Manoeuvre
 4 AB div (2 para/air aslt regt; 1 arty regt; 1 AD regt)
 1 indep AB bde
 3 air aslt bde
EQUIPMENT BY TYPE
ARMOURED FIGHTING VEHICLES
 IFV 20 BTR-82AM
 APC • APC (T) 712: 700 BTR-D; 12 BTR-MDM
 AUV GAZ *Tigr*
 ABCV 1,152: 100 BMD-1; 1,000 BMD-2; 10 BMD-3; 30 BMD-4; 12 BMD-4M
ENGINEERING & MAINTENANCE VEHICLES
 ARV BREM-D; BREhM-D
ANTI-TANK/ANTI-INFRASTRUCTURE
 MSL
  SP 100 BTR-RD
  MANPATS 9K111 *Fagot* (AT-4 *Spigot*); 9K113 *Konkurs* (AT-5 *Spandrel*); 9K115 *Metis* (AT-7 *Saxhorn*); 9K115-1 *Metis*-M (AT-13 *Saxhorn* 2); 9K135 *Kornet* (AT-14 *Spriggan*)

RCL 73mm SPG-9
GUNS • SP 125mm 36+ 2S25 *Sprut*-SD
ARTILLERY 600+
  TOWED 122mm 150 D-30
  GUN/MOR • SP 120mm 250 2S9 NONA-S (500 in store: 120mm 500 2S9 NONA-S)
  MOR • TOWED 200+ 82mm 150 2B14; 120mm 50+ 2B23 NONA-M1
AIR DEFENCE
  SAM • Point-defence 30+: 30 *Strela*-10MN; 9K310 *Igla*-1 (SA-16 *Gimlet*); 9K38 *Igla* (SA-18 *Grouse*); 9K333 *Verba*; 9K338 *Igla*-S (SA-24 *Grinch*); 9K34 *Strela*-3 (SA-14 *Gremlin*)
  GUNS • SP 23mm 150 BTR-ZD

Special Operations Forces ε1,000
FORCES BY ROLE
SPECIAL FORCES
  2 SF unit

Russian Military Districts

Western Military District
HQ at St Petersburg

Army
FORCES BY ROLE
COMMAND
  3 army HQ
SPECIAL FORCES
  2 (Spetsnaz) SF bde
MANOEUVRE
  Reconnaissance
  1 recce bde
  Armoured
  1 tk div
  1 tk bde
  1 tk bde(-)
  2 MR div (forming)
  1 MR bde(-)
  Mechanised
  1 MR div
  3 MR bde
SURFACE-TO-SURFACE MISSILE
  2 SRBM/GLCM bde with *Iskander*-M/K
  1 SRBM bde with *Tochka*-U
COMBAT SUPPORT
  2 arty bde
  1 MRL bde
  1 engr bde
  1 MP bde
  1 NBC bde
  2 NBC regt
COMBAT SERVICE SUPPORT
  2 log bde
AIR DEFENCE
  3 AD bde

Reserves
FORCES BY ROLE
  MANOEUVRE
  Mechanised
  2 MR bde

Northern Fleet
EQUIPMENT BY TYPE
SUBMARINES 32
  STRATEGIC 8 SSBN (of which 1 in refit)
  TACTICAL 25: 4 SSGN (of which 1 in refit); 12 SSN (of which 3 in refit); 6 SSK (of which 1 in refit)
PRINCIPAL SURFACE COMBATANTS 10: 1 CV; 2 CGHMN (of which one non-operational); 1 CGHM (in refit); 6 DDGHM
PATROL AND COASTAL COMBATANTS 10: 2 FSGM; 6 FSM; 2 PBM
MINE WARFARE • MINE COUNTERMEASURES 12: 1 MHO; 4 MSO; 7 MSC
AMPHIBIOUS 6: 4 LST; 2 LCM

Naval Aviation
FORCES BY ROLE
FIGHTER
  1 sqn with Su-33 *Flanker* D; Su-25UTG *Frogfoot*
FIGHTER/GROUND ATTACK
  1 regt with MiG-29KR/KUBR *Fulcrum*
FIGHTER/GROUND ATTACK/ISR
  1 regt with MiG-31BM *Foxhound*; Su-24M/M2/MR *Fencer*
ANTI-SUBMARINE WARFARE
  1 sqn with Il-38 *May*; Il-20RT *Coot* A; Tu-134
  3 sqn with Ka-27/Ka-29 *Helix*
  1 sqn with Tu-142MK/MZ/MR *Bear* F/J
AIR DEFENCE
  3 SAM regt
EQUIPMENT BY TYPE
AIRCRAFT
  FTR 38: 20 MiG-31BM *Foxhound*; 18 Su-33 *Flanker* D
  FGA 23: 19 MiG-29KR *Fulcrum*; 4 MiG-29KUBR *Fulcrum*
  ATK 18: 13 Su-24M *Fencer*; 5 Su-25UTG *Frogfoot* (trg role)
  ASW 21: 10 Il-38 *May*; 11 Tu-142MK/MZ/MR *Bear* F/J
  ISR 4 Su-24MR *Fencer**
  ELINT 3: 2 Il-20RT *Coot* A; 1 Il-22 *Coot* B
  TPT 9: 8 An-26 *Curl*; 1 Tu-134
HELICOPTERS
  ASW Ka-27 *Helix* A
  TPT • Medium Ka-29 *Helix* B; Mi-8 *Hip*

Naval Infantry
FORCES BY ROLE
MANOEUVRE
  Mechanised
  2 MR bde
  1 naval inf bde

Coastal Artillery and Missile Troops
FORCES BY ROLE
COASTAL DEFENCE
  1 AShM bde

Baltic Fleet
EQUIPMENT BY TYPE
SUBMARINES • TACTICAL • SSK 2 (of which 1 in refit)
PRINCIPAL SURFACE COMBATANTS 8: 2 DDGHM; 6 FFGHM
PATROL AND COASTAL COMBATANTS 23: 4 FSGM; 6 FSM; 7 PCFG; 5 PBF; 1 PBM
MINE WARFARE • MINE COUNTERMEASURES 12: 5 MSC; 7 MHI
AMPHIBIOUS 13: 4 LST; 6 LCU; 1 LCM; 2 LCAC

Naval Aviation
FORCES BY ROLE
FIGHTER
 1 sqn with Su-27 *Flanker*
ANTI-SURFACE WARFARE/ISR
 1 sqn with Su-24M/MR *Fencer*
ANTI-SUBMARINE WARFARE
 1 sqn with Ka-27/Ka-29 *Helix*
TRANSPORT
 1 sqn with An-26 *Curl*; Tu-134 *Crusty*
ATTACK/TRANSPORT HELICOPTER
 1 sqn with Mi-24P *Hind*; Mi-8 *Hip*
TRANSPORT HELICOPTER
 1 sqn with Mi-8 *Hip*
EQUIPMENT BY TYPE
AIRCRAFT
 FTR 18 Su-27/Su-27UB *Flanker*
 ATK 10 Su-24M *Fencer*
 ISR 4 Su-24MR *Fencer**
 TPT 8: 6 An-26 *Curl*; 2 Tu-134 *Crusty*
HELICOPTERS
 ATK Mi-24P *Hind*
 ASW Ka-27 *Helix*
 TPT • Medium Ka-29 *Helix*; Mi-8 *Hip*

Naval Infantry
FORCES BY ROLE
MANOEUVRE
 Mechanised
 1 MR bde
 1 MR regt
 1 naval inf bde
SURFACE-TO-SURFACE MISSILE
 1 SRBM bde with *Tochka*-U
COMBAT SUPPORT
 1 arty bde
AIR DEFENCE
 2 SAM regt

Coastal Artillery and Missile Troops
FORCES BY ROLE
COASTAL DEFENCE
 1 AShM regt

Military Air Force
6th Air Force & Air Defence Army
FORCES BY ROLE
FIGHTER
 1 regt with MiG-29SMT *Fulcrum*
 1 regt with MiG-31BM *Foxhound*; Su-27 *Flanker*
 1 regt with Su-27/Su-27SM *Flanker*; Su-35S *Flanker*
GROUND ATTACK
 1 regt with Su-34 *Fullback*
ISR
 1 sqn with Su-24MR *Fencer*
 1 flt with A-30 *Clank*
ELECTRONIC WARFARE
 1 sqn with Mi-8PPA *Hip*
TRANSPORT
 1 regt with An-12 *Cub*; An-26 *Curl*; Tu-134 *Crusty*
ATTACK HELICOPTER
 1 bde with Ka-52A *Hokum B*; Mi-28N *Havoc B*; Mi-35 *Hind*; Mi-26 *Halo*; Mi-8MTV-5 *Hip*
 1 sqn with Mi-24P *Hind*
 1 sqn with Mi-24P/Mi-35 *Hind*
 1 sqn with Mi-28N *Havoc B*
TRANSPORT HELICOPTER
 2 sqn with Mi-8 *Hip*
AIR DEFENCE
 1 SAM regt with 9K317 *Buk*-M1-2 (SA-11 *Gadfly*); S-300V (SA-12 *Gladiator/Giant*)
 5 SAM regt with S-300PM (SA-20 *Gargoyle*)
 1 SAM regt with S-400 (SA-21 *Growler*); 96K6 *Pantsir*-S1 (SA-22 *Greyhound*)
EQUIPMENT BY TYPE
AIRCRAFT
 FTR 61: 31 MiG-31B/BS/BM *Foxhound*; 30 Su-27/Su-27UB *Flanker*
 FGA 74: 28 MiG-29SMT *Fulcrum*; 6 MiG-29UBT *Fulcrum*; 12 Su-27SM *Flanker*; 24 Su-34 *Fullback*; 4 Su-35S *Flanker*
 ISR 19: 4 An-30 *Clank*; 15 Su-24MR *Fencer**
 TPT 12 An-12/An-26/Tu-134
HELICOPTERS
 ATK 64+: 12 Ka-52A *Hokum B*; 16 Mi-24P *Hind*; 24 Mi-28N *Havoc B*; 12+ Mi-35 *Hind*
 EW 10 Mi-8PPA *Hip*
 TPT • Medium 50 Mi-8 *Hip*
AIR DEFENCE • SAM
 Long-range S-300PM (SA-20 *Gargoyle*); S-300V (SA-12 *Gladiator/Giant*); S-400 (SA-21 *Growler*)
 Medium-range 9K317 *Buk*-M1-2 (SA-11 *Gadfly*)
 Short-range 96K6 *Pantsir*-S1 (SA-22 *Greyhound*)

Airborne Troops
FORCES BY ROLE
SPECIAL FORCES
 1 (AB Recce) SF bde
MANOEUVRE
 Air Manoeuvre
 3 AB div

Central Military District

HQ at Yekaterinburg

Army

FORCES BY ROLE
COMMAND
  2 army HQ
SPECIAL FORCES
  2 (Spetsnaz) SF bde
MANOEUVRE
  Armoured
  1 tk div (forming)
  1 tk bde(-)
  3 MR bde
  1 MR bde(-)
  Mechanised
  3 MR bde
  1 MR bde(-)
  1 (mtn) MR bde
SURFACE-TO-SURFACE MISSILE
  1 SRBM/GLCM bde with *Iskander*-M/K
  1 SRBM/GLCM bde with *Iskander*-M/K (forming)
COMBAT SUPPORT
  2 arty bde
  1 MRL bde
  1 engr bde
  2 NBC bde
  2 NBC regt
COMBAT SERVICE SUPPORT
  2 log bde
AIR DEFENCE
  3 AD bde

Reserves

FORCES BY ROLE
MANOEUVRE
  Mechanised
  3 MR bde

Military Air Force

14th Air Force & Air Defence Army

FORCES BY ROLE
FIGHTER
  1 regt with MiG-31BM *Foxhound*
  1 regt with MiG-31B/BS/BM *Foxhound*
GROUND ATTACK
  2 sqn with Su-24M *Fencer*
  1 sqn with Su-25SM *Frogfoot* (Kyrgyzstan)
ISR
  1 sqn with Su-24MR *Fencer* E
TRANSPORT
  1 regt with An-12 *Cub*; An-26 *Curl*; Tu-134 *Crusty*; Tu-154; Mi-8 *Hip*
ATTACK HELICOPTER
  1 sqn with Mi-24P *Hind*
ATTACK/TRANSPORT HELICOPTER
  1 sqn with Mi-24P *Hind*; Mi-8 *Hip*
TRANSPORT HELICOPTER
  1 sqn with Mi-8 *Hip*/Mi-26 *Halo*

AIR DEFENCE
  4 regt with S-300PS (SA-10B *Grumble*)
  1 regt with S-300PM (SA-20 *Gargoyle*)
  1 regt with S-400 (SA-21 *Growler*); 96K6 *Pantsir*-S1 (SA-22 *Greyhound*)
EQUIPMENT BY TYPE
AIRCRAFT
  FTR 40 MiG-31B/BS/BM *Foxhound*
  ATK 37: 26 Su-24M *Fencer*; 11 Su-25SM *Frogfoot*
  ISR 9 Su-24MR *Fencer* E
  TPT 36 An-12 *Cub*/An-26 *Curl*/Tu-134 *Crusty*/Tu-154 *Careless*
HELICOPTERS
  ATK 24 Mi-24 *Hind*
  TPT 46: 6 Mi-26 *Halo*; 40 Mi-8 *Hip*
AIR DEFENCE • SAM
  Long-range S-300PS (SA-10B *Grumble*); S-300PM (SA-20 *Gargoyle*); S-400 (SA-21 *Growler*)
  Short-range 96K6 *Pantsir*-S1 (SA-22 *Greyhound*)

Airborne Troops

FORCES BY ROLE
MANOEUVRE
  Air Manoeuvre
  1 AB bde

Southern Military District

HQ located at Rostov-on-Don

Army

FORCES BY ROLE
COMMAND
  2 army HQ
SPECIAL FORCES
  2 (Spetsnaz) SF bde
MANOEUVRE
  Reconnaissance
  1 recce bde
  Armoured
  1 MR div (forming)
  3 MR bde
  1 MR bde (Armenia)
  1 MR bde (South Ossetia)
  Mechanised
  3 MR bde
  1 MR bde (Abkhazia)
  2 (lt/mtn) MR bde
  1 (lt/mtn) MR bde(-)
SURFACE-TO-SURFACE MISSILE
  2 SRBM/GLCM bde with *Iskander*-M/K
COMBAT SUPPORT
  1 arty bde
  1 MRL bde
  1 MRL regt
  1 engr bde
  1 NBC bde
  2 NBC regt
COMBAT SERVICE SUPPORT
  2 log bde
AIR DEFENCE
  3 AD bde

Black Sea Fleet

The Black Sea Fleet is primarily based in Crimea, at Sevastopol, Karantinnaya Bay and Streletskaya Bay

EQUIPMENT BY TYPE
SUBMARINES • TACTICAL 4 SSK (3 more to follow)
PRINCIPAL SURFACE COMBATANTS 6: 1 CGHM; 1 DDGM; 2 FFGHM; 2 FFGM
PATROL AND COASTAL COMBATANTS 27: 6 FSGM; 6 FSM; 5 PCFG; 5 PBM; 5 PBF
MINE WARFARE • MINE COUNTERMEASURES 11: 1 MHO; 6 MSO; 3 MSC; 1 MHI
AMPHIBIOUS 10: 7 LST; 1 LCM; 2 LCU

Naval Aviation
FORCES BY ROLE
FIGHTER
ANTI-SURFACE WARFARE/ISR
  1 regt with Su-24M/MR *Fencer*; Su-30SM
ANTI-SUBMARINE WARFARE
  1 sqn with Ka-27 *Helix*
  1 sqn with Mi-14 *Haze*
MARITIME PATROL/TRANSPORT
  1 sqn with An-26 *Curl*; Be-12PS *Mail**; Mi-8
EQUIPMENT BY TYPE
AIRCRAFT
  FGA 9 Su-30SM
  ATK 13 Su-24M *Fencer*
  ISR 4 Su-24MR *Fencer* E
  MP 3 Be-12PS *Mail**
  TPT 6 An-26
HELICOPTERS
  ASW Ka-27 *Helix*
  TPT • **Medium** Mi-8 *Hip* (MP/EW/Tpt)

Naval Infantry
FORCES BY ROLE
MANOEUVRE
  Mechanised
  2 naval inf bde
COMBAT SUPPORT
  1 arty bde
AIR DEFENCE
  1 SAM regt

Coastal Artillery and Missile Troops
FORCES BY ROLE
COASTAL DEFENCE
  2 AShM bde

Caspian Sea Flotilla
EQUIPMENT BY TYPE
PRINCIPAL SURFACE COMBATANTS 2 FFGM
PATROL AND COASTAL COMBATANTS 12: 3 FSGM; 3 FSM; 1 PCFG; 1 PBM; 4 PBR
MINE WARFARE • MINE COUNTERMEASURES 3: 2 MSC; 1 MHI
AMPHIBIOUS 9: 2 LCM; 7 LCU

Military Air Force

4th Air Force & Air Defence Army

FORCES BY ROLE
FIGHTER
  1 regt with Su-30SM
  1 sqn with MiG-29 *Fulcrum* (Armenia)
FIGHTER/GROUND ATTACK
  1 regt with Su-27 *Flanker*
  1 regt with Su-27SM/SM3 *Flanker*; Su-30M2
GROUND ATTACK
  1 regt with Su-24M *Fencer*; Su-25SM *Frogfoot*
  2 regt with Su-25SM/SM3 *Frogfoot*
  1 regt with Su-34 *Fullback*
ISR
  1 regt with Su-24MR *Fencer* E
TRANSPORT
  1 regt with An-12 *Cub*/Mi-8 *Hip*
ATTACK/TRANSPORT HELICOPTER
  1 bde with Mi-28N *Havoc* B; Mi-35 *Hind*; Mi-8 *Hip*; Mi-26 *Halo*
  1 regt with Mi-28N *Havoc* B; Mi-35 *Hind*; Mi-8 *Hip*
  2 regt with Ka-52A *Hokum* B; Mi-28N *Havoc* B; Mi-35 *Hind*; Mi-8AMTSh *Hip*
AIR DEFENCE
  1 regt with 9K317 *Buk*-M2 (SA-17 *Grizzly*)
  2 regt with S-300PM (SA-20 *Gargoyle*)
  2 regt with S-400 (SA-21 *Growler*); 96K6 *Pantsir*-S1 (SA-22 *Greyhound*)
EQUIPMENT BY TYPE
AIRCRAFT
  FTR 46: 12 MiG-29 *Fulcrum*; 34 Su-27 *Flanker*
  FGA 86: 12 Su-27SM *Flanker*; 12 Su-27SM3 *Flanker*; 4 Su-30M2; 22 Su-30SM; 36 Su-34 *Fullback*
  ATK 125: 40 Su-24M *Fencer*; 85 Su-25SM/SM3 *Frogfoot*
  ISR 24 Su-24MR *Fencer**
  TPT 12 An-12 *Cub*
HELICOPTERS
  ATK 99: 25 Ka-52A *Hokum* B; 34 Mi-28N *Havoc* B; 40 Mi-35 *Hind*
  TPT 72: **Heavy** 10 Mi-26 *Halo*; **Medium** 62 Mi-8 *Hip*
AIR DEFENCE • SAM
  Long-range S-300PM (SA-20 *Gargoyle*); S-400 (SA-21 *Growler*)
  Medium-range 9K317 *Buk*-M2 (SA-17 *Grizzly*)
  Short-range 96K6 *Pantsir*-S1 (SA-22 *Greyhound*)

Airborne Troops
FORCES BY ROLE
MANOEUVRE
  Air Manoeuvre
  1 AB div
  1 air aslt bde

Eastern Military District
HQ located at Khabarovsk

Army
FORCES BY ROLE
COMMAND
  4 army HQ

SPECIAL FORCES
1 (Spetsnaz) SF bde
MANOEUVRE
  Armoured
    1 tk bde
    7 MR bde
  Mechanised
    3 MR bde
    1 MGA div
SURFACE-TO-SURFACE MISSILE
  3 SRBM/GLCM bde with *Iskander*-M/K
COMBAT SUPPORT
  3 arty bde
  1 MRL bde
  1 engr bde
  1 NBC bde
  4 NBC regt
COMBAT SERVICE SUPPORT
  4 log bde
AIR DEFENCE
  3 AD bde

Reserves
FORCES BY ROLE
MANOEUVRE
  Mechanised
    8 MR bde

Pacific Fleet
EQUIPMENT BY TYPE
SUBMARINES 23
  STRATEGIC 5 SSBN
  TACTICAL 18: 5 **SSGN** (of which 2 in refit); 5 **SSN** (of which 1 in refit); 8 **SSK**
PRINCIPAL SURFACE COMBATANTS 7: 1 **CGHM**; 6 **DDGHM** (of which 3 in refit)
PATROL AND COASTAL COMBATANTS 24: 4 **FSGM**; 8 **FSM**; 9 **PCFG**; 3 **PBM**
MINE WARFARE 8: 2 **MSO**; 6 **MSC**
AMPHIBIOUS 8: 4 **LST**; 3 **LCM**; 1 **LCU**

Naval Aviation
FORCES BY ROLE
FIGHTER
  1 sqn with MiG-31B/BS *Foxhound*
ANTI-SUBMARINE WARFARE
  3 sqn with Ka-27/Ka-29 *Helix*
  2 sqn with Il-38 *May**; Il-18D; Il-22 *Coot* B
  1 sqn with Tu-142MK/MZ/MR *Bear* F/J*
TRANSPORT
  2 sqn with An-12BK *Cub*; An-26 *Curl*; Tu-134
EQUIPMENT BY TYPE
AIRCRAFT
  FTR 12 MiG-31B/BS *Foxhound*
  ASW 23: 11 Tu-142MK/MZ/MR *Bear* F/J; 12 Il-38 *May*
  EW • ELINT 1 Il-22 *Coot* B
  TPT 6: 2 An-12BK *Cub*; 3 An-26 *Curl*; 1 Tu-134
HELICOPTERS
  ASW Ka-27 *Helix*
  TPT • Medium Ka-29 *Helix*; Mi-8 *Hip*

Naval Infantry
FORCES BY ROLE
MANOEUVRE
  Mechanised
    2 naval inf bde
AIR DEFENCE
  1 SAM regt

Coastal Artillery and Missile Troops
FORCES BY ROLE
COASTAL DEFENCE
  2 AShM bde

Military Air Force

11th Air Force & Air Defence Army
FORCES BY ROLE
FIGHTER/GROUND ATTACK
  1 regt with MiG-31BM *Foxhound*; Su-27SM *Flanker*; Su-30M2; Su-30SM; Su-35S *Flanker*
  1 regt with Su-35S *Flanker*; Su-30SM
  1 regt with Su-25 *Frogfoot*; Su-30SM
GROUND ATTACK
  1 regt with Su-24M/M2 *Fencer*; Su-34 *Fullback*
  1 regt with Su-25SM *Frogfoot*
ISR
  1 regt with Su-24MR *Fencer* E
TRANSPORT
  2 sqn with An-12 *Cub*/An-26 *Curl*/Tu-134 *Crusty*/Tu-154 *Careless*
ATTACK HELICOPTER
  1 sqn with Mi-24P *Hind*
  2 sqn with Ka-52A *Hokum* B
TRANSPORT HELICOPTER
  4 sqn with Mi-8 *Hip*/Mi-26 *Halo*
AIR DEFENCE
  2 regt with 9K317 *Buk*-M1-2/M2 (SA-11 *Gadfly*/SA-17 *Grizzly*); S-300V (SA-12 *Gladiator/Giant*)
  3 regt with S-300PS (SA-10B *Grumble*); S-300PM (SA-20 *Gargoyle*)
  1 regt with S-400 (SA-21 *Growler*); 96K6 *Pantsir*-S1 (SA-22 *Greyhound*)
EQUIPMENT BY TYPE
AIRCRAFT
  FTR 20 MiG-31B/BS/BM *Foxhound*
  FGA 100: 23 Su-27SM *Flanker*; 2 Su-30M2; 29 Su-30SM; 12 Su-34 *Fullback*; 34 Su-35S *Flanker*
  ATK 114: 32 Su-24M *Fencer*; 10 Su-24M2 *Fencer*; 72 Su-25/Su-25SM *Frogfoot*
  ISR 28 Su-24MR *Fencer* E
  TPT 24: 22 An-12 *Cub*/An-26 *Curl*; 1 Tu-134 *Crusty*; 1 Tu-154 *Careless*
HELICOPTERS
  ATK 36: 24 Ka-52A *Hokum* B; 12 Mi-24P *Hind*
  TPT 60: Heavy 4 Mi-26 *Halo*; Medium 56 Mi-8 *Hip*
AIR DEFENCE • SAM
  Long-range S-300PS (SA-10 *Grumble*); S-300V (SA-12 *Gladiator/Giant*); S-400 (SA-21 *Growler*)

Medium-range 9K317 *Buk*-M1-2 (SA-11 *Gadfly*); 9K317 *Buk*-M2 (SA-17 *Grizzly*)
Short-range 96K6 *Pantsir*-S1 (SA-22 *Greyhound*)

Airborne Troops
FORCES BY ROLE
MANOEUVRE
  Air Manoeuvre
  2 air aslt bde

Paramilitary 659,000

Federal Border Guard Service ε160,000
Directly subordinate to the president; now reportedly all contract-based personnel
FORCES BY ROLE
10 regional directorates
MANOEUVRE
  Other
  7 frontier gp
EQUIPMENT BY TYPE
ARMOURED FIGHTING VEHICLES
  IFV/APC (W) 1,000 BMP/BTR
ARTILLERY 90:
  SP 122mm 2S1 *Gvozdika*
  GUN/MOR • SP 120mm 2S9 NONA-S
  MOR 120mm 2S12 *Sani*
PRINCIPAL SURFACE COMBATANTS
  FRIGATES • FFHM 3 *Nerey* (*Krivak* III) with 1 twin lnchr with *Osa*-M (SA-N-4 *Gecko*) SAM, 2 quad 533mm TT lnchr, 2 RBU 6000 *Smerch* 2 A/S mor, 1 100mm gun (capacity 1 Ka-27 *Helix* A ASW hel)
PATROL AND COASTAL COMBATANTS 188
  PSO 4 *Komandor*
  PCO 18: 8 *Alpinist* (Project 503); 1 *Sprut*; 7 *Rubin* with 1 AK630 CIWS, 1 hel landing platform; 2 *Purga* with 1 hel landing platform
  PCC 50: 5 *Molnya* II (*Pauk* II); 3 *Svetljak* (Project 10410) with 1 AK306 CIWS; 20 *Svetljak* (Project 10410) with 1 AK630M CIWS; 8 *Svetljak* (Project 10410) with 1 AK630M CIWS; 13 *Tarantul* (*Stenka*) with 4 406mm TT, 2 twin AK630 CIWS; 1 *Yakhont* with 2 AK306 CIWS
  PCR 1 *Slepen* (*Yaz*) with 1 AK630 CIWS, 2 100mm guns
  PBF 73: 44 *Mangust*; 3 *Mirazh* (Project 14310); 4 *Mustang*-2 (Project 18623); 20 *Sobol*; 2 *Sokzhoi* with 1 AK306 CIWS
  PBR 30: 2 *Ogonek* with 1 AK306 CIWS; 2 *Ogonek* with 2 AK306 CIWS; 8 *Piyavka* with 1 AK630 CIWS; 18 *Moskit* (*Vosh*) with 1 AK630 CIWS, 1 100mm gun
  PB 12: 2 *Morzh* (Project 1496M); 10 *Lamantin* (Project 1496M1)
LOGISTICS AND SUPPORT 37
  AE 1 *Muna*
  AGB 3 *Ivan Susanin* (primarily used as patrol ships) with 2AK630 CIWS, 1 76mm gun, 1 hel landing platform
  AK 8 *Pevek* with 1 AK306 CIWS
  AKSL 5 *Kanin*
  AO 3: 1 *Ishim* (Project 15010); 2 *Envoron*
  ATF 17: 16 *Sorum* (primarily used as patrol ships) with 2 AK230M CIWS; 1 *Sorum* (primarily used as patrol ship) with 2 AK306 CIWS
AIRCRAFT • TPT ε86: 70 An-24 *Coke*/An-26 *Curl*/An-72 *Coaler*/Il-76 *Candid*/Tu-134 *Crusty*/Yak-40 *Codling*; 16 SM-92
HELICOPTERS: ε200 Ka-28 (Ka-27) *Helix* ASW/Mi-24 *Hind* Atk/Mi-26 *Halo* Spt/Mi-8 *Hip* Spt

Federal Agency for Special Construction (MoD) ε50,000

Federal Communications and Information Agency ε55,000
FORCES BY ROLE
MANOEUVRE
  Other
  4 paramilitary corps
  28 paramilitary bde

Federal Protection Service ε10,000–30,000 active
Org include elm of ground forces (mech inf bde and AB regt)
FORCES BY ROLE
MANOEUVRE
  Mechanised
  1 mech inf regt
  Air Manoeuvre
  1 AB regt
  Other
  1 (Presidential) gd regt

Federal Security Service ε4,000 active (armed)
FORCES BY ROLE
MANOEUVRE
  Other
  Some cdo unit (including Alfa and Vympel units)

National Guard ε340,000
FORCES BY ROLE
MANOEUVRE
  Other
  3 (55th, 59th & ODON) paramilitary div (2–5 paramilitary regt)
  18 (OBRON) paramilitary bde (3 mech bn, 1 mor bn)
  2 indep paramilitary bde (OBR/OSMBR)
  102 paramilitary regt/bn (incl special motorised units)
  11 (special) paramilitary unit
  Aviation
  8 sqn
COMBAT SUPPORT
  1 arty regt
EQUIPMENT BY TYPE
ARMOURED FIGHTING VEHICLES
  RECCE some BRDM-2A
  IFV/APC (W) 1,650 BMP-2/BTR-70M/BTR-80/BTR-82A/BTR-82AM
ARTILLERY 35
  TOWED 122mm 20 D-30

MOR 120mm 15 M-1938 (PM-38)
AIRCRAFT • TPT 29: Heavy 9 Il-76 *Candid*; Medium 2 An-12 *Cub*; Light 12 An-26 *Curl*; 6 An-72 *Coaler*
HELICOPTERS • TPT 70: Heavy 10 Mi-26 *Halo*; Medium 60 Mi-8 *Hip*

Railway Troops (MoD) ε20,000
4 regional commands
FORCES BY ROLE
COMBAT SERVICE SUPPORT
10 (railway) tpt bde

Cyber

The first official doctrinal statement on the role of the Russian military in cyberspace, the 'Conceptual Views on the Activity of the Russian Federation Armed Forces in Information Space', was released at the end of 2011, and described cyber-force tasks with little correlation to those of equivalent commands in the West. In particular, the document contains no mention of the possibility of offensive cyber activity. It is also entirely defensive in tone, and focuses on force protection and prevention of information war, including allowing for a military role in negotiating international treaties governing information security. In January 2012, then-CGS Makarov gave a different picture of the three main tasks for any new command: 'disrupting adversary information systems, including by introducing harmful software; defending our own communications and command systems'; and 'working on domestic and foreign public opinion using the media, Internet and more'. The third task is a reminder that, unlike some other nations with advanced cyber capabilities, Russia considers cyber warfare as an integral component of information warfare. Operations in Crimea from early 2014, and in the wider information space concerning the conflict in Ukraine, demonstrate that Russian thinking and capacity has matured in these areas. In 2012, it was reported that Russia was considering establishing a cyber-security command, with this possibly reaching FOC by 2017.

DEPLOYMENT

ARMENIA
3,300: 1 mil base with (1 MR bde; 74 T-72; 80 BMP-1; 80 BMP-2; 12 2S1; 12 BM-21); 1 sqn with 18 MiG-29 *Fulcrum*; 2 AD bty with S-300V (SA-12 *Gladiator/Giant*); 1 AD bty with 2K12 *Kub* (SA-6 *Gainful*)

BELARUS
1 radar station at Baranovichi (*Volga* system; leased); 1 naval comms site

BOSNIA-HERZEGOVINA
OSCE • Bosnia and Herzegovina 2

CÔTE D'IVOIRE
UN • UNOCI 4 obs

DEMOCRATIC REPUBLIC OF THE CONGO
UN • MONUSCO 1; 28 obs

GEORGIA
7,000; Abkhazia 1 mil base with (1 MR bde; 40 T-90A; 120 BTR-82A; 18 2S3; 12 2S12; 18 BM-21; some S-300 SAM; some atk hel); South Ossetia 1 mil base with (1 MR bde; 40 T-72; 120 BMP-2; 36 2S3; 12 2S12)

KAZAKHSTAN
1 radar station at Balkash (*Dnepr* system; leased)

KYRGYZSTAN
ε500; 13 Su-25SM *Frogfoot*; 2 Mi-8 *Hip* spt hel

LIBERIA
UN • UNMIL 2 obs

MEDITERRANEAN SEA
1 CV; 1 CGHMN; 2 DDGHM; 1 FFGHM

MIDDLE EAST
UN • UNTSO 5 obs

MOLDOVA/TRANSDNIESTR
ε1,500 (including 441 peacekeepers); 2 MR bn; 100 MBT/AIFV/APC; 7 Mi-24 *Hind*; some Mi-8 *Hip*

SOUTH SUDAN
UN • UNMISS 3; 3 obs

SUDAN
UN • UNISFA 1 obs

SYRIA
4,000: 1 l inf BG; 7 T-90; ε20 BTR-82A; 12 2A65; 4 9A52 *Smerch*; TOS-1A; 9K720 *Iskander*-M; 12 Su-24M *Fencer*; 4 Su-30SM; 4 Su-34; 4 Su-35S; 1 Il-20M; 4 Mi-28N *Havoc*; 4 Ka-52 Hokum B; 12 Mi-24P/Mi-35M *Hind*; 4 Mi-8AMTSh *Hip*; 3 *Pantsir*-S1/S2; 1 AShM bty with 3K55 *Bastion*; 1 SAM bty with S-400; 1 SAM bty with S-300V4; air base at Latakia; naval facility at Tartus

TAJIKISTAN
5,000; 1 (201st) mil base with (40 T-72B1; 60 BMP-2; 80 BTR-82A; 40 MT-LB; 18 2S1; 36 2S3; 6 2S12; 12 9P140 *Uragan*); 4 Mi-24P *Hind*; 4 Mi-8MTV *Hip*

UKRAINE
Crimea: 28,000; 1 recce bde, 2 naval inf bde; 1 arty bde; 1 NBC regt; 40 T-72B3 MBT; 80 BMP-2 AIFV; 200 BTR-82A; 20 BTR-80 APC: 150 MT-LB; 18 2S1 arty; 18 2S19 arty; 12 BM-21 MRL; 1 AShM bde with 3K60 *Bal*; 3K55 *Bastion*; 1 FGA regt with Su-24M/MR; Su-30SM; 1 FGA regt with Su-27SM2/3; Su-30M2; 1 FGA regt with Su-24M/Su-25SM; 1 atk/tpt hel regt; 1 ASW hel regt; 1 AD regt with S-300PM; 1 AD regt with S-400; 1 Fleet HQ located at Sevastopol; 2 radar stations located at Sevastopol (*Dnepr* system) and Mukachevo (*Dnepr* system)
Donetsk/Luhansk: 6,000 (reported)
OSCE • Ukraine 40

WESTERN SAHARA
UN • MINURSO 16 obs

Tajikistan TJK

Tajikistani Somoni Tr		2015	2016	2017
GDP	Tr	48.4bn	52.8bn	
	US$	7.82bn	6.61bn	
per capita	US$	922	764	
Growth	%	6	6	
Inflation	%	5.8	6.3	
Def bdgt	Tr	n.k.	n.k.	
	US$	n.k.	n.k.	
FMA (US)	US$		0.7m	
US$1=Tr			6.19	7.99

Population 8,330,946

Ethnic groups: Tajik 84.2%; Uzbek 12.2%; Kyrgyz 0.8%; Russian 0.5%; other or unspecified 2.3%

Age	0–14	15–19	20–24	25–29	30–64	65 plus
Male	16.6%	4.9%	4.7%	5.1%	17.0%	1.3%
Female	16.0%	4.8%	4.6%	5.0%	18.0%	1.9%

Capabilities

The small Tajik armed forces have little capacity to deploy other than token forces and almost all equipment is of Soviet-era origin. Without support they would face difficulties in the event of conflict or significant internal unrest, but Tajikistan's membership of the CSTO and the presence of a large Russian military deployment in Dushanbe offers reassurance. A 2014 deal on military modernisation with Russia has opened the possibility of military aid possibly worth over US$1bn, including platforms, weapons and personal equipment. The extended border with Afghanistan, and the possibility of a spillover of violence, is a priority concern, and border deployments have been stepped up in response. In August 2016, the US embassy in Tajikistan donated radios and vehicles to the Tajik Border Guard. Given the overall weaknesses of the Tajik armed and security forces – which include limited special-forces training, a high number of conscripts and only modest planning capacity – low-level militant activity linked to drug trafficking could continue to burden and challenge the armed forces.

ACTIVE 8,800 (Army 7,300 Air Force/Air Defence 1,500) **Paramilitary 7,500**
Conscript liability 24 months

ORGANISATIONS BY SERVICE

Army 7,300
FORCES BY ROLE
MANOEUVRE
  Mechanised
  3 MR bde
  Air Manoeuvre
  1 air aslt bde
COMBAT SUPPORT
  1 arty bde

AIR DEFENCE
  1 SAM regt
EQUIPMENT BY TYPE
ARMOURED FIGHTING VEHICLES
  MBT 37: 30 T-72; 7 T-62
  IFV 23: 8 BMP-1; 15 BMP-2
  APC • APC (W) 23 BTR-60/BTR-70/BTR-80
ARTILLERY 23
  TOWED 122mm 10 D-30
  MRL 122mm 3 BM-21 *Grad*
  MOR 120mm 10
AIR DEFENCE • SAM
  Medium-range S-75 *Dvina* (SA-2 *Guideline*); S-125 *Pechora*-2M (SA-26)
  Point-defence 9K32 *Strela*-2 (SA-7 *Grail*)‡

Air Force/Air Defence 1,500
FORCES BY ROLE
TRANSPORT
  1 sqn with Tu-134A *Crusty*
ATTACK/TRANSPORT HELICOPTER
  1 sqn with Mi-24 *Hind*; Mi-8 *Hip*; Mi-17TM *Hip* H
EQUIPMENT BY TYPE
AIRCRAFT
  TPT • Light 1 Tu-134A *Crusty*
  TRG 4+: 4 L-39 *Albatros*; some Yak-52
HELICOPTERS
  ATK 4 Mi-24 *Hind*
  TPT • Medium 11 Mi-8 *Hip*/Mi-17TM *Hip* H

Paramilitary 7,500

Internal Troops 3,800

National Guard 1,200

Emergencies Ministry 2,500

Border Guards

DEPLOYMENT

SERBIA
OSCE • Kosovo 1

UKRAINE
OSCE • Ukraine 11

FOREIGN FORCES

Russia 5,000; 1 (201st) mil base with (40 T-72B1; 60 BMP-2; 80 BTR-82A; 40 MT-LB; 18 2S1; 36 2S3; 6 2S12; 12 9P140 *Uragan*); 4 Mi-24P *Hind*; 4 Mi-8MTV *Hip*

Turkmenistan TKM

Turkmen New Manat TMM		2015	2016	2017
GDP	TMM	125bn	128bn	
	US$	35.9bn	36.6bn	
per capita	US$	6,655	6,694	
Growth	%	6.5	5.4	
Inflation	%	6.4	5.5	
Def exp	TMM	n.k.	n.k.	
	US$	n.k.	n.k.	
FMA (US)	US$		0.1m	
USD1=TMM		3.50	3.50	

Population 5,291,317

Ethnic groups: Turkmen 77%; Uzbek 9%; Russian 7%; Kazak 2%

Age	0–14	15–19	20–24	25–29	30–64	65 plus
Male	13.1%	4.5%	5.1%	5.0%	19.8%	2.0%
Female	12.8%	4.4%	5.1%	5.0%	20.6%	2.6%

Capabilities

Turkmenistan declared its neutrality in 1999 and enshrined this principle in its 2009 military doctrine; it is not a member of the Russian-backed CSTO. The country's largely conscript-based armed forces are poorly equipped and remain reliant on Soviet-era equipment and doctrine. Low levels of training and a lack of available spare parts further limit capability. While the ground forces are shifting from a Soviet divisional structure to an updated brigade system, progress is slow. The air force has a very modest capability, as most of the aircraft the country inherited from the Soviet Union have been stored or scrapped and no significant new procurement has occurred. In a bid to redress these issues, a new military doctrine was issued in January 2016. It aimed to increase defensive capability in order to safeguard national interests and territorial integrity. It confirmed the commitment to permanent neutrality. Plans to strengthen coastal naval forces resulted in the procurement of some assets, leading to a moderate improvement in the Caspian Sea naval presence.

ACTIVE 36,500 (Army 33,000 Navy 500 Air 3,000)

Conscript liability 24 months

ORGANISATIONS BY SERVICE

Army 33,000
5 Mil Districts

FORCES BY ROLE
SPECIAL FORCES
  1 spec ops regt
MANOEUVRE
  Armoured
  1 tk bde
  Mechanised
  1 (3rd) MR div (1 tk regt; 3 MR regt, 1 arty regt)
  1 (22nd) MR div (1 tk regt; 1 MR regt, 1 arty regt)
  4 MR bde
  1 naval inf bde
  Other
  1 MR trg div
SURFACE-TO-SURFACE MISSILE
  1 SRBM bde with SS-1 *Scud*
COMBAT SUPPORT
  1 arty bde
  1 (mixed) arty/AT regt
  1 MRL bde
  1 AT regt
  1 engr regt
AIR DEFENCE
  2 SAM bde

EQUIPMENT BY TYPE†
ARMOURED FIGHTING VEHICLES
  MBT 654: 4 T-90S; 650 T-72/T-72UMG
  RECCE 260: 200 BRDM-2; 60 BRM-1
  IFV 1,038: 600 BMP-1/BMP-1M; 430 BMP-2; 4 BMP-3; 4 BTR-80A
  APC 870+
    APC (W) 870: 120 BTR-60 (all variants); 300 BTR-70; 450 BTR-80
    PPV Kirpi
  ABCV 8 BMD-1
ANTI-TANK/ANTI-INFRASTRUCTURE
  MSL
    SP 54: 8 9P122 *Malyutka*-M (AT-3 *Sagger* on BRDM-2); 8 9P133 *Malyutka*-P (AT-3 *Sagger* on BRDM-2); 2 9P148 *Konkurs* (AT-5 *Spandrel* on BRDM-2); 36 9P149 *Shturm* (AT-6 *Spiral* on MT-LB)
    MANPATS 9K11 *Malyutka* (AT-3 *Sagger*); 9K111 *Fagot* (AT-4 *Spigot*); 9K111-1 *Konkurs* (AT-5 *Spandrel*); 9K115 *Metis* (AT-7 *Saxhorn*)
  GUNS 100mm 60 MT-12/T-12
ARTILLERY 765
  SP 122mm 40 2S1
  TOWED 457: **122mm** 350 D-30; **130mm** 6 M-46; **152mm** 101: 17 D-1; 72 D-20; 6 2A36 *Giatsint*-B; 6 2A65 *Msta*-B
  GUN/MOR 120mm 17 2S9 NONA-S
  MRL 154: **122mm** 88: 18 9P138; 70 BM-21 *Grad*; **220mm** 60 9P140 *Uragan*; **300mm** 6 9A52 *Smerch*
  MOR 97: **82mm** 31; **120mm** 66 M-1938 (PM-38)
SURFACE-TO-SURFACE MISSILE LAUNCHERS
  SRBM • Conventional 16 SS-1 *Scud*
UNMANNED AERIAL VEHICLES
  CISR • Heavy CH-3; WJ-600
  ISR • Medium *Falco*
AIR DEFENCE
  SAM
    Short-range: FM-90; 2K12 *Kub* (SA-6 *Gainful*)
    Point-defence 53+: 40 9K33 *Osa* (SA-8 *Gecko*); 13 9K35 *Strela*-10 mod. (SA-13 *Gopher*); 9K32 *Strela*-2 (SA-7 *Grail*)‡; 9K34 *Strela*-3 (SA-14 *Gremlin*); *Mistral* (reported)
  GUNS 70
    SP 23mm 48 ZSU-23-4
    TOWED 57mm 22 S-60

AIR-LAUNCHED MISSILES
ASM: CM-502KG

Navy 500
EQUIPMENT BY TYPE
PATROL AND COASTAL COMBATANTS 19
  PCFGM 2 *Edermen* (RUS *Molnya*) with 4 quad lnchr with 3M24E *Uran* AShM, 1 quad lnchr (manual aiming) with 9K32 *Strela*-2 (SA-N-5 *Grail*) SAM, 2 AK620 CIWS, 1 76mm gun
  PCC 4 *Arkadag*
  PBF 12: 5 *Grif*-T; 5 Dearsan 14: 2 *Sobol*
  PB 1 *Point*

Air Force 3,000
FORCES BY ROLE
FIGHTER
  2 sqn with MiG-29 *Fulcrum*; MiG-29UB *Fulcrum*;
GROUND ATTACK
  1 sqn with Su-25MK *Frogfoot*
TRANSPORT
  1 sqn with An-26 *Curl*; Mi-8 *Hip*; Mi-24 *Hind*
TRAINING
  1 unit with L-39 *Albatros*
AIR DEFENCE
  Some sqn with S-75 *Dvina* (SA-2 *Guideline*); S-125 *Pechora* (SA-3 *Goa*); S-125 *Pechora*-2M (SA-26); S-200 *Angara* (SA-5 *Gammon*); FD-2000 (HQ-9); KS-1A (HQ-12)
EQUIPMENT BY TYPE
AIRCRAFT 36 combat capable
  FTR 24: 22 MiG-29A/C *Fulcrum*; 2 MiG-29UB *Fulcrum*
  ATK 12 Su-25MK *Frogfoot*
  TPT • Light 2: 1 An-26 *Curl*; 1 An-74 *Coaler*
  TRG 2 L-39 *Albatros*
HELICOPTERS
  ATK 10 Mi-24P *Hind* F
  TPT • Medium 8 Mi-8 *Hip*
AIR DEFENCE • SAM
  Long-range S-200 *Angara* (SA-5 *Gammon*); FD-2000 (HQ-9)
  Medium-range S-75 *Dvina* (SA-2 *Guideline*); S-125 *Pechora*-2M (SA-26); KS-1A (HQ-12)
  Short-range S-125 *Pechora* (SA-3 *Goa*)

Paramilitary 5,000
Federal Border Guard Service ε5,000
EQUIPMENT BY TYPE
HELICOPTERS
  MRH 2 AW139
  TPT 3+: Medium some Mi-8 *Hip*; Light 3 AW109

Ukraine UKR

Ukrainian Hryvnia h		2015	2016	2017
GDP	h	1.98tr	2.28tr	
	US$	90.5bn	87.2bn	
per capita	US$	2,125	2,052	
Growth	%	-9.9	1.5	
Inflation	%	48.7	15.06	
Def bdgt	h	50.0bn	56.6bn	65.4bn
	US$	2.29bn	2.17bn	
FMA (US)	US$	47m	42m	42m
USD1=h		21.87	26.16	

Population   44,209,733

Age	0–14	15–19	20–24	25–29	30–64	65 plus
Male	7.8%	2.4%	3.1%	4.1%	23.5%	5.3%
Female	7.4%	2.3%	3.0%	3.9%	26.6%	10.5%

Capabilities

Ukraine was not able to offer any resistance to Russia's seizure of Crimea in March 2014, and the country's armed forces have since been fighting separatist forces in the east and contending with the activity of Russian military forces. Ukraine has since enlarged its armed forces and begun a modernisation process with the aim of bringing the Ukrainian military in line with NATO standards. The National Security Strategy of Ukraine, passed in 2015, set out a number of modernisation objectives to be achieved by 2020, including the aim of eventually joining NATO, which was also iterated in the 2016 white book. In 2016 the Ukrainian defence ministry established a Joint Operational Command to act as the permanent command-and-control body for the various arms of the military. A Special Operations Forces branch was established in 2016, with training and assistance provided by NATO countries. Ukraine also increased equipment funding in 2015, when compared to 2014. Meanwhile, reform of the logistical-support system began in 2015 and in July the Centre for Development and Support of Logistics was established, which is responsible for the development of new, NATO-standard logistical support. The centre also has control over the development and production of equipment. The defence ministry's switch to 'e-procurement' has also sped up the procurement process and saved money. The Ukrainian defence industry was consolidated under the state-owned Ukroboronprom organisation in 2010. It is able to provide almost all of the armed forces' equipment, in particular armoured vehicles and fixed-wing transport aircraft, and has even resumed delivery of export orders. Much of the focus of the Ukrainian defence industry in the past couple of years has been on repairing and modernising equipment for use by the newly expanded armed forces. Ukraine receives training and assistance from the US and other NATO countries. Ukraine conducted 500 training exercises in 2015, of which 225 were operational training exercises; a significant increase on 2014 numbers. Ukraine has also increased participation in multinational exercises. In 2015, Ukraine passed legislation increasing the size of the armed forces. New formations were created to achieve this, as well as incorporating volunteer units into the army and the national guard. The availability of flyable aircraft continues to be a problem, with L-39 training aircraft being attached to tactical-aviation brigades in order to increase flying hours for *Flanker* and *Fulcrum* pilots. The limited availability of fixed-wing transport aircraft and helicopters places restrictions on the rapid deployment of forces. (See pp. 196–98.)

ACTIVE 204,000 (Army 145,000 Navy 6,000 Air Force 45,000 Airborne 8,000 Special Operations Forces n.k.) Paramilitary 88,000+

Conscript liability Army, Air Force 18 months, Navy 2 years. Minimum age for conscription raised from 18 to 20 in 2015

RESERVE 900,000 (Joint 900,000)
Military service within 5 years

ORGANISATIONS BY SERVICE

Army 145,000

4 regional HQ

FORCES BY ROLE
MANOEUVRE
  Reconnaissance
  5 recce bn
  Armoured
  2 tk bde
  Mechanised
  9 mech bde
  2 mtn bde
  Light
  4 mot inf bde
SURFACE-TO-SURFACE MISSILES
  1 SSM bde
COMBAT SUPPORT
  5 arty bde
  3 MRL regt
  1 engr regt
  1 EW regt
  1 EW bn
  2 EW coy
  1 CBRN regt
  4 sigs regt
COMBAT SERVICE SUPPORT
  3 maint regt
  1 maint coy
HELICOPTERS
  4 avn bde
  1 avn regt
AIR DEFENCE
  4 AD regt

Reserves
FORCES BY ROLE
MANOEUVRE
  Light
  25+ inf bn

EQUIPMENT BY TYPE
ARMOURED FIGHTING VEHICLES
  MBT 802: 710 T-64/T-64BV/BM; 70 T-72; 22 T-80BV; (10 T-84 *Oplot*; 143 T-80; 530 T-72; 588 T-64; 20 T-55 all in store)
  RECCE 548: 433 BRDM-2; 115 BRM-1K (CP)
  IFV 1,087: 193 BMP-1; 890 BMP-2; 4 BMP-3; some BTR-3DA; some BTR-3E1; some BTR-4E *Bucephalus*
  APC 328
    APC (T) 15+: 15 BTR-D; some MT-LB
    APC (W) 313: 5 BTR-60; 215 BTR-70; 93 BTR-80
  ABCV 30: 15 BMD-1, 15 BMD-2
ENGINEERING & MAINTENANCE VEHICLES
  AEV 53 BAT-2; MT-LB
  ARV BREM-1; BREM-2; BREM-64; T-54/T-55
  VLB MTU-20
ANTI-TANK/ANTI-INFRASTRUCTURE
  MSL • MANPATS 9K111 *Fagot* (AT-4 *Spigot*); 9K113 *Konkurs* (AT-5 *Spandrel*); 9K114 *Shturm* (AT-6 *Spiral*); *Stugna*-P
  GUNS 100mm ε500 MT-12/T-12
ARTILLERY 1,737
  SP 532+: 122mm 238 2S1 *Gvozdika*; 152mm 288: 235 2S3 *Akatsiya*; 18 2S5 *Giatsint*-S; 35 2S19 *Msta*-S; 203mm 6+ 2S7 *Pion*; (up to 90 2S7 *Pion* in store)
  TOWED 515+: 122mm 75 D-30; 152mm 440: 180 2A36 *Giatsint*-B; 130 2A65 *Msta*-B; 130+ D-20
  GUN/MOR • 120mm • TOWED 2 2B16 NONA-K
  MRL 348: 122mm 203: 18 9P138; 185 BM-21 *Grad*; 220mm 70 9P140 *Uragan*; 300mm 75 9A52 *Smerch*
  MOR 120mm 340: 190 2S12 *Sani*; 30 M-1938 (PM-38); 120 M120-15
SURFACE-TO-SURFACE MISSILE LAUNCHERS
  SRBM • Conventional 90 9K79 *Tochka* (SS-21 *Scarab*)
  RADAR • LAND AN/TPQ-36 *Firefinder* (arty); *Small Fred/Small Yawn*/SNAR-10 *Big Fred* (arty)
HELICOPTERS
  ATK ε35 Mi-24 *Hind*
  MRH 1 *Lev*-1
  TPT • Medium ε24 Mi-8 *Hip*
AIR DEFENCE
  SAM
    Long-range (Some S-300V (SA-12 *Gladiator*) in store)
    Point-defence 9K35 *Strela*-10 (SA-13 *Gopher*); 9K33 *Osa* (SA-8 *Gecko*)
  GUNS
    SP 30mm 70 2S6
    TOWED 23mm ZU-23-2; 57mm S-60

Navy 6,000 (incl Naval Aviation and Naval Infantry)

After Russia's annexation of Crimea, HQ shifted to Odessa. Several additional vessels remain in Russian possession in Crimea

2 Regional HQ

EQUIPMENT BY TYPE
PRINCIPAL SURFACE COMBATANTS 1
  FRIGATES • FFHM 1 *Hetman Sagaidachny* (RUS *Krivak* III) with 1 twin lnchr with *Osa*-M (SA-N-4 *Gecko*) SAM,

2 quad 533mm ASTT with T-53 HWT, 1 100mm gun, (capacity 1 Ka-27 *Helix* ASW hel)
PATROL AND COASTAL COMBATANTS 4
  CORVETTES • FSM 1 *Grisha* (II/V) with 1 twin lnchr with *Osa*-M (SA-N-4 *Gecko*) SAM, 2 twin 533mm ASTT with SAET-60 HWT, 2 RBU 6000 *Smerch* 2 A/S mor, 1 76mm gun
  PCFGM 1 *Tarantul* II (FSU *Molnya*) with 2 twin lnchr with P-15 *Termit*-R (SS-N-2D *Styx*) AShM; 1 quad lnchr (manual aiming) with 9K32 *Strela*-2 (SA-N-5 *Grail*) SAM; 1 76mm gun
  PHG 1 *Matka* (FSU *Vekhr*) with 2 single lnchr with P-15 *Termit*-M/R (SS-N-2C/D *Styx*) AShM, 1 76mm gun
  PB 1 *Zhuk* (FSU *Grif*)
MINE WARFARE • MINE COUNTERMEASURES 1
  MHI 1 *Yevgenya* (FSU *Korund*)
AMPHIBIOUS
  LANDING SHIPS
    LSM 1 *Polnochny* C (capacity 6 MBT; 180 troops)
  LANDING CRAFT • LCU 3
LOGISTICS AND SUPPORT 10
  AG 1 *Bereza*
  AGI 1 *Muna*
  AGS 1 *Biya*
  AKL 1
  AO 2 *Toplivo*
  AWT 1 *Sudak*
  AXL 3 *Petrushka*

Naval Aviation ε1,000

EQUIPMENT BY TYPE
FIXED-WING AIRCRAFT
  ASW (2 Be-12 *Mail* non-operational)
  TPT • Light (2 An-26 *Curl* in store)
HELICOPTERS
  ASW 7+: 4+ Ka-27 *Helix* A; 3 Mi-14PS/PL *Haze* A/C
  TPT • Medium 1 Ka-29 *Helix*-B

Naval Infantry ε2,000

FORCES BY ROLE
MANOEUVRE
  Light
  1 nav inf bde
  1 nav inf bn
EQUIPMENT BY TYPE
ARMOURED FIGHTING VEHICLES
  MBT T-64BV
  IFV some BMP-1
  APC • APC (W) some BTR-60; some BTR-80
ARTILLERY
  SP 122mm 247 2S1 *Gvozdika*
  TOWED 152mm some 2A36 *Giatsint*-B

Air Forces 45,000

Flying hours 40 hrs/yr

3 Regional HQ

FORCES BY ROLE
FIGHTER
  4 bde with MiG-29 *Fulcrum*; Su-27 *Flanker*; L-39 *Albatros*
FIGHTER/GROUND ATTACK
  2 bde with Su-24M *Fencer*; Su-25 *Frogfoot*
ISR
  2 sqn with Su-24MR *Fencer* E*
TRANSPORT
  3 bde with An-24; An-26; An-30; Il-76 *Candid*; Tu-134 *Crusty*
TRAINING
  Some sqn with L-39 *Albatros*
TRANSPORT HELICOPTER
  Some sqn with Mi-8; Mi-9; PZL Mi-2 *Hoplite*
AIR DEFENCE
  6 bde with 9K37M *Buk*-M1 (SA-11 *Gadfly*); S-300P/PS/PT (SA-10 *Grumble*)
  4 regt with 9K37M *Buk*-M1 (SA-11); S-300P/PS/PT (SA-10)
EQUIPMENT BY TYPE
AIRCRAFT ε125 combat capable
  FTR 71: ε37 MiG-29 *Fulcrum*; ε34 Su-27 *Flanker*
  FGA ε14 Su-24M *Fencer*
  ATK ε31 Su-25 *Frogfoot*
  ISR 12: 3 An-30 *Clank*; ε9 Su-24MR *Fencer* E*
  TPT 30: **Heavy** 5 Il-76 *Candid*; **Medium** 1 An-70; **Light** ε24: 3 An-24 *Coke*; ε20 An-26 *Curl*; 1 Tu-134 *Crusty*
  TRG ε32 L-39 *Albatros*
HELICOPTERS
  C2 ε14 Mi-9
  TPT 33: **Medium** ε30 Mi-8 *Hip*; **Light** 3 PZL Mi-2 *Hoplite*
AIR DEFENCE • SAM 322:
  Long-range 250 S-300P/PS/PT (SA-10 *Grumble*)
  Medium-range 72 9K37M *Buk*-M1 (SA-11 *Gadfly*)
AIR-LAUNCHED MISSILES
  AAM • IR R-60 (AA-8 *Aphid*); R-73 (AA-11 *Archer*)
  SARH R-27 (AA-10A *Alamo*)
  ASM Kh-25 (AS-10 *Karen*); Kh-29 (AS-14 *Kedge*)
  ARM Kh-25MP (AS-12 *Kegler*); Kh-58 (AS-11 *Kilter*); Kh-28 (AS-9 *Kyle*)

High-Mobility Airborne Troops ε8,000

FORCES BY ROLE
MANOEUVRE
  Air Manoeuvre
  1 AB bde
  4 air mob bde
EQUIPMENT BY TYPE
ARMOURED FIGHTING VEHICLES
  IFV 75+: 30 BMD-1; 45 BMD-2; some BTR-3E1; some BTR-4 *Bucephalus*
  APC 160+
    APC (T) 25 BTR-D
    APC (W) 135+: 1 BTR-60; 2 BTR-70; 122 BTR-80; 10+ *Dozor*-B
ANTI-TANK/ANTI-INFRASTRUCTURE
  MSL • MANPATS 9K111 *Fagot* (AT-4 *Spigot*); 9K111-1 *Konkurs* (AT-5 *Spandrel*)
ARTILLERY 118
  TOWED • 122mm 54 D-30
  GUN/MOR • SP • 120mm 40 2S9 NONA-S
  MOR 120mm 24 2S12 *Sani*

AIR DEFENCE • GUNS • SP 23mm some ZU-23-2 (truck mounted)

Special Operations Forces n.k.
SPECIAL FORCES
2 SF regt

Paramilitary

National Guard ε46,000
Ministry of Internal Affairs; 5 territorial comd
FORCES BY ROLE
MANOEUVRE
Armoured
Some tk bn
Mechanised
Some mech bn
Light
Some lt inf bn
EQUIPMENT BY TYPE
ARMOURED FIGHTING VEHICLES
MBT T-64; T-64BV; T-64BM; T-72
IFV 83: BTR-3; 32+ BTR-3E1; ε50 BTR-4 Bucephalus; 1 BMP-2
APC
APC (W) BTR-70; BTR-80
PPV Streit *Cougar*; Streit *Spartan*
ANTI-TANK/ANTI-INFRASTRUCTURE
RCL 73mm some SPG-9
ARTILLERY
TOWED 122mm some D-30
MOR 120mm some
AIRCRAFT
TPT • Light 24: 20 An-26 *Curl*; 2 An-72 *Coaler*; 2 Tu-134 *Crusty*
HELICOPTERS • TPT Medium 7 Mi-8 *Hip*
AIR DEFENCE
SAM • Point-defence 9K38 *Igla* (SA-18 *Grouse*)
GUNS • SP 23mm some ZU-23-2 (truck mounted)

Border Guard ε42,000
FORCES BY ROLE
MANOEUVRE
Light
some mot inf gp

Maritime Border Guard
The Maritime Border Guard is an independent subdivision of the State Commission for Border Guards and is not part of the navy
FORCES BY ROLE
PATROL
4 (cutter) bde
2 rvn bde
MINE WARFARE
1 MCM sqn
TRANSPORT
3 sqn
TRANSPORT HELICOPTER
1 sqn

COMBAT SERVICE SUPPORT
1 trg div
1 (aux ships) gp
EQUIPMENT BY TYPE
PATROL AND COASTAL COMBATANTS 26
PCFT 6 *Stenka* with 4 single 406mm TT
PCT 3 *Pauk* I with 4 single 406mm TT, 2 RBU-1200 A/S mor, 1 76mm gun
PHT 1 *Muravey* with 2 single 406mm TT, 1 76mm gun
PB 12: 11 *Zhuk*; 1 *Orlan*
PBR 4 *Shmel*
LOGISTICS AND SUPPORT • AGF 1
AIRCRAFT • TPT Medium An-8 *Camp*; Light An-24 *Coke*; An-26 *Curl*; An-72 *Coaler*
HELICOPTERS • ASW: Ka-27 *Helix* A

Cyber
In June 2016 the Ukrainian National Cyber Security Coordination Centre was established, a year after the publication of the National Cyber Security Strategy. This centre will be based in the National Security and Defence Council and will consist of representatives from the defence ministry and the chief of the general staff of the armed forces.

DEPLOYMENT

Legal provisions for foreign deployment:
Constitution: Codified constitution (1996)
Specific legislation: 'On the procedures to deploy Armed Forces of Ukraine units abroad' (1518-III, March 2000)
Decision on deployment of troops abroad: Parliament authorised to approve decision to provide military assistance, deploy troops abroad and allow foreign military presence in Ukraine (Art. 85, para 23); also, in accordance with Art. 7 of the specific legislation (above), president is authorised to take a decision to deploy troops abroad and at the same time to submit a draft law to the Parliament of Ukraine for approval

AFGHANISTAN
NATO • *Operation Resolute Support* 8

ARMENIA/AZERBAIJAN
OSCE • Minsk Conference 1

CÔTE D'IVOIRE
UN • UNOCI 2

CYPRUS
UN • UNFICYP 2

DEMOCRATIC REPUBLIC OF THE CONGO
UN • MONUSCO 255; 11 obs; 2 atk hel sqn; 1 hel sqn

LIBERIA
UN • UNMIL 162; 3 obs; 1 hel sqn

MOLDOVA
10 obs

SERBIA
NATO • KFOR 40

OSCE • Kosovo 1
UN • UNMIK 2 obs

SOUTH SUDAN
UN • UNMISS 1; 3 obs

SUDAN
UN • UNISFA 2; 4 obs

FOREIGN FORCES

Albania OSCE 3
Armenia OSCE 2
Austria OSCE 19
Azerbaijan OSCE 1
Belarus OSCE 7
Belgium OSCE 4
Bosnia-Herzegovina OSCE 32
Bulgaria OSCE 32
Canada OSCE 21 • *Operation Unifier* 200
Croatia OSCE 11
Czech Republic OSCE 17
Denmark OSCE 13
Estonia OSCE 7
Finland OSCE 23
France OSCE 19
Georgia OSCE 11
Germany OSCE 40
Greece OSCE 21
Hungary OSCE 30
Ireland OSCE 14
Italy OSCE 25
Kazakhstan OSCE 4
Kyrgyzstan OSCE 16
Latvia OSCE 7
Lithuania OSCE 2 • JMTG-U 16
Luxembourg OSCE 2
Macedonia (FYROM) OSCE 23
Moldova OSCE 31
Montenegro OSCE 2
Netherlands OSCE 11
Norway OSCE 13
Poland OSCE 38
Portugal OSCE 5
Romania OSCE 55
Russia OSCE 40
Slovakia OSCE 9
Slovenia OSCE 2
Spain OSCE 17
Sweden OSCE 23
Switzerland OSCE 16
Tajikistan OSCE 11
Turkey OSCE 14
United Kingdom OSCE 48 • *Operation Orbital* 100
United States OSCE 73 • JMTG-U 310

TERRITORY WHERE THE GOVERNMENT DOES NOT EXERCISE EFFECTIVE CONTROL

Following the overthrow of Ukraine's President Yanukovich in February 2014, the region of Crimea requested to join the Russian Federation after a referendum regarded as unconstitutional by the new Ukrainian government. Data presented here represents the de facto situation and does not imply international recognition.

EASTERN UKRAINE SEPARATIST FORCES

ORGANISATIONS BY SERVICE

Donetsk People's Republic ε20,000
FORCES BY ROLE
SPECIAL FORCES
  2 (Spetsnaz) SF bn
MANOEUVRE
  Reconnaissance
  1 recce bn
  Armoured
  1 tk bn
  Light
  6 mot inf bde
COMBAT SUPPORT
  1 arty bde
  1 engr coy
  1 EW coy
COMBAT SERVICE SUPPORT
  1 log bn
AIR DEFENCE
  1 AD bn

Luhansk People's Republic ε14,000
FORCES BY ROLE
MANOEUVRE
  Reconnaissance
  1 recce bn
  Armoured
  1 tk bn
  Light
  4 mot inf bde
COMBAT SUPPORT
  1 arty bde
  1 engr coy
  1 EW coy
COMBAT SERVICE SUPPORT
  1 log bn
AIR DEFENCE
  1 AD bn
EQUIPMENT BY TYPE
ARMOURED FIGHTING VEHICLES
  MBT T-64BV; T-64B; T-64BM†; T-72B1; T-72BA
  RECCE BDRM-2
  IFV BMP-1; BMP-2; BTR-4
  APC
    APC (T) BTR-D; MT-LB; GT-MU
    APC (W) BTR-60; BTR-70; BTR-80
  ABCV BMD-1, BMD-2

ANTI-TANK/ANTI-INFRASTRUCTURE
MSL 9K115 *Metis* (AT-7 *Saxhorn*); 9K135 *Kornet* (AT-14 *Spriggan*)
RCL 73mm SPG-9
GUNS 100mm MT-12
ARTILLERY
SP 122mm 2S1 *Gvozdika*; 152mm 2S3 *Akatsiya*; 2S19 *Msta-S†*; 203mm 2S7 *Pion*
TOWED 122mm D-30; 152mm 2A65 *Msta-B*
GUN/MOR
  SP 120mm 2S9 NONA-S
  TOWED 120mm 2B16 NONA-K
MRL 122mm BM-21 *Grad*
MOR 82mm 2B14; 120mm 2B11 *Sani*
AIR DEFENCE
  SAM
    Short-range 9K332 *Tor-M2* (SA-15 *Gauntlet*)
    Point-defence 2K22 *Tunguska* (SA-19 *Grison*); 9K32M *Strela-2M* (SA-7B *Grail*); 9K33 *Osa* (SA-8 *Gecko*); 9K35 *Strela-10* (SA-13 *Gopher*); 9K38 *Igla* (SA-18 *Grouse*); GROM
  GUNS
    SP 23mm ZU-23-2 (tch/on MT-LB)
    TOWED 14.5mm ZPU-2; 57mm S-60

FOREIGN FORCES

Russia Crimea: 28,000; 1 recce bde, 2 naval inf bde; 1 arty bde; 1 NBC bde; 40 T-72B3 MBT; 80 BMP-2 AIFV; 200 BTR-82A; 20 BTR-80 APC: 150 MT-LB; 18 2S1 arty; 18 2S19 arty; 12 BM-21 MRL; 1 AShM bde with 3K60 *Bal*; 3K55 *Bastion*; 1 FGA regt with Su-24M/MR; Su-30SM; 1 FGA regt with Su-27SM2/3; Su-30M2; 1 FGA regt with Su-24M/Su-25SM; 1 atk/tpt hel regt; 1 ASW hel regt; 1 AD regt with S-300PM; 1 AD regt with S-400; 1 Fleet HQ located at Sevastopol; 2 radar stations located at Sevastopol (*Dnepr* system) and Mukachevo (*Dnepr* system)
Donetsk/Luhansk: 6,000 (reported)

Uzbekistan UZB

Uzbekistani Som s		2015	2016	2017
GDP	s	171tr	196tr	
	US$	65.5bn	66.8bn	
per capita	US$	2,115	2,131	
Growth	%	8	6	
Inflation	%	8.5	8.4	
Def exp	s	n.k.	n.k.	
	US$	n.k.	n.k.	
FMA (US)	US$	0.7m		
US$1=s		2,616.20	2,928.98	

Population 29,473,614

Ethnic groups: Uzbek 73%; Russian 6%; Tajik 5%; Kazakh 4%; Karakalpak 2%; Tatar 2%; Korean <1%; Ukrainian <1%

Age	0–14	15–19	20–24	25–29	30–64	65 plus
Male	12.4%	4.5%	5.2%	5.3%	20.2%	2.2%
Female	11.8%	4.3%	5.2%	5.2%	20.9%	2.9%

Capabilities

Although Uzbekistan maintains bilateral defence ties with Moscow, uses mainly Soviet-era equipment and is a member of the SCO, it suspended its membership of the CSTO in mid-2012. The security situation in neighbouring Afghanistan, and the possibility of instability spilling over across Uzbekistan's border, is a primary concern. A sizeable air capability was inherited from the Soviet Union, but without recapitalisation in the intervening period the active inventory has been substantially reduced. Flying hours are reported to be low, with logistical and maintenance shortcomings affecting the availability of the remaining aircraft.

ACTIVE 48,000 (Army 24,500 Air 7,500 Joint 16,000)
Paramilitary 20,000
Conscript liability 12 months

ORGANISATIONS BY SERVICE

Army 24,500

4 Mil Districts; 2 op comd; 1 Tashkent Comd
FORCES BY ROLE
SPECIAL FORCES
  1 SF bde
MANOEUVRE
  Armoured
    1 tk bde
  Mechanised
    11 MR bde
  Air Manoeuvre
    1 air aslt bde
    1 AB bde
  Mountain
    1 lt mtn inf bde
COMBAT SUPPORT
  3 arty bde
  1 MRL bde
EQUIPMENT BY TYPE
ARMOURED FIGHTING VEHICLES
  MBT 340: 70 T-72; 100 T-64; 170 T-62
  RECCE 19: 13 BRDM-2; 6 BRM-1
  IFV 270 BMP-2
  APC 359
    APC (T) 50 BTR-D
    APC (W) 259: 24 BTR-60; 25 BTR-70; 210 BTR-80
    PPV 50 *Maxxpro+*
  ABCV 129: 120 BMD-1; 9 BMD-2
  AUV 7 *Cougar*
ENGINEERING & MAINTENANCE VEHICLES
  ARV 20 *Maxxpro* ARV
ANTI-TANK/ANTI-INFRASTRUCTURE
  MSL • MANPATS 9K11 *Malyutka* (AT-3 *Sagger*); 9K111 *Fagot* (AT-4 *Spigot*)
  GUNS 100mm 36 MT-12/T-12
ARTILLERY 487+
  SP 83+: 122mm 18 2S1 *Gvozdika*; 152mm 17+: 17 2S3 *Akatsiya*; 2S5 *Giatsint-S* (reported); 203mm 48 2S7 *Pion*
  TOWED 200: 122mm 60 D-30; 152mm 140 2A36 *Giatsint-B*

GUN/MOR 120mm 54 2S9 NONA-S
MRL 108: **122mm** 60: 36 BM-21 *Grad*; 24 9P138; **220mm** 48 9P140 *Uragan*
MOR 120mm 42: 5 2B11 *Sani*; 19 2S12 *Sani*; 18 M-120

Air Force 7,500
FORCES BY ROLE
FIGHTER
  1 sqn with MiG-29/MiG-29UB *Fulcrum*;
  1 sqn with Su-27/Su-27UB *Flanker*
FIGHTER/GROUND ATTACK
  1 regt with Su-24 *Fencer*
GROUND ATTACK
  2 sqn with Su-25/Su-25BM *Frogfoot*
ELINT/TRANSPORT
  1 regt with An-12/An-12PP *Cub*; An-26/An-26RKR *Curl*
TRANSPORT
  Some sqn with An-24 *Coke*; C295; Tu-134 *Crusty*
TRAINING
  1 sqn with L-39 *Albatros*
ATTACK/TRANSPORT HELICOPTER
  1 regt with Mi-24 *Hind*; Mi-26 *Halo*; Mi-8 *Hip*;
  1 regt with Mi-6 *Hook*; Mi-6AYa *Hook* C
EQUIPMENT BY TYPE
AIRCRAFT 45 combat capable
  FTR 12 MiG-29/MiG-29UB *Fulcrum*; (18 more in store)
  FGA 13 Su-27/Su-27UB *Flanker*; (11 more in store); (26 Su-17M (Su-17MZ)/Su-17UM-3 (Su-17UMZ) *Fitter* C/G non-operational);
  ATK 20 Su-25/Su-25BM *Frogfoot*
  EW/Tpt 26 An-12 *Cub* (med tpt)/An-12PP *Cub* (EW)
  ELINT/Tpt 13 An-26 *Curl* (lt tpt)/An-26RKR *Curl* (ELINT)
  TPT • **Light** 4: 1 An-24 *Coke*; 2 C-295W; 1 Tu-134 *Crusty*
  TRG 14 L-39 *Albatros*
HELICOPTERS
  ATK 29 Mi-24 *Hind*
  C2 2 Mi-6AYa *Hook* C
  TPT 69 **Heavy** 9: 8 H225M *Caracal*; 1 Mi-26 *Halo*; **Medium** 52 Mi-8 *Hip*; **Light** 8 AS350 *Ecureuil*
AIR DEFENCE • SAM 45
  Long-range S-200 *Angara* (SA-5 *Gammon*)
  Medium-range S-75 *Dvina* (SA-2 *Guideline*)
  Short-range S-125 *Pechora* (SA-3 *Goa*)
AIR-LAUNCHED MISSILES
  AAM • **IR** R-60 (AA-8 *Aphid*); R-73 (AA-11 *Archer*); **IR/SARH** R-27 (AA-10 *Alamo*)
  ASM Kh-23 (AS-7 *Kerry*); Kh-25 (AS-10 *Karen*)
  ARM Kh-25P (AS-12 *Kegler*); Kh-28 (AS-9 *Kyle*); Kh-58 (AS-11 *Kilter*)

Paramilitary up to 20,000

Internal Security Troops up to 19,000
Ministry of Interior

National Guard 1,000
Ministry of Defence

Table 8 **Selected arms procurements and deliveries, Russia and Eurasia**

Designation	Type	Quantity (Current)	Contract Value	Prime Nationality	Prime Contractor	Order Date	First Delivery Due	Notes
Armenia (ARM)								
TOS-1A	Arty (MRL 220mm)	n.k.	n.k.	RUS	Uralvagonzavod (Omsk-transmash)	2015	n.k.	Purchased with Russian credit
9K58 *Smerch*	Arty (MRL 300mm)	n.k.	n.k.	RUS	PJSC MZ	2015	n.k.	Purchased with Russian credit
Azerbaijan (AZE)								
BMP-3	IFV	100+	n.k.	RUS	KMZ	n.k.	2015	Total number on order unclear. Deliveries delayed due to financial issues
Belarus (BLR)								
BTR-82A	APC (W)	n.k.	n.k.	RUS	VPK	n.k.	2016	For special forces. Deliveries expected to begin in 2016
Mi-8MTV-5 *Hip*	Med tpt hel	12	n.k.	RUS	Russian Helicopters	2015	2016	First batch of six delivered Oct 2016. Remainder expected in 2017
Tor-M2K	SAM	5	n.k.	RUS	Almaz-Antey	2015	2016	Deliveries expected to begin in 2016
Georgia (GEO)								
n.k.	SAM	1 Battery	n.k.	FRA	MBDA	2015	n.k.	–
Kazakhstan (KAZ)								
Su-30SM	FGA ac	7	n.k.	RUS	UAC (Sukhoi)	2015	n.k.	Second batch
Mi-35M *Hind*	Atk hel	n.k.	n.k.	RUS	Russian Helicopters	2016	2016	Deliveries expected to begin in late 2016
Russia (RUS)								
RS-26 *Rubezh*	ICBM	n.k.	n.k.	RUS	Moscow Institute of Thermal Technology	n.k.	2017	Road-mobile intercontinental ballistic missile. In test. To replace RS-12M (SS-25 *Sickle*)
Sarmat	ICBM	n.k.	n.k.	RUS	Makeyev Rocket Design Bureau	2011	n.k.	Silo-based intercontinental ballistic missile. Ejection tests under way. Flight tests to begin in 2018
T-72B3	MBT upgrade	n.k.	n.k.	RUS	Uralvagonzavod	n.k.	2013	Upgrade of existing T-72 fleet. 1,000 delivered to army and naval infantry by late 2016
Armata	AFV	n.k.	n.k.	RUS	Uralvagonzavod	2014	2017	Heavy tracked universal-combat-platform programme. Limited serial production scheduled to commence 2016/17
Kurganets-25	AFV	n.k.	n.k.	RUS	KMZ	2014	2017	Medium tracked universal-combat-platform programme. Limited serial production scheduled to commence 2016/17
Bumerang	AFV	n.k.	n.k.	RUS	VPK (AMZ)	2014	2017	Medium wheeled universal-combat-platform programme. Limited serial production scheduled to commence 2016/17
BTR-82A	IFV	n.k.	n.k.	RUS	VPK (AMZ)	n.k.	2011	Improved BTR-80A series

Table 8 **Selected arms procurements and deliveries, Russia and Eurasia**

Designation	Type	Quantity (Current)	Contract Value	Prime Nationality	Prime Contractor	Order Date	First Delivery Due	Notes
BMP-3	IFV	n.k.	n.k.	RUS	KMZ	2015	n.k.	To equip 150th Motor-rifle Division
BMD-4M	ABCV	n.k.	n.k.	RUS	KMZ	n.k.	2015	For Airborne Troops. Deliveries ongoing
BTR-MDM	APC (T)	n.k.	n.k.	RUS	KMZ	n.k.	2015	For Airborne Troops. Deliveries ongoing
2S35 *Koalitsiya-SV*	Arty (SP 152mm)	n.k.	n.k.	RUS	Uraltransmash	n.k.	2016	Vehicles being delivered for test
9A54 *Tornado-S*	Arty (MRL 300mm)	n.k.	n.k.	RUS	Rostec (NPO Splav)	2016	2017	To replace 9A52 *Smerch*
Sprut-SDM-1	AT (Guns SP 125mm)	n.k.	n.k.	RUS	Traksornyye Zavody (VgTZ)	n.k.	2017	For Airborne Troops; to replace 2S25. Vehicle in test in 2016
9K720/728 *Iskander*-M/K	SRBM/ GLCM	n.k.	n.k.	RUS	KBM	2005	2006	Ballistic- and cruise-missile variants. Ninth brigade began converting late 2016
3K55 *Bastion*-P (SSC-5 *Stooge*)	AShM	n.k.	n.k.	RUS	Tactical Missiles Corporation (NPO Mashino-stroyeniya)	n.k.	2010	Deliveries ongoing
Borey-A class	SSBN	5	n.k.	RUS	Sevmash Shipyard	2012	2015	Fourth of class laid down Dec 2015
Yasen class	SSGN	7	n.k.	RUS	Sevmash Shipyard	1993	2013	Sixth of class laid down Jul 2016
Varshavyanka class (*Kilo*)	SSK	12	n.k.	RUS	Admiralty Shipyards	2010	2014	Sixth of class commissioned Nov 2016. Six ordered for the Pacific Fleet in 2016
Lada class	SSK	3	n.k.	RUS	Admiralty Shipyards	1997	2010	Third of class laid down Mar 2015. Delivery of second and third of class postponed to 2019
Admiral Gorshkov class	DDGHM	8	n.k.	RUS	Severnaya Verf	2005	2014	First vessel in trials as of late 2016
Project 23550	DDGH	2	n.k.	RUS	Admiralty Shipyards	2016	n.k.	Arctic patrol ship with icebreaking capability. Will be armed with *Kalibr*-NK AShM/LACM
Steregushchiy class	FFGHM	10	n.k.	RUS	Severnaya Verf Shipyard/ Komosololsk Shipyard	2001	2008	Project 20380. Tenth of class laid down Jul 2016. Fifth of class expected to commission late 2016
Gremyashchiy class	FFGHM	2	n.k.	RUS	Severnaya Verf	2011	2015	Project 20385. First of class laid down Feb 2012. Second of class laid down Jul 2013
Derzkiy class	FFGM	1	n.k.	RUS	Severnaya Verf	2014	n.k.	Project 20386. First of class laid down Oct 2016
Admiral Grigorovich class (*Krivak* IV)	FFGHM	6	n.k.	RUS	Yantar Shipyard	2010	2015	Six vessels in build for Black Sea Fleet. Second of class commissioned Jul 2016. Third of class in trials as of late 2016
Grad Sviyazhsk class (*Buyan-M*)	FSGM	12	n.k.	RUS	Zelenodolsk Shipyard	2010	2014	Fitted with *Kalibr*-NK AShM/LACM. Fourth and fifth of class commissioned Dec 2015
Project 22800	PCGM	7	n.k.	RUS	Pella Shipyard/ More Shipbuilding Plant	2015	n.k.	Eighteen planned. Will be armed with *Kalibr*-NK AShM/LACM. Third of class laid down Jul 2016
Ivan Gren class	LST	2	n.k.	RUS	Yantar Shipyard	2004	2016	First of class in trials as of late 2016. Second of class laid down Jun 2015. Order has suffered from significant delays
MiG-29SMT *Fulcrum*	FGA ac	16	n.k.	RUS	UAC (MiG)	2014	2015	First aircraft from this order delivered Dec 2015. Deliveries ongoing

Table 8 **Selected arms procurements and deliveries, Russia and Eurasia**

Designation	Type	Quantity (Current)	Contract Value	Prime Nationality	Prime Contractor	Order Date	First Delivery Due	Notes
Su-30SM	FGA ac	116	n.k.	RUS	UAC (Sukhoi)	2012	2012	Six contracts totalling 20 for navy and 96 for air force. Deliveries under way for both services
Su-34 *Fullback*	FGA ac	92	εR140bn (US$4.5bn)	RUS	UAC (Sukhoi)	2012	2013	Third order. Deliveries ongoing
Su-35S *Flanker*	FGA ac	98	n.k.	RUS	UAC (Sukhoi)	2009	2012	Fifty more aircraft ordered in Dec 2015
Il-76MD-90A	Hvy tpt ac	39	US$4bn	RUS	Aviastar-SP	2012	2014	Deliveries ongoing
Il-96-400TZ	Tkr ac	16	n.k.	RUS	UAC	2014	n.k.	Ordered 14 in 2014 and two more in 2015
Yak-130	Trg ac	40	n.k.	RUS	UAC (Irkut)	2013	n.k.	Second and third orders. Ten for navy and 30 for air force
Ka-52 *Alligator* (*Hokum B*)	Atk hel	146	n.k.	RUS	Russian Helicopters (Kamov)	2011	n.k.	For air force. Deliveries ongoing
Ka-52K *Katran*	Atk hel	32	n.k.	RUS	Russian Helicopters (Kamov)	2014	n.k.	For navy. First helicopters in test
Mi-35M *Hind*	Atk hel	n.k.	n.k.	RUS	Russian Helicopters (Rostvertol)	2010	2011	Deliveries ongoing
Mi-28N *Havoc*	Atk hel	n.k.	n.k.	RUS	Russian Helicopters (Rostvertol)	2011	n.k.	Officially entered service Dec 2013. Deliveries ongoing
Mi-28UB	Atk hel	24	n.k.	RUS	Russian Helicopters (Rostvertol)	2016	2018	For air force. Will be used for training
Mi-8MTPR-1	EW hel	18	n.k.	RUS	Russian Helicopters (KRET/Ulan-Ude)	2011	2015	Deliveries ongoing
Mi-8AMTSh *Hip*	Med tpt hel	172	n.k.	Rus	Russian Helicopters (Ulan-Ude)	2010	2010	Deliveries ongoing
Mi-8MTV-5 *Hip*	Med tpt hel	140	n.k.	RUS	Russian Helicopters (Kazan)	2011	2014	Deliveries ongoing
Tor-M2U	SAM	n.k.	n.k.	RUS	Almaz-Antey	n.k.	n.k.	Deliveries ongoing
Buk-M2 (SA-17 *Grizzly*)	SAM	n.k.	n.k.	RUS	Almaz-Antey	n.k.	n.k.	At least three brigade sets delivered by late 2016
Buk-M3	SAM	n.k.	n.k.	RUS	Almaz-Antey	n.k.	2016	First battalion set delivered for operational test late 2016
S-400 *Triumf* (SA-21 *Growler*)	SAM	n.k.	n.k.	RUS	Almaz-Antey	n.k.	2007	Fourteen regiment sets delivered by late 2016
96K6 *Pantsir*-S1 (SA-22 *Greyhound*)	SAM	n.k.	n.k.	RUS	KBP Instrument Design Bureau	n.k.	2010	Delivery in progress to S-400 regiments
Pantsir-S2	SAM	n.k.	n.k.	RUS	KBP Instrument Design Bureau	n.k.	2015	Delivery in progress to S-400 regiments

Ukraine (UKR)

Designation	Type	Quantity (Current)	Contract Value	Prime Nationality	Prime Contractor	Order Date	First Delivery Due	Notes
BTR-4 *Bucephalus*	IFV	n.k.	n.k.	UKR	Ukroboronprom (KMDB)	2014	2015	Deliveries ongoing

Uzbekistan (UZB)

Designation	Type	Quantity (Current)	Contract Value	Prime Nationality	Prime Contractor	Order Date	First Delivery Due	Notes
C-295W	Tpt ac	4	n.k.	Int'l	Airbus Group (Airbus Defence & Space)	2014	2015	Second aircraft delivered Nov 2015. Third in test early 2016

Chapter Six
Asia

Regional military roles

Armed forces in the Asia-Pacific region typically undertake a broader range of roles than their Western equivalents. This is particularly true in Southeast Asia, where armed forces – and armies in particular – sometimes remain central players in national politics (notably in Myanmar and Thailand) and retain significant internal-security responsibilities (as is the case in Indonesia, Myanmar, the Philippines and Thailand). In the region's single-party states – China, Laos, North Korea and Vietnam – the institutional nature of civil–military relations and military doctrine means that the preservation of domestic stability and party rule are vital concerns of the armed forces. From a Western perspective, the wider role of Asian forces may often seem to detract from their military capabilities, particularly in terms of their capacity to deter and defeat external adversaries, and to mount expeditionary operations. However, it should be remembered that they and their governments often employ notions of capability that differ substantially from Western norms.

Nevertheless, the development of greater capacity for conventional warfare is the dominant theme in regional defence policymaking. While rising tensions in the East China and South China seas, as well as on the Korean Peninsula, may have bolstered the case for developing conventional military capabilities, recent military developments should be seen as the latest phase in long-term defence-modernisation programmes and as such do not simply reflect external security preoccupations. These programmes are also shaped by increased financial resources resulting from sustained economic growth, strategic cultures rooted in the awareness of past conflicts and the perceived dangers of military weakness, and a pervasive long-term sense of strategic uncertainty deriving in large part from real and anticipated changes in the regional-security roles of the major powers.

The South China Sea and Washington's regional role

However, it is clear that external-security concerns are increasingly preoccupying defence establishments in the region. Furthermore, these concerns are affecting defence planning and procurement, as well as deployments. Bolstering China's position in the South China Sea has in recent years emerged as a priority for the People's Liberation Army (PLA). This has been pursued in order to reinforce Beijing's extensive territorial claims, as well as to protect its *Jin*-class (Type-094) nuclear-powered ballistic-missile submarines (SSBNs). These boats will become an important element of China's nuclear deterrent and are due to carry the CSS-NX-14 (JL-2) submarine-launched ballistic missile (SLBM). It has been reported that the boats commenced operational patrols in 2015. The Pentagon's latest annual report to Congress on China's military power spoke of four boats of the class being 'operational', without giving details, and anticipated a first Chinese SSBN deterrent patrol 'sometime in 2016'. The previous report, however, anticipated the same in 2015.

Strengthening China's capacity to project military power into the Western Pacific and Indian Ocean has also been an objective of the PLA. Speaking in November 2015, Commander of US Pacific Command Admiral Harry Harris Jr said that China was 'building runways and … facilities to support possible militarization of an area vital to the global economy'. By early 2016, there had been significant construction activity on seven Chinese-occupied features in the Spratly Islands, with military facilities established on six of them. Mischief Reef and Fiery Cross Reef each had a 3km runway that could be used by combat aircraft, and a similar airstrip was under construction on Subi Reef. Moreover, in February 2016 China deployed two batteries of the HQ-9 surface-to-air missile system on Woody Island in the Paracels; in the following weeks, J-11 and JH-7 combat aircraft were also reported on the island. China's increasingly assertive role in the South China Sea was also demonstrated by the interception of fishing and supply vessels from other claimant states (the Philippines and Vietnam) in both the Paracel and the Spratly islands.

One important consequence of China's activities in the South China Sea was that they led the United States Navy to undertake freedom-of-navigation operational patrols (FONOPs), designed to assert the right of the US (and others) to fly and sail wherever

Map 5 US military dispositions in the Western Pacific

Republic of Korea (28,500)

Army (19,200)	• HQ US Forces Korea and HQ 8th Army at Yongsan ❶ • HQ 2nd Infantry Division at Camp Casey ❷ • 1 armoured brigade and 1 ISR helicopter battalion ❷
Navy (250)	• 1 x (fleet activities) HQ at Chinhae Naval Base ❸
Air Force (8,800)	• HQ 7th Air Force at Osan Air Base ❹ • Kunsan Air Base ❺
US Marine Corps (250)	• Marine Force Korea; Camp Mujak ❻

Thailand (300)

Joint	• Bangkok: Joint Military Advisory Group ❼

British Indian Ocean Territory (300) ❽

Strategic Forces/ Navy	• Camp Justice • 1 x *Spacetrack* Optical Tracker • 1 x deep-space surveillance system • 1 Maritime Prepositioning Ship squadron • 1 x support facility
Air Force	• 3 x B-2 bombers (deployed in Mar 2016; prev. deployed to Guam in Aug 2015)

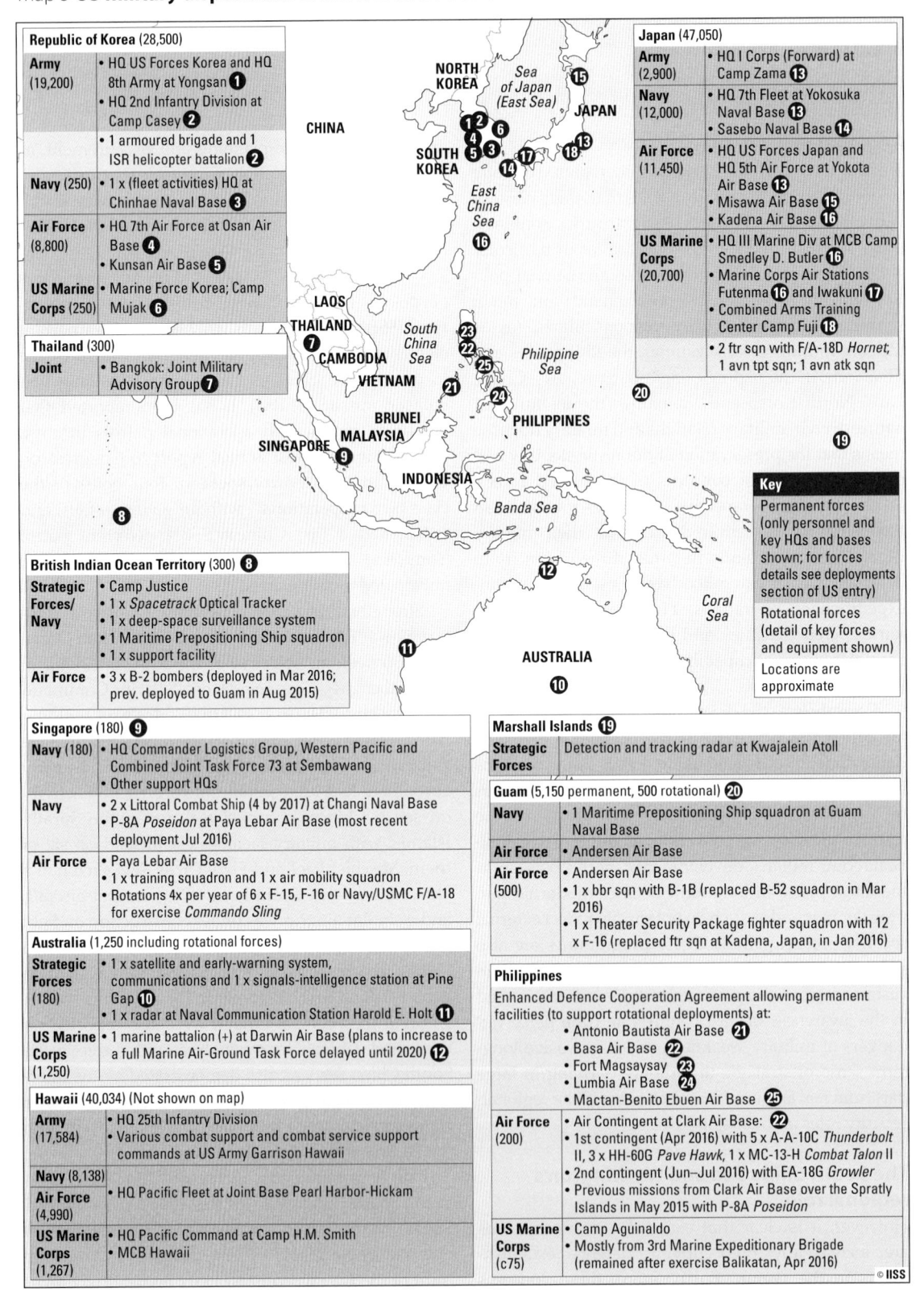

Singapore (180) ❾

Navy (180)	• HQ Commander Logistics Group, Western Pacific and Combined Joint Task Force 73 at Sembawang • Other support HQs
Navy	• 2 x Littoral Combat Ship (4 by 2017) at Changi Naval Base • P-8A *Poseidon* at Paya Lebar Air Base (most recent deployment Jul 2016)
Air Force	• Paya Lebar Air Base • 1 x training squadron and 1 x air mobility squadron • Rotations 4x per year of 6 x F-15, F-16 or Navy/USMC F/A-18 for exercise *Commando Sling*

Australia (1,250 including rotational forces)

Strategic Forces (180)	• 1 x satellite and early-warning system, communications and 1 x signals-intelligence station at Pine Gap ❿ • 1 x radar at Naval Communication Station Harold E. Holt ⓫
US Marine Corps (1,250)	• 1 marine battalion (+) at Darwin Air Base (plans to increase to a full Marine Air-Ground Task Force delayed until 2020) ⓬

Hawaii (40,034) (Not shown on map)

Army (17,584)	• HQ 25th Infantry Division • Various combat support and combat service support commands at US Army Garrison Hawaii
Navy (8,138) **Air Force** (4,990)	• HQ Pacific Fleet at Joint Base Pearl Harbor-Hickam
US Marine Corps (1,267)	• HQ Pacific Command at Camp H.M. Smith • MCB Hawaii

Japan (47,050)

Army (2,900)	• HQ I Corps (Forward) at Camp Zama ⓭
Navy (12,000)	• HQ 7th Fleet at Yokosuka Naval Base ⓭ • Sasebo Naval Base ⓮
Air Force (11,450)	• HQ US Forces Japan and HQ 5th Air Force at Yokota Air Base ⓭ • Misawa Air Base ⓯ • Kadena Air Base ⓰
US Marine Corps (20,700)	• HQ III Marine Div at MCB Camp Smedley D. Butler ⓰ • Marine Corps Air Stations Futenma ⓰ and Iwakuni ⓱ • Combined Arms Training Center Camp Fuji ⓲ • 2 ftr sqn with F/A-18D *Hornet*; 1 avn tpt sqn; 1 avn atk sqn

Marshall Islands ⓳

Strategic Forces	Detection and tracking radar at Kwajalein Atoll

Guam (5,150 permanent, 500 rotational) ⓴

Navy	• 1 Maritime Prepositioning Ship squadron at Guam Naval Base
Air Force	• Andersen Air Base
Air Force (500)	• Andersen Air Base • 1 x bbr sqn with B-1B (replaced B-52 squadron in Mar 2016) • 1 x Theater Security Package fighter squadron with 12 x F-16 (replaced ftr sqn at Kadena, Japan, in Jan 2016)

Philippines

Enhanced Defence Cooperation Agreement allowing permanent facilities (to support rotational deployments) at:
- Antonio Bautista Air Base ㉑
- Basa Air Base ㉒
- Fort Magsaysay ㉓
- Lumbia Air Base ㉔
- Mactan-Benito Ebuen Air Base ㉕

Air Force (200)	• Air Contingent at Clark Air Base: ㉒ • 1st contingent (Apr 2016) with 5 x A-A-10C *Thunderbolt II*, 3 x HH-60G *Pave Hawk*, 1 x MC-13-H *Combat Talon* II • 2nd contingent (Jun–Jul 2016) with EA-18G *Growler* • Previous missions from Clark Air Base over the Spratly Islands in May 2015 with P-8A *Poseidon*
US Marine Corps (c75)	• Camp Aguinaldo • Mostly from 3rd Marine Expeditionary Brigade (remained after exercise Balikatan, Apr 2016)

Key

Permanent forces (only personnel and key HQs and bases shown; for forces details see deployments section of US entry)

Rotational forces (detail of key forces and equipment shown)

Locations are approximate

© IISS

it was legally permissible. Following surveillance flights by US P-8A *Poseidon* maritime-patrol aircraft near Fiery Cross, Subi and Mischief reefs in May and July 2015, on 27 October the guided-missile destroyer USS *Lassen* passed within 12 nautical miles of Subi Reef. (Twelve nautical miles is the furthest extent of territorial waters, according to the UN Convention on the Law of the Sea.) In late January 2016 the destroyer USS *Curtis Wilbur* conducted a second FONOP, near Triton Island in the Paracels. A third FONOP in May 2016 involved another destroyer sailing close to Fiery Cross Reef. Overflights also continued, including one in December by a US Air Force (USAF) B-52 bomber within two miles of Chinese-occupied features.

Southeast Asian states' defence cooperation

Against this background of rising tension in the South China Sea, some Southeast Asian governments further strengthened their defence cooperation with the US in 2016.

Philippines
Most prominently, an Enhanced Defense Cooperation Agreement (EDCA), signed in 2014 by the US and the Philippines – which still lacks any significant domestic capacity for external defence – came into operation after the Supreme Court in Manila in January 2016 ruled that the agreement was constitutional. The EDCA, which will be in effect for at least ten years, supplements the 1951 bilateral defence treaty and the 1999 Visiting Forces Agreement. It allows US forces and defence contractors to operate from 'agreed locations' provided by the Philippines armed forces. In March 2016, the two governments agreed that rotational US deployments would operate from five locations: Antonio Bautista Air Base (Palawan); Basa Air Base (Pampanga, Central Luzon); Fort Magsaysay (Nueva Ecija, Central Luzon); Lumbia Airport (Cagayan de Oro, Central Luzon); and Benito Ebuen Air Base (Mactan, Cebu). In the same month, both countries' navies began joint maritime patrols and in April a US Air Contingent was inaugurated. The latter involved five A-10C ground-attack aircraft, three HH-60G combat search-and-rescue helicopters (all dispatched from bases in Japan and South Korea) and an MC-130H *Hercules* special-operations variant, which remained at Clark Air Base for 12 days following the annual bilateral exercise *Balikatan*.

In late April, four of the A-10Cs flew close to the disputed Scarborough Shoal amid speculation that China was set to commence dredging and construction there. In June, a new Air Contingent deployment included four US Navy EA-18G *Growler* electronic-warfare aircraft, which exercised with the Philippine Air Force's FA-50PH-equipped fighter/ground-attack squadron. However, the election of Rodrigo Duterte as Philippine president in May 2016 cast doubts over the future of defence cooperation with the US. Duterte made clear that he was 'not a fan of the Americans' and in September 2016 indicated that he wished to see the withdrawal of US special forces from Mindanao (where since 2002 they had supported Philippine military efforts to combat the Abu Sayyaf Group, a kidnapping-for-ransom gang operating under the guise of jihadism). He also said that his administration planned to halt joint maritime patrols with the US and was looking into the possibility of buying weapons from China and Russia. These statements may have contained a measure of bluster, but they did not bode well for bilateral talks scheduled for November 2016 on establishing 'implementation guidelines' for the EDCA.

Singapore
Meanwhile, defence relations with Singapore remained central to the continuing US 'rebalance' to the Asia-Pacific. In December 2015, Singapore Minister for Defence Dr Ng Eng Hen and US Secretary of Defense Ashton Carter signed an EDCA, building on a memorandum of understanding agreed in 1990 and a Strategic Framework Agreement (which included a DCA) signed in 2005. Under the new agreement, the two sides committed to enhance cooperation in 'the military, policy, strategic and technology spheres' and in combating 'non-conventional' threats including piracy and transnational terrorism. The EDCA also set out ambitions for cooperation in humanitarian assistance and disaster relief, cyber defence and biosecurity. Speaking in the US soon afterwards, Ng reiterated Singapore's long-held view that a continued US military presence in the Asia-Pacific was 'critical' for continued peace in the region. Concrete manifestations of this ever-closer defence relationship included the semi-permanent presence of a US Navy Littoral Combat Ship at Singapore's Changi Naval Base (although this vessel, USS *Forth Worth*, suffered serious accidental damage during maintenance in January 2016, which rendered it non-operational) and operational deployments of P-8A *Poseidon* aircraft to Paya Lebar Air Base from December 2015. By August 2016, there had been three P-8A deployments to Singapore, the latest lasting a month and involving two aircraft.

Indian Air Force: fleet-recapitalisation challenges remain

Nine years after India launched its competition for a Medium Multi-role Combat Aircraft (MMRCA), a contract was signed on 23 September 2016 for 36 French Dassault *Rafale* combat aircraft. However, this deal was for around one-quarter of the 126 aircraft stated in India's original requirement. Furthermore, the agreement was not with the preferred prime contractor, but made on a government-to-government basis. The MMRCA procurement failed because both governments could not agree on technology-transfer conditions for the *Rafale*, according to which 108 aircraft were to be built in India by state-owned manufacturer Hindustan Aeronautics Limited, following the construction of 18 aircraft in France. New Delhi wanted France to assume the risk for Indian-assembled aircraft. Within weeks of the *Rafale* contract being signed, reports emerged that India had begun to solicit information from at least three nations (Russia, Sweden and the US) for the purchase of more combat aircraft.

The *Rafale* was only one platform in the running for MMRCA. The United States' Boeing and Lockheed Martin, Russia's United Aircraft Corporation, Sweden's Saab and the United Kingdom (with the Eurofighter *Typhoon*) had also proposed aircraft for the requirement.

Prolonged and ultimately fruitless negotiations over the MMRCA requirement have further complicated the Indian Air Force's (IAF's) fleet-recapitalisation plans. The air force wants to be able to field 42 multi-role fighter squadrons by mid-2027; the IAF currently operates 32 squadrons. A considerable number of the air force's problems result from failed or delayed acquisitions and development programmes designed to replace ageing types such as the MiG-21 *Fishbed*, MiG-27 *Flogger* and *Jaguar*.

When it was first proposed, the MMRCA requirement called for the first aircraft to be delivered to the air force in the middle of this decade. What is now named the *Tejas*, previously the Light Combat Aircraft, was due to have entered service well over a decade ago. Instead, the first two *Tejas* aircraft were finally accepted into squadron service in July 2016. At the turn of this decade, then-defence minister A.K. Antony said that Russian Sukhoi T-50 aircraft, the platform intended to meet the IAF's Fifth Generation Fighter Aircraft (FGFA) project, would be introduced in 2017. At best, India can now hope only to sign the final contract for the FGFA, now called the Perspective Multirole Fighter (PMF), during 2017. However, even optimistically, deliveries are unlikely before the early 2020s.

The air force's target fleet strength is driven by its desire to be able to engage in a two-front conflict involving China and Pakistan. While India views Pakistan as the main source of external terrorist threat, the increasingly capable Chinese air force is the yardstick by which the IAF measures its own capacity.

Taking these concerns together, a likely outcome will be that India quickly acquires an F-16 or F/A-18 derivative from the US or the *Gripen* NG from Sweden to help cover the airframe shortfall following the failure of the MMRCA procurement. Past performance, however, suggests that the IAF still faces a considerable challenge in meeting its mid-2020s target for combat-aircraft-squadron numbers.

Vietnam

US defence relations with other Southeast Asian partners developed more slowly. In part, this indicated regional states' continuing wariness of more overt alignment as tensions between the region's major powers increased. In May 2016, when President Barack Obama visited Hanoi, the US announced it was removing the remaining restrictions on the sale of 'lethal arms' to Vietnam. This followed the inauguration of an annual Defense Policy Dialogue in 2010; a memorandum of understanding on defence cooperation in 2011; the inclusion of a defence element in the comprehensive partnership agreed in 2013; the partial lifting of the arms embargo in 2014; and a joint vision statement on defence relations including defence trade and industrial cooperation in 2015. In the medium term, US officials saw the potential for Vietnam to purchase F-16 combat aircraft, P-3C *Orion* maritime-patrol aircraft, radars and unmanned aerial vehicles. However, the immediate focus remained on capacity-building through the Pentagon's regional Maritime Security Initiative and the Global Peace Operations Initiative. In the context of growing competition with China in the South China Sea, the US has requested greater naval access to Vietnamese ports, particularly Cam Ranh Bay. However, Hanoi's caution on this matter will almost certainly mean that any dramatic opening to the US Navy is unlikely.

Southeast Asia: capability enhancements

Singapore

Incremental efforts by Southeast Asian states to improve their external-defence capabilities continue, notably in the maritime and air domains. Alongside Vietnam (see pp. 264–68), Singapore's military-modernisation programme remains the most determined. It has been financed by a defence budget that since the late 1990s had consistently been the largest in Southeast Asia and aimed at maintaining broad-based capability advantages over neighbouring states. At the most basic level, Singapore army infantry units are re-equipping with the ACMS iLite wearable digital system for section commanders and other key personnel; this is part of a larger Advanced Combat Man System, which is intended to transform soldiers into 'digitised warfighters'. In March 2016, Singapore's army brought into service a new Army Battlefield Internet system incorporating 'Software Defined Radio', which claims to provide 'secure, seamless and higher bandwidth connectivity' between division and brigade headquarters and their combat units. Commissioning the new system, Ng said that the Singapore Armed Forces' communications, command and computer-network systems were 'far superior and ahead of others in the region'.

The defence ministry also announced plans for two new army vehicles: a Protected Combat Support Vehicle (PCSV), and a new-generation Armoured Fighting Vehicle (AFV) to replace the *Ultra* (an upgraded M113 armoured personnel carrier). The PCSV and AFV will enter service in 2019 and 2017 respectively. Organisational changes were also intended to enhance the army's capability. In July 2016 a battalion-sized Army Deployment Force was established, primarily in response to heightened concerns over terrorism.

Singapore's navy continued to bring new vessels into service, including a new version of the Specialised Marine Craft – a fast interceptor boat for base defence, force protection and maritime-security operations – in conjunction with the new *Independence*-class Littoral Mission Vessels (LMVs), the first of which was commissioned in May 2016. All eight LMVs are due to be in service by 2020. Construction of two TKMS Type-218SG submarines for Singapore's navy proceeded in Germany: the boats are due to enter service from 2020. Meanwhile, plans to acquire a Joint Multi-Mission Ship to replace the navy's landing-platform docks appeared to firm up. It seems likely that the vessels will be based on the 14,500-tonne Multi-Role Support Ship developed by Singapore Technologies Marine. As such, it would be slightly smaller than the Korean *Dokdo*-class amphibious-assault ship, but could potentially act as a platform for CV-22 tilt-rotor aircraft and possibly even F-35B Joint Strike Fighters as well as helicopters. Amid plans for the eventual wholesale recapitalisation of Singapore's military-helicopter fleet, the CV-22 featured as a potential replacement for at least some of the air force's CH-47D transport helicopters.

In early 2016, following a protracted evaluation process, it was widely expected that Singapore would imminently order an initially small number of F-35s. But a report in the local *Straits Times* in August suggested that the city-state's defence ministry had informed the US Department of Defense in June that it would be 'delaying the final steps of the purchasing process'. In the meantime, in December 2015 Singapore awarded Lockheed Martin a US$914 million contract to upgrade the air force's F-16C/D force by 2023. Additional deliveries of F-15SG strike aircraft reportedly brought the overall size of the air force's F-15 fleet to 40, allowing formation of a second locally based squadron by early 2016. Air-force-infrastructure plans call for Paya Lebar Air Base to be closed around 2030 so that its site can be redeveloped for civilian purposes, while facilities at Changi and Tengah air bases will be expanded.

Malaysia
Elsewhere in Southeast Asia, recent defence-capability developments have been less far-reaching but nonetheless significant given the relatively low base of national capabilities. New security challenges since 2013 – evinced by the Lahad Datu incursion, the disappearance of flight MH370 and Chinese naval intrusions – have underlined the need for Malaysia to bolster many elements of its armed forces. But constraints on procurement funding – in 2015–16 the defence budget contracted by 2.6% in local currency – have meant that Malaysian defence planners have deferred procurements designed to fill long-standing requirements for new multi-role combat, maritime-patrol and airborne early-warning aircraft, as well as naval helicopters, in order to pay for immediate priorities. These include four Airbus A400M transport aircraft (the third of which was delivered in June 2016), six Second Generation Patrol Vessels (locally built versions of the DCNS *Gowind* frigate, which are scheduled to become operational from 2019) and the ForceSHIELD air-defence system (a first batch of this system's *Starstreak* man-portable air-defence weapons was delivered in March 2016).

Efforts to boost defences in the eastern Malaysian states of Sabah and Sarawak in Borneo have also continued. It was announced in October 2015 that the Airbus Defence and Space *Spexer* 2000 active electronically scanned array radar had been selected as a principal element of a new coastal-surveillance system for the Eastern Sabah Security Command based at Lahad Datu. This purchase will be financed by the national energy company Petronas, which has also funded two sea bases that were established off Sabah in 2015 – one a disused oil rig and another on a former merchant ship. In February 2016, the Malaysian Army stood up a second border brigade, located in Sarawak; it will eventually comprise five infantry battalions with more than 5,600 personnel. Plans call for a third such brigade in Sabah, as part of the army's yet-to-be-established 5th division there. Most of the 30 or so M109 self-propelled howitzers donated by the US in August 2016 under the Excess Defense Articles Program are reportedly likely to be based in Sabah.

Indonesia

In Indonesia, the emphasis remains on strengthening maritime and air defences. By September 2016, the first of two SIGMA 10514 multi-role frigates began sea trials ahead of delivery to the navy in early 2017. These were built in a 'collaborative modular process' in the Netherlands and Indonesia. While the first of three South Korean *Chang Bogo*-class submarines remained due for delivery from 2017, discussions took place between the local shipbuilder PT PAL and the French company DCNS as part of a government-to-government agreement about the possibility of acquiring *Scorpène* 1000 boats and overhauling the navy's existing German-built Type-206 submarines. These talks suggested that earlier plans to purchase Russian *Kilo*-class boats were not definite.

However, the latest effort to improve Indonesia's air capabilities involved the acquisition of Su-35 multi-role combat aircraft from Russia. In May 2016, Jakarta confirmed its intent to buy eight Su-35s in the first instance; however, the contract awaited an agreement on technology transfer to Indonesia. Approval by the US in March for a possible Foreign Military Sales transfer of AIM-120C-7 advanced medium-range air-to-air missiles and associated equipment to Indonesia was intended to provide modern weapons for the air force's refurbished ex-USAF F-16C/D fighters. To fulfil the Indonesian air force's longer-term combat-aircraft requirements, in January 2016 the state-owned aerospace company PT Dirgantara Indonesia formalised a partnership with Korea Aerospace Industries to develop and produce the KF-X combat aircraft. Indonesia plans to bring 80 of these aircraft into service from the late 2020s.

Philippines

Limited defence budgets meant that the previous Philippine administration of then-president Benigno Aquino III made only incremental progress in developing the country's capability for external defence, despite the incentive provided by adverse developments in the South China Sea. Nevertheless, delivery of 12 South Korean FA-50PH armed training aircraft began in November 2015; all were scheduled to be in service by early 2017. In October 2016, Japan's defence ministry finalised the lease of five ex-Japan Maritime Self-Defense Force TC-90 *King Air* twin-engine training aircraft to the Philippine Air Force for use as short-range maritime-patrol aircraft, while Italy-headquartered defence firm Leonardo announced that it would deliver two AW159 *Wildcat* helicopters to the Philippine Navy (PN) in 2018. The *Wildcat*s will be operated from three former US Coast Guard cutters transferred to the PN as patrol ships. The navy has a pressing requirement for new multi-mission frigates, and in August 2016 Duterte's administration awarded a contract to South Korea's Hyundai Heavy Industries to supply two 3,000-tonne ships based on the HDF-3000 design (in ROK Navy service as the *Incheon* class). The navy is also due to receive a donated *Po Hang*-class corvette from South Korea.

Northeast Asia

While the South China Sea was the principal regional focus for many observers of Asia-Pacific security during 2015–16, there remained three important potential flashpoints in Northeast Asia, each of which exerted important influence on the military programmes of regional states. Chinese probing around the Diaoyu/Senkaku Islands in the East China Sea escalated in early August 2016, when more than 300 Chinese fishing boats – believed by Japan's defence-intelligence staff to be part of an irregular maritime militia – supported by China Coast Guard vessels began a series of incursions into Japan's exclusive economic zone around the islands, raising fears in Tokyo that Beijing was promoting what amounted to a hybrid-warfare campaign intended incrementally to erode Japan's control of the features. Moreover, Chinese military aircraft approached Japanese airspace in record numbers – 571 times during the year to 31 March 2016, according to the defence ministry in Tokyo. In its 2016 annual defence white paper, published in August, Tokyo expressed 'deep concern' over China's behaviour, which it said

Table 9 **North Korea: ballistic-missile test launches in 2016**

The increasing number of ballistic-missile test launches in 2016 both reveals North Korea's current operational missile capabilities and demonstrates Pyongyang's progress in developing more capable systems that could in future be used to deliver a nuclear warhead, assuming the North is able to master warhead miniaturisation and re-entry challenges. The most significant such activity includes the first tests – and subsequent high failure rate – of the *Hwasong*-10 (*Musudan*) intermediate-range ballistic missile and the continuing progress of the *Bukkeukseong*-1 (KN-11) submarine-launched-ballistic-missile programme. Apparent 'lofted' trajectory launches of both systems (with an apogee greater than the minimum-energy trajectory) provide some indication of their theoretical operational ranges in the absence of full test flights. The longer-range *Hwasong*-13 (KN-08) intercontinental ballistic missile (ICBM) – which is potentially capable of reaching the mainland United States – and derivative *Hwasong*-14 (KN-14) ICBM remain untested.

Date	Type	Classification	Reported outcome[1]	Distance flown
20 Oct	*Musudan*	IRBM	Failure	n.k.
15 Oct	*Musudan*	IRBM	Failure	n.k.
20 Sep	Ground test of liquid-propellant engine			
09 Sep	5th nuclear test			
05 Sep	*Scud* ER	SRBM	Success	1,000km
	Scud ER	SRBM	Success	
	Scud ER	SRBM	Success	
24 Aug	KN-11	SLBM	Success	500km [2]
03 Aug	*NoDong*	MRBM	Success	1,000km
	NoDong	MRBM	Failure	n.k.
19 Jul	*NoDong*	MRBM	Two successes; one failure	500–600km
	NoDong	MRBM		
	Scud-C	SRBM		
09 Jul	KN-11	SLBM	Failure	10km
22 Jun	*Musudan*	IRBM	n.k.[3]	~250km
	Musudan	IRBM	Success	400km [4]
31 May	*Musudan*	IRBM	Failure	n.k.
28 Apr	*Musudan*	IRBM	Failure	n.k.
	Musudan	IRBM	Failure	
23 Apr	KN-11	SLBM	Success	30km
09 Apr	Ground test of liquid-propellant engine			
15 Apr	*Musudan*	IRBM	Failure	n.k.
24 Mar	Ground test of solid-propellant engine			
18 Mar	*NoDong*	MRBM	Success	800km
	NoDong	MRBM	Failure	n.k.
16 Mar	KN-11	SLBM	Success[5]	n.a.
15 Mar	Ground test simulating re-entry			
10 Mar	*Scud*-C	SRBM	Success	500km
	Scud-C	SRBM	Success	
07 Feb	*Unha*-4	Satellite-launch vehicle	Success	n.a.
06 Jan	4th nuclear test			

[1] Test objectives are unknown; published materials relate only to claimed successes. Outcomes are therefore an assessment of information released by, or reported from, DPRK, ROK and US officials.
[2] Lofted trajectory
[3] DPRK reported that the missile self-destructed
[4] Lofted trajectory
[5] Reported land-based ejection test

could have 'unintended consequences'. The white paper placed considerable weight on Japan's deepening alliance with the US and also emphasised the challenge posed by a new Russian military build-up in its Far East as well as the threat from North Korea's missile and nuclear-weapons programmes.

During 2016, the tempo of North Korea's missile and nuclear-weapons tests accelerated, heightening concern in Seoul and Tokyo. In February, Pyongyang claimed that it had successfully launched a satellite into orbit. In early August, it launched two intermediate-range ballistic missiles, one of which landed in the Sea of Japan (East Sea). Later in August, it claimed to have test-fired an SLBM for a second time. More worryingly, in January it conducted its fourth nuclear-weapons test, ostensibly of a hydrogen bomb, although experts were sceptical of this claim. In September, Pyongyang triggered a fifth nuclear device. Responses by Japan, South Korea and the US to these provocations from the North, which blatantly violated UN Security Council resolutions, were increasingly firm. While the three powers called for even tighter international economic sanctions with the aim of isolating North Korea, the military dimension of their responses became more prominent. In mid-January, following the North's fourth nuclear test, the USAF flew a B-52H bomber at low level over South Korea. As part of a 'theatre security package', the USAF also deployed other combat aircraft to strengthen its forces in the South. More importantly, in July 2016 Seoul and Washington finally agreed on the deployment of a Terminal High-Altitude Area Defense battery (see text box below). In September, South Korea's Defence Minister Han Min-koo confirmed that his country's armed forces had contingency plans to use precision weapons to 'eliminate' the DPRK's leadership in the event of a tangible threat of North Korea using nuclear weapons.

Meanwhile, South Korea's burgeoning defence budget supported a range of ambitious procurement projects aimed at substantially expanding the capabilities of its armed forces. With the intention that it should be a true blue-water force by 2020, and at the same time strengthening its capacity to deal with subsurface threats from North Korea, the South Korean Navy will bring a range of new vessels into service

THAAD deployment in South Korea

In July 2016, officials from South Korea and the United States agreed on the deployment of a US Army Terminal High-Altitude Area Defense (THAAD) battery in Seongju County, a rural area in the southeast of the country, after extensive discussions that began in mid-2014. Both sides stated that the deployment was intended 'as a defensive measure to ensure the security of the Republic of Korea and its people and to protect alliance military forces from North Korea's weapons of mass destruction and ballistic missile threats'.

However, China was opposed to the deployment of THAAD. This delayed South Korea's agreement to the deployment because of concerns in Seoul over what effect Beijing's opposition might have for the broader bilateral relationship with China. However, North Korea's fourth nuclear test in January 2016 – and its testing and deployment of increasingly sophisticated and long-range missiles – brought a change of heart in Seoul. While the US emphasised that the THAAD system in South Korea will focus entirely on threats from the North and is not directed at other countries' missile capabilities, the announced deployment accentuated China's opposition. Beijing claimed to be concerned that the radar system associated with a South Korea-based THAAD system (the AN/TPY-2 radar) might undermine its own nuclear deterrent.

By early October 2016, China was warning that South Korea and the US would 'pay the price' if a THAAD battery was deployed. There was also considerable domestic opposition in South Korea in July–August 2016, triggered by concerns over the deployment's possible impact on relations with China, as well as fears that the battery would be a threat to health in peacetime and a target in the event of war. However, Pyongyang's fifth nuclear test a month later dampened this opposition.

When deployed in South Korea, the THAAD system – which can destroy incoming warheads above the atmosphere – will provide the top tier of a layered missile-defence architecture, which also includes *Patriot* air-defence systems intended to intercept targets at relatively low altitudes. PAC-2 *Patriot*s operated by South Korean and US Forces in Korea were scheduled to be upgraded to the more capable PAC-3 standard or replaced by new PAC-3 systems by the end of 2016. In the longer term, South Korea's missile defences are expected to include SM-3 interceptor missiles paired with the Baseline-9 version of the *Aegis* combat system aboard the South Korean Navy's final three KDD-III *Sejong the Great*-class cruisers. In addition, South Korea is developing an indigenous upper-tier missile-defence system, known as L-SAM and equivalent to THAAD, with service entry scheduled for 2023–24.

over the next four years. These include a second *Dokdo*-class amphibious-assault ship, four additional *Son Won il*-class (Type-214) submarines, three more *Sejong the Great*-class guided-missile cruisers and further *Incheon*-class frigates. The navy is also strengthening its air capabilities: the first four of eight AW159 *Wildcat* multi-role naval helicopters were delivered in June 2016. The South Korean Air Force also plans major capability enhancements. Deliveries of the German–Swedish *Taurus* air-launched cruise missile, to arm the air force's F-15K strike aircraft, began during 2016. An order of 40 F-35A Joint Strike Fighters agreed in 2014 is scheduled for delivery during 2018–21. Between 2026 and 2031, the air force expects to bring into service 120 indigenously developed KF-X combat aircraft.

Tensions across the Taiwan Strait increased after Tsai Ing-wen of the Democratic Progressive Party – which favours independence from China – was elected as Taiwan's president in January 2016, highlighting the risk that China might use its military power to coerce or subjugate the island. Although the Obama administration approved in December 2015 the sale of a major weapons package for Taiwan, including frigates, amphibious armoured vehicles, anti-tank and short-range anti-aircraft missiles, and communications systems, this will be insufficient to redress the deteriorating cross-strait military balance, which moved steadily in China's favour during the tenure of the previous two Taiwanese governments. Electoral promises by these governments to increase defence spending went unfulfilled and the armed forces suffered from inadequate strategic guidance as well as serious morale, training and discipline problems. As a result, the Tsai administration has considered what the president called 'drastic' reforms in order to redress Taiwan's military weakness. Initiatives are likely to include establishing a cyber-warfare force to combat China's offensive cyber operations, even in peacetime; 'hardening' military headquarters and bases in response to the threat from PLA joint artillery strikes in time of conflict; reorientating military training away from disaster-relief preparations; and maintaining at least limited conscription despite earlier administrations' plans to end the draft.

DEFENCE ECONOMICS

Macroeconomics

In 2016, average economic growth in Asia slowed moderately to 4.0%, down from 4.2% in 2015. This weakening was mainly driven by reduced growth in China, which fell from 6.9% in 2015 to 6.6% in 2016. Given the importance of the Chinese market for Asian exporters, the deceleration in China's economy and the resulting reduction in imports helps explain the slowdown in the region more broadly: in 2014, for instance, China accounted for 37% of Australia's exports, 31% of South Korea's, 27% of the Philippines' and 22% of Japan's.

Slower Chinese growth was explained primarily by China's ongoing transition from increasingly unsustainable credit- and manufacturing-driven growth to domestic consumption and services. However, this shift did not necessarily mean increased Chinese imports. As China moves up the global value chain (by providing more added-value in international production processes), it imports a smaller amount of the intermediate goods that are now produced domestically. Not only does China produce more goods for its own consumption, but it increasingly competes internationally in sectors where it used to import goods, such as LCD screens. China's arrival on the international market for technologically advanced goods infringes upon the market share of other Asian exporters. The rebalancing of China's economy also means that its subsidised industrial state-owned enterprises (SOEs) are restructuring. These are locally called 'zombie' enterprises and often operate at overcapacity. China's slower growth and this restructuring of SOEs has led to lower demand in commodities, which in turn has driven global commodity prices down. This has proven a positive feature for commodity importers, but has had the opposite effect for commodity exporters in Asia.

Despite the Chinese slowdown, growth remained strong in most of the region, mainly because of domestic demand in the Philippines (6.4% in 2016), Vietnam (6.1%), Indonesia (4.9%) and Myanmar (8.1%). Economic activity was also robust in South Asia, where India's growth rate of 7.6% was sustained by domestic demand as well as by the liberalisation of foreign direct investments. Pakistan's improving security situation helped to boost its economy by 4.7%. Pakistan was also expected to benefit from the China–Pakistan Economic Corridor, which includes numerous infrastructure projects, such as the construction of highways, railways and pipelines. Conversely, Japan's economy stagnated, with 0.5% GDP growth in 2016 – the same level as in 2015. Singapore's growth also slowed, down from 3.3% in 2014 to 2.0% in 2015 and 1.6% in 2016. Singapore's

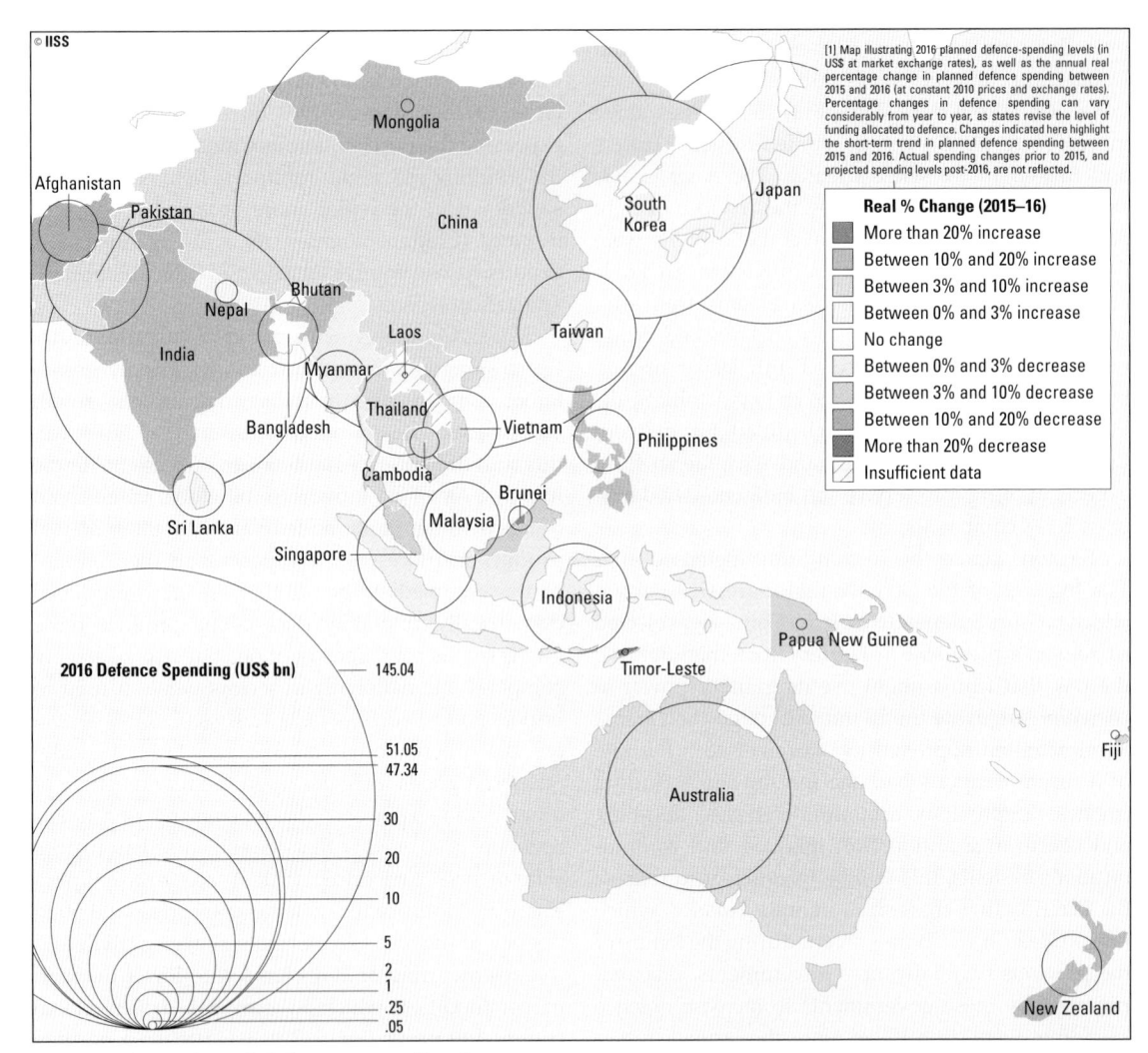

Map 6 **Asia regional defence spending**[1]

open economy has been vulnerable to China's economic deceleration and the slowdown in global trade. The shipbuilding and electronics sectors have been significantly affected, while Singapore's financial sector also experienced turbulence in the wake of the 1MDB Malaysian money-laundering scandal.

Asian defence spending

Sustained economic growth allowed Asian states to increase defence spending in 2016, in a region marked by rising tensions, such as over territorial issues in the South China Sea, simmering border disputes and enduring challenges from terrorism.

Taken together, Asian states spent US$367.7 billion in 2016, up by 5.3% when compared with the 2015 figure of US$349.1bn. In 2012–16, Asian real-terms defence spending grew by 5–6% each year. In 2016, China accounted for 39.4% of this total spend. Indeed, this figure is likely an underestimate, as it is based on the official Chinese defence budget, which according to the US Department of Defense is thought not to consider expenses such as research and development and weapons imports. When using constant 2010 US dollars, China's official defence spending grew by 6.5% in 2015–16, which was consistent with its GDP growth of 6.6%. However, the rate of increase in China's nominal defence budget has decelerated from 10.1% in 2015 to 7.6% in 2016. The countries with the second- and third-largest defence budgets in the region, India and Japan, accounted respectively for 13.9% and 12.9% of total regional defence spending in 2016. China spent 3.5 times more than Japan and 3.2 times more than India. South Korea was ranked fourth with 9.2% of total Asian defence spending,

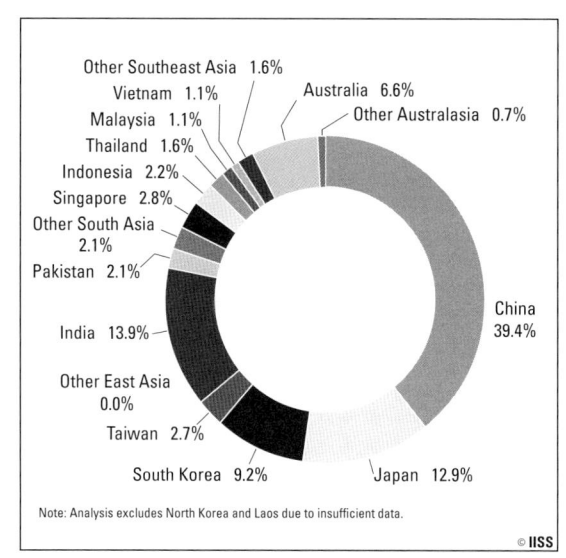

Figure 17 **Asia defence spending by country and sub-region**

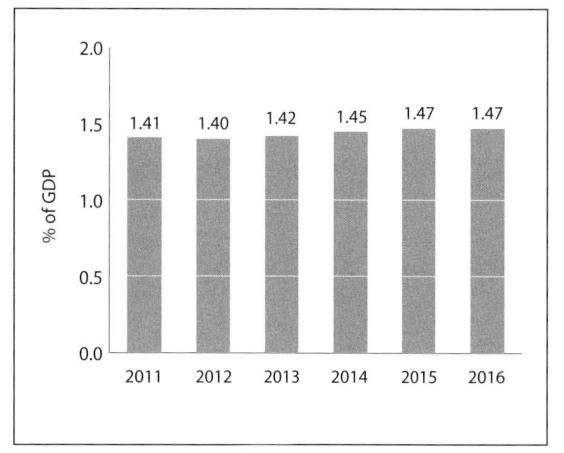

Figure 18 **Asia regional defence expenditure** as % of GDP

Australia was fifth at 6.6% and Singapore was sixth at 2.8%.

Among states increasing their defence spending, Singapore's share – when measured against total GDP – rose from 3.2% in 2014 to 3.5% in 2016, despite slower growth. Australia's increased too, with defence spending as a percentage of GDP growing from 1.7% in 2012 to 1.9% in 2016 – Australia's 2016 defence white paper aims to raise defence spending to 2% of GDP by 2020–21 (see pp. 249–51). Its northern neighbour Indonesia's percentage stagnated at around 0.9% in 2015–16, although this was still an increase from 0.7% five years before. With Jakarta aiming to tackle budget deficits, Indonesia's defence ministry has had to make savings. As a consequence, Indonesia's projected defence budget for 2017 is down by 4% compared with 2016 (in local currency terms). Indonesia's defence white paper, released in May 2016, sets out an objective for spending to rise above 1% of GDP in the next decade.

India's defence budget grew by 14% (in current US dollars) between 2015 and 2016, with 23.1% of the 2016 budget dedicated to procurement, while salaries and pensions accounted for 66.4%. The proportion of the budget allocated to pensions increased by 36.7% between 2015 and 2016, as a result of the introduction of the 'one rank one pension' scheme. India's 2016 defence budget (at US$51.1bn) was almost seven times higher than Pakistan's (US$7.7bn). However, the gap between the two rival countries was narrower in per capita terms, with the budgets equating to US$40.3 per inhabitant in India, against US$38.3 in Pakistan. In addition, Pakistan plans to increase its 2017 budget (FY2016/17, which runs from July 2016 to June 2017) by 11%. This includes a 155.6% increase from PKR900m (US$86m) to PKR2.3bn (US$221m) in the budget line for the 'Defence Production Division'. This is intended for investments in the state-owned Karachi Shipyard and Engineering Works Limited (KSEW).

Procurement

Pakistan's investment in KSEW reflects the fact that regional procurements remain dominated by maritime assets. Of 27 Asian states, 13 were undergoing or had completed procurements of patrol boats or patrol craft in 2016; nine for maritime-patrol/anti-submarine-warfare assets and nine for submarines (see Figure 19).

These included Australia's decision that DCNS of France would be the preferred partner for the delivery of 12 *Shortfin Barracuda* submarines (the first delivery is estimated in 2030); China's reported construction of Type-039C submarines, with at least one believed built and undergoing trials; India's six licence-built *Scorpène* submarines (with the first commissioning expected in late 2016); Indonesia's contract with South Korea for three Type-209s, with the first launched in spring 2016; Japan's 12 *Soryu*-class submarines, with the seventh having been commissioned in 2016; Pakistan's contract with China for eight submarines, which was confirmed in 2016; Singapore's procurement of the German-manufactured Type-218SG, with first delivery expected in 2020; and Vietnam's procurement of six Russian *Kilo*-class submarines,

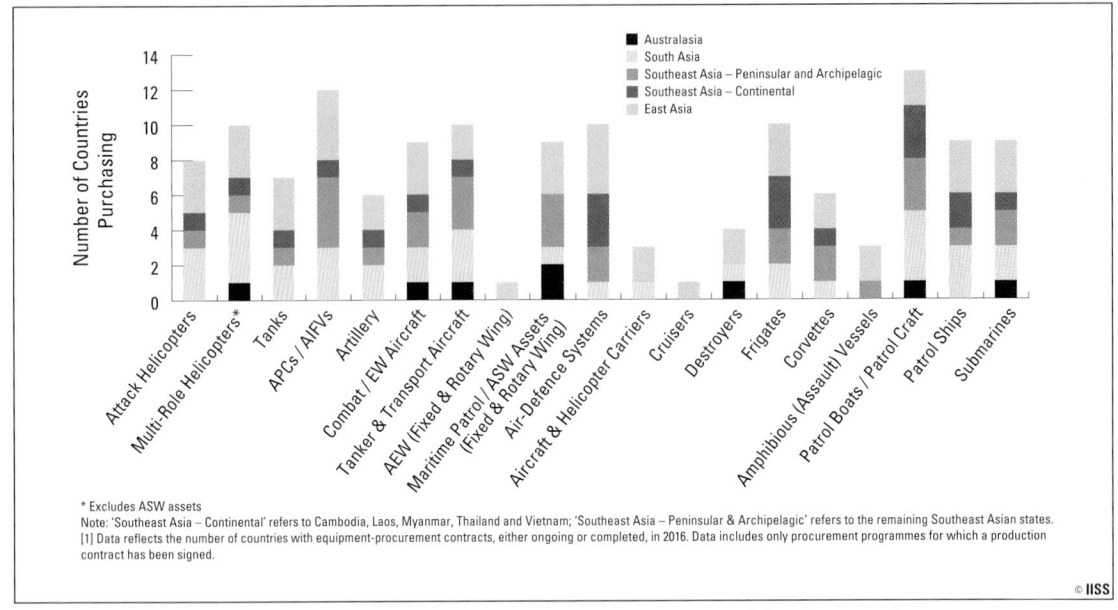

Figure 19 **Asia: selected ongoing or completed procurement priorities in 2016**[1]

with the fifth of class delivered in 2016. To this list can be added Thailand's announcement regarding the procurement of three conventionally powered Chinese submarines, with funding reportedly earmarked in the 2017 defence budget. Taiwan's newly elected government also announced the life-extension upgrade of its two *Hai Lung* submarines and announced its intention to move forward with the Indigenous Defense Submarine programme to build six to eight submarines domestically. Related to this, Taiwan's China Shipbuilding Corporation opened a new submarine-development centre in the southern port city of Kaohsiung in 2016. Japan also earmarked for its FY2017 budget the development of a new generation of locally produced submarines, designed by Mitsubishi Heavy Industries and Kawasaki Heavy Industries.

Nine Asian states procured combat or early-warning aircraft (see Figure 19). Among them, India eventually closed its decade-long Medium Multi-role Combat Aircraft requirement by signing a contract with France's Dassault Aviation for 36 *Rafale* combat aircraft, the first of which is expected to be delivered in 2019 (see textbox, p. 240). However, 36 combat aircraft will not cover the Indian Air Force's combat-aircraft needs, so a new tender is being considered for a single-engined fighter. Lockheed Martin's F-16 and Saab's *Gripen*-E may be leading competitors. If this procurement proceeds, the selected aircraft would become India's ninth type of fighter, alongside the Su-30MKI, *Mirage*-2000, *Jaguar*, MiG-29, MiG-27, MiG-21, the *Tejas* light combat aircraft and the *Rafale*.

Defence industry

Many regional states rely on the procurement of weapons from abroad to fulfil their equipment needs. As a consequence, some are making concerted efforts to develop their local defence industry; developments in 2016 exemplified this trend. Tsai Ing-wen, Taiwan's new president, committed to develop the local defence industry. Facing challenges in importing military equipment because of Chinese pressure on potential foreign suppliers, Taipei aims to locally develop submarines and training and combat aircraft, as well as unmanned aerial vehicles and the armed forces' 'information security capacities'. To support this policy, a new defence-technology department was set up.

Similarly, Australia plans to strengthen its defence industry, as was announced in the 'Defence Industry Policy Statement' published alongside the 2016 defence white paper; the shipbuilding sector will particularly benefit. A new Centre for Defence Industry Capability was created in order to direct this new defence-industrial policy.

Meanwhile, in India, a new Defence Procurement Procedure (DPP) was published in spring 2016, which placed renewed emphasis on Prime Minister Narendra Modi's 'Make in India' initiative. The new DPP prioritised the procurement of weapons that were locally designed, developed and manufactured. It also raised the threshold for foreign defence companies to engage in offsets, in order to enable international partnerships. At the same time, to encourage private Indian defence manufacturers to participate in tenders, the government also worked on a 'strategic partnership' regulation in 2016. The status of 'strategic partner' should allow selected private defence firms to bid on certain categories of equipment procurement.

In Indonesia, a law adopted in 2012 (UU16/2012) introduced offset obligations for foreign defence producers; this was designed to bolster the local defence industry. Jakarta's 2015 white paper, released in 2016, dedicated a chapter to the defence industry, outlining as priorities 'submarine construction and [the] propellant industry, also the development of rockets, missiles, national radars, medium tanks and fighter jets'.

In 2016 there was broader restructuring in countries with more mature defence-industrial and -technological bases. In China, the aero-engine sector was rationalised into a single company, Aero Engine Corp. of China, by merging several aero-engine factories within China's dominant aerospace conglomerate AVIC. There was also some restructuring in the military-shipbuilding sector within the China Shipbuilding Industry Corp (CSIC), one of the country's two naval conglomerates. As the global shipbuilding sector had experienced a crisis in recent years, CSIC announced the merger of six of its entities into three, including the merger of Dalian Shipbuilding Industry Co. (which is building China's first indigenously manufactured aircraft carrier) with Shanhaiguan Shipbuilding Industry.

South Korea's shipbuilding sector was also severely hit by the crisis – Daewoo Shipbuilding & Marine Engineering (DSME) was almost delisted from the Korean Stock Exchange in 2016. DSME plans to spin off its defence activities in 2017, as part of a bid to recover financial health. (DSME manufactures the Type-214 KSS-II and KSS-III classes of submarines.) While DSME was struggling, South Korea's Hanwha group fared better. As part of a consolidation process, it acquired various defence companies. In summer 2015, Hanwha Corp. acquired Samsung Techwin (manufacturers of the K9 self-propelled howitzer and aircraft engines) and Samsung Thales (a defence-electronics concern). In spring 2016, Hanwha bought Doosan DST (producer of the K21 infantry fighting vehicle). Later, in September 2016, Hanwha purchased a 30% stake in Pratt & Whitney's Singapore-based subsidiary. As a result of these acquisitions, Hanwha has become the main defence producer in South Korea, with products ranging from missiles and ammunition, unmanned systems and maritime systems, artillery systems, military-aircraft engines and C4ISR systems, to military vehicles.

AUSTRALIA

Prime Minister Malcolm Turnbull's administration has continued Canberra's long-term plan to improve the Australian Defence Force's (ADF's) capability for predominantly maritime expeditionary operations. Almost two years after it was commissioned by Turnbull's predecessor, Tony Abbott, the government released its long-awaited new defence white paper in February 2016. While the document contained no major surprises, there were some significant nuances in relation to defence-capability planning. As expected, it presented a more pessimistic strategic outlook for Australia caused by growing challenges to the international 'rules-based order', manifested in Australia's own region by China's actions. The white paper pointed to major US–China 'points of friction' and assessed that the South China Sea would 'continue to provide a source of tension that could undermine stability'. It also stated that Australia was 'particularly concerned by the unprecedented pace and scale of China's land reclamation activities' there.

The emergence of a more contested Asia-Pacific strategic environment has significantly influenced the 'strategic objectives' that the new white paper sets out for the ADF. In line with previous documents, it says that the force's primary strategic-defence objective continues to be to 'deter, deny and defeat' attacks against Australia. But in reality, the ADF is being primarily optimised for the second objective, which is to 'make effective military contributions to support the security of maritime South East Asia' and to support South Pacific states. This is apparent in the substantial investment in expeditionary capabilities detailed in the white paper, the further development of the military alliance with the United States and efforts to bolster regional defence cooperation.

The white paper announced investments of approximately A$195 billion (US$146bn) across six 'capability streams' in the decade up to 2025–26 (see Figure 20). Unsurprisingly, the Royal Australian Navy (RAN) is due to receive a significant boost to its capability. The Turnbull government reconfirmed the commitment to build 12 'regionally superior' submarines, the first of which is planned to enter service by the early 2030s. The document also announced a review in the late 2020s to 'consider whether the configuration of the submarines remains suitable or whether consideration of other specifications should commence'. In essence, this leaves the door open for a future nuclear-powered option. The government announced in April 2016 that French company DCNS was the preferred partner for its future boats, which lends weight to this argument: the selected *Shortfin Barracuda* is based on the French Navy's *Barracuda*-class 5,000-tonne nuclear-powered attack submarine.

The white paper also announced that the RAN would receive nine future frigates optimised for anti-submarine warfare from the late 2020s. The government selected BAE Systems, Fincantieri and Navantia as the final contenders for the programme in April 2016. The white paper also stated the intention to acquire 12 new large offshore-patrol vessels; the prime minister announced in April that two German companies (Fassmer and Lürssen) and one Dutch firm (Damen) had been shortlisted to build these ships. Furthermore, in May 2016 the RAN selected Navantia's bid for the construction of two large auxiliary oiler and replenishment vessels by the early 2020s. These will be based on the Spanish Navy's 19,800-tonne *Cantabria*-class oiler. Together with the acquisition of three *Hobart*-class air-warfare destroyers and two *Canberra*-class landing helicopter dock (LHD) amphibious platforms, Australia's naval capabilities will be significantly upgraded over the coming decades.

The white paper also committed to strengthening Australia's aerospace capability. The Royal Australian Air Force (RAAF) plans to receive 15 P-8A *Poseidon* maritime-patrol aircraft by the late 2020s, with the first eight to be acquired by the early 2020s. The P-8As are being procured to conduct surveillance and offensive operations against surface and undersea targets. The air force's surveillance assets will also be enhanced by the introduction of seven medium-altitude long-endurance MQ-4C *Triton* unmanned aerial vehicles (UAVs) from the early 2020s. Meanwhile, the white paper reconfirmed the plan to procure up to 72 F-35A Joint Strike Fighters. It also referred to the acquisition of 'high-speed long-range strike weapons for the air combat fleet capable of attacking land and maritime targets'.

However, the document remained vague on the replacement of the current fleet of 24 F/A-18F

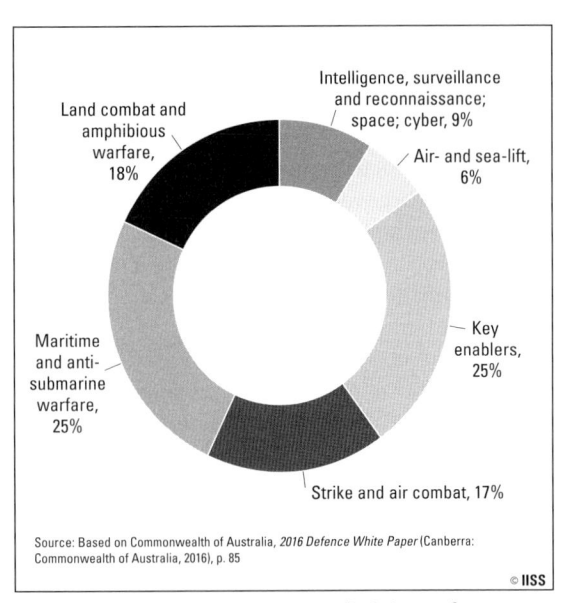

Figure 20 **Australia: ten-year division of investment stream to FY2025–26 (%)**

- Intelligence, surveillance and reconnaissance; space; cyber, 9%
- Air- and sea-lift, 6%
- Key enablers, 25%
- Strike and air combat, 17%
- Maritime and anti-submarine warfare, 25%
- Land combat and amphibious warfare, 18%

Source: Based on Commonwealth of Australia, *2016 Defence White Paper* (Canberra: Commonwealth of Australia, 2016), p. 85

Super Hornet combat aircraft, stating that options to replace these in the early 2020s would be considered 'in light of developments in technology and the strategic environment and will be informed by our experience in operating the Joint Strike Fighter'. This language could be interpreted as a weakening of Canberra's commitment to buy another batch of 25 F-35As, as originally envisaged under the air force's 'AIR 6000 Phase 2C' programme (for a fourth RAAF JSF squadron). It could also indicate a willingness to consider alternative aircraft, such as an additional tranche of F/A-18s or buying into a future US sixth-generation-fighter programme. Notably absent from the white paper was any mention of a possible order for the F-35B vertical/short take-off and landing variant, for operation from the RAN's LHDs.

The white paper also highlighted a planned increase in the Australian Army's expeditionary capabilities. In particular, the government decided to acquire 'deployable land-based anti-ship missiles to support operations to protect deployed forces and vital offshore assets such as oil and natural gas platforms'. The ground forces will also be equipped with armed medium-altitude UAVs, which will provide them with an organic, fixed-wing armed-reconnaissance capability. In combination with new armed-reconnaissance helicopters that are expected to replace the army's 22 *Tiger* helicopters from the mid-2020s, these assets will enhance the army's firepower and mobility in an expeditionary environment.

Finally, to manage the ADF's planned growth in capability, the defence white paper announced an increase in its personnel end strength to 62,400 over the next decade (the ADF last had an establishment strength of this size in 1993). In the coming decade, Australia will also invest significantly in defence infrastructure, including upgrades to HMAS Stirling, the naval base in Western Australia, and RAAF bases Darwin, Edinburgh, Pearce and Townsville, as well as the airfield at Cocos (Keeling) Island.

CHINA

China engaged in a series of legislative, physical and organisational actions in 2016, which were designed to upgrade and improve its military and security capability.

National-security legislation

In April 2016, China's National People's Congress formally passed a new law governing the operation of non-governmental organisations (NGOs) in China. The law set out various restrictions to ensure that foreign NGOs could operate only under the strict supervision of China's security services. This followed the approval of a new National Security Law in July 2015, which outlined areas that now fall under the rubric of 'national security', and the release of the second draft of a new cyber-security law. When finally enacted, this will further restrict access and freedom of expression in China's section of the internet. The draft cyber law, for example, requires that all personal and business data must be stored domestically in China.

These pieces of legislation provide a legal framework by which the Chinese Communist Party (CCP) can exercise control over a variety of exchanges, citing the defence of China's national security. They also provide a clear indication that, for the CCP, 'national security' includes far more than just the traditional military dimension, and includes ecological security and cultural and economic security, as well as cyber security and ensuring political stability.

These laws provide the basis for the conduct of 'legal warfare' – one of the 'three warfares' central to political warfare. In this regard, Beijing is providing the foundation for the conduct of actions that would enhance Chinese security, without necessarily undertaking kinetic operations consistent with traditional war-fighting concepts. It is also preparing for operations of the type recently labelled as 'hybrid warfare', albeit with Chinese characteristics.

China's interest in hybrid warfare is reflected in China's actions along its periphery. In constructing artificial islands in the South China Sea and dispatching flotillas of fishing boats into the waters around the Diaoyu/Senkaku Islands, Beijing is employing a variety of measures to underscore its territorial claims, while not crossing the line into open hostility. Such actions follow a trend evident since at least 2009, when Chinese vessels harassed the USNS *Impeccable* and USNS *Victorious*. Since then, China has employed its deep-sea oil-drilling platform Haiyang Shiyou 981 and China Coast Guard (CCG) ships to assert its claims to an extensive swathe of the East Asian littoral.

China also continued its island-building efforts in the South China Sea in 2016. On three of the artificial islands (Fiery Cross Reef, Subi Reef and Mischief Reef), not only has China constructed long runways, but it has also built aircraft hangars. China landed a military transport aircraft on the runway at Fiery Cross Reef early in 2016 and civilian aircraft have landed too, demonstrating that the runways are now potentially operational. However, as of late 2016, there were no indications that Beijing had begun large-scale reclamation efforts at Scarborough Shoal or the area of Macclesfield Bank.

China also renewed signalling activities concerning its claims to the Diaoyu/Senkaku Islands. Large flotillas of Chinese fishing boats have engaged in fishing activities around the islands, escorted by CCG vessels. It is believed that Chinese naval militia are also present, mixed with the fishing fleets. The CCG continued to expand in 2016, and the practice of providing the CCG with hulls based on warship designs continued. Japanese news reports from early 2016 indicated that Chinese oil-drilling platforms had been equipped with radars typically found on patrol vessels. This further blurs the line between military and civilian assets, and suggests a new means by which oil rigs can serve as 'mobile national territory', while further expanding China's maritime situational awareness.

Organisational reform

The most extensive, and far-reaching, change has been the overhaul of the People's Liberation Army (PLA)'s organisational structure. These changes were encapsulated in the statement that 'the Central

Military Commission manages the overall; the war zones are responsible for warfighting; the services are responsible for [military force] building [*junwei guanzong, zhanqu zhuzhan, junzhong zhujian*]'.

Role of the Central Military Commission
The Central Military Commission (CMC), not the Chinese defence ministry, oversees the PLA. Prior to 2016, the CMC was organised into four general departments (three, prior to 1999): the General Staff Department (GSD), the General Political Department (GPD), the General Logistics Department (GLD) and, since 1999, the General Armaments Department (GAD). The PLA Navy (PLAN), PLA Air Force (PLAAF) and Second Artillery branch were not represented on the commission until 2004.

In January 2016, China reorganised the CMC into 15 departments, commissions and offices (see Table 10).

One reason for this overhaul may relate to political rather than military factors. Given the approaching 19th Party Congress in October/November 2017, creating 11 additional slots (plus associated staff and support positions) provides President Xi Jinping with an opportunity to appoint a raft of additional senior-level officers. This is likely to strengthen his political grip over the top military leadership.

However, expanding the CMC to 15 offices is also intended to improve its efficiency. Relabelling the various departments and offices to include the prefix 'Central Military Commission' is reportedly intended to reverse the trend of the departments acting in an increasingly autonomous fashion. Creating new departments and reorganising their functions, as well as establishing new military services and reshaping the PLA's high-level organisation, would certainly disrupt the bureaucracy.

The functions of what had been the GPD, for example, are now divided among the CMC Political Work Department, the CMC Discipline Inspection Commission and the CMC Politics and Law Commission. This would suggest that the new CMC Political Work Department will focus on such tasks as the conduct of political warfare (including the 'three warfares' of public-opinion warfare, psychological warfare and legal warfare), while criminal and anti-corruption investigations (also previously a GPD responsibility) may now fall under the auspices of the CMC Discipline Inspection Commission.

It is also reported that the reorganisation will reduce the number of personnel assigned to the various political functions. The GPD had controlled military correspondents, bands, and musical and acting troupes, as well as military lawyers and political officers. There is likely to be a significant reduction in personnel assigned to these functions, forming part of the 300,000 reduction in personnel announced by Xi in 2015 at the ceremony marking the 70th anniversary of the end of the Second World War.

In addition, replacing the GSD with the CMC Joint Staff Department underscores the message that the CMC must be focused on the entire armed forces, and not just the ground component. (The previous four general departments had been responsible for the PLA as a whole, as well as the ground forces.) The title 'Joint Staff Department' arguably also reflects the centrality of joint operations to PLA military planning.

The creation of some of the new departments and commissions indicates the importance attached to certain key areas. For example, the establishment of the CMC National Defense Mobilisation Department reflects not only the growing prominence of mobilisation planning for the PLA, but also various efforts at integrating civilian and military efforts. Chinese concepts of mobilisation extend beyond personnel and defence-industrial facilities, to the ability to employ key infrastructure for military ends, as well as the mobilisation of key personnel, equipment and facilities to supplement military forces.

Similarly, military training now has its own CMC department, rather than being the responsibility of the military regions or armed services. This new entity, which is responsible for military training throughout the PLA, gives the top military leadership greater visibility into this important area. The CMC Science and Technology Commission likely takes the place of the previous GAD Science and Technology Commission, suggesting a similar effort to boost the introduction of advanced technologies across the entire force.

These efforts, however, also serve as a reminder that the Chinese armed forces are not formed along Western lines. The CMC, especially through its expanded organisational architecture, manages the entire PLA without relying upon a service-based structure. Instead, the CMC is intended to view the armed forces as a whole. The organisational changes, coupled with the creation of a new national-level army headquarters (see below), are likely intended to enhance this effort.

Table 10 **China: new Central Military Commission structure**

Name	Transliteration	Chinese characters
CMC General Office	*Junwei bangong ting*	军委办公厅
CMC Joint Staff Department	*Junwei lianhe canmou bu*	军委联合参谋部
CMC Political Work Department	*Junwei zhengzhi gongzuo bu*	军委政治工作部
CMC Logistics Support Department	*Junwei houqin baozhang bu*	军委后勤保障部
CMC Equipment Development Department	*Junwei zhuangbei fazhan bu*	军委装备发展部
CMC Training and Management Department	*Junwei xunlian guanli bu*	军委训练管理部
CMC National Defense Mobilisation Department	*Junwei guofang dongyuan bu*	军委国防动员部
CMC Discipline Inspection Commission	*Junwei jilu jiancha weiyaun hui*	军委记律检查委员会
CMC Politics and Law Commission	*Junwei zhengfa weiyuan hui*	军委政法委员会
CMC Science and Technology Commission	*Junwei kexue jishu weiyuan hui*	军委科学技术委员会
CMC Strategic Planning Office	*Junwei zhanlue guihua bangongshi*	军委战略规划办公室
CMC Reform and Organisation Office	*Junwei gaige he bianzhi bangongshi*	军委改革和编制办公室
CMC International Military Cooperation Office	*Junwei guoji junshi hezuo bangongshi*	军委国际军事合作办公室
CMC Audit Office	*Junwei shenjishu*	军委审计署
CMC Office Affairs and General Administration	*Junwei jiguan shiwu guanli zongju*	军委机关事务管理总局

Theatre commands: responsible for war fighting

A second major reform has been the reorganisation of the PLA's operational-command structure and the transition from seven 'military regions' to five 'theatre commands'. This marks the consolidation of the PLA's main war-fighting entities (see Table 11).

This is not the first time that the PLA has consolidated its military regions. In the late 1960s, 13 military regions were reduced to 11. These were further reduced to seven in the mid-1980s (at the same time as a major reorganisation of the PLA). The reduction from seven regions to five theatre commands provides another avenue for reducing the size of the PLA, as redundant senior staffs are eliminated. Two military-region command structures will be disbanded, including two military-region air forces.

The new theatre-command structure also introduces several PLA goals not highlighted previously. One is the streamlining of the operational-command process, paralleling Beijing's effort to produce greater efficiency through CMC reform. According to a Xinhua report on 1 February 2016, another objective of the new organisation is to establish a 'three-tier' command system, from the CMC to theatre commands and troops. This command system would operate alongside the reformed administrative system, and would move from the CMC, through the various military services, to the troops.

To this end, the theatre commands will be led by new permanent, joint headquarters. This marks a major change from the previous approach, whereby the military regions were the primary peacetime administrative bodies. Each region had a command structure, which was expected to transition in wartime to a 'joint campaign command headquarters'. These joint headquarters, however, were not permanent establishments, but instead drew from the various service commanders and staffs assigned to the military regions. Moreover, these peacetime headquarters were dominated by the ground forces. No military region was ever commanded by a naval or air-force officer. The deputy commanders (numbering around six) were also almost entirely drawn from the ground forces, joined by perhaps one naval and one air-force officer.

Under the new structure, the permanent joint headquarters will be smaller, which will assign more responsibility to the air and naval components (and probably the new PLA Rocket Force (PLARF) as well). At the same time, it is likely that the theatre-command headquarters will have a larger role in what the PLA terms 'informationised' operations, including cyber, electronic and space warfare.

Perhaps the most fundamental change, however, is that each theatre command is now not just responsible for China's immediate borders and territorial waters. Instead, they are clearly intended to support 'new historic missions', whereby the PLA is charged with not only defending the Chinese homeland but also ensuring Chinese interests, including in the maritime domain. This is reflected in another translation of *zhanqu* – that of 'war zones' rather than theatre commands – which some analysts choose to use in order to reflect the expectation of future wartime requirements. As the PLA increasingly engages in power-projection activities (such as air and maritime operations beyond the first island chain), as well as preparing for defensive operations farther afield (as part of its 'counter-intervention' or what has been termed an anti-access/area-denial strategy), it must extend its horizons beyond its traditional confines.

The navy has shifted over the past two decades from a 'near shore' strategy, first to a 'near sea' strategy and now to a 'far sea' strategy. Similarly, the PLAAF has changed its focus from the defence of Chinese territory and airspace increasingly to operations over water and farther from China's periphery. The new theatre-command organisation and headquarters will combine these efforts within a single planning and command structure. The new theatre commands are apparently expected to think in this extended context.

Significantly, the Northern Command includes two non-contiguous sections. This has allowed the PLAN to retain three fleets, with one assigned to each of the Northern, Eastern and Southern commands. This suggests that compromises based upon organisational and bureaucratic politics will exert some influence on how the reorganisation and reforms are ultimately implemented.

Armed services: responsible for building the force

Underpinning these changes is a radical reorganisation in the PLA's internal bureaucracy. The creation of several new services will fundamentally alter how the Chinese armed forces undertake operations, as well as the balance of power within the PLA as a whole.

The most marked shift is in the national-level army headquarters. As noted earlier, the ground forces have bureaucratically dominated the PLA, both in terms of the CMC and within the command structures of the previous military regions. There have been some efforts at diluting this power in the past. One of the two vice-chairmen of the CMC appointed in 2012, General Xu Qiliang, is the first vice-chairman drawn from the PLAAF. Non-ground-force officers have also been selected to head the PLA's Academy of Military Sciences, which is the combination of a top military think tank, an inspectorate general and a doctrinal-development centre.

This trend is likely to accelerate with the creation of a distinct ground-forces command, and a truly multi-service perspective is now more likely for the CMC. Indeed, the various general departments, commissions and offices comprising the new CMC can in theory now be led by officers drawn from the other services. Similarly, it is expected that some of the new theatre commands will be led by non-ground-force officers (the Eastern or Southern commands being the most likely). Supporting staffs will also have a higher proportion of non-ground-force officers (although that may be achieved by reducing the overall personnel complement, rather than adding additional non-ground-force officers).

Another major change has been the elevation of the Second Artillery, which is responsible for China's nuclear- and conventionally armed ballistic missiles, from a 'super-branch' to a full service – the PLARF. In theory, this means that the PLARF could be placed in charge of 'strategic missions', a role only accorded to the PLAAF in 2004. Furthermore, again in theory, this means that a PLARF officer could head one of the new theatre commands.

A final addition was the creation of the PLA Strategic Support Force (PLASSF). This is perhaps better labelled as the PLA's Information Warfare Force, as it brings under a single structure China's forces for space, electronic and network warfare. As one of the earliest adopters of the concept of 'integrated network and electronic warfare', the PLA has long held a holistic view of warfare in the electromagnetic domain. The creation of the PLASSF is consistent with two decades of evolving PLA views on the role of information and future warfare.

As the PLA prepares to fight and win 'informationized local wars', it has repeatedly emphasised the importance of establishing information dominance (*zhi xinxi quan*). This is achieved through a combination of space dominance (*zhi tian quan*), network dominance (*zhi wangluo quan*) and electronic dominance (*zhi dianzi quan*). That the forces associated with establishing dominance in these domains are now assigned to a single service is unlikely to be a coincidence. As important, by grouping them together,

Table 11 **China: PLA's new theatre commands**

Name	Likely focus
Northern Theatre Command	Korean Peninsula, Mongolia, Russia and possibly Japan
Eastern Theatre Command	Taiwan and possibly Japan
Southern Theatre Command	South China Sea and continental Southeast Asia
Western Theatre Command	Afghanistan, Central Asia, India and Pakistan
Central Theatre Command	Strategic reserve, and possibly space and cyber operations

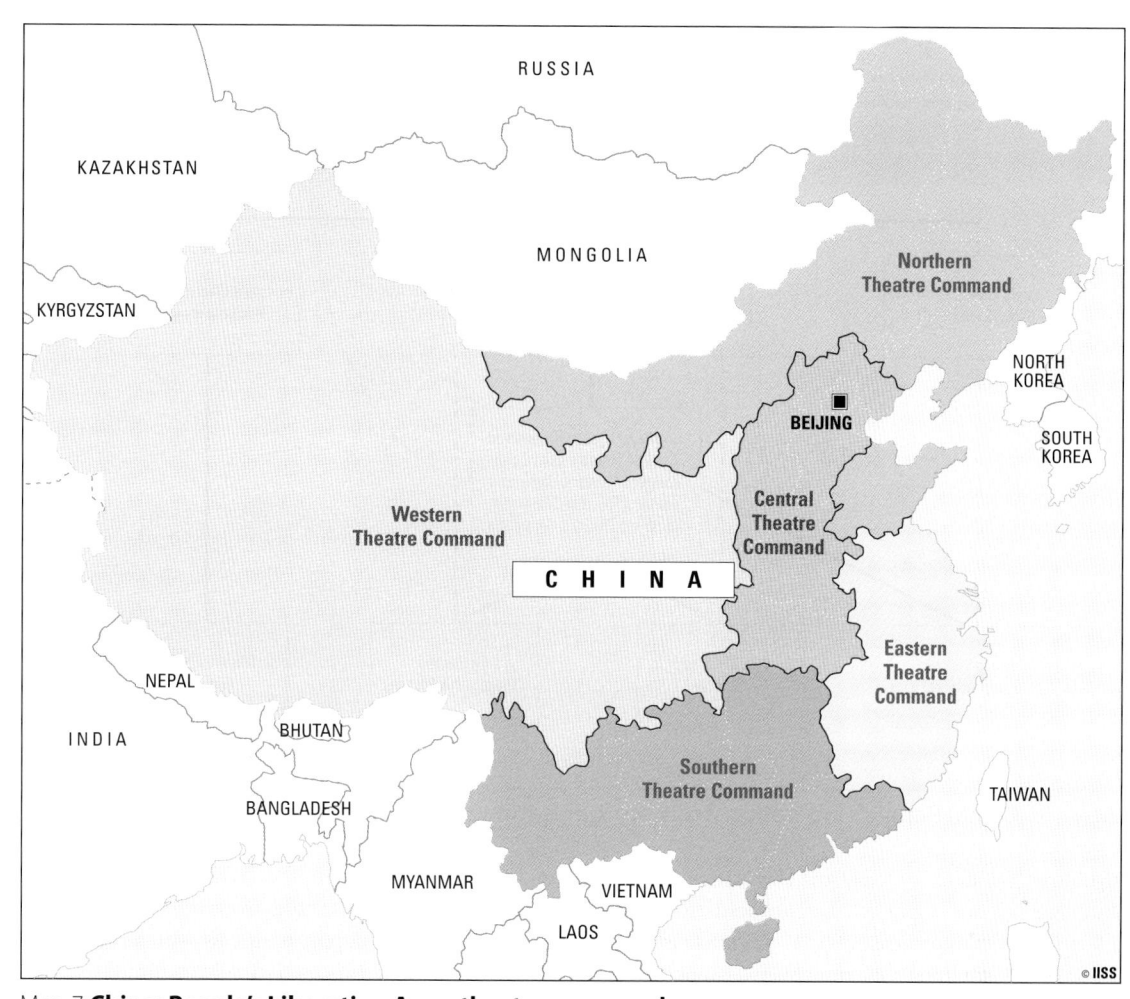

Map 7 **China: People's Liberation Army theatre commands**

Chinese doctrinal developers can look for synergies and areas of mutual support, again in pursuit of information dominance.

With the creation of the PLASSF, the PLA is pursuing an innovative approach to the challenges of information and modern warfare. For instance, there is no single service in the United States that combines space, electronic-warfare and computer-network-warfare operations. Space operations are largely the responsibility of Air Force Space Command, which reports to US Strategic Command (USSTRATCOM), as does Cyber Command – a sub-unified command. Electronic warfare, meanwhile, is the responsibility of the individual services.

Work in progress

This significant structural and command reorganisation is ongoing. Chinese statements make clear that the process will last several years, likely until 2020 (the end of the current five-year plan). During the process there remain issues requiring resolution. They include:

The composition of the CMC
Given the already expanded nature of the CMC, it is unclear whether the restructured body will necessarily include all of the new services. A CMC of over 20 officers has the potential to be unwieldy. At the same time, it remains to be seen what role the defence ministry will assume. This body has traditionally been largely focused on external military relations.

The structure of PLA intelligence
In the previous structure, the PLA had several intelligence agencies, largely subordinate to the GSD. These included the GSD 2nd Department

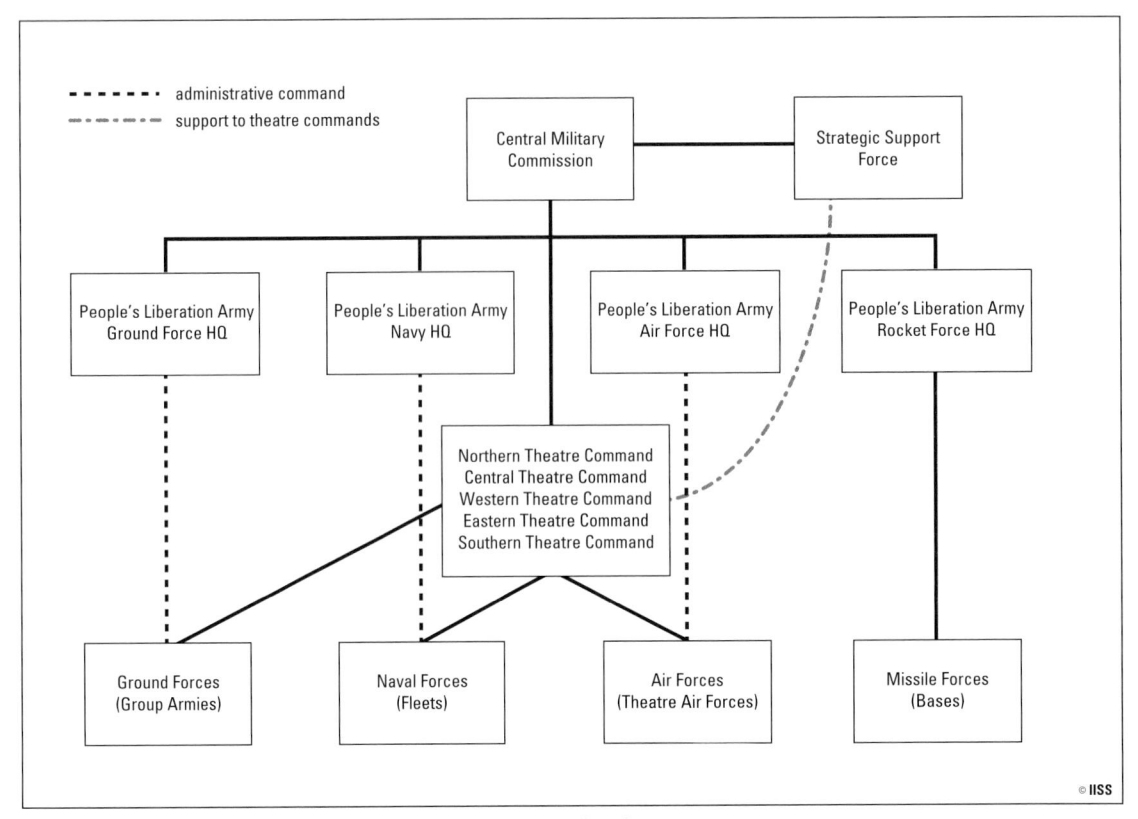

Figure 21 **China: People's Liberation Army reorganisation**

(Military Intelligence), GSD 3rd Department (Signals Intelligence) and GSD 4th Department (Radar and Electronic Countermeasures). It is unclear where these responsibilities have now been assigned.

Responsibilities of the Central Theatre Command
There appears to be a geographic division of responsibility for the other four theatre commands, but this leaves unclear the role of the Central Theatre Command. It is possible that this is intended to be an administrative headquarters for national strategic reserves, including the 15th Airborne Army. It is also possible that it is orientated towards internal security, to coordinate PLA support to civilian authorities and the People's Armed Police in the event of natural disaster or civil unrest. It is also possible, however, that it may have a functional, rather than geographic, responsibility. For example, it may be responsible for nuclear deterrence or for the conduct of space- and cyber-warfare activities.

Structure of the theatre-command headquarters
Military regions broadly repeated the structure of the CMC, with staff, political, logistics and armaments staffs all represented. Whether there will be comparable representations from the new mobilisation and training departments, as well as the other commissions and offices, is unclear. Similarly, it is unclear how the supporting-staff positions will be allocated in relation to the services. As important, it remains unclear how space-, cyber- and electronic-warfare activities will be planned and whether they will be planned and conducted at the theatre-command level, or whether these will be considered strategic activities to be undertaken at the CMC level.

Additional service restructuring
There does not appear to have been additional restructuring of the PLA's operational-level forces. While the PLA ground force remains embarked on its process of 'brigadisation', this does not appear to be the case with the PLAAF. The PLAN appears to remain structured around fleets, flotillas, groups and squadrons. Whether the effort to generate greater 'jointness' will translate into reforms at the lower-organisational levels of the armed forces remains to be seen.

PLA training in 2016

The pace of PLA joint training decelerated in 2016, when compared to the number of joint exercises held in 2015. Ironically, the creation of the five new joint theatre commands, which replaced the former seven military regions, was an important factor contributing to this slowdown. For much of the year the theatre commands focused on training newly assigned staff officers from all the services to perform their duties within these new organisations. As a result, the four service headquarters organised the majority of PLA training through the summer of 2016.

Since 2013, the annual unit-training cycle has generally started in December with individual- and small-unit training, expanding to training in larger formations in the spring, followed by regiment/brigade and higher-level combined-arms and joint training in the summer and autumn, culminating in evaluation and live-fire exercises. Due to the limited number of training areas, not all units participate in large-scale exercises every year. Instead they conduct lower-level training nearer to their garrisons, sometimes in conjunction with units from other services. When PLA units train at sea, the Chinese Maritime Safety Administration routinely issues notices for safety purposes. Army amphibious units and navy marines carry out landing exercises annually and in recent years these two marine brigades have travelled to inland training bases to operate in diverse climates and terrain. PLA Rocket Force units frequently practise multiple brigade operations and conduct multiple simultaneous missile launches on multiple vectors. Prior to deploying on major field exercises, Rocket Force units often conduct computer simulations of upcoming missions.

The number of joint exercises held during the 2015 training season was probably the highest in PLA history. Exercises with the greatest media profile included the series of army-centric, trans-regional, brigade-level joint confrontation exercises called *Stride–2015*, which took place sequentially at the Zhurihe, Taonan and Sanjie training bases and involved 15 infantry and armoured brigades from all of the military regions; *Firepower–2015 Qingtongxia*, which involved seven artillery brigades; and *Firepower–2015 Shandan*, which included seven air-defence brigades. The navy conducted at least three large-scale exercises in the Western Pacific in 2015, which brought together ships and aircraft from all three fleets, while the air force performed four long-range missions over the Western Pacific using multiple aircraft types, including H-6K bombers. Air-force and naval-aviation assets trained together under air-force command in exercise *Sharp Sword–2015*. Since 2013, navy and air-force headquarters have commanded joint exercises (respectively *Joint Action–2014A* and *Mission Action–2013C*), a task that was previously assigned primarily to military-region and lower-level army headquarters.

In 2016, the *Stride Zhurihe*, *Firepower Qingtongxia* and *Firepower Shandan* series of exercises were reduced to five brigades each, one per theatre command, and were organised by the newly formed national army headquarters in Beijing. These exercises were designed to address a problem identified by the PLA, that some commanders lacked 'five capabilities': to optimally appraise the operational situation; to understand the intent of higher authority; to make operational decisions; to deploy troops; and to deal with unexpected situations.

In summer 2016, the navy conducted multiple exercises integrating assets from all three fleets as well as a mobile-logistics-support exercise to defend 'strategic locations at sea'. In June, air-force H-6K bombers set new endurance records for flight times and ranges over the ocean, and transport aircraft conducted simulated airdrops on 'islands and reefs' in August. In July, Rocket Force brigades, armed with 'new model missiles', deployed to several areas in the Gobi Desert for multiple launches. Continuing a trend observed previously, military training in 2016 focused on improving realism, eliminating 'formalism' and cheating, and encouraging innovation in a complex electromagnetic environment.

Though PLA teams have participated in international military competitions before, in 2016 it sent 17 army, two navy and three air-force teams to Russia's International Army Games, as well as jungle-warfare specialists to Brazil and snipers to Kazakhstan. PLA units also took part in a number of exercises with foreign armed forces, mostly to practise non-traditional military tasks, such as disaster relief and counter-terrorism, including the 26-nation *Rim of the Pacific* exercise.

In the future, theatre-command headquarters will become increasingly involved in planning and directing joint exercises and operational deployments at sea and in the air.

PLA Army organisation

Part of the PLA's continuing reorganisation includes the creation of a new national-level army headquarters in Beijing and a new theatre-command army headquarters in each of the five joint theatre commands that replaced the seven military regions (see above).

Previously, four now-disbanded general departments served as the national-level army command, as well as performing joint functions for the other services. In bureaucratic terms, this configuration maintained army dominance among the forces. The new army headquarters in Beijing is organisationally equivalent to those of the navy, air force and rocket force. This has, in effect, lowered the prestige of the army and helped to better balance the four services. Eventually, the army is expected to bear the brunt of the personnel reduction (of 300,000 troops) that was announced in 2015.

The former military regions commanded most of the operational army units, such as group armies, as well as the system of provincial military districts and their subordinate headquarters and units. Now that the military regions have been replaced, most operational army units come under the command of the five theatre-command army headquarters, while most military districts report to the Central Military Commission's National Defense Mobilisation Department. However, in an important exception, the central army headquarters directly oversees the Xinjiang and Tibet military districts, both of which command significant combat forces. The relationship between these military districts and the Western Theatre Command, where they are located, is unclear at the time of writing.

The five theatre-command army headquarters are the principal link between the national-level army headquarters in Beijing and the joint theatre commands. They perform both 'construction' functions, such as personnel and organisation, as directed by the national-level army headquarters, as well as 'operational' tasks, including war fighting and military operations other than war, as directed by the theatre commands. Accordingly, theatre-command army headquarters may serve as 'campaign headquarters' in time of war or as 'emergency response headquarters' for non-traditional security missions.

Furthermore, prior to the reorganisation, army units wore the patches of the military region to which they were assigned. Now all army units wear generic army patches, which do not reflect the theatre-command areas in which they are stationed.

To date, all 18 group armies appear to be active and no divisions or brigades are known to have been eliminated as part of the reorganisation. The only major change announced is the transfer of the 27th Group Army headquarters from Shijiazhuang to Taiyuan.

There is also continued emphasis on developing 'new types of combat forces', which include army aviation, mechanised and light infantry units, special-operations forces, and cyber-/electronic-warfare units. Despite the trend toward 'brigadisation' of the army, about 20 divisions remain spread among half of the group armies, with four assigned to the Xinjiang Military District.

Group armies do not have a standard organisational structure. The number and type of mechanised, motorised and mountain/jungle infantry units within a group army ranges from two to five, along with a single armoured brigade/division. Army aviation and special-operations brigades or regiments are assigned to only about half the group armies. Smaller special-operations battalions or companies are being created in divisions and brigades, underscoring their primary focus on tactical and operational tasks rather than long-range strategic missions.

Though the pace may be uneven and the force is reducing in size, the PLA Army is being equipped with weapons and technologies that allow its units to move more rapidly over difficult terrain (including water), to engage targets faster and at greater range, and – more than ever before – integrate their capabilities with those found in the other services. However, training personnel and units to operate and maintain their new equipment and execute more complex operations will be as great a challenge as is restructuring the force.

People's Liberation Army Air Force
China's PLAAF continued to pursue broad modernisation aims during 2016, progressing developments in combat, transport and special-mission aircraft, as well as in air-launched weapons. For tactical aircraft, Beijing is pursuing a twin-track approach of upgrading in-service types at the same time as developing at least two new multi-role combat aircraft.

Following extended negotiations, early in 2016 the PLAAF signed a contract to purchase Russia's Su-35 *Flanker* E single-seat, multi-role combat aircraft, with the expectation that 24 aircraft would be purchased. The Su-35 is a development of the Su-27 *Flanker* design.

Meanwhile, China's Shenyang Aircraft Corporation, which manufactures domestic versions of the Su-27 family, continued work on the J-11D. This is an improved variant of the J-11B, a variant of the Su-27 with domestic avionics and weapons. In all likelihood, the PLAAF will want to compare the 'D' model with the Su-35 before deciding which of the two types to acquire in order to replace early-model Su-27/J-11s as these come to the end of their service lives over the next decade.

The PLAAF also continued its development of the Chengdu J-20 heavy fighter. Eight prototype aircraft have been built and are now being joined by production-standard aircraft. The type is likely to enter front-line service by the end of the decade. Work also continued on the Shenyang J-31 combat aircraft, though at a far slower pace than the Chengdu J-20, and as of the third quarter of 2016, no imagery of a second prototype had been released.

At the same time, the PLAAF continued its attempts to address its relative weakness in heavy transport, airborne early warning (AEW), air-to-air-refuelling, and intelligence, surveillance and reconnaissance platforms. The first two Xian Y-20 transport aircraft were delivered to the air force in June 2016 and, assuming the aircraft's performance is acceptable, the type will likely replace the Russian Il-76 *Candid* as the core of the airlift fleet. It is possible that tanker and AEW versions of the Y-20 may also emerge.

Reports also appeared in the Chinese media in 2016 that the PL-10 imaging infrared air-to-air missile was entering service with the air force. The PL-10 will likely replace the PL-8 and the R-73 (AA-11 *Archer*) as the PLAAF's primary short-range air-to-air missile; it is also likely that the PL-10 will be a credible offer in the export arena.

People's Liberation Army Navy

Beijing continued to consolidate its presence in the South China Sea in 2016, notwithstanding the judgements against China by the UN Permanent Court of Arbitration in July. China's comprehensive naval-modernisation programme continued to make steady progress, encompassing not just further additions to the fleet of modern, more capable combatants, but also logistic-support capabilities and developments in training and doctrine.

The Dalian Shipbuilding Industry Corporation is making rapid progress in building China's first domestically produced aircraft carrier, with the suggestion that the vessel could be ready for launch in 2017. The ship was only officially confirmed at the end of 2015, and it appears to be a close, although evolutionary, copy of the PLAN's first carrier, the *Liaoning*, which was built in Ukraine. The *Liaoning*'s capability remains limited. However, it has been observed with up to eight Shenyang J-15 naval combat aircraft embarked, as the PLAN continues to develop its operational carrier experience and the military concepts required to use this new capability.

There is now firm evidence that work is under way on the first of the anticipated Type-055 large destroyer/cruisers. Meanwhile, the PLAN's third and fourth Type-052D multi-mission destroyers were commissioned in December 2015 and June 2016. A fifth appeared close to completion, out of a total of at least 12 of these vessels now in service or under construction.

In addition, more Type-054A frigates and Type-056A corvettes were added to the PLAN's inventory. Other significant additions during 2016 included the commissioning of a fourth Type-071 landing platform dock, which will be assigned to the East Sea Fleet, boosting the PLAN's amphibious capabilities. (The South Sea Fleet received the first three Type-071s.) Speculation persisted in 2016 about plans for an amphibious-aviation ship, which would be a logical next step for the PLAN's growing amphibious capabilities.

Perhaps of equal significance was the commissioning of three more Type-903A large replenishment ships in 2016, as part of the modernisation and strengthening of the PLAN's logistic support. Beijing also announced the decision to construct a naval facility in Djibouti. These developments reinforce the impression that the PLAN's blue-water capabilities are maturing.

It remains more difficult to discern the Chinese submarine force's progress. It is still unclear whether the *Jin*-class Type-094 ballistic-missile submarines have begun regular patrols, and if not, why not, since the boats would seem to have been ready for some time. There is also uncertainty over the operational status of the latest, improved variant of the *Shang*-class Type-093 nuclear-powered attack submarine, which features a vertical-launch system believed capable of accommodating the YJ-18 advanced anti-ship cruise missile.

The China Coast Guard also continues to bolster its capabilities and appears to have adopted the basic design of the PLAN's Type-54A frigate (without weapons) for its latest ocean-going patrol vessel. It has also received modified former PLAN Type-

053H2G frigates, again with weapons removed, and completed a second 10,000-tonne patrol ship. Beijing continues to develop the different arms of its maritime capability in pursuit of broad policy goals, but these larger coastguard vessels will likely permit deployments of greater duration, at greater range and in larger sea states.

DEFENCE ECONOMICS

The administration of President Xi Jinping is accelerating its efforts to make science, technology and innovation (STI) a centrepiece of China's overhauled development model, and the defence sector looks likely to be one of the principal beneficiaries. A series of new medium- and long-term STI strategies, plans and reform initiatives were issued in 2016, which seek to transform China from a technological follower to a global-innovation leader within the next few decades, especially in strategic areas such as defence, dual-use systems, high-technology and advanced manufacturing.

Beijing unveiled in May a new innovation-directed development strategy (IDDS) with a three-stage strategic road map designed to transform China's STI out to 2050. The first stage sets a target of becoming an 'innovative country' by 2020, which means establishing an innovation-friendly environment with improved intellectual-property protection, better incentives, and a comprehensive set of policies and regulations. The second step is to join the leading ranks of advanced-innovation countries by 2030. The third stage is to become a 'strong' innovation power by 2050, which translates into reaching parity or even overtaking the US as the world's most advanced-technology country. While these are national targets, they are also likely to apply to the defence STI sector.

Overhauling defence R&D

Two major themes of the strategy are especially relevant for China's efforts to improve its defence-innovation capabilities. The first is an emphasis on the development of original and cutting-edge innovation instead of focusing on the absorption and improvement of foreign technologies, as in previous STI strategies. This will, however, require a major overhaul of the country's national and defence research-and-development (R&D) systems.

One important initiative is the establishment of large-scale national laboratories, modelled on foreign entities such as the US Los Alamos National Laboratory, in order to support the pursuit of scientific breakthroughs. Xi has pointed out that 'national laboratories are important vehicles in which developed countries seize the high ground in technological innovation'. For China, these national laboratories are viewed as critical platforms for accelerating the research needed to enable it to become a global scientific player. National-security topics are expected to be central to the research agendas of these new establishments.

The second theme is the pursuit of 'big science' turnkey projects that will enable China to make breakthroughs in core technological capabilities. At the Chinese Communist Party's 5th Plenum in November 2015, the president stressed that there must be more 'serious prioritisation' of 'technological innovation in key sectors and implementation of important technological projects that affect the national big picture and long-term future'.

A number of technological fields have been designated as suitable for turnkey projects. These include aero-engine and gas-turbine manufacture, quantum communications, information-network and cyber security, smart manufacturing and robotics, deep-space and deep-sea exploration, and vital materials and neurosciences.

At the same time, the Chinese defence-industrial bureaucracy, led by the State Administration for Science, Technology, and Industry for National Defence (SASTIND), has formulated new strategies and plans to significantly adjust the defence industry as well as to chart its medium- and long-term transformation. One of the key plans is the 13th Defence Science, Technology, and Industry Five Year Plan (13th FYP). This plan was issued at the beginning of 2016 and sets out six main tasks to be achieved by 2020: enabling the so-called 'leapfrog' development of weapons and military equipment; enhancing innovation capabilities in turnkey areas; improving overall quality and efficiency; optimising the structure of the defence industry and vigorously promoting civil–military integration; accelerating the export of armaments and military equipment; and supporting national economic and social construction.

Compared to its predecessor, the 13th FYP has a stronger focus on the development of high-technology weaponry and civil–military integration. It also signals a significant shift in the direction of defence-industry development from absorption and re-innovation towards greater emphasis on domestic innovation, conforming to the IDDS. The 13th FYP illustrates that China is seeking to build on the inroads it has been steadily making in the international arms market.

A major weakness of China's defence industry is a lack of higher-end manufacturing capability. SASTIND has reportedly been preparing a '2025 Defence Science and Technology Plan' that aligns closely with a national 'Made in China 2025 Advanced Manufacturing Plan' (MIC2025). This is aimed at lifting the overall level of the country's industrial-equipment-manufacturing base and curtailing excessive dependence on foreign suppliers for essential technology and products.

The defence industry features prominently in the MIC2025 plan, especially the development of the high-bypass-ratio turbofan engines that the Chinese aerospace industry has struggled to master. Shortly after the release of the MIC2025 plan, the aero-engine industry underwent a far-reaching consolidation in which scores of separate engine-research and -production facilities were merged into a new corporate vehicle called China Aircraft Engine Corp.

In a further sign of efforts by Chinese leaders to chart a long-term course for the country's defence STI development, SASTIND has established a defence Science and Technology Development Strategy Committee to conduct research and provide policy input to help the leadership in its decision-making on long-term defence R&D over the next 20–30 years. The key goals of this committee are to: implement the Communist Party leadership's strategic decisions and plans; focus on strategic, comprehensive and forward-looking studies; and provide policy recommendations and consultation on defence science and technology development and innovation.

SASTIND Director Xu Dazhe heads the Development Strategy Committee and its membership features many prominent figures in the Chinese national and defence scientific community, including academicians from the Chinese Academy of Sciences and the Chinese Academy of Engineering.

Realising the potential of civil–military integration

The government is making a concerted effort to make civil–military integration (CMI) a policy initiative. Although Beijing has been promoting CMI since the early 2000s, progress has been painfully slow. One problem is that the civil–military divide has proved far more difficult to overcome than was anticipated, while there has been poor coordination between defence and civilian agencies.

One of the new measures announced in March 2015 was to elevate CMI from an industry-level initiative into a national strategy. More powerful government agencies were brought into the CMI process, such as the National Development and Reform Commission. This has far more reach and experience in industrial-policy implementation than SASTIND and the Ministry of Industry and Information Industry, which have hitherto been in charge of CMI.

SASTIND has also overhauled its approach to CMI. It issued its first annual CMI Strategic Action Plan in 2015, which offered a more realistic and effective set of achievable near-term CMI policy measures. This revised strategy appears to have been successful and was followed by a second SASTIND action plan in 2016.

Diversifying defence-budget sources

The double-digit growth in the defence budget since the 1990s is a major factor underpinning the Chinese defence industry's improving performance. But as the country's overall economic growth has dropped, from over 10% annually to around 6–7% in the past one to two years, there are indications that this may also dampen defence-budget increases. This comes at a time when there is demand for yet more defence spending as new generations of weapons systems are finally moving from the development to the production phase.

Beijing slowed defence-budget growth to 7.6% in 2016, from 10.1% the previous year. This was the first single-digit increase since 2010, when the country was buffeted by the global financial crisis. But the official 2016 defence budget, at RMB954 billion (US$145bn), was not believed to include key categories such as R&D and foreign-weapons purchases.

Xi has hinted that this reduction in the pace of defence-budget growth may become the normal state of affairs. He was quoted by the *People's Liberation Army Daily*, the PLA's official newspaper, as saying that 'in the face of mounting pressure resulting from the economic downturn, with a slowdown in budgetary income and growing expenditure, it is not easy to secure a normal rise in the military budget any more'. Moreover, Xi complained that there was widespread waste of defence disbursements, pointing out that a number of costly but unnamed major projects had failed to meet operational requirements.

To mitigate this possible slowdown in defence funding, China's authorities have opened the domestic-capital markets to the country's major state-owned defence corporations. The hope is that they can take advantage of the financial opportunities that this may offer to help them better manage and leverage their assets. With strong order books, a pipeline full of developmental, new-generation equipment, and high-level leadership support, the defence industry is attracting significant interest from a growing range of domestic investment vehicles that have appeared in the past two decades, especially in the past few years.

Between 2010 and June 2016, the total funds raised in public- and private-equity offerings by the country's ten big defence corporations totalled RMB207.6bn (US$31.6bn). Most of these funds were specifically earmarked for weapons-development projects. The funds raised in 2016 are expected to register a significant increase on those in 2015 – in the first half of 2016, the total funds had already exceeded those raised in 2015 by RMB4.3bn (US$653 million).

The shipbuilding and aviation industries have been the most active defence sectors in using this fundraising opening. Between 2010 and June 2016, the shipbuilding industry raised RMB63bn (US$9.6bn), while the aviation sector brought in RMB65bn (US$9.9bn). Meanwhile, the space industry raised RMB31.9bn (US$4.8bn), the ordnance industry RMB27.1bn (US$4.1bn), the electronics industry RMB17.3bn (US$2.6bn) and the nuclear industry RMB3.4bn (US$517m).

Defence corporations will be able to continue to raise large amounts from asset-securitisation deals and bond issues, as well as from bank loans, in the coming years. As of March 2016, the big ten defence companies had 80 subsidiaries listed on China's stock exchanges, which accounted for around 25% of their total assets. Analysts estimate that if China follows the example of the US, which has around 70% of defence-industrial assets listed, it could allow Chinese firms to raise upwards of another RMB1 trillion (US$151.9bn) of funds.

China and the Third Offset Strategy

There is considerable debate among Chinese military analysts about the implications of the US Third Offset Strategy for China and what Beijing's strategic and programmatic responses should be. At the time of writing, the leading school of thought argued that the Third Offset is an attempt by the US to lure peer-competitors to compete in areas that are strategically advantageous to the US but place its rivals at a serious handicap.

An article in the *People's Liberation Army Daily* in May 2016 said that China should 'maintain strategic sobriety, make correct judgments on scientific and technological developments and military transformations in the future, not be confused or misled by the United States; we should strengthen our strategic steadfastness, persevere in taking our own development road, continue to stress and strengthen the domains where we enjoy superiority, and not be influenced by the United States'. This viewpoint is endorsed by Xi. In a speech at a meeting of the Central Economic Finance Leading Group in August 2014, Xi insisted that China 'needed to develop asymmetric capabilities and not just do exactly the same as developed countries are doing'.

JAPAN

In 2015, Japan's parliament passed security legislation designed to enable the country to exercise the right of collective self-defence. Following the political upheaval caused by this legislation, Prime Minister Shinzo Abe's administration looked in 2016 to consolidate its position on security matters, before considering further radical reforms. However, this strategy had mixed success.

With the government preparing to host the G7 Summit in May and to contest the Upper House elections in July, it was keen to avoid undue controversy over foreign policy – or issues relating to history – that could undermine the prime minister's position and affect domestic electoral support. The administration worked to improve ties with South Korea, having struck an agreement over the 'comfort women' issue in December 2015. It also reached out to China, with Abe meeting President Xi Jinping on the sidelines of international summits. Abe also slowed the pace of the relocation of the US Marine Corps' Futenma facility, in an attempt to minimise prefectural opposition in Okinawa and stem wider domestic controversy. Furthermore, Japanese diplomats engineered the visit of US President Barack Obama to Hiroshima after the G7 Summit, generating significant domestic and international prestige for Abe and displaying the strength of US–Japan ties. The summit passed smoothly, and Abe won another decisive victory for his Liberal Democratic Party–New Komeito coalition in the Upper House. The coalition increased its working majority, but the greater prize was that more

Myanmar's armed forces: privileges maintained

Myanmar transitioned to a democratic system of government following victory by the National League for Democracy in the November 2015 general election. A new administration was formed in March 2016, led by State Counsellor Aung San Suu Kyi. However, the Tatmadaw (Myanmar's armed forces), which dominated the country through various mechanisms from 1958 onwards, remains a vital player in the country's politics. Although the Tatmadaw leadership began the political-reform process, which commenced in 2010 with the release from house arrest of Aung San Suu Kyi – then the country's de facto opposition leader – the 2008 constitution gives political advantages to the armed forces in ways that constrain the powers of any elected government. Under the 2008 constitution, the armed forces retain 25% of the seats in both national legislative bodies, the 440-member People's Assembly and the 224-member House of Nationalities. Other military privileges include the control of important ministries (defence, home affairs and border affairs) and the provision for a military-led body to assume power should a state of emergency be declared. Moreover, in January 2016 the previous parliament, dominated by the military-backed Union Solidarity and Development Party, bequeathed a budget for the 2016–17 financial year that included a historically large allocation to the armed forces. (The new fiscal year began in March 2016.)

The Tatmadaw has made some efforts to increase its conventional-warfare capability, but it is still focused on internal-security operations against numerous ethnic-minority rebel groups, some of which have mounted the world's longest-running insurgencies. Eight of these groups signed a Nationwide Ceasefire Agreement (NCA) in October 2015, but others did not – notably the United Wa State Army, Kachin Independence Organisation, Shan State Army–North, Ta'ang National Liberation Army and Arakan Army – and are still involved in frequent armed clashes with the Tatmadaw. The Panglong Conference, which took place between August and September 2016 and aimed at securing a comprehensive nationwide peace agreement, excluded non-ceasefire armed groups. Though it achieved no concrete results, the conference laid the foundations for further talks and is scheduled to reconvene every six months. Some of these 'non-ceasefire' groups have indicated that they will begin negotiations to sign the NCA, thereby allowing their participation in future talks. In the meantime, continuing internal conflict led the European Union to renew its arms embargo on Myanmar for a further year in April 2016. This move may have contributed to the Tatmadaw's willingness to sign agreements that strengthen military cooperation with China and Russia in May and June 2016, respectively.

---

than two-thirds of the members of the Upper House were now in favour of revising the constitution. When combined with the coalition's outright two-thirds majority in the Lower House, this meant that forces in the National Diet were now potentially aligned for an attempt by Abe to push through revisions to Article IX of the constitution. (Among other points, Article IX states that Japan renounces 'the threat or use of force as means of settling international disputes'.) Abe and his supporters are likely to spend much of 2017 and 2018 looking to sweep away this post-war constitutional barrier to a greater international military role.

However, as 2016 wore on, Abe's strategy and Japan's security environment became progressively more challenging. North Korea posed new provocations to Japan with its nuclear- and ballistic-missile tests in January and February, and then further missile tests in July and August that landed in Japan's exclusive economic zone. Japan was especially disturbed by the failure of its ballistic-missile-defence (BMD) systems to detect the summer tests, which were launched from mobile platforms. Meanwhile, Sino-Japanese tensions rose again. Japan's apparent interference in the South China Sea disputes formed the background for renewed bilateral tensions with Beijing on the East China Sea. These included expressing approval at the end of 2015 for US freedom-of-navigation patrols, dispatching a Maritime Self-Defense Force (MSDF) destroyer and submarine on port visits to the Philippines and Vietnam in April, and clear support for the Philippines regarding the Permanent Court of Arbitration's South China Sea decision in July. In August, Japan protested to China about the rapid and persistent increase in intrusions by Chinese vessels into territorial waters around the disputed Senkaku/Diaoyu Islands.

The Abe administration's policy response to these challenges has been to continue to steadily augment Japan's defence capabilities. The Japan Ministry of Defense has continued to receive steady budget increases of between 1% and 2% a year since 2013 – firmly breaking from the pattern of stagnant budgets over the previous decade – and for FY2017 has requested a 2.3% increase that would enable the highest annual defence expenditure in the post-war period. The ministry has shown no retrenchment from the procurement plans laid out in the 2014 Mid-Term Defence Programme (MTDP). The Air Self-Defense Force released pictures in August of the first of its 42 F-35A Joint Strike Fighters, which is scheduled to be delivered in FY2017. The Ground Self-Defense Force (GSDF) continues to generate its amphibious force for the defence of outlying islands, awarding a contract in April 2016 to BAE Systems for 30 AAV-7 amphibious-assault vehicles. A further order for MV-22 *Osprey* tilt-rotor aircraft in July brought the number ordered to nine, out of the total requirement of 17. The MSDF maintained the plan to generate an *Aegis* BMD-capable cruiser/destroyer force of eight vessels (the MSDF currently has six, and budgeted for two more cruisers in FY2015 and FY2016), as well as to field helicopter carriers and expand its submarine fleet.

Looking to the latter period of the current MTDP, Japan is seeking to further expand its military capabilities. North Korea's missile tests in 2016 have strengthened calls for an increase in BMD assets and possible additional procurement of *Aegis*-capable vessels. China's activities in the East China Sea provided a trigger for the GSDF's announcement of plans to procure shore-to-ship missiles that could, in theory, be deployed to protect Japan's southern islands and close the straits across to Taiwan – thereby restricting the Chinese navy's movements – in a conflict situation. Meanwhile, Mitsubishi Heavy Industries (MHI) conducted test flights in April of its X-2 fifth-generation-fighter prototype. Japan is unlikely to develop an indigenous fifth-generation aircraft but the X-2's apparent stealth technologies may provide Tokyo with leverage in joining any future multinational fighter consortium.

Japan's recent attempts to internationalise its defence-industrial cooperation have had limited success. Kawasaki failed to sell the P-1 maritime-patrol aircraft to the United Kingdom in 2015, which instead chose Boeing's P-8A *Poseidon*. More strikingly, in 2016 MHI and Kawasaki Shipbuilding Corporation failed in their bid to export *Soryu*-class attack submarines to Australia. The Abe administration had hoped the bid would help kick-start Japan's export of military technology and cement the Australia–Japan strategic partnership. A number of factors contributed to Japan's failure to win the contract, including questions over the suitability of the *Soryu* technology for Australia's defence needs and, crucially, Japanese defence contractors' lack of experience in competing in international markets. However, Tokyo appears undeterred and, with negotiations over pricing and technology transfer apparently resolved in late 2016, is still looking to sell the ShinMaywa US-2 search-and-rescue aircraft to India. In an attempt to improve the coordination of these weapons-export efforts, the defence ministry established an Acquisition, Technology and Logistics Agency in 2015. However, Tokyo still needs to do more to encourage Japanese defence manufacturers to venture into international markets, and also learn the skills concerned with lobbying and the provision of offsets as incentives.

VIETNAM

New strategy document

In January 2016, Vietnam's cabinet approved the 'Overall Strategy for International Integration Through 2020, Vision to 2030', a document laying out strategic challenges and opportunities for Vietnam, and which charts paths to deepen the degree and effectiveness of Vietnam's integration in the international political and economic environment. It stated that Vietnam's strategic environment will, in the next half-decade, witness tension and the possibility of armed conflict between major powers as a result of the gradual shift towards a more multipolar balance of power. The Asia-Pacific region will witness competition among the major powers, an arms race, and more complicated territorial and maritime disputes. The Association of Southeast Asian Nations (ASEAN) will face difficult challenges both internally and externally arising from major-power rivalry and economic competition.

Vietnam's key objectives, as outlined in the strategy document, are to maintain a regional strategic environment conducive to 'peace, cooperation and development', ensure domestic security and stability, preserve one-party rule and defend national sovereignty, especially regarding features occupied by Vietnam and off-shore oil-production platforms in the South China Sea. In order to attain these objectives, Hanoi mapped out a long-term policy agenda aimed at ensuring that Vietnam becomes a modern and industrialised country by 2020, through proactive international and regional integration.

The strategy document also reviewed Vietnam's bilateral strategic and comprehensive partnerships with 25 countries, and concluded that the level of interdependence (and where interests coincide) 'is still low'; furthermore, many features of this cooperation are out of line with the frameworks for cooperation: 'there remain gaps between political commitments and implementation; cooperation in some areas have not … deepened [and] cooperation in security, intelligence and police [matters] with some countries' remains limited.

In order to address these gaps, Vietnam gave priority to upgrading relations with its major strategic partners 'in the areas of defence, security and development' as well as exploiting 'external resources in order to gradually modernize armed forces' and strengthen the country's capacity to ensure national security and defence. Hanoi intends for Vietnam to become a central player in regional security and defence cooperation mechanisms by 2030. In order to achieve these objectives, Vietnam plans to deepen, accelerate and diversify relations with its strategic partners and promote greater interdependence by enhancing 'bonds of interest'. Existing strategic partnerships with key countries in different regions are to be upgraded to comprehensive strategic partnerships.

Vietnam's strategy document gave priority to developing relations with India, Japan, Russia 'and some other potential partners like Australia and Israel'. (Vietnam signed comprehensive partnership agreements with Russia in 2001, India in 2007 and Japan in 2007.) It also called for Vietnam to 'gradually expand the content of defense and security cooperation … including joint patrol activities, joint exercises within ASEAN, working towards joint exercises between ASEAN and [its dialogue] partners'. The text did not specifically mention China, a comprehensive strategic-cooperative partner, or the United States, a comprehensive partner.

Given Vietnam's security concerns over the South China Sea, the strategy directed that Vietnam 'proactively and actively use ASEAN-led forums and mechanisms to create favorable conditions for partners to participate in and make contributions to the maintenance of peace, stability, security and safety of navigation and aviation in the East Sea [South China Sea] … [and] coordinate measures for trust building and preventive diplomacy in the region'. Specifically, Vietnam should work to increase the effectiveness of the ASEAN Regional Forum, ASEAN Defence Ministers' Meeting Plus (ADMM–Plus) and the East Asia Summit, as well as campaign for non-permanent membership on the United Nations Security Council by 2030. Furthermore, Hanoi should also 'proactively and actively beef up defense and security cooperation activities within the ASEAN Defense Ministerial Meeting and the ASEAN Defense Ministerial Meeting Plus', while at the same time attaching 'special importance to strengthening the capacity of air forces, towards participating in joint patrols in the East Sea, search and rescue work in the region; participate in joint exercises within ASEAN, and then between ASEAN and partners; [and also consider] participation in peace and security-keeping operations in the region, giving priority to less sensitive issues'.

Twelfth National Congress

In January 2016, the Twelfth National Congress of the Vietnam Communist Party approved the secretary-general's political report; this set broad policy guidelines for the period 2016–20. The section on 'Safeguarding the Homeland' called for a close link between national defence and security, with external relations by promoting international cooperation in defence and security in order to 'forge the People's Army [into a] standardized, elite and gradually modernized [force], with priority given step by step to modernizing a number of arms, services and forces'.

The twelfth congress saw sweeping changes to the leadership of the Vietnam People's Army (VPA). Two-term minister of national defence General Phung Quang Thanh stepped down and was replaced by General Ngo Xuan Lich, who vacated his post as head of the General Political Department. Senior Lt.-Gen. Luong Cuong replaced Lich as the army's chief political officer. Lt.-Gen. Phan Van Giang was appointed the new chief of the general staff and senior deputy minister. Senior Lt.-Gen. Nguyen Chi Vinh, who was responsible for international defence relations, was retained as deputy minister; his portfolio was expanded to include international defence-industry cooperation.

Defence policy and capability

Vietnam is a significant importer of military materiel. Its modernising armed forces operate a wide range of equipment of varying ages. In terms of some platform capabilities, Vietnam is on a par with regional peers, but this modern equipment is still low in numbers. Meanwhile, there are significant legacy fleets in need of replacement, particularly in terms of land equipment but also some naval and aviation assets. Upgrading all of these will be prohibitively expensive, so the incremental and highly targeted modernisation that is taking place is likely to continue. With

Vietnam having a significant littoral and a growing range of offshore energy and economic interests, it is unsurprising that capabilities are being procured that are suitable for the maritime and aerospace domains, such as submarines, advanced combat aircraft and domain-awareness capabilities, coupled with defensive assets like air- and coastal-defence capabilities.

In February 2016, Vietnam took delivery of its fifth *Varshavyanka* (enhanced *Kilo*-class) conventional submarine, HQ 186 *Da Nang*, from Russia. In September, the sixth and final submarine in this order, HQ 187 *Ba Ria-Vung Tau*, underwent sea trials and was expected to be delivered before the end of the year. In April and May, Russia's Zelenodolsk Shipyard launched two *Gepard*-class 3.9 (Project 11661E) frigates configured for anti-submarine warfare. They were expected to be delivered to Vietnam before the end of 2016. In September, Japan's prime minister Shinzo Abe promised to provide Vietnam with six new patrol boats for its coastguard through a soft loan. Three AgustaWestland SPA AW189 transport helicopters also entered service during the year.

In mid-2016, Vietnam confirmed its acquisition of the Israeli SPYDER-SR and the upgrade, reportedly by Belarus-based company Tetreaedr, to Vietnam's S-125 *Pechora*-2T air-defence systems. The country also acquired 20 Israeli Extended-Range Artillery Rocket (EXTRA) launchers, a potentially valuable capability development given the range and accuracy (ten metres' circular error probable) attributed to this 10–150km-range Israel-manufactured land-attack system. When combined with the incremental modernisation of Vietnam's air-defence capability, and the acquisition of systems like the *Bastion* coastal-defence system, as well as Vietnam's developing submarine force, Hanoi is gaining capabilities that could complicate the plans of any potential aggressor.

Foreign defence relations

Early in the year, Vietnam's General Political Department announced that 200 officers, a record number, would be sent abroad to attend professional military education and training courses. Fifty VPA officers were currently studying in Australia in late 2016 while another 150 were receiving training by Australian staff in Vietnam. In September, 20 Vietnamese officers and 40 submariners also completed the six-month basic submarine course at INS *Satavahana* in India. In addition, India agreed to provide pilot-conversion training for the Su-30MK combat aircraft. In a new development, around 50 Vietnamese assigned to the Defence Economic Technical Industry Corporation under the General Department of Defence Industry completed a five-month internship with Japan's Mukai Corporation.

In 2016 Vietnam intensified its efforts to prepare for the deployment of a level-two field hospital and engineering company for UN peacekeeping operations in the Central African Republic and South Sudan. Vietnam also approved the deployment of female officers for the first time. During the year, Military Hospital 175, in Ho Chi Minh City, received military medical delegations from Cuba, Japan, Singapore and South Korea to assist in pre-deployment training.

In March 2016, the International Committee of the Red Cross and the Vietnam Peacekeeping Centre jointly sponsored a training course on international humanitarian law. In August, the US Embassy's Defense Cooperation Office teamed up with the VPA's Engineering Corps Command and the Vietnam Mine Action Center to inaugurate a five-year course for instructors on the disposal of unexploded ordnance, field surveys and emergency first aid.

The year also saw Vietnam step up international defence engagement with its strategic partners. In February, Vietnam participated in its first International Fleet Review by dispatching HQ 011 *Dinh Tien Hoang*, a *Gepard*-class frigate, to India. The frigate paid a port call to Singapore en route.

In March, then-defence minister General Phung Quang Thanh met with his Chinese counterpart Senior Lt.-Gen. Chang Wanquan at the 3rd Vietnam–China Friendship Defence Border Exchange in Guanxi, China. Both ministers witnessed the signing of a memorandum of understanding on cooperation in UN peacekeeping missions. After assuming the ministerial portfolio, in April Defence Minister General Lich made his first official visit to Moscow to meet his Russian counterpart, Sergei Shoigu. Lich also addressed the 5th Moscow International Security Conference and conferred with his counterparts from Singapore and Thailand on the sidelines. Lich later visited Laos in May to attend the ADMM–Plus meeting, Cambodia in June and China in September and also hosted official visits by the defence ministers of India in June and France the same month.

In June 2016, Deputy Minister of National Defence Vinh addressed the IISS Shangri-La Dialogue in Singapore and used this opportunity to confer separately with the Canadian and Indian defence ministers, Singapore's permanent secretary of defence development, the US assistant secretary of defense,

Map 8 **Vietnam: military regions, air and naval bases**

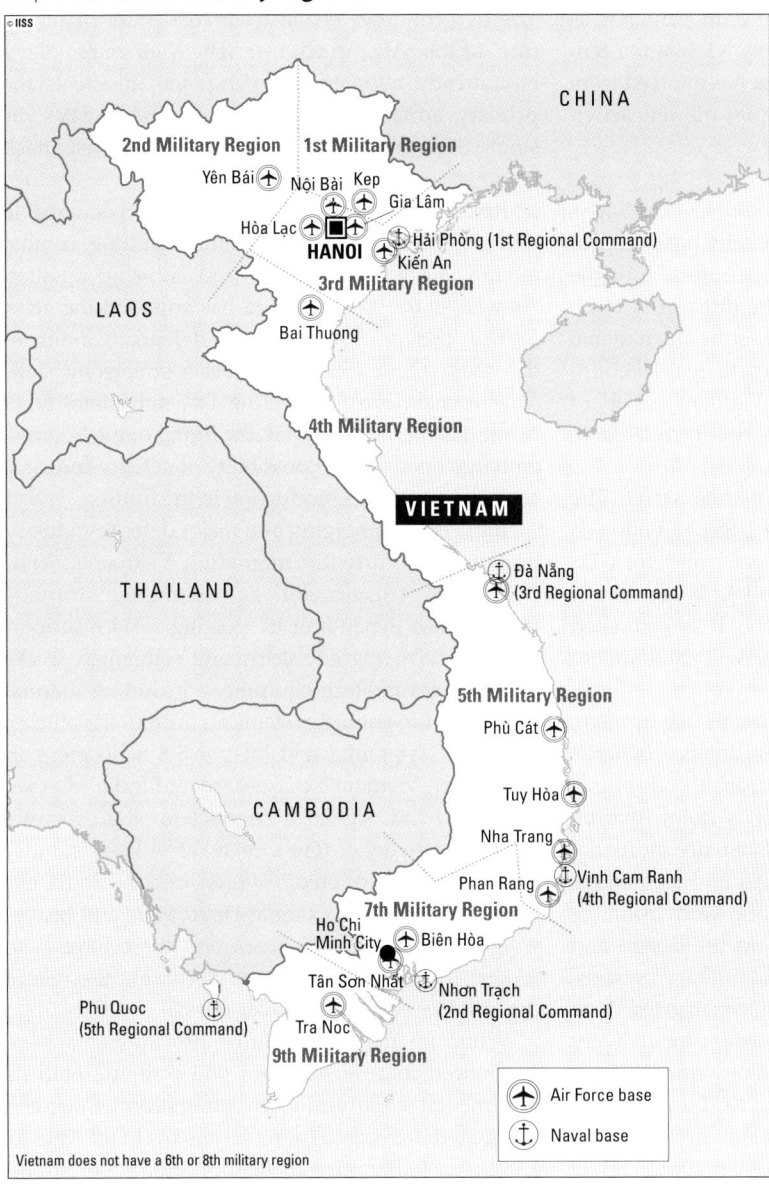

[Map showing Vietnam's military regions, air force bases and naval bases. Labeled locations include: 1st Military Region, 2nd Military Region (Yên Bái, Nội Bài, Kep, Gia Lâm, Hòa Lạc, HANOI), Hải Phòng (1st Regional Command), Kiến An, 3rd Military Region (Bai Thuong), 4th Military Region, 5th Military Region (Đà Nẵng – 3rd Regional Command, Phù Cát, Tuy Hòa, Nha Trang, Phan Rang, Vinh Cam Ranh – 4th Regional Command), 7th Military Region (Ho Chi Minh City, Biên Hòa, Tân Sơn Nhất, Nhơn Trạch – 2nd Regional Command), 9th Military Region (Phu Quoc – 5th Regional Command, Tra Noc). Vietnam does not have a 6th or 8th military region.]

fied defence purchases and US$5m to set up a military-information-technology software park in Nha Trang. Secondly, US President Barack Obama removed all restrictions on arms sales under the terms of the International Trafficking in Arms Regulations during his state visit to Vietnam in May.

Meanwhile, the VPA remained active in multilateral activities under the auspices of ASEAN. Vietnam and India, as co-chairs of the ADMM–Plus Experts' Working Group on Humanitarian Mine Action, hosted the Peacekeeping Operations and Humanitarian Mine Action field-training exercise in India in March. Vietnamese Navy personnel participated in the ADMM–Plus Maritime Security and Counterterrorism Exercise held in Brunei and Singapore in May, while Hanoi participated in the ADMM–Plus Experts' Working Group on Humanitarian Assistance and Disaster Relief/Military Medicine field-training exercise in Thailand in September. Additionally, Vietnamese naval personnel participated in the 6th Western Pacific Mine Countermeasures Exercise, co-hosted by Singapore and Indonesia in August 2016.

In March 2016, Vietnam officially opened the Cam Ranh Bay international port. During the year, warships from China, France, India, Japan, Singapore and the US visited the port. Vietnam also hosted a port call by an Australian warship in Ho Chi Minh City in May. In September, two US warships (the guided-missile destroyer USS *John S. McCain* and Littoral Combat Ship USS *Fort Worth*) visited Da Nang to participate in low-level naval-engagement activities including search-and-rescue practice and a Code of Unplanned Encounters at Sea exercise. A month later, and the Australian and New Zealand chiefs of defence force. Vinh also met the head of China's delegation, Admiral Sun Jianquo, and invited the People's Liberation Army Navy to visit Vietnam and hold maritime search-and-rescue exercises.

In terms of Vietnam's relations with its strategic and comprehensive partners, 2016 saw two key developments. Firstly, Vietnam and India raised bilateral relations to the level of a comprehensive strategic partnership during a visit by India's Prime Minister Narendra Modi in September. Modi offered Vietnam a US$500 million line of credit for unspeci-

the USS *John S. McCain*, together with the submarine tender USS *Frank Cable*, moored at Cam Ranh Bay as part of Naval Engagement Activity Vietnam, a ten-year-old US Navy programme that has evolved from port visits to including more complex training activities with the Vietnamese Navy.

Defence economics

For the past decade Vietnam's economy has grown at an average of 6.1% per year. In early August 2016, the cabinet concluded that it would be difficult to reach the target of 6.7% growth in 2016 set by the national assembly, and that economic growth was likely to fall between 6.27% and 6.5%. Vietnam's defence spending in 2014 and 2015 was closely related to growth in GDP.

Vietnam's defence budget is a state secret. The defence budget was estimated at US$4.31 billion in 2014 and US$3.84bn in 2015 (in 2014 and 2015 US dollars). This represented 8.0% and 7.0% of nominal government spending respectively. It is estimated that Vietnam's defence budget will amount to US$4.33bn in 2017.

As well as purchasing foreign equipment, Vietnam is looking to make more defence materiel itself and gain domestic benefit from the disbursement of procurement funding. It is doing this by gradually expanding its national defence-industrial base through overseas partnerships and technology transfers. For example, Damen Shipyard from the Netherlands is assisting Vietnam in the design and production of commercial and military vessels. In 2016, Vietnam successfully constructed and launched two 600-tonne troop carriers for delivery to Venezuela. As a result of technology transfer from Russia, Vietnam is developing the KCT-15 anti-ship missile. The KCT-15 is based on the Zvezda 3M24 (SS-N-25 *Switchblade*) anti-ship missile. Zvezda Strela is a subsidiary of the Moscow-headquartered Tactical *Strela* Missile System company. The missile was first displayed publicly in late 2015 as part of a defence-technology exhibition, although the precise status of the overall programme is unclear.

However, the nature of Vietnam's 'indigenous' capability to produce the KCT-15 has yet to be ascertained. It is possible that at least some of the main sub-assemblies for weapon production are provided by Russia, with final assembly carried out in Vietnam. The two countries began to discuss local 'manufacture' of the 3M24 in 2011–12. The Vietnamese Navy has already adopted the 3M24; the missile is the primary armament on its *Gepard*-class frigates, its single BPS-500 corvette and its *Tarantul*-V fast attack craft.

Russia remains the main supplier of capable military equipment to Vietnam, including combat aircraft, air-defence systems and anti-ship missiles. As well as the 3M24, Russia has supplied the 3K55 *Bastion* (SSC-5 *Stooge*) coastal-defence variant of the 3M55 *Onyx* (SS-N-26 *Strobile*) supersonic anti-ship missile developed by the TRV subsidiary NPO Mashinostroenia. That said, the lifting of the US arms embargo opens up the possibility of defence-industry cooperation and co-production in the future.

India is fast emerging as a major defence-industry partner. It is currently upgrading Vietnam's *Petya*-class light frigates for anti-submarine warfare. India is also expanding its existing service-support programme to upgrade all existing Vietnamese stocks of Soviet-era military equipment, including thermal sights and fire-control systems for armoured vehicles, T-54 and T-55 tanks, and Mi-17/Mi-8 helicopters. In September, Vietnam's coastguard and India's Larson & Toubro Ltd. signed a contract for the construction and delivery of four Ocean Patrol Vessels under a US$100m line of credit offered in 2014. India has offered to sell Light Combat Helicopters and heavyweight torpedoes to Vietnam and there have been reports that the two sides are discussing the sale of the *BrahMos* supersonic cruise missile.

While no major new arms procurements were announced in 2016, Vietnam will continue with its incremental military-modernisation process. Vietnam is engaged in a search for replacements to the MiG-21 and Su-22 fighter-aircraft fleets. Media reports indicate that Hanoi is looking at South Korea's T-50 *Golden Eagle*, Sweden's Saab JAS-39E/F *Gripen* NG, the Eurofighter *Typhoon* and Lockheed Martin's F-16. Vietnam has also expressed interest in acquiring maritime-patrol aircraft, such as Saab 340 or Saab 2000 twin-engine turboprops, the Airbus Group SE's C295, US-origin Lockheed Martin's P-3 *Orion*s and Japan's P-3Cs, as well as unmanned aerial vehicles for intelligence, surveillance and reconnaissance.

Afghanistan AFG

New Afghan Afghani Afs		2015	2016	2017
GDP	Afs	1.20tr	1.28tr	
	US$	19.7bn	18.4bn	
per capita	US$	615	562	
Growth	%	0.8	2	
Inflation	%	-1.5	4.5	
Def bdgt [a]	Afs	192bn	180bn	163bn
	US$	3.14bn	2.58bn	
US$1=Afs		61.14	69.75	

[a] Security expenditure. Includes expenditure on Ministry of Defence, Ministry of Interior, Ministry of Foreign Affairs, National Security Council and the General Directorate of National Security. Also includes donor funding

Population 33,332,025

Ethnic groups: Pashtun 38%; Tajik 25%; Hazara 19%; Uzbek 12%; Aimaq 4%; Baluchi 0.5%

Age	0–14	15–19	20–24	25–29	30–64	65 plus
Male	20.8%	6.2%	5.2%	4.1%	13.1%	1.2%
Female	20.2%	6.0%	5.0%	3.8%	12.7%	1.4%

Capabilities

The Afghan National Defence and Security Forces (ANDSF) are optimised for countering the threat posed by the Taliban, ISIS and other insurgent and terrorist groups. During the 2016 fighting season, the ANDSF largely succeeded in countering insurgent attacks, but territory under government control did not increase and the force was continually tested by Taliban activity. The forces continue to suffer a high attrition rate due to casualties and desertions. Insurgent forces retain significant influence in rural territories, while still demonstrating their ability to conduct attacks in population centres. NATO advisers remain embedded in the defence and interior ministries. The ANDSF are now responsible for the majority of their own training, albeit with high-level advisory support from NATO. They have sometimes found it difficult to balance individual and collective training with generating forces for operations, and training has often been the lower priority. Indigenous logistic support of Afghan forces is slowly improving but still represents a source of weakness. Considerable efforts are under way to improve leadership, intelligence, logistics and coordination between the different arms of the ANDSF. Air-force close-air support capability was improved by delivery of *Super Tucano* aircraft and MD-930F helicopters. Although the army and police have often been over-matched by the Taliban at the tactical level, they have eventually been able to organise tactical and operational-level counter-attacks. Army and police special-operations forces are well regarded by the US and NATO and have borne the brunt of intelligence-led strike operations against insurgent networks. Key constraints on US forces in Afghanistan were reduced in June 2016, giving them greater authority to support Afghan conventional forces with US firepower and to accompany and advise Afghan conventional forces.

ACTIVE 171,200 (Army 164,100 Air Force 7,100)
Paramilitary 148,200

ORGANISATIONS BY SERVICE

Afghan National Army (ANA) 164,100

5 regional comd

FORCES BY ROLE
SPECIAL FORCES
1 spec ops div (1 SF gp; 1 mech inf bn (2 mech inf coy), 2 cdo bde (1 mech inf coy, 4 cdo bn))
MANOEUVRE
Mechanised
2 (1st MSF) mech bde (2 mech inf bn)
1 (2nd MSF) mech bde (3 mech inf bn)
Light
1 (201st) corps (3 inf bde (4 inf bn, 1 sy coy, 1 cbt spt bn, 1 CSS bn), 1 inf bde (3 inf bn, 1 sy coy, 1 cbt spt bn, 1 CSS bn), 1 engr bn, 1 int bn, 2 MP coy, 1 sigs bn)
1 (203rd) corps (2 inf bde (5 inf bn, 1 sy coy, 1 cbt spt bn, 1 CSS bn), 2 inf bde (4 inf bn, 1 sy coy, 1 cbt spt bn, 1 CSS bn), 1 engr bn, 1 int bn, 2 MP coy, 1 sigs bn)
1 (205th) corps (4 inf bde (4 inf bn, 1 sy coy, 1 cbt spt bn, 1 CSS bn), 1 engr bn, 1 int bn, 2 MP coy, 1 sigs bn)
2 (207th & 209th) corps (3 inf bde (4 inf bn, 1 sy coy, 1 cbt spt bn, 1 CSS bn), 1 engr bn, 1 int bn, 2 MP coy, 1 sigs bn)
1 (215th) corps (3 inf bde (4 inf bn, 1 sy coy, 1 cbt spt bn, 1 CSS bn), 1 inf bde (2 inf bn, 1 cbt spt bn, 1 CSS bn), 1 engr bn, 1 int bn, 2 MP coy, 1 sigs bn)
1 (111st Capital) div (1 inf bde (1 tk bn, 1 mech inf bn, 2 inf bn, 1 sy coy, 1 cbt spt bn, 1 CSS bn), 1 inf bde (4 inf bn, 1 sy coy, 1 cbt spt bn, 1 CSS bn), 1 int bn)

EQUIPMENT BY TYPE
ARMOURED FIGHTING VEHICLES
MBT 20 T-55/T-62 (24 more in store†)
APC 951
 APC (T) 173 M113A2†
 APC (W) 623 MSFV (inc variants)
 PPV 200 *Maxxpro*
ENGINEERING & MAINTENANCE VEHICLES
 ARV 20 *Maxxpro* ARV
 MW *Bozena*
ARTILLERY 775
 TOWED 109: **122mm** 85 D-30†; **155mm** 24 M114A1†
 MOR 82mm 666: 521 2B14†; 105 M-69†; 40 M252†

Afghan Air Force (AAF) 7,100

Including Special Mission Wing

EQUIPMENT BY TYPE
AIRCRAFT 8 combat capable
 TPT 44: **Medium** 4 C-130H *Hercules*; **Light** 37: 24 Cessna 208B; 13 PC-12 (Special Mission Wing); **PAX** 3 B-727
 TRG 8 EMB-314 *Super Tucano**
HELICOPTERS
 ATK 3 Mi-35 *Hind*
 MRH 108: 3 *Cheetah*; 27 MD-530F (11 armed); 78 Mi-17 *Hip* H (incl 32 Special Mission Wing hel)

Paramilitary 148,200

Afghan National Police 148,200

Under control of Interior Ministry. Includes Afghan Uniformed Police (AUP), Afghan National Civil Order Police (ANCOP), Afghan Border Police (ABP), Police Special Forces (GDPSU) and Afghan Anti-Crime Police (AACP)

FOREIGN FORCES

All *Operation Resolute Support* unless otherwise specified
Albania 43
Armenia 65
Australia 270
Austria 10
Azerbaijan 94
Belgium 62
Bosnia-Herzegovina 55
Bulgaria 110
Croatia 105
Czech Republic 214 • UNAMA 2 obs
Denmark 90
Estonia 6
Finland 30
Georgia 861; 1 lt inf bn • UNAMA 3 obs
Germany 965; 1 bde HQ; CH-53G *Stallion*; *Heron* UAV • UNAMA 1 obs
Greece 4
Hungary 90
India Indo-Tibetan Border Police 335 (facilities protection)
Italy 827; 1 mech inf bde HQ; 1 mech inf regt(-); 1 avn bn(-); AW129 *Mangusta*; CH-47 *Chinook*; NH90
Latvia 18
Lithuania 21
Macedonia (FYROM) 39
Mongolia 120 • UNAMA 1 obs
Montenegro 14
Netherlands 120
New Zealand 8
Norway 50
Poland 198 • UNAMA 1 obs
Portugal 10 • UNAMA 1 obs
Romania 624 • UNAMA 2 obs
Slovakia 40
Slovenia 7
Spain 7
Sweden 23
Turkey 523
Ukraine 8
United Kingdom 450; 1 inf bn(-)
United States 7,006; 1 div HQ; 1 div HQ (fwd); 1 mech bde HQ; 1 lt inf bde HQ; 1 air aslt bde HQ; 1 armd recce bn, 2 mech bn; 2 inf bn; 1 cbt avn bde; RC-12X *Guardrail*; EC-130H *Compass Call*, C-130 *Hercules*, AH-64 *Apache*; CH-47 *Chinook*; UH-60 *Black Hawk*; HH-60 *Pave Hawk*; RQ-7B *Shadow*; MQ-1 *Predator*; MQ-9 *Reaper* • *Operation Freedom's Sentinel* 1,400

Australia AUS

Australian Dollar A$		2015	2016	2017
GDP	A$	1.63tr	1.68tr	
	US$	1.23tr	1.26tr	
per capita	US$	51,181	51,593	
Growth	%	2.4	2.9	
Inflation	%	1.5	1.3	
Def bdgt	A$	30.0bn	32.3bn	34.6bn
	US$	22.6bn	24.2bn	
US$1=A$		1.33	1.34	

Population 22,992,654

Age	0–14	15–19	20–24	25–29	30–64	65 plus
Male	9.2%	3.1%	3.5%	3.7%	23.4%	7.3%
Female	8.7%	3.0%	3.3%	3.5%	22.9%	8.5%

Capabilities

Australia possesses capable, well-trained and -equipped armed forces, with strong doctrine, logistic support, C4ISR and the capacity for deployment over long distances. They also have considerable recent operational experience. Canberra's primary ally remains the United States, but it is also forging closer defence ties with India, Japan and South Korea, while remaining committed to the Five Power Defence Arrangements in Southeast Asia and close defence relations with New Zealand. In March 2016, the government published Australia's third defence white paper in seven years. This identified China's growing regional role, regional military modernisation and interstate rivalry, the threat of terrorism from the Middle East and cyber attacks as important influences shaping Australia's defence policy. The defence of Australia, securing maritime Southeast Asia and the Pacific, and contributing to stability and the 'rules-based order' across the wider Indo-Pacific region are the country's three main 'defence objectives'. While the white paper indicated that Australia might be more reserved over involvement in distant military operations unless they involved 'core national interests', the Australian Defence Force (ADF) continued to be involved in the Middle East, with approximately 500 advisers and support personnel in Iraq and airstrikes continuing against ISIS targets in Iraq and Syria. Australia's government has promised to increase the defence budget to 2% of presently projected GDP by 2020–21, enabling the procurement of high-end equipment to strengthen ADF capabilities. In April 2016, the choice of French shipbuilder DCNS as winner of a competition to provide 12 new 'regionally superior' submarines was announced. These will all be built in Australia, and the first is expected in service around 2030. Due to be delivered from 2017–20, three *Aegis*-equipped destroyers will significantly reinforce naval anti-air capabilities, while nine new anti-submarine-warfare frigates will replace the existing *Anzac* class during the 2020s. The second of two *Canberra*-class LHDs, which will allow the ADF to create a significant amphibious capability, was commissioned in December 2015. The white paper confirmed that Australia is still committed to buying 72 F-35A Joint Strike Fighters, intended to boost offensive air capability, from 2020. In the meantime, the first of 15 P-8A maritime-patrol aircraft arrived in late 2016; the white paper also confirmed that from the early 2020s the air force will also acquire seven MQ-4C *Triton* unmanned aerial vehicles for maritime reconnaissance.

ACTIVE 57,800 (Army 29,000 Navy 14,400 Air 14,400)

RESERVE 21,100 (Army 13,200 Navy 3,150 Air 4,750)

Integrated units are formed from a mix of reserve and regular personnel. All ADF operations are now controlled by Headquarters Joint Operations Command (HQJOC)

ORGANISATIONS BY SERVICE

Space
EQUIPMENT BY TYPE
SATELLITES • COMMUNICATIONS 1 *Optus* C1 (dual use for civil/mil comms)

Army 29,000

Forces Command
FORCES BY ROLE
COMMAND
  1 (1st) div HQ (1 sigs regt)
MANOEUVRE
  Mechanised
  3 (1st, 3rd & 7th) mech inf bde (1 armd cav regt, 2 mech inf bn, 1 arty regt, 1 cbt engr regt, 1 sigs regt, 1 CSS bn)
  Amphibious
  1 (2nd RAR) amph bn
  Aviation
  1 (16th) avn bde (1 regt (2 ISR hel sqn), 1 regt (3 tpt hel sqn), 1 regt (2 spec ops hel sqn, 1 avn sqn))
COMBAT SUPPORT
  1 (6th) cbt spt bde (1 STA regt (1 STA bty, 1 UAV bty, 1 CSS bty), 1 AD/FAC regt (integrated), 1 engr regt (2 construction sqn, 1 EOD sqn), 1 EW regt, 1 int bn)
COMBAT SERVICE SUPPORT
  1 (17th) CSS bde (3 log bn, 3 med bn, 1 MP bn)

Special Operations Command
FORCES BY ROLE
SPECIAL FORCES
  1 (SAS) SF regt
  1 (SF Engr) SF regt
  2 cdo regt
COMBAT SUPPORT
  3 sigs sqn (incl 1 reserve sqn)
COMBAT SERVICE SUPPORT
  1 CSS sqn

Reserve Organisations 13,200 reservists

Force Command
FORCES BY ROLE
COMMAND
  1 (2nd) div HQ
MANOEUVRE
  Reconnaissance
  3 (regional force) surv unit (integrated)
  Light
  6 inf bde (total: 3 recce regt, 3 recce sqn, 12 inf bn, 6 arty bty)
COMBAT SUPPORT
  3 cbt engr regt
  1 sigs regt
COMBAT SERVICE SUPPORT
  6 CSS bn

Special Operations Command
FORCES BY ROLE
SPECIAL FORCES
  1 cdo regt
EQUIPMENT BY TYPE
ARMOURED FIGHTING VEHICLES
  MBT 59 M1A1 *Abrams*
  IFV 253 ASLAV-25 (all variants)
  APC • APC (T) 431 M113AS4
  AUV 1,020 *Bushmaster* IMV
ENGINEERING & MAINTENANCE VEHICLES
  ARV 45: 15 ASLAV-F; 17 ASLAV-R; 13 M88A2
  VLB 5 *Biber*
  MW 20: 12 *Husky*; 8 MV-10
ANTI-TANK/ANTI-INFRASTRUCTURE
  MSL • MANPATS FGM-148 *Javelin*
  RCL • 84mm *Carl Gustav*
ARTILLERY 239
  TOWED 155mm 54 M777A2
  MOR 81mm 185
RADAR • LAND 33: 3 *Giraffe*; 30 LCMR
AMPHIBIOUS 15 LCM-8 (capacity either 1 MBT or 200 troops)
HELICOPTERS
  ATK 22 *Tiger*
  TPT 105: **Heavy** 10 CH-47F *Chinook*; **Medium** 72: 38 NH90 TTH (MRH90 TTH); 34 S-70A *Black Hawk*; **Light** 23 Bell 206B1 *Kiowa*
UNMANNED AERIAL VEHICLES
  ISR • **Medium** 15 RQ-7B *Shadow* 200
AIR DEFENCE • SAM • Point-defence RBS-70

Navy 14,400
Fleet Comd HQ located at Sydney. Naval Strategic Comd HQ located at Canberra
EQUIPMENT BY TYPE
SUBMARINES • TACTICAL • SSK 6 *Collins* with 6 single 533mm TT with Mk48 *Sea Arrow* ADCAP HWT/UGM-84C *Harpoon* AShM
PRINCIPAL SURFACE COMBATANTS 11
  FRIGATES • FFGHM 11
    3 *Adelaide* (Mod) with 1 Mk13 GMLS with RGM-84C *Harpoon* AShM/SM-2 MR SAM, 1 8 cell Mk41 VLS with RIM-162 ESSM SAM, 2 triple Mk32 324mm

ASTT with MU90 LWT, 1 *Phalanx* Block 1B CIWS, 1 76mm gun (capacity 2 S-70B *Seahawk* ASW hel/MH-60R *Seahawk* ASW hel))

8 *Anzac* (GER MEKO 200) with 2 quad Mk141 lnchr with RGM-84C *Harpoon* Block 2 AShM, 1 8 cell Mk41 VLS with RIM-162 ESSM SAM, 2 triple 324mm ASTT with MU90 LWT, 1 127mm gun (capacity 1 S-70B *Seahawk* ASW hel) (capability upgrades in progress)

PATROL AND COASTAL COMBATANTS 15
  PCO 15: 13 *Armidale*; 2 *Cape*
MINE WARFARE • MINE COUNTERMEASURES •
MHO 6 *Huon* (of which 2 in reserve)
AMPHIBIOUS
  PRINCIPAL AMPHIBIOUS SHIPS 3
    LHD 2 *Canberra* (capacity 8 hel; 4 LCM; 100 veh; 1,000 troops)
    LSD 1 *Choules* (UK *Bay*) (capacity 1 med hel; 2 LCVP; 24 MBT; 350 troops)
  LANDING CRAFT 17
    LCM 12 LCM-1E
    LCVP 5
LOGISTICS AND SUPPORT 14
  AGHS 2 *Leeuwin* with 1 hel landing platform
  AGS 4 *Paluma*
  AORH 1 *Success*
  AOR 1 *Sirius*
The following vessels are operated by a private company, DMS Maritime:
  ASR 2: 1 *Besant*; 1 *Stoker*
  AX 2: 1 *Seahorse Horizon*; 1 *Seahorse Standard*
  AXL 1 *Seahorse Mercator*
  AXS 1 *Young Endeavour*

Naval Aviation 1,350

FORCES BY ROLE
ANTI SUBMARINE WARFARE
  1 sqn with NH90 (MRH90)
  1 sqn with S-70B2 *Seahawk*
TRAINING
  1 OCU sqn with MH-60R *Seahawk*
  1 sqn with AS350BA *Ecureuil*; Bell 429; H135

EQUIPMENT BY TYPE
HELICOPTERS
  ASW 33: 24 MH-60R *Seahawk*; 9 S-70B2 *Seahawk* (being withdrawn)
  TPT 17: **Medium** 6 NH90 (MRH90); **Light** 11: 6 AS350BA *Ecureuil*; 4 Bell 429; 1 H135

Clearance Diving Branch

FORCES BY ROLE
SPECIAL FORCES
  2 diving unit

Air Force 14,400

Flying hours   175 hrs/yr on F/A-18 *Hornet*

FORCES BY ROLE
FIGHTER/GROUND ATTACK
  3 sqn with F/A-18A/B *Hornet*
  2 sqn with F/A-18F *Super Hornet*
  1 sqn (forming) with F-35A *Lightning* II

ANTI SUBMARINE WARFARE
  1 sqn with AP-3C *Orion*
  1 sqn (forming) with P-8A *Poseidon*
ISR
  1 (FAC) sqn with PC-9/A(F)
AIRBORNE EARLY WARNING & CONTROL
  1 sqn with B-737-700 *Wedgetail* (E-7A)
TANKER/TRANSPORT
  1 sqn with A330 MRTT (KC-30A)
TRANSPORT
  1 VIP sqn with B-737BBJ; CL-604 *Challenger*
  1 sqn with Beech 350 *King Air*
  1 sqn with C-17A *Globemaster*
  1 sqn (forming) with C-27J *Spartan*
  1 sqn with C-130J-30 *Hercules*
TRAINING
  1 OCU with F/A-18A/B *Hornet*
  1 sqn with Beech 350 *King Air*
  2 (LIFT) sqn with *Hawk* MK127*
ISR UAV
  1 flt with *Heron*

EQUIPMENT BY TYPE
AIRCRAFT 147 combat capable
  FGA 97: 55 F/A-18A *Hornet*; 16 F/A-18B *Hornet*; 24 F/A-18F *Super Hornet*; 2 F-35A *Lightning* II (in test)
  ASW 16: 15 AP-3C *Orion*; 1 P-8A *Poseidon*
  EW 1 EA-18G *Growler**
  AEW&C 6 B-737-700 *Wedgetail* (E-7A)
  TKR/TPT 5 A330 MRTT (KC-30A)
  TPT 44: **Heavy** 8 C-17A *Globemaster*; **Medium** 15: 3 C-27J *Spartan*; 12 C-130J-30 *Hercules*; **Light** 16 Beech 300 *King Air*; **PAX** 5: 2 B-737BBJ (VIP); 3 CL-604 *Challenger* (VIP)
  TRG 97: 33 *Hawk* Mk127*; 62 PC-9/A (incl 4 PC-9/A(F) for tgt marking); 2 PC-21
UNMANNED AERIAL VEHICLES
  ISR • Heavy 8 *Heron*
RADAR • AD RADAR 7
  OTH-B 3 *Jindalee*
  Tactical 4 AN/TPS-77
AIR-LAUNCHED MISSILES
  AAM • IIR AIM-9X *Sidewinder* II; ASRAAM; **ARH** AIM-120B/C-5 AMRAAM
  ASM AGM-154 JSOW
  AShM AGM-84A *Harpoon*
  LACM Conventional AGM-158 JASSM
BOMBS
  Laser-guided *Paveway* II/IV; Laser JDAM (being delivered)
  INS/GPS-guided JDAM; JDAM-ER (in development)

Paramilitary

Maritime Border Command

Has responsibility for operational coordination and control of both civil and military maritime-enforcement activities within Australia's EEZ. At any one time, between 5 and 7 *Armidale*-class patrol boats and 2 AP-3C *Orion* aircraft are also assigned.

EQUIPMENT BY TYPE
PATROL AND COASTAL COMBATANTS 12
  PSO 2: 1 *Ocean Protector* with 1 hel landing platform; 1 *Ocean Shield* with 1 hel landing platform

PCO 8: 1 *Thaiyuk*; 1 *Triton* (leased) with 1 hel landing platform; 6 *Cape*
PCC 2 *Bay*
AIRCRAFT • **TPT** • **Light** 10 DHC-8
HELICOPTERS • **TPT** 2: **Medium** 1 Bell 214; **Light** 1 AS350 *Ecureuil*

Cyber

The Australian Cyber Security Centre was officially opened on 27 November 2014 and brings cyber-security capabilities from across the Australian government into a single location. It is the hub for private- and public-sector collaboration and information sharing to combat cyber-security threats. The department of defence is the first and largest contributor and works with other government agencies in the centre to ensure that Australia is both protected against emerging cyber threats and adequately positioned to meet the government's requirement to implement the Top 4 Strategies to Mitigate Targeted Cyber Intrusions. On 21 April 2016, the Australian Government Cyber Security Strategy was launched. The Australian Cyber Security Centre was a key contributor to this strategy. During the launch, the government publicly announced Australia's offensive cyber capabilities to respond to cyber intrusions against Australian networks. This capability is housed in the Australian Signals Directorate (ASD) and this public recognition brings Australia in line with international partners who have already announced their capability. The 2016 Defence White Paper acknowledges the importance of cyber security to the future of Australia's security environment and announced growth for the ASD's cyber capabilities.

DEPLOYMENT

Legal provisions for foreign deployment:
Constitution: Constitution (1900)
Decision on deployment of troops abroad: By government exercising its executive power under Section 61 of the Australian Constitution

AFGHANISTAN
NATO • ISAF (*Operation Highroad*) 270

ARABIAN SEA
Combined Maritime Forces • CTF-150 1 FFGHM

EGYPT
MFO (*Operation Mazurka*) 25

IRAQ
Operation Okra 380

MALAYSIA
120; 1 inf coy (on 3-month rotational tours); 2 AP-3C *Orion* (on rotation)

MIDDLE EAST
UN • UNTSO 13 obs

PAPUA NEW GUINEA
33; 1 trg unit

SOUTH SUDAN
UN • UNMISS 16; 1 obs

UNITED ARAB EMIRATES
Operation Accordion 400: 1 tpt det with 2 C-130J-30 *Hercules*
Operation Okra 400; 1 FGA det with 6 F/A-18A *Hornet*; 1 B-737-700 *Wedgetail* (E-7A); 1 A330 MRTT (KC-30A)

FOREIGN FORCES

New Zealand 9 (air navigation trg)
Singapore 230: 1 trg sqn at Pearce with PC-21 trg ac; 1 trg sqn at Oakey with 12 AS332 *Super Puma*; AS532 *Cougar*
United States US Pacific Command: 1,250; 1 SEWS at Pine Gap; 1 comms facility at NW Cape; 1 SIGINT stn at Pine Gap • US Strategic Command: 1 detection and tracking radar at Naval Communication Station Harold E. Holt

Bangladesh BGD

Bangladeshi Taka Tk		2015	2016	2017
GDP	Tk	16.2tr	18.6tr	
	US$	207bn	227bn	
per capita	US$	1,292	1,404	
Growth	%	6.8	6.9	
Inflation	%	6.4	6.7	
Def bdgt	Tk	207bn	221bn	
	US$	2.63bn	2.71bn	
FMA (US)	US$	2m	2m	2m
US$1=Tk		78.57	81.81	

Population   156,186,882

Religious groups: Muslim 90%; Hindu 9%; Buddhist 1%

Age	0–14	15–19	20–24	25–29	30–64	65 plus
Male	14.4%	5.2%	4.6%	4.1%	18.2%	2.9%
Female	13.9%	5.1%	4.7%	4.4%	19.5%	3.2%

Capabilities

Bangladesh has a limited military capability optimised for border and domestic security, and forces have shown themselves capable of mobilising and deploying quickly to tackle internal-security tasks. The country's long record of service in UN missions has brought it considerable peacekeeping experience. The armed forces also reportedly retain extensive business interests, in real estate, banks and other businesses. Over the past year, attacks by ISIS-linked and al-Qaeda-linked militant groups have continued, highlighting weaknesses in Bangladesh's preparedness and capacity to deal with terror attacks. Bangladesh is undertaking a major naval-recapitalisation and expansion programme in order to protect its large exclusive economic zone. In the recent past, Bangladesh has relied on Chinese and Russian aid and credit to overcome its limited procurement funding. UN payments for Bangladesh's contribution to peacekeeping operations reportedly provide important income for defence. Substantial efforts have been taken to strengthen a nascent shipbuilding industry with the assistance of foreign partners. The main Bangladeshi shipyard is now constructing high-speed patrol vessels with the firm Dockyard and Engineering

Works, itself owned by the Bangladeshi Navy. The patrol vessels are reportedly to equip the country's newly established naval special-forces unit. Work has also begun on a new submarine-support facility. The first two former Italian *Minerva*-class corvettes (converted by Fincantieri) were delivered to the coastguard in August, with a further two to follow. Two further Chinese-built *Swadhinota*-class guided-missile corvettes were commissioned in March 2016, while the delivery of two second-hand Chinese Type-035G submarines was scheduled for early 2017.

ACTIVE 157,050 (Army 126,150 Navy 16,900 Air 14,000) **Paramilitary 63,900**

ORGANISATIONS BY SERVICE

Army 126,150
FORCES BY ROLE
COMMAND
  7 inf div HQ
SPECIAL FORCES
  1 cdo bn
MANOEUVRE
  Armoured
  1 armd bde
  6 indep armd regt
  Light
  18 inf bde
  1 (composite) bde
COMBAT SUPPORT
  20 arty regt
  1 engr bde
  1 sigs bde
AVIATION
  1 avn regt (1 avn sqn; 1 hel sqn)
AIR DEFENCE
  1 AD bde
EQUIPMENT BY TYPE
ARMOURED FIGHTING VEHICLES
  MBT 276: 174 Type-59; 58 Type-69/Type-69G; 44 Type-90-II (MBT-2000)
  LT TK 8 Type-62
  RECCE 8+ BOV M11
  APC 306
    APC (T) 134 MT-LB
    APC (W) 172: 155 BTR-80; 17 *Cobra*
ENGINEERING & MAINTENANCE VEHICLES
  AEV MT-LB
  ARV 3+: T-54/T-55; Type-84; 3 Type-654
  VLB MTU
ANTI-TANK/ANTI-INFRASTRUCTURE
  MSL • MANPATS 9K115-2 *Metis* M1 (AT-13 *Saxhorn*-2)
  RCL 106mm 238 M40A1
ARTILLERY 853+
  SP 155mm 12 NORA B-52
  TOWED 363+: **105mm** 170 Model 56 pack howitzer; **122mm** 131: 57 Type-54/54-1 (M-30); 20 Type-83; 54 Type-96 (D-30), **130mm** 62 Type-59-1 (M-46)
  MRL 122mm 6 (PRC)
  MOR 472: **81mm** 11 M29A1; **82mm** 366 Type-53/type-87/M-31 (M-1937); **120mm** 95 AM-50/UBM 52
RADAR • LAND 2 SLC-2 (arty)
AMPHIBIOUS • LANDING CRAFT 3: 1 **LCT**; 2 **LCVP**
AIRCRAFT • TPT • Light 6: 5 Cessna 152; 1 PA-31T *Cheyenne*
HELICOPTERS
  MRH 2 AS365N3 *Dauphin*
  TPT 6: **Medium** 3 Mi-171Sh **Light** 3 Bell 206L-4 *Long Ranger*
AIR DEFENCE
  SAM
    Short-range FM-90
    Point-defence QW-2; HN-5A (being replaced by QW-2)
  GUNS • TOWED 166: **37mm** 132 Type-65/74; **57mm** 34 Type-59 (S-60)

Navy 16,900
EQUIPMENT BY TYPE
PRINCIPAL SURFACE COMBATANTS • FRIGATES 5
  FFGHM 1 *Bangabandhu* (ROK modified *Ulsan*) with 2 twin lnchr with *Otomat* Mk2 AShM, 1 octuple HQ-7 SAM, 2 triple 324mm TT with A244 LWT, 1 76mm gun (capacity: 1 AW109E hel)
  FFG 3:
    2 *Abu Bakr* (ex-PRC *Jianghu* III) with 2 twin lnchr with C-802A AShM, 2 RBU 1200 A/S mor, 2 twin 100mm gun
    1 *Osman* (ex-PRC *Jianghu* I) with 2 quad lnchr with C-802 (CSS-N-8 *Saccade*) AShM, 2 RBU 1200 A/S mor, 2 twin 100mm gun
  FF 1 *Umar Farooq*† (UK *Salisbury* – trg role) with 3 *Squid* A/S Mor, 1 twin 115mm gun
PATROL AND COASTAL COMBATANTS 56
  CORVETTES 6
  FSGM 2 *Shadhinota* (PRC C13B) with 2 twin lnchr with C-802 AShM, 1 octuple FL-3000N lnchr with HQ-10 SAM, 1 76mm gun, 1 hel landing platform
  FSG 4:
    2 *Durjoy* with 2 twin lnchr with C-704 AShM, 1 76mm gun
    2 *Bijoy* (ex-UK *Castle*) with 2 twin lnchr with C-704 AShM, 1 76mm gun, 1 hel landing platform
  PSOH 2 *Somudra Joy* (ex-USCG *Hero*) with 1 76mm gun, hel landing platform
  PCFG 4 *Durdarsha* (ex-PRC *Huangfeng*) with 4 single lnchr with HY-2 (CSS-N-2 *Safflower*) AShM
  PCO 6: 1 *Madhumati* (*Sea Dragon*) with 1 57mm gun; 5 *Kapatakhaya* (ex-UK *Island*)
  PCC 8:
    2 *Meghna* with 1 57mm gun (fishery protection)
    1 *Nirbhoy* (ex-PRC *Hainan*) with 4 RBU 1200 A/S mor; 2 twin 57mm gun
    5 *Padma*
  PBFG 5 *Durbar* (PRC *Hegu*) with 2 single lnchr with SY-1 AShM
  PBFT 4 *Huchuan* (PRC) with 2 single 533mm TT each with YU 1 Type-53 HWT
  PBF 4 *Titas* (ROK *Sea Dolphin*)

PB 11: 1 *Barkat* (ex-PRC *Shanghai III*); 2 *Karnaphuli*; 1 *Salam* (ex-PRC *Huangfen*); 7 *Shaheed Daulat* (PRC *Shanghai II*)

MINE WARFARE • MINE COUNTERMEASURES 5
MSO 5: 1 *Sagar*; 4 *Shapla* (ex-UK *River*)

AMPHIBIOUS
  LANDING SHIPS • LSL 1
  LANDING CRAFT 14
    LCT 2
    LCU 4 (of which 2†)
    LCVP 3†
    LCM 5 *Darshak* (*Yuchin*)

LOGISTICS AND SUPPORT 9
  AG 1
  AGHS 2: 1 *Agradoot*; 1 *Anushandhan*
  AOR 2 (coastal)
  AOT 1 *Khan Jahangir Ali*
  AR 1†
  ATF 1†
  AX 1 *Shaheed Ruhul Amin*

Naval Aviation
EQUIPMENT BY TYPE
AIRCRAFT • TPT • Light 2 Do-228NG (MP)
HELICOPTERS • TPT • Light 2 AW109E *Power*

Special Warfare and Diving Command 300

Air Force 14,000
FORCES BY ROLE
FIGHTER
  1 sqn with MiG-29B/UB *Fulcrum*
FIGHTER/GROUND ATTACK
  1 sqn with F-7MB/FT-7B *Airguard*
  1 sqn with F-7BG/FT-7BG *Airguard*
  1 sqn with F-7BGI/FT-7BGI *Airguard*
GROUND ATTACK
  1 sqn (forming) with Yak-130 *Mitten*
TRANSPORT
  1 sqn with An-32 *Cline*
  1 sqn with C-130B *Hercules*
  1 sqn with L-410UVP
TRAINING
  1 sqn with K-8W *Karakorum**; L-39ZA *Albatros**
  1 sqn with PT-6
TRANSPORT HELICOPTER
  1 sqn with AW139; Mi-17 *Hip* H; Mi-17-1V *Hip* H; Mi-171Sh
  1 sqn with Mi-17 *Hip* H; Mi-17-1V *Hip* H; Mi-171Sh
  1 sqn with Bell 212
  1 trg sqn with Bell 206L *Long Ranger*

EQUIPMENT BY TYPE†
AIRCRAFT 75 combat capable
  FTR 53: 9 F-7MB *Airguard*; 11 F-7BG *Airguard*; 12 F-7BGI *Airguard*; 5 FT-7B *Airguard*; 4 FT-7BG *Airguard*; 4 FT-7BGI *Airguard*; 6 MiG-29 *Fulcrum*; 2 MiG-29UB *Fulcrum*
  TPT 10: **Medium** 4 C-130B *Hercules*; **Light** 5: 3 An-32 *Cline*†; 3 L-410UVP
  TRG 32: 9 K-8W *Karakorum** being delivered; 7 L-39ZA *Albatros**; 10 PT-6; 6 Yak-130 *Mitten**

HELICOPTERS
  MRH 16: 2 AW139 (SAR); 12 Mi-17 *Hip* H; 2 Mi-17-1V *Hip* H (VIP)
  TPT 13: **Medium** 7 Mi-171Sh; **Light** 6: 2 Bell 206L *Long Ranger*; 4 Bell 212

AIR-LAUNCHED MISSILES
  AAM • IR R-3 (AA-2 *Atoll*)‡; R-73 (AA-11 *Archer*); PL-5; PL-7; **SARH** R-27R (AA-10A *Alamo*)

Paramilitary 63,900

Ansars 20,000+
Security Guards

Rapid Action Battalions 5,000
Ministry of Home Affairs
FORCES BY ROLE
MANOEUVRE
  Other
    14 paramilitary bn

Border Guard Bangladesh 38,000
FORCES BY ROLE
MANOEUVRE
  Amphibious
    1 rvn coy
  Other
    54 paramilitary bn

Coast Guard 900
EQUIPMENT BY TYPE
PATROL AND COASTAL COMBATANTS 11
  PSO 2 *Syed Nazrul* (ex-ITA *Minerva*) with 1 hel landing platform
  PB 4: 1 *Ruposhi Bangla*; 1 *Shaheed Daulat*; 2 *Shetgang*
  PBR 5 *Pabna*

DEPLOYMENT

CENTRAL AFRICAN REPUBLIC
UN • MINUSCA 1,073; 11 obs; 1 inf bn; 1 sigs coy; 1 med coy

CÔTE D'IVOIRE
UN • UNOCI 105; 7 obs; 1 fd hospital

DEMOCRATIC REPUBLIC OF THE CONGO
UN • MONUSCO 1,711; 17 obs; 1 inf bn; 1 engr coy; 1 avn coy; 2 hel coy

HAITI
UN • MINUSTAH 112; 1 hel sqn

LEBANON
UN • UNIFIL 276; 1 FFG; 1 FSG

LIBERIA
UN • UNMIL 4; 4 obs

MALI
UN • MINUSMA 1,414; 3 obs; 1 inf bn; 1 engr coy; 2 sigs coy; 1 tpt coy

SOMALIA
UN • UNSOM 1 obs

SOUTH SUDAN
UN • UNMISS 484; 6 obs; 2 engr coy; 2 rvn coy

SUDAN
UN • UNAMID 373; 7 obs; 2 inf coy

WESTERN SAHARA
UN • MINURSO 20; 5 obs; 1 fd hospital

Brunei BRN

Brunei Dollar B$		2015	2016	2017
GDP	B$	17.8bn	14.7bn	
	US$	12.9bn	10.5bn	
per capita	US$	30,993	24,713	
Growth	%	-0.6	0.4	
Inflation	%	-0.4	-0.3	
Def bdgt	B$	537m	565m	
	US$	391m	402m	
US$1=B$		1.37	1.41	

Population   436,620

Ethnic groups: Malay 65.7%; Chinese 10.3%; Indigenous 3.4%; other or unspecified 23.6%

Age	0–14	15–19	20–24	25–29	30–64	65 plus
Male	12.1%	4.1%	4.4%	4.6%	22.0%	2.2%
Female	11.4%	4.0%	4.6%	5.0%	23.3%	2.3%

Capabilities

While professional and well trained, the limited size of the Royal Brunei Armed Forces (RBAF) means they could offer little resistance on their own to a determined aggressor. Since 2015/16 (when defence spending was significantly reduced) funding shortfalls resulting primarily from the impact of declining energy prices on Brunei's national budget have challenged the RBAF's efforts to enhance its limited capabilities. While defence spending is projected to recover slightly in 2016/17, there are limited resources to enable the RBAF's Defence Capability Enhancement Project. However, Brunei has always depended on external support for its defence. The sultanate has long-established and close defence relations with the UK, and in February 2015 the UK and Brunei renewed for a further five years their long-standing agreement under which the sultanate hosts a British army garrison, including a Gurkha battalion and a jungle-warfare school. There is also a long-term Singapore Armed Forces presence in Brunei. Brunei continues to deploy small peacekeeping contingents, under Malaysian command, in Lebanon (UNIFIL) and the southern Philippines (IMT).

ACTIVE 7,000 (Army 4,900 Navy 1,000 Air 1,100)
Paramilitary 2,250

RESERVE 700 (Army 700)

ORGANISATIONS BY SERVICE

Army 4,900
FORCES BY ROLE
MANOEUVRE
  Light
  3 inf bn
COMBAT SUPPORT
  1 cbt spt bn (1 armd recce sqn, 1 engr sqn)

  Reserves 700
  FORCES BY ROLE
  MANOEUVRE
    Light
    1 inf bn
EQUIPMENT BY TYPE
ARMOURED FIGHTING VEHICLES
  LT TK 20 Scorpion (16 to be upgraded)
  APC • APC (W) 45 VAB
ENGINEERING & MAINTENANCE VEHICLES
  ARV 2 Samson
ARTILLERY • MOR 81mm 24

Navy 1,000
FORCES BY ROLE
SPECIAL FORCES
  1 SF sqn
EQUIPMENT BY TYPE
PATROL AND COASTAL COMBATANTS 12
  CORVETTES • FSG 4 Darussalam with 2 twin lnchr with MM-40 Exocet Block II AShM, 1 57mm gun, 1 hel landing platform
  PCC 4 Ijtihad
  PBF 1 Mustaed
  PB 3 Perwira
AMPHIBIOUS • **LANDING CRAFT** • **LCU** 4: 2 Teraban; 2 Cheverton Loadmaster

Air Force 1,100
FORCES BY ROLE
MARITIME PATROL
  1 sqn with CN-235M
TRAINING
  1 sqn with PC-7; Bell 206B Jet Ranger II
TRANSPORT HELICOPTER
  1 sqn with Bell 212; Bell 214 (SAR)
  1 sqn with Bo-105
  1 sqn with S-70i Black Hawk
AIR DEFENCE
  1 sqn with Rapier
  1 sqn with Mistral
EQUIPMENT BY TYPE
AIRCRAFT
  MP 1 CN-235M
  TRG 4 PC-7
HELICOPTERS
  TPT 23: **Medium** 5: 1 Bell 214 (SAR); 4 S-70i Black Hawk; **Light** 18: 2 Bell 206B Jet Ranger II; 10 Bell 212; 6 Bo-105 (armed, 81mm rockets)
AIR DEFENCE • SAM • Point-defence Rapier; Mistral

Paramilitary ε2,250

Gurkha Reserve Unit 400–500
FORCES BY ROLE
MANOEUVRE
Light
2 inf bn(-)

Royal Brunei Police 1,750
EQUIPMENT BY TYPE
PATROL AND COASTAL COMBATANTS • PB 10: 3 *Bendaharu*; 7 PDB-type

DEPLOYMENT

LEBANON
UN • UNIFIL 29

PHILIPPINES
IMT 8

FOREIGN FORCES

Singapore 1 trg camp with infantry units on rotation; 1 trg school; 1 hel det with AS332 *Super Puma*
United Kingdom 550; 1 Gurhka bn; 1 trg unit; 1 hel flt with 3 hel

Cambodia CAM

Cambodian Riel r		2015	2016	2017
GDP	r	73.4tr	82.0tr	
	US$	17.8bn	19.4bn	
per capita	US$	1,144	1,228	
Growth	%	7.0	7.0	
Inflation	%	1.2	3.1	
Def bdgt [a]	r	ε2.33tr	ε2.66tr	
	US$	ε565m	ε628m	
US$1=r		4,127.42	4,232.65	

[a] Defence and security budget

Population 15,957,223

Ethnic groups: Khmer 90%; Vietnamese 5%; Chinese 1%

Age	0–14	15–19	20–24	25–29	30–64	65 plus
Male	15.8%	4.4%	5.0%	5.1%	16.7%	1.6%
Female	15.5%	4.5%	5.1%	5.2%	18.5%	2.6%

Capabilities

Despite their name, which reflects Cambodia's formal status as a constitutional monarchy – and the integration in the early 1990s of two non-communist resistance armies – the Royal Cambodian Armed Forces (RCAF) are essentially the modern manifestation of the armed forces of the former People's Republic of Kampuchea, established in 1979 following Vietnam's invasion. In terms of organisation, the RCAF has an excessive number of senior officers, while many formations and units appear to be of only nominal status. Skirmishes on the border with Thailand since 2008 provide little indication of capacity for high-intensity combat. Cambodia's most important international links are with the Chinese and Vietnamese armed forces. A training relationship also exists with the US, and the latest iteration of the bilateral exercise *Angkor Sentinel* was held in March 2006 at the National Center for Peacekeeping Forces in Kampong Speu Province. Cambodia has contributed personnel to UN peacekeeping missions, including MINUSCA (Central African Republic) and MINUSMA (Mali).

ACTIVE 124,300 (Army 75,000 Navy 2,800 Air 1,500 Provincial Forces 45,000) **Paramilitary 67,000**

Conscript liability 18 months service authorised but not implemented since 1993

ORGANISATIONS BY SERVICE

Army ε75,000
6 Military Regions (incl 1 special zone for capital)
FORCES BY ROLE
SPECIAL FORCES
1 (911th) AB/SF Bde
MANOEUVRE
Light
2 (2nd & 3rd Intervention) inf div (3 inf bde)
5 (Intervention) indep inf bde
7 indep inf bde
Other
1 (70th) sy bde (4 sy bn)
17 (border) sy bn
COMBAT SUPPORT
2 arty bn
4 fd engr regt
COMBAT SERVICE SUPPORT
1 (construction) engr regt
2 tpt bde
AIR DEFENCE
1 AD bn
EQUIPMENT BY TYPE
ARMOURED FIGHTING VEHICLES
MBT 200+: 50 Type-59; 150+ T-54/T-55
LT TK 20+: Type-62; 20 Type-63
RECCE 4+ BRDM-2
IFV 70 BMP-1
APC 230+
  APC (T) M113
  APC (W) 230: 200 BTR-60/BTR-152; 30 OT-64
ENGINEERING & MAINTENANCE VEHICLES
ARV T-54/T-55
MW *Bozena*; RA-140 DS
ANTI-TANK/ANTI-INFRASTRUCTURE
RCL 82mm B-10; 107mm B-11
ARTILLERY 433+
  TOWED 400+ 76mm ZIS-3 (M-1942)/122mm D-30/122mm M-30 (M-1938)/130mm Type-59-I
  MRL 33+: 107mm Type-63; 122mm 13: 8 BM-21; 5 RM-70; 132mm BM-13-16 (BM-13); 140mm 20 BM-14-16 (BM-14)
  MOR 82mm M-37; 120mm M-43; 160mm M-160
AIR DEFENCE
SAM • Point-defence FN-6; FN-16 (reported)
GUNS • TOWED 14.5mm ZPU-1/ZPU-2/ZPU-4; 37mm M-1939; 57mm S-60

Navy ε2,800 (incl 1,500 Naval Infantry)
EQUIPMENT BY TYPE
PATROL AND COASTAL COMBATANTS 16
  PBF 3 Stenka
  PB 11: 4 (PRC 46m); 3 (PRC 20m); 2 Shershen; 2 Turya
  PBR 2 Kaoh Chhlam
AMPHIBIOUS • LANDING CRAFT
  LCU 1

Naval Infantry 1,500
FORCES BY ROLE
MANOEUVRE
  Light
  1 (31st) nav inf bde
COMBAT SUPPORT
  1 arty bn

Air Force 1,500
FORCES BY ROLE
ISR/TRAINING
  1 sqn with P-92 Echo; L-39 Albatros*
TRANSPORT
  1 VIP sqn (reporting to Council of Ministers) with An-24RV Coke; AS350 Ecureuil; AS355F2 Ecureuil II
  1 sqn with BN-2 Islander; Y-12 (II)
TRANSPORT HELICOPTER
  1 sqn with Mi-26 Halo; Mi-17 Hip H; Mi-8 Hip; Z-9
EQUIPMENT BY TYPE
AIRCRAFT 5 combat capable
  TPT • Light 10: 2 An-24RV Coke; 1 BN-2 Islander; 5 P-92 Echo (pilot trg/recce); 2 Y-12 (II)
  TRG 5 L-39 Albatros*
HELICOPTERS
  MRH 14: 3 Mi-17 Hip H; 11 Z-9
  TPT 10: **Heavy** 2 Mi-26 Halo; **Medium** 4 Mi-8 Hip; **Light** 4: 2 AS350 Ecureuil; 2 AS355F2 Ecureuil II

Provincial Forces 45,000+
Reports of at least 1 inf regt per province, with varying numbers of inf bn (with lt wpn)

Paramilitary
  Police 67,000 (including gendarmerie)

DEPLOYMENT

CENTRAL AFRICAN REPUBLIC
UN • MINUSCA 216; 6 obs; 1 engr coy

LEBANON
UN • UNIFIL 185; 1 engr coy

MALI
UN • MINUSMA 301; 1 engr coy; 1 EOD coy

SOUTH SUDAN
UN • UNMISS 149; 2 obs; 1 fd hospital

SUDAN
UN • UNAMID 2 obs
UN • UNISFA 1; 2 obs

China, People's Republic of PRC

Chinese Yuan Renminbi Y		2015	2016	2017
GDP	Y	69.6tr	75.0tr	
	US$	11.2tr	11.4tr	
per capita	US$	8,141	8,261	
Growth	%	6.9	6.6	
Inflation	%	1.4	2.1	
Def exp	Y	n.k.	n.k.	
	US$	n.k.	n.k.	
Def bdgt	Y	887bn	954bn	
	US$	142bn	145bn	
US$1=Y		6.23	6.58	

Population 1,381,306,106
Ethnic groups: Han 91.5%; Zhuang 1.3%; Hui 0.8%; Manchu 0.8%; Uighur 0.7%; Tibetan 0.5%; other or unspecified 4.4%

Age	0–14	15–19	20–24	25–29	30–64	65 plus
Male	9.2%	3.2%	3.8%	4.7%	25.5%	5.0%
Female	7.9%	2.8%	3.4%	4.5%	24.6%	5.4%

Capabilities

Despite slowing economic growth, China remains committed to developing and modernising its military capabilities. The latest 2014 defence white paper, published in English in 2015, outlined the importance of power-projection capabilities to the People's Liberation Army (PLA), emphasising the requirements for offensive and defensive air operations, and 'open seas protection'. A major restructuring of the PLA was announced in late 2015 and early 2016, along with a planned reduction in size by 300,000 personnel, including from front-line/teeth-arm units and formations. It remains unclear how effective the reorganisations will be at generating and controlling high-intensity combined-arms capabilities. A problem in improving operational effectiveness is that the recognised operational imperative to generate dynamic change in the armed forces will be tempered by the political requirement to maintain control. Establishment of the Strategic Support Force underscores the importance placed upon the further development of China's already advanced cyber, space and information-dominance capabilities. The navy and air force have continued to receive the majority of equipment investment. The navy has almost fully modernised its main 'surface action groups', while the air force is introducing into service improved indigenous aircraft designs, such as the J-10B. The PLA Rocket Force (formerly the Second Artillery but elevated to service level in the restructuring) is also undergoing a period of sustained modernisation, reflected in the introduction into service over the past two years of new missile types. Despite modernisation, however, significant amounts of old equipment remain in service. China has a robust domestic defence industry, capable of producing equipment across all domains, although questions persist over quality. Meanwhile, the deals with Russia for Su-35 combat aircraft and S-400 air-defence systems show continuing willingness to purchase from Russia in limited amounts in order to help further develop domestic industry. The armed forces have some experience with extended out-of-area maritime deployments, and China is constructing support facilities in Djibouti to support such missions, but there is less experience in the other services. However, incremental growth in limited deployments to UN peacekeeping missions indicates developing intent in this area. (See pp. 251–62.)

ACTIVE 2,183,000 (Ground Forces 1,150,000 Navy 235,000 Air Force 398,000 Strategic Missile Forces 100,000 Strategic Support Force 150,000 Other 150,000) Paramilitary 660,000

Conscript liability Selective conscription; all services 2 years

RESERVE ε510,000

ORGANISATIONS BY SERVICE

Strategic Missile Forces 100,000+

People's Liberation Army Rocket Force

The People's Liberation Army Rocket Force (formerly the Second Artillery Force) organises and commands its own troops to launch nuclear counter-attacks with strategic missiles and to conduct operations with conventional missiles. Organised as launch bdes subordinate to 6 army-level msl bases. Org varies by msl type

FORCES BY ROLE
SURFACE-TO-SURFACE MISSILE
  1 ICBM bde with DF-4
  2 ICBM bde with DF-5A
  1 ICBM bde with DF-5B
  1 ICBM bde with DF-31
  2 ICBM bde with DF-31A
  1 IRBM bde with DF-26
  1 MRBM bde with DF-16
  1 MRBM bde with DF-21
  5 MRBM bde with DF-21A
  3 MRBM bde with DF-21C
  2 MRBM bde with DF-21D
  4 SRBM bde with DF-11A
  3 SRBM bde with DF-15B
  2 GLCM bde with DH-10
  2 SSM trg bde

EQUIPMENT BY TYPE
SURFACE-TO-SURFACE MISSILE LAUNCHERS
  ICBM • Nuclear 62: ε10 DF-4 (CSS-3); ε20 DF-5A/B (CSS-4 Mod 2/3); ε8 DF-31 (CSS-10 Mod 1); ε24 DF-31A (CSS-10 Mod 2)
  IRBM • Dual-capable ε16 DF-26
  MRBM 146: **Nuclear** ε80 DF-21/DF-21A/DF-21E (CSS-5 Mod 1/2/6); **Conventional** 66: ε12 DF-16 (CSS-11 Mod 1); ε36 DF-21C (CSS-5 Mod 4); ε18 DF-21D (CSS-5 Mod 5 – ASBM)
  SRBM • Conventional 189: ε108 DF-11A (CSS-7 Mod 2); ε81 DF-15B (CSS-6 Mod 3)
  GLCM • Dual-capable ε54 DH-10

Navy
EQUIPMENT BY TYPE
SUBMARINES • STRATEGIC • SSBN 4:
  4 *Jin* (Type-094) with up to 12 JL-2 (CSS-NX-14) strategic SLBM (operational status unknown)

Air Force
FORCES BY ROLE
BOMBER
  3 regt with H-6K
EQUIPMENT BY TYPE
AIRCRAFT • BBR ε60 H-6K
AIR-LAUNCHED MISSILES
  ALCM • Dual-capable CJ-20

Defensive
EQUIPMENT BY TYPE
RADAR • STRATEGIC: 4+ large phased array radars; some detection and tracking radars

Space
EQUIPMENT BY TYPE
SATELLITES 72
  COMMUNICATIONS 6 *Zhongxing* (dual-use telecom satellites for civ/mil comms)
  NAVIGATION/POSITIONING/TIMING 21: 7 *Beidou-2*(M); 5 *Beidou-2*(G); 9 *Beidou-2*(IGSO)
  ISR 30: 29 *Yaogan Weixing* (remote sensing); 1 *Ziyuan* (ZY-2 – remote sensing)
  ELINT/SIGINT 15: 8 *Shijian* 6 (4 pairs – reported ELINT/SIGINT role); 7 *Shijian* 11 (reported ELINT/SIGINT role)

Ground Forces ε1,150,000

In late 2015, a single, separate, headquarters was established for the People's Liberation Army (PLA) ground forces, in place of the four general departments

FORCES BY ROLE
COMMAND
  18 (Group) army HQ
SPECIAL FORCES
  10 SF bde
  2 SF gp (regt)
MANOEUVRE
  Armoured
  1 armd div (3 armd regt, 1 arty regt, 1 AD regt)
  16 armd bde
  2 hy mech inf div (1 armd regt, 2 mech inf regt, 1 arty regt, 1 AD regt)
  6 hy mech inf bde
  Mechanised
  2 mech inf div (1 armd regt, 2 mech inf regt, 1 arty regt, 1 AD regt)
  2 mech inf div (1 lt armd regt, 2 mech inf regt, 1 arty regt, 1 AD regt)
  1 (high alt) mech inf div (1 armd regt, 2 mech inf regt, 1 arty regt, 1 AD regt)
  16 mech inf bde
  1 (high alt) mech inf bde
  Light
  1 mot inf div (1 armd regt, 3 mot inf regt, 1 arty regt, 1 AD regt)

4 mot inf div (1 armd regt, 2 mot inf regt, 1 arty regt, 1 AD regt)
4 (high alt) mot inf div (1 armd regt, 2 mot inf regt, 1 arty regt, 1 AD regt)
18 mot inf bde
2 (high alt) mot inf bde
5 mtn inf bde
Amphibious
1 amph armd bde
2 amph mech div (1 armd regt, 2 mech inf regt, 1 arty regt, 1 AD regt)
Other
1 (OPFOR) mech inf bde
1 mech gd div (1 armd regt, 2 mech inf regt, 1 arty regt, 1 AD regt)
1 sy gd div (4 sy regt)
59 (border) sy regt
1 (border) sy gp
COMBAT SUPPORT
19 arty bde
2 MRL bde
2 engr bde
19 engr regt
10 EW regt
50 sigs regt
COASTAL DEFENCE
19 AShM regt
AVIATION
1 mixed avn bde
HELICOPTER
6 hel bde
5 hel regt
TRAINING
4 hel trg regt
AIR DEFENCE
22 AD bde

Reserves

FORCES BY ROLE
MANOEUVRE
  Armoured
  2 armd regt
  Light
  18 inf div
  4 inf bde
  3 indep inf regt
COMBAT SUPPORT
  3 arty div
  7 arty bde
  15 engr regt
  1 ptn br bde
  3 ptn br regt
  10 chem regt
  10 sigs regt
COMBAT SERVICE SUPPORT
  9 log bde
  1 log regt
AIR DEFENCE
  17 AD div
  8 AD bde
  8 AD regt

EQUIPMENT BY TYPE
ARMOURED FIGHTING VEHICLES
  MBT 6,740: 1,600 ZTZ-59; 650 ZTZ-59-II; 600 ZTZ-59D; 200 ZTZ-79; 300 ZTZ-88A/B; 1,000 ZTZ-96; 1,500 ZTZ-96A; 40 ZTZ-98A; 600 ZTZ-99; 250 ZTZ-99A
  LT TK 650: 250 ZTD-05; 250 ZTQ-62; 150 ZTS-63A
  ASLT 400 ZTL-09
  IFV 3,800: 400 ZBD-04; 500 ZBD-04A; 500 ZBL-09; 600 ZBD-86; 650 ZBD-86A; 550 ZSL-92; 600 ZSL-92B
  APC 5,020+
    APC (T) 4,150: 2,400 ZSD-63/ZSD-63C; 1,750 ZSD-89
    APC (W) 870+: 700 ZSL-92A; 120 ZBL-09A; 50 ZSL-93; some EQ2050F
  AAV 300 ZBD-05
  AUV *Tiger* 4×4
ENGINEERING & MAINTENANCE VEHICLES
  ARV Type-73; Type-84; Type-85; Type-97; Type-654
  VLB KMM; MTU; TMM; Type-84A
  MW Type-74; Type-79; Type-81-II; Type-84
ANTI-TANK/ANTI-INFRASTRUCTURE
  MSL
    SP 924: 450 HJ-8 (veh mounted); 24 HJ-10; 450 ZSL-02B
    MANPATS HJ-73A/B/C; HJ-8A/C/E
  RCL 3,966: **75mm** PF-56; **82mm** PF-65 (B-10); PF-78; **105mm** PF-75; **120mm** PF-98
  GUNS 1,788
    SP 480: **100mm** 250 PTL-02; **120mm** 230 PTZ-89
    TOWED • **100mm** 1,308 PT-73 (T-12)/PT-86
ARTILLERY 13,218+
  SP 2,320: **122mm** 1,650: 700 PLZ-89; 300 PLZ-07; 150 PLZ-07B; 300 PLC-09; 200 PLL-09; **152mm** 350 PLZ-83A/B; **155mm** 320 PLZ-05
  TOWED 6,140: **122mm** 3,800 PL-54-1 (M-1938)/PL-83/PL-60 (D-74)/PL-96 (D-30); **130mm** 234 PL-59 (M-46)/PL-59-I; **152mm** 2,106 PL-54 (D-1)/PL-66 (D-20)
  GUN/MOR 120mm 300: 200 PLL-05; 100 PLZ-05A
  MRL 1,872+ **107mm** 54+ PH-63; **122mm** 1,643: 1,250 PHL-81/PHL-90/SR4; 375 PHZ-89; 18 PHZ-10; **300mm** 175 PHL-03
  MOR 2,586: **82mm** PP-53 (M-37)/PP-67/PP-82/PP-87; **100mm** PP-89
RADAR • LAND *Cheetah*; RASIT; Type-378
COASTAL DEFENCE
  AShM HY-1 (CSS-C-2 *Silkworm*); HY-2 (CSS-C-3 *Seersucker*); HY-4 (CSS-C-7 *Sadsack*); YJ-62
PATROL AND COASTAL COMBATANTS 25
  PB 25: 9 *Huzong*; 16 *Shenyang*
AMPHIBIOUS 148+
  LCM 117+: 1+ *Yunnan*; 100+ *Yunnan* II; 16+ *Yupen*
  LCU 31+: 30 *Yuwei*; 1 other
LOGISTICS AND SUPPORT 18
  AK 5 *Leizhuang*
  AKR 1 Type-901
  ARC 1
  AOT 8: 1 *Fuzhong*; 7 *Fubing*
  ATF 2 *Huntao*
  AX 1 *Haixun* III
AIRCRAFT • TPT 8: **Medium** 4 Y-8; **Light** 4 Y-7
HELICOPTERS
  ATK 240: 120 WZ-10; 120 WZ-19

MRH 351: 22 Mi-17 *Hip* H; 3 Mi-17-1V *Hip* H; 38 Mi-17V-5 *Hip* H; 25 Mi-17V-7 *Hip* H; 8 SA342L *Gazelle*; 21 Z-9A; 31 Z-9W; 10 Z-9WA; 193 Z-9WZ
TPT 362: **Heavy** 85: 9 Z-8A; 76 Z-8B; **Medium** 209: 50 Mi-8T *Hip*; 140 Mi-171; 19 S-70C2 (S-70C) *Black Hawk*; **Light** 68: 53 AS350 *Ecureuil*; 15 H120 *Colibri*
UNMANNED AERIAL VEHICLES
ISR • Heavy BZK-005; BZK-009 (reported); **Medium** BZK-006; BZK-007; BZK-008; **Light** *Harpy* (anti-radiation)
AIR DEFENCE
SAM
Medium-range 90: 72 HQ-16A; 18 HQ-17
Short-range 254: 24 9K331 *Tor*-M1 (SA-15 *Gauntlet*); 30 HQ-6D; 200 HQ-7A/B
Point-defence HN-5A/HN-5B; FN-6/QW-1/QW-2
GUNS 7,376+
SP 376: **25mm** 270 PGZ-04A; **35mm** 100 PGZ-07; **37mm** 6 PGZ-88
TOWED 7,000+: **25mm** PG-87; **35mm** PG-99 (GDF-002); **37mm** PG-55 (M-1939)/PG-65/PG-74; **57mm** PG-59 (S-60); **100mm** PG-59 (KS-19)
AIR-LAUNCHED MISSILES
ASM AKD-8; AKD-9; AKD-10

Navy ε235,000

The PLA Navy is organised into five service arms: submarine, surface, naval aviation, coastal defence and marine corps, as well as other specialised units. There are three fleets: the Beihai Fleet (North Sea), Donghai Fleet (East Sea) and Nanhai Fleet (South Sea)

EQUIPMENT BY TYPE
SUBMARINES 57
STRATEGIC • SSBN 4:
4 *Jin* (Type-094) with up to 12 JL-2 (CSS-NX-14) strategic SLBM (operational status unknown)
TACTICAL 53
SSN 5:
3 *Han* (Type-091) with 6 single 533mm TT with YJ-82 (CSS-N-7) AShM
2 *Shang* (Type-093) with 6 single 533mm TT with YJ-82 (CSS-N-7) AShM
SSK 47:
4 *Kilo* (2 Project 877 & 2 Project 636) with 6 single 533mm TT
8 *Kilo* (Project 636M) with 6 single 533mm TT with 3M54E *Klub* (SS-N-27B *Sizzler*) AShM
11 *Ming* (7 Type-035G, 4 Type-035B) with 8 single 533mm TT
12 *Song* (Type-039G) with 6 single 533mm TT with YJ-82 (CSS-N-7) AShM
4 *Yuan* (Type-039A) with 6 533mm TT with YJ-82 (CSS-N-7) AShM
8 *Yuan* II (Type-039B) with 6 533mm TT with YJ-82 (CSS-N-7) AShM
SSB 1 *Qing* (Type-032) (SLBM trials)
PRINCIPAL SURFACE COMBATANTS 79
AIRCRAFT CARRIERS • CV 1
1 *Liaoning* (RUS *Kuznetsov*) with 4 18-cell GMLS with HHQ-10 SAM, 2 RBU 6000 *Smerch* 2 A/S mor, 3 H/PJ-11 CIWS (capacity 18–24 J-15 ac; 17 Ka-28/Ka-31/Z-8S/Z-8JH/Z-8AEW hel)

DESTROYERS 21
DDGHM 19:
2 *Hangzhou* (RUS *Sovremenny*) with 2 quad lnchr with 3M80/3M82 *Moskit* (SS-N-22A/B *Sunburn*) AShM, 2 3K90 *Uragan* (SA-N-7 *Gadfly*) SAM, 2 twin 533mm ASTT, 2 RBU 1000 *Smerch* 3 A/S mor, 2 CADS-N-1 *Kashtan* CIWS, 2 twin 130mm gun (capacity 1 Z-9C/Ka-28 *Helix* A hel)
2 *Hangzhou* (RUS *Sovremenny*) with 2 quad lnchr with 3M80/3M82 *Moskit* (SS-N-22A/B *Sunburn*) AShM, 2 *Yezh* (SA-N-12 *Grizzly*) SAM, 2 twin 533mm ASTT, 2 RBU 1000 *Smerch* 3 A/S mor, 4 AK630 CIWS, 1 twin 130mm gun (capacity 1 Z-9C/Ka-28 *Helix* A hel) (both vessels in refit)
1 *Luhai* (Type-051B) with 4 quad lnchr with YJ-83 AShM, 1 octuple lnchr with HHQ-7 SAM, 2 triple 324mm ASTT with Yu-7 LWT, 1 twin 100mm gun (capacity 2 Z-9C/Ka-28 *Helix* A hel) (in refit)
2 *Luhu* (Type-052) with 4 quad lnchr with YJ-83 AShM, 1 octuple lnchr with HHQ-7 SAM, 2 triple 324mm ASTT with Yu-7 LWT, 2 FQF 2500 A/S mor, 2 H/PJ-12 CIWS, 1 twin 100mm gun (capacity 2 Z-9C hel)
2 *Luyang* (Type-052B) with 4 quad lnchr with YJ-83 AShM, 2 single lnchr with *Yezh* (SA-N-12 *Grizzly*) SAM, 2 triple 324mm TT with Yu-7 LWT, 2 H/PJ-12 CIWS, 1 100mm gun (capacity 1 Ka-28 *Helix* A hel)
6 *Luyang* II (Type-052C) with 2 quad lnchr with YJ-62 AShM, 8 sextuple VLS with HHQ-9 SAM, 2 triple 324mm TT with Yu-7 LWT, 2 H/PJ-12 CIWS, 1 100mm gun (capacity 2 Ka-28 *Helix* A hel)
4 *Luyang* III (Type-052D) with 8 octuple VLS with YJ-18 (CSS-N-13) AShM/LACM/HHQ-9ER SAM/CY-2 ASW msl, 1 24-cell GMLS with HHQ-10 SAM, 2 triple 324mm TT with Yu-7 LWT, 1 H/PJ-12 CIWS, 1 130mm gun (capacity 2 Ka-28 *Helix* A hel)
DDGM 2:
2 *Luzhou* (Type-051C) with 2 quad lnchr with YJ-83 AShM; 6 sextuple VLS with S-300FM (SA-N-20 *Grumble*) SAM, 2 H/PJ-12 CIWS, 1 100mm gun, 1 hel landing platform
FRIGATES 57
FFGHM 34:
2 *Jiangkai* (Type-054) with 2 quad lnchr with YJ-83 AShM, 1 octuple lnchr with HHQ-7 SAM, 2 triple 324mm TT with Yu-7 LWT, 2 RBU 1200 A/S mor, 4 AK630 CIWS, 1 100mm gun (capacity 1 Ka-28 *Helix* A/Z-9C hel)
16 *Jiangkai* II (Type-054A) with 2 quad lnchr with YJ-83 AShM, 1 32-cell VLS with HHQ-16 SAM, 2 triple 324mm TT with Yu-7 LWT, 2 RBU 1200 A/S mor, 2 H/PJ-12 CIWS, 1 76mm gun (capacity 1 Ka-28 *Helix* A/Z-9C hel)
6 *Jiangkai* II (Type-054A) with 2 quad lnchr with YJ-83 AShM, 1 32-cell VLS with HHQ-16 SAM, 2 triple 324mm TT with Yu-7 LWT, 2 RBU 1200 A/S mor, 2 H/PJ-11 CIWS, 1 76mm gun (capacity 1 Ka-28 *Helix* A/Z-9C hel)
10 *Jiangwei* II (Type-053H3) with 2 quad lnchr with YJ-83 AShM, 1 octuple lnchr with HHQ-7 SAM, 2 RBU 1200 A/S mor, 1 twin 100mm gun (capacity 2 Z-9C hel)

FFGH 1:
- 1 *Jianghu* IV (Type-053H1Q – trg role) with 1 triple lnchr with HY-2 (CSS-N-2) AShM, 4 RBU 1200 A/S mor, 1 100mm gun (capacity 1 Z-9C hel)

FFGM 4:
- 2 *Luda* IV (Type-051DT) with 4 quad lnchr with YJ-83 AShM, 1 octuple lnchr with HHQ-7 SAM, 2 FQF 2500 A/S mor, 2 130mm gun, 3 twin 57mm gun
- 2 *Luda* III (Type-051G) with 4 quad lnchr with YJ-83 AShM, 1 octuple lnchr with HHQ-7 SAM, 2 FQF 2500 A/S mor, 2 triple 324mm ASTT, 2 twin 100mm gun

FFG 17:
- 2 *Jianghu* I (Type-053H) with 2 twin lnchr with SY-1 (CSS-N-1) AShM, 4 RBU 1200 A/S mor, 2 100mm gun
- 6 *Jianghu* II (Type-053H1) with 2 twin lnchr with HY-2 (CSS-N-2) AShM, 2 RBU 1200 A/S mor, 1 twin 100mm gun (capacity 1 Z-9C hel)
- 1 *Jianghu* III (Type-053H2) with 2 quad lnchr with YJ-83 AShM, 2 RBU 1200, 2 twin 100mm gun
- 6 *Jianghu* V (Type-053H1G) with 2 quad lnchr with YJ-83 AShM, 2 RBU 1200, 2 twin 100mm gun
- 2 *Luda* II (Type-051) with 2 triple lnchr with HY-2 (CSS-N-2) AShM, 2 triple 324mm ASTT, 2 FQF 2500 A/S mor, 2 twin 130mm gun, (minelaying capability)

FF 1:
- 1 *Jianghu* I (Type-053H) with 5 122mm MRL, 4 RBU 1200 A/S mor, 2 100mm gun

PATROL AND COASTAL COMBATANTS ε207

CORVETTES • FSGM 27:
- 19 *Jiangdao* I (Type-056) with 2 twin lnchr with YJ-83 AShM, 1 8-cell GMLS with HHQ-10 SAM, 2 triple ASTT, 1 76mm gun, 1 hel landing platform
- 8 *Jiangdao* II (Type-056A) with 2 twin lnchr with YJ-83 AShM, 1 8-cell GMLS with HHQ-10 SAM, 2 triple ASTT, 1 76mm gun, 1 hel landing platform

PCFG ε65 *Houbei* (Type-022) with 2 quad lnchr with YJ-83 AShM

PCG 26
- 6 *Houjian* (Type-037-II) with 2 triple lnchr with YJ-8 (CSS-N-4) AShM, 1 76mm gun
- 20 *Houxin* (Type-037-IG) with 2 twin lnchr with YJ-8 (CSS-N-4) AShM

PCC 49
- 2 *Haijiu* (Type-037-I) with 4 RBU 1200 A/S mor, 1 twin 57mm gun
- 30 *Hainan* (Type-037) with ε4 RBU 1200 A/S mor, 2 twin 57mm gun
- 17 *Haiqing* (Type-037-IS) with 2 FQF-3200 A/S mor

PB ε40 *Shanghai* III (Type-062-1)

MINE WARFARE 41

MINE COUNTERMEASURES 40

MCO 1 *Rongcheng* (Type-082A)

MHO 14: 4 *Wochi* (Type-081); 6 *Wochi* mod (Type-081A); 4 *Wozang* (Type-082-II)

MSO ε5 T-43 (Type-010/6610)

MSC 14: 4 *Wosao* I (Type-082); 10 *Wosao* II (Type-082-II)

MSD 6 *Wonang* (Type-529)

MINELAYERS • ML 1 *Wolei* with 1 twin 57mm gun

AMPHIBIOUS

PRINCIPAL AMPHIBIOUS SHIPS • LPD 4 *Yuzhao* (Type-071) with 4 AK630 CIWS, 1 76mm gun (capacity 4 *Yuyi* LCAC plus supporting vehicles; 800 troops; 60 armoured vehs; 4 hel)

LANDING SHIPS 52

LSM 23:
- 1 *Yudeng* (Type-073-II) (capacity 5 tk or 500 troops)
- 12 *Yuhai* (Type-074) (capacity 2 tk; 250 troops)
- 10 *Yunshu* (Type-073A) (capacity 6 tk)

LST 29:
- 4 *Yukan* (Type-072-IIG) (capacity 10 tk; 200 troops)
- 10 *Yuting* I (Type-072-II/III) (capacity 10 tk; 250 troops; 2 hel)
- 9 *Yuting* II (Type-072A) (capacity 4 LCVP; 10 tk; 250 troops)
- 6 *Yuting* III (Type-072B) (capacity 4 LCVP; 10 tk; 250 troops)

LANDING CRAFT 84

LCU 67: 11 *Yubei* (Type-074A) (capacity 10 tanks or 150 troops); 56 *Yunnan*

LCAC 5: 3 *Yuyi*; 2 *Zubr*

UCAC 12 *Payi* (Type-724)

LOGISTICS AND SUPPORT ε180

ABU 4 *Yannan* (Type-744)

AFS 5: 2 *Dayun* (Type-904); 1 *Danyao* (Type-904A); 2 *Junshanhu* (Type-904B)

AG 5: 1 *Darong*; 3 *Kanhai*; 1 *Kanwu*

AGB 2: 1 *Haibing* (Type-272) with 1 hel landing platform; 1 *Yanha*

AGE 7: 2 *Dahua* (Type-909) with 1 hel landing platform; 1 *Kantan*; 2 *Shupang* (Type-636); 1 *Yanqian* (Type-904I); 1 *Yanqian* (Type-904II)

AGI 7: 1 *Dadie*; 1 *Dongdiao* (Type-815) with 1 hel landing platform; 4 *Dongdiao* (Type-815A) with 1 hel landing platform; 1 *Hai Yang* (Type-625C)

AGM 4 *Yuan Wang* (Type-718) (space and missile tracking)

AGOR 2 *Dahua*

AGS 13: 1 *Kandao*; 2 *Kanyang*; 4 *Shupang* (Type-636A) with 1 hel landing platform; 2 *Yanjiu*; 4 *Yanlai* (Type-635A/B/C)

AH 8: 5 *Ankang*; 1 *Anwei* (Type-920); 2 *Qiongsha* (hospital conversion)

AK 5: 4 *Hongqi*; 1 *Yudao*

AORH 11: 2 *Fuchi* (Type-903); 6 *Fuchi* mod (Type-903A); 2 *Fuqing* (Type-905); 1 *Fusu*

AOT 32: 4 *Fubai*; 6 *Fuchang*; 13 *Fujian* (Type-632); 8 *Fulin*; 1 *Shengli*

AP 1 *Daguan*

ARC 6 *Youdian* (Type-991)

ARS 11: 1 *Dadao*; 1 *Dadong*; 1 *Dalang* II (Type-922III); 3 *Dalang* III (Type-922IIIA); 3 *Dasan*; 2 *Dazhou*

ASR 6: 3 *Dalao* (Type-926); 3 *Dajiang* (Type-925) (capacity 2 Z-8)

ATF ε33: ε17 *Hujiu*; ε13 *Roslavl*; 3 *Tuqiang*

AWT 14: 3 *Fujian*; 4 *Fulin*; 3 *Fushi*; 3 *Guangzhou*; 1 *Jinyou*

AX 3:
- 1 *Dashi* (Type-0891A) with 2 hel landing platforms
- 1 *Daxin* with 2 FQF 1200 A/S mor, 2 Type-69 CIWS, 1 57mm gun, 1 hel landing platform
- 1 *Yudao*

ESD 1 *Donghaidao*
COASTAL DEFENCE • AShM 72 YJ-62 (3 regt)

Naval Aviation 26,000
FORCES BY ROLE
BOMBER
  1 regt with H-6DU/G
  1 regt with H-6G
FIGHTER
  1 regt with J-8F *Finback*
  1 regt with J-15 *Flanker*
FIGHTER/GROUND ATTACK
  1 regt with J-10A/S *Firebird*
  3 regt with J-11B/BS *Flanker* L
  1 regt with Su-30MK2 *Flanker* G
ATTACK
  2 regt with JH-7 *Flounder*
  3 regt with JH-7A *Flounder*
ANTI-SUBMARINE WARFARE
  1 unit forming with Y-8Q
ELINT/ISR/AEW
  1 regt with Y-8J/JB/W/X; Y-9JB
TRANSPORT
  1 regt with Y-7; Y-7H; Y-8
  1 regt with Y-7; Y-8; Z-8; Z-9
TRAINING
  1 regt with CJ-6A
  2 regt with HY-7
  1 regt with JL-8
  1 regt with JL-9
  1 regt with Mi-8 *Hip*; Z-9C
  1 regt with Y-5
HELICOPTER
  1 regt with Mi-8; Ka-28; Ka-31
  1 regt with SH-5; AS365; Ka-28; Z-9; Z-8A/JH/S
EQUIPMENT BY TYPE
AIRCRAFT 348 combat capable
  BBR 30 H-6G
  FTR 24 J-8F *Finback*
  FGA 132: 16 J-10A; 7 J-10S; 72 J-11B/BS; 13 J-15; 24 Su-30MK2 *Flanker* G
  ATK 120 JH-7/JH-7A *Flounder*
  ASW 7: 3 SH-5; 4 Y-8Q
  ELINT 7: 4 Y-8JB *High New* 2; 3 Y-8X
  AEW&C 14: 4 Y-8J *Mask*; 6 Y-8W *High New* 5; 4 Y-9JB
  ISR 7 HZ-5
  TKR 3 H-6DU
  TPT 66: **Medium** 4 Y-8; **Light** 62: 50 Y-5; 4 Y-7; 6 Y-7H; 2 Yak-42
  TRG 106+: 38 CJ-6; 5 HJ-5*; 21 HY-7; 14 JJ-6*; 4 JJ-7*; 12 JL-8*; 12+ JL-9
HELICOPTERS
  ASW 44: 19 Ka-28 *Helix* A; 25 Z-9C **AEW** 10+: 9 Ka-31; 1+ Z-18 AEW
  MRH: 1+ Z-9D
  SAR 6: 4 Z-8JH; 2 Z-8S
  TPT 43: **Heavy** 35: 15 SA321 *Super Frelon*; 20 Z-8/Z-8A; **Medium** 8 Mi-8 *Hip*
UNMANNED AERIAL VEHICLES
  ISR Heavy BZK-005; **Medium** BZK-007

AIR-LAUNCHED MISSILES
  AAM • IR PL-5; PL-8; PL-9; R-73 (AA-11 *Archer*); **IR/SARH** R-27 (AA-10 *Alamo*); **SARH** PL-11; **ARH** R-77 (AA-12 *Adder*); PL-12
  ASM Kh-31A (AS-17B *Krypton*); KD-88
  AShM YJ-12; YJ-61; YJ-8K; YJ-83K; YJ-9
  ARM YJ-91
BOMBS
  Laser-guided: LS-500J
  TV-guided: KAB-500KR; KAB-1500KR

Marines ε10,000
FORCES BY ROLE
MANOEUVRE
  Amphibious
  2 mne bde (1 spec ops bn, 1 SF amph recce bn, 1 recce bn, 1 tk bn, 2 mech inf bn, 1 arty bn, 1 AT/AD bn, 1 engr bn, 1 sigs bn)
EQUIPMENT BY TYPE
ARMOURED FIGHTING VEHICLES
  LT TK 73 ZTD-05
  AAV 152 ZBD-05
ANTI-TANK/ANTI-INFRASTRUCTURE
  MSL • MANPATS HJ-73; HJ-8
  RCL 120mm Type-98
ARTILLERY 40+
  SP 122mm 40+: 20+ PLZ-07; 20+ PLZ-89
  MRL 107mm PH-63
  MOR 82mm
AIR DEFENCE • SAM • Point-defence HN-5

Air Force 398,000

Flying hours Ftr, ground attack and bbr pilots average 100–150 hrs/yr. Tpt pilots average 200+ per year. Each regt has two quotas to meet during the year – a total number of hours, and the percentage of flight time dedicated to tactics trg

FORCES BY ROLE
BOMBER
  1 regt with H-6M
  2 regt with H-6H
  3 regt with H-6K
FIGHTER
  6 regt with J-7 *Fishbed*
  4 regt with J-7E *Fishbed*
  4 regt with J-7G *Fishbed*
  1 regt with J-8B *Finback*
  1 regt with J-8F *Finback*
  2 regt with J-8H *Finback*
  1 regt with J-11B/BS/Su-27SK/UBK *Flanker*
  6 regt with J-11/Su-27UBK *Flanker*
  2 regt with J-11B/BS *Flanker* L
  2 bde with J-7G *Fishbed*; J-10A/S *Firebird*
FIGHTER/GROUND ATTACK
  2 regt with Su-30MKK *Flanker*
  8 regt with J-10/J-10A/J-10S *Firebird*
  2 regt with J-10B/S *Firebird*
  2 bde with J-7E *Fishbed*; J-11B/BS; Q-5D/E *Fantan*
  2 bde with J-8H *Finback*; J-11B/BS; JH-7A

FIGHTER/GROUND ATTACK/ISR
2 bde with J-7E *Fishbed*; J-8H *Finback*; JZ-8F *Finback** Su-30MKK
GROUND ATTACK
5 regt with JH-7A
4 regt with Q-5C/D/E *Fantan*
ELECTRONIC WARFARE
1 regt with Y-8CB/G/XZ
1 regt with Y-8/Y-8CB/Y-8G
ISR
1 regt with JZ-8F *Finback**
1 regt with Y-8H1
AIRBORNE EARLY WARNING & CONTROL
1 regt with KJ-200 *Moth*; KJ-500; KJ-2000; Y-8T
COMBAT SEARCH & RESCUE
1 regt with Mi-171; Z-8
TANKER
1 regt with H-6U
TRANSPORT
1 (VIP) regt with B-737; CRJ-200/700
1 (VIP) regt with B-737; Tu-154M; Tu-154M/D
1 regt with Il-76MD/TD *Candid*
1 regt with Il-76MD *Candid*; Il-78 *Midas*
1 regt with Mi-17V-5; Y-7
1 regt with Y-5/Y-7/Z-9
1 regt with Y-5/Y-7
3 regt with Y-7
1 regt with Y-8
1 regt with Y-8; Y-9
TRAINING
2 regt with J-7; JJ-7
5 bde with CJ-6/6A/6B; JL-8*; Y-5; Y-7; Z-9
TRANSPORT HELICOPTER
1 regt with AS332 *Super Puma*; H225 (VIP)
ISR UAV
1 regt with *Gongji*-1
AIR DEFENCE
3 SAM div
2 mixed SAM/ADA div
9 SAM bde
2 mixed SAM/ADA bde
2 ADA bde
9 indep SAM regt
1 indep ADA regt
4 indep SAM bn
EQUIPMENT BY TYPE
AIRCRAFT 2,307 combat capable
BBR 120: ε60 H-6H/M; ε60 H-6K
FTR 819: 216 J-7 *Fishbed*; 192 J-7E *Fishbed*; 120 J-7G *Fishbed*; 24 J-8B *Finback*; 24 J-8F *Finback*; 96 J-8H *Finback*; 95 J-11; 20 Su-27SK *Flanker*; 32 Su-27UBK *Flanker*
FGA 510+: 78 J-10; 142 J-10A; 55+ J-10B; 48 J-10S; 110 J-11B/BS *Flanker* L; 2+ J-16 (in test); 2+ J-20 (in test) 73 Su-30MKK *Flanker*
ATK 260: 140 JH-7A; 120 Q-5C/D/E *Fantan*
EW 13: 4 Y-8CB *High New* 1; 7 Y-8G *High New* 3; 2 Y-8XZ *High New* 7
ELINT 4 Tu-154M/D *Careless*
ISR 51: 24 JZ-8 *Finback**; 24 JZ-8F *Finback**; 3 Y-8H1
AEW&C 10: 4 KJ-200 *Moth*; 2 KJ-500; 4 KJ-2000
C2 5: 2 B-737; 3 Y-8T *High New* 4

TKR 13: 10 H-6U; 3 Il-78 *Midas*
TPT 331+ **Heavy** 23: 20 Il-76MD/TD *Candid*; 3 Y-20; **Medium** 42+: 30 Y-8; 12+ Y-9; **Light** 239: 170 Y-5; 41 Y-7/Y-7H; 20 Y-11; 8 Y-12; **PAX** 27: 9 B-737 (VIP); 5 CRJ-200; 5 CRJ-700; 8 Tu-154M *Careless*
TRG 960+: 400 CJ-6/6A/6B; 200 JJ-7*; 350 JL-8*; some JL-9; 10+ JL-10
HELICOPTERS
MRH 22: 20 Z-9; 2 Mi-17V-5 *Hip* H
TPT 31+: **Heavy** 18+ Z-8 (SA321); **Medium** 13+: 6+ AS332 *Super Puma* (VIP); 3 H225 (VIP); 4+ Mi-171
UNMANNED AERIAL VEHICLES
ISR • Heavy 4+ *Gongji*-1
AIR DEFENCE
SAM 600+
  Long-range 192+: 32+ HQ-9; 32 S-300PMU (SA-20 *Gargoyle*); 64 S-300PMU1 (SA-20 *Gargoyle*); 64 S-300PMU2 (SA-20 *Gargoyle*)
  Medium-range 324: 300+ HQ-2/HQ-2A/HQ-2B(A); 24 HQ-12 (KS-1A)
  Short-range 84+: 24 HQ-6D; 60+ HQ-7
GUNS 16,000 100mm/85mm
AIR-LAUNCHED MISSILES
AAM • IR PL-5B/C; PL-8; R-73 (AA-11 *Archer*); **IIR** PL-10 (in service in small numbers); **IR/SARH** R-27 (AA-10 *Alamo*); **SARH** PL-11; **ARH** PL-12; R-77 (AA-12 *Adder*)
ASM AKD-9; AKD-10; KD-88; Kh-29 (AS-14 *Kedge*); Kh-31A/P (AS-17 *Krypton*); Kh-59M (AS-18 *Kazoo*); YJ-91 (Domestically produced Kh-31P variant)
ALCM • Dual-capable CJ-20; **Conventional** YJ(KD)-63
BOMBS
Laser-guided: LS-500J; LT-2
TV-guided: KAB-500KR; KAB-1500KR

15th Airborne Corps
FORCES BY ROLE
SPECIAL FORCES
1 SF unit
MANOEUVRE
Reconnaissance
1 recce regt
Air Manoeuvre
2 AB div (2 AB regt; 1 arty regt)
1 AB div (1 AB regt; 1 arty regt)
Aviation
1 hel regt
COMBAT SUPPORT
1 sigs gp
COMBAT SERVICE SUPPORT
1 log gp
TRANSPORT
1 regt with Y-7; Y-8
EQUIPMENT BY TYPE
ARMOURED FIGHTING VEHICLES
ABCV 180 ZBD-03
APC • APC (T) 4 ZZZ-03 (CP)
ANTI-TANK/ANTI-INFRASTRUCTURE
SP some HJ-9
ARTILLERY 162+
TOWED 122mm ε54 PL-96 (D-30)

MRL 107mm ε54 PH-63
MOR 54+: **82mm** some; **100mm** 54
AIRCRAFT • **TPT 8: Medium** 6 Y-8; **Light** 2 Y-7
HELICOPTERS
ATK 6 WZ-10
CSAR 8 Z-8KA
MRH 12 Z-9WZ
AIR DEFENCE
SAM • **Point-defence** QW-1
GUNS • **TOWED 25mm** 54 PG-87

Theatre Commands

In early 2016, the previous seven military regions were consolidated into five new theatre commands. Designated Rapid Reaction Units (RRU) are indicated

Northern Theatre Command
(Former Shenyang and parts of Beijing & Jinan MRs)

Northern Theatre Ground Forces
16th Group Army
(1 SF bde, 1 armd bde, 3 mech inf bde, 1 mot inf div, 1 mot inf bde, 1 arty bde, 1 AD bde, 1 engr regt)
26th Group Army
(1 SF bde, 1 armd bde, 1 mech inf bde, 3 mot inf bde, 1 arty bde, 1 AD bde, 1 engr regr, 1 EW rgt, 1 hel regt)
39th Group Army
(1 SF gp, 1 armd bde, 1 hy mech inf bde, 1 mech inf div, 1 mech inf bde, 2 mot inf bde, 1 arty bde, 1 AD bde, 1 engr regt, 1 EW regt, 1 hel bde)
40th Group Army
(1 armd bde, 1 mech inf bde, 2 mot inf bde, 1 arty bde, 1 AD bde, 1 engr regt)

North Sea Fleet
Coastal defence from the DPRK border (Yalu River) to south of Lianyungang (approx 35°10′N), and to seaward; HQ at Qingdao; support bases at Lushun, Qingdao. 9 coastal-defence districts
3 **SSN**; 15 **SSK**; 1 **CV**; 2 **DDGHM**; 2 **DDGM**; 10 **FFGHM**; 2 **FFGM**; 1 **FFGH**; 4 **FFG**; 7 **FSGM**; ε18 **PCFG/PCG**; ε6 **LS**; 1 **ML**; ε9 **MCMV**

North Sea Fleet Naval Aviation
2nd Naval Air Division
(1 EW/ISR/AEW regt with Y-8J/JB/W/X; Y-9JB; 1 MP/hel regt with SH-5; AS365; Ka-28; SA321; Z-8; Z-9; 1 tpt regt with Y-7/Y-8)
5th Naval Air Division
(2 FGA regt with JH-7A; 1 ftr regt with J-8F)
Other Forces
(1 ftr regt with J-15; 1 trg regt with CJ-6A; 2 trg regt with HY-7; 1 trg regt with JL-8; 1 trg regt with JL-9; 1 trg regt with Y-5; 1 hel trg regt with Mi-8; Z-9)

Nothern Theatre Air Force
1st Fighter Division
(1 ftr regt with J-11B; 1 FGA regt with J-10/J-10A/J-10S; 1 ftr regt with J-8F)
5th Attack Division
(2 atk regt with Q-5E; 1 atk regt with JH-7A)
11th Attack Division
(1 atk regt with JH-7A; 1 atk regt with Q-5)
12th Fighter Division
(1 ftr regt with J-10A/S; 1 ftr regt with J-8B; 1 ftr regt with J-7G)
16th Special Mission Division
(1 EW regt with Y-8/Y-8CB/Y-8G; 1 ISR regt with JZ-8F; 1 tpt regt with Y-5/Y-7)
21st Fighter Division
(1 ftr regt with J-10A/S; 1 ftr regt with J-8H; 1 ftr regt with J-7H)
Dalian Base
(2 FGA bde with J-7E; J-11B; Q-5)
Harbin Flying Academy
(2 trg bde with CJ-6; JL-8; Y-5; Y-7)
Other Forces
(1 (mixed) SAM/ADA bde; 1 SAM bde; 4 SAM bn)

Central Theatre Command
(Former Beijing & part Jinan MRs)

Central Theatre Ground Forces
20th Group Army
(1 armd bde, 2 mech inf bde, 1 arty bde, 1 AD bde, 1 engr regt)
27th Group Army
(1 armd bde, 1 hy mech inf bde, 1 mech inf bde, 2 mot inf bde, 1 arty bde, 1 AD bde, 1 engr regt)
38th Group Army
(1 SF bde, 1 armd div, 1 hy mech inf div, 1 mech inf div, 1 arty bde, 1 AD bde, 1 engr regt, 1 hel bde)
54th Group Army
(1 SF bde, 1 armd bde, 2 mech inf div (RRU), 1 mech bde, 1 arty bde, 1 AD bde, 1 engr regt, 1 hel regt)
65th Group Army
(1 armd bde, 1 hy mech inf bde, 1 mech inf bde, 2 mot inf bde, 1 arty bde, 1 AD bde, 1 engr regt)
Other Forces
(1 (OPFOR) mech inf bde; 2 (Beijing) gd div; 1 avn bde)

Central Theatre Air Force
7th Fighter Division
(1 ftr regt with J-11; 2 ftr regt with J-7)
15th Fighter/Attack Division
(1 FGA regt with J-10A/S; 1 ftr regt with J-7G)
19th Fighter Division
(1 ftr regt with Su-27SK; 1 ftr regt with J-10B/S; 1 trg regt with J-7/JJ-7)
24th Fighter Division
(1 ftr regt with J-7G; 1 FGA regt with J-10/J-10A/J-10S)
Shijiazhuang Flying Academy
(1 trg bde with CJ-6; JL-8; Y-5; Y-7)
Other Forces
(1 Flight Test Centre; 3 SAM div; 1 (mixed) SAM/ADA div)

Other Forces
34th VIP Transport Division
(1 tpt regt with B-737; CRJ200/700; 1 tpt regt with B-737; Tu-154M; Tu-154M/D; 1 tpt regt with Y-7; 1 hel regt with AS332; H225)

Western Theatre Command
(Former Lanzhou & part Chengdu MRs)

Western Theatre Ground Forces
(Command relationship between Western Theatre Command and Xinjiang/Xizang Military District forces unclear)
13th Group Army
(1 SF bde, 1 armd bde, 1 (high alt) mot inf div (RRU), 1 mot inf div, 1 arty bde, 1 AD bde, 1 engr regt, 1 EW regt, 1 hel bde)
21st Group Army
(1 SF bde, 1 armd bde, 1 mech inf bde, 1 mot inf div (RRU), 1 arty bde, 1 AD bde, 1 engr regt, 1 EW regt)
47th Group Army
(1 armd bde, 1 hy mech inf bde, 2 (high alt) mot inf bde, 1 arty bde, 1 AD bde, 1 engr regt)
Xinjiang Military District
(1 SF bde, 1 (high alt) mech div, 3 (high alt) mot div, 1 arty bde, 1 AD bde, 1 engr regt, 1 EW regt, 1 hel bde)
Xizang Military District
(1 SF gp; 1 (high alt) mech inf bde; 2 mtn inf bde; 1 arty regt, 1 AD bde, 1 engr bde, 1 EW regt)

Western Theatre Air Force
4th Transport Division
(1 tpt regt with Y-8/Y-9; 1 tpt regt with Y-7; 1 tpt regt with Mi-17V-5/Y-7)
6th Fighter Division
(1 ftr regt with J-11; 1 ftr regt with J-7E; 1 ftr regt with J-7)
33rd Fighter Division
(1 ftr regt with J-7E; 1 ftr regt with J-11)
36th Bomber Division
(1 surv regt with Y-8H1; 1 bbr regt with H-6M; 1 bbr regt with H-6H/M)
Urumqi Base
(2 FGA bde with J-8H; J-11B; JH-7A)
Xi'an Flying Academy
(2 trg bde with CJ-6; JL-8; Y-7; Z-9)
Other Forces
(1 (mixed) SAM/ADA div; 1 (mixed) SAM/ADA bde; 1 SAM bde; 4 indep SAM regt)

Eastern Theatre Command
(Former Nanjing MR)

Eastern Theatre Ground Forces
1st Group Army
(1 armd bde, 1 amph mech div, 1 hy mech inf bde, 1 mot inf bde, 1 arty bde, 1 MRL bde, 1 AD bde, 1 engr regt, 1 EW regt, 1 hel bde)
12th Group Army
(1 SF bde, 1 armd bde, 1 hy mech inf bde, 1 mech inf bde, 1 mot inf bde, 1 arty bde, 1 AD bde, 1 engr regt)
31st Group Army
(1 SF bde, 1 (amph) armd bde, 2 mot inf div (incl 1 RRU), 1 mot inf bde, 1 arty bde, 1 AD bde, 1 engr regt, 1 EW regt, 1 hel regt)

East Sea Fleet
Coastal defence from south of Lianyungang to Dongshan (approx. 35°10′N to 23°30′N), and to seaward; HQ at Ningbo; support bases at Fujian, Zhoushan, Ningbo. 7 coastal-defence districts
16 **SSK**; 8 **DDGHM**; 16 **FFGHM**; 3 **FFG**; 1 **FF**; 7 **FSGM**; ε30 **PCFG/PCG**; 1 **LPD**; ε24 **LS**; ε20 **MCMV**

East Sea Fleet Naval Aviation
4th Naval Aviation Division
(1 FGA regt with Su-30MK2; 1 hel regt with Mi-8; Ka-28; Ka-31; 1 FGA regt with J-10A)
6th Naval Aviation Division
(2 FGA regt with JH-7; 1 bbr regt with H-6G)

Eastern Theatre Air Force
3rd Fighter Division
(1 ftr regt with J-7G; 1 FGA regt with J-10/J-10A/J-10S; 1 FGA regt with Su-30MKK)
10th Bomber Division
(1 bbr regt with H-6H; 1 bbr regt with H-6K)
14th Fighter Division
(2 ftr regt with J-11; 1 ftr regt with J-7E)
26th Special Mission Division
(1 AEW&C regt with KJ-200; KJ-500; KJ-2000/Y-8T; 1 CSAR regt with M-171; Z-8)
28th Attack Division
(2 atk regt with JH-7A; 1 atk regt with Q-5D/E)
32nd Fighter Division
(1 ftr regt with J-11B; 1 tpt regt with Y-5/Y-7/Z-9; 1 trg regt with J-7/JJ-7)
Shanghai Base
(2 FGA/ISR bde with J-7E; J-8H; JZ-8F; Su-30MKK)
Other Forces
(3 SAM bde; 1 ADA bde; 2 indep SAM regt; 1 Flight Instructor Training Base with CJ-6; JL-8)

Southern Theatre Command
(Former Guangzhou and part Chengdu MRs)

Southern Theatre Ground Forces
14th Group Army
(1 armd bde, 1 mech inf bde, 1 mot inf bde, 2 mtn inf bde, 1 arty bde, 1 AD bde, 1 engr regt, 1 hel regt)
41st Group Army
(1 armd bde, 1 hy mech inf div (RRU), 1 mech inf bde, 1 mtn inf bde, 1 arty bde, 1 AD bde, 1 engr regt, 1 hel regt)
42nd Group Army
(1 SF bde, 1 armd bde, 1 amph mech div (RRU), 1 mech inf bde, 1 mot inf bde, 1 arty bde, 1 MRL bde, 1 AD bde, 1 engr regt, 1 EW regt, 1 hel bde)
Other Forces
(1 mot inf bde; 1 (composite) mot inf bde (composed of units drawn from across the PLA and deployed to Hong Kong on a rotational basis); 1 hel sqn (Hong Kong), 1 AD bn (Hong Kong))

South Sea Fleet
Coastal defence from Dongshan (approx. 23°30′N) to VNM border, and to seaward (including Paracel and Spratly islands); HQ at Zuanjiang; support bases at Yulin, Guangzhou
4 **SSBN**; 2 **SSN**; 16 **SSK**; 9 **DDGHM**; 8 **FFGHM**; 2 **FFGM**; 8 **FFG**; 13 **FSGM**; ε38 **PCFG/PCG**; 3 **LPD**; ε20 **LS**; ε11 **MCMV**

South Sea Fleet Naval Aviation
8th Naval Aviation Division
(2 FGA regt with J-11B; 1 bbr regt with H-6G)
9th Naval Aviation Division
(1 FGA regt with J-11B, 1 FGA regt with JH-7A; 1 tpt regt with Y-7; Y-8; Z-8; Z-8JH/S; Z-9)

Southern Theatre Air Force
2nd Fighter Division
(1 ftr regt with J-8H; 1 FGA regt with J-10B/S; 1 ftr regt with J-11)
8th Bomber Division
(1 tkr regt with H-6U; 2 bbr regt with H-6K)
9th Fighter Division
(1 FGA regt with J-10A/S; 2 ftr regt with J-7E)
13th Transport Division
(1 tpt regt with Y-8; 1 tpt regt with Il-76MD/TD; 1 tpt regt with Il-76MD; Il-78)
18th Fighter Division
(1 ftr regt with J-7; 1 FGA regt with Su-30MKK)
20th Special Mission Division
(1 tpt regt with Y-7; 1 EW regt with Y-8CB/G/XZ)
44th Fighter Division
(1 ftr regt with J-7; 1 FGA regt with J-10/J-10A/J-10S)
Nanning Base
(2 ftr bde with J-7G; J-10A/S)
Other Forces
(4 SAM Bde; 3 indep SAM regt; 1 ADA bde; 1 indep ADA regt)

Other Forces
Marines
(2 mne bde)
15th Airborne Corps
(3 AB div)

Strategic Support Force ε150,000
At the end of 2015, a new Strategic Support Force was established by drawing upon capabilites previously exercised by the PLA's 3rd and 4th departments and other central functions. It reports to the Central Military Commission and is believed to be responsible for the PLA's space and cyber capabilities

Paramilitary 660,000+ active

People's Armed Police ε660,000

Internal Security Forces ε400,000
FORCES BY ROLE
MANOEUVRE
Other
14 (mobile) paramilitary div
22 (mobile) indep paramilitary regt
Some (firefighting/garrison) unit

Border Defence Force ε260,000
FORCES BY ROLE
COMMAND
30 div HQ
MANOEUVRE
Other
110 (border) paramilitary regt
20 (marine) paramilitary regt

China Coast Guard
In March 2013, four of China's maritime law-enforcement agencies were unified under the State Oceanic Administration and renamed the China Coast Guard
EQUIPMENT BY TYPE
PATROL AND COASTAL COMBATANTS 462+
  PSOH 31
  PSO 35+
  PCC 120+
  PCO 54+
  PB/PBF 222+
AMPHIBIOUS • LST 7: 3 *Yukan*; 4 *Yuting* II
LOGISTICS AND SUPPORT 16
  AGOR 13
  AGS 1
  ATF 2

Maritime Safety Administration (MSA)
Various tasks, including aid to navigation
EQUIPMENT BY TYPE
PATROL AND COASTAL COMBATANTS 61+
  PSOH 2
  PSO 3
  PCO 10+
  PCC 22+
  PB 24+
LOGISTICS AND SUPPORT 31
  ABU 16
  AG 5
  AGF 5
  ATF 5

Cyber
The PLA has devoted much attention to information warfare over the past decade, in terms of both battlefield electronic warfare (EW) and wider cyber-warfare capabilities. The main doctrine is the 'Integrated Network Electronic Warfare' (INEW) document, which guides PLA computer-network operations. PLA thinking appears to have moved beyond INEW, towards a new concept of 'information confrontation' (*xinxi duikang*), which aims to integrate both electronic and non-electronic aspects of information warfare within a single command authority. PLA thinking sees warfare under informationised conditions as characterised by opposing sides using complete systems of ground, naval, air, space and electromagnetic forces. Since 2008, major PLA military exercises, including *Kuayue 2009* and *Lianhe 2011*, have all had cyber and information-operations components that have been both offensive

and defensive in nature. At the end of 2015, the Central Military Commission announced a reorganisation of the PLA, including the establishment of three new support branches, including the Strategic Support Force. Although precise responsibilities remain unclear, the Strategic Support Force may have three branches: the first dealing with intelligence and military operations in cyberspace (defensive and offensive); the second dealing with military space operations (surveillance and satellite); and the third in charge of defensive and offensive EW and electronic intelligence. It appears to be taking over the third and fourth PLA departments, merging cyber and space under the same command. In a February 2013 report, US security company Mandiant described a secret Chinese military unit, 'Unit 61398', subordinate to 3PLA that had, Mandiant alleged, systematically exfiltrated substantial amounts of data from 141 companies since 2007, when its facility was built in Shanghai. A December 2013 Science of Military Strategy document explicitly referenced China's network-warfare forces, reportedly dividing them into three groups: 'specialized military network warfare forces'; 'PLA-authorized forces'; and 'non-governmental forces'.

DEPLOYMENT

CÔTE D'IVOIRE
UN • UNOCI 2 obs

DEMOCRATIC REPUBLIC OF THE CONGO
UN • MONUSCO 219; 12 obs; 1 engr coy; 1 fd hospital

GULF OF ADEN
1 SSN (reported); 1 DDGHM; 1 FFGHM; 1 AORH; 1 ASR

LEBANON
UN • UNIFIL 412; 1 engr coy

LIBERIA
UN • UNMIL 127; 1 obs; 1 engr pl; 1 tpt coy

MALI
UN • MINUSMA 397; 1 sy coy; 1 engr coy; 1 fd hospital

MIDDLE EAST
UN • UNTSO 2 obs

SOUTH SUDAN
UN • UNMISS 1,051; 3 obs; 1 inf bn; 1 engr coy; 1 fd hospital

SUDAN
UN • UNAMID 230; 1 engr coy

WESTERN SAHARA
UN • MINURSO 10 obs

Fiji FJI

Fijian Dollar F$		2015	2016	2017
GDP	F$	9.21bn	9.75bn	
	US$	4.39bn	4.56bn	
per capita	US$	4,926	5,088	
Growth	%	4.3	2.5	
Inflation	%	1.4	3.3	
Def bdgt	F$	108m	105m	
	US$	52m	49m	
US$1=F$		2.10	2.14	

Population 915,303

Ethnic groups: Fijian 51%; Indian 44%; European/Others 5%

Age	0–14	15–19	20–24	25–29	30–64	65 plus
Male	14.2%	4.1%	4.3%	4.1%	21.1%	2.9%
Female	13.6%	4.0%	4.1%	3.9%	20.2%	3.4%

Capabilities

The Republic of Fiji Military Forces (RFMF) are an infantry-dominated defence force with a small naval element. The main roles of the Fiji Infantry Regiment are to provide units for international peacekeeping operations (an important revenue source for the government) and for home defence: of the three regular battalions, one is mainly deployed in Iraq with UNAMI and another is with the MFO in Sinai. Such international deployments have provided the RFMF with considerable operational experience, and its professionalism is widely recognised. However, the RFMF has also intervened heavily in Fiji's domestic politics and between a third coup in 2006 and 2014 – when coup leader Commodore Frank Bainimarama's FijiFirst party was elected to government – democracy was effectively suspended, leading to a rift in relations with Australia and other Western states. This opened the way for China (which signed a bilateral memorandum of understanding on defence cooperation in 2014) and Russia (which donated a ten-container shipment of arms in January 2016) to develop closer military relations with Fiji. In December 2014, Fiji's government announced that it planned to formulate a national-security strategy and publish a defence white paper, but neither had been published by October 2016.

ACTIVE 3,500 (Army 3,200 Navy 300)

RESERVE ε6,000
(to age 45)

ORGANISATIONS BY SERVICE

Army 3,200 (incl 300 recalled reserves)
FORCES BY ROLE
SPECIAL FORCES
  1 spec ops coy
MANOEUVRE
  Light
  3 inf bn

COMBAT SUPPORT
  1 arty bty
  1 engr bn
COMBAT SUPPORT
  1 log bn

Reserves 6,000
FORCES BY ROLE
MANOEUVRE
  Light
    3 inf bn
EQUIPMENT BY TYPE
ARTILLERY 16
  TOWED 85mm 4 25-pdr (ceremonial)
  MOR 81mm 12

Navy 300
EQUIPMENT BY TYPE
PATROL AND COASTAL COMBATANTS • PB 5: 3 *Kula* (AUS *Pacific*); 2 *Levuka*

DEPLOYMENT

EGYPT
MFO 201; elm 1 inf bn

IRAQ
UN • UNAMI 168; 2 sy unit

LEBANON
UN • UNIFIL 143; 1 inf coy

MIDDLE EAST
UN • UNTSO 2 obs

SOUTH SUDAN
UN • UNMISS 4: 2 obs

SYRIA/ISRAEL
UN • UNDOF 255; 1 inf coy; elm 1 log bn

India IND

Indian Rupee Rs		2015	2016	2017
GDP	Rs	136tr	150tr	
	US$	2.07tr	2.25tr	
per capita	US$	1,604	1,719	
Growth	%	7.6	7.6	
Inflation	%	4.9	5.5	
Def bdgt [a]	Rs	2.94tr	3.41tr	
	US$	44.8bn	51.1bn	
US$1=Rs		65.49	66.78	

[a] Includes defence civil estimates, which include military pensions

Population 1,266,883,598
Religious groups: Hindu 80%; Muslim 14%; Christian 2%; Sikh 2%

Age	0–14	15–19	20–24	25–29	30–64	65 plus
Male	14.7%	4.9%	4.7%	4.3%	20.4%	2.9%
Female	13.0%	4.3%	4.1%	3.9%	19.5%	3.2%

Capabilities

India has the third-largest armed forces in the world by personnel strength, and is continuing a substantial drive to modernise its military capabilities. The armed forces are orientated against both Pakistan and China. Internal security is the responsibility of civilian police at state level, and large numbers of paramilitary forces are employed in this role. The armed forces offer significant support to police and paramilitary forces in both Kashmir and eastern India. The Indian military is subordinated to the country's civilian political leadership. Development and procurement programmes across the services are aimed at replacing ageing equipment, largely of Soviet-era and Russian origin, but many projects have experienced significant delays and cost overruns, particularly indigenous systems. India continues to modernise its strategic forces, particularly its delivery systems, evidenced by the ongoing SLBM programme. The overall capability of India's army is limited by inadequate logistics, and shortages of ammunition and spare parts. The navy funded upgrades of its diesel-electric submarines and ordered four more Boeing P-8I maritime-patrol aircraft. A deal for the purchase of 36 *Rafale* combat aircraft was signed with France in September 2016, but the air force's programme to acquire the A330 transport/tanker aircraft was suspended. All three services aspire to acquire UAVs. The government's 'Make in India' policy aims to strengthen the indigenous defence-industrial base through measures including reforming the cap on foreign direct investment. The government announced that all restrictions on the employment of women in the military would be removed. Indian personnel participate in numerous bilateral and multilateral exercises, and the country is one of the top troop contributors to UN peacekeeping operations. The armed forces are capable of internal deployment for stabilisation operations, but it is not clear if they can rapidly mobilise and deploy in strength to either the border with Pakistan or with China. The lack of joint command and control may militate against effective tactical-level inter-service cooperation.

ACTIVE 1,395,100 (Army 1,200,000 Navy 58,350 Air 127,200 Coast Guard 9,550) **Paramilitary 1,403,700**

RESERVE 1,155,000 (Army 960,000 Navy 55,000 Air 140,000) **Paramilitary 987,800**
Army first-line reserves (300,000) within 5 years of full-time service, further 500,000 have commitment to the age of 50

ORGANISATIONS BY SERVICE

Strategic Forces Command

Strategic Forces Command (SFC) is a tri-service command established in 2003. The commander-in-chief of SFC, a senior three-star military officer, manages and administers all strategic forces through separate army and air-force chains of command

FORCES BY ROLE
SURFACE-TO-SURFACE MISSILE
  1 SRBM gp with *Agni* I
  1 MRBM gp with *Agni* II
  1 IRBM gp (reported forming) with *Agni* III
  2 SRBM gp with SS-250 *Prithvi* II
EQUIPMENT BY TYPE
SURFACE-TO-SURFACE MISSILE LAUNCHERS 54
  ICBM • **Nuclear** *Agni* V (in test)
  IRBM • **Nuclear** *Agni* III (entering service); *Agni* IV (in test)
  MRBM • **Nuclear** ε12 *Agni* II
  SRBM • **Nuclear** 42: ε12 *Agni* I; ε30 SS-250 *Prithvi* II; some SS-350 *Dhanush* (naval testbed)
AIR-LAUNCHED MISSILES
  ALCM • **Nuclear** *Nirbhay* (likely nuclear capable; in development)
Some Indian Air Force assets (such as *Mirage* 2000H or Su-30MKI) may be tasked with a strategic role

Space
EQUIPMENT BY TYPE
SATELLITES 12
  NAVIGATION, POSITONING, TIMING: 7 IRNSS
  COMMUNICATIONS: 2 GSAT
  ISR 3: 1 *Cartosat* 2C; 2 RISAT

Army 1,200,000
6 Regional Comd HQ (Northern, Western, Central, Southern, Eastern, Southwestern), 1 Training Comd (ARTRAC)
FORCES BY ROLE
COMMAND
  4 (strike) corps HQ
  10 (holding) corps HQ
SPECIAL FORCES
  8 SF bn
MANOEUVRE
  Armoured
  3 armd div (2–3 armd bde, 1 arty bde (2 arty regt))
  8 indep armd bde
  Mechanised
  6 (RAPID) mech inf div (1 armd bde, 2 mech inf bde, 1 arty bde)
  2 indep mech bde
  Light
  15 inf div (2–5 inf bde, 1 arty bde)
  1 inf div (forming)
  7 indep inf bde
  12 mtn div (3-4 mtn inf bde, 3–4 art regt)
  2 indep mtn bde
  Air Manoeuvre
  1 para bde
SURFACE-TO-SURFACE MISSILE
  2 SSM gp with *Agni* I/II
  2 SSM gp with SS-250 *Prithvi* I/II
  3 GLCM regt with PJ-10 *Brahmos*
COMBAT SUPPORT
  3 arty div (2 arty bde (3 med art regt, 1 STA/MRL regt))
  4 engr bde

HELICOPTER
  14 hel sqn
AIR DEFENCE
  8 AD bde

Reserve Organisations
Reserves 300,000 reservists (first-line reserve within 5 years full time service); 500,000 reservists (commitment until age of 50) (total 800,000)

Territorial Army 160,000 reservists (only 40,000 regular establishment)
FORCES BY ROLE
MANOEUVRE
  Light
  42 inf bn
COMBAT SUPPORT
  6 (Railway) engr regt
  2 engr regt
  1 sigs regt
COMBAT SERVICE SUPPORT
  6 ecological bn
EQUIPMENT BY TYPE
ARMOURED FIGHTING VEHICLES
  MBT 3,024+: 124 *Arjun*; 1,950 T-72M1; 950+ T-90S; (ε1,100 various models in store)
  RECCE *Ferret* (used for internal-security duties along with some indigenously built armd cars)
  IFV 2,500: 700 BMP-1; 1,800 BMP-2 *Sarath* (incl some BMP-2K CP)
  APC 336+
    APC (W) 157+ OT-64
    PPV 179: 165 *Casspir*; 14+ *Yukthirath* MPV
ENGINEERING & MAINTENANCE VEHICLES
  AEV BMP-2; FV180
  ARV T-54/T-55; VT-72B; WZT-2; WZT-3
  VLB AM-50; BLG-60; BLG T-72; *Kartik*; MTU-20; MT-55; *Sarvatra*
  MW 24 910 MCV-2
ANTI-TANK/ANTI-INFRASTRUCTURE
  MSL
    SP 110 9P148 *Konkurs* (AT-5 *Spandrel*)
    MANPATS 9K11 *Malyutka* (AT-3 *Sagger*) (being phased out); 9K111 *Fagot* (AT-4 *Spigot*); 9K113 *Konkurs* (AT-5 *Spandrel*); Milan 2
  RCL 84mm *Carl Gustav*; **106mm** 3,000+ M40A1 (10 per inf bn)
ARTILLERY 9,682+
  TOWED 2,970+: **105mm** 1,350+: 600+ IFG Mk1/Mk2/Mk3 (being replaced); up to 700 LFG; 50 M-56; **122mm** 520 D-30; **130mm** ε600 M-46; (500 in store) **155mm** 500: ε300 FH-77B; ε200 M-46 (mod)
  MRL 192: **122mm** ε150 BM-21/LRAR **214mm** 14 *Pinaka* (non operational) **300mm** 28 9A52 *Smerch*
  MOR 6,520+: **81mm** 5,000+ E1; **120mm** ε1,500 AM-50/E1; **SP 120mm** E1; **160mm** 20 M-58 *Tampella*
SURFACE-TO-SURFACE MISSILE LAUNCHERS
  IRBM • **Nuclear** some *Agni*-III (entering service)
  MRBM • **Nuclear** ε12 *Agni*-II
  SRBM • **Nuclear** 42: ε12 *Agni*-I; ε30 250 *Prithvi* II
  GLCM • **Conventional** 15 PJ-10 *Brahmos*

RADAR • LAND 38+: 14 AN/TPQ-37 *Firefinder*; BSR Mk.2; 24 *Cymbeline*; EL/M-2140; M113 A1GE *Green Archer* (mor); MUFAR; *Stentor*
AMPHIBIOUS 2 LCVP
HELICOPTERS
  MRH 275+: 80 *Dhruv*; 12 *Lancer*; 3+ *Rudra*; 120 SA315B *Lama* (*Cheetah*); 60 SA316B *Alouette* III (*Chetak*)
UNMANNED AERIAL VEHICLES
  ISR • Medium 25: 13 *Nishant*; 12 *Searcher* Mk I/II
AIR DEFENCE
  SAM
    Medium-range *Akash*
    Short-range 180 2K12 *Kub* (SA-6 *Gainful*)
    Point-defence 500+: 50+ 9K33 *Osa* (SA-8B *Gecko*); 200 9K31 *Strela*-1 (SA-9 *Gaskin*); 250 9K35 *Strela*-10 (SA-13 *Gopher*); 9K32 *Strela*-2 (SA-7 *Grail* – being phased out)‡; 9K310 *Igla*-1 (SA-16 *Gimlet*); 9K38 *Igla* (SA-18 *Grouse*)
  GUNS 2,395+
    SP 155+: 23mm 75 ZSU-23-4; ZU-23-2 (truck-mounted); 30mm 20-80 2S6 *Tunguska*
    TOWED 2,240+: 20mm Oerlikon (reported); 23mm 320 ZU-23-2; 40mm 1,920 L40/70

Navy 58,350 (incl 7,000 Naval Avn and 1,200 Marines)

Fleet HQ New Delhi. Commands located at Mumbai, Vishakhapatnam, Kochi & Port Blair

EQUIPMENT BY TYPE
SUBMARINES • TACTICAL 14
  SSN 1 *Chakra* (ex-RUS *Akula* II) with 4 single 533mm TT with 3M54E *Klub* (SS-N-27B *Sizzler*) AShM, 4 single 650mm TT with T-65 HWT (RUS lease agreement)
  SSK 13:
    4 *Shishumar* (GER T-209/1500) with 8 single 533mm TT
    2 *Sindhughosh* (FSU *Kilo*) with 6 single 533mm TT
    7 *Sindhughosh* (FSU *Kilo*) with 6 single 533mm TT with 3M54E *Klub* (SS-N-27B *Sizzler*) AShM
PRINCIPAL SURFACE COMBATANTS 28
  AIRCRAFT CARRIERS 1
    CV 1 *Vikramaditya* (ex-FSU *Kiev* mod) (capacity: 12 MiG-29K/KUB *Fulcrum* FGA ac; 6 Ka-28 *Helix* A ASW hel/Ka-31 *Helix* B AEW hel)
  DESTROYERS 14
    DDGHM 9:
      3 *Delhi* with 4 quad lnchr with 3M24E *Uran* (SS-N-25 *Switchblade*) AShM, 2 single lnchr with 3K90 *Uragan* (SA-N-7 *Gadfly*) SAM, 4 octuple VLS with *Barak*-1 SAM, 5 single 533mm ASTT, 2 RBU 6000 A/S mor; 2 AK630 CIWS, 1 100mm gun (capacity either 2 *Dhruv* hel/*Sea King* Mk42A ASW hel)
      3 *Kolkata* with 2 octuple VLS with *Brahmos* AShM; 4 octuple VLS fitted for *Barak*-8 SAM; 2 twin 533mm TT with SET-65E HWT, 2 RBU 6000 *Smerch* 2 A/S mor, 4 AK630 CIWS, 1 76mm gun (capacity 2 *Dhruv*/*Sea King* Mk42B hel)
      3 *Shivalik* with 1 octuple VLS with 3M54 *Klub* (SS-N-27 *Sizzler*) AShM; *Brahmos* AShM/LACM 4 octuple VLS with *Barak*-1 SAM, 1 single lnchr with 3K90 *Uragan* (SA-N-7 *Gadfly*) SAM, 2 triple 324mm ASTT, 2 RBU 6000 *Smerch* 2 A/S mor, 2 AK630 CIWS, 1 76mm gun (capacity 1 *Sea King* Mk42B ASW hel)
    DDGM 5:
      2 *Rajput* (FSU *Kashin*) with 2 twin lnchr with P-15M *Termit* (SS-N-2C *Styx*) AShM, 2 twin lnchr with M-1 *Volna* (SA-N-1 *Goa*) SAM, 5 single 533mm ASTT, 2 RBU 6000 *Smerch* 2 A/S mor, 2 AK630 CIWS, 1 76mm gun (capacity Ka-28 *Helix* A hel)
      1 *Rajput* (FSU *Kashin*) with 2 twin lnchr with *Brahmos* AShM, 2 single lnchr with P-15M *Termit* (SS-N-2C *Styx*) AShM, 2 twin lnchr with M-1 *Volna* (SA-N-1 *Goa*) SAM, 5 single 533mm ASTT, 2 RBU 6000 *Smerch* 2 A/S mor, 4 AK630 CIWS, 1 76mm gun (capacity 1 Ka-28 *Helix* A hel)
      2 *Rajput* (FSU *Kashin*) with 1 octuple VLS with *Brahmos* AShM, 2 twin lnchr with P-15M *Termit* (SS-N-2C *Styx*) AShM, 2 octuple VLS with *Barak* SAM. 1 twin lnchr with M-1 *Volna* (SA-N-1 *Goa*) SAM, 5 single 533mm ASTT, 2 RBU 6000 *Smerch* 2 A/S mor, 4 AK630 CIWS, 1 76mm gun (capacity 1 Ka-28 *Helix* A hel)
  FRIGATES 13
    FFGHM 11:
      3 *Brahmaputra* with 4 quad lnchr with 3M24E *Uran* (SS-N-25 *Switchblade*) AShM, 3 octuple VLS with *Barak*-1 SAM, 2 triple 324mm ASTT with A244 LWT, 4 AK630 CIWS, 1 76mm gun (capacity 2 SA316B *Alouette* III (*Chetak*)/*Sea King* Mk42 ASW hel)
      2 *Godavari* with 4 single lnchr with P-15M *Termit* (SS-N-2D *Styx*) AShM, 1 octuple VLS with *Barak*-1 SAM, 2 triple 324mm ASTT with A244 LWT, 4 AK630 CIWS, 1 76mm gun (capacity 2 SA316B *Alouette* III (*Chetak*)/*Sea King* Mk42 ASW hel)
      3 *Talwar* I with 1 octuple VLS with 3M54E *Klub* (SS-N-27B *Sizzler*) AShM, 1 single lnchr with 3K90 *Uragan* (SA-N-7 *Gadfly*) SAM, 2 twin 533mm ASTT, 2 RBU 6000 *Smerch* 2 A/S mor, 2 *Kashtan* (CADS-N-1) CIWS, 1 100mm gun (capacity 1 *Dhruv*/Ka-28 *Helix* A ASW hel)
      3 *Talwar* II with 1 octuple VLS with *Brahmos* AShM/LACM, 1 single lnchr with 3K90 *Uragan* (SA-N-7 *Gadfly*) SAM, 2 twin 533mm ASTT, 2 RBU 6000 *Smerch* 2 A/S mor, 2 AK630 CIWS, 1 100mm gun (capacity 1 *Dhruv*/Ka-28 *Helix* A ASW hel)
    FFH 2:
      2 *Kamorta* with 2 twin 533mm TT, 2 RBU 6000 *Smerch* 2 A/S mor, 2 AK630 CIWS, 1 76mm gun (capacity 1 *Dhruv*/Ka-28 *Helix* A ASW hel)
  PATROL AND COASTAL COMBATANTS 107
    CORVETTES • FSGM 8:
      4 *Khukri* with 2 twin lnchr with P-15M *Termit* (SS-N-2C *Styx*) AShM, 2 twin lnchr (manual aiming) with 9K32M *Strela*-2M (SA-N-5 *Grail*) SAM, 2 AK630 CIWS, 1 76mm gun, 1 hel landing platform (for *Dhruv*/SA316 *Alouette* III (*Chetak*))
      4 *Kora* with 4 quad lnchr with 3M24E *Uran* (SS-N-25 *Switchblade*) AShM, 1 quad lnchr (manual aiming) with 9K32M *Strela*-2M (SA-N-5 *Grail*) SAM, 2 AK630 CIWS, 1 76mm gun, 1 hel landing platform (for *Dhruv*/SA316 *Alouette* III (*Chetak*))

PSOH 10: 4 *Saryu* with 2 AK630 CIWS, 1 76mm gun (capacity 1 *Dhruv*); 6 *Sukanya* with 4 RBU 2500 A/S mor (capacity 1 SA316 *Alouette* III (*Chetak*))
PCFGM 10
  8 *Veer* (FSU *Tarantul*) with 4 single lnchr with P-15M *Termit* (SS-N-2D *Styx*) AShM, 2 quad lnchr (manual aiming) with 9K32M *Strela*-2M (SA-N-5 *Grail*), 2 AK630 CIWS, 1 76mm gun
  2 *Prabal* (mod *Veer*) each with 4 quad lnchr with 3M24E *Uran* (SS-N-25 *Switchblade*) AShM, 1 quad lnchr (manual aiming) with 9K32M *Strela*-2M (SA-N-5 *Grail*) SAM, 2 AK630 CIWS, 1 76mm gun
PCM 4 *Abhay* (FSU *Pauk* II) with 1 quad lnchr (manual aiming) with 9K32M *Strela*-2M (SA-N-5 *Grail*) SAM, 2 twin 533mm ASTT, 2 RBU 1200 A/S mor, 1 76mm gun
PCC 17: 4 *Bangaram*; 10 *Car Nicobar*; 2 *Tarmugli* (*Car Nicobar* mod); 1 *Trinkat* (SDB Mk5)
PBF 58: 9 Immediate Support Vessel (Rodman 78); 13 Immediate Support Vessel (Craftway); 15 Plascoa 1300 (SPB); 5 *Super Dvora*; 16 Solas Marine Interceptor (additional vessels in build)
MINE WARFARE • MINE COUNTERMEASURES 6
  MSO 6 *Pondicherry* (FSU *Natya*) with 2 RBU 1200 A/S mor
AMPHIBIOUS
  PRINCIPAL AMPHIBIOUS VESSELS 1
    LPD 1 *Jalashwa* (ex-US Austin) with 1 *Phalanx* CIWS, (capacity up to 6 med spt hel; either 9 LCM or 4 LCM and 2 LCAC; 4 LCVP; 930 troops)
  LANDING SHIPS 9
    LSM 4 *Kumbhir* (FSU *Polnocny* C) (capacity 5 MBT or 5 APC; 160 troops)
    LST 5:
      2 *Magar* (capacity 15 MBT or 8 APC or 10 trucks; 500 troops)
      3 *Magar* mod (capacity 11 MBT or 8 APC or 10 trucks; 500 troops)
  LANDING CRAFT 32
    LCM 4 LCM-8 (for use in *Jalashwa*)
    LCU 8: 2 LCU Mk4; 6 *Vasco de Gama* Mk2/3 LC (capacity 2 APC; 120 troops)
    LCVP 20 (for use in *Magar*)
LOGISTICS AND SUPPORT 34
  AGOR 1 *Sagardhwani* with 1 hel landing platform
  AGHS 8 *Sandhayak*
  AGS 2 *Makar*
  AH 1
  AOL 7: 6 *Poshak*; 1 *Ambika*
  AOR 1 *Jyoti* with 1 hel landing platform
  AORH 3: 1 *Aditya* (mod *Deepak*); 2 *Deepak* with 4 AK630 CIWS
  AP 3 *Nicobar* with 1 hel landing platform
  ASR 1
  ATF 1
  AWT 2
  AX 1 *Tir*
  AXS 3

Naval Aviation 7,000

Flying hours 125–150 hrs/yr on *Sea Harrier*

FORCES BY ROLE
FIGHTER/GROUND ATTACK
  2 sqn with MiG-29K/KUB *Fulcrum*
ANTI-SUBMARINE WARFARE
  4 sqn with Ka-28 *Helix* A; SA316B *Alouette* III (*Chetak*); *Sea King* Mk42A/B
MARITIME PATROL
  2 sqn with BN-2 *Islander*; Do-228-101; Il-38SD *May*; Tu-142M *Bear* F
  1 sqn with P-8I *Neptune*
AIRBORNE EARLY WARNING & CONTROL
  1 sqn with Ka-31 *Helix* B
SEARCH & RESCUE
  1 sqn with SA316B *Alouette* III (*Chetak*); *Sea King* Mk42C
  1 sqn with *Dhruv*
TRANSPORT
  1 (comms) sqn with Do-228
  1 sqn with HS-748M (HAL-748M)
TRAINING
  1 sqn with HJT-16 *Kiran* MkI/II, *Hawk* Mk132
TRANSPORT HELICOPTER
  1 sqn with UH-3H *Sea King*
ISR UAV
  1 sqn with *Heron*; *Searcher* MkII
EQUIPMENT BY TYPE
AIRCRAFT 73 combat capable
  FTR 45 MiG-29K/KUB *Fulcrum*
  ASW 17: 5 Il-38SD *May*; 4 Tu-142M *Bear* F; 8 P-8I *Neptune*
  MP 13 Do-228-101
  TPT 37: Light 27: 17 BN-2 *Islander*; 10 Do-228; PAX 10 HS-748M (HAL-748M)
  TRG 23: 6 HJT-16 *Kiran* MkI; 6 HJT-16 *Kiran* MkII; 11 *Hawk* Mk132*
HELICOPTERS
  ASW 47: 12 Ka-28 *Helix* A; 21 *Sea King* Mk42A; 14 *Sea King* Mk42B
  MRH 58: 10 *Dhruv*; 25 SA316B *Alouette* III (*Chetak*); 23 SA319 *Alouette* III
  AEW 9 Ka-31 *Helix* B
  TPT • Medium 11: 5 *Sea King* Mk42C; up to 6 UH-3H *Sea King*
UNMANNED AERIAL VEHICLES
  ISR 10: Heavy 4 *Heron*; Medium 6 *Searcher* Mk II
AIR-LAUNCHED MISSILES
  AAM • IR R-550 *Magic*/*Magic* 2; R-73 (AA-11 *Archer*) IR/SARH R-27 (AA-10 *Alamo*); ARH: R-77 (AA-12 *Adder*)
  AShM AGM-84 *Harpoon* (on P-8I ac); Kh-35 (AS-20 *Kayak*; on *Bear* and *May* ac); *Sea Eagle* (service status unclear); *Sea Skua*

Marines ε1,200 (Additional 1,000 for SPB duties)

After the Mumbai attacks, the Sagar Prahari Bal (SPB), with 80 PBF, was established to protect critical maritime infrastructure

FORCES BY ROLE
SPECIAL FORCES
  1 (marine) cdo force

MANOEUVRE
  Amphibious
  1 amph bde

Air Force 127,200

5 regional air comds: Western (New Delhi), Southwestern (Gandhinagar), Eastern (Shillong), Central (Allahabad), Southern (Trivandrum). 2 support comds: Maintenance (Nagpur) and Training (Bangalore)

Flying hours   180 hrs/yr

FORCES BY ROLE
FIGHTER
  3 sqn with MiG-29 *Fulcrum*; MiG-29UB *Fulcrum*
FIGHTER/GROUND ATTACK
  4 sqn with *Jaguar* IB/IS
  6 sqn with MiG-21 *Bison*
  1 sqn with MiG-21M/MF *Fishbed*
  4 sqn with MiG-27ML *Flogger*
  3 sqn with *Mirage* 2000E/ED/I/IT (2000H/TH – secondary ECM role)
  10 sqn with Su-30MKI *Flanker*
ANTI SURFACE WARFARE
  1 sqn with *Jaguar* IM
ISR
  1 unit with Gulfstream IV SRA-4
AIRBORNE EARLY WARNING & CONTROL
  1 sqn with Il-76TD *Phalcon*
TANKER
  1 sqn with Il-78 *Midas*
TRANSPORT
  1 sqn with C-130J-30 *Hercules*
  1 sqn with C-17A *Globemaster* III
  5 sqn with An-32/An-32RE *Cline*
  1 (comms) sqn with B-737; B-737BBJ; EMB-135BJ
  4 sqn with Do-228; HS-748
  1 sqn with Il-76MD *Candid*
  1 flt with HS-748
TRAINING
  1 OCU sqn with Su-30MKI *Flanker*
  1 sqn (forming) with *Tejas*
  Some units with An-32; Do-228; *Hawk* Mk 132*; HJT-16 *Kiran* MkI/II; *Jaguar* IS/IM; MiG-21bis; MiG-21FL; MiG-21M/MF; MiG-27ML; PC-7 *Turbo Trainer* MkII; SA316B *Alouette* III (*Chetak*)
ATTACK HELICOPTER
  2 sqn with Mi-25 *Hind*; Mi-35 *Hind*
TRANSPORT HELICOPTER
  5 sqn with *Dhruv*
  1 sqn with Mi-8 *Hip*
  7 sqn with Mi-17/Mi-17-1V *Hip* H
  12 sqn with Mi-17V-5 *Hip* H
  2 sqn with SA316B *Alouette* III (*Chetak*)
  1 flt with Mi-8 *Hip*
  1 flt with Mi-26 *Halo*
  2 flt with SA315B *Lama* (*Cheetah*)
  2 flt with SA316B *Alouette* III (*Chetak*)
ISR UAV
  5 sqn with *Heron*; *Searcher* MkII
AIR DEFENCE
  25 sqn with S-125 *Pechora* (SA-3B *Goa*)
  6 sqn with 9K33 *Osa*-AK (SA-8B *Gecko*)
  2 sqn with *Akash*
  10 flt with 9K38 *Igla*-1 (SA-18 *Grouse*)

EQUIPMENT BY TYPE
AIRCRAFT 803 combat capable
  FTR 62: 55 MiG-29 *Fulcrum* (incl 12+ MiG-29UPG); 7 MiG-29UB *Fulcrum*
  FGA 551: 115 MiG-21 *Bison*; 20 MiG-21M/MF *Fishbed*; 39 MiG-21U/UM *Mongol*; 90 MiG-27ML *Flogger* J2; 40 *Mirage* 2000E/I (2000H); 10 *Mirage* 2000ED/IT (2000TH); ε235 Su-30MKI *Flanker*; 2 *Tejas*
  ATK 101: 12 *Jaguar* IB; 79 *Jaguar* IS; 10 *Jaguar* IM
  ISR 3 Gulfstream IV SRA-4
  AEW&C 6: 3 EMB-145AEW; 3 Il-76TD *Phalcon*
  TKR 6 Il-78 *Midas*
  TPT 244: **Heavy** 34: 10 C-17A *Globemaster* III; 24 Il-76MD *Candid*; **Medium** 5 C-130J-30 *Hercules*; **Light** 141: 63 An-32; 39 An-32RE *Cline*; 35 Do-228; 4 EMB-135BJ; **PAX** 64: 1 B-707; 4 B-737; 3 B-737BBJ; 56 HS-748
  TRG 339: 89 *Hawk* Mk132*; 120 HJT-16 *Kiran* MkI; 55 HJT-16 *Kiran* MkII; 75 PC-7 *Turbo Trainer* MkII
HELICOPTERS
  ATK 19 Mi-25/Mi-35 *Hind*
  MRH 389: 60 *Dhruv*; 80 Mi-17/Mi-17-1V *Hip* H; 150 Mi-17V-5 *Hip* H; 59 SA315B *Lama* (*Cheetah*); 40 SA316B *Alouette* III (*Chetak*)
  TPT 34: **Heavy** 4 Mi-26 *Halo*; **Medium** 30 Mi-8 *Hip*
UNMANNED AERIAL VEHICLES
  ISR • Heavy 9 *Heron*; **Medium** some *Searcher* MkII
AIR DEFENCE • SAM
  Medium-range *Akash*
  Short-range S-125 *Pechora* (SA-3B *Goa*)
  Point-defence 9K33 *Osa*-AK (SA-8B *Gecko*); 9K38 *Igla* (SA-18 *Grouse*)
AIR-LAUNCHED MISSILES
  AAM • IR R-60 (AA-8 *Aphid*); R-73 (AA-11 *Archer*) R-550 *Magic*; **IR/SARH** R-27 (AA-10 *Alamo*); **SARH** Super 530D **ARH** R-77 (AA-12 *Adder*)
  AShM AGM-84 *Harpoon*; AM-39 *Exocet*; *Sea Eagle*†
  ASM Kh-29 (AS-14 *Kedge*); Kh-59 (AS-13 *Kingbolt*); Kh-59M (AS-18 *Kazoo*); Kh-31A (AS-17B *Krypton*); AS-30; Kh-23 (AS-7 *Kerry*)‡
  ARM Kh-25MP (AS-12 *Kegler*); Kh-31P (AS-17A *Krypton*)
  ALCM • Nuclear *Nirbhay* (likely nuclear capable; in development)
  BOMBS • Laser-guided *Paveway* II

Coast Guard 9,550

EQUIPMENT BY TYPE
PATROL AND COASTAL COMBATANTS 106
  PSOH 12: 2 *Sankalp* (capacity 1 *Chetak*/*Dhruv* hel); 4 *Samar* with 1 76mm gun (capacity 1 *Chetak*/*Dhruv* hel); 3 *Samarth*; 3 *Vishwast* (capacity 1 *Dhruv* hel)
  PSO 3 *Samudra Prahari* with 1 hel landing platform
  PCO 4 *Vikram* with 1 hel landing platform
  PCC 38: 19 *Aadesh*; 8 *Rajshree*; 4 *Rani Abbakka*; 7 *Sarojini Naidu*
  PBF 40: 2 C-141; 11 C-143; 27 C-401
  PB 9: 5 C-154; 4 *Priyadarshini*

AMPHIBIOUS
UCAC 18: 6 H-181 (*Griffon* 8000TD); 12 H-187 (*Griffon* 8000TD)
AIRCRAFT • TPT • Light 23 Do-228
HELICOPTERS • MRH 21: 4 *Dhruv*; 17 SA316B *Alouette III* (*Chetak*)

Paramilitary 1,403,700

Rashtriya Rifles 65,000
Ministry of Defence. 15 sector HQ
FORCES BY ROLE
MANOEUVRE
  Other
    65 paramilitary bn

Assam Rifles 63,900
Ministry of Home Affairs. Security within northeastern states, mainly army-officered; better trained than BSF
FORCES BY ROLE
Equipped to roughly same standard as an army inf bn
COMMAND
  7 HQ
MANOEUVRE
  Other
    46 paramilitary bn
EQUIPMENT BY TYPE
ARTILLERY • MOR 81mm 252

Border Security Force 230,000
Ministry of Home Affairs
FORCES BY ROLE
MANOEUVRE
  Other
    178 paramilitary bn
EQUIPMENT BY TYPE
Small arms, lt arty, some anti-tank weapons
ARTILLERY • MOR 81mm 942+
AIRCRAFT • TPT some (air spt)
HELICOPTERS • MRH 2 Mi-17V-5 *Hip*

Central Industrial Security Force 134,100 (lightly armed security guards)
Ministry of Home Affairs. Guards public-sector locations

Central Reserve Police Force 229,700
Ministry of Home Affairs. Internal-security duties, only lightly armed, deployable throughout the country
FORCES BY ROLE
MANOEUVRE
  Other
    203 paramilitary bn
    10 (rapid action force) paramilitary bn
    10 (CoBRA) paramilitary bn
    5 (Mahila) paramilitary bn (female)

Defence Security Corps 31,000
Provides security at Defence Ministry sites

Indo-Tibetan Border Police 36,300
Ministry of Home Affairs. Tibetan border security SF/guerrilla-warfare and high-altitude-warfare specialists
FORCES BY ROLE
MANOEUVRE
  Other
    56 paramilitary bn

National Security Guards 7,350
Anti-terrorism contingency deployment force, comprising elements of the armed forces, CRPF and Border Security Force

Railway Protection Forces 70,000

Sashastra Seema Bal 73,350
Guards the borders with Nepal and Bhutan

Special Frontier Force 10,000
Mainly ethnic Tibetans

Special Protection Group 3,000
Protection of ministers and senior officials

State Armed Police 450,000
For duty primarily in home state only, but can be moved to other states. Some bn with GPMG and army-standard infantry weapons and equipment
FORCES BY ROLE
MANOEUVRE
  Other
    24 (India Reserve Police) paramilitary bn (cdo trained)

Reserve Organisations

Civil Defence 500,000 reservists
Operate in 225 categorised towns in 32 states. Some units for NBC defence

Home Guard 487,800 reservists (515,000 authorised str)
In all states except Arunachal Pradesh and Kerala; men on reserve lists, no trg. Not armed in peacetime. Used for civil defence, rescue and firefighting provision in wartime; 6 bn (created to protect tea plantations in Assam)

Cyber
National agencies include the Computer Emergency Response Team (CERT-In), which has authorised designated individuals to carry out penetration tests against infrastructure. The Defence Information Assurance and Research Agency (DIARA) is mandated to deal with cyber-security-related issues for the armed services. All services have their own cyber-security policies and CERT teams, and headquarters maintain information-security policies. The Indian Army raised the Army Cyber Security Establishment in 2005 and set up the Cyber Security Laboratory at the Military College of Telecommunication Engineering (under the Corps of Signals) in April 2010. The services have their own cyber cells, but the government is

reportedly considering a suggestion from the Task Force on National Security to establish three tri-service commands, including one for cyberspace.

DEPLOYMENT

AFGHANISTAN
335 (Indo-Tibetan Border Police paramilitary: facilities protection)

CÔTE D'IVOIRE
UN • UNOCI 3 obs

DEMOCRATIC REPUBLIC OF THE CONGO
UN • MONUSCO 3,111; 43 obs; 3 mech inf bn; 1 inf bn; 1 fd hospital

LEBANON
UN • UNIFIL 900; 1 inf bn; 1 fd hospital

MIDDLE EAST
UN • UNTSO 1 obs

SOUTH SUDAN
UN • UNMISS 2,277; 10 obs; 2 inf bn; 1 engr coy; 1 fd hospital

SUDAN
UN • UNISFA 4 obs

SOMALIA
UN • UNSOM 1 obs

SYRIA/ISRAEL
UN • UNDOF 189; 1 log bn(-)

WESTERN SAHARA
UN • MINURSO 3 obs

FOREIGN FORCES

Total numbers for UNMOGIP mission in India and Pakistan
Chile 2 obs
Croatia 9 obs
Finland 6 obs
Korea, Republic of 7 obs
Philippines 4 obs
Sweden 5 obs
Switzerland 3 obs
Thailand 3 obs
Uruguay 2 obs

Indonesia IDN

Indonesian Rupiah Rp		2015	2016	2017
GDP	Rp	11,541tr	12,553tr	
	US$	859bn	941bn	
per capita	US$	3,362	3,636	
Growth	%	4.8	4.9	
Inflation	%	6.4	3.7	
Def bdgt	Rp	106tr	109tr	105tr
	US$	7.88bn	8.17bn	
FMA (US)	US$	14m	14m	10m
US$1=Rp		13,435.88	13,341.05	

Population 258,316,051

Ethnic groups: Jawa 40.2%; Sunda, Priangan 15.5%; Banjar, Melayu Banjar 4%; other or unspecified 40.5%

Age	0–14	15–19	20–24	25–29	30–64	65 plus
Male	12.9%	4.5%	4.2%	4.0%	21.5%	3.0%
Female	12.5%	4.3%	4.1%	3.8%	21.5%	3.9%

Capabilities

Indonesia's armed forces have traditionally been concerned primarily with internal security and counter-insurgency. The army remains the dominant service and is deployed operationally in West Papua (where resistance to Indonesian rule continues) and on counter-terrorist operations in Poso regency (central Sulawesi) and elsewhere. However, Indonesia's post-1998 transformation from a military-dominated dictatorship to a democracy, and the emergence of clearer threats to its extensive maritime interests, have contributed to a drive to restructure and modernise the TNI (Indonesian National Defence Force). The modernisation plan adopted in 1999 calls for the establishment by 2024 of a 'Minimum Essential Force' including strengthened naval and air capabilities. The government's ambition for Indonesia to become a 'global maritime fulcrum' has reinforced the emphasis on developing the navy as well as maritime paramilitary forces. Increased defence spending has enabled the TNI's modernisation and restructuring, and has allowed not only significant equipment acquisition for all three services, but also the construction of new military infrastructure, notably in the Natuna Islands in the South China Sea. However, budget cuts announced in August 2016 are likely to slow down efforts to strengthen capabilities. Indonesia has bought military equipment from diverse international sources, while using technology-transfer agreements with foreign suppliers to develop its national defence industry. The TNI has contributed to UN and other international peacekeeping operations, and exercises with the Australian and US armed forces and those of several other Southeast Asian states.

ACTIVE 395,500 (Army 300,400 Navy 65,000 Air 30,100) **Paramilitary 280,000**

Conscription liability 2 years selective conscription authorised (not required by law)

RESERVE 400,000
Army cadre units; numerical str n.k., obligation to age 45 for officers

ORGANISATIONS BY SERVICE

Army ε300,400

Mil Area Commands (KODAM)
13 comd (I, II, III, IV, V, VI, VII, IX, XII, XVI, XVII, Jaya & Iskandar Muda)
FORCES BY ROLE
MANOEUVRE
　Mechanised
　　3 armd cav bn
　　5 cav bn
　Light
　　1 inf bde (1 cav bn, 3 inf bn)
　　4 inf bde (1 cdo bn, 2 inf bn)
　　3 inf bde (3 inf bn)
　　38 indep inf bn
　　13 cdo bn
COMBAT SUPPORT
　12 fd arty bn
　7 cbt engr bn
COMBAT SERVICE SUPPORT
　4 construction bn
AVIATION
　1 composite avn sqn
HELICOPTER
　1 hel sqn
AIR DEFENCE
　1 AD regt (2 ADA bn, 1 SAM unit)
　6 ADA bn
　3 SAM unit

Special Forces Command (KOPASSUS)
FORCES BY ROLE
SPECIAL FORCES
　3 SF gp (total: 2 cdo/para unit, 1 CT unit, 1 int unit)

Strategic Reserve Command (KOSTRAD)
FORCES BY ROLE
COMMAND
　2 div HQ
MANOEUVRE
　Armoured
　　2 armd bn (forming)
　Light
　　3 inf bde (total: 1 mech inf bn; 6 cdo bn; 1 inf bn)
　Air Manoeuvre
　　3 AB bde (3 AB bn)
COMBAT SUPPORT
　2 fd arty regt (total: 6 arty bn)
　1 arty bn
　2 cbt engr bn
AIR DEFENCE
　2 AD bn
EQUIPMENT BY TYPE
ARMOURED FIGHTING VEHICLES
　MBT 49: 41 *Leopard* 2A4; 8 *Leopard* 2RI
　LT TK 350: 275 AMX-13 (partially upgraded); 15 PT-76; 60 *Scorpion* 90
　RECCE 142: 55 *Ferret* (13 upgraded); 69 *Saladin* (16 upgraded); 18 VBL
　IFV 59: 22 *Black Fox*; 37 *Marder* 1A3
　APC 544+
　　APC (T) 177+: 75 AMX-VCI; 34 BTR-50PK; 15 FV4333 *Stormer*; 53+ M113A1-B
　　APC (W) 367+: ε150 *Anoa*; some *Barracuda*; 40 BTR-40; 45 FV603 *Saracen* (14 upgraded); 100 LAV-150 *Commando*; 32 VAB-VTT
　　PPV some *Casspir*
　AUV 39: 14 APR-1; 3 *Bushmaster*; 22 *Commando Ranger*;
ENGINEERING & MAINTENANCE VEHICLES
　AEV 3: 2 *Leopard* 2; 1 M113A1-B-GN
　ARV 11+: 2 AMX-13; 6 AMX-VCI; 3 BREM-2; 2 *Leopard* 2; *Stormer*; T-54/T-55
　VLB 13+: 10 AMX-13; *Leguan*; 1 *Leopard* 2; 2 *Stormer*
ANTI-TANK/ANTI-INFRASTRUCTURE
　MSL • MANPATS SS.11; *Milan*; 9K11 *Malyutka* (AT-3 *Sagger*)
　RCL 90mm M67; **106mm** M40A1
　RL 89mm LRAC
ARTILLERY 1,110+
　SP 155mm 9 CAESAR
　TOWED 133+: **105mm** 110+: some KH-178; 60 M101; 50 M-56; **155mm** 23: 5 FH-88; 18 KH-179
　MRL 127mm 36 ASTROS II Mk6
　MOR 955: **81mm** 800; **120mm** 155: 75 Brandt; 80 UBM 52
AMPHIBIOUS • LCU 17
　1 ADRI XXXII
　4 ADRI XXXIII
　1 ADRI XXXIX
　1 ADRI XL
　3 ADRI XLI
　2 ADRI XLIV
　2 ADRI XLVI
　2 ADRI XLVIII
　1 ADRI L
AIRCRAFT • TPT • Light 9: 1 BN-2A *Islander*; 6 C-212 *Aviocar* (NC-212); 2 *Turbo Commander* 680
HELICOPTERS
　ATK 6 Mi-35P *Hind*
　MRH 35: 1 AS550 *Fennec*; 17 Bell 412 *Twin Huey* (NB-412); 17 Mi-17V-5 *Hip H*
　TPT • Light 29: 7 Bell 205A; 20 Bo-105 (NBo-105); 2 H120 *Colibri*
　TRG 12 Hughes 300C
AIR DEFENCE
　SAM • Point-defence 95+: 2 *Kobra* (with 125 GROM-2 msl); TD-2000B (*Giant Bow II*); 51 *Rapier*; 42 RBS-70; QW-3
　GUNS • TOWED 411: **20mm** 121 Rh 202; **23mm** *Giant Bow*; **40mm** 90 L/70; **57mm** 200 S-60

Navy ε65,000 (including Marines and Aviation)
Two fleets: East (Surabaya), West (Jakarta). It is currently planned to change to three commands: Riau (West); Papua (East); Makassar (Central). Two Forward Operating Bases at Kupang (West Timor) and Tahuna (North Sulawesi)

EQUIPMENT BY TYPE
SUBMARINES • TACTICAL • SSK 2 *Cakra*† (Type-209/1300) with 8 single 533mm TT with SUT HWT
PRINCIPAL SURFACE COMBATANTS 12
  FRIGATES 12
    FFGHM 7:
      3 *Ahmad Yani* (ex-NLD *Van Speijk*) fitted for 2 quad Mk 141 lnchr with RGM-84A *Harpoon* AShM, 2 SIMBAD twin lnchr (manual) with *Mistral* SAM, 2 triple 324mm ASTT with Mk46 LWT, 1 76mm gun (capacity 1 Bo-105 (NBo-105) hel)
      1 *Ahmad Yani* (ex-NLD *Van Speijk*) with 2 twin-cell VLS with 3M55E *Yakhont* (SS-N-26 *Strobile*) AShM; 2 SIMBAD twin lnchr (manual) with *Mistral* SAM, 2 triple 324mm ASTT with Mk46 LWT, 1 76mm gun (capacity 1 Bo-105 (NBo-105) hel)
      2 *Ahmad Yani* (ex-NLD *Van Speijk*) with 2 single lnchr with C-802 AShM, 2 SIMBAD twin lnchr (manual) with *Mistral* SAM, 2 triple 324mm ASTT with Mk46 LWT, 1 76mm gun (capacity 1 Bo-105 (NBo-105) hel)
      1 *Hajar Dewantara* (trg role) with 2 twin lnchr with MM-38 *Exocet* AShM, 2 single 533mm ASTT with SUT HWT, 1 57mm gun (capacity 1 Bo-105 (NBo-105) hel)
    FFGM 5:
      4 *Diponegoro* (NLD SIGMA 9113) with 2 twin lnchr with MM-40 *Exocet* Block II AShM, 2 quad *Tetral* lnchr with *Mistral* SAM, 2 triple 324mm ASTT with MU90 LWT, 1 76mm gun, 1 hel landing platform
      1 *Hajar Dewantara* (trg role) with 2 twin lnchr with MM-38 *Exocet* AShM, 2 single 533mm ASTT with SUT HWT, 1 57mm gun (capacity 1 Bo-105 (NBo-105) hel)
PATROL AND COASTAL COMBATANTS 84
  CORVETTES 20
    FSGHM 3 *Bung Tomo* with 2 quad lnchr with MM-40 *Exocet* AShM, 1 18-cell VLS with *Sea Wolf* SAM, 2 triple 324mm ASTT, 1 76mm gun (capacity: 1 Bo-105 hel)
    FSGH 1 *Nala* with 2 twin lnchr with MM-38 *Exocet* AShM, 1 twin 375mm A/S mor, 1 120mm gun (capacity 1 lt hel)
    FSG 2 *Fatahillah* with 2 twin lnchr with MM-38 *Exocet* AShM, 2 triple B515 *ILAS-3/Mk32* 324mm ASTT with A244/Mk46 LWT, 1 twin 375mm A/S mor, 1 120mm gun
    FS 14 *Kapitan Pattimura* (GDR *Parchim* I) with 4 single 400mm ASTT, 2 RBU 6000 *Smerch* 2 A/S mor, 1 twin 57mm gun
  PCFG 4 *Mandau* with 4 single lnchr with MM-38 *Exocet* AShM, 1 57mm gun
  PCG 3 *Sampari* (KCR-60M) with 2 twin lnchr for C-705 AShM,
  PCT 2 *Singa* with 2 single 533mm TT, 1 57mm gun
  PCC 13: 4 *Kakap*; 2 *Pandrong*; 3 *Pari* with 1 57mm gun; 4 *Todak* with 1 57mm gun
  PBG 10:
    2 *Clurit* with 2 twin lnchr with C-705 AShM, 1 AK630 CIWS
    6 *Clurit* with 2 twin lnchr with C-705 AShM

    2 *Badau* (ex-BRN *Waspada*) with 2 twin lnchr for MM-38 *Exocet* AShM
  PB 32: 9 *Boa*; 1 *Cucut* (ex-SGP *Jupiter*); 4 *Kobra*; 1 *Krait*; 8 *Sibarau*; 5 *Viper*; 4 *Tarihu*
MINE WARFARE • MINE COUNTERMEASURES 8
  MCO 2 *Pulau Rengat*
  MSC 6 *Pulau Rote* (ex-GDR *Wolgast*)
AMPHIBIOUS
  PRINCIPAL AMPHIBIOUS VESSELS • LPD 5:
    1 *Dr Soeharso* (Ex-*Tanjung Dalpele*; capacity 2 LCU/LCVP; 13 tanks; 500 troops; 2 AS332L *Super Puma*) (used in AH role)
    4 *Makassar* (capacity 2 LCU or 4 LCVP; 13 tanks; 500 troops; 2 AS332L *Super Puma*)
  LANDING SHIPS • LST 19
    1 *Teluk Amboina* (capacity 16 tanks; 800 troops)
    1 *Teluk Bintuni* (capacity 10 MBT)
    10 *Teluk Gilimanuk* (ex-GDR *Frosch*)
    2 *Teluk Langsa* (capacity 16 tanks; 200 troops)
    5 *Teluk Semangka* (capacity 17 tanks; 200 troops)
  LANDING CRAFT 55
    LCM 20
    LCU 5
    LCVP 30
LOGISTICS AND SUPPORT 23
  AGF 1 *Multatuli* with 1 hel landing platform
  AGOR 2 *Rigel*
  AGOS 1 *Leuser*
  AGHS 1
  AGS 3 *Pulau Rote* (ex-GDR *Wolgast*)
  AKSL 4
  AORLH 1 *Arun* (ex-UK *Rover*)
  AOT 3: 2 *Khobi*; 1 *Sorong*
  AP 4: 1 *Tanjung Kambani* (troop transport) with 1 hel landing platform; 1 *Tanjung Nusanive* (troop transport); 2 *Karang Pilang* (troop transport)
  ATF 1
  AXS 2

Naval Aviation ε1,000

EQUIPMENT BY TYPE
AIRCRAFT
  MP 23: 3 CN-235 MPA; 14 N-22B *Searchmaster* B; 6 N-22SL *Searchmaster* L
  TPT • Light 38: 8 Beech G36 *Bonanza*; 2 Beech G38 *Baron*; 21 C-212-200 *Aviocar*; 2 DHC-5D *Buffalo*; 3 TB-9 *Tampico*; 2 TB-10 *Tobago*
HELICOPTERS
  MRH 4 Bell 412 (NB-412) *Twin Huey*
  TPT 15: **Medium** 3 AS332L *Super Puma* (NAS322L); **Light** 12: 3 H120 *Colibri*; 9 Bo-105 (NBo-105)

Marines ε20,000

FORCES BY ROLE
SPECIAL FORCES
  1 SF bn
MANOEUVRE
  Amphibious
    2 mne gp (1 cav regt, 3 mne bn, 1 arty regt, 1 cbt spt regt, 1 CSS regt)
    1 mne bde (3 mne bn)

EQUIPMENT BY TYPE
ARMOURED FIGHTING VEHICLES
LT TK 65: 10 AMX-10 PAC 90; 55 PT-76†
RECCE 21 BRDM-2
IFV 112: 24 AMX-10P; 22 BMP-2; 54 BMP-3F; 12 BTR-80A
APC • APC (T) 100 BTR-50P
AAV 10 LVTP-7A1
ARTILLERY 67+
TOWED 50: 105mm 22 LG1 MK II; 122mm 28 M-38
MRL 122mm 17: 9 RM-70; 8 RM-70 *Vampir*
MOR 81mm
AIR DEFENCE • GUNS • 40mm 5 L/60/L/70; 57mm S-60

Air Force 30,100

2 operational comd (East and West) plus trg comd
FORCES BY ROLE
FIGHTER
  1 sqn with F-5E/F *Tiger* II
  1 sqn with F-16A/B/C/D *Fighting Falcon*
FIGHTER/GROUND ATTACK
  1 sqn with F-16C/D *Fighting Falcon*
  1 sqn with Su-27SK/SKM *Flanker*; Su-30MK/MK2 *Flanker*
  2 sqn with *Hawk* Mk109*/Mk209*
  1 sqn with T-50i *Golden Eagle**
GROUND ATTACK
  1 sqn with EMB-314 (A-29) *Super Tucano**
MARITIME PATROL
  1 sqn with B-737-200; CN-235M-220 MPA
TANKER/TRANSPORT
  1 sqn with C-130B/KC-130B *Hercules*
TRANSPORT
  1 VIP sqn with B-737-200; C-130H/H-30 *Hercules*; L-100-30; F-27-400M *Troopship*; F-28-1000/3000; AS332L *Super Puma* (NAS332L); SA330SM *Puma* (NAS300SM)
  1 sqn with C-130H/H-30 *Hercules*; L-100-30
  1 sqn with C-212 *Aviocar* (NC-212)
  1 sqn with CN-235M-110; C-295M
TRAINING
  1 sqn with Grob 120TP
  1 sqn with KT-1B
  1 sqn with SF-260M; SF-260W *Warrior*
TRANSPORT HELICOPTER
  2 sqn with AS332L *Super Puma* (NAS332L); SA330J/L *Puma* (NAS330J/L); H120 *Colibri*
EQUIPMENT BY TYPE
Only 45% of ac op
AIRCRAFT 111 combat capable
FTR 22: 8 F-5E *Tiger* II; 4 F-5F *Tiger* II; 7 F-16A *Fighting Falcon*; 3 F-16B *Fighting Falcon*
FGA 29: 9 F-16C *Fighting Falcon*; 4 F-16D *Fighting Falcon*; 2 Su-27SK *Flanker*; 3 Su-27SKM *Flanker*; 2 Su-30MK *Flanker*; 9 Su-30MK2
MP 6: 3 B-737-200; 3 CN-235M-220 MPA
TKR 1 KC-130B *Hercules*
TPT 50: **Medium** 17: 4 C-130B *Hercules*; 5 C-130H *Hercules*; 6 C-130H-30 *Hercules*; 2 L-100-30; **Light** 24: 9 C-295; 9 C-212 *Aviocar* (NC-212); 5 CN-235-110; 1 F-27-400M *Troopship*; **PAX** 9: 1 B-737-200; 3 B-737-400; 1 B-737-500; 1 B-737-800BBJ; 1 F-28-1000; 2 F-28-3000
TRG 109: 15 EMB-314 (A-29) *Super Tucano**; 18 Grob 120TP; 7 *Hawk* Mk109*; 23 *Hawk* Mk209*; 14 KT-1B; 10 SF-260M; 7 SF-260W *Warrior*; 15 T-50i *Golden Eagle**
HELICOPTERS
TPT 30: **Medium** 18: 9 AS332 *Super Puma* (NAS332L) (VIP/CSAR); 1 SA330SM *Puma* (NAS330SM) (VIP); 4 SA330J *Puma* (NAS330J); 4 SA330L *Puma* (NAS330L); **Light** 12 H120 *Colibri*
AIR-LAUNCHED MISSILES
AAM • IR AIM-9P *Sidewinder*; R-73 (AA-11 *Archer*); IR/SARH R-27 (AA-10 *Alamo*)
ASM AGM-65G *Maverick*
ARM Kh-31P (AS-17A *Krypton*)

Special Forces (Paskhasau)

FORCES BY ROLE
SPECIAL FORCES
  3 (PASKHASAU) SF wg (total: 6 spec ops sqn)
  4 indep SF coy
EQUIPMENT BY TYPE
AIR DEFENCE
SAM • Point QW-3
GUNS • TOWED 35mm 6 Oerlikon *Skyshield*

Paramilitary 280,000+

Customs

EQUIPMENT BY TYPE
PATROL AND COASTAL COMBATANTS 65
PBF 15
PB 50

Marine Police

EQUIPMENT BY TYPE
PATROL AND COASTAL COMBATANTS 37
PSO 2 *Bisma*
PCC 5
PBF 3 *Gagak*
PB 27: 14 *Bango*; 13 (various)
LOGISTICS AND SUPPORT • AP 1

Police ε280,000 (including 14,000 police 'mobile bde' (BRIMOB) org in 56 coy, incl CT unit (Gegana))
EQUIPMENT BY TYPE
ARMOURED FIGHTING VEHICLES
APC (W) 34 *Tactica*
AIRCRAFT • TPT • **Light** 5: 2 Beech 18; 2 C-212 *Aviocar* (NC-212); 1 Turbo Commander 680
HELICOPTERS • TPT • **Light** 22: 3 Bell 206 *Jet Ranger*; 19 Bo-105 (NBo-105)

KPLP (Coast and Seaward Defence Command)

Responsible to Military Sea Communications Agency
EQUIPMENT BY TYPE
PATROL AND COASTAL COMBATANTS 31
PCO 4: 2 *Arda Dedali*; 2 *Trisula*

PB 27: 4 *Golok* (SAR); 5 *Kujang*; 3 *Rantos*; 15 (various)
LOGISTICS AND SUPPORT • ABU 1 *Jadayat*

Bakamla (Maritime Security Agency)
EQUIPMENT BY TYPE
PATROL AND COASTAL COMBATANTS 6
PB 6 *Bintang Laut* (KCR-40 mod)

Reserve Organisations

Kamra People's Security ε40,000 (report for 3 weeks' basic training each year; part-time police auxiliary)

DEPLOYMENT

CENTRAL AFRICAN REPUBLIC
UN • MINUSCA 207; 6 obs; 1 engr coy

DEMOCRATIC REPUBLIC OF THE CONGO
UN • MONUSCO 176; 14 obs; 1 engr coy

LEBANON
UN • UNIFIL 1,296; 1 inf bn; 1 log bn(-); 1 FSGHM

LIBERIA
UN • UNMIL 1 obs

MALI
UN • MINUSMA 147; 1 hel sqn

PHILIPPINES
IMT 5

SOUTH SUDAN
UN • UNMISS 1; 3 obs

SUDAN
UN • UNAMID 812; 4 obs; 1 inf bn UN • UNISFA 2; 2 obs

WESTERN SAHARA
UN • MINURSO 5 obs

Japan JPN

Japanese Yen ¥		2015	2016	2017
GDP	¥	499tr	505tr	
	US$	4.12tr	4.73tr	
per capita	US$	32,479	37,304	
Growth	%	0.5	0.5	
Inflation	%	0.8	-0.2	
Def bdgt	¥	4.98tr	5.05tr	5.17tr
	US$	41.1bn	47.3bn	
US$1=¥		121.04	106.76	

Population 126,702,133
Ethnic groups: Korean <1%

Age	0–14	15–19	20–24	25–29	30–64	65 plus
Male	6.7%	2.5%	2.5%	2.5%	22.3%	11.9%
Female	6.3%	2.3%	2.3%	2.5%	22.7%	15.4%

Capabilities

Japan's alliance with the United States remains the cornerstone of its defence policy, reflected by continued US basing on Honshu, Kyushu and Okinawa; the widespread use of US equipment across all three services; and regular training with US forces. While the Self-Defense Forces' offensive capacity remains weak, the navy has strengths in anti-submarine warfare and air defence. Tokyo's concerns over its deteriorating regional security environment, in which it perceives an emerging threat from China, as well as its established concern over North Korea, have escalated. This has stimulated budget increases and defence-policy and legislative reforms to enable it to play a more active international security role, as well as to strengthen the US–Japan alliance. A new military-procurement drive has, for the first time, focused on power projection, mobility and ISR, with the first F-35 combat aircraft scheduled for delivery in 2017 and Japan continuing its plans to develop an amphibious force. Japan also continues its efforts to develop a more internationally focused defence industry, although two recent failed sales attempts (P-1 aircraft to the UK and *Soryu* submarines to Australia) highlighted Japanese defence contractors' lack of experience in competing in international markets. (See pp. 262–64.)

ACTIVE 247,150 (Ground Self-Defense Force 150,850 Maritime Self-Defense Force 45,350 Air Self-Defense Force 46,950 Central Staff 4,000) Paramilitary 12,650

RESERVE 56,000 (General Reserve Army (GSDF) 46,000 Ready Reserve Army (GSDF) 8,100 Navy 1,100 Air 800)

ORGANISATIONS BY SERVICE

Space
EQUIPMENT BY TYPE
SATELLITES • ISR 6 IGS

Ground Self-Defense Force 150,850
FORCES BY ROLE
COMMAND
 5 army HQ (regional comd)
SPECIAL FORCES
 1 spec ops unit (bn)
MANOEUVRE
 Armoured
 1 (7th) armd div (1 armd recce sqn, 3 tk regt, 1 armd inf regt, 1 avn sqn, 1 SP arty regt, 1 AD regt, 1 cbt engr bn, 1 sigs bn, 1 NBC bn, 1 log regt)
 Mechanised
 1 (2nd) inf div (1 armd recce sqn, 1 tk regt, 1 mech inf regt, 2 inf regt, 1 avn sqn, 1 SP arty regt, 1 AT coy, 1 AD bn, 1 cbt engr bn, 1 sigs bn, 1 NBC bn, 1 log regt)
 1 (4th) inf div (1 armd recce sqn, 1 tk bn, 1 mech inf regt, 2 inf regt, 1 inf coy, 1 avn sqn, 1 arty regt, 1 AT coy, 1 AD bn, 1 cbt engr bn, 1 sigs bn, 1 NBC bn, 1 log regt)

1 (9th) inf div (1 armd recce sqn, 1 tk bn, 3 mech inf regt, 1 avn sqn, 1 arty regt, 1 AD bn, 1 cbt engr bn, 1 sigs bn, 1 NBC bn, 1 log regt) 2 (5th & 11th) inf bde (1 armd recce sqn, 1 tk bn, 3 mech inf regt, 1 avn sqn, 1 SP arty bn, 1 AD coy, 1 cbt engr coy, 1 sigs coy, 1 NBC coy, 1 log bn)

Light
1 (8th) inf div (1 recce sqn, 1 tk bn, 4 inf regt, 1 avn sqn, 1 arty regt, 1 AD bn, 1 cbt engr bn, 1 sigs bn, 1 NBC bn, 1 log regt)
4 (1st, 3rd, 6th & 10th) inf div (1 recce sqn, 1 tk bn, 3 inf regt, 1 avn sqn, 1 arty regt, 1 AD bn, 1 cbt engr bn, 1 sigs bn, 1 NBC bn, 1 log regt)
1 (13th) inf bde (1 recce sqn, 1 tk coy, 3 inf regt, 1 avn sqn, 1 arty bn, 1 AD coy, 1 cbt engr coy, 1 NBC coy, 1 sigs coy, 1 log bn)
1 (14th) inf bde (1 recce sqn, 1 tk coy, 2 inf regt, 1 avn sqn, 1 arty bn, 1 AD coy, 1 cbt engr coy, 1 NBC coy, 1 sigs coy, 1 log bn)
1 (15th) inf bde (1 recce sqn, 1 inf regt, 1 avn sqn, 1 AD regt, 1 cbt engr coy, 1 NBC coy, 1 sigs coy, 1 log bn)

Air Manoeuvre
1 (1st) AB bde (3 AB bn, 1 arty bn, 1 cbt engr coy, 1 sigs coy, 1 log bn)
1 (12th) air mob inf bde (1 recce sqn, 3 inf regt, 1 avn sqn, 1 SP arty bn, 1 AD coy, 1 cbt engr coy, 1 NBC coy, 1 sigs coy, 1 log bn)

COMBAT SUPPORT
1 arty bde
2 arty unit (bde)
4 engr bde
1 engr unit
1 EW bn
5 int bn
1 MP bde
1 sigs bde

COMBAT SERVICE SUPPORT
5 log unit (bde)
5 trg bde

HELICOPTER
1 hel bde
5 hel gp (1 atk hel bn, 1 hel bn)

AIR DEFENCE
2 AD bde
4 AD gp

EQUIPMENT BY TYPE
ARMOURED FIGHTING VEHICLES
  MBT 690: 66 Type-10; 283 Type-74; 341 Type-90
  RECCE 111 Type-87
  IFV 68 Type-89
  APC 795
    APC (T) 226 Type-73
    APC (W) 569: 204 Type-82; 365 Type-96
  AAV 4 AAV-7
  AUV 4 *Bushmaster*
ENGINEERING & MAINTENANCE VEHICLES
  ARV 70: 4 Type-11; 36 Type-78; 30 Type-90
  VLB 22 Type-91
NBC VEHICLES 52 Chemical Reconnaissance Vehicle
ANTI-TANK/ANTI-INFRASTRUCTURE
  MSL
    SP 37 Type-96 MPMS
    MANPATS Type-79 *Jyu*-MAT; Type-87 *Chu*-MAT; Type-01 LMAT
  RCL • 84mm *Carl Gustav*
ARTILLERY 1,774
  SP 172: **155mm** 105 Type-99; **203mm** 67 M110A2
  TOWED 155mm 398 FH-70
  MRL 227mm 99 M270 MLRS
  MOR 1,105: **81mm** 652 L16 **120mm** 429; **SP 120mm** 24 Type-96
COASTAL DEFENCE • AShM 88: 6 Type-12; 82 Type-88
AIRCRAFT
  TPT • Light 7 Beech 350 *King Air* (LR-2)
HELICOPTERS
  ATK 104: 59 AH-1S *Cobra*; 12 AH-64D *Apache*; 33 OH-1
  ISR 44 OH-6D
  TPT 259: **Heavy** 56: 24 CH-47D *Chinook* (CH-47J); 32 CH-47JA *Chinook*; **Medium** 42: 3 H225 *Super Puma* MkII+ (VIP); 39 UH-60L *Black Hawk* (UH-60JA); **Light** 161: 131 Bell-205 (UH-1J); 30 Enstrom 480B (TH-480B)
AIR DEFENCE
  SAM
    Medium-range 163: 43 Type-03 *Chu*-SAM; 120 MIM-23B I-*Hawk*
    Short-range 5 Type-11 *Tan*-SAM
    Point-defence 159+: 46 Type-81 *Tan*-SAM; 113 Type-93 *Kin*-SAM; Type-91 *Kei*-SAM
  GUNS • SP 35mm 52 Type-87

Maritime Self-Defense Force 45,350

Surface units organised into 4 Escort Flotillas with a mix of 8 warships each. Bases at Yokosuka, Kure, Sasebo, Maizuru, Ominato. SSK organised into two flotillas with bases at Kure and Yokosuka

EQUIPMENT BY TYPE
SUBMARINES • TACTICAL • SSK 19:
  1 *Harushio* (trg role) with 6 single 533mm TT with T-89 HWT/UGM-84C *Harpoon* AShM
  1 *Oyashio* (trg role) with 6 single 533mm TT with T-89 HWT/UGM-84C *Harpoon* AShM
  10 *Oyashio* with 6 single 533mm TT with T-89 HWT/UGM-84C *Harpoon* AShM
  7 *Soryu* (AIP fitted) with 6 single 533mm TT with T-89 HWT/UGM-84C *Harpoon* AShM
PRINCIPAL SURFACE COMBATANTS 47
  AIRCRAFT CARRIERS • CVH 3:
    2 *Hyuga* with 1 16-cell Mk41 VLS with ASROC/RIM-162 ESSM SAM, 2 triple 324mm ASTT with Mk46/Type-97 LWT, 2 *Phalanx* Block 1B CIWS (normal ac capacity 3 SH-60 *Seahawk* ASW hel; plus additional ac embarkation up to 7 SH-60 *Seahawk* or 7 MCH-101)
    1 *Izumo* with 2 11-cell SeaRAM lnchr with RIM-116 SAM, 2 *Phalanx* Block 1B CIWS (normal ac capacity 7 SH-60 *Seahawk* ASW hel; plus additional ac embarkation up to 5 SH-60 *Seahawk*/MCH-101 hel)
  CRUISERS • CGHM 2 *Atago* with *Aegis* Baseline 7 C2, 2 quad lnchr with SSM-1B AShM, 1 64-cell Mk41 VLS with SM-2 MR SAM/ASROC, 1 32-cell Mk41 VLS with SM-2 MR SAM, 2 triple 324mm ASTT with Mk46 LWT, 2 *Phalanx* Block 1B CIWS, 1 127mm gun (capacity 1 SH-60 *Seahawk* ASW hel)

DESTROYERS 33
  DDGHM 26:
    8 *Asagiri* with 2 quad Mk141 lnchr with RGM-84C *Harpoon* AShM, 1 octuple Mk29 lnchr with *Sea Sparrow* SAM, 2 triple 324mm ASTT with Mk46 LWT, 1 octuple Mk112 lnchr with ASROC, 2 *Phalanx* CIWS, 1 76mm gun (capacity 1 SH-60 *Seahawk* ASW hel)
    4 *Akizuki* with 2 quad lnchr with SSM-1B AShM, 1 32-cell Mk41 VLS with ASROC/ESSM SAM, 2 triple 324mm ASTT with Type-97 LWT, 2 *Phalanx* CIWS, 1 127mm gun (capacity 1 SH-60 *Seahawk* ASW hel)
    9 *Murasame* with 2 quad lnchr with SSM-1B AShM, 1 16-cell Mk48 VLS with ESSM SAM, 2 triple 324mm TT with Mk46 LWT, 1 16-cell Mk41 VLS with ASROC, 2 *Phalanx* CIWS, 2 76mm gun (capacity 1 SH-60 *Seahawk* ASW hel)
    5 *Takanami* (improved *Murasame*) with 2 quad lnchr with SSM-1B AShM, 1 32-cell Mk41 VLS with ASROC/RIM-7M/ESSM SAM, 2 triple 324mm TT with Mk46 LWT, 2 *Phalanx* CIWS, 1 127mm gun (capacity 1 SH-60 *Seahawk* ASW hel)
  DDGM 6:
    2 *Hatakaze* with 2 quad Mk141 lnchr with RGM-84C *Harpoon* AShM, 1 Mk13 GMLS with SM-1 MR SAM, 2 triple 324mm ASTT with Mk46 LWT, 1 octuple Mk112 lnchr with ASROC, 2 *Phalanx* CIWS, 2 127mm gun, 1 hel landing platform
    4 *Kongou* with *Aegis* Baseline 4/5 C2, 2 quad Mk141 lnchr with RGM-84C *Harpoon* AShM, 1 29-cell Mk41 VLS with SM-2/3 SAM/ASROC, 1 61-cell Mk41 VLS with SM-2/3 SAM/ASROC, 2 triple 324mm ASTT, 2 *Phalanx* Block 1B CIWS, 1 127mm gun
  DDHM 1 *Shirane* with 1 octuple Mk112 lnchr with ASROC, 1 octuple Mk29 lnchr with RIM-7M *Sea Sparrow* SAM, 2 triple ASTT with Mk46 LWT, 2 *Phalanx* CIWS, 2 127mm gun (capacity 3 SH-60 *Seahawk* ASW hel)
FRIGATES 9
  FFGHM 3 *Hatsuyuki* with 2 quad Mk141 lnchr with RGM-84C *Harpoon* AShM, 1 octuple Mk29 lnchr with RIM-7F/M *Sea Sparrow* SAM, 2 triple ASTT with Mk46 LWT, 1 octuple Mk112 lnchr with ASROC, 2 *Phalanx* CIWS, 1 76mm gun (capacity 1 SH-60 *Seahawk* ASW hel)
  FFGM 6 *Abukuma* with 2 quad Mk141 lnchr with RGM-84C *Harpoon* AShM, 2 triple ASTT with Mk 46 LWT, 1 octuple Mk112 lnchr with ASROC, 1 *Phalanx* CIWS, 1 76mm gun
PATROL AND COASTAL COMBATANTS 6
  PBFG 6 *Hayabusa* with 4 SSM-1B AShM, 1 76mm gun
MINE WARFARE • MINE COUNTERMEASURES 27
  MCCS 4:
    2 *Ieshima*
    1 *Uraga* with 176mm gun, 1 hel landing platform (for MH-53E)
    1 *Uraga* with 1 hel landing platform (for MH-53E)
  MSC 20: 3 *Hirashima*; 12 *Sugashima*; 2 *Uwajima*; 3 *Enoshima*
  MSO 3 *Yaeyama*

AMPHIBIOUS
  LANDING SHIPS • LST 3 *Osumi* with 2 *Phalanx* CIWS, 1 hel landing platform (for 2 CH-47 hel) (capacity 10 Type-90 MBT; 2 LCAC(L) ACV; 330 troops)
  LANDING CRAFT 8
    LCU 2 *Yusotei*
    LCAC 6 LCAC(L) (capacity either 1 MBT or 60 troops)
LOGISTICS AND SUPPORT 21
  AGH 1 *Asuka* with 1 8-cell VLS (wpn trials) (capacity 1 SH-60 *Seahawk* hel)
  AGBH 1 *Shirase* (capacity 2 AW101 *Merlin* hel)
  AGOS 2 *Hibiki* with 1 hel landing platform
  AGS 3: 1 *Futami*; 1 *Nichinan*; 1 *Shonan*
  AOE 5: 2 *Mashu* (capacity 1 MH-53 hel); 3 *Towada* with 1 hel landing platform
  ARC 1 *Muroto*
  ASR 2: 1 *Chihaya* with 1 hel landing platform; 1 *Chiyoda* with 1 hel landing platform
  AX 6:
    1 *Kashima* with 2 triple 324mm ASTT, 1 76mm gun, 1 hel landing platform
    1 *Kurobe* with 1 76mm gun (trg spt ship)
    3 *Shimayuki* with 2 quad lnchr with RGM-84 *Harpoon* AShM, 1 octuple Mk29 lnchr with RIM-7M *Sea Sparrow* SAM, 1 octuple Mk112 lnchr with ASROC, 2 triple 324mm ASTT with Mk46 LWT, 2 *Phalanx* CIWS, 1 76mm gun
    1 *Tenryu* (trg spt ship); with 1 76mm gun (capacity: 1 med hel)

Naval Aviation ε9,800

7 Air Groups
FORCES BY ROLE
ANTI SUBMARINE/SURFACE WARFARE
  5 sqn with SH-60B (SH-60J)/SH-60K *Seahawk*
MARITIME PATROL
  4 sqn with P-3C *Orion*
ELECTRONIC WARFARE
  1 sqn with EP-3 *Orion*
MINE COUNTERMEASURES
  1 sqn with MH-53E *Sea Dragon*; MCH-101
SEARCH & RESCUE
  1 sqn with *Shin Meiwa* US-1A/US-2
  2 sqn with UH-60J *Black Hawk*
TRANSPORT
  1 sqn with AW101 *Merlin* (CH-101); Beech 90 *King Air* (LC-90); KC-130R *Hercules*
TRAINING
  1 sqn with Beech 90 *King Air* (TC-90)
  1 sqn with P-3C *Orion*
  1 sqn with T-5J
  1 hel sqn with H135 (TH-135); OH-6DA; SH-60B (SH-60J) *Seahawk*

EQUIPMENT BY TYPE
AIRCRAFT 80 combat capable
  ASW 75: 9 P-1; 66 P-3C *Orion*
  ELINT 5 EP-3C *Orion*
  SAR 5: 1 *Shin Meiwa* US-1A; 4 *Shin Meiwa* US-2
  TPT 28: **Medium** 5 C-130R *Hercules*; **Light** 23: 5 Beech 90 *King* Air (LC-90); 18 Beech 90 *King Air* (TC-90)
  TRG 30 T-5J

HELICOPTERS
ASW 85: 37 SH-60B *Seahawk* (SH-60J); 48 SH-60K *Seahawk*
MCM 10: 2 MH-53E *Sea Dragon*; 8 MCH-101
SAR 15 UH-60J *Black Hawk*
TPT 17: **Medium** 2 AW101 *Merlin* (CH-101) (additional ac being delivered); **Light** 15 H135 (TH-135)

Air Self-Defense Force 46,950

Flying hours 150 hrs/yr

7 cbt wg

FORCES BY ROLE
FIGHTER
7 sqn with F-15J *Eagle*
2 sqn with F-4EJ (F-4E) *Phantom* II
3 sqn with Mitsubishi F-2
ELECTRONIC WARFARE
2 sqn with Kawasaki EC-1; YS-11E
ISR
1 sqn with RF-4EJ (RF-4E) *Phantom* II*
AIRBORNE EARLY WARNING & CONTROL
2 sqn with E-2C *Hawkeye*
1 sqn with E-767
SEARCH & RESCUE
1 wg with U-125A *Peace Krypton*; UH-60J *Black Hawk*
TANKER
1 sqn with KC-767J
TRANSPORT
1 (VIP) sqn with B-747-400
3 sqn with C-1; C-130H *Hercules*; YS-11
Some (liaison) sqn with Gulfstream IV (U-4); T-4*
TRAINING
1 (aggressor) sqn with F-15J *Eagle*
TEST
1 wg with F-15J *Eagle*; T-4*
TRANSPORT HELICOPTER
4 flt with CH-47 *Chinook*

EQUIPMENT BY TYPE
AIRCRAFT 556 combat capable
FTR 201 F-15J *Eagle*
FGA 146: 92 F-2A/B; 54 F-4E *Phantom* II (F-4EJ)
EW 3: 1 Kawasaki EC-1; 2 YS-11EA
ISR 17: 13 RF-4E *Phantom* II* (RF-4J); 4 YS-11EB
AEW&C 17: 13 E-2C *Hawkeye*; 4 E-767
SAR 26 U-125A *Peace Krypton*
TKR 4 KC-767J
TPT 59: **Medium** 16: 15 C-130H *Hercules*; 1 C-2; **PAX** 43: 2 B-747-400; 13 Beech T-400; 19 C-1; 5 Gulfstream IV (U-4); 4 YS-11
TRG 245: 196 T-4*; 49 T-7
HELICOPTERS
SAR 36 UH-60J *Black Hawk*
TPT • **Heavy** 15 CH-47 *Chinook*
AIR-LAUNCHED MISSILES
AAM • **IR** AAM-3 (Type-90); AIM-9 *Sidewinder*; **IIR** AAM-5 (Type-04); **SARH** AIM-7 *Sparrow*; **ARH** AAM-4 (Type-99)
ASM ASM-1 (Type-80); ASM-2 (Type-93)

Air Defence

Ac control and warning. 4 wg; 28 radar sites

FORCES BY ROLE
AIR DEFENCE
6 SAM gp (total: 24 SAM bty with MIM-104D/F *Patriot* PAC-2/3)
1 AD gp with Type-81 *Tan-SAM*; M167 *Vulcan*

EQUIPMENT BY TYPE
AIR DEFENCE
SAM
Long-range 120 MIM-104D/F *Patriot* PAC-2 GEM/PAC-3
Point-defence Type-81 *Tan-SAM*
GUNS • **TOWED 20mm** M167 *Vulcan*

Paramilitary 12,650

Coast Guard 12,650

Ministry of Land, Transport, Infrastructure and Tourism (no cbt role)

EQUIPMENT BY TYPE
PATROL AND COASTAL COMBATANTS 368
PSOH 14: 2 *Mizuho* (capacity 2 hels); 2 *Shikishima* (capacity 2 hels); 10 *Soya* (capacity 1 hel)
PSO 45:
3 *Hida* with 1 hel landing platform
1 *Izu* with 1 hel landing platform
9 *Hateruma* with 1 hel landing platform
6 *Iwami*
1 *Kojima* (trg) with 1 hel landing platform
2 *Kunigami* with 1 hel landing platform
1 *Miura* with 1 hel landing platform
1 *Nojima* with 1 hel landing platform
7 *Ojika* with 1 hel landing platform
4 *Shiretoko*
10 *Taketomi* with 1 hel landing platform
PCO 16: 3 *Aso*; 2 *Takatori*; 11 *Teshio*
PCC 26: 4 *Amami*; 22 *Tokara*
PBF 47: 20 *Hayagumo*; 5 *Mihashi*; 14 *Raizan*; 2 *Takatsuki*; 6 *Tsuruugi*
PB 50: 2 *Akizuki*; 4 *Asogiri*; 4 *Hamagumo*; 11 *Hayanami*; 8 *Katonami*; 1 *Matsunami*; 5 *Murakumo*; 2 *Natsugiri*; 3 *Shimagiri*; 10 *Yodo*
PBI 168: 2 *Hakubai*; 1 *Hayagiku*; 163 *Himegiku*; 2 *Nadaka*
LOGISTICS AND SUPPORT 17
ABU 1 *Teshio*
AGS 13: 7 *Hamashio*; 1 *Jinbei*; 2 *Meiyo*; 1 *Shoyo*; 1 *Takuyo*; 1 *Tenyo*
AX 3
AIRCRAFT
MP 2 *Falcon* 900 MPAT
TPT 27: **Light** 18: 9 Beech 350 *King Air* (LR-2); 9 DHC Dash-7 (Bombardier 300) (MP) **PAX** 9: 3 CL-300; 2 Gulfstream V (MP); 4 Saab 340B
HELICOPTERS
MRH 5 Bell 412 *Twin Huey*
SAR 5 S-76D
TPT 38: **Medium** 8: 3 AS332 *Super Puma*; 5 H225 *Super Puma*; **Light** 30: 18 AW139; 3 Bell 206B *Jet Ranger* II; 6 Bell 212; 3 S-76C

Cyber

In 2012 a 'Cyber Planning Office' was established in the C4 Systems Planning Division, Joint Staff Office (JSO) of the Ministry of Defense to consolidate the cyber-planning functions of the JSO and to create a more systematic structure for responding to cyber attacks. The National Defense Program Guidelines for FY2014 and beyond stated that 'Japan will build up persistent ISR [intelligence, surveillance and reconnaissance] capabilities to prevent any acts that could impede efficient action by the SDF'. The 2014 Mid-Term Defense Program (FY2014–18) said that the Self-Defense Forces would develop specialist training for cyber personnel. The document also said that 'through its efforts to secure response capabilities in cyberspace where attackers have an overwhelming advantage, the SDF may consider the acquisition of capabilities to prevent them from using cyberspace'. A Cyber Defense Group was launched in March 2014 to respond to cyber threats. The group monitors defence-ministry and SDF networks, and provides responses to cyber attacks. A revised Cybersecurity Strategy was developed in mid-2015.

DEPLOYMENT

DJIBOUTI
170; 2 P-3C *Orion*

GULF OF ADEN & INDIAN OCEAN
2 DDGHM

SOUTH SUDAN
UN • UNMISS 272; 1 engr coy

FOREIGN FORCES

United States
US Pacific Command: 47,050
    Army 2,900; 1 SF gp; 1 avn bn; 1 SAM regt
    Navy 12,000; 1 CVN; 3 CGHM; 3 DDGHM; 5 DDGM; 1 LCC; 4 MCO; 1 LHD; 1 LPD; 2 LSD; 1 base at Sasebo; 1 base at Yokosuka
    USAF: 11,450; 1 HQ (5th Air Force) at Okinawa–Kadena AB; 1 ftr wg at Misawa AB (2 ftr sqn with 22 F-16C/D *Fighting Falcon*); 1 ftr wg at Okinawa–Kadena AB (2 ftr sqn with total of 54 F-15C/D *Eagle*; 1 tkr sqn with 15 KC-135R *Stratotanker*; 1 AEW sqn with 2 E-3B *Sentry*; 1 CSAR sqn with 10 HH-60G *Pave Hawk*); 1 tpt wg at Yokota AB with 10 C-130H *Hercules*; 2 C-12J; 1 spec ops gp at Okinawa–Kadena AB with (1 sqn with 5 MC-130H *Combat Talon*; 1 sqn with 5 MC-130J *Commando* II); 1 ISR sqn with RC-135 *Rivet Joint*
    USMC 20,700; 1 Marine div (3rd); 1 ftr sqn at Iwakuni with 12 F/A-18D *Hornet*; 1 tkr sqn at Iwakuni with 15 KC-130J *Hercules*; 2 tpt sqn at Futenma with 12 MV-22B *Osprey*
US Strategic Command: 1 AN/TPY-2 X-band radar at Shariki; 1 AN/TPY-2 X-Band radar at Kyogamisaki

Korea, Democratic People's Republic of DPRK

North Korean Won		2015	2016	2017
GDP	US$			
per capita	US$			
Def exp	won			
	US$			

US$1=won

*definitive economic data not available

Population   25,115,311

Age	0–14	15–19	20–24	25–29	30–64	65 plus
Male	10.7%	3.9%	4.1%	3.9%	22.6%	3.3%
Female	10.3%	3.8%	4.1%	3.8%	23.1%	6.4%

Capabilities

In spite of international sanctions, North Korea continues to define the development of nuclear weapons and ballistic missiles as central to its military power and survival. While questions remain over the extent of progress in the miniaturisation and integration of warheads, fourth and fifth nuclear tests conducted in January and September 2016 coupled with enduring regime rhetoric indicate ongoing ambitions. North Korea has also increased the number of ballistic-missile tests compared to previous years alongside ground tests of associated technologies (see p. 243). This includes the long-anticipated – albeit troubled – launches of the *Hwasong*-10 (*Musudan*) IRBM and further firings of the *Bukkeukseong*-1 (KN-11) SLBM, the latter with apparent integration of a new solid-fuel motor. However, longer-range ballistic-missile systems such as the *Hwasong*-13 (KN-08) ICBM – assessed by the US as having operational capability – and its *Hwasong*-14 (KN-04) derivative remain untested. While ongoing testing and associated failures suggest that some notional operational capabilities have yet to be achieved, North Korea has shown clear progress towards developing more capable and credible delivery systems. In contrast, the country's conventional forces remain reliant on increasingly obsolete equipment, with little evidence of widespread modernisation across the armed services. Their capability is arguably more reliant on personnel strength and the potential for asymmetric warfare. Exercises are regularly conducted, but they often appear staged and as such are not necessarily representative of wider operational capability.

ACTIVE 1,190,000 (Army ε1,020,000 Navy 60,000 Air 110,000) **Paramilitary 189,000**

Conscript liability Army 5–12 years, Navy 5–10 years, Air Force 3–4 years, followed by compulsory part-time service to age 40. Thereafter service in the Worker/Peasant Red Guard to age 60

RESERVE ε600,000 (Armed Forces ε600,000), **Paramilitary 5,700,000**

Reservists are assigned to units (see also Paramilitary)

ORGANISATIONS BY SERVICE

Strategic Forces

North Korea's ballistic missiles and obsolete H-5 (Il-28) bombers could in future be used to deliver nuclear warheads or bombs. At present, however, there is no conclusive evidence to suggest that North Korea has successfully produced a warhead or bomb capable of being delivered by these systems

Army ε1,020,000
FORCES BY ROLE
COMMAND
  2 mech corps HQ
  9 inf corps HQ
  1 (Capital Defence) corps HQ
MANOEUVRE
  Armoured
  1 armd div
  15 armd bde
  Mechanised
  4 mech div
  Light
  27 inf div
  14 inf bde
SURFACE-TO-SURFACE MISSILE
  1 SSM bde with *Scud*
  1 SSM bde with FROG-7
COMBAT SUPPORT
  1 arty div
  21 arty bde
  9 MRL bde
  5–8 engr river crossing/amphibious regt
  1 engr river crossing bde

Special Purpose Forces Command 88,000
FORCES BY ROLE
SPECIAL FORCES
  8 (Reconnaissance General Bureau) SF bn
MANOEUVRE
  Reconnaissance
  17 recce bn
  Light
  9 lt inf bde
  6 sniper bde
  Air Manoeuvre
  3 AB bde
  1 AB bn
  2 sniper bde
  Amphibious
  2 sniper bde

Reserves 600,000
FORCES BY ROLE
MANOEUVRE
  Light
  40 inf div
  18 inf bde

EQUIPMENT BY TYPE (ε)
ARMOURED FIGHTING VEHICLES
  MBT 3,500+ T-34/T-54/T-55/T-62/Type-59/*Chonma/Pokpoong*
  LT TK 560+: 560 PT-76; M-1985
  IFV 32 BTR-80A
  APC 2,500+
    APC (T) BTR-50; Type-531 (Type-63); VTT-323
    APC (W) 2,500 BTR-40/BTR-60/M-1992/1/BTR-152/M-2010 (6×6)/M-2010 (8×8)
ANTI-TANK/ANTI-INFRASTRUCTURE
  MSL
    SP 9K11 *Malyutka* (AT-3 *Sagger*)
    MANPATS 2K15 *Shmel* (AT-1 *Snapper*); 9K111 *Fagot* (AT-4 *Spigot*); 9K113 *Konkurs* (AT-5 *Spandrel*)
  RCL 82mm 1,700 B-10
ARTILLERY 21,100+
  SP/TOWED 8,500: **SP 122mm** M-1977/M-1981/M-1985/M-1991; **130mm** M-1975/M-1981/M-1991; **152mm** M-1974/M-1977; **170mm** M-1978/M-1989
  TOWED 122mm D-30/D-74/M-1931/37; **130mm** M-46; **152mm** M-1937/M-1938/M-1943
  GUN/MOR 120mm (reported)
  MRL 5,100: **107mm** Type-63; **122mm** BM-11/M-1977 (BM-21)/M-1985/M-1992/M-1993; **200mm** BMD-20; **240mm** BM-24/M-1985/M-1989/M-1991; **300mm** some
  MOR 7,500: **82mm** M-37; **120mm** M-43; **160mm** M-43
SURFACE-TO-SURFACE MISSILE LAUNCHERS
  ICBM 6+ *Hwasong*-13 (KN-08) (reported operational)
  MRBM ε10 *Nodong* (ε90+ msl); some *Musudan*
  SBRM 54+: 24 FROG-3/5/7; some KN-02; 30+ *Scud*-B/*Scud*-C (ε200+ msl)
AIR DEFENCE
  SAM • Point-defence 9K35 *Strela*-10 (SA-13 *Gopher*); 9K310 *Igla*-1 (SA-16 *Gimlet*); 9K32 *Strela*-2 (SA-7 *Grail*)‡
  GUNS 11,000
    SP 14.5mm M-1984; **23mm** M-1992; **37mm** M-1992; **57mm** M-1985
    TOWED 11,000: **14.5mm** ZPU-1/ZPU-2/ZPU-4; **23mm** ZU-23; **37mm** M-1939; **57mm** S-60; **85mm** M-1939 KS-12; **100mm** KS-19

Navy ε60,000
EQUIPMENT BY TYPE
SUBMARINES • TACTICAL 73
  SSB 1 *Sinpo* with 1 *Bukkeukseong*-1 (KN-11) SLBM (under development)
  SSK 20 PRC Type-033/FSU *Romeo*† with 8 single 533mm TT with 14 SAET-60 HWT
  SSC 32+:
    30 *Sang-O* with 2 single 533mm TT with Type-53–65 HWT
    2+ *Sang-O* II with 4 single 533mm TT with Type-53–65 HWT
  SSW 20† (some *Yugo* with 2 single 406mm TT; some *Yeono* with 2 single 533mm TT)
PRINCIPAL SURFACE COMBATANTS 2
  FRIGATES • FFG 2:
    1 *Najin* with 2 single lnchr with P-15 *Termit* (SS-N-2) AShM, 2 RBU 1200 A/S mor, 2 100mm gun, 2 twin 57mm gun

1 *Najin* with 2 twin lnchr with KN-01 AShM (reported), 2 RBU 1200 A/S mor, 2 100mm gun, 2 twin 57mm gun (operational status unclear)

PATROL AND COASTAL COMBATANTS 383+
  PCG 18:
    8 *Osa* I with 4 single lnchr with P-15 *Termit* (SS-N-2) AShM, 2 twin AK230 CIWS
    10 *Soju* with 4 single lnchr with P-15 *Termit* (SS-N-2) AShM
  PCO 5:
    4 *Sariwon* with 2 twin 57mm gun
    1 *Tral* with 1 85mm gun
  PCC 18:
    6 *Hainan* with 4 RBU 1200 A/S mor, 2 twin 57mm gun
    7 *Taechong* I with 2 RBU 1200 A/S mor, 1 85mm gun, 1 twin 57mm gun
    5 *Taechong* II with 2 RBU 1200 A/S mor, 1 100mm gun, 1 twin 57mm gun
  PBFG 17+:
    4 *Huangfen* with 4 single lnchr with P-15 *Termit* (SS-N-2) AShM, 2 twin AK230 CIWS
    6 *Komar* with 2 single lnchr with P-15 *Termit* (SS-N-2) AShM
    6 *Sohung* with 2 single lnchr with P-15 *Termit* (SS-N-2) AShM
    1+ *Nongo* with 2 twin lnchr with KN-01 AShM, 2 30mm CIWS (operational status unknown)
  PBF 229:
    54 *Chong-Jin* with 1 85mm gun
    142 *Ku Song/Sin Hung/Sin Hung* (mod)
    33 *Sinpo*
  PB 96:
    59 *Chaho*
    6 *Chong-Ju* with 2 RBU 1200 A/S mor, 1 85mm gun
    13 *Shanghai* II
    18 SO-1 with 4 RBU 1200 A/S mor, 2 twin 57mm gun

MINE WARFARE • MINE COUNTERMEASURES 24
  MSC 24: 19 *Yukto* I; 5 *Yukto* II

AMPHIBIOUS
  LANDING SHIPS • LSM 10 *Hantae* (capacity 3 tanks; 350 troops)
  LANDING CRAFT 257
    LCPL 96 *Nampo* (capacity 35 troops)
    LCM 25
    UCAC 136 *Kongbang* (capacity 50 troops)

LOGISTICS AND SUPPORT 23:
  AGI 14 (converted fishing vessels)
  AS 8 (converted cargo ships)
  ASR 1 *Kowan*

Coastal Defence

FORCES BY ROLE
COASTAL DEFENCE
  2 AShM regt with HY-1/KN-01 (6 sites, and probably some mobile launchers)

EQUIPMENT BY TYPE
COASTAL DEFENCE
  ARTY 130mm M-1992; SM-4-1
  AShM HY-1; KN-01
ARTILLERY • TOWED 122mm M-1931/37; **152mm** M-1937

Air Force 110,000

4 air divs. 1st, 2nd and 3rd Air Divs (cbt) responsible for N, E and S air defence sectors respectively; 8th Air Div (trg) responsible for NE sector. The AF controls the national airline

Flying hours 20 hrs/yr on ac

FORCES BY ROLE
BOMBER
  3 lt regt with H-5; Il-28 *Beagle*
FIGHTER
  1 regt with MiG-15 *Fagot*
  6 regt with J-5; MiG-17 *Fresco*
  4 regt with J-6; MiG-19 *Farmer*
  5 regt with J-7; MiG-21F-13/PFM *Fishbed*
  1 regt with MiG-21bis *Fishbed*
  1 regt with MiG-23ML/P *Flogger*
  1 regt with MiG-29A/S/UB *Fulcrum*
GROUND ATTACK
  1 regt with Su-25/Su-25UBK *Frogfoot*
TRANSPORT
  Some regt with An-2 *Colt*/Y-5 (to infiltrate 2 air-force sniper brigades deep into ROK rear areas); An-24 *Coke*; Il-18 *Coot*; Il-62M *Classic*; Tu-134 *Crusty*; Tu-154 *Careless*
TRAINING
  Some regt with CJ-6; FT-2; MiG-21U/UM
TRANSPORT HELICOPTER
  Some regt with Hughes 500D/E; Mi-8 *Hip*; Mi-17 *Hip* H; Mil-26 *Halo*; PZL Mi-2 *Hoplite*; Z-5
AIR DEFENCE
  19 bde with S-125 *Pechora* (SA-3 *Goa*); S-75 *Dvina* (SA-2 *Guideline*); S-200 *Angara* (SA-5 *Gammon*); 9K36 *Strela-3* (SA-14 *Gremlin*); 9K310 *Igla-1* (SA-16 *Gimlet*); 9K32 *Strela-2* (SA-7 *Grail*)‡; KN-06

EQUIPMENT BY TYPE
AIRCRAFT 545 combat capable
  BBR 80 Il-28 *Beagle*/H-5†
  FTR 401+: MiG-15 *Fagot*; 107 MiG-17 *Fresco*/J-5; 100 MiG-19 *Farmer*/J-6; 120 MiG-21F-13 *Fishbed*/J-7; MiG-21PFM *Fishbed*; 46 MiG-23ML *Flogger*; 10 MiG-23P *Flogger*; 18+ MiG-29A/S/UB *Fulcrum*
  FGA 30 MiG-21bis *Fishbed*; (18 Su-7 *Fitter* in store)
  ATK 34 Su-25/Su-25UBK *Frogfoot*
  TPT 217+: **Heavy** some Il-76 (operated by state airline); **Light** 208: 6 An-24 *Coke*; 2 Tu-134 *Crusty*; ε200 An-2 *Colt*/Y-5; **PAX** 9: 2 Il-18 *Coot*; 2 Il-62M *Classic*; 4 Tu-154 *Careless*; 1 Tu-204-300
  TRG 215+: 180 CJ-6; 35 FT-2; some MiG-21U/UM
HELICOPTERS
  MRH 80 Hughes 500D/E†
  TPT 206: **Heavy** 4 Mi-26 *Halo*; **Medium** 63: 15 Mi-8 *Hip*/Mi-17 *Hip* H; 48 Mi-4 *Hound*/Z-5; **Light** 139 PZL Mi-2 *Hoplite*
UNMANNED AERIAL VEHICLES
  ISR • Medium some (unidentified indigenous type); **Light** *Pchela-1* (*Shmel*) (reported)
AIR DEFENCE • SAM
  Long-range 38 S-200 *Angara* (SA-5 *Gammon*)
  Medium-range 179+: some KN-06 (status unknown); 179+ S-75 *Dvina* (SA-2 *Guideline*)
  Short-range 133 S-125 *Pechora* (SA-3 *Goa*)

Point-defence 9K32 *Strela*-2 (SA-7 *Grail*)‡; 9K36 *Strela*-3 (SA-14 *Gremlin*); 9K310 Igla-1 (SA-16 *Gimlet*)
AIR-LAUNCHED MISSILES
AAM • IR R-3 (AA-2 *Atoll*)‡; R-60 (AA-8 *Aphid*); R-73 (AA-11 *Archer*); PL-5; PL-7; **SARH** R-23/24 (AA-7 *Apex*); R-27R/ER (AA-10 A/C *Alamo*)
ASM Kh-23 (AS-7 *Kerry*)‡; Kh-25 (AS-10 *Karen*)

Paramilitary 189,000 active

Security Troops 189,000 (incl border guards, public safety personnel)
Ministry of Public Security

Worker/Peasant Red Guard ε5,700,000 reservists
Org on a province/town/village basis; comd structure is bde–bn–coy–pl; small arms with some mor and AD guns (but many units unarmed)

Cyber
Since the 1970s, the North Korean military (the Korean People's Army or KPA) has maintained a modest electronic-warfare (EW) capability. As a result of strategic reviews following *Operation Desert Storm*, the KPA established an information-warfare (IW) capability under the concept of 'electronic intelligence warfare' (EIW). In 1998, Unit 121 was reportedly established within the Reconnaissance Bureau of the General Staff Department to undertake offensive cyber operations. Experts assess North Korea as conceiving of cyber capabilities as useful tools for 'coercive diplomacy' and 'disruptive actions' in the South in the case of war. North Korea has launched distributed-denial-of-service attacks on South Korean institutions and pursues cyber infiltration against military and other government agencies. The attack on Sony Pictures in 2014 was attributed to North Korea. In response, US President Obama said that the US 'will respond. We will respond proportionally, and we'll respond in a place and time and manner that we choose.' North Korea's internet service was shut down, for a time, four days later. However, the incident illustrated that while attribution of North Korean activity may have been possible in this case, the country has also invested significant capacity in cyber operations.

Korea, Republic of ROK

South Korean Won		2015	2016	2017
GDP	won	1,559tr	1,613tr	
	US$	1,38tr	1,40tr	
per capita	US$	27,222	27,633	
Growth	%	2.6	2.7	
Inflation	%	0.7	1.0	
Def bdgt	won	37.5tr	38.8tr	40.3tr
	US$	33.2bn	33.8bn	
US$1=won		1,131.16	1,148.65	

Population 50,924,172

Age	0–14	15–19	20–24	25–29	30–64	65 plus
Male	6.9%	3.2%	3.7%	3.4%	27.1%	5.7%
Female	6.5%	2.9%	3.3%	3.0%	26.4%	7.8%

Capabilities

South Korea's primary military concern remains its troubled relationship with North Korea. This has led to a defence policy that seeks to recapitalise conventional military capabilities in order to maintain Seoul's qualitative edge, while simultaneously pursuing the niche capabilities required to deter North Korea's artillery, ballistic-missile and littoral-submarine threats. Military procurement is therefore currently both extensive and widely spread, and includes new armoured vehicles and artillery, tactical and tanker aircraft, UAVs, precision munitions, ballistic and cruise missiles, satellites, and cyber- and missile-defence equipment. While most of these acquisitions are from indigenous defence industry, the lengthy timelines of key programmes such as Korean Air and Missile Defence and 'Kill Chain' (intended to give Seoul the ability to detect and destroy North Korean ballistic missiles prior to their launch) have led to imports of key items. The US alliance remains a major element of defence strategy, and the transfer of wartime operational control of forces to Seoul, planned for the end of 2015, is now 'conditions based' with no firm date set. Nuclear tests by North Korea in 2016 and continued missile tests led Washington and Seoul to finally reach agreement on the long-discussed deployment to South Korea of the US THAAD missile-defence system. (See p. 244.)

ACTIVE 630,000 (Army 495,000 Navy 70,000 Air 65,000) **Paramilitary 4,500**

Conscript liability 20–24 months depending on branch

RESERVE 4,500,000

Reserve obligation of three days per year. First Combat Forces (Mobilisation Reserve Forces) or Regional Combat Forces (Homeland Defence Forces) to age 33

Reserve Paramilitary 3,000,000

Being reorganised

ORGANISATIONS BY SERVICE

Army 495,000
FORCES BY ROLE
COMMAND
 2 army HQ
 8 corps HQ
 1 (Capital Defence) comd HQ
SPECIAL FORCES
 1 (Special Warfare) SF comd
 6 SF bde
 1 indep SF bn
 2 cdo bde
 6 cdo regt
 2 indep cdo bn
MANOEUVRE
 Armoured
 5 armd bde
 Mechanised
 6 mech inf div (1 recce bn, 1 armd bde, 2 mech inf bde, 1 fd arty bde, 1 engr bn)
 Light
 16 inf div (1 recce bn, 1 tk bn, 3 inf regt, 1 arty regt (4 arty bn), 1 engr bn)
 2 indep inf bde
 Air Manoeuvre
 1 air aslt bde
 Other
 5 sy regt
SURFACE-TO-SURFACE MISSILE
 3 SSM bn
COMBAT SUPPORT
 6 engr bde
 5 engr gp
 1 CBRN defence bde
 8 sigs bde
COMBAT SERVICE SUPPORT
 4 log spt comd
HELICOPTER
 1 (army avn) comd
AIR DEFENCE
 1 ADA bde
 5 ADA bn

Reserves
FORCES BY ROLE
COMMAND
 1 army HQ
MANOEUVRE
 Light
 24 inf div

EQUIPMENT BY TYPE
ARMOURED FIGHTING VEHICLES
 MBT 2,434: 1,000 K1; 484 K1A1; 100 K2; 253 M48; 597 M48A5; (80 T-80U; 400 M47 in store)
 IFV ε350 K21 (40 BMP-3 in store)
 APC 2,790
  APC (T) 2,560: 300 Bv 206; 1,700 KIFV; 420 M113; 140 M577 (CP)
  APC (W) 220; 20 BTR-80; 200 KM-900/-901 (Fiat 6614)
  PPV 10 *MaxxPro*
ENGINEERING & MAINTENANCE VEHICLES
 AEV 207 M9
 ARV 238: 200 K1; K288A1; M47; 38 M88A1
 VLB 56 K1
ANTI-TANK/ANTI-INFRASTRUCTURE
 MSL • MANPATS 9K115 *Metis* (AT-7 *Saxhorn*); TOW-2A
 RCL 57mm; 75mm; 90mm M67; 106mm M40A2
 GUNS 58
  SP 90mm 50 M36
  TOWED 76mm 8 M18 *Hellcat* (AT gun)
ARTILLERY 11,038+
 SP 1,353+: 155mm 1,340: ε300 K9 *Thunder*; 1,040 M109A2 (K55/K55A1); 175mm some M107; 203mm 13 M110
 TOWED 3,500+: 105mm 1,700 M101/KH-178; 155mm/203mm 1,800+ KH-179/M114/M115
 MRL 185+: 130mm 156 K136 *Kooryong*; 227mm 48 M270 MLRS; 10 M270A1 MLRS; 239mm some *Chunmoo*
 MOR 6,000: 81mm KM29 (M29); 107mm M30
SURFACE-TO-SURFACE MISSILE LAUNCHERS
 SRBM • Conventional 30 *Hyonmu* I/IIA/IIB; MGM-140A/B ATACMS (launched from M270/M270A1 MLRS)
 GLCM • Conventional *Hyonmu* III
RADAR • LAND AN/TPQ-36 *Firefinder* (arty, mor); AN/TPQ-37 *Firefinder* (arty); RASIT (veh, arty)
HELICOPTERS
 ATK 64: 60 AH-1F/J *Cobra*; 4 AH-64E *Apache*
 MRH 175: 130 Hughes 500D; 45 MD-500
 TPT 276: Heavy 37: 31 CH-47D *Chinook*; 6 MH-47E *Chinook*; Medium 147: 60 KUH-1 *Surion*; 87 UH-60P *Black Hawk*; Light 112: ε100 Bell-205 (UH-1H *Iroquois*); 12 Bo-105
AIR DEFENCE
 SAM • Point-defence *Chun Ma* (*Pegasus*); FIM-92 *Stinger*; *Javelin*; *Mistral*; 9K310 *Igla*-1 (SA-16 *Gimlet*)
 GUNS 330+
  SP 170: 20mm ε150 KIFV *Vulcan* SPAAG; 30mm 20 BIHO *Flying Tiger*
  TOWED 160: 20mm 60 M167 *Vulcan*; 35mm 20 GDF-003; 40mm 80 L/60/L/70; M1

Navy 70,000 (incl marines)
Three separate fleet elements; 1st Fleet Donghae (East Sea/Sea of Japan); 2nd Fleet Pyeongtaek (West Sea/Yellow Sea); 3rd Fleet Busan (South Sea/Korea Strait); independent submarine command; three additional flotillas (incl SF, mine warfare, amphibious and spt elements) and 1 Naval Air Wing (3 gp plus spt gp)
EQUIPMENT BY TYPE
SUBMARINES • TACTICAL 23
 SSK 14:
  6 *Chang Bogo* (GER Type-209/1200; KSS-1) with 8 single 533mm TT with SUT HWT
  3 *Chang Bogo* (GER Type-209/1200; KSS-1) with 8 single 533mm TT with SUT HWT/UGM-84B *Harpoon* AShM
  5 *Son Won-il* (GER Type-214; KSS-2; AIP fitted) with 8 single 533mm TT with SUT HWT/*Hae Sung* AShM
 SSC 9 *Cosmos*

PRINCIPAL SURFACE COMBATANTS 23
CRUISERS • CGHM 3:
3 *Sejong* (KDD-III) with *Aegis* Baseline 7 C2, 2 quad Mk141 lnchr with RGM-84 *Harpoon* AShM, 1 48-cell Mk41 VLS with SM-2MR SAM, 1 32-cell Mk41 VLS with SM-2MR SAM, 1 Mk49 GMLS with RIM-116 SAM, 2 triple Mk32 324mm ASTT with K745 LWT, 1 32-cell VLS with ASROC, 1 *Goalkeeper* CIWS, 1 127mm gun (capacity 2 *Lynx* Mk99 hel)
DESTROYERS • DDGHM 6:
6 *Chungmugong Yi Sun-Sin* (KDD-II) with 2 quad Mk141 lnchr with RGM-84C *Harpoon* AShM (some may be fitted with *Hae Sung* AShM), 1 32-cell Mk41 VLS with SM-2MR SAM/ASROC, 1 Mk49 GMLS with RIM-116 SAM, 2 triple Mk32 324mm ASTT with Mk46 LWT, 1 *Goalkeeper* CIWS, 1 127mm gun (capacity 1 *Lynx* Mk99 hel)
FRIGATES 14
FFGHM 7:
3 *Gwanggaeto Daewang* (KDD-I) with 2 quad Mk141 lnchr with RGM-84 *Harpoon* AShM, 1 16 cell Mk48 VLS with *Sea Sparrow* SAM, 2 triple Mk32 324mm ASTT with Mk46 LWT, 1 *Goalkeeper* CIWS, 1 127mm gun (capacity 1 *Lynx* Mk99 hel)
4 *Incheon* with 2 quad lnchr with *Hae Sung* AShM, 1 21-cell Mk49 lnchr with RIM-116 SAM, 2 triple 324mm ASTT with K745 *Blue Shark* LWT, 1 Mk15 1B *Phalanx* CIWS, 1 127 mm gun
FFGM 7 *Ulsan* with 2 quad Mk141 lnchr with RGM-84C *Harpoon* AShM, 2 triple Mk32 324mm ASTT with Mk46 LWT, 2 76mm gun
PATROL AND COASTAL COMBATANTS ε109
CORVETTES • FSG 35:
17 *Gumdoksuri* with 2 twin lnchr with *Hae Sung* AShM, 1 76mm gun
18 *Po Hang* with 2 twin lnchr with RGM-84 *Harpoon* AShM, 2 triple 324mm ASTT with Mk46 LWT, 2 76mm gun
PBF ε74 *Sea Dolphin*
MINE WARFARE 10
MINE COUNTERMEASURES 9
MHO 6 *Kan Kyeong*
MSO 3 *Yang Yang*
MINELAYERS • ML 1 *Won San* with 2 triple Mk32 324mm ASTT, 1 76mm gun, 1 hel landing platform
AMPHIBIOUS
PRINCIPAL AMPHIBIOUS SHIPS 2
LHD
1 *Dokdo* with 1 Mk49 GMLS with RIM-116 SAM, 2 *Goalkeeper* CIWS (capacity 2 LCAC; 10 tanks; 700 troops; 10 UH-60 hel)
LPD 2:
1 *Cheonwangbong* (LST-II) (capacity 2 LCM; 300 troops; 2 UH-60 hel)
LANDING SHIPS • LST 4 *Go Jun Bong* with 1 hel landing platform (capacity 20 tanks; 300 troops)
LANDING CRAFT 41
LCAC 5: 3 *Tsaplya* (capacity 1 MBT; 130 troops); 2 LSF-II
LCM 10 LCM-8
LCT 6
LCVP 20

LOGISTICS AND SUPPORT 8
AG 1 *Sunjin* (trials spt)
AORH 3 *Chun Jee*
ARS 3: 1 *Cheong Hae Jin*; 2 *Pyong Taek* (ex-US *Edenton*)
ASR 1 *Tongyeong*

Naval Aviation
EQUIPMENT BY TYPE
AIRCRAFT 16 combat capable
ASW 16: 8 P-3C *Orion*; 8 P-3CK *Orion*
TPT • Light 5 Cessna F406 *Caravan* II
HELICOPTERS
ASW 27: 11 *Lynx* Mk99; 12 *Lynx* Mk99A; 4 AW159 *Wildcat*
MRH 3 SA319B *Alouette* III
TPT 15: **Medium** 8 UH-60P *Black Hawk* **Light** 7 Bell 205 (UH-1H *Iroquois*)

Marines 29,000
FORCES BY ROLE
SPECIAL FORCES
1 SF regt
MANOEUVRE
Amphibious
2 mne div (1 recce bn, 1 tk bn, 3 mne regt, 1 amph bn, 1 arty regt, 1 engr bn)
1 mne bde
COMBAT SUPPORT
Some cbt spt unit
EQUIPMENT BY TYPE
ARMOURED FIGHTING VEHICLES
MBT 100: 50 K1A1; 50 M48
AAV 166 AAV-7A1
ANTI-TANK/ANTI-INFRASTRUCTURE
MSL • SP *Spike* NLOS
ARTILLERY • TOWED 105mm; 155mm
COASTAL DEFENCE • AShM RGM-84A *Harpoon* (truck mounted)

Naval Special Warfare Flotilla

Air Force 65,000
4 Comd (Ops, Southern Combat, Logs, Trg)
FORCES BY ROLE
FIGHTER/GROUND ATTACK
3 sqn with F-4E *Phantom* II
6 sqn with F-5E/F *Tiger* II
3 sqn with F-15K *Eagle*
10 sqn with F-16C/D *Fighting Falcon* (KF-16C/D)
1 sqn with FA-50 *Fighting Eagle*
1 sqn with FA-50 *Fighting Eagle* (forming)
ISR
1 wg with KO-1
SIGINT
1 sqn with Hawker 800RA/XP
SEARCH & RESCUE
2 sqn with AS332L *Super Puma*; Bell 412EP; HH-47D *Chinook*; HH-60P *Black Hawk*; Ka-32 *Helix* C
TRANSPORT
1 VIP sqn with B-737-300; B-747; CN-235-220; S-92A *Superhawk*; VH-60P *Black Hawk* (VIP)

3 sqn (incl 1 Spec Ops) with C-130H/H-30/J-30 *Hercules*
2 sqn with CN-235M-100/220
TRAINING
2 sqn with F-5E/F *Tiger* II
1 sqn with F-16C/D *Fighting Falcon*
4 sqn with KT-1
1 sqn with Il-103
3 sqn with T-50/TA-50 *Golden Eagle**
TRANSPORT HELICOPTER
1 sqn with UH-60P *Black Hawk* (Spec Ops)
AIR DEFENCE
3 AD bde (total: 3 SAM bn with MIM-23B I-HAWK; 2 SAM bn with MIM-104E *Patriot* PAC-2 GEM-T)
EQUIPMENT BY TYPE
AIRCRAFT 567 combat capable
  FTR 174: 142 F-5E *Tiger* II; 32 F-5F *Tiger* II
  FGA 313: 70 F-4E *Phantom* II; 60 F-15K *Eagle*; 118 F-16C *Fighting Falcon* (KF-16C); 45 F-16D *Fighting Falcon* (KF-16D); 20 FA-50 *Fighting Eagle*
  AEW&C 4 B-737 AEW
  ISR 24: 4 Hawker 800RA; 20 KO-1
  SIGINT 4 Hawker 800SIG
  TPT 38: **Medium** 16: 8 C-130H *Hercules*; 4 C-130H-30 *Hercules*; 4 C-130J-30 *Hercules*; **Light** 20: 12 CN-235M-100; 8 CN-235M-220 (incl 2 VIP); **PAX** 2: 1 B-737-300; 1 B-747
  TRG 186: 23 Il-103; 83 KT-1; 49 T-50 *Golden Eagle**; 9 T-50B *Black Eagle** (aerobatics); 22 TA-50 *Golden Eagle**
HELICOPTERS
  SAR 16: 5 HH-47D *Chinook*; 11 HH-60P *Black Hawk*
  MRH 3 Bell 412EP
  TPT • **Medium** 30: 2 AS332L *Super Puma*; 8 Ka-32 *Helix* C; 3 S-92A *Super Hawk*; 7 UH-60P *Black Hawk*; 10 VH-60P *Black Hawk* (VIP)
UNMANNED AERIAL VEHICLES • **ISR** 103+: **Medium** 3+: some *Night Intruder*; 3 *Searcher* **Light** 100 *Harpy* (anti-radiation)
AIR DEFENCE • **SAM** 206
  Long-range 48 MIM-104E *Patriot* PAC-2 GEM-T
  Medium-range 158 MIM-23B I-HAWK
AIR-LAUNCHED MISSILES
  AAM • **IR** AIM-9 *Sidewinder*; **IIR** AIM-9X *Sidewinder* II; **SARH** AIM-7 *Sparrow*; **ARH** AIM-120B/C-5 AMRAAM
  ASM AGM-65A *Maverick*; AGM-130
  AShM AGM-84 *Harpoon*; AGM-142 *Popeye*
  ARM AGM-88 HARM
  ALCM AGM-84H SLAM-ER; KEPD-350 *Taurus*
BOMBS • **Laser-guided** *Paveway* II

Paramilitary 9,000 active

Civilian Defence Corps 3,000,000 reservists (to age 50)

Coast Guard 9,000
Part of the Ministry of Public Safety and Secuity. Five regional headquarters and 17 coastguard stations
EQUIPMENT BY TYPE
PATROL AND COASTAL COMBATANTS 84
  PSOH 2: 1 *Lee Cheong-ho* with 1 76mm gun; 1 *Sambongho*
  PSO 34: 3 *Han Kang* with 1 76mm gun, 1 hel landing platform; 5 *Han Kang* II with 1 76mm gun, 1 hel landing pllatform; 12 *Jaemin* with 1 hel landing platform; 1 *Sumjinkang*; 13 *Tae Pung Yang* with 1 hel landing platform
  PCO 15 *Tae Geuk*
  PCC 10: 4 *Bukhansan*; 6 (430 tonne)
  PB 23: 5 Hyundai Type; 14 *Hae Uri*; ε4 (various)
AMPHIBIOUS
  LANDING CRAFT • **UCAC** 8: 1 BHT-150; 4 *Griffon* 470TD; 3 *Griffon* 8000TD
AIRCRAFT
  MP 5: 1 C-212-400 MP; 4 CN-235-110 MPA
  TPT • **PAX** 1 CL-604
HELICOPTERS
  MRH 7: 5 AS565MB *Panther*; 1 AW139; 1 Bell 412SP
  TPT • **Medium** 8 Ka-32 *Helix* C

Cyber

South Korea established a Cyber Warfare Command Centre with over 200 personnel in early 2010, in the wake of a substantial distributed-denial-of-service attack in 2009. In early 2015, the Korea–US National Cyber Defense Cooperation Working Group was convened for the second time to share information and enhance cooepration in relation to policy, strategy, doctrine and training. The 2014 defence white paper referenced several changes, including the development of a master plan for defence cyber policy, the implementation of a joint cyber-operations manual and the creation of a new office for cyber operations in the Joint Chiefs of Staff office.

DEPLOYMENT

AFGHANISTAN
NATO • ISAF 50

ARABIAN SEA
Combined Maritime Forces • CTF-151: 1 DDGHM

CÔTE D'IVOIRE
UN • UNOCI 1 obs

INDIA/PAKISTAN
UN • UNMOGIP 7 obs

LEBANON
UN • UNIFIL 333; 1 mech inf bn

SOUTH SUDAN
UN • UNMISS 273; 2 obs; 1 engr coy

SUDAN
UN • UNAMID 2

UAE
128 (trg activities at UAE Spec Ops School)

WESTERN SAHARA
UN • MINURSO 4 obs

FOREIGN FORCES

Sweden NNSC: 5 obs

Switzerland NNSC: 5 obs

United States US Pacific Command: 28,500

Army 19,200; 1 HQ (8th Army) at Seoul; 1 div HQ (2nd Inf) at Tongduchon; 1 armd bde with M1 *Abrams*; M2/M3 *Bradley*; M109; 1 (cbt avn) hel bde with AH-64 *Apache*; CH-47 *Chinook*; UH-60 *Black Hawk*; 1 ISR hel bn with OH-58D *Kiowa Warrior*; 1 MRL bde with M270 MLRS; 1 AD bde with MIM 104 *Patriot*/FIM-92A *Avenger*; 1 (APS) armd bde eqpt set

Navy 250

USAF 8,800; 1 HQ (7th Air Force) at Osan AB; 1 ftr wg at Kunsan AB (2 ftr sqn with 20 F-16C/D *Fighting Falcon*); 1 ftr wg at Osan AB (1 ftr sqn with 20 F-16C/D *Fighting Falcon*, 1 atk sqn with 24 A-10C *Thunderbolt* II); 1 ISR sqn at Osan AB with U-2S

USMC 250

Laos LAO

New Lao Kip		2015	2016	2017
GDP	kip	103tr	113tr	
	US$	12.6bn	13.8bn	
per capita	US$	1,787	1,921	
Growth	%	7.6	7.5	
Inflation	%	5.3	-3.3	
Def exp	kip	n.k.	n.k.	
	US$	n.k.	n.k.	
FMA	US$	0.2m	0.2m	
US$1=kip		8,163.60	8,193.27	

Population 7,019,073

Ethnic groups: Lao 55%; Khmou 11%; Hmong 8%

Age	0–14	15–19	20–24	25–29	30–64	65 plus
Male	16.9%	5.6%	5.0%	4.4%	16.0%	1.7%
Female	16.5%	5.6%	5.1%	460.0%	16.5%	2.1%

Capabilities

The Lao People's Armed Forces (LPAF) have considerable military experience from the Second Indo-China War and the 1988 border war with Thailand. However, Laos is one of the world's poorest countries, and defence spending and military procurement have been limited for more than 20 years. The armed forces remain closely linked to the ruling Communist Party, and their primary role is internal security. Contacts with the Chinese and Vietnamese armed forces continue, but the LPAF have made no international deployments and have little capacity for sustained high-intensity operations. Laos participates in ADMM–Plus military exercises, and in 2014–15 was co-chair of the ADMM–Plus expert working group on HA/DR with Japan.

ACTIVE 29,100 (Army 25,600 Air 3,500) **Paramilitary 100,000**

Conscript liability 18 months minimum

ORGANISATIONS BY SERVICE

Space
EQUIPMENT BY TYPE
SATELLITES • ISR 1 LaoSat-1

Army 25,600
FORCES BY ROLE
4 mil regions
MANOEUVRE
  Armoured
  1 armd bn
  Light
  5 inf div
  7 indep inf regt
  65 indep inf coy
COMBAT SUPPORT
  5 arty bn
  1 engr regt
  2 (construction) engr regt
AIR DEFENCE
  9 ADA bn

EQUIPMENT BY TYPE
ARMOURED FIGHTING VEHICLES
  MBT 25: 15 T-54/T-55; 10 T-34/85
  LT TK 10 PT-76
  APC • APC (W) 50: 30 BTR-40/BTR-60; 20 BTR-152
ENGINEERING & MAINTENANCE VEHICLES
  ARV T-54/T-55
  VLB MTU
ANTI-TANK/ANTI-INFRASTRUCTURE • RCL 57mm M18/A1; **75mm** M20; **106mm** M40; **107mm** B-11
ARTILLERY 62+
  TOWED 62: **105mm** 20 M101; **122mm** 20 D-30/M-30 M-1938; **130mm** 10 M-46; **155mm** 12 M114
  MOR **81mm**; **82mm**; **107mm** M-1938/M2A1; **120mm** M-43
AIR DEFENCE
  SAM • Point-defence 9K32 *Strela*-2 (SA-7 *Grail*)‡; 25 9K310 *Igla*-1 (SA-16 *Gimlet*)
  GUNS
    SP **23mm** ZSU-23-4
    TOWED **14.5mm** ZPU-1/ZPU-4; **23mm** ZU-23; **37mm** M-1939; **57mm** S-60

Army Marine Section ε600
EQUIPMENT BY TYPE
PATROL AND COASTAL COMBATANTS • PBR 52†
AMPHIBIOUS LCM 4†

Air Force 3,500
FORCES BY ROLE
TRANSPORT
  1 sqn with An-2 *Colt*; An-26 *Curl*; An-74 *Coaler*; Y-7; Y-12; Yak-40 *Codling* (VIP)
TRAINING
  1 sqn with Yak-18 *Max*
TRANSPORT HELICOPTER
  1 sqn with Ka-32T *Helix* C; Mi-6 *Hook*; Mi-8 *Hip*; Mi-17 *Hip* H; Mi-26 *Halo*; SA360 *Dauphin*

EQUIPMENT BY TYPE
AIRCRAFT
TPT • **Light** 15: 4 An-2 *Colt*; 3 An-26 *Curl*; 1 An-74 *Coaler*; 5 Y-7; 1 Y-12; 1 Yak-40 *Codling* (VIP)
TRG 8 Yak-18 *Max*
HELICOPTERS
MRH 15: 11 Mi-17 *Hip* H; 4 Z-9A
TPT 15: **Heavy** 2: 1 Mi-6 *Hook*; 1 Mi-26 *Halo* **Medium** 10: 1 Ka-32T *Helix* C; 9 Mi-8 *Hip*
Light 3 SA360 *Dauphin*
AIR-LAUNCHED MISSILES • **AAM** • **IR** R-3 (AA-2 *Atoll*)†

Paramilitary

Militia Self-Defence Forces 100,000+
Village 'home guard' or local defence

Malaysia MYS

Malaysian Ringgit RM		2015	2016	2017
GDP	RM	1.16tr	1.24tr	
	US$	296bn	303bn	
per capita	US$	9,501	9,546	
Growth	%	5.0	4.3	
Inflation	%	2.1	2.1	
Def bdgt	RM	17.8bn	17.3bn	15.1bn
	US$	4.55bn	4.22bn	
US$1=RM		3.91	4.10	

Population 30,949,962

Ethnic groups: Malay 50.1%; Chinese 22.5%; Indian 6.5%; other or unspecified 20.9%

Age	0–14	15–19	20–24	25–29	30–64	65 plus
Male	14.5%	4.4%	4.2%	3.9%	21.0%	2.8%
Female	13.7%	4.2%	4.1%	3.9%	20.4%	3.1%

Capabilities

Over the last 30 years, substantial modernisation programmes have developed the Malaysian armed forces' capacity for external defence, notably by strengthening air and naval capabilities and moving the army's operational focus away from counter-insurgency and towards conventional warfare. The 2013 armed intrusion at Lahad Datu in Sabah state, the aftermath of the March 2014 disappearance of Malaysia Airlines flight MH370 and Chinese naval intrusions into Malaysia's EEZ in 2015–16 all revealed serious capability shortcomings, particularly in air and maritime surveillance. Addressing these capability gaps is a high priority for the armed forces, but budgetary constraints resulting from the Najib government's domestic priorities and low oil prices have slowed equipment procurement and infrastructural improvements. Army units have deployed on UN peacekeeping operations and the navy has achieved well-publicised successes with its anti-piracy patrols in the Gulf of Aden. Malaysian forces regularly participate in Five Power Defence Arrangements, ADMM–Plus and other exercises with regional and international partners, including the US. While senior naval officers may nominally support plans revealed in October 2016 to purchase Chinese naval vessels, they may also be concerned over the implications of buying arms from a country whose claims over and activities in regional waters are assessed to threaten Malaysian security interests.

ACTIVE 109,000 (Army 80,000 Navy 14,000 Air 15,000) Paramilitary 24,600

RESERVE 51,600 (Army 50,000, Navy 1,000 Air Force 600) Paramilitary 244,700

ORGANISATIONS BY SERVICE

Army 80,000 (to be 60–70,000)
2 mil region, 4 area comd (div)

FORCES BY ROLE
SPECIAL FORCES
  1 SF bde (3 SF bn)
MANOEUVRE
  Armoured
  1 tk regt (5 armd bn)
  Mechanised
  5 armd regt
  1 mech inf bde (3 mech bn, 1 cbt engr sqn)
  Light
  1 inf bde (4 inf bn, 1 arty regt)
  5 inf bde (3 inf bn, 1 arty regt)
  2 inf bde (2 inf bn)
  1 inf bde (2 inf bn)
  Air Manoeuvre
  1 (Rapid Deployment Force) AB bde (1 lt tk sqn, 3 AB bn, 1 lt arty regt, 1 engr sqn)
  Other
  1 (border) sy bde (5 bn)
  1 (border) sy bde (forming)
COMBAT SUPPORT
  9 arty regt
  1 STA regt
  1 MRL regt
  1 cbt engr sqn
  3 fd engr regt (total: 7 cbt engr sqn, 3 engr spt sqn)
  1 construction regt
  1 int unit
  4 MP regt
  1 sigs regt
HELICOPTER
  1 hel sqn
AIR DEFENCE
  3 ADA regt
EQUIPMENT BY TYPE
ARMOURED FIGHTING VEHICLES
  MBT 48 PT-91M *Twardy*
  LT TK 21 *Scorpion*-90
  RECCE 214: 130 AML-60/90; 74 SIBMAS (some†); 10 VBL
  IFV 71+: 31 ACV300 *Adnan* (25mm *Bushmaster*); 13 ACV300 *Adnan* AGL; 27+ AV8 *Gempita* IFV25

APC 777
   APC (T) 265: 149 ACV300 *Adnan* (incl 69 variants); 13 FV4333 *Stormer* (upgraded); 63 K-200A; 40 K-200A1
   APC (W) 512: 32 *Anoa*; 300 *Condor* (incl variants); 150 LAV-150 *Commando*; 30 M3 Panhard
ENGINEERING & MAINTENANCE VEHICLES
   AEV 9: 3 MID-M; 6 WZT-4
   ARV 41+: *Condor*; 15 ACV300; 4 K-288A1; 22 SIBMAS
   VLB 5+: *Leguan*; 5 PMCz-90
NBC VEHICLES K216A1
ANTI-TANK/ANTI-INFRASTRUCTURE • MSL
   SP 8 ACV300 *Baktar Shikan*; K263
   MANPATS 9K115 *Metis* (AT-7 *Saxhorn*); 9K115-2 *Metis*-M (AT-13 *Saxhorn* 2); *Eryx*; *Baktar Shihan* (HJ-8); SS.11
   RCL 260: **84mm** 236 *Carl Gustav*; **106mm** 24 M40
ARTILLERY 424
   TOWED 134: **105mm** 100 Model 56 pack howitzer; **155mm** 34: 12 FH-70; 22 G-5
   MRL 36 ASTROS II (equipped with 127mm SS-30)
   MOR 254: **81mm** 232; **SP 81mm** 14: 4 K281A1; 10 ACV300-S; **SP 120mm** 8 ACV-S
AMPHIBIOUS • LANDING CRAFT
   LCA 165 Damen Assault Craft 540 (capacity 10 troops)
HELICOPTERS • TPT • Light 10 AW109
AIR DEFENCE
   SAM • Point-defence 15+: 15 *Jernas* (*Rapier* 2000); *Anza*; HY-6 (FN-6); 9K38 *Igla* (SA-18 *Grouse*); QW-1 *Vanguard*;
   GUNS • TOWED 52: **35mm** 16 GDF-005; **40mm** 36 L40/70

Reserves

Territorial Army
Some paramilitary forces to be incorporated into a re-organised territorial organisation
FORCES BY ROLE
MANOEUVRE
   Mechanised
      4 armd sqn
   Light
      16 inf regt (3 inf bn)
   Other
      5 (highway) sy bn
COMBAT SUPPORT
   5 arty bty
   2 fd engr regt
   1 int unit
   3 sigs sqn
COMBAT SUPPORT
   4 med coy
   5 tpt coy

Navy 14,000

3 Regional Commands; Kuantan (East Coast); Kinabalu (Borneo) & Langkawi (West Coast)
EQUIPMENT BY TYPE
SUBMARINES • TACTICAL • SSK 2 *Tunku Abdul Rahman* (FRA *Scorpene*) with 6 single 533mm TT with WASS *Black Shark* HWT/SM-39 *Exocet* AShM

PRINCIPAL SURFACE COMBATANTS 10
   FRIGATES 10
   FFGHM 2:
      2 *Lekiu* with 2 quad lnchr with MM-40 *Exocet* Block II AShM, 1 16-cell VLS with *Sea Wolf* SAM, 2 B515 ILAS-3 triple 324mm ASTT with *Sting Ray* LWT, 1 57mm gun (capacity 1 *Super Lynx* hel)
   FFG 2:
      2 *Kasturi* with 2 quad lnchr with MM-40 *Exocet* Block II AShM, 1 twin 375mm A/S mor, 1 100mm gun, 1 57mm gun, 1 hel landing platform
   FF 6:
      6 *Kedah* (GER MEKO) with 1 76mm gun, 1 hel landing platform, (fitted for MM-40 *Exocet* AShM & RAM CIWS)
PATROL AND COASTAL COMBATANTS 37
   CORVETTES • FSGM 4 *Laksamana* with 3 twin lnchr with Mk 2 *Otomat* AShM, 1 *Albatros* quad lnchr with *Aspide* SAM, 1 76mm gun
   PCFG 4 *Perdana* (FRA *Combattante* II) with 2 single lnchr with MM-38 *Exocet* AShM, 1 57mm gun
   PBG 4 *Handalan* (SWE *Spica*-M) with 2 twin lnchr with MM-38 *Exocet* AShM, 1 57mm gun
   PBF 17 *Tempur* (SWE CB90)
   PB 8: 6 *Jerong* (Lurssen 45) with 1 57mm gun; 2 *Sri Perlis*
MINE WARFARE • MINE COUNTERMEASURES 4
   MCO 4 *Mahamiru* (ITA *Lerici*)
LOGISTICS AND SUPPORT 13
   AG 2 *Bunga Mas Lima* with 1 hel landing platform
   AGS 2: 1 *Mutiara* with 1 hel landing platform; 1 *Perantau*
   AP 2 *Sri Gaya*
   AOR 2: 1 *Mahawangsa* with 2 57mm guns; 1 *Sri Indera Sakti* with 1 57mm gun
   ASR 1 *Mega Bakti*
   ATF 2
   AX 1 *Hang Tuah* with 1 57mm gun, 1 hel landing platform
   AXS 1

Naval Aviation 160

EQUIPMENT BY TYPE
HELICOPTERS
   ASW 6 *Super Lynx* 300
   MRH 6 AS555 *Fennec*
AIR-LAUNCHED MISSILES • AShM *Sea Skua*

Special Forces

FORCES BY ROLE
SPECIAL FORCES
   1 (mne cdo) SF unit

Air Force 15,000

1 air op HQ, 2 air div, 1 trg and log comd, 1 Intergrated Area Def Systems HQ
Flying hours 60 hrs/yr
FORCES BY ROLE
FIGHTER
   2 sqn with MiG-29/MiG-29UB *Fulcrum*

FIGHTER/GROUND ATTACK
  1 sqn with F/A-18D *Hornet*
  1 sqn with Su-30MKM *Flanker*
  2 sqn with *Hawk* Mk108*/Mk208*
FIGHTER/GROUND ATTACK/ISR
  1 sqn with F-5E/F *Tiger* II; RF-5E *Tigereye**
MARITIME PATROL
  1 sqn with Beech 200T
TANKER/TRANSPORT
  2 sqn with KC-130H *Hercules*; C-130H *Hercules*;
  C-130H-30 *Hercules*; Cessna 402B
TRANSPORT
  1 (VIP) sqn with A319CT; AW109; B-737-700 BBJ; BD700 *Global Express*; F-28 *Fellowship*; *Falcon* 900
  1 sqn with CN-235
TRAINING
  1 unit with PC-7; SA316 *Alouette* III
TRANSPORT HELICOPTER
  4 (tpt/SAR) sqn with H225M *Super Cougar*; S-61A-4 *Nuri*; S-61N; S-70A *Black Hawk*
AIR DEFENCE
  1 sqn with *Starburst*
SPECIAL FORCES
  1 (Air Force Commando) unit (airfield defence/SAR)
EQUIPMENT BY TYPE
AIRCRAFT 67 combat capable
  FTR 21: 8 F-5E *Tiger* II; 3 F-5F *Tiger* II; 8 MiG-29 *Fulcrum* (MiG-29N); 2 MiG-29UB *Fulcrum* (MIG-29NUB)
  FGA 26: 8 F/A-18D *Hornet*; 18 Su-30MKM
  ISR 6: 4 Beech 200T; 2 RF-5E *Tigereye**
  TKR 4 KC-130H *Hercules*
  TPT 36: **Heavy** 3 A400M *Atlas*; **Medium** 10: 2 C-130H *Hercules*; 8 C-130H-30 *Hercules*; **Light** 18: 9 CN-235M-220 (incl 1 VIP); 9 Cessna 402B (2 modified for aerial survey); **PAX** 5: 1 A319CT; 1 B-737-700 BBJ; 1 BD700 *Global Express*; 1 F-28 *Fellowship*; 1 *Falcon* 900
  TRG 79: 6 *Hawk* Mk108*; 12 *Hawk* Mk208*; 7 MB-339C; 7 MD3-160 *Aero Tiga*; 30 PC-7; 17 PC-7 Mk II *Turbo Trainer*
HELICOPTERS
  MRH 17 SA316 *Alouette* III
  TPT 44: **Heavy** 12 H225M *Super Cougar*; **Medium** 31: 27 S-61A-4 *Nuri*; 2 S-61N; 2 S-70A *Black Hawk*; **Light** 1 AW109
UNMANNED AERIAL VEHICLES
  ISR • **Medium** *Aludra*
AIR DEFENCE • **SAM** • **Point-defence** *Starburst*
AIR-LAUNCHED MISSILES
  AAM • **IR** AIM-9 *Sidewinder*; R-73 (AA-11 *Archer*); **IIR** AIM-9X *Sidewinder* II; **IR/SARH** R-27 (AA-10 *Alamo*); **SARH** AIM-7 *Sparrow*; **ARH** AIM-120C AMRAAM; R-77 (AA-12 *Adder*)
  ASM AGM-65 *Maverick*
  AShM AGM-84D *Harpoon*
BOMBS • **Laser-guided** *Paveway* II

Paramilitary ε24,600

Police–General Ops Force 18,000
FORCES BY ROLE
COMMAND
  5 bde HQ

SPECIAL FORCES
  1 spec ops bn
MANOEUVRE
  Other
  19 paramilitary bn
  2 (Aboriginal) paramilitary bn
  4 indep paramilitary coy
EQUIPMENT BY TYPE
ARMOURED FIGHTING VEHICLES
  RECCE 192: ε100 S52 *Shorland*; 92 FV701 *Ferret* (60 mod)
  APC • **APC (W)** 170: 140 AT105 *Saxon*
  AUV ε30 SB-301

Malaysian Maritime Enforcement Agency (MMEA) ε4,500

Controls 5 Maritime Regions (Northern Peninsula; Southern Peninsula; Eastern Peninsula; Sarawak; Sabah), subdivided into a further 18 Maritime Districts. Supported by one provisional MMEA Air Unit

EQUIPMENT BY TYPE
PATROL AND COASTAL COMBATANTS 185
  PSO 2 *Langkawi* with 1 57mm gun, 1 hel landing platform
  PBF 57: 18 *Penggalang* 17 (TUR MRTP 16); 2 *Penggalang* 18; 6 *Penyelamat* 20; 16 *Penggalang* 16; 15 *Tugau*
  PB 126: 15 *Gagah*; 4 *Malawali*; 2 *Nusa*; 3 *Nusa* 28; 1 *Peninjau*; 7 *Ramunia*; 2 *Rhu*; 4 *Semilang*; 9 *Sipadan* (ex-*Kris*/*Sabah*); 8 *Icarus* 1650; 10 *Pengawal*; 10 *Pengawal* 13; 27 *Pengawal* 23; 4 *Penyelamat*; 2 *Perwira*; 9 *Sipadan Steel*; 9 *Sipadan Kayu*
LOGISTICS AND SUPPORT • **AX** 1 *Marlin*
AIRCRAFT • **MP** 2 Bombardier 415MP
HELICOPTERS • **MRH** 3 AS365 *Dauphin*

Marine Police 2,100
EQUIPMENT BY TYPE
PATROL AND COASTAL COMBATANTS 132
  PBF 12: 6 *Sangitan*; 6 Stan Patrol 1500
  PB/PBR 120

Police Air Unit
EQUIPMENT BY TYPE
AIRCRAFT
  TPT • **Light** 17: 4 Cessna 206 *Stationair*; 6 Cessna 208 *Caravan*; 7 PC-6 *Turbo-Porter*
HELICOPTERS
  TPT • **Light** 2: 1 Bell 206L *Long Ranger*; 1 AS355F *Ecureuil* II

Area Security Units (R) 3,500
(Auxiliary General Ops Force)
FORCES BY ROLE
MANOEUVRE
  Other
  89 paramilitary unit

Border Scouts (R) 1,200
in Sabah, Sarawak

People's Volunteer Corps 240,000 reservists (some 17,500 armed)

RELA

Customs Service

EQUIPMENT BY TYPE
PATROL AND COASTAL COMBATANTS 23
　PBF 10
　PB 13

DEPLOYMENT

DEMOCRATIC REPUBLIC OF THE CONGO
UN • MONUSCO 5; 10 obs

LEBANON
UN • UNIFIL 818; 1 mech inf bn

LIBERIA
UN • UNMIL 1; 2 obs

PHILIPPINES
IMT 11

SUDAN
UN • UNAMID 9; 1 obs
UN • UNISFA 1 obs

WESTERN SAHARA
UN • MINURSO 5 obs

FOREIGN FORCES

Australia 130; 1 inf coy (on 3-month rotational tours); 1 AP-3C *Orion* on occasion

Mongolia MNG

Mongolian Tugrik t		2015	2016	2017
GDP	t	23.1tr	24.0tr	
	US$	11.7bn	11.2bn	
per capita	US$	3,946	3,704	
Growth	%	2.4	0.0	
Inflation	%	5.9	2.4	
Def bdgt	t	201bn	251bn	224bn
	US$	102m	117m	
FMA (US)	US$	2m	1.6m	1.6m
US$1=t		1,974.23	2,149.53	

Population 3,031,330

Ethnic groups: Khalkh 81.9%; Kazak 3.8%; Dorvod 2.7%; other or unspecified 11.6%

Age	0–14	15–19	20–24	25–29	30–64	65 plus
Male	13.7%	4.1%	4.4%	5.2%	19.8%	1.7%
Female	13.2%	4.0%	4.3%	5.3%	21.7%	2.5%

Capabilities

Mongolia's small armed forces remain reliant on Soviet-era equipment, although this has been supplemented by recent deliveries of second-hand Russian armaments. Positioned between much stronger neighbours, territorial integrity would be difficult to maintain in the event of an inter-state conflict. This has encouraged Mongolia to pursue strong defence ties and bilateral training with multiple regional powers, as well as the US. The army has focused its development on peacekeeping operations, and the country hosts *Khaan Quest*, an annual multilateral peacekeeping exercise.

ACTIVE 9,700 (Army 8,900 Air 800) **Paramilitary 7,500**

Conscript liability One year for males aged 18–25

RESERVE 137,000 (Army 137,000)

ORGANISATIONS BY SERVICE

Army 5,600; 3,300 conscript (total 8,900)

FORCES BY ROLE
MANOEUVRE
　Mechanised
　1 MR bde
　Light
　1 (rapid deployment) lt inf bn (2nd bn to form)
　Air Manoeuvre
　1 AB bn
COMBAT SUPPORT
　1 arty regt
EQUIPMENT BY TYPE
ARMOURED FIGHTING VEHICLES
　MBT 420: 370 T-54/T-55; 50 T-72A
　RECCE 120 BRDM-2
　IFV 310 BMP-1
　APC • APC (W) 210: 150 BTR-60; 40 BTR-70M; 20 BTR-80
ENGINEERING & MAINTENANCE VEHICLES
　ARV T-54/T-55
ANTI-TANK/ANTI-INFRASTRUCTURE
　GUNS • TOWED 200: 85mm D-44/D-48; 100mm M-1944/MT-12
ARTILLERY 570
　TOWED ε300: 122mm D-30/M-30 (M-1938); 130mm M-46; 152mm ML-20 (M-1937)
　MRL 122mm 130 BM-21
　MOR 140: 120mm; 160mm; 82mm
AIR DEFENCE • SAM • Medium-range 2+ S-125 *Pechora-2M* (SA-26)

Air Force 800

FORCES BY ROLE
TRANSPORT
　1 sqn with An-24 *Coke*; An-26 *Curl*
ATTACK/TRANSPORT HELICOPTER
　1 sqn with Mi-8 *Hip*; Mi-171
AIR DEFENCE
　2 regt with S-60/ZPU-4/ZU-23
EQUIPMENT BY TYPE
AIRCRAFT • TPT • Light 3: 2 An-24 *Coke*; 1 An-26 *Curl*
HELICOPTERS
　TPT • Medium 12: 10 Mi-8 *Hip*; 2 Mi-171

AIR DEFENCE • GUNS • TOWED 150: **14.5mm** ZPU-4; **23mm** ZU-23; **57mm** S-60

Paramilitary 7,500 active

Border Guard 1,300; 4,700 conscript (total 6,000)

Internal Security Troops 400; 800 conscript (total 1,200)
FORCES BY ROLE
MANOEUVRE
Other
4 gd unit

Construction Troops 300

DEPLOYMENT

AFGHANISTAN
NATO • *Operation Resolute Support* 120
UN • UNAMA 1 obs

DEMOCRATIC REPUBLIC OF THE CONGO
UN • MONUSCO 1 obs

SOUTH SUDAN
UN • UNMISS 863; 7 obs; 1 inf bn

SUDAN
UN • UNAMID 70; 1 fd hospital
UN • UNISFA 2 obs

WESTERN SAHARA
UN • MINURSO 4 obs

Myanmar MMR

Myanmar Kyat K			2015	2016	2017
GDP		K	72.2tr	86.8tr	
		US$	62.9bn	68.3bn	
per capita		US$	1,213	1,307	
Growth		%	7.0	8.1	
Inflation		%	11.4	9.8	
Def bdgt		K	2.61tr	2.88tr	
		US$	2.27bn	2.26bn	
US$1=K			1,147.98	1,270.56	

Population 56,890,418

Ethnic groups: Burman 68%; Shan 9%; Karen 7%; Rakhine 4%; Chinese 3+%; Other Chin, Kachin, Kayan, Lahu, Mon, Palaung, Pao, Wa, 9%

Age	0–14	15–19	20–24	25–29	30–64	65 plus
Male	13.1%	4.4%	4.5%	4.5%	20.7%	2.4%
Female	12.6%	4.3%	4.4%	4.4%	21.4%	3.1%

Capabilities

Myanmar's large, army-dominated Tatmadaw (armed forces) have, since the country's independence struggle in the 1940s, been intimately involved in domestic politics. Even though the National League for Democracy (NLD) won the November 2015 election, the armed forces remain politically important, with control of key ministries (including defence) and the automatic right to 25% of parliamentary seats. The primary focus of the *Tatmadaw* has always been maintaining internal security, particularly in the face of the world's longest-running insurgencies, conducted by the Karen, Kachin, Mon, Shan and other ethnic-minority groups. In late 2016, fighting continued with several 'non-ceasefire groups', including Karen Independence Army, Shan State Army–North and Ta'ang National Liberation Army. Morale among ordinary soldiers (mainly conscripts) is reportedly low. While the army grew substantially after the military seized power in 1988, its counter-insurgency focus means it remains essentially a light-infantry force. Nevertheless, since the 1990s, the armed forces have attempted to develop limited conventional-warfare capabilities and have brought into service new armoured vehicles, air-defence weapons, artillery, combat aircraft and ships, procured from China, Russia and other diverse sources. The NLD government's dependence on military goodwill implies that defence spending is likely to continue increasing. However, Western arms embargoes are unlikely to be lifted in the absence of a comprehensive peace settlement with the ethnic-minority armed groups. (See p. 263.)

ACTIVE 406,000 (Army 375,000 Navy 16,000 Air 15,000) Paramilitary 107,250
Conscript liability 24–36 months

ORGANISATIONS BY SERVICE

Army ε375,000
14 military regions, 7 regional op comd
FORCES BY ROLE
COMMAND
  20 div HQ (military op comd)
  10 inf div HQ
  34+ bde HQ (tactical op comd)
MANOEUVRE
  Armoured
  10 armd bn
  Light
  100 inf bn (coy)
  337 inf bn (coy) (regional comd)
COMBAT SUPPORT
  7 arty bn
  37 indep arty coy
  6 cbt engr bn
  54 fd engr bn
  40 int coy
  45 sigs bn
AIR DEFENCE
  7 AD bn
EQUIPMENT BY TYPE
ARMOURED FIGHTING VEHICLES
  MBT 185+: 10 T-55; 50 T-72S; 25+ Type-59D; 100 Type-69-II
  LT TK 105 Type-63 (ε60 serviceable)

ASLT 24 PTL-02 mod
RECCE 87+: 12+ EE-9 *Cascavel*; 45 *Ferret*; 30 Mazda
IFV 10+ BTR-3U
APC 391+
  APC (T) 331: 26 MT-LB; 250 Type-85; 55 Type-90
  APC (W) 90+: 20 Hino; 40 Humber *Pig*; 30+ Type-92
  PPV 10 MPV
ENGINEERING & MAINTENANCE VEHICLES
  ARV Type-72
  VLB MT-55A
ANTI-TANK/ANTI-INFRASTRUCTURE
  RCL 1,000+: **84mm** ε1,000 *Carl Gustav*; **106mm** M40A1
  GUNS • TOWED 60: **57mm** 6-pdr; **76mm** 17-pdr
ARTILLERY 419+
  SP 155mm 42: 30 NORA B-52; 12 SH-1
  TOWED 264+: **105mm** 132: 36 M-56; 96 M101; **122mm** 100 D-30; **130mm** 16 M-46; **140mm**; **155mm** 16 Soltam M-845P
  MRL 36+: **107mm** 30 Type-63; **122mm** BM-21 *Grad* (reported); Type-81; **240mm** 6+ M-1985 mod
  MOR 80+: **82mm** Type-53 (M-37); **120mm** 80+: 80 Soltam; Type-53 (M-1943)
SURFACE-TO-SURFACE MISSILE LAUNCHERS
  SRBM • Conventional some *Hwasong*-6 (reported)
AIR DEFENCE
  SAM
    Medium-range 4+: 4 KS-1A (HQ-12); S-125 *Pechora*-2M (SA-26); 2K12 *Kvadrat*-M (SA-6 *Gainful*)
    Point-defence Some 2K22 *Tunguska* (SA-19 *Grison*); HN-5 *Hong Nu/Red Cherry* (reported); 9K310 *Igla*-1 (SA-16 *Gimlet*)
  GUNS 46 **SP 57mm** 12 Type-80
  TOWED 34: **37mm** 24 Type-74; **40mm** 10 M1

Navy ε16,000
EQUIPMENT BY TYPE
PRINCIPAL SURFACE COMBATANTS • FRIGATES 5
  FFGH 2 *Kyansitthar* with 2 twin lnchr with DPRK AShM (possibly KN-01), 4 AK630 CIWS, 1 76mm gun (capacity 1 med hel)
  FFG 3:
    1 *Aung Zeya* with 2 twin lnchr with DPRK AShM (possibly KN-01), 4 AK630 CIWS, 1 76mm gun, 1 hel landing platform
    2 *Mahar Bandoola* (PRC Type-053H1) with 2 quad lnchr with C-802 (CSS-N-8 *Saccade*) AShM, 2 RBU 1200 A/S mor, 2 twin 100mm gun
PATROL AND COASTAL COMBATANTS 113
  CORVETTES • FSG 2 *Anawrahta* with 2 twin lnchr with C-802 (CSS-N-8 *Saccade*) AShM; 1 76mm gun, 1 hel landing platform
  PCG 7: 6 *Houxin* with 2 twin lnchr with C-801 (CSS-N-4 *Sardine*) AShM; 1 Type-491 with 2 twin lnchr with C-802 (CSS-N-8 *Saccade*) AShM
  PCO 2 *Indaw*
  PCC 9 *Hainan* with 4 RBU 1200 A/S mor, 2 twin 57mm gun
  PBG 4 *Myanmar* with 2 twin lnchr with C-801 (CSS-N-4 *Sardine*) AShM
  PBF 1 Type-201
  PB 31: 3 PB-90; 6 PGM 401; 6 PGM 412; 13 *Myanmar*; 3 *Swift*
  PBR 57: 4 *Sagu*; 9 Y-301†; 1 Y-301 (Imp); 43 (various)
AMPHIBIOUS • CRAFT 9: 3 LCU 6 **LCM**
LOGISTICS AND SUPPORT 19
  ABU 1; **AGS** 1; **AH** 2; **AK** 1; **AKSL** 5; **AP** 9

Naval Infantry 800
FORCES BY ROLE
MANOEUVRE
  Light
  1 inf bn

Air Force ε15,000
FORCES BY ROLE
FIGHTER
  4 sqn with F-7 *Airguard*; FT-7; MiG-29B *Fulcrum*; MiG-29UB *Fulcrum*
GROUND ATTACK
  2 sqn with A-5M *Fantan*
TRANSPORT
  1 sqn with An-12 *Cub*; F-27 *Friendship*; FH-227; PC-6A/B *Turbo Porter*
TRAINING
  2 sqn with G-4 *Super Galeb**; PC-7 *Turbo Trainer**; PC-9*
  1 (trg/liaison) sqn with Cessna 550 *Citation* II; Cessna 180 *Skywagon*; K-8 *Karakorum**
TRANSPORT HELICOPTER
  4 sqn with Bell 205; Bell 206 *Jet Ranger*; Mi-17 *Hip* H; Mi-35P *Hind*; PZL Mi-2 *Hoplite*; PZL W-3 *Sokol*; SA316 *Alouette* III
EQUIPMENT BY TYPE
AIRCRAFT 167 combat capable
  FTR 88: 49 F-7 *Airguard*; 10 FT-7; 18 MiG-29 *Fulcrum*; 6 MiG-29SE *Fulcrum*; 5 MiG-29UB *Fulcrum*
  ATK 22 A-5M *Fantan*
  TPT 24: **Medium** 6: 4 Y-8D; 2 Y-8F-200W **Light** 16: 3 Beech 1900D; 4 Cessna 180 *Skywagon*; 1 Cessna 550 *Citation* II; 3 F-27 *Friendship*; 5 PC-6A/B *Turbo Porter*; **PAX** 4 FH-227
  TRG 87: 12 G-4 *Super Galeb**; 20 Grob G120; 24+ K-8 *Karakorum**; 12 PC-7 *Turbo Trainer**; 9 PC-9*
HELICOPTERS
  ATK 12 Mi-35P *Hind*
  MRH 23: 3 AS365; 11 Mi-17 *Hip* H; 9 SA316 *Alouette* III
  TPT 45: **Medium** 10 PZL W-3 *Sokol*; **Light** 35: 12 Bell 205; 6 Bell 206 *Jet Ranger*; 17 PZL Mi-2 *Hoplite*
AIR-LAUNCHED MISSILES • AAM • IR PL-5; R-73 (AA-11 *Archer*); **IR/SARH** R-27 (AA-10 *Alamo*)

Paramilitary 107,250

People's Police Force 72,000

People's Militia 35,000

People's Pearl and Fishery Ministry ε250
EQUIPMENT BY TYPE
PATROL AND COASTAL COMBATANTS • PBR 6 *Carpentaria*

DEPLOYMENT

LIBERIA
UN • UNMIL 2 obs

SOUTH SUDAN
UN • UNMISS 2

Nepal NPL

Nepalese Rupee NR		2015	2016	2017
GDP	NR	2.12tr	2.25tr	
	US$	21.3bn	21.2bn	
per capita	US$	748	734	
Growth	%	2.7	0.6	
Inflation	%	7.2	10.0	
Def bdgt	NR	33.4bn	35.9bn	39.5bn
	US$	336m	338m	
FMA (US)	US$	3.8m	5m	1.7m
US$1=NR		99.49	106.30	

Population 29,033,914

Religious groups: Hindu 90%; Buddhist 5%; Muslim 3%

Age	0–14	15–19	20–24	25–29	30–64	65 plus
Male	16.0%	5.6%	5.3%	3.8%	15.4%	2.5%
Female	15.0%	5.5%	5.4%	4.7%	18.3%	2.5%

Capabilities

The principal role of Nepal's armed forces is maintaining territorial integrity, but they have also traditionally focused on internal security. The army's pre-eminence reflects the country's history of counter-insurgency operations in the 1990s and 2000s, as well as explosive-ordnance-disposal activities. Nepal's logistic capability appears to be sufficient for internal-security operations, however its contingents on UN peacekeeping operations appear to largely depend on contracted logistic support. The US recently donated modern HF and VHF radios to the armed forces for disaster-relief operations. Training support is provided by several countries, including China, India and the US. Following a 2006 peace accord with the Maoist People's Liberation Army, Maoist personnel underwent a process of demobilisation or integration into the armed forces. Gurkhas continue to be recruited by the Indian and British armed forces and the Singaporean police. In 2016, India increased the size of its Gurkha Rifles unit, comprising Gurkhas resident in India. The small air wing provides a limited transport and support capacity but mobility remains a challenge, in part because of the country's difficult topography. This deficit was highlighted by the country's considerable dependence on foreign military assistance following the earthquake in April 2015.

ACTIVE 96,600 (Army 96,600) Paramilitary 62,000

ORGANISATIONS BY SERVICE

Army 96,600

FORCES BY ROLE
COMMAND
  6 inf div HQ
  1 (valley) comd
SPECIAL FORCES
  1 bde (1 SF bn, 1 AB bn, 1 cdo bn, 1 ranger bn, 1 mech inf bn)
MANOEUVRE
  Light
  16 inf bde (total: 62 inf bn; 32 indep inf coy)
COMBAT SUPPORT
  4 arty regt
  5 engr bn
AIR DEFENCE
  2 AD regt
  4 indep AD coy
EQUIPMENT BY TYPE
ARMOURED FIGHTING VEHICLES
  RECCE 40 *Ferret*
  APC 253
    APC (W) 13: 8 OT-64C; 5 WZ-551
    PPV 240: 90 *Casspir*; 150 MPV
ARTILLERY 92+
  TOWED 105mm 22: 8 L118 Light Gun; 14 Pack Howitzer (6 non-operational)
  MOR 70+: 81mm; 120mm 70 M-43 (est 12 op)
AIR DEFENCE • GUNS • TOWED 32+: 14.5mm 30 Type-56 (ZPU-4); 37mm (PRC); 40mm 2 L/60

Air Wing 320

EQUIPMENT BY TYPE†
AIRCRAFT • TPT 3: Light 3: 1 BN-2T *Islander*; 2 M-28 *Skytruck*;
HELICOPTERS
  MRH 12: 2 *Dhruv*; 2 *Lancer*; 3 Mi-17-1V *Hip* H; 2 Mi-17V-5 *Hip*; 1 SA315B *Lama* (*Cheetah*); 2 SA316B *Alouette* III
  TPT 3: Medium 1 SA330J *Puma*; Light 2 AS350B2 *Ecureuil*

Paramilitary 62,000

Armed Police Force 15,000
Ministry of Home Affairs

Police Force 47,000

DEPLOYMENT

CENTRAL AFRICAN REPUBLIC
UN • MINUSCA 65; 3 obs; 1 MP pl

CÔTE D'IVOIRE
UN • UNOCI 1; 3 obs

DEMOCRATIC REPUBLIC OF THE CONGO
UN • MONUSCO 1,029; 189 obs; 1 inf bn; 1 engr coy

HAITI
UN • MINUSTAH 2

IRAQ
UN • UNAMI 76; 1 sy unit

LEBANON
UN • UNIFIL 867; 1 mech inf bn

LIBERIA
UN • UNMIL 17; 2 obs

MALI
UN • MINUSMA 146; 3 obs; 1 EOD coy

SOMALIA
UN • UNSOM 1 obs

SOUTH SUDAN
UN • UNMISS 1,579; 12 obs; 2 inf bn

SUDAN
UN • UNAMID 362; 8 obs; 1 SF coy; 1 inf coy
UN • UNISFA 2; 3 obs

SYRIA/ISRAEL
UN • UNDOF 200; 1 inf coy

WESTERN SAHARA
UN • MINURSO 2 obs

FOREIGN FORCES

United Kingdom 60 (Gurkha trg org)

New Zealand NZL

New Zealand Dollar NZ$		2015	2016	2017
GDP	NZ$	246bn	257bn	
	US$	172bn	179bn	
per capita	US$	37,066	38,066	
Growth	%	3.0	2.8	
Inflation	%	0.3	0.7	
Def bdgt	NZ$	3.12bn	3.70bn	3.18bn
	US$	2.18bn	2.58bn	
US$1=NZ$		1.43	1.43	

Population 4,474,549

Age	0–14	15–19	20–24	25–29	30–64	65 plus
Male	10.1%	3.4%	3.5%	3.4%	22.4%	6.9%
Female	9.6%	3.3%	3.3%	3.4%	22.6%	8.0%

Capabilities

Reflecting its geographical isolation and the absence of immediate threats, limited defence spending has kept the New Zealand Defence Force (NZDF) small and, according to critics, in some respects under-equipped. Nevertheless, New Zealand has a strong military tradition and the NZDF is well trained and has operational experience. More than 3,500 New Zealand military personnel served in Afghanistan in 2003–13 and, since 2015, around 100 NZDF troops have been based in Iraq in a capacity-building role. The June 2016 defence white paper – the first since 2010 – foresaw a range of challenges likely to affect New Zealand's security in the period to 2040, including increased activity by a range of actors in the country's EEZ, the Southern Ocean and the South Pacific; an increased risk of terrorist attacks; and rising tension in the South and East China seas. In response, New Zealand's 'refreshed' defence policy will place greater emphasis on awareness of and capacity to respond to activity in its maritime domain; the country's interests in Antarctica and the Southern Ocean; and the need to maintain the international 'rules-based order'. The white paper indicated there would be future investment in improved maritime air-surveillance capability; an ice-strengthened third OPV for patrolling the Southern Ocean; 'enhanced littoral operations support capability' in the form of a more capable support vessel; new cyber-support capability for deployed operations; and additional intelligence personnel. While the white paper claimed that these additional capabilities were 'costed and funded', it also made clear that until 2030 defence spending was expected to remain pegged at around 1% of GDP. New Zealand's closest defence partner is Australia. While there is little prospect of New Zealand's role in the trilateral ANZUS alliance being restored (this was suspended in 1986), the country has since 2010 revived defence relations with the United States. In 2012, the two countries agreed to cooperate in developing 'deployable capabilities' for the South Pacific. In July 2015, New Zealand participated for the first time in the bilateral US–Australia exercise *Talisman Sabre*. In July 2016, defence minister Gerry Brownlee indicated a further strengthening of defence links with the US when he announced that a US warship would visit the country for the first time in three decades the following November: the USS *Sampson* subsequently assisted local authorities in New Zealand's South Island after the November 2016 earthquake.

ACTIVE 8,950 (Army 4,500 Navy 2,050 Air 2,400)

RESERVE 2,200 (Army 1,550 Navy 450 Air Force 200)

ORGANISATIONS BY SERVICE

Army 4,500
FORCES BY ROLE
SPECIAL FORCES
  1 SF gp
MANOEUVRE
  Light
  1 inf bde (1 armd recce regt, 2 lt inf bn, 1 arty regt (2 arty bty, 1 AD tp), 1 engr regt(-), 1 MI coy, 1 MP coy, 1 sigs regt, 2 log bn, 1 med bn)
COMBAT SUPPORT
  1 EOD sqn

EQUIPMENT BY TYPE
ARMOURED FIGHTING VEHICLES
  IFV 95 NZLAV-25
ENGINEERING & MAINTENANCE VEHICLES
  AEV 7 NZLAV
  ARV 3 LAV-R

ANTI-TANK/ANTI-INFRASTRUCTURE
MSL • MANPATS 24 FGM-148 *Javelin*
RCL 84mm 42 *Carl Gustav*
ARTILLERY 74
TOWED 105mm 24 L118 Light Gun
MOR 81mm 50

Reserves

Territorial Force 1,550 reservists
Responsible for providing trained individuals for augmenting deployed forces
FORCES BY ROLE
COMBAT SERVICE SUPPORT
3 (Territorial Force Regional) trg regt

Navy 2,050
Fleet HQ at Auckland
EQUIPMENT BY TYPE
PRINCIPAL SURFACE COMBATANTS • FRIGATES • FFHM 2:
2 *Anzac* (GER MEKO 200) with 1 octuple Mk41 VLS with RIM-7M *Sea Sparrow* SAM, 2 triple Mk32 324mm TT, 1 Mk15 *Phalanx* Block 1B CIWS, 1 127mm gun (capacity 1 SH-2G(I) *Super Seasprite* ASW hel)
PATROL AND COASTAL COMBATANTS 6
PSOH 2 *Otago* (capacity 1 SH-2G(I) *Super Seasprite* ASW hel)
PCC 4 *Rotoiti*
AMPHIBIOUS • LANDING CRAFT • LCM 2
LOGISTICS AND SUPPORT 2 AKRH 1 *Canterbury* (capacity 4 NH90 tpt hel; 1 SH-2G(I) *Super Seasprite* ASW hel; 2 LCM; 16 NZLAV; 14 NZLAV; 20 trucks; 250 troops)
AOR 1 *Endeavour* with 1 hel landing platform

Air Force 2,400
Flying hours 190 hrs/yr

FORCES BY ROLE
MARITIME PATROL
1 sqn with P-3K2 *Orion*
TRANSPORT
1 sqn with B-757-200 (upgraded); C-130H *Hercules* (upgraded)
ANTI-SUBMARINE/SURFACE WARFARE
1 (RNZAF/RNZN) sqn with SH-2G(I) *Super Seasprite*
TRAINING
1 sqn with T-6C *Texan* II
1 sqn with Beech 200 *King Air* (leased)
TRANSPORT HELICOPTER
1 sqn with AW109; NH90
EQUIPMENT BY TYPE
AIRCRAFT 6 combat capable
ASW 6 P-3K2 *Orion*
TPT 11: **Medium** 5 C-130H *Hercules* (upgraded); **Light** 4 Beech 200 *King Air* (leased); **PAX** 2 B-757-200 (upgraded)
TRG 11 T-6C *Texan* II
HELICOPTERS
ASW 8 SH-2G(I) *Super Seasprite*
TPT 13: **Medium** 8 NH90; **Light** 5 AW109

AIR-LAUNCHED MISSILES • AShM AGM-119 *Penguin* Mk2 mod7

DEPLOYMENT

AFGHANISTAN
NATO • Operation Resolute Support 8

EGYPT
MFO 26; 1 trg unit; 1 tpt unit

IRAQ
Operation Inherent Resolve 143

MIDDLE EAST
UN • UNTSO 8 obs

SOUTH SUDAN
UN • UNMISS 1; 2 obs

Pakistan PAK

Pakistani Rupee Rs		2015	2016	2017
GDP	Rs	27.5tr	29.6tr	
	US$	271bn	n.k.	
per capita	US$	1,428	n.k.	
Growth	%	4.0	4.7	
Inflation	%	4.5	2.9	
Def bdgt [a]	Rs	725bn	779bn	865bn
	US$	7.15bn	7.47bn	
FMA (US)	US$	265m	265m	265m
US$1=Rs		101.43	104.29	

[a] Includes defence allocations to the Public Sector Development Programme (PSDP), including funding to the Defence Division and the Defence Production Division

Population 201,995,540
Religious groups: Hindu less than 3%

Age	0–14	15–19	20–24	25–29	30–64	65 plus
Male	16.4%	5.6%	5.4%	4.8%	17.0%	2.0%
Female	15.6%	5.3%	5.0%	4.5%	15.9%	2.4%

Capabilities

Pakistan's nuclear and conventional forces have traditionally been oriented and structured against a prospective threat from India. Since 2008, however, counter-insurgency and counter-terrorism have been of increasing importance and are now the forces' main effort, despite an increase in cross-border incidents with Indian forces since summer 2015. The air force is modernising its inventory while improving its precision-strike and ISR capabilities. Pakistan produces the Chinese JF-17 combat aircraft and a third squadron transitioned to this newer aircraft in 2016. Pakistan has declared that its 'short-range low-yield' battlefield nuclear capability based on the *Nasr* missile has become operational. Major investment in this programme continues. As part of the China–Pakistan Economic Corridor initiative the army is to raise a 15,000-strong dedicated security force to protect the project. Major defence-industry partners include China and Turkey, with a number of programmes in their early stages. However, according to Pakistan's minister for defence production, Pakistan has significantly reduced its reliance on external sources for defence procurement. The navy is currently too small to sustain a long campaign against a significant competitor, but recent and likely future investment in Chinese-supplied frigates, missile craft and submarines could improve sea-denial capabilities. 2016 saw the start of a number of upgrades to maritime capabilities, including the development with Turkey of the navy's new fleet tanker, which should form the backbone of Pakistan's naval-auxiliary support. The army continues to contribute to UN peacekeeping operations. The Pakistan Navy took over the rotational command of the Combined Maritime Forces' Task Force 150 maritime-security operation in August 2016.

ACTIVE 653,800 (Army 560,000 Navy 23,800 Air 70,000) **Paramilitary 282,000**

ORGANISATIONS BY SERVICE

Strategic Forces

Operational control rests with the National Command Authority. The Strategic Plans Directorate (SPD) manages and commands all of Pakistan's military nuclear capability. The SPD also commands a reportedly 25,000-strong military security force responsible for guarding military nuclear infrastructure

Army Strategic Forces Command 12,000–15,000

Commands all land-based strategic nuclear forces
EQUIPMENT BY TYPE
SURFACE-TO-SURFACE MISSILE LAUNCHERS 60+
  MRBM • Nuclear ε30 *Ghauri/Ghauri* II (*Hatf-5*)/ *Shaheen-2* (*Hatf-6* – in test); *Shaheen-3* (in test)
  SRBM • Nuclear 30+: ε30 *Ghaznavi* (*Hatf-3* – PRC M-11)/*Shaheen-1* (*Hatf-4*); some *Abdali* (*Hatf-2*); some *Nasr* (*Hatf-9*)
  GLCM • Nuclear *Babur* (*Hatf-7*); *Ra'ad* (*Hatf-8* – in test)

Air Force

1–2 sqn of F-16A/B or *Mirage* 5 may be assigned a nuclear-strike role

Army 560,000

FORCES BY ROLE
COMMAND
  9 corps HQ
  1 (area) comd
SPECIAL FORCES
  2 SF gp (total: 4 SF bn)
MANOEUVRE
  Armoured
  2 armd div
  7 indep armd bde
  Mechanised
  2 mech inf div
  1 indep mech bde
  Light
  18 inf div
  5 indep inf bde
  Other
  1 sy div (1 more div forming)
COMBAT SUPPORT
  1 arty div
  14 arty bde
  7 engr bde
AVIATION
  1 VIP avn sqn
  4 avn sqn
HELICOPTER
  3 atk hel sqn
  2 ISR hel sqn
  2 SAR hel sqn
  2 tpt hel sqn
  1 spec ops hel sqn
AIR DEFENCE
  1 AD comd (3 AD gp (total: 8 AD bn))

EQUIPMENT BY TYPE
ARMOURED FIGHTING VEHICLES
  MBT 2,561+: 415 *Al-Khalid* (MBT 2000); 320 T-80UD; 51 T-54/T-55; 1,100 Type-59/*Al-Zarrar*; 400 Type-69; 275+ Type-85; (270 M48A5 in store)
  APC 1,422
    APC (T) 1,260: 1,160 M113/*Talha*; ε100 Type-63
    APC (W) 120 BTR-70/BTR-80
    PPV 42 *Maxxpro*
    AUV 10 *Dingo* 2
ENGINEERING & MAINTENANCE VEHICLES
  ARV 117+: 65 Type-653; *Al-Hadeed*; 52 M88A1; T-54/T-55
  VLB M47M; M48/60
  MW *Aardvark* Mk II
ANTI-TANK/ANTI-INFRASTRUCTURE
  MSL
    SP M901 TOW
    MANPATS HJ-8; TOW
  RCL 75mm Type-52; **106mm** M40A1
  RL 89mm M20
  GUNS 85mm 200 Type-56 (D-44)
ARTILLERY 4,472+
  SP 375: **155mm** 315: 200 M109A2; ε115 M109A5 **203mm** 60 M110/M110A2
  TOWED 1,659: **105mm** 329: 216 M101; 113 M-56; **122mm** 570: 80 D-30 (PRC); 490 Type-54 (M-1938); **130mm** 410 Type-59-I; **155mm** 322: 144 M114; 148 M198; ε30 *Panter*; **203mm** 28 M115
  MRL 88+: **107mm** Type-81; **122mm** 52+: 52 *Azar* (Type-83); some KRL-122; **300mm** 36 A100
  MOR 2,350+: **81mm**; **120mm** AM-50
SURFACE-TO-SURFACE MISSILE LAUNCHERS
  MRBM • Nuclear ε30 *Ghauri/Ghauri* II (*Hatf-5*); some *Shaheen-2* (*Hatf-6* – in test); *Shaheen-3* (in test)
  SRBM 135+: **Nuclear** 30+: ε30 *Ghaznavi* (*Hatf-3* – PRC M-11)/*Shaheen-1* (*Hatf-4*); some *Abdali* (*Hatf-2*); some *Nasr* (*Hatf-9*); **Conventional** 105 *Hatf*-1
  GLCM • Nuclear some *Babur* (*Hatf-7*)
RADAR • LAND AN/TPQ-36 *Firefinder* (arty, mor); RASIT (veh, arty); SLC-2

AIRCRAFT
TPT • **Light** 14: 1 Beech 200 *King Air*; 1 Beech 350 *King Air*; 3 Cessna 208B; 1 Cessna 421; 1 Cessna 550 *Citation*; 1 Cessna 560 *Citation*; 2 Turbo Commander 690; 4 Y-12(II)
TRG 87 MFI-17B *Mushshak*
HELICOPTERS
ATK 38 AH-1F/S *Cobra* with TOW (1 Mi-24 *Hind* in store)
MRH 115+: 10 H125M *Fennec*; 6 AW139; 26 Bell 412EP *Twin Huey*; 38+ Mi-17 *Hip* H; 2 Mi-171E *Hip*; 12 SA315B *Lama*; 20 SA319 *Alouette* III
TPT 76: **Medium** 36: 31 SA330 *Puma*; 4 Mi-171; 1 Mi-172; **Light** 40: 17 H125 *Ecureuil* (SAR); 5 Bell 205 (UH-1H *Iroquois*); 5 Bell 205A-1 (AB-205A-1); 13 Bell 206B *Jet Ranger* II
TRG 10 Hughes 300C
UNMANNED AERIAL VEHICLES
ISR • **Light** *Bravo*; *Jasoos*; *Vector*
AIR DEFENCE
SAM • **Point-defence** some M113 with RBS-70; *Anza* Mk1/Mk2; FIM-92 *Stinger*; HN-5A; *Mistral*; RBS-70
GUNS • TOWED 1,933: **14.5mm** 981; **35mm** 248 GDF-002/GDF-005 (with 134 *Skyguard* radar units); **37mm** 310 Type-55 (M-1939)/Type-65; **40mm** 50 L/60; **57mm** 144 Type-59 (S-60); **85mm** 200 Type-72 (M-1939) KS-12

Navy 23,800 (incl ε3,200 Marines and ε2,000 Maritime Security Agency (see Paramilitary))

EQUIPMENT BY TYPE
SUBMARINES • TACTICAL 8
SSK 5:
  2 *Hashmat* (FRA *Agosta* 70) with 4 single 533mm ASTT with F17P HWT/UGM-84 *Harpoon* AShM
  3 *Khalid* (FRA *Agosta* 90B – 1 with AIP) with 4 single 533mm ASTT with F17 Mod 2 HWT/SM-39 *Exocet* AShM
SSI 3 MG110 (SF delivery) each with 2 single 533mm TT
PRINCIPAL SURFACE COMBATANTS • FRIGATES 10
FFGHM 4 *Sword* (F-22P) with 2 quad lnchr with C-802A AShM, 1 octuple lnchr with HHQ-7 SAM, 2 triple 324mm ASTT with Mk 46 LWT, 2 sextuple Type 87 A/S mor, 1 Type 730B CIWS, 1 76mm gun (capacity 1 Z-9C *Haitun* hel)
FFGH 2:
  1 *Tariq* (UK *Amazon*) with 2 twin Mk141 lnchr with RGM-84D *Harpoon* AShM, 2 triple 324mm ASTT with Mk 46 LWT, 1 *Phalanx* Block 1B CIWS, 1 114mm gun (capacity 1 hel)
  1 *Tariq* (UK *Amazon*) with 2 quad Mk141 lnchr with RGM-84D *Harpoon* AShM, 2 single 400mm TT with TP 45 LWT, 1 *Phalanx* Block 1B CIWS, 1 114mm gun (capacity 1 hel)
FFHM 3 *Tariq* (UK *Amazon*) with 1 sextuple lnchr with LY-60 (*Aspide*) SAM, 2 single 400mm TT with TP 45 LWT, 1 *Phalanx* Block 1B CIWS, 1 114mm gun (capacity 1 hel)
FFH 1 *Alamgir* (US *Oliver Hazard Perry*) with 2 triple 324mm ASTT with Mk46 LWT, 1 *Phalanx* CIWS, 1 76mm gun
PATROL AND COASTAL COMBATANTS 16
PCG 2 *Azmat* (PRC *Houjian* mod) with 2 quad lnchr with C-802A AShM, 1 AK630 CIWS
PBFG 2 *Zarrar* (33) with 4 single lnchr each with RGM-84 *Harpoon* AShM
PBG 4:
  2 *Jalalat* with 2 twin lnchr with C-802 (CSS-N-8 *Saccade*) AShM
  2 *Jurrat* with 2 twin lnchr with C-802 (CSS-N-8 *Saccade*) AShM
PBF 2 *Kaan* 15
PB 6: 1 *Larkana*; 1 *Rajshahi*; 4 LCP
MINE WARFARE • MINE COUNTERMEASURES
MHC 3 *Munsif* (FRA *Eridan*)
AMPHIBIOUS • LANDING CRAFT 8
LCM 2
LCAC 2 *Griffon* 8100TD
UCAC 4 *Griffon* 2000
LOGISTICS AND SUPPORT 9
AGS 1 *Behr Paima*
AOL 2 *Madagar*
AORH 2:
  1 *Fuqing* with 1 *Phalanx* CIWS (capacity 1 SA319 *Alouette* III hel)
  1 *Moawin* with 1 *Phalanx* CIWS (capacity 1 *Sea King* Mk45 ASW hel)
AOT 3: 1 *Attock*; 2 *Gwadar*
AXS 1

Marines ε3,200

FORCES BY ROLE
SPECIAL FORCES
  1 cdo gp
MANOEUVRE
  Amphibious
  3 mne bn
AIR DEFENCE
  1 AD bn

Naval Aviation

EQUIPMENT BY TYPE
AIRCRAFT 7 combat capable
  ASW 7 P-3B/C *Orion*
  MP 6 F-27-200 MPA
  TPT 4: **Light** 3 ATR-72-500 (MP); **PAX** 1 Hawker 850XP
HELICOPTERS
  ASW 12: 5 *Sea King* Mk45; 7 Z-9C *Haitun*
  MRH 6 SA319B *Alouette* III
AIR-LAUNCHED MISSILES • AShM AM-39 *Exocet*

Air Force 70,000

3 regional comds: Northern (Peshawar), Central (Sargodha), Southern (Masroor). The Composite Air Tpt Wg, Combat Cadres School and PAF Academy are Direct Reporting Units

FORCES BY ROLE
FIGHTER
  1 sqn with F-7P/FT-7P *Skybolt*
  3 sqn with F-7PG/FT-7PG *Airguard*
  1 sqn with F-16A/B MLU *Fighting Falcon*
  1 sqn with F-16A/B ADF *Fighting Falcon*
  1 sqn with *Mirage* IIID/E (IIIOD/EP)

FIGHTER/GROUND ATTACK
  2 sqn with JF-17 *Thunder*
  1 sqn with JF-17 *Thunder* Block II
  1 sqn with F-16C/D Block 52 *Fighting Falcon*
  3 sqn with *Mirage* 5 (5PA)
ANTI-SURFACE WARFARE
  1 sqn with *Mirage* 5PA2/5PA3 with AM-39 *Exocet* AShM
ELECTRONIC WARFARE/ELINT
  1 sqn with *Falcon* 20F
AIRBORNE EARLY WARNING & CONTROL
  1 sqn with Saab 2000; Saab 2000 *Erieye*
  1 sqn with ZDK-03
SEARCH & RESCUE
  1 sqn with Mi-171Sh (SAR/liaison)
  6 sqn with SA316 *Alouette* III
TANKER
  1 sqn with Il-78 *Midas*
TRANSPORT
  1 sqn with C-130B/E *Hercules*; CN-235M-220; L-100-20
  1 VIP sqn with B-707; Cessna 560XL *Citation Excel*; CN-235M-220; F-27-200 *Friendship*; *Falcon* 20E; Gulfstream IVSP
  1 (comms) sqn with EMB-500 *Phenom* 100; Y-12 (II)
TRAINING
  1 OCU sqn with F-7P/FT-7P *Skybolt*
  1 OCU sqn with *Mirage* III/*Mirage* 5
  1 OCU sqn with F-16A/B MLU *Fighting Falcon*
  2 sqn with K-8 *Karakorum**
  2 sqn with MFI-17
  2 sqn with T-37C *Tweet*
AIR DEFENCE
  1 bty with HQ-2 (SA-2 *Guideline*); 9K310 *Igla*-1 (SA-16 *Gimlet*)
  6 bty with *Crotale*
  10 bty with SPADA 2000
EQUIPMENT BY TYPE
AIRCRAFT 451 combat capable
  FTR 195: 48 F-7PG *Airguard*; 60 F-7P *Skybolt*; 24 F-16A MLU *Fighting Falcon*; 21 F-16B MLU *Fighting Falcon*; 9 F-16A ADF *Fighting Falcon*; 4 F-16B ADF *Fighting Falcon*; 21 FT-7; 6 FT-7PG; 2 *Mirage* IIIB
  FGA 208: 12 F-16C Block 52 *Fighting Falcon*; 6 F-16D Block 52 *Fighting Falcon*; 49 JF-17 *Thunder* (FC-1 Block 1); 20 JF-17 *Thunder* (FC-1 Block 2); 7 *Mirage* IIID (*Mirage* IIIOD); 63 *Mirage* IIIE (IIIEP); 39 *Mirage* 5 (5PA)/5PA2; 2 *Mirage* 5D (5DPA)/5DPA2; 10 *Mirage* 5PA3 (ASuW)
  ISR 10 *Mirage* IIIR* (*Mirage* IIIRP)
  ELINT 2 *Falcon* 20F
  AEW&C 5: 1 Saab 2000 *Erieye* (2 more non-op); 4 ZDK-03
  TKR 4 Il-78 *Midas*
  TPT 35: **Medium** 16: 5 C-130B *Hercules*; 10 C-130E *Hercules*; 1 L-100-20; **Light** 14: 2 Cessna 208B; 1 Cessna 560XL *Citation Excel*; 4 CN-235M-220; 4 EMB-500 *Phenom* 100; 1 F-27-200 *Friendship*; 2 Y-12 (II); **PAX** 5: 1 B-707; 1 *Falcon* 20E; 2 Gulfstream IVSP; 1 Saab 2000
  TRG 142: 38 K-8 *Karakorum**; 80 MFI-17B *Mushshak*; 24 T-37C *Tweet*
HELICOPTERS
  MRH 15 SA316 *Alouette* III
  TPT • **Medium** 4 Mi-171Sh

UNMANNED AERIAL VEHICLES
  CSIR • **Heavy** CH-3 (*Burraq*)
AIR DEFENCE • SAM 190+
  Medium-range 6 HQ-2 (SA-2 *Guideline*)
  Short-range 184: 144 *Crotale*; ε40 SPADA 2000
  Point-defence 9K310 *Igla*-1 (SA-16 *Gimlet*)
RADAR • AD 6+: 6 AR-1 (AD radar low level); some *Condor* (AD radar high level); some FPS-89/100 (AD radar high level); MPDR 45/MPDR 60/MPDR 90 (AD radar low level); Type-514 (AD radar high level)
AIR-LAUNCHED MISSILES
  AAM • **IR** AIM-9L/P *Sidewinder*; U-*Darter*; PL-5; **SARH** Super 530; **ARH** PL-12 (SD-10 – likely on order for the JF-17); AIM-120C AMRAAM
  ASM AGM-65 *Maverick*; *Raptor* II
  AShM AM-39 *Exocet*
  ARM MAR-1
  ALCM • **Nuclear** Ra'ad (in test)
BOMBS • **Laser-guided** *Paveway* II

Paramilitary 282,000 active

Coast Guard
EQUIPMENT BY TYPE
PATROL AND COASTAL COMBATANTS 5
  PBF 4
  PB 1

Frontier Corps 70,000
Ministry of Interior
FORCES BY ROLE
MANOEUVRE
  Reconnaissance
  1 armd recce sqn
  Other
  11 paramilitary regt (total: 40 paramilitary bn)
EQUIPMENT BY TYPE
ARMOURED FIGHTING VEHICLES
  APC (W) 45 UR-416

Maritime Security Agency ε2,000
EQUIPMENT BY TYPE
PRINCIPAL SURFACE COMBATANTS 1
  DESTROYERS • DD 1 *Nazim* (ex-US *Gearing*) with 2 triple 324mm ASTT, 1 twin 127mm gun
PATROL AND COASTAL COMBATANTS 15
  PCC 4 *Barkat*
  PBF 5
  PB 6: 2 *Subqat* (PRC *Shanghai* II); 1 *Sadaqat* (ex-PRC *Huangfen*); 3 *Guns*

National Guard 185,000
Incl Janbaz Force; Mujahid Force; National Cadet Corps; Women Guards

Pakistan Rangers 25,000
Ministry of Interior

DEPLOYMENT

CENTRAL AFRICAN REPUBLIC
UN • MINUSCA 1,127; 10 obs; 1 inf bn; 1 engr coy; 1 hel sqn

CÔTE D'IVOIRE
UN • UNOCI 9; 8 obs

DEMOCRATIC REPUBLIC OF THE CONGO
UN • MONUSCO 3,446; 44 obs; 3 mech inf bn; 1 inf bn; 1 hel sqn

LIBERIA
UN • UNMIL 95; 4 obs; 1 fd hospital

SUDAN
UN • UNAMID 2,120; 4 obs; 2 inf bn, 1 engr coy; 1 engr pl; 1 med pl

WESTERN SAHARA
UN • MINURSO 14 obs

FOREIGN FORCES
Figures represent total numbers for UNMOGIP mission in India and Pakistan
Chile 2 obs
Croatia 9 obs
Finland 6 obs
Korea, Republic of 7 obs
Philippines 4 obs
Sweden 5 obs
Switzerland 3 obs
Thailand 3 obs
Uruguay 2 obs

Papua New Guinea PNG

Papua New Guinea Kina K		2015	2016	2017
GDP	K	59.0bn	61.7bn	
	US$	21.2bn	19.9bn	
per capita	US$	2,745	2,517	
Growth	%	6.6	2.5	
Inflation	%	6.0	6.9	
Def bdgt	K	261m	256m	275m
	US$	94m	83m	
US$1=K		2.79	3.10	

Population	6,791,317					
Age	0–14	15–19	20–24	25–29	30–64	65 plus
Male	17.3%	5.3%	4.7%	4.1%	17.5%	2.1%
Female	16.7%	5.2%	4.6%	4.0%	16.5%	2.0%

Capabilities

Since independence in 1975, the Papua New Guinea Defence Force (PNGDF) has suffered from chronic underfunding, ill-discipline and lack of capacity to perform its core roles. During the 1990s, the force operated in a counter-insurgency role against a secessionist movement on the island of Bougainville, but without distinction. Mainly for budgetary reasons, a PNGDF Reform Program reduced personnel strength from around 4,000 to 2,100 between 2002 and 2007. However, during the current decade, the government has made efforts to revive PNGDF capability, increasing defence spending from 2010. The 2013 defence white paper identified core PNGDF roles as: defending the state; civil-emergency assistance; nation-building; and meeting international obligations, while noting that 'our defence capabilities have deteriorated to the extent that we have alarming gaps in our land, air and maritime borders'. The white paper called for the strengthening of defence capability on an ambitious scale, with personnel increases projected by 2017, while longer-term plans call for a 'division-sized force' of 10,000 personnel by 2030. The likelihood of these plans will largely depend on whether further substantial increases in defence spending are possible. In the meantime, the PNGDF continues to receive substantial external military assistance, not only from Australia but also from China, which in 2015 donated 40 new trucks, buses and other vehicles.

ACTIVE 1,900 (Army 1,600 Maritime Element 200 Air 100)

ORGANISATIONS BY SERVICE

Army ε1,600
FORCES BY ROLE
MANOEUVRE
Light
2 inf bn
COMBAT SUPPORT
1 engr bn
1 EOD unit
1 sigs sqn
EQUIPMENT BY TYPE
ARTILLERY • MOR 3+: **81mm** Some; **120mm** 3

Maritime Element ε200
1 HQ located at Port Moresby
EQUIPMENT BY TYPE
PATROL AND COASTAL COMBATANTS • PB 4 *Rabaul* (*Pacific*)
AMPHIBIOUS • LANDING SHIPS • LCH 3 *Salamaua* (ex-AUS *Balikpapan*) (of which 1 in trg role)

Air Force ε100
FORCES BY ROLE
TRANSPORT
1 sqn with CN-235M-100; IAI-201 *Arava*
TRANSPORT HELICOPTER
1 sqn with Bell 205 (UH-1H *Iroquois*)†
EQUIPMENT BY TYPE
AIRCRAFT • TPT • **Light** 4: 1 CN-235M-100; 3 IAI-201 *Arava*
HELICOPTERS • TPT • **Light** 7: 4 Bell 205 (UH-1H *Iroquois*)†; 2 Bell 412 (leased); 1 Bell 212 (leased)

DEPLOYMENT

SOUTH SUDAN
UN • UNMISS 2 obs

SUDAN
UN • UNAMID 1; 1 obs

FOREIGN FORCES
Australia 38; 1 trg unit

Philippines PHL

Philippine Peso P		2015	2016	2017
GDP	P	13.3tr	14.4tr	
	US$	292bn	312bn	
per capita	US$	2,863	2,991	
Growth	%	5.9	6.4	
Inflation	%	1.4	2.0	
Def bdgt [a]	P	99.9bn	118bn	134bn
	US$	2.20bn	2.54bn	
FMA (US)	US$	50m	40m	40m
US$1=P		45.50	46.30	

[a] Excludes military pensions

Population 102,624,209

Age	0–14	15–19	20–24	25–29	30–64	65 plus
Male	17.2%	5.1%	4.7%	4.3%	17.1%	1.8%
Female	16.5%	4.9%	4.4%	4.0%	17.3%	2.6%

Capabilities

Despite modest increases in defence funding over the last two years, mainly in response to rising tensions in the South China Sea, the capabilities and procurement plans of the Armed Forces of the Philippines (AFP) remain limited. Since the 1990s, when the US withdrew its substantial military presence, Philippine military-modernisation budgets have consistently failed to provide the resources needed to fulfil procurement plans. Although the armed forces have benefited from minor purchases of new equipment such as advanced jet trainers, as well as the transfer of surplus US helicopters and coastguard cutters, it remains unlikely that the Philippines would be able to provide more than a token national capability to defend its maritime claims. For this reason, under the administration led by Benigno Aquino III in 2010–16, the country relied heavily on revived alliance relations with the US for its external defence. However, the new president, Rodrigo Duterte, announced a 'separation' from the US and the pursuit of closer relations with China, including in the defence sphere. However, it was confirmed in November that joint training would continue with the US and that the US–Philippines Enhanced Defense Coooperation Agreement would be implemented. The army and marines continue to be deployed extensively, with air-force support, on internal-security duties in the face of continuing challenges from the Abu Sayyaf Group and other Muslim insurgents in the south. Under the previous administration, the AFP had continued its low-key counter-insurgency campaign against the communist New People's Army (NPA). However, Duterte has made a peace settlement with the NPA a priority and emphasised the need for the AFP to focus on defeating Muslim rebels.

ACTIVE 125,000 (Army 86,000 Navy 24,000 Air 15,000) Paramilitary 40,500

RESERVE 131,000 (Army 100,000 Navy 15,000 Air 16,000) Paramilitary 50,000 (to age 49)

ORGANISATIONS BY SERVICE

Army 86,000
5 Area Unified Comd (joint service), 1 National Capital Region Comd

FORCES BY ROLE
SPECIAL FORCES
  1 spec ops comd (1 ranger regt, 1 SF regt, 1 CT regt)
MANOEUVRE
  Mechanised
  1 mech inf div (2 mech bde (total: 3 lt armd sqn; 7 armd cav tp; 4 mech inf bn; 1 cbt engr coy; 1 avn bn; 1 cbt engr coy, 1 sigs coy))
  Light
  1 div (4 inf bde; 1 arty bn, 1 int bn, 1 sigs bn)
  9 div (3 inf bde; 1 arty bn, 1 int bn, 1 sigs bn)
  Other
  1 (Presidential) gd gp
COMBAT SUPPORT
  1 arty regt HQ
  5 engr bde

EQUIPMENT BY TYPE
ARMOURED FIGHTING VEHICLES
  LT TK 7 FV101 Scorpion
  IFV 36: 2 YPR-765; 34 M113A1 FSV
  APC 413
    APC (T) 190: 6 ACV300; 70 M113; 114 M113A2
    APC (W) 223: 77 LAV-150 Commando; 146 Simba
ENGINEERING & MAINTENANCE VEHICLES
  ARV ACV-300; Samson; M578
ANTI-TANK-ANTI-INFRASTRUCTURE • RCL 75mm M20; **90mm** M67; **106mm** M40A1
ARTILLERY 254+
  TOWED 214: **105mm** 204 M101/M102/Model 56 pack howitzer; **155mm** 10 M114/M-68
  MOR 40+: **81mm** M29; **107mm** 40 M30
AIRCRAFT
  TPT • Light 4: 1 Beech 80 Queen Air; 1 Cessna 170; 1 Cessna 172; 1 Cessna P206A
UNMANNED AERIAL VEHICLES • ISR • Medium Blue Horizon

Navy 24,000
EQUIPMENT BY TYPE
PRINCIPAL SURFACE COMBATANTS • FRIGATES
  FF 1 Rajah Humabon (ex-US Cannon) with 3 76mm gun
PATROL AND COASTAL COMBATANTS 66
  PSOH 3 Gregorio del Pilar (ex-US Hamilton) with 1 76mm gun, (capacity 1 Bo 105)
  PCF 1 General Mariano Alvares (ex-US Cyclone)
  PCO 11:
    3 Emilio Jacinto (ex-UK Peacock) with 1 76mm gun
    6 Miguel Malvar (ex-US) with 1 76mm gun

2 *Rizal* (ex-US *Auk*) with 2 76mm gun
PBF 15: 2 *Conrado Yap* (ex-ROK *Sea Hawk*); 7 *Tomas Batilo* (ex-ROK *Chamsuri*); 6 MPAC
PB 31: 1 *Aguinaldo*; 22 *Jose Andrada*; 2 *Kagitingan*; 2 *Point* (ex-US); 4 *Swift* Mk3 (ex-US)
PBR 6 Silver Ships
AMPHIBIOUS
  PRINCIPAL AMPHIBIOUS SHIPS 1
    LPD 1 *Tarlac* (IDN *Makassar*) (capacity 2 LCU; 2 hels; 13 tanks; 500 troops)
  LANDING SHIPS • LST 4:
    2 *Bacolod City* (US *Besson*) with 1 hel landing platform (capacity 32 tanks; 150 troops)
    2 *Zamboanga del Sur* (LST-1/542) (capacity 16 tanks; 200 troops)
  LANDING CRAFT 35
    LCH 5 *Ivatan* (ex-AUS *Balikpapan*)
    LCU 12
    LCVP 2
    LCM 16
LOGISTICS AND SUPPORT 16
  AFD 4
  AGOR 1 *Gregorio Velasquez* (ex-US *Melville*)
  AK 1
  AOL 2
  AOT 3
  AO 1 *Lake Caliraya*
  AP 1
  AR 1
  AWT 2

Naval Aviation
EQUIPMENT BY TYPE
AIRCRAFT • TPT • Light 6: 4 BN-2A *Defender*; 2 Cessna 177 *Cardinal*
HELICOPTERS • TPT 13: **Medium** 4 Mi-171Sh; **Light** 9: 3 AW109; 2 AW109E; 4 Bo-105

Marines 8,300
FORCES BY ROLE
SPECIAL FORCES
  1 (force recon) spec ops bn
MANOEUVRE
  Amphibious
  4 mne bde (total: 12 mne bn)
COMBAT SUPPORT
  1 CSS bde (6 CSS bn)
EQUIPMENT BY TYPE
ARMOURED FIGHTING VEHICLES
  APC • APC (W) 42: 19 LAV-150 *Commando*; 23 LAV-300
  AAV 59: 4 LVTH-6†; 55 LVTP-7
ARTILLERY 31+
  TOWED 105mm 31: 23 M101; 8 M-26
  MOR 107mm M30

Naval Special Operations Group
FORCES BY ROLE
SPECIAL FORCES
  1 SEAL unit
  1 diving unit
  10 naval spec ops unit
  1 special boat unit
COMBAT SUPPORT
  1 EOD unit

Air Force 15,000
FORCES BY ROLE
FIGHTER
  1 sqn with FA-50PH *Fighting Eagle*; S-211*
GROUND ATTACK
  1 sqn with OV-10A/C *Bronco*
ISR
  1 sqn with *Turbo Commander* 690A
SEARCH & RESCUE
  4 (SAR/Comms) sqn with Bell 205 (UH-1M *Iroquois*); AUH-76
TRANSPORT
  1 sqn with C-130B/H/T *Hercules*; L-100-20
  1 sqn with N-22B *Nomad*; N-22SL *Searchmaster*
  1 sqn with F-27-200 MPA; F-27-500 *Friendship*
  1 VIP sqn with F-28 *Fellowship*
TRAINING
  1 sqn with SF-260F/TP
  1 sqn with T-41B/D/K *Mescalero*
ATTACK HELICOPTER
  1 sqn with MD-520MG
TRANSPORT HELICOPTER
  1 sqn with AUH-76
  1 sqn with W-3 *Sokol*
  4 sqn with Bell 205 (UH-1H *Iroquois*)
  1 (VIP) sqn with Bell 412EP *Twin Huey*; S-70A *Black Hawk* (S-70A-5)
EQUIPMENT BY TYPE
AIRCRAFT 24 combat capable
  FGA 2 FA-50PH *Fighting Eagle*
  MP 2: 1 F-27-200 MPA; 1 N-22SL *Searchmaster*
  ISR 10 OV-10A/C *Bronco**
  TPT 13: **Medium** 6: 1 C-130B *Hercules*; 3 C-130H *Hercules*; 2 C-130T *Hercules* **Light** 6: 3 C-295; 1 F-27-500 *Friendship*; 1 N-22B *Nomad*; 1 *Turbo Commander* 690A; **PAX** 1 F-28 *Fellowship* (VIP)
  TRG 39: 12 S-211*; 7 SF-260F; 10 SF-260TP; 10 T-41B/D/K *Mescalero*
HELICOPTERS
  MRH 32: 8 W-3 *Sokol*; 3 AUH-76; 8 Bell 412EP *Twin Huey*; 2 Bell 412HP *Twin Huey*; 11 MD-520MG
  TPT 48: **Medium** 1 S-70A *Black Hawk* (S-70A-5); **Light** 47: 2 AW109E; 45 Bell 205 (UH-1H *Iroquois*)
UNMANNED AERIAL VEHICLES
  ISR • Medium 2 *Blue Horizon* II
AIR-LAUNCHED MISSILES
  AAM • IR AIM-9 *Sidewinder*

Paramilitary

Philippine National Police 40,500
Department of Interior and Local Government. 15 regional & 73 provincial comd. 62,000 auxiliaries
EQUIPMENT BY TYPE
AIRCRAFT
  TPT • Light 5: 2 BN-2 *Islander*; 3 Lancair 320

Coast Guard
EQUIPMENT BY TYPE
Rodman 38 and Rodman 101 owned by Bureau of Fisheries and Aquatic Resources
PATROL AND COASTAL COMBATANTS 72
   PCO 5: 4 *San Juan*; 1 *Balsam*
   PCC 2 *Tirad*
   PB 54: 3 *De Haviland*; 4 *Ilocos Norte*; 1 *Palawan*; 12 PCF 50 (US *Swift* Mk1/2); 10 PCF 46; 10 PCF 65 (US *Swift* Mk3); 4 Rodman 38; 10 Rodman 101
   PBR 11
AMPHIBIOUS • LANDING CRAFT 2
   LCM 1
   LCVP 1
LOGISTICS AND SUPPORT • ABU 3
AIRCRAFT • TPT • Light 2 BN-2 *Islander*
HELICOPTERS • TPT • Light 2 Bo-105

Citizen Armed Force Geographical Units
50,000 reservists
MANOEUVRE
   Other
     56 militia bn (part-time units which can be called up for extended periods)

DEPLOYMENT

CÔTE D'IVOIRE
UN • UNOCI 1 obs

HAITI
UN • MINUSTAH 137; 1 HQ coy

INDIA/PAKISTAN
UN • UNMOGIP 4 obs

FOREIGN FORCES
Brunei IMT 8
Indonesia IMT 5
Malaysia IMT 11

Singapore SGP

Singapore Dollar S$		2015	2016	2017
GDP	S$	402bn	404bn	
	US$	293bn	297bn	
per capita	US$	52,888	53,053	
Growth	%	2.0	1.7	
Inflation	%	-0.5	-0.3	
Def bdgt	S$	13.1bn	14.0bn	
	US$	9.54bn	10.2bn	
US$1=S$		1.37	1.36	

Population 5,781,728

Ethnic groups: Chinese 74.1%; Malay 13.4%; Indian 9.2%; other or unspecified 3.3%

Age	0–14	15–19	20–24	25–29	30–64	65 plus
Male	6.6%	3.5%	4.9%	5.3%	24.4%	4.2%
Female	6.3%	3.4%	5.2%	5.7%	25.3%	5.0%

Capabilities

The Singapore Armed Forces (SAF) are the best equipped in Southeast Asia. They are organised essentially along Israeli lines, with the air force and navy being staffed mainly by professional personnel while, apart from a small core of regulars, the much larger army is based on conscripts and reservists. It is widely presumed that the SAF's primary role is to deter attacks on the city-state or interference with its vital interests – particularly its sea lines of communication – by potential regional adversaries. There is now an additional focus on counter-terrorist operations, and dedicated units have been formed for that purpose. There is a significant personnel challenge ahead, with an ageing population and declining conscript cohort, which the defence ministry is addressing with lean manning and increased use of technology. Tracking its economic growth, Singapore's defence budget has increased to the extent that the city-state outspends all its Southeast Asian counterparts. Training is routinely carried out overseas, notably in Australia, Brunei, Germany, Taiwan, Thailand and the United States. The SAF also engages extensively in bilateral and multilateral exercises with regional and international partners, including through the Five Power Defence Arrangements and ADMM–Plus. Singaporean forces have gradually become more involved in multinational operations including the US-led air offensive against ISIS, to which Singapore has contributed a tanker aircraft and planning staff. While such deployments have provided some operational experience, and training standards and operational readiness are high, the army's reliance on conscripts and reservists limits its capacity for sustained operations away from Singapore.

ACTIVE 72,500 (Army 50,000 Navy 9,000 Air 13,500)
Paramilitary 75,100
Conscription liability 22–24 months

RESERVE 312,500 (Army 300,000 Navy 5,000 Air 7,500) **Paramilitary 44,000**
Annual trg to age of 40 for army other ranks, 50 for officers

ORGANISATIONS BY SERVICE

Army 15,000; 35,000 conscript (total 50,000)
FORCES BY ROLE
COMMAND
  3 (combined arms) div HQ
  1 (rapid reaction) div HQ
  3 armd bde HQ
  9 inf bde HQ
  1 air mob bde HQ
  1 amph bde HQ
SPECIAL FORCES
  1 cdo bn
MANOEUVRE
  Reconnaissance
  3 lt armd/recce bn
  Armoured
  1 armd bn
  Mechanised
  6 mech inf bn
  Light
  2 (gds) inf bn
  Other
  2 sy bn
COMBAT SUPPORT
  2 arty bn
  1 STA bn
  2 engr bn
  1 EOD bn
  1 ptn br bn
  1 int bn
  2 ISR bn
  1 CBRN bn
  3 sigs bn
COMBAT SERVICE SUPPORT
  3 med bn
  2 tpt bn
  3 spt bn

Reserves
Activated units form part of divisions and brigades listed above; 1 op reserve div with additional inf bde; People's Defence Force Comd (homeland defence) with 12 inf bn
FORCES BY ROLE
SPECIAL FORCES
  1 cdo bn
MANOEUVRE
  Reconnaissance
  6 lt armd/recce bn
  Mechanised
  6 mech inf bn
  Light
  ε56 inf bn
COMBAT SUPPORT
  ε12 arty bn
  ε8 engr bn

EQUIPMENT BY TYPE
ARMOURED FIGHTING VEHICLES
  MBT 96 *Leopard* 2SG; (80–100 *Tempest* (upgraded *Centurion*) reported in store)
  LT TK 372: 22 AMX-10 PAC 90; ε350 AMX-13 SM1
  IFV 572+: 22 AMX-10P; 250 *Bionix* IFV-25; 250 *Bionix* IFV-40/50; 50+ M113A1/A2 (some with 40mm AGL, some with 25mm gun)
  APC 1,530+
    APC (T) 1,100+: 700+ M113A1/A2; 400+ ATTC *Bronco*
    APC (W) 415: 250 LAV-150 *Commando*/V-200 *Commando*; 135 *Terrex* ICV; 30 V-100 *Commando*
    PPV 20: 15 *MaxxPro Dash*; 5 *Peacekeeper*
ENGINEERING & MAINTENANCE VEHICLES
  AEV 94: 18 CET; 54 FV180; 14 *Kodiak*; 8 M728
  ARV *Bionix*; *Büffel*; LAV-150; LAV-300
  VLB 72+: *Bionix*; LAB 30; *Leguan*; M2; 60 M3; 12 M60
  MW 910-MCV-2; *Trailblazer*
ANTI-TANK/ANTI-INFRASTRUCTURE
  MSL • MANPATS 60: 30 *Milan*; 30 *Spike* MR
  RCL 290: **84mm** ε200 *Carl Gustav*; **106mm** 90 M40A1
ARTILLERY 798+
  SP 155mm 54 SSPH-1 *Primus*
  TOWED 88: **105mm** (37 LG1 in store); **155mm** 88: 18 FH-2000; ε18 *Pegasus*; 52 FH-88
  MRL 227mm 18 M142 HIMARS
  MOR 638+
    SP 90+: **81mm**; **120mm** 90: 40 on *Bronco*; 50 on M113
    TOWED 548: **81mm** 500 **120mm** 36 M-65; **160mm** 12 M-58 Tampella
  RADAR • LAND AN/TPQ-36 *Firefinder*; AN/TPQ-37 *Firefinder* (arty, mor); 3 ARTHUR (arty)
UNMANNED AERIAL VEHICLES • ISR • Light *Skylark*

Navy 3,000; 1,000 conscript; ε5,000 active reservists (total 9,000)
EQUIPMENT BY TYPE
SUBMARINES • TACTICAL • SSK 4:
  2 *Challenger* (ex-SWE *Sjoormen*) with 4 single 533mm TT
  2 *Archer* (ex-SWE *Västergötland*) (AIP fitted) with 6 single 533mm TT for WASS *Black Shark* HWT
PRINCIPAL SURFACE COMBATANTS 6:
  FRIGATES • FFGHM 6 *Formidable* with 2 quad lnchr with RGM-84 *Harpoon* AShM, 4 octuple VLS with *Aster* 15 SAM, 2 triple 324mm ASTT with A244 LWT, 1 76mm gun (capacity 1 S-70B *Sea Hawk* hel)
PATROL AND COASTAL COMBATANTS 35
  CORVETTES • FSGM 6 *Victory* with 2 quad Mk140 lnchr with RGM-84C *Harpoon* AShM, 2 octuple lnchr with *Barak* SAM, 2 triple 324mm ASTT with A244 LWT, 1 76mm gun
  PCO 11 *Fearless* with 2 sextuple *Sadral* lnchr with *Mistral* SAM, 1 76mm gun
  PBF 6
  PB 12
MINE WARFARE • MINE COUNTERMEASURES
  MHC 4 *Bedok*
AMPHIBIOUS
  PRINCIPAL AMPHIBIOUS SHIPS • LPD 4 *Endurance* with 2 twin lnchr with *Mistral* SAM, 1 76mm gun (capacity 2 hel; 4 LCVP; 18 MBT; 350 troops)
  LANDING CRAFT 34 LCU 100 LCVP
LOGISTICS AND SUPPORT 2
  ASR 1 *Swift Rescue*
  AX 1

Naval Diving Unit
FORCES BY ROLE
SPECIAL FORCES
1 SF gp
1 (diving) SF gp
COMBAT SUPPORT
1 EOD gp

Air Force 13,500 (incl 3,000 conscript)
5 comds
FORCES BY ROLE
FIGHTER/GROUND ATTACK
1 sqn with F-5S/T *Tiger II*
2 sqn with F-15SG *Eagle*
3 sqn with F-16C/D *Fighting Falcon* (some used for ISR with pods)
ANTI-SUBMARINE WARFARE
1 sqn with S-70B *Seahawk*
MARITIME PATROL/TRANSPORT
1 sqn with F-50
AIRBORNE EARLY WARNING & CONTROL
1 sqn with G550-AEW
TANKER
1 sqn with KC-135R *Stratotanker*
TANKER/TRANSPORT
1 sqn with KC-130B/H *Hercules*; C-130H *Hercules*
TRAINING
1 (FRA-based) sqn with M-346 *Master*
4 (US-based) units with AH-64D *Apache*; CH-47D *Chinook*; F-15SG: F-16C/D
1 (AUS-based) sqn with PC-21
1 hel sqn with H120 *Colibri*
ATTACK HELICOPTER
1 sqn with AH-64D *Apache*
TRANSPORT HELICOPTER
1 sqn with CH-47SD *Super D Chinook*
2 sqn with AS332M *Super Puma*; AS532UL *Cougar*
ISR UAV
1 sqn with *Hermes* 450
1 sqn with *Heron* 1
1 sqn with *Searcher* MkII
AIR DEFENCE
1 AD bn with *Mistral* opcon Army
3 AD bn with RBS-70; 9K38 *Igla* (SA-18 *Grouse*) opcon Army
1 ADA sqn with Oerlikon
1 AD sqn with MIM-23 HAWK
1 AD sqn with *Spyder*
1 radar sqn with radar (mobile)
1 radar sqn with LORADS
MANOEUVRE
Other
4 (field def) sy sqn
EQUIPMENT BY TYPE
AIRCRAFT 134 combat capable
FTR 29: 20 F-5S *Tiger* II; 9 F-5T *Tiger* II
FGA 100: 40 F-15SG *Eagle*; 20 F-16C *Fighting Falcon*; 40 F-16D *Fighting Falcon* (incl reserves)
ATK (4 A-4SU *Super Skyhawk*; 10 TA-4SU *Super Skyhawk* in store)
MP 5 F-50 *Maritime Enforcer**
AEW&C 4 G550-AEW
TKR 5: 1 KC-130H *Hercules*; 4 KC-135R *Stratotanker*
TKR/TPT 4 KC-130B *Hercules*
TPT 9: **Medium** 5 C-130H *Hercules* (2 ELINT); **PAX** 4 F-50
TRG 31: 12 M-346 *Master*; 19 PC-21
HELICOPTERS
ATK 19 AH-64D *Apache*
ASW 10 S-70B *Seahawk*
TPT 51: **Heavy** 16: 6 CH-47D *Chinook*; 10 CH-47SD *Super D Chinook*; **Medium** 30: 18 AS332M *Super Puma* (incl 5 SAR); 12 AS532UL *Cougar*; **Light** 5 H120 *Colibri* (leased)
UNMANNED AERIAL VEHICLES
ISR 37+: **Heavy** 8+ *Heron* 1; **Medium** 29: 9+ *Hermes* 450; 20 *Searcher* MkII
AIR DEFENCE
SAM
Medium-range MIM-23 *Hawk*
Short-range *Spyder*-SR
Point-defence 9K38 *Igla* (SA-18 *Grouse*) (some on V-200/M113); *Mistral*; RBS-70
GUNS 34
SP 20mm GAI-C01
TOWED 34 **20mm** GAI-C01; **35mm** 34 GDF (with 25 *Super-Fledermaus* fire control radar)
AIR-LAUNCHED MISSILES
AAM • **IR** AIM-9N/P *Sidewinder*; *Python* 4 (reported); **IIR** AIM-9X *Sidewinder* II; **SARH** AIM-7P *Sparrow*; **ARH** (AIM-120C AMRAAM in store in US)
ASM: AGM-65B/G *Maverick*; AGM-114 *Hellfire*
AShM AGM-84 *Harpoon*; AM-39 *Exocet*
ARM AGM-45 *Shrike*
BOMBS • **Laser-guided** *Paveway* II

Paramilitary 19,900 active

Civil Defence Force 5,600 (incl conscripts); 500 auxiliaries; (total 6,100)

Singapore Police Force (including Coast Guard) 8,500; 3,500 conscript (total 12,000)
EQUIPMENT BY TYPE
PATROL AND COASTAL COMBATANTS 102
PBF 81: 25 *Angler Ray*; 2 *Atlantic Ray*; 1 *Marlin*; 11 *Sailfish*; 10 *Shark*; 32 other
PB 21: 19 *Amberjack*; 2 *Manta Ray*

Singapore Gurkha Contingent (under police) 1,800
FORCES BY ROLE
MANOEUVRE
Other
6 paramilitary coy

Cyber
The Singapore Ministry of Defence has long identified the potential damage that could be caused by cyber attacks, with this concern perhaps more acute following its adoption of the Integrated Knowledge-based Command-and-Control (IKC2) doctrine, designed to aid the transition of Singapore's Armed Forces to a 'third-generation' force.

A Cyber Defence Operations Hub was set up within the armed forces in 2013 and in 2016 it was announced that the number of personnel assigned to this hub would double by 2020. In 2015 the government established the Cyber Security Agency Singapore to act as a national body overseeing cyber-security strategy, outreach and industrial development.

DEPLOYMENT

AUSTRALIA
2 trg schools – 1 with 12 AS332 *Super Puma*/AS532 *Cougar* (flying trg) located at Oakey; 1 with PC-21 (flying trg) located at Pearce. Army: prepositioned AFVs and heavy equipment at Shoalwater Bay training area

BRUNEI
1 trg camp with inf units on rotation; 1 hel det with AS332 *Super Puma*

FRANCE
200: 1 trg sqn with 12 M-346 *Master*

QATAR
1 KC-135R (on rotation)

TAIWAN
3 trg camp (incl inf and arty)

THAILAND
1 trg camp (arty, cbt engr)

UNITED STATES
Trg units with F-16C/D; 12 F-15SG; AH-64D *Apache*; 6+ CH-47D *Chinook*

FOREIGN FORCES
United States US Pacific Command: 180; 1 naval spt facility at Changi naval base; 1 USAF log spt sqn at Paya Lebar air base

Sri Lanka LKA

Sri Lankan Rupee Rs		2015	2016	2017
GDP	Rs	11.2tr	12.1tr	
	US$	81.2bn	82.2bn	
per capita	US$	3,849	3,870	
Growth	%	4.8	5.0	
Inflation	%	6.9	4.1	
Def bdgt	Rs	277bn	289bn	297bn
	US$	2.01bn	1.96bn	
FMA (US)	US$			0.4m
US$1=Rs		137.64	147.70	

Population 22,235,000

Age	0–14	15–19	20–24	25–29	30–64	65 plus
Male	12.4%	3.7%	3.8%	3.6%	21.4%	4.0%
Female	11.9%	3.5%	3.7%	3.6%	23.0%	5.4%

Capabilities

Since the defeat of the Tamil Tigers, the armed forces have reoriented to a peacetime internal-security role. The army is reducing in size, but overall plans remain unclear. India considers Sri Lanka an increasingly important security partner, and is anxious to counter Pakistani and Chinese defence links with Colombo. There appears to have been little spending on new equipment since the end of the civil war, although Sri Lanka is looking to begin a series of procurements to fill key capability gaps. The navy's littoral capability, based on fast-attack and patrol boats, is being strengthened with the acquisition of offshore-patrol vessels. Military support has been provided by China, in an indication of a growing military-to-military relationship. However, India reportedly exerted pressure on Colombo to suspend the purchase of JF-17 fighters from Pakistan, stalling Sri Lanka's combat-aircraft-procurement programme. Sri Lanka has also taken delivery of its first offshore-patrol vessel from India. The US has eased its long-standing military-trade restrictions on Sri Lanka, and US foreign-military financing is expected to rise over the coming years. Sri Lanka's defence industry achieved an important milestone in securing its first export in 2016 – an order for nine patrol craft to Nigeria. Sri Lanka has little capacity for force projection beyond its national territory, but has sent small numbers of troops on UN missions.

ACTIVE 243,000 (Army 200,000 Navy 15,000 Air 28,000) Paramilitary 62,200

RESERVE 5,500 (Army 1,100 Navy 2,400 Air Force 2,000) Paramilitary 30,400

ORGANISATIONS BY SERVICE

Army 140,000; 60,00 active reservists (recalled) (total 200,000)

Regt are bn sized
FORCES BY ROLE
COMMAND
　7 region HQ
　21 div HQ
SPECIAL FORCES
　1 indep SF bde
MANOEUVRE
　Reconnaissance
　3 armd recce regt
　Armoured
　1 armd bde(-)
　Mechanised
　1 mech inf bde
　Light
　55 inf bde
　1 cdo bde
　Air Manoeuvre
　1 air mob bde
COMBAT SUPPORT
　7 arty regt
　1 MRL regt

8 engr regt
6 sigs regt

EQUIPMENT BY TYPE
ARMOURED FIGHTING VEHICLES
MBT 62 T-55A/T-55AM2
RECCE 15 *Saladin*
IFV 62: 13 BMP-1; 49 BMP-2
APC 211+
APC (T) 30+: some Type-63; 30 Type-85; some Type-89
APC (W) 181: 25 BTR-80/BTR-80A; 31 *Buffel*; 20 Type-92; 105 *Unicorn*
ENGINEERING & MAINTENANCE VEHICLES
ARV 16 VT-55
VLB 2 MT-55
ANTI-TANK/ANTI-INFRASTRUCTURE
RCL 40: **105mm** ε10 M-65; **106mm** ε30 M40
GUNS **85mm** 8 Type-56 (D-44)
ARTILLERY 908
TOWED 96: **122mm** 20; **130mm** 30 Type-59-I; **152mm** 46 Type-66 (D-20)
MRL **122mm** 28: 6 KRL-122; 22 RM-70
MOR 784: **81mm** 520; **82mm** 209; **120mm** 55 M-43
RADAR • LAND 4 AN/TPQ-36 *Firefinder* (arty)
UNMANNED AERIAL VEHICLES
ISR • **Medium** 1 *Seeker*

Navy 15,000 (incl 2,400 recalled reservists)

EQUIPMENT BY TYPE
PATROL AND COASTAL COMBATANTS 131
PSOH 1 *Sayura* (IND *Vigraha*)
PCG 2 *Nandimithra* (ISR *Sa'ar* 4) with 3 single lnchr with *Gabriel* II AShM, 1 76mm gun
PCO 2: 1 *Samadura* (ex-US *Reliance*); 1 *Sagara* (IND *Vikram*)
PCC 1 *Jayesagara*
PBF 79: 26 *Colombo*; 2 *Dvora*; 3 *Killer* (ROK); 6 *Shaldag*; 10 *Super Dvora* MkII/III; 5 *Trinity Marine*; 27 *Wave Rider*
PB 20: 4 *Cheverton*; 2 *Oshadi* (ex-AUS *Bay*); 2 *Prathapa* (PRC mod *Haizhui*); 3 *Ranajaya* (PRC *Haizhui*); 1 *Ranarisi* (PRC mod *Shanghai* II); 5 *Weeraya* (PRC *Shanghai* II); 3 (various)
PBR 26
AMPHIBIOUS
LANDING SHIPS • LSM 1 *Shakthi* (PRC *Yuhai*) (capacity 2 tanks; 250 troops)
LANDING CRAFT 8
LCM 2
LCP 3 *Hansaya*
LCU 2 *Yunnan*
UCAC 1 M 10 (capacity 56 troops)
LOGISTICS AND SUPPORT 2: 1 AP; 1 AX

Air Force 28,000 (incl SLAF Regt)

FORCES BY ROLE
FIGHTER
1 sqn with F-7BS/G; FT-7
FIGHTER/GROUND ATTACK
1 sqn with MiG-23UB *Flogger* C; MiG-27M *Flogger* J2
1 sqn with *Kfir* C-2/C-7/TC-2
1 sqn with K-8 *Karakorum**

TRANSPORT
1 sqn with An-32B *Cline*; C-130K *Hercules*; Cessna 421C *Golden Eagle*
1 sqn with Beech B200 *King Air*; Y-12 (II)
TRAINING
1 wg with PT-6, Cessna 150L
ATTACK HELICOPTER
1 sqn with Mi-24V *Hind* E; Mi-35P *Hind*
TRANSPORT HELICOPTER
1 sqn with Mi-17 *Hip* H; Mi-171Sh
1 sqn with Bell 206A/B (incl basic trg), Bell 212
1 (VIP) sqn with Bell 212; Bell 412 *Twin Huey*
ISR UAV
1 sqn with *Blue Horizon* II
1 sqn with *Searcher* MkII
MANOEUVRE
Other
1 (SLAF) sy regt
EQUIPMENT BY TYPE
AIRCRAFT 30 combat capable
FTR 8: 3 F-7BS; 4 F-7GS; 1 FT-7
FGA 15: 4 *Kfir* C-2; 2 *Kfir* C-7; 2 *Kfir* TC-2; 6 MiG-27M *Flogger* J2; 1 MiG-23UB *Flogger* C (conversion trg)
TPT 21: **Medium** 2 C-130K *Hercules*; **Light** 19: 3 An-32B *Cline*; 6 Cessna 150L; 1 Cessna 421C *Golden Eagle*; 7 Y-12 (II); 2 Y-12 (IV)
TRG 14: 7 K-8 *Karakoram**; 7 PT-6
HELICOPTERS
ATK 11: 6 Mi-24P *Hind*; 3 Mi-24V *Hind* E; 2 Mi-35V *Hind*
MRH 18: 6 Bell 412 *Twin Huey* (VIP); 2 Bell 412EP (VIP); 10 Mi-17 *Hip* H
TPT 16: **Medium** 4 Mi-171Sh; **Light** 12: 2 Bell 206A *Jet Ranger*; 2 Bell 206B *Jet Ranger*; 8 Bell 212
UNMANNED AERIAL VEHICLES
ISR • **Medium** 2+: some *Blue Horizon* II; 2 *Searcher* MkII
AIR DEFENCE • GUNS • TOWED 27: **40mm** 24 L/40; **94mm** 3 (3.7in)

Paramilitary ε62,200

Home Guard 13,000

National Guard ε15,000

Police Force 30,200; 1,000 (women) (total 31,200) 30,400 reservists

Ministry of Defence Special Task Force 3,000
Anti-guerrilla unit

Coast Guard n/k
EQUIPMENT BY TYPE
PATROL AND COASTAL COMBATANTS 11
PBF 8: 1 *Dvora*; 4 *Super Dvora* MkI; 3 *Killer* (ROK)
PB 2 Simonneau Type-508
PBR 1

DEPLOYMENT

CENTRAL AFRICAN REPUBLIC
UN • MINUSCA 116; 5 obs; 1 hel sqn

DEMOCRATIC REPUBLIC OF THE CONGO
UN • MONUSCO 4 obs

HAITI
UN • MINUSTAH 3

LEBANON
UN • UNIFIL 151; 1 inf coy

SOUTH SUDAN
UN • UNMISS 177; 2 obs; 1 hel sqn; 1 fd hospital

SUDAN
UN • UNISFA 1

WESTERN SAHARA
UN • MINURSO 3 obs

Taiwan (Republic of China) ROC

New Taiwan Dollar NT$		2015	2016	2017
GDP	NT$	16.7tr	16.9tr	
	US$	523	519	
per capita	US$	22,263	22,044	
Growth	%	0.6	1.0	
Inflation	%	-0.3	1.1	
Def bdgt	NT$	319bn	320bn	322bn
	US$	10.0bn	9.82bn	
US$1=NT$		31.91	32.58	

Population 23,464,787

Ethnic groups: Taiwanese 84%; mainland Chinese 14%

Age	0–14	15–19	20–24	25–29	30–64	65 plus
Male	6.8%	3.2%	3.5%	3.5%	26.6%	6.0%
Female	6.4%	3.1%	3.4%	3.4%	27.1%	7.1%

Capabilities

Taiwan's relationship with China and its attempts to sustain a credible military capability dominate its security policy. The armed forces remain well trained and exercise regularly, but Beijing's ongoing military recapitalisation continues to undermine Taipei's historic qualitative military advantage over the PLA. As a result, procurement efforts have been directed towards asymmetric and defensive items, such as development programmes for indigenous anti-ship missiles (*Hsiung-Feng* III) and cruise missiles (*Hsiung-Feng* IIE). Despite persistent US refusal to sanction the transfer of new combat aircraft, Taiwan has still been able to acquire modern US equipment to help it recapitalise in other areas, notably in anti-submarine warfare, helicopters, and air and missile defence. Under its indigenous submarine programme, it was reported in 2016 that the local China Shipbuilding Corporation had opened a centre to design the projected new submarine capability. Demographic pressure has influenced plans for force reductions and a shift towards an all-volunteer force; however, recruitment difficulties mean that conscription will remain in force in the near term, although the period of service for those born after 1994 has been reduced to four months.

ACTIVE 215,000 (Army 130,000 Navy 40,000 Air 45,000) **Paramilitary 17,000**

Conscript liability (19–40 years) 12 months for those born before 1993; four months for those born after 1994 (alternative service available)

RESERVE 1,657,000 (Army 1,500,000 Navy 67,000 Air Force 90,000)
Some obligation to age 30

ORGANISATIONS BY SERVICE

Army ε130,000 (incl ε10,000 MP)
FORCES BY ROLE
COMMAND
  3 corps HQ
  5 defence comd HQ
SPECIAL FORCES/HELICOPTER
  1 SF/hel comd (2 spec ops gp, 2 hel bde)
MANOEUVRE
  Armoured
  4 armd bde
  Mechanised
  3 mech inf bde
  Light
  6 inf bde
COMBAT SUPPORT
  3 arty gp
  3 engr gp
  3 CBRN gp
  3 sigs gp
COASTAL DEFENCE
  1 AShM bn

Reserves
FORCES BY ROLE
MANOEUVRE
  Light
  21 inf bde
EQUIPMENT BY TYPE
ARMOURED FIGHTING VEHICLES
  MBT 565: 200 M60A3; 100 M48A5; 265 M48H *Brave Tiger*
  LT TK 625 M41/Type-64; (230 M24 *Chaffee* (90mm gun); in store)
  IFV 225 CM-25 (M113 with 20–30mm cannon)
  APC 1,220
    APC (T) 650 M113
    APC (W) 570: ε270 CM-32 *Yunpao*; 300 LAV-150 *Commando*
ENGINEERING & MAINTENANCE VEHICLES
  AEV 18 M9
  ARV CM-27/A1; 37 M88A1
  VLB 22 M3; M48A5
NBC VEHICLES 48+: BIDS; 48 K216A1; KM453
ANTI-TANK/ANTI-INFRASTRUCTURE
  MSL
    SP TOW
    MANPATS FGM-148 *Javelin*; TOW
  RCL 500+: **90mm** M67; **106mm** 500+: 500 M40A1; Type-51

ARTILLERY 2,254
SP 488: **105mm** 100 M108; **155mm** 318: 225 M109A2/A5; 48 M44T; 45 T-69; **203mm** 70 M110
TOWED 1,060+: **105mm** 650 T-64 (M101); **155mm** 340+: 90 M59; 250 T-65 (M114); M44; XT-69; **203mm** 70 M115
MRL 330: **117mm** 120 *Kung Feng* VI; **126mm** 210: 60 *Kung Feng* III/*Kung Feng* IV; 150 RT 2000 *Thunder* (KF towed and SP)
MOR 322+
  SP 162+: **81mm** 72+: M29; 72 M125; **107mm** 90 M106A2
  TOWED 81mm 160 M29; T-75; **107mm** M30; **120mm** K5; XT-86
RADAR 1 AN/TPQ-37 *Firefinder*
COASTAL DEFENCE
  ARTY 54: **127mm** ε50 US Mk32 (reported); **240mm** 4 M1
  AShM *Ching Feng*
HELICOPTERS
  ATK 96: 67 AH-1W *Cobra*; 29 AH-64E *Apache*
  MRH 38 OH-58D *Kiowa Warrior*
  TPT 96: **Heavy** 8 CH-47SD *Super D Chinook*; **Medium** 12 UH-60M *Black Hawk*; **Light** 76 Bell 205 (UH-1H *Iroquois*)
  TRG 29 TH-67 *Creek*
UNMANNED AERIAL VEHICLES
  ISR • Light *Mastiff* III
AIR DEFENCE
  SAM • Point-defence 76: 74 M1097 *Avenger*; 2 M48 *Chaparral*; FIM-92 *Stinger*
  GUNS 400
    SP 40mm M42
    TOWED 20: 35mm 20 GDF-001 (30 systems with 20 guns) **40mm** L/70

Navy 40,000

3 district; 1 (ASW) HQ located at Hualien; 1 Fleet HQ located at Tsoying; 1 New East Coast Fleet

EQUIPMENT BY TYPE
SUBMARINES • TACTICAL • SSK 4:
  2 *Hai Lung* with 6 single 533mm TT with SUT HWT/ UGM-84L *Harpoon* AShM
  2 *Hai Shih*† (ex-US *Guppy* II – trg role) with 10 single 533mm TT (6 fwd, 4 aft) with SUT HWT
PRINCIPAL SURFACE COMBATANTS 26
  CRUISERS • CGHM 4 *Keelung* (ex-US *Kidd*) with 1 quad lnchr with RGM-84L *Harpoon* AShM, 2 twin Mk26 lnchr with SM-2MR SAM, 2 triple Mk32 324mm ASTT with Mk46 LWT, 2 *Phalanx* Block 1B CIWS, 2 127mm gun (capacity 1 S-70 ASW hel)
  FRIGATES 22
    FFGHM 20:
      8 *Cheng Kung* with 2 quad lnchr with *Hsiung Feng* II/III AShM, 1 Mk13 GMLS with SM-1MR SAM, 2 triple 324mm ASTT with Mk 46 LWT, 1 *Phalanx* Block 1B CIWS, 1 76mm gun (capacity 2 S-70C ASW hel)
      6 *Chin Yang* (ex-US *Knox*) with 1 octuple Mk112 lnchr with ASROC/RGM-84C *Harpoon* AShM, 2 triple lnchr with SM-1MR SAM, 2 twin lnchr with SM-1MR SAM, 2 twin 324mm ASTT with Mk 46 LWT, 1 *Phalanx* Block 1B CIWS, 1 127mm gun (capacity 1 MD-500 hel)
      6 *Kang Ding* with 2 quad lnchr with *Hsiung Feng* II AShM, 1 quad lnchr with *Sea Chaparral* SAM, 2 triple 324mm ASTT with Mk 46 LWT, 1 *Phalanx* Block 1B CIWS, 1 76mm gun (capacity 1 S-70C ASW hel)
    FFGH 2:
      2 *Chin Yang* (ex-US *Knox*) with 1 octuple Mk112 lnchr with ASROC/RGM-84C *Harpoon* AShM, 2 twin 324mm ASTT with Mk 46 LWT, 1 *Phalanx* Block 1B CIWS, 1 127mm gun (capacity 1 MD-500 hel)
PATROL AND COASTAL COMBATANTS 51
  CORVETTES • FSG 1 *Tuo Jiang* (*Hsun Hai*) with 8 twin lnchr with *Hsiung Feng* III AShM, 1 *Phalanx* Block 1B CIWS; 1 76mm gun
  PCG 12:
    10 *Jin Chiang* with 1 quad lnchr with *Hsiung Feng* II/III AShM
    2 *Jin Chiang* with 1 quad lnchr with *Hsiung Feng* III AShM, 1 76mm gun
  PBG 31 *Kwang Hua* with 2 twin lnchr with *Hsiung Feng* II AShM
  PBF 8 *Ning Hai*
MINE WARFARE • MINE COUNTERMEASURES 14
  MHC 2 *Yung Jin* (ex-US *Osprey*)
  MSC 8: 4 *Yung Chuan* (ex-US *Adjutant*); 4 *Yung Feng*
  MSO 4 *Yung Yang* (ex-US *Aggressive*)
COMMAND SHIPS • LCC 1 *Kao Hsiung*
AMPHIBIOUS
  PRINCIPAL AMPHIBIOUS SHIPS • LSD 1 *Shiu Hai* (ex-US *Anchorage*) with 2 *Phalanx* CIWS, 1 hel landing platform (capacity either 2 LCU or 18 LCM; 360 troops)
  LANDING SHIPS
    LST 12:
      10 *Chung Hai* (capacity 16 tanks; 200 troops)
      2 *Chung Ho* (ex-US *Newport*) with 1 *Phalanx* CIWS , 1 hel landing platform (capacity 3 LCVP, 400 troops)
  LANDING CRAFT 278: 8 **LCU**; 100 **LCVP**; 170 **LCM**
LOGISTICS AND SUPPORT 10
  AGOR 1 *Ta Kuan*
  AK 1 *Wu Kang* with 1 hel landing platform (capacity 1,400 troops)
  AOEH 1 *Panshih*
  AOE 1 *Wu Yi* with 1 hel landing platform
  ARS 6

Marines 10,000
FORCES BY ROLE
MANOEUVRE
  Amphibious
  3 mne bde
COMBAT SUPPORT
  Some cbt spt unit
EQUIPMENT BY TYPE
ARMOURED FIGHITNG VEHICLES
  AAV 202: 52 AAV-7A1; 150 LVTP-5A1
ENGINEERING & MAINTENANCE VEHICLES
  ARV 2 AAVR-7
ANIT-TANK/ANTI-INFRASTRUCTURE
  RCL 106mm
ARTILLERY • TOWED 105mm; 155mm

Naval Aviation
FORCES BY ROLE
ANTI SUBMARINE WARFARE
3 sqn with S-70C *Seahawk* (S-70C *Defender*)
EQUIPMENT BY TYPE
HELICOPTERS • ASW 20 S-70C *Seahawk* (S-70C *Defender*)

Air Force 45,000
Flying hours 180 hrs/yr
FORCES BY ROLE
FIGHTER
3 sqn with *Mirage* 2000-5E/D (2000-5EI/DI)
FIGHTER/GROUND ATTACK
3 sqn with F-5E/F *Tiger* II
6 sqn with F-16A/B *Fighting Falcon*
5 sqn with F-CK-1A/B *Ching Kuo*
ANTI-SUBMARINE WARFARE
1 sqn with S-2T *Turbo Tracker*/P-3C *Orion*
ELECTRONIC WARFARE
1 sqn with C-130HE *Tien Gian*
ISR
1 sqn with RF-5E *Tigereye*
AIRBORNE EARLY WARNING & CONTROL
1 sqn with E-2T *Hawkeye*
SEARCH & RESCUE
1 sqn with H225; S-70C *Black Hawk*
TRANSPORT
2 sqn with C-130H *Hercules*
1 (VIP) sqn with B-727-100; B-737-800; Beech 1900; F-50; S-70C *Black Hawk*
TRAINING
1 sqn with AT-3A/B *Tzu-Chung**
1 sqn with Beech 1900
1 (basic) sqn with T-34C *Turbo Mentor*
EQUIPMENT BY TYPE
AIRCRAFT 493 combat capable
FTR 287: 87 F-5E/F *Tiger* II (some in store); 144 F-16A/B *Fighting Falcon*; 9 *Mirage* 2000-5D (2000-5DI); 47 *Mirage* 2000-5E (2000-5EI)
FGA 128 F-CK-1A/B *Ching Kuo*
ASW 23: 11 S-2T *Tracker*; 12 P-3C *Orion*
EW 1 C-130HE *Tien Gian*
ISR 7 RF-5E *Tigereye*
AEW&C 6 E-2T *Hawkeye*
TPT 34: **Medium** 20 C-130H *Hercules*; **Light** 10 Beech 1900; **PAX** 4: 1 B-737-800; 3 F-50
TRG 97: 55 AT-3A/B *Tzu-Chung**; 42 T-34C *Turbo Mentor*
HELICOPTERS
TPT • Medium 19: 3 H225; 16 S-70C *Black Hawk*
AIR DEFENCE • SAM • Point-defence *Antelope*
AIR-LAUNCHED MISSILES
AAM • IR AIM-9J/P *Sidewinder*; R-550 *Magic* 2; *Shafrir*; *Sky Sword* I; **IR/ARH** *Mica*; **ARH** AIM-120C *AMRAAM*; *Sky Sword* II
ASM AGM-65A *Maverick*
AShM AGM-84 *Harpoon*
ARM *Sky Sword* IIA
BOMBS • Laser-guided *Paveway* II

Missile Command
FORCES BY ROLE
SURFACE-TO-SURFACE MISSILE
3 SSM bty with *Hsiung Feng* IIE
AIR DEFENCE
2 AD/SAM gp (total: 13 bty with MIM-23 HAWK; 4 bty with MIM-104F *Patriot* PAC-3; 6 bty with *Tien Kung* I *Sky Bow*/*Tien Kung* II *Sky Bow*)
EQUIPMENT BY TYPE
SURFACE-TO-SURFACE MISSILE LAUNCHERS
GLCM • **Conventional** ε12 *Hsiung Feng* IIE
AIR DEFENCE • SAM • Medium-range 600+: 100 MIM-23 HAWK; ε500 *Tien Kung* I *Sky Bow*/*Tien Kung* II *Sky Bow*
MISSILE DEFENCE • Medium-range 24+ MIM-104F *Patriot* PAC-3

Paramilitary 17,000

Coast Guard 17,000
EQUIPMENT BY TYPE
PATROL AND COASTAL COMBATANTS 146
PSOH 2 *Yilan*
PSO 7: 2 *Ho Hsing*; 3 *Shun Hu* 7; 2 *Tainan*
PCO 14: 1 *Teh Hsing*; 2 *Kinmen*; 2 *Mou Hsing*; 1 *Shun Hu* 1; 2 *Shun Hu* 2/3; 4 *Taichung*; 2 *Taipei*
PBF 63 (various)
PB 60: 1 *Shun Hu* 5; 1 *Shun Hu* 6; 58 (various)

Directorate General (Customs)
EQUIPMENT BY TYPE
PATROL AND COASTAL COMBATANTS 9
PCO 1 *Yun Hsing*
PB 8: 4 *Hai Cheng*; 4 *Hai Ying*

Cyber
Although Taiwan has a highly developed civilian IT sector, the Taiwanese government has been relatively slow to exploit this advantage for national-defence purposes. But for the past decade, Taipei has worked on its *Po Sheng – Broad Victory –* C4ISR programme, an all-hazards-defence system with a significant defence component located in the Hengshan Command Center, which also houses the Tri-Service Command. The main focus of the military component of this programme is countering PLA IW and EW attacks. The authorities responsible for cyber activity include the National Security Bureau (NSB), the defence ministry, and the Research, Development and Evaluation Commission (RDEC). In 2015, it was reported that the National Security Bureau was to establish a cyber-security department to improve surveillance capacity.

FOREIGN FORCES
Singapore 3 trg camp (incl inf and arty)

Thailand THA

Thai Baht b		2015	2016	2017
GDP	b	13.5tr	14.1tr	
	US$	395bn	391bn	
per capita	US$	5,742	5,662	
Growth	%	2.8	3.2	
Inflation	%	-0.9	0.3	
Def bdgt	b	193bn	206bn	211bn
	US$	5.63	5.72	
FMA (US)	US$	1m		
US$1=b		34.25	36.11	

Population 68,200,824

Ethnic and religious groups: Thai 75%; Chinese 14%; Muslim 4%

Age	0–14	15–19	20–24	25–29	30–64	65 plus
Male	8.8%	3.5%	3.9%	3.6%	24.8%	4.5%
Female	8.4%	3.3%	3.8%	3.5%	26.2%	5.7%

Capabilities

Thailand has large, well-funded armed forces. In particular, its air force is one of the best equipped and trained in Southeast Asia: the introduction into service of *Gripen* combat aircraft and Saab 340 airborne early-warning platforms has significantly boosted the effectiveness of Thailand's airpower. However, despite the fact that the armed forces have benefited from substantially increased budgets during the present decade and from engagement in bilateral and multinational exercises with regional partners and the US, they remain army-dominated. The army, and marines, have continued counter-insurgency operations against ethnic-Malay separatists in Thailand's three southernmost provinces, where peace talks have made no significant progress. Meanwhile, the armed forces' entanglement in domestic politics has often overshadowed efforts to sustain and modernise operational capability. The May 2014 coup again brought the armed forces into a central political role, undermining Thailand's defence relations with the US, which reduced its participation in the annual exercise *Cobra Gold* in 2015 and 2016. Defence relations with Beijing have warmed: the military government has expressed interest in buying Chinese submarines, and there was a bilateral air-combat exercise in November 2015. However, the approval of a new constitution (in an August 2016 referendum) and the likelihood of elections for a new government in late 2017 appear likely to provide a basis for restored defence ties with the US.

ACTIVE 360,850 (Army 245,000 Navy 69,850 Air 46,000) **Paramilitary 93,700**

Conscription liability 2 years

RESERVE 200,000 Paramilitary 45,000

ORGANISATIONS BY SERVICE

Army 130,000; ε115,000 conscript (total 245,000)

FORCES BY ROLE
COMMAND
4 (regional) army HQ
3 corps HQ
SPECIAL FORCES
1 SF div
1 SF regt
MANOEUVRE
Armoured
3 cav div (1 recce bn; 3 tk regt (3 tk bn); 1 indep tk bn; 1 sigs bn; 1 maint bn; 1 hel sqn)
Mechanised
1 mech inf div (1 recce coy; 1 recce sqn; 1 tk bn; 1 inf regt (4 inf bn); 3 inf regt; 1 engr bn; 1 sigs bn)
Light
8 inf div (1 recce sqn; 3 inf regt (3 inf bn); 1 engr bn; 1 sigs bn)
COMBAT SUPPORT
1 arty div
1 engr div
COMBAT SERVICE SUPPORT
4 economic development div
HELICOPTER
Some hel flt
AIR DEFENCE
1 ADA div (6 bn)

EQUIPMENT BY TYPE
ARMOURED FIGHTING VEHICLE
MBT 303: 53 M60A1; 125 M60A3; (50 Type-69 in store); 105 M48A5; 20 T-84 *Oplot*
LT TK 194: 24 M41; 104 *Scorpion* (50 in store); 66 *Stingray*
RECCE 32 S52 *Shorland*
IFV 223 BTR-3E1 (incl variants)
APC 1,140
 APC (T) 880: *Bronco*; 430 M113A1/A3; 450 Type-85
 APC (W) 160: 18 *Condor*; 142 LAV-150 *Commando*
PPV 100 REVA
ENGINEERING & MAINTENANCE VEHICLES
ARV 48: 5 BTR-3BR; 22 M88A1; 6 M88A2; 10 M113; 5 Type-653; WZT-4
VLB Type-84
MW *Bozena*; *Giant Viper*
ANTI-TANK/ANTI-INFRASTRUCTURE
MSL
 SP 24+: 18+ M901A5 (TOW); 6 BTR-3RK
 MANPATS M47 *Dragon*
RCL 180: **75mm** 30 M20; **106mm** 150 M40
ARTILLERY 2,547
SP 155mm 32: 6 ATMOS-2000; 6 CAESAR; 20 M109A5
TOWED 617: **105mm** 340: 24 LG1 MkII; 12 M-56; 200 M101/M425; 12 M102; 32 M618A2; 60 L119 Light Gun; **155mm** 277: 90 GHN-45 A1; 48 M114; 118 M198; 21 M-71
MRL 84: **122mm** 4 SR-4; **130mm** 60 Type-85; **302mm** 4: 1 DTI-1 (WS-1B); 3 DTI-1G (WS-32)
MOR 1,900+: SP **81mm** 21 M125A3; SP **107mm** M106A3; SP **120mm** 12 M1064A3; 1,867 **81mm/107mm/120mm**
RADAR • LAND AN/TPQ-36 *Firefinder* (arty, mor); RASIT (veh, arty)
AIRCRAFT
TPT • Light 20: 2 Beech 200 *King Air*; 2 Beech 1900C; 1 C-212 *Aviocar*; 1 C-295W; 10 Cessna A185E (U-17B); 2 ERJ-135LR; 2 *Jetstream* 41

TRG 33: 11 MX-7-235 *Star Rocket*; 22 T-41B *Mescalero*
HELICOPTERS
ATK 7 AH-1F *Cobra*
MRH 13: 8 AS550 *Fennec*; 2 AW139; 3 Mi-17V-5 *Hip* H
TPT 211: **Heavy** 5 CH-47D *Chinook*; **Medium** 12: 9 UH-60L *Black Hawk*; 3 UH-60M *Black Hawk*; **Light** 194: 93 Bell 205 (UH-1H *Iroquois*); 27 Bell 206 *Jet Ranger*; 52 Bell 212 (AB-212); 16 Enstrom 480B; 5 UH-72 *Lakota*
TRG 53 Hughes 300C
UNMANNED AERIAL VEHICLES
ISR • **Medium** *Searcher*; *Searcher* II
AIR DEFENCE
SAM
Short-range *Aspide*
Point-defence 8+: 8 *Starstreak*; 9K338 *Igla-S* (SA-24 *Grinch*)
GUNS 184
SP 54: **20mm** 24 M163 *Vulcan*; **40mm** 30 M1/M42 SP
TOWED 130: **20mm** 24 M167 *Vulcan*; **37mm** 52 Type-74; **40mm** 48 L/70; **57mm** ε6 Type-59 (S-60); (18+ more non-operational)

Reserves

FORCES BY ROLE
COMMAND
1 inf div HQ

Navy 44,000 (incl Naval Aviation, Marines, Coastal Defence); 25,850 conscript (total 69,850)

EQUIPMENT BY TYPE
PRINCIPAL SURFACE COMBATANTS 10
AIRCRAFT CARRIERS • CVH 1:
1 *Chakri Naruebet* with 2 sextuple *Sadral* lnchr with *Mistral* SAM (capacity 6 S-70B *Seahawk* ASW hel)
FRIGATES 9
FFGHM 2:
2 *Naresuan* with 2 quad Mk141 lnchr with RGM-84A *Harpoon* AShM, 1 8 cell Mk41 VLS with RIM-7M *Sea Sparrow* SAM, 2 triple Mk32 324mm TT, 1 127mm gun (capacity 1 *Super Lynx* 300 hel)
FFGM 4:
2 *Chao Phraya* with 4 twin lnchr with C-802A AShM, 2 twin lnchr with HHQ-61 (CSA-N-2) SAM (non-operational), 2 RBU 1200 A/S mor, 2 twin 100mm gun
2 *Kraburi* with 4 twin lnchr with C-802A AShM, 2 twin lnchr with HHQ-61 (CSA-N-2) SAM, 2 RBU 1200 A/S mor, 1 twin 100mm gun, 1 hel landing platform
FFGH 1 *Phuttha Yotfa Chulalok* (ex-US *Knox*) with 1 octuple Mk112 lnchr with RGM-84C *Harpoon* AShM/ASROC, 2 twin 324mm ASTT with Mk 46 LWT, 1 *Phalanx* CIWS, 1 127mm gun (capacity 1 Bell 212 (AB-212) hel)
FF 2:
1 *Makut Rajakumarn* with 2 triple 324mm ASTT, 2 114mm gun
1 *Pin Klao* (trg role) with 6 single 324mm ASTT, 3 76mm gun

PATROL AND COASTAL COMBATANTS 84
CORVETTES 7
FSG 2 *Rattanakosin* with 2 quad Mk140 lnchr with RGM-84A *Harpoon* AShM, 1 octuple *Albatros* lnchr with *Aspide* SAM, 2 triple Mk32 324mm ASTT with *Stingray* LWT, 1 76mm gun
FS 5:
3 *Khamronsin* with 2 triple 324mm ASTT with *Stingray* LWT, 1 76mm gun
2 *Tapi* with 2 triple 324mm ASTT with Mk46 LWT, 1 76mm gun
PSO 1 *Krabi* (UK *River* mod) with 1 76mm gun
PCFG 6:
3 *Prabparapak* with 2 single lnchr with *Gabriel* I AShM, 1 triple lnchr with *Gabriel* I AShM, 1 57mm gun
3 *Ratcharit* with 2 twin lnchr with MM-38 *Exocet* AShM, 1 76mm gun
PCOH 2 *Pattani* with 1 76mm gun
PCO 3 *Hua Hin* with 1 76mm gun
PCC 9: 3 *Chon Buri* with 2 76mm gun; 6 *Sattahip* with 1 76mm gun
PBF 4
PB 52: 7 T-11; 4 *Swift*; 3 T-81; 9 T-91; 3 T-111; 3 T-210; 13 T-213; 1 T-227; 3 T-228; 3 T-991; 3 T-994
MINE WARFARE • MINE COUNTERMEASURES 17
MCM SPT 1 *Thalang*
MCO 2 *Lat Ya*
MCC 2 *Bang Rachan*
MSR 12
AMPHIBIOUS
PRINCIPAL AMPHIBIOUS SHIPS 1
LPD 1 *Anthong* (SGP *Endurance*) with 1 76mm gun (capacity 2 hel; 19 MBT; 500 troops)
LANDING SHIPS 2
LST 2 *Sichang* with 2 hel landing platform (capacity 14 MBT; 300 troops)
LANDING CRAFT 56
LCU 13: 3 *Man Nok*; 6 *Mataphun* (capacity either 3–4 MBT or 250 troops); 4 *Thong Kaeo*
LCM 24
LCVP 12
LCA 4
UCAC 3 *Griffon* 1000TD
LOGISTICS AND SUPPORT 13
ABU 1
AGOR 1
AGS 2
AOL 6: 1 *Matra* with 1 hel landing platform; 4 *Prong*; 1 *Samui*
AOR 1 *Chula*
AORH 1 *Similan* (capacity 1 hel)
AWT 1

Naval Aviation 1,200

EQUIPMENT BY TYPE
AIRCRAFT 3 combat capable
ASW 2 P-3A *Orion* (P-3T)
ISR 9 *Sentry* O-2-337
MP 1 F-27-200 MPA*
TPT • Light 15: 7 Do-228-212; 2 ERJ-135LR; 2 F-27-400M *Troopship*; 3 N-24A *Searchmaster*; 1 UP-3A *Orion* (UP-3T)

HELICOPTERS
  ASW 8: 6 S-70B *Seahawk*; 2 *Super Lynx* 300
  MRH 2 MH-60S *Knight Hawk*
  TPT 15: **Medium** 2 Bell 214ST (AB-214ST); **Light** 13: 6 Bell 212 (AB-212); 2 H145M; 5 S-76B
  AIR-LAUNCHED MISSILES • AShM AGM-84 *Harpoon*

Marines 23,000
FORCES BY ROLE
COMMAND
  1 mne div HQ
MANOEUVRE
  Reconnaissance
  1 recce bn
  Light
  2 inf regt (total: 6 bn)
  Amphibious
  1 amph aslt bn
COMBAT SUPPORT
  1 arty regt (3 fd arty bn, 1 ADA bn)
EQUIPMENT BY TYPE
ARMOURED FIGHTING VEHICLES
  IFV 14 BTR-3E1
  APC (W) 24 LAV-150 *Commando*
  AAV 33 LVTP-7
ENGINEERING & MAINTENANCE VEHICLES
  ARV 1 AAVR-7
ANTI-TANK/ANTI-INFRASTRUCTURE • MSL
  SP 10 M1045A2 HMMWV with TOW
  MANPATS M47 *Dragon*; TOW
ARTILLERY • TOWED 48: **105mm** 36 (reported); **155mm** 12 GC-45
AIR DEFENCE • GUNS 12.7mm 14

Naval Special Warfare Command

Air Force ε46,000
4 air divs, one flying trg school
Flying hours 100 hrs/yr
FORCES BY ROLE
FIGHTER
  2 sqn with F-5E/5F *Tiger* II
  3 sqn with F-16A/B *Fighting Falcon*
FIGHTER/GROUND ATTACK
  1 sqn with Gripen C/D
GROUND ATTACK
  1 sqn with *Alpha Jet**
  1 sqn with AU-23A *Peacemaker*
  1 sqn with L-39ZA *Albatros**
ELINT/ISR
  1 sqn with DA42 MPP *Guardian*;
AIRBORNE EARLY WARNING & CONTROL
  1 sqn with Saab 340B; Saab 340 *Erieye*
TRANSPORT
  1 (Royal Flight) sqn with A310-324; A319CJ; B-737-800
  1 sqn with ATR-72; BAe-748
  1 sqn with BT-67
  1 sqn with C-130H/H-30 *Hercules*
TRAINING
  1 sqn with L-39ZA *Albatros**
  1 sqn with CT-4A/B *Airtrainer*; T-41D *Mescalero*
  1 sqn with CT-4E *Airtrainer*
  1 sqn with PC-9
TRANSPORT HELICOPTER
  1 sqn with Bell 205 (UH-1H *Iroquois*)
  1 sqn with Bell 412 *Twin Huey*; S-92A
EQUIPMENT BY TYPE
AIRCRAFT 150 combat capable
  FTR 78: 1 F-5B *Freedom Fighter*; 21 F-5E *Tiger* II; 3 F-5F *Tiger* II (F-5E/F being upgraded); 38 F-16A *Fighting Falcon*; 15 F-16B *Fighting Falcon*
  FGA 12: 8 *Gripen* C; 4 *Gripen* D
  ATK 17 AU-23A *Peacemaker*
  ISR 5 DA42 MPP *Guardian*
  AEW&C 2 Saab 340 *Erieye*
  TPT 48: **Medium** 14: 6 C-130H *Hercules*; 6 C-130H-30 *Hercules*; 2 Saab 340B; **Light** 21: 3 ATR-72; 3 Beech 200 *King Air*; 8 BT-67; 1 *Commander* 690; 6 DA42M; **PAX** 13: 1 A310-324; 1 A319CJ; 1 A320CJ; 1 B-737-800; 5 BAe-748; 2 SSJ-100-95LR **TRG** 110: 16 *Alpha Jet**; 13 CT-4A *Airtrainer*; 6 CT-4B *Airtrainer*; 20 CT-4E *Airtrainer*; 27 L-39ZA *Albatros**; 21 PC-9; 7 T-41D *Mescalero*
HELICOPTERS
  MRH 11: 2 Bell 412 *Twin Huey*; 2 Bell 412SP *Twin Huey*; 1 Bell 412HP *Twin Huey*; 6 Bell 412EP *Twin Huey*
  CSAR 4 H225M *Super Cougar*
  TPT 20: **Medium** 3 S-92A *Super Hawk*; **Light** 17 Bell 205 (UH-1H *Iroquois*)
AIR-LAUNCHED MISSILES
  AAM • IR AIM-9B/J *Sidewinder*; *Python* 3; **ARH** AIM-120 AMRAAM
  ASM AGM-65 *Maverick*
BOMBS • Laser-guided *Paveway* II

Paramilitary ε93,700

Border Patrol Police 20,000

Marine Police 2,200
EQUIPMENT BY TYPE
PATROL AND COASTAL COMBATANTS 94
  PCO 1 *Srinakrin*
  PCC 2 *Hameln*
  PB 45: 2 *Chasanyabadee*; 3 *Cutlass*; 2 *Ratayapibanbancha* (*Reef Ranger*); 1 *Sriyanont*; 1 *Yokohama*; 36 (various)
  PBR 46

National Security Volunteer Corps 45,000 – Reserves

Police Aviation 500
EQUIPMENT BY TYPE
AIRCRAFT 6 combat capable
  ATK 6 AU-23A *Peacemaker*
  TPT 16: **Light** 15: 2 CN-235; 8 PC-6 *Turbo-Porter*; 3 SC-7 3M *Skyvan*; 2 Short 330UTT; **PAX** 1 F-50
HELICOPTERS
  MRH 6 Bell 412 *Twin Huey*
  TPT • Light 61: 27 Bell 205A; 14 Bell 206 *Jet Ranger*; 20 Bell 212 (AB-212)

Provincial Police 50,000 (incl ε500 Special Action Force)

Thahan Phran (Hunter Soldiers) 21,000
Volunteer irregular force
FORCES BY ROLE
MANOEUVRE
 Other
  22 paramilitary regt (total: 275 paramilitary coy)

DEPLOYMENT

Legal provisions for foreign deployment:
Constitution: In addition to the below, government has to ensure no violation of Para. 1 and 2 of Provision 190 of the Constitution of the Kingdom of Thailand, BE 2550
Decision on deployment of troops abroad: Depends on operation. In case of PSO or HADR, cabinet resolution endorsing deployment and defence-council concurrence would constitute legislation. Legal provisions for foreign deployment generally under the Defence Act, BE 2551 (2008). Justification for overseas missions is in accordance with following sections of the Act: Provision 37, Art. 4: Minister of Defence has exclusive authority to arrange and deploy armed forces to areas considered appropriate; Provision 38, Art. 4: Employment of armed forces for peace operations shall be endorsed by council of ministers with concurrence of defence council. No terms of reference on 'the foreign deployment of forces for combat operations in [a] conventional war area are stipulated' in the Act, so deployment purpose and operation type should be clearly determined

INDIA/PAKISTAN
UN • UNMOGIP 3 obs

SUDAN
UN • UNAMID 7; 4 obs

FOREIGN FORCES

United States US Pacific Command: 300

Timor-Leste TLS

US$		2015	2016	2017
GDP	US$	2.87bn	2.50bn	
per capita	US$	2,462	2,104	
Growth	%	4.3	5.0	
Inflation	%	0.6	-0.6	
Def bdgt	US$	72m	26m	27m
FMA (US)	US$	0.3m		

Population 1,261,072

Age	0–14	15–19	20–24	25–29	30–64	65 plus
Male	21.3%	5.7%	4.5%	3.6%	13.2%	1.8%
Female	20.1%	5.4%	4.5%	3.9%	14.0%	2.0%

Capabilities

The small Timor-Leste Defence Force (F-FDTL) has been plagued by inadequate funding, personnel shortages, poor morale and ill-discipline since it was established in 2001. While the F-FDTL is responsible for external defence, its parallel internal-security role has sometimes brought it into conflict with the national police force, which has an overlapping responsibility. Following the dismissal in 2006 of half of the defence force's personnel, there was a general collapse of the security forces. With external assistance – mainly from Australia and Portugal – the F-FDTL has been reconstituted but is still a long way from meeting the ambitious force-structure goals set out in the controversial Force 2020 plan published in 2007. The origins of the F-FDTL in the Falintil national resistance force (which waged a successful insurgency against occupying Indonesian forces in 1975–99) and a continuing training and doctrinal emphasis on low-intensity infantry tactics mean that the force provides a deterrent to invasion. However, the two regular infantry battalions are believed to remain under-strength. In 2014, and again in early 2016, Australia offered to boost the F-FDTL naval component's capability by providing 'a complete patrol boat capability', but there was no response from Timor-Leste's government, almost certainly because of the dispute between Dili and Canberra over maritime-boundary delimitation.

ACTIVE 1,330 (Army 1,250 Naval Element 80)

ORGANISATIONS BY SERVICE

Army 1,250

Training began in January 2001 with the aim of deploying 1,500 full-time personnel and 1,500 reservists. Authorities are engaged in developing security structures with international assistance
FORCES BY ROLE
MANOEUVRE
 Light
  2 inf bn
COMBAT SUPPORT
 1 MP pl
COMBAT SERVICE SUPPORT
 1 log spt coy

Naval Element 80
EQUIPMENT BY TYPE
PATROL AND COASTAL COMBATANTS 7
 PB 7: 2 *Albatros*; 2 *Dili* (ex-ROK); 2 *Shanghai* II; 1 *Kamenassa* (ex-ROK *Chamsuri*)

DEPLOYMENT

SOUTH SUDAN
UN • UNMISS 3 obs

Vietnam VNM

Vietnamese Dong d		2015	2016	2017
GDP	d	4193tr	4555tr	
	US$	191bn	200bn	
per capita	US$	2,088	2,164	
Growth	%	6.7	6.1	
Inflation	%	0.6	2.0	
Def bdgt	d	ε83.9tr	ε91.1tr	
	US$	ε3.83bn	ε4.01bn	
FMA (US)	US$	11m	12m	10m
US$1=d		21,900.10	22,718.55	

Population 95,261,021

Ethnic groups: Kinh 85.7%; Tay 1.9%; Thai 1.8%; Khome 1.4%; Hmong 1.3%; other or unspecified 7.1%

Age	0–14	15–19	20–24	25–29	30–64	65 plus
Male	12.5%	4.1%	4.6%	4.8%	21.7%	2.3%
Female	11.3%	3.7%	4.3%	4.6%	22.3%	3.7%

Capabilities

Vietnam has a stronger military tradition and its armed forces have more operational experience than any of its Southeast Asian neighbours. Its defence efforts and conscript-based armed forces also benefit from broad popular support, particularly in the context of current tensions with China over conflicting claims in the South China Sea. With rapid economic growth over the last decade, defence spending has increased, and particular efforts have been made to re-equip the navy and air force, mainly with a view to deterring Chinese military pressure in the disputed Spratly Islands. While Hanoi cannot hope to balance China's power on its own, the ongoing development of a submarine capability, based on six *Kilo*-class boats, and the procurement of additional Su-30MK2 combat aircraft and new air-defence capabilities would complicate Beijing's military options. Vietnam is now turning to Western defence suppliers. However, residual sensitivities and restrictions on both sides have meant that US–Vietnam defence relations have been slow to develop, although the 'joint vision statement' of June 2015 declared the intent to expand defence trade and to strengthen maritime-security collaboration. (See pp. 264–68.)

ACTIVE 482,000 (Army 412,000 Navy 40,000 Air 30,000) Paramilitary 40,000

Conscript liability 2 years army and air defence, 3 years air force and navy, specialists 3 years, some ethnic minorities 2 years

RESERVES 5,000,000

ORGANISATIONS BY SERVICE

Space
EQUIPMENT BY TYPE
SATELLITES • ISR 1 VNREDSat

Army ε412,000
8 Mil Regions (incl capital)

FORCES BY ROLE
COMMAND
 4 corps HQ
SPECIAL FORCES
 1 SF bde (1 AB bde, 1 demolition engr regt)
MANOEUVRE
 Armoured
 6 armd bde
 3 armd regt
 Mechanised
 2 mech inf div
 Light
 23 inf div
SURFACE-TO-SURFACE MISSILE
 1 SRBM bde
COMBAT SUPPORT
 13 arty bde
 1 arty regt
 10 engr bde
 1 engr regt
 1 EW unit
 3 sigs bde
 2 sigs regt
COMBAT SERVICE SUPPORT
 9 economic construction div
 1 log regt
 1 med unit
 1 trg regt
AIR DEFENCE
 11 AD bde

Reserve
MANOEUVRE
 Light
 9 inf div

EQUIPMENT BY TYPE
ARMOURED FIGHTING VEHICLES
 MBT 1,270: 70 T-62; 350 Type-59; 850 T-54/T-55; (45 T-34† in store)
 LT TK 620: 300 PT-76; 320 Type-62/Type-63
 RECCE 100 BRDM-1/BRDM-2
 IFV 300 BMP-1/BMP-2
 APC 1,380+
  APC (T) 280+: Some BTR-50; 200 M113 (to be upgraded); 80 Type-63
  APC (W) 1,100 BTR-40/BTR-60/BTR-152
ANTI-TANK/ANTI-INFRASTRUCTURE
 MSL • MANPATS 9K11 *Malyutka* (AT-3 *Sagger*)
 RCL 75mm Type-56; **82mm** Type-65 (B-10); **87mm** Type-51
 GUNS
  SP 100mm SU-100; **122mm** SU-122
  TOWED 100mm T-12 (arty); M-1944
ARTILLERY 3,040+
 SP 30+: **122mm** 2S1 *Gvozdika*; **152mm** 30 2S3 *Akatsiya*; **175mm** M107

TOWED 2,300: **105mm** M101/M102; **122mm** D-30/Type-54 (M-1938)/Type-60 (D-74); **130mm** M-46; **152mm** D-20; **155mm** M114
MRL 710+: **107mm** 360 Type-63; **122mm** 350 BM-21 *Grad*; **140mm** BM-14
MOR **82mm**; **120mm** M-1943; **160mm** M-1943
SURFACE-TO-SURFACE MISSILE LAUNCHERS
SRBM • Coventional *Scud*-B/C
AIR DEFENCE
SAM • Point-defence 9K32 *Strela*-2 (SA-7 *Grail*)‡; 9K310 *Igla*-1 (SA-16 *Gimlet*); 9K38 *Igla* (SA-18 *Grouse*)
GUNS 12,000
SP **23mm** ZSU-23-4
TOWED **14.5mm/30mm/37mm/57mm/85mm/100mm**

Navy ε40,000 (incl ε27,000 Naval Infantry)

EQUIPMENT BY TYPE
SUBMARINES • TACTICAL 7
SSK 5 *Hanoi* (RUS *Varshavyanka*) with 6 533mm TT with TEST-71ME HWT/3M54E (SS-N-27B *Sizzler*) AShM/3M14E (SS-N-30) LACM
SSI 2 *Yugo*† (DPRK)
PRINCIPAL SURFACE COMBATANTS 2
FRIGATES • FFGM 2
2 *Dinh Tien Hoang* (RUS *Gepard* 3.9) with 2 quad lnchr with Kh-35 *Uran* (SS-N-25 *Switchblade*) AShM, 1 *Palma* lnchr with *Sosna*-R SAM, 2 twin 533mm TT, 1 RBU 6000 *Smerch* 2 A/S mor, 2 AK630 CIWS, 1 76mm gun
PATROL AND COASTAL COMBATANTS 71
CORVETTES 6:
FSG 1 BPS-500 with 2 quad lnchr with 3M24 *Uran* (SS-N-25 *Switchblade*) AShM, 9K32 *Strela*-2M (SA-N-5 *Grail*) SAM (manually operated), 2 twin 533mm TT, 1 RBU-1600 A/S mor, 1 AK630 CIWS, 1 76mm gun
FS 5:
3 *Petya* II (FSU) with 1 quintuple 406mm ASTT, 4 RBU 6000 *Smerch* 2 A/S mor, 2 twin 76mm gun
2 *Petya* III (FSU) with 1 triple 533mm ASTT, 4 RBU 2500 *Smerch* 1 A/S mor, 2 twin 76mm gun
PCFGM 10:
4 *Tarantul* (FSU) with 2 twin lnchr with P-15 *Termit* (SS-N-2D *Styx*) AShM, 1 quad lnchr with 9K32 *Strela*-2M (SA-N-5 *Grail*) SAM (manually operated), 2 AK630 CIWS, 1 76mm gun
6 *Tarantul* V with 4 quad lnchr with 3M24 *Uran* (SS-N-25 *Switchblade*) AShM; 1 quad lnchr with 9K32 *Strela*-2M (SA-N-5 *Grail*) SAM (manually operated), 2 AK630 CIWS, 1 76mm gun
PCC 10: 6 *Svetlyak* with 1 AK630 CIWS, 1 76mm gun; 4 TT-400TP with 2 AK630 CIWS, 1 76mm gun
PBFG 8 *Osa* II with 4 single lnchr with P-15 *Termit* AShM
PBFT 2 *Shershen*† (FSU) with 4 single 533mm TT
PH 2 *Turya*† with 1 twin 57mm gun
PHT 3 *Turya*† with 4 single 533mm TT, 1 twin 57mm gun
PB 26: 2 *Poluchat* (FSU); 14 *Zhuk*†; 4 *Zhuk* (mod); 6 (various)
PBR 4 *Stolkraft*
MINE WARFARE • MINE COUNTERMEASURES 13
MSO 2 *Yurka*
MSC 4 *Sonya*
MHI 2 *Yevgenya*
MSR 5 K-8
AMPHIBIOUS
LANDING SHIPS 8
LSM 5:
1 *Polnochny* A† (capacity 6 MBT; 180 troops)
2 *Polnochny* B† (capacity 6 MBT; 180 troops)
2 *Nau Dinh*
LST 3 LST-510-511 (US) (capacity 16 tanks; 200 troops)
LANDING CRAFT 30: 15 LCU; 12 LCM; 3 LCVP
LOGISTICS AND SUPPORT 27
AFD 2; AGS 1; AGSH 1; AKSL 18; AP 1; AT 2; AWT 1; AXS 1
COASTAL DEFENCE • AShM 4K44 *Redut* (SS-C-1B *Sepal*); 4K51 *Rubezh* (SS-C-3 *Styx*); K-300P *Bastion*-P (SS-C-5 *Stooge*)

Naval Infantry ε27,000

EQUIPMENT BY TYPE
ARMOURED FIGHTING VEHICLES
LT TK PT-76; Type-63
APC • APC (W) BTR-60
ARTILLERY • MRL **306mm** EXTRA

Navy Air Wing

FORCES BY ROLE
ASW/SAR
1 regt with H225; Ka-28 (Ka-27PL) *Helix* A; Ka-32 *Helix* C
EQUIPMENT BY TYPE
AIRCRAFT • TPT • Light 6 DHC-6-400 *Twin Otter*
HELICOPTERS
ASW 10 Ka-28 *Helix* A
TPT • Medium 4: 2 H225; 2 Ka-32 *Helix* C

Air Force 30,000

3 air div, 1 tpt bde
FORCES BY ROLE
FIGHTER
4 regt with MiG-21bis *Fishbed* L; MiG-21UM *Mongol* B
FIGHTER/GROUND ATTACK
1 regt with Su-22M3/M4/UM *Fitter* (some ISR)
1 regt with Su-27SK/Su-27UBK *Flanker*
1 regt with Su-27SK/Su-27UBK *Flanker*; Su-30MK2
1 regt with Su-30MK2
TRANSPORT
2 regt with An-2 *Colt*; An-26 *Curl*; Bell 205 (UH-1H *Iroquois*); Mi-8 *Hip*; Mi-17 *Hip* H; M-28 *Bryza*
TRAINING
1 regt with L-39 *Albatros*
1 regt with Yak-52
ATTACK/TRANSPORT HELICOPTER
2 regt with Mi-8 *Hip*; Mi-17 *Hip* H; Mi-171; Mi-24 *Hind*
AIR DEFENCE
4 ADA bde
Some (People's Regional) force (total: ε1,000 AD unit, 6 radar bde with 100 radar stn)
EQUIPMENT BY TYPE
AIRCRAFT 107 combat capable

FGA 107: 25 MiG-21bis *Fishbed* L & N; 8 MiG-21UM *Mongol* B; 28 Su-22M3/M4/UM *Fitter* (some ISR); 6 Su-27SK *Flanker*; 5 Su-27UBK *Flanker*; 35 Su-30MK2 *Flanker*
TPT • **Light** 23: 6 An-2 *Colt*; 12 An-26 *Curl*; 3 C-295M; 1 M-28 *Bryza*
TRG 47: 17 L-39 *Albatros*; 30 Yak-52
HELICOPTERS
ATK 26 Mi-24 *Hind*
MRH 6 Mi-17 *Hip* H
TPT 28: **Medium** 17: 14 Mi-8 *Hip*; 3 Mi-171; **Light** 11 Bell 205 (UH-1H *Iroquois*)
AIR DEFENCE
SAM 12+:
  Long-range 12 S-300PMU1 (SA-20 *Gargoyle*)
  Medium-range S-75 *Dvina* (SA-2 *Guideline*); S-125-2TM *Pechora* (SA-26), *Spyder*-MR
  Short-range 2K12 *Kub* (SA-6 *Gainful*);
  Point-defence 9K32 *Strela*-2 (SA-7 *Grail*)‡; 9K310 *Igla*-1 (SA-16 *Gimlet*)
GUNS 37mm; 57mm; 85mm; 100mm; 130mm
AIR-LAUNCHED MISSILES
AAM • **IR** R-3 (AA-2 *Atoll*)‡; R-60 (AA-8 *Aphid*); R-73 (AA-11 *Archer*); **IR/SARH** R-27 (AA-10 *Alamo*); **ARH** R-77 (AA-12 *Adder*)
ASM Kh-29L/T (AS-14 *Kedge*); Kh-31A (AS-17B *Krypton*); Kh-59M (AS-18 *Kazoo*)
ARM Kh-28 (AS-9 *Kyle*); Kh-31P (AS-17A *Krypton*)

Paramilitary 40,000+ active

Border Defence Corps ε40,000

Coast Guard
EQUIPMENT BY TYPE
PATROL AND COASTAL COMBATANTS 56+
  PSO 4 DN2000 (Damen 9014)
  PCO 13+: 1 *Mazinger* (ex-ROK); 9 TT-400; 3+ other
  PBF 10: 8 MS-50S; 2 *Shershen*
  PB 29: 2 *Hae Uri* (ex-ROK); 1 MS-50; 12 TT-200; 13 TT-120; 1 other
LOGISTICS AND SUPPORT 5
AFS 1
ATF 4
AIRCRAFT • MP 3 C-212-400 MPA

Fisheries Surveillance Force
EQUIPMENT BY TYPE
PATROL AND COASTAL COMBATANTS 22
  PSO 3 DN2000 (Damen 9014)
  PCO 2
  PB 17

Local Forces ε5,000,000 reservists
Incl People's Self-Defence Force (urban units), People's Militia (rural units); comprises static and mobile cbt units, log spt and village protection pl; some arty, mor and AD guns; acts as reserve

DEPLOYMENT

CENTRAL AFRICAN REPUBLIC
UN • MINUSCA 3

SOUTH SUDAN
UN • UNMISS 2 obs

Table 12 **Selected arms procurements and deliveries, Asia**

Designation	Type	Quantity	Contract Value (Current)	Supplier Country	Prime Contractor	Order Date	First Delivery Due	Notes
Afghanistan (AFG)								
EMB-314 *Super Tucano*	Trg ac	20	US$427m	BRZ	Embraer	2013	2014	USAF Light Air Support programme. First aircraft arrived in AFG in 2016
Australia (AUS)								
Hawkei	AUV	1,100	A$1.3bn (US$980m)	FRA (AUS)	Thales (Thales Australia)	2015	2016	Low-rate production began in 2016; full-rate production to begin 2018
Shortfin Barracuda class	SSK	12	See notes	FRA (AUS)	DCNS (t.b.c.)	2016	2030s	SEA 1000 project for *Collins*-class replacement. Entire programme estimated to cost A$50bn (US$38.5bn)
Hobart class	DDGHM	3	US$8bn	AUS/ESP	AWD Alliance	2007	2016	Air Warfare Destroyer programme. Option on fourth ship. All to be fitted with *Aegis* system. First of class began sea trials in late 2016
n.k. (ESP *Cantabria* class)	AORH	2	A$640m (US$484.8m)	ESP	Navantia	2016	2021	SEA 1654 Phase 3. To replace the *Durance*- and *Sirius*-class vessels
F-35A *Lightning II*	FGA ac	2	n.k.	US	Lockheed Martin	2012	2014	Programme of record for 100 aircraft. First two test and training aircraft delivered by end of 2014. Two ordered in Low-rate Initial Production 6
EA-18G *Growler*	EW ac	12	n.k.	US	Boeing	2013	2017	Initial operating capability planned for 2018. Training has begun at US Naval Air Station Whidbey Island. First aircraft rolled out in the US in 2015
P-8A *Poseidon*	ASW ac	8	A$4bn (US$3.6bn)	US	Boeing	2014	2016	AIR 7000 Phase 2. Programme of record for 15 aircraft. All to be in service by 2020. A further four aircraft approved in 2015. First aircraft due to be delivered Nov 2016
G550	ISR ac	2	US$93.6m	US	L-3 Communications	2015	2016	Programme of record for five aircraft
KC-30A (A330 MRTT)	Tkr/Tpt ac	2	A$408m (US$309m)	Int'l	Airbus Group (Airbus Defence & Space)	2015	2018	-
C-27J *Spartan*	Med tpt ac	10	A$1.4bn (US$1.4bn)	US/ITA	L-3 Communications	2012	2015	Deliveries ongoing
NH90 NFH/TTH	ASW/Med tpt hel	47	A$2bn (US$1.47bn)	FRA/GER/ITA/NLD	NHIndustries	2005	2007	Twelve ordered 2005, 34 more in 2006 and one added in 2013. First four built in Europe; remainder in AUS. Deliveries ongoing
Bangladesh (BGD)								
BTR-80	APC (W)	330	n.k.	RUS	VPK (AMZ)	2014	2016	For UN peacekeeping tasks. First batch en route for delivery in late 2016
NORA B-52	Arty (SP 155mm)	18	n.k.	SER	Yugoimport	2011	2013	Deliveries ongoing

Table 12 **Selected arms procurements and deliveries, Asia**

Designation	Type	Quantity	Contract Value (Current)	Supplier Country	Prime Contractor	Order Date	First Delivery Due	Notes
Nabajatra class (ex-PRC *Ming* class, Type-035G)	SSK	2	εUS$203m	PRC	Government surplus	n.k.	2016	Pair of boats handed over in PRC Nov 2016. Will go into trials before commissioning in early 2017
Syed Nazrul class (ex-ITA *Minerva* class)	PSO	4	n.k.	ITA	Government surplus/ Fincantieri	2015	2016	Fincantieri to refit ships before delivery to BGD Coast Guard. First pair of vessels delivered late 2016
Yak-130	Trg ac	16	US$800m	RUS	UAC (Irkut)	2013	2015	Part of arms order made from εUS$1bn loan from RUS. Deliveries ongoing
Mi-171	Med tpt hel	See notes	n.k.	RUS	Russian Helicopters	2015	2016	Financed by US$1bn loan from Russia. Six Mi-171Sh and one Mi-171E
China (PRC)								
JL-2 (CSS-NX-14)	SLBM	n.k.	n.k.	PRC	n.k.	1985	n.k.	In development; reported range of 8,000km. To equip Type-094 nuclear-powered ballistic-missile submarine. In-service date uncertain
Type-96A	MBT	n.k.	n.k.	PRC	NORINCO	n.k.	n.k.	Delivery in progress
Type-99A	MBT	n.k.	n.k.	PRC	NORINCO	n.k.	n.k.	In limited production
Type-05 (ZBD-05)	IFV	n.k.	n.k.	PRC	NORINCO	n.k.	n.k.	Amphibious-assault-vehicle family. Issued to marine and amphibious army units
Type-04A (ZBD-04A)	IFV	n.k.	n.k.	PRC	NORINCO	n.k.	2011	Infantry-fighting-vehicle family. Improved version of Type-04 with extra armour
Type-09 (ZBL-09)	IFV	n.k.	n.k.	PRC	NORINCO	n.k.	n.k.	Family of vehicles including assault-gun (ZTL-09) and 122mm self-propelled-howitzer (PLL-09) variants. Being issued to light mechanised units
Type-07 (PLZ-07)	Arty (SP 122mm)	n.k.	n.k.	PRC	n.k.	n.k.	n.k.	122mm tracked self-propelled howitzer. First displayed in public at 2009 parade
Type-09 (PLC-09)	Arty (SP 122mm)	n.k.	n.k.	PRC	n.k.	n.k.	n.k.	Truck-mounted 122mm howitzer. Also referred to as AH2
Type-05 (PLZ-05)	Arty (SP 155mm)	n.k.	n.k.	PRC	n.k.	n.k.	n.k.	155mm tracked self-propelled howitzer. First displayed in public at 2009 parade
Type-03 (PHL-03)	MRL (SP 300mm)	n.k.	n.k.	PRC	n.k.	n.k.	n.k.	8x8-truck-mounted multiple-rocket launcher; also referred to as AR2
Type-07 (PGZ-07)	AD	n.k.	n.k.	PRC	n.k.	n.k.	n.k.	Twin 35mm-armed tracked self-propelled anti-aircraft gun
Shang II class (Type-093 mod)	SSGN	4	n.k.	PRC	CSIC (Bohai Shipbuilding Heavy Industry Co.)	n.k.	n.k.	Fitted with vertical-launch system. All vessels built; service status unclear
Yuan III class (Type-039C)	SSK	1	n.k.	PRC	CSIC (Wuchang Shipbuilding Industry Co.)	n.k.	2017	Production believed to have switched from Type-039B to C variant. At least one boat reported in trials in late 2016

Asia 343

Table 12 **Selected arms procurements and deliveries, Asia**

Designation	Type	Quantity	Contract Value (Current)	Supplier Country	Prime Contractor	Order Date	First Delivery Due	Notes
Type-001A	CV	1	n.k.	PRC	CSIC (Dalian Shipbuilding Industry Offshore Co.)	n.k.	n.k.	Construction of the first domestically built aircraft carrier under way since 2015
n.k. (Type-055)	CGHM	1	n.k.	PRC	CSIC (Jiangnan Shipyard)	n.k.	n.k.	First of class under construction
Luyang III class (Type-052D)	DDGHM	13	n.k.	PRC	CSIC (Dalian Shipbuilding Industry Offshore Co.)/CSSC (Jiangnan Shipyard)	n.k.	2014	Fourth of class commissioned Jul 2016
Jiangkai II class (Type-054A)	FFGHM	25	n.k.	PRC	CSSC (Huangpu Wenchong Shipbuilding Co./Hudong-Zhonghua Shipbuilding Co.)	2005	2008	Twenty-second of class commissioned Feb 2016
Jiangdao I/II class (Type-056/Type-056A)	FSGM	38	n.k.	PRC	CSSC (Huangpu Wenchong Shipbuilding Co./Hudong-Zhonghua Shipbuilding Co.)/CSIC (Wuchang Shipbuilding Industry Co.)/Southern Liaoning Dalian Shipyard	n.k.	2013	Replacing *Hainan*-class patrol craft. Type-056A is an anti-submarine-warfare variant. Twenty-seventh vessel commissioned Aug 2016
Yuzhao class (Type-071)	LPD	6	n.k.	PRC	CSSC (Hudong-Zhonghua Shipbuilding Co.)	n.k.	2007	Fourth of class commissioned Feb 2016
Wozang class (Type-082-II)	MHO	n.k.	n.k.	PRC	CSIC (Jiangnan Shipyard)	n.k.	2005	Fourth of class commissioned Jan 2016
J-10B	FGA ac	n.k.	n.k.	PRC	AVIC (Shenyang)	n.k.	2014	First batch of 55 aircraft delivered. Status of subsequent production unclear
J-11B/BS *Flanker* L	FGA ac	n.k.	n.k.	PRC	AVIC (Shenyang)	n.k.	2007	Upgraded J-11; now fitted with indigenous WS-10 engines. In service with PLAAF and PLANAF
J-15/J-15S	FGA ac	n.k.	n.k.	PRC	AVIC (Shenyang)	n.k.	2012	For PLANAF. To operate from *Liaoning* CV
J-16	FGA ac	n.k.	n.k.	PRC	AVIC (Shenyang)	n.k.	n.k.	For PLAAF. Entering serial production
Su-35 *Flanker*	FGA ac	24	n.k.	RUS	UAC (Sukhoi)	2015	2017	–
J-20	FGA ac	n.k.	n.k.	PRC	AVIC (Chengdu)	n.k.	2016	Low-rate initial production believed to have begun in 2016
Y-8Q	ASW ac	n.k.	n.k.	PRC	AVIC (Shaanxi)	n.k.	2015	Four aircraft delivered by late 2016
Y-20 *Kunpeng*	Hvy tpt ac	n.k.	n.k.	PRC	AVIC (Xian Aircraft Corporation)	n.k.	2016	First aircraft delivered to PLAAF 4th Division Jul 2016
WZ-10	Atk hel	n.k.	n.k.	PRC	AVIC (Harbin)	n.k.	2010	In service with ten army-aviation brigades/regiments

Table 12 **Selected arms procurements and deliveries, Asia**

Designation	Type	Quantity	Contract Value (Current)	Supplier Country	Prime Contractor	Order Date	First Delivery Due	Notes
WZ-19	Atk hel	n.k.	n.k.	PRC	AVIC (Harbin)	n.k.	n.k.	In service with ten army-aviation brigades/regiments
HQ-16A	SAM	n.k.	n.k.	PRC	n.k.	n.k.	2011	At least seven battalion sets delivered by late 2016
S-400 *Triumf* (SA-21 *Growler*)	SAM	32	n.k.	RUS	Almaz-Antey	2014	n.k.	Two regiment sets. First delivery expected Dec 2017; to be complete by Jun 2019
BeiDou	Satellite (Navigation)	n.k.	n.k.	PRC	CAST		2000	BeiDou G7 launched Jun 2016
PL-10	Msl (AAM IIR)	n.k.	n.k.	PRC	LEOC	n.k.	n.k.	In low-rate production
India (IND)								
Agni-V	ICBM	n.k.	n.k.	IND	DRDO	n.k.	2012	In development. Estimated range 5,000km. Some technical problems in development
Sagarika K-15	SLBM	n.k.	n.k.	IND	DRDO	1991	n.k.	Test-firing-programme under way. Estimated 700km range with one-ton payload
K-4	SLBM	n.k.	n.k.	IND	DRDO	n.k.	n.k.	3,500km-range submarine-launched ballistic missile in tests
K-5	SLBM	n.k.	n.k.	IND	DRDO	n.k.	n.k.	5,000km-range submarine-launched ballistic missile under development
BrahMos Block II (Land Attack)	AShM/LACM	n.k.	n.k.	IND/RUS	Brahmos Aerospace	2010	n.k.	In service with three army regiments. Government approved funding for fourth regiment in late 2016. Being integrated with Su-30MKI aircraft
Nirbhay	ALCM	n.k.	n.k.	IND	DRDO	n.k.	n.k.	In test
T-90S *Bhishma*	MBT	236	INR60bn (US$991.7m)	IND/RUS	Ordnance Factory Board	2013	2016	Second contract for indigenous production of T-90S. Deliveries expected to have begun by end of 2016
Arjun II	MBT	118	n.k.	IND	CVRDE	2014	2017	Upgraded variant. Currently in trials. To be delivered by 2017
Arihant class	SSBN	5	n.k.	IND	DRDO	n.k.	2016	First of class in trials. In-service date now expected 2016/17. Second keel laid down mid-2011
Kalvari class (Project 75)	SSK	6	INR180bn (US$4.07bn)	FRA/IND	DCNS/Mazagon Dock	2005	2016	*Scorpene* class built under licence in IND. First delivery delayed again; expected by end of 2016. Option for a further six boats. First of class launched late 2015 and now in trials
Vikrant class (Project 71)	CV	1	US$730m	IND	Cochin Shipyard	2001	2018	Formerly known as Air Defence Ship. Launched Aug 2013. Expected in-service date has slipped to 2018. Second vessel of class anticipated

Table 12 **Selected arms procurements and deliveries, Asia**

Designation	Type	Quantity	Contract Value (Current)	Supplier Country	Prime Contractor	Order Date	First Delivery Due	Notes
Improved *Shivalik* class (Project 17A)	DDGHM	7	INR450bn (US$9.24 bn)	IND	Mazagon Dock/ GRSE	2009	2017	Follow-up to Project 17. Requires shipyard upgrade; construction yet to begin
Kolkata II class (Project 15B)	DDGHM	4	US$6.5bn	IND	Mazagon Dock	2011	2017	Follow-on from *Kolkata* class with improved stealth capabilites. Second of class launched Sep 2016
Kamorta class (Project 28)	FFH	4	εINR78bn (εUS$1.28bn)	IND	GRSE	2003	2014	Anti-submarine-warfare role. Second of class commissioned Jan 2016
Su-30MKI	FGA ac	182	INR 382.7bn (US$6.83bn)	IND/RUS	HAL/UAC (Sukhoi)	2000	2004	Mixture of locally built, locally assembled and RUS-built aircraft. Delivery schedule changed in 2006 to meet new completion target of 2015/16. Production suffered significant delays and is still ongoing
Tejas	FGA ac	20	INR20bn (US$445m)	IND	HAL	2005	2016	Limited series production. To be delivered in initial op config. Option for a further 20 in full op config. First pair entered service Jun 2016
Rafale	FGA ac	36	€7.8bn (US$8.7bn)	FRA	Dassault	2016	2018	–
P-8I *Neptune*	ASW ac	4	US$1bn	US	Boeing	2016	n.k.	To replace Il-38 and Tu-142M. Second order
C-130J-30 *Hercules*	Med tpt ac	7	US$564.7m	US	Lockheed Martin	2014	n.k.	Follow-up to initial order for six. To be based at Panagargh. Attrition replacement approved in 2015
Hawk Mk132 Advanced Jet Trainer	Trg ac	57	US$780m	IND	HAL	2010	2013	Forty for air force; 17 for navy. Delivery to be complete by end of 2016
AH-64E *Apache Guardian*	Atk hel	22	n.k.	US	Boeing	2015	2018	For air force
CH-47F *Chinook*	Tpt hel	15	n.k.	US	Boeing	2015	2019	For air force
Dhruv	MRH hel	191	n.k.	IND	HAL	2004	2004	Includes additional 32 ordered Jul 2014; to be split equally between navy and coastguard
Indonesia (IDN)								
Leopard 2A4/2RI	MBT	103	See notes	GER	Rheinmetall	2012	2013	Ex-Bundeswehr surplus. Forty-two 2A4 and 61 2 Revolution. Part of US$280m deal including 42 *Marder* 1A3 AIFVs and 11 ARV/AEVs. First *Leopard* 2RI MBTs delivered 2016
Marder 1A3	IFV	42	See notes	GER	Rheinmetall	2012	2013	Ex-Bundeswehr surplus. Part of US$280m deal including 103 *Leopard* 2 MBTs and 11 ARV/AEVs. Deliveries ongoing
Badak 6x6	Wheeled Asslt Gun (90mm)	50	n.k.	IDN	PT Pindad	2016	2016	Based on *Anoa* platform. Deliveries expected to begin 2016
M113A1-BE	APC (T)	150	n.k.	BEL	Government surplus	n.k.	2016	Deliveries ongoing
Anoa 6x6	APC (W)	n.k.	n.k.	IDN	PT Pindad	2012	2014	Deliveries ongoing

Table 12 **Selected arms procurements and deliveries, Asia**

Designation	Type	Quantity	Contract Value (Current)	Supplier Country	Prime Contractor	Order Date	First Delivery Due	Notes
CAESAR	Arty (SP 155mm)	37	€115m (US$152.7m)	FRA	Nexter	2012	2014	Deliveries ongoing
RM-70 *Vampire*	Arty (MRL 122mm)	36	n.k.	CZE	Excalibur Group (Excalibur Army)	n.k.	2016	For marines. Improved version of RM-70
Nagabanda class (Type-209/1400)	SSK	3	US$1.1bn	IDN/ROK	PT PAL/DSME	2012	2015	First to be built in ROK; second to be partially assembled in IDN; and third to be largely built in IDN. First of class launched Mar 2016; second launched Oct 2016
SIGMA 10514	FFGHM	2	n.k.	NLD	Damen Schelde Naval Shipbuilding	2012	2016	Further acquisitions expected, with technology transfers allowing greater proportion to be built in IDN. First of class completed sea trials late 2016
F-16C/D *Fighting Falcon*	FGA ac	24	US$670m	US	Government surplus	2012	2014	Nineteen F-16C and five F-16D. All ex-US Air Force aircraft. Deliveries ongoing
C-130H *Hercules*	Med tpt ac	5	Donation	AUS	Government surplus	2013	2016	Second batch of AUS surplus aircraft. First delivered Feb 2016
AH-64E *Apache Guardian*	Atk hel	8	US$295.86m	US	Boeing	2015	2017	Deliveries to be complete by Feb 2018
AS565 Mbe *Panther*	ASW hel	11	n.k.	Int'l	Airbus Group (Airbus Helicopters)	2014	2016	For navy. Deliveries accelerated; first batch handed over in FRA in Nov 2016
H225M *Caracal* (EC725 *Super Cougar*)	Hvy tpt hel	6	n.k.	Int'l	Airbus Group (Airbus Helicopters)	2012	2014	First delivered to PT Digrantara for modification before final delivery
AS550 *Fennec*	MRH hel	12	n.k.	Int'l	Airbus Group (Airbus Helicopters)	n.k.	2014	First delivered Nov 2014

Japan (JPN)

Designation	Type	Quantity	Contract Value (Current)	Supplier Country	Prime Contractor	Order Date	First Delivery Due	Notes
Type-10	MBT	82	JPY83.9bn (US$896.46m)	JPN	MHI	2010	2011	Six budgeted for in FY2016
AAV7 RAM/RS	AAV	41	JPY28.1bn (US$240.77m)	UK (USA)	BAE Systems (BAE Systems Land & Armaments)	2015	2016	Eleven budgeted for in FY2016
Mobile Combat Vehicle	Wheeled Asslt Gun (105mm)	36	JPY25.2bn (US$236m)	JPN	MHI	2016	2017	Thirty-six budgeted for in FY2016
Type-12	AShM	26	JPY55.1bn (US$538.9m)	JPN	MHI	2012	2016	One set budgeted for in FY2016
Soryu class	SSK	12	JPY673.7bn (US$6.64bn)	JPN	KHI/MHI	2004	2009	Seventh of class commissioned Mar 2016
Izumo class	CVH	2	JPY229.4bn (US$2.75bn)	JPN	IHI Marine United/JMU	2010	2015	First vessel commissioned Mar 2015; second of class launched Aug 2015
Improved *Atago* class	CGHM	2	JPY341bn (US$3.01bn)	JPN	MHI	2015	n.k.	Second of class and *Aegis* system budgeted for in FY2016
Asahi class (Improved *Akizuki* class)	DDGHM	2	JPY143bn (US$1.41bn)	JPN	MHI	2013	2017	First of class launched Oct 2016
Awaji class	MSO	2	JPY36bn (US$354.58m)	JPN	JMU	2013	2017	First of class launched Oct 2015

Table 12 **Selected arms procurements and deliveries, Asia**

Designation	Type	Quantity	Contract Value (Current)	Supplier Country	Prime Contractor	Order Date	First Delivery Due	Notes
F-35A *Lightning II*	FGA ac	4	n.k.	US	Lockheed Martin	2012	2017	Programme of record for 42 aircraft. First unveiled in the US Sep 2016. Pilot training due to begin Nov 2016 at Luke Air Force Base
P-1	ASW ac	29	JPY526.2bn (US$4.8bn)	JPN	KHI	2010	2013	Deliveries ongoing
E-2D *Hawkeye*	AEW&C ac	2	JPY26bn (US$435.2m)	US	Northrop Grumman	2015	n.k.	Second aircraft budgeted for in FY2016
KC-130R	Tkr ac	6	US$42m	US	Government surplus	2012	2014	Ex-USMC aircraft
C-2	Hvy tpt ac	6	JPY118.8bn (US$1.34bn)	JPN	KHI	2011	2016	First production aircraft delivered Jun 2016
AH-64D *Apache*	Atk hel	13	JPY88.9bn (US$822.4m)	US/JPN	Boeing/Fuji Heavy Industries	2002	2006	Deliveries ongoing
SH-60K	ASW hel	74	εJPY482.3bn (εUS$4.63bn)	US/JPN	Lockheed Martin (Sikorsky)/MHI	2002	2005	Seventeen budgeted for in FY2016
MCH-101	MCM hel	10	εJPY63.2bn (εUS$727.15m)	ITA/JPN	Leonardo/KHI	2003	2006	To replace MH-53E
V-22B Blk C *Osprey*	Tilt-rotor ac	9	JPY93.6bn (US$845m)	US	Bell Helicopter/ Boeing Rotorcraft Systems	2015	n.k.	For Ground Self-Defense Force. Includes four budgeted for in FY2016
Republic of Korea (ROK)								
Hyonmu IIB	SRBM	n.k.	n.k.	ROK	Agency for Defense Development	2012	n.k.	In test
K2 *Black Panther*	MBT	100	KRW901.5bn (US$891.62m)	ROK	Hyundai Rotem	2014	2015	Second order. To use locally built engines
K21	IFV	ε500	n.k.	ROK	Hanwha Defense	2008	2009	Delivery resumed after accident investigation
Chunmoo	MRL (239mm)	58	n.k.	ROK	Hanwha Defense	n.k.	2015	To replace K136 *Kooryong*
Son Won-il class	SSK	6	εUS$3bn	ROK	DSME	2008	2014	A second batch of six KSS-II (with AIP). Second batch to be fitted with *Hae Sung* submarine-launched cruise missile. Second vessel of batch, fifth of class, commissioned Jun 2016
KSS-III	SSG	n.k.	n.k.	ROK	DSME/Hyundai Heavy Industries	2007	2017	Contract for design signed in 2007. Second of class keel laid Jul 2016
Incheon class	FFGHM	6	n.k.	ROK	Hyundai Heavy Industries/ STX Offshore & Shipbuilding	2006	2013	To replace current *Ulsan*-class frigates. First batch. Fifth of class commissioned Jan 2016; fourth of class delayed due to damage in trials. Sixth of class delivered Nov 2016 and will enter service early 2017
Daegu class (*Incheon* class mod)	FFGHM	1	n.k.	ROK	DSME	n.k.	2017	To replace current *Ulsan*-class frigate. Second batch follow-on to *Incheon* class. First of class launched Jun 2016
Nanpo class	ML	1	n.k.	ROK	Hyundai Heavy Industries	n.k.	2016	First of class expected to commission 2017
Dokdo class	LHD	1	US$355.1m	ROK	Hanjin Heavy Industries	2015	n.k.	Order for second of class

Table 12 **Selected arms procurements and deliveries, Asia**

Designation	Type	Quantity	Contract Value (Current)	Supplier Country	Prime Contractor	Order Date	First Delivery Due	Notes
Cheonwangbong class	LPD	2	n.k.	ROK	Hanjin Heavy Industries	2013	2016	Order for second and third of class. Second of class launched Dec 2015
F-35A *Lightning II*	FGA ac	See notes	See notes	US	Lockheed Martin	2014	n.k.	Programme of record for 40 aircraft for US$6.2bn
FA-50 *Fighting Eagle*	FGA ac	ε60	US$1.6bn	ROK	KAI	2012	2013	To replace F-5E/F. Deliveries ongoing
KF-X	FGA ac	See notes	See notes	ROK	KAI	2015	2026	Contract awarded for development and construction of KF-X prototypes. Estimated cost of entire programme is KRW8.5trn (US$7.99bn) for development and KRW10trn (US$9.41bn) for six prototypes and 120 production aircraft. IDN signed in Jan 2016 a KRW1.6trn (US$1.3bn) deal to take part in development and receive a prototype
AH-64E *Apache Guardian*	Atk hel	36	KRW1.8tr (US$1.6bn)	US/ROK	Boeing/KAI	2013	2016	First batch delivered May 2016
Light Armed Helicopter	Atk hel	See notes	KRW1.6tr (US$1.4bn)	Int'l/ROK	Airbus Group (Airbus Helicopters)/KAI	2015	2022	214 Light Armed Helicopters and 100 civilian versions. Based on H155
AW159 *Wildcat*	MRH hel	8	€270m (US$358m)	ITA	Leonardo	2013	2016	Part of US$560m contract including support and training. To be equipped with *Spike* NLOS missiles. First batch of four delivered Jun 2016
KUH-1 *Surion*	Med tpt hel	80	KRW2.35bn (US$2.11bn)	ROK	KAI	2010	2013	Army to procure up to 245. Second production contract signed in 2013
RQ-4B *Global Hawk*	UAV	4	US$657.4m	USA	Northrop Grumman	2014	2018	–
Malaysia (MYS)								
AV8 *Gempita* 8x8	APC (W)	257	US$559m	TUR	FNSS	2011	2013	To include 12 variants. Deliveries have slowed but are ongoing
Gowind 2500	FFGHM	6	MYR9bn (US$2.8bn)	MYS	Boustead Naval Shipyard	2011	2017	Second Generation Patrol Vessel programme. Licence-built from DCNS in MYS. First in-service date expected to be 2019. First of class keel laid Mar 2016
A400M *Atlas*	Hvy tpt ac	4	MYR907m (US$246m)	Int'l	Airbus Group (Airbus Defence & Space)	2006	2015	In development. Third aircraft delivered Jun 2016
Myanmar (MMR)								
JF-17 *Thunder* (FC-1)	FGA ac	n.k.	n.k.	PAK/PRC	PAC	2015	n.k.	Contract reportedly signed in 2015
Yak-130	Trg ac	16	n.k.	RUS	UAC (Irkut)	2015	2016	First three reportedly due for delivery by end of 2016
KS-1A (HQ-12)	SAM	24	n.k.	PRC	China Jiangnan Space and Industry Company	n.k.	2015	For army. Deliveries ongoing

Table 12 Selected arms procurements and deliveries, Asia

Designation	Type	Quantity	Contract Value (Current)	Supplier Country	Prime Contractor	Order Date	First Delivery Due	Notes
New Zealand (NZL)								
n.k.	AORH	1	NZ$493m (US$345.91m)	ROK	Hyundai Heavy Industries	2016	2020	To replace HMNZS *Endeavour*
Pakistan (PAK)								
Hatf-8 (*Raad*)	ALCM	n.k.	n.k.	PAK	n.k.	n.k.	n.k.	In development. Last known test-firing Feb 2015
Al Khalid I	MBT	ε110	n.k.	PAK/PRC	Heavy Industries Taxila/NORINCO	2012	n.k.	Version unclear. Will move on to *Al Khalid* II production and upgrade earlier models to that standard
S20	SSK	8	n.k.	PAK/PRC	Karachi Shipyard/CSIC (Wuchang Shipbuilding Industry Co.)	2015	n.k.	Believed to be based on *Yuan*-class submarine but variant unclear. Pakistan and China to build four each
n.k.	AOR	1	n.k.	TUR/PAK	STM/Karachi Shipyards	2013	2017	Fleet Tanker programme. STM to provide designs and support. Keel laid Mar 2014
JF-17 *Thunder* (FC-1)	FGA ac	150	n.k.	PAK/PRC	PAC	2006	2008	150 currently on order; Block 3 in development. Third squadron transferred to JF-17 in Apr 2016
AH-1Z	Atk hel	9	US$170.1m	US	Textron (Bell Helicopter)	2016	n.k.	Delivery to be complete by Sep 2018
Philippines (PHL)								
KAAV7A1	AAV	8	PHP2.42bn (US$52.5m)	ROK	Hanwha Techwin	2016	n.k.	For marines
n.k.	FFGHM	2	PHP15.7bn (US$339.1m)	ROK	Hyundai Heavy Industries	2016	2020	–
Tarlac class (IDN *Makassar* class mod)	LPD	2	PHP3.87bn (US$87.17m)	IDN	PT PAL	2014	2016	Strategic Sealift Vessel programme. First of class commissioned Jun 2016
FA-50PH *Fighting Eagle*	FGA ac	12	US$420m	ROK	KAI	2014	2015	Delivery to be complete by 2018
AW159 *Wildcat*	ASW hel	2	PHP5.36bn (US$110m)	ITA	Leonardo	2016	2018	For navy. Includes support and training package
Singapore (SGP)								
Peacekeeper PRV	APC (PPV)	n.k.	n.k.	SGP	DSTA	n.k.	2015	To replace V200s. Three variants
Type-218SG	SSK	2	n.k.	GER	TKMS	2013	2020	To replace remaining *Challenger*-class boats. Construction of first of class began mid-2015
Independence class	FSM	8	n.k.	SGP	ST Engineering	2013	2017	Littoral Mission Vessel to replace *Fearless*-class PCOs. First of class expected to commission 2017
A330 MRTT	Tkr/Tpt ac	6	n.k.	Int'l	Airbus Group (Airbus Defence & Space)	2014	n.k.	First aircraft conversion completed Sep 2016
CH-47F *Chinook*	Hvy tpt hel	n.k.	n.k.	US	Boeing	2016	n.k.	Unknown number ordered. To replace older *Chinook*s in service
H225M *Caracal* (EC725 *Super Cougar*)	Med tpt hel	n.k.	n.k.	Int'l	Airbus Group (Airbus Helicopters)	2016	n.k.	Unknown number ordered. To replace *Super Puma*s in service

Table 12 **Selected arms procurements and deliveries, Asia**

Designation	Type	Quantity	Contract Value (Current)	Supplier Country	Prime Contractor	Order Date	First Delivery Due	Notes
Sri Lanka (LKA)								
Sayurala class (IND *Samarth* class)	PSOH	2	n.k.	IND	Goa Shipyard	2013	2017	First of class launched Jun 2016
Taiwan (ROC)								
CM-32 *Yunpao*	APC (W)	up to 650	n.k.	ROC	Ordnance Readiness Development Centre	2010	2011	Replacement of M113 fleet
Tuo Jiang class mod	FSM	3	n.k.	ROC	Lung Teh Shipbuilding	2016	n.k.	Air-defence corvette based on the *Tuo Jiang* class
UH-60M *Black Hawk*	Med tpt hel	60	US$3.1bn	US	Lockheed Martin (Sikorsky)	2011	2014	Deliveries ongoing
Hsiung Feng IIE	LACM	n.k.	n.k.	ROC	CSIST	2005	n.k.	In production
Hsiung Feng III	AShM	n.k.	n.k.	ROC	CSIST	n.k.	n.k.	In production. Upgraded version reportedly to be developed
Thailand (THA)								
T-84 *Oplot*	MBT	49	THB7bn (US$241m)	UKR	Ukroboronprom (KMDB)	2011	2013	Deliveries have suffered delays. Third batch delivered May 2016
VT-4 (MBT-3000)	MBT	28	εUS$150m	PRC	NORINCO	2016	2017	–
BTR-3E1 8x8	IFV	142	n.k.	UKR	Ukroboronprom (KMDB)	2011	2013	Second batch of 121 ordered in 2011 and third batch of 21 in 2013. Deliveries delayed as a result of conflict in Ukraine
ATMOS 2000	Arty (SP 155mm)	n.k.	n.k.	ISR	Elbit Systems	2012	2015	First batch ordered 2012; second batch believed ordered in 2015
DTI-1G	Arty (MRL 302mm)	3 Systems	n.k.	THA	Defence Technology Institute	n.k.	2016	Deliveries ongoing
DW3000H	FFGHM	1	KRW520bn (US$464m)	ROK	DSME	2013	2018	Order for second vessel anticipated. Based on KDD-I derivative. First of class laid down May 2016
Oliver Hazard Perry class	FFH	2	Donation	US	Government surplus	2014	n.k.	Donation approved by US Congress Dec 2014
T-50 *Golden Eagle*	Trg ac	4	US$110m	ROK	KAI	2015	n.k.	For air force. To replace L-39
H225M *Caracal* (EC725 *Super Cougar*)	Hvy tpt hel	4	n.k.	Int'l	Airbus Group (Airbus Helicopters)	2014	2016	Search-and-rescue configuration. For air force. Ordered second batch of two in 2014; third batch of two in 2016
Vietnam (VNM)								
Varshavyanka class (*Kilo*)	SSK	6	εUS$1.8bn	RUS	Admiralty Shipyards	2009	2014	Sixth of class in sea trials in late 2016
Dinh Tien Hoang class (*Gepard* 3.9)	FFGM	2	n.k.	RUS	Zelenodolsk Shipyard	2014	2017	Second batch. Both vessels in sea trials in late 2016
VNREDSat-1b	Satellite (ISR)	1	€60m (US$77.13m)	FRA/VNM	Airbus Group/ VAST	2012	2017	–

Chapter Seven
Middle East and North Africa

Four major conflicts raged in the Middle East in late 2016, in Iraq, Libya, Syria and Yemen. Conflict resolution appeared distant in each, although of the four, the campaign against the Islamic State, also known as ISIS or ISIL, in Iraq and Syria seemed to be gaining the most traction, with the jihadi group losing significant territory and personnel. In contrast, the Syrian civil war continued to defy UN and international diplomatic efforts and appeared too complex for immediate resolution. The slow retreat by ISIS in Iraq and Syria was balanced by the emergence of volatile post-ISIS fault lines, illustrated most notably by Turkey's intervention in northern Syria to contain Kurdish ambitions.

The crisis in Yemen also challenged regional diplomacy. The Saudi-led coalition struggled to translate military advances into political gains at the failed peace talks in Kuwait and faced the task of fighting a hardened enemy while containing a jihadi threat. In Libya, a UN-backed government struggled to impose its authority in the face of militarily superior armed factions, demonstrating that international consensus was not enough to re-establish state control in fractured societies.

These wars and their related human, economic and security costs cast a long shadow across the region. Competition between Iran and Saudi Arabia, jihadi activity across the region, a sense of retrenchment by the United States and concern about further instability created anxiety. As a result, there was further investment in the region's defence and security sectors. In recent years, military service made a return in Kuwait, Qatar and the United Arab Emirates; these nations, with Saudi Arabia, remain involved in active military operations. The sense of regional military and strategic extroversion seen since 2011 continues, with these states now willing to take military action not just as part of a Western-led coalition, but as part of regional coalitions organised in pursuit of their own security interests.

Regional and international intervention remained central to each of the region's conflicts, adding layers of complexity to already convoluted crises. In Iraq, Syria and Yemen, foreign powers that were ostensibly in agreement about combating ISIS pursued conflicting agendas or saw the jihadi group as a secondary concern. The forceful Russian entry on the Syrian battlefield and the sense of American disengagement recalibrated regional views of both these powers. Once hard to conceive, an operational Russia–Iran military partnership began to take form, though it was possibly short-lived.

Russia changes the battlefield

The Russian intervention in Syria, beginning in September 2015, restored the Assad regime's dimming military fortunes. Despite US assessments and a difficult early phase, the Russian operation changed the trajectory of the conflict, enhancing Moscow's diplomatic and military leverage. Russia deployed combat aircraft including Su-25 *Frogfoot*, Su-24 *Fencer* and Su-34 *Fullback* and (after a Russian aircraft was shot down by a Turkish F-16 in late 2015) improved fighter cover with advanced Su-35 combat aircraft armed with air-to-air missiles. Su-25s were withdrawn (at least for a time) in 2016; some observers assessed that this was because of their relative vulnerability when compared to the higher- and faster-flying Su-24. Helicopter deployment included the Mi-24 and the newer Mi-28, while the Ka-52K was seen on the deck of the *Kuznetsov* aircraft carrier en route to the Mediterranean in late 2016. If this helicopter, together with the embarked fixed-wing complement of MiG-29KRs, was deployed in the carrier-strike role to Syria it would also serve a key mission of the campaign: to demonstrate Russia's military capabilities to the world, as well as act as an operational testing ground for these capabilities. This objective was also evidenced by the deployment of missile defences, the continued (though less, in 2016) use of stand-off guided weapons and upgrades to Russia's military bases in Tartus and Humeimim. Russia also deployed military advisers as well as small numbers of military contractors and troops. These capabilities have transformed the battlefield. At the same time, the addition of Iranian troops and Shia fighters from Afghanistan, Iraq, Lebanon and Pakistan provided the personnel numbers that Assad's forces lacked. In an unprecedented move, the Russian Air Force even used an Iranian base at

Hamadan to conduct airstrikes, although the revelation of this event led to an outcry inside Iran – unlike Russia, Iran has generally preferred to minimise international publicity surrounding its involvement in the Syrian war.

In 2016, Russian firepower, combined with regime airstrikes, tended to target Islamist and nationalist rebel groups instead of ISIS. As a result, within months the rebel advances in northwest Syria were reversed. Rebel-held areas in Damascus, Deraa, Hama, Homs and Idlib provinces came under sustained bombardment and shrank in size. Meanwhile, a Russian strike killed the head of the powerful Jaysh al-Islam group in Damascus in December, weakening the faction. The Russian intervention also neutralised or raised the cost of options for intervention by other powers. One example that served to deter such intervention was the shooting down of a Russian Su-24 by the Turkish Air Force in November 2015. In response, Moscow hit Turkish-allied rebels in Syria, imposed painful economic sanctions and put considerable pressure on Ankara. By summer 2016, Ankara and Moscow had reconciled.

With conflict dynamics on the ground rapidly changing, in February regime forces and Shia auxiliaries managed to cut the Azzaz corridor that linked rebel-held parts of Aleppo to the Turkish border. The regime laid siege to eastern Aleppo in July and it became increasingly likely that the regime would succeed in securing all major cities located in the central corridor. By late 2016, Iranian, Russian and Shia jihadi support had helped the regime neutralise the strategic threat to its survival and turn the rebellion into a largely rural insurgency.

Lacking any anti-aircraft missiles to blunt the regime's advantage, the rebel forces deployed anti-tank missiles and organised themselves into broader coalitions. However, as a result of greater Western risk-aversion and sharpened focus on defeating ISIS, the ideological centre of gravity shifted even more toward the Islamist hardliners. As a result, the jihadi Jabhat al-Nusra (rebranded Jabhat Fateh al-Sham during summer 2016) and the hardline Ahrar al-Sham became the most prominent groups; they led a successful, if short-lived, break of the Aleppo siege, gaining credibility among civilians and respect among fighters.

Meanwhile, the US has struggled to adapt to this new military reality. Initially dismissive of Russian efforts and Moscow's offers of military collaboration, the US focused on its anti-ISIS effort, agreeing to a simple de-confliction mechanism to avoid accidents between coalition and Russian aircraft. But intensified fighting in western Syria and the worsening humanitarian situation in Syria overall – as well as Russian military successes – led US diplomats to reach out to Moscow.

The US and Russia cooperated diplomatically to ostensibly reduce violence and facilitate political talks, even though Russia's actions undermined both objectives. Moscow and Washington agreed on a political process (enshrined in UN Resolution 2254), pledged to cooperate against jihadi groups and announced their intention to compel their local allies to abide by ceasefires. They negotiated a cessation of hostilities in February 2016 but this only temporarily reduced fighting. The US continued to pursue plans for greater military cooperation with Russia, hoping that the latter would in return pressure the Assad regime to respect the ceasefire. In summer 2016, Moscow and Washington agreed on a plan to share targeting information against Jabhat al-Nusra. However, this deal provoked scepticism within the US armed forces and intelligence community and was rebuffed by Syrian rebel and opposition groups.

For all of Russia's investment in Syria, there was little sign of any reorganisation or greater professionalisation among Assad's forces; these remained a mixture of units of varying readiness and capability. Elite troops such as the Republican Guard continued to secure the capital, but elsewhere a combination of regular military, competing and rapacious local militias such as the Tiger Forces and the Desert Hawks, as well as Shia mercenaries, engaged in operations to conquer or defend territory. Even then, personnel shortages were ever-present. Russian air support helped Damascus conduct offensives, but regime forces struggled to hold conquered territory. It appeared difficult, if not impossible, for the regime to properly staff several front lines at once, a fact illustrated by reversals in southern Aleppo. Maintaining unity of effort among such disparate forces further complicated military effectiveness.

In this context, local ceasefires – mostly imposed through sieges and starvation – served to freeze fighting in one place in order to allocate military resources to ongoing combat elsewhere. Rebel-held areas such as Daraya agreed to surrender and residents were sent to regions in the northern parts of the country, leading the UN and foreign governments to warn against sectarian cleansing.

The campaign against ISIS

By mid-2015, the US-led international effort against ISIS in Iraq and Syria began to score important territorial and qualitative victories. The tempo of operations increased later in the year and throughout 2016. Airstrikes against ISIS facilities, command posts, leadership targets and income-generating installations weakened the group and threatened its logistics.

In Iraq, the liberation of Tikrit in March 2015 and the subsequent battle for Baiji exposed the difficulties faced by the Iraq Security Forces (ISF) and the complexity of the terrain, where Iranian-supported militias operated in parallel to, but not in coordination with, the US-led coalition. The US denied air support to militias backed by Iran, to the benefit of the ISF and non-Iran-affiliated militias operating as part of the government-endorsed Hashd al-Shaabi (also known as Popular Mobilisation Forces or PMF).

Tough urban battles to recover Ramadi in February 2016 and Falluja in June 2016 resulted in some progress but highlighted enduring operational and logistical challenges. Managing the rivalry and tensions between the various government forces and PMF militias, and maximising coalition input, proved to be complex. ISIS offered intense resistance in Ramadi, which suffered considerable damage. In Falluja, the elite, US-backed Counter-Terrorism Service played the leading role, seizing the city faster and with less destruction than anticipated thanks to a considerably better designed and conducted operation. The combined-arms operations first seen in late 2015 began to be heavily employed, with armoured bulldozers often in the vanguard of any advance into an urban area. This tactic was designed to blunt the effectiveness of ISIS ambushes and their use of improvised explosive devices and vehicle-borne improvised explosive devices, and to create relatively safe passage for the armour and infantry following the bulldozers. Nevertheless, these battles exposed a lack of government preparedness for the humanitarian consequences of the fighting, with tens of thousands of civilians displaced as a result.

Importantly, a pattern emerged whereby the government forces that conducted most of the fighting were later replaced by Shia militias who held the territory, with these sometimes reported as committing abuses and seeking to dominate and punish the Sunni population. This perpetuated Sunni resentment against Baghdad, with the significant risk that it will hinder the political goal of reconciliation.

In parallel with advances against ISIS, a debate unfolded over the future of the PMF and the ambitions of militia leaders who sought to institutionalise these armed groups, likely as a means of securing political influence. Grand Ayatollah Ali Sistani, who inspired popular mobilisation in 2014, resisted such schemes, but Iranian-backed militias and leaders, notably Hadi al-Ameri and Qais al-Khazali, were prominent in supporting them. In reality, due to deficiencies in logistics, leadership and discipline, the performance of Shia militias on the battlefield was poor. Instead, the US and coalition members sought to shore up the government forces; they also planned to bolster Sunni forces, including tribal militias, which was a goal enshrined in the US$1.6 billion Train and Equip fund. However, the National Guard bill, which was intended to legalise and bring into the government fold all the militias, continued to face opposition from Shia parties in Iraq's parliament.

In Syria, the principal ground partner of the international coalition remained the Kurdish-dominated Syrian Democratic Forces (SDF). The SDF steadily conquered and cleared territory along the Syria–Turkey border, extending from the border with Iraq to the Euphrates. With the goal of isolating and retaking Raqqa, these forces, which included Arab factions, sought to cut important supply routes from the Turkish border. In summer 2016, the SDF freed the town of Manbij after almost three months of fighting. Nevertheless, ISIS showed stiff resistance, managing to withstand assaults in Deir Ezzor and Taqba by Assad's forces and in Abu Kamal by US-backed rebel groups.

Predictably, successes against ISIS exposed other fault lines in both countries. In Iraq, tensions between Kurdish fighters and Shia militiamen in the town of Tuz Khormatu, north of Baghdad, escalated into deadly firefights. Sunni residents of freed cities complained about abuse and discrimination at the hands of Shia militias. Meanwhile, Kurdish successes against ISIS motivated Turkey to launch an intervention: in August, Turkish armoured troops and special forces, supported by Syrian Arab rebel forces, rapidly seized the town of Jarablus within two weeks, expelling ISIS from the border area. For the first time since 2013, ISIS was denied direct access to the Syrian border. At the request of the Turkish government, US special forces and coalition airpower supported the operation.

Turkey's intervention was primarily a result of anxiety at the Kurdish expansion in Syria. Ankara

The Iraqi Army

The Iraqi Army's cohesion was shattered by the 2014 fall of Mosul, Iraq's second city. The capture of Mosul by Islamic State, also known as ISIS or ISIL, and that group's subsequent rapid advance, revealed the army to be a force hollowed out by political cronyism, corruption and poor training. Were it not for airstrikes by the US-led coalition and the rapid mobilisation of Shia militias, many actively supported by Iran, ISIS could have captured more territory and perhaps threatened Baghdad.

Since autumn 2014 the Iraqi Army has been fighting ISIS while receiving training, advice and some equipment from the US and its coalition allies. Its operations gradually transitioned from the strategic defensive to local offensives and then a large campaign to evict ISIS from Iraq, culminating in the start of operations to recapture Mosul in October 2016. This mission saw a high level of coordination between three Iraqi division-sized formations and Kurdish Peshmerga units.

The Mosul operation showed that the Iraqi Army's capability had greatly improved since 2014. It was capable of deploying some 30,000–40,000 troops for a sustained period. These were capable of combined-arms operations that were able to drive ISIS from its well-prepared defences in villages, towns and cities. Iraqi Army tactics included the use of infantry deploying in armoured vehicles, principally armoured HMMWVs and tanks, often with armoured bulldozers in the vanguard to destroy ISIS berms and field fortifications and, in towns, simultaneously construct defensive lines to stop flanking attacks by ISIS including by vehicle-borne improvised explosive devices (IEDs). Iraq's army demonstrated improved counter-IED capability. Extensive use was made of US and coalition airstrikes, and there was increasing use of artillery, including precision artillery fired by US Army and Marine Corps units. French forces also deployed fire support using their CAESAR howitzers.

However, military tactics often resulted in considerable damage to urban areas. This was partially mitigated by information operations that encouraged the civilian population to flee, although this exodus compounded the country's humanitarian crisis. In recognition of this, army operations exhibited a degree of synchronisation with relief agencies' efforts to assist internally displaced civilians, including the designation of 'safe routes' and the movement of displaced persons in army vehicles. The army's information-operations capability was also demonstrated by embedding members of international media in advancing brigades. The extent to which this depended on the presence of US advisers was unclear.

In 2016, the leading counter-ISIS role was usually assumed by Iraq special-operations forces, especially the Counter-Terrorism Services, acting as elite infantry. These are well trained, highly motivated and the most effective of all Iraq's government units. However, there was a risk that extensive use of such units could lead to excessive civilian casualties. The Iraqi Army's 9th Division and Rapid Intervention Division also played leading roles in the early stages of the Mosul campaign.

The Iraqi Air Force was also increasingly involved in supporting ground operations. In September 2016 alone, 1,200 sorties were reportedly flown. Elements of the air force's inventory of F-16, L-159 and Su-25 aircraft are employed in the air campaign, as are the army's Mi-28, Mi-35 and IA407 helicopters. The F-16s are based at Balad and on current operations, the main armament observed on this type when used in the ground-attack role is the GBU-12 laser-guided bomb. The L-159s appeared to be used only with free-fall Mk-82 bombs. Meanwhile, the air force's AC-208 *Combat Caravan* turboprop aircraft are used in the intelligence, surveillance and reconnaissance role and to provide targeting information.

A significant role in these military operations was also played by the Popular Mobilisation Forces. Although some of these represented Sunni militias and tribal fighters, most were Shia militias that had mobilised themselves in 2014. Many received Iranian training, advice and equipment. This was channelled through Iran's Islamic Revolutionary Guard Corps' Quds Force. Its commander, General Qassem Soleimani, played a prominent advisory role in the coordination of militia operations.

---

sought to pre-empt and even reverse Kurdish advances, insisting that People's Protection Units (YPG) leave Jarablus and turn over its governance to Arab factions.

The war in Yemen

The war in Yemen entered its second year in 2016 without much hope for resolution. The Saudi-led coalition supporting President Abd Rabbo Mansour Hadi made some progress, but seemed unable to translate military gains into political leverage. The rebel Houthis and their allies proved well entrenched and hardened, resisting incessant coalition strikes and isolation. Meanwhile, Yemeni forces supported by the coalition were only nominally under Hadi's command. The disparate militias fighting the Houthis have not coalesced into a national force, with their military efforts based on local alliances. As a result,

Saudi Arabia and the United Arab Emirates have had to strike deals with local tribes and politicians.

This scenario proved problematic for Saudi Arabia and the UAE. Having decided on a minimal presence of their own and heavy reliance on local partners, there were not enough troops to secure Sana'a and contain the rise of al-Qaeda in the Arabian Peninsula (AQAP) by late 2015. The UAE took a proactive role in organising proxy forces. It resourced this effort well, paying generous salaries to fighters and providing leadership. It also orchestrated an intervention to expel AQAP from Mukalla, the port-capital of Hadhramaut Province. But for all parties involved in the conflict, the greater challenge will come when a deal has been signed or the parties have fought to exhaustion. Both Saudi Arabia and the UAE were aware of the looming cost of post-conflict stabilisation in Yemen; this country had before the conflict been the poorest on the Arabian Peninsula, and even then it had only a fragile sense of unity.

Yemen and GCC military cooperation

The members of the Gulf Cooperation Council (GCC) have sought to develop closer defence cooperation for decades, but until 2013 progress in this area was modest at best. Cooperation was closest when states contributed to US CENTCOM-led headquarters and through occasional set-piece exercises; meanwhile, the Peninsula Shield Force – established in 1984 – remained moribund until it was used as the vehicle to deploy forces to Bahrain in 2011. But a flurry of recent announcements detailing closer defence cooperation, coupled with a deteriorating regional security situation, have indicated greater attention to this issue; developing effective combined capability among a number of states that struggle to operate on a joint basis internally is, however, a harder task.

Regional extroversion
In late 2013 the GCC agreed, at its December ministerial meeting, to form a Joint Military Command headquarters in Riyadh. Until that time, the GCC only had a small military secretariat. September 2014 saw Bahrain, Qatar, Saudi Arabia and the UAE committed to airstrikes against ISIS in Syria as part of an international coalition. This was followed in March 2015 by the generation of the ad hoc Saudi-led coalition and the start of the campaign in Yemen, under UN Security Council Resolution 2216 and at the invitation of Yemen's embattled President Hadi. About the same time, Egypt's President Abdel Fattah Al-Sisi announced the establishment of an Arab League military force. Subsequently, Saudi Defence Minister Mohammed bin Salman announced the formation of a 34-nation (now 39) Islamic Coalition against terrorism.

These activities have taken place against the backdrop of a worsening regional security situation, perceived Western inaction in relation to Syria and concerns over Iran, sharpened by the signing in mid-2015 of the Joint Comprehensive Plan of Action, designed to curb Iran's nuclear ambitions. At the same time, US efforts to encourage GCC countries into a more joined-up approach to procurement have so far been largely overlooked, notwithstanding the factors – such as the benefits of missile-defence cooperation – that should impel greater cooperation.

These factors have combined to impede progress towards the development of a collective GCC approach to defence. A principal challenge in developing effective collective-defence structures is the generation of a common political view regarding, for instance, threat perceptions and the use of force; this is far from evident in the region at present. Saudi Arabia, the UAE and, to a lesser extent, Bahrain have demonstrated their willingness to project force into Yemen; these states contrast with the more measured and established approaches of Kuwait and particularly Oman.

Towards greater cohesion
However, the intervention in Yemen and the campaign against ISIS have significantly changed the situation. All participants in the operation will have learned tactical lessons from the deployment of forces and the employment of equipment and, in many cases, the loss of troops in combat; the progressive and far-sighted states will act on these lessons. A priority will be to increase coherence between military services that have traditionally been stove-piped, as well as the need to share intelligence and develop common standards in order to ensure future interoperability. This will have been a stark lesson within Saudi Arabia, with forces reporting to the Ministry of Defence, the Ministry of the Interior and the National Guard having deployed alongside each other on the Yemeni border with different standard operating procedures and communications systems. This challenge is amplified when operating as part of a coalition, although, with the exception of special forces and artillery, ensuring that forces in Yemen operated in discrete areas of operation has somewhat alleviated the issue.

The lack of internal cohesion makes the challenge of building a GCC military coalition even more clear. For instance, the Yemen campaign seems to be running without a nominated campaign commander or coalition headquarters. While there is an Air Operations Centre in Riyadh, its practical effect in coordinating national contributions remains open to question. While the GCC has had a number of staff officers operating in potential areas of cooperation, such as communications, missile defence and logistics, there has been little progress. If there is little standardisation between services, it would be surprising to find a great deal between nations. As things stand, the Yemen mission has not led to firm statements advocating a more collective defence stance: financial issues mean that the region's states are examining their own policies, structures and procurements first, while traction in the GCC arena may be influenced by Oman's position.

However, the move to greater cohesion has started. One example was the agreement to build a GCC joint military command headquarters in Riyadh. This headquarters continues to develop, as does a smaller naval HQ (Task Force 81) alongside the coalition/US NAVCENT HQ in Bahrain. An option to boost effective defence cooperation would be to continue to form these headquarters, but in parallel capturing and applying the coalition lessons from current operations.

The most significant challenge will be in ensuring that no one state seeks to dominate such initiatives. Saudi Arabia, for instance, might have the largest regional military force, but the military competence and experience of some of its neighbours should not be overlooked. At the same time, regional states could benefit from better sharing the burden of trying to convince increasingly doubtful US and UK governments as to the need, and required safeguards, to ensure future weapons sales.

One view is that the dust should be allowed to settle, and individual member states encouraged to implement lessons from the Yemen and Syria operations. But the continuing evolution of security threats and the broader geopolitical environment mean that nations should act sooner. Saudi Arabia and the UAE have already secured outside consultants to advise on defence restructuring, and regional states have a good balance of ambitious young leaders and ministers and no shortage of talent amongst their various armed forces, who might welcome the chance to redesign forces. These processes would need to be accompanied by independent external support, complemented by or including some senior mentors, in order for these processes to stand the best chances of success.

Despite regional states' growing military extroversion since the end of 2013, the case is stronger than ever for a regional collective-defence organisation. Saudi Arabia's size and military power will inevitably give it significant weight in any such arrangement, but Riyadh needs to recognise that the support and counsel of close neighbours will come at an affordable price, including learning from others, as well as listening to partners and developing plans and procurements jointly. As coalition members consider how best to scale back their commitments to Yemen and draw a line under the campaign, a real chance exists to move ahead with plans for greater regional cooperation.

Regional capabilities increase

With many of the region's states either engaged in domestic-security operations and counter-terrorism tasks, or engaged in the regions conflicts, it is unsurprising that procurements continue apace. In some cases this results from modernisation drives, and in some instances there have been deals related either to equipment attrition or munitions resupply. Qatar appears to have accelerated equipment purchases in order to continue its military-modernisation drive. In April 2016, Qatar signed a deal with Turkey for MRTP-20 patrol boats. In June 2016, Doha ordered four corvettes, one landing-platform dock amphibious-warfare vessel and two offshore-patrol vessels from the Italian company Fincantieri. A related order for *Exocet* Block III, *Aster* 30 and VL-MICA missiles went to MBDA. Also in June 2016, Qatar signed a deal for AH-64E *Apache* attack helicopters. In late 2016, Washington also approved after two years the sale of combat aircraft to Kuwait and Qatar, for Boeing F/A-18E/Fs and F-15Es respectively. In addition, Qatar, like Kuwait, has introduced mandatory military service, which will affect defence budgets; the UAE introduced military service in 2015. While this is in part a means of offsetting the shortage of staff in the armed forces, and ensuring that these are from the local population, these moves have also been designed to inculcate a greater sense of statehood among the young population in the region. Meanwhile, amid continuing worries about Iran's ballistic-missile arsenal, regional states have continued plans to boost missile-defence capabilities. These capabilities are now being used: Saudi Arabia's *Patriot* systems have been deployed to engage *Scud* systems fired by rebel forces in Yemen. Egypt and Iran ordered the Russian S-300 system. Egypt is believed to have ordered the S-300VM (SA-23 *Gladiator/Giant*), though delivery status is unclear, while Iran completed the receipt of its S-300PMU-2 (SA-20 *Gargoyle*) in 2016.

Qatar's maritime orders in 2016, coming in the same year that Egypt acquired two *Mistral*-class vessels from France, are reflective of the broader military extroversion seen across the region. With increased purchases of strategic-airlift aircraft and longer-range guided munitions, states are acquiring military equipment of a broader range than previously. Some of these capabilities are suitable for power projection, and purchasers are likely mindful that some of them have recently engaged in military operations of a type – and in locations – that they would not previously have considered.

DEFENCE ECONOMICS

Macroeconomics

Although overall GDP growth in the Middle East and North Africa rose to 2.9% in 2016, up from 2.3% in 2015, this figure masked some divergence across the region. While GCC states' growth decreased from 3.3% in 2015 to 1.8% in 2016, Iran's increased from 0.4% to 4.5%. Hydrocarbon exporters in particular struggled with low market prices in 2016. Oil prices were set to remain low into 2017, due to the combination of slow global demand, continued high output from OPEC members and high non-OPEC oil production, particularly in the United States. The International Energy Agency (IEA) projected that OPEC members' oil-export revenues would fall from US$1.2 trillion in 2012 to US$320bn in 2016, if prices remained at the level they were when the IEA report was released in February 2016. At its meeting in November 2016, OPEC indicated that it might cut production in a bid to reduce oversupply and stabilise prices.

Crude-oil prices averaged US$43 per barrel in the six-month period up to July 2016. This was less than half the 2016 fiscal break-even oil price (the minimum price per barrel a state needs to balance its budget), which was estimated on average for Middle Eastern and North African oil-producing states at US$107.2. Consequently, oil-producing states remained under serious economic pressure in 2016. The World Bank estimated that in 2016 public-spending cuts amounted to 14% of the budget in Saudi Arabia, 11% in Oman, 9% in Algeria and 8% in Iraq.

Oil revenue accounted for three-quarters of Saudi Arabia's budget in 2015, and the continued fall in prices increased the kingdom's deficit, which amounted to 13.5% of GDP in 2016. As part of measures resulting from tighter government finances, Saudi Arabia announced pay cuts for government employees. Recognising the kingdom's dependence on the oil sector, the government launched the 'Vision 2030' programme in April 2016, which aims to diversify the economy. It highlights planned reductions in government subsidies for electricity, fuel and water, and taxes on luxury products and tobacco, among others. To tackle unemployment, Vision 2030 aims to increase private-sector employment in Saudi Arabia and favours the recruitment of Saudi nationals over migrant workers. Furthermore, the plan envisages the sale of 5% of Aramco, the national oil company, on the stock market and the creation of a public-investment fund. The government also sees tourism as a potential new source of revenue, with the ambition to quintuple the number of visitors to Saudi Arabia, rising to 30 million per year.

Further east, the United Arab Emirates' economic growth declined from 4.0% in 2015 to 2.3% in 2016, while Bahrain's growth declined from 2.9% in 2015 to 2.1% in 2016, and Oman's from 3.3% in 2015 to 1.8% in 2016. These states also took measures to compensate for the loss of oil revenues: Oman increased corporation tax and Bahrain raised tobacco and alcohol taxes; elsewhere, Algeria increased fuel, electricity and natural-gas prices. Iran fared better than the GCC countries. As a result of the nuclear deal, Iran's economy increased oil production, but production rates in the oil and gas sector have a long way to recover after years of underinvestment in the sector. Iran also regained access to foreign markets and capital as part of the deal. Meanwhile, Iraq's general budget declined by 13% compared to 2015, with oil income accounting for 85% of total revenue.

The situation was different for the region's oil importers. GDP growth increased in Egypt (3.8%), Jordan (2.8%) and Mauritania (3.2%), but there was only moderate growth in Lebanon (1.0%), Morocco (1.8%) and Tunisia (1.5%). Security challenges and social issues affected economic growth in these countries. For instance, terrorist attacks in Tunisia limited tourism and general economic confidence, while Jordan and Lebanon remain exposed to the effects of the civil war in Syria.

358 THE MILITARY BALANCE 2017

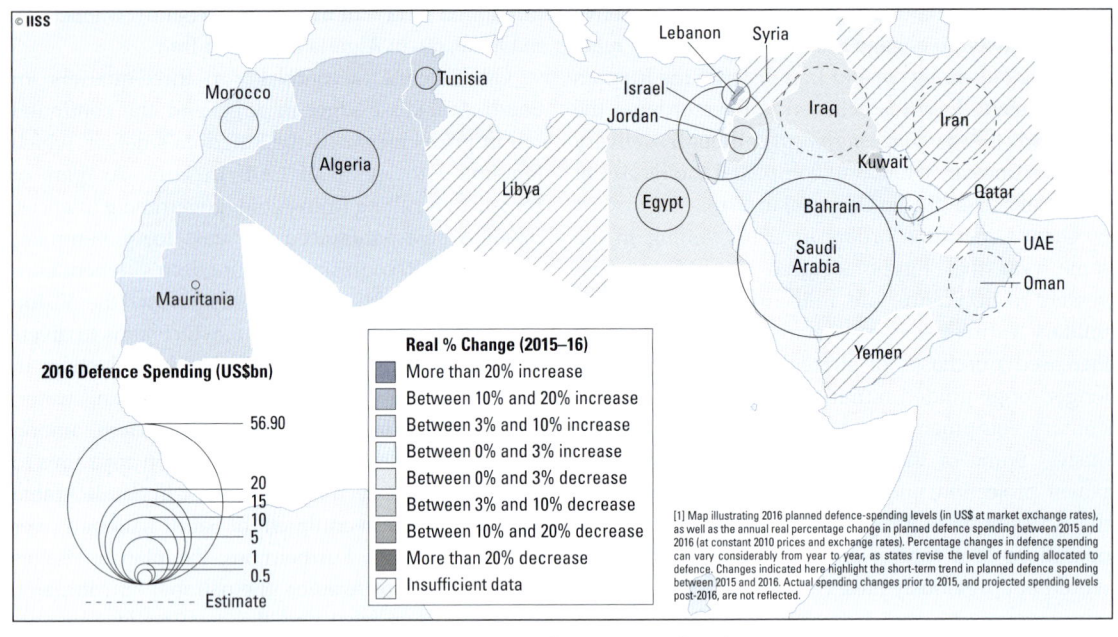

Map 9 **Middle East and North Africa regional defence spending**[1]

[1] Map illustrating 2016 planned defence-spending levels (in US$ at market exchange rates), as well as the annual real percentage change in planned defence spending between 2015 and 2016 (at constant 2010 prices and exchange rates). Percentage changes in defence spending can vary considerably from year to year, as states revise the level of funding allocated to defence. Changes indicated here highlight the short-term trend in planned defence spending between 2015 and 2016. Actual spending changes prior to 2015, and projected spending levels post-2016, are not reflected.

Despite its strong growth, Egypt's economy remained fragile. In August 2016, the IMF agreed to loan Cairo US$12bn over three years on the condition of economic reforms. Along with foreign-currency shortages and high inflation (at 10.2% in 2016), which were a burden on Egypt's economy, the effect of the government's currency flotation in November 2016 (which reduced the value of the Egyptian pound, making imports more expensive), combined with cuts to subsidies on bread, petrol and diesel, meant that the cost of living for Egyptians would rise. In response, the government was reportedly planning to distribute basic supplies to poorer members of society. It was hoped that this economic rebalancing would not only secure the IMF loan but would, in time, begin to attract greater inward investment. Meanwhile, Morocco's downward growth trend appeared temporary, owing much to a contraction in agricultural production.

Figure 22 **Estimated Middle East and North Africa defence expenditure 2016: sub-regional breakdown**

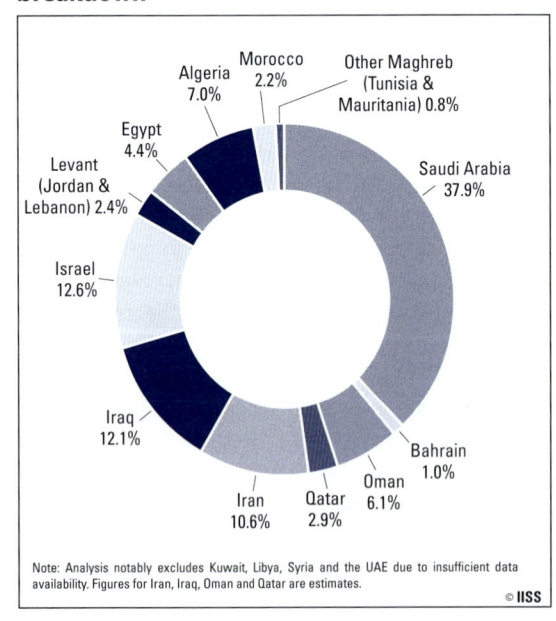

- Saudi Arabia 37.9%
- Israel 12.6%
- Iraq 12.1%
- Iran 10.6%
- Algeria 7.0%
- Oman 6.1%
- Egypt 4.4%
- Qatar 2.9%
- Levant (Jordan & Lebanon) 2.4%
- Morocco 2.2%
- Bahrain 1.0%
- Other Maghreb (Tunisia & Mauritania) 0.8%

Note: Analysis notably excludes Kuwait, Libya, Syria and the UAE due to insufficient data availability. Figures for Iran, Iraq, Oman and Qatar are estimates.

Defence spending and procurement

As a result of varying drivers for state-security and defence-policy priorities across the region, in many cases driven by direct involvement in regional conflicts, low oil prices have not affected the defence spending of all regional states in the same way. (However, limited transparency around defence disbursements in some states undermines overall regional assessments.) On the one hand, oil-producing states had limited fiscal space to increase defence budgets in 2016. For those countries dependent on hydrocarbon prices, and where data was available, defence budgets either decreased or stagnated. The decline in spending was most apparent in Saudi Arabia, where official defence spending declined from US$81.9bn to US$56.9bn between 2015 and 2016, which was a reduction of 30.5% (in current US dollars). Nonetheless, Saudi Arabia remains by far the region's largest defence spender. Meanwhile, Oman's defence budget decreased by 7.9% (US$9.9bn in 2015 to US$9.1bn in 2016) and Iraq's declined by 14.6% (US$21.1bn in 2015 to US$18.1bn in 2016). Bahrain's defence budget decreased by only 0.2%. However, Algeria, although it is an oil-producing state, was able to increase its defence budget by 1.6%, from US$10.4bn in 2015 to US$10.6bn in 2016.

On the whole, the region's non-oil producers have had the most economic freedom to dedicate more funds to defence. Israel's defence budget expanded by 3.0% (US$15.4bn in 2015 to US$15.9bn in 2016), Jordan's by 11.1% and Morocco's by 3.0%. In September 2016, Washington renewed the financial-aid package, granting Israel US$38bn between 2019 and 2028 – around US$3.8bn per year. Of this sum, US$5bn will be used for missile-defence systems. Nonetheless, constrained defence budgets have not limited oil-producing countries' procurement ambitions. This may be due to the high priority some states give to defence programmes if they are engaged in, or feel threatened by, military challenges. However, the continuation of large procurement programmes in the face of economic difficulty may also reflect the existence of other sources of funding over and above the official defence budget. For example, the Kuwaiti government announced a defence supplement budget in 2016 estimated at US$10bn. The money reportedly will be placed in a fund outside the budget, with the capital coming from state reserves. This additional funding is intended to be spent on new equipment and upgrades over a ten-year period.

As illustrated in Figure 24, in 2016 air-defence systems were being procured by ten out of the 12 countries in the region. While Gulf countries sought to acquire US systems, other states in the region purchased Russian equipment. Rotary-wing mobility was also a priority in the region. Spending by GCC states is likely driven in part by military operations

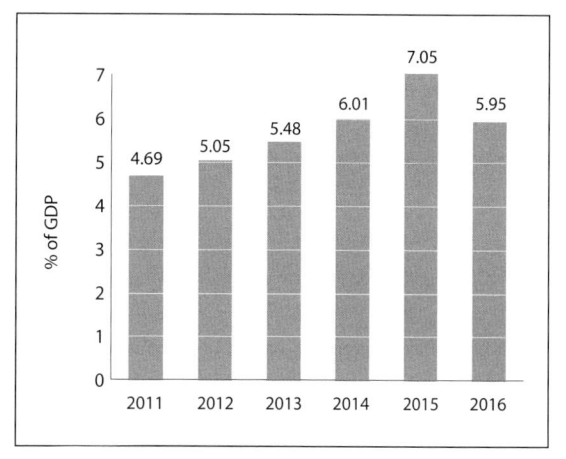

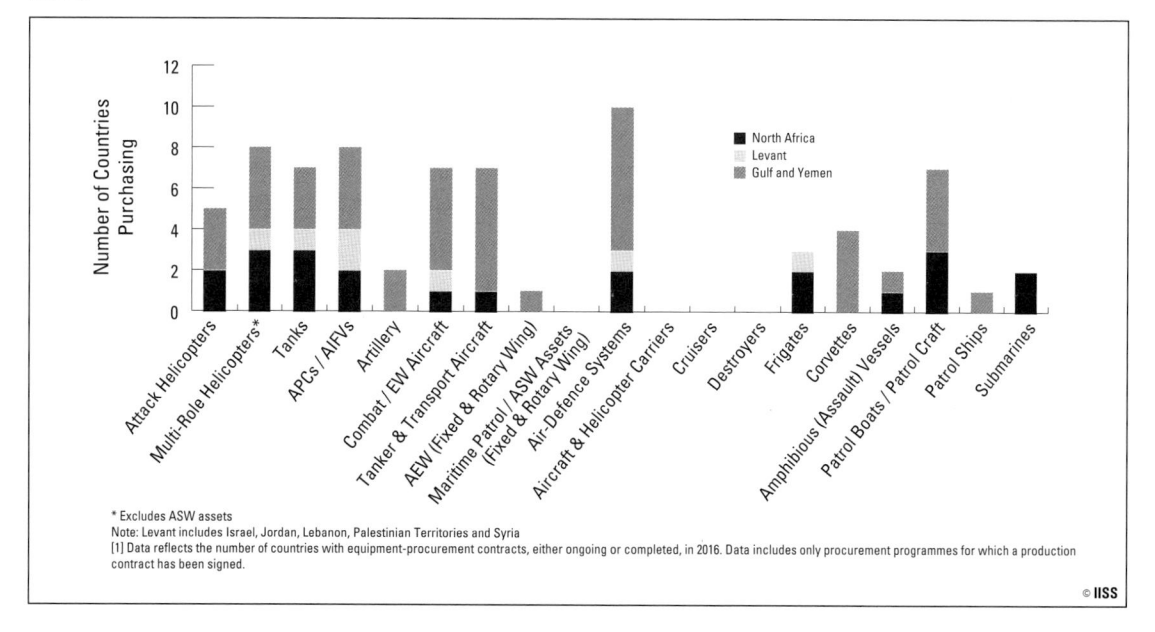

Figure 23 **Middle East and North Africa regional defence expenditure** as % of GDP

Figure 24 **Middle East and North Africa: selected ongoing or completed procurement priorities in 2016**[1]

* Excludes ASW assets
Note: Levant includes Israel, Jordan, Lebanon, Palestinian Territories and Syria
[1] Data reflects the number of countries with equipment-procurement contracts, either ongoing or completed, in 2016. Data includes only procurement programmes for which a production contract has been signed.

in Yemen and against ISIS, but it is also driven by concerns over Iran's ballistic-missile inventory, as evidenced by the purchase of air-defence systems by Gulf states.

GCC defence budgets remain higher than that of Iran. Saudi Arabia's official 2016 budget alone is US$56.9bn, 3.5 times higher than Iran's (US$15.9bn). Furthermore, GCC states purchase advanced defence equipment from the West, while Iran, under sanctions, has had to rely on its own defence industry for incremental upgrades and the maintenance of legacy platforms. However, although Iran might seek to improve its armed forces after the nuclear deal, a range of embargos remain in place. For example, even after the nuclear deal was signed, the embargo on the sale of conventional weapons to Iran was due to stay in place for five years from 'adoption day', while the UN Security Council's ban on Iran's ballistic-missile developments is supposed to be lifted after eight years. Meanwhile, the US also maintains a range of sanctions due to concerns about Iran and terrorism. Meanwhile, Russia, which in 2010 had interpreted the Security Council ban on exports to Iran to include an air-defence system it had agreed to export, reversed that decision and Tehran finally received the first deliveries of the S-300 system in 2016.

Defence industry

Countries across the region have renewed efforts to develop domestic defence industries. This is part of

Emirates Defence Industries Company

The United Arab Emirates has one of the most developed and ambitious defence-industry portfolios in the Middle East. Until 2014, the management of defence-industrial programmes within the UAE was divided across three holding companies: Emirates Advanced Investments (which is privately owned), Mubadala and Tawazun. In order to reduce unnecessary competition and streamline the UAE's strategic manufacturing and service capabilities for the UAE armed forces and prospective customers, the Emirates Defence Industries Company (EDIC) was formed on 2 December 2014 (the UAE's National Day).

The incorporation of assets occurred in two stages. The first saw the integration of 11 firms: Al Taif; Bayanat; C4 Advanced Solutions; Global Aerospace Logistics; Horizon International Flight Academy; Naval Advanced Solutions; NIMR Automotive; Secure Communications; Tawazun Dynamics; Tawazun Precision Industries (TPI); and Thales Advanced Solutions. The second absorption cycle included Abu Dhabi Autonomous Systems Investments; Advanced Military Maintenance Repair and Overhaul Centre (AMMROC); Burkan; Caracal; and Caracal Light Ammunition.

The senior executive board is chaired by Mubadala Chief Executive of Aerospace and Engineering Hommaid al Shemmari. Also on this board are Saif al Hajeri, Tawzun CEO and chairman of the Critical Infrastructure and Coastal Protection Authority; Major General Pilot Fares Khalaf al Mazrouei, Executive Director of Aerospace and Defence Mubadala; Cyril Arar; and Major General Saif al-Masafri. The CEO of EDIC is the former chairman and CEO of Thales Group, Luc Vigneron. Each commercial entity within EDIC retains its own leadership and management, but after their integration now report directly to the EDIC CEO.

The firm says its mission is twofold: to provide capability and support to the UAE armed forces and to help develop the UAE's engineering and manufacturing capabilities. As such, it is hoped that EDIC will help develop the skills of the local workforce and contribute to the plan for economic diversification. EDIC forms a part of the UAE's modernisation strategy and, as a result, is supervised by a number of entities including the UAE armed forces and the Ministry of Defence (MoD). It was hoped that creating a vertical hierarchy would enable a unified UAE defence industry to complement not only the armed forces, but also the Joint Logistic Programme (established in 2012 to coordinate tri-service logistics support) and the wider economy.

EDIC firms carry out three principal tasks: maintenance, repair and overhaul; manufacturing; and assembly. The institutional relationship between the UAE armed forces, EDIC and original equipment manufacturers (OEMs) has led to a range of public–private partnerships, which provide services to the armed forces. Indeed, the firm's primary focus is on the local market, not least because of its emphasis on developing local talent and incubating local research and development (R&D), engineering and manufacturing, as well as providing the best capabilities to the UAE armed forces.

The UAE's Gulf Cooperation Council neighbours and other countries in the Middle East and North Africa, as well as in South Asia, are seen as secondary markets. However, EDIC's projected growth remains central to its strategy as the firm not only looks to offer its services and products for sale, but also to acquire new technology and

a diversification strategy, whereby the defence sector is intended to be a high-tech growth area as part of national economic-development strategies. It is also a means of ensuring that defence funding is re-invested within the local economy. However, these expansion programmes are also pursued in a bid to develop more secure supply chains and because of concerns over external political factors that could affect defence imports – such as the criticism in the West in recent years regarding some weapons sales to Middle Eastern states.

In common with defence importers worldwide, regional states request technology transfers when signing contracts, in order to foster domestic competences. In August 2016, Algeria and Leonardo (formerly Finmeccanica) signed a deal to create a joint venture for helicopter production. In September 2016 the first of the *Gowind* 2500 corvettes ordered by Egypt from France was launched, with another three to be built in an Egyptian shipyard under a technology-transfer deal. The UAE's defence industry has also developed in recent years, as reflected in the establishment of the Emirates Defence Industries Company (EDIC) (see below). UAE defence firms are most advanced in the shipbuilding sector, through Abu Dhabi Shipbuilding (ADSB). ADSB locally produced the *Ghannatha*-class patrol boat, which was based on the *Combatboat* 60 design from Swede Ship Marine; three ships were built in Sweden and nine in the UAE. Some of these are missile boats, some will

expertise. Most of its portfolio stems from joint ventures with OEMs and, in other cases, is the result of the co-development of new technologies.

Tawazun Economic Council (TEC) (formerly the Offset Program Bureau) directs much of the large-scale investment and cooperation between the UAE and its commercial partners, mainly OEMs. TEC creates, manages and executes the UAE's offset policy and in doing so works closely with the armed forces, EDIC and the government to implement strategic policies benefiting the UAE. Currently, for defence and aerospace sales over US$10 million, the UAE requires 60% of the purchase-contract value to be re-invested in the country through a combination of direct and indirect offsets. Indeed, the UAE offset programme has coordinated what are now seen as some of EDIC's greatest successes, such as AMMROC, Tawazun Dynamics and TPI. Due to this desire to bring skills into the UAE, foreign entities looking to enter the market could consider strategies related to the development of local industrial expertise (such as joint ventures, training, partnerships and technology transfer), areas such as risk-share proposals with local partners, and investments in local human capital. The last area is one where EDIC may face its most significant challenge in producing a more self-sufficient defence sector.

The UAE's small population means that EDIC will face competition from other sectors of the economy for the best candidates, while retaining these staff will require careful nurturing and good incentive structures. Meanwhile, the development of local high-tech R&D centres will also be important, as will further development of the higher-education sector more broadly, in order to ensure that the skills presently gained abroad can either be locally grown or developed in the UAE.

While the creation of an indigenous defence industry has resulted from the procurement of foreign equipment, domestic production will have to replace foreign imports in order for EDIC to fully succeed. However, if the UAE is not able to indigenously generate innovative technology, EDIC may well become more reliant on foreign defence equipment for the domestic production of technology.

Emirates Defence Industries Company (EDIC): commercial structure

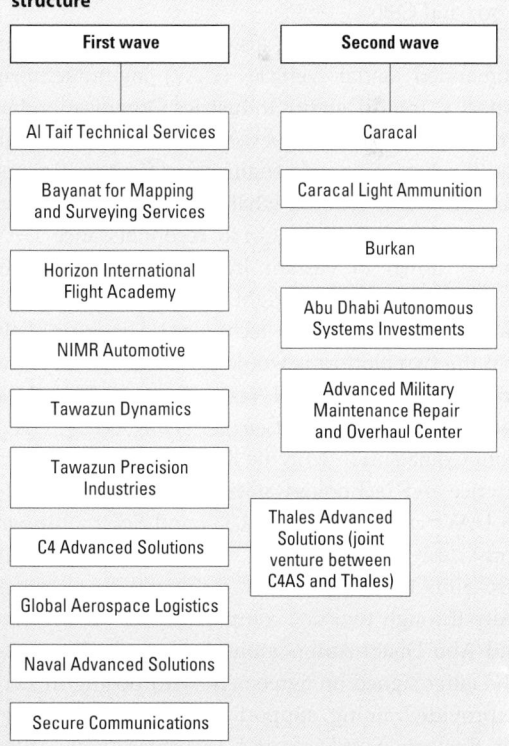

First wave:
- Al Taif Technical Services
- Bayanat for Mapping and Surveying Services
- Horizon International Flight Academy
- NIMR Automotive
- Tawazun Dynamics
- Tawazun Precision Industries
- C4 Advanced Solutions
- Global Aerospace Logistics
- Naval Advanced Solutions
- Secure Communications

Second wave:
- Caracal
- Caracal Light Ammunition
- Burkan
- Abu Dhabi Autonomous Systems Investments
- Advanced Military Maintenance Repair and Overhaul Center
- Thales Advanced Solutions (joint venture between C4AS and Thales)

carry mortars and some will be used in the landing/amphibious role. Similarly, ADSB has produced *Baynunah* corvettes based on a design by French firm CMN. The first *Baynunah* was built in France and another five were built in the UAE; there is one left to construct.

Somewhat lagging behind regionally, Saudi Arabia launched an initiative to reinforce its domestic defence-technological and -industrial base. In its Vision 2030 strategy, the Saudi government announced an objective to localise 50% of its military-equipment spending by 2030. The document stated that Saudi Arabia only spends 2% of its budget within the kingdom. To reach this goal, Riyadh was due to launch a government-owned military holding company in late 2016 or early 2017. Offset requirements in arms-import contracts will include partnerships with local firms. Another announced objective is for the Saudi defence industry to become able to manufacture military aircraft.

Due to the arms embargo, Iran had incentives to develop its local defence industry, notably in the missiles sector. For example, the Aerospace Industries Organisation unveiled the *Soumar* ground-launched cruise missile in March 2015 and also displayed missiles based on Chinese designs, including the C-701 and C-802.

Regional states have also begun to develop an unmanned aerial vehicle (UAV) manufacturing capacity. Iran's Defence Industries Organisation has stressed the importance of UAV technology, although it still relies on reverse-engineering foreign designs. Iran has demonstrated what it says are derivatives of the United States' RQ-170 reconnaissance UAV forced down in eastern Iran in 2011. However, without access to the right engine, materials and hardware and software technologies it is unlikely that the two platforms would be similar in any way other than by outward resemblance. Meanwhile, Saudi Arabia procured *Gongji-1* (*Wing Loong*) UAVs from China and in 2013 the King Abdulaziz City for Science and Technology stated that it had produced 38 UAVs called *Saker* 2, *Saker* 3 and *Saker* 4, apparently designed for border- control tasks. The UAE also aims to set up a UAV industrial base, principally through two key companies, Adcom Systems and Abu Dhabi Autonomous Systems Investments. The latter signed an agreement with Boeing in 2013 to provide training, support and marketing services for Boeing's *ScanEagle* and *Integrator* (now called *Blackjack*) UAV systems.

Israel still possesses the region's most advanced defence industry, including for UAV technology. However, Israel will no longer be able to use a significant proportion of the US military-financing package to buy defence equipment from Israeli firms for the Israel Defense Forces. The domestic-procurement clause will be phased out in the first six years of the new agreement and that relating to fuel expenditure at the start of the package. While the larger Israeli firms may be able to circumvent the new regulations through US-based subsidiaries, the consequences could be more significant for small- and medium-sized enterprises.

SAUDI ARABIA

Saudi Arabia is now over two years into its first sustained military operations, with air missions continuing over Syria targeting the Islamic State, also known as ISIS or ISIL, and air and limited ground operations continuing as part of *Operation Restoring Hope* in Yemen, the latter designed to aid the restoration to power of Yemen's President Abd Rabbo Mansour Hadi. Meanwhile, the air force remains active on operations over Syria to target ISIS.

The lack of a Western commitment to intervene in Syria in September 2014 proved the catalyst for a substantive shift in military thinking and defence postures in the Middle East. Regional military dynamics had been drifting this way for some time. In 2011, when primarily Western military operations began to halt the threat to Libyan civilians from Muammar Gadhafi, Qatar and the United Arab Emirates deployed combat air assets, while other regional states deployed capacities including airlift support. Regional states were displaying growing, if cautious, military and strategic extroversion.

This shift in thinking was most profound in the largest military power among the Gulf states, Saudi Arabia. The kingdom's armed forces do not have a history of offensive operations beyond their borders. There had been a brief air campaign against Houthi targets in Yemen in 2009 and elements of Saudi land forces and National Guard deployed to Bahrain in 2011. Saudi naval forces also take part in maritime-security operations in the Gulf as part of Combined Task Forces 151 and 152. However, there has been no enduring, multi-service deployment since the First Gulf War in 1991. In line with the challenges Riyadh faced at that time, Saudi forces have generally focused on maintaining territorial integrity. Nonetheless, since 2014 they have rapidly been projected externally, firstly in September that year as part of the United States-led coalition airstrikes in Syria and then in March 2015 at the request of Hadi and under UN Security Council Resolution 2216 in the largely unexpected Saudi-led coalition intervention in Yemen.

Today the Saudis and their coalition partners face a situation with stark similarities to that of US-led coalitions in Iraq and Afghanistan – an external intervention that, for the time being, is increasingly deadlocked without political or military end in sight, and requires the commitment of substantial military resources. Alongside efforts to resolve problems in Yemen and a commitment to counter-ISIS operations, concerns over a Western accommodation with Iran preoccupies Saudi Arabia.

Defence policy

Like its neighbours, Saudi Arabia has not formally published a defence and security policy or any associated official budget to underpin force structures and activities. However, the Ministry of Defence (MoD) has recently engaged consultants to help with this process. It is likely that there will be some effort made to generate this type of policy documentation and, related to this process, to examine current and future Saudi force structures and military capabilities, even if such work is not publicly released. This is particularly likely as the kingdom launched a broad programme called 'Vision 2030' in April 2016, which is designed to serve as a road map for Saudi Arabia's development and economic objectives until 2030 and which has already projected far-reaching reforms to Saudi Arabia's defence-industrial ambitions.

While developing a basic policy should not be difficult, the greatest challenge will come in operationalising it. Indeed, the first versions of a defence policy will be unlikely to have a significant impact across all of the 'defence lines of development' (UK terminology to describe a way of coordinating the elements needed to generate military capability: training, equipment, personnel information, concepts and doctrine, organisation, infrastructure, logistics). This is because legacy capability and procurement decisions, and many years of operating in relative isolation, will take time to 'work through' the system.

A useful indication of policy parameters can be seen in the document prepared in 2014 by former Saudi official Nawaf Obaid (in a Belfer Center Paper) and that was subsequently refined and presented, unofficially, by Obaid and HRH Sultan bin Khaled Al Faisal, former commander of Saudi Naval Special Forces and son of the governor of Mecca. Their work suggests five main principles: defence of the homeland; protect Saudi citizens; secure national security and interests; bolster partners' defence; and strengthen inter-agency partnerships. Obaid attempted to allocate resources to some of these categories in his early work but some areas of focus were missing. In light of Saudi Arabia's recent (and potential) ground, naval and air-force activities, it should now be possible to offer a more evidential basis for policy, concept and capability recommendations.

The armed forces

Saudi Arabia has the third-largest armed forces in the Gulf region after Iraq and Iran. At its core is a conventional MoD headquarters (MoD HQ) with five armed services: the Royal Saudi land, naval and air forces together with separate air-defence and strategic-rocket forces. There are few truly 'joint' organisations, apart from a joint-operations centre in the MoD HQ and an embryonic 'J6' (communications) branch. Two other armed forces, the Ministry of the National Guard and the Royal Guard, are independent of MoD command. All these individual services retain considerable autonomy, as indeed do some procurement programmes. Nonetheless, there has been some quick adaption since the start of *Operation Decisive Edge/Restoring Hope*, with military operations demonstrating the advantages of joint structures and closer integration. An example of this has been the need to coordinate closely between MoD land forces, national-guard elements and the border guard (reporting to the Ministry of the Interior); these forces have been operating in very close proximity to each other on the Yemeni border. In contrast to most other Gulf states, recruitment and retention is less of a challenge due to a comparatively large proportion of Saudi nationals in the population. As a result, the armed forces comprise almost exclusively Saudi nationals.

Air Force
The Royal Saudi Air Force (RSAF) remains at the vanguard of Saudi capability. Many years of close cooperation with the United Kingdom and the US due to major capability-development and -integration programmes, and associated training, have worked to the advantage of the RSAF. So too has careful husbandry by some far-sighted individuals. Today it has a large fleet of modern combat aircraft based on

the older F-15 *Strike Eagle* and *Tornado* but with over 60 Eurofighter *Typhoon*s and large numbers of F-15SA variants in the pipeline; for the air force, these types indicate a significant move into multi-role capability. The RSAF has also benefited from good funding and programme management as well as considerable bilateral and multilateral training activities, such as participation in the NATO-led *Anatolian Eagle* and US *Red Flag* exercises. The strong training line of development associated with these programmes has had the added effect of developing middle- and senior-ranking officers whose experience and English-language ability have enabled them to benefit further from external training opportunities.

Development of combat air capability continues with deliveries of Eurofighter *Typhoon*s (a total order of 72), the imminent arrival of the F-15SA, a recent upgrade of training aircraft to the Cirrus and Pilatus PC21 airframes and an order for 22 *Hawk* T-165 trainers. Weapons upgrades include smart weapons such as the *Brimstone* air-to-ground missile and the *Paveway* IV dual-mode GPS/INS-guided bomb. The replacement of the ageing *Tornado* fleet with further deliveries of Eurofighter *Typhoon* aircraft is also being considered. The air force is also procuring more support aircraft, including Beechcraft *King Air*, A330 multi-role tanker transports and Saab 2000 *Erieye* airborne early-warning and control aircraft, with the latter commissioned and flying since 2015.

However, there has been little progress on unmanned aerial vehicle (UAV) programmes, despite a clear operational need. Much of this may be down to concerns over stated ambitions for armed UAVs. A number of platforms were assessed and the Chinese-manufactured *Gongji-1* is in service in limited numbers; this allows the air force to develop experience of their use on operations, not least in relation to their value as intelligence platforms and the challenge of airspace integration. This is in stark contrast to their Emirati neighbours who are already manufacturing these systems. UAV acquisition and integration are likely to form part of Saudi procurement programmes in the near future.

Air defence
The Royal Saudi Air Defence Force (RSADF) is similar to the RSAF in terms of funding and operational experience. It was formed in 1970, when then-deputy defence minister HRH Khalid bin Sultan moved air defence out of the land forces and into a separate command. The RSADF has enjoyed good funding levels and has seen the acquisition of principally US and French equipment, the latter leading to numerous RSADF officers training in France. However, US-supplied *Patriot* systems are the principal air-defence system. The force was formed in response to a clear requirement, given the growing number of capable combat air platforms in the region, as well as the growth in guided and unguided weapons, including those capable of delivering 'weapons of mass destruction'. Its traditional roles include the protection of airfields and major military bases, as well as the defence of major petrochemical and desalination facilities.

The recent Yemen operation has tested the RSADF, during which its units successfully engaged *Scud* missiles fired into Saudi Arabia from Yemen. Concerns over Iran and its ballistic-missile arsenal will mean that the Saudi air-defence force will remain well funded. Indeed, Iran's growing ballistic-missile inventory, a common concern among Gulf states, has led some – including sequential US administrations – to press for greater integration between the missile-defence capabilities of Gulf Cooperation Council (GCC) states, some of which operate similar US-supplied equipment. The proximity of Iran's missile systems and the challenge of regional geography would seem to make cooperation on early warning and engagement a useful way of developing a more effective defence, but real progress remains elusive.

Navy
The Royal Saudi Naval Forces (RSNF) are a clear step behind the other armed services, with some dated equipment in the inventory. The Red Sea-based, French-supplied frigate and destroyer fleet has started a major upgrade programme but the Arabian Gulf-based inventory of patrol boats and corvettes is now close to obsolete and has proved hard to support on the Yemen operation. Assuming that the destroyer and frigate upgrades proceed according to plan, the next priority will be to acquire an appropriate Gulf-based capability. Talk of a 'Saudi Naval Expansion Programme' with the US has been under way for over five years. The UK-manufactured fibreglass-hull *Sandown*-class minehunter fleet is now well into an upgrade programme that will prolong the life of what is judged by experts an essential and capable platform. Meanwhile, specialist training with coalition partners coordinated with the 31-nation Combined Maritime Forces HQ in Bahrain continues.

The Saudi navy also has strong training relationships with France, Pakistan, the UK and the US. Most recently, the UK Royal Navy and the RSNF began an upgraded officer-training programme for RSNF cadets at the UK's Royal Naval College that complements the UK-instructor cadre at the King Fahd Naval Academy in Jubail.

Land Forces
The Royal Saudi Land Forces (RSLF) are the largest component of the MoD's service structure, and they have faced many challenges in the Yemen campaign. Equipment modernisation has been incremental, with piecemeal upgrades to tank and infantry-fighting-vehicle fleets. With the exception of some special-forces operations and the training of loyalist Yemeni forces, the land forces have been employed on largely static border-security tasks against incursions by Houthi rebels, alongside the national guard and border guard. These static tasks, which stem from the nature of Yemen's terrain and the legacy of the military operations of 2009, coupled with a desire not to become an army of occupation in Yemen, have made the land forces vulnerable. These missions have stretched logistics, forced the rapid development of force-protection tactics, techniques and procedures, and put enormous pressure on the attack-helicopter fleet, which, in the absence of effective intelligence, surveillance and reconnaissance (ISR) platforms across all the services, has become the 'go to' platform during these operations. However, these operations will have resulted in a significant number of lessons that could inform modernisation programmes.

Other forces
Once largely a secret, the principal capability of the Saudi Strategic Rocket Forces were openly displayed at the large-scale exercise *Saif Abdallah* in May 2014 at Hafr al-Batin. The Forces' Chinese-made DF-3 systems are now 30 years old and there have been rumours regarding upgrades and/or renewal; there have been a number of reports that the Saudi inventory now includes the Chinese DF-21 missile, though this remains unconfirmed.

The Ministry of the National Guard remains independent of the MoD, although some Saudi Arabian National Guard (SANG) force elements are deployed under MoD command and control due to the Yemen operations. SANG's principal commitment to current operations is the French-supplied CAESAR self-propelled 155mm wheeled artillery piece, which is more advanced than other artillery systems currently in the ground forces' inventory. SANG has also deployed to bolster security on Saudi Arabia's northern border. It is also slowly building an air wing, based on AH6i *Little Bird*, *Blackhawk* and *Apache* helicopters, and has pilots trained and on exchange operations in the land forces. Plans for a major expansion of the force were first mooted in 2014, but these now seem to have been paused and the future size, shape and command-and-control reporting lines for this force remain unanswered. SANG funding continues to be reduced, making it closely examine its programmes and related costs, while some analysts believe that some of its capabilities may, in time, be devolved to the MoD and interior ministry. SANG continues to benefit from close training ties through the US Office of Program Management and the British Military Mission.

The Royal Guard Regiment also sits outside of the MoD's command-and-control system. It provides close protection for senior members of the royal family and major royal palaces. Despite effectively being a personal-security force, there have been reports in recent years that the purchase of light armoured vehicles is under consideration.

Defence and security cooperation and coalitions

Saudi Arabia maintains an extensive network of bilateral agreements and sends its personnel to countries across the globe for training. It has strong ties with Pakistan, and Islamabad boosted training support at the start of Yemen operations – mainly, but not exclusively, with the land forces. Riyadh has a growing appetite for bilateral collective training, which has taken place with French, UK and US forces both inside and outside the kingdom. Meanwhile, China is quietly engaged with Saudi Arabia and has been supporting the kingdom's embryonic armed-UAV capability.

For the time being, multilateral engagement is largely limited to the maritime and air domains. The naval forces are particularly prominent in this type of engagement, having commanded a naval combined task force for the first time in 2015. With the exception of periodic set-piece GCC events, Saudi Arabia does not engage in any multinational joint exercises. However, Defence Minister HRH Mohammed bin Salman is keen to expand training cooperation, although without any particular preference for specific partners. Meanwhile, regional coalition cooperation has recently developed. Slow moves towards GCC and Arab League military forces were overtaken by the rapid formation of the ad hoc 11-nation coalition to conduct *Operation Decisive Storm* and the subsequent announcement, by the Saudi defence minister, of the Muslim counter-terrorism coalition in December 2015. The latter has established a headquarters just outside Riyadh, but as of late 2016 was still in the early stages of defining its role. Meanwhile, although some Gulf partners have shown an interest in NATO cooperation, Saudi Arabia has not.

Operations in Yemen

At home, there has been a sense of national pride in how the armed forces have risen to the challenge of the operations in Yemen. Saudi Arabia's military will be gathering valuable lessons as the result of these missions, as they confront the requirements for joint operations by forces that had previously been mainly autonomous. This requirement has implications in terms of equipment procurement across the armed forces. It has become necessary to understand the difficulties of operating with weapons and communications systems from multiple sources and the need to develop standardisation plans – these will be vital for effective joint operations. Furthermore, the requirement for ground–air support and precise air operations has highlighted the forces' requirement for tactical air controllers, which, although emphasised in the 2009 campaign against the Houthis, had not received significant attention. This deficiency has proven as much an issue for the air force as the ground forces. At the start of the Yemen operation, the number of pilots with high levels of flying hours was reportedly limited, likely meaning that some pilots were comparatively inexperienced. Saudi Arabia's *Patriot* air-defence systems, meanwhile, have reportedly operated effectively against incoming targets.

However, effective progress in the broader Yemen campaign remains harder to gauge. The alliance of convenience between the Houthi forces and those loyal to former president Ali Abdullah Saleh persists, and military forces reporting to these factions remain in control of much of the capital and of northern Yemen (terrorist groups hold territory elsewhere). They also retain significant military capability, as has been demonstrated by intermittent ballistic-missile launches aimed at Saudi Arabia, but most significantly by the anti-ship-missile attack on the former HSV *Swift* in the Red Sea, which had been chartered by the UAE. Meanwhile, Saudi Arabia's air campaign has attracted significant criticism internationally, particularly over targeting. While the air mission continues, the activity of special-forces detachments and the training of local Yemeni forces has – together with negotiations with Yemeni tribal groups – also proven effective on the ground.

Defence economics and industry

After a period of growth, the official defence budget fell in 2016, placing Saudi Arabia behind Russia as the fourth-largest budget in the world. However, this is probably a conservative figure given the added requirements of Yemen operations where considerable additional expenditure will have been needed to restock munitions and service the deployed force, and the possible availability of other off-budget revenues. Funding levels have come under pressure as a result of factors including the fall in revenues resulting from lower oil prices. While national threat perceptions and the requirements of ongoing operations will likely mean that defence still receives significant sums, the fall was nonetheless stark, down from US$81.9 billion in 2015 to US$56.9bn in 2016 (in current dollars and taking into account exchange-rate fluctuations). Defence and security spending will likely come under further scrutiny in future, not least if it is to be consistent with the reform agenda of King Salman's Vision 2030.

Virtually all of the kingdom's equipment and materiel is imported, with only modest amounts of ammunition and uniforms and some weapons manufactured locally; this represents barely 2% of overall spending. Vision 2030 has clear and ambitious goals for defence, and sets a target 'to localize 50% of [defence] expenditure by 2030 moving towards higher value and more complex tasks', recognising that direct investment and strategic partnerships are likely to be the main routes to success. This will put pressure on major international defence companies to consider how they can participate in this initiative; progress through offsets and other joint-venture and partnering programmes has been patchy. It is not yet clear what role a revitalised state-owned Military Industries Corporation (MIC) may play in this, although the appointment in 2015 of Mohammed Al Mathy (former chief executive of the Saudi Arabian Basic Industries Corporation) and discussion of a revised constitution (to make MIC the supplier of choice) gives some indication. Saudi Arabia's fledgling defence industries will face the challenge of competing in a constrained regional market where extra-regional suppliers will want to retain their market share. However, given the increasing pressure on governments to place arms sales to Saudi Arabia under greater scrutiny, moves to create a viable domestic defence industry are timely, even if it remains challenging.

It is likely that some major equipment programmes will need to be revisited to see if the required outputs can be delivered in different ways or with fewer platforms. Each service will have its own funding priorities, yet there is an urgent need to take some major capabilities into a joint environment, notably ISR; it is likely that prioritisation judgements will need to be applied vigorously. The air force has a compelling argument for maintaining the F-15SA programme, but it also needs to make improvements in air support and to consider the need for a *Tornado* replacement. The navy urgently needs to decide on the type of capability required for operations in the Arabian Gulf and the land forces need to rationalise their equipment holdings. The air-defence force is looking to modernise, and may be subject to pressure to meet US calls for greater regional integration. These pressures will bring the national guard into sharper focus, specifically whether it can continue as a separate force with duplicate capabilities, including some costly and effective artillery and aviation equipment.

Taken together, the challenges of low oil prices, a changing defence posture and lessons from Yemen will impose significant demands on an MoD that has so far had a relatively conservative and limited outlook. These factors highlight the need for significant, though gradual, defence reform. Although a number of consultancies have been engaged by Riyadh, a defence ministry is not a commercial enterprise and care will be needed to produce the right approach – nor can such change be implemented immediately. The objectives of the military-reform process need to be ambitious, but the first steps ought to be relatively conservative in order to grow the human capital required for success. It will not be possible to produce a cadre of expert capability managers overnight, but years of training overseas mean that the building blocks are in place.

Algeria ALG

Algerian Dinar D		2015	2016	2017
GDP	D	16.8tr	17.8tr	
	US$	167bn	168bn	
per capita	US$	4,175	4,129	
Growth	%	3.9	3.6	
Inflation	%	4.8	5.9	
Def bdgt	D	1.05tr	1.12tr	
	US$	10.4bn	10.6bn	
US$1=D		100.69	105.73	

Population 40,263,711

Age	0–14	15–19	20–24	25–29	30–64	65 plus
Male	14.9%	3.7%	4.5%	4.6%	20.5%	2.5%
Female	14.2%	3.5%	4.3%	4.4%	20.1%	3.0%

Capabilities

Algerian defence planners remain concerned by the conflict in Mali; instability in Libya; regional terrorist activity, including that of the Islamic State; and porous eastern and southern borders. These threats have motivated change in policy priorities, structures and deployments, increasing focus on professionalisation and regional cooperation. Al-Qaeda in the Islamic Maghreb targeted Algerian petroleum plants in 2016, leading to the armed forces being placed on high alert, increased surveillance activity and heightened attention on border security. There is also a focus on equipment upgrades and modernisation. Algeria has ordered a significant amount of Russian equipment, including armoured vehicles, surface ships, submarines, combat aircraft and attack helicopters. Algeria has been a leading proponent of combined training with neighbouring powers – in particular Mali, Mauritania and Niger – partially to build counter-terrorist capacity in the Sahel and Maghreb regions. The armed forces have substantial counter-insurgency experience and took over the counter-narcotics-trafficking role in 2013. The army plans to build an electronic-surveillance system on the border. Algeria is part of the African Union's North African Regional Capability Standby Force, hosting the force's logistics base in Algiers.

ACTIVE 130,000 (Army 110,000 Navy 6,000 Air 14,000) **Paramilitary 187,200**

Conscript liability 18 months, only in the army (6 months basic, 12 months with regular army often involving civil projects)

RESERVE 150,000 (Army 150,000) to age 50

ORGANISATIONS BY SERVICE

Army 35,000; 75,000 conscript (total 110,000)
FORCES BY ROLE
6 Mil Regions; re-org into div structure on hold
MANOEUVRE
  Armoured
  2 (1st & 8th) armd div (3 tk regt; 1 mech regt, 1 arty gp)
  1 indep armd bde
  Mechanised
  2 (12th & 40th) mech div (1 tk regt; 3 mech regt, 1 arty gp)
  3 indep mech bde
  Light
  2 indep mot bde
  Air Manoeuvre
  1 AB div (4 para regt; 1 SF regt)
COMBAT SUPPORT
  2 arty bn
  4 engr bn
AIR DEFENCE
  7 AD bn
EQUIPMENT BY TYPE
ARMOURED FIGHTING VEHICLES
  MBT 1,262: 367 T-90SA; 325 T-72; 300 T-62; 270 T-54/T-55
  RECCE 134: 44 AML-60; 26 BRDM-2; 64 BRDM-2M with 9M133 *Kornet* (AT-14 *Spriggan*)
  IFV 1,089: 685 BMP-1; 304 BMP-2M with 9M133 *Kornet* (AT-14 *Spriggan*); 100 BMP-3
  APC 883+
    APC (W) 881+: 250 BTR-60; 150 BTR-80; 150 OT-64; 55 M3 Panhard; 176+ *Fuchs* 2; 100 *Fahd*
    PPV 2 *Marauder*
ANTI-TANK/ANTI-INFRASTRUCTURE
  MSL • MANPATS 9K11 *Malyutka* (AT-3 *Sagger*); 9K111 *Fagot* (AT-4 *Spigot*); 9K111-1 *Konkurs* (AT-5 *Spandrel*); 9K115-2 *Metis*-M1 (AT-13 *Saxhorn*-2); 9K135 *Kornet*-E (AT-14 *Spriggan*); *Milan*
  RCL 180: 82mm 120 B-10; 107mm 60 B-11
  GUNS 250: 57mm 160 ZIS-2 (M-1943); 85mm 80 D-44; 100mm 10 T-12
ARTILLERY 1,091
  SP 224: 122mm 140 2S1 *Gvozdika*; 152mm 30 2S3 *Akatsiya*; 155mm ε54 PLZ-45
  TOWED 393: 122mm 345: 160 D-30; 25 D-74; 100 M-1931/37; 60 M-30; 130mm 10 M-46; 152mm 20 M-1937 (ML-20); 155mm 18 Type-88 (PLL-01)
  MRL 144: 122mm 48 BM-21 *Grad*; 140mm 48 BM-14; 240mm 30 BM-24; 300mm 18 9A52 *Smerch*
  MOR 330: 82mm 150 M-37; 120mm 120 M-1943; 160mm 60 M-1943
AIR DEFENCE
  SAM 106+
    Short-range 38 96K6 *Pantsir*-S1 (SA-22 *Greyhound*)
    Point-defence 68+: ε48 9K33M *Osa* (SA-8B *Gecko*); ε20 9K31 *Strela*-1 (SA-9 *Gaskin*); 9K32 *Strela*-2 (SA-7A/B *Grail*)‡
  GUNS ε830
    SP 23mm ε225 ZSU-23-4
    TOWED ε605: 14.5mm 100: 60 ZPU-2; 40 ZPU-4; 23mm 100 ZU-23; 37mm ε150 M-1939; 57mm 75 S-60; 85mm 20 M-1939 (KS-12); 100mm 150 KS-19; 130mm 10 KS-30

Navy ε6,000
EQUIPMENT BY TYPE
SUBMARINES • TACTICAL • SSK 4:
  2 *Kilo* (FSU *Paltus*) with 6 single 533mm TT with Test-71ME HWT/3M54 *Klub*-S (SS-N-27B) AShM

2 Improved *Kilo* (RUS *Varshavyanka*) with 6 single 533mm TT with Test-71ME HWT/3M54E *Klub*-S (SS-N-27B) AShM

PRINCIPAL SURFACE COMBATANTS • FRIGATES 7
FFGHM 4:
3 *Adhafer* (C28A) with 2 quad lnchr with C-802 (CSS-N-8 *Saccade*) AShM, 1 FM-90 lnchr with HQ-7 SAM, 2 triple 324mm ASTT, 2 Type-730B CIWS, 1 76mm gun (capacity 1 hel)
1 *Erradii* (MEKO 200AN) with 2 octuple lnchrs with RBS-15 Mk3 AShM, 4 8-cell VLS with *Umkhonto*-IR SAM, 2 twin 324mm TT with MU90 LWT, 1 127mm gun (capacity 1 *Super Lynx* 300)
FF 3 *Mourad Rais* (FSU *Koni*) with 2 twin 533mm TT, 2 RBU 6000 *Smerch* 2 A/S mor, 2 twin 76mm gun

PATROL AND COASTAL COMBATANTS 24
CORVETTES 6
FSGM 3 *Rais Hamidou* (FSU *Nanuchka* II) with up to 4 twin lnchr with 3M24 *Uran* (SS-N-25 *Switchblade*) AShM, 1 twin lnchr with 9M33 *Osa-M* (SA-N-4 *Gecko*) SAM, 1 AK630 CIWS, 1 twin 57mm gun
FSG 3 *Djebel Chenoua* with 2 twin lnchr with C-802 (CSS-N-8 *Saccade*) AShM, 1 AK630 CIWS, 1 76mm gun
PBFG 9 *Osa* II (3†) with 4 single lnchr with P-15 *Termit* (SS-N-2B *Styx*) AShM
PB 9 *Kebir* with 1 76mm gun

AMPHIBIOUS 7
PRINCIPAL AMPHIBIOUS SHIPS • LHD 1 *Kalaat Beni Abbes* with 1 8-cell A50 VLS with *Aster*-15 SAM, 1 76mm gun (capacity 5 med hel; 3 LCVP; 15 MBT; 350 troops)
LANDING SHIPS 3:
LSM 1 *Polnochny* B with 1 twin AK230 CIWS (capacity 6 MBT; 180 troops)
LST 2 *Kalaat beni Hammad* (capacity 7 MBT; 240 troops) with 1 med hel landing platform
LANDING CRAFT • LCVP 3

LOGISTICS AND SUPPORT 2
AGS 1 *El Idrissi*
AX 1 *Daxin* with 2 twin AK230 CIWS, 1 76mm gun, 1 hel landing platform

Naval Aviation

EQUIPMENT BY TYPE
HELICOPTERS
MRH 6 *Super Lynx* 300
SAR 12: 6 AW101 SAR; 4 *Super Lynx* Mk130

Coast Guard ε500

EQUIPMENT BY TYPE
PATROL AND COASTAL COMBATANTS 55
PBF 6 *Baglietto* 20
PB 49: 6 *Baglietto Mangusta*; 12 *Jebel Antar*; 21 *Deneb*; 4 *El Mounkid*; 6 *Kebir* with 1 76mm gun
LOGISTICS AND SUPPORT 9
AR 1 *El Mourafek*
ARS 3 *El Moundjid*
AXL 5 *El Mouderrib* (PRC *Chui-E*) (2 more in reserve†)

Air Force 14,000

Flying hours 150 hrs/yr

FORCES BY ROLE
FIGHTER
1 sqn with MiG-25PDS/RU *Foxbat*
4 sqn with MiG-29C/UB *Fulcrum*
FIGHTER/GROUND ATTACK
3 sqn with Su-30MKA *Flanker*
GROUND ATTACK
2 sqn with Su-24M/MK *Fencer D*
ELINT
1 sqn with Beech 1900D
MARITIME PATROL
2 sqn with Beech 200T/300 *King Air*
ISR
1 sqn with Su-24MR *Fencer* E*; MiG-25RBSh *Foxbat* D*
TANKER
1 sqn with Il-78 *Midas*
TRANSPORT
1 sqn with C-130H/H-30 *Hercules*; L-100-30
1 sqn with C-295M
1 sqn with Gulfstream IV-SP; Gulfstream V
1 sqn with Il-76MD/TD *Candid*
TRAINING
2 sqn with Z-142
1 sqn with Yak-130 *Mitten*
2 sqn with L-39C/ZA *Albatros*
1 hel sqn with PZL Mi-2 *Hoplite*
ATTACK HELICOPTER
3 sqn with Mi-24 *Hind* (one re-equipping with Mi-28NE *Havoc*)
TRANSPORT HELICOPTER
1 sqn with AS355 *Ecureuil*
5 sqn with Mi-8 *Hip*; Mi-17 *Hip* H
1 sqn with Ka-27PS *Helix* D; Ka-32T *Helix*
AIR DEFENCE
3 ADA bde
3 SAM regt with S-75 *Dvina* (SA-2 *Guideline*); S-125 *Neva* (SA-3 *Goa*); 2K12 *Kub* (SA-6 *Gainful*); S-300PMU2 (SA-20 *Gargoyle*)

EQUIPMENT BY TYPE
AIRCRAFT 119 combat capable
FTR 34: 11 MiG-25 *Foxbat*; 23 MiG-29C/UB *Fulcrum*
FGA 44 Su-30MKA
ATK 33 Su-24M/MK *Fencer D*
ISR 8: 4 MiG-25RBSh *Foxbat* D*; 4 Su-24MR *Fencer* E*
TKR 6 Il-78 *Midas*
TPT 67: **Heavy** 12: 3 Il-76MD *Candid* B; 9 Il-76TD *Candid*; **Medium** 17: 9 C-130H *Hercules*; 6 C-130H-30 *Hercules*; 2 L-100-30; **Light** 32: 3 Beech C90B *King Air*; 5 Beech 200T *King Air*; 6 Beech 300 *King Air*; 12 Beech 1900D (electronic surv); 5 C-295M; 1 F-27 *Friendship*; **PAX** 6: 1 A340; 4 Gulfstream IV-SP; 1 Gulfstream V
TRG 99: 36 L-39ZA *Albatros*; 7 L-39C *Albatros*; 16 Yak-130 *Mitten*; 40 Z-142
HELICOPTERS
ATK 37: 31 Mi-24 *Hind*; 6 Mi-28NE *Havoc*
SAR 3 Ka-27PS *Helix* D
MRH 8: 5 AW139 (SAR); 3 Bell 412EP
MRH/TPT 74 Mi-8 *Hip* (med tpt)/Mi-17 *Hip* H
TPT 44: **Heavy** 4 Mi-26T2 *Halo*; **Medium** 4 Ka-32T *Helix*; **Light** 36: 8 AS355 *Ecureuil*; 28 PZL Mi-2 *Hoplite*

UNMANNED AERIAL VEHICLES
ISR • Medium *Seeker* II
AIR DEFENCE
Long-range S-300PMU2 (SA-20 *Gargoyle*)
Medium-range S-75 *Dvina* (SA-2 *Guideline*); S-125 *Pechora*-M (SA-3 *Goa*)
Short-range 2K12 *Kvadrat* (SA-6 *Gainful*)
GUNS 725 100mm/130mm/85mm
AIR-LAUNCHED MISSILES
AAM • IR R-3 (AA-2 *Atoll*)‡; R-60 (AA-8 *Aphid*); R-73 (A-11 *Archer*); **IR/SARH** R-40/46 (AA-6 *Acrid*); R-23/24 (AA-7 *Apex*); R-27 (AA-10 *Alamo*); **ARH** R-77 (AA-12 *Adder*); **ASM** Kh-25 (AS-10 *Karen*); Kh-29 (AS-14 *Kedge*); Kh-23 (AS-7 *Kerry*); Kh-31P/A (AS-17A/B *Krypton*); Kh-59ME (AS-18 *Kazoo*); ZT-35 *Ingwe*
ARM Kh-25MP (AS-12 *Kegler*)

Paramilitary ε187,200

Gendarmerie 20,000
Ministry of Defence control; 6 regions
EQUIPMENT BY TYPE
ARMOURED FIGHTING VEHICLES
  RECCE AML-60
  APC • APC (W) 210: 100 TH-390 *Fahd*; 110 Panhard M3
HELICOPTERS • TPT • Light Some PZL Mi-2 *Hoplite*

National Security Forces 16,000
Directorate of National Security. Small arms

Republican Guard 1,200
EQUIPMENT BY TYPE
ARMOURED FIGHTING VEHICLES
  RECCE AML-60
  APC • APC (T) M3 half-track

Legitimate Defence Groups ε150,000
Self-defence militia, communal guards (60,000)

Bahrain BHR

Bahraini Dinar D		2015	2016	2017
GDP	D	11.7bn	12bn	
	US$	31.1bn	31.8bn	
per capita	US$	24,058	24,119	
Growth	%	2.9	2.1	
Inflation	%	1.8	3.6	
Def bdgt [a]	D	574m	573m	
	US$	1.53bn	1.52bn	
FMA (US)	US$	7.5m	7.5m	5m
US$1=D		0.38	0.38	

[a] Excludes funds allocated to the Ministry of the Interior

Population   1,378,904

Ethnic groups: Nationals 46%; Asian 45.5%; African 1.5%; other or unspecified 7%

Age	0–14	15–19	20–24	25–29	30–64	65 plus
Male	9.8%	3.8%	5.1%	6.3%	34.2%	1.4%
Female	9.5%	3.2%	3.6%	3.9%	17.7%	1.5%

Capabilities

Bahrain has small but comparatively well-equipped and -trained armed forces. The core role of the military is to protect the territorial integrity of Bahrain, although this is fundamentally underpinned by the presence of the US 5th Fleet and Bahrain's membership of the Gulf Cooperation Council (GCC). It has contributed both ground and air units to the Saudi-led coalition of GCC states that intervened in Yemen in 2015 to counter the Houthi-led insurgency, notably units from the Royal Guard. Bahraini ground forces suffered combat losses during the operation. Later in the year, the navy sent a frigate to take part in the naval blockade. The Royal Bahrain Air Force has also supported the air campaign against ISIS in Syria. The air force was reported in 2016 to have submitted a request for F-16s to replace its elderly F-5 combat aircraft. Prior to its recent involvement in the campaign against ISIS and the war in Yemen, it and other elements of the security forces had been focused on internal-security tasks. The armed forces took part in the 20-nation *Northern Thunder* counter-terrorism exercise in Saudi Arabia in March 2016. Bahrain does not possess a strategic-airlift capability, and would be dependent on its partners for significant mobility requirements.

ACTIVE 8,200 (Army 6,000 Navy 700 Air 1,500)
Paramilitary 11,260

ORGANISATIONS BY SERVICE

Army 6,000
FORCES BY ROLE
SPECIAL FORCES
  1 SF bn
MANOEUVRE
  Armoured
  1 armd bde(-) (1 recce bn, 2 armd bn)
  Mechanised
  1 inf bde (2 mech bn, 1 mot bn)
  Light
  1 (Amiri) gd bn
COMBAT SUPPORT
  1 arty bde (1 hvy arty bty, 2 med arty bty, 1 lt arty bty, 1 MRL bty)
  1 engr coy
COMBAT SERVICE SUPPORT
  1 log coy
  1 tpt coy
  1 med coy
AIR DEFENCE
  1 AD bn (1 ADA bty, 2 SAM bty)
EQUIPMENT BY TYPE
ARMOURED FIGHTING VEHICLES
  MBT 180 M60A3
  RECCE 22 AML-90
  IFV 67: 25 YPR-765 PRI; 42 AIFV-B-C25
  APC 203+
    APC (T) 203: 200 M113A2; 3 AIFV-B
    APC (W) *Arma* 6×6

ENGINEERING & MAINTENANCE VEHICLES
ARV 53 *Fahd* 240
ANTI-TANK/ANTI-INFRASTRUCTURE
  MSL
    SP 5 AIFV-B-*Milan*; HMMWV with BGM-71A TOW
    MANPATS BGM-71A TOW
  RCL 31: **106mm** 25 M40A1; **120mm** 6 MOBAT
ARTILLERY 151
  SP 82: **155mm** 20 M109A5; **203mm** 62 M110A2
  TOWED 36: **105mm** 8 L118 Light Gun; **155mm** 28 M198
  MRL 227mm 9 M270 MLRS
  MOR 24: **SP 120mm** 12 M113A2; **81mm** 12 L16
SURFACE-TO-SURFACE MISSILE LAUNCHERS
  SRBM • **Conventional** MGM-140A ATACMS (launched from M270 MLRS)
AIR DEFENCE
  SAM
    Medium-range 6 MIM-23B I-*Hawk*
    Short-range 7 *Crotale*
    Point-defence FIM-92 *Stinger*; RBS-70
  GUNS 24: **35mm** 12 Oerlikon; **40mm** 12 L/70

Navy 700

EQUIPMENT BY TYPE
PRINCIPAL SURFACE COMBATANTS 1
  FRIGATES • **FFGHM** 1 *Sabha* (ex-US *Oliver Hazard Perry*) with 1 Mk13 GMLS with SM-1MR SAM/RGM-84C *Harpoon* AShM, 2 triple 324mm Mk32 ASTT with Mk46 LWT, 1 *Phalanx* Block 1B CIWS, 1 76mm gun (capacity 1 Bo-105 hel)
PATROL AND COASTAL COMBATANTS 12
  CORVETTES • **FSG** 2 *Al Manama* (GER Lurssen 62m) with 2 twin lnchr with MM-40 *Exocet* AShM, 2 76mm guns, 1 hel landing platform
  PCFG 4 *Ahmed el Fateh* (GER Lurssen 45m) with 2 twin lnchr with MM-40 *Exocet* AShM, 1 76mm gun
  PB 4: 2 *Al Jarim* (US *Swift* FPB-20); 2 *Al Riffa* (GER Lurssen 38m)
  PBF 2 Mk V SOC
AMPHIBIOUS • **LANDING CRAFT** 9
  LCU 7: 1 *Loadmaster*; 4 *Mashtan*; 2 *Dinar* (ADSB 42m)
  LCVP 2 *Sea Keeper*

Naval Aviation
EQUIPMENT BY TYPE
HELICOPTERS • **TPT** • **Light** 2 Bo-105

Air Force 1,500

FORCES BY ROLE
FIGHTER
  2 sqn with F-16C/D *Fighting Falcon*
FIGHTER/GROUND ATTACK
  1 sqn with F-5E/F *Tiger* II
TRANSPORT
  1 (Royal) flt with B-727; B-747; BAe-146; Gulfstream II; Gulfstream IV; Gulfstream 450; Gulfstream 550; S-92A
TRAINING
  1 sqn with *Hawk* Mk129*
  1 sqn with T-67M *Firefly*
ATTACK HELICOPTER
  2 sqn with AH-1E/F *Cobra*; TAH-1P *Cobra*

TRANSPORT HELICOPTER
  1 sqn with Bell 212 (AB-212)
  1 sqn with UH-60M *Black Hawk*
  1 (VIP) sqn with Bo-105; S-70A *Black Hawk*; UH-60L *Black Hawk*

EQUIPMENT BY TYPE
AIRCRAFT 39 combat capable
  FTR 12: 8 F-5E *Tiger* II; 4 F-5F *Tiger* II
  FGA 20: 16 F-16C *Fighting Falcon*; 4 F-16D *Fighting Falcon*
  TPT • **PAX** 10: 1 B-727; 2 B-747; 1 Gulfstream II; 1 Gulfstream IV; 1 Gulfstream 450; 1 Gulfstream 550; 3 BAe-146
  TRG 9: 6 *Hawk* Mk129*; 3 T-67M *Firefly*
HELICOPTERS
  ATK 28: 16 AH-1E *Cobra*; 12 AH-1F *Cobra*
  TPT 27: **Medium** 13: 3 S-70A *Black Hawk*; 1 S-92A (VIP); 1 UH-60L *Black Hawk*; 8 UH-60M *Black Hawk*; **Light** 14: 11 Bell 212 (AB-212); 3 Bo-105
  TRG 6 TAH-1P *Cobra*
AIR-LAUNCHED MISSILES
  AAM • **IR** AIM-9P *Sidewinder*; **SARH** AIM-7 *Sparrow*; **ARH** AIM-120 AMRAAM
  ASM AGM-65D/G *Maverick*; some TOW
BOMBS
  Laser-guided GBU-10/12 *Paveway* II

Paramilitary ε11,260

Police 9,000
Ministry of Interior

EQUIPMENT BY TYPE
ARMOURED FIGHTING VEHICLES
  RECCE 8 S52 *Shorland*
  APC • **APC (W)** Otokar ISV; *Cobra*
HELICOPTERS
  MRH 2 Bell 412 *Twin Huey*
  ISR 2 Hughes 500
  TPT • **Light** 1 Bo-105

National Guard ε2,000
FORCES BY ROLE
MANOEUVRE
  Other
    3 paramilitary bn
EQUIPMENT BY TYPE
ARMOURED FIGHTING VEHICLES
  APC • **APC (W)** Arma 6×6; *Cobra*

Coast Guard ε260
Ministry of Interior
PATROL AND COASTAL COMBATANTS 52
  PBF 23: 2 *Ares* 18; 4 *Jaris*; 6 *Saham*; 6 *Fajr*; 5 *Jarada*
  PB 29: 6 *Haris*; 1 *Al Muharraq*; 10 *Deraa* (of which 4 *Halmatic* 20, 2 *Souter* 20, 4 *Rodman* 20); 10 *Saif* (of which 4 *Fairey Sword*, 6 *Halmatic* 160); 2 *Hawar*
AMPHIBIOUS • **LANDING CRAFT** • **LCU** 1 *Loadmaster* II

DEPLOYMENT

SAUDI ARABIA
Operation Restoring Hope 6 F-16C *Fighting Falcon*

FOREIGN FORCES
Saudi Arabia GCC (SANG): Peninsula Shield ε1,500
United Kingdom Air Force 80: 1 BAe-146
United States US Central Commmand 5,000; 1 HQ (5th Fleet); 2 AD bty with MIM-104E/F *Patriot* PAC-2/3

Egypt EGY

Egyptian Pound E£		2015	2016	2017
GDP	E£	2.43tr	2.78tr	
	US$	330bn	n/a	
per capita	US$	3,710	n/a	
Growth	%	4.2	3.8	
Inflation	%	11.0	10.2	
Def bdgt	E£	39.3bn	43.2bn	47.1bn
	US$	5.34bn	5.33bn	
FMA (US)	US$	1.3bn	1.3bn	1.3bn
US$1=E£		7.36	8.10	

Population   94,666,993

Age	0–14	15–19	20–24	25–29	30–64	65 plus
Male	17.2%	4.9%	5.0%	4.9%	17.1%	2.0%
Female	16.0%	4.6%	4.8%	4.7%	16.8%	2.1%

Capabilities

Increased jihadist activity, including by ISIS-affiliated groups in Sinai, has led to substantial troop deployments and military operations, whilst insurgent activity on Egypt's borders has led to closer security cooperation with other North African states. State breakdown in Libya and Syria, and smuggling across the border, is of particular concern. In 2015 Egypt was part of the Saudi-led coalition in Yemen, supplying troops and warships to enforce a maritime blockade in the Bab el-Mandeb. While training is at a high standard for many troops within the armed forces, the large number of conscripts – and reports of conscripts being employed in expanding military-owned business concerns – makes effectiveness across the entire force difficult to estimate. Egypt's relationship with the US came under strain after army chief Abdel Fattah Al-Sisi took power in 2013. Equipment deliveries were delayed, but recommenced in March 2015 with the release of F-16 aircraft, among others. In July 2015, the possible sale of a US$100m mobile surveillance-sensor security system to bolster the Egyptian Border Guard's limited capabilities on the border with Libya was approved by the US, while the donation in 2016 of a large number of surplus US armoured vehicles should enhance the armed forces' protected-patrol capability. Egypt also has a significant number of equipment orders in place with European, Russian and US firms, including for armoured vehicles, submarines, frigates, surface-to-air missiles and combat aircraft. The second *Mistral*-class amphibious assault vessel was delivered from France in late 2016. Cairo agreed the purchase of *Rafale* combat aircraft from France in 2015 (reportedly with funding support from the Gulf); a second batch was delivered in early 2016.

ACTIVE 438,500 (Army 310,000 Navy 18,500 Air 30,000 Air Defence Command 80,000) **Paramilitary 397,000**

Conscription liability 12 months–3 years (followed by refresher training over a period of up to 9 years)

RESERVE 479,000 (Army 375,000 Navy 14,000 Air 20,000 Air Defence 70,000)

ORGANISATIONS BY SERVICE

Army 90,000–120,000; 190,000–220,000 conscript (total 310,000)

FORCES BY ROLE
SPECIAL FORCES
  5 cdo gp
  1 counter-terrorist unit
MANOEUVRE
  Armoured
  4 armd div (2 armd bde, 1 mech bde, 1 arty bde)
  4 indep armd bde
  1 Republican Guard bde
  Mechanised
  8 mech div (1 armd bde, 2 mech bde, 1 arty bde)
  4 indep mech bde
  Light
  1 inf div
  2 indep inf bde
  Air Manoeuvre
  2 air mob bde
  1 para bde
SURFACE-TO-SURFACE MISSILE
  1 SRBM bde with FROG-7
  1 SRBM bde with *Scud*-B
COMBAT SUPPORT
  15 arty bde
  6 engr bde (3 engr bn)
  2 spec ops engr bn
  6 salvage engr bn
  24 MP bn
  18 sigs bn
COMBAT SERVICE SUPPORT
  36 log bn
  27 med bn

EQUIPMENT BY TYPE
ARMOURED FIGHTING VEHICLES
  MBT 2,710: 1,360 M1A1 *Abrams*; 300 M60A1; 850 M60A3; 200 T-62; (260 *Ramses* II (mod T-54/55); 840 T-54/T-55; 300 T-62 all in store)
  RECCE 412: 300 BRDM-2; 112 *Commando Scout*
  IFV 390 YPR-765 25mm; (220 BMP-1 in store)
  APC 4,720+
    APC (T) 2,700: 2,000 M113A2/YPR-765 (incl variants); 500 BTR-50; 200 OT-62

APC (W) 1,560: 250 BMR-600P; 250 BTR-60; 410 *Fahd-30/TH* 390 *Fahd*; 650 *Walid*
PPV 460+: 110+ *Caiman*; some REVA III; some REVA V LWB; 350+ RG-33L
AUV *Panthera* T6; *Sherpa* Light Scout

ENGINEERING & MAINTENANCE VEHICLES
ARV 367+: *Fahd* 240; BMR 3560.55; 12 *Maxxpro* ARV; 220 M88A1; 90 M88A2; M113 ARV; 45 M578; T-54/55 ARV
VLB KMM; MTU; MTU-20
MW *Aardvark* JFSU Mk4

ANTI-TANK/ANTI-INFRASTRUCTURE • MSL
SP 352+: 52 M901, 300 YPR-765 PRAT; HMMWV with TOW-2
MANPATS 9K11 *Malyutka* (AT-3 *Sagger*) (incl BRDM-2); HJ-73; *Milan*; TOW-2

ARTILLERY 4,468
SP 492+: **122mm** 124+: 124 SP 122; D-30 mod; **130mm** M-46 mod; **155mm** 368: 164 M109A2; 204 M109A5
TOWED 962: **122mm** 526: 190 D-30M; 36 M-1931/37; 300 M-30; **130mm** 420 M-46; **155mm** 16 GH-52
MRL 450: **122mm** 356: 96 BM-11; 60 BM-21; 50 *Sakr*-10; 50 *Sakr*-18; 100 *Sakr*-36; **130mm** 36 K136 *Kooryong*; **140mm** 32 BM-14; **227mm** 26 M270 MLRS; **240mm** (48 BM-24 in store)
MOR 2,564: **81mm** 50 M125A2; **82mm** 500; **SP 107mm** 100: 65 M106A1; 35 M106A2; **120mm** 1,848: 1,800 M-1943; 48 Brandt; **SP 120mm** 36 M1064A3; **160mm** 30 M-160

SURFACE-TO-SURFACE MISSILE LAUNCHERS
SRBM • **Conventional** 42+: 9 FROG-7; 24 *Sakr*-80; 9 *Scud*-B

RADAR • LAND AN/TPQ-36 *Firefinder*; AN/TPQ-37 *Firefinder* (arty/mor)

UNMANNED AERIAL VEHICLES
ISR • **Medium** R4E-50 *Skyeye*; ASN-209

AIR DEFENCE
SAM
Point-defence 96+: 50 M1097 *Avenger*; 26 M48 *Chaparral*; 20 9K31 *Strela*-1 (SA-9 *Gaskin*); *Ayn al-Saqr*; 9K32 *Strela*-2 (SA-7 *Grail*)‡; FIM-92 *Stinger*; 9K38 *Igla* (SA-18 *Grouse*)
GUNS
SP 205: **23mm** 165: 45 *Sinai*-23; 120 ZSU-23-4; **57mm** 40 ZSU-57-2
TOWED 700: **14.5mm** 300 ZPU-4; **23mm** 200 ZU-23-2; **57mm** 200 S-60

Navy ε8,500 (incl 2,000 Coast Guard); 10,000 conscript (total 18,500)

EQUIPMENT BY TYPE
SUBMARINES • TACTICAL • SSK 4 *Romeo*† (PRC Type-033) with 8 single 533mm TT with UGM-84C *Harpoon* AShM/Mk37 HWT

PRINCIPAL SURFACE COMBATANTS 9
DESTROYERS • DDGHM 1 *Tahya Misr* (FRA *Aquitaine*) with 2 quad lnchr with MM-40 *Exocet* Block 3 AShM, 2 octuple A43 VLS with *Aster* 15 SAM, 2 twin B515 324mm ASTT with MU90 LWT, 1 76mm gun (capacity 1 med hel)

FRIGATES 8
FFGHM 4 *Alexandria* (ex-US *Oliver Hazard Perry*) with 1 Mk13 GMLS with RGM-84C *Harpoon* AShM/SM-1MP SAM, 2 triple 324mm ASTT with Mk 46 LWT, 1 *Phalanx* CIWS, 1 76mm gun (capacity 2 SH-2G *Super Seasprite* ASW hel)
FFGH 2 *Damyat* (ex-US *Knox*) with 1 octuple Mk16 GMLS with RGM-84C *Harpoon* AShM/ASROC, 2 twin 324mm Mk 32 TT with Mk 46 LWT, 1 *Phalanx* CIWS, 1 127mm gun, (capacity 1 SH-2G *Super Seasprite* ASW hel)
FFG 2 *Najim Al Zaffer* (PRC *Jianghu* I) with 2 twin lnchr with HY-2 (CSS-N-2 *Safflower*) AShM, 4 RBU 1200 A/S mor, 2 twin 57mm guns

PATROL AND COASTAL COMBATANTS 60
CORVETTES • FSGM 2:
2 *Abu Qir* (ESP *Descubierta* – 1†) with 2 quad Mk141 lnchr with RGM-84C *Harpoon* AShM, 1 octuple *Albatros* lnchr with *Aspide* SAM, 2 triple Mk32 324mm ASTT with *Sting Ray* LWT, 1 twin 375mm A/S mor, 1 76mm gun
PCFGM 4:
4 *Ezzat* (US *Ambassador* IV) with 2 quad lnchr with RGM-84L *Harpoon* Block II AShM, 1 21-cell Mk49 lnchr with RAM Block 1A SAM, 1 Mk15 Mod 21 Block 1B *Phalanx* CIWS 1 76mm gun
PCFG 12:
1 *Molnya* (RUS *Tarantul* IV) with 2 twin lnchr with 3M80E *Moskit* (SS-N-22 *Sunburn*), 2 AK630 CIWS, 1 76mm gun
6 *Ramadan* with 4 single lnchr with *Otomat* MkII AShM, 1 76mm gun
5 *Tiger* with 2 twin lnchr with MM-38 *Exocet* AShM, 1 76mm gun
PCC 5:
5 *Al-Nour* (ex-PRC *Hainan* – 3 more in reserve†) with 2 triple 324mm TT, 4 RBU 1200 A/S mor, 2 twin 57mm guns
PBFG 17:
4 *Hegu* (PRC – *Komar* type) with 2 single lnchr with SY-1 AShM (2 additional vessels in reserve)
5 *October* (FSU *Komar* – 1†) with 2 single lnchr with *Otomat* MkII AShM (1 additional vessel in reserve)
8 *Osa* I (ex-YUG – 3†) with 1 9K32 *Strela*-2 (SA-N-5 *Grail*) SAM (manual aiming), 4 single lnchr with P-15 *Termit* (SS-N-2A *Styx*) AShM
PBFM 4:
4 *Shershen* (FSU) with 1 9K32 *Strela*-2 (SA-N-5 *Grail*) SAM (manual aiming), 1 12-tube BM-24 MRL
PBF 10:
6 *Kaan* 20 (TUR MRTP 20)
4 *Osa* II (ex-FIN)
PB 6:
4 *Shanghai* II (PRC)
2 *Shershen* (FSU – 1†) with 4 single 533mm TT, 1 8-tube BM-21 MRL

MINE WARFARE • MINE COUNTERMEASURES 14
MHC 5: 2 *Al Siddiq* (ex-US *Osprey*); 3 *Dat Assawari* (US Swiftships)
MSI 2 *Safaga* (US Swiftships)
MSO 7: 3 *Assiout* (FSU T-43 class); 4 *Aswan* (FSU *Yurka*)

AMPHIBIOUS 20
 PRINCIPAL AMPHIBIOUS SHIPS • LHD 2 *Gamal Abdel Nasser* (FRA *Mistral*) (capacity 16 med hel; 2 LCT or 4 LCM; 13 MBTs; 50 AFVs; 450 troops)
 LANDING SHIPS • LSM 3 *Polnochny* A (FSU) (capacity 6 MBT; 180 troops)
 LANDING CRAFT 15:
 LCM 4 CTM NG
 LCT 2 EDA-R
 LCU 9 *Vydra* (FSU) (capacity either 3 AMX-30 MBT or 100 troops)
LOGISTICS AND SUPPORT 24
 AOT 7 *Ayeda* (FSU *Toplivo* – 1 additional in reserve)
 AE 1 *Halaib* (ex-GER *Westerwald*-class)
 AKR 3 *Al Hurreya*
 AR 1 *Shaledin* (ex-GER *Luneberg*-class)
 ARS 2 *Al Areesh*
 ATF 5 *Al Maks†* (FSU *Okhtensky*)
 AX 5: 1 *El Fateh†* (ex-UK 'Z' class); 1 *El Horriya* (also used as the presidential yacht); 1 *Al Kousser*; 1 *Intishat*; 1 other

Coastal Defence

Army tps, Navy control
EQUIPMENT BY TYPE
COASTAL DEFENCE
 ARTY 100mm; 130mm SM-4-1; 152mm
 AShM 4K87 (SS-C-2B *Samlet*); *Otomat* MkII

Naval Aviation

All aircraft operated by Air Force
AIRCRAFT • TPT • Light 4 Beech 1900C (maritime surveillance)
HELICOPTERS
 ASW 10 SH-2G *Super Seasprite* with Mk 46 LWT
 MRH 5 SA342L *Gazelle*
UNMANNED AERIAL VEHICLES
 ISR • Light 2 *Camcopter* 5.1

Coast Guard 2,000

EQUIPMENT BY TYPE
PATROL AND COASTAL COMBATANTS 79
 PBF 14: 6 *Crestitalia*; 5 *Swift Protector*; 3 *Peterson*
 PB 65: 5 *Nisr*; 12 *Sea Spectre* MkIII; 15 *Swiftships*; 21 *Timsah*; 3 Type-83; 9 *Peterson*

Air Force 30,000 (incl 10,000 conscript)

FORCES BY ROLE
FIGHTER
 1 sqn with F-16A/B *Fighting Falcon*
 8 sqn with F-16C/D *Fighting Falcon*
 4 sqn with J-7/MiG-21 *Fishbed*/MiG-21U *Mongol* A
 2 sqn with *Mirage* 5D/E
 1 sqn with *Mirage* 2000B/C
FIGHTER/GROUND ATTACK
 2 sqn with F-4E *Phantom* II
 1 sqn with *Mirage* 5E2
 1 sqn (forming) with *Rafale* DM
ANTI-SUBMARINE WARFARE
 1 sqn with SH-2G *Super Seasprite*
MARITIME PATROL
 1 sqn with Beech 1900C
ELECTRONIC WARFARE
 1 sqn with Beech 1900 (ELINT); *Commando* Mk2E (ECM)
ELECTRONIC WARFARE/TRANSPORT
 1 sqn with C-130H/VC-130H *Hercules*
AIRBORNE EARLY WARNING
 1 sqn with E-2C *Hawkeye*
SEARCH & RESCUE
 1 unit with AW139
TRANSPORT
 1 sqn with An-74TK-200A
 1 sqn with C-130H/C-130H-30 *Hercules*
 1 sqn with C-295M
 1 sqn with DHC-5D *Buffalo*
 1 sqn with B-707-366C; B-737-100; Beech 200 *Super King Air*; *Falcon* 20; Gulfstream III; Gulfstream IV; Gulfstream IV-SP
TRAINING
 1 sqn with *Alpha Jet**
 1 sqn with DHC-5 *Buffalo*
 3 sqn with EMB-312 *Tucano*
 1 sqn with Grob 115EG
 ε6 sqn with K-8 *Karakorum**
 1 sqn with L-39 *Albatros*; L-59E *Albatros**
ATTACK HELICOPTER
 2 sqn with AH-64D *Apache*
 2 sqn with SA-342K *Gazelle* (with HOT)
 1 sqn with SA-342L *Gazelle*
TRANSPORT HELICOPTER
 1 sqn with CH-47C/D *Chinook*
 1 sqn with Mi-8
 1 sqn with Mi-8/Mi-17-V1 *Hip*
 1 sqn with S-70 *Black Hawk*; UH-60A/L *Black Hawk*
UAV
 Some sqn with R4E-50 *Skyeye*; Teledyne-Ryan 324 *Scarab*
EQUIPMENT BY TYPE
AIRCRAFT 586 combat capable
 FTR 62: 26 F-16A *Fighting Falcon*; 6 F-16B *Fighting Falcon*; ε30 J-7
 FGA 328: 29 F-4E *Phantom* II; 139 F-16C *Fighting Falcon*; 37 F-16D *Fighting Falcon*; 3 *Mirage* 2000B; 15 *Mirage* 2000C; 36 *Mirage* 5D/E; 12 *Mirage* 5E2; ε50 MiG-21 *Fishbed*/MiG-21U *Mongol* A; 6 *Rafale* DM
 ELINT 2 VC-130H *Hercules*
 ISR 6 *Mirage* 5R (5SDR)*
 AEW&C 7 E-2C *Hawkeye*
 TPT 77: **Medium** 24: 21 C-130H *Hercules*; 3 C-130H-30 *Hercules*; **Light** 42: 3 An-74TK-200A; 1 Beech 200 *King Air*; 4 Beech 1900 (ELINT); 4 Beech 1900C; 21 C-295M; 9 DHC-5D *Buffalo* **PAX** 11: 1 B-707-366C; 3 *Falcon* 20; 2 Gulfstream III; 1 Gulfstream IV; 4 Gulfstream IV-SP
 TRG 329: 36 *Alpha Jet**; 54 EMB-312 *Tucano*; 74 Grob 115EG; 120 K-8 *Karakorum**; 10 L-39 *Albatros*; 35 L-59E *Albatros**
HELICOPTERS
 ATK 45 AH-64D *Apache*
 ASW 10 SH-2G *Super Seasprite* (opcon Navy)
 ELINT 4 *Commando* Mk2E (ECM)
 MRH 72: 2 AW139 (SAR); 65 SA342K *Gazelle* (some with HOT); 5 SA342L *Gazelle* (opcon Navy)

TPT 96: **Heavy** 19: 3 CH-47C *Chinook*; 16 CH-47D *Chinook*; **Medium** 77: 2 AS-61; 24 *Commando* (of which 3 VIP); 40 Mi-8T *Hip*; 3 Mi-17-1V *Hip*; 4 S-70 *Black Hawk* (VIP); 4 UH-60L *Black Hawk* (VIP)
TRG 17 UH-12E
UNMANNED AERIAL VEHICLES
  ISR • Medium R4E-50 *Skyeye*; Teledyne-Ryan 324 *Scarab*
AIR LAUNCHED MISSILES
  AAM • IR R-3 (AA-2 *Atoll*)‡; AIM-9FL/P *Sidewinder*; R-550 *Magic*; **SARH** AIM-7E/F/M *Sparrow*; R-530
  ASM AGM-65A/D/F/G *Maverick*; AGM-114F/K *Hellfire*; AS-30L; HOT
  AShM AGM-84 *Harpoon*; AM-39 *Exocet*;
  ARM *Armat*; Kh-25MP (AS-12 *Kegler*)
BOMBS
  Laser-guided GBU-10/12 *Paveway* II

Air Defence Command 80,000 conscript; 70,000 reservists (total 150,000)

FORCES BY ROLE
AIR DEFENCE
  5 AD div (geographically based) (total: 12 SAM bty with M48 *Chaparral*, 12 radar bn, 12 ADA bde (total: 100 ADA bn), 12 SAM bty with MIM-23B I-*Hawk*, 14 SAM bty with *Crotale*, 18 AD bn with RIM-7M *Sea Sparrow* with *Skyguard*/GDF-003 with *Skyguard*, 110 SAM bn with S-125 *Pechora*-M (SA-3A *Goa*); 2K12 *Kub* (SA-6 *Gainful*); S-75M *Volkhov* (SA-2 *Guideline*))

EQUIPMENT BY TYPE
AIR DEFENCE
  SAM 832+
    Medium-range 612+: 40+ *Buk*-M1-2/M2E (SA-11/SA-17); 78+ MIM-23B I-*Hawk*; 282 S-75M *Volkhov* (SA-2 *Guideline*); 212+ S-125 *Pechora*-M (SA-3A *Goa*)
    Short-range 170+: 56+ 2K12 *Kub* (SA-6 *Gainful*); 10 9K331M *Tor*-M1 (SA-15 *Gauntlet*); 24+ *Crotale*; 80 RIM-7M *Sea Sparrow* with *Skyguard*
    Point-defence 50+ M48 *Chaparral*
  GUNS 1,646+
    SP • 23mm 266+: 36+ *Sinai*-23 with *Ayn al-Saqr* MANPAD; 230 ZSU-23-4
    TOWED 1,380: **35mm** 80 GDF-003 with *Skyguard*; **57mm** 600 S-60; **85mm** 400 M-1939 (KS-12); **100mm** 300 KS-19

Paramilitary ε397,000 active

Central Security Forces ε325,000

Ministry of Interior; includes conscripts
ARMOURED FIGHTING VEHICLES
  APC • APC (W) *Walid*

National Guard ε60,000

Lt wpns only
FORCES BY ROLE
MANOEUVRE
  Other
    8 paramilitary bde (cadre) (3 paramilitary bn)
EQUIPMENT BY TYPE
  ARMOURED FIGHTING VEHICLES APC • APC (W) 250 *Walid*

Border Guard Forces ε12,000

Ministry of Interior; lt wpns only
FORCES BY ROLE
MANOEUVRE
  Other
    18 Border Guard regt

DEPLOYMENT

CENTRAL AFRICAN REPUBLIC
UN • MINUSCA 1,019; 5 obs; 1 inf bn; 1 tpt coy

CÔTE D'IVOIRE
UN • UNOCI 14

DEMOCRATIC REPUBLIC OF THE CONGO
UN • MONUSCO 155; 23 obs; 1 SF coy

LIBERIA
UN • UNMIL 5 obs

MALI
UN • MINUSMA 64; 3 obs; 1 MP coy

SOUTH SUDAN
UN • UNMISS 1; 3 obs

SUDAN
UN • UNAMID 865; 13 obs; 1 inf bn

UNITED ARAB EMIRATES
Operation Restoring Hope 6 F-16C *Fighting Falcon*

WESTERN SAHARA
UN • MINURSO 20 obs

FOREIGN FORCES

Australia MFO (*Operation Mazurka*) 25
Canada MFO 70
Colombia MFO 354; 1 inf bn
Czech Republic MFO 18; 1 C-295M
Fiji MFO 203; elm 1 inf bn
France MFO 1
Italy MFO 78; 3 PB
New Zealand MFO 26; 1 trg unit; 1 tpt unit
Norway MFO 3
United Kingdom MFO 2
United States MFO 401; elm 1 ARNG inf bn; 1 ARNG spt bn (1 EOD coy, 1 medical coy, 1 hel coy)
Uruguay MFO 58 1 engr/tpt unit

Iran IRN

Iranian Rial r		2015	2016	2017
GDP	r	11,563tr	12,962tr	
	US$	390bn	412bn	
per capita	US$	4,908	5,124	
Growth	%	0.4	4.5	
Inflation	%	11.9	7.4	
Def bdgt	r	ε420tr	ε499tr	
	US$	ε14.2bn	ε15.9bn	
US$1=r		29,645.48	31,437.36	

Population 82,801,633

Ethnic groups: Persian 51%; Azeri 24%; Gilaki/Mazandarani 8%; Kurdish 7%; Arab 3%; Lur 2%; Baloch 2%; Turkman 2%

Age	0–14	15–19	20–24	25–29	30–64	65 plus
Male	12.1%	3.7%	4.8%	5.8%	21.8%	2.5%
Female	11.5%	3.5%	4.5%	5.4%	21.3%	2.9%

Capabilities

Iran continues to rely on a mix of ageing combat equipment, reasonably well-trained regular and Islamic Revolutionary Guard Corps (IRGC) forces, and its ballistic-missile inventory to underpin the security of the state. The IRGC, including senior military leaders, has been increasingly involved in the civil war in Syria, supporting President Bashar al-Assad's regular and irregular forces; it was first deployed to Syria in an 'advisory' role in 2012. The IRGC's Quds Force is a principal element of Iran's military power abroad, while elements of the Basij militia also play a foreign role (as well as operating domestically) – as do Iranian-supported contingents of other nationalities. Russia used Iran's Hamadan Air Base for bombing missions in 2016, though this reportedly halted after Russia publicised the agreement in the media. The military continues to struggle with an ageing inventory of primary combat equipment that ingenuity and asymmetric-warfare techniques can only partially offset. Sectors of its defence industry continue to develop, including those for missiles and guided weapons. In regional terms, Iran has a well-developed defence-industrial base and has shown the capacity to support and sustain equipment when access to the original equipment manufacturer is blocked. However, although Iran has a sizeable defence sector, this is incapable of meeting the armed forces' need for modern weapons systems, which Iran will increasingly seek through imports; co-development and technology transfer will likely also feature in major deals. The 2015 nuclear agreement with the P5+1 and the European Union also begins to open the way for Iran to revamp its equipment inventory, with China and Russia potentially major suppliers, although sales of conventional systems remain embargoed for five years. Following the nuclear agreement, Tehran and Moscow re-engaged on the sale of a version of the S-300 surface-to-air missile (SAM) system, and delivery from Russia of a variant of the S-300PMU2 (SA-20 *Gargoyle*) long-range SAM is now assessed as complete.

ACTIVE 523,000 (Army 350,000 Islamic Revolutionary Guard Corps 125,000 Navy 18,000 Air 30,000) **Paramilitary 40,000**

Armed Forces General Staff coordinates two parallel organisations: the regular armed forces and the Islamic Revolutionary Guard Corps

Conscript liability 21 months (reported, with variations depending on location in which service is performed)

RESERVE 350,000 (Army 350,000, ex-service volunteers)

ORGANISATIONS BY SERVICE

Army 130,000; 220,000 conscript (total 350,000)
FORCES BY ROLE
5 corps-level regional HQ
COMMAND
 1 cdo div HQ
 4 armd div HQ
 2 mech div HQ
 4 inf div HQ
SPECIAL FORCES
 1 cdo div (3 cdo bde)
 6 cdo bde
 1 SF bde
MANOEUVRE
 Armoured
 8 armd bde
 Mechanised
 14 mech bde
 Light
 12 inf bde
 Air Manoeuvre
 1 AB bde
 Aviation
 Some avn gp
COMBAT SUPPORT
 5 arty gp
EQUIPMENT BY TYPE
Totals incl those held by IRGC Ground Forces. Some equipment serviceability in doubt
ARMOURED FIGHTING VEHICLES
 MBT 1,513+: 480 T-72S; 150 M60A1; 75+ T-62; 100 Chieftain Mk3/Mk5; 540 T-54/T-55/Type-59/*Safir*-74; 168 M47/M48; *Zulfiqar*
 LT TK 80+: 80 *Scorpion*; *Towsan*
 RECCE 35 EE-9 *Cascavel*
 IFV 610: 210 BMP-1; 400 BMP-2 with 9K111 *Fagot* (AT-4 *Spigot*)
 APC 640+
  APC (T) 340+: 140 *Boragh* with 9K111 *Fagot* (AT-4 *Spigot*); 200 M113; BMT-2 *Cobra*
  APC (W) 300+: 300 BTR-50/BTR-60; *Rakhsh*
ENGINEERING & MAINTENANCE VEHICLES
 ARV 20+: BREM-1 reported; 20 *Chieftain* ARV; M578; T-54/55 ARV reported
 VLB 15: 15 *Chieftain* AVLB
 MW *Taftan* 1

ANTI-TANK/ANTI-INFRASTRUCTURE
MSL • MANPATS 9K11 *Malyutka* (AT-3 *Sagger*/I-*Raad*); 9K111 *Fagot* (AT-4 *Spigot*); 9K111-1 *Konkurs* (AT-5 *Spandrel/Towsan*-1); *Saeqhe* 1; *Saeqhe* 2; *Toophan*; *Toophan* 2
RCL 200+: **75mm** M20; **82mm** B-10; **106mm** ε200 M40; **107mm** B-11
ARTILLERY 6,798+
SP 292+: **122mm** 60+: 60 2S1 *Gvozdika*; *Raad*-1 (*Thunder* 1); **155mm** 150+: 150 M109; *Raad*-2 (*Thunder* 2); **170mm** 30 M-1978; **175mm** 22 M107; **203mm** 30 M110
TOWED 2,030+; **105mm** 150: 130 M101A1; 20 M-56; **122mm** 640: 540 D-30; 100 Type-54 (M-30); **130mm** 985 M-46; **152mm** 30 D-20; **155mm** 205: 120 GHN-45; 70 M114; 15 Type-88 WAC-21; **203mm** 20 M115
MRL 1,476+: **107mm** 1,300: 700 Type-63; 600 HASEB *Fadjr* 1; **122mm** 157: 7 BM-11; 100 BM-21 *Grad*; 50 *Arash/Hadid/Noor*; **240mm** 19: ε10 *Fadjr* 3; 9 M-1985; **330mm** *Fadjr* 5
MOR 3,000: **81mm**; **82mm**; **107mm** M30; **120mm** M-65
SURFACE-TO-SURFACE MISSILE LAUNCHERS
SRBM • **Conventional** ε30 CSS-8 (175 msl); *Shahin*-1/*Shahin*-2; *Nazeat*; *Oghab*
AIRCRAFT • TPT 17 **Light** 16: 10 Cessna 185; 2 F-27 *Friendship*; 4 Turbo Commander 690; **PAX** 1 Falcon 20
HELICOPTERS
ATK 50 AH-1J *Cobra*
TPT 173: **Heavy** 20 CH-47C *Chinook*; **Medium** 75: 50 Bell 214; 25 Mi-171; **Light** 78: 68 Bell 205A (AB-205A); 10 Bell 206 *Jet Ranger* (AB-206)
UNMANNED AERIAL VEHICLES
ISR • **Medium** *Mohajer* 3/4; *Shahed* 129; **Light** *Mohajer* 2; *Ababil*
AIR DEFENCE
SAM
Short-range FM-80
Point-defence 9K36 *Strela*-3 (SA-14 *Gremlin*); 9K32 *Strela*-2 (SA-7 *Grail*)‡; *Misaq* 1 (QW-1 *Vanguard*); *Misaq* 2 (QW-18); 9K338 *Igla-S* (SA-24 *Grinch* – reported); HN-5A
GUNS 1,122
SP 180: **23mm** 100 ZSU-23-4; **57mm** 80 ZSU-57-2
TOWED 942 **14.5mm** ZPU-2; ZPU-4; **23mm** 300 ZU-23-2; **35mm** 92 *Skyguard*; **37mm** M-1939; **40mm** 50 L/70; **57mm** 200 S-60; **85mm** 300 M-1939

Islamic Revolutionary Guard Corps 125,000+

Islamic Revolutionary Guard Corps Ground Forces 100,000+

Controls Basij paramilitary forces. Lightly manned in peacetime. Primary role: internal security; secondary role: external defence, in conjunction with regular armed forces

FORCES BY ROLE
COMMAND
31 provincial corps HQ (2 in Tehran)
SPECIAL FORCES
3 spec ops div
MANOEUVRE
Armoured
2 armd div
3 armd bde

Light
8+ inf div
5+ inf bde
Air Manoeuvre
1 AB bde

Islamic Revolutionary Guard Corps Naval Forces 20,000+ (incl 5,000 Marines)

FORCES BY ROLE
COMBAT SUPPORT
Some arty bty
Some AShM bty with HY-2 (CSS-C-3 *Seersucker*) AShM

EQUIPMENT BY TYPE
In addition to the vessels listed, the IRGC operates a substantial number of patrol boats with a full-load displacement below 10 tonnes, including ε40 *Boghammar*-class vessels and small *Bavar*-class wing-in-ground effect air vehicles
PATROL AND COASTAL COMBATANTS 113
PBFG 46:
5 *China Cat* with 2 twin lnchr with C-701/*Kosar* AShM
10 *Thondor* (PRC *Houdong*) with 2 twin lnchr with C-802 (CSS-N-4 *Sardine*) AShM, 2 twin AK230 CIWS
25 *Peykaap* II (IPS-16 mod) with 2 single lnchr with C-701 (*Kosar*) AShM, 2 single 324mm TT
6 *Zolfaghar* (*Peykaap* III/IPS-16 mod) with 2 single lnchr with C-701 (*Kosar*)/C-704 (*Nasr*) AShM
PBF 35: 15 *Peykaap* I (IPS -16) with 2 single 324mm TT; 10 *Tir* (IPS-18); ε10 *Pashe* (MIG-G-1900)
PB ε 20 *Ghaem*
PTG 12
AMPHIBIOUS
LANDING SHIPS • LST 4:
2 *Hejaz* (minelaying capacity)
2 MIG-S-5000 (*Hejaz* design for commercial use)
LOGISTICS AND SUPPORT • AP 3 *Naser*
COASTAL DEFENCE • AShM C-701 (*Kosar*); C-704 (*Nasr*); C-802; HY-2 (CSS-C-3 *Seersucker*)

Islamic Revolutionary Guard Corps Marines 5,000+

FORCES BY ROLE
MANOEUVRE
Amphibious
1 marine bde

Islamic Revolutionary Guard Corps Air Force

Controls Iran's strategic-missile force
FORCES BY ROLE
MISSILE
ε1 bde with *Shahab*-1/2
ε1 bn with *Shahab*-3; *Ghadr*-1; *Sajjil*-2 (in devt)
EQUIPMENT BY TYPE
SURFACE-TO-SURFACE MISSILE LAUNCHERS
MRBM • **Conventional** 22+: 12+ *Shahab*-3/*Ghadr*-1 (mobile); 10 *Shahab*-3/*Ghadr*-1 (silo); some *Sajjil*-2 (in devt)

SRBM • **Conventional** 18+: some *Fateh* 110; 12–18 *Shahab*-1/2 (ε200–300 msl); some *Zelzal*

Navy 18,000
HQ at Bandar Abbas
EQUIPMENT BY TYPE
In addition to the vessels listed, the Iranian Navy operates a substantial number of patrol boats with a full-load displacement below 10 tonnes
SUBMARINES 21
  TACTICAL 21
    SSK 3 *Taregh* (RUS *Paltus* Type 877EKM) with 6 single 533mm TT
    SSC 1 *Fateh*
    SSW 17: 16 *Qadir* with 2 single 533mm TT (additional vessels in build); 1 *Nahang*
PATROL AND COASTAL COMBATANTS 81 (+ε50 small craft under 10 tonnes)
  CORVETTES 7
    FSGM 2 *Jamaran* (UK Vosper Mk 5 – 1 more undergoing sea trials) with 2 twin lnchr with C-802 (CSS-N-8 *Saccade*) AShM, 2 single lnchr with SM-1 SAM, 2 triple 324mm Mk32 ASTT, 1 76mm gun, 1 hel landing platform
    FSG 5:
      3 *Alvand* (UK Vosper Mk 5) with 2 twin lnchr with C-802 (CSS-N-8 *Saccade*) AShM, 2 triple Mk32 324mm ASTT, 1 114mm gun
      2 *Bayandor* (US PF-103) with 2 twin lnchr with C-802 (CSS-N-8 *Saccade*) AShM, 2 triple 324mm Mk32 ASTT, 1 76mm gun
  PCFG 14 *Kaman* (FRA *Combattante* II) with 1–2 twin lnchr with C-802 (CSS-N-4 *Saccade*) AShM, 1 76mm gun
  PBFG 8:
    ε4 Mk13 with 2 single lnchr with C-704 (*Nasr*) AShM, 2 single 324mm TT
    4 *China Cat* with 2 single lnchr with C-701 (*Kosar*) AShM
  PBG 15: 12 *Hendijan* (also used for coastal patrol) with 2 twin lnchr with C-802 (*Noor*) AShM; *Parvin* with 2 single lnchr with C-704 (*Nasr*) AShM
  PBF 16: 15 *Kashdom* II; 1 MIL55
  PB 22: 3 *Kayvan*; 6 MkII; 10 MkIII
  PTF 3 *Kajami* (semi-submersible)
MINE WARFARE • MINE COUNTERMEASURES 5
  MSC 3: 2 Type-292; 1 *Shahrokh* (in Caspian Sea as trg ship)
  MSI 2 *Riazi* (US *Cape*)
AMPHIBIOUS
  LANDING SHIPS 13
    LSM 3 *Farsi* (ROK) (capacity 9 tanks; 140 troops)
    LST 4 *Hengam* with 1 hel landing platform (capacity 9 tanks; 225 troops)
    LSL 6 *Fouque*
  LANDING CRAFT 11
    UCAC 8: 6 *Wellington*; 2 *Tondar* (UK *Winchester*)
    LCT 2
    LCU 1 *Liyan* 110
LOGISTICS AND SUPPORT 18
  AE 2 *Delvar*
  AFD 2 *Dolphin*
  AG 1 *Hamzah* with 2 single lnchr with C-802 (*Noor*) AShM
  AK 3 *Delvar*
  AORH 3: 2 *Bandar Abbas*; 1 *Kharg* with 1 76mm gun
  AWT 5: 4 *Kangan*; 1 *Delvar*
  AX 2 *Kialas*
COASTAL DEFENCE • AShM C-701 (*Kosar*); C-704 (*Nasr*); C-802 (*Noor*); C-802A (*Ghader*); *Ra'ad* (reported)

Marines 2,600
FORCES BY ROLE
MANOEUVRE
  Amphibious
  2 marine bde

Naval Aviation 2,600
EQUIPMENT BY TYPE
AIRCRAFT 3 combat capable
  ASW 3 P-3F *Orion*
  TPT 16: **Light** 13: 5 Do-228; 4 F-27 *Friendship*; 4 *Turbo Commander* 680; **PAX** 3 *Falcon* 20 (ELINT)
HELICOPTERS
  ASW ε10 SH-3D *Sea King*
  MCM 3 RH-53D *Sea Stallion*
  TPT • Light 17: 5 Bell 205A (AB-205A); 2 Bell 206 *Jet Ranger* (AB-206); 10 Bell 212 (AB-212)

Air Force 30,000 (incl 12,000 Air Defence)
FORCES BY ROLE
Serviceability probably about 60% for US ac types and about 80% for PRC/Russian ac. Includes IRGC Air Force equipment.
FIGHTER
  1 sqn with F-7M *Airguard*; JJ-7*
  2 sqn with F-14 *Tomcat*
  2 sqn with MiG-29A/UB *Fulcrum*
FIGHTER/GROUND ATTACK
  1 sqn with *Mirage* F-1E; F-5E/F *Tiger* II
  5 sqn with F-4D/E *Phantom* II
  3 sqn with F-5E/F *Tiger* II
GROUND ATTACK
  1 sqn with Su-24MK *Fencer* D
MARITIME PATROL
  1 sqn with P-3MP *Orion**
ISR
  1 (det) sqn with RF-4E *Phantom* II*
SEARCH & RESCUE
  Some flt with Bell-214C (AB-214C)
TANKER/TRANSPORT
  1 sqn with B-707; B-747; B-747F
TRANSPORT
  1 sqn with B-707; *Falcon* 50; L-1329 *Jetstar*; Bell 412
  2 sqn with C-130E/H *Hercules*
  1 sqn with F-27 *Friendship*; *Falcon* 20
  1 sqn with Il-76 *Candid*; An-140 (Iran-140 *Faraz*)
TRAINING
  1 sqn with Beech F33A/C *Bonanza*
  1 sqn with F-5B *Freedom Fighter*
  1 sqn with PC-6
  1 sqn with PC-7 *Turbo Trainer*

Some units with EMB-312 *Tucano*; MFI-17 *Mushshak*; TB-21 *Trinidad*; TB-200 *Tobago*

TRANSPORT HELICOPTER
1 sqn with CH-47 *Chinook*
Some units with Bell 206A *Jet Ranger* (AB-206A); *Shabaviz* 2-75; *Shabaviz* 2061

AIR DEFENCE
16 bn with MIM-23B I-*Hawk*/*Shahin*
4 bn with S-300PMU (SA-20 *Gargoyle*)
5 sqn with FM-80 (*Crotale*); *Rapier*; *Tigercat*; S-75M *Volkhov* (SA-2 *Guideline*); S-200 *Angara* (SA-5 *Gammon*); FIM-92A *Stinger*; 9K32 *Strela*-2 (SA-7 *Grail*)‡; 9K331 *Tor*-M1 (SA-15 *Gauntlet*) (reported)

EQUIPMENT BY TYPE
AIRCRAFT 333 combat capable
  FTR 184+: 20 F-5B *Freedom Fighter*; 55+ F-5E/F *Tiger* II 24 F-7M *Airguard*; 43 F-14 *Tomcat*; 36 MiG-29A/U/UB *Fulcrum*; up to 6 *Azarakhsh* (reported)
  FGA 80: 64 F-4D/E *Phantom* II; 10 *Mirage* F-1E; up to 6 *Saegheh* (reported)
  ATK 39: 29 Su-24MK *Fencer D*; 7 Su-25K *Frogfoot*; 3 Su-25UBK *Frogfoot* (incl 4+ Su-25K/UBK deployed in Iraq; status unclear)
  ASW 5 P-3MP *Orion*
  ISR 6+ RF-4E *Phantom* II*
  TKR/TPT 3: ε1 B-707; ε2 B-747
  TPT 117: **Heavy** 12 Il-76 *Candid*; **Medium** ε19 C-130E/H *Hercules*; **Light** 75: 11 An-74TK-200; 5 An-140 (Iran-140 *Faraz*) (45 projected); 10 F-27 *Friendship*; 1 L-1329 *Jetstar*; 10 PC-6B *Turbo Porter*; 8 TB-21 *Trinidad*; 4 TB-200 *Tobago*; 3 *Turbo Commander* 680; 14 Y-7; 9 Y-12; **PAX** 11: 2 B-707; 1 B-747; 4 B-747F; 1 *Falcon* 20; 3 *Falcon* 50
  TRG 151: 25 Beech F33A/C *Bonanza*; 15 EMB-312 *Tucano*; 15 JJ-7*; 25 MFI-17 *Mushshak*; 12 *Parastu*; 15 PC-6; 35 PC-7 *Turbo Trainer*; 9 T-33

HELICOPTERS
  MRH 2 Bell 412
  TPT 34+: **Heavy** 2+ CH-47 *Chinook*; **Medium** 30 Bell 214C (AB-214C); **Light** 2+: 2 Bell 206A *Jet Ranger* (AB-206A); some *Shabaviz* 2-75 (indigenous versions in production); some *Shabaviz* 2061

AIR DEFENCE •
  SAM 514+:
    Long-range 10 S-200 *Angara* (SA-5 *Gammon*); 32 S-300PMU2 (SA-20 *Gargoyle*) (unit forming)
    Medium-range 195+: 150+ MIM-23B I-*Hawk*/*Shahin*; 45 S-75 *Dvina* (SA-2 *Guideline*);
    Short-range 279: 250 FM-80 (*Crotale*); 29 9K331 *Tor*-M1 (SA-15 *Gauntlet*) (reported)
    Point-defence 30+: 30 *Rapier*; FIM-92 *Stinger*; 9K32 *Strela*-2 (SA-7 *Grail*)‡
  GUNS • **TOWED 23mm** ZU-23-2; **35mm** Oerlikon

AIR-LAUNCHED MISSILES
  AAM • **IR** PL-2A‡; PL-7; R-60 (AA-8 *Aphid*); R-73 (AA-11 *Archer*); AIM-9 *Sidewinder*; **IR/SARH** R-27 (AA-10 *Alamo*); **SARH** AIM-7 *Sparrow*; **ARH** AIM-54 *Phoenix*†
  ASM AGM-65A *Maverick*; Kh-25 (AS-10 *Karen*); Kh-29 (AS-14 *Kedge*)
  AShM C-801K
  ARM Kh-58 (AS-11 *Kilter*)

Air Defence Command
Established to coordinate army, air-force and IRGC air-defence assets. Precise composition unclear

Paramilitary 40,000–60,000

Law-Enforcement Forces 40,000–60,000 (border and security troops); 450,000 on mobilisation (incl conscripts)
Part of armed forces in wartime

EQUIPMENT BY TYPE
PATROL AND COASTAL COMBATANTS • **PB** ε90
AIRCRAFT • **TPT** • **Light** 2+: 2 An-140; some Cessna 185/Cessna 310
HELICOPTERS • **TPT** • **Light** ε24 AB-205 (Bell 205)/AB-206 (Bell 206) *Jet Ranger*

Basij Resistance Force up to ε1,000,000 on mobilisation
Paramilitary militia with claimed membership of 12.6 million; perhaps 1 million combat capable; in the process of closer integration with IRGC Ground Forces

FORCES BY ROLE
MANOEUVRE
  Other
  2,500 militia bn(-) (claimed, limited permanent membership)

Cyber
Iran has a well-developed capacity for cyber operations. It has a well-educated and computer-literate young population. In September 2015, Ayatollah Ali Khamenei appointed members to a Supreme Council for Cyberspace, reportedly a policymaking and supervisory body. The Stuxnet incident in 2010 is reported to have been a turning point in Iran's approach to cyber capabilities. In 2011–12, Tehran established a Joint Chiefs of Staff Cyber Command with emphasis on thwarting attacks against Iranian nuclear facilities and coordinating national cyber-warfare and information security. The IRGC has its own Cyber Defence Command; IRGC civilian business interests will aid its activities in this area. The precise relationship of groups such as the 'Iranian Cyber Army' to regime and military organisations is unclear, but the former has launched hacking attacks against a number of foreign organisations. There are continued reports of increasing investment in cyber capabilities, used not only for propaganda and intelligence exploitation but also as a means for Iran to attempt to offset its conventional military weakness vis-à-vis its neighbours and the US. But Iran also remains aware of its own potential vulnerabilities, not least in terms of infrastructure protection: it was reported in May that a senior official was advising that Iran should identify 'vital points' in infrastructure so as to boost passive defences, while another leader said in February that Iran should 'adopt a pre-emptive approach towards future cyber risks'.

DEPLOYMENT

GULF OF ADEN AND SOMALI BASIN
Navy: 1 FSG; 1 AORH

SUDAN
UN • UNAMID 4 obs

SYRIA
IRGC: up to 2,000

Iraq IRQ

Iraqi Dinar D		2015	2016	2017
GDP	D	193tr	184tr	
	US$	165bn	156bn	
per capita	US$	4,696	4,334	
Growth	%	-2.4	10.3	
Inflation	%	1.4	2	
Def bdgt [a]	D	24.6tr	ε21.1tr	
	US$	21.2bn	ε18.1bn	
US$1=D		1,166.00	1,180.00	

[a] Defence and security budget

Population 38,146,025

Ethnic and religious groups: Arab 75–80% (of which Shi'a Muslim 55%, Sunni Muslim 45%) Kurdish 20–25%

Age	0–14	15–19	20–24	25–29	30–64	65 plus
Male	20.4%	5.3%	4.4%	4.0%	14.9%	1.5%
Female	19.5%	5.1%	4.3%	3.9%	14.8%	1.9%

Capabilities

The Iraqi Army has slowly been rebuilt after a number of divisions collapsed in the face of attacks by ISIS in 2014. Combat performance against ISIS has grown incrementally, although there is still reliance on the numerous popular mobilisation forces (PMF) that have, with Shia militia, bolstered the defence of key areas and helped in retaking some territory from ISIS. Kurdish forces in the north performed a range of combat missions and received training and materiel support from Western states; for a time, they were the bulwark against further ISIS expansion. In the Mosul operation in 2016, there was a level of coordination between Kurdish and Iraqi government forces. Personnel from Iraq's coalition-trained Counter-terrorism Service proved effective as the campaign progressed, and were heavily employed in the operation to retake the city. Nonetheless, there remain significant challenges ahead, not just in rebuilding an inclusive Iraqi Army, but in decisions about demobilising or integrating the PMF into the armed forces, ensuring wider Sunni representation in the forces and tackling corruption. Training provided by coalition forces (worth US$1.6bn since 2015) has proved important in developing Iraqi combat capabilities, while training has also been provided to Kurdish forces. Iraq has also deployed combat airpower to support ground operations against ISIS, using its F-16s with laser-guided bombs and L-159s with free-fall bombs, and has increasingly used its own reconnaissance and surveillance assets as part of ongoing operations. (See pp. 353–54.)

ACTIVE 64,000 (Army 54,000 Navy 3,000 Air 4,000 Air Defence 3,000) **Paramilitary 145,000**

ORGANISATIONS BY SERVICE

Army 54,000

Due to ongoing conflict with ISIS insurgents, there have been significant personnel and equipment losses in the Iraqi Army. Many formations are now under-strength. Military capability has been bolstered by the activity of Shia militias and Kurdish Peshmerga forces

FORCES BY ROLE
SPECIAL FORCES
  2 SF bde
MANOEUVRE
  Armoured
  1 armd div (2 armd bde, 2 mech bde, 1 engr bn, 1 sigs regt, 1 log bde)
  Mechanised
  2 mech div (4 mech inf bde, 1 engr bn, 1 sigs regt, 1 log bde)
  1 mech div (3 mech inf bde, 1 engr bn, 1 sigs regt, 1 log bde)
  1 mech div (2 mech inf bde, 1 inf bde, 1 engr bn, 1 sigs regt, 1 log bde)
  Light
  1 mot div (1 mech bde, 3 mot inf bde, 2 inf bde, 1 engr bn, 1 sigs regt, 1 log bde)
  1 mot div (2 mot inf bde, 3 inf bde, 1 engr bn, 1 sigs regt, 1 log bde)
  1 inf div (4 lt inf bde, 1 engr bn, 1 sigs regt, 1 log bde)
  1 inf div (3 inf bde)
  1 inf div (2 inf bde)
  1 inf div (1 inf bde)
  1 cdo div (5 lt inf bde, 1 engr bn, 1 sigs regt, 1 log bde)
  1 inf bde
  Aviation
  1 atk hel sqn (forming) with Mi-28NE *Havoc*
  1 atk hel sqn with Mi-35M *Hind*
  1 sqn with Bell 205 (UH-1H *Huey* II)
  3 atk hel sqn with Bell T407; H135M
  3 sqn with Mi-17 *Hip* H; Mi-171Sh
  1 ISR sqn with SA342M *Gazelle*
  2 trg sqn with Bell 206; OH-58C *Kiowa*
  1 trg sqn with Bell 205 (UH-1H *Huey* II)
  1 trg sqn with Mi-17 *Hip*
EQUIPMENT BY TYPE
ARMOURED FIGHTING VEHICLES
  MBT 318+: ε100 M1A1 *Abrams*; 168+ T-72; ε50 T-55;
  RECCE 453: ε400 *Akrep*; 18 BRDM 2; 35 EE-9 *Cascavel*;
  IFV 240: ε80 BMP-1; ε60 BTR-4 (inc variants); 100 BTR-80A
  APC 2,102+
    APC (T) 900: ε500 M113A2/*Talha*; ε400 MT-LB
    APC (W) 10 *Cobra*
    PPV 1,192+: 12 *Barracuda*; 250 *Caiman*; ε500 *Dzik*-3; ε400 ILAV *Badger*; *Mamba*; 30 *Maxxpro*
  AUV M-ATV
ENGINEERING & MAINTENANCE VEHICLES
  ARV 215+: 180 BREM; 35+ M88A1/2; T-54/55 ARV; Type-653; VT-55A
NBC VEHICLES 20 *Fuchs* NBC

ANTI-TANK/ANTI-INFRASTRUCTURE
MSL • MANPATS 9K135 Kornet (AT-14 Spriggan) (reported)
ARTILLERY 1,061+
SP 48+: **152mm** 18+ Type-83; **155mm** 30: 6 M109A1; 24 M109A5
TOWED 60+: **130mm** M-46/Type-59; **152mm** D-20; Type-83; **155mm** ε60 M198
MRL 3+: **122mm** some BM-21 Grad; **220mm** 3+ TOS-1A
MOR 950+: **81mm** ε500 M252; **120mm** ε450 M120; **240mm** M-240
HELICOPTERS
ATK 29: 11 Mi-28NE Havoc; 4 Mi-28UB Havoc; 14 Mi-35M Hind
MRH 51+: 4+ SA342 Gazelle; 24 Bell IA407; 23 H135M
MRH/TPT ε19 Mi-17 Hip H/Mi-171Sh
ISR 10 OH-58C Kiowa
TPT • **Light** 45: 16 Bell 205 (UH-1H Huey II); 10 Bell 206B3 Jet Ranger; ε19 Bell T407
UNMANNED AERIAL VEHICLES • **CISR Heavy** CH-4
AIR-LAUNCHED MISSILES • **ASM** 9K114 Shturm (AT-6 Spiral); AR-1; Ingwe

Navy 3,000
EQUIPMENT BY TYPE
PATROL AND COASTAL COMBATANTS 32+
PCO 2 Al Basra (US River Hawk)
PCC 4 Fateh (ITA Diciotti)
PB 20: 12 Swiftships 35; 5 Predator (PRC-27m); 3 Al Faw
PBR 6: 2 Type-200; 4 Type-2010

Marines 1,000
FORCES BY ROLE
MANOEUVRE
Amphibious
2 mne bn

Air Force ε4,000
FORCES BY ROLE
FIGHTER/GROUND ATTACK
1 sqn with F-16C/D Fighting Falcon
GROUND ATTACK
1 sqn with Su-25/Su-25K/Su-25UBK Frogfoot
1 sqn with L-159
ISR
1 sqn with CH-2000 Sama; SB7L-360 Seeker
1 sqn with Cessna 208B Grand Caravan; Cessna AC-208B Combat Caravan*
1 sqn with Beech 350 King Air
TRANSPORT
1 sqn with An-32B Cline
1 sqn with C-130E/J-30 Hercules
TRAINING
1 sqn with Cessna 172, Cessna 208B
1 sqn with Lasta-95
1 sqn with T-6A
EQUIPMENT BY TYPE
AIRCRAFT 29 combat capable
FGA 10: 7 F-16C Fighting Falcon; 3 F-16D Fighting Falcon
ATK 15+: 4 L-159; 11+ Su-25/Su-25K/Su-25UBK Frogfoot

ISR 10: 2 Cessna AC-208B Combat Caravan*; 2 SB7L-360 Seeker; 6 Beech 350ER King Air
TPT 29: **Medium** 15: 3 C-130E Hercules; 6 C-130J-30 Hercules; 6 An-32B Cline (of which 2 combat capable); **Light** 17: 1 Beech 350 King Air; 5 Cessna 208B Grand Caravan; 8 Cessna 172
TRG 33+: 8 CH-2000 Sama; 10+ Lasta-95; 15 T-6A
AIR-LAUNCHED MISSILES • **ASM** AGM-114 Hellfire
BOMBS • **Laser-Guided** GBU-12 Paveway II

Air Defence Command ε3,000
FORCES BY ROLE
AIR DEFENCE
1 bn with 96K6 Pantsir-S1 (SA-22 Greyhound)
1 bn with M1097 Avenger
1 bn with 9K338 Igla-S (SA-24 Grinch)
1 bn with ZU-23-2; S-60
EQUIPMENT BY TYPE
AIR DEFENCE
SAM
Short-range 24 96K6 Pantsir-S1 (SA-22 Greyhound)
Point-defence M1097 Avenger; 9K338 Igla-S (SA-24 Grinch)
GUNS • **TOWED 23mm** ZU-23-2; **57mm** S-60

Paramilitary ε145,000

Iraqi Federal Police ε36,000

Border Enforcement ε9,000

Militias ε100,000
Popular Mobilisation Forces include: Kata'ib Sayyid al-Shuhada Brigade; Kata'ib Hizbullah; Badr Brigades; Peace Brigades and Imam Ali Battalions

FOREIGN FORCES
Australia Operation Okra 380
Belgium Operation Valiant Phoenix 16
Canada Operation Impact 207; 3 Bell 412 (CH-146 Griffon)
Czech Republic Operation Inherent Resolve 31
Denmark Operation Inherent Resolve 220
Estonia Operation Inherent Resolve 10
Fiji UNAMI 168; 2 sy unit
Finland Operation Inherent Resolve 100
France Operation Chammal 550; 1 SP arty bty with 4 CAESAR
Germany Operation Inherent Resolve 123
Hungary Operation Inherent Resolve 139
Italy Operation Inherent Resolve 1,120; 1 inf regt; 1 hel sqn with 4 AW129 Mangusta; 4 NH90
Latvia Operation Inherent Resolve 6
Nepal UNAMI 76; 1 sy unit
Netherlands Operation Inherent Resolve 130
New Zealand Operation Inherent Resolve 143
Norway Operation Inherent Resolve 120
Poland Operation Inherent Resolve 60
Portugal Operation Inherent Resolve 32

Romania *Operation Inherent Resolve* 50
Slovenia *Operation Inherent Resolve* 6
Spain *Operation Inherent Resolve* 300
Sweden *Operation Inherent Resolve* 35
Turkey Army 2,000; 1 armd BG
United Kingdom *Operation Shader* 550
United States *Operation Inherent Resolve* 5,262; 1 air aslt div HQ; 1 mne coy; 1 SP arty bty with 4 M109A6; 1 fd arty bty with 4 M777A2; 1 MRL bty with 4 M142 HIMARS; 1 atk hel sqn with AH-64D *Apache*

Israel ISR

New Israeli Shekel NS		2015	2016	2017
GDP	NS	1.16tr	1.2tr	
	US$	299bn	312bn	
per capita	US$	35,743	36,557	
Growth	%	2.5	2.8	
Inflation	%	-0.6	-0.6	
Def bdgt	NS	59.9bn	60.9bn	
	US$	15.4bn	15.9bn	
FMA (US)	US$	3.1bn	3.1bn	3.1bn
US$1=NS		3.89	3.84	

Population 8,174,527

Age	0–14	15–19	20–24	25–29	30–64	65 plus
Male	14.2%	4.1%	3.8%	3.6%	19.5%	5.0%
Female	13.5%	3.9%	3.6%	3.5%	19.0%	6.1%

Capabilities

The Israel Defense Forces (IDF) remain the most capable forces in the region, with the motivation, equipment and training to considerably overmatch the conventional capability of other regional armed forces. Israel's defence policy prioritises homeland defence but with the ability to intervene in Lebanon and Syria. The requirement for power projection further afield appears limited to ISR, precision strikes and special-forces operations as far away as Iran. Senior Israeli personnel have declared training and readiness the IDF's foremost priority amid budget cuts. Currently preoccupied by threats posed by Hamas, Hizbullah and Iran's proxies in Syria, the IDF continues to launch strikes in Syria. Israel must also be assumed to have the military capability for a unilateral attack on Iran. There is an emphasis on maintaining Israel's technological superiority, especially in missile defence, intelligence gathering, precision weapons and cyber capabilities. Israel also continues to improve its missile- and rocket-defence network. 2016 saw the IDF start to implement its five-year Gideon modernisation plan to improve combat capability and administrative efficiency while reducing costs and overhead. This includes eliminating two army divisions and the retirement of an air-force squadron (as part of the transition to the F-35 aircraft), and the early retirement of older F-16 combat aircraft. The plan also calls for a reduction in the number of career soldiers to 40,000, as well as a decrease in the length of compulsory service for men from 36 to 32 months. The army has recently introduced a new artillery doctrine focused on swift precision strikes, and has formed a new artillery brigade with an integrated intelligence unit. It is forming a joint cyber command, consolidating various cyber-defence capabilities. Israel's logistics capability appears to be adequate to support its military operations and plans. Israel also has a capable defence industry. The aerospace, ISR, missile and armoured-vehicles sectors are particular strengths, as are counter-rocket systems and active-protection systems for armoured vehicles. The modernisation and production of indigenous armoured vehicles continues, while the navy is trialling indigenous patrol craft.

ACTIVE 176,500 (Army 133,000 Navy 9,500 Air 34,000) **Paramilitary 8,000**
Conscript liability Officers 48 months, other ranks 36 months, women 24 months (Jews and Druze only; Christians, Circassians and Muslims may volunteer)

RESERVE 465,000 (Army 400,000 Navy 10,000 Air 55,000)
Annual trg as cbt reservists to age 40 (some specialists to age 54) for male other ranks, 38 (or marriage/pregnancy) for women

ORGANISATIONS BY SERVICE

Strategic Forces
Israel is widely believed to have a nuclear capability – delivery means include F-15I and F-16I ac, *Jericho* 2 IRBM and, reportedly, *Dolphin/Tanin*-class SSKs with LACM

FORCES BY ROLE
SURFACE-TO-SURFACE MISSILE
3 IRBM sqn with *Jericho* 2

EQUIPMENT BY TYPE
SURFACE-TO-SURFACE MISSILE LAUNCHERS
IRBM • **Nuclear**: ε24 *Jericho* 2

Strategic Defences
FORCES BY ROLE
AIR DEFENCE
3 bty with *Arrow/Arrow* 2 ATBM with *Green Pine/Super Green Pine* radar and *Citrus Tree* command post
10 bty with *Iron Dome* (incl reserve bty)
17 bty with MIM-23B I-*Hawk*
6 bty with MIM-104 *Patriot*

Space
EQUIPMENT BY TYPE
SATELLITES 9
COMMUNICATIONS 3 *Amos*
ISR 6: 1 EROS; 4 *Ofeq* (7, 9, 10 & 11); 1 TecSAR-1 (*Polaris*)

Army 26,000; 107,000 conscript (total 133,000)
Organisation and structure of formations may vary according to op situations. Equipment includes that required for reserve forces on mobilisation

FORCES BY ROLE
COMMAND
3 (regional comd) corps HQ
2 armd div HQ
5 (territorial) inf div HQ
SPECIAL FORCES
3 SF bn
1 spec ops bde (4 spec ops unit)
MANOEUVRE
Reconnaissance
1 indep recce bn
Armoured
3 armd bde (1 armd recce coy, 3 armd bn, 1 AT coy, 1 cbt engr bn)
Mechanised
3 mech inf bde (3 mech inf bn, 1 cbt spt bn,1 sigs coy)
1 mech inf bde (5 mech inf bn)
1 indep mech inf bn
Light
2 indep inf bn
Air Manoeuvre
1 para bde (3 para bn,1 cbt spt bn, 1 sigs coy)
Other
1 armd trg bde (3 armd bn)
COMBAT SUPPORT
3 arty bde
3 engr bn
1 EOD coy
1 CBRN bn
1 int bde (3 int bn)
2 MP bn

Reserves 400,000+ on mobilisation
FORCES BY ROLE
COMMAND
3 armd div HQ
1 AB div HQ
MANOEUVRE
Armoured
9 armd bde
Mechanised
8 mech inf bde
Light
16 (territorial/regional) inf bde
Air Manoeuvre
4 para bde
Mountain
1 mtn inf bn
COMBAT SUPPORT
5 arty bde
COMBAT SERVICE SUPPORT
6 log unit

EQUIPMENT BY TYPE
ARMOURED FIGHTING VEHICLES
 MBT 500: ε40 *Merkava* MkII; ε160 *Merkava* MkIII; ε300 *Merkava* MkIV (ε330 *Merkava* MkII; ε570 *Merkava* MkIII; ε160 *Merkava* MkIV all in store)
 RECCE ε300 RBY-1 RAMTA
 APC • APC (T) 1,200: ε100 *Namer*; ε200 *Achzarit* (modified T-55 chassis); 500 M113A2; ε400 *Nagmachon* (*Centurion* chassis); *Nakpadon* (5,000 M113A1/A2 in store)
 AUV 100 *Ze'ev*

ENGINEERING & MAINTENANCE VEHICLES
 AEV D9R; *Puma*
 ARV *Centurion* Mk2; *Eyal*; *Merkava*; M88A1; M113 ARV
 VLB *Alligator* MAB; M48/60; MTU
NBC VEHICLES ε8 TPz-1 *Fuchs* NBC
ANTI-TANK/ANTI-INFRASTRUCTURE • MSL
 SP M113 with *Spike*; *Tamuz* (*Spike* NLOS); *Magach* mod with *Spike*
 MANPATS IMI MAPATS; *Spike* MR/LR/ER
ARTILLERY 530
 SP 250: **155mm** 250 M109A5 (**155mm** 148 Soltam L-33; 30 M109A1; 50 M-50; **175mm** 36 M107; **203mm** 36 M110 all in store)
 TOWED (**122mm** 5 D-30; **130mm** 100 M-46; **155mm** 171: 40 M-46 mod; 50 M-68/M-71; 81 M-839P/M-845P all in store)
 MRL 30: **227mm** 30 M270 MLRS (**122mm** 58 BM-21 *Grad*; **160mm** 50 LAR-160; **227mm** 18 M270 MLRS; **240mm** 36 BM-24; **290mm** 20 LAR-290 all in store)
 MOR 250: **81mm** 250; (**81mm** 1,100; **120mm** 650; **160mm** 18 Soltam M-66 all in store)
SURFACE-TO-SURFACE MISSILE LAUNCHERS
 IRBM • Nuclear ε24 *Jericho* 2
 SRBM • Dual-capable (7 *Lance* in store)
RADAR • LAND AN/PPS-15 (arty); AN/TPQ-37 *Firefinder* (arty); EL/M-2140 (veh)
AIR DEFENCE • SAM • Point-defence 20 *Machbet*; FIM-92 *Stinger*

Navy 7,000; 2,500 conscript (total 9,500)
EQUIPMENT BY TYPE
SUBMARINES • TACTICAL
 SSK 5:
  3 *Dolphin* (GER HDW design) with 6 single 533mm TT with UGM-84C *Harpoon* AShM/HWT, 4 single 650mm TT
  2 *Tanin* (GER HDW design with AIP) with 6 single 533mm TT with UGM-84C *Harpoon* AShM/HWT, 4 single 650mm TT
PATROL AND COASTAL COMBATANTS 53
 CORVETTES • FSGHM 3:
  2 *Eilat* (*Sa'ar* 5) with 2 quad Mk140 lnchr with RGM-84C *Harpoon* AShM, 2 32-cell VLS with *Barak*-1 SAM (being upgraded to *Barak*-8), 2 triple 324mm TT with Mk 46 LWT, 1 *Sea Vulcan* CIWS, 1 76mm gun (capacity 1 AS565SA *Panther* ASW hel)
  1 *Eilat* (*Sa'ar* 5) with 2 quad Mk140 lnchr with RGM-84C *Harpoon* AShM, 2 32-cell VLS with *Barak*-8 SAM, 2 triple 324mm TT with Mk 46 LWT, 1 *Sea Vulcan* CIWS, 1 76mm gun (capacity 1 AS565SA *Panther* ASW hel)
 PCGM 8 *Hetz* (*Sa'ar* 4.5) with 6 single lnchr with *Gabriel* II AShM, 2 twin Mk140 lnchr with RGM-84C *Harpoon* AShM, 1 16-32-cell Mk56 VLS with *Barak*-1 SAM, 1 *Vulcan* CIWS, 1 *Typhoon* CIWS, 1 76mm gun
 PBF 18: 5 *Shaldag* with 1 *Typhoon* CIWS; 3 *Stingray*; 10 *Super Dvora* MK III (AShM & TT may be fitted)
 PBFT 13: 9 *Super Dvora* MkI with 2 single 324mm TT with Mk 46 LWT (AShM may also be fitted); 4 *Super Dvora*

MkII with 2 single 324mm TT with Mk 46 LWT (AShM may also be fitted)
  PBT 11 *Dabur* with 2 single 324mm TT with Mk 46 LWT
AMPHIBIOUS • LANDING CRAFT • LCT 3: 1 *Ashdod*; 2 others
LOGISTICS AND SUPPORT 3
  AG 2 *Bat Yam* (ex German Type-745)
  AX 1 *Queshet*

Naval Commandos ε300

Air Force 34,000

Responsible for Air and Space Coordination
FORCES BY ROLE
FIGHTER & FIGHTER/GROUND ATTACK
  1 sqn with F-15A/B/D *Eagle*
  1 sqn with F-15B/C/D *Eagle*
  1 sqn with F-15I *Ra'am*
  6 sqn with F-16A/B/C/D *Fighting Falcon*
  4 sqn with F-16I *Sufa*
  (2 sqn with F-4 *Phantom II/Kfir* C-7 in reserve)
ANTI-SUBMARINE WARFARE
  1 sqn with AS565SA *Panther* (missions flown by IAF but with non-rated aircrew)
MARITIME PATROL/TANKER/TRANSPORT
  1 sqn with IAI-1124 *Seascan*; KC-707
ELECTRONIC WARFARE
  2 sqn with RC-12D *Guardrail*; Beech A36 *Bonanza* (*Hofit*); Beech 200 *King Air*; Beech 200T *King Air*; Beech 200CT *King Air*
AIRBORNE EARLY WARNING & CONTROL
  1 sqn with Gulfstream G550 *Eitam*; Gulfstream G550 *Shavit*
TANKER/TRANSPORT
  1 sqn with C-130E/H *Hercules*; KC-130H *Hercules*
  1 sqn with C-130J-30 *Hercules*
TRAINING
  1 OPFOR sqn with F-16A/B *Fighting Falcon*
  1 sqn with M-346 *Master* (*Lavi*)
ATTACK HELICOPTER
  1 sqn with AH-64A *Apache*
  1 sqn with AH-64D *Apache*
TRANSPORT HELICOPTER
  2 sqn with CH-53D *Sea Stallion*
  2 sqn with S-70A *Black Hawk*; UH-60A *Black Hawk*
  1 medevac unit with CH-53D *Sea Stallion*
UAV
  1 ISR sqn with *Hermes* 450
  1 ISR sqn with *Searcher* MkII
  1 ISR sqn with *Heron* (*Shoval*); *Heron* TP (*Eitan*)
AIR DEFENCE
  3 bty with *Arrow/Arrow* 2
  10 bty with *Iron Dome*
  17 bty with MIM-23 I-HAWK
  6 bty with MIM-104 *Patriot*
EQUIPMENT BY TYPE
AIRCRAFT 431 combat capable
  FTR 151: 16 F-15A *Eagle*; 6 F-15B *Eagle*; 17 F-15C *Eagle*; 19 F-15D *Eagle*; 77 F-16A *Fighting Falcon*; 16 F-16B *Fighting Falcon*
  FGA 250: 25 F-15I *Ra'am*; 78 F-16C *Fighting Falcon*; 49 F-16D *Fighting Falcon*; 98 F-16I *Sufa*
  FTR/FGA/ATK (Some A-4N *Skyhawk*/F-4 *Phantom* II/F-15A *Eagle*/F-16A/B *Fighting Falcon*/*Kfir* C-7 in store)
  MP 3 IAI-1124 *Seascan*
  ISR 6 RC-12D *Guardrail*
  ELINT 4: 1 EC-707; 3 Gulfstream G550 *Shavit*
  AEW 4: 2 B-707 *Phalcon*; 2 Gulfstream G550 *Eitam* (1 more on order)
  TKR/TPT 11: 4 KC-130H *Hercules*; 7 KC-707
  TPT 62: Medium 15: 5 C-130E *Hercules*; 6 C-130H *Hercules*; 4 C-130J-30 *Hercules*; Light 47: 3 AT-802 *Air Tractor*; 9 Beech 200 *King Air*; 8 Beech 200T *King Air*; 5 Beech 200CT *King Air*; 22 Beech A36 *Bonanza* (*Hofit*)
  TRG 67: 17 Grob G-120; 30 M-346 *Master* (*Lavi*)*; 20 T-6A
HELICOPTERS
  ATK 44: 27 AH-64A *Apache*; 17 AH-64D *Apache* (*Sarat*)
  ASW 7 AS565SA *Panther* (missions flown by IAF but with non-rated aircrew)
  ISR 12 OH-58B *Kiowa*
  TPT 81: Heavy 26 CH-53D *Sea Stallion*; Medium 49: 39 S-70A *Black Hawk*; 10 UH-60A *Black Hawk*; Light 6 Bell 206 *Jet Ranger*
UNMANNED AERIAL VEHICLES
  ISR 24+: Heavy 2+: *Heron* (*Shoval*); 3 *Heron* TP (*Eitan*); RQ-5A *Hunter*; Medium 22+: *Hermes* 450; *Hermes* 900; 22 *Searcher* MkII (22+ in store); Light *Harpy*
AIR DEFENCE
  SAM 54+:
    Long-range MIM-104C *Patriot* PAC-2
    Medium-range 24 *Arrow/Arrow* 2; some MIM-23B *I-Hawk*;
    Short-range ε30 *Iron Dome*
  GUNS 920
    SP 165: 20mm 105 M163 *Machbet Vulcan*; 23mm 60 ZSU-23-4
    TOWED 755: 23mm 150 ZU-23-2; 20mm/37mm 455 M167 *Vulcan* towed 20mm/M-1939 towed 37mm/TCM-20 towed 20mm; 40mm 150 L/70
AIR-LAUNCHED MISSILES
  AAM • IR AIM-9 *Sidewinder*; *Python* 4; IIR *Python* 5; ARH AIM-120C AMRAAM; *Derby*
  ASM AGM-114 *Hellfire*; AGM-62B *Walleye*; AGM-65 *Maverick*; *Popeye* I/*Popeye* II; *Delilah* AL
BOMBS
  IIR guided *Opher*
  Laser-guided *Griffin*; *Lizard*; *Paveway* II
  INS/GPS guided GBU-31 JDAM; GBU-39 Small Diameter Bomb (*Barad Had*); *Spice*

Airfield Defence 3,000 active (15,000 reservists)

Paramilitary ε8,000

Border Police ε8,000

Cyber

Israel has a substantial capacity for cyber operations. In early 2012, the National Cyber Bureau (NCB) was created in the prime minister's office to develop technology, human resources and international collaboration. In late October 2012, the NCB and the defence ministry's Directorate for Research and Development announced a dual cyber-security programme called MASAD 'to promote R&D projects that serve both civilian and defense goals at the national level'. It is reported that the IDF's 'Unit 8200' is responsible for ELINT and some cyber operations. In 2012, according to the IDF, the C4I Directorate and Unit 8200 were combined into a new task force 'tasked with developing offensive capabilities and operations'. Specialist training courses exist, including the four-month 'Cyber Shield' activity. The IDF's Gideon plan calls for a Joint Cyber Command that integrates defensive capabilities provided by the C4I branch with military intelligence. In April 2016, the National Cyber Defense Authority was created, consolidating cyber defences in one body.

FOREIGN FORCES

UNTSO unless specified. UNTSO figures represent total numbers for mission.
Argentina 3 obs
Australia 13 obs
Austria 4 obs
Belgium 2 obs
Bhutan 1 obs • UNDOF 2
Canada 4 obs
Chile 2 obs
China 2 obs
Czech Republic UNDOF 3
Denmark 10 obs
Estonia 6 obs
Fiji 2 obs • UNDOF 255; 1 inf coy; elm 1 log bn
Finland 17 obs • UNDOF 2
France 1 obs
India 1 obs • UNDOF 189; 1 log bn(-)
Ireland 11 obs • UNDOF 136; 1 inf coy
Nepal 3 obs • UNDOF 200; 1 inf coy
Netherlands 11 obs • UNDOF 2
New Zealand 8 obs
Norway 13 obs
Russia 5 obs
Serbia 1 obs
Slovakia 2 obs
Slovenia 3 obs
Sweden 7 obs
Switzerland 15 obs
United States 2 obs • US Strategic Command; 1 AN/TPY-2 X-band radar at Mount Keren

Jordan JOR

Jordanian Dinar D		2015	2016	2017
GDP	D	26.6bn	28bn	
	US$	37.6bn	39.5bn	
per capita	US$	4,947	5,092	
Growth	%	2.4	2.8	
Inflation	%	-0.9	-0.5	
Def bdgt [a]	D	936m	1.03bn	
	US$	1.32bn	1.45bn	
FMA (US)	US$	385m	300m	350m
US$1=D		0.71	0.71	

[a] Excludes expenditure on public order and safety

Population 8,185,384
Ethnic groups: Palestinian ε50–60%

Age	0–14	15–19	20–24	25–29	30–64	65 plus
Male	18.0%	5.4%	4.9%	4.4%	15.9%	1.8%
Female	17.1%	5.1%	4.7%	4.3%	16.2%	2.1%

Capabilities

Jordan's armed forces benefit from a high level of defence spending relative to GDP, and strong defence relationships with the US and the UK that have boosted training. The main roles of Jordan's fully professional armed forces are border and internal security, and the services are combat capable and contribute to international expeditionary operations. Jordan's main security preoccupations are the threat from ISIS, the complex conflicts in Syria and Iraq, and the resulting flow of refugees. In 2016 a new Quick Reaction Force was formed to support activity by Jordanian special forces. The country is reliant on external support for the majority of its military equipment, although the state-owned KADDB indigenously produces some light armoured vehicles for the army. Personnel are well trained, particularly aircrew and special forces, who are highly regarded, served alongside ISAF forces in Afghanistan and participated in various UN missions. The country has developed a bespoke special-forces-training centre, which regularly plays host to various special-forces contingents and continues to host annual exercise *Eager Lion*. US and UK forces also regularly exercise in the country. Jordan has significantly stepped up border security in light of the continued presence of ISIS on its periphery, including a complex border-security project funded by the US, which includes a C3 package, sensors, watchtowers and a command centre.

ACTIVE 100,500 (Army 74,000 Navy 500 Air 12,000 Special Operations 14,000) **Paramilitary 15,000**

RESERVE 65,000 (Army 60,000 Joint 5,000)

ORGANISATIONS BY SERVICE

Army 74,000

FORCES BY ROLE
MANOEUVRE
  Armoured
  1 (strategic reserve) armd div (3 armd bde, 1 arty bde, 1 AD bde)
  1 armd bde
  Mechanised
  5 mech bde
  Light
  3 lt inf bde
COMBAT SUPPORT
  3 arty bde
  3 AD bde
  1 MRL bn

EQUIPMENT BY TYPE
ARMOURED FIGHTING VEHICLES
  MBT 572: 390 FV4034 *Challenger 1 (Al Hussein)*; 182 M60 *Phoenix*; (274 FV4030/2 *Khalid* in store)
  LT TK (19 FV101 *Scorpion* in store)
  ASLT 141 B1 *Centauro*
  RECCE 153: 103 FV107 *Scimitar*; 50 FV701 *Ferret*
  IFV 678: 13 AIFV-B-C25; 31 BMP-2; 321 *Ratel-20*; 311 YPR-765 PRI
  APC 800+
    APC (T) 650+: 370 M113A1/A2 Mk1J; 200 M577A2 (CP); some *Temsah*; 77 YPR-765 PRCO (CP); 3 AIFV-B
    PPV 150: 25 *Marauder*; 25 *Matador*; 100 *MaxxPro*
  AUV 35 *Cougar*
ENGINEERING & MAINTENANCE VEHICLES
  ARV 155+: *Al Monjed*; 55 *Chieftain* ARV; *Centurion* Mk2; 20 M47; 32 M88A1; 30 M578; 18 YPR-806
  MW 12 *Aardvark* Mk2
ANTI-TANK/ANTI-INFRASTRUCTURE • MSL
  SP 115: 70 M901; 45 AIFV-B-*Milan*
  MANPATS FGM-148 *Javelin*; TOW/TOW-2A; 9K135 *Kornet* (AT-14 *Spriggan*)
ARTILLERY 1,429+
  SP 556: **105mm** 30 M52; **155mm** 390: 358 M109A1/A2; 20 M44; **203mm** 148 M110A2
  TOWED 100: **105mm** 72: 54 M102; 18 MOBAT; **155mm** 28: 10 M1/M59; 18 M114; **203mm** (4 M115 in store)
  MRL 14+: **227mm** 12 M142 HIMARS; **273mm** 2+ WM-80
  MOR 759: **81mm** 359; **SP 81mm** 50; **107mm** 50 M30; **120mm** 300 Brandt
RADAR • LAND 7 AN/TPQ-36 *Firefinder*/AN/TPQ-37 *Firefinder* (arty, mor)
AIR DEFENCE
  SAM • Point-defence 140+: 92 9K35 *Strela-10* (SA-13 *Gopher*); 48 9K33 *Osa-M* (SA-8 *Gecko*); 9K32M *Strela-2M* (SA-7B *Grail*)‡; 9K36 *Strela-3* (SA-14 *Gremlin*); 240 9K310 *Igla-1* (SA-16 *Gimlet*); 9K38 *Igla* (SA-18 *Grouse*)
  GUNS • SP 356: **20mm** 100 M163 *Vulcan*; **23mm** 40 ZSU-23-4; **35mm** 60 *Cheetah* (*Gepard*); **40mm** 216 M42 (not all op)

Navy ε500
EQUIPMENT BY TYPE
PATROL AND COASTAL COMBATANTS 7
  PB 7: 3 *Al Hussein* (UK Vosper 30m); 4 *Abdullah* (US *Dauntless*)

Air Force 12,000
Flying hours 180 hrs/yr

FORCES BY ROLE
FIGHTER/GROUND ATTACK
  2 sqn with F-16AM/BM *Fighting Falcon*
GROUND ATTACK
  1 sqn with AC-235
ISR
  1 sqn with AT-802U *Air Tractor*; Cessna 208B
TRANSPORT
  1 sqn with C-130E/H *Hercules*
  1 unit with Il-76MF *Candid*
TRAINING
  1 OCU with F-16AM/BM *Fighting Falcon*
  1 OCU with *Hawk* Mk63
  1 sqn with C-101 *Aviojet*
  1 sqn with T-67M *Firefly*
  1 hel sqn with AS350B3; Hughes 500
ATTACK HELICOPTER
  2 sqn with AH-1F *Cobra* (with TOW)
TRANSPORT HELICOPTER
  1 sqn with AS332M *Super Puma*
  1 sqn with Bell 205 (UH-1H *Iroquois*); UH-60A *Black Hawk*
  1 sqn with H135M (Tpt/SAR)
  1 (Royal) flt with S-70A *Black Hawk*; UH-60L/M *Black Hawk*; AW139
AIR DEFENCE
  2 bde with MIM-104C *Patriot* PAC-2; MIM-23B Phase III I-*Hawk*

EQUIPMENT BY TYPE
AIRCRAFT 63 combat capable
  FGA 43: 30 F-16AM *Fighting Falcon*; 13 F-16BM *Fighting Falcon*
  ATK 2 AC-235
  ISR 6 AT-802U *Air Tractor**
  TPT 21: **Heavy** 2 Il-76MF *Candid*; **Medium** 7: 3 C-130E *Hercules*; 4 C-130H *Hercules*; **Light** 6: 5 Cessna 208B; 1 M-28 *Skytruck* (2 C-295M in store being converted into gunships)
  TRG 36: 12 *Hawk* Mk63*; 14 T-67M *Firefly*; 10 C-101 *Aviojet*
HELICOPTERS
  ATK 24+ AH-1F *Cobra*
  MRH 14: 3 AW139; 11 H135M (Tpt/SAR)
  TPT 41: **Medium** 26: 10 AS332M *Super Puma*; 3 S-70A *Black Hawk*; 8 UH-60A *Black Hawk*; 3 UH-60L *Black Hawk*; 2 VH-60M *Black Hawk*; **Light** 10: 4+ Bell 205 (UH-1H *Iroquois*); 6 AS350B3; 8 R-44 *Raven* II
UNMANNED AERIAL VEHICLES
  ISR • Light some *Falco*; S-100 *Camcopter*
AIR DEFENCE • SAM 64:
  Long-range 40 MIM-104C *Patriot* PAC-2
  Medium-range 24 MIM-23B Phase III I-*Hawk*
AIR-LAUNCHED MISSILES
  AAM • IR AIM-9J/N/P *Sidewinder*; R-550 *Magic*; **SARH** AIM-7 *Sparrow*; R-530; **ARH** AIM-120C AMRAAM
  ASM AGM-65D/G *Maverick*; BGM-71 TOW
BOMBS
  Laser-guided GBU-10/12 *Paveway* II

Joint Special Operations Command 14,000
FORCES BY ROLE
SPECIAL FORCES
  1 (Royal Guard) SF bde (1 SF regt, 2 SF bn, 1 CT bn)
  1 ranger bde (1 SF bn, 3 ranger bn)
MANOEUVRE
  Air Manoeuvre
  1 AB bde (2 SF bn, 2 AB bn, 1 AB arty bn, 1 psyops unit)
ISR
  1 sqn with AT-802U *Air Tractor*
TRANSPORT
  1 sqn with An-32B
TRANSPORT HELICOPTER
  1 sqn with MD-530F
  1 sqn with UH-60L *Black Hawk*
EQUIPMENT BY TYPE
AIRCRAFT
  ISR 10 AT-802U *Air Tractor*
  TPT **Light** 3 An-32B
HELICOPTERS
  MRH 6 MD-530F
  TPT • **Medium** 8 UH-60L *Black Hawk*

Paramilitary ε15,000 active

Gendarmerie ε15,000 active
3 regional comd
FORCES BY ROLE
SPECIAL FORCES
  2 SF unit
MANOEUVRE
  Other
  10 sy bn
EQUIPMENT BY TYPE
ARMOURED FIGHTING VEHICLES
  APC • **APC (W)** 25+: AT105 *Saxon* (reported); 25+ EE-11 *Urutu*
  AUV AB2 *Al-Jawad*

Reserve Organisations ε35,000 reservists

Civil Militia 'People's Army' ε35,000 reservists
Men 16–65, women 16–45

DEPLOYMENT

CENTRAL AFRICAN REPUBLIC
UN • MINUSCA 7; 3 obs

CÔTE D'IVOIRE
UN • UNOCI 6; 4 obs

DEMOCRATIC REPUBLIC OF THE CONGO
UN • MONUSCO 9; 15 obs

HAITI
UN • MINUSTAH 3

MALI
UN • MINUSMA 1

SOUTH SUDAN
UN • UNMISS 3

SUDAN
UN • UNAMID 15; 5 obs

UNITED ARAB EMIRATES
Operation Restoring Hope 6 F-16C *Fighting Falcon*

FOREIGN FORCES

Belgium Operation Desert Falcon 106: 6 F-16AM *Fighting Falcon*
France Operation Chammal 6 *Rafale* F3; 1 *Atlantique* 2
Netherlands Operation Inherent Resolve 35
Norway Operation Inherent Resolve 60
United States Central Command: Operation Inherent Resolve 2,000; 1 FGA sqn with 12 F-16C *Fighting Falcon*; 1 AD bty with MIM-104E/F *Patriot* PAC-2/3

Kuwait KWT

Kuwaiti Dinar D		2015	2016	2017
GDP	D	34.3bn	33.5bn	
	US$	114bn	110bn	
per capita	US$	27,756	26,145	
Growth	%	1.1	2.5	
Inflation	%	3.2	3.4	
Def bdgt	D	1.3bn	n.k.	
	US$	4.31bn	n.k.	
US$1=D		0.30	0.30	

Population 2,832,776

Ethnic groups: Nationals 35.5%; other non-Arab Asian countries 37.7%; other Arab countries 17.5%; other or unspecified 9.3%

Age	0–14	15–19	20–24	25–29	30–64	65 plus
Male	13.1%	3.2%	5.1%	7.3%	28.6%	1.1%
Female	12.1%	3.0%	3.9%	4.4%	17.0%	1.3%

Capabilities

The armed forces' primary role is ensuring the territorial integrity of the state, though their small size means they would struggle to defeat a committed attack from a larger neighbouring state. Kuwait's membership of the Gulf Cooperation Council and its relationship with Washington are intended to guarantee its security. In 2015 the National Guard launched a 2015–20 strategic plan that will, it was reported, review its structure and procedures so as to increase readiness. The armed forces and the National Guard exercise regularly, including with US forces deployed in the country. Kuwait continues to revamp core elements of its equipment inventory. A government-to-government memorandum with Italy covering the acquisition of the Eurofighter *Typhoon* was signed in April 2016. Approval by the US State Department for the sale of F/A-18E/F *Super Hornet* combat aircraft was granted in November 2016, which, along with the *Typhoon*, should effectively complete the recapitalisation of the air force's combat-aircraft inventory. An order for Airbus Helicopters H225M *Caracal*s will boost combat search and rescue, medevac and rotary-lift capacity. The air force also took delivery of the last of three KC-130J tanker/transport aircraft it had on order. Kuwait has also contributed to the Saudi-led operation in Yemen, with air-force F/A-18s taking part.

ACTIVE 15,500 (Army 11,000 Navy 2,000 Air 2,500)
Paramilitary 7,100

RESERVE 23,700 (Joint 23,700)
Reserve obligation to age 40; 1 month annual trg

ORGANISATIONS BY SERVICE

Army 11,000
FORCES BY ROLE
SPECIAL FORCES
 1 SF unit (forming)
MANOEUVRE
 Reconnaissance
 1 mech/recce bde
 Armoured
 3 armd bde
 Mechanised
 2 mech inf bde
 Light
 1 cdo bn
 Other
 1 (Amiri) gd bde
COMBAT SUPPORT
 1 arty bde
 1 engr bde
 1 MP bn
COMBAT SERVICE SUPPORT
 1 log gp
 1 fd hospital

Reserve
FORCES BY ROLE
MANOEUVRE
 Mechanised
 1 bde
EQUIPMENT BY TYPE
ARMOURED FIGHTING VEHICLES
 MBT 293: 218 M1A2 *Abrams*; 75 M-84 (75 more in store)
 IFV 465: 76 BMP-2; 153 BMP-3; 236 *Desert Warrior*† (incl variants)
 APC 260
  APC (T) 260: 230 M113A2; 30 M577 (CP)
  APC (W) (40 TH 390 *Fahd* in store)
ENGINEERING & MAINTENANCE VEHICLES
 ARV 24+: 24 M88A1/2; Type-653A; *Warrior*
 MW *Aardvark* Mk2
NBC VEHICLES 11 TPz-1 *Fuchs* NBC
ARTY 211
 SP 155mm 106: 37 M109A3; 18 Mk F3; 51 PLZ-45; (18 AU-F-1 in store)
 MRL 300mm 27 9A52 *Smerch*
 MOR 78: **81mm** 60; **107mm** 6 M30; **120mm** ε12 RT-F1
ANTI-TANK/ANTI-INFRASTRUCTURE
 MSL
  SP 74: 66 HMMWV TOW; 8 M901
  MANPATS TOW-2; M47 *Dragon*
 RCL 84mm ε200 *Carl Gustav*
AIR DEFENCE
 SAM
  Short-range 12 *Aspide*
  Point-defence *Starburst*; FIM-92 *Stinger*
 GUNS • TOWED 35mm 12+ Oerlikon

Navy ε2,000 (incl 500 Coast Guard)
EQUIPMENT BY TYPE
PATROL AND COASTAL COMBATANTS 20
 PCFG 2:
  1 *Al Sanbouk* (GER Lurssen TNC-45) with 2 twin lnchr with MM-40 *Exocet* AShM, 1 76mm gun
  1 *Istiqlal* (GER Lurssen FPB-57) with 2 twin lnchr with MM-40 *Exocet* AShM, 1 76mm gun
 PBF 10 *Al Nokatha* (US Mk V *Pegasus*)
 PBG 8 *Um Almaradim* (FRA P-37 BRL) with 2 twin lnchr with *Sea Skua* AShM, 1 sextuple lnchr (lnchr only)
LOGISTICS AND SUPPORT • AG 1 *Sawahil* with 1 hel landing platform

Air Force 2,500
Flying hours 210 hrs/yr
FORCES BY ROLE
FIGHTER/GROUND ATTACK
 2 sqn with F/A-18C/D *Hornet*
TRANSPORT
 1 sqn with C-17A *Globemaster*; KC-130J *Hercules*; L-100-30
TRAINING
 1 unit with EMB-312 *Tucano**; *Hawk* Mk64*
ATTACK HELICOPTER
 1 sqn with AH-64D *Apache*
 1 atk/trg sqn with SA342 *Gazelle* with HOT
TRANSPORT HELICOPTER
 1 sqn with AS532 *Cougar*; SA330 *Puma*; S-92
EQUIPMENT BY TYPE
AIRCRAFT 66 combat capable
 FGA 39: 31 F/A-18C *Hornet*; 8 F/A-18D *Hornet*
 TKR 3 KC-130J *Hercules*
 TPT 5: **Heavy** 2 C-17A *Globemaster*; **Medium** 3 L-100-30
 TRG 27: 11 *Hawk* Mk64*; 16 EMB-312 *Tucano**
HELICOPTERS
 ATK 16 AH-64D *Apache*
 MRH 13 SA342 *Gazelle* with HOT
 TPT • Medium 13: 3 AS532 *Cougar*; 7 SA330 *Puma*; 3 S-92
AIR-LAUNCHED MISSILES
 AAM • IR AIM-9L *Sidewinder*; R-550 *Magic*; **SARH** AIM-7F *Sparrow*; **ARH** AIM-120C7 AMRAAM
 ASM AGM-65G *Maverick*; AGM-114K *Hellfire*
 AShM AGM-84A *Harpoon*

Air Defence Command
FORCES BY ROLE
AIR DEFENCE
1 SAM bde with (7 SAM bty with MIM-104D *Patriot* PAC-2 GEM)
1 SAM bde with (6 SAM bty with *Skyguard/Aspide*)
EQUIPMENT BY TYPE
AIR DEFENCE • SAM 52:
Long-range 40 MIM-104D *Patriot* PAC-2 GEM
Short-range 12 *Skyguard/Aspide*

Paramilitary ε7,100 active

National Guard ε6,600 active
FORCES BY ROLE
SPECIAL FORCES
1 SF bn
MANOEUVRE
Reconnaissance
1 armd car bn
Other
3 security bn
COMBAT SUPPORT
1 MP bn
EQUIPMENT BY TYPE
ARMOURED FIGHTING VEHICLES
RECCE 20 VBL
APC • APC (W) 97+: 5+ *Desert Chameleon*; 70 *Pandur*; 22 S600 (incl variants)
ENGINEERING & MAINTENANCE VEHICLES
ARV *Pandur*

Coast Guard 500
EQUIPMENT BY TYPE
PATROL AND COASTAL COMBATANTS 32
PBF 12 *Manta*
PB 20: 3 *Al Shaheed*; 4 *Inttisar* (Austal 31.5m); 3 *Kassir* (Austal 22m); 10 *Subahi*
AMPHIBIOUS • LANDING CRAFT • LCU 4: 2 *Al Tahaddy*; 1 *Saffar*; 1 other
LOGISTICS AND SUPPORT • AG 1 *Sawahil*

DEPLOYMENT

SAUDI ARABIA
Operation Restoring Hope 4 F/A-18A *Hornet*

FOREIGN FORCES
Canada *Operation Impact* 2 P-3 *Orion* (CP-140); 1 A310 MRTT (C-150T)
Italy *Operation Inherent Resolve* 4 AMX; 1 KC-767A
Poland *Operation Inherent Resolve* 4 F-16C *Fighting Falcon*
United Kingdom 40 • *Operation Shader* MQ-9A *Reaper*
United States Central Command: 13,000; 1 armd bde; 1 ARNG cbt avn bde; 1 spt bde; 4 AD bty with MIM-104E/F *Patriot* PAC-2/3; 1 (APS) armd bde eqpt set; 1 (APS) inf bde eqpt set

Lebanon LBN

Lebanese Pound LP		2015	2016	2017
GDP	LP	76.6tr	78.1tr	
	US$	50.807	51.815	
per capita	US$	11,157	11,270	
Growth	%	1	1	
Inflation	%	-3.7	-0.7	
Def bdgt	LP	2.25tr	2.62tr	
	US$	1.5bn	1.74bn	
FMA (US)	US$	84m	80m	105m
US$1=LP		1,507.50	1,507.50	

Population 6,237,738

Ethnic and religious groups: Christian 30%; Druze 6%; Armenian 4%, excl ε300,000 Syrians and ε350,000 Palestinian refugees

Age	0–14	15–19	20–24	25–29	30–64	65 plus
Male	12.6%	4.2%	4.3%	4.5%	21.5%	2.9%
Female	12.0%	4.0%	4.2%	4.3%	21.7%	3.7%

Capabilities

The destabilising effects of the complex war in Syria have seen the Lebanese armed forces increasingly tested in their principal roles of internal and border security. Hizbullah plays a key role in Lebanese politics and controls much of southern Lebanon; the group has also been involved in pro-regime military operations in Syria since 2013. In 2016 there was an increasing number of attacks in Lebanon by ISIS and affiliated groups due to Hizbullah's growing involvement in Syria. The Lebanese Army has been stretched by internal-security operations and relies on outdated weapons for these tasks; should Lebanon's fragile internal balance of power shift, it would struggle to overmatch Hizbullah. Modernisation efforts are under way, but ambitions are likely to be reduced to match diminished funding. Saudi Arabia cancelled US$3bn of military aid in early 2016, resulting in the termination of some equipment-procurement plans, including those for French APCs. However, some deliveries of French equipment had already taken place. The US provides an aid package to Lebanon, and in 2016 delivered an instalment of M198 towed howitzers, ammunition and TOW missiles; the US had earlier provided armed Cessna 208B aircraft. The UK has pledged US$28m in military aid for training, as well as secure-communications equipment, light vehicles and body armour. These equipment deliveries are aimed at boosting the armed forces' firepower and counter-insurgency capabilities in order to better combat jihadist militants.

ACTIVE 60,000 (Army 56,600 Navy 1,800 Air 1,600)
Paramilitary 20,000

ORGANISATIONS BY SERVICE

Army 56,600

FORCES BY ROLE
5 regional comd (Beirut, Bekaa Valley, Mount Lebanon, North, South)
SPECIAL FORCES
 1 cdo regt
MANOEUVRE
 Armoured
  2 armd regt
 Mechanised
  11 mech inf bde
 Air Manoeuvre
  1 AB regt
 Amphibious
  1 mne cdo regt
 Other
  1 Presidential Guard bde
  5 intervention regt
  2 border sy regt
COMBAT SUPPORT
 2 arty regt
 1 cbt spt bde (1 engr regt, 1 AT regt, 1 sigs regt)
 1 MP bde
COMBAT SERVICE SUPPORT
 1 log bde
 1 med regt
 1 construction regt
EQUIPMENT BY TYPE
MBT 324: 92 M48A1/A5; 185 T-54; 47 T-55
RECCE 55 AML
IFV 16 AIFV-B-C25
APC 1,360
 APC (T) 1,274 M113A1/A2 (incl variants)
 APC (W) 86 VAB VCT
ENGINEERING & MAINTENANCE VEHICLES
 ARV M113 ARV; T-54/55 ARV reported
 VLB MTU-72 reported
 MW Bozena
ARTILLERY 571
 SP 155mm 12 M109
 TOWED 313: **105mm** 13 M101A1; **122mm** 35: 9 D-30; 26 M-30; **130mm** 15 M-46; **155mm** 250: 18 M114A1; 218 M198; 14 Model-50
 MRL 122mm 11 BM-21
 MOR 275: **81mm** 134; **82mm** 112; **120mm** 29 Brandt
ANTI-TANK/ANTI-INFRASTRUCTURE
 MSL • MANPATS Milan; TOW
 RCL 106mm 113 M40A1
UNMANNED AERIAL VEHICLES
 ISR • Medium 8 Mohajer 4
AIR DEFENCE
 SAM • Point-defence 9K32 Strela-2/2M (SA-7A Grail/SA-7B Grail)‡
 GUNS • TOWED 77: **20mm** 20; **23mm** 57 ZU-23-2

Navy 1,800
EQUIPMENT BY TYPE
PATROL AND COASTAL COMBATANTS 13
 PCC 1 Trablous
 PB 11: 1 Aamchit (ex-GER Bremen); 1 Al Kalamoun (ex-FRA Avel Gwarlarn); 7 Tripoli (ex-UK Attacker/Tracker Mk 2); 1 Naquora (ex-GER Bremen); 1 Tabarja (ex-GER Bergen)
 PBF 1
AMPHIBIOUS • LANDING CRAFT • LCT 2 Sour (ex-FRA Edic – capacity 8 APC; 96 troops)

Air Force 1,600
4 air bases
FORCES BY ROLE
FIGHTER/GROUND ATTACK
 1 sqn with Hunter Mk6/Mk9/T66†; Cessna AC-208 Combat Caravan*
ATTACK HELICOPTER
 1 sqn with SA342L Gazelle
TRANSPORT HELICOPTER
 4 sqn with Bell 205 (UH-1H)
 1 sqn with SA330/IAR330SM Puma
 1 trg sqn with R-44 Raven II
EQUIPMENT BY TYPE
AIRCRAFT 9 combat capable
 FGA 4: 3 Hunter Mk6/Mk9†; 1 Hunter T66†
 ISR 3 Cessna AC-208 Combat Caravan*
 TRG 3 Bulldog
HELICOPTERS
 MRH 9: 1 AW139; 8 SA342L Gazelle (5 SA342L Gazelle; 5 SA316 Alouette III; 1 SA318 Alouette II all non-operational)
 TPT 35: **Medium** 13: 3 S-61N (fire fighting); 10 SA330/IAR330 Puma; **Light** 22: 18 Bell 205 (UH-1H Huey) 4 R-44 Raven II (basic trg); (11 Bell 205; 7 Bell 212 all non-operational)

Paramilitary ε20,000 active

Internal Security Force ε20,000
Ministry of Interior
FORCES BY ROLE
Other Combat Forces
 1 (police) judicial unit
 1 regional sy coy
 1 (Beirut Gendarmerie) sy coy
EQUIPMENT BY TYPE
ARMOURED FIGHTING VEHICLES
 APC • APC (W) 60 V-200 Chaimite

Customs
EQUIPMENT BY TYPE
PATROL AND COASTAL COMBATANTS 7
 PB 7: 5 Aztec; 2 Tracker

FOREIGN FORCES
Unless specified, figures refer to UNTSO and represent total numbers for the mission
Argentina 3 obs
Armenia UNIFIL 33
Australia 13 obs
Austria 4 obs • UNIFIL 183: 1 log coy
Bangladesh UNIFIL 276: 1 FFG; 1 FSG
Belarus UNIFIL 5

Belgium 2 obs • UNIFIL 1
Bhutan 1 obs
Brazil UNIFIL 279: 1 FFGHM
Brunei UNIFIL 29
Cambodia UNIFIL 185: 1 engr coy
Canada 4 obs (*Operation Jade*)
Chile 2 obs
China, People's Republic of 2 obs • UNIFIL 412: 1 engr coy
Croatia UNIFIL 1
Cyprus UNIFIL 2
Denmark 10 obs
El Salvador UNIFIL 52: 1 inf pl
Estonia 6 obs • UNIFIL 50
Fiji 2 obs • UNIFIL 143; 1 inf coy
Finland 17 obs • UNIFIL 308; elm 1 mech inf bn
France 1 obs • UNIFIL 779: 1 mech BG; VBL; VBCI; VAB; *Mistral*
Germany UNIFIL 126: 1 FFGM
Ghana UNIFIL 870: 1 mech inf bn
Greece UNIFIL 46: 1 PCFG
Guatemala UNIFIL 2
Hungary UNIFIL 4
India 1 obs • UNIFIL 900: 1 inf bn; 1 fd hospital
Indonesia UNIFIL 1,296: 1 mech inf bn; 1 log bn(-); 1 MP coy; 1 FSGHM
Ireland 11 obs • UNIFIL 218: elm 1 mech inf bn
Italy UNIFIL 1,112: 1 cav bde HQ; 1 cav BG; 1 engr coy; 1 sigs coy; 1 hel bn
Kenya UNIFIL 1
Korea, Republic of UNIFIL 333: 1 mech inf bn
Macedonia (FYROM) UNIFIL 1
Malaysia UNIFIL 818: 1 mech inf bn; 1 mech inf coy
Mexico UNIFIL 2
Nepal 3 obs • UNIFIL 867: 1 inf bn
Netherlands 11 obs
New Zealand 8 obs
Nigeria UNIFIL 1
Norway 13 obs
Qatar UNIFIL 3
Russia 5 obs
Serbia 1 obs • UNIFIL 177; 1 mech inf coy
Sierra Leone UNIFIL 3
Slovakia 2 obs
Slovenia 3 obs • UNIFIL 15
Spain UNIFIL 609: 1 armd inf bde HQ; 1 mech inf BG
Sri Lanka UNIFIL 151: 1 inf coy
Sweden 7 obs
Switzerland 15 obs
Tanzania UNIFIL 159: 2 MP coy
Turkey UNIFIL 50: 1 PCFG
United States 2 obs

Libya LBY

Libyan Dinar D		2015	2016	2017
GDP	D	54.8bn	55.1bn	
	US$	39.7bn	39.4bn	
per capita	US$	6,277	6,169	
Growth	%	-6.4	-3.3	
Inflation	%	14.1	14.2	
Def exp	D	n.k.	n.k.	
	US$	n.k.	n.k.	
US$1=D			1.38	1.40

Population	6,541,948					
Age	0–14	15–19	20–24	25–29	30–64	65 plus
Male	13.4%	4.5%	4.5%	4.9%	22.4%	2.1%
Female	12.8%	4.2%	4.2%	4.4%	20.5%	2.1%

Capabilities

Libya remains in a state of civil war and political uncertainty, with the new UN-backed Government of National Accord (GNA) in Tripoli yet to unite the main political and military factions in the country. Forces loyal to the GNA have emerged, including elements of the former Libya Dawn militia alliance, and are contributing to renewed anti-ISIS operations in the central Sirte region. However, the Libyan National Army (LNA), under the command of Khalifa Haftar, remains aligned to the Tobruk-based House of Representatives (HoR). The HoR, although now the recognised legislative body of the GNA, does not support the new government nor plans for integration. Although reportedly in receipt of foreign assistance, these two principal armed forces remain dependent on the former arms stockpiles of the Gadhafi regime, often improvising to enhance capability. While both functioning air forces continue to reactivate aircraft, their operations remain hampered by poor serviceability and high attrition levels. Libya's instability has contributed to the Mediterranean refugee and migrant crisis, with the enduring EU naval mission (EUNAVFOR–MED/*Operation Sophia*) expanding to include the training of Libyan Navy and coastguard personnel, as well as enforcement of the UN arms embargo. This instability has also sustained the presence of ISIS and other Islamist extremist groups, despite the efforts of the opposing internal and intervening external military forces – the US element of which conducted an increasing number of airstrikes in 2016.

Forces loyal to the Government of National Accord (Tripoli-based)

ACTIVE n.k.

ORGANISATIONS BY SERVICE

Ground Forces n.k.
EQUIPMENT BY TYPE
ARMOURED FIGHTING VEHICLES
 MBT T-55; T-72

IFV BMP-2
APC • **APC (T)** 4K-7FA *Steyr*
AUV Nimr *Ajban*
ENGINEERING & MAINTENANCE VEHICLES
 ARV *Centurion* 105 AVRE
ANTI-TANK/ANTI-INFRASTRUCTURE
 MSL • **SP** 9P157-2 *Khryzantema*-S (AT-15 *Springer*)
ARTILLERY
 SP 155mm *Palmaria*
 TOWED 122mm D-30

Navy n.k.

A number of intact naval vessels remain in Tripoli, although serviceability is questionable

EQUIPMENT BY TYPE
PRINCIPAL SURFACE COMBATANTS 1
FRIGATES • FFGM 1 *Al Hani* (FSU *Koni*) (in Italy for refit since 2013) with 2 twin lnchr with P-15 *Termit*-M (SS-N-2C *Styx*) AShM, 1 twin lnchr with 9K33 *Osa*-M (SA-N-4 *Gecko*) SAM, 2 twin 406mm ASTT with USET-95 Type-40 LWT, 1 RBU 6000 *Smerch* 2 A/S mor, 2 twin 76mm gun† **PATROL AND COASTAL COMBATANTS** 4+
PBFG 1 *Sharaba* (FRA *Combattante* II) with 4 single lnchr with *Otomat* Mk2 AShM, 1 76mm gun†
PB 1 *Hamelin*; 2+ PV30
AMPHIBIOUS
 LANDING SHIPS • LST 1 *Ibn Harissa* with 3 twin 40mm DARDO CIWS† (capacity 1 hel; 11 MBT; 240 troops)
LOGISTICS AND SUPPORT 2
 AFD 1
 ARS 1 *Al Munjed* (YUG *Spasilac*)†

Air Force n.k.

EQUIPMENT BY TYPE
AIRCRAFT
 FGA 2 MiG-23ML
 ATK 1 J-21 *Jastreb*†
 TRG 11+: 3 G-2 *Galeb**; up to 8 L-39ZO *Albatros**; some SF-260
HELICOPTERS
 ATK Mi-24 *Hind*
 TPT • **Medium** Mi-17 *Hip*
AIR-LAUNCHED MISSILES • AAM • IR R-3 (AA-2 *Atoll*)‡; R-60 (AA-8 *Aphid*); R-24 (AA-7 *Apex*)

Paramilitary n.k.

Coast Guard n.k.

EQUIPMENT BY TYPE
PATROL AND COASTAL COMBATANTS
 PB 1 *Burdi* (Damen Stan 1605); 1 *Ikrimah* (FRA RPB 20)
 PC Damen Stan 2909 (YTB armed with with 14.5mm ZSU-2 AD GUNS and 122mm MRL)

TERRITORY WHERE THE RECOGNISED AUTHORITY DOES NOT EXERCISE EFFECTIVE CONTROL

Data here represents the de facto situation. This does not imply international recognition

ACTIVE n.k.

ORGANISATIONS BY SERVICE

Libya National Army n.k.

EQUIPMENT BY TYPE
ARMOURED FIGHTING VEHICLES
 MBT T-55; T-72
 RECCE BRDM-2; EE-9 *Cascavel*
 IFV BMP-1; *Ratel*-20
 APC
  APC (T) M113
  APC (W) BTR-60PB; *Puma*
  PPV Streit *Typhoon*
 AUV *Panthera* T6
ANTI-TANK/ANTI-INFRASTRUCTURE
 MSL
  SP 10 9P157-2 *Khryzantema*-S (status unknown)
  MANPATS 9K11 *Malyutka* (AT-3 *Sagger*); 9K111 *Fagot* (AT-4 *Spigot*); 9K111-1 *Konkurs* (AT-5 *Spandrel*); *Milan*
 RCL some: **106mm** M40A1; **84mm** *Carl Gustav*
ARTILLERY
 TOWED 122mm D-30
 MRL 107mm Type-63; **122mm** BM-21 *Grad*
 MOR M106
AIR DEFENCE
 SAM • **Point-defence** 9K338 *Igla*-S (SA-24 *Grinch*)
 GUNS • **SP 14.5mm** ZPU-2 (on tch); **23mm** ZSU-23-4 *Shilka*; ZU-23-2 (on tch)

Navy n.k.

EQUIPMENT BY TYPE
PATROL AND COASTAL COMBATANTS 7+
 PB: 7+: 1 *Burdi* (Damen Stan 1605) with 1 23mm gun; 1 *Burdi* (Damen Stan 1605) with 1 76mm gun; 1 *Burdi* (Damen Stan 1605); 2 *Ikrimah* (FRA RPB20); 1 *Hamelin*; 1+ PV30
LOGISTICS AND SUPPORT 1
 AFD 1

Air Force n.k.

EQUIPMENT BY TYPE
AIRCRAFT
 FTR MiG-23 *Flogger*
 FGA 6+: 4+ MiG-21bis/MF *Fishbed*; 1 *Mirage* F-1ED; 1 Su-22UM-3K
 TRG 1+ MiG-21UM
HELICOPTERS
 ATK Mi-24/35 *Hind*
 TPT **Medium** Mi-8/Mi-17 *Hip*
AIR-LAUNCHED MISSILES • AAM • IR R-3 (AA-2 *Atoll*)‡; R-60 (AA-8 *Aphid*)

FOREIGN FORCES

Italy UNSMIL 300; 1 inf coy; 1 log unit; 1 fd hospital
United Arab Emirates 6 *Archangel*; 2 UH-60M; 2 *Gongji*-1 UAV

Mauritania MRT

Mauritanian Ouguiya OM		2015	2016	2017
GDP	OM	1.57tr	1.64tr	
	US$	4.86bn	4.72bn	
per capita	US$	1,312	1,244	
Growth	%	1.2	3.2	
Inflation	%	0.5	1.3	
Def bdgt	OM	44.29bn	48.37bn	
	US$	137m	139m	
US$1=OM		323.90	347.36	

Population 3,677,293

Age	0–14	15–19	20–24	25–29	30–64	65 plus
Male	19.5%	5.2%	4.5%	3.9%	13.5%	1.6%
Female	19.3%	5.3%	4.8%	4.3%	16.0%	2.1%

Capabilities

The armed forces' readiness levels appear to be low and they have little combat experience. Patrol craft donated by the EU and purchased from China have enhanced the navy's littoral capabilities but limited airlift hinders mobility. The armed forces' ISR capability was boosted in late 2014 by the delivery of a sensor-equipped aircraft. Mauritania's limited capability to secure borders, territory and resources, combined with the perceived regional threat from jihadist groups, has encouraged the US to provide training through the special-operations *Flintlock* programme. Exercise *Flintlock 2016* was co-hosted in February 2016 by Mauritania, and military personnel attended a US-led intelligence-training session in Morocco in March. In response to Mauritania's request for NATO assistance, a new 'Partnership for Peace Trust Fund' began in early 2016. Led by the US, this activity is intended to enhance army efficiency through improved physical security and stockpile management; destruction and demilitarisation of old ammunition and equipment; and broader defence-reform initiatives. Joint Force Command Naples and NATO Special Forces HQ also provide support, guidance and counter-insurgency training. France provides training, funding and support to strengthen Mauritania's internal-security capability and has a forward-operating base in Atar as part of *Operation Barkhane*, in which Mauritania is a partner nation.

ACTIVE 15,850 (Army 15,000 Navy 600 Air 250)
Paramilitary 5,000
Conscript liability 24 months authorised

ORGANISATIONS BY SERVICE

Army 15,000
FORCES BY ROLE
6 mil regions
MANOEUVRE
   Reconnaissance
   1 armd recce sqn
   Armoured
   1 armd bn
   Light
   7 mot inf bn
   8 (garrison) inf bn
   Air Manoeuvre
   1 cdo/para bn
   Other
   2 (camel corps) bn
   1 gd bn
COMBAT SUPPORT
3 arty bn
4 ADA bty
1 engr coy
EQUIPMENT BY TYPE
ARMOURED FIGHTING VEHICLES
   MBT 35 T-54/T-55
   RECCE 70: 20 AML-60; 40 AML-90; 10 *Saladin*
   APC • APC (W) 25: 5 FV603 *Saracen*; ε20 Panhard M3
ENGINEERING & MAINTENANCE VEHICLES
   ARV T-54/55 ARV reported
ANTI-TANK/ANTI-INFRASTRUCTURE
   MSL • MANPATS *Milan*
   RCL 114: **75mm** ε24 M20; **106mm** ε90 M40A1
ARTILLERY 180
   TOWED 80: **105mm** 36 HM-2/M101A1; **122mm** 44: 20 D-30; 24 D-74
   MRL 10: **107mm** 4 Type-63; **122mm** 6 Type-81
   MOR 90: **81mm** 60; **120mm** 30 Brandt
AIR DEFENCE
   SAM • Point-defence ε4 SA-9 *Gaskin* (reported); 9K32 *Strela*-2 (SA-7 *Grail*)‡
   GUNS • TOWED 82: **14.5mm** 28: 16 ZPU-2; 12 ZPU-4; **23mm** 20 ZU-23-2; **37mm** 10 M-1939; **57mm** 12 S-60; **100mm** 12 KS-19

Navy ε600
EQUIPMENT BY TYPE
PATROL AND COASTAL COMBATANTS 19
   PCO 1 *Voum-Legleita*
   PCC 7: 1 *Abourbekr Ben Amer* (FRA OPV 54); 1 *Arguin*; 2 *Conejera*; 1 *Limam El Hidran* (PRC *Huangpu*); 2 *Timbédra* (PRC *Huangpu* Mod)
   PB 11: 1 *El Nasr*† (FRA *Patra*); 4 *Mandovi*; 2 Rodman 55M; 2 *Saeta*-12; 2 *Megsem Bakkar* (FRA RPB20 – for SAR duties)

Air Force 250
EQUIPMENT BY TYPE
AIRCRAFT 4 combat capable
   ISR 2 Cessna 208B *Grand Caravan*
   TPT 8: **Light** 7: 2 BN-2 *Defender*; 1 C-212; 2 PA-31T *Cheyenne* II; 2 Y-12(II); **PAX** 1 BT-67 (with sensor turret)
   TRG 11: 3 EMB-312 *Tucano*; 4 EMB-314 *Super Tucano**; 4 SF-260E
HELICOPTERS • MRH 3: 1 SA313B *Alouette* II; 2 Z-9

Paramilitary ε5,000 active

Gendarmerie ε3,000
Ministry of Interior

FORCES BY ROLE
MANOEUVRE
  Other
    6 regional sy coy
EQUIPMENT BY TYPE
ARMOURED FIGHTING VEHICLES
  APC • APC (W) 12 *Cobra*

National Guard 2,000
Ministry of Interior

Customs
EQUIPMENT BY TYPE
PATROL AND COASTAL COMBATANTS • PB 2: 1 *Dah Ould Bah* (FRA *Amgram* 14); 1 *Yaboub Ould Rajel* (FRA RPB18)

DEPLOYMENT

CENTRAL AFRICAN REPUBLIC
UN • MINUSCA 746; 5 obs; 1 inf bn

MALI
UN • MINUSMA 4

Morocco MOR

Moroccan Dirham D		2015	2016	2017
GDP	D	982bn	1.02tr	
	US$	101bn	105bn	
per capita	US$	3,003	3,101	
Growth	%	4.5	1.8	
Inflation	%	1.5	1.3	
Def bdgt	D	31.9bn	32.6bn	
	US$	3.27bn	3.37bn	
FMA (US)	US$	5m	5m	5m
US$1=D		9.76	9.70	
Population	33,655,786			

Age	0–14	15–19	20–24	25–29	30–64	65 plus
Male	13.3%	4.3%	4.2%	4.2%	20.1%	3.0%
Female	12.8%	4.3%	4.3%	4.4%	21.4%	3.6%

Capabilities

The armed forces are well trained and relatively mobile. They have gained extensive experience in counter-insurgency operations in Western Sahara, which have given them expertise in desert warfare and combined air–land operations. The defence budget has increased in order to modernise and re-equip the services, partly in response to regional security contingencies; orders for US Army surplus M1A1 *Abrams* MBTs, refurbished to SA standard, were placed in 2015 and deliveries began in 2016. Air-force equipment is ageing overall, bar the delivery of 24 F-16s in 2012. Significant investment in the navy is now taking place. Exercise *African Lion 2016* took place in April, with Moroccan troops training with US, European and select regional forces. Moroccan troops also participate in a biannual parachute exercise, *Jebel Sahara*, with the UK armed forces. While Moroccan forces have taken part in peacekeeping operations, they have little experience in state-on-state warfare, although in 2015 Morocco took part in the Saudi-led coalition operation in Yemen, deploying its F-16s in combat. In December 2015, it was reported that Saudi Arabia had pledged US$22bn of financing over 2015–19 to develop Morocco's defence industry, as well as to provide training and exercises. Western defence companies such as Airbus and Thales have a presence in the country. Meanwhile, in early 2016 the Moroccan armed forces were incorporated into NATO's Interoperability Platform, in order to strengthen Morocco's defence and security sectors and to bring its forces up to NATO standard, enabling them to participate in joint regional counter-terrorist operations.

ACTIVE 195,800 (Army 175,000 Navy 7,800 Air 13,000) **Paramilitary 50,000**
Conscript liability 18 months authorised; most enlisted personnel are volunteers

RESERVE 150,000 (Army 150,000)
Reserve obligation to age 50

ORGANISATIONS BY SERVICE

Army ε75,000; 100,000 conscript (total 175,000)
FORCES BY ROLE
2 comd (Northern Zone, Southern Zone)
MANOEUVRE
  Armoured
    1 armd bde
    11 armd bn
  Mechanised
    3 mech inf bde
  Mechanised/Light
    8 mech/mot inf regt (2–3 bn)
  Light
    1 lt sy bde
    3 (camel corps) mot inf bn
    35 lt inf bn
    4 cdo unit
  Air Manoeuvre
    2 para bde
    2 AB bn
  Mountain
    1 mtn inf bn
COMBAT SUPPORT
  11 arty bn
  7 engr bn
AIR DEFENCE
  1 AD bn

Royal Guard 1,500
FORCES BY ROLE
MANOEUVRE
  Other
    1 gd bn
    1 cav sqn

EQUIPMENT BY TYPE
ARMOURED FIGHTING VEHICLES
  MBT 402: 22 M1A1SA *Abrams*; 220 M60A1 *Patton*; 120 M60A3 *Patton*; 40 T-72; (ε200 M48A5 *Patton* in store)
  LT TK 116: 5 AMX-13; 111 SK-105 *Kuerassier*
  ASLT 80 AMX-10RC
  RECCE 284: 38 AML-60-7; 190 AML-90; 40 EBR-75; 16 *Eland*
  IFV 70: 10 AMX-10P; 30 *Ratel* Mk3-20; 30 *Ratel* Mk3-90
  APC 851
    APC (T) 486: 400 M113A1/A2; 86 M577A2 (CP)
    APC (W) 365: 45 VAB VCI; 320 VAB VTT
ENGINEERING & MAINTENANCE VEHICLES
  ARV 48+: 10 *Greif*; 18 M88A1; M578; 20 VAB-ECH
ANTI-TANK/ANTI-INFRASTRUCTURE
  MSL
    SP 80 M901
    MANPATS 9K11 *Malyutka* (AT-3 *Sagger*); M47 *Dragon*; *Milan*; TOW
  RCL 106mm 350 M40A1
  RL 89mm 200 M20
  GUNS • **SP** 36: **90mm** 28 M56; **100mm** 8 SU-100
ARTILLERY 2,141
  SP 282: **105mm** 5 AMX Mk 61; **155mm** 217: 84 M109A1/A1B; 43 M109A2; 90 Mk F3; **203mm** 60 M110
  TOWED 118: **105mm** 50: 30 L118 *Light Gun*; 20 M101; **130mm** 18 M-46; **155mm** 50: 30 FH-70; 20 M114
  MRL 122mm 35 BM-21 *Grad*
  MOR 1,706: **81mm** 1,100 Expal model LN; **SP 107mm** 32–36 M106A2; **120mm** 550 Brandt; **SP 120mm** 20 (VAB APC)
RADAR • **LAND** RASIT (veh, arty)
UNMANNED AERIAL VEHICLES
  ISR • **Medium** R4E-50 *Skyeye*
AIR DEFENCE
  SAM
    SP 49: 12 2K22M *Tunguska*-M (SA-19 *Grison*) SPAAGM; 37 M48 *Chaparral*
    MANPAD 9K32 *Strela*-2 (SA-7 *Grail*)‡
  GUNS 407
    SP 20mm 60 M163 *Vulcan*
    TOWED 347: **14.5mm** 200: 150–180 ZPU-2; 20 ZPU-4; **20mm** 40 M167 *Vulcan*; **23mm** 75–90 ZU-23-2; **100mm** 17 KS-19

Navy 7,800 (incl 1,500 Marines)

EQUIPMENT BY TYPE
PRINCIPAL SURFACE COMBATANTS 6
  DESTROYERS 1
    DDGHM 1 *Mohammed VI*-class (FRA FREMM) with 2 quad lnchr with MM40 *Exocet* Block III AShM, 2 octuple A43 VLS with *Aster* 15 SAM, 2 triple B515 324mm ASTT with MU90 LWT, 1 76mm gun (capacity 1 AS565SA *Panther*)
  FRIGATES 5
    FFGHM 3 *Tarik ben Ziyad* (NLD SIGMA 9813/10513) with 4 single lnchr with MM-40 *Exocet* Block II/III AShM, 2 sextuple lnchr with *Mica* SAM, 2 triple 324mm ASTT with MU90 LWT, 1 76mm gun (capacity 1 AS565SA *Panther*)
    FFGH 2 *Mohammed V* (FRA *Floreal*) with 2 single lnchr with MM-38 *Exocet* AShM, 1 76mm gun (can be fitted with *Simbad* SAM) (capacity 1 AS565SA *Panther*)
PATROL AND COASTAL COMBATANTS 50
  CORVETTES • **FSGM** 1
    1 *Lt Col Errhamani* (ESP *Descubierto*) with 2 twin lnchr with MM-38 *Exocet* AShM, 1 octuple *Albatros* lnchr with *Aspide* SAM, 2 triple 324mm ASTT with Mk46 LWT, 1 76mm gun
  PSO 1 *Bin an Zaran* (OPV 70) with 1 76mm gun
  PCG 4 *Cdt El Khattabi* (ESP *Lazaga* 58m) with 4 single lnchr with MM-38 *Exocet* AShM, 1 76mm gun
  PCO 5 *Rais Bargach* (under control of fisheries dept)
  PCC 12:
    4 *El Hahiq* (DNK *Osprey* 55, incl 2 with customs)
    6 *LV Rabhi* (ESP 58m B-200D)
    2 *Okba* (FRA PR-72) each with 1 76mm gun
  PB 27: 6 *El Wacil* (FRA P-32); 10 VCSM (RPB 20); 10 Rodman 101; 1 other (UK *Bird*)
AMPHIBIOUS 5
  LANDING SHIPS 4:
    LSM 3 *Ben Aicha* (FRA *Champlain* BATRAL) (capacity 7 tanks; 140 troops)
    LST 1 *Sidi Mohammed Ben Abdallah* (US *Newport*) (capacity 3 LCVP; 400 troops)
  LANDING CRAFT 2:
    LCM 1 CTM (FRA CTM-5)
    LCT 1 *Sidi Ifni*
LOGISTICS AND SUPPORT 8
  AG 1 Damen 3011
  AGOR 1 *Abou Barakat Albarbari*† (ex-US *Robert D. Conrad*)
  AGS 1 Stan 1504
  AK 2
  AX 1 *Essaouira*
  AXS 2

Marines 1,500

FORCES BY ROLE
MANOEUVRE
  Amphibious
  2 naval inf bn

Naval Aviation

EQUIPMENT BY TYPE
HELICOPTERS • **ASW/ASUW** 3 AS565SA *Panther*

Air Force 13,000

Flying hours 100 hrs/yr on *Mirage* F-1/F-5E/F *Tiger* II/F-16C/D *Fighting Falcon*

FORCES BY ROLE
FIGHTER/GROUND ATTACK
  2 sqn with F-5E/F-5F *Tiger* II
  3 sqn with F-16C/D *Fighting Falcon*
  1 sqn with *Mirage* F-1C (F-1CH)
  1 sqn with *Mirage* F-1E (F-1EH)
ELECTRONIC WARFARE
  1 sqn with EC-130H *Hercules*; *Falcon* 20 (ELINT)
MARITIME PATROL
  1 flt with Do-28

TANKER/TRANSPORT
1 sqn with C-130/KC-130H *Hercules*
TRANSPORT
1 sqn with CN-235
1 VIP sqn with B-737BBJ; Beech 200/300 *King Air*; *Falcon* 50; Gulfstream II/III/V-SP
TRAINING
1 sqn with *Alpha Jet**
1 sqn T-6C
ATTACK HELICOPTER
1 sqn with SA342L *Gazelle* (some with HOT)
TRANSPORT HELICOPTER
1 sqn with Bell 205A (AB-205A); Bell 206 *Jet Ranger* (AB-206); Bell 212 (AB-212)
1 sqn with CH-47D *Chinook*
1 sqn with SA330 *Puma*
EQUIPMENT BY TYPE
AIRCRAFT 90 combat capable
  FTR 22: 19 F-5E *Tiger* II; 3 F-5F *Tiger* II
  FGA 49: 15 F-16C *Fighting Falcon*; 8 F-16D *Fighting Falcon*; 15 *Mirage* F-1C (F-1CH); 11 *Mirage* F-1E (F-1EH)
  ELINT 1 EC-130H *Hercules*
  TKR/TPT 2 KC-130H *Hercules*
  TPT 45: **Medium** 17: 4 C-27J *Spartan*; 13 C-130H *Hercules*; **Light** 19: 4 Beech 100 *King Air*; 2 Beech 200 *King Air*; 1 Beech 200C *King Air*; 2 Beech 300 *King Air*; 3 Beech 350 *King Air*; 5 CN-235; 2 Do-28; **PAX** 9: 1 B-737BBJ; 2 *Falcon* 20; 2 *Falcon* 20 (ELINT); 1 *Falcon* 50 (VIP); 1 Gulfstream II (VIP); 1 Gulfstream III; 1 Gulfstream V-SP
  TRG 80: 12 AS-202 *Bravo*; 19 *Alpha Jet**; 2 CAP-10; 24 T-6C *Texan*; 9 T-34C *Turbo Mentor*; 14 T-37B *Tweet*
  FF 4 CL-415
HELICOPTERS
  MRH 19 SA342L *Gazelle* (7 with HOT, 12 with cannon)
  TPT 73: **Heavy** 10 CH-47D *Chinook*; **Medium** 24 SA330 *Puma*; **Light** 39: 25 Bell 205A (AB-205A); 11 Bell 206 *Jet Ranger* (AB-206); 3 Bell 212 (AB-212)
AIR-LAUNCHED MISSILES
  AAM • **IR** AIM-9J *Sidewinder*; R-550 *Magic*; **IIR** AIM-9X *Sidewinder* II; **SARH** R-530; **ARH** AIM-120C7 AMRAAM
  ASM AASM; AGM-62B *Walleye* (for F-5E); HOT
BOMBS • **Laser-guided** *Paveway* II

Paramilitary 50,000 active

Gendarmerie Royale 20,000
FORCES BY ROLE
MANOEUVRE
  Air Manoeuvre
  1 para sqn
  Other
  1 paramilitary bde
  4 (mobile) paramilitary gp
  1 coast guard unit
TRANSPORT HELICOPTER
  1 sqn
EQUIPMENT BY TYPE
PATROL AND COASTAL COMBATANTS • **PB** 15 Arcor 53
AIRCRAFT • **TRG** 2 R-235 *Guerrier*

HELICOPTERS
  MRH 14: 3 SA315B *Lama*; 2 SA316 *Alouette* III; 3 SA318 *Alouette* II; 6 SA342K *Gazelle*
  TPT 8: **Medium** 6 SA330 *Puma*; **Light** 2 SA360 *Dauphin*

Force Auxiliaire 30,000 (incl 5,000 Mobile Intervention Corps)

Customs/Coast Guard
EQUIPMENT BY TYPE
PATROL AND COASTAL COMBATANTS • **PB** 36: 4 *Erraid*; 18 *Arcor* 46; 14 (other SAR craft)

DEPLOYMENT

CENTRAL AFRICAN REPUBLIC
UN • MINUSCA 760; 2 obs; 1 inf bn

CÔTE D'IVOIRE
UN • UNOCI 4; 2 obs

DEMOCRATIC REPUBLIC OF THE CONGO
UN • MONUSCO 836; 3 obs; 1 mech inf bn; 1 fd hospital

UNITED ARAB EMIRATES
Operation Restoring Hope 5 F-16C *Fighting Falcon*

Oman OMN

Omani Rial R		2015	2016	2017
GDP	R	24.7bn	22.9bn	
	US$	64.1bn	59.7bn	
per capita	US$	16,699	15,080	
Growth	%	3.3	1.8	
Inflation	%	0.1	1.1	
Def bdgt	R	3.8bn	ε3.5bn	
	US$	9.88bn	ε9.10bn	
FMA (US)	US$	4m	2m	0m
US$1=R		0.38	0.38	

Population 3,355,262
Expatriates: 27%

Age	0–14	15–19	20–24	25–29	30–64	65 plus
Male	15.4%	4.7%	5.3%	6.0%	21.2%	1.7%
Female	14.7%	4.4%	4.7%	4.7%	15.4%	1.7%

Capabilities

Oman supports small but well-trained and -equipped armed forces whose principal task is ensuring the territorial integrity of the state. Membership of the GCC and ties with the UK and the US are also intended to act as security guarantors. The forces are in the process of recapitalising core inventory elements with air- and naval-systems purchases. The air force has taken delivery of the last of a batch of F-16 Block 40s that have replaced the *Jaguar*, while it also has 12 Eurofighter *Typhoon* multi-role combat aircraft on order. Recapitalisation of naval platforms is under way. Four patrol vessels and two high-speed support vessels were delivered in 2016. Oman is making a significant investment in infrastructure, such as the port of Duqm, which in 2014 saw a US submarine and aircraft-carrier dock; the US reportedly sees Duqm as a potential logistics hub and maintenance facility. Although a GCC member, Oman has not contributed any forces to the Saudi-led military intervention in Yemen.

ACTIVE 42,600 (Army 25,000 Navy 4,200 Air 5,000 Foreign Forces 2,000 Royal Household 6,400) Paramilitary 4,400

ORGANISATIONS BY SERVICE

Army 25,000
FORCES BY ROLE
(Regt are bn size)
MANOEUVRE
  Armoured
  1 armd bde (2 armd regt, 1 recce regt)
  Light
  1 inf bde (5 inf regt, 1 arty regt, 1 fd engr regt, 1 engr regt, 1 sigs regt)
  1 inf bde (3 inf regt, 2 arty regt)
  1 indep inf coy (Musandam Security Force)
  Air Manoeuvre
  1 AB regt
COMBAT SERVICE SUPPORT
  1 tpt regt
AIR DEFENCE
  1 ADA regt (2 ADA bty)
EQUIPMENT BY TYPE
ARMOURED FIGHTING VEHICLES
  MBT 117: 38 *Challenger* 2; 6 M60A1 *Patton*; 73 M60A3 *Patton*
  LT TK 37 FV101 *Scorpion* **RECCE** 137: 13 FV105 *Sultan* (CP); 124 VBL
  APC 200
    APC (T) 10 FV4333 *Stormer*
    APC (W) 190: 175 *Piranha* (incl variants); 15 AT-105 *Saxon*
  AUV 6 FV103 *Spartan*
ENGINEERING & MAINTENANCE VEHICLES
  ARV 11: 4 *Challenger*; 2 M88A1; 2 *Piranha*; 3 *Samson*
ARTILLERY 233
  SP 155mm 24 G-6
  TOWED 108: **105mm** 42 L118 Light Gun; **122mm** 30 D-30; **130mm** 24: 12 M-46; 12 Type-59-I; **155mm** 12 FH-70
  MOR 101: **81mm** 69; **107mm** 20 M30; **120mm** 12 Brandt
ANTI-TANK/ANTI-INFRASTRUCTURE • MSL
  SP 8 VBL with TOW
  MANPATS FGM-148 *Javelin*; Milan; TOW/TOW-2A
AIR DEFENCE
  SAM • Point-defence 8 *Mistral* 2; FGM-148 *Javelin*; 9K32 *Strela*-2 (SA-7 *Grail*)‡
  GUNS 26: **23mm** 4 ZU-23-2; **35mm** 10 GDF-005 (with *Skyguard*); **40mm** 12 L/60 (Towed)

Navy 4,200
EQUIPMENT BY TYPE
PRIMARY SURFACE COMBATANTS 3
  FFGHM 3 *Al-Shamikh* with 2 twin lnchr with MM-40 *Exocet* Block III AShM, 2 6-cell VLS with VL MICA SAM, 1 76mm gun
PATROL AND COASTAL COMBATANTS 12
  CORVETTES • FSGM 2:
    2 *Qahir Al Amwaj* with 2 quad lnchr with MM-40 *Exocet* AShM, 1 octuple lnchr with *Crotale* SAM, 1 76mm gun, 1 hel landing platform
  PCFG 3 *Dhofar* with 2 quad lnchr with MM-40 *Exocet* AShM, 1 76mm gun
  PCO 4 *Al Ofouq* with 1 76mm gun, 1 hel landing platform
  PCC 3 *Al Bushra* (FRA P-400) with 1 76mm gun
AMPHIBIOUS 6
  LANDING SHIPS • LST 1 *Nasr el Bahr* with 1 hel landing platform (capacity 7 tanks; 240 troops)
  LANDING CRAFT 5: 1 **LCU**; 3 **LCM**; 1 **LCT**
LOGISTICS AND SUPPORT 8
  AGS 1 *Al Makhirah*
  AK 1 *Al Sultana*
  AP 2 *Shinas* (commercial tpt – auxiliary military role only) (capacity 56 veh; 200 tps)
  AXS 1 *Shabab Oman II*
  EPF 2 *Al Mubshir* (High Speed Support Vessel 72) with 1 hel landing platform (capacity 260 troops)

Air Force 5,000
FORCES BY ROLE
FIGHTER/GROUND ATTACK
  2 sqn with F-16C/D Block 50 *Fighting Falcon*
  1 sqn with *Hawk* Mk103; *Hawk* Mk203
MARITIME PATROL
  1 sqn with C-295MPA; SC.7 3M *Skyvan*
TRANSPORT
  1 sqn with C-130H/J/J-30 *Hercules*
  1 sqn with C-295M
TRAINING
  1 sqn with MFI-17B *Mushshak*; PC-9*; Bell 206 (AB-206) *Jet Ranger*
TRANSPORT HELICOPTER
  4 (med) sqn; Bell 212 (AB-212); NH-90; *Super Lynx* Mk300 (maritime/SAR)
AIR DEFENCE
  2 sqn with *Rapier*; *Blindfire*; S713 *Martello*
EQUIPMENT BY TYPE
AIRCRAFT 53 combat capable
  FGA 24: 18 F-16C Block 50 *Fighting Falcon*; 6 F-16D Block 50 *Fighting Falcon*
  MP 4 C-295MPA
  TPT 20: **Medium** 6: 3 C-130H *Hercules*; 2 C-130J *Hercules*; 1 C-130J-30 *Hercules* (VIP); **Light** 12: 5 C-295M; 7 SC.7 3M *Skyvan* (radar-equipped, for MP); **PAX** 2 A320-300
  TRG 36: 4 *Hawk* Mk103*; 12 *Hawk* Mk203*; 8 MFI-17B *Mushshak*; 12 PC-9*
HELICOPTERS
  MRH 15 *Super Lynx* Mk300 (maritime/SAR)
  TPT 36+ **Medium** 20 NH90 TTH; **Light** 6: 3 Bell 206 (AB-206) *Jet Ranger*; 3 Bell 212 (AB-212)

AIR DEFENCE • SAM • Point-defence 40 *Rapier*
RADAR • AIR DEFENCE 6+: 6 *Blindfire*; S713 *Martello*
MSL
   AAM • IR AIM-9N/M/P *Sidewinder*; ARH AIM-120C7 AMRAAM
   ASM AGM-65D/G *Maverick*
   AShM AGM-84D *Harpoon*
BOMBS
   Laser-guided EGBU-10 *Paveway* II; EGBU-12 *Paveway* II
   INS/GPS guided GBU-31 JDAM

Royal Household 6,400
(incl HQ staff)
FORCES BY ROLE
SPECIAL FORCES
   2 SF regt

Royal Guard bde 5,000
FORCES BY ROLE
MANOEUVRE
   Other
   1 gd bde (1 armd sqn, 2 gd regt, 1 cbt spt bn)
EQUIPMENT BY TYPE
ARMOURED FIGHTING VEHICLES
   ASLT 9 *Centauro* MGS (9 VBC-90 in store)
   APC • APC (W) 73: ε50 Type-92; 14 VAB VCI; 9 VAB VDAA
ANTI-TANK/ANTI-INFRASTRUCTURE
   MSL • MANPATS *Milan*
ARTILLERY • MRL 122mm 6 Type-90A
AIR DEFENCE
   SAM • Point-defence 14 *Javelin*
   GUNS • SP 9: 20mm 9 VAB VDAA

Royal Yacht Squadron 150
EQUIPMENT BY TYPE
LOGISTICS AND SUPPORT 3
   AP 1 *Fulk Al Salamah* (also veh tpt) with up to 2 AS332 *Super Puma* hel

Royal Flight 250
EQUIPMENT BY TYPE
AIRCRAFT • TPT • PAX 5: 2 B-747SP; 1 DC-8-73CF; 2 Gulfstream IV
HELICOPTERS • TPT • Medium 6: 3 SA330 (AS330) *Puma*; 2 AS332F *Super Puma*; 1 AS332L *Super Puma*

Paramilitary 4,400 active

Tribal Home Guard 4,000
org in teams of ε100

Police Coast Guard 400
EQUIPMENT BY TYPE
PATROL AND COASTAL COMBATANTS 33
   PCO 2 *Haras*
   PBF 3 *Haras* (US Mk V *Pegasus*)
   PB 27: 3 Rodman 101; 1 *Haras* (SWE CG27); 3 *Haras* (SWE CG29); 14 Rodman 58; 1 D59116; 5 *Zahra*

Police Air Wing
EQUIPMENT BY TYPE
AIRCRAFT • TPT • Light 4: 1 BN-2T *Turbine Islander*; 2 CN-235M; 1 Do-228
HELICOPTERS • TPT • Light 5: 2 Bell 205A; 3 Bell 214ST (AB-214ST)

FOREIGN FORCES
United Kingdom 70

Palestinian Territories PT

New Israeli Shekel NS	2015	2016	2017
GDP	US$		
per capita	US$		
Growth	%		
Inflation	%		

*definitive economic data unavailable

US$1=NS

Population   4,451,014

Age	0–14	15–19	20–24	25–29	30–64	65 plus
Male	20.7%	5.8%	5.1%	4.2%	13.6%	1.4%
Female	19.6%	5.5%	5.0%	4.2%	13.3%	1.6%

Capabilities

The Palestinian Authority's National Security Force (NSF) is a paramilitary organisation designed to provide internal-security support within Gaza and the West Bank. The NSF only has real authority within the West Bank, where it has generally proved capable of maintaining internal security. Since 2007 Gaza has been run by Hamas. Its military wing has a strong, well-developed rocket-artillery capability – which includes manufacturing, development and testing – but this is increasingly countered by Israel's *Iron Dome* missile-defence system. Hamas brigades also engage in innovative asymmetric attacks. Israel's military actions in recent years have periodically degraded the command and control of, as well as the physical infrastructure used by, Hamas forces, but have seemingly had little effect on the long-term ability of the brigades to produce, import, store and launch rockets. International partners remain engaged in support and development of the security sector; the EU, for instance, has maintained a police-support mission headquarted in Ramallah since 2006.

ACTIVE 0 Paramilitary n.k.
Precise personnel-strength figures for the various Palestinian groups are not known

ORGANISATIONS BY SERVICE

There is little available data on the status of the organisations mentioned below. Following internal fighting in June 2007, Gaza is under the de facto control of Hamas, while the West Bank is controlled by the Palestinian Authority; both participate in a unity government

Paramilitary

Palestinian Authority n.k.

Presidential Security ε3,000

Special Forces ε1,200

Police ε9,000

National Security Force ε10,000
FORCES BY ROLE
MANOEUVRE
Light
9 inf bn

Preventative Security ε4,000

Civil Defence ε1,000

The al-Aqsa Brigades n.k.
Profess loyalty to the Fatah group that dominates the Palestinian Authority

Hamas n.k.

Izz al-Din al-Qassam Brigades ε15,000–20,000
FORCES BY ROLE
COMMAND
6 bde HQ (regional)
MANOEUVRE
Light
1 cdo unit (Nukhba)
27 bn
100 cbt coy
COMBAT SUPPORT
Some engr units
COMBAT SERVICE SUPPORT
Some log units
EQUIPMENT BY TYPE
ANTI-TANK/ANTI-INFRASTRUCTURE • MSL • MANPATS 9K11 *Malyutka* (AT-3 *Sagger*) (reported)
ARTILLERY
MRL • *Qassam* rockets (multiple calibres); **122mm** *Grad*
MOR some (multiple calibres)

Qatar QTR

Qatari Riyal R		2015	2016	2017
GDP	R	608bn	570bn	
	US$	167bn	157bn	
per capita	US$	68,940	60,733	
Growth	%	3.7	2.6	
Inflation	%	1.8	3.0	
Def exp	R	ε17.3bn	ε16bn	
	US$	ε4.75bn	ε4.40bn	
US$1=R		3.64	3.64	

Population 2,258,283

Ethnic groups: Nationals 25%; expatriates 75% of which Indian 18%; Iranian 10%; Pakistani 18%

Age	0–14	15–19	20–24	25–29	30–64	65 plus
Male	6.4%	2.5%	6.7%	11.7%	49.5%	0.6%
Female	6.2%	1.5%	1.9%	2.9%	9.8%	0.3%

Capabilities

Qatar continues its ambitious re-equipment and expansion programme and has procured, and plans to procure, platforms with potentially significant power-projection capability. Now that the delivery of C-17s is complete, only the UAE has a larger strategic-transport fleet in the Gulf Cooperation Council (GCC). In 2015 Qatar also ordered 24 *Rafale* multi-role combat aircraft, which may be operated alongside rather than instead of the air force's *Mirage* 2000s. The air force also harbours ambitions for a further fighter purchase of notionally around the same number again. This would in effect triple the size of the air force, and would require an investment in infrastructure, maintenance and personnel. The navy is also experiencing significant growth: four corvettes, two offshore-patrol vessels and an amphibious platform were ordered from Italy in June 2016, while *Marte* ER and *Exocet* MM40 Block 3 missiles are being acquired for coastal defence; these would provide a layered engagement field out to 200km (using the MM40). The armed forces are designed to assure the sovereignty of the state, although, given the small number of uniformed personnel, Qatar's membership of the GCC and the relationship with the US also serve to underwrite security. It supported the Saudi-led combat operation in Yemen, initially with *Mirage* 2000 fighter aircraft and later reportedly with a contingent of ground troops.

ACTIVE 11,800 (Army 8,500 Navy 1,800 Air 1,500)
Conscript liability 4 months national service for those aged 18–35; reduced to 3 months for graduates. Reserve commitment for 10 years or to age 40

ORGANISATIONS BY SERVICE

Army 8,500
FORCES BY ROLE
SPECIAL FORCES
1 SF coy

MANOEUVRE
Armoured
1 armd bde (1 tk bn, 1 mech inf bn, 1 mor sqn, 1 AT bn)
Mechanised
3 mech inf bn
Light
1 (Royal Guard) bde (3 inf regt)
COMBAT SUPPORT
1 fd arty bn
EQUIPMENT BY TYPE
ARMOURED FIGHTING VEHICLES
  MBT 60: 30 AMX-30; ε30 Leopard 2A7
  ASLT 48: 12 AMX-10RC; 36 Piranha II 90mm
  RECCE 44: 20 EE-9 Cascavel; 8 V-150 Chaimite; 16 VBL
  IFV 40 AMX-10P
  APC 190
    APC (T) 30 AMX-VCI
    APC (W) 160 VAB
ENGINEERING & MAINTENANCE VEHICLES
  ARV 3: 1 AMX-30D; 2 Piranha
ANTI-TANK/ANTI-INFRASTRUCTURE
  MSL
    SP 24 VAB VCAC HOT
    MANPATS Milan
  RCL 84mm ε40 Carl Gustav
ARTILLERY 94+
  SP 155mm 33: 28 Mk F3; 5 PzH 2000
  TOWED 155mm 12 G-5
  MRL 6+: 122mm 2+ (30-tube); 127mm 4 ASTROS II Mk3
  MOR 45: 81mm 26 L16; SP 81mm 4 VAB VPM 81; 120mm 15 Brandt

Navy 1,800 (incl Coast Guard)
EQUIPMENT BY TYPE
PATROL AND COASTAL COMBATANTS 11
  PCFGM 7:
    4 *Barzan* (UK *Vita*) with 2 quad lnchr with MM-40 *Exocet* Block III AShM, 1 sextuple lnchr with *Mistral* SAM, 1 *Goalkeeper* CIWS, 1 76mm gun 3 *Damsah* (FRA *Combattante* III) with 2 quad lnchr with MM-40 *Exocet* AShM, 1 76mm gun
  PBF 3 MRTP 16
  PB 1 MRTP 34
AMPHIBIOUS • LANDING CRAFT • LCT 1 *Rabha* (capacity 3 MBT; 110 troops)

Coast Guard
EQUIPMENT BY TYPE
PATROL AND COASTAL COMBATANTS 12
  PBF 4 DV 15
  PB 8: 4 *Crestitalia* MV-45; 3 *Halmatic* M160; 1 other

Coastal Defence
FORCES BY ROLE
COASTAL DEFENCE
  1 bty with 3 quad lnchr with MM-40 *Exocet* AShM
EQUIPMENT BY TYPE
COASTAL DEFENCE • AShM 12 MM-40 *Exocet* AShM

Air Force 1,500
FORCES BY ROLE
FIGHTER/GROUND ATTACK
  1 sqn with *Alpha Jet**
  1 sqn with *Mirage* 2000ED; *Mirage* 2000D
TRANSPORT
  1 sqn with C-17A *Globemaster*; C-130J-30 *Hercules*
  1 sqn with A340; B-707; B-727; *Falcon* 900
ATTACK HELICOPTER
  1 ASuW sqn with *Commando* Mk3 with *Exocet*
  1 sqn with SA341 *Gazelle*; SA342L *Gazelle* with HOT
TRANSPORT HELICOPTER
  1 sqn with *Commando* Mk2A; *Commando* Mk2C
  1 sqn with AW139
EQUIPMENT BY TYPE
AIRCRAFT 18 combat capable
  FGA 12: 9 *Mirage* 2000ED; 3 *Mirage* 2000D
  TPT 18: **Heavy** 8 C-17A *Globemaster*; **Medium** 4 C-130J-30 *Hercules*; **PAX** 6: 1 A340; 2 B-707; 1 B-727; 2 *Falcon* 900
  TRG 27: 6 *Alpha Jet**; 21 PC-21
HELICOPTERS
  ASuW 8 *Commando* Mk3
  MRH 34: 21 AW139 (incl 3 for medevac); 2 SA341 *Gazelle*; 11 SA342L *Gazelle*
  TPT • **Medium** 4: 3 *Commando* Mk2A; 1 *Commando* Mk2C
AIR DEFENCE • SAM
  Long-Range MIM-104E *Patriot* PAC-2 GEM-T
  Short-Range 9 *Roland* II
  Point-defence *Mistral*; *Blowpipe*; FIM-92 *Stinger*; 9K32 *Strela-2* (SA-7 *Grail*)‡
AIR-LAUNCHED MISSILES
  AAM • IR R-550 *Magic* 2; ARH *Mica* RF
  ASM *Apache*; HOT
  AShM AM-39 *Exocet*

DEPLOYMENT

LEBANON
UN • UNIFIL 3

SAUDI ARABIA
Operation Restoring Hope 4 *Mirage* 2000ED

YEMEN
Operation Restoring Hope 1,000; *Piranha* II 90mm; VAB; VAB VCAC HOT

FOREIGN FORCES
Singapore 1 KC-135R (on rotation)
Turkey 150 (trg team)
United Kingdom Operation Shader 1 RC-135W *Rivet Joint*
United States US Central Command: 8,000; USAF CAOC; 1 bbr sqn with 6 B-52H *Stratofortress*; 1 ISR sqn with 4 RC-135 *Rivet Joint*; 1 ISR sqn with 4 E-8C JSTARS; 1 tkr sqn with 24 KC-135R/T *Straotanker*; 1 tpt sqn with 4 C-17A *Globemaster*; 4 C-130H/J-30 *Hercules*; 2 AD bty with MIM-104E/F *Patriot* PAC-2/3 • US Strategic Command: 1 AN/TPY-2 X-band radar

Saudi Arabia SAU

Saudi Riyal R		2015	2016	2017
GDP	R	2.42tr	2.39tr	
	US$	646bn	638bn	
per capita	US$	20,583	19,922	
Growth	%	3.5	1.2	
Inflation	%	2.2	4.0	
Def exp	R	307bn	213bn	
	US$	81.9bn	56.9bn	
US$1=R		3.75	3.75	

Population 28,160,273

Ethnic groups: Nationals 73% of which Bedouin up to 10%, Shia 6%; Expatriates 27% of which Asians 20%, Arabs 6%, Africans 1%, Europeans <1%

Age	0–14	15–19	20–24	25–29	30–64	65 plus
Male	13.6%	4.7%	5.4%	6.0%	23.0%	1.7%
Female	12.8%	4.3%	4.5%	4.6%	17.7%	1.6%

Capabilities

Saudi Arabia's armed forces remain the best equipped of all states in the region except Israel. The role of the military is to protect the territorial integrity of the state and to ensure internal security. Operations against the Houthis in Yemen since 2015 showed improvements in command and control, and in operational planning, although gaps were apparent in tactical air control and the missions highlighted the requirement to develop a truly joint approach to operations among Saudi forces. Saudi air, land and naval forces have been committed to *Operation Restoring Hope*, with coalition operations coordinated in Riyadh, where there is an Air Operations Centre. However, the degree of close cooperation between nations remains open to question. Saudi *Patriot* PAC-2 units have continued to successfully engage the few *Scud*-B missiles fired individually by Houthi forces. National Guard aviation modernisation continues, although future roles for the National Guard remain uncertain. While the US and the UK are principal suppliers, the armed forces have historically also sourced equipment from other countries, leading to cases – for instance, in artillery – where there is a wide range of types in single-calibre groups. This has led to reports of unfamiliarity with certain equipment due to the need for training on multiple types, as well as maintenance challenges across a diverse fleet. Saudi Arabia has demonstrated its ability to support deployed forces over land within the region. Continued US and UK contractor support is reportedly important for maintenance of combat aircraft and other modern platforms. However, as part of the government's Vision 2030 programme, conceived amid an environment of declining oil prices and consequent financial pressures, there is an ambitious plan to localise 50% of equipment spending by 2030, which would involve a significant development of the local defence sector. (See pp. 362–67.)

ACTIVE 227,000 (Army 75,000 Navy 13,500 Air 20,000 Air Defence 16,000 Strategic Missile Forces 2,500 National Guard 100,000) Paramilitary 24,500

ORGANISATIONS BY SERVICE

Army 75,000
FORCES BY ROLE
MANOEUVRE
Armoured
4 armd bde (1 recce coy, 3 tk bn, 1 mech bn, 1 fd arty bn, 1 AD bn, 1 AT bn,1 engr coy, 1 log bn, 1 maint coy, 1 med coy)
Mechanised
5 mech bde (1 recce coy, 1 tk bn, 3 mech bn, 1 fd arty bn, 1 AD bn, 1 AT bn, 1 engr coy, 1 log bn, 1 maint coy, 1 med coy)
Light
2 lt inf bde
1 (Royal Guard) regt (3 lt inf bn)
Air Manoeuvre
1 AB bde (2 AB bn, 3 SF coy)
Aviation
1 comd (3 hel gp)
COMBAT SUPPORT
3 arty bde

EQUIPMENT BY TYPE
MBT 900: 140 AMX-30; 370 M1A2/A2S *Abrams*; 390 M60A3 *Patton*
RECCE 300 AML-60/AML-90
IFV 765: 380 AMX-10P; 385 M2A2 *Bradley*
APC 1,573
  APC (T) 1,190 M113A1/A2/A3 (incl variants)
  APC (W) 150 Panhard M3; (ε40 AF-40-8-1 *Al-Fahd* in store)
AUV 233: 73 *Aravis*; 160 M-ATV
ENGINEERING & MAINTENANCE VEHICLES
AEV 15 M728
ARV 278+: 8 ACV ARV; AMX-10EHC; 55 AMX-30D; *Leclerc* ARV; 125 M88A1; 90 M578
VLB 10 AMX-30
MW *Aardvark* Mk2
NBC VEHICLES 10 TPz-1 *Fuchs* NBC
ANTI-TANK/ANTI-INFRASTRUCTURE
  MSL
    SP 290+: 90+ AMX-10P (HOT); 200 VCC-1 ITOW
    MANPATS M47 *Dragon*; TOW-2A
  RCL **84mm** *Carl Gustav*; **90mm** M67; **106mm** M40A1
ARTILLERY 761
  SP 155mm 224: 60 AU-F-1; 110 M109A1B/A2; 54 PLZ-45
  TOWED 110: **105mm** (100 M101/M102 in store); **155mm** 110: 50 M114; 60 M198; **203mm** (8 M115 in store)
  MRL 127mm 60 ASTROS II Mk3
  MOR 367: **SP 81mm** 70; **SP 107mm** 150 M30; **120mm** 147: 110 Brandt; 37 M12-1535
RADAR • **LAND** AN/TPQ-36 *Firefinder*/AN/TPQ-37 *Firefinder* (arty, mor)
HELICOPTERS
ATK 35: 11 AH-64D *Apache*; 24 AH-64E *Apache*

MRH 21: 6 AS365N *Dauphin* 2 (medevac); 15 Bell 406CS *Combat Scout*
TPT • **Medium** 58: 12 S-70A1 *Desert Hawk*; 22 UH-60A *Black Hawk* (4 medevac); 24 UH-60L *Black Hawk*
AIR DEFENCE • SAM
Short-range *Crotale*
Point-defence FIM-92 *Stinger*

Navy 13,500

Navy HQ at Riyadh; Eastern Fleet HQ at Jubail; Western Fleet HQ at Jeddah

EQUIPMENT BY TYPE
PRINCIPAL SURFACE COMBATANTS 7
DESTROYERS • DDGHM 3 *Al Riyadh* (FRA *La Fayette* mod) with 2 quad lnchr with MM-40 *Exocet* Block II AShM, 2 8-cell A43 VLS with *Aster* 15 SAM, 4 single 533mm TT with F17P HWT, 1 76mm gun (capacity 1 AS365N *Dauphin* 2 hel)
FRIGATES • FFGHM 4 *Madina* (FRA F-2000) with 2 quad lnchr with *Otomat* Mk2 AShM, 1 octuple lnchr with *Crotale* SAM, 4 single 533mm TT with F17P HWT, 1 100mm gun (capacity 1 AS365N *Dauphin* 2 hel)
PATROL AND COASTAL COMBATANTS 30
CORVETTES • FSG 4 *Badr* (US *Tacoma*) with 2 quad Mk140 lnchr with RGM-84C *Harpoon* AShM, 2 triple 324mm ASTT with Mk 46 LWT, 1 *Phalanx* CIWS, 1 76mm gun
PCFG 9 *Al Siddiq* (US 58m) with 2 twin Mk140 lnchr with RGM-84C *Harpoon* AShM, 1 *Phalanx* CIWS, 1 76mm gun
PB 17 (US *Halter Marine*)
MINE WARFARE • MINE COUNTERMEASURES 3
MHC 3 *Al Jawf* (UK *Sandown*)
AMPHIBIOUS • LANDING CRAFT 2
LCU 2 *Al Qiaq* (US LCU 1610) (capacity 120 troops)
LOGISTICS AND SUPPORT 2
AORH 2 *Boraida* (mod FRA *Durance*) (capacity either 2 AS365F *Dauphin* 2 hel or 1 AS332C *Super Puma*)

Naval Aviation
EQUIPMENT BY TYPE
HELICOPTERS
MRH 34: 6 AS365N *Dauphin* 2; 15 AS565 with AS-15TT AShM; 13 Bell 406CS *Combat Scout*
TPT • Medium 12 AS332B/F *Super Puma* with AM-39 *Exocet* AShM

Marines 3,000
FORCES BY ROLE
MANOEUVRE
Amphibious
1 inf regt with (2 inf bn)
EQUIPMENT BY TYPE
ARMOURED FIGHTING VEHICLES
APC • APC (W) 140 BMR-600P

Air Force 20,000
FORCES BY ROLE
FIGHTER
1 sqn with F-15S *Eagle*
4 sqn with F-15C/D *Eagle*

FIGHTER/GROUND ATTACK
2 sqn with F-15S *Eagle*
3 sqn with *Tornado* IDS; *Tornado* GR1A
2 sqn with *Typhoon*
AIRBORNE EARLY WARNING & CONTROL
1 sqn with E-3A *Sentry*; 2 Saab 2000 *Erieye*
ELINT
1 sqn with RE-3A/B; Beech 350ER *King Air*
TANKER
1 sqn with KE-3A
TANKER/TRANSPORT
1 sqn with KC-130H/KC-130J *Hercules*
1 sqn with A330 MRTT
TRANSPORT
3 sqn with C-130H *Hercules*; C-130H-30 *Hercules*; CN-235; L-100-30HS (hospital ac)
2 sqn with Beech 350 *King Air* (forming)
TRAINING
3 sqn with *Hawk* Mk65*; *Hawk* Mk65A*; *Hawk* Mk165*
1 sqn with *Jetstream* Mk31
1 sqn with MFI-17 *Mushshak*; SR22T
2 sqn with PC-9; PC-21
TRANSPORT HELICOPTER
4 sqn with AS532 *Cougar* (CSAR); Bell 212 (AB-212); Bell 412 (AB-412) *Twin Huey* (SAR)

EQUIPMENT BY TYPE
AIRCRAFT 338 combat capable
FTR 81: 56 F-15C *Eagle*; 25 F-15D *Eagle*
FGA 134: 70 F-15S *Eagle*; 64 *Typhoon*
ATK 69 *Tornado* IDS
ISR 14+: 12 *Tornado* GR1A*; 2+ Beech 350ER *King Air*
AEW&C 7: 5 E-3A *Sentry*; 2 Saab 2000 *Erieye*
ELINT 2: 1 RE-3A; 1 RE-3B
TKR/TPT 15: 6 A330 MRTT; 7 KC-130H *Hercules*; 2 KC-130J *Hercules*
TKR 7 KE-3A
TPT 51+: **Medium** 32: 30 C-130H *Hercules*; 3 C-130H-30 *Hercules*; 3 L-100-30; **Light** 15+: 10+ Beech 350 *King Air*; 1 *Jetstream* Mk31
TRG 161: 24 *Hawk* Mk65* (incl aerobatic team); 16 *Hawk* Mk65A*; 2 *Hawk* Mk165*; 20 MFI-17 *Mushshak*; 20 PC-9; 55 PC-21; 24 SR22T
HELICOPTERS
MRH 15 Bell 412 (AB-412) *Twin Huey* (SAR)
TPT 30: **Medium** 10 AS532 *Cougar* (CSAR); **Light** 20 Bell 212 (AB-212)
UNMANNED AERIAL VEHICLES
CISR • Heavy some *Gongji*-1 (reported)
AIR-LAUNCHED MISSILES
AAM • IR AIM-9P/L *Sidewinder*; **IIR** AIM-9X *Sidewinder* II; IRIS-T; **SARH** AIM-7 *Sparrow*; AIM-7M *Sparrow*; **ARH** AIM-120C AMRAAM
ASM AGM-65 *Maverick*
AShM *Sea Eagle*
ARM ALARM
ALCM *Storm Shadow*
BOMBS
Laser-guided GBU-10/12 *Paveway* II; *Paveway* IV
INS/GPS-guided GBU-31 JDAM

Royal Flt
EQUIPMENT BY TYPE
AIRCRAFT • TPT 24: **Medium** 8: 5 C-130H *Hercules*; 3 L-100-30; **Light** 3: 1 Cessna 310; 2 Learjet 35; **PAX** 13: 1 A340; 1 B-737-200; 2 B-737BBJ; 2 B-747SP; 4 BAe-125-800; 2 Gulfstream III; 1 Gulfstream IV
HELICOPTERS • TPT 3+: **Medium** 3: 2 AS-61; 1 S-70 *Black Hawk*; **Light** some Bell 212 (AB-212)

Air Defence Forces 16,000
FORCES BY ROLE
AIR DEFENCE
6 bn with MIM-104D/F *Patriot* PAC-2 GEM/PAC-3
17 bty with *Shahine*/AMX-30SA
16 bty with MIM-23B I-*Hawk*
73 units (static defence) with *Crotale*/*Shahine*
EQUIPMENT BY TYPE
AIR DEFENCE
  SAM
    Long-range 108 MIM-140D/F *Patriot* PAC-2 GEM/PAC-3
    Medium-range 128 MIM-23B I-*Hawk*
    Short-range 181: 40 *Crotale*; 73 *Shahine*; 68 *Crotale*/*Shahine*
    Point-defence 400+: 400 M1097 *Avenger*; *Mistral*
  GUNS 1,070
    SP 942: **20mm** 92 M163 *Vulcan*; **30mm** 850 AMX-30SA
    TOWED 128: **35mm** 128 GDF Oerlikon; **40mm** (150 L/70 in store)
RADARS • AIR DEFENCE 80: 17 AN/FPS-117; 28 AN/TPS-43; AN/TPS-59; 35 AN/TPS-63; AN/TPS-70

Strategic Missile Forces 2,500
EQUIPMENT BY TYPE
MSL • TACTICAL
  IRBM 10+ DF-3 (CSS-2) (service status unclear)
  MRBM Some DF-21 (CSS-5 – variant unclear) (reported)

National Guard 73,000 active; 27,000 (tribal levies) (total 100,000)
FORCES BY ROLE
MANOEUVRE
  Mechanised
  5 mech bde (1 recce coy, 3 mech inf bn, 1 SP arty bn, 1 cbt engr coy, 1 sigs coy, 1 log bn)
  Light
  5 inf bde (3 combined arms bn, 1 arty bn, 1 log bn)
  3 indep lt inf bn
  Other
  1 (Special Security) sy bde (3 sy bn)
  1 (ceremonial) cav sqn
COMBAT SUPPORT
  1 MP bn
EQUIPMENT BY TYPE
ARMOURED FIGHTING VEHICLES
  ASLT 214 LAV-AG (90mm)
  IFV 647 LAV-25
  APC • APC (W): 808: 119 LAV-A; 30 LAV-AC; 296 LAV-CC; 73 LAV-PC; 290 V-150 *Commando* (810 in store)

ENGINEERING & MAINTENANCE VEHICLES
  AEV 58 LAV-E
  ARV 111 LAV-R; V-150 ARV
ANTI-TANK/ANTI-INFRASTRUCTURE
  MSL
    SP 183 LAV-AT
    MANPATS TOW-2A; M47 *Dragon*
  RCL • 106mm M40A1
ARTILLERY 359+
  SP 155mm 132 CAESAR
  TOWED 108: **105mm** 50 M102; **155mm** 58 M198
  MOR 119+: **81mm** some; **120mm** 119 LAV-M
AIR DEFENCE
  GUNS • TOWED 160: **20mm** 30 M167 *Vulcan*; **90mm** 130 M2
HELICOPTERS • ATK ε4 AH-64E *Apache*

Paramilitary 24,500+ active

Border Guard 10,500
FORCES BY ROLE
Subordinate to Ministry of Interior. HQ in Riyadh. 9 subordinate regional commands
MANOEUVRE
  Other
  Some mobile def (long-range patrol/spt) units
  2 border def (patrol) units
  12 infrastructure def units
  18 harbour def units
  Some coastal def units
COMBAT SUPPORT
  Some MP units

Coast Guard 4,500
EQUIPMENT BY TYPE
PATROL AND COASTAL COMBATANTS 14
  PBF 6: 4 *Al Jouf*; 2 *Sea Guard*
  PB 8: 6 Stan Patrol 2606; 2 *Al Jubatel*
AMPHIBIOUS • LANDING CRAFT 8: 3 UCAC; 5 UCAC *Griffin* 8000
LOGISTICS AND SUPPORT 4: 1 AXL; 3 AO

Facilities Security Force 9,000+
Subordinate to Ministry of Interior

General Civil Defence Administration Units
EQUIPMENT BY TYPE
HELICOPTERS • TPT • Medium 10 Boeing *Vertol* 107

Special Security Force 500
EQUIPMENT BY TYPE
ARMOURED FIGHTING VEHICLES
  APC • APC (W): UR-416

DEPLOYMENT

BAHRAIN
GCC • *Peninsula Shield* ε1,500 (National Guard)

TURKEY
Operation Inherent Resolve 6 F-15S *Eagle*

YEMEN
Operation Restoring Hope 750; M-ATV; 2+ MIM-104D/F Patriot PAC-2/3

FOREIGN FORCES
Bahrain *Operation Restoring Hope* 6 F-16C *Fighting Falcon*
Kuwait *Operation Restoring Hope* 4 F/A-18A *Hornet*
Qatar *Operation Restoring Hope* 4 *Mirage* 2000ED
Sudan *Operation Restoring Hope* 3 Su-24 *Fencer*
United Arab Emirates *Operation Restoring Hope* 12 F-16E *Fighting Falcon*
United States US Central Command: 350

Syria SYR

Syrian Pound S£		2015	2016	2017
GDP	S£			
	US$			
per capita	US$			
Growth	%			
Inflation	%			
Def exp	S£			
	US$			

US$1=S£
*definitive economic data unavailable

Population	17,185,170					
Age	0–14	15–19	20–24	25–29	30–64	65 plus
Male	16.4%	5.3%	4.7%	4.6%	17.5%	1.9%
Female	15.6%	5.1%	4.6%	4.7%	17.6%	2.3%

Capabilities

After over five years of war, Syrian government forces have suffered considerable attrition. The army is short of personnel, resulting in increased efforts to conscript young men, many of whom try to avoid service. In many areas, conventional forces have been supplanted by militias over which the government often has limited control. During 2016 support from Lebanese Hizbullah, Iran and particularly Russia allowed Syrian forces to regain some strategic, operational and tactical initiative, pushing back rebels around Damascus and recapturing Palmyra from ISIS. Russia and Iran have provided financial support. There is also strong evidence of Iran and Hizbullah having helped field militia forces and the transfer of, and training on, Russian equipment. Russian airstrikes have been decisive in reversing rebel momentum. Even so, the limited capabilities of Syrian government ground forces and militias mean that advances against rebel positions are usually limited, slow and dependent on fire support from artillery and airstrikes. Nonetheless, government forces have displayed an ability to move elite formations around territory it controls. Both Russia and Iran have assisted with fixed- and rotary-wing airlift. Most army formations are believed to be under-strength. Syrian government forces are capable of air–land cooperation and combined-arms tactics. Their ability to coordinate operations has been greatly improved by Russian advisers. (See pp. 351–54.)

ACTIVE 127,500 (Army 90,000 Navy 2,500 Air 15,000 Air Defence 20,000) **Paramilitary 150,000**
Conscript liability 30 months (there is widespread avoidance of military service)

ORGANISATIONS BY SERVICE

Army ε90,000
FORCES BY ROLE
The army can be split into two groups: the first composed of approximately 25,000 fighters from the 4th Armoured Division, the Republican Guard and the Special Forces comprises the majority of the regime's effective military power; the remaining approximately 65,000 personnel are largely tasked with holding government territory. Many formations are under-strength, at an estimated 500–1,000 personnel in brigades and regiments
PRINCIPAL FORCES
COMMAND
  4 corps HQ
SPECIAL FORCES
  2 SF div (total: 11 SF regt; 1 tk regt)
MANOEUVRE
  Armoured
  1 (4th) armd div (1 SF regt, 2 armd bde, 2 mech bde, 1 arty regt, 1 SSM bde (3 SSM bn with *Scud*-B/C))
  Mechanised
  1 (Republican Guard) mech div (3 mech bde, 2 sy regt, 1 arty regt)
SUPPORTING FORCES (CADRE ORGANISATION)
MANOEUVRE
  Armoured
  5 armd div
  Mechanised
  3 mech div
  2 indep inf bde
COMBAT SUPPORT
  2 arty bde
  2 AT bde
  1 SSM bde (3 SSM bn with FROG-7)
  1 SSM bde (3 SSM bn with SS-21)
EQUIPMENT BY TYPE
Attrition during the civil war has severely reduced equipment numbers for almost all types. It is unclear how much remains available for operations
ARMOURED FIGHTING VEHICLES
  MBT T-55A; T-55AM; T-55AMV; T-62; T-72; T-72AV; T-72B; T-72M1
  RECCE BRDM-2
  IFV BMP-1; BMP-2; BTR-82A
  APC
    APC (T) BTR-50
    APC (W) BTR-152; BTR-60; BTR-70; BTR-80
ENGINEERING & MAINTENANCE VEHICLES
  ARV BREM-1 reported; T-54/55
  MW UR-77
  VLB MTU; MTU-20

ANTI-TANK/ANTI-INFRASTRUCTURE • MSL
SP 9P133 *Malyutka*-P (BRDM-2 with AT-3C *Sagger*); 9P148 *Konkurs* (BRDM-2 with AT-5 *Spandrel*)
MANPATS 9K111 *Fagot* (AT-4 *Spigot*); 9K111-1 *Konkurs* (AT-5 *Spandrel*); 9K115 *Metis* (AT-7 *Saxhorn*); 9K115-2 *Metis*-M (AT-13 *Saxhorn* 2); 9K116-1 *Bastion* (AT-10 *Stabber*); 9K135 *Kornet* (AT-14 *Spriggan*); *Milan*
ARTILLERY
SP 122mm 2S1 *Gvozdika*; D-30 (mounted on T34/85 chassis); **130mm** M-46 (truck–mounted); **152mm** 2S3 *Akatsiya*
TOWED 122mm D-30; M-30 (M1938); **130mm** M-46; **152mm** D-20; ML-20 (M-1937); **180mm** S-23
MRL 107mm Type-63; **122mm** BM-21 *Grad*; **140mm** BM-14; **220mm** 9P140 *Uragan*; **300mm** 9A52 *Smerch*; **330mm** some
MOR 82mm some; **120mm** M-1943; **160mm** M-160; **240mm** M-240
SURFACE-TO-SURFACE MISSILE LAUNCHERS
SRBM • Conventional *Scud*-B/C/D; *Scud* look-a-like; 9K79 *Tochka* (SS-21 *Scarab*); *Fateh*-110/M-600
UNMANNED AERIAL VEHICLES
ISR • Medium *Mohajer* 3/4; **Light** *Ababil*
AIR DEFENCE
SAM
Medium-range 9K37 *Buk* (SA-11 *Gadfly*); 9K317 *Buk*-M2 (SA-17 *Grizzly*)
Short-range 96K6 *Pantsir*-S1 (SA-22 *Greyhound*)
Point-defence 9K31 *Strela*-1 (SA-9 *Gaskin*); 9K33 *Osa* (SA-8 *Gecko*); 9K35 *Strela*-10 (SA-13 *Gopher*); 9K32 *Strela*-2 (SA-7 *Grail*)‡; 9K38 *Igla* (SA-18 *Grouse*); 9K36 *Strela*-3 (SA-14 *Gremlin*); 9K338 *Igla*-S (SA-24 *Grinch*)
GUNS
SP 23mm ZSU-23-4; **57mm** ZSU-57-2; S-60 (on 2K12 chassis)
TOWED 23mm ZU-23-2; **37mm** M-1939; **57mm** S-60; **100mm** KS-19

Navy ε4,000
Some personnel are likely to have been drafted into other services
EQUIPMENT BY TYPE
PATROL AND COASTAL COMBATANTS 32†:
CORVETTES • FS 2 *Petya* III (1†) with 1 triple 533mm ASTT with SAET-60 HWT, 4 RBU 2500 *Smerch* 1† A/S mor, 2 twin 76mm gun
PBFG 22:
16 *Osa* I/II with 4 single lnchr with P-15M *Termit*-M (SS-N-2C *Styx*) AShM
6 *Tir* with 2 single lnchr with C-802 (CSS-N-8 *Saccade*) AShM
PB 8 *Zhuk*†
MINE WARFARE • MINE COUNTERMEASURES 7
MHC 1 *Sonya* with 2 quad lnchr with 9K32 *Strela*-2 (SA-N-5 *Grail*)‡ SAM, 2 AK630 CIWS
MSO 1 *Natya* with 2 quad lnchr with 9K32 *Strela*-2 (SA-N-5 *Grail*)‡ SAM
MSI 5 *Yevgenya*
AMPHIBIOUS • LANDING SHIPS • LSM 3 *Polnochny* B (capacity 6 MBT; 180 troops)
LOGISTICS AND SUPPORT • AX 1 *Al Assad*

Coastal Defence
FORCES BY ROLE
COASTAL DEFENCE
1 AShM bde with P-35 (SS-C-1B *Sepal*); P-15M *Termit*-R (SS-C-3 *Styx*); C-802; K-300P *Bastion* (SS-C-5 *Stooge*)
EQUIPMENT BY TYPE
COASTAL DEFENCE • AShM P-35 (SS-C-1B *Sepal*); P-15M *Termit*-R (SS-C-3 *Styx*); C-802; K-300P *Bastion* (SS-C-5 *Stooge*)

Naval Aviation
All possibly non-operational after vacating base for Russian deployment
EQUIPMENT BY TYPE
HELICOPTERS • ASW 10: 4 Ka-28 *Helix* A; 6 Mi-14 *Haze*

Air Force ε15,000 (-)
FORCES BY ROLE
FIGHTER
2 sqn with MiG-23 MF/ML/UM *Flogger*
2 sqn with MiG-29A/U *Fulcrum*
FIGHTER/GROUND ATTACK
4 sqn with MiG-21MF/bis *Fishbed*; MiG-21U *Mongol* A
2 sqn with MiG-23BN/UB *Flogger*
GROUND ATTACK
4 sqn with Su-22 *Fitter* D
1 sqn with Su-24 *Fencer*
1 sqn with L-39 *Albatros**
TRANSPORT
1 sqn with An-24 *Coke*; An-26 *Curl*; Il-76 *Candid*
1 sqn with Falcon 20; Falcon 900
1 sqn with Tu-134B-3
1 sqn with Yak-40 *Codling*
ATTACK HELICOPTER
3 sqn with Mi-25 *Hind* D
2 sqn with SA342L *Gazelle*
TRANSPORT HELICOPTER
6 sqn with Mi-8 *Hip*/Mi-17 *Hip* H
EQUIPMENT BY TYPE
Heavy use of both fixed- and rotary-wing assets has likely reduced readiness and availability to very low levels
AIRCRAFT It is estimated that 30–40% of the inventory is combat capable
FTR 75: 39 MiG-23MF/ML/UM *Flogger*; 30 MiG-29A/SM/UB *Fulcrum*
FGA 130: 70 MiG-21MF/bis *Fishbed*; 9 MiG-21U *Mongol* A; 41 MiG-23BN/UB *Flogger*;
ATK 36 Su-22 *Fitter* D; 11 Su-24 *Fencer*
TPT 23: **Heavy** 3 Il-76 *Candid*; **Light** 13: 1 An-24 *Coke*; 6 An-26 *Curl*; 2 PA-31 *Navajo*; 4 Yak-40 *Codling*; **PAX** 7: 2 Falcon 20; 1 Falcon 900; 4 Tu-134B-3
TRG 17 L-39 *Albatros**
HELICOPTERS
ATK 24 Mi-25 *Hind* D
MRH 57: 27 Mi-17 *Hip* H; 30 SA342L *Gazelle*
TPT • Medium 27 Mi-8 *Hip*
AIR-LAUNCHED MISSILES
AAM • IR R-3 (AA-2 *Atoll*)‡; R-60 (AA-8 *Aphid*); R-73

(AA-11 *Archer*); **IR/SARH**; R-23/24 (AA-7 *Apex*); R-27 (AA-10 *Alamo*); **ARH**; R-77 (AA-12 *Adder*) reported
ASM Kh-25 (AS-10 *Karen*); Kh-29T/L (AS-14 *Kedge*) HOT
ARM Kh-31P (AS-17A *Krypton*)

Air Defence Command ε20,000 (-)

FORCES BY ROLE
AIR DEFENCE
    4 AD div with S-125 *Pechora* (SA-3 *Goa*); 2K12 *Kub* (SA-6 *Gainful*); S-75 *Dvina* (SA-2 *Guideline*)
    3 AD regt with S-200 *Angara* (SA-5 *Gammon*)

EQUIPMENT BY TYPE
AIR DEFENCE • SAM
    Long-range S-200 *Angara* (SA-5 *Gammon*)
    Medium-range S-75 *Dvina* (SA-2 *Guideline*)
    Short-range 2K12 *Kub* (SA-6 *Gainful*); S-125 *Pechora* (SA-3 *Goa*)
    Point-defence 9K32 *Strela-2/2M* (SA-7A/B *Grail*)‡

Paramilitary ε150,000

National Defence Force ε100,000
Have received training from Hizbullah and the Islamic Revolutionary Guard Corps

Other Militias ε50,000
In addition to the regular forces and the National Defence Force, there are a number of other, smaller military organisations fighting for the Assad regime, including sectarian, Iraqi and Afghan organisations

Coast Guard
EQUIPMENT BY TYPE
PATROL AND COASTAL COMBATANTS 6
    PBF 2 *Mawani*
    PB 4

TERRITORY WHERE THE GOVERNMENT DOES NOT EXERCISE EFFECTIVE CONTROL

Data here represents the de facto situation. Observed equipments; selected armed opposition groups

Free Syrian Army (Coalition)
The Free Syrian Army (FSA) is a broad coalition which includes all FSA affiliates not associated with the FSA Southern Front. The FSA is a broad anti-regime grouping comprising local defence forces, anti-regime militias, moderate Islamists, hardline Islamists, secularists and others

ACTIVE ε20,000

EQUIPMENT BY TYPE
ARMOURED FIGHTING VEHICLES
    MBT some T-55; T-72AV
    IFV BMP-1
ANTI-TANK/ANTI-INFRASTRUCTURE
    MSL • MANPATS 9K11 *Malyutka* (AT-3 *Sagger*); 9K111 *Fagot* (AT-4 *Spigot*); 9K113 *Konkurs* (AT-5 *Spandrel*); 9K115-2 *Metis-M* (AT-13 *Saxhorn* 2); 9K135 *Kornet* (AT-14 *Spriggan*); BGM-71 TOW; *Milan*
ARTILLERY
    SP 122mm 2+ BM-21 *Grad*
    TOWED 122mm D-30
    MRL 107mm Type-63
    MOR 82mm some
AIR DEFENCE
    SAM
        Point-defence MANPADS some
    GUNS
    SP 14.5mm ZPU-1 **23mm** ZU-23-2; ZSU-23-4 *Shilka*

Free Syrian Army – Southern Front (Coalition)
The FSA Southern Front is a capable coalition almost entirely concentrated in the provinces of Daraa and Quneitra, south of Damascus. The majority of the coalition consists of mainstream Islamist factions

ACTIVE ε25,000

EQUIPMENT BY TYPE
ARMOURED FIGHTING VEHICLES
    MBT T-55; T-54B/M; T-54-3; T-72AV
    IFV BMP-1
ANTI-TANK/ANTI-INFRASTRUCTURE
    MSL • MANPATS 9K11 *Malyutka* (AT-3 *Sagger*); 9K111 *Fagot* (AT-4 *Spigot*); 9K115-2 *Metis-M* (AT-13 *Saxhorn* 2); BGM-71 TOW
    RCL 106mm M40
ARTILLERY
    SP 122mm 2S1 *Gvozdika*
    TOWED 122mm D-30
    MOR 120mm some; others of varying calibre
AIR DEFENCE
    SAM
        Point-defence 9K32 *Strela-2* (SA-7 *Grail*) MANPAD
    GUNS
    SP 14.5mm ZPU-2 **23mm** ZU-23-2

Syrian Democratic Forces (Coalition)
The Syrian Democratic Forces (SDF) extensively benefit from US and coalition air support, and embedded US special forces. The main combat power within the SDF is provided by the Kurdish YPG/J (People's Protection Units/ Women's Protection Units). An estimated 40% of the SDF's strength is from ethnically mixed and Arab militias

ACTIVE ε2,000

EQUIPMENT BY TYPE
ARMOURED FIGHTING VEHICLES
    MBT T-72 (reported); T-55
    IFV BMP-1
ANTI-TANK/ANTI-INFRASTRUCTURE
    MSL • MANPATS 9K111-1 *Konkurs*
    RCL 73mm SPG-9; **90mm** M-79 *Osa*
ARTILLERY
    MRL 122mm 9K132 *Grad-P*
    MOR 82mm 82-BM-37; M1938; **120mm** M1943; improvised mortars of varying calibre

AIR DEFENCE
    GUNS
    SP 14.5mm ZPU-4 (tch); ZPU-2 (tch); ZPU-1 (tch); 1 ZPU-2 (tch/on T-55); **23mm** ZSU-23-4 *Shilka*; ZU-23-2 (tch); **57mm** AZP S-60
    TOWED 14.5mm ZPU-2; ZPU-1; **23mm** ZU-23-2

Syrian Turkmen Brigades

The Syrian Turkmen Brigades are affiliated with the FSA and work with other opposition armed groups, including Jabhat Fateh al-Sham and the Islamist Ahrar al-Sham. They comprise smaller groups operating mostly in Aleppo and Latakia

ACTIVE ε5,000

EQUIPMENT BY TYPE
ARMOURED FIGHTING VEHICLES
    MBT T-55; T-54; T-62
    IFV BMP-1
ANTI-TANK/ANTI-INFRASTRUCTURE
    MSL • MANPATS BGM-71 TOW; 9K115 *Metis* (AT-7 *Saxhorn*)
    RCL 73mm SPG-9; **82mm** B-10
ARTILLERY
    MRL 107mm Type-63; **122mm** 9K132 *Grad*-P
    MOR 82mm 2B9 *Vasilek*; improvised mortars of varying calibre
AIR DEFENCE
    GUNS
    SP 14.5mm ZPU-4 (tch); ZPU-2 (tch); ZPU-1 (tch); **23mm** ZU-23-2 (tch); **57mm** AZP S-60
    TOWED 14.5mm ZPU-4; ZPU-2; ZPU-1; **23mm** ZU-23-2

Jabhat Fateh al-Sham

Formerly known as Jabhat al-Nusra, has long been one of the most effective and capable rebel groups, and has been designated a terrorist organisation by the US and the UK for its links to al-Qaeda. It is active throughout Syria, particularly in the north

ACTIVE ε6,000

EQUIPMENT BY TYPE
ARMOURED FIGHTING VEHICLES
    MBT T-55; T-62; T-72; T-72AV
    IFV BMP-1
ANTI-TANK/ANTI-INFRASTRUCTURE
    MSL • MANPATS 9K11 *Malyutka* (AT-3 *Sagger*); 9K113 *Konkurs* (AT-5 *Spandrel*); 9K115-2 *Metis*-M (AT-13 *Saxhorn* 2); 9K135 *Kornet* (AT-14 *Spriggan*)
    RCL 73mm SPG-9; **106mm** M-40
ARTILLERY
    SP 122mm 2S1 *Gvozdika*
    TOWED 122mm D-30; **130mm** M-46
    MRL 107mm Type-63
    MOR 120mm some; improvised mortars of varying calibres
AIR DEFENCE
    SAM
        Point-defence 9K327 *Strela*-2 (SA-7 *Grail*)
    GUNS
    SP 14.5mm ZPU-1; ZPU-2; **23mm** ZU-23-2; **57mm** AZP S-60

Jaysh al-Islam

Jaysh al-Islam is among the largest and most capable opposition actors in Syria. The bulk of its forces are thought to be based in the East Ghouta suburbs of Damascus

ACTIVE ε12,000

EQUIPMENT BY TYPE
ARMOURED FIGHTING VEHICLES
    MBT T-72; T-55
    IFV BMP-1
ANTI-TANK/ANTI-INFRASTRUCTURE
    MSL • MANPATS 9K113 *Konkurs* (AT-5 *Spandrel*)
    RCL 106mm M-40
ARTILLERY
    SP 122mm 2S1 *Gvozdika*
    MRL 107mm 5+ Type-63; **122mm** 2 BM-21 *Grad*
AIR DEFENCE
    SAM
        Point-defence 9K33 *Osa* (SA-8 *Gecko*)

Ahrar al-Sham

Ahrar al-Sham is one of the few groups with the manpower and resources to carry out operations nationwide. The group is composed of hardline Sunni Salafist Islamists and borderline jihadists

ACTIVE ε15,000

EQUIPMENT BY TYPE
ARMOURED FIGHTING VEHICLES
    MBT T-55
    IFV 1 BMP-1
ANTI-TANK/ANTI-INFRASTRUCTURE
    MSL • MANPATS 9K113 *Konkurs* (AT-5 *Spandrel*); 9K115-2 *Metis*-M (AT-13 *Saxhorn* 2); 9K135 *Kornet* (AT-14 *Spriggan*)
    RCL 106mm M40
ARTILLERY
    SP 122mm 2S1 *Gvozdika*
    TOWED 130mm some M-46
    MRL 107mm 5+ Type-63
    MOR improvised mortars of varying calibre

FOREIGN FORCES

Hizbullah 4,000–8,000

Iran IRGC up to 2,000

Russia 4,000: 1 inf BG; 7 T-90; ε20 BTR-82A; 12 2A65; 4 9A52 *Smerch*; TOS-1A; 9K720 *Iskander*-M; 12 Su-24M *Fencer*; 4 Su-30SM; 4 Su-34; 4 Su-35S; 1 Il-20M; 4 Mi-28N *Havoc*; 4 Ka-52 *Hokum* B; 12 Mi-24P/Mi-35M *Hind*; 4 Mi-8AMTSh *Hip*; 3 *Pantsir*-S1/S2; 1 AShM bty with 3K55 *Bastion* (SS-C-5 *Stooge*); 1 SAM bty with S-400 (SA-21 *Growler*); 1 SAM bty with S-300V4 (SA-23); air base at Latakia; naval facility at Tartus

Turkey Operation Euphrates Shield 350; 1 SF coy; 1 armd coy(+); 1 arty unit

Tunisia TUN

Tunisian Dinar D		2015	2016	2017
GDP	D	85.5bn	90.7bn	
	US$	43.6bn	42.4bn	
per capita	US$	3,923	3,777	
Growth	%	0.8	1.5	
Inflation	%	4.9	3.7	
Def bgt	D	1.92bn	2.09bn	2.02bn
	US$	979m	979m	
FMA (US)	US$	25m	63m	45m
US$1=D		1.96	2.14	

Population 11,134,588

Age	0–14	15–19	20–24	25–29	30–64	65 plus
Male	11.9%	3.6%	4.0%	3.9%	22.4%	4.0%
Female	11.2%	3.5%	4.0%	4.1%	23.4%	4.2%

Capabilities

Tunisia's small armed forces rely on conscripts for their personnel strength, and much equipment is ageing. The National Guard takes the lead on domestic stability and internal security, although in the wake of a March 2015 terrorist attack the army deployed to major cities. The armed forces are suited to such constabulary roles, and more traditional military roles, such as high-tempo war fighting, would likely prove a challenge. The armed forces have struggled with the Islamist spillover through the porous borders with Algeria and Libya, but have carried out operations against insurgents and arms traffickers in remote areas. In response to this threat, the government has boosted the defence budget. There are also plans to reform and professionalise the armed forces. In early 2016, the defence minister announced that a national defence-and-security-policy white paper would be drafted. In mid-2016, NATO announced its intention to establish an 'intelligence fusion' centre in Tunisia, to support special-operations forces. Tunisia is also erecting a fortified security fence that will cover almost half of its border with Libya, and will include observation towers and sensors. The armed forces have also taken delivery of a range of equipment purchases enabled by defence-budget increases, including multi-role and transport helicopters from the US and armoured vehicles from Turkey. US–Tunisia relations have been strengthened recently; the US has supplied counter-terrorism equipment and aircraft, as well as donations of patrol boats, which have bolstered maritime security and aided in policing Tunisia's exclusive economic zone. In 2015 the US said Tunisia was a major non-NATO ally, enabling access to increased defence cooperation. Washington announced it would provide technical support and border-management training, and increase military aid. Tunisia is also a member of NATO's Mediterranean Dialogue. Coordination with Algeria has also increased on common security threats, while the UK extended its training mission to Tunisia's Explosive Ordnance Device School into 2017. The UK provided commando training to the national guard in 2016, focusing on medical training, small-boat handling and security operations.

ACTIVE 35,800 (Army 27,000 Navy 4,800 Air 4,000)
Paramilitary 12,000

Conscript liability 12 months selective

ORGANISATIONS BY SERVICE

Army 5,000; 22,000 conscript (total 27,000)

FORCES BY ROLE
SPECIAL FORCES
1 SF bde
1 (Sahara) SF bde
MANOEUVRE
Reconnaissance
1 recce regt
Mechanised
3 mech bde (1 armd regt, 2 mech inf regt, 1 arty regt, 1 AD regt, 1 engr regt, 1 sigs regt, 1 log gp)
COMBAT SUPPORT
1 engr regt
EQUIPMENT BY TYPE
ARMOURED FIGHTING VEHICLES
MBT 84: 30 M60A1; 54 M60A3
LT TK 48 SK-105 *Kuerassier*
RECCE 60: 40 AML-90; 20 FV601 *Saladin*
APC 280
  APC (T) 140 M113A1/A2
  APC (W) 110 Fiat 6614
  PPV 30+ *Kirpi*
ENGINEERING & MAINTENANCE VEHICLES
  AEV 2 *Greif*
  ARV 3 *Greif*; 6 M88A1
ANTI-TANK/ANTI-INFRASTRUCTURE • MSL
  SP 35 M901 ITV TOW
  MANPATS *Milan*; TOW
ARTILLERY 276
  TOWED 115: **105mm** 48 M101A1/A2; **155mm** 67: 12 M114A1; 55 M198
  MOR 161: **81mm** 95; **107mm** 48 (some SP); **120mm** 18 Brandt
RADAR • LAND RASIT (veh, arty)
AIR DEFENCE
  SAM • Point-defence 26 M48 *Chaparral*; RBS-70
  GUNS 127
    SP 40mm 12 M42
    TOWED 115: **20mm** 100 M-55; **37mm** 15 Type-55 (M-1939)/Type-65

Navy ε4,800

EQUIPMENT BY TYPE
PATROL AND COASTAL COMBATANTS 29
  PCFG 3 *La Galite* (FRA *Combattante* III) with 2 quad Mk140 lnchr with MM-40 *Exocet* AShM, 1 76mm gun
  PCG 3 *Bizerte* (FRA P-48) with 8 SS 12M AShM
  PCF 6 *Albatros* (GER Type-143B) with 2 single 533mm TT, 2 76mm guns
  PBF 2 20m Fast Patrol Boat

PB 15: 1 *Istiklal*; 3 *Utique* (mod PRC *Haizhui* II); 5 *Joumhouria*; 6 V Series

LOGISTICS AND SUPPORT 7:
ABU 3: 2 *Tabarka* (ex-US *White Sumac*); 1 *Sisi Bou Said*
AGE 1 *Hannibal*
AGS 1 *Khaireddine* (ex-US *Wilkes*)
AWT 1 *Ain Zaghouan* (ex-ITA *Simeto*)
AX 1 *Salambo* (ex-US *Conrad*, survey)

Air Force 4,000

FORCES BY ROLE
FIGHTER/GROUND ATTACK
1 sqn with F-5E/F-5F *Tiger* II
TRANSPORT
1 sqn with C-130B/H/J-30 *Hercules*; G-222; L-410 *Turbolet*
1 liaison unit with S-208A
TRAINING
2 sqn with L-59 *Albatros**; MB-326B; SF-260
1 sqn with MB-326K; MB-326L
TRANSPORT HELICOPTER
2 sqn with AS350B *Ecureuil*; AS365 *Dauphin* 2; AB-205 (Bell 205); SA313; SA316 *Alouette* III; UH-1H *Iroquois*; UH-1N *Iroquois*
1 sqn with HH-3E

EQUIPMENT BY TYPE
AIRCRAFT 24 combat capable
FTR 12: 10 F-5E *Tiger* II; 2 F-5F *Tiger* II
ATK 3 MB-326K
ISR 12 Maule MX-7-180B
TPT 18: **Medium** 13: 5 C-130B *Hercules*; 1 C-130H *Hercules*; 2 C-130J-30 *Hercules*; 5 G-222; **Light** 5: 3 L-410 *Turbolet*; 2 S-208A
TRG 30: 9 L-59 *Albatros**; 4 MB-326B; 3 MB-326L; 14 SF-260
HELICOPTERS
MRH 10: 1 AS365 *Dauphin* 2; 6 SA313; 3 SA316 *Alouette* III
SAR 11 HH-3E
TPT • Light 32: 6 AS350B *Ecureuil*; 15 Bell 205 (AB-205); 9 Bell 205 (UH-1H *Iroquois*); 2 Bell 212 (UH-1N *Iroquois*)
AIR-LAUNCHED MISSILES • AAM • IR AIM-9P *Sidewinder*

Paramilitary 12,000

National Guard 12,000
Ministry of Interior

EQUIPMENT BY TYPE
ARMOURED FIGHTING VEHICLES
ASLT 2 EE-11 *Urutu* FSV
APC • APC (W) 16 EE-11 *Urutu* (anti-riot)
PATROL AND COASTAL COMBATANTS 24
PCC 6 *Rais el Blais* (ex-GDR *Kondor* I)
PBF 7: 4 *Gabes*; 3 *Patrouiller*
PB 11: 5 *Breitla* (ex-GDR *Bremse*); 4 Rodman 38; 2 *Socomena*
HELICOPTERS
MRH 8 SA318 *Alouette* II/SA319 *Alouette* III

DEPLOYMENT

CÔTE D'IVOIRE
UN • UNOCI 3; 6 obs

DEMOCRATIC REPUBLIC OF THE CONGO
UN • MONUSCO 31 obs

United Arab Emirates UAE

Emirati Dirham D		2015	2016	2017
GDP	D	1.36tr	1.38tr	
	US$	370bn	375bn	
per capita	US$	38,650	38,050	
Growth	%	4.0	2.3	
Inflation	%	4.1	3.6	
Def exp	D	n.k.	n.k.	
	US$	n.k.	n.k.	
US$1=D		3.67	3.67	

Population   5,927,482

Ethnic groups: Nationals 24%; expatriates 76% of which Indian 30%, Pakistani 20%; other Arab 12%; other Asian 10%; UK 2%; other European 1%

Age	0–14	15–19	20–24	25–29	30–64	65 plus
Male	10.7%	2.8%	5.3%	10.6%	38.5%	0.6%
Female	10.2%	2.3%	3.2%	3.4%	11.4%	0.4%

Capabilities

The United Arab Emirates' armed forces are arguably the best trained and most capable among the GCC states. In recent years, the UAE has shown a growing willingness to take part in operations, including supporting an F-16 detachment to Afghanistan, and participating in the air campaign in Libya, the counter-ISIS air campaign and the Saudi-led effort to defeat Houthi rebels in Yemen. In the last case, it has committed air and ground forces, particularly but not exclusively the Presidential Guard, and has incurred significant casualties. UAE involvement in the Yemen campaign is offering combat lessons, not least of all in littoral operations and the threat from coastal-defence missiles after a High Speed Support Vessel was hit by an anti-ship missile in late 2016. Reports emerged in 2016 alleging that the UAE might be using the Eritrean port of Assab as a staging base. The operations are also demonstrating the country's developing approach to the use of force. A war memorial is planned, and the deaths on operations are subject to significant press coverage, indicative of an acceptance of military risk but also demonstrating that the casualties come from across the Emirates. The UAE has deployed armour and demonstrated the use of a range of air munitions, including the Denel *Umbani* precision-guidance kit. Two C-17s ordered in 2015 will, when delivered, bring its fleet up to eight aircraft. However, efforts to purchase a successor to the *Mirage* 2000 have slowed – although the French *Rafale* is the preferred aircraft. At the end of 2015, the UAE began to receive US-manufactured THAAD ballistic-missile-defence batteries to improve the country's missile defences. The UAE continues to develop its defence-industrial base to maintain and support military equipment; parent company EDIC oversees a variety of subsidiaries, including in the UAV, support, munitions, guided weapons and defence-electronic sectors. The UAE remains reliant, however, on external providers for major weapons systems. (See pp. 360–61.)

ACTIVE 63,000 (Army 44,000 Navy 2,500 Air 4,500 Presidential Guard 12,000)

Conscript liability 2 years National Service for men aged 18–30; reduced to 9 months for those completing secondary school. Voluntary 9 months service for women

ORGANISATIONS BY SERVICE

Space
EQUIPMENT BY TYPE
SATELLITES • COMMUNICATIONS 2 *Yahsat*

Army 44,000
FORCES BY ROLE
MANOEUVRE
  Armoured
  2 armd bde
  Mechanised
  2 mech bde
  Light
  1 inf bde
COMBAT SUPPORT
  1 arty bde (3 SP arty regt)
  1 engr gp
EQUIPMENT BY TYPE
ARMOURED FIGHTING VEHICLES
  MBT 421: 45 AMX-30; 340 *Leclerc*; 36 OF-40 Mk2 (*Lion*)
  LT TK 76 FV101 *Scorpion*
  RECCE 73: 49 AML-90; 24 VBL; (20 FV701 *Ferret* in store); (20 FV601 *Saladin* in store)
  IFV 405: 15 AMX-10P; 390 BMP-3
  APC 766
    APC (T) 136 AAPC (incl 53 engr plus other variants)
    APC (W) 630: 40 AMV 8×8; 120 EE-11 *Urutu*; 370 Panhard M3; 80 VCR (incl variants); 20 VAB
  AUV 750 M-ATV; Nimr
ENGINEERING & MAINTENANCE VEHICLES
  AEV 53 ACV-AESV
  ARV 143: 8 ACV-AESV Recovery; 4 AMX-30D; 85 BREM-L; 46 *Leclerc* ARV
  NBC VEHICLES 32 TPz-1 *Fuchs* NBC
ANTI-TANK/ANTI-INFRASTRUCTURE
  MSL
    SP 20 HOT
    MANPATS FGM-148 *Javelin*; *Milan*; TOW; (*Vigilant* in store)
  RCL 262: **84mm** 250 *Carl Gustav*; **106mm** 12 M40
ARTILLERY 584+
  SP 155mm 181: 78 G-6; 85 M109A3; 18 Mk F3
  TOWED 93: **105mm** 73 L118 Light Gun; **130mm** 20 Type-59-I
  MRL 74+: **122mm** 48+: 48 Firos-25 (est 24 op); Type-90 (reported); **227mm** 20 M142 HIMARS; **300mm** 6 9A52 *Smerch*
  MOR 236: **81mm** 134: 20 Brandt; 114 L16; **120mm** 21 Brandt; **SP 120mm** 81 RG-31 MMP *Agrab* Mk2
SURFACE-TO-SURFACE MISSILE LAUNCHERS
  SRBM • Conventional 6 Scud-B (up to 20 msl); MGM-140A/B ATACMS (launched from M142 HIMARS)
UNMANNED AERIAL VEHICLES
  ISR • Medium *Seeker* II
AIR DEFENCE
  SAM • Point-defence *Blowpipe*; *Mistral*
  GUNS 62
    SP 20mm 42 M3 VDAA
    TOWED 30mm 20 GCF-BM2

Navy 2,500
EQUIPMENT BY TYPE
PRINCIPAL SURFACE COMBATANTS 1
  FRIGATES • FFGH 1
    1 *Abu Dhabi* with 2 twin lnchr with MM-40 *Exocet* Block III AShM, 1 76mm gun
PATROL AND COASTAL COMBATANTS 41
  CORVETTES 9
    FSGHM 5:
      5 *Baynunah* with 2 quad lnchr with MM-40 *Exocet* Block III AShM, 1 8-cell Mk56 VLS with RIM-162 ESSM SAM, 1 21-cell Mk49 GMLS with RIM-116B SAM, 1 76mm gun
    FSGM 4:
      2 *Muray Jib* (GER Lurssen 62m) with 2 quad lnchr with MM-40 *Exocet* Block II AShM, 1 octuple lnchr with *Crotale* SAM, 1 *Goalkeeper* CIWS, 1 76mm gun, 1 hel landing platform
      2 *Ganthoot* with 2 twin lnchr with MM-40 *Exocet* Block III AShM, 2 3-cell VLS with VL *Mica* SAM, 1 76mm gun, 1 hel landing platform
  PCFGM 2 *Mubarraz* (GER Lurssen 45m) with 2 twin lnchr with MM-40 *Exocet* AShM, 1 sextuple lnchr with *Mistral* SAM, 1 76mm gun
  PCFG 6 *Ban Yas* (GER Lurssen TNC-45) with 2 twin lnchr with MM-40 *Exocet* Block III AShM, 1 76mm gun
  PBFG 12 *Butinah* (*Ghannatha* mod) with 4 single lncher with *Marte* Mk2/N AShM
  PBF 12: 6 *Ghannatha* with 120mm mor (capacity 42 troops); 6 *Ghannatha* (capacity 42 troops)
MINE WARFARE • MINE COUNTERMEASURES 2
  MHO 2 *Al Murjan* (ex-GER *Frankenthal*-class Type-332)
AMPHIBIOUS 29
  LANDING SHIPS • LST 2 *Alquwaisat* with 1 hel landing platform
  LANDING CRAFT 16
    LCP 4 Fast Supply Vessel (multi-purpose)
    LCU 5: 3 *Al Feyi* (capacity 56 troops); 2 (capacity 40 troops and additional vehicles)
    LCT 7
LOGISTICS AND SUPPORT 2:
  AFS 2 *Rmah* with 4 single 533mm TT

Air Force 4,500

Flying hours 110 hrs/yr

FORCES BY ROLE
FIGHTER/GROUND ATTACK
  3 sqn with F-16E/F Block 60 *Fighting Falcon*
  3 sqn with *Mirage* 2000-9DAD/EAD/RAD
AIRBORNE EARLY WARNING AND CONTROL
  1 flt with Saab 340 *Erieye*
SEARCH & RESCUE
  2 flt with AW109K2; AW139
TANKER
  1 flt with A330 MRTT
TRANSPORT
  1 sqn with C-17A *Globemaster*
  1 sqn with C-130H/H-30 *Hercules*; L-100-30
  1 sqn with CN-235M-100
TRAINING
  1 sqn with Grob 115TA
  1 sqn with *Hawk* Mk102*
  1 sqn with PC-7 *Turbo Trainer*
  1 sqn with PC-21
TRANSPORT HELICOPTER
  1 sqn with Bell 412 *Twin Huey*
EQUIPMENT BY TYPE
AIRCRAFT 156 combat capable
  FGA 137: 54 F-16E Block 60 *Fighting Falcon* (*Desert Eagle*); 24 F-16F Block 60 *Fighting Falcon* (13 to remain in US for trg); 15 *Mirage* 2000-9DAD; 44 *Mirage* 2000-9EAD
  ISR 7 *Mirage* 2000 RAD*
  AEW&C 2 Saab 340 *Erieye*
  TPT/TKR 3 A330 MRTT
  TPT 23: **Heavy** 7 C-17 *Globemaster*; **Medium** 6: 3 C-130H *Hercules*; 1 C-130H-30 *Hercules*; 2 L-100-30; **Light** 10: 6 CN235; 4 DHC-8 *Dash 8* (MP)
  TRG 79: 12 Grob 115TA; 12 *Hawk* Mk102*; 30 PC-7 *Turbo Trainer*; 25 PC-21
HELICOPTERS
  MRH 21: 12 AW139; 9 Bell 412 *Twin Huey*
  TPT • **Light** 4: 3 AW109K2; 1 Bell 407
UNMANNED AERIAL VEHCILES
  ISR • **Heavy** some *Gongji*-1 (reported)
AIR-LAUNCHED MISSILES
  AAM • **IR** AIM-9L *Sidewinder*; R-550 *Magic*; **IIR/ARH** *Mica*; **ARH** AIM-120C AMRAAM
  ASM AGM-65G *Maverick*; *Hakeem* 1/2/3 (A/B)
  ARM AGM-88C HARM
  ALCM *Black Shaheen* (*Storm Shadow*/SCALP EG variant)
BOMBS
  Laser-guided GBU-12/58 *Paveway* II

Air Defence

FORCES BY ROLE
AIR DEFENCE
  2 AD bde (3 bn with MIM-23B *I-Hawk*; MIM-104F *Patriot* PAC-3)
  3 (short range) AD bn with *Crotale*; *Mistral*; *Rapier*; RB-70; *Javelin*; 9K38 *Igla* (SA-18 *Grouse*); 96K6 *Pantsir*-S1
EQUIPMENT BY TYPE
AIR DEFENCE • **SAM**
  Medium-range MIM-23B *I-Hawk*; MIM-104F *Patriot* PAC-3
  Short-range *Crotale*; 50 96K6 *Pantsir*-S1
  Point-defence RBS-70; *Rapier*; *Javelin*; 9K38 *Igla* (SA-18 *Grouse*); *Mistral*

Presidential Guard Command 12,000

FORCES BY ROLE
MANOEUVRE
  Reconaissance
  1 recce sqn
  Mechanised
  1 mech bde (1 tk bn, 4 mech inf bn, 1 AT coy, 1 cbt engr coy, 1 CSS bn)
  Amphibious
  1 mne bn
EQUIPMENT BY TYPE
ARMOURED FIGHTING VEHICLES
  MBT 50 *Leclerc*
  IFV 290: 200 BMP-3; 90 BTR-3U *Guardian*
ANTI-TANK/ANTI-INFRASTRUCTURE
  MSL • **SP** HMMWV with 9M133 *Kornet*

Joint Aviation Command

FORCES BY ROLE
GROUND ATTACK
  1 sqn with *Archangel*; AT802 *Air Tractor*
ANTI-SURFACE/ANTI-SUBMARINE WARFARE
  1 sqn with AS332F *Super Puma*; AS565 *Panther*
TRANSPORT
  1 (Spec Ops) gp with AS365F *Dauphin 2*; H125M *Fennec*; AW139; Bell 407MRH; Cessna 208B *Grand Caravan*; CH-47C/F *Chinook*; DHC-6-300/400 *Twin Otter*; UH-60L/M *Black Hawk*
ATTACK HELICOPTER
  1 gp with AH-64D *Apache*
EQUIPMENT BY TYPE
AIRCRAFT 36 combat capable
  ATK 20 *Archangel*
  ISR 8 AT802 *Air Tractor**
  TPT • **Light** 15: 2 Beech 350 *King Air*; 8 Cessna 208B *Grand Caravan**; 1 DHC-6-300 *Twin Otter*; 4 DHC-6-400 *Twin Otter*
HELICOPTERS
  ATK 29 AH-64D *Apache*
  ASW 7 AS332F *Super Puma* (5 in ASuW role)
  MRH 55: 4 AS365F *Dauphin 2* (VIP); 18 H125M *Fennec*; 7 AS565 *Panther*; 3 AW139 (VIP); 20 Bell 407MRH; 4 SA316 *Alouette* III
  TPT 63+: **Heavy** 22 CH-47F *Chinook*; **Medium** 41+: 11 UH-60L *Black Hawk*; 30+ UH-60M *Black Hawk*
AIR-LAUNCHED MISSILES
  ASM AGM-114 *Hellfire*; *Cirit* (reported); *Hydra*-70; HOT
  AShM AS-15TT; AM-39 *Exocet*

Paramilitary

Coast Guard
Ministry of Interior
EQUIPMENT BY TYPE
PATROL AND COASTAL COMBATANTS 112
  PSO 1 *Al Watid*

PBF 58: 6 *Baglietto* GC23; 3 *Baglietto* 59; 15 DV-15; 34 MRTP 16

PB 53: 2 *Protector;* 16 (US Camcraft 65); 5 (US Camcraft 77); 6 Watercraft 45; 12 *Halmatic Work*; 12 *Al Saber*

DEPLOYMENT

ERITREA
Operation Restoring Hope 9 Mirage 2000-9EAD

LIBYA
6 *Archangel*; 2 UH-60M; 2 *Gongji*-1 UAV

SAUDI ARABIA
Operation Restoring Hope 12 F-16E *Fighting Falcon*

YEMEN
Operation Restoring Hope 4,000 1 bde HQ; 2–3 armd BG; *Leclerc*; BMP-3; M-ATV; G-6; M109A3; *Agrab* Mk2; 4 AH-64D *Apache*; 2 CH-47F *Chinook*; 4 UH-60M *Black Hawk*; 96K6 *Pantsir*-S1; 4 MIM-104F *Patriot* PAC-3

FOREIGN FORCES

Australia 800; 1 FGA det with 6 F/A-18A *Hornet*; 1 B-737-700 *Wedgetail* (E-7A); 1 A330 MRTT (KC-30A); 1 tpt det with 2 C-130J-30 *Hercules*

Egypt Operation Restoring Hope 6 F-16C *Fighting Falcon*

France 650: 1 armd BG (1 tk sqn, 1 aty bty); *Leclerc*; VBCI; CASEAR; 8 *Rafale*, 1 C-135FR

Jordan Operation Restoring Hope 6 F-16C *Fighting Falcon*

Korea, Republic of: 128 (trg activities at UAE Spec Ops School)

Morocco Operation Restoring Hope 5 F-16C *Fighting Falcon*

United Kingdom 1 tkr/tpt flt with C-17A *Globemaster*; C-130J *Hercules*; A330 MRTT *Voyager*

United States: 5,000; 1 ftr sqn with 6 F-22A *Raptor*; 1 FGA sqn with 12 F-15E *Strike Eagle*; 1 ISR sqn with 4 U-2; 1 AEW&C sqn with 4 E-3 *Sentry*; 1 tkr sqn with 12 KC-10A; 1 ISR UAV sqn with RQ-4 *Global Hawk*; 2 AD bty with MIM-104E/F *Patriot* PAC-2/3

Yemen, Republic of YEM

Yemeni Rial R		2015	2016	2017
GDP	R	8,11tr	8,14tr	
	US$	37.7bn	31.3bn	
per capita	US$	1,334	1,075	
Growth	%	-28.1	-4.2	
Inflation	%	39.4	5	
Def bdgt	R	n.k.	n.k.	
	US$	n.k.	n.k.	
US$1=R		214.89	260.00	

Population 27,392,779

Ethnic groups: Majority Arab, some African and South Asian

Age	0–14	15–19	20–24	25–29	30–64	65 plus
Male	20.6%	5.7%	5.0%	4.4%	13.7%	1.2%
Female	19.9%	5.6%	4.8%	4.3%	13.4%	1.5%

Capabilities

The civil war in Yemen continued throughout 2016 with Houthi rebels and troops loyal to the former president, Ali Abdullah Saleh, continuing to fight the armed forces of President Abd Rabbo Mansour Hadi's government, allied militias and the Saudi-led coalition supporting his regime. Opposition forces remained strongest in the northwest of the country, while the government controlled the central and eastern areas of Yemen. Al-Qaeda affiliates were active in the central and southern regions, while ISIS claimed responsibility for a number of suicide bombings in Aden, as well as other cities such as Mukalla (although ISIS was reportedly ejected from Mukalla). The Saudi-led coalition continued to provide ground and air support for the Hadi government. Civilian casualties resulting from coalition air and artillery strikes have been an increasing focus of international attention and concern. Sana'a remains in rebel hands, and was a focus of air attacks during the third quarter of 2016. Greater use was reportedly being made of strategies designed to secure the allegiance of local militias and tribal groupings; given the difficulty of moving on Yemen's highly canalised road network, securing ground by gaining the support of populations may prove fruitful. The US was further involved in the conflict when it mounted missile strikes against coastal radar following the launch by opposition forces of coastal-defence anti-ship missiles at *Arleigh Burke*-class destroyer USS *Mason* in October 2016. The failed attack on the *Mason* followed soon after a high-speed support vessel being used by the UAE to supply its forces in-theatre was hit and badly damaged by a coastal-defence anti-ship missile. Government forces are numerically inferior to the Houthis and the Republican Guard, with both sides operating at up to 'brigade'-strength-size units. The insurgents appear to retain the bulk of the more capable heavy armour and armoured fighting vehicles, with government forces relying on the older equipment that was not in the Republican Guard inventory. The air force has effectively ceased to function, except for a small number of aircraft apparently stored at Al-Anad Air Base and AT-802 aircraft provided by the UAE.

ACTIVE 10,000–20,000 (Army 10,000–20,000 Navy n.k. Air Force n.k., Air Defence n.k.) Paramilitary n.k.

ORGANISATIONS BY SERVICE

Army 10,000–20,000 (incl militia)
FORCES BY ROLE
MANOEUVRE
 Mechanised
  up to 10 bde(-)
EQUIPMENT BY TYPE
ARMOURED FIGHTING VEHICLES
 MBT Some M60A1; T-34†; T-54/55; T-62; T-72
 RECCE some BRDM-2
 APC • APC (W) BTR-60
ANTI-TANK/ANTI-INFRASTRUCTURE
 MSL • MANPATS 9K11 *Malyutka* (AT-3 *Sagger*); M47 *Dragon*; TOW
 GUNS • SP 100mm SU-100†
ARTILLERY • SP 122mm 2S1 *Gvozdika*
AIR DEFENCE • **SAM** systems heavily degraded during coalition air attacks

Navy n.k.
Yemen's naval forces have no operational capability

Air Force n.k.
The air force has no operational capability, and most of its aircraft appear to have been destroyed. Coalition forces have provided the AT-802s and training for Yemeni pilots
EQUIPMENT BY TYPE
AIRCRAFT
 FTR/FGA 8: 6 MiG-21 *Fishbed*; 2 Su-22 *Fitter*
 ISR 6 AT-802 *Air Tractor**
 TRG 3 L-39C

TERRITORY WHERE THE GOVERNMENT DOES NOT EXERCISE EFFECTIVE CONTROL

Insurgent forces 20,000 (incl Republican Guard, Houthi and tribes)
FORCES BY ROLE
MANOEUVRE
 Mechanised
  up to 20 bde(-)
EQUIPMENT BY TYPE
ARMOURED FIGHTING VEHICLES
 MBT Some T-72; T-55; T-80
 IFV BTR-80A; *Ratel*
 APC • APC (W) Some BTR-40; BTR-60
ANTI-TANK/ANTI-INFRASTRUCTURE
 MSL • MANPATS M47 *Dragon*; 9K111-1 *Konkurs* (AT-5B *Spandrel/Towsan*-1); 9K115 *Metis* (AT-7 *Saxhorn*)
SURFACE-TO-SURFACE MISSILE LAUNCHERS
 SRBM • Conventional (most fired or destroyed) 9K79 *Tochka* (SS-21 *Scarab*); *Scud*-B/*Hwasong*-5; *Borkan*-1 (possible extended-range *Scud* derivative); *Qaher*-1 (possible *Tondar*-69 derivative)
COASTAL DEFENCE • **AShM** some C-801/C-802 (reported)

DEPLOYMENT

CENTRAL AFRICAN REPUBLIC
UN • MINUSCA 5 obs

CÔTE D'IVOIRE
UN • UNOCI 4 obs

DEMOCRATIC REPUBLIC OF THE CONGO
UN • MONUSCO 6 obs

MALI
UN • MINUSMA 6

SOUTH SUDAN
UN • UNMISS 6; 9 obs

SUDAN
UN • UNAMID 21; 23 obs
UN • UNISFA 2

WESTERN SAHARA
UN • MINURSO 10 obs

FOREIGN FORCES

All *Operation Restoring Hope* unless stated
Qatar 1,000; *Piranha* II 90mm; VAB; VAB VCAC HOT
Saudi Arabia 750; M-ATV; AH-64 *Apache*; 2+ MIM-104D/F *Patriot* PAC-2/3
Sudan 950; 1 mech BG; BTR-70M *Kobra* 2
United Arab Emirates 4,000 1 bde HQ; 2–3 armd BG; *Leclerc*; BMP-3; M-ATV; G-6; M109A3; *Agrab* Mk2; 4 AH-64D *Apache*; 2 CH-47F *Chinook*; 4 UH-60M *Black Hawk*; 96K6 *Pantsir*-S1; 4 MIM-104F *Patriot* PAC-3

Table 13 **Selected arms procurements and deliveries, Middle East and North Africa**

Designation	Type	Quantity (Current)	Contract Value	Prime Nationality	Prime Contractor	Order Date	First Delivery Due	Notes
Algeria (ALG)								
T-90SA	MBT	200	n.k.	RUS	Uralvagonzavod	2014	2015	Deliveries ongoing
Fuchs 2	APC (W)	1,200	€2.7bn (US$3.59bn)	GER/ALG	Rheinmetall (Rheinmetall-Algerie-SPA)	2014	2015	ALG to licence produce 980 of the total
Varshavyanka class (Kilo)	SSK	2	εUS$1.2bn	RUS	Admiralty Shipyards	2014	2018	Construction yet to begin
Erradii class (MEKO A200)	FFGHM	2	See notes	GER	TKMS	2012	2016	Part of €2.1bn (US$2.7bn) deal including six Super Lynx 300 helicopters. First of class commissioned Apr 2016
Project 20382	FFGHM	2	n.k.	RUS	Severnaya Verf	n.k.	2017	Both vessels under construction
Su-30MKI	FGA ac	14	n.k.	RUS	UAC (Sukhoi)	2015	2016	First aircraft made first flight in Nov 2016. First delivery planned to begin in 2016
Mi-28NE Havoc	Atk hel	42	n.k.	RUS	Russian Helicopters (Rostvertol)	2013	2016	First four helicopters delivered Jun 2016
Egypt (EGY)								
M1A1 Abrams	MBT	1,130	US$3.7bn+	US (EGY)	General Dynamics (Egyptian Tank Plant 200)	1988	1992	M1A1 Co-production Program. EGY licenced assembly of kits supplied by GDLS
Type-209/1400	SSK	2	€920m (US$1.28bn)	GER	TKMS	2011	2016	First of class launched Dec 2015
El Fateh class (Gowind 2500)	FFGHM	4	€1bn (US$1.33bn)	FRA/EGY	DCNS/ Alexandria Shipyard	2014	2017	First to be built in FRA; remainder in EGY. First of class launched Sep 2016. Construction begun in EGY on second of class Apr 2016
Rafale	FGA ac	24	n.k.	FRA	Dassault	2015	2015	First three aircraft delivered Jul 2015. Three more delivered Jan 2016
MiG-29M/M2 Fulcrum	FGA ac	50	US$2bn	RUS	UAC (MiG)	2015	2016	First aircraft due to be delivered by end of 2016
Ka-52 Hokum B	Atk hel	46	n.k.	RUS	Russian Helicopters	2015	2016	First deliveries due by end of 2016
S-300VM	SAM	n.k.	US$1bn+	RUS	Almaz-Antey	2014	2016	First deliveries due by end of 2016
Iran (IRN)								
Mowj class	FSGM	5	n.k.	IRN	n.k.	2004	2010	Second vessel commissioned Mar 2015
Iraq (IRQ)								
F-16C/D Fighting Falcon	FGA ac	36	US$1bn	US	Lockheed Martin	2011	2015	24 C and 12 D models. Deliveries ongoing
FA-50	FGA ac	24	US$1.1bn	ROK	KAI	2013	2016	Deliveries to occur 2016–17
Mi-35M Hind	Atk hel	28	n.k.	RUS	Russian Helicopters (Rostvertol)	2013	2013	Deliveries ongoing
Israel (ISR)								
Merkava Mk IV	MBT	Up to 400	n.k.	ISR	MANTAK	2001	2003	Tenth battalion equipped by late 2016

Table 13 **Selected arms procurements and deliveries, Middle East and North Africa**

Designation	Type	Quantity (Current)	Contract Value	Prime Nationality	Prime Contractor	Order Date	First Delivery Due	Notes
Namer	APC (T)	n.k.	n.k.	US	General Dynamics (GDLS)	2011	2012	ISR to acquire fewer than originally planned due to high cost
Dolphin II class (Type-800)	SSK	1	€400m (US$500m)	GER	TKMS (HDW)	2012	2017	With AIP system. Order for third boat
Sa'ar 6	FFGHM	4	€430m (US$477.14m)	GER	TKMS	2015	n.k.	GER to pay €115m (US$127.6m) of the order cost
F-35A *Lightning* II	FGA ac	2	n.k.	US	Lockheed Martin	2010	2016	Programme of record for 33 aircraft. Low-rate Initial Production 8 contains two for ISR
Arrow 2	SAM (BMD)	n.k.	n.k.	ISR/US	IAI/Boeing	1991	1998	Number and cost undisclosed
Arrow 3	SAM (BMD)	n.k.	n.k.	ISR/US	IAI/Boeing	2008	2017	In-service date expected in 2017
David's Sling (*Magic Wand*)	SAM	n.k.	n.k.	ISR/US	Rafael/ Raytheon	2006	2016	Initial operating capability yet to be declared
Jordan (JOR)								
Mbombe	APC (W)	50	n.k.	JOR/RSA	ADI	2015	n.k.	Production began Jun 2016
Kuwait (KWT)								
Eurofighter *Typhoon*	FGA ac	28	£6.4bn (US$9.26bn)	Int'l	Eurofighter (Leonardo)	2016	n.k.	Tranche-three aircraft
H225M *Caracal* (EC725 *Super Cougar*)	Hvy tpt hel	30	ε€1bn (εUS$1.1bn)	Int'l	Airbus Group (Airbus Helicopters)	2016	2019	Twenty-four for army; six for national guard
Patriot PAC-3	SAM upgrade	6 fire units	US$523.39m	US	Raytheon	2016	n.k.	Modernisation of six fire units to 3+ standard. To be complete by 2022
Lebanon (LBN)								
A-29 *Super Tucano*	Trg ac	6	US$172.5m	US	Sierra Nevada	2015	2017	Delivery to be complete by 2019
Morocco (MOR)								
M1A1SA *Abrams*	MBT	222	n.k.	US	General Dynamics	2011	2016	Ex-US Army surplus. M1A1s being refitted by General Dynamics to M1A1SA standard
Oman (OMN)								
Eurofighter *Typhoon*	FGA ac	12	See notes	GER/ITA/ ESP/UK	Eurofighter (BAE Systems)	2012	2017	Part of GB£2.5bn (US$3.9bn) deal including eight *Hawk* Mk128s. Construction of first aircraft began 2016
Hawk Mk128 Advanced Jet Trainer	Trg ac	8	See notes	UK	BAE Systems	2012	n.k.	Part of GB£2.5bn (US$3.9bn) deal including 12 Eurofighter *Typhoon*s
Qatar (QTR)								
Leopard 2A7	MBT	62	See notes	GER	KMW	2013	2015	Part of €1.66bn (US$2.47bn) contract including 24 PzH 2000. Deliveries ongoing
PzH 2000	Arty (SP 155mm)	24	See notes	GER	KMW	2013	2015	Part of €1.66bn (US$2.47bn) contract including 62 *Leopard* 2A7. Deliveries ongoing
Coastal Defence System	AShM	n.k.	ε€640m (US$715m)	Int'l	MBDA	2016	n.k.	Coastal Defence System including *Exocet* MM40 Blk 3 and *Marte* ER anti-ship missiles

Table 13 Selected arms procurements and deliveries, Middle East and North Africa

Designation	Type	Quantity (Current)	Contract Value	Prime Nationality	Prime Contractor	Order Date	First Delivery Due	Notes
n.k.	FSGHM	4	See notes	ITA	Fincantieri	2016	n.k.	Part of €4bn (US$4.46bn) contract including two PSO and one LPD
n.k.	PSO	2	See notes	ITA	Fincantieri	2016	n.k.	See above
n.k.	LPD	1	See notes	ITA	Fincantieri	2016	n.k.	See above
Rafale	FGA ac	24	€6.4bn (US$7.5bn)	FRA	Dassault	2016	n.k.	–
B-737 AEW	AEW&C ac	3	n.k.	US	Boeing	2014	n.k.	–
AH-64E Apache Guardian	Atk hel	24	US$667.5m	US	Boeing	2016	2019	–
Patriot PAC-3	SAM	10 fire units	US$2.4bn	US	Raytheon	2014	2015	Deliveries ongoing

Saudi Arabia (SAU)

Designation	Type	Quantity (Current)	Contract Value	Prime Nationality	Prime Contractor	Order Date	First Delivery Due	Notes
LAV	APC (W)	n.k.	C$15bn (US$10bn)	CAN	General Dynamics Land Systems – Canada	2014	n.k.	SAU light armoured vehicle, will be manufactured in CAN
Eurofighter Typhoon	FGA ac	72	GB£4.43bn (US$8.9bn)	GER/ITA/ESP/UK	Eurofighter (BAE Systems)	2005	2009	Project Salam. Original plan to complete final assembly of remaining 48 in SAU dropped
F-15E Strike Eagle	FGA ac	84	US$11.4bn	US	Boeing	2012	2015	F-15SA variant. Part of a package including F-15S upgrades, and AH-64 and AH-6i helicopters that could total US$24bn
Hawk Mk128 Advanced Jet Trainer	Trg ac	44	n.k.	UK	BAE Systems	2012	2016	Twenty-two more ordered in 2015
AH-64E Apache Guardian	Atk hel	36	US$1.27bn	US	Boeing	2011	2012	Twenty-four for RSLF and 12 for national guard. Deliveries ongoing
AH-6i Little Bird	MRH hel	24	n.k.	US	Boeing	2014	n.k.	For national guard
Patriot PAC-3	SAM	n.k.	US$2bn	US	Raytheon	2015	n.k.	Including ground systems, training package and support equipment

Tunisia (TUN)

Designation	Type	Quantity (Current)	Contract Value	Prime Nationality	Prime Contractor	Order Date	First Delivery Due	Notes
OH-58D Kiowa Warrior	MRH hel	24	n.k.	US	Government surplus	2016	2017	First helicopters in test late 2016

United Arab Emirates (UAE)

Designation	Type	Quantity (Current)	Contract Value	Prime Nationality	Prime Contractor	Order Date	First Delivery Due	Notes
M142 HIMARS	Arty (MRL 227mm)	12	US$142.75m	US	Lockheed Martin	2015	2016	Deliveries to be complete by Dec 2017
Baynunah class	FSGHM	6	AED3bn (US$820m)	UAE (FRA)	ADSB (CMN)	2003	2006	First of class built in FRA; others to be built in UAE. Fifth of class entered service 2016
Global 6000 SRSS	ISR ac	2	US$1.27bn	SWE	Saab	2015	n.k.	–
C-17A Globemaster III	Hvy tpt ac	2	US$618m	US	Boeing	2015	2015	Delivery status of final aircraft unclear
Piaggio P.1HH Hammerhead	UAV (ISR Med)	8	€316m (US$350m)	ITA	Piaggio Aerospace	2016	n.k.	–
Terminal High-Altitude Area Defense (THAAD)	SAM	12	n.k.	US	Lockheed Martin	2011	2015	Two batteries. First battery delivered 2015
Falcon Eye	Satellite (ISR)	2	€800m (US$1.1bn)	Int'l	Airbus Group/Thales	2013	2017	First satellite due to launch 2017; second 2018

Chapter Eight
Latin America and the Caribbean

Caribbean security challenges

The Caribbean region has for some years grappled with a range of ongoing security crises, including organised crime and narcotics trafficking, but the convergence of a number of factors is now raising particular issues for Caribbean Basin states. Three key countries – Colombia, Cuba and Venezuela – are each facing complex political and strategic challenges that will influence regional stability. At the same time, there has been a significant increase in drug trafficking and other transnational criminal activities, including human trafficking and arms smuggling. Meanwhile, a number of long-standing border disputes have resurfaced. This combination of challenges will not only concern regional states; it will in all likelihood demand more attention from the United States.

The security situation in Colombia is facing fundamental change, marked by the challenge of implementing the peace agreement with FARC and the implications this has for the role of the armed forces. However, there was at the time of writing some uncertainty over the deal, after voters rejected it in a 2 October referendum. Undaunted, the government around the same time scheduled peace talks with the second-largest rebel group, the National Liberation Army (ELN), for later that month. Other complications for Bogota include an expansion in cocaine production and a tough economic climate that led to budget cuts in 2016 and maintained downward pressure on defence spending (see pp. 429–30).

Meanwhile, Venezuela is facing three concurrent crises, with a spiral of criminal violence (Caracas's 119 homicides per 100,000 inhabitants make it one of the world's most violent cities), an economic debacle that has brought its population to the brink of famine, and a political deadlock between government and opposition. In these circumstances, President Nicolás Maduro has sought to bolster the armed forces' support by appointing senior military officials to key government positions and making them responsible for food distribution. By increasing their political role, these military leaders now have a crucial role in determining the future of the regime.

Further east, the recent thawing of relations between Cuba and the US may have reduced strategic tensions, but has not alleviated the island's parlous economic situation. To a large extent, the Cuban economy had stayed above water because of the daily delivery of 100,000 barrels of Venezuelan oil. However, Venezuela's economic implosion has forced a radical reduction in aid. At the same time, with the retirement of President Raúl Castro already announced for 2018, there is a significant risk of political vacuum in a country that has been ruled by Raúl and his elder brother Fidel before him for more than half a century.

In these circumstances, the Cuban armed forces' political and economic role has become more significant. On the one hand, the armed forces retain a certain level of prestige among the population; on the other, they are known to control some of the most dynamic sectors of the economy through a business conglomerate known as Grupo de Administracion Empresarial SA (GAESA). As such, the transition to a post-Castro era will likely be influenced by the position of the Cuban armed forces.

Narcotics trafficking: on the up

The region has seen a resurgence in drug trafficking as a result of increased cocaine production in Colombia and the ease with which narcotics transit Venezuela (a process for which corruption is a key enabler). There are now two principal drug routes to the US through the Caribbean. The first is the route from Colombia through Panama, Guatemala and Mexico, and the second is either directly from the Venezuelan coast or through the Lesser Antilles to the Dominican Republic and Haiti, before transiting Central America and from there to Mexico.

This increase in narcotics trafficking in the Caribbean is evidenced by the dramatic surge in cocaine seizures by regional countries. From 2014 to 2015, the amount of cocaine seized by Panama's security forces rose from just over 35 tonnes to 53 tonnes. In the same period, the amount confiscated in the Dominican Republic and adjacent waters rose from 7.5 tonnes to just under 15 tonnes. Meanwhile, in July 2016, the Guatemalan authorities announced that they had so far that year intercepted about 7.4 tonnes of cocaine, the same amount that they seized in the whole of 2015.

This expansion of drug trafficking is taking place at the same time as significant change to the structure of the drug-smuggling gangs. In recent years, arrests in Central America have disrupted the groups that acted as intermediaries between producers in Colombia and the Mexican cartels, dismantling gangs such as the Guatemalan Los Mendoza or the Honduran Los Cachiros. This has created a vacuum that groups such as Mara Salvatrucha – as well as emerging criminal networks in Costa Rica and Panama – are hoping to fill. It is unlikely that such change in the smuggling networks will come about peaceably.

The expansion of other illegal business has created more complex security concerns. Criminal networks linked to Mexican cartels and Central American *maras* (gangs) are now accruing enormous profits from intra- and extra-regional human trafficking while the region more broadly grapples with weapons smuggling. Although the US was traditionally the origin of much of the illicit arms market, Venezuela is an increasingly common source. This highlights the possible risk of proliferation of illegal weapons should Venezuela's crisis worsen such that law and order – and the security of armouries – is challenged.

Caribbean security sector adapts

Following years of counter-narcotics activity, security structures in many regional states have been adapted to fight organised crime. From Guatemala to the Dominican Republic and Jamaica, efforts have focused on reducing the role of the armed forces in internal security, and on modernising the police by reducing corruption, introducing community-policing skills and strengthening key capabilities such as intelligence or criminal investigation.

In some cases, efforts to maintain a dominant role for police forces in internal-security missions have suffered from institutional weakness, particularly among those forces that are still too under-strength to face heavily armed criminal groups alone. As a consequence, several governments have looked to develop closer cooperation between the police and the armed forces. For example, Guatemala and the Dominican Republic have created inter-agency task forces, bringing together military and police personnel for counter-crime operations.

Meanwhile, there has been increased emphasis on strengthening regional security-cooperation mechanisms. Examples include the 15 states of the Caribbean Community (CARICOM) approving a Regional Security Strategy in 2013; this includes lines of effort such as strengthening border controls, combating human trafficking and tackling money laundering. Within this framework, CARICOM's Implementation Agency for Crime and Security has been highlighted as a useful instrument in facilitating information exchanges and joint security-force training.

However, the Caribbean also faces renewed inter-state tension. There has been friction between Nicaragua and Colombia caused by the demarcation of their territorial waters, while Venezuela's claim to an extensive region in western Guyana has also raised tensions. In addition, there is evidence of emerging friction associated with the deterioration of security and social conditions in border areas. Tensions between the Dominican Republic and Haiti have been caused by a combination of migratory pressures, drug trafficking and the smuggling of consumer goods. There are similar challenges in areas bordering Colombia and Venezuela, where guerrillas and criminal gangs control drug trafficking and fuel smuggling.

The US has increased security cooperation with Central American and Caribbean states in light of this rise in instability. *The Military Balance* has long highlighted some of Washington's security- and military-assistance measures within Central America. In 2010 Washington established the Central America Regional Security Initiative (having renamed the Central America element of the Merida Initiative), which provides advice and resources to strengthen police forces and tackle criminality in the region. In parallel, it launched the Caribbean Basin Security Initiative, seeking similar objectives in CARICOM countries and the Dominican Republic. But it remains to be seen whether these efforts will be enough to stop any possible deterioration in inter-state relations or further expansion of organised crime in the region.

Mexico

Mexico's forthcoming National Defence Policy remains under internal discussion. It is the first such document to be drafted jointly by the Ministry of National Defence (which controls the army and the air force) and the Ministry of the Navy, and it is expected to reflect a redefinition of Mexico's regional and international security role, with a shift in Mexico's military posture towards greater participation in international security operations. Since the September 2014 announcement of a shift in the country's foreign-policy stance, Mexico has increased its contribution to UN peacekeeping operations. It now has observers deployed to the UN missions in Haiti, Lebanon and Western Sahara. The armed forces also announced plans to contribute observers to the proposed UN-sponsored force to monitor the ceasefire in Colombia, and to prepare for the establishment of a new peacekeeping training centre, allowing for the formation of battalion-level peacekeeping units. In addition, Mexico expanded its network of overseas military attachés.

Despite this new external role, internal-security functions – including law-enforcement support and natural-disaster response – remain a high priority for Mexico's armed forces. Indeed, given the failure to implement national-level police reform and grow the civilian-led National Gendarmerie beyond its original 5,000-personnel strength, the army's and navy's homeland-security profiles continue to increase.

The army is expanding and re-tasking its Military Police (MP) units to undertake law-enforcement-support duties. Each MP brigade is composed of three standard MP battalions and a special-operations battalion. These specially tasked and trained forces will form the first line of support for state and local law-enforcement agencies battling organised criminal groups. Meanwhile, to cope with the continued and expanding need for disaster response, engineering units are being redeployed from their main base in Mexico City and re-equipped to serve as first responders in areas frequently affected by natural disasters. At the same time, programmes to modernise the armoured fleet and to modernise and expand artillery are at the planning stage and scheduled to move ahead in 2017.

The navy is also in the process of redefining its structure. Plans to reorganise the navy into coastal-protection and blue-water forces are under way. The coastguard force will monitor the exclusive economic zone and include coastal-patrol and interceptor craft, as well as search-and-rescue stations and port-security units. The navy assumed all port-security responsibilities in June 2016, further expanding its internal-security mandate, and also took over from civilian authorities in ports throughout the country. The Marina de Guerra – the more conventional naval force – will comprise forces on each coast consisting of Mexico's ageing frigates, as well as missile boats and support vessels, and two amphibious marine forces; these units will have a greater external role, but will require significant funding. Local construction of ocean, coastal and interceptor patrol vessels, plus auxiliaries, continues, with the sixth 1,700-tonne *Oaxaca*-class offshore patrol vessel (OPV) launched in August and the seventh *Tenochtitlan*-class (Damen Stan Patrol 4207) vessel commissioned in the same month. Meanwhile, a programme for the local construction of two Damen SIGMA 105 frigates remains in the planning stage.

Chile

Chile also received deliveries of naval equipment in 2016. In August, the fourth *Piloto Pardo*-class OPV was launched by Chilean shipbuilder ASMAR. This maritime-patrol ship (OPV 84 *Cabo Odger*) is scheduled for delivery to the navy in August 2017. *Cabo Odger* and her sister-ship *Marinero Fuentealba* are armed with 76mm cannons and are reinforced for Antarctic patrol operations. Negotiations are under way concerning a mid-life upgrade to Chile's (ex-UK) Type-23 frigates, and plans should be further refined in 2017. The air force has shelved its combat and advanced trainer requirements, as replacing the F-5E *Tiger* II or A-36 fleets with a new lead-in fighter/trainer is no longer considered a priority for 2017. Meanwhile, it was reported in early September 2016 that the air force had selected the *Black Hawk* to meet the medium multi-role helicopter requirement.

Central America

In Central America, the most notable equipment delivery was to Nicaragua, with an initial batch of 20 T-72B1 main battle tanks delivered from Russian surplus stocks. A further 30 will be delivered during 2017, and Nicaragua also announced that it will procure new helicopters and patrol vessels. Military modernisation in Venezuela is on hold because of the economic crisis that continues to place significant strain on the country's finances. Nonetheless, the Venezuelan armed forces continued receiving the last batches of equipment contracted from Russia and China between 2009 and 2014, including VN-18 infantry fighting vehicles, VN-1 armoured personnel carriers and AVIC K-8W lead-in fighter/trainers. The navy is taking delivery of a new patrol fleet including six Damen 5009 OPVs; deliveries like these are the last vestiges of the Venezuelan military's high spending levels in the pre-crisis years.

DEFENCE ECONOMICS

The macroeconomic outlook for the region remained bleak in 2016. Although the regional economy stagnated the previous year (a figure of 0.0% was recorded), 2016 was marked by negative growth of -0.6%, according to the IMF. The current slowdown stems from a confluence of internal and external factors. Weak global trade, coupled with low Chinese demand, kept commodity prices down. With many Latin American countries significant exporters of commodities, including metals and agricultural products, this means reduced revenues for state coffers.

Meanwhile, still-low oil prices continued to affect Colombia, Ecuador and Venezuela in particular. At the same time, Latin American currencies remained weak against the dollar. As a whole, fiscal policy in many countries was constrained by this fall in revenue, and public debt rose. However, this general slowdown masked divergent economic trends across the region. Although South American growth was moderated by poor economic performance in Argentina, Brazil and Venezuela, Central America and the Caribbean fared better.

Brazil's economy contracted by 3.8% in 2015 and 3.3% in 2016. The fall in commodity prices since

Map 10 **Latin America and the Caribbean regional defence spending**[1]

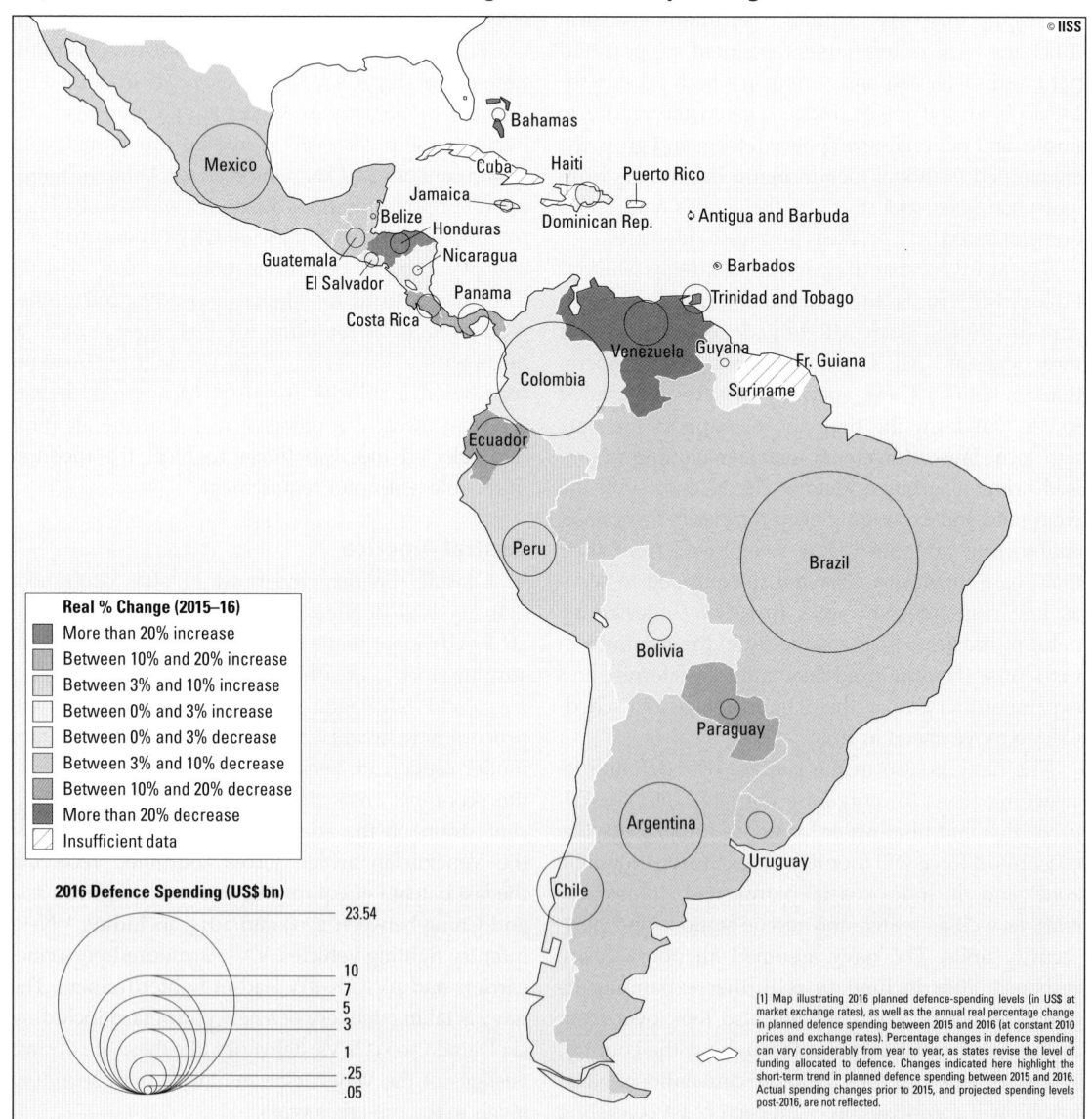

[1] Map illustrating 2016 planned defence-spending levels (in US$ at market exchange rates), as well as the annual real percentage change in planned defence spending between 2015 and 2016 (at constant 2010 prices and exchange rates). Percentage changes in defence spending can vary considerably from year to year, as states revise the level of funding allocated to defence. Changes indicated here highlight the short-term trend in planned defence spending between 2015 and 2016. Actual spending changes prior to 2015, and projected spending levels post-2016, are not reflected.

2011 has reduced government revenues, but Brazil did not reduce public expenditures over this period. Meanwhile, unemployment rose to more than 11% in 2016, with inflation also on the up. To help address this situation, the government reduced unemployment insurance and increased taxes on fuel, while water and electricity prices rose. As a result, real income has fallen, limiting private consumption. In addition, political upheaval during the year increased uncertainty and undermined confidence in the economy.

Further south, a year after it expanded by 2.5%, Argentina's economy contracted by 1.8% in 2016. This was mostly due to the government's economic-austerity policies. Taking office in December 2015, the administration of President Mauricio Macri announced a goal to limit public deficits and to boost international trade. Macri settled Argentina's decade-long dispute with foreign creditors and also reduced foreign-exchange controls and agricultural-export tariffs. Furthermore, a 30% devaluation of the peso favoured Argentine exporters. These various measures have helped reintegrate Argentina into the global trading system and have re-ignited the interest of foreign investors. However, challenges remain. Inflation rose by 30–40% in 2016, and there was a deficit accounting for around 5% of GDP. As part of a bid to limit public spending, the government cut the previous administration's electricity, gas and water subsidies. As a consequence, gas prices rocketed during the winter by over 700%. After demonstrations, the government backed down and it was agreed that new gas prices should be decided through public consultations. Nonetheless, the IMF projected that Argentina's GDP will grow by 2.7% in 2017.

Venezuela remains mired in recession. After growth declined by 3.9% in 2014 and 6.2% in 2015, 2016 growth was forecast to contract by 10%, with a negative forecast of -4.5% for 2017. The IMF estimated that inflation was 720% in 2016.

In contrast, Central America and the Caribbean were in a good economic position, and growing at a steady pace, in 2016. Economic recovery in the US meant sustained external demand for Central American and Caribbean economies, which are more dependent on their northern neighbour than South American states. They also benefited from lower oil prices. Furthermore, growing exports and higher tourism receipts contributed to economic development in many countries. For example, Mexico's economy grew by 2.1% in 2016, the Dominican Republic's by 5.9%, Costa Rica's by 4.2%, Guatemala's by 3.5% and Nicaragua's by 4.5%.

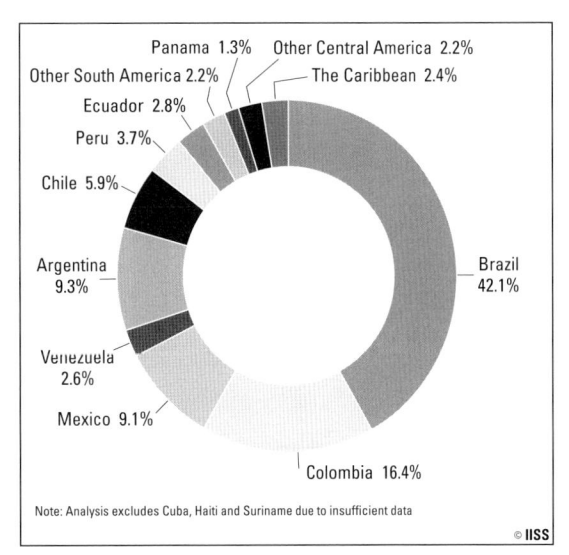

Figure 25 **Latin America and the Caribbean defence spending by country & sub-region**

Panama 1.3%
Other Central America 2.2%
Other South America 2.2%
The Caribbean 2.4%
Ecuador 2.8%
Peru 3.7%
Chile 5.9%
Argentina 9.3%
Venezuela 2.6%
Mexico 9.1%
Colombia 16.4%
Brazil 42.1%

Note: Analysis excludes Cuba, Haiti and Suriname due to insufficient data

Defence spending

With no Latin American or Caribbean states facing major external threats or engaging in inter-state military clashes (even if disputes flared on occasion), the drivers for defence spending remained muted in the region. Overall, Latin America and the Caribbean spent about 1.1% of GDP on defence in 2016, the lowest proportion of any region. However, regional states are improving their capabilities for counter-criminal and counter-narcotics tasks, as well as, in some cases, newer outward-facing defence tasks. Investment has therefore focused on improving and expanding homeland-security capabilities, including through procurements of armoured vehicles, coastal patrol vessels, radars and armed training aircraft employed for aerial-sovereignty patrols. Although these capabilities tend to dominate, some states are still pursuing significant enhancements to their conventional military capability.

Until 2013, Brazil and Venezuela accounted for more than half of the region's overall defence spending, so the decline in available government revenues in these states, combined with political crises there, has had a direct effect on regional defence spending. Several of Brazil's multi-billion, multi-year investments have been shelved, although those at an advanced stage – or that were linked to significant foreign direct investment or programmes to deliver

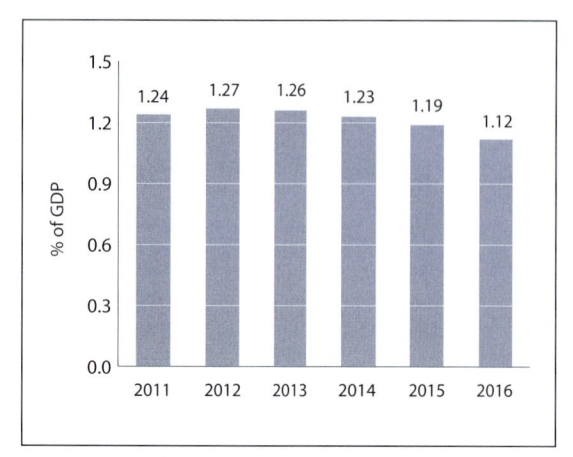

Figure 26 **Latin America and the Caribbean regional defence expenditure** as % of GDP

Year	% of GDP
2011	1.24
2012	1.27
2013	1.26
2014	1.23
2015	1.19
2016	1.12

the transfer of technology or industrial expertise – have managed to survive.

Venezuela is approaching the end of a major multi-service equipment-recapitalisation programme, but plans to follow this up with additional procurements have been shelved because of the country's parlous economic situation. As a result, further procurement spending is unlikely; with the country having so recently received a significant amount of modern equipment, there is a risk that sustaining optimum maintenance levels will prove challenging.

Peru's economic growth has been higher than expected, with 3.7% growth in GDP in 2016, and it is projected to increase by 4.1% in 2017, according to the IMF. Defence spending, however, has not increased at the same rate, and no major procurement programmes were announced in 2016.

Colombia's growth decelerated to 2.2% in 2016, down from 4.9% in 2013. However, the IMF has projected that growth will rise to 2.7% in 2017. Defence spending in 2016 still amounted to 3.3% of GDP, a significant figure by regional standards.

Positive economic indicators in Mexico and Central America have been mostly linked to recovery in the US, but this has not had an impact on regional defence spending, with regional countries traditionally allocating a low percentage of GDP to defence. Defence spending in Mexico has not grown at the same rate as broader economic growth, principally due to the effect of low oil prices (oil makes up a significant proportion of government revenues). Meanwhile, in the Caribbean, Trinidad and Tobago increased its defence spending by some 54.2%, from US$394 million to US$608m, as part of a drive to modernise its naval, coastguard and military capabilities.

Procurement

Few large defence-procurement programmes were announced in the region in 2016. This is principally because national budgets were still struggling with the effects of rising inflation, decreasing exchange rates and continued low oil prices. While Brazil's procurements decreased significantly, some have been reduced or redrafted. Among these, the US$300m procurement of three Boeing 767-300ERs, modified by Israel Aerospace Industries to the multi-role tanker/transport configuration, is on hold and has been replaced by the US$20m three-year lease of a Boeing 767-300ER for the air force. Meanwhile, the air force offered for sale eight of its now retired *Mirage 2000C*s, and the navy announced it was considering offering for sale several defence estates.

Colombia's largest procurement in 2016 was an order for 60 Textron *Commando* armoured infantry fighting vehicles for US$65m. Meanwhile, the first Bell TH-67 training helicopters arrived for air-force service in 2016; these were procured second-hand from the US Army. The Peruvian armed forces had received by late 2015 three of the four C-27J *Spartan* medium transport aircraft ordered in two batches in 2013 and 2015. Other ongoing contracts include that with Korea Aerospace Industries for 24 KT-1P armed trainers (most of which are to be built in Peru), as well as deals with Russian Helicopters for 37 Mi-171Sh medium transport helicopters and with General Dynamics for five Kaman SH-2G *Super Seasprite* anti-submarine-warfare helicopters. However, no major defence-procurement programmes were announced in 2016, an election year in Peru.

In Central America, Nicaragua has announced a boost to its military capabilities, which so far includes 50 T-72B1 main battle tanks and, although they have not yet been confirmed, patrol craft – also from Russia. Other states in Central America continue to procure small vessels and light aircraft for border security and the protection of exclusive economic zones, mostly against smuggling and illegal fishing. For instance, Costa Rica was expected to take delivery in 2017 of two *Island*-class patrol craft donated by the US Coast Guard. The donation of two UH-1H helicopters by Taiwan in 2016, as well as the confiscation of a single Bell 407 abandoned by presumed drug traffickers in 2015, has also significantly increased Belize's air-mobility capabilities. Honduras for its part procured

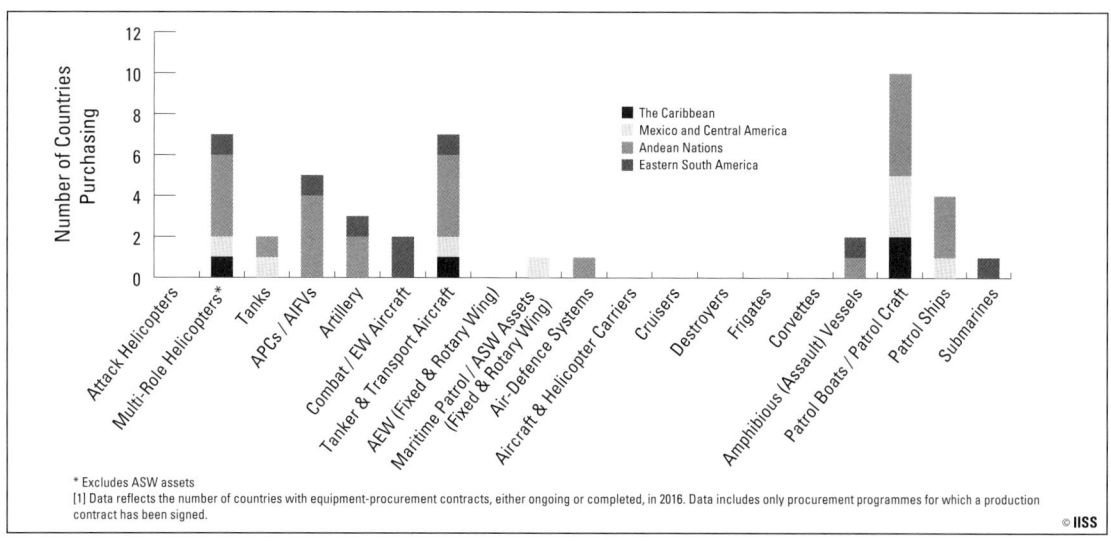

Figure 27 **Latin America and the Caribbean: selected ongoing or completed procurement priorities in 2016**[1]

a single landing craft from Colombia's COTECMAR shipyards and reportedly signalled its intention to procure an ocean-patrol vessel.

ARGENTINA

The election of centre-right candidate Mauricio Macri in Argentina's October 2015 presidential contest, coming after 12 years of left-wing administrations under Néstor Kirchner (2003–07) and Cristina Fernández de Kirchner (2007–15), indicated that the country was about to make a significant change in political direction. On assuming power in December 2015, the Macri administration faced challenges on several fronts, including an economy with high inflation, unstable exchange rates and significant social discontent. While the government acknowledges that the defence sector requires significant investment and reorganisation, it is prioritising the economy by attempting to reduce the fiscal deficit, and eliminating exchange-rate restrictions in order to boost exports. The government has also looked to settle outstanding disputes with holdout bondholders (following Argentina's 2014 selective default) to begin to attract foreign investment again.

The establishment of the Macri administration also heralds potentially profound change for Argentina's defence sector. After a long period of relative neglect and underinvestment, there is a requirement to modernise the country's defence policy, update its doctrine, reorganise and revitalise the defence industry, and replace a large number of ageing, inoperable or retired platforms. By late 2015, the operational capabilities of the Argentine armed forces had declined significantly due to these factors, as well as a lack of equipment investment and a general erosion of maintenance practices, particularly since the turn of this century. Defence-industrial capacity also declined over this period. In January 2016, Defence Minister Julio Martinez announced that the new government's plans for the country did not include 'an Air Force which could not fly or a Navy that could not sail' and reiterated that the Macri administration would seek to remedy operational deficiencies. Martinez emphasised that the country's equipment needs were wide-ranging, and that the armed forces had long suffered from a lack of attention predating the Kirchner administrations.

Argentina's armed forces are a shadow of those that were defeated in a limited war with the United Kingdom in 1982. After the fall of the military government, the 1983 general election confirmed a return to multi-party democracy and a period in which the armed forces were de-prioritised, while at the same time undergoing a far-reaching process aimed at investigating their role in the 'dirty war' against political opponents in the 1970s and early 1980s. Military and defence-industrial capacity declined further in the 1990s, with the defence budget falling in relation to the overall budget and hovering at under 1% of GDP. While the administrations of Néstor and Cristina Kirchner both saw a significant increase in

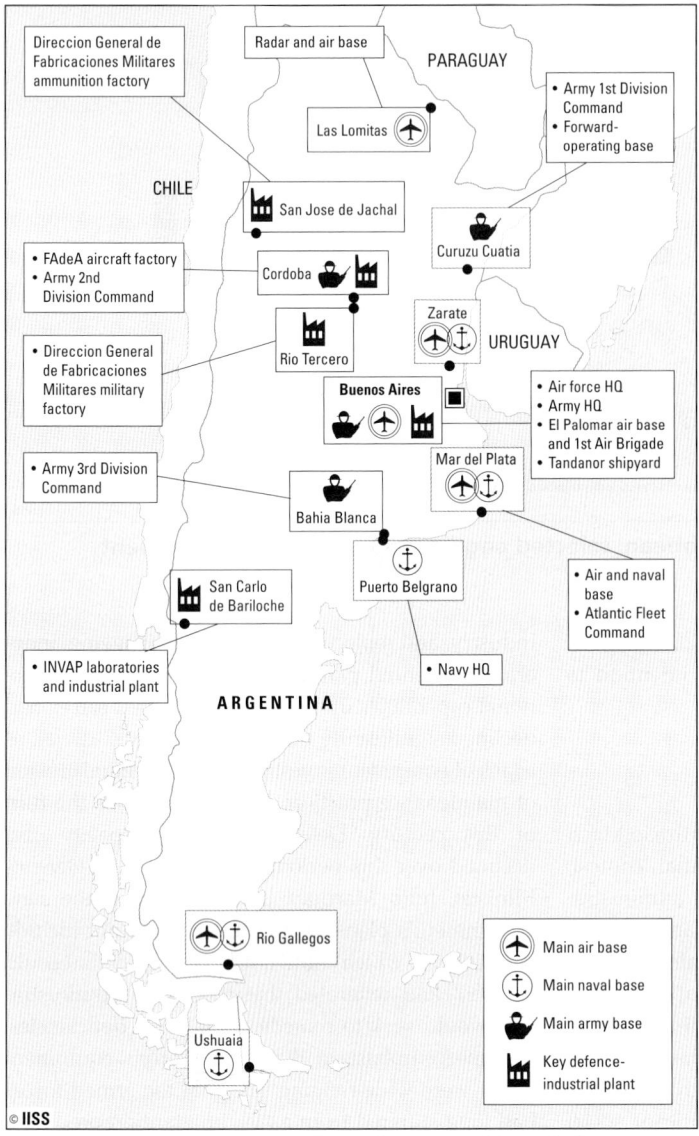

Map 11 **Argentina's main military bases and key defence-industrial sites**

eration within South America are visible in the 2015 book. So too is Argentina's claim to the Falkland Islands, which remains a significant issue in foreign- and defence-policy dynamics, although there has been an improvement in bilateral relations with the UK since the election of the Macri government. Antarctic sovereignty is another key concern, as is maintenance of the logistics capacity necessary to support relevant tasks on that continent. Border protection is a growing theme, and the most likely shift in Argentina's defence policy will centre on the possibility of employing the armed forces in internal-security operations – mainly counter-narcotics missions. An increase in narcotics smuggling prompted Argentina to institute in 2011 its *Northern Shield* monitoring and interdiction mission. This led to the procurement and deployment of new radar facilities and, in January 2016, the issue of security procedures that would, among other measures, allow the air force to force down aircraft suspected of involvement in organised criminal activity.

Alongside continuing defence cooperation with Brazil on land- and air-platform development and production, Argentina's other significant regional defence initiative has been further rapprochement with long-time rival Chile. This cooperation began in the late 1990s and was embodied by the establishment

government rhetoric over Argentina's claim to the Falkland Islands, this was not followed by measures that would have led to a concomitant increase in military capabilities to enforce these claims. Funding may have nominally increased, but the effect of this was eroded by inflation.

Throughout this period, however, the Ministry of Defence published defence documentation, including white papers in 1999 and 2010, and again in 2015. Strategic priorities for defence display continuity but also reflect current security imperatives. Territorial-defence considerations and greater regional coop-

of the bilateral *Cruz del Sur* combined peacekeeping force in 2005, a two-battalion formation that includes air, land and sea elements from both nations.

Service developments

For a country its size, Argentina's defence procurement has been limited since the turn of this century. The army has since received only a few conventional systems, including four WMZ-551B1 armoured personnel carriers (APCs) from China, which were destined for trials with the *Cruz del Sur* force, and a small number of 105mm howitzers. Inflation effects and other economic difficulties prevented even modest budget hikes from translating into increased defence investments.

Army

The army resorted to indigenous upgrade programmes to maintain minimum combat capability. In most cases, these programmes were cut short due to funding shortfalls, and as such there was only a limited impact on ground-force capabilities. Examples include Project *Patagon*, which called for the local remanufacture of up to 40 AMX-13 light tank turrets (the AMX-13s had been withdrawn from service some years before) and fitting these on new SK105A2 chassis, four of which were procured. There were also two attempts, in 2010 and 2015, to upgrade the TAM main battle tank, although neither progressed beyond the prototype stage. Plans to procure an initial 14 Iveco VBTP-MR *Guarani* APCs from the Brazilian production line have been announced several times since 2012, but have failed to materialise. Likewise, a co-development project for a light air-transportable vehicle known as the VLEGA *Gaucho*, which included pre-production of some 35 vehicles in 2007–08, failed to reach series production.

Army aviation has also experienced significant challenges. Project *Hornero*, launched in 2004, called for the upgrade of 20 of the army's Bell UH-1H helicopters to *Huey* 2 standard; this has proceeded at a very slow pace, with the 20th *Huey* 2 expected by 2020. In 2007 attention shifted towards a local-assembly agreement with China for up to 40 Z-11 light helicopters. However, the programme only resulted in one CZ-11 *Pampero* being received in kit form and assembled at the government-run Fabrica Argentina de Aviones (FAdeA) aircraft factory. The project was later cancelled. Meanwhile, a procurement process was initiated in 2012 for up to 20 former Italian AB206B1 light helicopters, half of which were to be equipped with miniguns to fulfil an armed-escort role. This acquisition was not finalised until May 2016.

Navy

Naval procurement was also limited during the Kirchner era. The navy's only major new vessel programme during 2003–15 involved the procurement of new patrol vessels, ideally from local shipyards. Based on a regional-cooperation project initially conceived with Chile for the selection of a common offshore-patrol vessel (OPV) platform, the navy launched in 2005 the *Patrullero de Alta Mar* (High Seas Patrol) programme, which envisioned local production of five Fassmer OPV80s. Funding delays forced the navy to shelve the plan, which in 2010 was relaunched as the *Patrullero Oceánico Multipropósito* (Multi-purpose Ocean Patrol) programme, with the number of OPVs reduced to four. Local production was due to begin in 2012, with first delivery from 2013, but this programme has also experienced difficulties. The only 'new' vessels procured by the navy are four second-hand *Neftegaz*-class oil-rig tugs from Russia, which arrived in December 2015.

Naval-aviation procurement has also been minimal, limited to four UH-3H *Sea King* helicopters from US Navy stocks. Two of the Argentinian Navy's fleet of these helicopters had been lost in a 2007 fire on the *Almirante Irizar* icebreaker. Meanwhile, the intended purchase of ten Dassault *Super Etendard Modernisé* fighters from the French Navy as attrition replacements did not materialise, nor did a plan for mid-life updates to the *Super Etendard* fleet; as a consequence, this fleet was inoperable from the mid-2000s. Indeed, the retirement of the last EMB-326 *Xavante* light attack aircraft in 2008 left the navy without a real air-combat capability.

The strain on the fleet is evident, with a lack of investment leaving anti-submarine-warfare capability moribund; effectively ending mine-warfare and airborne-early-warning capacity; severely depleting surface- and aerial-patrol capability; and failing to replace obsolete electronic-warfare systems. This has led to a reduction in both capability and morale; to outsiders, the fleet's relative decline was encapsulated in one of its former principal surface vessels, ARA *Santisima Trinidad*, capsizing in 2013 at its berth in Puerto Belgrano. (The vessel was raised in 2015 and is under consideration as a museum ship.)

Air force

The air force has also experienced procurement challenges, despite multiple announcements of upgrades and increased production of the IA-63 *Pampa* lead-in fighter/trainer. (A 2007 plan called for production of up to 40 new IA-63s – including enhanced combat variants – that would partially replace the then-ageing, now almost-vanished, fighter fleet.) However, the only successful air-force procurement has been of rotary-wing, rather than fixed-wing, assets. Two Mi-171 medium helicopters specifically outfitted for Antarctic operations were procured in 2011 and two Bell 412s (one new and one a search-and-rescue variant from a civilian operator) in 2013–14. At the same time as the 2016 announcement concerning the AB206B1 helicopters for army aviation, the Ministry of Defence's logistics chief, Walter Ceballos, said that Argentina might discuss the possible purchase of AW169 helicopters to replace the SA315. At the same time, Ceballos indicated that a study was under way on C-27J *Spartan* or C295M medium transport aircraft, possibly with an eye to a replacement for Argentina's Fokker *Friendships*.

As of late 2016, Argentina's fixed-wing combat capability was greatly reduced, with only a limited number of operational A-4AR *Fighting Hawk*s (upgraded A-4M *Skyhawk*s) out of a fleet of 36 delivered in the mid-1990s. These aircraft were due to retire by 2018, and the defence ministry was considering second-hand and new-build options. In August, *La Nacion* reported that air-force officers had visited South Korea to evaluate the Korea Aerospace Industries FA-50, perhaps as a replacement for the A-4ARs.

Meanwhile, Argentina's supersonic-fighter capability ceased with the ceremonial retirement of the air force's iconic *Mirage* fleet in late November 2015. The search for a new (or second-hand) fighter to replace the *Mirage* has been particularly challenging, with several options – including new, used and upgraded aircraft – evaluated, reportedly selected and even budgeted. So far, there has been no firm progress on any of the discussed options. This saga began with a 2013 expression of interest in a squadron of 16 former Spanish *Mirage* F1M interceptors, for which a budget of 1.1 billion pesos (US$200.9 million) was included in the 2013 defence budget. After no progress was made on that proposal, in 2014 attention shifted to 14 former Israeli *Kfir* multi-role fighters, upgraded to Block 60 standard, at a price of 4.1bn pesos (US$504.6m).

In October 2014 the focus moved towards potential new-build fighters, with then-defence minister Agustin Rossi announcing that Argentina was interested in procuring up to 24 *Gripen* E/F multi-role fighters from Brazil's production line. However, UK export restrictions regarding British components and systems in the *Gripen* prohibited further negotiations. In late December 2014, reports in the Russian and UK media indicated that Argentina was considering a Russian offer of 12 Sukhoi Su-24 *Fencer* ground-attack aircraft, and in February 2015 Buenos Aires announced the establishment of a bilateral working group to analyse options offered by China. The FC-1 (JF-17 *Thunder*) and J-10 were both evaluated, with 14 of the former reportedly selected. In September 2015, the offer of *Kfir* Block 60s resurfaced with a revised cost of 3.6bn pesos (US$388.4m). After all that, outgoing defence minister Rossi announced in November 2015 that a decision on fighter procurement would be left for the incoming government.

In mid-2016, Defence Minister Martinez announced discussions on a potential purchase of second-hand *Mirage* F1Cs or *Mirage* 2000Cs from France, and in July he revisited the idea of procuring *Gripen* from the Brazilian production line, this time requesting that British components be replaced so that the UK could not veto the deal. Given the large number of UK-derived components in *Gripen*, this would not be a viable option unless there is a political shift over Argentina's claim on sovereignty of the Falklands. UK-origin components are particularly prevalent in the *Gripen's* active electronically scanned radar, but the cost of retrofitting another radar onto the platform would make an order for such a small number of aircraft prohibitive for Argentina on its own.

While the search for a new supersonic fighter might gain more attention than other procurement efforts, the air force is looking to set in place the building blocks of a future capability. Indeed, the priority is now focused on procuring a new generation of training aircraft to replace the ageing fleet of B-45 *Mentor* and EMB-312 *Tucano* basic trainers; light fighters that can be used to intercept illegal flights; medium- and long-range transport aircraft; and helicopters that can replenish Argentina's Antarctic bases. Although actual purchases might still prove problematic, Argentina is exploring other avenues to deliver capability; the use of innovative financing options is one approach, and four Grob G120TP primary trainers have been leased using funding from FAdeA.

DEFENCE ECONOMICS

On taking power in late 2015, the new Argentinian government was confronted by high inflation and unstable exchange rates. To some degree, these problems continued in 2016. Indeed, the economy contracted by -1.8% during the year, principally due to austerity policies initiated by the government. That said, the IMF predicted that the economy will grow by 2.7% in 2017. But there is currently reduced fiscal space for defence disbursements as the government weathers the domestic buffeting caused by issues

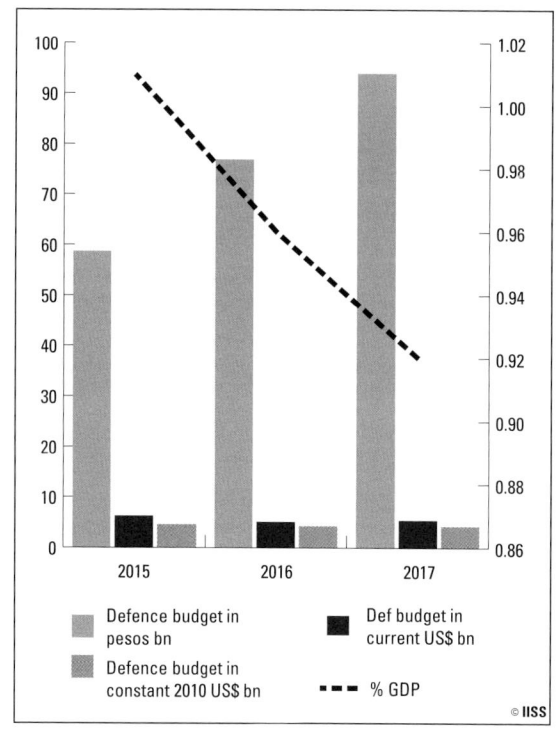

Figure 28 **Argentina's defence budgets, 2015–17**

including the lifting of subsidies on gas, electricity and water; this means that the receipts received on these utilities covered only a small proportion of the production costs. IMF figures on GDP growth are indicative of the bumpy ride that Argentina's economy has endured in recent years – at 6% in 2011; -1% in 2012; 2.4% in 2013; -2.5% in 2014; and 2.5% in 2015. However, the government hopes that structural reform and measures such as encouraging investment (and access to foreign credit markets once outstanding legal cases are settled) will increase Argentina's attractiveness as an investment destination and also stimulate domestic consumption.

During the presidential campaign, Macri said that Argentinian defence spending had fallen to 0.8% of GDP and that the armed forces required increased spending of at least 1.2% of GDP. Argentinian defence budgets increased nominally between 2015 and the latest 2017 budget proposal. However, these increases were not sufficient to compensate for inflation, estimated at between 30% and 40% in 2016 and forecast at 23% for 2017.

As a consequence, the defence budget decreased in current US dollars (from US$6.3bn in 2015 to US$5.2bn in 2017), as well as in constant 2010 US dollars (US$4.6bn in 2015 to US$4.3bn in 2016). Year-on-year, the defence budget declined by 6.5% in real-terms spending between 2015 and 2016, and by 0.7% between 2016 and 2017; it also fell as a share of the country's GDP (from 1.01% in 2015 to 0.92% in 2017). With the government keen to rein in public spending in its bid to balance the economy, it is likely that future rises might be moderate even amid an obvious need for equipment investment. Meanwhile, more important than the overall figure is what the country spends it on. In Argentina's case, a significant proportion of the defence budget is allocated to personnel-related costs, not to research and development (R&D) or new equipment purchases. In its 2015 defence white paper, the ministry noted that 77.7% of the 2014 budget went on personnel costs, with 16.9% on operations and maintenance, 5.2% on R&D and 0.2% on 'investments'. With increased disbursements on mortgage assistance for service personnel and also – as was again announced in 2016 – salaries, the personnel proportion of spending will continue to constitute a significant portion of the budget.

Defence industry

Argentina possesses an indigenous defence-manufacturing capacity covering land, sea and air systems, albeit one that has been degraded in recent years by underinvestment and fading skills as the workforce has been depleted, with upgrades and new builds generally proceeding glacially. However, the 2016 budget included measures to strengthen defence-industrial production through Fabricaciones Militares (FM, the principal state-owned defence-manufacturing company), bolstering military shipbuilding and the provision of Antarctic logistic capacities. The army was to focus on the modernisation of UH-1H helicopters and the TAM main battle tank. Navy refurbishment priorities include the *Almirante Brown* (MEKO 360) destroyers and the submarine *Santa Cruz*. Unsurprisingly, given the focus on *Northern Shield* activities, the 2016 budget also prioritised the air force's airspace-control capabilities. FM is making some improvement to its industrial capacity, including through the acquisition of machinery, infrastructure upgrades and the opening of new production lines. Following discussions between Argentina and Italy, it is possible that two small-arms systems will be produced under licence at FM factories.

The FAdeA aircraft plant is also the subject of renewed attention. As of August 2016, four of Argentina's C-130s were among the aircraft undergoing maintenance at the plant, which was reportedly under scrutiny by its new director over both the size of its workforce and its programme focus. It is possible that Argentina will push for FAdeA to be involved in any future combat-aircraft deal in order to secure long-term work for the plant, although this would be subject to intense discussion and would in all likelihood be limited to component manufacture. FAdeA established relations with Brazil's Embraer following a 2011 partnership contract between them to locally produce the spoilers, flap fairings and ramp doors – among other parts – for the Embraer KC-390 transport aircraft.

The domestic shipbuilding industry is a target for development. Complejo Industrial y Naval Argentino (Argentine Naval Industrial Complex), comprising the Tandanor and Almirante Storni shipyards, is the focus of attention. Key priorities to revitalise the naval sector include the refurbishment and modernisation of the *Almirante Irizar* following the 2007 fire, and mid-life upgrades to submarines, including the *Santa Cruz*. Again, rebuilding a skilled workforce is a priority. According to Tandanor, the yard had only 150 workers in 2007; expanding workflow (partly through the repair of private vessels) necessitated an expanded workforce, some of which was secured by retraining naval veterans, particularly for submarine work.

BRAZIL

With Brazil experiencing its worst recession in decades, major defence projects suffered further delays in 2016. Budgetary restrictions affected some of the country's most strategically significant projects, including the SISFRON border-monitoring programme – although the importance of the effort was highlighted after a congressional committee criticised security policies on Brazil's porous western borders. Despite the poor economic context, the administration of President Michel Temer – sworn in following Dilma Rousseff's impeachment in September 2016 – is viewed as being more favourably disposed to the armed forces, given his statements about the strategic importance of Brazil's defence projects.

Amid the general economic gloom, the defence budget for 2016 saw a nominal increase (4.1%) on 2015, reaching R$82.1 billion (US$23.5bn). But, similar to previous years in the Brazilian federal government, several ministries in March suffered budgetary restrictions. The defence ministry was one of the most heavily affected, with R$2.8bn (US$803 million) of its budget officially 'frozen' – meaning that the resources may or may not be released during the year.

Budgetary constraints limit the armed forces' procurement plans. By law, salaries and pensions are considered mandatory expenditures, which means that the adjustments required to comply with budget cuts fall entirely on its investment component. In 2016 this comprised just 9.7% of the total resources forecast for the year. As a result, current procurement programmes are proceeding at a slow pace and there are very few announcements of significant new projects.

Another possible reason for the slow progress in procurements may relate to the fact that significant costs were incurred hosting the Olympic and Paralympic games (two years after Brazil hosted the football World Cup) amid ongoing concerns over armed activity in urban areas by organised criminal groups. The 2016 events saw 38,000 personnel deployed on security tasks during August and September. Between 2014 and 2016, preparing and carrying out these security plans cost some R$854.4m (US$245m).

The practice of restricting significant portions of the defence budget, which by 2015 had become an annual fixture, led the senate's Foreign Relations Committee (CRE) to release a report in December of that year criticising the government's approach to defence. The report found that the budgetary restrictions and cuts had affected 'strategic projects' deemed essential to Brazil's sovereignty, adding that the national defence industry's production capacity had been compromised as a result. The CRE report proposed that a National Defence Fund be created. The fund should be managed by the defence ministry, the report continued, in order to give these strategic projects greater financial security. This recommendation may have influenced the National Bank of Economic and Social Development's initiative to create a study group tasked with improving state credit to private defence companies.

The severe budget restrictions in 2016 delayed the PROSUB project, which includes the construction of four conventional and one nuclear-powered submarine. This project is seen as a defence priority, as it is intended to transfer technology to Brazil's naval industry and involves technical and military capacities that are in line with the country's global political ambitions. Nonetheless, the head of the navy, Admiral Eduardo Leal Ferreira, said in 2016 that the resources allotted to PROSUB had that year been cut by half, to R$200m (US$57m). According to Admiral Ferreira, this would delay the delivery of the nuclear-powered submarine by four years, until 2027.

Another priority defence project is the Embraer KC-390 transport aircraft, developed in partnership with the Brazilian Air Force. Although this too has been delayed, Embraer decided to proceed with the programme despite not receiving R$1.4bn (US$402bn) that the government was due to transfer over the second half of 2015 and the beginning of 2016. The aircraft made its first international appearance in July 2016, at the Farnborough International Air Show in the United Kingdom.

However, the procurement project most severely affected by budgetary constraints is the SISFRON border-monitoring system. With a projected cost of R$12bn (US$3.4bn), SISFRON has in recent years received just R$300m (US$86m) per year. This comes despite the change in the armed forces' strategic orientation – towards the border – under the Strategic Border Plan. Launched in 2011, this consists of ad hoc military operations and a permanent police presence in border areas in order to combat criminality. SISFRON is designed to aid in this effort by implementing a network of monitoring systems along Brazil's 16,800-kilometre land border using geostationary satellites, sensors, intelligence aircraft and command-and-communications hubs.

This inconsistency between the discourse over border protection and the practical implementation of the border-protection initiatives has attracted criticism from the National Budgetary Ombudsman. In November 2015, this body said that 'the lack of human, material and financial resources' for the armed forces' border operations 'highlight the vulnerability' of those spaces to threats such as drug- and arms-trafficking groups.

A central component of the ombudsman's censure was the lack of a coherent and coordinated approach towards the border. It criticised the fact that the police, military and customs service had separate border projects, each with different names and little coordination between them. The armed forces' *Ágata* operations consist of periodic large-scale deployments to the border for monitoring, inspections (of vehicles and land crossings, for example) and patrols. In June 2016, the 11th *Ágata* operation took place for ten days at key points along the western border. This led to the seizure of 5.7 tonnes of explosive material, 168 small arms and 123 kilograms of cocaine. However, it remains unclear if these operations help in dealing strategic blows to transnational criminal organisations or their leadership structures.

The presidential transition from the left-wing Rousseff to Temer, her centre-right vice-president, was seen as potentially positive in terms of securing resources for the armed forces. Temer is regarded as being more familiar with the requirements for such strategic projects – not least because as vice-president he was responsible for overseeing Brazil's border-security efforts. Indeed, when the Temer government sent its 2017 budget plan to congress in August 2016, the total amount assigned for defence reached R$93.3bn (US$27.7bn), a 13.7% increase on the 2016 budget. However, at the time of writing it remained unclear whether broader economic conditions would, as before, lead to a reduction in the resources allocated for defence.

COLOMBIA

Peace agreement, economic crisis and military transformation

On 26 September 2016, the government of Colombia signed a peace deal with FARC rebels, marking the end of a decades-long conflict. Although the deal was rejected by referendum on 2 October, both sides were at the time of writing trying to continue with the peace process. This agreement, and the subsequent start of negotiations with another rebel group, the National Liberation Army (ELN), marked the beginning of a strategic transformation for Colombia. It is in this context that the armed forces and police will have to undergo a profound transformation, including an overall reduction in size amid defence-budget cuts and persistent security threats. The challenge will lie in balancing these issues and managing force reductions while minimising any decrease in operational capability.

At the same time, Colombia is experiencing economic difficulty. The global fall in oil prices badly affected a country that depends on oil for most of its hard currency. This situation could worsen in the near future as the fall in prices has not only cut government revenues but also discouraged the search for new oil deposits. The consequence has been a rapid decline in Colombian crude reserves, challenging Colombia's oil economy.

At the same time, notwithstanding the uncertainty caused by the referendum result, the peace agreement between the government and FARC far from guarantees an end to violence in Colombia. Although the text signed by both parties includes the commitment that the guerrilla group will disarm, doubts persist about whether FARC will completely dismantle its military capability. In fact, under the agreement a number of the former guerrillas will retain their weapons in order to provide security for their leaders. In addition, dissension in the FARC ranks is becoming apparent, and the possibility exists that some members could reject the peace agreement.

Although the ELN escalated its attacks in 2016, it too was in negotiations with the government, and peace talks were announced for the end of October. However, Los Urabenos and other, smaller criminal organisations continue to pose a significant threat in a number of regions. At the same time, coca cultivation has grown; this now encompasses an area of around 1,590 square kilometres. With potential cocaine production of around 426 tonnes, this increase in coca cultivation could provide criminal groups with the finances necessary to strengthen their military capabilities.

As noted in previous editions of *The Military Balance*, Colombia's armed forces have in recent years been planning for a new security role and new organisational structures in the post-FARC era. In this context, the Ministry of Defence, the armed forces and the police have developed a series of plans that seek to reconfigure their structure and missions. For instance, in August 2016 the army adopted a new doctrine called 'Damascus'. This doctrine emphasises roles such as disaster relief or assistance to rural communities (the army announced in early 2016 a plan to create 12 new reserve battalions tasked for the disaster-relief role), but it does not lose sight of the need to maintain combat capability. These new doctrinal shifts include the adoption of a new command structure that includes the creation of four new branches, including a special-forces branch, and an effort to strengthen the Joint Special Operations Command.

Meanwhile, the navy has increased its international activities. The second OPV80-class ocean-patrol vessel, ARC *7 de Agosto*, took part in the EU-led *Operation Atalanta* in 2015, proving the navy can contribute to international security operations. As a result of this focus on taking on new roles overseas, the third of class, ARC *Santander*, which is due to be delivered in 2017, has been up-gunned with a 76mm cannon and the capacity to operate a medium helicopter. Colombian shipyards are gearing up for the local development and construction of a light frigate under the *Plataforma Estrategica de Superficie* (PES) programme. PES is expected to be defined in 2017, with subcontractors selected in 2018 and initial deliveries expected in 2023. In August, the air force announced that it too would undergo a transformation that, while stressing air mobility within Colombia, would focus on enhancing technology, communications, meteorology and climate change, among other areas.

The success of these transformation efforts depends in large part on predictable defence budgets, although these are not guaranteed. The Colombian armed forces have already felt the effects of the economic crisis. A reduction in investment budgets has led to the cancellation or delay of many procurement programmes, including air-defence and naval-helicopter upgrades. At the same time, restrictions on fuel and spare parts limit air and riverine operations.

This transformation process will also lead to a reduction in establishment strength; the trend will be underlined by increasing political pressure to transfer resources from defence to social spending in order to gain economic dividends from the peace agreement with FARC. The effects of this process will be very different for each branch of the Colombian armed services, but the conscript-heavy army will bear the brunt of the reductions. The government is focusing on two mechanisms to reduce force levels. It has eased the legal sanctions for young people who do not comply with compulsory military service; as such, the number of conscript recruits for the army has reduced by about one-third. The army has also slowed its recruitment of new professional soldiers.

The navy will likely see its large force of marines reduced, although the need to strengthen interdiction capacity to curb drug trafficking by sea, as well as to deal with the maritime dispute with Nicaragua, are likely to limit cuts in naval capability. The air force's relatively small establishment, meanwhile, will make it difficult to reduce its numbers significantly, although budget cuts will likely lead to the postponement or cancellation of modernisation projects – possibly including the replacement of the *Kfir* fighter/ground-attack aircraft fleet.

However, the National Police Force appears to be faring better. As part of the broader transformation of Colombia's security apparatus, it is likely that control of the police will transfer from the defence ministry to the interior ministry. In addition, it is possible that the police will receive new equipment, including helicopters and unmanned aerial vehicles, and that their personnel numbers will increase.

Antigua and Barbuda ATG

East Caribbean Dollar EC$		2015	2016	2017
GDP	EC$	3.4bn	3.52bn	
	US$	1.26bn	1.3bn	
per capita	US$	14,100	14,432	
Growth	%	2.2	2.0	
Inflation	%	1.0	1.4	
Def bdgt [a]	EC$	72m	71m	
	US$	26m	26m	
US$1=EC$		2.70	2.70	

[a] Budget for the Ministry of Legal Affairs, Public Safety, Immigration & Labour

Population 93,581

Age	0–14	15–19	20–24	25–29	30–64	65 plus
Male	11.9%	4.5%	4.0%	3.5%	20.2%	3.4%
Female	11.5%	4.4%	4.1%	3.8%	24.4%	4.5%

Capabilities

Internal-security and counter-narcotics operations are the main focus of the state's small armed forces. Regional cooperation is evident in Antigua and Barbuda's long-standing participation in the *Tradewinds* exercise series and in ongoing efforts to counter the illicit narcotics trade. The defence forces also maintain a disaster-response capability. China has donated equipment to the armed forces, including vehicles, motorbikes and general materiel. Although the US radar-tracking and telemetry air station based in-country closed in 2015, both Washington and the Antiguan authorities stressed that there would be future opportunities for defence cooperation.

ACTIVE 180 (Army 130 Coast Guard 50)
(all services form combined Antigua and Barbuda Defence Force)

RESERVE 80 (Joint 80)

ORGANISATIONS BY SERVICE

Army 130
FORCES BY ROLE
MANOEUVRE
  Light
  1 inf bn HQ
  1 inf coy
COMBAT SERVICE SUPPORT
  1 spt gp (1 engr unit, 1 med unit)

Coast Guard 50
EQUIPMENT BY TYPE
PATROL AND COASTAL COMBATANTS • PB 2: 1 *Dauntless*; 1 *Swift*

Argentina ARG

Argentine Peso P		2015	2016	2017
GDP	P	5.84tr	8.04tr	
	US$	630bn	542bn	
per capita	US$	14,617	12,425	
Growth	%	2.5	-1.8	
Inflation	%	n.k.	n.k.	
Def bdgt	P	58.7bn	76.9bn	94bn
	US$	6.3bn	5.2bn	
US$1=P		9.27	14.85	

Population 43,886,748

Age	0–14	15–19	20–24	25–29	30–64	65 plus
Male	12.7%	4.0%	3.9%	3.8%	20.2%	4.8%
Female	12.0%	3.8%	3.7%	3.8%	20.6%	6.7%

Capabilities

Argentina's armed forces principally focus on border security, surveillance and counter-narcotics operations, in part due to the increase in drug-trafficking activity in and around the country. Buenos Aires cooperates with Bolivia and Paraguay on border-security and counter-narcotics operations. The *Northern Shield* mission was extended to December 2016 and the defence ministry has increased air-force flying hours to enable more frequent ISR operations. Argentina's equipment inventory is increasingly obsolete, with modernisation hampered by limited funding. According to the 2016 defence-spending review and 2017 projections, most of the budget will be allocated to aircraft maintenance and modernisation and for the procurement of new types. Air-force capability is declining: in January 2016 the entire A-4 *Skyhawk* fleet was grounded due to technical problems and is expected to be permanently retired from service by 2018. The defence ministry aims to upgrade the entire fleet of ageing IA-58H *Pucara* ground-attack aircraft. The *Mirage* III fleet has not yet been replaced. The naval fleet has also seen its capability decline in areas like anti-submarine warfare, mine warfare and AEW, although ship maintenance also came under scrutiny when the ARA *Santisima Trinidad* capsized at berth in 2012. However, there is some naval maintenance and limited shipbuilding capacity at the country's yards. Argentina relies on foreign suppliers for most of its equipment, although domestic firm Fabricaciones Militares signed an agreement with Italy's Beretta to produce weapons on licence. Aviation concern FAdeA conducts some aircraft maintenance, including to Argentina's *Hercules* transports, but its efficiency has been questioned. The armed forces train with Brazil and Chile and participate in UN peacekeeping missions. A 'State Partnership' agreement was inked with the US Georgia National Guard in late 2016; this military-to-military relationship will include sharing expertise in enhancing readiness as well as in disaster response, border security and peacekeeping missions. (See pp. 423–28.)

ACTIVE 74,200 (Army 42,800 Navy 18,500 Air 12,900) **Paramilitary 31,250**

ORGANISATIONS BY SERVICE

Army 42,800; 7,000 civilian
Regt and gp are usually bn-sized
FORCES BY ROLE
SPECIAL FORCES
1 SF gp
MANOEUVRE
Mechanised
1 (1st) div (1 armd bde (4 tk regt, 1 mech inf regt, 1 SP arty gp, 1 cbt engr bn, 1 int coy, 1 sigs coy, 1 log coy), 1 (3rd) jungle bde (2 jungle inf regt, 1 arty gp, 1 engr bn, 1 int coy, 1 sigs coy, 1 log coy, 1 med coy); 1 (12th) jungle bde (3 jungle inf regt, 1 arty gp, 1 engr bn, 1 int coy, 1 sigs coy, 1 log coy, 1 med coy), 2 engr bn, 1 sigs bn, 1 log coy)
1 (3rd) div (1 mech bde (1 armd recce regt, 1 tk regt, 2 mech inf regt, 1 SP arty gp, 1 cbt engr bn, 1 int coy, 1 sigs coy, 1 log coy), 1 mech bde (1 armd recce tp, 1 tk regt, 2 mech inf regt, 1 SP arty gp, 1 cbt engr bn, 1 int coy, 1 sigs coy, 1 log coy), 1 int bn, 1 sigs bn, 1 log coy)
1 (Rapid Deployment) force (1 armd bde (1 recce sqn, 3 tk regt, 1 mech inf regt, 1 SP arty gp, 1 cbt engr coy, 1 int coy, 1 sigs coy, 1 log coy), 1 mech bde (1 armd recce regt, 3 mech inf regt, 1 arty gp, 1 cbt engr coy, 1 int coy, 1 sigs coy,1 log coy), 1 AB bde (1 recce tp, 2 para regt, 1 arty gp, 1 cbt engr coy, 1 sigs coy, 1 log coy), 1 AD gp (2 AD bn))
Light
1 (2nd) mtn inf div (2 mtn inf bde (1 armd recce regt, 3 mtn inf regt, 2 arty gp, 1 cbt engr bn, 1 sigs coy, 1 log coy), 1 mtn inf bde (1 armd recce bn, 2 mtn inf regt, 1 jungle inf regt, 2 arty gp, 1 cbt engr bn, 1 sigs coy, 1 construction coy, 1 log coy), 1 AD gp, 1 sigs bn)
1 mot cav regt (presidential escort)
Air Manoeuvre
1 air aslt regt
COMBAT SUPPORT
1 arty gp (bn)
1 engr bn
1 sigs gp (1 EW bn, 1 sigs bn, 1 maint bn)
1 sigs bn
1 sigs coy
COMBAT SERVICE SUPPORT
5 maint bn
HELICOPTER
1 avn gp (bde) (1 avn bn, 1 hel bn)
EQUIPMENT BY TYPE
ARMOURED FIGHTING VEHICLES
MBT 231: 225 TAM, 6 TAM S21
LT TK 117: 107 SK-105A1 *Kuerassier*; 6 SK-105A2 *Kuerassier*; 4 *Patagón*
RECCE 47 AML-90
IFV 232: 118 VCTP (incl variants); 114 M113A2 (20mm cannon)
APC 278
  APC (T) 274: 70 M113A1-ACAV; 204 M113A2
  APC (W) 4 WZ-551B1
ENGINEERING & MAINTENANCE VEHICLES
ARV *Greif*
ANTI-TANK/ANTI-INFRASTRUCTURE
MSL • SP 3 M1025 HMMWV with TOW-2A
RCL 105mm 150 M-1968
ARTILLERY 1,085
SP 155mm 19 VCA 155 *Palmaria*
TOWED 172: **105mm** 64 Model 56 pack howitzer; **155mm** 108: 28 CITEFA M-77/CITEFA M-81; 80 SOFMA L-33
MRL 8: **105mm** 4 SLAM *Pampero*; **127mm** 4 CP-30
MOR 886: **81mm** 492; **SP 107mm** 25 M106A2; **120mm** 330 Brandt; **SP 120mm** 39 TAM-VCTM
RADAR • LAND 18+: M113A1GE *Green Archer* (mor); 18 RATRAS (veh, arty)
AIRCRAFT
TPT • Light 23: 1 Beech 80 *Queen Air*; 3 C-212-200 *Aviocar*; 3 Cessna 207 *Stationair*; 2 Cessna 208EX *Grand Caravan*; 1 Cessna 500 *Citation* (survey); 1 Cessna 550 *Citation Bravo*; 3 DA42 (to be converted to ISR role); 2 DHC-6 *Twin Otter*; 3 SA-226 *Merlin* IIIA; 3 SA-226AT *Merlin* IVA; 1 Sabreliner 75A (*Gaviao* 75A)
TRG 5 T-41 *Mescalero*
HELICOPTERS
MRH 5: 4 SA315B *Lama*; 1 Z-11
TPT 47: **Medium** 3 AS332B *Super Puma*; **Light** 44: 1 Bell 212; 25 Bell 205 (UH-1H *Iroquois* – 6 armed); 5 Bell 206B3; 13 UH-1H-II *Huey* II
AIR DEFENCE
SAM • Point-defence RBS-70
GUNS • TOWED 229: **20mm** 200 GAI-B01; **30mm** 21 HS L81; **35mm** 8 GDF Oerlikon (*Skyguard* fire control)
RADAR • AIR DEFENCE 11: 5 Cardion AN/TPS-44; 6 *Skyguard*

Navy 18,500; 7,200 civilian
Commands: Surface Fleet, Submarines, Naval Avn, Marines
FORCES BY ROLE
SPECIAL FORCES
1 (diver) SF gp
EQUIPMENT BY TYPE
SUBMARINES • TACTICAL • SSK 3:
  1 *Salta* (GER T-209/1100) with 8 single 533mm TT with Mk 37/SST-4 HWT
  2 *Santa Cruz* (GER TR-1700) with 6 single 533mm TT with SST-4 HWT (one undergoing MLU)
PRINCIPAL SURFACE COMBATANTS 11
  DESTROYERS 5
    DDGHM 4 *Almirante Brown* (GER MEKO 360) with 2 quad lnchr with MM-40 *Exocet* AShM, 1 octuple *Albatros* lnchr with *Aspide* SAM, 2 triple B515 ILAS-3 324mm TT with A244 LWT, 1 127mm gun (capacity 1 AS555 *Fennec* hel)
    DDH 1 *Hercules* (UK Type-42 – utilised as a fast troop-transport ship), with 1 114mm gun (capacity 2 SH-3H *Sea King* hel)
  FRIGATES • FFGHM 6:
    6 *Espora* (GER MEKO 140) with 2 twin lnchr with MM-38 *Exocet* AShM, 2 triple B515 ILAS-3 324mm

ASTT with A244 LWT, 1 76mm gun (capacity 1 AS555 *Fennec* hel) (1 vessel damaged in 2016, in repair)

PATROL AND COASTAL COMBATANTS 16
  CORVETTES • FSG 3 *Drummond* (FRA A-69) with 2 twin lnchr with MM-38 *Exocet* AShM, 2 triple Mk32 324mm ASTT with A244 LWT, 1 100mm gun
  PSO 3:
    2 *Irigoyen* (ex-US *Cherokee*)
    1 *Teniente Olivieri* (ex-US oilfield tug)
  PCO 2:
    1 *Murature* (ex-US *King* – trg/river patrol role) with 3 105mm gun
    1 *Sobral* (ex-US *Sotoyomo*)
  PCGT 1 *Intrepida* (GER Lurssen 45m) with 2 single lnchr with MM-38 *Exocet* AShM, 2 single 533mm TT with SST-4 HWT, 1 76mm gun
  PCC 1 *Intrepida* (GER Lurssen 45m) with 1 76mm gun
  PB 6: 4 *Baradero* (*Dabur*); 2 *Point*
AMPHIBIOUS 6 LCVP
LOGISTICS AND SUPPORT 18
  ABU 3 *Red*
  AFS 4 *Puerto Argentina* (ex-RUS *Neftegaz*)
  AGB 1 *Almirante Irizar* (damaged by fire in 2007; now expected to return to service in 2016–17)
  AGHS 3: 1 *Austral*; 1 *Cormoran*; 1 *Puerto Deseado* (ice-breaking capability, used for polar research)
  AGOR 1 *Commodoro Rivadavia*
  AK 3 *Costa Sur* (capacity 4 LCVP)
  AOR 1 *Patagonia* (FRA *Durance*) with 1 hel platform
  AORL 1 *Ingeniero Julio Krause*
  AXS 1 *Libertad*

Naval Aviation 2,000
EQUIPMENT BY TYPE
AIRCRAFT 20 combat capable
  FGA 2 *Super Etendard* (9 more in store)
  ATK 1 AU-23 *Turbo Porter*
  ASW 7: 3 S-2T *Tracker*†; 4 P-3B *Orion*
  TPT • Light 7 Beech 200F/M *King Air*
  TRG 10 T-34C *Turbo Mentor**
HELICOPTERS
  ASW 2 SH-3H (ASH-3H) *Sea King*
  MRH 4 AS555 *Fennec*
  TPT • Medium 4 UH-3H *Sea King*
AIR-LAUNCHED MISSILES
  AAM • IR R-550 *Magic*
  AShM AM-39 *Exocet*

Marines 2,500
FORCES BY ROLE
MANOEUVRE
  Amphibious
    1 (fleet) force (1 cdo gp, 1 (AAV) amph bn, 1 mne bn, 1 arty bn, 1 ADA bn)
    1 (fleet) force (2 mne bn, 2 navy det)
    1 force (1 mne bn)
EQUIPMENT BY TYPE
ARMOURED FIGHTING VEHICLES
  RECCE 12 ERC-90F *Sagaie*
  APC • APC (W) 31 VCR

  AAV 24: 13 LARC-5; 11 LVTP-7
ENGINEERING & MAINTENANCE VEHICLES
  ARV AAVR 7
ANTI-TANK/ANTI-INFRASTRUCTURE
  RCL 105mm 30 M-1974 FMK-1
ARTILLERY 89
  TOWED 19: **105mm** 13 Model 56 pack howitzer; **155mm** 6 M114
  MOR 70: **81mm** 58; **120mm** 12
AIR DEFENCE
  SAM • Point-defence RBS-70
  GUNS 40mm 4 Bofors 40L

Air Force 12,900; 6,900 civilian
4 Major Comds – Air Operations, Personnel, Air Regions, Logistics, 8 air bde

Air Operations Command
FORCES BY ROLE
GROUND ATTACK
  2 sqn with A-4/OA-4 (A-4AR/OA-4AR) *Skyhawk*
  2 (tac air) sqn with IA-58 *Pucara*; EMB-312 *Tucano* (on loan for border surv/interdiction)
ISR
  1 sqn with Learjet 35A
SEARCH & RESCUE/TRANSPORT HELICOPTER
  2 sqn with Bell 212; Bell 212 (UH-1N); Mi-171, SA-315B *Lama*
TANKER/TRANSPORT
  1 sqn with C-130B/E/H *Hercules*; KC-130H *Hercules*; L-100-30
TRANSPORT
  1 sqn with B-707
  1 sqn with DHC-6 *Twin Otter*; Saab 340
  1 sqn with F-27 *Friendship*
  1 sqn with F-28 *Fellowship*; Learjet 60
  1 (Pres) flt with B-757-23ER; S-70A *Black Hawk*, S-76B
TRAINING
  1 sqn with AT-63 *Pampa*
  1 sqn with EMB-312 *Tucano*
  1 sqn with Grob 120TP
  1 hel sqn with Hughes 369; SA-315B *Lama*
TRANSPORT HELICOPTER
  1 sqn with Hughes 369; MD-500; MD500D
EQUIPMENT BY TYPE
AIRCRAFT 64 combat capable
  ATK 52: 20 A-4 (A-4AR) *Skyhawk*†; 2 OA-4 (OA-4AR) *Skyhawk*†; 21 IA-58 *Pucara*; 9 IA-58M *Pucara*
  ELINT 1 Cessna 210
  TKR 2 KC-130H *Hercules*
  TPT 38: **Medium** 7: 1 C-130B *Hercules*; 1 C-130E *Hercules*; 4 C-130H *Hercules*; 1 L-100-30; **Light** 22: 1 Cessna 310; 8 DHC-6 *Twin Otter*; 4 F-27 *Friendship*; 4 Learjet 35A (test and calibration); 1 Learjet 60; 4 Saab 340; **PAX** 9: 1 B-737; 1 B-757-23ER; 7 F-28 *Fellowship*
  TRG 49: 20 AT-63 *Pampa** (LIFT); 19 EMB-312 *Tucano*; 10 Grob 120TP
HELICOPTERS
  MRH 29: 2 Bell 412EP; 15 Hughes 369; 3 MD-500; 4 MD-500D; 5 SA315B *Lama*

TPT 11 **Medium** 3: 2 Mi-171E; 1 S-70A *Black Hawk*;
Light 8: 7 Bell 212; 1 S-76B
AIR DEFENCE
 GUNS 88: **20mm**: 86 Oerlikon/Rh-202 with 9 Elta
 EL/M-2106 radar; **35mm**: 2 Oerlikon GDF-001 with
 Skyguard radar
RADAR • AIR DEFENCE 6: 5 AN/TPS-43; 1 BPS-1000
AIR-LAUNCHED MISSILES
 AAM • IR AIM-9L *Sidewinder*; R-550 *Magic*; *Shafrir* 2‡

Paramilitary 31,250

Gendarmerie 18,000
Ministry of Security
FORCES BY ROLE
COMMAND
 7 regional comd
SPECIAL FORCES
 1 SF unit
MANOEUVRE
 Other
 17 paramilitary bn
 Aviation
 1 (mixed) avn bn
EQUIPMENT BY TYPE
ARMOURED FIGHTING VEHICLES
 RECCE S52 *Shorland*
 APC (W) 87: 47 *Grenadier*; 40 UR-416
ARTILLERY • MOR 81mm
AIRCRAFT
 TPT • Light 12: 3 Cessna 152; 3 Cessna 206; 1 Cessna 336; 1 PA-28 *Cherokee*; 2 PC-6B *Turbo Porter*; 2 PC-12
HELICOPTERS
 MRH 2 MD-500C
 TPT • Light 16: 5 Bell 205 (UH-1H *Iroquois*); 7 AS350 *Ecureuil*; 1 H135; 3 R-44 *Raven* II
 TRG 1 S-300C

Prefectura Naval (Coast Guard) 13,250
Ministry of Security
EQUIPMENT BY TYPE
PATROL AND COASTAL COMBATANTS 67
 PCO 7: 1 *Correa Falcon*; 1 *Delfin*; 5 *Mantilla* (F30 *Halcón* – undergoing modernisation)
 PCC 1 *Mariano Moreno*
 PB 58: 1 *Dorado*; 25 *Estrellemar*; 2 *Lynch* (US *Cape*); 18 *Mar del Plata* (Z-28); 1 *Surel*; 8 Damen Stan 2200; 3 Stan Tender 1750
 PBR 1 *Tonina*
LOGISTICS & SUPPORT 11
 AAR 1 *Tango*
 AFS 1 *Prefecto Garcia*
 AG 2
 ARS 1 *Prefecto Mansilla*
 AX 5: 1 *Mandubi*; 4 other
 AXS 1 *Dr Bernardo Houssay*
AIRCRAFT
 MP 1 Beech 350ER *King Air*
 TPT • Light 6: 5 C-212 *Aviocar*; 1 Beech 350ER *King Air*
 TRG 2 Piper PA-28 *Archer* III

HELICOPTERS
 SAR 3 AS565MA *Panther*
 MRH 1 AS365 *Dauphin 2*
 TPT 5: Medium 3: 1 H225 *Puma*; 2 SA330L (AS330L) *Puma*; **Light** 2 AS355 *Ecureuil* II
 TRG 4 S-300C

DEPLOYMENT

CYPRUS
UN • UNFICYP 362; 2 inf coy; 1 hel flt; 2 Bell 212

HAITI
UN • MINUSTAH 73; 1 fd hospital

MIDDLE EAST
UN • UNTSO 3 obs

WESTERN SAHARA
UN • MINURSO 3 obs

Bahamas BHS

Bahamian Dollar B$		2015	2016	2017
GDP	B$	8.85bn	9.05bn	
	US$	8.85bn	9.05bn	
per capita	US$	24,310	24,567	
Growth	%	-1.7	0.3	
Inflation	%	1.9	1.0	
Def bdgt	B$	152m	121m	99m
	US$	152m	121m	
US$1=B$		1.00	1.00	

Population 327,316

Age	0–14	15–19	20–24	25–29	30–64	65 plus
Male	11.5%	4.1%	4.4%	4.0%	22.1%	2.9%
Female	11.2%	4.0%	4.3%	3.9%	23.0%	4.6%

Capabilities

The Royal Bahamas Defence Force's primary role is maintaining maritime security and countering narcotics trafficking, as well as having a major disaster-relief remit. The country is a regular participant in the *Tradewinds* exercise series and has a training relationship with the US armed forces. In the recent past, the *Coral Cays* table-top exercise, run with US Northern Command, has focused on maritime-security tasks and military assistance to the civilian authorities in cases of unrest. Counter-terrorism exercises have also been conducted with US support. The government is continuing the 'Sandy Bottom' project to address these tasks by undertaking a substantial fleet upgrade and investing in infrastructure at the main base at Coral Harbour and at forward locations. As part of upgrade activities associated with the Sandy Bottom project, the Bahamas commissioned two offshore-patrol vessels and one support vessel in the first half of 2016, while other vessels are being refitted.

ACTIVE 1,300

ORGANISATIONS BY SERVICE

Royal Bahamian Defence Force 1,300

FORCES BY ROLE
MANOEUVRE
Amphibious
1 mne coy (incl marines with internal- and base-security duties)

EQUIPMENT BY TYPE
PATROL AND COASTAL COMBATANTS 22
PCC 2 *Bahamas*
PBF 6 *Nor-Tech*
PB 14: 4 *Arthur Dion Hanna*; 2 *Dauntless*; 1 *Eleuthera*; 2 *Lignum Vitae* (Damen 3007); 1 *Protector*; 2 Sea Ark 12m; 2 Sea Ark 15m
LOGISTICS & SUPPORT 1
AKR 1 *Lawrence Major* (Damen 5612)
AIRCRAFT • TPT • Light 3: 1 Beech A350 *King Air*; 1 Cessna 208 *Caravan*; 1 P-68 *Observer*

FOREIGN FORCES

Guyana Navy: Base located at New Providence Island

Barbados BRB

Barbados Dollar B$		2015	2016	2017
GDP	B$	8.77bn	8.95bn	
	US$	4.39bn	4.47bn	
per capita	US$	15,677	15,955	
Growth	%	0.9	1.7	
Inflation	%	-1.1	0.3	
Def bdgt [a]	B$	67m	73m	79m
	US$	33m	36m	
US$1=B$		2.00	2.00	

[a] Defence & security expenditure

Population 291,495

Age	0–14	15–19	20–24	25–29	30–64	65 plus
Male	9.1%	3.1%	3.4%	3.5%	24.8%	4.5%
Female	9.1%	3.2%	3.4%	3.5%	25.8%	6.8%

Capabilities

Maritime security and resource protection are the main tasks of the Barbados Defence Force. It also has a limited ability to participate in regional peacekeeping and disaster-relief operations. The country takes part in the *Tradewinds* exercise series. Barbados is home to the headquarters of the Regional Security System, a grouping of Caribbean nations' police and security forces – and military capabilities – which can be called on to address threats to regional security and to undertake counter-narcotics and disaster-relief tasks, among others. Local media reports have indicated that the defence force is experiencing some recruitment problems, including in the officer corps.

ACTIVE 610 (Army 500 Coast Guard 110)
RESERVE 430 (Joint 430)

ORGANISATIONS BY SERVICE

Army 500

FORCES BY ROLE
MANOEUVRE
Light
1 inf bn (cadre)

Coast Guard 110

HQ located at HMBS Pelican, Spring Garden
EQUIPMENT BY TYPE
PATROL AND COASTAL COMBATANTS • PB 6:
1 *Dauntless*; 2 *Enterprise* (Damen Stan 1204); 3 *Trident* (Damen Stan 4207)
LOGISTICS & SUPPORT • AX 1

Belize BLZ

Belize Dollar BZ$		2015	2016	2017
GDP	BZ$	3.51bn	3.54bn	
	US$	1.75bn	1.77bn	
per capita	US$	4,785	4,693	
Growth	%	1.0	0.0	
Inflation	%	-0.9	1.0	
Def bdgt [a]	BZ$	39m	42m	43m
	US$	19m	21m	
FMA (US)	US$	0.8m	1m	1m
US$1=BZ$		2.00	2.00	

[a] Excludes funds allocated to Coast Guard and Police Service

Population 353,858

Age	0–14	15–19	20–24	25–29	30–64	65 plus
Male	17.6%	5.4%	5.1%	4.6%	16.1%	1.8%
Female	16.8%	5.2%	4.9%	4.4%	15.9%	2.0%

Capabilities

The principal task for Belize's small armed forces is territorial defence, particularly along the border with Guatemala, along which there were a number of security incidents in 2016. Recent military support to law-enforcement authorities has been steadily downscaled, freeing up troops for border patrolling. Most recent activity has focused on countering narcotics smuggling, although the ability to carry this out is hampered by insufficient maritime patrol or aerial-surveillance and interdiction capacity. However, US SOUTHCOM deployed US Army personnel to Belize in 2016 to carry out training with the BDF to improve the latter's counter-narcotics-smuggling capability. Plans outlined in 2015 included infrastructure refurbishment and the procurement of additional vehicles. A defence security review was planned for 2014 and is believed to be still under way. Assistance has been reported from Canada, the UK and the US in progressing the tasks required for a defence-review process. There has recently been a modest increase in BDF personnel numbers but operations are entirely limited to national territory.

There are established training relationships with the US (including maintenance support), the UK and regional states. Future plans for training include inviting countries to carry out jungle training in Belize with the defence force. Prior to the delivery of a pair of light helicopters in 2016, which has significantly increased the BDF's logistics and deployment capability, the BDF was without rotary-wing assets, making jungle operations more problematic.

ACTIVE 1,500 (Army 1,500)

RESERVE 700 (Joint 700)

ORGANISATIONS BY SERVICE

Army ε1,500
FORCES BY ROLE
MANOEUVRE
　Light
　　2 inf bn (3 inf coy)
COMBAT SERVICE SUPPORT
　1 spt gp
EQUIPMENT BY TYPE
ANTI-TANK/ANTI-INFRASTRUCTURE • RCL 84mm
　8 *Carl Gustav*
ARTILLERY • MOR 81mm 6

Air Wing
EQUIPMENT BY TYPE
AIRCRAFT
　TPT • Light 3: 1 BN-2A *Defender*; 1 BN-2B *Defender*; 1 Cessna 182 *Skylane*
　TRG 1 T-67M-200 *Firefly*
HELICOPTERS
　TPT • Light 3: 2 Bell 205 (UH-1H *Iroquois*); 1 Bell 407

Reserve
FORCES BY ROLE
MANOEUVRE
　Light
　　1 inf bn (3 inf coy)

Paramilitary 150

Coast Guard 150
EQUIPMENT BY TYPE
All Operational patrol vessels under 10t FLD

FOREIGN FORCES
United Kingdom Army 17

Bolivia BOL

Bolivian Boliviano B		2015	2016	2017
GDP	B	228bn	245bn	
	US$	33.2bn	35.7bn	
per capita	US$	3,099	3,276	
Growth	%	4.8	3.7	
Inflation	%	4.1	3.9	
Def bdgt	B	2.99bn	3.04bn	
	US$	435m	443m	
US$1=B		6.86	6.86	

Population　10,969,649

Age	0–14	15–19	20–24	25–29	30–64	65 plus
Male	16.5%	5.1%	4.8%	4.5%	16.4%	2.3%
Female	15.9%	5.0%	4.7%	4.4%	17.7%	2.9%

Capabilities

Counter-narcotics and internal and border security are the main tasks of the armed forces. Modest procurement programmes are intended to improve the services' ability to undertake these roles. A new defence white paper remains in progress. Defence spending has been increasing in recent years, helped by an increase in revenues accruing from a hydrocarbon tax. This has enabled sufficient funding for Bolivia's procurement programmes. In September 2016 Bolivia signed an agreement with Russia on defence-technology cooperation, but China remains a significant supplier of military materiel. Airspace control is an emerging strategic priority, and Bolivia is acquiring 13 radars to help address this requirement. The radars are due to be installed by 2018 and placed along the border with Brazil. There is also increasing cooperation with Peru on matters of border security and countering narcotics trafficking, while exercises in this area have taken place with Argentina's air force. There is some local maintenance capacity for the services, with refurbished aircraft delivered in late 2016. Bolivian personnel deploy on UN peacekeeping missions.

ACTIVE 34,100 (Army 22,800 Navy 4,800 Air 6,500)
Paramilitary 37,100
Conscript liability 12 months (18–22 years of age)

ORGANISATIONS BY SERVICE

Army 9,800; 13,000 conscript (total 22,800)
FORCES BY ROLE
COMMAND
　6 mil region HQ
　10 div HQ
SPECIAL FORCES
　3 SF regt
MANOEUVRE
　Reconnaissance
　　1 mot cav gp
　Armoured
　　1 armd bn

Mechanised
1 mech cav regt
2 mech inf regt
Light
1 (aslt) cav gp
5 (horsed) cav gp
3 mot inf regt
21 inf regt
Air Manoeuvre
2 AB regt (bn)
Other
1 (Presidential Guard) inf regt
COMBAT SUPPORT
6 arty regt (bn)
6 engr bn
1 int coy
1 MP bn
1 sigs bn
COMBAT SERVICE SUPPORT
2 log bn
AVIATION
2 avn coy
AIR DEFENCE
1 ADA regt

EQUIPMENT BY TYPE
ARMOURED FIGHTING VEHICLES
LT TK 54: 36 SK-105A1 *Kuerassier*; 18 SK-105A2 *Kuerassier*
RECCE 24 EE-9 *Cascavel*
APC 148+
APC (T) 87+: 50+ M113, 37 M9 half-track
APC (W) 61: 24 EE-11 *Urutu*; 22 MOWAG *Roland*; 15 V-100 *Commando*
AUV 19 *Tiger* 4×4
ENGINEERING & MAINTENANCE VEHICLES
ARV 4 *Greif*; M578 LARV
ANTI-TANK/ANTI-INFRASTRUCTURE
MSL
SP 2 *Koyak* with HJ-8
MANPATS HJ-8
RCL 90mm M67; 106mm M40A1
ARTILLERY 311+
TOWED 61: 105mm 25 M101A1; 122mm 36 M-30 (M-1938)
MOR 250+: 81mm 250 M29; Type-W87; 107mm M30; 120mm M120
AIRCRAFT
TPT • Light 4: 1 Fokker F-27-200; 1 Beech 90 *King Air*; 1 C-212 *Aviocar*; 1 Cessna 210 *Centurion*
HELICOPTERS
MRH 6 H425
TRG 1 Robinson R55
AIR DEFENCE • GUNS • TOWED 37mm 18 Type-65

Navy 4,800
Organised into six naval districts with HQ located at Puerto Guayaramerín.
EQUIPMENT BY TYPE
PATROL AND COASTAL COMBATANTS • PBR 3: 1 *Santa Cruz*; 2 others

LOGISTICS AND SUPPORT 3
AG 1
AH 2

Marines 1,700 (incl 1,000 Naval Military Police)
FORCES BY ROLE
MANOEUVRE
Mechanised
1 mech inf bn
Amphibious
6 mne bn (1 in each Naval District)
COMBAT SUPPORT
4 (naval) MP bn

Air Force 6,500 (incl conscripts)
FORCES BY ROLE
GROUND ATTACK
2 sqn with AT-33AN *Shooting Star*
1 sqn with K-8WB *Karakorum*
ISR
1 sqn with Cessna 206; Cessna 402; Learjet 25B/25D (secondary VIP role)
SEARCH & RESCUE
1 sqn with AS332B *Super Puma*; H125 *Ecureuil*; H145
TRANSPORT
1 sqn with BAe-146-100; CV-580; MA60
1 (TAB) sqn with C-130A *Hercules*; MD-10-30F
1 sqn with C-130B/H *Hercules*
1 sqn with F-27-400M *Troopship*
1 (VIP) sqn with Beech 90 *King Air*; Beech 200 *King Air*; Beech 1900; Falcon 900EX; Sabreliner 60
6 sqn with Cessna 152/206; IAI-201 *Arava*; PA-32 *Saratoga*; PA-34 *Seneca*
TRAINING
1 sqn with DA40; T-25
1 sqn with Cessna 152/172
1 sqn with PC-7 *Turbo Trainer*
1 hel sqn with R-44 *Raven* II
TRANSPORT HELICOPTER
1 (anti-drug) sqn with Bell 205 (UH-1H *Iroquois*)
AIR DEFENCE
1 regt with Oerlikon; Type-65
EQUIPMENT BY TYPE
AIRCRAFT 38 combat capable
ATK 15 AT-33AN *Shooting Star*
TPT 85: **Heavy** 1 MD-10-30F; **Medium** 4: 1 C-130A *Hercules*; 2 C-130B *Hercules*; 1 C-130H *Hercules*; **Light** 70: 1 *Aero Commander* 690; 3 Beech 90 *King Air*; 2 Beech 200 *King Air*; 1 Beech 1900; 5 C-212-100; 10 Cessna 152; 2 Cessna 172; 19 Cessna 206; 1 Cessna 402; 1 CV-580; 9 DA40; 3 F-27-400M *Troopship*; 4 IAI-201 *Arava*; 2 Learjet 25B/D; 2 MA60†; 1 PA-32 *Saratoga*; 3 PA-34 *Seneca*; 1 Sabreliner 60; **PAX** 10: 1 B-727; 3 B-737-200; 5 BAe-146-100; 1 Falcon 900EX (VIP)
TRG 29: 6 K-8W *Karakorum**; 6 T-25; 17 PC-7 *Turbo Trainer**
HELICOPTERS
MRH 1 SA316 *Alouette* III

TPT 32: **Medium** 3 H215 *Super Puma*; **Light** 29: 2 H125 *Ecureuil*; 19 Bell 205 (UH-1H *Iroquois*); 2 H145; 6 R-44 *Raven* II
AIR DEFENCE • GUNS 18+: **20mm** Oerlikon; **37mm** 18 Type-65

Paramilitary 37,100+

National Police 31,100+
FORCES BY ROLE
MANOEUVRE
  Other
    27 frontier sy unit
    9 paramilitary bde
    2 (rapid action) paramilitary regt

Narcotics Police 6,000+
FOE (700) – Special Operations Forces

DEPLOYMENT

CENTRAL AFRICAN REPUBLIC
UN • MINUSCA 2; 3 obs

CÔTE D'IVOIRE
UN • UNOCI 1 obs

DEMOCRATIC REPUBLIC OF THE CONGO
UN • MONUSCO 8 obs

LIBERIA
UN • UNMIL 1 obs

SOUTH SUDAN
UN • UNMISS 2; 2 obs

Brazil BRZ

Brazilian Real R		2015	2016	2017
GDP	R	5.90tr	6.17tr	
	US$	1.77tr	1.77tr	
per capita	US$	8,670	8,587	
Growth	%	-3.8	-3.3	
Inflation	%	9.0	9.0	
Def bdgt [a]	R	78.8bn	82.1bn	93.3bn
	US$	23.7bn	23.5bn	
US$1=R		3.33	3.49	

[a] Includes military pensions

Population   205,823,665

Age	0–14	15–19	20–24	25–29	30–64	65 plus
Male	11.6%	4.3%	4.1%	4.1%	21.8%	3.4%
Female	11.2%	4.1%	4.0%	4.1%	22.7%	4.6%

Capabilities

Brazil retains ambitions to enhance its power-projection capabilities, improve surveillance of the Amazon region and coastal waters, and further develop its defence industry. However, economic difficulties have significantly affected its ability to develop these ambitions, procurements have been reduced and modernisation plans slowed. Funding and internal deployments associated with the major sporting events of the past four years have also had a budgetary impact. In 2016, the Senate Foreign Relations Committee suggested the creation of a National Defence Fund to guarantee financial support to current projects. Although a budget increase was planned for 2017, continuing economic difficulties may reduce available funds. In May the new defence minister endorsed the previous administration's plans. Nevertheless, the KC-390, FX-2, SISFRON and PROSUB programmes all suffered funding problems. Brazil has a well-developed defence-industrial base, across the land, sea and air domains, and is looking to further its capabilities in terms of aerospace manufacturing and shipbuilding through the *Gripen* combat-aircraft procurement and the PROSUB programme, which is intended to lead to the construction in Brazil of nuclear- and conventionally powered submarines. The armed forces continue to work towards a national cyber-defence capability, regularly participate in domestic and international exercises, and provide the largest contingent of troops for the UN peacekeeping mission in Haiti. (See pp. 428–29.)

ACTIVE 334,500 (Army 198,000 Navy 69,000 Air 67,500) **Paramilitary 395,000**
Conscript liability 12 months (can go to 18; often waived)

RESERVE 1,340,000

ORGANISATIONS BY SERVICE

Army 128,000; 70,000 conscript (total 198,000)
FORCES BY ROLE
COMMAND
  8 mil comd HQ
  12 mil region HQ
  7 div HQ (2 with regional HQ)
SPECIAL FORCES
  1 SF bde (1 SF bn, 1 cdo bn)
  1 SF coy
MANOEUVRE
  Reconnaissance
  3 mech cav regt
  Armoured
  1 (5th) armd bde (1 mech cav sqn, 2 armd bn, 2 armd inf bn, 1 SP arty bn, 1 engr bn, 1 sigs coy, 1 log bn)
  1 (6th) armd bde (1 mech cav sqn, 2 armd bn, 2 armd inf bn, 1 SP arty bn, 1 AD bty, 1 engr bn, 1 sigs coy, 1 log bn)
  Mechanised
  3 (1st, 2nd & 4th) mech cav bde (1 armd cav bn, 3 mech cav bn, 1 arty bn, 1 engr coy, 1 sigs coy, 1 log bn)
  1 (3rd) mech cav bde (1 armd cav bn, 2 mech cav bn, 1 arty bn, 1 engr coy, 1 sigs coy, 1 log bn)
  1 (15th) mech inf bde (3 mech inf bn, 1 arty bn, 1 engr coy, 1 log bn)
  Light
  1 (3rd) mot inf bde (1 mech cav sqn, 2 mot inf bn, 1 inf bn, 1 arty bn, 1 engr coy, 1 sigs coy, 1 log bn)

1 (4th) mot inf bde (1 mech cav sqn, 1 mot inf bn, 1 inf bn, 1 mtn inf bn, 1 arty bn, 1 sigs coy, 1 log bn)
1 (7th) mot inf bde (3 mot inf bn, 1 arty bn)
1 (8th) mot inf bde (1 mech cav sqn, 3 mot inf, 1 arty bn, 1 log bn)
1 (10th) mot inf bde (1 mech cav sqn, 4 mot inf bn, 1 inf coy, 1 arty bn, 1 engr coy, 1 sigs coy)
1 (13th) mot inf bde (1 mot inf bn, 2 inf bn, 1 inf coy, 1 arty bn)
1 (14th) mot inf bde (1 mech cav sqn, 3 inf bn, 1 arty bn)
1 (11th) lt inf bde (1 mech cav regt, 3 inf bn, 1 arty bn, 1 engr coy, 1 sigs coy, 1 MP coy, 1 log bn)
11 inf bn
1 (1st) jungle inf bde (1 mech cav sqn, 2 jungle inf bn, 1 arty bn)
3 (2nd, 16th & 17th) jungle inf bde (3 jungle inf bn)
1 (23rd) jungle inf bde (1 cav sqn, 4 jungle inf bn, 1 arty bn, 1 sigs coy, 1 log bn)
2 jungle inf bn

Air Manoeuvre
1 AB bde (1 cav sqn, 3 AB bn, 1 arty bn, 1 engr coy, 1 sigs coy, 1 log bn)
1 (12th) air mob bde (1 cav sqn, 3 air mob bn, 1 arty bn, 1 engr coy, 1 sigs coy, 1 log bn)

Other
1 (9th) mot trg bde (3 mot inf bn, 1 arty bn, 1 log bn)
1 (18th) sy bde (2 sy bn, 2 sy coy)
1 sy bn
7 sy coy
3 gd cav regt
1 gd inf bn

COMBAT SUPPORT
3 SP arty bn
6 fd arty bn
1 MRL bn
1 STA bty
6 engr bn
1 engr gp (1 engr bn, 4 construction bn)
1 engr gp (4 construction bn, 1 construction coy)
2 construction bn
1 EW coy
1 int coy
6 MP bn
3 MP coy
4 sigs bn
2 sigs coy

COMBAT SERVICE SUPPORT
5 log bn
1 tpt bn
4 spt bn

HELICOPTER
1 avn bde (3 hel bn, 1 maint bn)
1 hel bn

AIR DEFENCE
1 ADA bde (5 ADA bn)

EQUIPMENT BY TYPE
ARMOURED FIGHTING VEHICLES
 MBT 393: 128 *Leopard* 1A1BE; 220 *Leopard* 1A5BR; 45 M60A3/TTS
 LT TK 50 M41C
 RECCE 408 EE-9 *Cascavel*
 APC 1,013
  APC (T) 630: 584 M113; 12 M113A2; 34 M577A2
  APC (W) 383: 223 EE-11 *Urutu*; 160 VBTP-MR *Guarani* 6×6
ENGINEERING & MAINTENANCE VEHICLES
 AEV 4+: *Greif*; HART; 4+ *Leopard* 1
 ARV 4+: *Leopard* 1; 4 M88A1; M578 LARV
 VLB 4+: XLP-10; 4 *Leopard* 1
ANTI-TANK/ANTI-INFRASTRUCTURE
 MSL • MANPATS *Eryx*; *Milan*; MSS-1.2 AC
 RCL 343: **84mm** 149 *Carl Gustav*; **106mm** 194 M40A1
ARTILLERY 1,853
 SP 147: **105mm** 72 M7/108; **155mm** 75: 37 M109A3; 38 M109A5
 TOWED 431
  105mm 336: 233 M101/M102; 40 L118 Light Gun; 63 Model 56 pack howitzer
  155mm 95 M114
 MRL 127mm 30: 12 ASTROS II Mk3; 6 ASTROS II Mk3M; 12 ASTROS II Mk6
 MOR 1,245: **81mm** 1,168: 453 L16, 715 M936 AGR; **120mm** 77 M2
HELICOPTERS
 MRH 51: 29 AS565 *Panther* (HM-1); 5 AS565 K2 *Panther* (HM-1); 17 AS550U2 *Fennec* (HA-1 – armed)
 TPT 35: **Heavy** 8 H225M *Caracal* (HM-4); **Medium** 12: 8 AS532 *Cougar* (HM-3); 4 S-70A-36 *Black Hawk* (HM-2); **Light** 15 AS350L1 *Ecureuil* (HA-1)
AIR DEFENCE
 SAM • Point-defence RBS-70; 9K38 *Igla* (SA-18 *Grouse*); 9K338 *Igla*-S (SA-24 *Grinch*)
 GUNS 100:
  SP 35mm 34 *Gepard* 1A2
  TOWED 66: **35mm** 39 GDF-001 towed (some with *Super Fledermaus* radar); **40mm** 27 L/70 (some with BOFI)
RADAR • AIR DEFENCE 5 SABER M60

Navy 69,000

Organised into 9 districts with HQ I Rio de Janeiro, HQ II Salvador, HQ III Natal, HQ IV Belém, HQ V Rio Grande, HQ VI Ladario, HQ VII Brasilia, HQ VIII Sao Paulo, HQ IX Manaus

FORCES BY ROLE
SPECIAL FORCES
 1 (diver) SF gp
EQUIPMENT BY TYPE
SUBMARINES • TACTICAL • SSK 5:
 4 *Tupi* (GER T-209/1400) with 8 single 533mm TT with Mk48 HWT
 1 *Tikuna* with 8 single 533mm TT with Mk48 HWT
PRINCIPAL SURFACE COMBATANTS 14
 AIRCRAFT CARRIERS • CV 1:
  1 *São Paulo*† (FRA *Clemenceau*) with 2 sextuple *Sadral* lnchr with *Mistral* SAM (capacity 15–18 A-4 *Skyhawk* atk ac; 4–6 SH-3D/A *Sea King*/S-70B *Seahawk* ASW hel; 3 AS355/AS350 *Ecureuil* hel; 2 AS532 *Cougar* hel)
 DESTROYERS • DDGHM 3:
  3 *Greenhalgh* (UK *Broadsword*, 1 low readiness) with 4 single lnchr with MM-40 *Exocet* Block II AShM, 2

sextuple lnchr with *Sea Wolf* SAM, 6 single STWS Mk2 324mm ASTT with Mk 46 LWT (capacity 2 *Super Lynx* Mk21A hel)

FRIGATES 10

FFGHM 6 *Niterói* with 2 twin lnchr with MM-40 *Exocet* Block II AShM, 1 octuple *Albatros* lnchr with *Aspide* SAM, 2 triple Mk32 324mm ASTT with Mk 46 LWT, 1 twin 375mm A/S mor, 2 *Sea Trinity* Mk3 CIWS, 1 115mm gun (capacity 1 *Super Lynx* Mk21A hel)

FFGH 4:

3 *Inhaúma* with 2 twin lnchr with MM-40 *Exocet* Block II AShM, 2 triple Mk32 324mm ASTT with Mk 46 LWT, 1 115mm gun (1 *Super Lynx* Mk21A hel)

1 *Barroso* with 2 twin lnchr with MM-40 *Exocet* Block II AShM, 2 triple 324mm ASTT with Mk 46 LWT, 1 *Sea Trinity* CIWS, 1 115mm gun (capacity 1 *Super Lynx* Mk21A hel)

PATROL AND COASTAL COMBATANTS 44

PSO 3 *Amazonas*

PCO 6: 4 *Bracui* (UK *River*); 1 *Imperial Marinheiro* with 1 76mm gun; 1 *Parnaiba* with 1 hel landing platform

PCC 2 *Macaé*

PCR 5: 2 *Pedro Teixeira*; 3 *Roraima*

PB 24: 12 *Grajau*; 6 *Marlim*; 6 *Piratini* (US PGM)

PBR 4 LPR-40

MINE WARFARE • MINE COUNTERMEASURES •

MSC 5 *Aratu* (GER *Schutze*)

AMPHIBIOUS

PRINCIPAL AMPHIBIOUS SHIPS 2

LPD 1 *Bahia*-class (ex-FRA *Foudre*) (capacity 4 hels; 8 LCM, 450 troops)

LSD 1 *Ceará* (US *Thomaston*) with 3 twin 76mm guns (capacity either 21 LCM or 6 LCU; 345 troops)

LANDING SHIPS 3

LST 1 *Mattoso Maia* (US *Newport*) with 1 *Phalanx* CIWS (capacity 3 LCVP; 1 LCPL; 400 troops)

LSLH 2: 1 *Garcia D'Avila* (UK *Sir Galahad*) (capacity 1 hel; 16 MBT; 340 troops); 1 *Almirante Saboia* (UK *Sir Bedivere*) (capacity 1 med hel; 18 MBT; 340 troops)

LANDING CRAFT 32: 3 **LCU**; 8 **LCVP**; 21 **LCM**

LOGISTICS AND SUPPORT 87+

ABU 35+: 4 *Comandante Varella*; 1 *Faroleiro Mario Seixas*; 30+ others

ABUH 1 *Almirante Graca Aranah* (lighthouse tender)

AFD 4

AFS 1 *Potengi*

AGHS 5: 1 *Caravelas* (riverine); 4 *Rio Tocantin*

AGOS 2: 1 *Ary Rongel* with 1 hel landing platform; 1 *Almirante Maximiano* (capacity 2 AS350/AS355 *Ecureuil* hel)

AGS 8: 1 *Aspirante Moura*; 1 *Cruzeiro do Sul*; 1 *Antares*; 3 *Amorim do Valle* (ex-UK *Rover*); 1 *Rio Branco*; 1 *Vital de Oliveira*

AGSH 1 *Sirius*

AH 5: 2 *Oswaldo Cruz* with 1 hel landing platform; 1 *Dr Montenegro*; 1 *Tenente Maximianol* with 1 hel landing platform; 1 *Soares de Meirelles*

AK 5

AOR 2: 1 *Almirante Gastão Motta*; 1 *Marajó*

AP 7: 1 *Almirante Leverger*; 1 *Paraguassu*; 1 *Pará* (all river transports); 4 *Rio Pardo*

ASR 1 *Felinto Perry* (NOR *Wildrake*) with 1 hel landing platform

ATF 5: 3 *Triunfo*; 2 *Almirante Guihem*

AX 1 *Brasil* with 1 hel landing platform

AXL 3 *Nascimento*

AXS 1 *Cisne Barco*

Naval Aviation 2,100

FORCES BY ROLE

GROUND ATTACK

1 sqn with A-4/4M (AF-1) *Skyhawk*; TA-4/4M (AF-1A) *Skyhawk*

ANTI SURFACE WARFARE

1 sqn with *Super Lynx* Mk21A

ANTI SUBMARINE WARFARE

1 sqn with S-70B *Seahawk* (MH-16)

TRAINING

1 sqn with Bell 206B3 *Jet Ranger* III

TRANSPORT HELICOPTER

1 sqn with AS332 *Super Puma*; AS532 *Cougar*

4 sqn with AS350 *Ecureuil* (armed); AS355 *Ecureuil* II (armed)

EQUIPMENT BY TYPE

AIRCRAFT 11 combat capable

ATK 11: 8 A-4/4M (AF-1/1B) *Skyhawk*; 3 TA-4/4M (AF-1A) *Skyhawk*

HELICOPTERS

ASW 18: 12 *Super Lynx* Mk21A; 6 S-70B *Seahawk* (MH-16)

TPT 51: **Heavy** 6 H225M *Caracal* (UH-15); **Medium** 7: 5 AS332 *Super Puma*; 2 AS532 *Cougar* (UH-14); **Light** 38: 15 AS350 *Ecureuil* (armed); 8 AS355 *Ecureuil* II (armed); 15 Bell 206B3 *Jet Ranger* III (IH-6B)

AIR-LAUNCHED MISSILES • AShM: AM-39 *Exocet*; *Sea Skua*; AGM-119 *Penguin*

Marines 16,000

FORCES BY ROLE

SPECIAL FORCES

1 SF bn

MANOEUVRE

Amphibious

1 amph div (1 lt armd bn, 3 mne bn, 1 arty bn)

1 amph aslt bn

7 (regional) mne gp

1 rvn bn

COMBAT SUPPORT

1 engr bn

COMBAT SERVICE SUPPORT

1 log bn

EQUIPMENT BY TYPE

ARMOURED FIGHTING VEHICLES

LT TK 18 SK-105 *Kuerassier*

APC 60

APC (T) 30 M113A1 (incl variants)

APC (W) 30 *Piranha* IIIC

AAV 25: 13 AAV-7A1; 12 LVTP-7

ENGINEERING VEHICLES • ARV 1 AAVR-7

ANTI-TANK/ANTI-INFRASTRUCTURE

MSL• MANPATS RB-56 *Bill*; MSS-1.2 AC

ARTILLERY 65
　TOWED 41: **105mm** 33: 18 L118 Light Gun; 15 M101; **155mm** 8 M114
　MRL **127mm** 6 ASTROS II Mk6
　MOR **81mm** 18 M29
　AIR DEFENCE • GUNS **40mm** 6 L/70 (with BOFI)

Air Force 67,500

Brazilian airspace is divided into 7 air regions, each of which is responsible for its designated air bases. Air assets are divided among 4 designated air forces (I, II, III & V) for operations (IV Air Force temporarily deactivated)

FORCES BY ROLE
FIGHTER
　4 sqn with F-5EM/FM *Tiger* II
FIGHTER/GROUND ATTACK
　2 sqn with AMX (A-1A/B)
GROUND ATTACK/ISR
　4 sqn with EMB-314 *Super Tucano* (A-29A/B)*
MARITIME PATROL
　1 sqn with P-3AM *Orion*
　2 sqn with EMB-111 (P-95A/B/M)
ISR
　1 sqn with AMX-R (RA-1)*
　1 sqn with Learjet 35 (R-35A); EMB-110B (R-95)
AIRBORNE EARLY WARNING & CONTROL
　1 sqn with EMB-145RS (R-99); EMB-145SA (E-99)
TANKER/TRANSPORT
　1 sqn with C-130H/KC-130H *Hercules*
TRANSPORT
　1 VIP sqn with A319 (VC-1A); EMB-190 (VC-2); AS355 *Ecureuil* II (VH-55); H135M (VH-35); H225M *Caracal* (VH-36)
　1 VIP sqn with EMB-135BJ (VC-99B); ERJ-135LR (VC-99C); ERJ-145LR (VC-99A); Learjet 35A (VU-35); Learjet 55C (VU-55C)
　2 sqn with C-130E/H *Hercules*
　2 sqn with C-295M (C-105A)
　7 (regional) sqn with Cessna 208/208B (C-98); Cessna 208-G1000 (C-98A); EMB-110 (C-95); EMB-120 (C-97)
　1 sqn with ERJ-145 (C-99A)
　1 sqn with EMB-120RT (VC-97), EMB-121 (VU-9)
TRAINING
　1 sqn with EMB-110 (C-95)
　2 sqn with EMB-312 *Tucano* (T-27) (incl 1 air show sqn)
　1 sqn with T-25A/C
ATTACK HELICOPTER
　1 sqn with Mi-35M *Hind* (AH-2)
TRANSPORT HELICOPTER
　1 sqn with H225M *Caracal* (H-36)
　1 sqn with AS350B *Ecureuil* (H-50); AS355 *Ecureuil* II (H-55)
　1 sqn with Bell 205 (H-1H); H225M *Caracal* (H-36)
　2 sqn with UH-60L *Black Hawk* (H-60L)
ISR UAV
　1 sqn with *Hermes* 450/900

EQUIPMENT BY TYPE
AIRCRAFT 220 combat capable
　FTR 56: 6 F-5E *Tiger* II; 50 F-5EM/FM *Tiger* II
　FGA 49: 38 AMX (A-1); 11 AMX-T (A-1B)
　ASW 9 P-3AM *Orion*

　MP 19: 10 EMB-111 (P-95A *Bandeirulha*)*; 8 EMB-111 (P-95B *Bandeirulha*)*; 1 EMB-111 (P-95M *Bandeirulha*)
　ISR: 8: 4 AMX-R (RA-1)*; 4 EMB-110B (R-95)
　ELINT 6: 3 EMB-145RS (R-99); 3 Learjet 35A (R-35A)
　AEW&C 5 EMB-145SA (E-99)
　SAR 7: 2 C-295M *Amazonas* (SC-105); 4 EMB-110 (SC-95B), 1 SC-130E *Hercules*
　TKR/TPT 2 KC-130H
　TPT 197: **Medium** 20: 4 C-130E *Hercules*; 16 C-130H *Hercules*; **Light** 169: 10 C-295M (C-105A); 7 Cessna 208 (C-98); 9 Cessna 208B (C-98); 13 Cessna 208-G1000 (C-98A); 52 EMB-110 (C-95A/B/C/M); 16 EMB-120 (C-97); 4 EMB-120RT (VC-97); 5 EMB-121 (VU-9); 7 EMB-135BJ (VC-99B); 3 EMB-201R *Ipanema* (G-19); 2 EMB-202A *Ipanema* (G-19A); 2 ERJ-135LR (VC-99C); 7 ERJ-145 (C-99A); 1 ERJ-145LR (VC-99A); 9 Learjet 35A (VU-35); 1 Learjet 55C (VU-55); 9 PA-34 *Seneca* (U-7); 12 U-42 *Regente*; **PAX** 8: 1 A319 (VC-1A); 3 EMB-190 (VC-2); 4 Hawker 800XP (EU-93A – calibration)
　TRG 264: 100 EMB-312 *Tucano* (T-27); 39 EMB-314 *Super Tucano* (A-29A)*; 44 EMB-314 *Super Tucano* (A-29B)*; 81 T-25A/C
HELICOPTERS
　ATK 12 Mi-35M *Hind* (AH-2)
　MRH 2 H135M (VH-35)
　TPT 80: **Heavy** 12 H225M *Caracal* (10 H-36 & 2 VH-36); **Medium** 16 UH-60L *Black Hawk* (H-60L); **Light** 52: 24 AS350B *Ecureuil* (H-50); 4 AS355 *Ecureuil* II (H-55/VH-55); 24 Bell 205 (H-1H)
UNMANNED AERIAL VEHICLES
　ISR • **Medium** 5: 4 *Hermes* 450; 1 *Hermes* 900
AIR-LAUNCHED MISSILES
　AAM • **IR** MAA-1 *Piranha*; R-550 *Magic* 2; *Python* 3; **IIR** *Python* 4; **SARH** Super 530F; **ARH** *Derby*
　ARM MAR-1 (in development)

Paramilitary 395,000 opcon Army

Public Security Forces 395,000

State police organisation technically under army control. However, military control is reducing, with authority reverting to individual states

EQUIPMENT BY TYPE
UNMANNED AERIAL VEHICLES
　ISR • **Heavy** 3 *Heron* (deployed by Federal Police for Amazon and border patrols)

Cyber

Cyber was a key component of the 2008 National Defence Strategy and the July 2012 Defence White Paper. In 2011, the army inaugurated Brazil's cyber-defence centre (CDCiber) to coordinate the existing activities of the army, navy and air force. There is an active training programme, run by the Institute of Cyber Defence among others, while in 2013 the country's first Cyber Operations Simulator (SIMOC) was set up. The Integrated Electronic Warfare Centre houses the SIMOC. In 2014 the MoD said it would create a National Cyber Defense School and Cyber Defense Command, which will supervise, coordinate and provide technical and regulatory guidance for the national cyber-defence system.

DEPLOYMENT

CENTRAL AFRICAN REPUBLIC
UN • MINUSCA 2; 4 obs

CÔTE D'IVOIRE
UN • UNOCI 2; 2 obs

CYPRUS
UN • UNFICYP 3

HAITI
UN • MINUSTAH 982; 1 inf bn; 1 engr coy

LEBANON
UN • UNIFIL 279; 1 FFGHM

LIBERIA
UN • UNMIL 1; 1 obs

SOUTH SUDAN
UN • UNMISS 5; 5 obs

SUDAN
UN • UNISFA 2 obs

WESTERN SAHARA
UN • MINURSO 10 obs

Chile CHL

Chilean Peso pCh		2015	2016	2017
GDP	pCh	157tr	165tr	
	US$	240bn	235bn	
per capita	US$	13,342	12,910	
Growth	%	2.3	1.7	
Inflation	%	4.3	4.0	
Def bdgt [a]	pCh	2.25tr	2.33tr	2.60tr
	US$	3.44bn	3.32bn	
US$1=pCh		654.07	702.70	

[a] Includes military pensions

Population   17,650,114

Age	0–14	15–19	20–24	25–29	30–64	65 plus
Male	10.3%	3.8%	4.1%	4.2%	22.4%	4.4%
Female	9.9%	3.6%	3.9%	4.0%	23.2%	6.1%

Capabilities

Assuring sovereignty, territorial integrity and internal security remain core roles, and the armed forces have spent the past decade recapitalising the equipment of all three services with second-hand US and European equipment. However, there is an increasing focus on non-traditional military roles, such as disaster relief, illustrated by deployments in response to flooding and an earthquake in 2015. A new defence white paper is scheduled for 2017. Procurement priorities have changed to reflect this, focusing on littoral and blue-water surveillance capabilities and new helicopters, although slower economic growth may delay or reduce the scope of some of these plans. Chile has a developed defence-industrial base, with ENAER conducting aircraft maintenance. In late 2016, ENAER signed an agreement with Airbus designed to further cooperation in maintenance and manufacturing. ASMAR and FAMAE are key industries in the maritime and land sectors, respectively. Training takes place regularly on a national basis, and the armed forces also routinely participate in exercises with international and regional partners. Chile has announced that it will withdraw its troops from the UN peacekeeping mission in Haiti in 2017, although Santiago is looking to increase its contributions to international peace operations more generally.

ACTIVE 64,750 (Army 37,850 Navy 19,100 Air 7,800)
Paramilitary 44,700
Conscript liability Army 1 year; Navy 21 months; Air Force 18 months. Legally, conscription can last for 2 years

RESERVE 40,000 (Army 40,000)

ORGANISATIONS BY SERVICE

Space
EQUIPMENT BY TYPE
SATELLITES
  ISR 1 SSOT (Sistema Satelital del la Observación del la Tierra)

Army 37,850
6 military administrative regions
FORCES BY ROLE
Currently being reorganised into 4 armd, 2 mot, 2 mtn and 1 SF brigade. Standard regt/gp are single bn strength, reinforced regt comprise multiple bn
COMMAND
  6 div HQ
SPECIAL FORCES
  1 SF bde (1 SF bn, 1 (mtn) SF gp, 1 para bn, 1 cdo coy, 1 log coy)
  2 cdo coy
MANOEUVRE
  Reconnaissance
  1 armd recce pl
  3 cav sqn
  4 recce pl
  Armoured
  3 (1st, 2nd & 3rd) armd bde (1 armd recce pl, 1 armd cav gp, 1 mech inf bn, 1 arty gp, 1 AT coy, 1 engr coy, 1 sigs coy)
  1 (4th) armd bde (1 armd recce pl, 1 armd cav gp, 1 mech inf bn, 1 arty gp, 1 engr coy)
  Mechanised
  1 (1st) mech inf regt
  Light
  1 (1st) reinforced regt (1 mot inf bn, 1 arty gp, 2 AT coy, 1 engr bn)
  1 (4th) reinforced regt (1 mot inf bn, 1 MRL gp, 1 mor coy, 1 AT coy, 1 engr bn)
  1 (5th) reinforced regt (1 armd cav gp, 1 mech inf coy, 1 arty gp, 1 engr coy)

1 (7th) reinforced regt (1 mot inf bn, 1 arty gp, 1 sigs coy)
1 (10th) reinforced regt (1 mot inf bn, 1 AT coy, 1 engr bn, 1 sigs bn)
2 (11th & 24th) reinforced mot inf regt (1 mot inf bn, 1 arty gp, 1 AT coy)
1 (14th) reinforced mot inf regt (1 mot inf bn, 1 sigs coy, 1 AT coy)
7 mot inf regt
1 (3rd) reinforced mtn regt (1 mtn inf bn, 1 arty gp, 1 engr coy)
1 (9th) reinforced mtn regt (1 mtn inf bn, 1 engr bn)
1 (17th) reinforced mtn regt (1 mtn inf bn, 1 engr coy)
2 mtn inf regt

COMBAT SUPPORT
3 arty regt
1 engr regt
2 sigs regt
1 int regt
1 MP bn

COMBAT SERVICE SUPPORT
1 log div (2 log regt)
4 log regt
6 log coy
1 maint div (1 maint regt)

AVIATION
1 avn bde (1 tpt avn bn, 1 hel bn, 1 maint bn, 1 spt bn, 1 log coy)

EQUIPMENT BY TYPE
ARMOURED FIGHTING VEHICLES
MBT 245: 114 *Leopard* 1; 131 *Leopard* 2A4
IFV 197: 173 *Marder* 1A3; 24 YPR-765 PRI
APC 548
APC (T) 369 M113A1/A2
APC (W) 179 *Piranha*

ENGINEERING & MAINTENANCE VEHICLES
AEV 8 *Leopard* 1
ARV 21 *Leopard* 1
VLB 13 *Leopard* 1
MW 3 *Leopard* 1

ANTI-TANK/ANTI-INFRASTRUCTURE
MSL • MANPATS *Spike*-LR; *Spike*-ER
RCL 84mm *Carl Gustav*; 106mm 213 M40A1

ARTILLERY 1,391
SP 155mm 48: 24 M109A3; 24 M109A5+
TOWED 233: 105mm 193: 89 M101; 104 Model 56 pack howitzer; 155mm 40 M-68
MRL 160mm 12 LAR-160
MOR 1,098: 81mm 744: 303 ECIA L65/81; 175 FAMAE; 266 Soltam; 120mm 282: 173 ECIA L65/120; 16 FAMAE; 93 M-65; SP 120mm 72: 36 FAMAE (on *Piranha* 6x6); 36 Soltam (on M113A2)

AIRCRAFT
TPT • Light 8: 2 C-212-300 *Aviocar*; 3 Cessna 208 *Caravan*; 3 CN-235

HELICOPTERS
ISR 9 MD-530F *Lifter* (armed)
TPT 17: Medium 12: 8 AS532AL *Cougar*; 1 AS532ALe *Cougar*; 3 SA330 *Puma*; Light 5: 4 H125 *Ecureuil*; 1 AS355F *Ecureuil* II

AIR DEFENCE
SAM • Point-defence *Mistral*
GUNS 41:
SP 20mm 16 *Piranha*/TCM-20
TOWED 20mm 25 M167 *Vulcan*

Navy 19,100

5 Naval Zones; 1st Naval Zone and main HQ at Valparaiso; 2nd Naval Zone at Talcahuano; 3rd Naval Zone at Punta Arenas; 4th Naval Zone at Iquique; 5th Naval Zone at Puerto Montt

FORCES BY ROLE
SPECIAL FORCES
1 (diver) SF comd

EQUIPMENT BY TYPE
SUBMARINES • TACTICAL • SSK 4:
2 *O'Higgins* (*Scorpene*) with 6 single 533mm TT with A-184 *Black Shark* HWT/SUT HWT/SM-39 *Exocet* Block II AShM (1 currently in repair)
2 *Thompson* (GER T-209/1300) with 8 single 533mm TT A-184 *Black Shark* HWT/SUT HWT/SM-39 *Exocet* Block II AShM

PRINCIPAL SURFACE COMBATANTS 8
DESTROYERS • DDGHM 1 *Almirante Williams* (UK Type-22) with 2 quad Mk141 lnchr with RGM-84 *Harpoon* AShM, 2 octuple VLS with *Barak* SAM; 2 triple 324mm ASTT with Mk46 LWT, 1 76mm gun (capacity 1 AS532SC *Cougar*)
FRIGATES 7:
FFGHM 5:
3 *Almirante Cochrane* (UK *Duke*-class Type-23) with 2 quad Mk141 lnchr with RGM-84C *Harpoon* AShM, 1 32-cell VLS with *Sea Wolf* SAM, 2 twin 324mm ASTT with Mk46 Mod 2 LWT, 1 114mm gun (capacity 1 AS-532SC *Cougar*)
2 *Almirante Riveros* (NLD *Karel Doorman*-class) with 2 quad lnchr with MM-40 *Exocet* Blk 3 AShM, 1 octuple Mk48 lnchr with RIM-7P *Sea Sparrow* SAM, 4 single Mk32 Mod 9 324mm ASTT with Mk46 Mod 5 HWT, 1 76mm gun (capacity 1 AS532SC *Cougar*)
FFGM 2:
2 *Almirante Lattore* (NLD *Jacob Van Heemskerck*-class) with 2 twin Mk141 lnchr with RGM-84 *Harpoon* AShM, 1 Mk13 GMLS with SM-1MR SAM, 1 octuple Mk48 lnchr with RIM-7P *Sea Sparrow* SAM, 2 twin Mk32 324mm ASTT with Mk46 LWT, 1 *Goalkeeper* CIWS

PATROL AND COASTAL COMBATANTS 13
PSOH 3 *Piloto Pardo*
PCG 5:
3 *Casma* (ISR *Sa'ar* 4) with 4 GI *Gabriel* I AShM, 2 76mm guns
2 *Tiger* (GER Type-148) with 4 single lnchr with MM-38 *Exocet* AShM, 1 76mm gun
PCO 5 *Micalvi*

AMPHIBIOUS
PRINCIPAL AMPHIBIOUS SHIPS
LPD 1 *Sargento Aldea* (FRA *Foudre*) with 3 twin *Simbad* lnchr with *Mistral* SAM (capacity 4 med hel; 1 LCT; 2 LCM; 22 tanks; 470 troops)

LANDING SHIPS 3
  LSM 1 *Elicura*
  LST 2 *Maipo* (FRA *Batral*) with 1 hel landing platform (capacity 7 tanks; 140 troops)
LANDING CRAFT 3
  LCT 1 CDIC (for use in *Sargento Aldea*)
  LCM 2 (for use in *Sargento Aldea*)
LOGISTICS AND SUPPORT 14
  ABU 1 *George Slight Marshall* with 1 hel landing platform
  AFD 3
  AG 1 *Almirante Jose Toribio Merino Castro* (also used as general spt ship) with 1 hel landing platform
  AGOR 1 *Cabo de Hornos*
  AGHS 1 *Micalvi*
  AGS 1 Type-1200 (ice-strengthened hull, ex-CAN) with 1 hel landing platform
  AOR 2: 1 *Almirante Montt* with 1 hel landing platform; 1 *Araucano*
  AP 1 *Aguiles* (1 hel landing platform)
  ATF 2 *Veritas*
  AXS 1 *Esmeralda*
MSL • **AShM** MM-38 *Exocet*

Naval Aviation 600
EQUIPMENT BY TYPE
AIRCRAFT 17 combat capable
  ASW 4: 2 C-295ASW *Persuader*; 2 P-3ACH *Orion*
  MP 4: 1 C-295MPA *Persuader*; 3 EMB-111 *Bandeirante**
  ISR 4: 2 Cessna O-2A *Skymaster**; 2 P-68 *Observer*
  TRG 7 PC-7 *Turbo Trainer**
HELICOPTERS
  ASW 5 AS532SC *Cougar*
  MRH 8 AS365 *Dauphin*
  TPT • **Light** 7: 3 Bell 206 *Jet Ranger*; 4 Bo-105S
AIR-LAUNCHED MISSILES • **AShM** AM-39 *Exocet*

Marines 3,600
FORCES BY ROLE
MANOEUVRE
  Amphibious
  1 amph bde (2 mne bn, 1 cbt spt bn, 1 log bn)
  2 coastal def unit
EQUIPMENT BY TYPE
ARMOURED FIGHTING VEHICLES
  LT TK 15 FV101 *Scorpion*
  APC • **APC (W)** 25 MOWAG *Roland*
  AAV 12 AAV-7
ARTILLERY 39
  TOWED 23: **105mm** 7 KH-178; **155mm** 16 M-71
  MOR 81mm 16
COASTAL DEFENCE • **AShM** MM-38 *Exocet*
AIR DEFENCE • **SAM** • **Point-defence** 14: 4 M998 *Avenger*; 10 M1097 *Avenger*

Coast Guard
Integral part of the Navy
EQUIPMENT BY TYPE
PATROL AND COASTAL COMBATANTS 55
  PBF 26 *Archangel*
  PB 29: 18 *Alacalufe* (*Protector*-class); 4 *Grumete Diaz* (*Dabor*-class); 6 *Pelluhue*; 1 *Ona*

Air Force 7,800
Flying hours 100 hrs/yr
FORCES BY ROLE
FIGHTER
  1 sqn with F-5E/F *Tiger* III+
  2 sqn with F-16AM/BM *Fighting Falcon*
FIGHTER/GROUND ATTACK
  1 sqn with F-16C/D Block 50 *Fighting Falcon* (*Puma*)
ISR
  1 (photo) flt with; DHC-6-300 *Twin Otter*; Learjet 35A
AIRBORNE EARLY WARNING
  1 flt with B-707 *Phalcon*
TANKER/TRANSPORT
  1 sqn with B-737-300; C-130B/H *Hercules*; KC-130R *Hercules*; KC-135 *Stratotanker*
TRANSPORT
  3 sqn with Bell 205 (UH-1H *Iroquois*); C-212-200/300 *Aviocar*; Cessna O-2A; Cessna 525 *Citation* CJ1; DHC-6-100/300 *Twin Otter*; PA-28-236 *Dakota*; Bell 205 (UH-1H *Iroquois*)
  1 VIP flt with B-737-500 (VIP); Gulfstream IV
TRAINING
  1 sqn with EMB-314 *Super Tucano**
  1 sqn with PA-28-236 *Dakota*; T-35A/B *Pillan*
TRANSPORT HELICOPTER
  1 sqn with Bell 205 (UH-1H *Iroquois*); Bell 206B (trg); Bell 412 *Twin Huey*; Bo-105CBS-4; S-70A *Black Hawk*
AIR DEFENCE
  1 AD regt (5 AD sqn) with *Crotale*; *Mistral*; M163/M167 *Vulcan*; Oerlikon GDF-005
EQUIPMENT BY TYPE
AIRCRAFT 79 combat capable
  FTR 48: 10 F-5E *Tigre* III+; 2 F-5F *Tigre* III+; 29 F-16AM *Fighting Falcon*; 7 F-16BM *Fighting Falcon*
  FGA 10: 6 F-16C Block 50 *Fighting Falcon*; 4 F-16D Block 50 *Fighting Falcon*
  ATK 9 C-101CC *Aviojet* (A-36 *Halcón*)
  ISR 2 Cessna O-2A
  AEW&C 1 B-707 *Phalcon*
  TKR 5: 2 KC-130R *Hercules*: 3 KC-135 *Stratotanker*
  TPT 38: **Medium** 3: 1 C-130B *Hercules*; 2 C-130H *Hercules*; **Light** 30: 2 C-212-200 *Aviocar*; 1 C-212-300 *Aviocar*; 4 Cessna 525 *Citation* CJ1; 3 DHC-6-100 *Twin Otter*; 7 DHC-6-300 *Twin Otter*; 2 Learjet 35A; 11 PA-28-236 *Dakota*; **PAX** 5: 1 B-737-300; 1 B-737-500; 1 B-767-300ER; 2 Gulfstream IV
  TRG 46: 4 Cirrus SR-22T; 12 EMB-314 *Super Tucano**; 30 T-35A/B *Pillan*
HELICOPTERS
  MRH 12 Bell 412EP *Twin Huey*
  TPT 22: **Medium** 1 S-70A *Black Hawk*; **Light** 21: 13 Bell 205 (UH-1H *Iroquois*); 5 Bell 206B (trg); 2 BK-117; 1 Bo-105CBS-4
UNMANNED AERIAL VEHICLES
  ISR • **Medium** 3 *Hermes* 900
AIR DEFENCE
  SAM
    Short-range 5 *Crotale*
    Point-defence *Mistral* (including some *Mygale/Aspic*)

GUNS • TOWED 20mm M163/M167 *Vulcan*; 35mm Oerlikon GDF-005
AIR-LAUNCHED MISSILES
AAM • IR AIM-9J/M *Sidewinder*; Python 3; *Shafrir*‡; IIR *Python* 4; ARH AIM-120C AMRAAM; *Derby*
ASM AGM-65G *Maverick*
BOMBS
Laser-guided *Paveway* II
INS/GPS guided JDAM

Paramilitary 44,700

Carabineros 44,700
Ministry of Interior; 15 zones, 36 districts, 179 *comisaria*
EQUIPMENT BY TYPE
ARMOURED FIGHTING VEHICLES
APC • APC (W) 20 MOWAG *Roland*
ARTILLERY • MOR 81mm
AIRCRAFT
TPT • Light 4: 1 Beech 200 *King Air*; 1 Cessna 208; 1 Cessna 550 *Citation* V; 1 PA-31T *Cheyenne* II
HELICOPTERS • TPT • Light 15: 5 AW109E *Power*; 1 Bell 206 *Jet Ranger*; 2 BK-117; 5 Bo-105; 2 H135

Cyber
The Joint Staff coordinates cyber-security policies for the Ministry of Defense and the armed forces. Each service has a cyber-security organisation within their security structure. The Ministry of Interior and Public Security (Internal Affairs) is the national coordination authority for cyber security and is currently developing a National Cyber Security Strategy.

DEPLOYMENT
Legal provisions for foreign deployment:
Constitution: Constitution (1980, since amended)
Decision on deployment of troops abroad: Article 63, number 13 of the constitution, concerning matters of law, states that the procedures for foreign deployment are a matter that must be established by law by congress. Law Number 19.067 regulates matters concerning the foreign deployment of Chilean troops and deployment of foreign troops in Chile. It states that the government needs to request congressional approval

BOSNIA-HERZEGOVINA
EU • EUFOR • *Operation Althea* 15

CENTRAL AFRICAN REPUBLIC
UN • MINUSCA 4

CYPRUS
UN • UNFICYP 14

HAITI
UN • MINUSTAH 392; 1 inf bn HQ; 2 inf coy; 1 hel sqn

INDIA/PAKISTAN
UN • UNMOGIP 2 obs

MIDDLE EAST
UN • UNTSO 2 obs

Colombia COL

Colombian Peso pC		2015	2016	2017
GDP	pC	801tr	861tr	
	US$	292	274	
per capita	US$	6,059	5,623	
Growth	%	3.1	2.2	
Inflation	%	5.0	7.6	
Def bdgt [a]	pC	27.3tr	28.1tr	29.6tr
	US$	9.96bn	8.95bn	
FMA (US)	US$	27m	25m	39m
US$1=pC		2,741.78	3,140.00	

[a] Includes defence and security

Population   47,220,856

Age	0–14	15–19	20–24	25–29	30–64	65 plus
Male	12.6%	4.4%	4.5%	4.3%	20.6%	3.0%
Female	12.0%	4.2%	4.4%	4.2%	21.6%	4.2%

Capabilities

Colombia's security and defence requirements continue to be dominated by counter-insurgency and counter-narcotics operations, although the ongoing peace talks with FARC guerrillas (and with the ELN) is leading the defence ministry to consider a shift towards more conventional military structures and inventories. At the same time, the fall in oil prices has had an effect on state finances. This period of transformation will see a reduction in personnel and likely see the police transferring from the defence ministry to the interior ministry. This is not new: Colombia's armed forces have in recent years been planning for new security roles, and new organisational structures for the post-FARC era. In August 2016 the army adopted a new doctrine, 'Damascus'. This doctrine emphasises roles such as disaster relief or assistance to rural communities, but a strong focus on combat capabilities remains. The navy has increased its international activities, but it will likely see its marine forces reduce as part of transformation plans. Air-force-modernisation plans might be affected by financial challenges, though the force's small size may insulate it from heavy personnel cuts. Colombia has a defence industry active across all domains, with COTECMAR building vessels, including amphibious ships and patrol boats, CIAC active in the aerospace sector as a maintenance and manufacturing firm, and INDUMIL manufacturing arms and ammunition. The strong relationship with the US continues and has been particularly valuable in terms of training and equipment support, although this has reduced in recent years due to an improved security situation. (See pp. 429–30.)

ACTIVE 293,200 (Army 223,150, Navy 56,400 Air 13,650) **Paramilitary 187,900**

RESERVE 34,950 (Army 25,050 Navy 6,500 Air 3,400)

ORGANISATIONS BY SERVICE

Army 223,150
FORCES BY ROLE
SPECIAL FORCES
1 anti-terrorist SF bn
MANOEUVRE
Mechanised
1 (1st) div (1 (2nd) mech bde (2 mech inf bn, 1 mtn inf bn, 1 engr bn, 1 MP bn, 1 cbt spt bn, 1 log bn, 1 Gaula anti-kidnap gp); 1 (10th) mech bde (1 armd recce bn, 1 mech cav bn, 1 mech inf bn, 1 mtn inf bn, 2 sy bn, 2 arty bn, 1 engr bn, 1 cbt spt bn, 2 Gaula anti-kidnap gp); 2 sy bn; 1 log bn)
Light
1 (2nd) div (1 (5th) lt inf bde (2 lt inf bn, 1 jungle inf bn, 1 sy bn, 1 arty bn, 1 AD bn, 1 engr bn, 1 cbt spt bn, 1 Gaula anti-kidnap gp); 1 (30th) lt inf bde (1 cav recce bn, 2 lt inf bn, 1 sy bn, 1 arty bn, 1 engr bn, 1 cbt spt bn, 1 log bn); 1 rapid reaction force (3 mobile sy bde))
1 (3rd) div (1 (3rd) lt inf bde (2 lt inf bn, 1 mtn inf bn, 1 COIN bn, 1 arty bn, 1 engr bn, 1 cbt spt bn, 1 MP bn, 1 log bn, 1 Gaula anti-kidnap gp); 1 (23rd) lt inf bde (1 cav gp, 1 lt inf bn, 1 jungle inf bn, 1 cbt spt bn, 1 log bn); 1 (29th) mtn bde (1 mtn inf bn, 1 lt inf bn, 2 COIN bn, 1 cbt spt bn, 1 log bn); 2 rapid reaction force (total: 7 mobile sy bde))
1 (4th) div (1 (7th) air mob bde (2 air mob inf bn, 1 lt inf bn, 1 COIN bn, 1 engr bn, 1 cbt spt bn, 1 log bn, 1 Gaula anti-kidnap gp); 1 (22nd) jungle bde (1 air mob inf bn, 1 lt inf bn, 1 jungle inf bn, 1 COIN bn, 1 cbt spt bn, 1 log bn); 1 (31st) jungle bde (1 lt inf bn, 1 jungle inf bn))
1 (5th) div (1 (6th) lt inf bde (2 lt inf bn,1 mtn inf bn, 2 COIN bn, 1 cbt spt bn, 1 log bn, 1 Gaula anti-kidnap gp); 1 (8th) lt inf bde (1 lt inf bn, 1 mtn inf bn, 1 arty bn, 1 engr bn, 1 cbt spt bn, 1 Gaula anti-kidnap gp); 1 (9th) lt inf bde (1 SF bn, 2 lt inf bn, 1 arty bn, 1 COIN bn, 1 cbt spt bn, 1 sy bn, 1 log bn, 1 Gaula anti-kidnap gp); 1 (13th) lt inf bde (2 cav recce bn, 1 airmob inf bn, 3 lt inf bn, 1 COIN bn, 1 arty bn, 1 engr bn, 1 cbt spt bn, 2 MP bn, 1 log bn, 2 Gaula anti-kidnap gp); 1 rapid reaction force (3 mobile sy bde))
1 (6th) div (1 (12th) lt inf bde (2 lt inf bn, 2 jungle inf bn, 1 COIN bn, 1 engr bn, 1 cbt spt bn, 1 Gaula anti-kidnap gp); 1 (13th) mobile sy bde (4 COIN bn); 1 (26th) jungle bde (1 lt jungle inf bn, 1 COIN bn, 1 cbt spt bn); 1 (27th) lt inf bde (2 lt inf bn, 1 jungle inf bn, 1 sy bn, 1 arty bn, 1 cbt spt bn, 1 log bn))
1 (7th) div (1 (4th) lt inf bde (1 cav recce bn, 3 lt inf bn, 1 sy bn, 1 arty bn, 1 engr bn, 1 MP bn, 1 cbt spt bn, 1 log bn); 1 (11th) lt inf bde (2 lt inf bn, 1 sy bn, 1 engr bn, 1 cbt spt bn, 1 log bn); 1 (14th) lt inf bde (3 lt inf bn, 1 sy bn, 1 engr bn, 1 cbt spt bn, 1 log bn); 1 (15th) jungle bde (1 lt inf bn, 1 COIN bn, 1 engr bn, 1 log bn); 1 (17th) lt inf bde (2 lt inf bn, 1 COIN bn, 1 engr bn, 1 cbt spt bn, 1 log bn); 1 rapid reaction force (1 (11th) mobile sy bde (3 COIN bn)))
1 (8th) div (1 (16th) lt inf bde (1 mech cav recce bn, 1 lt inf bn, 1 log bn, 1 Gaula anti-kidnap gp); 1 (18th) lt inf bde (1 air mob gp, 1 sy bn, 1 arty bn, 1 engr bn, 1 cbt spt bn, 1 log bn); 1 (28th) jungle bde (2 inf, 2 COIN, 1 cbt spt bn); 1 rapid reaction force (1 (5th) mobile sy bde (3 COIN bn); 1 (31st) mobile sy bde (5 COIN bn)))
3 COIN mobile bde (each: 4 COIN bn, 1 cbt spt bn)
Other
1 indep rapid reaction force (1 SF bde, 3 mobile sy bde)
COMBAT SUPPORT
1 cbt engr bde (1 SF engr bn, 1 (emergency response) engr bn, 1 EOD bn, 1 construction bn, 1 demining bn, 1 maint bn)
1 int bde (2 SIGINT bn, 1 kog bn, 1 maint bn)
COMBAT SERVICE SUPPORT
2 spt/log bde (each: 1 spt bn, 1 maint bn, 1 supply bn, 1 tpt bn, 1 medical bn, 1 log bn)
AVIATION
1 air aslt div (1 SF bde (2 SF bn); 1 counter-narcotics bde (3 counter-narcotics bn, 1 spt bn); 1 (25th) avn bde (4 hel bn; 5 avn bn; 1 avn log bn); 1 (32nd) avn bde (1 avn bn, 2 maint bn, 1 trg bn, 1 spt bn); 1 SF avn bn)

EQUIPMENT BY TYPE
ARMOURED FIGHTING VEHICLES
RECCE 121 EE-9 *Cascavel*
IFV 60: 28 *Commando Advanced*; 32 LAV III
APC 114
　APC (T) 54: 28 M113A1 (TPM-113A1); 26 M113A2 (TPM-113A2)
　APC (W) 56 EE-11 *Urutu*
　PPV 4 RG-31 *Nyala*
AUV 38 M1117 *Guardian*
ANTI-TANK/ANTI-INFRASTRUCTURE
MSL
　SP 77 *Nimrod*
　　MANPATS TOW; *Spike*-ER
RCL 106mm 73 M40A1
ARTILLERY 1,796
TOWED 120: **105mm** 107: 22 LG1 MkIII; 85 M101; **155mm** 13 155/52 APU SBT-1
MOR 1,676: **81mm** 1,507; **120mm** 169
AIRCRAFT
ELINT 3: 2 Beech B200 *King Air*; 1 Beech 350 *King Air*
TPT • Light 23: 2 An-32B; 2 Beech B200 *King Air*; 2 Beech 350 *King Air*; 2 Beech 200 *King Air* (Medevac); 1 Beech C90 *King Air*; 2 C-212 *Aviocar* (Medevac); 8 Cessna 208B *Grand Caravan*; 4 Turbo Commander 695A
HELICOPTERS
MRH 20: 8 Mi-17-1V *Hip*; 8 Mi-17MD; 4 Mi-17V-5 *Hip*
TPT 97: **Medium** 57: 50 UH-60L *Black Hawk*; 7 S-70i *Black Hawk*; **Light** 40: 24 Bell 205 (UH-1H *Iroquois*); 16 Bell 212 (UH-1N *Twin Huey*)
AIR DEFENCE • GUNS • TOWED 40mm 4 M1A1

Navy 56,400 (incl 12,100 conscript)
HQ located at Puerto Carreño.
EQUIPMENT BY TYPE
SUBMARINES • TACTICAL • SSK 4:
2 *Pijao* (GER T-209/1200) each with 8 single 533mm TT each with HWT
2 *Intrepido* (GER T-206A) each with 8 single 533mm TT each with HWT

PRINCIPAL SURFACE COMBATANTS 4
 FRIGATES • FFGHM 4 *Almirante Padilla* with 2 twin lnchr with MM-40 *Exocet* AShM, 2 twin *Simbad* lnchr with *Mistral* SAM, 2 triple B515 *ILAS-3* 324mm ASTT each with A244 LWT, 1 76mm gun (capacity 1 Bo-105/ AS555SN *Fennec* hel)
PATROL AND COASTAL COMBATANTS 54
 CORVETTES • FS 1 *Narino* (ex-ROK *Dong Hae*) with 2 triple 324mm ASTT with Mk46 LWT, 1 76mm gun
 PSOH 2 *20 de Julio*
 PCO 2: 1 *Valle del Cauca Durable* (ex-US *Reliance*) with 1 hel landing platform; 1 *San Andres* (ex-US *Balsam*)
 PCC 3 *Punta Espada* (CPV-46)
 PCR 10: 2 *Arauca* with 2 76mm guns; 8 *Nodriza* (PAF-II) with hel landing platform
 PB 12: 1 *11 de Noviembre* (CPV-40) with 1 *Typhoon* CIWS; 2 *Castillo y Rada* (Swiftships 105); 2 *Jaime Gomez*; 1 *José Maria Palas* (Swiftships 110); 4 *Point*; 2 *Toledo*
 PBR 27: 6 *Diligente*; 7 LPR-40; 3 Swiftships; 9 *Tenerife*; 2 PAF-L
AMPHIBIOUS 22
 LCM 3 LCM-8
 LCU 11: 4 *Golfo de Tribuga*; 7 *Morrosquillo* (LCU 1466)
 UCAC 8 *Griffon* 2000TD
LOGISTICS AND SUPPORT 8
 ABU 1 *Quindio*
 AG 3: 1 *Inirida*; 2 *Luneburg* (ex-GER, depot ship for patrol vessels)
 AGOR 2 *Providencia*
 AGS 1 *Gorgona*
 AXS 1 *Gloria*

Naval Aviation 150
EQUIPMENT BY TYPE
AIRCRAFT
 MP 3 CN-235 MPA *Persuader*
 ISR 1 PA-31 *Navajo* (upgraded for ISR)
 TPT • Light 11: 1 C-212 (Medevac); 4 Cessna 206; 3 Cessna 208 *Caravan*; 1 PA-31 *Navajo*; 1 PA-34 *Seneca*; 1 Beech 350 *King Air*
HELICOPTERS
 MRH 9: 2 AS555SN *Fennec*; 3 Bell 412 *Twin Huey*; 4 Bell 412EP *Twin Huey*
 TPT • Light 9: 1 Bell 212; 5 Bell 212 (UH-1N); 1 BK-117; 2 Bo-105

Marines 22,250
FORCES BY ROLE
SPECIAL FORCES
 1 SF bde (4 SF bn)
MANOEUVRE
 Amphibious
 1 mne bde (1 SF (Gaula) bn, 5 mne bn, 2 rvn bn, 1 spt bn)
 1 mne bde (1 SF bn, 2 mne bn, 2 rvn bn, 1 spt bn)
 1 rvn bde (1 SF bn, 1 mne bn, 2 rvn bn, 1 spt bn)
 1 rvn bde (4 rvn bn)
 1 rvn bn (3 rvn bn)
COMBAT SERVICE SUPPORT
 1 log bde (6 spt bn)
 1 trg bde (7 trg bn, 1 spt bn)

EQUIPMENT BY TYPE
 ARTILLERY • MOR 82: 81mm 74; 120mm 8

Air Force 13,650
FORCES BY ROLE
FIGHTER/GROUND ATTACK
 1 sqn with *Kfir* C-10/C-12/TC-12
GROUND ATTACK/ISR
 1 sqn with A-37B/OA-37B *Dragonfly*
 1 sqn with AC-47T
 1 sqn with EMB-312 *Tucano**
 2 sqn with EMB-314 *Super Tucano** (A-29)
EW/ELINT
 2 sqn with Beech 350 *King Air*; Cessna 208; Cessna 560; C-26B *Metroliner*; SA 2-37; 1 *Turbo Commander* 695
TRANSPORT
 1 (Presidential) sqn with B-737BBJ; EMB-600 *Legacy*; Bell 412EP; F-28 *Fellowship*; UH-60L *Black Hawk*
 1 sqn with B-727; B-737-400; C-130B/H *Hercules*; C-212; C-295M; CN-235M; ; IAI *Arava*; KC-767
 1 sqn with Beech C90 *King Air*; Beech 350C *King Air*; Cessna 208B; Cessna 550; EMB-110P1 (C-95)
TRAINING
 1 sqn with Lancair *Synergy* (T-90 *Calima*)
 1 sqn with T-37B
 1 hel sqn with Bell 206B3
 1 hel sqn with TH-67
HELICOPTER
 1 sqn with AH-60L *Arpia* III
 1 sqn with UH-60L *Black Hawk* (CSAR)
 1 sqn with Hughes 500M
 1 sqn with Bell 205 (UH-1H)
 1 sqn with Bell 212
EQUIPMENT BY TYPE
AIRCRAFT 69 combat capable
 FGA 19: 9 *Kfir* C-10; 9 *Kfir* C-12; 1 *Kfir* TC-12
 ATK 12: 6 A-37B/OA-37B *Dragonfly*; 6 AC-47T *Spooky* (*Fantasma*)
 ISR 13: 1 Beech C90 *King Air*; 1 C-26B *Metroliner*; 5 Cessna 560 *Citation* II; 6 SA 2-37
 ELINT 13: 4 Beech 350 *King Air*; 6 Cessna 208 *Grand Caravan*; 2 Cessna 337G; 1 *Turbo Commander* 695
 TKR/TPT 1 KC-767
 TPT 64: **Medium** 7: 3 C-130B *Hercules* (3 more in store); 3 C-130H *Hercules*; 1 B-737F; **Light** 49: 10 ATR-42; 2 Beech 300 *King Air*; 2 Beech 350C *King Air*; 1 Beech 350i *King Air* (VIP); 4 Beech C90 *King Air*; 4 C-212; 6 C-295M; 1 Cessna 182R; 12 Cessna 208B (medevac); 1 Cessna 550; 2 CN-235M; 2 EMB-110P1 (C-95); 1 EMB-170-100LR; 1 IAI-201 *Arava*; **PAX** 8: 2 B-727; 1 B-737-400; 1 B-737BBJ; 1 EMB-600 *Legacy*; 1 F-28-1000 *Fellowship*; 1 F-28-3000 *Fellowship*; 1 Learjet 60
 TRG 79: 14 EMB-312 *Tucano**; 24 EMB-314 *Super Tucano* (A-29)*; 24 Lancair *Synergy* (T-90 *Calima*); 17 T-37B
HELICOPTERS
 MRH 18: 13 AH-60L *Arpia* III; 1 AH-60L *Arpia* IV; 2 Bell 412EP *Twin Huey* (VIP); 2 Hughes 500M

TPT 48: **Medium** 13 UH-60L *Black Hawk* (incl 1 VIP hel); **Light** 35: 12 Bell 205 (UH-1H *Iroquois*); 12 Bell 206B3 *Jet Ranger* III; 11 Bell 212
TRG 30 TH-67
UNAMMED AERIAL VEHICLES • ISR • Medium 8: 6 *Hermes 450*; 2 *Hermes 900*
AIR-LAUNCHED MISSILES
 AAM • IR *Python* 3; **IIR** *Python* 4; **ARH** *Derby*;
 ASM *Spike*-ER; *Spike*-NLOS
BOMBS • Laser-guided *Paveway* II

Paramilitary 187,900

National Police Force 187,900
EQUIPMENT BY TYPE
AIRCRAFT
 ELINT 5 C-26B *Metroliner*
 TPT • Light 40: 3 ATR-42; 3 Beech 200 *King Air*; 2 Beech 300 *King Air*; 2 Beech 1900; 1 Beech C99; 4 BT-67; 2 C-26 *Metroliner*; 3 Cessna 152; 3 Cessna 172; 9 Cessna 206; 2 Cessna 208 *Caravan*; 2 DHC-6 *Twin Otter*; 1 DHC-8; 3 PA-31 *Navajo*
HELICOPTERS
 MRH 3: 1 Bell 412EP; 2 MD-500D
 TPT 67: **Medium** 9 UH-60L *Black Hawk*; **Light** 58: 34 Bell 205 (UH-1H-II *Huey II*); 6 Bell 206B; 5 Bell 206L/L3/L4 *Long Ranger*; 8 Bell 212; 5 Bell 407

Cyber

Colombia publicised policy guidelines for cyber security and cyber defence in 2011. There are three main organisations: the CERT team (colCERT); the Police Cyber Centre; and the armed forces' Joint Cyber Command. The defence ministry is the coordinating body for cyber defence, and Colombia has an active training and simulation programme in cyber defence, with the Higher War College also organising courses in cyber warfare for military (a staff course) and civil personnel. The armed forces are reported to be in the process of devolving cyber capability to the tactical level. An initial cyber cell was formed by linking the Joint Cyber Command, the National Police Cyber Center and the MoD's CERT team.

DEPLOYMENT

EGYPT
MFO 354; 1 inf bn

FOREIGN FORCES

United States US Southern Command: 50

Costa Rica CRI

Costa Rican Colon C		2015	2016	2017
GDP	C	28.3tr	30.8tr	
	US$	52.9bn	57.7bn	
per capita	US$	10,905	11,749	
Growth	%	3.7	4.3	
Inflation	%	0.8	0.7	
Sy Bdgt [a]	C	238bn	220bn	220bn
	US$	445m	413m	
FMA (US)	US$	1m	1m	1m
US$1=C		534.60	533.92	

[a] Paramilitary budget

Population 4,872,543

Age	0–14	15–19	20–24	25–29	30–64	65 plus
Male	11.7%	4.2%	4.4%	4.5%	22.0%	3.5%
Female	11.2%	4.0%	4.2%	4.4%	22.0%	4.0%

Capabilities

The Costa Rican armed forces were constitutionally abolished in 1949, and the country relies on paramilitary-type police organisations for internal security, counter-narcotics and counter-criminal tasks, as well as participation in regional peacekeeping operations. More recently, Costa Rica has utilised these organisations to counter illegal immigration on its southern border with Panama. In May 2014 the country launched a joint-services initiative (known as OPMAT) to develop closer cooperation between the Public Force, Coast Guard and Air Surveillance Unit. With internal security the principal focus of activity, little significant logistical support is required. Some elements, such as the Special Intervention Unit (UEI), have received training from non-regional states, including the US. The UEI has also conducted small-scale training with regional allies. The air wing is relatively well equipped with light aircraft. The vessels currently in the coastguard's inventory have a relatively limited range, impeding operations at reach. However, the delivery of two ex-US Coast Guard patrol boats in 2017 will significantly increase the service's operational capability.

PARAMILITARY 9,800

ORGANISATIONS BY SERVICE

Paramilitary 9,800

Special Intervention Unit
FORCES BY ROLE
SPECIAL FORCES
 1 spec ops unit

Public Force 9,000
11 regional directorates

Coast Guard Unit 400
EQUIPMENT BY TYPE
PATROL AND COASTAL COMBATANTS 8:
  PB 8: 2 *Cabo Blanco* (US *Swift* 65); 1 *Isla del Coco* (US *Swift* 105); 3 *Point*; 1 *Primera Dama* (US *Swift* 42); 1 *Puerto Quebos* (US *Swift* 36)

Air Surveillance Unit 400
EQUIPMENT BY TYPE
AIRCRAFT • TPT • Light 17: 4 Cessna T210 *Centurion*; 4 Cessna U206G *Stationair*; 1 DHC-7 *Caribou*; 2 PA-31 *Navajo*; 2 PA-34 *Seneca*; 1 Piper PA-23 *Aztec*; 1 Cessna 182RG; 2 Y-12E
HELICOPTERS • MRH 3: 2 MD-500E; 1 MD-600N

Cuba CUB

Cuban Peso P		2015	2016	2017
GDP	P			
	US$			
per capita	US$			
Growth	%			
Inflation	%			
Def bdgt	P			
	US$			

US$1=P

*definitive economic data unavailable

Population	11,179,995					
Age	0–14	15–19	20–24	25–29	30–64	65 plus
Male	8.6%	3.2%	3.2%	3.8%	24.2%	6.7%
Female	8.1%	3.0%	3.0%	3.5%	24.6%	7.9%

Capabilities

Cuba's defence focus is on protecting territorial integrity, as well as sustaining ties to some regional military partners, such as Venezuela. Although numerically significant, the Cuban armed forces are hampered by an ageing and predominantly Soviet-era equipment inventory and by a reliance on continual maintenance instead of modernisation. It is unlikely that Havana will be in a position to finance significant equipment recapitalisation in the near term. The US embargo on Cuba remains despite the re-establishment of diplomatic relations, with the future of the US base at Guantanamo Bay also uncertain. New US regulations in January 2015, and in January and March 2016, gradually eased restrictions on travel and trade. The Cuban armed forces are benefiting from the ensuing increase in economic activity by taking control of elements of the economy, including transport facilities such as ports, as well as hotels and restaurants. Cuba maintains military ties with China and Russia. The Russian government is reportedly considering re-opening its signals-intelligence facility in Cuba, having closed its base there in 2002.

ACTIVE 49,000 (Army 38,000 Navy 3,000 Air 8,000)
Paramilitary 26,500
Conscript liability 3 years (or 2 if studying for a profession)

RESERVE 39,000 (Army 39,000) **Paramilitary 1,120,000**
Ready Reserves (serve 45 days per year) to fill out Active and Reserve units; see also Paramilitary

ORGANISATIONS BY SERVICE

Army ε38,000
FORCES BY ROLE
COMMAND
  3 regional comd HQ
  3 army comd HQ
MANOEUVRE
  Armoured
  up to 5 armd bde
  Mechanised
  9 mech inf bde (1 armd regt, 3 mech inf regt, 1 arty regt, 1 ADA regt)
  Light
  1 (frontier) bde
  Air Manoeuvre
  1 AB bde
AIR DEFENCE
  1 ADA regt
  1 SAM bde

Reserves 39,000
FORCES BY ROLE
MANOEUVRE
  Light
  14 inf bde
EQUIPMENT BY TYPE†
ARMOURED FIGHTING VEHICLES
  MBT ε900 T-34/T-54/T-55/T-62
  LT TK PT-76
  ASLT BTR-60 100mm
  RECCE BRDM-2;
  AIFV ε50 BMP-1/1P
  APC ε500 BTR-152/BTR-50/BTR-60
ANTI-TANK/ANTI-INFRASTRUCTURE
  MSL
    SP 2K16 *Shmel* (AT-1 *Snapper*)
    MANPATS 9K11 *Malyutka* (AT-3 *Sagger*)
  GUNS 600+: **57mm** 600 ZIS-2 (M-1943); **85mm** D-44
ARTILLERY 1,715+
  SP 40+: **100mm** AAPMP-100; CATAP-100; **122mm** 2S1 *Gvozdika*; AAP-T-122; AAP-BMP-122; *Jupiter* III; *Jupiter* IV; **130mm** AAP-T-130; *Jupiter* V; **152mm** 2S3 *Akatsiya*
  TOWED 500: **122mm** D-30; M-30 (M-1938); **130mm** M-46; **152mm** D-1; M-1937 (ML-20)
  MRL • SP 175: **122mm** BM-21 *Grad*; **140mm** BM-14
  MOR 1,000: **82mm** M-41; **82mm** M-43; **120mm** M-43; M-38
AIR DEFENCE
  SAM
    Short-range 2K12 *Kub* (SA-6 *Gainful*)
    Pont-defence 200+: 200 9K35 *Strela*-10 (SA-13 *Gopher*); 9K33 *Osa* (SA-8 *Gecko*); 9K31 *Strela*-1 (SA-9 *Gaskin*);

9K36 *Strela-3* (SA-14 *Gremlin*); 9K310 *Igla-1* (SA-16 *Gimlet*); 9K32 *Strela-2* (SA-7 *Grail*)‡
GUNS 400
SP 23mm ZSU-23-4; **30mm** BTR-60P SP; **57mm** ZSU-57-2
TOWED 100mm KS-19/M-1939/**85mm** KS-12/**57mm** S-60/**37mm** M-1939/**30mm** M-53/**23mm** ZU-23

Navy ε3,000
Western Comd HQ at Cabanas; Eastern Comd HQ at Holquin
EQUIPMENT BY TYPE
PATROL AND COASTAL COMBATANTS 8
  PSO 1 *Rio Damuji* with two single P-15M *Termit* (SS-N-2C *Styx*) AShM, 2 57mm guns, 1 hel landing platform
  PCM 1 *Pauk II†* (FSU) with 1 quad lnchr (manual aiming) with 9K32 *Strela-2* (SA-N-5 *Grail*) SAM, 4 single ASTT, 2 RBU 1200 A/S mor, 1 76mm gun
  PBF 6 *Osa II†* (FSU) each with 4 single lnchr (for P-15 *Termit* (SS-N-2B *Styx*) AShM – missiles removed to coastal defence units)
MINE WARFARE AND MINE COUNTERMEASURES 5
  MHI 3 *Yevgenya†* (FSU)
  MSC 2 *Sonya†* (FSU)
LOGISTICS AND SUPPORT 2
  ABU 1
  AX 1

Coastal Defence
ARTILLERY • TOWED 122mm M-1931/37; **130mm** M-46; **152mm** M-1937
COASTAL DEFENCE • AShM 4+: *Bandera* IV (reported); 4 4K51 *Rubezh* (SS-C-3 *Styx*)

Naval Infantry 550+
FORCES BY ROLE
MANOEUVRE
  Amphibious
    2 amph aslt bn

Anti-aircraft Defence and Revolutionary Air Force ε8,000 (incl conscripts)
Air assets divided between Western Air Zone and Eastern Air Zone

Flying hours 50 hrs/yr
FORCES BY ROLE
FIGHTER/GROUND ATTACK
  3 sqn with MiG-21ML *Fishbed*; MiG-23ML/MF/UM *Flogger*; MiG-29A/UB *Fulcrum*
TRANSPORT
  1 (VIP) tpt sqn with An-24 *Coke*; Mi-8P *Hip*; Yak-40
ATTACK HELICOPTER
  2 sqn with Mi-17 *Hip H*; Mi-35 *Hind*
TRAINING
  2 (tac trg) sqn with L-39C *Albatros* (basic); Z-142 (primary)
EQUIPMENT BY TYPE
AIRCRAFT 45 combat capable
  FTR 33: 16 MiG-23ML *Flogger*; 4 MiG-23MF *Flogger*; 4 MiG-23U *Flogger*; 4 MiG-23UM *Flogger*; 2 MiG-29A *Fulcrum*; 3 MiG-29UB *Fulcrum* (6 MiG-15UTI *Midget*; 4+ MiG-17 *Fresco*; 4 MiG-23MF *Flogger*; 6 MiG-23ML *Flogger*; 2 MiG-23UM *Flogger*; 2 MiG-29 *Fulcrum* in store)
  FGA 12: 4 MiG-21ML *Fishbed*; 8 MiG-21U *Mongol* A (up to 70 MiG-21bis *Fishbed*; 30 MiG-21F *Fishbed*; 28 MiG-21PFM *Fishbed*; 7 MiG-21UM *Fishbed*; 20 MiG-23BN *Flogger* in store)
  ISR 1 An-30 *Clank*
  TPT 11: **Heavy** 2 Il-76 *Candid*; **Light** 9: 1 An-2 *Colt*; 3 An-24 *Coke*; 2 An-32 *Cline*; 3 Yak-40 (8 An-2 *Colt*; 18 An-26 *Curl* in store)
  TRG 45: 25 L-39 *Albatros*; 20 Z-326 *Trener Master*
HELICOPTERS
  ATK 4 Mi-35 *Hind* (8 more in store)
  ASW (5 Mi-14 in store)
  MRH 8 Mi-17 *Hip H* (12 more in store)
  TPT • Medium 2 Mi-8P *Hip*
AIR DEFENCE • SAM
  Medium-range S-75 *Dvina* (SA-2 *Guideline*); S-75 *Dvina* mod (SA-2 *Guideline* – on T-55 chassis)
  Short-range S-125 *Pechora* (SA-3 *Goa*); S-125 *Pechora* mod (SA-3 *Goa* – on T-55 chassis)
AIR-LAUNCHED MISSILES
  AAM • IR R-3‡ (AA-2 *Atoll*); R-60 (AA-8 *Aphid*); R-73 (AA-11 *Archer*); **IR/SARH** R-23/24‡ (AA-7 *Apex*); R-27 (AA-10 *Alamo*)
  ASM Kh-23‡ (AS-7 *Kerry*)

Paramilitary 26,500 active

State Security 20,000
Ministry of Interior

Border Guards 6,500
Ministry of Interior
PATROL AND COASTAL COMBATANTS 20
  PCC 2 *Stenka*
  PB 18 *Zhuk*

Youth Labour Army 70,000 reservists

Civil Defence Force 50,000 reservists

Territorial Militia ε1,000,000 reservists

FOREIGN FORCES
United States US Southern Command: 950 (JTF-GTMO) at Guantanamo Bay

Dominican Republic DOM

Dominican Peso pRD		2015	2016	2017
GDP	pRD	3.02tr	3.31tr	
	US$	67.2bn	71.5bn	
per capita	US$	6,733	7,083	
Growth	%	7.0	5.9	
Inflation	%	0.8	2.3	
Def bdgt	pRD	20bn	21.1bn	
	US$	444m	455m	
US$1=pRD		44.99	46.37	

Population   10,606,865

Age	0–14	15–19	20–24	25–29	30–64	65 plus
Male	13.8%	4.8%	4.6%	4.2%	19.9%	3.4%
Female	13.3%	4.6%	4.4%	4.0%	19.1%	4.0%

Capabilities

The principal tasks for the Dominican armed forces include internal- and border-security missions, as well as disaster relief. However, counter-narcotics activity is an increasing focus of training and operations. The armed forces also collaborate with the police in a counter-narcotics inter-agency task force. The shared border with Haiti continues to be a focus of attention. The country also engages in regional military and security cooperation. A military-partnership agreement signed with the US in 2015 represents a new level of formalised cooperation between the two countries; this will include temporary deployments of US personnel to the Dominican Republic for training and exercises. The *New Horizons 2016* exercises focused on humanitarian-assistance and disaster-relief operations and featured the deployment of US engineering and medical personnel. Dominican naval personnel have received training in Colombia and exercise with regional partners. The country has strengthened its presence on the border with Haiti, establishing new surveillance posts and increasing its monitoring activities.

ACTIVE 56,050 (Army 28,750 Navy 11,200 Air 16,100) **Paramilitary 15,000**

ORGANISATIONS BY SERVICE

Army 28,750
5 Defence Zones
FORCES BY ROLE
SPECIAL FORCES
  3 SF bn
MANOEUVRE
  Light
  4 (1st, 2nd, 3rd & 4th) inf bde (3 inf bn)
  2 (5th & 6th) inf bde (2 inf bn)
  Air Manoeuvre
  1 air cav bde (1 cdo bn, 1 (6th) mtn bn, 1 hel sqn with Bell 205 (op by Air Force); OH-58 *Kiowa*; R-22; R-44 *Raven* II)

Other
  1 (Presidential Guard) gd regt
  1 (MoD) sy bn
COMBAT SUPPORT
  1 cbt spt bde (1 lt armd bn; 1 arty bn; 1 engr bn; 1 sigs bn)
EQUIPMENT BY TYPE
ARMOURED FIGHTING VEHICLES
  LT TK 12 M41B (76mm)
  APC • APC (W) 8 LAV-150 *Commando*
ANTI-TANK/ANTI-INFRASTRUCTURE
  RCL 106mm 20 M40A1
  GUNS 37mm 20 M3
ARTILLERY 104
  TOWED 105mm 16: 4 M101; 12 *Reinosa* 105/26
  MOR 88: **81mm** 60 M1; **107mm** 4 M30; **120mm** 24 Expal Model L
HELICOPTERS
  ISR 8: 4 OH-58A *Kiowa*; 4 OH-58C *Kiowa*
  TPT • Light 6: 4 R-22; 2 R-44 *Raven* II

Navy 11,200
HQ located at Santo Domingo
FORCES BY ROLE
SPECIAL FORCES
  1 (SEAL) SF unit
MANOEUVRE
  Amphibious
  1 mne sy unit
EQUIPMENT BY TYPE
PATROL AND COASTAL COMBATANTS 17
  PCO 1 *Almirante Didiez Burgos* (ex-US *Balsam*)
  PCC 2 *Tortuguero* (ex-US *White Sumac*)
  PB 14: 2 *Altair* (Swiftships 35m); 4 *Bellatrix* (US Sewart Seacraft); 2 *Canopus* (Swiftships 101); 3 *Hamal* (Damen Stan 1505); 3 *Point*
AMPHIBIOUS • LCU 1 *Neyba* (ex-US LCU 1675)
LOGISTICS AND SUPPORT 8
  AG 8

Air Force 16,100
Flying hours   60 hrs/yr
FORCES BY ROLE
GROUND ATTACK
  1 sqn with EMB-314 *Super Tucano**
SEARCH & RESCUE
  1 sqn with Bell 205 (UH-1H *Huey II*); Bell 205 (UH-1H *Iroquois*); Bell 430 (VIP); OH-58 *Kiowa* (CH-136); S-333
TRANSPORT
  1 sqn with C-212-400 *Aviocar*; PA-31 *Navajo*
TRAINING
  1 sqn with T-35B *Pillan*
AIR DEFENCE
  1 ADA bn with 20mm guns
EQUIPMENT BY TYPE
AIRCRAFT 8 combat capable
  ISR 1 AMT-200 *Super Ximango*
  TPT • Light 13: 3 C-212-400 *Aviocar*; 1 Cessna 172; 1 Cessna 182; 1 Cessna 206; 1 Cessna 207; 1 *Commander* 690; 3 EA-100; 1 PA-31 *Navajo*; 1 P2006T

TRG 13: 8 EMB-314 *Super Tucano**; 5 T-35B *Pillan*
HELICOPTERS
ISR 9 OH-58 *Kiowa* (CH-136)
TPT • **Light** 16: 8 Bell 205 (UH-1H *Huey* II); 5 Bell 205 (UH-1H *Iroquois*); 1 H155 (VIP); 2 S-333
AIR DEFENCE • **GUNS 20mm** 4

Paramilitary 15,000

National Police 15,000

Ecuador ECU

United States Dollar $		2015	2016	2017
GDP	US$	100.9bn	99.1bn	
per capita	US$	6,196	5,997	
Growth	%	0.3	-2.3	
Inflation	%	4.0	2.4	
Def bdgt	US$	1.91bn	1.57bn	
Population	16,080,778			

Age	0–14	15–19	20–24	25–29	30–64	65 plus
Male	14.0%	4.8%	4.6%	4.2%	18.6%	3.4%
Female	13.5%	4.6%	4.4%	4.2%	19.7%	3.8%

Capabilities

Defence policy is aimed at guaranteeing sovereignty and territorial integrity, and also allows the armed forces to participate in international peacekeeping operations. In 2015, the armed forces' role was expanded to include law-enforcement support. Border security has long been a priority but there has been a growing emphasis on maritime security in recent years, although there remains little capacity for sustained power projection beyond national borders. A modernisation programme announced in 2014 is intended to reduce bases and units, and reduce personnel numbers to 34,500 by 2025. An earthquake in April 2016 devastated areas on Ecuador's Pacific coast, and prompted a large-scale military response from Ecuador with the assistance of other regional states. Extra-regional states including China also provided assistance, with Beijing donating materiel in August to help the affected population and to enhance the capability of Ecuador's armed forces. The same month saw China and Ecuador also sign an agreement concerning greater defence-industrial cooperation. The defence ministry announced that an integrated radar system was due to go into service in 2016, and that Ecuador was making progress in the field of cyber defence. The services take part in regular exercises, both domestically and with international partners.

ACTIVE 40,250 (Army 24,750 Navy 9,100 Air 6,400)
Paramilitary 500
Conscript liability Voluntary conscription

RESERVE 118,000 (Joint 118,000)
Ages 18–55

ORGANISATIONS BY SERVICE

Army 24,750
FORCES BY ROLE
gp are bn sized
COMMAND
4 div HQ
SPECIAL FORCES
1 (9th) SF bde (3 SF gp, 1 SF sqn, 1 para bn, 1 sigs sqn, 1 log comd)
MANOEUVRE
Mechanised
1 (11th) armd cav bde (3 armd cav gp, 1 mech inf bn, 1 SP arty gp, 1 engr gp)
1 (5th) inf bde (1 SF sqn, 2 mech cav gp, 2 inf bn, 1 cbt engr coy, 1 sigs coy, 1 log coy)
Light
1 (1st) inf bde (1 SF sqn, 1 armd cav gp, 1 armd recce sqn, 3 inf bn, 1 med coy)
1 (3rd) inf bde (1 SF gp, 1 mech cav gp, 1 inf bn, 1 arty gp, 1 hvy mor coy, 1 cbt engr coy, 1 sigs coy, 1 log coy)
1 (7th) inf bde (1 SF sqn, 1 armd recce sqn, 1 mech cav gp, 3 inf bn, 1 jungle bn, 1 arty gp, 1 cbt engr coy, 1 sigs coy, 1 log coy, 1 med coy)
1 (13th) inf bde (1 SF sqn, 1 armd recce sqn, 1 mot cav gp, 3 inf bn, 1 arty gp, 1 hvy mor coy, 1 cbt engr coy, 1sigs coy, 1 log coy)
2 (17th & 21st) jungle bde (3 jungle bn, 1 cbt engr coy, 1 sigs coy, 1 log coy)
1 (19th) jungle bde (3 jungle bn, 1 jungle trg bn, 1 cbt engr coy, 1 sigs coy, 1 log coy)
COMBAT SUPPORT
1 (27th) arty bde (1 SP arty gp, 1 MRL gp, 1 ADA gp, 1 cbt engr coy, 1 sigs coy, 1 log coy)
1 (23rd) engr bde (3 engr bn)
2 indep MP coy
1 indep sigs coy
COMBAT SERVICE SUPPORT
1 (25th) log bde
2 log bn
2 indep med coy
AVIATION
1 (15th) avn bde (2 tpt avn gp, 2 hel gp, 1 mixed avn gp)
AIR DEFENCE
1 ADA gp
EQUIPMENT BY TYPE
ARMOURED FIGHTING VEHICLES
LT TK 24 AMX-13
RECCE 67: 25 AML-90; 10 EE-3 *Jararaca*; 32 EE-9 *Cascavel*
APC 123
  APC (T) 95: 80 AMX-VCI; 15 M113
  APC (W) 28: 18 EE-11 *Urutu*; 10 UR-416
ANTI-TANK/ANTI-INFRASTRUCTURE
RCL 404: **90mm** 380 M67; **106mm** 24 M40A1
ARTILLERY 541+
SP **155mm** 5 Mk F3
TOWED 100: **105mm** 78: 30 M101; 24 M2A2; 24 Model 56 pack howitzer; **155mm** 22: 12 M114; 10 M198

MRL 122mm 24: 18 BM-21 *Grad*; 6 RM-70
MOR 412+: **81mm** 400 M29; **107mm** M30; **160mm** 12 M-66
AIRCRAFT
TPT • **Light** 14: 1 Beech 200 *King Air*; 2 C-212; 1 CN-235; 4 Cessna 172; 2 Cessna 206; 1 Cessna 500 *Citation* I; 3 IAI-201 *Arava*
TRG 6: 2 MX-7-235 *Star Rocket*; 2 T-41D *Mescalero*; 2 CJ-6A
HELICOPTERS
MRH 32: 5 H125M *Fennec*; 6 Mi-17-1V *Hip*; 3 SA315B *Lama*; 18 SA342L *Gazelle* (13 with HOT for anti-armour role)
TPT 13: **Medium** 7: 5 AS332B *Super Puma*; 2 Mi-171E; (3 SA330 *Puma* in store); **Light** 6: 2 AS350B *Ecureuil*; 4 AS350B2 *Ecureuil*
AIR DEFENCE
SAM • Point-defence *Blowpipe*; 9K32 *Strela*-2 (SA-7 *Grail*)‡; 9K38 *Igla* (SA-18 *Grouse*)
GUNS 240
SP 20mm 44 M163 *Vulcan*
TOWED 196: **14.5mm** 128 ZPU-1/-2; **20mm** 38: 28 M-1935, 10 M167 *Vulcan*; **40mm** 30 L/70/M1A1

Navy 9,100 (incl Naval Aviation, Marines and Coast Guard)

EQUIPMENT BY TYPE
SUBMARINES • TACTICAL • SSK 2:
2 *Shyri* (GER T-209/1300, 1 undergoing refit in Chile) each with 8 single 533mm TT each with SUT HWT
PRINCIPAL SURFACE COMBATANTS • FRIGATES 1
FFGHM 1 *Moran Valverde*† (ex-UK *Leander* batch II) with 4 single lnchr with MM-40 *Exocet* AShM, 3 twin lnchr with *Mistral* SAM, 1 *Phalanx* CIWS, 1 twin 114mm gun (capacity 1 Bell 206B *Jet Ranger* II hel)
PATROL AND COASTAL COMBATANTS 9
CORVETTES • FSGM 6 *Esmeraldas* (3†) with 2 triple lnchr with MM-40 *Exocet* AShM, 1 quad *Albatros* lnchr with *Aspide* SAM, 2 triple B515 ILAS-3 324mm ASTT with A244 LWT (removed from two vessels), 1 76mm gun, 1 hel landing platform (upgrade programme ongoing)
PCFG 3 *Quito* (GER Lurssen TNC-45 45m) with 4 single lnchr with MM-38 *Exocet* AShM, 1 76mm gun (upgrade programme ongoing)
LOGISTICS AND SUPPORT 8
AE 1 *Calicuchima*
AGOS 1 *Orion* with 1 hel landing platform
AGS 1 *Sirius*
AK 1 *Galapagos*
ATF 1
AWT 2: 1 *Quisquis*; 1 *Atahualpa*
AXS 1 *Guayas*

Naval Aviation 380

EQUIPMENT BY TYPE
AIRCRAFT
MP 1 CN-235-300M
ISR 3: 2 Beech 200T *King Air*; 1 Beech 300 *Catpass King Air*
TPT • **Light** 3: 1 Beech 200 *King Air*; 1 Beech 300 *King Air*; 1 CN-235-100
TRG 6: 2 T-34C *Turbo Mentor*; 4 T-35B *Pillan*
HELICOPTERS
TPT • **Light** 9: 3 Bell 206A; 3 Bell 206B; 1 Bell 230; 2 Bell 430
UNMANNED AERIAL VEHICLES
ISR 5: **Heavy** 2 *Heron*; **Medium** 3 *Searcher* Mk.II

Marines 2,150

FORCES BY ROLE
SPECIAL FORCES
1 cdo unit
MANOEUVRE
Amphibious
5 mne bn (on garrison duties)
EQUIPMENT BY TYPE
ARTILLERY • MOR 32+ 60mm/81mm/120mm
AIR DEFENCE • SAM • Point-defence *Mistral*; 9K38 *Igla* (SA-18 *Grouse*)

Air Force 6,400

Operational Command

FORCES BY ROLE
FIGHTER
1 sqn with *Cheetah* C/D
FIGHTER/GROUND ATTACK
2 sqn with EMB-314 *Super Tucano**
1 sqn with *Kfir* C-10 (CE); *Kfir* C-2; *Kfir* TC-2

Military Air Transport Group

FORCES BY ROLE
SEARCH & RESCUE/TRANSPORT HELICOPTER
1 sqn with Bell 206B *Jet Ranger* II
1 sqn with PA-34 *Seneca*
TRANSPORT
1 sqn with C-130/H *Hercules*; L-100-30
1 sqn with HS-748
1 sqn with DHC-6-300 *Twin Otter*
1 sqn with B-727; EMB-135BJ *Legacy* 600; Sabreliner 40
TRAINING
1 sqn with Cessna 206; DA20-C1; MXP-650; T-34C *Turbo Mentor*
EQUIPMENT BY TYPE
AIRCRAFT 42 combat capable
FGA 25: 10 *Cheetah* C; 2 *Cheetah* D; 4 *Kfir* C-2; 7 *Kfir* C-10 (CE); 2 *Kfir* TC-2
TPT 28: **Medium** 4: 2 C-130B *Hercules*; 1 C-130H *Hercules*; 1 L-100-30; **Light** 15: 1 Beech E90 *King Air*; 3 C-295M; 1 Cessna 206; 3 DHC-6 *Twin Otter*; 1 EMB-135BJ *Legacy* 600; 2 EMB-170; 2 EMB-190; 1 MXP-650; 1 PA-34 *Seneca*; **PAX** 9: 2 A320; 2 B-727; 5 HS-748
TRG 39: 11 DA20-C1; 17 EMB-314 *Super Tucano**; 11 T-34C *Turbo Mentor*
HELICOPTERS • TPT • **Light** 7 Bell 206B *Jet Ranger* II
AIR-LAUNCHED MISSILES • AAM • IR *Python* 3; R-550 *Magic*; *Shafrir*‡; IIR *Python* 4; SARH *Super* 530

AIR DEFENCE
    SAM • **Point-defence** 13+: 6 9K33 *Osa* (SA-8 *Gecko*); 7 M48 *Chaparral*; *Blowpipe*; 9K32 *Strela*-2 (SA-7 *Grail*)‡; 9K310 *Igla*-1 (SA-16 *Gimlet*); 9K38 *Igla* (SA-18 *Grouse*)
    GUNS
        SP 20mm 28 M35
        TOWED 64: **23mm** 34 ZU-23; **35mm** 30 GDF-002 (twin)
RADAR • AIR DEFENCE 2 CFTC gap fillers; 2 CETC 2D

Paramilitary
All police forces; 39,500

Police Air Service
EQUIPMENT BY TYPE
HELICOPTERS
    ISR 3 MD-530F *Lifter*
    TPT • Light 6: 2 AS350B *Ecureuil*; 1 Bell 206B *Jet Ranger*; 3 R-44

Coast Guard 500
EQUIPMENT BY TYPE
PATROL AND COASTAL COMBATANTS 21
    PCC 3 *Isla Fernandina* (*Vigilante*)
    PB 15: 1 *10 de Agosto*; 2 *Espada*; 1 *Isla Isabela*; 2 *Manta* (GER Lurssen 36m); 1 *Point*; 4 *Rio Coca*; 4 *Isla Santa Cruz* (Damen Stan 2606)
    PBR 3: 2 *Río Esmeraldas*; 1 *Rio Puyango*

DEPLOYMENT

CÔTE D'IVOIRE
UN • UNOCI 2 obs

HAITI
UN • MINUSTAH 1

SUDAN
UN • UNAMID 1; 3 obs
UN • UNISFA 1; 2 obs

El Salvador SLV

United States Dollar $		2015	2016	2017
GDP	US$	25.85	26.61	
per capita	US$	4,219	4,330	
Growth	%	2.5	2.4	
Inflation	%	-0.7	1.0	
Def bdgt	US$	148m	146m	
FMA (US)	US$	2m	2m	2m

Population 6,156,670

Age	0–14	15–19	20–24	25–29	30–64	65 plus
Male	13.6%	5.3%	5.0%	4.2%	16.8%	3.2%
Female	13.0%	5.1%	5.1%	4.4%	20.3%	4.1%

Capabilities

Principal roles for El Salvador's armed forces include territorial defence, support to civilian authorities, disaster relief and combating non-traditional threats, as well as periodic deployments to counter organised criminal groups. In 2016 El Salvador, Honduras and Guatemala signed a memorandum of understanding to increase cooperation in counter-gang operations. Security measures taken in 2016 saw the police and Ministry of National Defence receive an additional US$120m of funding. The armed forces have long-standing internal and external training programmes. While the forces are reasonably well equipped, there is a desire to upgrade equipment, including that held by the small (self-sustaining) Salvadorian contingent to the UN's MINUSMA mission in Mali. El Salvador also deployed small units to both Iraq and Afghanistan. Current challenges include boosting professionalisation – conscription accounts for a little under half of recruits – and tackling organised crime and narcotics trafficking.

ACTIVE 24,500 (Army 20,500 Navy 2,000 Air 2,000)
Paramilitary 17,000
Conscript liability 12 months (selective); 11 months for officers and NCOs

RESERVE 9,900 (Joint 9,900)

ORGANISATIONS BY SERVICE

Army 20,500
FORCES BY ROLE
SPECIAL FORCES
    1 spec ops gp (1 SF coy, 1 para bn, 1 (naval inf) coy)
MANOEUVRE
    Reconnaissance
    1 armd cav regt (2 armd cav bn)
    Light
    6 inf bde (3 inf bn)
    Other
    1 (special) sy bde (2 border gd bn, 2 MP bn)
COMBAT SUPPORT
    1 arty bde (2 fd arty bn, 1 AD bn)
    1 engr comd (2 engr bn)
EQUIPMENT BY TYPE
ARMOURED FIGHTING VEHICLES
    RECCE 5 AML-90; (4 more in store)
    APC • APC (W) 38: 30 VAL *Cashuat* (mod); 8 UR-416
ANTI-TANK/ANTI-INFRASTRUCTURE
    RCL 399: **106mm** 20 M40A1 (incl 16 SP); **90mm** 379 M67
ARTILLERY 217+
    TOWED 105mm 54: 36 M102; 18 M-56 (FRY)
    MOR 163+: **81mm** 151 M29; **120mm** 12+: 12 UBM 52; (some M-74 in store)
AIR DEFENCE • GUNS 35: **20mm** 31 M-55; 4 TCM-20

Navy 2,000
EQUIPMENT BY TYPE
PATROL AND COASTAL COMBATANTS 10
    PB 10: 3 Camcraft (30m); 1 *Point*; 1 Swiftships 77; 1 Swiftships 65; 4 Type-44 (ex-USCG)
AMPHIBIOUS • LANDING CRAFT • LCM 4

Naval Inf (SF Commandos) 90

FORCES BY ROLE
SPECIAL FORCES
 1 SF coy

Air Force 2,000

Flying hours 90 hrs/yr on A-37 *Dragonfly*

FORCES BY ROLE
FIGHTER/GROUND ATTACK/ISR
 1 sqn with A-37B/OA-37B *Dragonfly*; O-2A/B *Skymaster**
TRANSPORT
 1 sqn with BT-67; Cessna 210 *Centurion*; Cessna 337G; Commander 114; IAI-202 *Arava*; SA-226T *Merlin* IIIB
TRAINING
 1 sqn with R-235GT *Guerrier*; T-35 *Pillan*; T-41D *Mescalero*; TH-300
TRANSPORT HELICOPTER
 1 sqn with Bell 205 (UH-1H *Iroquois*); Bell 407; Bell 412EP *Twin Huey*; MD-500E; UH-1M *Iroquois*

EQUIPMENT BY TYPE
AIRCRAFT 25 combat capable
 ATK 14 A-37B *Dragonfly*
 ISR 11: 6 O-2A/B *Skymaster**; 5 OA-37B *Dragonfly**
 TPT • Light 10: 2 BT-67; 2 Cessna 210 *Centurion*; 1 Cessna 337G *Skymaster*; 1 Commander 114; 3 IAI-201 *Arava*; 1 SA-226T *Merlin* IIIB
 TRG 11: 5 R-235GT *Guerrier*; 5 T-35 *Pillan*; 1 T-41D *Mescalero*
HELICOPTERS
 MRH 14: 4 Bell 412EP *Twin Huey*; 8 MD-500E; 2 UH-1M *Iroquois*
 TPT• Light 19: 18 Bell 205 (UH-1H *Iroquois*) (incl 4 SAR); 1 Bell 407 (VIP tpt, govt owned)
 TRG 5 TH-300
AIR-LAUNCHED MISSILES • AAM • IR *Shafrir*‡

Paramilitary 17,000

National Civilian Police 17,000
Ministry of Public Security
AIRCRAFT
 ISR 1 O-2A *Skymaster*
 TPT • Light 1 Cessna 310
HELICOPTERS
 MRH 2 MD-520N
 TPT • Light 3: 1 Bell 205 (UH-1H *Iroquois*); 2 R-44 *Raven* II

DEPLOYMENT

HAITI
UN • MINUSTAH 44

LEBANON
UN • UNIFIL 52; 1 inf pl

MALI
UN • MINUSMA 91; 1 obs; 1 hel sqn

SOUTH SUDAN
UN • UNMISS 1; 1 obs

SUDAN
UN • UNISFA 1 obs

WESTERN SAHARA
UN • MINURSO 3 obs

FOREIGN FORCES

United States US Southern Command: 1 Forward Operating Location (Military, DEA, USCG and Customs personnel)

Guatemala GUA

Guatemalan Quetzal q		2015	2016	2017
GDP	q	488bn	530bn	
	US$	63.8bn	68.4bn	
per capita	US$	3,922	4.102	
Growth	%	4.1	3.5	
Inflation	%	2.4	4.5	
Def bdgt	q	2.1bn	2.08bn	2.12bn
	US$	274m	268m	
FMA (US)	US$	1m	2m	2m
US$1=q		7.65	7.75	

Population 15,189,958

Age	0–14	15–19	20–24	25–29	30–64	65 plus
Male	17.9%	5.7%	5.3%	4.5%	14.0%	2.0%
Female	17.2%	5.5%	5.3%	4.6%	15.7%	2.4%

Capabilities

Whilst the primary task of Guatemala's armed forces is territorial defence, they also retain a limited capability to participate in international operations and disaster-relief tasks. These are two areas identified in the country's 2015 white paper as being of importance to the country's armed forces. In 2016, El Salvador, Honduras and Guatemala signed a memorandum of understanding to increase cooperation in counter-gang operations. The National Defence Policy of Guatemala, released in late 2013, identified organised crime as a key security concern for the nation in addition to the need to respond to natural disasters. Rising levels of organised crime and narcotics trafficking have resulted in proposals to increase the defence budget, and boost recruitment and procurement. Given the transnational nature of organised crime in Central America, there is close cooperation with counterparts from neighbouring countries and the army has recently trained with Colombia in riverine operations and the US on counter-narcotics tasks. Guatemala has also conducted humanitarian training with US SOUTHCOM and the Dominican Republic, whilst Brazil is conducting 'train the trainer' activities in HA/DR with Guatemalan Army personnel. Equipment requirements include aerial-surveillance radars and coastal-patrol craft to monitor littoral waters, light armoured vehicles and light attack/training aircraft.

ACTIVE 18,050 (Army 15,550 Navy 1,500 Air 1,000)
Paramilitary 25,000

RESERVE 63,850 (Navy 650 Air 900 Armed Forces 62,300)

(National Armed Forces are combined; the army provides log spt for navy and air force)

ORGANISATIONS BY SERVICE

Army 15,550
15 Military Zones
FORCES BY ROLE
SPECIAL FORCES
  1 SF bde (1 SF bn, 1 trg bn)
  1 SF bde (1 SF coy, 1 ranger bn)
  1 SF mtn bde
MANOEUVRE
  Light
  1 (strategic reserve) mech bde (1 inf bn, 1 cav regt, 1 log coy)
  6 inf bde (1 inf bn)
  Air Manoeuvre
  1 AB bde with (2 AB bn)
  Amphibious
  1 mne bde
  Other
  1 (Presidential) gd bde (1 gd bn, 1 MP bn, 1 CSS coy)
COMBAT SUPPORT
  1 engr comd (1 engr bn, 1 construction bn)
  2 MP bde with (1 MP bn)

Reserves
FORCES BY ROLE
MANOEUVRE
  Light
    ε19 inf bn
EQUIPMENT BY TYPE
ARMOURED FIGHTING VEHICLES
  RECCE (7 M8 in store)
  APC 47
    APC (T) 10 M113 (5 more in store)
    APC (W) 37: 30 *Armadillo*; 7 V-100 *Commando*
ANTI-TANK/ANTI-INFRASTRUCTURE
  RCL 120+: **75mm** M20; **105mm** 64 M-1974 FMK-1 (ARG); **106mm** 56 M40A1
ARTILLERY 149
  TOWED **105mm** 76: 12 M101; 8 M102; 56 M-56
  MOR 73: **81mm** 55 M1; **107mm** (12 M30 in store); **120mm** 18 ECIA
AIR DEFENCE • GUNS • TOWED 32: **20mm** 16 GAI-D01; 16 M-55

Navy 1,500
EQUIPMENT BY TYPE
PATROL AND COASTAL COMBATANTS 10
  PB 10: 6 *Cutlass*; 1 *Dauntless*; 1 *Kukulkan* (US *Broadsword* 32m); 2 *Utatlan* (US *Sewart*)

AMPHIBIOUS • LANDING CRAFT • LCP 2 *Machete*
LOGISTICS AND SUPPORT • AXS 3

Marines 650 reservists
FORCES BY ROLE
MANOEUVRE
  Amphibious
  2 mne bn(-)

Air Force 1,000
2 air comd
FORCES BY ROLE
FIGHTER/GROUND ATTACK/ISR
  1 sqn with A-37B *Dragonfly*
  1 sqn with PC-7 *Turbo Trainer**
TRANSPORT
  1 sqn with BT-67; Beech 90/100/200/300 *King Air*; IAI-201 *Arava*
  1 (tactical support) sqn with Cessna 206; PA-31 *Navajo*
TRAINING
  1 sqn with Cessna R172K *Hawk* XP; T-35B *Pillan*
TRANSPORT HELICOPTER
  1 sqn with Bell 206 *Jet Ranger*; Bell 212 (armed); Bell 412 *Twin Huey* (armed); UH-1H *Iroquois*
EQUIPMENT BY TYPE
Serviceability of ac is less than 50%
AIRCRAFT 9 combat capable
  ATK 2 A-37B *Dragonfly*
  TPT • Light 27: 5 Beech 90 *King Air*; 1 Beech 100 *King Air*; 2 Beech 200 *King Air*; 2 Beech 300 *King Air*; 4 BT-67; 2 Cessna 206; 1 Cessna 208B; 5 Cessna R172K *Hawk* XP; 4 IAI-201 *Arava*; 1 PA-31 *Navajo*
  TRG 11: 7 PC-7 *Turbo Trainer**; 4 T-35B *Pillan*
HELICOPTERS
  MRH 2 Bell 412 *Twin Huey* (armed)
  TPT • Light 17: 2 Bell 205 (UH-1H *Iroquois*); 8 Bell 206 *Jet Ranger*; 7 Bell 212 (armed)

Tactical Security Group
Air Military Police

Paramilitary 25,000 active

National Civil Police 25,000
FORCES BY ROLE
SPECIAL FORCES
  1 SF bn
MANOEUVRE
  Other
  1 (integrated task force) paramilitary unit (incl mil and treasury police)

DEPLOYMENT

CENTRAL AFRICAN REPUBLIC
UN • MINUSCA 2; 2 obs

CÔTE D'IVOIRE
UN • UNOCI 4 obs

DEMOCRATIC REPUBLIC OF THE CONGO
UN • MONUSCO 151; 1 obs; 1 SF coy

HAITI
UN • MINUSTAH 54

LEBANON
UN • UNIFIL 2

SOUTH SUDAN
UN • UNMISS 4; 3 obs

SUDAN
UN • UNISFA 1; 2 obs

Guyana GUY

Guyanese Dollar G$		2015	2016	2017
GDP	G$	653bn	717bn	
	US$	3.16bn	3.46bn	
per capita	US$	4,125	4,492	
Growth	%	3.2	4.0	
Inflation	%	-0.3	0.2	
Def bdgt	G$	9.02bn	9.58bn	
	US$	44m	46m	
US$1=G$		206.49	207.53	

Population 735,909

Age	0–14	15–19	20–24	25–29	30–64	65 plus
Male	13.8%	5.0%	5.2%	4.1%	19.1%	2.4%
Female	13.3%	5.6%	4.9%	3.7%	18.6%	3.4%

Capabilities

The Guyana Defence Force (GDF) has minimal military capability and its activities are limited to border control and support to law-enforcement operations. It also assists the civilian authorities and contributes to economic development. Guyana has close ties with Brazil, with whom it cooperates on safeguarding the security of the shared border via the annual military regional exchange meeting. The country also has bilateral agreements with France and China, who provide military training and equipment. Guyana is also part of the Caribbean Basin Security Initiative. Disputes over border demarcation between Guyana and Venezuela flared up in 2016. In 2015, the president highlighted the need to modernise and reorganise the defence force in order to better protect Guyana's sovereignty. This reform will mean reorganising some units, more training, infrastructure improvements, and the procurement of new equipment for the air force, coastguard and army engineering corps. In December 2015 the government officially re-established the *Milicia Popular de Guyana* reserve force. The defence ministry plans to make increasing use of reservists in order to bolster the GDF and increase its ability to patrol Guyana's territory. Representatives from Russia's Rosoboronexport met senior Guyanese officials in June 2016 to discuss possible military-technical cooperation and to promote its products in light of the modernisation programme. The GDF held the *Home Guard 2016* exercise in Tacama in August and also took part in the US-led *Tradewinds 2016* exercise.

ACTIVE 3,400 (Army 3,000 Navy 200 Air 200)
Active numbers combined Guyana Defence Force

RESERVE 670 (Army 500 Navy 170)

ORGANISATIONS BY SERVICE

Army 3,000
FORCES BY ROLE
SPECIAL FORCES
 1 SF coy
MANOUEVRE
 Light
 1 inf bn
 Other
 1 (Presidential) gd bn
COMBAT SUPPORT
 1 arty coy
 1 (spt wpn) cbt spt coy
 1 engr coy
EQUIPMENT BY TYPE
ARMOURED FIGHTING VEHICLES
 RECCE 9: 6 EE-9 *Cascavel* (reported); 3 S52 *Shorland*
ARTILLERY 54
 TOWED 130mm 6 M-46†
 MOR 48: 81mm 12 L16A1; 82mm 18 M-43; 120mm 18 M-43

Navy 200
EQUIPMENT BY TYPE
PATROL AND COASTAL COMBATANTS 5
 PCO 1 *Essequibo* (ex-UK *River*)
 PB 4 *Barracuda* (ex-US Type-44)

Air Force 200
FORCES BY ROLE
TRANSPORT
 1 unit with Bell 206; Cessna 206; Y-12 (II)
EQUIPMENT BY TYPE
AIRCRAFT • TPT • Light 2: 1 Cessna 206; 1 Y-12 (II)
HELICOPTERS
 MRH 1 Bell 412 *Twin Huey*†
 TPT • **Light** 2 Bell 206

Haiti HTI

Haitian Gourde G		2015	2016	2017
GDP	G	426bn	484bn	
	US$	8.71bn	8.26bn	
per capita	US$	813	761	
Growth	%	1.2	1.5	
Inflation	%	7.5	13.3	
Def bdgt	G	n/a	420m	
	US$	n/a	7m	
FMA (US)	US$	1m	1m	1m
US$1=G		48.85	58.66	

Population   10,485,800

Age	0–14	15–19	20–24	25–29	30–64	65 plus
Male	16.6%	5.5%	5.1%	4.5%	15.9%	1.2%
Female	16.7%	5.5%	5.2%	4.5%	16.3%	2.3%

Capabilities

Haiti formally re-established its defence ministry and a small army at the end of 2015. The country is seeking external assistance from other countries in the region in forming its new defence force, including from Brazil and Ecuador. Plans for military expansion were outlined in the country's first White Paper on Security and Defence, which was published in 2015. The embryonic army has focused on providing an engineering capability for disaster-relief tasks, although other requirements have been identified, including for a border-patrol capability. Political violence and civil unrest are an increasing concern. The mandate of the UN Multinational Stabilisation Mission (MINUSTAH), which held armed gangs and other non-state actors in check, was in October 2016 renewed for six months. The devastation in the southeast from Hurricane Matthew challenged Haiti's embryonic defence institutions, as well as the MINUSTAH force, and saw international military and civil assistance arrive in-country.

ACTIVE 70 (Army 70) **Paramilitary 50**

ORGANISATIONS BY SERVICE

Army 70

Paramilitary 50

Coast Guard ε50
EQUIPMENT BY TYPE
PATROL AND COASTAL COMBATANTS • PB 8: 5 *Dauntless*; 3 3812-VCF

FOREIGN FORCES

Argentina 73; 1 fd hospital
Bangladesh 112; 1 hel sqn
Bhutan 1
Brazil 982; 1 inf bn; 1 engr coy
Canada 4
Chile 392; 1 inf bn HQ; 2 inf coy; 1 hel sqn
Ecuador 1
El Salvador 44
Guatemala 54
Honduras 47
Jordan 3
Mexico 6
Nepal 2
Paraguay 83; 1 engr coy
Peru 161; 1 inf coy
Philippines 137; 1 HQ coy
Sri Lanka 3
United States 4
Uruguay 249; 1 inf bn HQ; 1 inf coy

Honduras HND

Honduran Lempira L		2015	2016	2017
GDP	L	451bn	482bn	
	US$	20.5bn	21bn	
per capita	US$	2,530	2,551	
Growth	%	3.6	3.6	
Inflation	%	3.2	3.1	
Def bdgt [a]	L	5.42bn	6.78bn	7bn
	US$	246m	295m	
FMA (US)	US$	3m	5m	5m
US$1=L		22.07	23.01	

[a] Defence & national-security budget

Population   8,893,259

Age	0–14	15–19	20–24	25–29	30–64	65 plus
Male	17.1%	5.6%	5.2%	4.6%	16.1%	1.8%
Female	16.4%	5.4%	5.0%	4.4%	16.1%	2.4%

Capabilities

Honduras retains a broad range of capabilities, although in many cases equipment is ageing, with serviceability in doubt. In 2011, the armed forces began to deploy in a paramilitary role, in conjunction with the police, to combat organised crime and narcotics trafficking. To this end, a new maritime special-forces unit was established in 2012, as were two new security agencies in 2014 – the Public Order Military Police and the TIGRES. The US maintains a small military presence at Soto Cano air base. The Honduran Navy is also active in counter-narcotics activities and operates in coordination with Colombia on *Operation Swordfish*, among other multilateral security initiatives. In 2016, El Salvador, Honduras and Guatemala signed a memorandum of understanding to increase cooperation in counter-gang operations. In late 2016 the president announced plans to create two new battalions of riot police. Equipment maintenance and procurement accounts for a small proportion of the defence budget. Donations of helicopters by South Korea and Cessna *Grand Caravan* aircraft from the US have gone some way to increasing the air force's light-transport capability, although the Cessnas can also be used for surveillance and counter-narcotics operations.

ACTIVE 10,700 (Army 7,300 Navy 1,100 Air 2,300)
Paramilitary 8,000

RESERVE 60,000 (Joint 60,000; Ex-servicemen registered)

ORGANISATIONS BY SERVICE

Army 7,300
FORCES BY ROLE
SPECIAL FORCES
  1 (special tac) spec ops gp (2 spec ops bn, 1 inf bn; 1 AB bn; 1 arty bn)
MANOEUVRE
  Mechanised
  1 inf bde (1 mech cav regt, 1 inf bn, 1 arty bn)
  Light
  1 inf bde (3 inf bn, 1 arty bn)
  3 inf bde (2 inf bn)
  1 indep inf bn
  Other
  1 (Presidential) gd coy
COMBAT SUPPORT
  1 engr bn
  3 MP bn
  1 sigs bn
AIR DEFENCE
  1 ADA bn
EQUIPMENT BY TYPE
ARMOURED FIGHTING VEHICLES
  LT TK 12 FV101 *Scorpion*
  RECCE 57: 1 FV105 *Sultan* (CP); 3 FV107 *Scimitar*; 40 FV601 *Saladin*; 13 RBY-1
ANTI-TANK/ANTI-INFRASTRUCTURE
  RCL 170: **84mm** 120 *Carl Gustav*; **106mm** 50 M40A1
ARTILLERY 118+
  TOWED 28: **105mm**: 24 M102; **155mm**: 4 M198
  MOR 90+: **81mm**; **120mm** 60 FMK-2; **160mm** 30 M-66
AIR DEFENCE • GUNS 20mm 48: 24 M-55A2; 24 TCM-20

Navy 1,100
EQUIPMENT BY TYPE
PATROL AND COASTAL COMBATANTS 17
  PB 17: 2 *Lempira* (Damen Stan 4207 – leased); 1 *Chamelecon* (Swiftships 85); 1 *Tegucilgalpa* (US *Guardian* 32m); 4 *Guanaja* (ex-US Type-44); 3 *Guaymuras* (Swiftships 105); 5 *Nacaome* (Swiftships 65*)*; 1 *Rio Coco* (US PB Mk III)
AMPHIBIOUS • LANDING CRAFT 3
  LCU 1 *Punta Caxinas*
  LCM 2

Marines 830
FORCES BY ROLE
MANOEUVRE
  Amphibious
  1 mne bn

Air Force 2,300
FORCES BY ROLE
FIGHTER/GROUND ATTACK
  1 sqn with A-37B *Dragonfly*
  1 sqn with F-5E/F *Tiger* II
GROUND ATTACK/ISR/TRAINING
  1 unit with Cessna 182 *Skylane*; EMB-312 *Tucano*; MXT-7-180 *Star Rocket*
TRANSPORT
  1 sqn with Beech 200 *King Air*; C-130A *Hercules*; Cessna 185/210; IAI-201 *Arava*; PA-42 *Cheyenne*; Turbo Commander 690
  1 VIP flt with PA-31 *Navajo*; Bell 412EP/SP *Twin Huey*
TRANSPORT HELICOPTER
  1 sqn with Bell 205 (UH-1H *Iroquois*); Bell 412SP *Twin Huey*
EQUIPMENT BY TYPE
AIRCRAFT 17 combat capable
  FTR 11: 9 F-5E *Tiger* II†; 2 F-5F *Tiger* II†
  ATK 6 A-37B *Dragonfly*
  TPT 18: **Medium** 1 C-130A *Hercules*; **Light** 17: 1 Beech 200 *King Air*; 2 Cessna 172 *Skyhawk*; 2 Cessna 182 *Skylane*; 1 Cessna 185; 2 Cessna 208B *Grand Caravan*; 2 Cessna 210; 1 EMB-135 *Legacy* 600; 1 IAI-201 *Arava*; 2 L-410 (leased); 1 PA-31 *Navajo*; 1 PA-42 *Cheyenne*; 1 Turbo Commander 690
  TRG 16: 9 EMB-312 *Tucano*; 7 MXT-7-180 *Star Rocket*
HELICOPTERS
  MRH 7: 1 Bell 412EP *Twin Huey* (VIP); 5 Bell 412SP *Twin Huey*; 2 Hughes 500
  TPT • **Light** 7: 6 Bell 205 (UH-1H *Iroquois*); 1 H125 *Ecureuil*
AIR-LAUNCHED MISSILES • AAM • IR *Shafrir*‡

Paramilitary 8,000

Public Security Forces 8,000
Ministry of Public Security and Defence; 11 regional comd

DEPLOYMENT

HAITI
UN • MINUSTAH 47

WESTERN SAHARA
UN • MINURSO 12 obs

FOREIGN FORCES

United States US Southern Command: 410; 1 avn bn with CH-47 *Chinook*; UH-60 *Black Hawk*

Jamaica JAM

Jamaican Dollar J$		2015	2016	2017
GDP	J$	1.67tr	1.76tr	
	US$	14.2bn	13.8bn	
per capita	US$	5,053	4,870	
Growth	%	0.9	1.5	
Inflation	%	3.7	4.4	
Def bdgt	J$	13.9bn	14.6bn	
	US$	119m	115m	
US$1=J$		117.26	127.56	

Population 2,970,340

Age	0–14	15–19	20–24	25–29	30–64	65 plus
Male	14.0%	5.2%	5.4%	4.8%	16.6%	3.6%
Female	13.5%	5.1%	5.4%	4.9%	17.2%	4.4%

Capabilities

The Jamaican Defence Force focuses on its maritime-security and internal-security capability, including providing some support to police operations. Although Jamaica maintains relatively small military forces, these benefit from training with larger armed services, including those of Canada, the UK and the US. Jamaica hosted phase two of the *Tradewinds* exercise in mid-2016, with a focus on maritime security, having earlier in the year hosted the 14th Caribbean Nations Security Conference in Kingston along with US Southern Command, with a focus on strengthening regional capacity and developing cooperation to tackle regional threats.

ACTIVE 3,450 (Army 2,900 Coast Guard 300 Air 250) (combined Jamaican Defence Force)

RESERVE 980 (Army 900 Coast Guard 60 Air 20)

ORGANISATIONS BY SERVICE

Army 2,900
FORCES BY ROLE
MANOEUVRE
  Mechanised
    1 (PMV) lt mech inf coy
  Light
    2 inf bn
COMBAT SUPPORT
  1 engr regt (4 engr sqn)
COMBAT SERVICE SUPPORT
  1 spt bn (1 MP coy, 1 med coy, 1 log coy, 1 tpt coy)
EQUIPMENT BY TYPE
ARMOURED FIGHTING VEHICLES
  AUV 12 *Bushmaster*
ARTILLERY • MOR 81mm 12 L16A1

Reserves
FORCES BY ROLE
MANOEUVRE
  Light
    1 inf bn

Coast Guard 300
EQUIPMENT BY TYPE
PATROL AND COASTAL COMBATANTS 11
  PBF 3
  PB 8: 3 *Cornwall* (Damen Stan 4207); 4 *Dauntless*; 1 *Paul Bogle* (US 31m)

Air Wing 250
Plus National Reserve
FORCES BY ROLE
MARITIME PATROL/TRANSPORT
  1 flt with BN-2A *Defender*; Cessna 210M *Centurion*
SEARCH & RESCUE/TRANSPORT HELICOPTER
  1 flt with Bell 407
  1 flt with Bell 412EP
TRAINING
  1 unit with Bell 206B3; DA40-180FP *Diamond Star*
EQUIPMENT BY TYPE
AIRCRAFT
  TPT • Light 4: 1 BN-2A *Defender*; 1 Cessna 210M *Centurion*; 2 DA40-180FP *Diamond Star*
HELICOPTERS
  MRH 2 Bell 412EP
  TPT • Light 5: 2 Bell 206B3 *Jet Ranger*; 3 Bell 407

Mexico MEX

Mexican Peso NP		2015	2016	2017
GDP	NP	18.1tr	19.3tr	
	US$	1.14tr	1.06tr	
per capita	US$	9,452	8,699	
Growth	%	2.5	2.1	
Inflation	%	2.7	2.8	
Def bdgt [a]	NP	95.3bn	91.8bn	86.4bn
	US$	6.02bn	5.06bn	
FMA (US)	US$	5m	7m	3m
US$1=NP		15.85	18.14	

[a] National-security expenditure

Population 123,166,749

Age	0–14	15–19	20–24	25–29	30–64	65 plus
Male	13.9%	4.6%	4.4%	4.2%	18.9%	3.1%
Female	13.3%	4.4%	4.3%	4.2%	20.9%	3.8%

Capabilities

Mexico has the most capable armed forces in Central America. Main tasks for the armed forces include defending state sovereignty and territorial integrity, internal security and extending aid to civilian authorities. Under the previous Calderón administration, operations against drug cartels became the army's primary activity, involving about a quarter of its active strength at any given time. A national-defence-policy document remains under discussion, and is expected to reflect a redefined security role towards greater participation in international security operations. A new National Gendarmerie was activated in

August 2014, although plans for an initial establishment of 10,000 were subsequently reduced to 5,000. The navy retains well-equipped frigates, but the majority of its forces are dedicated to maritime security, though there are plans to reorganise the navy into coastal and blue-water forces. Mexico relies on foreign suppliers for the majority of its equipment, in particular the US. But the state-owned ASTIMAR shipyards are able to provide several classes of patrol vessels for the Mexican Navy. However, ASTIMAR has yet to build any vessels with a military capability greater than seen on these patrol vessels. Mexico made its largest contribution to the RIMPAC exercise in 2016, sending 470 personnel including marines and special forces, as well as surveillance aircraft and one amphibious landing ship. During the exercise Mexico was able to practice amphibious landings and increase interoperability with partner nations. Mexico regularly features in US-led exercises. A continuing problem with desertion has prompted efforts to improve benefits, training and conditions for serving personnel. Measures taken in the last few years, such as subsidies and better housing, have significantly decreased levels of desertion. The recent retirement of the remaining F-5 fighter aircraft in late 2016 has left the country without any airborne air-defence capability. In 2014, the purchase of *King Air* surveillance aircraft was announced. There exists a significant air- and sea-lift capability that would allow for some regional deployment if necessary. Since the announcement in September 2014 of a shift in the country's foreign-policy stance, Mexico has increased its participation in UN peacekeeping operations.

ACTIVE 277,150 (Army 208,350 Navy 60,300 Air 8,500) **Paramilitary 58,900**

RESERVE 81,500 (National Military Service)

ORGANISATIONS BY SERVICE

Space
EQUIPMENT BY TYPE
SATELLITES • COMMUNICATIONS 2 *Mexsat*

Army 208,350
12 regions (total: 46 army zones)
FORCES BY ROLE
SPECIAL FORCES
   1 (1st) SF bde (5 SF bn)
   1 (2nd) SF bde (7 SF bn)
   1 (3rd) SF bde (4 SF bn)
MANOEUVRE
   Reconnaissance
   3 (2nd, 3rd & 4th Armd) mech bde (2 armd recce bn, 2 lt mech bn, 1 arty bn, 1 (Canon) AT gp)
   25 mot recce regt
   Light
   1 (1st) inf corps (1 (1st Armd) mech bde (2 armd recce bn, 2 lt mech bn, 1 arty bn, 1 (Canon) AT gp), 3 (2nd, 3rd & 6th) inf bde (each: 3 inf bn, 1 arty regt, 1 (Canon) AT gp), 1 cbt engr bde (3 engr bn))
   3 (1st, 4th & 5th) indep lt inf bde (2 lt inf bn, 1 (Canon) AT gp)
   92 indep inf bn
   25 indep inf coy
Air Manoeuvre
   1 para bde with (1 (GAFE) SF gp, 3 bn, 1 (Canon) AT gp)
Other
   1 (Presidential) gd corps (1 SF gp, 1 mech inf bde (2 inf bn, 1 aslt bn), 1 mne bn (Navy), 1 cbt engr bn, 1 MP bde (3 bn, 1 special ops anti-riot coy))
COMBAT SUPPORT
   1 indep arty regt
   2 MP bde (3 MP bn)
EQUIPMENT BY TYPE
ARMOURED FIGHTING VEHICLES
   RECCE 255: 19 DN-5 *Toro*; 127 ERC-90F1 *Lynx* (7 trg); 40 M8; 37 MAC-1; 32 VBL
   APC 699
      APC (T) 463: 390 DNC-1 (mod AMX-VCI); 40 HWK-11; 33 M5A1 half-track
      APC (W) 236: 95 BDX; 16 DN-4; 2 DN-6; 28 LAV-100 (*Pantera*); 26 LAV-150 ST; 25 MOWAG *Roland*; 44 VCR (3 amb; 5 cmd post)
ENGINEERING & MAINTENANCE VEHICLES
   ARV 7: 3 M32 *Recovery Sherman*; 4 VCR ARV
ANTI-TANK/ANTI-INFRASTRUCTURE
   MSL • SP 8 VBL with *Milan*
   RCL • 106mm 1,187+ M40A1 (incl some SP)
   GUNS 37mm 30 M3
ARTILLERY 1,390
   TOWED 123: 105mm 123: 40 M101; 40 M-56; 16 M2A1; 14 M3; 13 NORINCO M90
   MOR 1,267: 81mm 1,100: 400 M1; 400 Brandt; 300 SB
   120mm 167: 75 Brandt; 60 M-65; 32 RT-61
AIR DEFENCE • GUNS • TOWED 80: 12.7mm 40 M55; 20mm 40 GAI-B01

Navy 60,300
Two Fleet Commands: Gulf (6 zones), Pacific (11 zones)
EQUIPMENT BY TYPE
PRINCIPAL SURFACE COMBATANTS 6
   FRIGATES 6
      FFGHM 4 *Allende* (US *Knox*) with 1 octuple Mk16 lnchr with ASROC/RGM-84C *Harpoon* AShM, 1 Mk25 GMLS with RIM-7 *Sea Sparrow* SAM, 2 twin Mk32 324mm ASTT with Mk46 LWT, 1 127mm gun (capacity 1 MD-902 hel)
      FF 2 *Bravo* (US *Bronstein*) with 1 octuple Mk112 lnchr with ASROC†, 2 triple Mk32 324mm ASTT with Mk46 LWT, 1 twin 76mm gun, 1 hel landing platform
PATROL AND COASTAL COMBATANTS 122
   PSOH 4 *Oaxaca* with 1 76mm gun (capacity 1 AS565MB *Panther* hel)
   PCOH 16:
      4 *Durango* with 1 57mm gun (capacity 1 Bo-105 hel)
      4 *Holzinger* (capacity 1 MD-902 *Explorer*)
      3 *Sierra* with 1 57mm gun (capacity 1 MD-902 *Explorer*)
      5 *Uribe* (ESP *Halcon*) (capacity 1 Bo-105 hel)
   PCO 10 *Leandro Valle* (US *Auk* MSF) with 1 76mm gun

PCG 2 *Huracan* (ISR *Aliya*) with 4 single lnchr with *Gabriel* II AShM, 1 *Phalanx* CIWS
PCC 2 *Democrata*
PBF 73: 6 *Acuario*; 2 *Acuario B*; 48 *Polaris* (SWE CB90); 17 *Polaris* II (SWE IC 16M)
PB 15: 3 *Azteca*; 3 *Cabo* (US *Cape Higgon*); 2 *Punta* (US *Point*); 7 *Tenochtitlan* (Damen Stan Patrol 4207)
AMPHIBIOUS • LS • LST 4: 2 *Monte Azule*s with 1 hel landing platform; 2 *Papaloapan* (US *Newport*) with 4 76mm guns, 1 hel landing platform
LOGISTICS AND SUPPORT 22
  AG 2
  AGOR 3: 2 *Altair* (ex-US *Robert D. Conrad*); 1 *Humboldt*
  AGS 8: 4 *Arrecife*; 1 *Onjuku*; 1 *Rio Hondo*; 1 *Rio Tuxpan*; 1 *Moctezuma* II (also used as AXS)
  AK 2: 1 *Tarasco*; 1 *Rio Suchiate*
  ATF 4 *Otomi* with 1 76mm gun
  AX 2 *Huasteco* (also serve as troop transport, supply and hospital ships)
  AXS 1 *Cuauhtemoc* with 2 65mm saluting guns

Naval Aviation 1,250
FORCES BY ROLE
MARITIME PATROL
  5 sqn with Cessna 404 *Titan*; MX-7 *Star Rocket*; Lancair IV-P; T-6C+ *Texan* II
  1 sqn with Beech 350ER *King Air*; C-212PM *Aviocar*; CN-235-300 MPA *Persuader*
  1 sqn with L-90 *Redigo*
TRANSPORT
  1 sqn with An-32B *Cline*
  1 (VIP) sqn with DHC-8 *Dash 8*; Learjet 24; *Turbo Commander* 1000
TRANSPORT HELICOPTER
  2 sqn with AS555 *Fennec*; AS565MB/AS565MBe *Panther*; MD-902
  2 sqn with Bo-105 CBS-5
  5 sqn with Mi-17-1V/V-5 *Hip*
TRAINING
  1 sqn with Z-242L
EQUIPMENT BY TYPE
  AIRCRAFT 9 combat capable
    MP 6 CN-235-300 MPA *Persuader*
    ISR 2 C-212PM *Aviocar*
    TPT 30: **Light** 28: 1 An-32B *Cline*; 5 Beech 350ER *King Air* (4 used for ISR); 4 C-295M; 2 C-295W; 1 Cessna 404 *Titan*; 1 DHC-8 *Dash 8*; 6 Lancair IV-P; 3 Learjet 24; 5 *Turbo Commander* 1000; **PAX** 2: 1 CL-605 *Challenger*; 1 Gulfstream 550
    TRG 40: 3 L-90TP *Redigo**; 4 MX-7 *Star Rocket*; 6 T-6C+ *Texan* II; 27 Z-242L
  HELICOPTERS
    MRH 29: 2 AS555 *Fennec*; 4 MD-500E; 19 Mi-17-1V *Hip*; 4 Mi-17V-5 *Hip*
    SAR 5: 4 AS565MB *Panther*; 1 AS565MBe *Panther*
    TPT 34: **Heavy** 3 H225M *Caracal*; **Medium** 3 UH-60M *Black Hawk*; **Light** 28: 1 AW109SP; 11 Bo-105 CBS-5; 5 MD-902 (SAR role); 1 R-44; 10 S-333
    TRG 4 Schweizer 300C

Marines 21,500 (Expanding to 26,560)
FORCES BY ROLE
SPECIAL FORCES
  3 SF unit
MANOEUVRE
  Light
    32 inf bn(-)
  Air Manoeuvre
    1 AB bn
  Amphibious
    2 amph bde (4 inf bn, 1 amph bn, 1 arty gp)
  Other
    1 (Presidential) gd bn (included in army above)
COMBAT SERVICE SUPPORT
  2 spt bn
EQUIPMENT BY TYPE
ARMOURED FIGHTING VEHICLES
  APC • APC (W) 29: 3 BTR-60 (APC-60); 26 BTR-70 (APC-70)
ANTI-TANK/ANTI-INFRASTRUCTURE
  RCL 106mm M40A1
ARTILLERY 22+
  TOWED 105mm 16 M-56
  MRL 122mm 6 Firos-25
  MOR 81mm some
AIR DEFENCE • SAM • Point-defence 9K38 *Igla* (SA-18 *Grouse*)

Air Force 8,500
FORCES BY ROLE
GROUND ATTACK/ISR
  4 sqn with PC-7*
  1 sqn with PC-7*/PC-9M
ISR/AEW
  1 sqn with Beech 350ER *King Air*; EMB-145AEW *Erieye*; EMB-145RS; SA-2-37B; SA-227-BC *Metro* III (C-26B)
TRANSPORT
  1 sqn with C-295M; PC-6B
  1 sqn with B-727; Beech 90
  1 sqn with C-27J *Spartan*; C-130E/K-30 *Hercules*; L-100-30
  6 (liaison) sqn with Cessna 182/206
  1 (anti-narcotic spraying) sqn with Bell 206; Cessna T206H;
  1 (Presidential) gp with AS332L *Super Puma*; AW109SP; B-737; B-757; Gulfstream III; H225; Learjet 35A; Learjet 36; *Turbo Commander* 680
  1 (VIP) gp with B-737; Beech 200 *King Air*; Beech 350i *King Air*; Cessna 500 *Citation*; CL-605 *Challenger*; Gulfstream 150/450/550; S-70A-24
TRAINING
  1 sqn with Cessna 182
  1 sqn with PC-7*; T-6C+ *Texan* II
  1 sqn with Beech F33C *Bonanza*; Grob G120TP; SF-260EU
TRANSPORT HELICOPTER
  4 sqn with Bell 206B; Bell 212; Bell 407GX
  1 sqn with MD-530MF/MG
  1 sqn with Mi-8T *Hip*; Mi-17 *Hip*
  1 sqn with H225M *Caracal*; Bell 412EP *Twin Huey*; S-70A-24 *Black Hawk*

ISR UAV
1 unit with *Hermes* 450; S4 *Ehécatl*

EQUIPMENT BY TYPE
AIRCRAFT 65 combat capable
 ISR 6: 2 SA-2-37A; 4 SA-227-BC *Metro* III (C-26B)
 ELINT 8: 6 Beech 350ER *King Air*; 2 EMB-145RS
 AEW&C 1 EMB-145AEW *Erieye*
 TPT 111: **Medium** 9: 4 C-27J *Spartan*; 2 C-130E *Hercules*; 2 C-130K-30 *Hercules*; 1 L-100-30; **Light** 89: 2 Beech 90 *King Air*; 1 Beech 200 *King Air*; 1 Beech 350i *King Air*; 6 C-295M; 59 Cessna 182; 3 Cessna 206; 8 Cessna T206H; 1 Cessna 500 *Citation*; 2 Learjet 35A; 1 Learjet 36; 1 Learjet 45XP; 3 PC-6B; 1 *Turbo Commander* 680; **PAX** 9: 2 B-737; 1 B-757; 1 CL-605 *Challenger*; 2 Gulfstream III; 1 Gulfstream 150; 1 Gulfstream 450; 1 Gulfstream 550
 TRG 135: 4 Beech F33C *Bonanza*; 25 Grob G120TP; 54 PC-7*; 1 PC-9M*; 4 PT-17; 25 SF-260EU; 22 T-6C+ *Texan* II
HELICOPTERS
 MRH 46: 15 Bell 407GXP; 12 Bell 412EP *Twin Huey*; 19 Mi-17 *Hip* H
 ISR 13: 4 MD-530MF; 9 MD-530MG
 TPT 114: **Heavy** 11 H225M *Caracal*; **Medium** 19: 3 AS332L *Super Puma*; 2 H225 (VIP); 2 Mi-8T *Hip*; 6 S-70A-24 *Black Hawk*; 6 UH-1M *Black Hawk* **Light** 83: 5 AW109SP; 45 Bell 206; 13 Bell 206B *Jet Ranger* II; 7 Bell 206L; 13 Bell 212
UNMANNED AERIAL VEHICLES • ISR 8: **Medium** 3 *Hermes* 450; **Light** 5 S4 *Ehécatl*
AIR-LAUNCHED MISSILES • AAM • IR AIM-9J *Sidewinder*

Paramilitary 62,900

Federal Police 41,000 (Incl 5,000 Gendarmerie)
Public Security Secretariat
EQUIPMENT BY TYPE
AIRCRAFT
 TPT 13: **Light** 7: 2 CN-235M; 2 Cessna 182 *Skylane*; 1 Cessna 500 *Citation*; 2 *Turbo Commander* 695; **PAX** 6: 4 B-727; 1 *Falcon* 20; 1 Gulfstream II
HELICOPTERS
 MRH 3 Mi-17 *Hip* H
 TPT 27: **Medium** 13: 1 SA330J *Puma*; 6 UH-60L *Black Hawk*; 6 UH-60M *Black Hawk*; **Light** 14: 2 AS350B *Ecureuil*; 1 AS355 *Ecureuil* II; 6 Bell 206B; 5 H120 *Colibri*
UNMANNED AERIAL VEHICLES
 ISR 12: **Medium** 2 *Hermes* 900; **Light** 10 S4 *Ehécatl*

Federal Ministerial Police 4,500
EQUIPMENT BY TYPE
HELICOPTERS
 TPT • **Light** 25: 18 Bell 205 (UH-1H); 7 Bell 212
UNMANNED AERIAL VEHICLES
 ISR • **Heavy** 2 *Dominator* XP

Rural Defense Militia 17,400
FORCES BY ROLE
MANOEUVRE
Light
 13 inf unit
 13 (horsed) cav unit

Cyber

It was announced that two Cyberspace Operations centres would be created by 2018, one for the army and one for the navy, to address and better coordinate defence work on cyber security and in cyberspace. Key documentation includes the 2013–18 National Defence Sector Programme, the 2013–18 National Development Programme and the 2014–18 National Security Programme. In 2013 it was reported that a Center for Cyber Security and Cyber Defense Control would be created within naval intelligence.

DEPLOYMENT

HAITI
UN • MINUSTAH 6

LEBANON
UN • UNIFIL 2

WESTERN SAHARA
UN • MINURSO 4 obs

Nicaragua NIC

Nicaraguan Gold Cordoba Co		2015	2016	2017
GDP	Co	346bn	384bn	
	US$	12.7bn	13.4bn	
per capita	US$	2,024	2,115	
Growth	%	4.9	4.5	
Inflation	%	4.0	6.2	
Def bdgt	Co	1.95bn	2.08bn	2.51bn
	US$	72m	73m	
US$1=Co		27.26	28.62	

Population	5,966,798					
Age	0–14	15–19	20–24	25–29	30–64	65 plus
Male	14.2%	5.3%	5.6%	4.6%	16.8%	2.3%
Female	13.7%	5.2%	5.6%	4.8%	19.1%	2.8%

Capabilities

Nicaragua's armed forces provide assistance to border- and internal-security operations, with a central reserve focused on a single mechanised brigade, although there is increasing focus on disaster-relief, coastal-security and counter-narcotics activities. Nicaragua maintains a good relationship with Russia from whom it has sourced most of its equipment. Training relationships exist with Moscow as well as with regional states, where there is also cooperation in the fight against transnational narcotics trafficking and other organised crime. Most equipment is of Cold War-era vintage and, although there has been some recent modernisation and refurbishment, there has been little in the way of broad defence procurement. However, Nicaragua is now recapitalising its main-battle-tank fleet with the acquisition of new vehicles from Russia. There are currently no procurement plans for broader assets such as fixed- and rotary-wing aircraft and coastal-patrol vessels suitable for the border- and maritime-security roles. The army coordinates its counter-narcotics activities with the National Police.

ACTIVE 12,000 (Army 10,000 Navy 800 Air 1,200)

ORGANISATIONS BY SERVICE

Army ε10,000
FORCES BY ROLE
SPECIAL FORCES
  1 SF bde (2 SF bn)
MANOEUVRE
  Mechanised
  1 mech inf bde (1 armd recce bn, 1 tk bn, 1 mech inf bn, 1 arty bn, 1 MRL bn, 1 AT coy)
  Light
  1 regional comd (3 lt inf bn)
  1 regional comd (2 lt inf bn; 1 arty bn)
  3 regional comd (2 lt inf bn)
  2 indep lt inf bn
  Other
  1 comd regt (1 inf bn, 1 sy bn, 1 int unit, 1 sigs bn)
  1 (ecological) sy bn
COMBAT SUPPORT
  1 engr bn
COMBAT SERVICE SUPPORT
  1 med bn
  1 tpt regt
EQUIPMENT BY TYPE
ARMOURED FIGHTING VEHICLES
  MBT 82: 62 T-55 (65 more in store); 20 T-72B1
  LT TK (10 PT-76 in store)
  RECCE 20 BRDM-2
  IFV 17+ BMP-1
  APC • APC (W) 90+: 41 BTR-152 (61 more in store); 45 BTR-60 (15 more in store); 4+ BTR-70M
ENGINEERING & MAINTENANCE VEHICLES
  AEV T-54/T-55
  VLB TMM-3
ANTI-TANK/ANTI-INFRASTRUCTURE
  MSL
    SP 12 9P133 *Malyutka* (AT-3 *Sagger*)
    MANPATS 9K11 *Malyutka* (AT-3 *Sagger*)
  RCL 82mm B-10
  GUNS 281: **57mm** 174 ZIS-2; (90 more in store); **76mm** 83 ZIS-3; **100mm** 24 M-1944
ARTILLERY 766
  TOWED 12: **122mm** 12 D-30; (**152mm** 30 D-20 in store)
  MRL 151: **107mm** 33 Type-63; **122mm** 118: 18 BM-21 *Grad*; 100 *Grad* 1P (BM-21P) (single-tube rocket launcher, man portable)
  MOR 603: **82mm** 579; **120mm** 24 M-43; (**160mm** 4 M-160 in store)
AIR DEFENCE • SAM • Point-defence 9K36 *Strela*-3 (SA-14 *Gremlin*); 9K310 *Igla*-1 (SA-16 *Gimlet*); 9K32 *Strela*-2 (SA-7 *Grail*)‡

Navy ε800
EQUIPMENT BY TYPE
PATROL AND COASTAL COMBATANTS • PB 8: 3 *Dabur*; 4 Rodman 101, 1 *Zhuk*

Marines
FORCES BY ROLE
MANOEUVRE
  Amphibious
  1 mne bn

Air Force 1,200
FORCES BY ROLE
TRANSPORT
  1 sqn with An-26 *Curl*; Beech 90 *King Air*; Cessna U206; Cessna 404 *Titan* (VIP)
TRAINING
  1 unit with Cessna 172; PA-18 *Super Cub*; PA-28 *Cherokee*
TRANSPORT HELICOPTER
  1 sqn with Mi-17 *Hip* H (armed)
AIR DEFENCE
  1 gp with ZU-23
EQUIPMENT BY TYPE
AIRCRAFT
  TPT • Light 9: 3 An-26 *Curl*; 1 Beech 90 *King Air*; 1 Cessna 172; 1 Cessna U206; 1 Cessna 404 *Titan* (VIP); 2 PA-28 *Cherokee*
  TRG 2 PA-18 *Super Cub*
HELICOPTERS
  MRH 7 Mi-17 *Hip* H (armed)†
  TPT • Medium 2 Mi-171E
AIR DEFENCE • GUNS 23mm 18 ZU-23
AIR-LAUNCHED MISSILES • ASM 9M17 *Skorpion* (AT-2 *Swatter*)

Panama PAN

Panamanian Balboa B		2015	2016	2017
GDP	B	52.1bn	55.2bn	
	US$	52.1bn	55.2bn	
per capita	US$	13,013	13,515	
Growth	%	5.8	5.2	
Inflation	%	0.1	0.7	
Def bdgt [a]	B	654m	751m	
	US$	654m	751m	
FMA (US)	US$	2m	2m	2m
US$1=B		1.00	1.00	

[a] Public-security expenditure

Population 3,705,246

Age	0–14	15–19	20–24	25–29	30–64	65 plus
Male	13.6%	4.5%	4.2%	4.0%	20.2%	3.7%
Female	13.1%	4.3%	4.1%	3.9%	19.9%	4.4%

Capabilities

Panama's armed forces were abolished in 1990, however a police force and an air/maritime organisation were retained for low-level security activities. Disaster relief, internal security and combating narcotics trafficking and other transnational organised crime are key priorities. Panama's forces are built around core capabilities including transport aircraft and small patrol craft, with some interceptor vessels for interdiction operations. There are also light-armoured and other urban vehicles. In a bid to improve information gathering on the activity of transnational narcotics gangs, there are plans to create a broader information-gathering and -sharing network. The Panamanian government has a goal of a no-deficit budget and as such the security budget has seen substantial fluctuations in recent years. However, in May the president announced the intention to purchase equipment to help counter drug trafficking. There have been some exercises with neighbouring countries, such as Colombia. In mid-2016, Panama launched *Operation Escudo* to tackle drug smuggling and closed the border with Colombia.

Paramilitary 22,050

ORGANISATIONS BY SERVICE

Paramilitary 22,050

National Border Service 3,600
FORCES BY ROLE
SPECIAL FORCES
  1 SF gp
MANOEUVRE
  Other
  1 sy bde (5 sy bn(-))
  1 indep sy bn

National Police Force 16,150
No hvy mil eqpt, small arms only
FORCES BY ROLE
SPECIAL FORCES
  1 SF unit
MANOEUVRE
  Other
  1 (presidential) gd bn(-)

National Aeronaval Service ε2,300
FORCES BY ROLE
TRANSPORT
  1 sqn with C-212M *Aviocar*; Cessna 210; PA-31 *Navajo*; PA-34 *Seneca*
  1 (Presidential) flt with ERJ-135BJ; S-76C
TRAINING
  1 unit with Cessna 152; Cessna 172; T-35D *Pillan*
TRANSPORT HELICOPTER
  1 sqn with AW139; Bell 205; Bell 205 (UH-1H *Iroquois*); Bell 212; Bell 407; Bell 412EP; H145; MD-500E
EQUIPMENT BY TYPE
PATROL AND COASTAL COMBATANTS 17
  PCO 1 *Independencia* (ex-US *Balsam*)
  PCC 2 *Saettia*
  PB 14: 1 *Cocle*; 1 *Chiriqui* (ex-US PB MkIV); 2 *Panquiaco* (UK Vosper 31.5m); 5 3 *De Noviembre* (ex-US *Point*), 1 *Taboga*; 4 Type-200
AMPHIBIOUS • LANDING CRAFT • LCU 1 *General Estaban Huertas*
LOGISTICS AND SUPPORT • AG 2

AIRCRAFT
TPT • Light 10: 3 C-212M *Aviocar*; 1 Cessna 152, 1 Cessna 172; 1 Cessna 210; 1 ERJ-135BJ; 1 PA-31 *Navajo*; 2 PA-34 *Seneca*
TRG 6 T-35D *Pillan*
HELICOPTERS
MRH 8: 6 AW139; 1 Bell 412EP; 1 MD-500E
TPT • Light 21: 2 Bell 205; 13 Bell 205 (UH-1H *Iroquois*); 2 Bell 212; 2 Bell 407; 1 H145; 1 S-76C

Paraguay PRY

Paraguayan Guarani Pg		2015	2016	2017
GDP	Pg	144tr	155tr	
	US$	27.7bn	27.3bn	
per capita	US$	4,102	3,986	
Growth	%	3.1	3.5	
Inflation	%	3.1	4.1	
Def bdgt	Pg	1.63tr	1.52tr	
	US$	313m	267m	
US$1=Pg		5,204.93	5,679.96	

Population 6,862,812

Age	0–14	15–19	20–24	25–29	30–64	65 plus
Male	12.7%	4.8%	5.1%	4.6%	19.7%	3.2%
Female	12.3%	4.7%	5.1%	4.6%	19.4%	3.7%

Capabilities

The armed forces are small by regional standards and the equipment inventory for all services is ageing and largely obsolete. The forces are mainly involved in internal-security operations and humanitarian UN peacekeeping missions. Paraguay's most recent defence white paper was published in 2013. Although landlocked, the country supports a small force of river-patrol craft, reflecting the importance of its riverine systems, and the navy has also contributed a small force of personnel – along with army personnel and troops from the air force's airborne formation – to the National Anti-Drug Secretariat's Joint Special Forces Battalion, a unit organised for counter-narcotics missions. The country signed military-cooperation agreements with Brazil, Peru and South Korea in 2016. Paraguay is reportedly interested in acquiring radars and aircraft from South Korea, although the mooted acquisition of South Korea's KT-1P turboprop aircraft has not yet taken place. The army is trialling and evaluating for purchase Spanish VAMTAC ST5 multi-purpose vehicles. The US has trained Paraguayan troops since 2001 as part of the State Partnership Program. As of late 2016, Paraguay was participating in eight UN peacekeeping operations, though the largest contribution is just under 80 troops to the mission in Haiti.

ACTIVE 10,650 (Army 7,600 Navy 1,950 Air 1,100)
Paramilitary 14,800
Conscript liability 12 months

RESERVE 164,500 (Joint 164,500)

ORGANISATIONS BY SERVICE

Army 6,100; 1,500 conscript (total 7,600)

Much of the Paraguayan army is maintained in a cadre state during peacetime; the nominal inf and cav divs are effectively only at coy strength. Active gp/regt are usually coy sized

FORCES BY ROLE
MANOEUVRE
  Light
  3 inf corps (total: 6 inf div(-), 3 cav div(-), 6 arty bty)
  Other
  1 (Presidential) gd regt (1 SF bn, 1 inf bn, 1 sy bn, 1 log gp)
COMBAT SUPPORT
  1 arty bde with (2 arty gp, 1 ADA gp)
  1 engr bde with (1 engr regt, 3 construction regt)
  1 sigs bn

Reserves
FORCES BY ROLE
MANOEUVRE
  Light
  14 inf regt (cadre)
  4 cav regt (cadre)
EQUIPMENT BY TYPE
ARMOURED FIGHTING VEHICLES
  MBT 3 M4A3 *Sherman*
  RECCE 28 EE-9 *Cascavel*
  APC • APC (W) 12 EE-11 *Urutu*
ARTILLERY 99
  TOWED 105mm 19 M101
  MOR 81mm 80
AIR DEFENCE • GUNS 22:
  SP 20mm 3 M9 half track
  TOWED 19: 40mm 13 M1A1, 6 L/60

Navy 1,100; 850 conscript (total 1,950)
EQUIPMENT BY TYPE
PATROL AND COASTAL COMBATANTS 22
  PCR 3: 1 *Itaipú*; 1 *Nanawa*†; 1 *Paraguay*† with 2 twin 120mm gun, 3 76mm gun
  PBR 19: 1 *Capitan Cabral*; 2 *Capitan Ortiz* (ROC *Hai Ou*); 2 *Novatec*; 6 Type-701; 3 Croq 15; 5 others
AMPHIBIOUS • LANDING CRAFT • LCVP 3

Naval Aviation 100
FORCES BY ROLE
TRANSPORT
  1 (liaison) sqn with Cessna 150; Cessna 210 *Centurion*; Cessna 310; Cessna 401
TRANSPORT HELICOPTER
  1 sqn with AS350 *Ecureuil* (HB350 *Esquilo*)
EQUIPMENT BY TYPE
AIRCRAFT • TPT • Light 6: 2 Cessna 150; 1 Cessna 210 *Centurion*; 2 Cessna 310; 1 Cessna 401
HELICOPTERS • TPT • Light 2 AS350 *Ecureuil* (HB350 *Esquilo*)

Marines 700; 200 conscript (total 900)
FORCES BY ROLE
MANOEUVRE
  Amphibious
  3 mne bn(-)
ARTILLERY • TOWED 105mm 2 M101

Air Force 900; 200 conscript (total 1,100)
FORCES BY ROLE
GROUND ATTACK/ISR
  1 sqn with EMB-312 *Tucano**
TRANSPORT
  1 gp with C-212-200/400 *Aviocar*; DHC-6 *Twin Otter*
  1 VIP gp with Beech 58 *Baron*; Bell 427; Cessna U206 *Stationair*; Cessna 208B *Grand Caravan*; Cessna 210 *Centurion*; Cessna 402B; PA-32R *Saratoga* (EMB-721C *Sertanejo*); PZL-104 *Wilga* 80
TRAINING
  1 sqn with T-25 *Universal*; T-35A/B *Pillan*
TRANSPORT HELICOPTER
  1 gp with AS350 *Ecureuil* (HB350 *Esquilo*); Bell 205 (UH-1H *Iroquois*)
MANOEUVRE
  Air Manoeuvre
  1 AB bde
EQUIPMENT BY TYPE
AIRCRAFT 6 combat capable
  TPT • Light 18: 1 Beech 58 *Baron*; 4 C-212-200 *Aviocar*; 1 C-212-400 *Aviocar*; 2 Cessna 208B *Grand Caravan*; 1 Cessna 210 *Centurion*; 1 Cessna 310; 2 Cessna 402B; 2 Cessna U206 *Stationair*; 1 DHC-6 *Twin Otter*; 1 PA-32R *Saratoga* (EMB-721C *Sertanejo*); 2 PZL-104 *Wilga* 80
  TRG 21: 6 EMB-312 *Tucano**; 6 T-25 *Universal*; 6 T-35A *Pillan*; 3 T-35B *Pillan*
HELICOPTERS • TPT • Light 9: 3 AS350 *Ecureuil* (HB350 *Esquilo*); 5 Bell 205 (UH-1H *Iroquois*); 1 Bell 427 (VIP)

Paramilitary 14,800

Special Police Service 10,800; 4,000 conscript (total 14,800)

DEPLOYMENT

CENTRAL AFRICAN REPUBLIC
UN • MINUSCA 3; 1 obs

CÔTE D'IVOIRE
UN • UNOCI 1; 1 obs

CYPRUS
UN • UNFICYP 14

DEMOCRATIC REPUBLIC OF THE CONGO
UN • MONUSCO 15 obs

HAITI
UN • MINUSTAH 83; 1 engr coy

SOUTH SUDAN
UN • UNMISS 2 obs

Peru PER

Peruvian Nuevo Sol NS		2015	2016	2017
GDP	NS	612bn	649bn	
	US$	192bn	180bn	
per capita	US$	6,168	5,727	
Growth	%	3.3	3.7	
Inflation	%	3.5	3.6	
Def bdgt	NS	7.06bn	7.51bn	7.06bn
	US$	2.22bn	2.09bn	
FMA (US)	US$	2m	1m	1m
US$1=NS		3.19	3.60	

Population 30,741,062

Age	0–14	15–19	20–24	25–29	30–64	65 plus
Male	13.5%	4.6%	4.8%	4.2%	18.7%	3.4%
Female	13.1%	4.5%	4.8%	4.4%	20.3%	3.8%

Capabilities

The armed forces remain primarily orientated towards internal-security tasks, undertaking operations against guerrillas and narcotics traffickers, as well as tackling other challenges, such as illegal mining. As part of the fight against drug trafficking, the defence ministry is planning to improve military bases in the VRAEM region, which encompasses the Apurimac, Ene and Mantaro rivers and is associated with coca production. The most recent military doctrine dates back to 2015, but the new government released a statement endorsing the previous administration's armed-forces-modernisation plan, identifying the war on drugs and transnational criminal activity as new strategic tasks. Peru plans to reduce the FY2017 defence budget, while increasing the funding for the Ministry of the Interior. The SIVAN monitoring-and-surveillance system, intended to cover Peru's Amazon border regions, received government approval in late 2014; Peru's Earth-observation satellite (PERUSAT-1) was successfully launched in September 2016. Some modernisation of conventional equipment has also been possible in recent years, but a substantial proportion of the inventories of all three services remain unmodernised. No replacement has been selected so far for the army's ageing T-55 main battle tanks and armoured fighting vehicles, although a number of platforms were being assessed in late 2016. Airlift capability has been enhanced by the delivery of C-27J *Spartan* medium transport aircraft and Mi-17Sh medium transport helicopters, for which Russian technicians are providing training. A naval-modernisation programme is also under way, including the construction of landing-platform-dock ships, while Peru's amphibious capability has been bolstered by the delivery of LAV II 8x8 vehicles to the marines. In cooperation with Korean Aerospace Industries, Peru manufactures the KT-1 turboprop aircraft at its Las Palmas facility; South Korea is also interested in marketing its FA-50 combat aircraft to Peru. The armed forces continue to train regularly, and participate in multinational exercises and UN deployments.

ACTIVE 81,000 (Army 47,500 Navy 24,000 Air 9,500)
Paramilitary 77,000

RESERVE 188,000 (Army 188,000)

ORGANISATIONS BY SERVICE

Space
EQUIPMENT BY TYPE
SATELLITES • ISR PERÚSAT-1

Army 47,500
4 mil region

FORCES BY ROLE
SPECIAL FORCES
 1 (1st) SF bde (4 cdo bn, 1 airmob arty gp, 1 MP Coy, 1 cbt spt bn)
 1 (3rd) SF bde (3 cdo bn, 1 airmob arty gp, 1 MP coy)
 1 SF gp (regional troops)
MANOEUVRE
 Armoured
 1 (3rd) armd bde (2 tk bn, 1 armd inf bn, 1 arty gp, 1 AT coy, 1 AD gp, 1 engr bn, 1 cbt spt bn)
 1 (9th) armd bde (forming - 1 tk bn)
 Mechanised
 1 (3rd) armd cav bde (3 mech cav bn, 1 mot inf bn, 1 arty gp, 1 AD gp, 1 engr bn, 1 cbt spt bn)
 1 (1st) cav bde (4 mech cav bn, 1 MP coy, 1 cbt spt bn)
 Light
 2 (2nd & 31st) mot inf bde (3 mot inf bn, 1 arty gp, 1 MP coy, 1 log bn)
 3 (1st, 7th & 32nd) inf bde (3 inf bn, 1 MP coy, 1 cbt spt bn)
 1 (4th) mtn bde (1 armd regt, 3 mot inf bn, 1 arty gp, 1 MP coy, 1 cbt spt bn)
 1 (5th) mtn bde (1 armd regt, 2 mot inf bn, 3 jungle coy, 1 arty gp, 1 MP coy, 1 cbt spt bn)
 1 (5th) jungle inf bde (1 SF gp, 3 jungle bn, 3 jungle coy, 1 jungle arty gp, 1 AT coy, 1 AD gp, 1 jungle engr bn)
 1 (6th) jungle inf bde (4 jungle bn, 1 engr bn, 1 MP coy, 1 cbt spt bn)
 Other
 1 (18th) armd trg bde (1 mech cav regt, 1 armd regt, 2 tk bn, 1 armd inf bn, 1 engr bn, 1 MP coy, 1 cbt spt bn)
COMBAT SUPPORT
 1 (1st) arty bde (4 arty gp, 2 AD gp, 1 sigs gp)
 1 (3rd) arty bde (4 arty gp, 1 AD gp, 1 sigs gp)
 1 (22nd) engr bde (3 engr bn, 1 demining coy)
AVIATION
 1 (1st) avn bde (1 atk hel/recce hel bn, 1 avn bn, 2 aslt hel/tpt hel bn)
AIR DEFENCE
 1 AD gp (regional troops)
EQUIPMENT BY TYPE
ARMOURED FIGHTING VEHICLES
 MBT 165 T-55; (75† in store)
 LT TK 96 AMX-13
 RECCE 95: 30 BRDM-2; 15 Fiat 6616; 50 M9A1
 APC 295
  APC (T) 120 M113A1
  APC (W) 175: 150 UR-416; 25 Fiat 6614

ENGINEERING & MAINTENANCE VEHICLES
  ARV M578
ANTI-TANK-ANTI-INFRASTRUCTURE
  MSL
    SP 22 M1165A2 HMMWV with 9K135 *Kornet* E (AT-14 *Spriggan*)
    MANPATS 9K11 *Malyutka* (AT-3 *Sagger*); HJ-73C; 9K135 *Kornet* E (AT-14 *Spriggan*); *Spike*-ER
  RCL 106mm M40A1
ARTILLERY 1,011
  SP 155mm 12 M109A2
  TOWED 290: **105mm** 152: 44 M101; 24 M2A1; 60 M-56; 24 Model 56 pack howitzer; **122mm**; 36 D-30; **130mm** 36 M-46; **155mm** 66: 36 M114, 30 Model 50
  MRL 122mm 35: 22 BM-21 *Grad*; 13 Type-90B
  MOR 674+ **81mm/107mm** 350; **SP 107mm** 24 M106A1; **120mm** 300+ Brandt/Expal Model L
AIRCRAFT
  TPT • Light 16: 2 An-28 *Cash*; 3 An-32B *Cline*; 1 Beech 350 *King Air*; 1 Beech 1900D; 4 Cessna 152; 1 Cessna 208 *Caravan* I; 2 Cessna U206 *Stationair*; 1 PA-31T *Cheyenne* II; 1 PA-34 *Seneca*
  TRG 4 IL-103
HELICOPTERS
  MRH 8 Mi-17 *Hip* H
  TPT 24: **Heavy** (3 Mi-26T *Halo* in store); **Medium** 11 Mi-171Sh; **Light** 13: 2 AW109K2; 9 PZL Mi-2 *Hoplite*; 2 R-44
  TRG 5 F-28F
AIR DEFENCE
  SAM • Point-defence 9K36 *Strela*-3 (SA-14 *Gremlin*); 9K310 *Igla*-1 (SA-16 *Gimlet*); 9K32 *Strela*-2 (SA-7 *Grail*)‡
  GUNS 165
    SP 23mm 35 ZSU-23-4
    TOWED 23mm 130: 80 ZU-23-2; 50 ZU-23

Navy 24,000 (incl 1,000 Coast Guard)

Commands: Pacific, Lake Titicaca, Amazon River
EQUIPMENT BY TYPE
SUBMARINES • TACTICAL • SSK 6:
  4 *Angamos* (GER T-209/1200) with 8 single 533mm TT with AEG SST-4 HWT
  2 *Islay* (GER T-209/1100) with 8 single 533mm TT with AEG SUT-264 HWT
PRINCIPAL SURFACE COMBATANTS 8
  CRUISERS • CG 1 *Almirante Grau*† (NLD *De Ruyter*) with 8 single lnchr with *Otomat* Mk2 AShM, 4 twin 152mm guns (in reserve)
  FRIGATES 7
    FFGHM 6:
      3 *Aguirre* (ITA *Lupo*) with 8 single lnchr with *Otomat* Mk2 AShM, 1 octuple Mk29 lnchr with RIM-7P *Sea Sparrow* SAM, 2 triple 324mm ASTT with A244 LWT, 1 127mm gun (capacity 1 Bell 212 (AB-212)/SH-3D *Sea King*)
      3 *Carvajal* (mod ITA *Lupo*) with 8 single lnchr with *Otomat* Mk2 AShM, 1 octuple *Albatros* lnchr with *Aspide* SAM, 2 triple 324mm ASTT with A244 LWT, 1 127mm gun (capacity 1 Bell 212 (AB-212)/SH-3D *Sea King*)
    FFHM 1:
      1 *Aguirre* (ITA *Lupo*) with 1 octuple Mk29 lnchr with RIM-7P *Sea Sparrow* SAM, 2 triple 324mm ASTT with A244 LWT, 1 127mm gun (capacity 1 Bell 212 (AB-212)/SH-3D *Sea King*) (is being fit with MM-40 *Exocet* Block III)
PATROL AND COASTAL COMBATANTS 12
  CORVETTES • FSG 6 *Velarde* (FRA PR-72 64m) with 4 single lnchr with MM-38 *Exocet* AShM, 1 76mm gun
  PCR 6:
    2 *Amazonas* with 1 76mm gun
    2 *Manuel Clavero*
    2 *Marañon* with 2 76mm guns
AMPHIBIOUS
  LANDING SHIPS • LST 2 *Paita* (capacity 395 troops) (US *Terrebonne Parish*)
  LANDING CRAFT • UCAC 7 *Griffon* 2000TD (capacity 22 troops)
LOGISTICS AND SUPPORT 23
  AG 4 *Rio Napo*
  AGOR 1 *Humboldt*
  AGS 5: 1 *Carrasco*; 2 *Van Straelen*; 1 *La Macha*, 1 *Stiglich* (river survey vessel for the upper Amazon)
  AH 4 (river hospital craft)
  AO 2 *Noguera*
  AOR 1 *Mollendo*
  AORH 1 *Tacna* (ex-NLD *Amsterdam*)
  AOT 2 *Bayovar*
  ATF 1
  AWT 1 *Caloyeras*
  AXS 2: 1 *Marte*; 1 *Union*

Naval Aviation ε800

FORCES BY ROLE
MARITIME PATROL
  1 sqn with Beech 200T; Bell 212 ASW (AB-212 ASW); F-27 *Friendship*; Fokker 60; SH-3D *Sea King*
TRANSPORT
  1 flt with An-32B *Cline*; Cessna 206; Fokker 50
TRAINING
  1 sqn with F-28F; T-34C *Turbo Mentor*
TRANSPORT HELICOPTER
  1 (liaison) sqn with Bell 206B *Jet Ranger* II; Mi-8 *Hip*
EQUIPMENT BY TYPE
AIRCRAFT
  MP 8: 4 Beech 200T; 4 Fokker 60
  ELINT 1 F-27 *Friendship*
  TPT • Light 6: 3 An-32B *Cline*; 1 Cessna 206; 2 Fokker 50
  TRG 5 T-34C *Turbo Mentor*
HELICOPTERS
  ASW 5: 2 Bell 212 ASW (AB-212 ASW); 3 SH-3D *Sea King*
  MRH 3 Bell 412SP
  TPT 11: **Medium** 8: 2 Mi-8 *Hip*; 6 UH-3H *Sea King*; **Light** 3 Bell 206B *Jet Ranger* II
  TRG 5 F-28F
MSL • AShM AM-39 *Exocet*

Marines 4,000

FORCES BY ROLE
SPECIAL FORCES
  3 cdo gp

MANOEUVRE
Light
2 inf bn
1 inf gp
Amphibious
1 mne bde (1 SF gp, 1 recce bn, 2 inf bn, 1 amph bn, 1 arty gp)
Jungle
1 jungle inf bn
EQUIPMENT BY TYPE
ARMOURED FIGHTING VEHICLES
APC • APC (W) 47+: 32 LAV II; V-100 *Commando*; 15 V-200 *Chaimite*
ANTI-TANK/ANTI-INFRASTRUCTURE
RCL 84mm *Carl Gustav*; 106mm M40A1
ARTILLERY 18+
TOWED 122mm D-30
MOR 18+: 81mm some; 120mm ε18
AIR DEFENCE • GUNS 20mm SP (twin)

Air Force 9,500

Divided into five regions – North, Lima, South, Central and Amazon

FORCES BY ROLE
FIGHTER
1 sqn with MiG-29S/SE *Fulcrum* C; MiG-29UB *Fulcrum* B
FIGHTER/GROUND ATTACK
1 sqn with *Mirage* 2000E/ED (2000P/DP)
2 sqn with A-37B *Dragonfly*
1 sqn with Su-25A *Frogfoot* A†; Su-25UB *Frogfoot* B†
ISR
1 (photo-survey) sqn with Learjet 36A; SA-227-BC *Metro III* (C-26B)
TRANSPORT
1 sqn with B-737; An-32 *Cline*
1 sqn with DHC-6 *Twin Otter*; DHC-6-400 *Twin Otter*; PC-6 *Turbo Porter*
1 sqn with L-100-20
TRAINING
2 (drug interdiction) sqn with EMB-312 *Tucano*
1 sqn with MB-339A*
1 sqn with Z-242
1 hel sqn with Schweizer 300C
ATTACK HELICOPTER
1 sqn with Mi-25/Mi-35P *Hind*
TRANSPORT HELICOPTER
1 sqn with Mi-17 *Hip* H
1 sqn with Bell 206 *Jet Ranger*; Bell 212 (AB-212); Bell 412 *Twin Huey*
1 sqn with Bo-105C/LS
AIR DEFENCE
6 bn with S-125 *Pechora* (SA-3 *Goa*)
EQUIPMENT BY TYPE
AIRCRAFT 78 combat capable
FTR 20: 9 MiG-29S *Fulcrum* C; 3 MiG-29SE *Fulcrum* C; 6 MiG-29SMP *Fulcrum*; 2 MiG-29UBM *Fulcrum* B
FGA 12: 2 *Mirage* 2000ED (2000DP); 10 *Mirage* 2000E (2000P) (some†)
ATK 36: 18 A-37B *Dragonfly*; 10 Su-25A *Frogfoot* A†; 8 Su-25UB *Frogfoot* B†
ISR 6: 2 Learjet 36A; 4 SA-227-BC *Metro* III (C-26B)
TPT 32: **Medium** 5: 3 C-27J *Spartan*; 2 L-100-20; **Light** 23: 4 An-32 *Cline*; 3 Cessna 172 *Skyhawk*; 3 DHC-6 *Twin Otter*; 12 DHC-6-400 *Twin Otter*; 1 PC-6 *Turbo-Porter*; **PAX** 4 B-737
TRG 54: 19 EMB-312 *Tucano*; 5 KT-1P; 10 MB-339A*; 6 T-41A/D *Mescalero*; 14 Z-242
HELICOPTERS
ATK 18: 16 Mi-25 *Hind* D; 2 Mi-35P *Hind* E
MRH 21: 2 Bell 412 *Twin Huey*; 19 Mi-17 *Hip* H
TPT • **Light** 21: 8 Bell 206 *Jet Ranger*; 6 Bell 212 (AB-212); 1 Bo-105C; 6 Bo-105LS
TRG 4 Schweizer 300C
AIR DEFENCE • SAM
Short-range S-125 *Pechora* (SA-3 *Goa*)
Point-defence *Javelin*
AIR-LAUNCHED MISSILES
AAM • IR R-3 (AA-2 *Atoll*)‡; R-60 (AA-8 *Aphid*)‡; R-73 (AA-11 *Archer*); R-550 *Magic*; IR/SARH R-27 (AA-10 *Alamo*); ARH R-77 (AA-12 *Adder*)
ASM AS-30; Kh-29L (AS-14A *Kedge*)
ARM Kh-58 (AS-11 *Kilter*)

Paramilitary 77,000

National Police 77,000 (100,000 reported)
EQUIPMENT BY TYPE
APC (W) 120: 20 BMR-600; 100 MOWAG *Roland*

General Police 43,000

Security Police 21,000

Technical Police 13,000

Coast Guard 1,000
Personnel included as part of Navy
EQUIPMENT BY TYPE
PATROL AND COASTAL COMBATANTS 37
PSOH 1 *Carvajal* (mod ITA *Lupo*) with 1 127mm gun (capacity 1 Bell 212 (AB-212)/SH-3D *Sea King*)
PCC 7: 2 *Río Cañete* (ROK *Tae Geuk*); 5 *Río Nepena*
PB 10: 6 *Chicama* (US *Dauntless*); 1 *Río Chira*; 3 *Río Santa*
PBR 19: 1 *Río Viru*; 8 *Parachique*; 10 *Zorritos*
LOGISTICS AND SUPPORT • AH 1 *Puno*
AIRCRAFT
TPT • **Light** 3: 1 DHC-6 *Twin Otter*; 2 F-27 *Friendship*

Rondas Campesinas
Peasant self-defence force. Perhaps 7,000 rondas 'gp', up to pl strength, some with small arms. Deployed mainly in emergency zone

DEPLOYMENT

CENTRAL AFRICAN REPUBLIC
UN • MINUSCA 206; 4 obs; 1 maint coy

CÔTE D'IVOIRE
UN • UNOCI 1 obs

DEMOCRATIC REPUBLIC OF THE CONGO
UN • MONUSCO 1; 11 obs

HAITI
UN • MINUSTAH 161; 1 inf coy

SOUTH SUDAN
UN • UNMISS 2

SUDAN
UN • UNAMID 2 obs

UN • UNISFA 1 obs

Suriname SUR

Suriname Dollar srd		2015	2016	2017
GDP	srd	17.6bn	26.2bn	
	US$	5.15bn	4.14bn	
per capita	US$	9,231	7,347	
Growth	%	-0.3	-7.0	
Inflation	%	6.9	67.1	
Def exp	srd	n.k.	n.k.	
	US$	n.k.	n.k.	
US$1=srd			3.42	6.34
Population	585,824			

Age	0–14	15–19	20–24	25–29	30–64	65 plus
Male	12.8%	4.7%	4.2%	4.2%	21.9%	2.5%
Female	12.3%	4.5%	4.0%	4.1%	21.4%	3.3%

Capabilities

The armed forces are principally intended to assure sovereignty and territorial integrity, but amid limited capability to defend against a well-armed and concerted attack, in practice their main activities are related to border security and tackling transnational criminal and terrorist activity. They have no ability to project power beyond the country's borders. Suriname has bilateral agreements with the US and other regional and extra-regional states regarding maritime counter-narcotics activities. Ties with larger countries, particularly Brazil, China and India, have been crucial to the supply of more costly equipment, including a limited number of armoured vehicles and helicopters, as well as training activity. Training is also delivered through participation in multinational exercises like the *Tradewinds* series, in which Suriname participated in 2016. Infantry troops have conducted jungle-warfare training with US South Dakota National Guard personnel in order to enhance readiness. Suriname is also part of the US-led Caribbean Basin Security Initiative. Cyber attack has also been identified as a growing security threat.

ACTIVE 1,840 (Army 1,400 Navy 240 Air 200)
Paramilitary 100
(All services form part of the army)

ORGANISATIONS BY SERVICE

Army 1,400
FORCES BY ROLE
MANOEUVRE
  Mechanised
    1 mech cav sqn
  Light
    1 inf bn (4 coy)
COMBAT SUPPORT
  1 MP bn (coy)
EQUIPMENT BY TYPE
ARMOURED FIGHTING VEHICLES
  RECCE 6 EE-9 *Cascavel*
  APC • APC (W) 15 EE-11 *Urutu*
ANTI-TANK/ANTI-INFRASTRUCTURE
  RCL 106mm M40A1
ARTILLERY • MOR 81mm 6

Navy ε240
EQUIPMENT BY TYPE
  PATROL AND COASTAL COMBATANTS 10 PB 5: 3 Rodman 101†; 2 others
  PBR 5 Rodman 55

Air Force ε200
EQUIPMENT BY TYPE
  AIRCRAFT 2 combat capable
    TPT • Light 2: 1 BN-2 *Defender**; 1 Cessna 182
    TRG 1 PC-7 *Turbo Trainer**
  HELICOPTERS • MRH 3 SA316B *Alouette* III (*Chetak*)

Paramilitary ε100

Coast Guard ε100
Formed in November 2013; 3 Coast Guard stations to be formed; HQ at Paramaribo
EQUIPMENT BY TYPE
PATROL AND COASTAL COMBATANTS • PB 3: 1 OCEA FPB 98; 2 OCEA FPB 72 MkII

Trinidad and Tobago TTO

Trinidad and Tobago Dollar TT$		2015	2016	2017
GDP	TT$	157bn	151bn	
	US$	24.6bn	22.8bn	
per capita	US$	18,143	16,717	
Growth	%	-2.1	-2.8	
Inflation	%	4.7	4.8	
Def bdgt	TT$	2.52bn	4.04bn	4.09bn
	US$	394m	608m	
US$1=TT$		6.38	6.64	
Population	1,220,479			

Age	0–14	15–19	20–24	25–29	30–64	65 plus
Male	9.9%	3.1%	3.3%	4.0%	25.9%	4.5%
Female	9.5%	2.9%	3.0%	3.8%	24.4%	5.8%

Capabilities

The Trinidad and Tobago Defence Force focuses on providing border and maritime security, as well as undertaking counter-narcotics tasks. The army is intended to play a greater role in countering criminal activity. Closer diplomatic and military ties with Beijing are evident in the army's receipt of light utility vehicles from China in 2015. This relationship has resulted in other equipment procurements and the provision of training. Renewed efforts to recapitalise coastguard equipment resulted in an order for 12 new vessels from Dutch firm Damen. The order includes two utility vessels, four patrol vessels and six interceptors, which will bolster the country's maritime-security capacity. Trinidad and Tobago was one of the first Caribbean states to publish a cyber strategy, in 2012, which noted potential defence vulnerabilities arising from compromised critical national infrastructure.

ACTIVE 4,050 (Army 3,000 Coast Guard 1,050)
(All services form the Trinidad and Tobago Defence Force)

ORGANISATIONS BY SERVICE

Army ε3,000
FORCES BY ROLE
SPECIAL FORCES
  1 SF unit
MANOEUVRE
  Light
  2 inf bn
COMBAT SUPPORT
  1 engr bn
COMBAT SERVICE SUPPORT
  1 log bn
EQUIPMENT BY TYPE
ANTI-TANK/ANTI-INFRASTRUCTURE
  RCL 84mm ε24 *Carl Gustav*
ARTILLERY • MOR 81mm 6 L16A1

Coast Guard 1,050
FORCES BY ROLE
COMMAND
  1 mne HQ
EQUIPMENT BY TYPE
PATROL AND COASTAL COMBATANTS 22
  PCO 1 *Nelson II* (ex-PRC)
  PCC 2 *Speyside* (Damen Stan Patrol 5009)
  PB 19: 2 *Gasper Grande*; 1 *Matelot*; 4 *Plymouth*; 4 *Point*; 6 *Scarlet Ibis* (Austal 30m); 2 *Wasp*; (1 *Cascadura* (SWE *Karlskrona* 40m) non-operational)
  LOGISTICS AND SUPPORT • AG 2 *Point Lisas* (Damen Fast Crew Supply 5009)

Air Wing 50
EQUIPMENT BY TYPE
AIRCRAFT
  TPT • Light 2 SA-227 *Metro* III (C-26)

HELICOPTERS
  MRH 2 AW139
  TPT • Light 1 S-76

Uruguay URY

Uruguayan Peso pU		2015	2016	2017
GDP	pU	1.46tr	1.62tr	
	US$	53.1bn	54.4bn	
per capita	US$	15,547	15,864	
Growth	%	1.0	0.1	
Inflation	%	8.7	10.2	
Def bdgt	pU	14.0bn	14.8bn	14.8bn
	US$	510m	494m	
US$1=pU		27.50	29.85	

Population 3,351,016

Age	0–14	15–19	20–24	25–29	30–64	65 plus
Male	10.4%	4.0%	4.0%	3.8%	20.5%	5.6%
Female	10.0%	3.9%	3.9%	3.7%	21.7%	8.5%

Capabilities

While the principal tasks for the armed forces are assuring sovereignty and territorial integrity, they have in recent years deployed on peacekeeping missions, most notably in Haiti, as well as on domestic disaster-relief missions. Much of the equipment inventory is second-hand, which increases the maintenance burden, and there is little capacity for independent power projection. Much maintenance work is outsourced to foreign companies, such as Chile's ENAER, which has conducted maintenance on the A37 and C-130 platforms. The air force is focused on a counter-insurgency role, but ambitions to purchase a light fighter aircraft remain hampered by funding problems. While the acquisition of air-defence radars may have improved the military's ability to monitor domestic airspace, the lack of interdiction capability will continue to limit the ability to respond to contingencies. The armed forces train regularly and participate in multinational exercises and deployments – notably on UN missions.

ACTIVE 24,650 (Army 16,250 Navy 5,400 Air 3,000)
Paramilitary 800

ORGANISATIONS BY SERVICE

Army 16,250

Uruguayan units are substandard size, mostly around 30%. Div are at most bde size, while bn are of reinforced coy strength. Regts are also coy size, some bn size, with the largest formation being the 2nd armd cav regt

FORCES BY ROLE
COMMAND
  4 mil region/div HQ
MANOEUVRE
  Mechanised
  2 armd regt

1 armd cav regt
5 mech cav regt
8 mech inf regt
Light
1 mot inf bn
5 inf bn
Air Manoeuvre
1 para bn
COMBAT SUPPORT
1 (strategic reserve) arty regt
5 fd arty gp
1 (1st) engr bde (2 engr bn)
4 cbt engr bn
AIR DEFENCE
1 AD gp
EQUIPMENT BY TYPE
ARMOURED FIGHTING VEHICLES
MBT 15 *Tiran-5*
LT TK 38: 16 M24 *Chaffee*; 22 M41A1UR
RECCE 15 EE-9 *Cascavel*
IFV 18 BMP-1
APC 376
  APC (T) 27: 24 M113A1UR; 3 MT-LB
  APC (W) 349: 54 *Condor*; 48 GAZ-39371 *Vodnik*; 53 OT-64: 47 OT-93; 147 *Piranha*
ENGINEERING & MAINTENANCE VEHICLES
  AEV MT-LB
ANTI-TANK/ANTI-INFRASTRUCTURE
  MSL • MANPATS *Milan*
  RCL 69: **106mm** 69 M40A1
ARTILLERY 185
  SP 122mm 6 2S1 *Gvozdika*
  TOWED 44: **105mm** 36: 28 M101A1; 8 M102; **155mm** 8 M114A1
  MOR 135: **81mm** 91: 35 M1, 56 Expal Model LN; **120mm** 44 Model SL
UNMANNED AERIAL VEHICLES • ISR • Light 1 *Charrua*
AIR DEFENCE • GUNS • TOWED 14: **20mm** 14: 6 M167 *Vulcan*; 8 TCM-20 (w/Elta M-2016 radar)

Navy 5,400 (incl 1,800 Prefectura Naval Coast Guard)

HQ at Montevideo
EQUIPMENT BY TYPE
PRINCIPAL SURFACE COMBATANTS • FRIGATES 2
  FF 2 *Uruguay* (PRT *Joao Belo*) with 2 triple Mk32 324mm ASTT with Mk46 LWT, 2 100mm gun
PATROL AND COASTAL COMBATANTS 15
  PB 15: 2 *Colonia* (US *Cape*); 1 *Paysandu*; 9 Type-44 (coast guard); 3 PS (coast guard)
MINE WARFARE • MINE COUNTERMEASURES 3
  MSO 3 *Temerario* (*Kondor* II)
AMPHIBIOUS 3: 2 LCVP; 1 LCM
LOGISTICS AND SUPPORT 9
  ABU 2
  AG 2: 1 *Artigas* (GER *Freiburg*, general spt ship with replenishment capabilities); 1 *Maldonado* (also used as patrol craft)
  AGS 2: 1 *Helgoland*; 1 *Trieste*

ARS 1 *Vanguardia*
AXS 2: 1 *Capitan Miranda*; 1 *Bonanza*

Naval Aviation 210
FORCES BY ROLE
ANTI-SUBMARINE WARFARE
  1 flt with Beech 200T*; *Jetstream* Mk2
SEARCH & RESCUE/TRANSPORT HELICOPTER
  1 sqn with AS350B2 *Ecureuil* (*Esquilo*); Bo-105M
TRANSPORT/TRAINING
  1 flt with T-34C *Turbo Mentor*
EQUIPMENT BY TYPE
AIRCRAFT 2 combat capable
  MP 2 *Jetstream* Mk2
  ISR 2 Beech 200T*
  TRG 2 T-34C *Turbo Mentor*
HELICOPTERS
  MRH 6 Bo-105M
  TPT • Light 1 AS350B2 *Ecureuil* (*Esquilo*)

Naval Infantry 450
FORCES BY ROLE
MANOEUVRE
  Amphibious
  1 mne bn(-)

Air Force 3,000

Flying hours   120 hrs/yr
FORCES BY ROLE
FIGHTER/GROUND ATTACK
  1 sqn with A-37B *Dragonfly*
  1 sqn with IA-58B *Pucará*
ISR
  1 flt with EMB-110 *Bandeirante*
TRANSPORT
  1 sqn with C-130B *Hercules*; C-212 *Aviocar*; EMB–110C *Bandeirante*; EMB-120 *Brasilia*
  1 (liaison) sqn with Cessna 206H; T-41D
  1 (liaison) flt with Cessna 206H
TRAINING
  1 sqn with PC-7U *Turbo Trainer*
  1 sqn with Beech 58 *Baron* (UB-58); SF-260EU
TRANSPORT HELICOPTER
  1 sqn with AS365 *Dauphin*; Bell 205 (UH–1H *Iroquois*); Bell 212
EQUIPMENT BY TYPE
AIRCRAFT 18 combat capable
  ATK 17: 12 A-37B *Dragonfly*; 5 IA-58B *Pucará*
  ISR 1 EMB-110 *Bandeirante**
  TPT 23: **Medium** 2 C-130B *Hercules*; **Light** 21: 2 Beech 58 *Baron* (UB-58); 6 C-212 *Aviocar*; 9 Cessna 206H; 1 Cessna 210; 2 EMB-110C *Bandeirante*; 1 EMB-120 *Brasilia*
  TRG 21: 5 PC-7U *Turbo Trainer*; 12 SF-260EU; 4 T-41D *Mescalero*
HELICOPTERS
  MRH 2 AS365N2 *Dauphin* II
  TPT • Light 9: 5 Bell 205 (UH–1H *Iroquois*); 4 Bell 212

Paramilitary 800

  Guardia de Coraceros 350 (under Interior Ministry)

  Guardia de Granaderos 450

DEPLOYMENT

CÔTE D'IVOIRE
UN • UNOCI 1; 1 obs

DEMOCRATIC REPUBLIC OF THE CONGO
UN • MONUSCO 1,175; 13 obs; 1 inf bn; 1 mne coy; 1 hel flt

EGYPT
MFO 58; 1 engr/tpt unit

HAITI
UN • MINUSTAH 249; 1 inf bn HQ; 1 inf coy

INDIA/PAKISTAN
UN • UNMOGIP 2 obs

Venezuela VEN

Venezuelan Bolivar Fuerte Bs		2015	2016	2017
GDP	Bs	6.03tr	29.7tr	
	US$	261bn	334bn	
per capita	US$	8,494	10,755	
Growth	%	-6.2	-10	
Inflation	%	121.7	475.8	
Def bdgt	Bs	52bn	128bn	
	US$ [a]	2.24bn	1.44bn	
US$1=Bs		23.17	88.89	

[a] US dollar figures should be treated with caution due to high levels of currency volatility as well as wide differentials between official and parallel exchange rates

Population   30,912,302

Age	0–14	15–19	20–24	25–29	30–64	65 plus
Male	14.2%	4.4%	4.4%	4.2%	19.6%	3.1%
Female	13.5%	4.2%	4.3%	4.2%	20.3%	3.7%

Capabilities

The armed forces, including the National Guard, are tasked with protecting the sovereignty of the state, assuring territorial integrity and assisting with internal-security and counter-narcotics operations. The National Guard has seen its resources grow as it has become more involved in internal-security and counter-narcotics operations. Most of the funds in the 2016 budget were allocated to strengthen the National Guard and the armed forces' capabilities, to improve the military-intelligence sector and to procure military – mainly air-force – equipment. Despite serious economic difficulties, the armed and security forces continue to receive significant funding, due to their role in regime protection and in helping suppress anti-government protests. A series of contracts with China and Russia have overhauled ageing army, marine and air-force inventories and are key for training as well as procurement; Venezuela now possesses one of the region's most capable air and air-defence structures.

ACTIVE 115,000 (Army 63,000 Navy 17,500 Air 11,500 National Guard 23,000) **Paramilitary 150,000**
Conscript liability 30 months selective, varies by region for all services

RESERVE 8,000 (Army 8,000)

ORGANISATIONS BY SERVICE

Space
EQUIPMENT BY TYPE
SATELLITES • COMMUNICATIONS 1 *Venesat-1*

Army ε63,000
FORCES BY ROLE
MANOEUVRE
  Armoured
  1 (4th) armd div (1 armd bde, 1 lt armd bde, 1 AB bde, 1 arty bde)
  Mechanised
  1 (9th) mot cav div (1 mot cav bde, 1 ranger bde, 1 sy bde)
  Light
  1 (1st) inf div (1 SF bn, 1 armd bde, 1 mech inf bde, 1 ranger bde, 1 inf bde, 1 arty unit, 1 spt unit)
  1 (2nd) inf div (1 mech inf bde, 1 inf bde, 1 mtn inf bde)
  1 (3rd) inf div (1 inf bde, 1 ranger bde, 1 sigs bde, 1 MP bde)
  1 (5th) inf div (1 SF bn, 1 cav sqn, 2 jungle inf bde, 1 engr bn)
COMBAT SUPPORT
  1 cbt engr corps (3 engr regt)
COMBAT SERVICE SUPPORT
  1 log comd (2 log regt)
AVIATION
  1 avn comd (1 tpt avn bn, 1 atk hel bn, 1 ISR avn bn)

Reserve Organisations 8,000
FORCES BY ROLE
MANOEUVRE
  Armoured
  1 armd bn
  Light
  4 inf bn
  1 ranger bn
COMBAT SUPPORT
  1 arty bn
  2 engr regt
EQUIPMENT BY TYPE
ARMOURED FIGHTING VEHICLES
  MBT 173: 81 AMX-30V; 92 T-72B1
  LT TK 109: 31 AMX-13; 78 *Scorpion*-90
  RECCE 121: 42 *Dragoon* 300 LFV2; 79 V-100/V-150
  IFV 237: 123 BMP-3 (incl variants); 114 BTR-80A (incl variants)

APC 81
   APC (T) 45: 25 AMX-VCI; 12 AMX-PC (CP); 8 AMX-VCTB (Amb)
   APC (W) 36 Dragoon 300
ENGINEERING & MAINTENANCE VEHICLES
   ARV 5: 3 AMX-30D; BREM-1; 2 Dragoon 300RV; Samson
   VLB Leguan
NBC VEHICLES 10 TPz-1 Fuchs NBC
ANTI-TANK/ANTI-INFRASTRUCTURE
   MSL • MANPATS IMI MAPATS
   RCL 106mm 175 M40A1
   GUNS • SP 76mm 75 M18 Hellcat
ARTILLERY 515+
   SP 60: 152mm 48 2S19 Msta-S (replacing Mk F3s); 155mm 12 Mk F3
   TOWED 92: 105mm 80: 40 M101A1; 40 Model 56 pack howitzer; 155mm 12 M114A1
   MRL 56: 122mm 24 BM-21 Grad; 160mm 20 LAR SP (LAR-160); 300mm 12 9A52 Smerch
   GUN/MOR 120mm 13 2S23 NONA-SVK
   MOR 294+: 81mm 165; SP 81mm 21 Dragoon 300PM; AMX-VTT; 120mm 108: 60 Brandt; 48 2S12
RADAR • LAND RASIT (veh, arty)
AIRCRAFT
   TPT • Light 28: 1 Beech 90 King Air; 1 Beech 200 King Air; 1 Beech 300 King Air; 1 Cessna 172; 6 Cessna 182 Skylane; 2 Cessna 206; 2 Cessna 207 Stationair; 1 IAI-201 Arava; 2 IAI-202 Arava; 11 M-28 Skytruck
HELICOPTERS
   ATK 10 Mi-35M2 Hind
   MRH 33: 10 Bell 412EP; 2 Bell 412SP; 21 Mi-17V-5 Hip H
   TPT 9: Heavy 3 Mi-26T2 Halo; Medium 2 AS-61D; Light 4: 3 Bell 206B Jet Ranger, 1 Bell 206L3 Long Ranger II

Navy ε14,300; ε3,200 conscript (total ε17,500)

EQUIPMENT BY TYPE
SUBMARINES • TACTICAL • SSK 2:
   2 Sabalo (GER T-209/1300) with 8 single 533mm TT with SST-4 HWT
PRINCIPAL SURFACE COMBATANTS • FRIGATES 6
   FFGHM 6 Mariscal Sucre (ITA mod Lupo) with 8 single lnchr with Otomat Mk2 AShM, 1 octuple Albatros lnchr with Aspide SAM, 2 triple 324mm ASTT with A244 LWT, 1 127mm gun (capacity 1 Bell 212 (AB-212) hel)
PATROL AND COASTAL COMBATANTS 10
   PSOH 4 Guaiqueri with 1 Millennium CIWS, 1 76mm gun (2 vessels damaged following collision in 2012, awaiting repairs)
   PBG 3 Federación (UK Vosper 37m) with 2 single lnchr with Otomat Mk2 AShM
   PB 3 Constitucion (UK Vosper 37m) with 1 76mm gun; 1 Fernando Gomez de Saa (Damen 4207)
AMPHIBIOUS
   LANDING SHIPS • LST 4 Capana (capacity 12 tanks; 200 troops) (FSU Alligator)
   LANDING CRAFT 3:
      LCU 2 Margarita (river comd)
      UCAC 1 Griffon 2000TD
LOGISTICS AND SUPPORT 10
   AGOR 1 Punta Brava

AGS 2
AKL 4 Los Frailes
AORH 1 Ciudad Bolivar
ATF 1
AXS 1 Simon Bolivar

Naval Aviation 500

FORCES BY ROLE
ANTI-SUBMARINE WARFARE
   1 sqn with Bell 212 (AB-212)
MARITIME PATROL
   1 flt with C-212-200 MPA
TRANSPORT
   1 sqn with Beech 200 King Air; C-212 Aviocar; Turbo Commander 980C
TRAINING
   1 hel sqn with Bell 206B Jet Ranger II; TH-57A Sea Ranger
TRANSPORT HELICOPTER
   1 sqn with Bell 412EP Twin Huey; Mi-17V-5 Hip H
EQUIPMENT BY TYPE
AIRCRAFT 2 combat capable
   MP 2 C-212-200 MPA*
   TPT • Light 7: 1 Beech C90 King Air; 1 Beech 200 King Air; 4 C-212 Aviocar; 1 Turbo Commander 980C
HELICOPTERS
   ASW 5 Bell 212 ASW (AB-212 ASW)
   MRH 12: 6 Bell 412EP Twin Huey; 6 Mi-17V-5 Hip
   TPT • Light 1 Bell 206B Jet Ranger II (trg)
   TRG 1 TH-57A Sea Ranger

Marines ε7,000

FORCES BY ROLE
COMMAND
   1 div HQ
SPECIAL FORCES
   1 spec ops bde
MANOEUVRE
   Amphibious
   1 (rvn) mne bde
   2 (landing) mne bde
COMBAT SUPPORT
   1 arty gp (1 arty bty, 1 MRL bty, 1 mor bty)
   1 cbt engr bn
   1 MP bde
   1 sigs bn
COMBAT SERVICE SUPPORT
   1 log bn
EQUIPMENT BY TYPE
ARMOURED FIGHTING VEHICLES
   LT TK 5+ VN-16
   IFV 15+: 10 VN-1; 5+ VN-18
   APC • APC (W) 37 EE-11 Urutu
   AAV 11 LVTP-7
ENGINEERING & MAINTENANCE VEHICLES
   AEV 1 AAVR7
ANTI-TANK/ANTI-INFRASTRUCTURE
   RCL 84mm Carl Gustav; 106mm M40A1
ARTILLERY 30
   TOWED 105mm 18 M-56
   MOR 120mm 12 Brandt

PATROL AND COASTAL COMBATANTS • PBR 23:
18 *Constancia*; 2 *Manaure*; 3 *Terepaima* (*Cougar*)
AMPHIBIOUS • LANDING CRAFT • 1 **LCM**; 1 **LCU**;
12 **LCVP**

Coast Guard 1,000

EQUIPMENT BY TYPE
PATROL AND COASTAL COMBATANTS 22
  PSOH 3 *Guaicamacuto* with 1 *Millennium* CIWS, 1 76 mm gun (capacity 1 Bell 212 (AB-212) hel) (1 additional vessel in build)
  PB 19: 12 *Gavion*; 1 *Pagalo* (Damen Stan 2606); 4 *Petrel* (*US Point*); 2 *Protector*
LOGISTICS AND SUPPORT 5
  AG 2 *Los Tanques* (salvage ship)
  AKSL 1
  AP 2

Air Force 11,500

Flying hours 155 hrs/yr

FORCES BY ROLE
FIGHTER/GROUND ATTACK
  1 sqn with F-5 *Freedom Fighter* (VF-5)
  2 sqn with F-16A/B *Fighting Falcon*
  4 sqn with Su-30MKV
  2 sqn with K-8W *Karakorum**
GROUND ATTACK/ISR
  1 sqn with EMB-312 *Tucano**; OV-10A *Bronco*
ELECTRONIC WARFARE
  1 sqn with Falcon 20DC; SA-227 *Metro* III (C-26B)
TRANSPORT
  1 sqn with Y-8; C-130H *Hercules*; KC-137
  1 sqn with A319CJ; B-737
  4 sqn with Cessna T206H; Cessna 750
  1 sqn with Cessna 500/550/551; Falcon 20F; Falcon 900
  1 sqn with G-222; Short 360 *Sherpa*
TRAINING
  1 sqn with Cessna 182N; SF-260E
  2 sqn with DA40NG; DA42VI
  1 sqn with EMB-312 *Tucano**
TRANSPORT HELICOPTER
  1 VIP sqn with AS532UL *Cougar*; Mi-172
  3 sqn with AS332B *Super Puma*; AS532 *Cougar*
  2 sqn with Mi-17 *Hip* H

EQUIPMENT BY TYPE
AIRCRAFT 103 combat capable
  FTR 31: 5 F-5 *Freedom Fighter* (VF-5), 4 F-5B *Freedom Fighter* (NF-5B); 1 CF-5D *Freedom Fighter* (VF-5D); 17 F-16A *Fighting Falcon*; 4 F-16B *Fighting Falcon*
  FGA 23 Su-30MKV
  ATK 7 OV-10A *Bronco*
  EW 4: 2 Falcon 20DC; 2 SA-227 *Metro* III (C-26B)
  TKR 1 KC-137
  TPT 74: **Medium** 14: 5 C-130H *Hercules* (some in store); 1 G-222; 8 Y-8; **Light** 55: 6 Beech 200 *King Air*; 2 Beech 350 *King Air*; 10 Cessna 182N *Skylane*; 12 Cessna 206 *Stationair*; 4 Cessna 208B *Caravan*; 1 Cessna 500 *Citation* I; 3 Cessna 550 *Citation* II; 1 Cessna 551; 1 Cessna 750 *Citation* X; 2 Do-228-212; 11 Quad City *Challenger* II; 2 Short 360 *Sherpa*; **PAX** 5: 1 A319CJ; 1 B-737; 1 Falcon 20F; 2 Falcon 900
  TRG 75: 24 DA40NG; 6 DA42VI; 18 EMB-312 *Tucano**; 24 K-8W *Karakorum** ; 12 SF-260E
HELICOPTERS
  MRH 8 Mi-17 (Mi-17VS) *Hip* H
  TPT • Medium 15: 3 AS332B *Super Puma*; 8 AS532 *Cougar*; 2 AS532UL *Cougar*; 2 Mi-172 (VIP)
AIR-LAUNCHED MISSILES
  AAM • IR AIM-9L/P *Sidewinder*; R-73 (AA-11 *Archer*); PL-5E; R-27T/ET (AA-10B/D *Alamo*); **IIR** *Python* 4; **SARH** R-27R/ER (AA-10A/C *Alamo*); **ARH** R-77 (AA-12 *Adder*)
  ASM Kh-29L/T (AS-14A/B *Kedge*); Kh-31A (AS-17B *Krypton*); Kh-59M (AS-18 *Kazoo*)
  AShM AM-39 *Exocet*
  ARM Kh-31P (AS-17A *Krypton*)

Air Defence Command (CODAI)

Joint service command with personnel drawn from other services

FORCES BY ROLE
AIR DEFENCE
  5 AD bde
COMBAT SERVICE SUPPORT
  1 log bde (5 log gp)

EQUIPMENT BY TYPE
AIR DEFENCE
  SAM
    Long-range S-300VM
    Medium-range 9K317M2 *Buk*-M2E (SA-17 *Grizzly*); S-125 *Pechora*-2M (SA-26)
    Point-defence 9K338 *Igla*-S (SA-24 *Grinch*); ADAMS; *Mistral*; RBS-70
  GUNS 440+
    SP 40mm 12+: 6+ AMX-13 *Rafaga*; 6 M42
    TOWED 428+: **20mm**: 114 TCM-20; **23mm** ε200 ZU-23-2; **35mm**; **40mm** 114+: 114+ L/70; Some M1
  RADARS • AIR DEFENCE *Flycatcher*

National Guard (Fuerzas Armadas de Cooperacion) 23,000

(Internal sy, customs) 9 regional comd

EQUIPMENT BY TYPE
ARMOURED FIGHTING VEHICLES
  APC • APC (W) 44: 24 Fiat 6614; 20 UR-416
ARTILLERY • MOR 50 81mm
PATROL AND COASTAL COMBATANTS • PB 34: 12 *Protector*; 12 *Punta*; 10 *Rio Orinoco* II
AIRCRAFT
  TPT • Light 34: 1 Beech 55 *Baron*; 1 Beech 80 *Queen Air*; 1 Beech 90 *King Air*; 1 Beech 200C *King Air*; 3 Cessna 152 *Aerobat*; 2 Cessna 172; 2 Cessna 402C; 4 Cessna U206 *Stationair*; 6 DA42 MPP; 1 IAI-201 *Arava*; 12 M-28 *Skytruck*
  TRG 3: 1 PZL 106 *Kruk*; 2 PLZ M2-6 *Isquierka*
HELICOPTERS
  MRH 13: 8 Bell 412EP; 5 Mi-17V-5 *Hip* H
  TPT • Light 19: 9 AS355F *Ecureuil* II; 4 AW109; 5 Bell 206B/L *Jet Ranger/Long Ranger*; 1 Bell 212 (AB 212);
  TRG 5 F-280C

Paramilitary ε150,000

Bolivarian National Militia ε150,000

Table 14 **Selected arms procurements and deliveries, Latin America and the Caribbean**

Designation	Type	Quantity (Current)	Contract Value	Prime Nationality	Prime Contractor	Order Date	First Delivery Due	Notes
Argentina (ARG)								
VN-1	APC (W)	110	n.k.	PRC/ARG	NORINCO/ Tandanor-CINAR	2015	n.k.	For bi-national Southern Cross Force and the army's 10th Infantry Brigade
IA-63 *Pampa* III	Trg ac	18	n.k.	ARG	FAdeA	2010	n.k.	First flight in 2015; final pre-production aircraft rolled out Apr 2016 for test
AB-206	Lt tpt hel	20	€2.6m (US$2.9m)	ITA	Government surplus	2016	n.k.	Ex-ITA Carabinieri helicopters, to be exchanged for three surplus ARG G-222s
H225M *Caracal* (EC725 *Super Cougar*)	Med tpt hel	2	n.k.	Int'l	Airbus Group (Airbus Helicopters)	2013	2014	First helicopter entered service Feb 2016
Bolivia (BOL)								
H215 (AS332 *Super Puma*)	Med tpt hel	6	n.k.	Int'l	Airbus Group (Airbus Helicopters)	2014	2014	Third helicopter delivered Feb 2016
Brazil (BRZ)								
VBTP-MR *Guarani*	APC (W)	172	R504.4m (US$238m)	BRZ/ITA	IVECO Latin America	2009	2014	BRZ has a requirement for 2,044 *Guarani* to replace EE-9 *Cascavel* and EE-11 *Urutu*. Delivery to be complete by 2030
AAV-7A1	APC (W)	23	US$82m	UK (US)	BAE Systems (BAE Systems Land & Armaments)	2015	n.k.	For marine corps. Delivery to be complete by end of 2018
ASTROS II Mk6	MRL (SP 127mm)	18	n.k.	BRZ	Avibras	2011	2014	For army. Three batteries ordered. First battery set delivered Mar 2014; second set expected late 2016
SN-BR (Submarino Nuclear Brasileiro)	SSN	1	See notes	FRA/BRZ	DCNS/ Odebrecht (Itaguaí Construções Navais)	2009	2027	Part of €6.7bn (US$8.3bn) PROSUB naval programme. Contract covers work on the non-nuclear sections of the submarine
Scorpene class	SSK	4	See notes	FRA/BRZ	DCNS/ Odebrecht (Itaguaí Construções Navais)	2009	2018	Part of €6.7bn (US$8.3bn) PROSUB naval programme. To be built by Itaguaí Construções Navais (joint venture between DCNS and Odebrecht). Delivery to be completed 2022
Gripen E/F	FGA ac	36	US$4.78bn	SWE	Saab	2014	2019	Twenty-eight E and eight F aircraft. The latter are to be manufactured in Brazil
C-295M (SC-105)	SAR ac	3	US$200m	Int'l	Airbus Group (Airbus Defence & Space)	2014	2017	Search-and-rescue configuration
KC-390	Tkr/Tpt ac	28	US$3.25bn	BRZ	Embraer	2014	2018	First aircraft rolled out Oct 2014. Entry into service delayed until 2018. Serial production began mid-2016
H225M *Caracal* (EC725 *Super Cougar*)	Hvy tpt hel	50	€1.9bn (US$2.7bn)	Int'l/BRZ	Airbus Group (Airbus Helicopters)/ Helibras	2008	2010	H-XBR programme. First three built in FRA. Remainder being manufactured in BRZ by Helibras. Delivery completion date postponed from 2017 to 2022 due to funding problems. Twenty-five delivered by end of 2016

Table 14 **Selected arms procurements and deliveries, Latin America and the Caribbean**

Designation	Type	Quantity (Current)	Contract Value	Prime Nationality	Prime Contractor	Order Date	First Delivery Due	Notes
A-*Darter*	AAM IIR	n.k.	n.k.	BRZ/RSA	Denel Dynamics	2007	n.k.	Co-funded project between Brazil and South Africa. Brazilian production contract yet to be signed. Project hampered by budget cuts
SGDC	Satellite (Comms)	1	n.k.	FRA & ITA/BRZ	Thales Alenia Space/Visiona	2013	2017	Geostationary Defense and Strategic Communications Satellite
Chile (CHL)								
Piloto Pardo class	PSOH	4	n.k.	CHL	ASMAR	2005	2008	Fassmer OPV 80 design. Fourth of class launched Aug 2016
Colombia (COL)								
20 de Julio class	PSO	1	n.k.	COL	COTECMAR	2014	n.k.	Order for third of class. Vessel laid down Dec 2014
Costa Rica (CRI)								
Ex-US *Island* class	PB	2	Donation	US	Government surplus	2016	2017	For coastguard
Ecuador (ECU)								
Damen Stan Patrol 5009	PCC	2	n.k.	NLD/ECU	Damen Schelde Naval Shipbuilding/ASTINAVE	2014	n.k.	For coastguard; both vessels under construction
H125M (AS550C3 *Fennec*)	MRH hel	7	n.k.	Int'l	Airbus Group (Airbus Helicopters)	2010	2011	Contract included two AS250B2 *Ecureuils*, both of which have been delivered. First two *Fennecs* in service by late 2013; delivery status of remainder unclear
Honduras (HND)								
EMB-314 *Super Tucano*	Trg ac	2	n.k.	BRZ	Embraer	2014	n.k.	Order includes upgrade of six *Tucano*s currently in service
Mexico (MEX)								
Ex-US *Oliver Hazard Perry* class	FFH	2	Donation	US	Government surplus	2014	n.k.	Donation approved by US Congress Dec 2014
Oaxaca class	PSOH	4	n.k.	MEX	ASTIMAR	2014	2016	Second batch of four; sixth of class launched Aug 2016
T-6C+ *Texan* II	Trg ac	77	n.k.	US	Textron (Beechcraft)	2012	2012	Series of orders. Sixty for air force; 17 for navy. Deliveries ongoing
UH-60M *Black Hawk*	Med tpt hel	25	US$285.5m	US	Lockheed Martin (Sikorsky)	2014	2016	For air force. First order for 18; second for seven. First batch delivered Feb 2016
AS565MBe *Panther*	ASW hel	10	US$433m	Int'l	Airbus Group (Airbus Helicopters)	2014	2016	First helicopter delivered Sep 2016
Nicaragua (NIC)								
T-72B1	MBT	50	n.k.	RUS	Government surplus	2015	2016	Deliveries ongoing

Table 14 **Selected arms procurements and deliveries, Latin America and the Caribbean**

Designation	Type	Quantity (Current)	Contract Value	Prime Nationality	Prime Contractor	Order Date	First Delivery Due	Notes
Peru (PER)								
Paita class (IDN *Makassar* class)	LPD	2	n.k.	ROK/PER	Dae Sun Shipbuilding & Engineering/ SIMA Callao	2012	2015	Construction of first vessel commenced Jul 2013
C-27J *Spartan*	Med tpt ac	2	€100m (US$122m)	ITA	Leonardo	2015	2015	Second order for two; first aircraft from this order delivered Dec 2015
KT-1P	Trg ac	20	US$200m	ROK	KAI	2012	2014	Ten KT-1 and ten KA-1 variants. First four manufactured in ROK; remainder in PER. All ROK-manufactured aircraft delivered; PER-manufactured-aircraft deliveries ongoing
SH-2G *Super Seasprite*	ASW hel	5	US$80m	US (CAN)	General Dynamics (General Dynamics Mission Systems – Canada)	2014	n.k.	For navy. Ex-RNZAF SH-2Gs to be refurbished and modified in CAN
Trinidad and Tobago (TTO)								
Speyside class (Damen Stan Patrol 5009)	PCC	4	US$189m	NLD	Damen Schelde Naval Shipbuilding	2015	2015	Order includes supply of two Damen Fast Crew Supplier 5009 utility vessels. Utility vessels and the first patrol vessel delivered Aug 2015. Second patrol vessel commissioned Mar 2016
Venezuela (VEN)								
VN16	Lt tk	25	n.k.	PRC	NORINCO	2012	2015	Export version of Type-05 (ZTD-05). For marines. Deliveries ongoing
VN1	IFV	40	n.k.	PRC	NORINCO	2012	2014	Export version of Type-09 (ZBL-09). For marines. Deliveries ongoing
VN18	IFV	25	n.k.	PRC	NORINCO	2012	2015	Export version of Type-05 (ZBD-05). For marines. Deliveries ongoing
SR5	Arty (MRL 220mm)	18	n.k.	PRC	NORINCO	2012	2017	–
Guaicamacuto class	PSOH	4	n.k.	ESP/VEN	Navantia/ DIANCA	2005	2010	For coastguard. Fourth vessel, *Comandante Eterno Hugo Chávez*, launched Jul 2014. In-service date delayed until late 2017
L-15	Trg ac	24	n.k.	PRC	AVIC (Hongdu)	2014	n.k.	Order status unclear

Chapter Nine
Sub-Saharan Africa

Active conflicts, state fragility and enduring development issues combine to create significant challenges for governments in sub-Saharan Africa; they impel the factors that absorb the day-to-day focus of many of the continent's military forces. In some cases, as nations grapple with current threats, addressing these challenges has the effect of forestalling moves towards defence-reform processes, even though engaging in these processes might make regional armed forces' responses to security problems more efficient. Meanwhile, the international community (including other African states) remains vital to tackling the security crises in and across nations on the continent. This is not just in terms of generating diplomatic traction and help in enabling renewed efforts at conflict and dispute resolution, but also involves continuing material support to Africa's nations and multilateral institutions as they look to develop greater local capacity to tackle these crises themselves.

The broad parameters of this international assistance remain similar in nature to those of recent years; from extra-regional states and institutions it can range from financial assistance to advice and assistance missions as well as external private-sector support. It also still includes targeted defence support. Indeed, there remains a significant international military presence on the continent. Principally, this takes the form of contributions to UN peacekeeping missions; at the end of 2016, nine of the 16 UN peacekeeping operations were based on the continent. But these contributions also take the form of combat forces. One example is in the contribution of African states to military operations such as the African Union's AMISOM mission in Somalia and the UN's Force Intervention Brigade – part of the MONUSCO mission in the Democratic Republic of the Congo. Perhaps the most robust international military presence is that of the French forces engaged in counter-terrorism operations in the Sahel, although US forces based in Djibouti can also call on significant combat assets. (The US established the Combined Joint Task Force – Horn of Africa in 2002 to conduct regional capacity-building activities, among other tasks. Other nations base forces out of Djibouti, principally on counter-piracy operations.) A more recent development concerns the agreement between Eritrea and the Saudi-led coalition engaged in operations against Houthi rebels in Yemen; this has led to imagery emerging of military forces, allegedly from the United Arab Emirates, present in 2016 at military facilities close to the Eritrean port of Assab.

As well as combat capabilities, military assistance includes (more often, in most cases) training and capacity-building, such as in the UK's Peace Support Training Teams as well as the varied training programmes and exercises organised with the participation of US Africa Command. The provision of targeted capability support, such as in command-and-control systems, airlift (capable of moving equipment as well as people), and greater intelligence and surveillance capacity are also important. High-end capabilities like this will often be unaffordable for local militaries, with them often engaged in, and assuming related costs for, infantry-heavy ground operations. Meanwhile, the structures of local armed forces, and the historical predominance given to certain sections of the force deriving from local historical and political factors, can make it more likely that personnel-intensive ground forces may continue to be a focus for investment. Nonetheless, as a result of day-to-day needs, the 'enablers' seen in Western armed forces may be on local defence ministries' wish lists, but they are often unaffordable.

However, as technology proliferates, the cost of entry falls. For instance, unmanned systems are now nearly ubiquitous in Western armed forces, although not all states can afford or need to operate long-endurance high-altitude, or armed, unmanned aerial vehicles (UAVs). However, as unmanned technologies become commercially available and progressively smaller, and easier to use, these have been seen increasingly in the inventories of African armed forces. In the main these are smaller, tactical UAVs. But some African states – Nigeria is the principal example – are also integrating higher-end

UAV capability, in this case China's CH-3 armed UAV. With China now one of the few countries manufacturing armed UAVs, and selling these in Africa, it is possible that states unable to procure Western systems for varying reasons may be able to secure similar capability from non-Western sources.

As Western military forces learned when growing this capability, integrating the intelligence, surveillance and reconnaissance (ISR) output from unmanned systems creates a range of new technical and operational as well as, in deciding whether and how to act on it, legal challenges for armed forces. This will be mitigated somewhat as many of these systems will, in Africa, likely remain at the tactical level (in other words, the information is held, and used locally and rapidly, by small units), but over time the costs of higher-end systems may fall, and states may direct more funding in their direction or smaller-scale airframes may become capable of delivering payloads. In October 2016, in response to growing concern about the proliferation of armed UAVs, 51 states signed a 'Joint Declaration for the Export and Subsequent Use of Armed or Strike-Enabled Unmanned Aerial Vehicles', aiming to restrict the export of such technologies; this idea was developed earlier in the year as part of the Arms Trade Treaty process. Neither China nor Russia were among the signatories.

At present, although some states might have recently bought or might be looking at high-end capabilities – examples include Su-27 combat aircraft in Angola and Su-30s in Uganda, and South Africa's wide range of capable land, sea and air assets (even if the country's military effectiveness has been somewhat eroded by equipment and personnel-readiness issues) – most procurement requirements derive more from the everyday challenges of insurgency, terrorism and criminality than the potential demands of inter-state warfare. It is, however, these 'lower-tier' military capabilities that are often precisely those most required, especially with the continent's security problems continuing to exhibit transnational characteristics.

A year after the end of the Ebola crisis in West Africa, the most prominent example of these transnational challenges is that from Boko Haram (see map 12). The group remains active not just in northeast Nigeria but now also across the border into Cameroon and Niger, particularly as Nigeria and the regional Multinational Joint Task Force have exerted greater pressure on the group. There is also the continuing instability in the Sahel, fuelled by a nexus of criminal–terrorist activity able to cross porous borders, compounded by problems relating to governance and extending the rule of law in a region where terrorist activity had so seriously confronted state institutions. Similar concerns exist on the other side of the continent where al-Shabaab continues not just to demonstrate its resilience in Somalia, but also its ability to attack neighbouring states such as Kenya. These continuing crises illustrate how important it is for military gains in unstable parts of Africa to be accompanied by rapid improvements not just in livelihoods, infrastructure and the economy, but also in governance and broader administrative effectiveness, such that any narratives on these themes employed by insurgent groups are invalidated, state institutions become more effective, and local populations develop greater faith in these same institutions.

Improving local security and military capacity remains vital. However, this is often best achieved not solely by improving platform capabilities, but also by improving military institutions and personnel. For instance, international governments and non-governmental organisations have long supported security-sector reform activities, as well as more post-conflict-related demobilisation, disarmament and reintegration programmes. Many of these missions tackle broader issues too: some contain training packages aimed at gender sensitisation for the armed forces or support to the judiciary and the broader arms of government. Developing security forces' skills in these broad areas may promote longer-term stability by increasing the chance of developing accountable and resilient armed and security forces. Such forces may develop greater capability to exert more effective control over potentially ungoverned space or, at a minimum, extend forms of governance so as to reassure and support vulnerable populations. But this support requires long-term engagement. Assistance is sometimes also required to be more rapid and to be focused on the capacity deficits that still hamper some African armed forces in terms of logistics; maintenance; airlift; ISR; command and control; and mission funding – particularly for states whose armed forces have traditionally had little requirement to deploy and sustain at distance. This kind of support, which has in recent years been vital in enabling operations on the continent, is helping those African states who wish to do more for the continent's security.

Map 12 **Support to the campaign against Boko Haram in northeast Nigeria and the Lake Chad region, Jan 2015–Aug 2016**

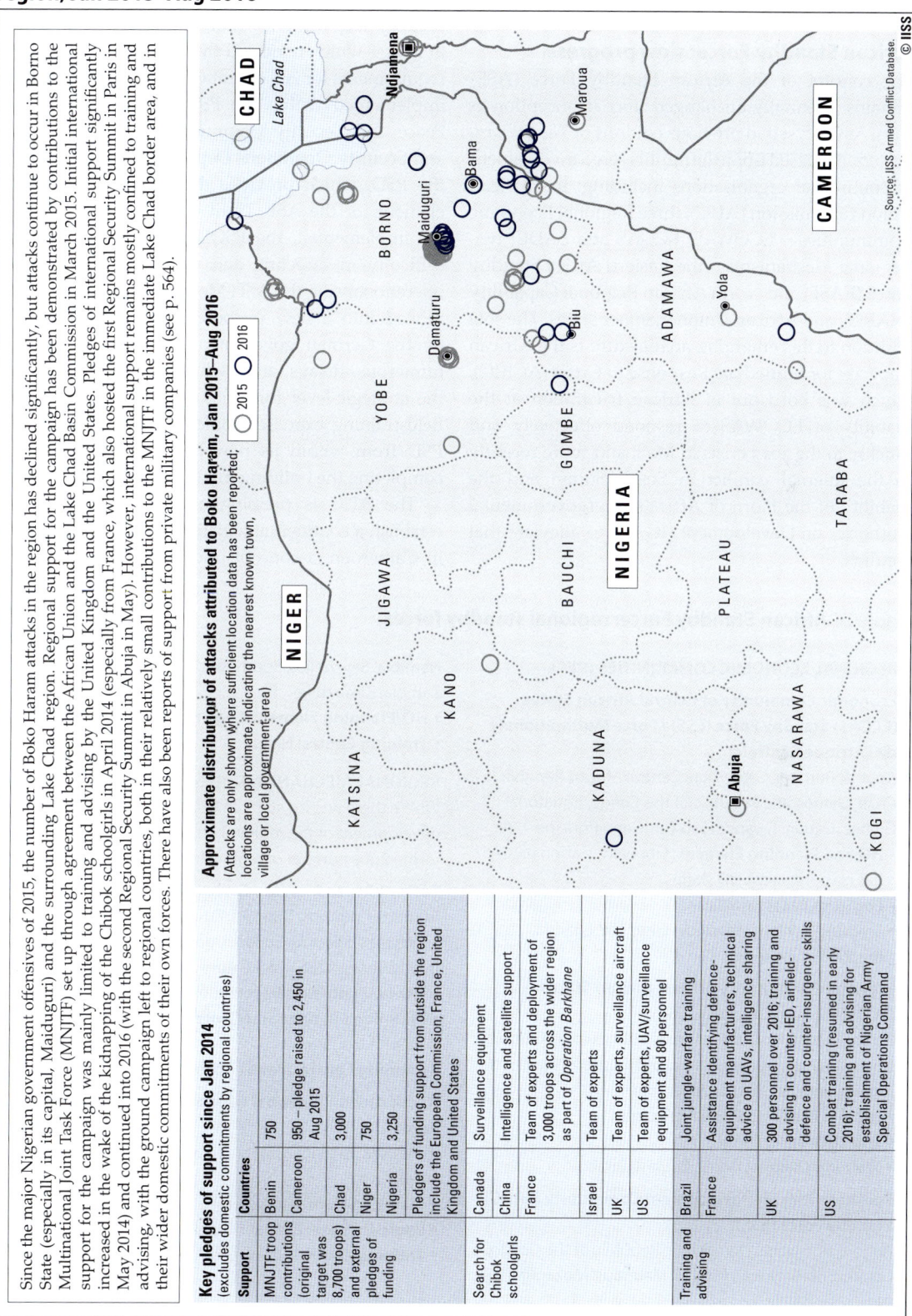

Since the major Nigerian government offensives of 2015, the number of Boko Haram attacks in the region has declined significantly, but attacks continue to occur in Borno State (especially in its capital, Maiduguri) and the surrounding Lake Chad region. Regional support for the campaign has been demonstrated by contributions to the Multinational Joint Task Force (MNJTF) set up through agreement between the African Union and the Lake Chad Basin Commission in March 2015. Initial international support for the campaign was mainly limited to training and advising by the United Kingdom and the United States. Pledges of international support significantly increased in the wake of the kidnapping of the Chibok schoolgirls in April 2014 (especially from France, which also hosted the first Regional Security Summit in Paris in May 2014) and continued into 2016 (with the second Regional Security Summit in Abuja in May). However, international support remains mostly confined to training and advising, with the ground campaign left to regional countries, both in their relatively small contributions to the MNJTF in the immediate Lake Chad border area, and in their wider domestic commitments of their own forces. There have also been reports of support from private military companies (see p. 564).

Approximate distribution of attacks attributed to Boko Haram, Jan 2015–Aug 2016
(Attacks are only shown where sufficient location data has been reported; locations are approximate, indicating the nearest known town, village or local government area)

○ 2015 ○ 2016

Source: IISS Armed Conflict Database.

Key pledges of support since Jan 2014
(excludes domestic commitments by regional countries)

Support	Countries	
MNJTF troop contributions (original target was 8,700 troops) and external pledges of funding	Benin	750
	Cameroon	950 – pledge raised to 2,450 in Aug 2015
	Chad	3,000
	Niger	750
	Nigeria	3,250
	Pledgers of funding support from outside the region include the European Commission, France, United Kingdom and United States	
Search for Chibok schoolgirls	Canada	Surveillance equipment
	China	Intelligence and satellite support
	France	Team of experts and deployment of 3,000 troops across the wider region as part of *Operation Barkhane*
	Israel	Team of experts
	UK	Team of experts, surveillance aircraft
	US	Team of experts, UAV/surveillance equipment and 80 personnel
Training and advising	Brazil	Joint jungle-warfare training
	France	Assistance identifying defence-equipment manufacturers, technical advice on UAVs, intelligence sharing
	UK	300 personnel over 2016; training and advising in counter-IED, airfield-defence and counter-insurgency skills
	US	Combat training (resumed in early 2016); training and advising for establishment of Nigerian Army Special Operations Command

CONTINENTAL SECURITY DEVELOPMENTS

African Standby Force: slow progress

The concept of the African Standby Force (ASF) remains essentially unchanged since its inception in 2003. As analysed in previous editions of *The Military Balance*, it is based upon the multilayered involvement of continental organisations including: the African Union Commission (AUC); three Regional Economic Communities – ECOWAS, ECCAS and SADC; two Regional Mechanisms – the Eastern Africa Standby Force (EASF) and North African Regional Capability (NARC); and African Union member states. The sole addition to this emerging architecture is the African Capacity for Immediate Response to Crisis (ACIRC), which was born out of African frustration at the inability of ECOWAS to respond effectively and quickly to the 2013 crisis in Mali, and more recently to the internal conflict in South Sudan and the inability of the Horn of Africa's Intergovernmental Authority on Development (IGAD) to alleviate that conflict.

On the administrative level, the personnel structures recommended at the AU Peace and Security Department's (PSD's) conference in Abuja in 2011 – which reviewed the strategic-headquarters requirements for AU operations – have yet to be fully implemented within the PSD, which supports the Peace and Security Commissioner, and the Peace and Security Operations Department (PSOD) within the PSD, which provides the continental-planning element for the ASF. Until these recommendations are implemented, the PSOD will continue to have difficulty in directing and completing the task of operationalising the ASF. Meanwhile, the whole PSD moved into a new purpose-built building funded by the German government. The project suffered numerous delays and, while it was hoped that the strategic-level functions for the *Amani Africa* II field-training exercise would be carried out by the PSD from within its new headquarters, delays in completing the building made this impossible.

The AUC is pressing ahead with its plan to establish a continental logistics base (CLB) at Douala in Cameroon, a concept unchanged since 2003 and

Figure 29 African Standby Force: regional standby forces

REGIONAL ECONOMIC COMMUNITIES (RECs)

Economic Community of Central African States (ECCAS) Standby Force (ESF) / Force Multinationale de l'Afrique Centrale:
Angola, Burundi, Cameroon, Central African Republic, Chad, Democratic Republic of the Congo, Equatorial Guinea, Gabon, Rwanda, São Tomé and Príncipe
- **HQ and Planning Element:** Libreville, Gabon (ECCAS has no permanent HQ staff.)
- **Logistics Base:** Douala
- **Training Centres:** Yaounde, Libreville, Luanda, Brazzaville, Awae

Economic Community of West African States (ECOWAS) Standby Force (ESF):
Benin, Burkina Faso, Cape Verde, Côte d'Ivoire, Gambia, Ghana, Guinea, Guinea Bissau, Liberia, Mali, Niger, Nigeria, Senegal, Sierra Leone, Togo
- **HQ and Planning Element:** Abuja
- **Logistics Base:** Lungi
- **Training Centres:** Accra, Abuja, Bamako

Southern African Development Community (SADC) Standby Force (SSF):
Angola, Botswana, Democratic Republic of the Congo, Lesotho, Madagascar, Malawi, Mauritius, Mozambique, Namibia, Seychelles, South Africa, Swaziland, Tanzania, Zambia, Zimbabwe
- **HQ/Planning Element/Logistics Base:** Gabarone
- **Training Centre:** Harare

REGIONAL MECHANISMS (RMs)
Where there was no suitable REC to act as the lead in the development of the regional standby forces an RM was formed of a number of regional states.

Eastern Africa Standby Force (EASF):
Burundi, Comoros, Djibouti, Ethiopia, Kenya, Rwanda, Seychelles, Somalia, Sudan, Uganda (South Sudan has had 'observer' status since April 2013.)
- **HQ and Logistics Base:** Addis Ababa
- **Planning Element and Coordinating Mechanism:** Nairobi, Ethiopia
- **Training Centres:** Addis Ababa, Nairobi

North African Regional Capability (NARC) Standby Force
Algeria, Egypt, Libya, Mauritania, Tunisia, Western Sahara
- **HQ:** Cairo
- **Planning Element:** Algiers
- **Logistics Base:** Elements in Algiers and Cairo
- **Training Centres:** Cairo and Algeria

modelled on the UN base in Brindisi, Italy. Critics argue that a base with a pool of maintained standby equipment is an outdated concept that will do little to enable rapid deployment in case of crisis and that will require significant resources in return for limited benefit. Those resources either do not exist in Africa or are not being made available, while donors have been reluctant to support the project. Detractors assert that without a review of the CLB concept, alternative methods of equipping and sustaining forces, such as dormant support contracts and a contract to provide strategic and tactical communications to whatever becomes the next theatre for an AU peace-support operation, are not receiving the attention they require. In addition, slow progress has been made on the intended multidimensional composition of the ASF, which would combine military, police and civilian personnel. As it stands, the ASF and its Rapid Deployment Capability, as well as the ACIRC, remain dependent on military assets, and military staff remain predominant. In particular, the regional economic communities and regional mechanisms are reported as having difficulty in coordinating police and civilian training and deployment scheduling.

But for all that, the ASF concept and its aspirations are unchanged – to create a tool flexible enough to address the full range of issues and challenges presented by African instability and insecurity. The *Amani Africa* II exercise cycle was seen as the opportunity to demonstrate and declare the full operational capability of the ASF. But while the cycle continues to provide a mechanism for engaging the AUC and donors (particularly the UN, the European Union and the United States), a schedule that was intended to include *Amani* II in 2013 and *Amani* III in 2015 slipped. Instead, *Amani Africa* II moved to November 2015, and there is uncertainty over the value of a third exercise. Meanwhile, the political pressure to declare full operational capability, even if it has not been demonstrated, was eased by the development of the ACIRC and its inclusion in *Amani Africa* II.

Results of *Amani Africa* II

According to the AU, a major achievement of the *Amani Africa* II field-training exercise (FTX) was that it brought together personnel from different AU member states and that the doctrine of a 'framework region' was exercised. As with *Amani Africa* I, this was not an insignificant achievement in itself, even if the donor community criticised the exercise for failing to address many of the lessons of the first exercise. The exercise was seen to validate the ASF's operational readiness, albeit without the declaration of 'full operational capability' that might have been expected. The exercise also re-emphasised the importance of the multidimensional character of the ASF, comprising police, civil and military components. Strategic airlift was seen as one of the best-practised areas during the FTX. Inputs from the after-action review process were fed into a draft five-year ASF work plan (2016–20), which is expected to be validated by member states and to be the basis for more attempts to enhance the ASF.

Regional developments

At the regional level, ASF progress has been – as noted above – hindered by the concept's complex multilayered structure, and the difficulty that this causes for generating rapid decision-making and effective engagement from contributing states. Furthermore, the regional standby forces (see Figure 29) remain at differing levels of maturity. The EASF and SADC standby forces are the most advanced, primarily due to consistent political will to operationalise them among each of the respective region's member states.

For EASF nations, the need to coordinate and develop regional military capability has been highlighted by ongoing operations in Somalia, the crisis in South Sudan, and threats to stability and peace among states in the Horn of Africa. These states are also among those most engaged in the ACIRC process – underlining their frustration at the ASF's slow progress in East Africa. SADC states, meanwhile, responded to the security challenge posed by the M23 rebels in the eastern Democratic Republic of the Congo (DRC) in late 2012, as did the International Conference on the Great Lakes Region (ICGLR). However, readiness issues, coupled with the ICGLR's non-inclusion in the ASF/Banjul mechanisms that established the ASF, combined with the UN's desire not to have to deal with a separate AU force in eastern DRC, meant that an African solution was not available to African decision-makers. As such, the creation of the UN Force Intervention Brigade offered a compromise solution acceptable to both the UN and the AU. ECCAS also continues to develop, as does ECOWAS, though the latter suffered a setback over Mali where it proved to be incapable of taking the lead in managing a regional response to the crisis there. Meanwhile, the establishment of the

Multinational Joint Task Force (MNJTF) against Boko Haram through the Lake Chad Basin Commission rather than through ECOWAS demonstrated not just ECOWAS's difficulty in generating military capacity, but also the AU's flexible approach to peace-support operations – one that is not necessarily tied to the fixed ASF layered structure.

African Capacity for Immediate Response to Crisis

Following the lesson from Mali that the ASF was not yet a rapid-response capability, the January 2014 AU Assembly in Addis Ababa established the ACIRC as a transitional arrangement. The initial participating countries were Algeria, Angola, Chad, Ethiopia, Guinea, Mauritania, Niger, Senegal, South Africa, Sudan, Tanzania and Uganda. In accordance with articles 4.h and 4.j of the African Union Constitutive Act, deployment of an ACIRC force can be authorised by the Peace and Security Council, at summit level.

A number of significant steps have been taken since the first ACIRC conceptualisation, including the establishment of an ACIRC 'cell' in the PSOD, staffed by ACIRC volunteering nations, and the completion of a command-post exercise (CPX) in Tanzania. Principal tasks for this cell include managing the ACIRC sub-working groups on Force Generation; Operations and Command-and-Control; Logistics and Strategic Lift; and on Command, Control, Communication and Information Systems (C3IS). In addition, it is tasked with developing a database for the ACIRC Table of Organisations and Equipment; developing contingency plans for its development; and, most importantly, harmonising the deployment and employment concepts of both the ACIRC and the ASF Rapid Deployment Capability (RDC).

The first ACIRC CPX, exercise *Utulivu Africa*, was considered a success. Held in Dar es Salaam on 25–28 November 2014, it was expected to practise operational readiness and interoperability in the planning and execution of intervention operations. Initial operating capability for the ACIRC was declared after the exercise, and it was agreed to hold a further exercise in 2015 in order to assess and declare full operational capability. Unlike the *Amani Africa* exercise series, the ACIRC CPX avoided the involvement of the regional economic communities and the regional mechanisms, as well as external donor support. While this might have led to a less comprehensive exercise, it resulted in a significantly faster execution cycle for activities. Voluntary contributors to the ACIRC have agreed to self-sustain and self-fund their deployments to ACIRC operations for the first 31 days, while the AUC has undertaken to provide all support from that point on. However, the AU has yet to identify and set up a system to meet this requirement, the likely outcome of which will be continued engagement from external donors.

AU documentation has always stressed the interim nature of the ACIRC, and that it will complement other institutions. The Declaration of the Eighth Ordinary Meeting of the AU Specialised Technical Committee on Defence, Safety and Security, dated 15 May 2015 (the annual African CHODs meeting), 'commends ACIRC Volunteering Nations for their contributions towards ensuring full operational readiness of the ACIRC Force. And further note that ACIRC should begin drawing down as ASF and its RDC become operational by December 2015.' This interim nature has not always been so clear to those international donors heavily engaged in ASF development. Indeed, this has led some to question in particular the AUC's plan for the RDC concept, which is seen as essential if the ASF is to develop an effective response capability. Perhaps in recognition of this, the second ACIRC CPX was merged with *Amani Africa* II. During *Amani Africa* II, elements of both the ACIRC and the RDC concepts were exercised simultaneously and operated alongside each other – offering an opportunity to combine lessons from both processes. Nonetheless, the RDC concept, set within the framework of the five regional standby forces, remains the AU's stated preference for early-intervention arrangements.

AU–UN cooperation

Current operations in both East and West Africa (respectively AMISOM and the counter-Lord's Resistance Army (LRA) initiative and the MNJTF) and the newly authorised regional protection force for South Sudan under UN Security Council Resolution 2304 (2016) highlight the link between those capabilities still absent in the ASF construct and the pragmatic approach being adopted by both the AU and UN in finding ways to mount and sustain peacekeeping and peace-support operations in Africa.

For instance, AMISOM relies upon ad hoc arrangements for command and control, namely meetings of troop contributing countries' (TCC) defence ministers and the Military Operations Coordination Committee of TCC Chiefs of Defence. The mission is still almost totally reliant on donor funding and donor provision of strategic airlift, service support, C3IS, medical evacuation and tactical airlift. Meanwhile, the MNJTF was established under the Lake Chad Basin Commission, with the UN Security Council calling for international donor support under UNSCR Statement SC/11983. This is illustrative of the current state of AU–UN planning and preparation for peace-support operations in Africa, which includes the assistance of regional and Addis Ababa-based UN staff as well as verbal endorsement by the UN for, and limited coordination of, wider external support to AU operations. There has also been significant progress in establishing liaison and coordination mechanisms, such as the UN Office to the AU in Addis Ababa, and better direct relationships between the AU PSD and the Department for Political Affairs, the Department for Peacekeeping Operations (DPKO) and the Department of Field Support at the UN Headquarters in New York, including the recent recruitment in December 2015 of the former director of the AU PSD, El Ghassim Wane, as an under-secretary-general in the DPKO.

UN–AU relations in peacekeeping and peace-support operations have matured considerably over the past ten years. The AU's previous insistence that the UN should directly fund the AU to conduct peace-support operations in Africa has been eased, if not dropped altogether. But operational relationships first developed during the hybrid operation in Darfur, and then through support to AMISOM, have had both positive and negative outcomes. On the positive side, the UN is able to bring a fully mature and well-resourced capacity to support peacekeeping operations. AU troops have benefited significantly from UN support in terms of basic operating requirements, such as functioning command and control, helicopter medevac and Level 2+ medical facilities, and in terms of operational living standards. In 2009, AU troops in Mogadishu lived on a diet of dried staples flown in from Uganda and what fresh produce was available on the local market, and lived in what tented accommodation was available from donors. Today they have a comprehensive diet and many are living in UN-standard accommodation.

However, peace-support operations in Africa require a different level of resourcing than traditional UN peacekeeping operations. Ammunition is rarely fired during peacekeeping missions, so no combat-resupply system exists; casualties are limited and most of the time incurred in a permissive or semi-permissive environment. AU peace-support operations, on the other hand, regularly expend large amounts of ammunition and incur significant casualties in a combat setting. Further work is therefore required to define when, how and with what the UN can, should and could support ASF operations. This work has effectively started, particularly as a result of ongoing operations, but could now be developed through bilateral discussions related specifically to ASF operations, whether initiated through regional standby forces, the ACIRC or a pragmatic approach to a specific crisis. The ongoing relationship between the AU counter-LRA initiative and UNMISS in South Sudan, and the AU's human-rights experts and military observers deployed in Burundi in 2015 with the UN country mission there, provide useful opportunities to explore modalities in the lower-intensity ASF scenarios. Meanwhile, operations in the Central African Republic, the DRC, Mali, Somalia and South Sudan – and against Boko Haram – offer a test bed for future relationships in higher-intensity scenarios.

Recent developments

In South Sudan in summer 2016, the already parlous relationship between the Sudan People's Liberation Movement (SPLM, led by Salva Kiir) and the SPLM–In Opposition (led by Riek Machar) deteriorated rapidly. This led to the consideration by both IGAD and the AU of an intervention/protection force for South Sudan. Although early international speculation was that the ASF might take up a role in planning for such an intervention, neither the AU nor IGAD favoured such an approach. The mechanism eventually agreed was for a series of meetings between the chiefs of defence of Ethiopia, Kenya, Rwanda, Sudan and Uganda under the political umbrella of IGAD. Subsequent endorsement of the IGAD approach by the AU PSC and the UN Security Council resulted in the agreement to form a regional intervention/protection force to secure Juba, comprising three battalions from Ethiopia, Kenya and Rwanda and fully under UNMISS command and control.

Some analysts would argue that coming so soon after exercise *Amani Africa* II, which had validated the operational readiness of the ASF, the failure by the AU and the regional economic communities to use the ASF mechanism for South Sudan is a sign of serious shortcomings – both political and operational – in the ASF construct. Others would argue that without the years of close work on ASF issues between the five chiefs of defence, there would never have been the necessary understanding and goodwill between them to address such a difficult regional issue. The reality is likely to be somewhere between the two.

The AU Summit in Kigali, Rwanda, in June 2016 agreed to institute and implement a 0.2% levy on all eligible imported goods into the continent in order to finance the African Union Operational Program and Peace Support Operations budgets, starting in 2017. The amounts collected from the levy would be automatically paid by the national administration in accordance with each member state's assessed contribution. The AUC was charged with establishing an oversight and accountability mechanism in order to ensure the effective and prudent use of these resources. It was further agreed that the AU Peace Fund (AUPF) would be endowed from the 0.2% levy with US$325 million in 2017, rising to US$400m in 2020. This total amount would be raised from equal contributions from each of the five ASF regions. The AUPF was planned to have three thematic windows – Mediation and Preventive Diplomacy; Institutional Capacity; and Peace Support Operations – as well as clear governance structures and an independent fund-management body. The summit requested that the AUC chairperson implement all aspects related to the operationalisation of the AUPF, in particular the legal, operational and financial rules and regulations. Additionally, the AUC will undertake consultations with the UN secretary-general, the UN General Assembly, the UN Security Council and other relevant partners on the envisaged funding arrangements for the provision of the UN-assessed contributions for AU-led peace operations, following the funding arrangements for the AUPF.

Should the AUC succeed in establishing the AUPF with an annual fund of US$400m for African peace-support operations by 2020, the AU will have achieved a significant degree of freedom from the current constraints on its ability to operationalise its peace and security decisions. Its total reliance on the EU, UN and other smaller bilateral donors for its peace-support-operation budget means that even for small deployments, such as the proposed High-Level Panel for Libya in 2011 and the counter-LRA mission in 2012, it is dependent upon financing and political agreement by outside bodies. Although this new initiative is in its infancy, the AUC has in the past found it impossible to raise such funds from member states. The chairperson of the AUC was charged with reporting to the assembly in January 2017 on the progress made in implementing this decision.

Looking to the future, it should be remembered that in general there are two philosophical approaches to the ASF. On the one hand, the AUC, and the PSD in particular, take a flexible view of the concept. In their view, there should be a number of useful capabilities to plan, to mandate and to intervene, but these should not be limited to the hierarchal construct of the AUC; regional economic communities or regional mechanisms; and regional member states. On the other hand, donors and the staff in the regional economic communities or regional mechanisms (encouraged by donor advisers) tend to view the architecture as a more formal set of relationships that are not useful or useable until all of the elements are in place and all of the enabling agreements and memorandums of understanding are signed.

This difference in approach underlies some of the confusion caused by the ACIRC initiative – flexibility and pragmatism from the AUC, African chiefs of defence and African member states is seen (by the donor/ASF-supporting international community) as undermining the procedural steps necessary to establish ASF regional forces and RDCs operating under clear, legal, continental/regional mandates and memorandums. However, the AUC said in 2016 that these two concepts are for the moment complementary, with the ACIRC providing an interim solution until the RDC concept matures and is established. This enabled the two concepts to combine in exercise *Amani Africa* II and clarified that the main challenges for them remain the same, including mandates, funding, and logistics and sustainment.

DEFENCE ECONOMICS

Macroeconomics

Average economic growth in sub-Saharan Africa has slowed to its lowest level since the 2008 financial crisis, to 3.1% in 2015 and 3.0% in 2016, down from 5.0% in 2013 and 4.7% in 2014. However, this regional overview masks significant variations, with the IMF noting that 'multispeed growth' exists in nations across the continent. As in previous years, the region's economic divergence derived principally from each nation's degree of reliance on natural commodities, between states that relied heavily on oil or mineral exports for their revenues, and states characterised as commodity importers. As revenues from energy exports remained weak, resulting from the international oversupply of petroleum products, which depressed prices, this continued to have a significant impact on the public finances of the continent's energy exporters. However, low prices for these products continued to benefit those states that might not extract and sell commodities to a significant degree, but that would benefit from low import costs. For instance, Côte d'Ivoire's economy grew by 8.0% in 2016, Senegal's by 6.6%, Ethiopia's by 6.5% and Kenya's by 6.0%. Sound economic management also helped: states in the West African Economic and Monetary Union fared particularly well due to infrastructure investments, domestic consumption and increased agricultural output.

The picture was different for the region's commodity exporters. These states, which include the continent's biggest economies, suffered as a result of low prices for oil and other natural resources but also from a weakened global trading environment. For instance, the region exported significant quantities of commodities to China (the largest trading partner for the region, according to the IMF). But, as China's economy has slowed and it has imported less, this has negatively affected Africa's exporters. As a result, revenues significantly decreased in the oil- and mineral-exporting states, which has constrained budgets. For example, Nigeria's GDP decreased by 1.7% during 2016, while South Africa's stagnated at 0.1% growth. These countries remain sub-Saharan Africa's largest economies, although electricity shortages impeded manufacturing activity in both in 2016, depressing economic growth.

Other factors constrained economic growth in sub-Saharan Africa. In 2015–16, severe drought in the Horn of Africa and southern Africa lowered agricultural production and resulted in a food crisis in Botswana, Lesotho, Malawi, Namibia, Swaziland and Zimbabwe, and parts of South Africa. Not only did this drought limit agricultural output for domestic consumption and export, but, when combined with currency depreciation in many states, it generated increased inflation; this, in turn, limited purchasing power. For instance, inflation reached 33.7% in Angola in 2016, 19.8% in Malawi, 19.1% in Zambia and 15.4% in Nigeria.

Defence economics and procurement

The region continued to face complex crises, including environmental, economic and social challenges that combine with threats from state and non-state actors to preoccupy many regional capitals. Terrorism remains a significant threat in the Sahel with continued activity by the Islamic State, also known as ISIS or ISIL, and al-Qaeda affiliates in the region, as well as al-Shabaab in Somalia and Boko Haram, which was still centred on Nigeria. Piracy in the Gulf of Guinea and the Horn of Africa also continued to pose a threat. These dangers continue to drive local and international military and security responses. At the same time, many states are grappling with requirements to recapitalise ageing military inventories, while reshaping their defence institutions to better address the security threats they face. In some cases, these processes take place with assistance from international partners or private-sector firms, with this assistance also channelled into training and other military activity. Added to this, regional countries are increasingly aware of the economic benefits that can accrue from their defence disbursements if they are able to produce more defence materiel in-country – by developing a local defence-industrial base, either for manufacturing or maintenance – rather than simply buying equipment from abroad. Even so, in time, importing more advanced military equipment will have the effect of incrementally upskilling local personnel simply by exposure to these technologies.

Nonetheless, overall sub-Saharan African defence spending fell by 12.8% (in current US dollars) between 2015 and 2016, so mirroring the economic slowdown in the region as well as currency depreciations across the continent.

In 2016, South Africa, Angola and Nigeria had the three highest defence budgets in the region, with these accounting for respectively 18.3%, 16.4% and 10.2% of the overall total – together, 45%. However, these

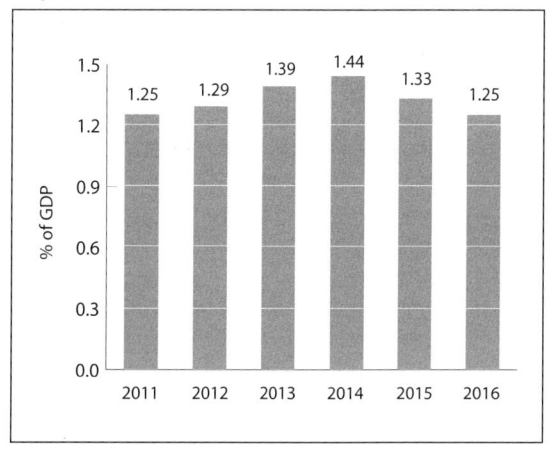

Figure 30 **Sub-Saharan Africa regional defence expenditure** as % of GDP

Year	% of GDP
2011	1.25
2012	1.29
2013	1.39
2014	1.44
2015	1.33
2016	1.25

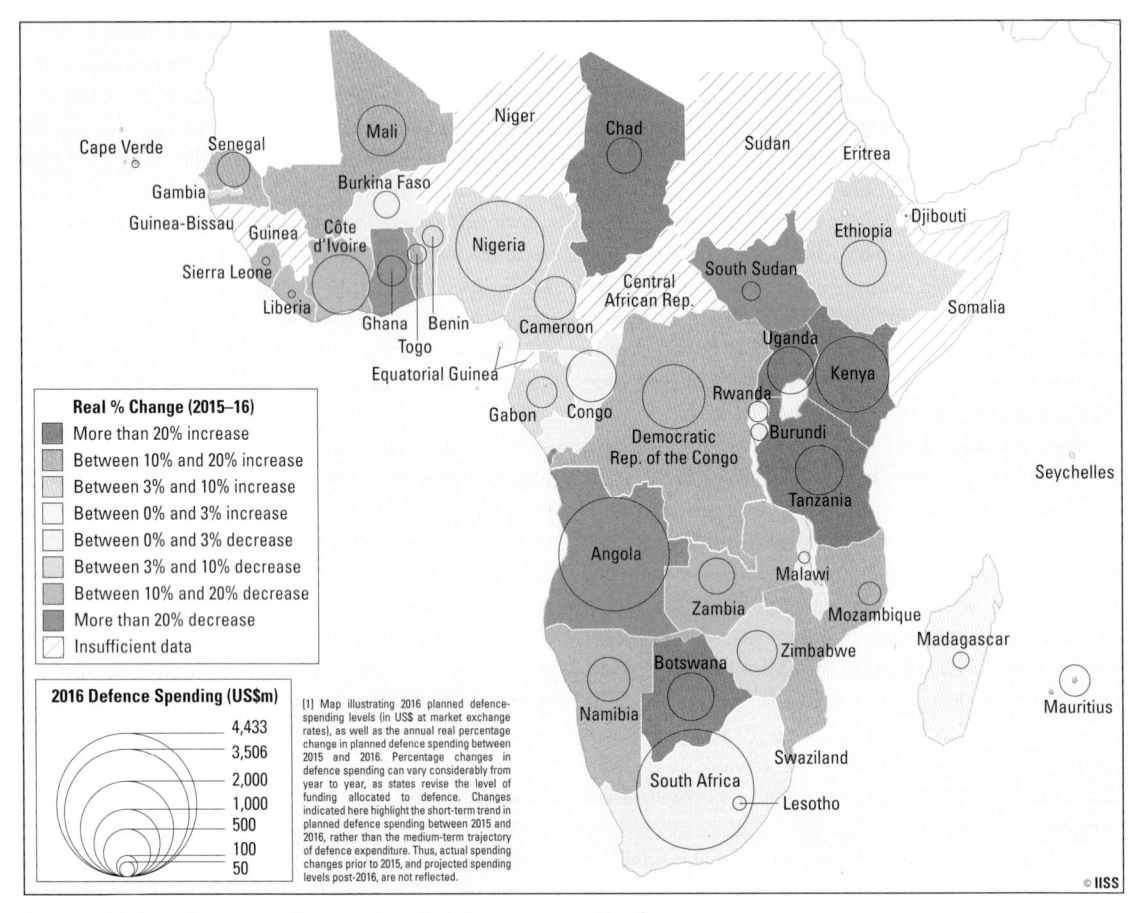

Map 13 **Sub-Saharan Africa regional defence spending**[1]

states have faced economic challenges from factors including low commodity and energy prices. In turn, this affected disbursements, meaning that reduced spending slowed defence spending in sub-Saharan Africa as a whole in 2016, when measured in US dollars. In local-currency terms, Angola's defence budget decreased by 8.6% between 2015 and 2016. In current US dollars, this amounted to a 37% reduction. South Africa's defence budget increased by 4.6% when measured in Rand, but exchange-rate movements resulted in this being a decline, in US dollar terms, of 13%. Although Nigeria's nominal defence budget increased by 18%, this translated into a fall of 11% when measured in US dollars. In contrast, the biggest increases in defence spending included Chad (57.9% between 2015 and 2016), Uganda (34.4%) and Kenya (31.9%). While Kenya's and Uganda's robust economic growth of 6% and 4.9% respectively might allow for increases in defence spending, it is less the case for Chad, whose GDP contracted by 1.1% in 2016. However, all three of these countries are currently engaged in military operations, which is likely to have led their governments to prioritise defence and security spending. In another key military power, Ethiopia, the defence budget grew by 13.1%, when measured in US dollars, between 2015 and 2016.

As Figure 31 shows, defence budgets in southern African states, including Angola and South Africa, have declined sharply since 2014, while the budgets of West African states have generally been on an upward trajectory since 2012. Economic difficulties in southern Africa are largely responsible for this; meanwhile, West African states have had to confront growing threats from extremism and terrorism in recent years.

For example, although South Africa remains one of the continent's leading military powers, its armed forces again saw funding reductions because of the country's ongoing economic crisis. While funding declined in general terms, it is significant that 57% of the 2016 budget's resources were directed to personnel costs, a proportion projected to fall to 53.5%

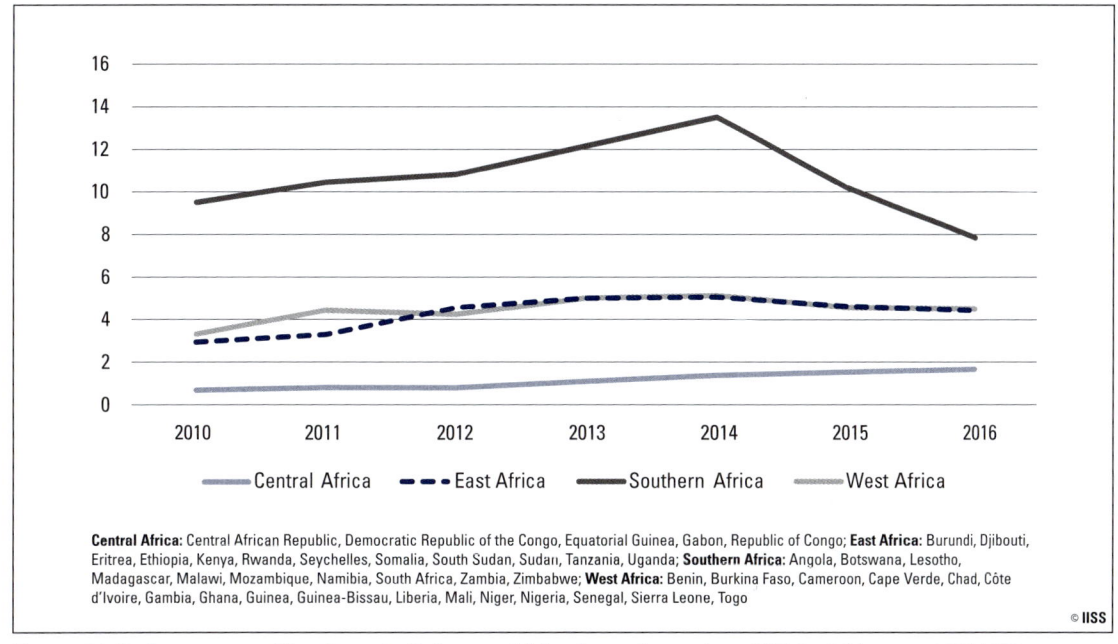

Figure 31 **Defence spending in sub-Saharan Africa by sub-region, 2010–16** (current US billion dollars)

Central Africa: Central African Republic, Democratic Republic of the Congo, Equatorial Guinea, Gabon, Republic of Congo; **East Africa:** Burundi, Djibouti, Eritrea, Ethiopia, Kenya, Rwanda, Seychelles, Somalia, South Sudan, Sudan, Tanzania, Uganda; **Southern Africa:** Angola, Botswana, Lesotho, Madagascar, Malawi, Mozambique, Namibia, South Africa, Zambia, Zimbabwe; **West Africa:** Benin, Burkina Faso, Cameroon, Cape Verde, Chad, Côte d'Ivoire, Gambia, Ghana, Guinea, Guinea-Bissau, Liberia, Mali, Niger, Nigeria, Senegal, Sierra Leone, Togo

in 2018. At the same time, the share of goods and services (including equipment-maintenance costs) was at 25.9% in 2016, and was projected to increase to 26.9% over the same time period, with the share dedicated to capital assets (which includes machinery, equipment and 'specialised military assets') moving from 0.6% to 0.9%. The lack of available funds for equipment procurement stalled several projects, in particular for the navy. The acquisition plan for six patrol vessels (Project *Biro*) was postponed from 2018 to 2024. In the coming years, the army is set to receive the majority of the funding, up to almost 35% of total expenditure in 2018, versus 14.3% for the air force and 8.7% for the navy (see Table 15). These continuing funding challenges contrast to the operational commitments undertaken by the defence forces, which have included in recent years combat missions in the Central African Republic and as part of the UN's Force Intervention Brigade in the MONUSCO mission in the Democratic Republic of the Congo, as well as missions closer to home, such as in the Mozambique Channel. But these tasks have seldom been accompanied by higher funding allocations. At the same time, reports of readiness challenges persist, notably in the air force, where questions continue over aircraft – and aircrew – availability.

Nigeria's armed forces also face budget pressures, with 0.42% of the country's GDP spent on defence

Table 15 **South Africa's defence budget by service**

	2015	2016	2017	2018
Landward defence	33.21%	33.18%	34.54%	34.92%
Air defence	15.81%	14.59%	13.53%	14.27%
Maritime defence	8.34%	9.23%	9.35%	8.73%

Source: South Africa National Treasury, Estimates of National Expenditure 2016, 24 February 2016

in 2016 – a slight increase compared with 0.39% in 2015. In the 2016 budget, 33.5% of the funding was earmarked for the army, 19.3% for the navy and 20.5% for the air force. The 2016 budget laid out some capability increases for the air force, including projected acquisitions of ten *Super Mushshak* trainer aircraft (at 2.1 billion naira or US$8.1m) and three JF-17 *Thunder* combat aircraft from Pakistan (5bn naira or US$19.6m), and two Mi-35 attack helicopters from Russia (11.7bn naira or US$45.7m). It is possible that on delivery the JF-17s and Mi-35s may be directed to the fight against Boko Haram in the northern part of the country.

Conversely, countries not overly reliant on oil or other mineral resources for their budget revenues had greater capacity to increase defence spending. For example, Senegal's defence budget jumped by 18.7% in current US dollars, from US$215m in 2015 to US$256m in 2016. This was justified, at the time

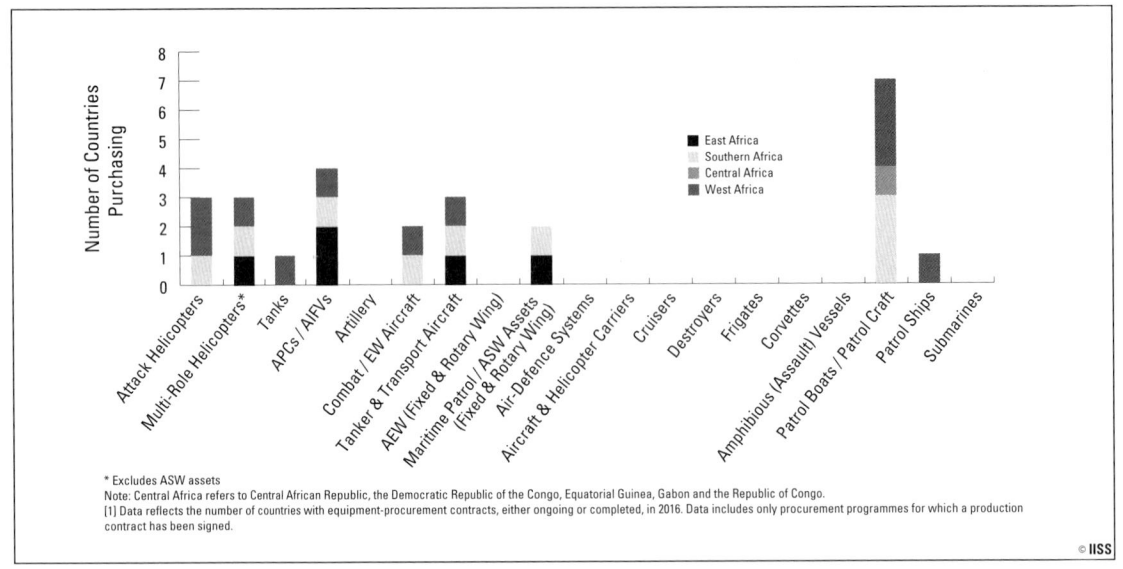

Figure 32 **Sub-Saharan Africa: selected ongoing or completed procurement priorities in 2016**[1]

the budget was approved, by terrorist activities in neighbouring countries, notably the November 2015 attack on the Radisson Blu hotel in Bamako, Mali. The budget increase was particularly directed towards the recruitment of additional police and military personnel. Similarly, Mali's budget rose by 17.4% in current US dollars, from US$467m in 2015 to US$549m in 2016.

Procurement priorities across the continent included patrol boats and patrol craft, with ongoing procurement in seven states (see Figure 32).

For example, Angola signed a contract in early 2016 for two fast attack craft from Leonardo (formerly Finmeccanica) to bolster its capability to defend its territorial waters. Although Gabon bought one P400-class patrol vessel and one offshore-patrol vessel (OPV) from France in 2014, it appeared that there had been no deliveries by the end of 2016. Senegal also purchased an OPV 190 Mk II from French company OCEA in 2014. The ship was launched in summer 2016 and was en route to Senegal at the time of writing. In 2016, Mauritius took delivery of patrol craft and fast interceptor boats for its coastguard from India's Goa Shipyard Ltd; India is the main supplier of military equipment to Mauritius. Nigeria is also locally building 30 gunboats at the Nigerian naval dockyard and one 38-metre patrol vessel, the second vessel in the Seaward Defence project. The Nigerian Navy also received a second Chinese P18N OPV, the first having been delivered in 2015. The procurement of patrol ships should strengthen sub-Saharan African states' anti-piracy and anti-smuggling capacities, the security of commercial ports, and help in the fight against illegal fishing.

Attack helicopters and multi-role/transport helicopters were another priority in sub-Saharan Africa (see above). Nigeria announced its intention to deploy H135 and AS365 *Dauphin* helicopters (acquired from the Nigerian National Petroleum Corporation) for intelligence and surveillance missions in the north of the country. This came on top of the provision of funds in the 2016 budget for the procurement of Russian Mi-35 helicopters. Nigeria established a helicopter-maintenance centre in 2016, in an attempt to localise the maintenance, repair and operations of its military-helicopter fleet. Angola signed a contract in late 2015 for the procurement of six AW109E helicopters from Leonardo for a reported €90m (US$100m). Angola had previously purchased four Mi-171Sh transport helicopters from Russian Helicopters.

ERITREA

Defence policy

The development of Eritrea's national-security policy is driven by three principal factors. Firstly, and probably the most important to policymakers, is simply the survival of the regime in Asmara and of its head, President Isaias Afewerki. Secondly, there is the need to counter what is presumed to be at least a partially existential threat from Ethiopia, not least given the strong call in some parts of Ethiopian society for the return to Ethiopia of the port city of Assab, as well as Eritrea's Southern Red Sea region (formerly Aseb province). Thirdly, there is the desire to be a major regional player, as befits Eritrea's important strategic position on the Red Sea and as one of the two states controlling the Bab-el-Mandeb Strait (Yemen is the other). These factors result in a policy that can seem at first to be ad hoc: since its independence in 1991, Eritrea has fought with all of its neighbours and has been linked with military activity as far away as the DRC and South Sudan.

In order to address the first and second priorities, the Eritrean regime maintains the image of an external threat (i.e., Ethiopia) and uses that to influence the population through universal conscription and into open-ended national service. The third priority, to be recognised as a major regional player, has resulted in pragmatic engagement with and against neighbouring and regional countries. Eritrea joined the Libyan-initiated Community of Sahel-Saharan States in April 1999 and has made efforts to develop and/or strengthen its ties with the Arab world. For example, it was granted observer status to the Arab League in 2003. Eritrea's strategic position at the mouth of the Red Sea has meant a strong security relationship with Egypt – for whom free transit through the Red Sea is essential to the Suez Canal's continued viability as a commercial shipping route. Having supported the Houthi rebels in Yemen for many years by training them at Assab – with some alleged involvement of Iranian trainers, money and equipment – the strategic opportunity was taken in early 2015 to support the Saudi-led *Operation Decisive Storm* against the Houthis by offering air- and sea-port facilities at Assab to forces from Saudi Arabia and the United Arab Emirates. In return for a 30-year lease of the deep-water port at Assab and the nearby hard-surfaced airfield, the Gulf states agreed to provide financial aid (the precise amount is unknown) to Eritrea and to modernise Asmara International Airport, as well as build new infrastructure and provide oil products. Furthermore, Yemeni anti-Houthi forces are reportedly being trained and equipped by the UAE armed forces at Assab, while rumours persist of Israeli electronic listening posts in the Dahlak archipelago and on Mount Amba Soira to the south of Asmara.

The Eritrean military strategy to counter the perceived Ethiopian threat has remained the same for many years and reportedly follows a four-pronged strategy in response to this 'frozen conflict': firstly, to strengthen Assab against any Ethiopian attempt to seize the port and surrounding territory in order to regain access to the sea; secondly, to strengthen the area to the south of Asmara in order to deny the Ethiopian armed forces fast access to the capital and seat of government; thirdly, to leave the western border between Badme and the border with Sudan weakly defended, on the assumption that the Ethiopian forces will become bogged down and unable to reach Asmara; and fourthly, to support any Ethiopian armed opposition groups. To this end the UN panel assesses Eritrea as extending support to groups such as Ginbot 7 and the Tigray People's Democratic Movement (TPDM), with support alleged for others including the Benishangul People's Liberation Movement, the Ethiopian People's Patriotic Front, the Oromo Liberation Front and the Ogaden National Liberation Front. In the past, Eritrean support was also given to al-Shabaab in Somalia as a proxy means of engaging Ethiopian forces, although the UN Somalia and Eritrea Monitoring Group (SEMG) stated in 2016 that it can find 'no compelling evidence that Eritrea was providing support to al-Shabaab'.

The activities of the Ethiopian opposition sometimes result in retaliatory 'proportionate' attacks on Eritrea (three in 2016, in the nine months to September). In these retaliatory operations, Ethiopia's forces appear to be able to gain local superiority and, having done so, to operate at will at distances of up to 25 kilometres inside Eritrea for limited periods. The lack of any Eritrean response to Ethiopian artillery strikes in 2015 and 2016 may be a sign of Asmara's need to conserve scarce stocks of useable artillery ammunition.

Armed forces

The Eritrean armed forces are manned by conscripts and there is only a small regular cadre of troops. National service begins in the last year of schooling through the 'maetot' national campaign, before formal entry into military service. Through this system all schoolchildren spend some time working on projects such as road drainage, farm terracing and reforestation. All pupils then spend the last year of school at the Sawa military training centre close to the Sudanese border. During this time they complete their education, including the national competition for university places, and undergo six months of basic military training. The official Eritrean government position on national service is that 'its sole objective is to cultivate capable, hard-working and alert individuals'. Those selected to join active units of the army, navy or air force are then sent on specialist training courses at a number of centres around the country before joining their units (see map 14).

National service is notionally 18 months in duration and is universal for all Eritreans between the ages of 18 and 40. However, in reality, once in the national-service system, it is difficult to leave. For many of those who remain in service, refresher courses take place at Kiloma camp near Assab. A commitment made by the government in 2014 to restrict national service to 18 months has never been fulfilled. Not all national-service obligations are carried out in the armed forces; many national-service personnel take a second job in order to bring in additional funds. Recently, those in the 40–65 age range have been called up as reservists and armed, in order to form local security militias across the country under the army's intelligence command structure.

Many of those migrating from Eritrea quote the lack of choice in the country, and in particular national service, as their main reason for leaving. A steady trickle of Eritrean soldiers cross the border into Ethiopia, entering Eritrean refugee camps – at its peak, more than a battalion's worth of soldiers were arriving in Ethiopia every month. The preferential 'out of camp policy' for Eritrean refugees in Ethiopia, which allows refugees to continue schooling and in some cases to attend Ethiopian universities, is a positive incentive for desertion from the Eritrean armed forces. Morale amongst the majority, but by no means all, of the Eritrean conscripts is said to be very low. Ethiopian sources have quoted that in a recent strike into Eritrea the Ethiopians withdrew when

Map 14 **Eritrean armed forces: military zones and basing**

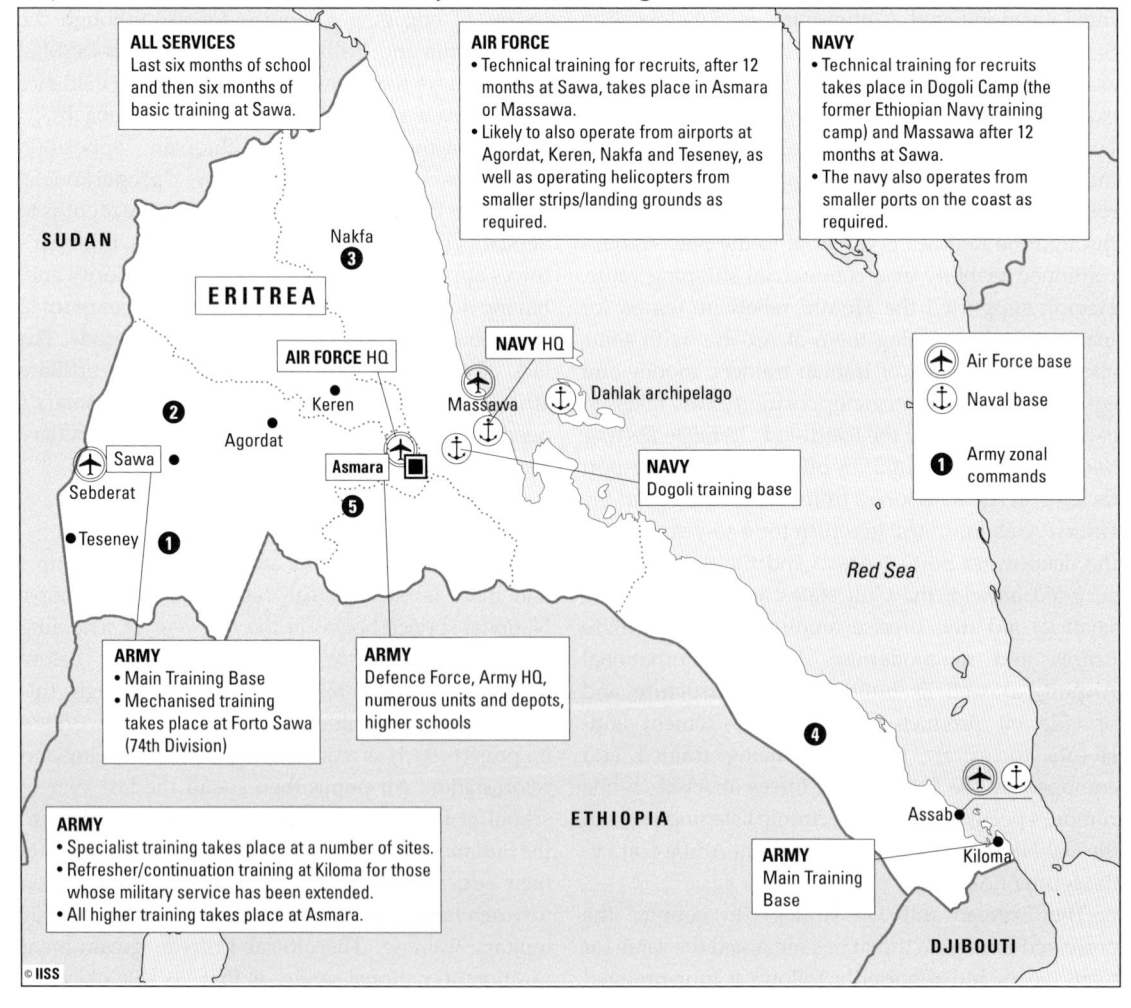

ALL SERVICES
Last six months of school and then six months of basic training at Sawa.

AIR FORCE
- Technical training for recruits, after 12 months at Sawa, takes place in Asmara or Massawa.
- Likely to also operate from airports at Agordat, Keren, Nakfa and Teseney, as well as operating helicopters from smaller strips/landing grounds as required.

NAVY
- Technical training for recruits takes place in Dogoli Camp (the former Ethiopian Navy training camp) and Massawa after 12 months at Sawa.
- The navy also operates from smaller ports on the coast as required.

ARMY
- Main Training Base
- Mechanised training takes place at Forto Sawa (74th Division)

ARMY
Defence Force, Army HQ, numerous units and depots, higher schools

ARMY
- Specialist training takes place at a number of sites.
- Refresher/continuation training at Kiloma for those whose military service has been extended.
- All higher training takes place at Asmara.

ARMY
Main Training Base

NAVY
Dogoli training base

© IISS

it was clear that Asmara was sending half-trained recruits against them.

The size of the Eritrean armed forces is difficult to gauge. Figures of a standing army of 250,000 have been quoted but are probably too high; *The Military Balance* estimates the forces' personnel strength at around 200,000. It seems likely that many units are cadreised and reliant upon national-service personnel to fill the ranks when required. This is more likely to be the case in the army than in the smaller navy and air force – the predominance of more technical equipment in these services (and their smaller personnel strength) might help Asmara exert more choice over recruits, while the incentives to stay may accordingly be higher. Of the army's five zonal/corps commands, those facing the Ethiopian border (1 and 4) and the one with responsibility for Asmara (5) are likely to have the majority of the effective equipment and the best personnel. Given the size of the available national-service force and the limited amount of heavy equipment (various assessments quote fewer than 150 tanks and 150 artillery pieces as operational, though actual holdings are reportedly slightly higher), units are likely to be infantry-heavy and only well supported by indirect fire on the border with Ethiopia. The ability of the Eritrean forces to respond to any attack with mobile reserves is also likely to be very limited. There are unconfirmed reports of up to 400 Eritrean soldiers operating in Yemen within the UAE contingent. If this is the case, they are likely to be drawn from the most capable forces, probably the commandos. Reports emerged that a coup attempt had taken place in Asmara in January 2013. Since then, other reporting has indicated that Isaias has been using the TPDM, a Tigrayan/Ethiopian armed opposition group, as a security force in Asmara and as an attempt to forestall any further coup attempts. If this is indeed the case, the defection in September 2015 of a large contingent of several hundred TPDM fighters back to Ethiopia, in a move coordinated by Ethiopian intelligence services and apparently with Sudanese assistance, will likely have had an impact on Eritrea's security system.

Defence economics and industry

Although no official budget figures have been released for several years, Eritrea's economy is estimated by the IMF to have taken significant strides since the negative growth that followed the 1998–2000 war with Ethiopia. GDP was estimated by the IMF at US$5.4bn in 2016 and growth has been steady, at between 3% and 5%; this trajectory is expected to hold. However, minerals, in particular the Bisha goldmine operated by Nevsun – which contributed about US$800m to the economy between 2011 and 2016 – accounts for a disproportionate percentage of GDP while generating few jobs, as does the service sector (estimated at 55%). Meanwhile, agriculture employs about 80% of the working population but accounts for only 12% of GDP.

Remittances from the Eritrean diaspora account for a large, but declining, component of GDP. In 2005 these remittances were estimated at 30% of GDP. According to some sources the fall is caused by diaspora money now being spent on helping people to leave Eritrea rather than helping them to live in the country. An additional important element of foreign currency flowing into the country is a compulsory 'diaspora tax' of 2% on the foreign income of non-resident citizens. This is reported to be enforced by denial of passports, denial of entry or exit, confiscation of assets in Eritrea and harassment of relatives in the country.

In late 2015 a new nakfa, Eritrea's currency, was introduced at an exchange rate of one-for-one, in a bid to control smuggling, the black-market economy and human trafficking. The effect on the local economy was to inflate prices and to reduce savings, while also reducing the black-market exchange rate from nearly 60 nakfa to the dollar to 18–20 nakfa to the dollar. Perhaps reflecting the increase in prices caused by the new nakfa, the government has said that it will raise the pay of national-service conscripts from the current US$50 per month to between US$130 and US$300 per month, although the timescale for this is unclear. Defence-budget figures are not published but the last figures, given in 2003, showed defence expenditure at 20.9% of GDP. It is likely that defence expenditure remains high, given the compulsory national service for all 18–40-year-olds and the still-unresolved border conflict with Ethiopia, which requires the maintenance of a high-readiness force on the border. Experts believe that defence expenditure is probably still over 10% of GDP, though the lack of data makes it difficult to be definitive. Should the promised rise in national-service pay materialise, this is likely to push defence expenditure even higher. It is unclear how much the Saudi-led coalition in Yemen is paying for the use of Assab by its forces. This could be a considerable sum and is likely to be allocated to defence rather than other segments of domestic spending. Other aspects of Saudi and UAE forces' basing at Assab, such as the refurbishment of port and airfield facilities, may release parts of the defence budget for other military uses. What industrial infrastructure there was in Eritrea during the Derg regime (Ethiopia's military leadership of 1974–91) was largely dismantled and re-established before 1991 in what is now Ethiopia. The consequent lack of a heavy industrial base means that there is no capacity for armaments production in Eritrea and only limited capacity for repair and maintenance. Under the Derg regime's '40,000 program' of defence capacity-building (all projects had a number in the 40,000s), a medium-repair facility was established in Asmara as Project 40720. This facility is thought to still be in use and to have been expanded to form the main maintenance facility for the Eritrean armed forces. Before Eritrea's independence, the Ethiopian Air Force established a maintenance facility at Asmara airport capable of handling jet-fighter aircraft. Although this was less capable than the Dejen Aircraft Engineering Establishment at Debre Zeit in Ethiopia, it is also assumed to have become the principal repair and maintenance facility of the Eritrean Air Force. Until 2010, the Eritrean Air Force had a number of Russian and Belarussian technicians at Asmara under a servicing contract with a Russian parastatal company. This is assumed to have stopped following the imposition of UN Security Council Resolution (UNSCR) 1907 (2009), which imposed an arms embargo and asset freezes on Eritrea following its activities in Somalia and Djibouti. The Ethiopian Navy's repair facilities at Massawa and Assab were entirely inherited by the Eritrean Navy on independence, as were some of their vessels. There was evidence of improvements to the small boat-repair facilities at Assab as reported in 2010.

Key priorities for Eritrea's limited defence maintenance and repair capacity are likely to include the maintenance of essential equipment for the defence of the land border (small arms, tanks and artillery, including anti-aircraft artillery and missiles) and of the air force's capacity to deny Eritrean airspace to the Ethiopian Air Force (fighters and anti-aircraft systems). The increasing challenges to the security of the Red Sea and Bab-el-Mandeb Strait caused by the war in Yemen are likely to have raised the priority for operational ships, boats and naval command-and-control systems. The lack of a local defence industry means that Eritrea is wholly dependent on imports for new stocks of vehicles, weapons, aircraft, ammunition and ships. The UN SEMG has published evidence of the purchase and delivery of armaments from eastern Sudan, both by land from Kassala to Tesenay in southwestern Eritrea and by ship from Port Sudan to Massawa on the northern coast. These movements are in contravention of UNSCR 1907 (2009) and are reportedly coordinated by the Eritrean-government-owned Red Sea Corporation. It is also alleged that Iran, Israel and Saudi Arabia have provided defence equipment in the past. This unusual grouping reflects the changing alliances formed by Isaias, while he looks to maintain an overall consistent security policy.

Angola ANG

New Angolan Kwanza AOA		2015	2016	2017
GDP	AOA	12.3tr	16.1tr	
	US$	103bn	91.9bn	
per capita	US$	3,876	3,360	
Growth	%	3.0	0	
Inflation	%	10.3	33.7	
Def bdgt	AOA	531bn	486bn	
	US$	4.44bn	2.78bn	
USD1=AOA		119.67	174.88	

Population 20,172,332

Ethnic groups: Ovimbundu 37%; Kimbundu 25%; Bakongo 13%

Age	0–14	15–19	20–24	25–29	30–64	65 plus
Male	21.8%	5.8%	4.8%	3.8%	13.0%	1.4%
Female	21.0%	5.5%	4.6%	3.7%	13.0%	1.6%

Capabilities

The armed forces' role is to ensure sovereignty and territorial integrity, although maritime security and the protection of offshore resources will also rank highly. The principal security concern comes from secessionists in the Cabinda enclave; there was a surge of violent acts in late 2016. Angola chaired the African Capacity for Immediate Response to Crises (ACIRC) in the final quarter of 2016. Force health and education have been investment priorities. Improving the military's logistics system was identified as a key requirement several years ago. However, it is not clear that many improvements have been made. The armed forces train regularly and in the past year have participated in multinational exercises with the US and others, including *Obangame/Saharan Express 2016*. Angola also participated in the Military Games 2016 in Russia and Kazakhstan and *Utulivu Africa* II with the ACIRC. On paper the army and air force constitute a significant force, but equipment availability and serviceability remain questionable; nonetheless, Angola is the only state in the region with strategic-airlift capacity in the form of Il-76s. There are plans to modernise equipment, particularly maritime-security capability in light of security concerns in the Gulf of Guinea, but these ambitions have been hit by the fall in the oil price, which led negotiations with Brazil regarding patrol-boat acquisitions to stall.

ACTIVE 107,000 (Army 100,000 Navy 1,000 Air 6,000) Paramilitary 10,000

ORGANISATIONS BY SERVICE

Army 100,000

FORCES BY ROLE
MANOEUVRE
  Armoured
    1 tk bde
  Light
    1 SF bde
    1 (1st) div (1 mot inf bde, 2 inf bde)
    1 (2nd) div (3 mot inf bde, 3 inf bde, 1 arty regt)
    1 (3rd) div (2 mot inf bde, 3 inf bde)
    1 (4th) div (1 tk regt, 5 mot inf bde, 2 inf bde, 1 engr bde)
    1 (5th) div (2 inf bde)
    1 (6th) div (3 inf bde, 1 engr bde)
COMBAT SUPPORT
  Some engr units
COMBAT SERVICE SUPPORT
  Some log units

EQUIPMENT BY TYPE†
ARMOURED FIGHTING VEHICLES
  MBT 300: ε200 T-54/T-55; 50 T-62; 50 T-72
  LT TK 10 PT-76
  RECCE 600 BRDM-2
  IFV 250 BMP-1/BMP-2
  APC 178
    APC (T) 8 MT-LB
    APC (W) ε170 BTR-152/BTR-60/BTR-80
  ABCV BMD-3
ENGINEERING & MAINTENANCE VEHICLES
  ARV T-54/T-55
  MW *Bozena*
ARTILLERY 1,408+
  SP 16+: **122mm** 2S1 *Gvozdika*; **152mm** 4 2S3 *Akatsiya*; **203mm** 12 2S7 *Pion*
  TOWED 552: **122mm** 500 D-30; **130mm** 48 M-46; **152mm** 4 D-20
  MRL 90+: **122mm** 90: 50 BM-21 *Grad*; 40 RM-70; **240mm** BM-24
  MOR 750: **82mm** 250; **120mm** 500
ANTI-TANK/ANTI-INFRASTRUCTURE
  MSL • MANPATS 9K11 (AT-3 *Sagger*)
  RCL 500: 400 **82mm** B-10/**107mm** B-11†; **106mm** 100†
  GUNS • SP 100mm SU-100†
AIR DEFENCE
  SAM • Point-defence 9K32 *Strela*-2 (SA-7 *Grail*)‡; 9K36 *Strela*-3 (SA-14 *Gremlin*); 9K310 *Igla*-1 (SA-16 *Gimlet*)
  GUNS • TOWED 450+: **14.5mm** ZPU-4; **23mm** ZU-23-2; **37mm** M-1939; **57mm** S-60

Navy ε1,000

EQUIPMENT BY TYPE
PATROL AND COASTAL COMBATANTS 22
  PCO 2 *Ngola Kiluange* with 1 hel landing platform (Ministry of Fisheries)
  PCC 5 *Rei Bula Matadi* (Ministry of Fisheries)
  PBF 5 PVC-170
  PB 10: 4 *Mandume*; 5 *Comandante Imperial Santana* (Ministry of Fisheries); 1 Damen 2810 (Ministry of Fisheries)

Coastal Defence

EQUIPMENT BY TYPE
COASTAL DEFENCE • AShM 4K44 *Utyos* (SS-C-1B *Sepal* – at Luanda)

Air Force/Air Defence 6,000

FORCES BY ROLE
FIGHTER
  1 sqn with MiG-21bis/MF *Fishbed*
  1 sqn with Su-27/Su-27UB *Flanker*
FIGHTER/GROUND ATTACK
  1 sqn with MiG-23BN/ML/UB *Flogger*
  1 sqn with Su-22 *Fitter* D
  1 sqn with Su-25 *Frogfoot*
MARITIME PATROL
  1 sqn with F-27-200 MPA; C-212 *Aviocar*
TRANSPORT
  3 sqn with An-12 *Cub*; An-26 *Curl*; An-32 *Cline*; An-72 *Coaler*; BN-2A *Islander*; C-212 *Aviocar*; Do-28D *Skyservant*; EMB-135BJ *Legacy* 600 (VIP); Il-76TD *Candid*
TRAINING
  1 sqn with Cessna 172K/R
  1 sqn with EMB-312 *Tucano*
  1 sqn with L-29 *Delfin*; L-39 *Albatros*
  1 sqn with PC-7 *Turbo Trainer*; PC-9*
  1 sqn with Z-142
ATTACK HELICOPTER
  2 sqn with Mi-24/Mi-35 *Hind*; SA342M *Gazelle* (with HOT)
TRANSPORT HELICOPTER
  2 sqn with AS565; SA316 *Alouette* III (IAR-316) (trg)
  1 sqn with Bell 212
  1 sqn with Mi-8 *Hip*; Mi-17 *Hip* H
  1 sqn with Mi-171sH
AIR DEFENCE
  5 bn/10 bty with S-125 *Pechora* (SA-3 *Goa*); 9K35 *Strela*-10 (SA-13 *Gopher*)†; 2K12 *Kub* (SA-6 *Gainful*); 9K33 *Osa* (SA-8 *Gecko*); 9K31 *Strela*-1 (SA-9 *Gaskin*); S-75M *Volkhov* (SA-2 *Guideline*)

EQUIPMENT BY TYPE†
AIRCRAFT 86 combat capable
  FTR 24: 6 Su-27/Su-27UB *Flanker*; 18 MiG-23ML *Flogger*
  FGA 42+: 20 MiG-21bis/MF *Fishbed*; 8 MiG-23BN/UB *Flogger*; 13 Su-22 *Fitter* D; 1+ Su-24 *Fencer*
  ATK 10: 8 Su-25 *Frogfoot*; 2 Su-25UB *Frogfoot*
  ELINT 1 B-707
  TPT 56: **Heavy** 4 Il-76TD *Candid*; **Medium** 6 An-12 *Cub*; **Light** 46: 12 An-26 *Curl*; 2 An-32 *Cline*; 8 An-72 *Coaler*; 8 BN-2A *Islander*; 2 C-212; 5 Cessna 172K; 6 Cessna 172R; 1 Do-28D *Skyservant*; 1 EMB-135BJ *Legacy* 600 (VIP); 1 Yak-40
  TRG 42: 13 EMB-312 *Tucano*; 6 EMB-314 *Super Tucano**; 6 L-29 *Delfin*; 2 L-39C *Albatros*; 5 PC-7 *Turbo Trainer*; 4 PC-9*; 6 Z-142
HELICOPTERS
  ATK 44: 22 Mi-24 *Hind*; 22 Mi-35 *Hind*
  MRH 25: 8 AS565 *Panther*; 9 SA316 *Alouette* III (IAR-316) (incl trg); 8 SA342M *Gazelle*
  MRH/TPT 35: 27 Mi-8 *Hip*/Mi-17 *Hip* H; 8 Mi-171Sh *Terminator*
  TPT • **Light** 8 Bell 212
AIR DEFENCE • **SAM** 122
  Medium-range 40 S-75M *Volkhov* (SA-2 *Guideline*)‡
  Short-range 37: 25 2K12 *Kub* (SA-6 *Gainful*); 12 S-125 *Pechora* (SA-3 *Goa*)

Point-defence 45: 10 9K35 *Strela*-10 (SA-13 *Gopher*)†; 15 9K33 *Osa* (SA-8 *Gecko*); 20 9K31 *Strela*-1 (SA-9 *Gaskin*)
AIR-LAUNCHED MISSILES
  AAM • **IR** R-3 (AA-2 *Atoll*)‡; R-60 (AA-8 *Aphid*); R-73 (AA-11 *Archer*); **IR/SARH** R-23/24 (AA-7 *Apex*)‡; R-27 (AA-10 *Alamo*)
  ASM AT-2 *Swatter*; HOT
  ARM Kh-28 (AS-9 *Kyle*)

Paramilitary 10,000

Rapid-Reaction Police 10,000

Benin BEN

CFA Franc BCEAO fr		2015	2016	2017
GDP	fr	5.01tr	5.26tr	
	US$	8.48bn	8.93bn	
per capita	US$	780	803	
Growth	%	5.0	4.6	
Inflation	%	0.3	0.6	
Def bdgt	fr	53.8bn	58.2bn	
	US$	91m	99m	
US$1=fr		591.17	589.42	

Population   10,741,458

Age	0–14	15–19	20–24	25–29	30–64	65 plus
Male	22.0%	5.6%	4.7%	3.9%	12.9%	1.1%
Female	21.1%	5.4%	4.6%	3.8%	13.2%	1.7%

Capabilities

The country's small armed forces mainly focus on border and internal security, as well as combating illicit trafficking. Benin has taken steps to increase border patrols and security in line with increased concern over the threat from Boko Haram and al-Qaeda in the Islamic Maghreb. Maritime security is a priority in light of continuing piracy in the Gulf of Guinea. Benin's small navy has been trying to bolster its anti-piracy capability by acquiring further high-speed craft, with assistance from the US. The air force has a limited number of light transport aircraft and helicopters for intra-theatre airlift, and is also developing a surveillance role. The army and national police have received training from the US to boost border-surveillance capacity, while French forces based out of Senegal are also heavily involved in similar assistance; in 2016 this included parachute and artillery training (on mortars). In March 2016, it was announced that Benin would deploy 150 troops with the Nigerian-led Multi-National Joint Task Force fighting Boko Haram. Benin earlier, in 2013, deployed troops to Mali. 2016 saw the government propose a second pre-deployment training centre at Cana air base, in addition to the centre at Bembereke Military Training Centre.

ACTIVE 7,250 (Army 6,500 Navy 500 Air 250)
Paramilitary 2,500
Conscript liability 18 months (selective)

ORGANISATIONS BY SERVICE

Army 6,500
FORCES BY ROLE
MANOEUVRE
  Armoured
  2 armd sqn
  Light
  1 (rapid reaction) mot inf bn
  8 inf bn
  Air Manoeuvre
  1 AB bn
COMBAT SUPPORT
  2 arty bn
  1 engr bn
  1 sigs bn
COMBAT SERVICE SUPPORT
  1 log bn
  1 spt bn
EQUIPMENT BY TYPE
ARMOURED FIGHTING VEHICLES
  LT TK 18 PT-76†
  RECCE 34: 3 AML-90; 14 BRDM-2; 7 M8; 10 VBL
  APC 34
    APC (T) 22 M113
    PPV 12: 2 *Bastion* APC; 10 *Casspir* NG
ARTILLERY 16+
  TOWED 105mm 16: 12 L118 Light Gun; 4 M101
  MOR 81mm some; 120mm some

Navy ε500
EQUIPMENT BY TYPE
PATROL AND COASTAL COMBATANTS
  PB 5: 2 *Matelot Brice Kpomasse* (ex-PRC); 3 FPB 98

Air Force 250
EQUIPMENT BY TYPE
AIRCRAFT
  TPT 4: Light 1 DHC-6 *Twin Otter*†; PAX 3: 2 B-727; 1 HS-748†
  TRG 2 LH-10 *Ellipse*
HELICOPTERS
  TPT • Light 5: 4 AW109BA; 1 AS350B *Ecureuil*†

Paramilitary 2,500

Gendarmerie 2,500
FORCES BY ROLE
MANOEUVRE
  Other
  4 (mobile) paramilitary coy

DEPLOYMENT

CENTRAL AFRICAN REPUBLIC
UN • MINUSCA 75; 3 obs; 1 sigs coy

CHAD
Lake Chad Basin Commission • MNJTF 750

CÔTE D'IVOIRE
UN • UNOCI 4; 4 obs

DEMOCRATIC REPUBLIC OF THE CONGO
UN • MONUSCO 454; 6 obs; 1 inf bn(-)

LIBERIA
UN • UNMIL 1; 1 obs

MALI
UN • MINUSMA 257; 3 obs; 1 mech inf coy

SOUTH SUDAN
UN • UNMISS 2; 1 obs

SUDAN
UN • UNISFA 2 obs

Botswana BWA

Botswana Pula P		2015	2016	2017
GDP	P	146bn	138bn	
	US$	14.4bn	10.9bn	
per capita	US$	6,771	5,082	
Growth	%	-0.3	3.1	
Inflation	%	3.0	3.2	
Def bdgt [a]	P	4.09bn	6.11bn	
	US$	404m	486m	
US$1=P		10.11	12.59	

[a] Defence, justice and security budget

Population 2,209,208

Age	0–14	15–19	20–24	25–29	30–64	65 plus
Male	16.5%	5.4%	5.2%	5.0%	17.2%	1.7%
Female	15.9%	5.3%	5.4%	5.1%	15.0%	2.5%

Capabilities

Key tasks for the Botswana Defence Force (BDF) include ensuring territorial integrity, coupled with domestic tasks such as anti-poaching, and there is a history of involvement in peacekeeping operations. Botswana has a good relationship with the US and regularly sends its officers to train there. The new BDF commander, appointed in September 2016, identified a number of priorities, including improving conditions of service and capability. The BDF has been working on a doctrine that is believed to be heavily influenced by US concepts and practice. Local reports suggest that the BDF has a very limited capacity, if any, to maintain its armoured vehicles. Growing relations with Beijing have seen some military personnel travel to China for training. The operations centre for the SADC Standby Force is located in Gaborone. Botswana holds biannual exercises with Namibia; the most recent was in 2016 and practised joint peacekeeping missions and other support operations for the SADC.

ACTIVE 9,000 (Army 8,500 Air 500)

ORGANISATIONS BY SERVICE

Army 8,500
FORCES BY ROLE
MANOEUVRE
  Armoured
    1 armd bde(-)
  Light
    2 inf bde (1 armd recce regt, 4 inf bn, 1 cdo unit, 1 engr regt, 1 log bn, 2 ADA regt)
COMBAT SUPPORT
  1 arty bde
  1 engr coy
  1 sigs coy
COMBAT SERVICE SUPPORT
  1 log gp
AIR DEFENCE
  1 AD bde(-)
EQUIPMENT BY TYPE
ARMOURED FIGHTING VEHICLES
  LT TK 55: ε30 SK-105 *Kuerassier*; 25 FV101 *Scorpion*
  RECCE 72+: RAM-V-1; ε8 RAM-V-2; 64 VBL
  APC • APC (W) 150: 50 BTR-60; 50 LAV-150 *Commando* (some with 90mm gun); 50 MOWAG *Piranha* III
  AUV 6 FV103 *Spartan*
ENGINEERING & MAINTENANCE VEHICLES
  ARV *Greif*; M578
ANTI-TANK/ANTI-INFRASTRUCTURE
  MSL
    SP V-150 TOW
    MANPATS TOW
  RCL 84mm *Carl Gustav*
ARTILLERY 78
  TOWED 30: **105mm** 18: 12 L118 *Light Gun*; 6 Model 56 pack howitzer; **155mm** 12 Soltam
  MRL 122mm 20 APRA-40
  MOR 28: **81mm** 22; **120mm** 6 M-43
AIR DEFENCE
  SAM • Point-defence *Javelin*; 9K310 *Igla*-1 (SA-16 *Gimlet*); 9K32 *Strela*-2 (SA-7 *Grail*)‡
  GUNS • TOWED 20mm 7 M167 *Vulcan*

Air Wing 500
FORCES BY ROLE
FIGHTER/GROUND ATTACK
  1 sqn with F-5A *Freedom Fighter*; F-5D *Tiger* II
ISR
  1 sqn with O-2 *Skymaster*
TRANSPORT
  2 sqn with BD-700 *Global Express*; BN-2A/B *Defender**; Beech 200 *Super King Air* (VIP); C-130B *Hercules*; C-212-300 *Aviocar*; CN-235M-100; Do-328-110 (VIP)
TRAINING
  1 sqn with PC-7 MkII *Turbo Trainer**
TRANSPORT HELICOPTER
  1 sqn with AS350B *Ecureuil*; Bell 412EP/SP *Twin Huey*; EC225LP *Super Puma*
EQUIPMENT BY TYPE
AIRCRAFT 29 combat capable
  FTR 14: 9 F-5A *Freedom Fighter*; 5 F-5D *Tiger* II
  ISR 5 O-2 *Skymaster*
  TPT 20: **Medium** 3 C-130B *Hercules*; **Light** 16: 4 BN-2 *Defender**; 6 BN-2B *Defender**; 1 Beech 200 *King Air* (VIP); 2 C-212-300 *Aviocar*; 2 CN-235M-100; 1 Do-328-110 (VIP); **PAX** 1 BD700 *Global Express*
  TRG 5 PC-7 MkII *Turbo Trainer**
HELICOPTERS
  MRH 7: 2 Bell 412EP *Twin Huey*; 5 Bell 412SP *Twin Huey*
  TPT 9: **Medium** 1 EC225LP *Super Puma* **Light** 8 AS350B *Ecureuil*

Burkina Faso BFA

CFA Franc BCEAO fr		2015	2016	2017
GDP	fr	6.51tr	7.02tr	
	US$	11bn	12bn	
per capita	US$	615	652	
Growth	%	4.0	5.2	
Inflation	%	0.9	1.6	
Def bdgt	fr	87.5bn	88.6bn	
	US$	148m	152m	
US$1=fr		591.15	584.31	

Population 19,512,533

Age	0–14	15–19	20–24	25–29	30–64	65 plus
Male	22.6%	5.4%	4.6%	3.8%	12.4%	0.9%
Female	22.5%	5.4%	4.6%	3.8%	12.5%	1.5%

Capabilities

On 15 January 2016, a significant Islamist attack in Ouagadougou and an alleged coup attempt underscored the country's continuing security challenges. Following the Ouagadougou attacks, Burkina Faso has been collaborating with Malian and French security forces. President Kabore has stated that overhauling the army is a priority, in order to ensure that it is independent, apolitical and more effective, particularly in the counter-terrorism role. The armed forces have struggled with funding issues, which is reflected in the equipment inventory. Training and support for the armed forces and gendarmerie have been provided by the US and France, among others; furthermore, France has a significant military presence in the country to provide support. The army has deployed personnel on a range of UN peacekeeping operations, including in Mali. But in 2016 Burkina Faso announced the withdrawal of forces deployed to the UN mission in Darfur in order to help deal with domestic-security challenges.

ACTIVE 11,200 (Army 6,400 Air 600 Gendarmerie 4,200) **Paramilitary 250**

ORGANISATIONS BY SERVICE

Army 6,400

Three military regions. In 2011, several regiments were disbanded and merged into other formations, including the new 24th and 34th *régiments interarmes*

FORCES BY ROLE
MANOEUVRE
Mechanised
  1 cbd arms regt
Light
  1 cbd arms regt
  6 inf regt
Air Manoeuvre
  1 AB regt (1 CT coy)
COMBAT SUPPORT
  1 arty bn (2 arty tp)
  1 engr bn

EQUIPMENT BY TYPE
ARMOURED FIGHTING VEHICLES
  RECCE 91+: 19 AML-60/AML-90; 8+ *Bastion Patsas*; 24 EE-9 *Cascavel*; 30 *Ferret*; 2 M20; 8 M8
  APC 44+
    APC (W) 13+: 13 Panhard M3; Some *Bastion* APC
    PPV 31 *Puma* M26-15
ANTI-TANK/ANTI-INFRASTRUCTURE
  RCL 75mm Type-52 (M20); 84mm *Carl Gustav*
ARTILLERY 50+
  TOWED 14: 105mm 8 M101; 122mm 6
  MRL 9: 107mm ε4 Type-63; 122mm 5 APR-40
  MOR 27+: 81mm Brandt; 82mm 15; 120mm 12
AIR DEFENCE
  SAM • Point-defence 9K32 *Strela-2* (SA-7 *Grail*)‡
  GUNS • TOWED 42: 14.5mm 30 ZPU; 20mm 12 TCM-20

Air Force 600
FORCES BY ROLE
GROUND ATTACK/TRAINING
  1 sqn with SF-260WL *Warrior**; Embraer EMB-314 *Super Tucano**
TRANSPORT
  1 sqn with AT-802 *Air Tractor*; B-727 (VIP); Beech 200 *King Air*; CN-235-220; PA-34 *Seneca*
ATTACK/TRANSPORT HELICOPTER
  1 sqn with AS350 *Ecureuil*; Mi-8 *Hip*; Mi-17 *Hip* H; Mi-35 *Hind*

EQUIPMENT BY TYPE
AIRCRAFT 5 combat capable
  ISR 1 DA42M (reported)
  TPT 9: Light 8: 1 AT-802 *Air Tractor*; 2 Beech 200 *King Air*; 1 CN-235-220; 1 PA-34 *Seneca*; 3 *Tetras*; PAX 1 B-727 (VIP)
  TRG 5: 3 EMB-314 *Super Tucano**; 2 SF-260WL *Warrior**
HELICOPTERS
  ATK 2 Mi-35 *Hind*
  MRH 3: 2 Mi-17 *Hip* H; 1 AW139
  TPT 2: Medium 1 Mi-8 *Hip*; Light 1 AS350 *Ecureuil*

Gendarmerie 4,200

Paramilitary 250

People's Militia (R) 45,000 reservists (trained)

Security Company 250

DEPLOYMENT

CENTRAL AFRICAN REPUBLIC
UN • MINUSCA 4; 1 obs

DEMOCRATIC REPUBLIC OF THE CONGO
UN • MONUSCO 1; 7 obs

MALI
UN • MINUSMA 1,721; 2 inf bn

SUDAN
UN • UNAMID 804; 5 obs; 1 inf bn

FOREIGN FORCES
France Operation Barkhane 220; 1 SF gp

Burundi BDI

Burundi Franc fr		2015	2016	2017
GDP	fr	4.51tr	4.91tr	
	US$	2.87bn	2.74bn	
per capita	US$	304	284	
Growth	%	-4.0	-0.5	
Inflation	%	5.6	6.3	
Def bdgt	fr	100bn	109.9bn	
	US$	64m	61m	
US$1=fr		1,571.95	1,790.49	

Population 11,099,298

Ethnic groups: Hutu 85%; Tutsi 14%

Age	0–14	15–19	20–24	25–29	30–64	65 plus
Male	22.9%	5.2%	4.3%	3.8%	12.4%	1.1%
Female	22.7%	5.2%	4.4%	3.8%	12.7%	1.5%

Capabilities

Burindi's armed forces retain a limited capability to deploy externally, and maintain a deployment to the AMISOM mission in Somalia. In 2015, the cohesiveness of the armed forces and the wider security and intelligence machinery was tested by the attempted coup against incumbent President Nkurunziza in May. Previous military training activity with international partners largely stalled in 2015 as a result of this situation. Notwithstanding the effect of the coup attempt on the armed forces, they have benefited from this training support as well as from their recent deployments, including to the UN mission in the Central African Republic and to AMISOM, where they gained valuable combat experience and specialist military skills. However, EU concern over human-rights issues meant that Brussels reportedly routed payments for Burundi's AMISOM mission through the African Union, rather than Bujumbura, which prompted protests from the AU. Other foreign donors have curtailed or cut aid following the 2015 election result.

ACTIVE 30,000 (Army 30,000) **Paramilitary 21,000**

DDR efforts continue, while activities directed at professionalising the security forces have taken place, some sponsored by BNUB, the UN mission

ORGANISATIONS BY SERVICE

Army 30,000
FORCES BY ROLE
MANOEUVRE
  Mechanised
    2 lt armd bn (sqn)
  Light
    7 inf bn
    Some indep inf coy
COMBAT SUPPORT
  1 arty bn
  1 engr bn
AIR DEFENCE
  1 AD bn

Reserves
FORCES BY ROLE
MANOEUVRE
  Light
    10 inf bn (reported)
EQUIPMENT BY TYPE
ARMOURED FIGHTING VEHICLES
  RECCE 55: 6 AML-60; 12 AML-90; 30 BRDM-2; 7 S52 *Shorland*
  APC 82
    APC (W) 60: 20 BTR-40; 10 BTR-80; 9 Panhard M3; 15 Type-92; 6 *Walid*
    PPV 22: 12 RG-31 *Nyala*; 10 RG-33L
  AUV 15 *Cougar* 4×4
ARTILLERY 120
  TOWED 122mm 18 D-30
  MRL 122mm 12 BM-21 *Grad*
  MOR 90: 82mm 15 M-43; 120mm ε75
ANTI-TANK/ANTI-INFRASTRUCTURE
  MSL • MANPATS *Milan* (reported)
  RCL 75mm Type-52 (M20)
AIR DEFENCE
  SAM • Point-defence 9K32 *Strela-2 (SA-7 Grail)*‡
  GUNS • TOWED 150+: **14.5mm** 15 ZPU-4; 135+ **23mm** ZU-23/**37mm** Type-55 (M-1939)

Naval detachment 50
EQUIPMENT BY TYPE
AMPHIBIOUS • LCT 2
LOGISTICS AND SUPPORT • AG 2

Air Wing 200
EQUIPMENT BY TYPE
AIRCRAFT 1 combat capable
  TPT 4: **Light** 2 Cessna 150L†; **PAX** 2 DC-3
  TRG 1 SF-260W *Warrior**
HELICOPTERS
  ATK 2 Mi-24 *Hind*
  MRH 2 SA342L *Gazelle*
  TPT • **Medium** (2 Mi-8 *Hip* non-op)

Paramilitary ε21,000

General Administration of State Security ε1,000

Imbonerakure ε20,000

DEPLOYMENT

CENTRAL AFRICAN REPUBLIC
UN • MINUSCA 826; 8 obs; 1 inf bn

SOMALIA
AU • AMISOM 5,432; 6 inf bn

SUDAN
UN • UNAMID 3; 5 obs
UN • UNISFA 1 obs

Cameroon CMR

CFA Franc BEAC fr		2015	2016	2017
GDP	fr	16.9tr	18tr	
	US$	28.5bn	30.9bn	
per capita	US$	1,235	1,303	
Growth	%	5.8	4.8	
Inflation	%	2.8	2.2	
Def bdgt	fr	209bn	230bn	
	US$	354m	393m	
US$1=fr		591.16	584.32	

Population 24,360,803

Age	0–14	15–19	20–24	25–29	30–64	65 plus
Male	21.5%	5.2%	4.6%	4.1%	13.3%	1.5%
Female	21.1%	5.2%	4.5%	4.0%	13.3%	1.7%

Capabilities

Although internal stability was long a focus for Cameroon's armed forces, the threat from Boko Haram has generated a significant defence response from Cameroon, particularly where Boko Haram is active, in the northern area of the country bordering Nigeria. Significant elements of Cameroon's equipment inventory are ageing, but infantry fighting vehicles and other armour were in recent years acquired from China and South Africa. Improving ISR capability is a priority that the government is hoping to address by buying from the US a Cessna C-208B *Caravan* aircraft, as well as UAV systems. The US, France and others continue to provide support and training for the armed forces and gendarmerie. In 2016, French forces conducted counter-IED and mine-clearance training in the north of the country. A US Marine detachment conducted small-unit training in 2016. The US has also trained naval personnel from Cameroon as part of the Africa Maritime Law Enforcement Partnership, designed to build maritime-security capacity. The army has contributed personnel to UN peacekeeping operations and Cameroon announced a further 750 troops for peacekeeping operations in the Central African Republic in July 2016. However, the ability to conduct active security and combat operations on domestic territory will likely require further training and capability-development assistance.

ACTIVE 14,400 (Army 12,500 Navy 1,500 Air 400)
Paramilitary 9,000

ORGANISATIONS BY SERVICE

Army 12,500
3 Mil Regions
FORCES BY ROLE
MANOEUVRE
  Light
  1 rapid reaction bde (1 armd recce bn, 1 AB bn, 1 amph bn)
  3 mot inf bde (3 mot inf bn, 1 spt bn)
  1 mot inf bde (2 mot inf bn, 1 spt bn)
  3 (rapid reaction) inf bn
  Air Manoeuvre
  1 cdo/AB bn
  Other
  1 (Presidential Guard) gd bn
COMBAT SUPPORT
  1 arty regt (5 arty bty)
  3 engr regt
AIR DEFENCE
  1 AD regt (6 AD bty)
EQUIPMENT BY TYPE
ARMOURED FIGHTING VEHICLES
  ASLT 18: 6 AMX-10RC; ε12 PTL-02 mod (Cara 105)
  RECCE 64: 31 AML-90; 15 *Ferret*; 8 M8; 5 RAM Mk3; 5 VBL
  IFV 42: 8 LAV-150 *Commando* with 20mm gun; 14 LAV-150 *Commando* with 90mm gun; 12 *Ratel*-20 (Engr); ε8 Type-07P
  APC 33
    APC (T) 12 M3 half-track
    APC (W) 21 LAV-150 *Commando*
  AUV 6 *Cougar* 4×4
ENGINEERING & MAINTENANCE VEHICLES
  ARV WZ-551 ARV
ANTI-TANK/ANTI-INFRASTRUCTURE
  MSL
    SP 24 TOW (on Jeeps)
    MANPATS *Milan*
  RCL 53: **75mm** 13 Type-52 (M20); **106mm** 40 M40A2
ARTILLERY 106+
  SP 155mm 18 ATMOS 2000
  TOWED 52: **105mm** 20 M101; **130mm** 24: 12 M-1982 (reported); 12 Type-59 (M-46); **155mm** 8 M-71
  MRL 122mm 20 BM-21 *Grad*
  MOR 16+: **81mm** (some SP); **120mm** 16 Brandt
AIR DEFENCE • GUNS
  SP 20mm RBY-1 with TCM-20
  TOWED 54: **14.5mm** 18 Type-58 (ZPU-2); **35mm** 18 GDF-002; **37mm** 18 Type-63

Navy ε1,500
HQ located at Douala
EQUIPMENT BY TYPE
PATROL AND COASTAL COMBATANTS 17
  PCC 4: 1 *Bakassi* (FRA P-48); 1 *Dipikar* (ex-FRA *Flamant*); 2 Polytechnologies 60m with 1 76mm gun
  PB 11: 2 Aresa 2400; 2 Aresa 3200; 2 Rodman 101; 4 Rodman 46; 1 *Quartier Maître Alfred Motto*
  PBR 2 *Swift*-38
AMPHIBIOUS • LANDING CRAFT 2
  LCM 1 Aresa 2300
  LCU 2 *Yunnan*

Fusiliers Marin
FORCES BY ROLE
MANOEUVRE
  Amphibious
  3 mne bn

Air Force 300–400
FORCES BY ROLE
FIGHTER/GROUND ATTACK
  1 sqn with MB-326K; *Alpha Jet*†
TRANSPORT
  1 sqn with C-130H/H-30 *Hercules*; DHC-4 *Caribou*; DHC-5D *Buffalo*; IAI-201 *Arava*; PA-23 *Aztec*
  1 VIP unit with AS332 *Super Puma*; AS365 *Dauphin* 2; Bell 206B *Jet Ranger*; Gulfstream III
TRAINING
  1 unit with *Tetras*
ATTACK HELICOPTER
  1 sqn with SA342 *Gazelle* (with HOT); Mi-24 *Hind*
TRANSPORT HELICOPTER
  1 sqn with Bell 206L-3; Bell 412; SA319 *Alouette* III
EQUIPMENT BY TYPE
AIRCRAFT 9 combat capable
  ATK 5: 1 MB-326K *Impala* I; 4 MB-326K *Impala* II
  TPT 20: **Medium** 3: 2 C-130H *Hercules*; 1 C-130H-30 *Hercules*; **Light** 16: 1 CN-235; 1 DHC-4 *Caribou*; 1 DHC-5D *Buffalo*; 1 IAI-201 *Arava*; 2 J.300 *Joker*; 1 MA60; 2 PA-23 *Aztec*; 7 *Tetras*; **PAX** 1 Gulfstream III
  TRG 4 *Alpha Jet**†
HELICOPTERS
  ATK 1 Mi-24 *Hind*
  MRH 13: 1 AS365 *Dauphin* 2; 1 Bell 412 *Twin Huey*; 2 Mi-17 *Hip* H; 2 SA319 *Alouette* III; 4 SA342 *Gazelle* (with HOT); 3 Z-9
  TPT 7: **Medium** 4: 2 AS332 *Super Puma*; 2 SA330J *Puma*; **Light** 3: 2 Bell 206B *Jet Ranger*; 1 Bell 206L3 *Long Ranger*

Fusiliers de l'Air
FORCES BY ROLE
MANOEUVRE
  Other
  1 sy bn

Paramilitary 9,000

Gendarmerie 9,000

FORCES BY ROLE
MANOEUVRE
  Reconnaissance
    3 (regional spt) paramilitary gp

DEPLOYMENT

CENTRAL AFRICAN REPUBLIC
UN • MINUSCA 761; 4 obs; 1 inf bn

MALI
UN • MINUSMA 2; 1 obs

DEMOCRATIC REPUBLIC OF THE CONGO
UN • MONUSCO 3; 3 obs

FOREIGN FORCES
United States 300

Cape Verde CPV

Cape Verde Escudo E		2015	2016	2017
GDP	E	159bn	167bn	
	US$	1.6bn	1.68bn	
per capita	US$	3,056	3,170	
Growth	%	1.5	3.6	
Inflation	%	0.1	0.1	
Def bdgt	E	995m	1.05bn	
	US$	10m	11m	
US$1=E		99.38	99.08	

Population   553,432

Age	0–14	15–19	20–24	25–29	30–64	65 plus
Male	14.9%	5.1%	5.1%	4.8%	16.6%	1.9%
Female	14.7%	5.1%	5.1%	4.8%	18.5%	3.2%

Capabilities

In its Legislative Programme for 2016–21, the government outlined the priorities for Cape Verde's defence forces, including territorial defence and maritime security, EEZ and airspace protection. Although the armed forces are small and presently have limited capability, the government has suggested reorganising around a marines, engineering and paramilitary national-guard unit. The government is interested in greater regional and international defence engagement; some maritime-security training support is provided by international partners.

ACTIVE 1,200 (Army 1,000 Coast Guard 100 Air 100)
Conscript liability Selective conscription (14 months)

ORGANISATIONS BY SERVICE

Army 1,000
FORCES BY ROLE
MANOEUVRE
  Light
    2 inf bn (gp)

COMBAT SUPPORT
  1 engr bn
EQUIPMENT BY TYPE
ARMOURED FIGHTING VEHICLES
  RECCE 10 BRDM-2
ARTILLERY • MOR 18: **82mm** 12; **120mm** 6 M-1943
AIR DEFENCE
  SAM • **Point-defence** 9K32 *Strela* (SA-7 *Grail*)‡
  GUNS • TOWED 30: **14.5mm** 18 ZPU-1; **23mm** 12 ZU-23

Coast Guard ε100
EQUIPMENT BY TYPE
PATROL AND COASTAL COMBATANTS 5
  PCC 2: 1 *Guardião*; 1 *Kondor I*
  PB 2: 1 *Espadarte*; 1 *Tainha* (PRC-27m)
  PBF 1 *Archangel*

Air Force up to 100
FORCES BY ROLE
MARITIME PATROL
  1 sqn with Do-228
EQUIPMENT BY TYPE
AIRCRAFT • TPT • **Light** 4: 1 Do-228; 3 An-26 *Curl*†

Central African Republic CAR

CFA Franc BEAC fr		2015	2016	2017
GDP	fr	937bn	1.04tr	
	US$	1.59bn	1.78bn	
per capita	US$	332	365	
Growth	%	4.8	5.2	
Inflation	%	4.5	4.0	
Def exp	fr	15.8bn	n.k.	
	US$	27m	n.k.	
US$1=fr		588.03	584.86	

Population   5,507,257

Age	0–14	15–19	20–24	25–29	30–64	65 plus
Male	20.2%	5.3%	4.7%	4.2%	13.7%	1.4%
Female	20.0%	5.2%	4.7%	4.2%	14.1%	2.1%

Capabilities

Effective military and security organisations still remain largely absent in the wake of the violence in 2013. Violence continued in 2016 between Seleka and anti-Balaka groups. Some military equipment remains, but inventory numbers are difficult to verify. The May 2015 Bangui Forum on National Reconciliation agreed principles governing disarmament, demobilisation, reintegration and repatriation (DDRR). Reform of the security forces was seen as a longer-term objective, but the provision of adequate international funding for the DDRR proposals was, stated the UN Development Programme in 2015, vital in the near term, as was development of improved vetting, and better security and defence infrastructure. An agreement was also reached to stop child-soldier recruitment. An EU mission to advise the authorities on higher defence-management functions and systematic reform of the armed forces began in early 2015. France's *Sangaris* mission ended in 2016, leaving the UN's MINUSCA mission as the principal security provider in the country.

ACTIVE 7,150 (Army 7,000 Air 150) **Paramilitary 1,000**

Conscript liability Selective conscription 2 years; reserve obligation thereafter, term n.k.

ORGANISATIONS BY SERVICE

Army ε7,000
EQUIPMENT BY TYPE
ARMOURED FIGHTING VEHICLES
 MBT 3 T-55†
 RECCE 9: 8 *Ferret*†; 1 BRDM-2
 IFV 18 *Ratel*
 APC • APC (W) 14+: 4 BTR-152†; 10+ VAB†
ARTILLERY • MOR 12+: **81mm**†; **120mm** 12 M-1943†
ANTI-TANK/ANTI-INFRASTRUCTURE
 RCL **106mm** 14 M40†
PATROL AND COASTAL COMBATANTS • PBR 9†

Air Force 150
EQUIPMENT BY TYPE
AIRCRAFT • **TPT** 7: **Medium** 1 C-130A *Hercules*; **Light** 6: 3 BN-2 *Islander*; 1 Cessna 172RJ *Skyhawk*; 2 J.300 *Joker*
HELICOPTERS • **TPT** • **Light** 1 AS350 *Ecureuil*

FOREIGN FORCES
MINUSCA unless stated
Austria EUTM RCA 3
Bangladesh 1,084; 11 obs; 1 inf bn; 1 sigs coy; 1 med coy
Belgium EUTM RCA 9
Benin 75; 3 obs; 1 sigs coy
Bhutan 2; 2 obs
Bolivia 2; 3 obs
Brazil 2; 4 obs
Burkina Faso 4; 1 obs
Burundi 826; 8 obs; 1 inf bn
Cambodia 216; 6 obs; 1 engr coy
Cameroon 761; 4 obs; 1 inf bn
Chile 4
Congo 628; 6 obs; 1 inf bn
Czech Republic 3 obs
Egypt 1,019; 5 obs; 1 inf bn; 1 tpt coy
France 9 • Operation Sangaris 350; 1 mech coy(+); 1 AS555UN *Fennec* • EUTM RCA 80
Gabon 445; 1 inf bn(-)
Gambia 2; 2 obs
Georgia EUTM RCA 5
Ghana 4; 4 obs
Guatemala 2; 2 obs
Hungary 2; 2 obs
Indonesia 207; 6 obs; 1 engr coy
Jordan 7; 3 obs
Kenya 8; 6 obs
Mauritania 746; 5 obs; 1 inf bn
Moldova 1; 2 obs
Morocco 760; 2 obs; 1 inf bn
Nepal 65; 3 obs; 1 MP pl
Niger 129; 4 obs; 1 sigs coy
Pakistan 1,127; 10 obs; 1 inf bn; 1 hel sqn; 1 engr coy
Paraguay 3; 1 obs
Peru 206; 4 obs; 1 maint coy
Poland EUTM RCA 2
Portugal EUTM RCA 11
Romania EUTM RCA 2
Rwanda 835; 11 obs; 1 inf bn; 1 fd hospital
Senegal 105; 1 hel sqn
Serbia 70; 2 obs; 1 med coy • EUTM RCA 4
Spain EUTM RCA 22
Sri Lanka 116; 5 obs; 1 hel sqn
Tanzania 1
Togo 6; 4 obs
United States 6
Vietnam 3
Yemen, Republic of 5 obs
Zambia 765; 9 mil obs; 1 inf bn

Chad CHA

CFA Franc BEAC fr		2015	2016	2017
GDP	fr	6.44tr	6.16tr	
	US$	10.9bn	10.4bn	
per capita	US$	942	881	
Growth	%	1.8	-1.1	
Inflation	%	3.7	0.0	
Def bdgt	fr	101bn	159bn	
	US$	170m	269m	
US$1=fr		591.14	589.86	

Population 11,852,462

Age	0–14	15–19	20–24	25–29	30–64	65 plus
Male	22.2%	5.8%	4.5%	3.7%	10.9%	1.2%
Female	21.5%	5.9%	4.9%	4.1%	13.5%	1.8%

Capabilities

Chad's most pressing security concerns are instability in Western Africa and the Sahel and the need to prosecute counter-insurgency operations against Boko Haram. Chad engaged in extensive joint operations with Niger and Nigeria against Boko Haram in 2016. The country is part of the 'G5 Sahel' nations, and has encouraged African armed forces to take greater ownership of regional security. The country's ISR capability should be improved by the receipt of Cessna *Caravan* aircraft from the US, coming shortly after improvements in ground-attack and medium airlift capability. Chad's ground forces have recent combat experience, having partnered French forces in Mali at the start of the *Operation Serval* in 2013. France's *Operation Barkhane* is headquartered in N'Djamena. As part of its involvement in the mission against Boko Haram, Chad reportedly deployed 2,000 troops to Niger in mid-2016.

ACTIVE 30,350 (Army 25,000 Air 350 Republican Guard 5,000) **Paramilitary 9,500**
Conscript liability Conscription authorised

ORGANISATIONS BY SERVICE

Army ε25,000
7 Mil Regions
FORCES BY ROLE
MANOEUVRE
　Armoured
　　1 armd bn
　Light
　　7 inf bn
COMBAT SUPPORT
　1 arty bn
　1 engr bn
　1 sigs bn
COMBAT SERVICE SUPPORT
　1 log gp
EQUIPMENT BY TYPE
ARMOURED FIGHTING VEHICLES
　MBT 60 T-55
　ASLT 30 PTL-02 *Assaulter*
　RECCE 309+: 132 AML-60/AML-90; 22 *Bastion Patsas*; ε100 BRDM-2; 20 EE-9 *Cascavel*; 4 ERC-90F *Sagaie*; 31+ RAM Mk3
　IFV 92: 83 BMP-1; 9 LAV-150 *Commando* with 90mm gun
　APC • APC (W) 95: 24 BTR-80; 8 BTR-3E; ε20 BTR-60; ε10 *Black Scorpion*; 25 VAB-VTT; 8 WZ-523
ARTILLERY 26+
　SP 122mm 10 2S1 *Gvozdika*
　TOWED 105mm 5 M2
　MRL 11+: **107mm** some Type-63; **122mm** 11: 6 BM-21 *Grad*; 5 Type-81
　MOR 81mm some; **120mm** AM-50
ANTI-TANK/ANTI-INFRASTRUCTURE
　MSL • MANPATS *Eryx*; *Milan*
　RCL 106mm M40A1
AIR DEFENCE
　SAM
　　Short-range 2K12 *Kub* (SA-6 *Gainful*)
　　Point-defence 9K310 *Igla-1* (SA-16 *Gimlet*)
　GUNS • TOWED 14.5mm ZPU-1/ZPU-2/ZPU-4; **23mm** ZU-23

Air Force 350
FORCES BY ROLE
GROUND ATTACK
　1 unit with PC-7; PC-9*; SF-260WL *Warrior**; Su-25 *Frogfoot*
TRANSPORT
　1 sqn with An-26 *Curl*; C-130H-30 *Hercules*; Mi-17 *Hip H*; Mi-171
　1 (Presidential) Flt with B-737BBJ; Beech 1900; DC-9-87; Gulfstream II

ATTACK HELICOPTER
　1 sqn with AS550C *Fennec*; Mi-24V *Hind*; SA316 *Alouette III*
EQUIPMENT BY TYPE
AIRCRAFT 14 combat capable
　FTR 1 MiG-29 *Fulcrum*
　ATK 10: 8 Su-25 *Frogfoot*; 2 Su-25UB *Frogfoot B*
　TPT 10: **Medium** 3: 2 C-27J *Spartan*; 1 C-130H-30 *Hercules*; **Light** 4: 3 An-26 *Curl*; 1 Beech 1900; **PAX** 3: 1 B-737BBJ; 1 DC-9-87; 1 Gulfstream II
　TRG 4: 2 PC-7 (only 1*); 1 PC-9 *Turbo Trainer**; 1 SF-260WL *Warrior**
HELICOPTERS
　ATK 5 Mi-24V *Hind*
　MRH 11: 6 AS550C *Fennec*; 3 Mi-17 *Hip H*; 2 SA316 *Alouette III*
　TPT • Medium 2 Mi-171

Paramilitary 9,500 active

State Security Service General Direction (DGSSIE) 5,000

Gendarmerie 4,500

DEPLOYMENT

CÔTE D'IVOIRE
UN • UNOCI 4 obs

MALI
UN • MINUSMA 1,440; 1 SF coy; 2 inf bn

FOREIGN FORCES

Benin MNJTF 750
France Operation Barkhane 1,250; 1 mech inf BG; 1 air unit with 1 C-130H *Hercules*; 1 C-160 *Transall*; 1 hel det with 4 *Tiger*; 2 SA330 *Puma*

Congo, Republic of COG

CFA Franc BEAC fr		2015	2016	2017
GDP	fr	5.23tr	5.21tr	
	US$	8.84bn	8.83bn	
per capita	US$	2,024	1,981	
Growth	%	2.3	1.7	
Inflation	%	2.0	4.0	
Def bdgt	fr	349bn	333bn	
	US$	590m	565m	
US$1=fr		591.17	589.42	

Population　4,852,412

Age	0–14	15–19	20–24	25–29	30–64	65 plus
Male	21.0%	4.5%	4.1%	3.6%	15.6%	1.3%
Female	20.6%	4.5%	4.1%	3.9%	15.1%	1.7%

Capabilities

Congo's armed forces are small, utilise aged equipment, and have low levels of training and limited overall capability. They have struggled to recover from the brief but devastating civil war in the late 1990s. Though the defence budget is not small in relation to those of its neighbours, the air force is effectively grounded for lack of spares and serviceable equipment and the navy is little more than a riverine force, despite the need for maritime security on the country's small coastline.

ACTIVE 10,000 (Army 8,000 Navy 800 Air 1,200)
Paramilitary 2,000

ORGANISATIONS BY SERVICE

Army 8,000
FORCES BY ROLE
MANOEUVRE
 Armoured
  2 armd bn
 Light
  2 inf bn (gp) each with (1 lt tk tp, 1 arty bty)
  1 inf bn
 Air Manoeuvre
  1 cdo/AB bn
COMBAT SUPPORT
 1 arty gp (with MRL)
 1 engr bn
EQUIPMENT BY TYPE†
ARMOURED FIGHTING VEHICLES
 MBT 40: 25 T-54/T-55; 15 Type-59; (some T-34 in store)
 LT TK 13: 3 PT-76; 10 Type-62
 RECCE 25 BRDM-1/BRDM-2
 APC 105+
  APC (W) 50+: 20 BTR-152; 30 BTR-60; Panhard M3
  PPV 55: 18 *Mamba*; 37 *Marauder*
 ARTILLERY 56+
  SP 122mm 3 2S1 *Gvozdika*
  TOWED 15+: **122mm** 10 D-30; **130mm** 5 M-46; **152mm** D-20
  MRL 10+: **122mm** 10 BM-21 *Grad*; **140mm** BM-14; **140mm** BM-16
  MOR 28+: **82mm**; **120mm** 28 M-43
 ANTI-TANK/ANTI-INFRASTRUCTURE
  RCL 57mm M18
  GUNS 15: **57mm** 5 ZIS-2 (M-1943); **100mm** 10 M-1944
 AIR DEFENCE • GUNS
  SP 23mm ZSU-23-4
  TOWED 14.5mm ZPU-2/ZPU-4; **37mm** 28 M-1939; **57mm** S-60; **100mm** KS-19

Navy ε800
EQUIPMENT BY TYPE
PATROL AND COASTAL COMBATANTS 8
 PCC 4 *Février*
 PBR 4

Air Force 1,200
FORCES BY ROLE
FIGHTER/GROUND ATTACK
 1 sqn with *Mirage* F-1AZ
TRANSPORT
 1 sqn with An-24 *Coke*; An-32 *Cline*; CN-235M-100
ATTACK/TRANSPORT HELICOPTER
 1 sqn with Mi-8 *Hip*; Mi-35P *Hind*
EQUIPMENT BY TYPE†
AIRCRAFT
 FGA 2 *Mirage* F-1AZ
 TPT • Light 4: 1 An-24 *Coke*; 2 An-32 *Cline*; 1 CN-235M-100
HELICOPTERS†
 ATK (2 Mi-35P *Hind* in store)
 TPT • Medium (3 Mi-8 *Hip* in store)
AIR-LAUNCHED MISSILES • AAM • IR R-3 (AA-2 *Atoll*)‡

Paramilitary 2,000 active

Gendarmerie 2,000
FORCES BY ROLE
MANOEUVRE
 Other
  20 paramilitary coy

Presidential Guard some
FORCES BY ROLE
MANOEUVRE
 Other
  1 paramilitary bn

DEPLOYMENT

CENTRAL AFRICAN REPUBLIC
UN • MINUSCA 628; 6 obs; 1 inf bn

Côte d'Ivoire CIV

CFA Franc BCEAO fr		2015	2016	2017
GDP	fr	18.6tr	20.4tr	
	US$	31.4bn	34.7bn	
per capita	US$	1,325	1,424	
Growth	%	8.5	8.0	
Inflation	%	1.2	1.0	
Def bdgt [a]	fr	499bn	446bn	
	US$	844m	759m	
US$1=fr		591.15	587.34	

[a] Defence, order and security expenses

Population 23,740,424

Age	0–14	15–19	20–24	25–29	30–64	65 plus
Male	18.9%	5.6%	5.0%	4.5%	15.0%	1.6%
Female	18.6%	5.5%	4.9%	4.4%	14.3%	1.8%

Capabilities

The Ivorian armed forces are still undergoing reconstruction, and security-sector reform (SSR) initiatives remain in place. A law on the organisation of defence forces was enacted in 2015. This detailed defence zones and military regions, the creation of a general staff and general inspectorate for the armed forces, and stressed the armed forces' role in assisting Ivorian society. A national-security council and authority for disarmament, demobilisation and reintegration have been created. In April 2016, the United Nations lifted the arms embargo that had previously been imposed on the country. The air force has no combat capability and a very limited capacity for transport, and there remain questions as to serviceability, though as part of the SSR process an Abidjan aircraft academy was established, with limited rotary-wing pilot and maintenance training. The latter is also an issue for the small naval unit. The UN reported in May 2015 that the armed forces 'continued to face institutional gaps in terms of training, discipline and low public confidence', while both the police and gendarmerie faced operational shortcomings. France has a significant training mission in the country, and planned to increase its presence to 900 personnel during summer 2016 following an al-Qaeda in the Islamic Maghreb attack. The administration has moved to regulate promotion and salary structures in a bid to aid professionalisation, as well as improving military infrastructure. In February 2016, the navy commissioned the third of three French-built patrol craft as part of ongoing attempts to rebuild the service. The UN peacekeeping mission is due to end in April 2017.

ACTIVE 25,400 (Army 23,000 Navy 1,000 Air 1,400)
Paramilitary n.k.

Moves to restructure and reform the armed forces continue.

ORGANISATIONS BY SERVICE

Army ε23,000
FORCES BY ROLE
MANOEUVRE
  Armoured
  1 armd bn
  Light
  4 inf bn
  Air Manoeuvre
  1 cdo/AB bn
COMBAT SUPPORT
  1 arty bn
  1 engr bn
COMBAT SERVICE SUPPORT
  1 log bn
AIR DEFENCE
  1 AD bn
EQUIPMENT BY TYPE
ARMOURED FIGHTING VEHICLES
  MBT 10 T-55†
  LT TK 5 AMX-13
  RECCE 34: 15 AML-60/AML-90; 13 BRDM-2; 6 ERC-90F4 *Sagaie*
  IFV 10 BMP-1/BMP-2†
  APC • APC (W) 31: 12 Panhard M3; 13 VAB; 6 BTR-80
ENGINEERING & MAINTENANCE VEHICLES
  VLB MTU
ANTI-TANK/ANTI-INFRASTRUCTURE
  MSL • MANPATS 9K111-1 *Konkurs* (AT-5 *Spandrel*) (reported); 9K135 *Kornet* (AT-14 *Spriggan*) (reported)
  RCL 106mm ε12 M40A1
ARTILLERY 36+
  TOWED 4+: 105mm 4 M-1950; 122mm (reported)
  MRL 122mm 6 BM-21
  MOR 26+: 81mm; 82mm 10 M-37; 120mm 16 AM-50
AIRCRAFT • TPT • Medium 1 An-12 *Cub*†
AIR DEFENCE
  SAM • Point-defence 9K32 *Strela*-2 (SA-7 *Grail*)‡ (reported)
  GUNS 21+
    SP 20mm 6 M3 VDAA
    TOWED 15+: 20mm 10; 23mm ZU-23-2; 40mm 5 L/60

Navy ε1,000
EQUIPMENT BY TYPE
PATROL AND COASTAL COMBATANTS 6
  PB 4: 3 *L'Emergence*; 1 *Intrepide*† (FRA *Patra*)
  PBR 2 Rodman (fishery-protection duties)
AMPHIBIOUS • LANDING CRAFT • LCM 2 *Aby*†

Air Force ε1,400
EQUIPMENT BY TYPE†
AIRCRAFT
  ATK (2 Su-25 *Frogfoot* in store)
  TPT • PAX 1 B-727
HELICOPTERS
  ATK 1 Mi-24 (reported)
  TPT • Medium 3 SA330L *Puma* (IAR-330L)

Paramilitary n.k.

Republican Guard n.k.
EQUIPMENT BY TYPE†
ARMOURED FIGHTING VEHICLES
  APC • APC (W) 4 *Mamba*

Gendarmerie n.k.
EQUIPMENT BY TYPE†
ARMOURED FIGHTING VEHICLES
  APC • APC (W) some VAB
PATROL AND COASTAL COMBATANTS • PB 1 *Bian*

DEPLOYMENT

DEMOCRATIC REPUBLIC OF THE CONGO
UN • MONUSCO 1

MALI
UN • MINUSMA 6

FOREIGN FORCES

All forces part of UNOCI unless otherwise stated.
Bangladesh 112; 1 fd hospital
Benin 4; 4 obs
Bolivia 1 obs
Brazil 2; 2 obs
Chad 4 obs
China, People's Republic of 2 obs
Ecuador 2 obs
Egypt 14
Ethiopia 2 obs
France 5 • Forces Francaises en Côte d'Ivoire: 900; 1 (Marine) inf bn
Gambia 1 obs
Ghana 95; 3 obs; 1 hel sqn
Guatemala 4 obs
Guinea 2 obs
India 3 obs
Ireland 2 obs
Jordan 6; 4 obs
Kazakhstan 1 obs
Korea, Republic of 1 obs
Malawi 1; 1 obs
Moldova 1 obs
Morocco 4; 2 obs
Namibia 1 obs
Nepal 1; 3 obs
Niger 652; 2 obs; 1 mech inf bn
Nigeria 2 obs
Pakistan 9; 8 obs
Paraguay 1; 1 obs
Peru 1 obs
Philippines 1 obs
Poland 1 obs
Romania 3 obs
Russia 4 obs
Senegal 735; 5 obs; 1 inf bn; 1 hel sqn
Serbia 1 obs
Tanzania 2; 2 obs
Togo 303; 6 obs; 1 inf bn(-)
Tunisia 3; 6 obs
Uganda 1; 2 obs
Ukraine 2
Uruguay 1; 1 obs
Yemen, Republic of 4 obs
Zambia 1 obs
Zimbabwe 1 obs

Democratic Republic of the Congo DRC

Congolese Franc fr		2015	2016	2017
GDP	fr	35.6tr	37.2tr	
	US$	38.4bn	39.8bn	
per capita	US$	470	473	
Growth	%	6.9	3.9	
Inflation	%	1.0	1.7	
Def bdgt	fr	684bn	817bn	844bn
	US$	738m	875m	
US$1=fr		926.82	933.78	

Population 81,331,050

Age	0–14	15–19	20–24	25–29	30–64	65 plus
Male	21.3%	5.7%	5.0%	4.0%	12.7%	1.1%
Female	21.0%	5.7%	5.0%	4.0%	13.0%	1.5%

Capabilities

On paper, the DRC has the largest armed forces in Central Africa. However, given the country's size and the poor levels of training, morale and equipment, the armed forces are unable to provide security throughout the country. The DRC has suffered the most protracted conflict since the end of the Cold War. Much of its military equipment is in a poor state of repair and the armed forces, which have since incorporated a number of non-state armed groups, struggle with conflicting loyalties. The UN's Force Intervention Brigade (FIB) remains active in the east of the country. Training will have improved for units operating with the FIB, while external-partner training and capacity-building assistance is also commonplace. When conflict finally abates in the east, significant attention to wide-ranging disarmament, demobilisation and reintegration and security-sector reform will be required, to continue the work intermittently undertaken over the past decade.

ACTIVE ε134,250 (Central Staffs ε14,000, Army 103,000 Republican Guard 8,000 Navy 6,700 Air 2,550)

ORGANISATIONS BY SERVICE

Army (Forces du Terre) ε103,000

The DRC has 11 Military Regions. In 2011, all brigades in North and South Kivu provinces were consolidated into 27 new regiments, the latest in a sequence of reorganisations designed to integrate non-state armed groups. The actual combat effectiveness of many formations is doubtful

FORCES BY ROLE
MANOEUVRE
  Light
  6 (integrated) inf bde
  ε3 inf bde (non-integrated)
  27+ inf regt
COMBAT SUPPORT
  1 arty regt
  1 MP bn

EQUIPMENT BY TYPE†
(includes Republican Guard eqpt)
ARMOURED FIGHTING VEHICLES
  MBT 149: 12–17 Type-59†; 32 T-55; 100 T-72AV
  LT TK 40: 10 PT-76; 30 Type-62† (reportedly being refurbished)
  RECCE up to 52: up to 17 AML-60; 14 AML-90; 19 EE-9 *Cascavel*; 2 RAM-V-2
  IFV 20 BMP-1
  APC 144:
    APC (T) 9: 3 BTR-50; 6 MT-LB
    APC (W) 135: 30-70 BTR-60PB; 58 Panhard M3†; 7 TH 390 *Fahd*
ANTI-TANK/ANTI-INFRASTRUCTURE
  RCL 57mm M18; **73mm**; **75mm** M20; **106mm** M40A1
  GUNS 85mm 10 Type-56 (D-44)
ARTILLERY 720+
  SP 16: **122mm** 6 2S1 *Gvozdika*; **152mm** 10 2S3 *Akatsiya*
  TOWED 119: **122mm** 77 M-30 (M-1938)/D-30/Type-60; **130mm** 42 Type-59 (M-46)/Type-59-I
  MRL 57+: **107mm** 12 Type-63; **122mm** 24+: 24 BM-21 *Grad*; some RM-70; **128mm** 6 M-51; **130mm** 3 Type-82; **132mm** 12
  MOR 528+: **81mm** 100; **82mm** 400; **107mm** M30; **120mm** 28: 10 Brandt; 18 other
AIR DEFENCE
  SAM • Point-defence 9K32 *Strela*-2 (SA-7 *Grail*)‡
  GUNS • TOWED 114: **14.5mm** 12 ZPU-4; **37mm** 52 M-1939; **40mm** ε50 L/60† (probably out of service)

Republican Guard 8,000
FORCES BY ROLE
MANOEUVRE
  Armoured
    1 armd regt
  Light
    3 gd bde
COMBAT SUPPORT
  1 arty regt

Navy 6,700 (incl infantry and marines)
EQUIPMENT BY TYPE
  PATROL AND COASTAL COMBATANTS 16
    PB 16: 1 *Shanghai* II; ε15 various (all under 15m)

Air Force 2,550
EQUIPMENT BY TYPE
AIRCRAFT 4 combat capable
  ATK 4 Su-25 *Frogfoot*
  TPT 5: **Medium** 1 C-130H *Hercules*; **Light** 2 An-26 *Curl*; **PAX** 2 B-727
HELICOPTERS
  ATK 9: 4 Mi-24 *Hind*; 5 Mi-24V *Hind*
  TPT • Medium 3: 1 AS332L *Super Puma*; 2 Mi-8 *Hip*

Paramilitary
National Police Force
Incl Rapid Intervention Police (National and Provincial forces)
People's Defence Force

FOREIGN FORCES
All part of MONUSCO unless otherwise specified
Bangladesh 1,711; 17 obs; 1 inf bn; 1 engr coy; 1 avn coy; 2 hel coy
Belgium 1; 1 obs • 52 (national deployment – trg)
Benin 454; 6 obs; 1 inf bn(-)
Bolivia 8 obs
Bosnia-Herzegovina 5 obs
Burkina Faso 1; 7 obs
Cameroon 3; 3 obs
Canada (*Operation Crocodile*) 9
China, People's Republic of 219; 12 obs; 1 engr coy; 1 fd hospital
Côte d'Ivoire 1
Czech Republic 3 obs
Egypt 155; 23 obs; 1 SF coy
France 2
Ghana 466; 21 obs; 1 mech inf bn(-)
Guatemala 151; 1 obs; 1 SF coy
Guinea 1
India 3,111; 43 obs; 3 mech inf bn; 1 inf coy; 1 fd hospital
Indonesia 176; 14 obs; 1 engr coy
Ireland 3
Jordan 9; 15 obs
Kenya 13; 15 obs
Malawi 857; 5 obs; 1 inf bn
Malaysia 5; 10 obs
Mali 1; 10 obs
Mongolia 1 obs
Morocco 836; 3 obs; 1 mech inf bn; 1 fd hospital
Nepal 1,029; 19 obs; 1 inf bn; 1 engr coy
Niger 4; 8 obs
Nigeria 1; 19 obs
Pakistan 3,446; 44 obs; 3 mech inf bn; 1 inf bn; 1 hel sqn
Paraguay 15 obs
Peru 1; 11 obs
Poland 2 obs
Romania 22 obs
Russia 1; 28 obs
Senegal 2; 2 obs
Serbia 8
South Africa (*Operation Mistral*) 1,355; 4 obs; 1 inf bn; 1 atk hel sqn; 1 hel sqn; 1 engr coy
Sri Lanka 4 obs
Sweden 2 obs
Switzerland 3
Tanzania 1,262; 1 SF coy; 1 inf bn; 1 arty coy
Tunisia 31 obs
Ukraine 255; 11 obs; 2 atk hel sqn; 1 hel sqn
United Kingdom 5
United States 3
Uruguay 1,175; 13 obs; 1 inf bn; 1 mne coy; 1 hel flt
Yemen, Republic of 6 obs
Zambia 2; 17 obs

Djibouti DJB

Djiboutian Franc fr		2015	2016	2017
GDP	fr	307bn	337bn	
	US$	1.73bn	1.89bn	
per capita	US$	1,788	1,908	
Growth	%	6.5	6.5	
Inflation	%	2.1	3	
Def exp	fr	n.k.	n.k.	
	US$	n.k.	n.k.	
FMA (US)	US$	0.7m	0.7m	0.5m
US$1=fr		177.70	177.74	

Population 846,687

Ethnic groups: Somali 60%; Afar 35%

Age	0–14	15–19	20–24	25–29	30–64	65 plus
Male	15.9%	5.2%	4.9%	4.4%	13.7%	1.7%
Female	15.8%	5.5%	5.9%	5.7%	19.2%	2.0%

Capabilities

The small armed forces of this strategically significant country are almost entirely dominated by the army. Recent ground-forces acquisitions have focused on mobility and artillery; armoured-warfare capability remains limited. Intra-theatre airlift capability improved in 2016 with the arrival of Y-12E aircraft and *Dauphin* helicopters. Training support and external security are bolstered by the presence of the US Combined Joint Task Force–Horn of Africa at Camp Lemonnier, as well as a French base with air-combat and transport assets. Other states base forces in Djibouti to participate in counter-piracy missions, including Japan, which opened its first overseas base there in 2010. A strategic-defence partnership was signed with China in February 2014 and China is now building naval-support facilities in Djibouti. Despite concerns about the country's ability to self-sustain on operations, Djibouti in 2015 agreed to deploy a second battalion group to AMISOM.

ACTIVE 10,450 (Army 8,000 Navy 200 Air 250 Gendarmerie 2,000) **Paramilitary 2,500**

ORGANISATIONS BY SERVICE

Army ε8,000
FORCES BY ROLE
4 military districts (Tadjourah, Dikhil, Ali-Sabieh and Obock)
MANOEUVRE
 Mechanised
  1 armd regt (1 recce sqn, 3 armd sqn, 1 (anti-smuggling) sy coy)
 Light
  4 inf regt (3-4 inf coy, 1 spt coy)
  1 rapid reaction regt (4 inf coy, 1 spt coy)
 Other
  1 (Republican Guard) gd regt (1 sy sqn, 1 (close protection) sy sqn, 1 cbt spt sqn (1 recce pl, 1 armd pl, 1 arty pl), 1 spt sqn)

COMBAT SUPPORT
 1 arty regt
 1 demining coy
 1 sigs regt
 1 CIS sect
COMBAT SERVICE SUPPORT
 1 log regt
 1 maint coy
EQUIPMENT BY TYPE
ARMOURED FIGHTING VEHICLES
 ASLT 1 PTL-02 *Assaulter*
 RECCE 36: 4 AML-60†; 17 AML-90; 15 VBL
 IFV 28: 8 BTR-80A; 16-20 *Ratel*
 APC 32+
  APC (W) 22+: 12 BTR-60†; 4+ AT-105 *Saxon*; 6 *Puma*
  PPV 10 RG-33L
 AUV 12 *Cougar* 4×4
ANTI-TANK/ANTI-INFRASTRUCTURE
 RCL 106mm 16 M40A1
ARTILLERY 71
 SP 155mm 10 M109L
 TOWED 122mm 6 D-30
 MRL 122mm 10: 6 (6-tube Toyota Land Cruiser 70 series); 2 (30-tube Iveco 110-16); 2 (30-tube)
 MOR 45: **81mm** 25; **120mm** 20 Brandt
AIR DEFENCE • GUNS 15+
 SP 20mm 5 M693
 TOWED 10: **23mm** 5 ZU-23; **40mm** 5 L/70

Navy ε200
EQUIPMENT BY TYPE
PATROL AND COASTAL COMBATANTS 12
 PBF 2 Battalion-17
 PB 10: 1 *Plascoa*†; 2 Sea Ark 1739; 1 *Swari*†; 6 others
AMPHIBIOUS • LCT 1 EDIC 700

Air Force 250
EQUIPMENT BY TYPE
AIRCRAFT
 TPT • Light 6: 1 Cessna U206G *Stationair*; 1 Cessna 208 *Caravan*; 2 Y-12E; 1 L-410UVP *Turbolet*; 1 MA60
HELICOPTERS
 ATK (2 Mi-35 *Hind* in store)
 MRH 5: 1 Mi-17 *Hip* H; 4 AS365 *Dauphin*
 TPT 3: **Medium** 1 Mi-8T *Hip*; **Light** 2 AS355F *Ecureuil* II

Gendarmerie 2,000+
Ministry of Defence
FORCES BY ROLE
MANOEUVRE
 Other
  1 paramilitary bn
EQUIPMENT BY TYPE
PATROL AND COASTAL COMBATANTS 1 PB

Paramilitary ε2,500

National Police Force ε2,500
Ministry of Interior

Coast Guard 145
EQUIPMENT BY TYPE
PATROL AND COASTAL COMBATANTS 11
    PB 11: 2 *Khor Angar*; 9 other

DEPLOYMENT

SOMALIA
AU • AMISOM 1,850; 2 inf bn

WESTERN SAHARA
UN • MINURSO 1

FOREIGN FORCES

France 1,450: 1 (Marine) combined arms regt (2 recce sqn, 2 inf coy, 1 arty bty, 1 engr coy); 1 hel det with 2 SA330 *Puma*; 1 SA342 *Gazelle*; 1 LCM; 1 air sqn with 4 *Mirage* 2000-5/D; 1 C-160 *Transall*; 2 SA330 *Puma*
Germany Operation Atalanta 1 AP-3C *Orion*
Japan 170; 2 P-3C *Orion*
New Zealand 1 P-3K2 *Orion*
Spain Operation Atalanta 1 P-3A *Orion*
United States US Africa Command: 3,150; 1 tpt sqn with C-130H/J-30 *Hercules*; 1 spec ops sqn with MC-130H; PC-12 (U-28A); 1 CSAR sqn with HH-60G *Pave Hawk*; 1 naval air base

Equatorial Guinea EQG

CFA Franc BEAC fr		2015	2016	2017
GDP	fr	8.17tr	6.86tr	
	US$	13.8bn	11.6bn	
per capita	US$	17,287	14,176	
Growth	%	-7.4	-9.9	
Inflation	%	1.7	1.5	
Def exp	fr	n.k.	n.k.	
	US$	n.k.	n.k.	
US$1=fr		591.14	589.37	

Population   759,451

Age	0–14	15–19	20–24	25–29	30–64	65 plus
Male	20.4%	5.4%	4.6%	3.8%	13.9%	1.7%
Female	19.8%	5.2%	4.4%	3.8%	14.6%	2.3%

Capabilities

The armed forces are dominated by the army, the principal role of which is internal security; there is only limited capability for power projection. There has been significant naval investment in recent years, including both equipment and onshore infrastructure at Malabo and Bata, although naval capabilities still remain limited in scope. Maritime-security concerns in the Gulf of Guinea have resulted in an increased emphasis on bolstering the country's coastal-patrol capacity, with new offshore-patrol vessels commissioned and the armed forces taking part in international exercises, including *Obangame Express 2016*.

ACTIVE 1,450 (Army 1,100 Navy 250 Air 100)

ORGANISATIONS BY SERVICE

Army 1,100
FORCES BY ROLE
MANOEUVRE
  Light
    3 inf bn(-)
EQUIPMENT BY TYPE
ARMOURED FIGHTING VEHICLES
  MBT 3 T-55
  RECCE 6 BRDM-2
  IFV 20 BMP-1
  APC 22
    APC (W) 10 BTR-152
    PPV 12 *Reva* (reported)

Navy ε250
EQUIPMENT BY TYPE
PATROL AND COASTAL COMBATANTS 11
  PSO 2:
    1 *Bata* with 1 76mm gun, 1 hel landing platform
    1 *Wele Nzas* with 2 AK630M 30mm CIWS, 2 76mm gun, 1 hel landing platform
  PCC 2 OPV 62
  PBF 2 *Shaldag* II
  PB 5: 1 *Daphne*; 2 *Estuario de Muni*; 2 *Zhuk*
LOGISTICS AND SUPPORT
  AKRH 1 *Capitan David Eyama Angue Osa* with 1 76mm gun

Air Force 100
EQUIPMENT BY TYPE
AIRCRAFT 4 combat capable
  ATK 4: 2 Su-25 *Frogfoot*; 2 Su-25UB *Frogfoot* B
  TPT 4: **Light** 3: 1 An-32B *Cline*; 2 An-72 *Coaler*; **PAX** 1 *Falcon* 900 (VIP)
  TRG 2 L-39C *Albatros*
HELICOPTERS
  ATK 5 Mi-24P/V *Hind*
  MRH 1 Mi-17 *Hip* H
  TPT 4: **Heavy** 1 Mi-26 *Halo*; **Medium** 1 Ka-29 *Helix*; **Light** 2 Enstrom 480

Paramilitary

Guardia Civil
FORCES BY ROLE
MANOEUVRE
  Other
    2 paramilitary coy

Coast Guard n.k.

Eritrea ERI

Eritrean Nakfa ERN		2015	2016	2017
GDP	ERN	71.7bn	82.3bn	
	US$	4.67bn	5.35bn	
per capita	US$	695	771	
Growth	%	4.8	3.7	
Inflation	%	9	9	
Def exp	ERN	n.k.	n.k.	
	US$	n.k.	n.k.	
USD1=ERN		15.38	15.37	

Population 5,869,869

Ethnic groups: Tigrinya 50%; Tigre and Kunama 40%

Age	0–14	15–19	20–24	25–29	30–64	65 plus
Male	20.4%	5.3%	4.4%	3.7%	13.8%	1.7%
Female	20.2%	5.3%	4.5%	3.8%	14.7%	2.2%

Capabilities

Eritrea maintains a large, mostly conscript, standing army. Its primary task is to defend the border with Ethiopia, where clashes occurred in 2016. Many troops are also used for civilian development and construction tasks. Significant numbers of conscripts choose to flee the country rather than serve, or evade service in other ways, which may have some effect on military cohesion and effectiveness. An ongoing UN arms embargo will have contributed to leaving the inventory dominated by outdated but numerous platforms, and it is likely that many will be slowly cannibalised for parts. There has been some investment in the nascent air force to produce a regionally comparable fighter wing, though this lacks experienced and trained pilots, while the navy remains capable of only limited coastal-patrol and interception operations. The port and airfield at Assab have been refurbished under an agreement with the Gulf states participating in military operations in Yemen; there were reports in 2016 of Gulf states training Yemeni forces in Eritrea and also basing (at least temporarily) some military equipment at Assab. (See pp. 490–94.)

ACTIVE 201,750 (Army 200,000 Navy 1,400 Air 350)
Conscript liability 18 months (4 months mil trg) between ages of 18 and 40

RESERVE 120,000 (Army ε120,000)

ORGANISATIONS BY SERVICE

Army ε200,000
Heavily cadreised
FORCES BY ROLE
COMMAND
  4 corps HQ
MANOEUVRE
  Mechanised
  1 mech bde
  Light
  19 inf div
  1 cdo div

Reserve ε120,000
FORCES BY ROLE
MANOEUVRE
  Light
  1 inf div
EQUIPMENT BY TYPE
ARMOURED FIGHTING VEHICLES
  MBT 270 T-54/T-55
  RECCE 40 BRDM-1/BRDM-2
  IFV 15 BMP-1
  APC 35
    APC (T) 10 MT-LB†
    APC (W) 25 BTR-152/BTR-60
ENGINEERING & MAINTENANCE VEHICLES
  ARV T-54/T-55 reported
  VLB MTU reported
ANTI-TANK/ANTI-INFRASTRUCTURE
  MSL • MANPATS 9K11 *Malyutka* (AT-3 *Sagger*); 9K111-1 *Konkurs* (AT-5 *Spandrel*)
  GUNS 85mm D-44
ARTILLERY 208+
  SP 45: **122mm** 32 2S1 *Gvozdika*; **152mm** 13 2S5 *Giatsint*-S
  TOWED 19+: **122mm** D-30; **130mm** 19 M-46
  MRL 44: **122mm** 35 BM-21 *Grad*; **220mm** 9 9P140 *Uragan*
  MOR 120mm/160mm 100+
AIR DEFENCE
  SAM • Point-defence 9K32 *Strela*-2 (SA-7 *Grail*)‡
  GUNS 70+
    SP 23mm ZSU-23-4
    TOWED 23mm ZU-23

Navy 1,400
EQUIPMENT BY TYPE
PATROL AND COASTAL COMBATANTS 12
  PBF 9: 5 *Battalion*-17; 4 *Super Dvora*
  PB 3 *Swiftships*
AMPHIBIOUS 3
  LS • LST 2: 1 *Chamo*† (Ministry of Transport); 1 *Ashdod*†
  LC • LCU 1 T-4† (in harbour service)

Air Force ε350
FORCES BY ROLE
FIGHTER/GROUND ATTACK
  1 sqn with MiG-29/MiG-29SMT/MiG-29UB *Fulcrum*
  1 sqn with Su-27/Su-27UBK *Flanker*
TRANSPORT
  1 sqn with Y-12(II)
TRAINING
  1 sqn with L-90 *Redigo*
  1 sqn with MB-339CE*
TRANSPORT HELICOPTER
  1 sqn with Bell 412 *Twin Huey*
  1 sqn with Mi-17 *Hip H*
EQUIPMENT BY TYPE
AIRCRAFT 20 combat capable

FTR 14: 4 MiG-29 *Fulcrum*; 2 MiG-29UB *Fulcrum*; 5 Su-27 *Flanker*; 3 Su-27UBK *Flanker*
FGA 2 MiG-29SMT *Fulcrum*
TPT • Light 5: 1 Beech 200 *King Air*; 4 Y-12(II)
TRG 12: 8 L-90 *Redigo*; 4 MB-339CE*
HELICOPTERS
MRH 8: 4 Bell 412 *Twin Huey* (AB-412); 4 Mi-17 *Hip* H
AIR-LAUNCHED MISSILES
AAM • IR R-60 (AA-8 *Aphid*); R-73 (AA-11 *Archer*); **IR/SARH** R-27 (AA-10 *Alamo*)

FOREIGN FORCES
United Arab Emirates *Operation Restoring Hope* 9 Mirage 2000-9EAD

Ethiopia ETH

Ethiopian Birr EB		2015	2016	2017
GDP	EB	1.24tr	1.46tr	
	US$	61.6bn	69.2bn	
per capita	US$	687	759	
Growth	%	10.2	6.5	
Inflation	%	10.1	7.7	
Def bdgt	EB	8bn	9.5bn	11bn
	US$	399m	451m	
FMA (US)	US$	0.7m	0.7m	0.5m
US$1=EB		20.07	21.07	

Population 102,374,044

Ethnic groups: Oromo 34.4%; Amhara 27%; Somalie 6.2%; Tigray 6.1%; Sidama 4%; Guragie 2.5%; other or unspecified 19.2%

Age	0–14	15–19	20–24	25–29	30–64	65 plus
Male	21.9%	5.4%	4.5%	3.8%	12.7%	1.3%
Female	21.8%	5.5%	4.6%	3.9%	12.9%	1.5%

Capabilities

Principal security concerns relate to Eritrea and also the activities of al-Shabaab. The 2016 state of emergency will, however, be absorbing the attention of the security forces. Ethiopia maintains one of the region's most effective armed forces, which have become battle-hardened and experienced following a history of combat operations. Ethiopia is at the end of a ten-year (2005–15) modernisation plan, designed to create flexible armed forces able to respond to regional contingencies. The country has enough deployable capability to make significant contributions to the UN missions in Darfur and South Sudan, as well as the AMISOM mission in Somalia, though these – and standing deployments on the Eritrean border – have meant it has had to transform while on operations. As of November 2015, Ethiopia was the second-largest troop contributor to UN peacekeeping missions. The country's arsenal remains focused on Soviet-era equipment, but there is adequate maintenance capability within the local defence industry, although there is more limited capacity to support the more advanced platforms. There is increasing procurement of Chinese systems.

ACTIVE 138,000 (Army 135,000 Air 3,000)

ORGANISATIONS BY SERVICE

Army 135,000
4 Mil Regional Commands (Northern, Western, Central and Eastern) each acting as corps HQ

FORCES BY ROLE
MANOEUVRE
  Light
  1 (Agazi Cdo) SF comd
  1 (Northern) corps (1 mech div, 4 inf div)
  1 (Western) corps (1 mech div, 3 inf div)
  1 (Central) corps (1 mech div, 5 inf div)
  1 (Eastern) corps (1 mech div, 5 inf div)

EQUIPMENT BY TYPE
ARMOURED FIGHTING VEHICLES
  MBT 461+: 246+ T-54/T-55/T-62; 215 T-72
  RECCE ε100 BRDM-1/BRDM-2
  IFV ε20 BMP-1
  APC 300+
    APC (T) some Type-89
    APC (W) 300+: ε300 BTR-60/BTR-152; some Type-92
  AUV some *Ze'ev*
ENGINEERING & MAINTENANCE VEHICLES
  ARV T-54/T-55 reported; 4 BTS-5B
  VLB MTU reported
  MW *Bozena*
ANTI-TANK/ANTI-INFRASTRUCTURE
  MSL • MANPATS 9K11 *Malyutka* (AT-3 *Sagger*); 9K111 *Fagot* (AT-4 *Spigot*); 9K135 *Kornet*-E (AT-14 *Spriggan*)
  RCL 82mm B-10; **107mm** B-11
  GUNS 85mm D-44
ARTILLERY 524+
  SP 10+: **122mm** 2S1 *Gvozdika*; **152mm** 10 2S19 *Msta*-S
  TOWED 464+: **122mm** 464 D-30/M-30 (M-1938); **130mm** M-46; **155mm** AH2
  MRL 122mm ε50 BM-21 *Grad*
  MOR 81mm M1/M29; **82mm** M-1937; **120mm** M-1944
AIR DEFENCE
  SAM
    Medium-range S-75 *Dvina* (SA-2 *Guideline*)
    Short-range S-125 *Pechora* (SA-3 *Goa*)
    Point-defence 9K32 *Strela*-2 (SA-7 *Grail*)‡
  GUNS
    SP 23mm ZSU-23-4
    TOWED 23mm ZU-23; **37mm** M-1939; **57mm** S-60

Air Force 3,000
FORCES BY ROLE
FIGHTER/GROUND ATTACK
  1 sqn with MiG-21MF *Fishbed* J†; MiG-21UM *Mongol* B†
  1 sqn with Su-27/Su-27UB *Flanker*
TRANSPORT
  1 sqn with An-12 *Cub*; An-26 *Curl*; An-32 *Cline*; C-130B *Hercules*; DHC-6 *Twin Otter*; L-100-30; Yak-40 *Codling* (VIP)
TRAINING
  1 sqn with L-39 *Albatros*
  1 sqn with SF-260

ATTACK/TRANSPORT HELICOPTER
2 sqn with Mi-24/Mi-35 *Hind*; Mi-8 *Hip*; Mi-17 *Hip* H; SA316 *Alouette* III

EQUIPMENT BY TYPE
AIRCRAFT 26 combat capable
  FTR 11: 8 Su-27 *Flanker*; 3 Su-27UB *Flanker*
  FGA 15 MiG-21MF *Fishbed* J/MiG-21UM *Mongol* B†
  TPT 12: **Medium** 8: 3 An-12 *Cub*; 2 C-130B *Hercules*; 1 C-130E *Hercules*; 2 L-100-30; **Light** 4: 1 An-26 *Curl*; 1 An-32 *Cline*; 1 DHC-6 *Twin Otter*; 1 Yak-40 *Codling* (VIP)
  TRG 16: 12 L-39 *Albatros*; 4 SF-260
HELICOPTERS
  ATK 18: 15 Mi-24 *Hind*; 3 Mi-35 *Hind*
  MRH 7: 1 AW139; 6 SA316 *Alouette* III
  MRH/TPT 12 Mi-8 *Hip*/Mi-17 *Hip* H
AIR-LAUNCHED MISSILES
  AAM • IR R-3 (AA-2 *Atoll*)‡; R-60 (AA-8 *Aphid*); R-73 (AA-11 *Archer*); **IR/SARH** R-23/R-24 (AA-7 *Apex*); R-27 (AA-10 *Alamo*)

DEPLOYMENT

CÔTE D'IVOIRE
UN • UNOCI 2 obs

LIBERIA
UN • UNMIL 2; 3 obs

SOMALIA
AU • AMISOM 4,395; 6 inf bn

SOUTH SUDAN
UN • UNMISS 1,267; 10 obs; 2 inf bn

SUDAN
UN • UNAMID 2,537; 11 obs; 3 inf bn
UN • UNISFA 4,371; 78 obs; 1 recce coy; 3 mech inf bn; 1 hel sqn; 2 arty coy; 1 engr coy; 1 sigs coy; 1 fd hospital

Gabon GAB

CFA Franc BEAC fr		2015	2016	2017
GDP	fr	8.44tr	8.58tr	
	US$	14.3bn	14.6bn	
per capita	US$	7,692	7,741	
Growth	%	4.0	3.2	
Inflation	%	0.1	2.5	
Def bdgt [a]	fr	116bn	120bn	
	US$	197m	204m	
US$1=fr		591.16	589.385	

[a] Includes funds allocated to Republican Guard

Population 1,738,541

Age	0–14	15–19	20–24	25–29	30–64	65 plus
Male	21.1%	5.5%	4.7%	4.1%	12.8%	1.6%
Female	20.9%	5.5%	4.7%	4.1%	12.9%	2.2%

Capabilities

Gabon's small armed forces are reasonably well equipped for their size. There is sufficient airlift to ensure mobility within the country and even a limited capability to project power by sea and air. The country has benefited from the long-term presence of French troops acting as a security guarantor, while oil revenues have allowed the government to support, in regional terms, capable armed forces. There is regular training with international partners. Military medicine is well regarded. Gabon contributed a field hospital to the ECCAS *Loango 2014* exercise and engaged in field medical training with US forces in 2015. Gabon hosted US AFRICOM's *Central Accord 2016* exercise, which focused on peacekeeping operations.

ACTIVE 4,700 (Army 3,200 Navy 500 Air 1,000)
Paramilitary 2,000

ORGANISATIONS BY SERVICE

Army 3,200

Republican Guard under direct presidential control
FORCES BY ROLE
MANOEUVRE
  Light
  1 (Republican Guard) gd gp (bn)
    (1 armd/recce coy, 3 inf coy, 1 arty bty, 1 ADA bty)
  8 inf coy
  Air Manoeuvre
  1 cdo/AB coy
COMBAT SUPPORT
  1 engr coy
EQUIPMENT BY TYPE
ARMOURED FIGHTING VEHICLES
  RECCE 77: 24 AML-60/AML-90; 12 EE-3 *Jararaca*; 14 EE-9 *Cascavel*; 6 ERC-90F4 *Sagaie*; 7 RAM V-2; 14 VBL
  IFV 12 EE-11 *Urutu* (with 20mm gun)
  APC 64
    APC (W) 30: 9 LAV-150 *Commando*; 5 Bastion APC; 3 WZ-523; 12 VXB-170; 1 *Pandur*
    PPV 34 Ashok Leyland MPV
  AUV 12 *Aravis*
ANTI-TANK/ANTI-INFRASTRUCTURE
  MSL • MANPATS *Milan*
  RCL 106mm M40A1
ARTILLERY 51
  TOWED 105mm 4 M101
  MRL 140mm 8 *Teruel*
  MOR 39: **81mm** 35; **120mm** 4 Brandt
AIR DEFENCE • GUNS 41
  SP 20mm 4 ERC-20
  TOWED 37: **23mm** 24 ZU-23-2; **37mm** 10 M-1939; **40mm** 3 L/70

Navy ε500

HQ located at Port Gentil
EQUIPMENT BY TYPE
PATROL AND COASTAL COMBATANTS 11

PCC 2 *General Ba'Oumar* (FRA P-400) with 1 57mm gun
PBG 1 *Patra* with 4 SS 12M AShM
PB 8: 4 *Port Gentil* (FRA VCSM); 4 Rodman 66
AMPHIBIOUS 14
　LANDING SHIPS • LST 1 *President Omar Bongo* (FRA *Batral*) (capacity 1 LCVP; 7 MBT; 140 troops) with 1 hel landing platform **LANDING CRAFT** 13
　　LCU 1 Mk 9 (ex-UK)
　　LCVP 12

Air Force 1,000
FORCES BY ROLE
FIGHTER/GROUND ATTACK
　1 sqn with *Mirage* F-1AZ
TRANSPORT
　1 (Republican Guard) sqn with AS332 *Super Puma*; ATR-42F; *Falcon* 900; Gulfstream IV-SP/G650ER
　1 sqn with C-130H *Hercules*; CN-235M-100
ATTACK/TRANSPORT HELICOPTER
　1 sqn with Bell 412 *Twin Huey* (AB-412); SA330C/H *Puma*; SA342M *Gazelle*
EQUIPMENT BY TYPE
AIRCRAFT 8 combat capable
　FGA 6 *Mirage* F-1AZ
　ATK 2 MB-326 *Impala* I
　MP (1 EMB-111* in store)
　TPT 6: **Medium** 1 C-130H *Hercules*; (1 L-100-30 in store); **Light** 2: 1 ATR-42F; 1 CN-235M-100; **PAX** 3: 1 *Falcon* 900; 1 Gulfstream IV-SP; 1 Gulfstream G650ER
　TRG (4 CM-170 *Magister* in store)
HELICOPTERS
　MRH 2: 1 Bell 412 *Twin Huey* (AB-412); 1 SA342M *Gazelle*; (2 SA342L *Gazelle* in store)
　TPT 7: **Medium** 4: 1 AS332 *Super Puma*; 3 SA330C/H *Puma*; **Light** 3: 2 H120 *Colibri*; 1 H135
AIR-LAUNCHED MISSILES • AAM • IR *U-Darter* (reported)

Paramilitary 2,000

Gendarmerie 2,000
FORCES BY ROLE
MANOEUVRE
　Armoured
　　2 armd sqn
　Other
　　3 paramilitary bde
　　11 paramilitary coy
　Aviation
　　1 unit with AS350 *Ecureuil*; AS355 *Ecureuil* II
EQUIPMENT BY TYPE
HELICOPTERS • TPT • Light 4: 2 AS350 *Ecureuil*; 2 AS355 *Ecureuil* II

DEPLOYMENT

CENTRAL AFRICAN REPUBLIC
UN • MINUSCA 445; 1 inf bn(-)

FOREIGN FORCES
France 450; 1 AB bn

Gambia GAM

Gambian Dalasi D		2015	2016	2017
GDP	D	38.2bn	42.2bn	
	US$	893m	886m	
per capita	US$	451	435	
Growth	%	4.4	2.3	
Inflation	%	6.8	8.3	
Def bdgt	D	591m	n.k.	
	US$	14m	n.k.	
US$1=D		42.79	47.66	

Population　2,009,648

Age	0–14	15–19	20–24	25–29	30–64	65 plus
Male	19.0%	5.3%	4.9%	4.3%	14.3%	1.6%
Female	18.9%	5.4%	5.1%	4.5%	14.9%	1.8%

Capabilities

Maritime security and human trafficking are security concerns. A National Maritime Security Committee was inaugurated in 2015. The country has a small army supported by air and marine units. Its forces have been deployed in support of UN missions, and have received training assistance from the US.

ACTIVE 800 (Army 800)

ORGANISATIONS BY SERVICE

Gambian National Army 800
FORCES BY ROLE
MANOEUVRE
　Light
　　2 inf bn
　Other
　　1 (Presidential Guard) gd coy
COMBAT SUPPORT
　1 engr sqn

Marine Unit ε300
EQUIPMENT BY TYPE
PATROL AND COASTAL COMBATANTS 9
　PBF 4: 2 Rodman 55; 2 *Fatimah* I
　PB 5: 1 *Bolong Kanta*†; 4 *Taipei* (ROC *Hai Ou*) (of which one damaged and in reserve)

Air Wing
EQUIPMENT BY TYPE
AIRCRAFT
　TPT 5: **Light** 2 AT-802A *Air Tractor*; **PAX** 3: 1 B-727; 1 CL-601; 1 Il-62M *Classic* (VIP)

DEPLOYMENT

CENTRAL AFRICAN REPUBLIC
UN • MINUSCA 2; 2 obs

CÔTE D'IVOIRE
UN • UNOCI 1 obs

LIBERIA
UN • UNMIL 3 obs

MALI
UN • MINUSMA 4

SUDAN
UN • UNAMID 213; 1 inf coy

Ghana GHA

Ghanaian New Cedi C		2015	2016	2017
GDP	C	140bn	167bn	
	US$	37.7bn	42.8bn	
per capita	US$	1,402	1,551	
Growth	%	3.9	3.3	
Inflation	%	17.2	17.0	
Def bdgt	C	880m	761m	790m
	US$	237m	195m	
FMA (US)	US$	0.3m	0.3m	0.3m
US$1=C		3.71	3.90	

Population 26,908,262

Age	0–14	15–19	20–24	25–29	30–64	65 plus
Male	19.2%	5.0%	4.3%	3.9%	15.0%	1.9%
Female	19.0%	5.0%	4.4%	4.0%	16.0%	2.3%

Capabilities

Ghana's armed forces are some of the most capable in the region, with a long-term development plan covering both the current and the next decade. The ability to control its maritime EEZ is of increasing importance to Ghana because of growing piracy and resource exploitation, and this underpins the navy's expansion ambitions. Internal and maritime security are the forces' central roles, along with participation in peacekeeping missions. Ghana hosted joint readiness exercise *Epic Guardian* with the US in April–May 2016 and Ghanaian and US units also conducted joint maritime-law-enforcement and interoperability activities as part of the Africa Maritime Law Enforcement Partnership. In November 2015, the air force announced plans to expand its training and close-air-support capabilities with *Super Tucano*s from Brazil. The air force also continues to build its airlift capacity and took delivery of a third C295 light transport aircraft in November 2015. The army is a regular contributor to UN peacekeeping operations, and has pledged to maintain 1,000 personnel in readiness for missions, including a mechanised infantry battalion, a level-two hospital, a signals company, an aviation unit and a riverine unit.

ACTIVE 15,500 (Army 11,500 Navy 2,000 Air 2,000)

ORGANISATIONS BY SERVICE

Army 11,500
FORCES BY ROLE
COMMAND
  2 comd HQ
MANOEUVRE
  Reconnaissance
  1 armd recce regt (3 recce sqn)
  Light
  1 (rapid reaction) mot inf bn
  6 inf bn
  Air Manoeuvre
  2 AB coy
COMBAT SUPPORT
  1 arty regt (1 arty bty, 2 mor bty)
  1 fd engr regt (bn)
  1 sigs regt
  1 sigs sqn
COMBAT SERVICE SUPPORT
  1 log gp
  1 tpt coy
  2 maint coy
  1 med coy
  1 trg bn
EQUIPMENT BY TYPE
ARMOURED FIGHTING VEHICLES
  RECCE 3 EE-9 *Cascavel*
  IFV 39: 24 *Ratel*-90; 15 *Ratel*-20
  APC • APC (W) 56: 50 *Piranha*; 6 Type-05P
  ARTY 87+
    TOWED 122mm 6 D-30
    MRL 3+: **107mm** Type-63; **122mm** 3 Type-81
    MOR 78: **81mm** 50; **120mm** 28 *Tampella*
ENGINEERING & MAINTENANCE VEHICLES
  ARV *Piranha* reported
ANTI-TANK/ANTI-INFRASTRUCTURE
  RCL **84mm** 50 *Carl Gustav*
AIR DEFENCE
  SAM • **Point-defence** 9K32 *Strela*-2 (SA-7 *Grail*)‡
  GUNS • TOWED 8+: **14.5mm** 4+: 4 ZPU-2; ZPU-4; **23mm** 4 ZU-23-2

Navy 2,000
Naval HQ located at Accra; Western HQ located at Sekondi; Eastern HQ located at Tema
EQUIPMENT BY TYPE
PATROL AND COASTAL COMBATANTS 14
  PCO 2 *Anzone* (US)
  PCC 10: 2 *Achimota* (GER Lurssen 57m) with 1 76mm gun; 2 *Dzata* (GER Lurssen 45m); 2 *Warrior* (GER *Gepard*); 4 *Snake* (PRC 47m)
  PBF 1 *Stephen Otu* (ROK *Sea Dolphin*)
  PB 1 *David Hansen* (US)

Air Force 2,000
FORCES BY ROLE
GROUND ATTACK
  1 sqn with K-8 *Karakorum**; L-39ZO*; MB-326K; MB-339A*

ISR
  1 unit with DA-42
TRANSPORT
  1 sqn with BN-2 *Defender*; C-295; Cessna 172; F-28 *Fellowship* (VIP)
TRANSPORT HELICOPTER
  1 sqn with AW109A; Bell 412SP *Twin Huey*; Mi-17V-5 *Hip* H; SA319 *Alouette* III; Z-9EH

EQUIPMENT BY TYPE†
AIRCRAFT 11 combat capable
  ATK 3 MB-326K
  TPT 11: **Light** 10: 1 BN-2 *Defender*; 3 C-295; 3 Cessna 172; 3 DA42; **PAX** 1 F-28 *Fellowship* (VIP)
  TRG 8: 4 K-8 *Karakorum**; 2 L-39ZO*; 2 MB-339A*
HELICOPTERS
  MRH 10: 1 Bell 412SP *Twin Huey*; 3 Mi-17V-5 *Hip* H; 2 SA319 *Alouette* III; 4 Z-9EH
  TPT 6: **Medium** 4 Mi-171Sh; **Light** 2 AW109A

DEPLOYMENT

CENTRAL AFRICAN REPUBLIC
UN • MINUSCA 4; 4 obs

CÔTE D'IVOIRE
UN • UNOCI 95; 3 obs; 1 hel sqn

DEMOCRATIC REPUBLIC OF THE CONGO
UN • MONUSCO 466; 21 obs; 1 mech inf bn(-)

LEBANON
UN • UNIFIL 870; 1 mech inf bn

LIBERIA
UN • UNMIL 58; 7 obs; 1 log coy

MALI
UN • MINUSMA 214; 3 obs; 1 engr coy; 1 hel sqn

SOUTH SUDAN
UN • UNMISS 715; 3 obs; 1 inf bn

SUDAN
UN • UNAMID 18; 4 obs
UN • UNISFA 2; 4 obs

WESTERN SAHARA
UN • MINURSO 4; 10 obs

Guinea GUI

Guinean Franc fr		2015	2016	2017
GDP	fr	51.3tr	58.2tr	
	US$	6.85bn	6.75bn	
per capita	US$	555	534	
Growth	%	0.1	3.8	
Inflation	%	8.2	8.2	
Def exp	fr	n.k.	n.k.	
	US$	n.k.	n.k.	
US$1=fr		7,489.02	8,617.21	

Population 12,093,349

Age	0–14	15–19	20–24	25–29	30–64	65 plus
Male	21.1%	5.4%	4.5%	3.8%	13.6%	1.6%
Female	20.6%	5.3%	4.5%	3.8%	13.8%	2.0%

Capabilities

Much of the country's military equipment is ageing and of Soviet-era vintage; serviceability will be questionable for some types. A military-programming law for 2015–20 is reportedly examining operational capacities. There is no fixed-wing airlift capacity and very limited rotary-wing airlift. China donated a small amount of non-lethal military and civilian equipment following an international appeal by Guinea after seven personnel serving with the UN mission in Mali were killed in an attack.

ACTIVE 9,700 (Army 8,500 Navy 400 Air 800)
Paramilitary 2,600
Conscript liability 2 years

ORGANISATIONS BY SERVICE

Army 8,500
FORCES BY ROLE
MANOEUVRE
  Armoured
  1 armd bn
  Light
  1 SF bn
  5 inf bn
  1 ranger bn
  1 cdo bn
  Air Manoeuvre
  1 air mob bn
  Other
  1 (Presidential Guard) gd bn
COMBAT SUPPORT
  1 arty bn
  1 AD bn
  1 engr bn
EQUIPMENT BY TYPE
ARMOURED FIGHTING VEHICLES
  MBT 38: 30 T-34; 8 T-54
  LT TK 15 PT-76
  RECCE 27: 2 AML-90; 25 BRDM-1/BRDM-2

IFV 2 BMP-1
APC 50
  APC (T) 10 BTR-50
  APC (W) 30: 16 BTR-40; 8 BTR-60; 6 BTR-152
  PPV 10 Mamba†
ENGINEERING & MAINTENANCE VEHICLES
  ARV T-54/T-55 reported
ANTI-TANK/ANTI-INFRASTRUCTURE
  MSL • MANPATS 9K11 *Malyutka* (AT-3 *Sagger*); 9K111-1 *Konkurs* (AT-5 *Spandrel*)
  RCL 82mm B-10
  GUNS 6+: **57mm** ZIS-2 (M-1943); **85mm** 6 D-44
ARTILLERY 47+
  TOWED 24: **122mm** 12 M-1931/37; **130mm** 12 M-46
  MRL 220mm 3 9P140 *Uragan*
  MOR 20+: **82mm** M-43; **120mm** 20 M-1938/M-1943
AIR DEFENCE
  SAM • Point-defence 9K32 *Strela*-2 (SA-7 *Grail*)‡
  GUNS • TOWED 24+: **30mm** M-53 (twin); **37mm** 8 M-1939; **57mm** 12 Type-59 (S-60); **100mm** 4 KS-19

Navy ε400
EQUIPMENT BY TYPE
PATROL AND COASTAL COMBATANTS • PB 4: 1 Swiftships†; 3 RPB 20

Air Force 800
EQUIPMENT BY TYPE†
AIRCRAFT
  FGA (3 MiG-21 *Fishbed* non-op)
  TPT • Light 4: 2 An-2 *Colt*; 2 Tetras
HELICOPTERS
  ATK 4 Mi-24 *Hind*
  MRH 5: 2 MD-500MD; 2 Mi-17-1V *Hip* H; 1 SA342K *Gazelle*
  TPT 2: **Medium** 1 SA330 *Puma*; **Light** 1 AS350B *Ecureuil*
AIR-LAUNCHED MISSILES
  AAM • IR R-3 (AA-2 *Atoll*)‡

Paramilitary 2,600 active

Gendarmerie 1,000

Republican Guard 1,600

People's Militia 7,000 reservists

DEPLOYMENT

CÔTE D'IVOIRE
UN • UNOCI 2 obs

DEMOCRATIC REPUBLIC OF THE CONGO
UN • MONUSCO 1

MALI
UN • MINUSMA 858; 3 obs; 1 inf bn

SOUTH SUDAN
UN • UNMISS 1; 1 obs

SUDAN
UN • UNISFA 1

WESTERN SAHARA
UN • MINURSO 5 obs

Guinea-Bissau GNB

CFA Franc BCEAO fr		2015	2016	2017
GDP	fr	625bn	689bn	
	US$	1.06bn	1.17bn	
per capita	US$	594	643	
Growth	%	4.8	4.8	
Inflation	%	1.5	2.6	
Def exp	fr	n.k.	n.k.	
	US$	n.k.	n.k.	
US$1=fr		591.41	589.479	

Population 1,759,159

Age	0–14	15–19	20–24	25–29	30–64	65 plus
Male	19.6%	5.3%	4.7%	4.1%	13.9%	1.3%
Female	19.7%	5.4%	4.8%	4.2%	15.0%	2.1%

Capabilities

The armed forces have often played a direct role in domestic politics. Narcotics trafficking and organised crime remain substantial problems for the security forces. Previous attempts at security-sector reform have largely been unsuccessful, and long-term international support is necessary for future attempts to gain traction. Political instability continues, and the UN in late 2016 pressed for the armed forces to maintain their independence. ECOWAS maintains a security mission in Guinea-Bissau (ECOMIB), with EU funding support. The parlous state of the economy limits any ability to replace its ageing inventory of mainly Soviet-era equipment.

ACTIVE 4,450 (Army 4,000 Navy 350 Air 100)
Conscript liability Selective conscription
Manpower and eqpt totals should be treated with caution. A number of draft laws to restructure the armed services and police have been produced

ORGANISATIONS BY SERVICE

Army ε4,000 (numbers reducing)
FORCES BY ROLE
MANOEUVRE
  Reconnaissance
    1 recce coy
  Armoured
    1 armd bn (sqn)
  Light
    5 inf bn
COMBAT SUPPORT
  1 arty bn
  1 engr coy

EQUIPMENT BY TYPE
ARMOURED FIGHTING VEHICLES
  MBT 10 T-34
  LT TK 15 PT-76
  RECCE 10 BRDM-2
  APC • APC (W) 55: 35 BTR-40/BTR-60; 20 Type-56 (BTR-152)
ANTI-TANK/ANTI-INFRASTRUCTURE
  RCL 75mm Type-52 (M20); 82mm B-10
  GUNS 85mm 8 D-44
ARTILLERY 26+
  TOWED 122mm 18 D-30/M-30 (M-1938)
  MOR 8+: 82mm M-43; 120mm 8 M-1943
AIR DEFENCE
  SAM • Point-defence 9K32 *Strela*-2 (SA-7 *Grail*)‡
  GUNS • TOWED 34: 23mm 18 ZU-23; 37mm 6 M-1939; 57mm 10 S-60

Navy ε350
EQUIPMENT BY TYPE
PATROL AND COASTAL COMBATANTS • PB 2 *Alfeite*†

Air Force 100
EQUIPMENT BY TYPE
AIRCRAFT • TPT • Light 1 Cessna 208B

DEPLOYMENT

MALI
UN • MINUSMA 1

FOREIGN FORCES
Nigeria ECOMIB 160

Kenya KEN

Kenyan Shilling sh		2015	2016	2017
GDP	sh	6.22tr	7.04tr	
	US$	63.4bn	69.2bn	
per capita	US$	1,434	1,522	
Growth	%	5.6	6.0	
Inflation	%	6.6	6.2	
Def bdgt [a]	sh	90.7bn	124bn	123bn
	US$	924m	1.22bn	
FMA (US)	US$	1.2m	1m	1m
US$1=sh		98.18	101.75	

[a] Includes national-intelligence funding

Population 46,790,758

Age	0–14	15–19	20–24	25–29	30–64	65 plus
Male	20.5%	5.0%	4.4%	4.2%	14.5%	1.3%
Female	20.4%	5.0%	4.4%	4.2%	14.4%	1.7%

Capabilities

Kenya's armed forces are a leading element of the East African Standby Force, and AMISOM in Somalia. Combat units that have rotated through Somalia have a higher level of confidence and capability, which is also reflected in Kenya's contribution to UN peacekeeping missions. In tandem with the police, the armed forces have been involved in internal-security tasks in the wake of al-Shabaab terrorist attacks in recent years. The threat of attack from al-Shabaab remains a significant security concern. Modernisation is focused on helicopters, armoured vehicles, UAVs and border-surveillance equipment. The navy undertakes coastguard and counter-piracy roles. The country has the ability to project power beyond its own territory, on a limited basis, and after operations in Somalia is well versed in managing deployment cycles. The air force set up a combat search-and-rescue unit in late 2016 following the loss of an F-5 aircraft two years earlier. The armed forces regularly join UK troops training in Kenya (a new defence-cooperation agreement was signed with the UK in September 2016) and take part in international exercises in Africa. There are significant defence ties with the US and a developing relationship with the Chinese armed forces.

ACTIVE 24,100 (Army 20,000 Navy 1,600 Air 2,500)
Paramilitary 5,000

ORGANISATIONS BY SERVICE

Army 20,000
FORCES BY ROLE
MANOEUVRE
  Armoured
  1 armd bde (1 armd recce bn, 2 armd bn)
  Light
  1 spec ops bn
  1 ranger bn
  1 inf bde (3 inf bn)
  1 inf bde (2 inf bn)
  1 indep inf bn
  Air Manoeuvre
  1 air cav bn
  1 AB bn
COMBAT SUPPORT
  1 arty bde (2 arty bn, 1 mor bty)
  1 ADA bn
  1 engr bde (2 engr bn)
EQUIPMENT BY TYPE
ARMOURED FIGHTING VEHICLES
MBT 78 Vickers Mk 3
RECCE 92: 72 AML-60/AML-90; 12 *Ferret*; 8 S52 *Shorland*
APC 189
  APC (W) 84: 52 UR-416; 32 Type-92; (10 M3 Panhard in store)
  PPV 105 *Puma* M26-15
ENGINEERING & MAINTENANCE VEHICLES
  ARV 7 Vickers ARV
  MW *Bozena*
ARTILLERY 110
  TOWED 105mm 48: 40 L118 Light Gun; 8 Model 56 pack howitzer
  MOR 62: 81mm 50; 120mm 12 Brandt

ANTI-TANK/ANTI-INFRASTRUCTURE
 MSL • MANPATS *Milan*
 RCL **84mm** 80 *Carl Gustav*
HELICOPTERS
 MRH 37: 2 Hughes 500D†; 12 Hughes 500M†; 10 Hughes 500MD *Scout Defender*† (with TOW); 10 Hughes 500ME†; 3 Z-9W
AIR DEFENCE • GUNS • TOWED 94: **20mm** 81: 11 Oerlikon; ε70 TCM-20; **40mm** 13 L/70
AIR-LAUNCHED MISSILES • ASM TOW

Navy 1,600 (incl 120 marines)
EQUIPMENT BY TYPE
PATROL AND COASTAL COMBATANTS 7
 PCO 1 *Jasiri* (to be fitted with 1 76mm gun)
 PCFG 2 *Nyayo*
 PCC 3: 1 *Harambee II* (ex-FRA P400); 2 *Shupavu* with 1 76mm gun
 PBF 1 *Archangel*
AMPHIBIOUS • LCM 2 *Galana*
LOGISTICS AND SUPPORT • AP 2

Air Force 2,500
FORCES BY ROLE
FIGHTER/GROUND ATTACK
 2 sqn with F-5E/F *Tiger* II
TRANSPORT
 Some sqn with DHC-5D *Buffalo*†; DHC-8†; F-70† (VIP); Y-12(II)†
TRAINING
 Some sqn with *Bulldog* 103/*Bulldog* 127†; EMB-312 *Tucano*†*; *Hawk* Mk52†*; Hughes 500D†
TRANSPORT HELICOPTER
 1 sqn with SA330 *Puma*†
EQUIPMENT BY TYPE†
AIRCRAFT 38 combat capable
 FTR 22: 18 F-5E *Tiger* II; 4 F-5F *Tiger* II
 TPT 17 **Light** 16: 4 DHC-5D *Buffalo*†; 3 DHC-8†; 9 Y-12(II)†; (6 Do-28D-2† in store); **PAX** 1 F-70 (VIP)
 TRG 30: 8 *Bulldog* 103/127†; 11 EMB-312 *Tucano*†*; 6 Grob 120A; 5 *Hawk* Mk52†*
HELICOPTERS
 TPT • **Medium** 12: 2 Mi-171; 10 SA330 *Puma*†
AIR-LAUNCHED MISSILES
 AAM • IR AIM-9 *Sidewinder*
 ASM AGM-65 *Maverick*

Paramilitary 5,000

Police General Service Unit 5,000
EQUIPMENT BY TYPE
PATROL AND COASTAL COMBATANTS • PB 5 (2 on Lake Victoria)

Air Wing
EQUIPMENT BY TYPE
AIRCRAFT • TPT • **Light** 6: 2 Cessna 208B *Caravan*; 3 Cessna 310; 1 Cessna 402
HELICOPTERS
 MRH 3 Mi-17 *Hip* H
 TPT • **Light** 2: 1 Bell 206L *Long Ranger*; 1 Bo-105
 TRG 1 Bell 47G

DEPLOYMENT

CENTRAL AFRICAN REPUBLIC
UN • MINUSCA 8; 6 obs

DEMOCRATIC REPUBLIC OF THE CONGO
UN • MONUSCO 13; 13 obs

LEBANON
UN • UNIFIL 1

MALI
UN • MINUSMA 4; 3 obs

SOMALIA
AU • AMISOM 3,664: 3 inf bn

SOUTH SUDAN
UN • UNMISS 1,027; 12 obs; 1 inf bn

SUDAN
UN • UNAMID 112; 3 obs; 1 MP coy

FOREIGN FORCES
United Kingdom Army 260

Lesotho LSO

Lesotho Loti M		2015	2016	2017
GDP	M	26.1bn	28.9bn	
	US$	2.04bn	1.81bn	
per capita	US$	1,057	933	
Growth	%	2.8	2.4	
Inflation	%	5.3	8.6	
Def bdgt	M	555m	642m	
	US$	44m	40m	
US$1=M		12.75	16.00	

Population 1,953,070

Age	0–14	15–19	20–24	25–29	30–64	65 plus
Male	16.3%	4.8%	4.5%	4.5%	16.5%	2.8%
Female	16.1%	5.1%	5.1%	5.3%	16.2%	2.7%

Capabilities

Lesotho's small armed forces are charged with protecting territorial integrity and sovereignty. The country contains significant water resources, which form a significant portion of its foreign trade. The armed forces' cohesion has suffered following an attempted military coup in September 2014, which prompted South Africa, which effectively acts as Lesotho's security guarantor, to deploy 140 police officers late that year. Continued political instability throughout 2015, notably the killing in mid-year of a former army commander, led South Africa to deploy a fact-finding mission, and the Southern African Development Community (SADC) to organise a commission of inquiry. Despite recommendations from the SADC at the end of 2015 for Lesotho to make constitutional and security reforms, these have not been realised.

ACTIVE 2,000 (Army 2,000)

ORGANISATIONS BY SERVICE

Army ε2,000
FORCES BY ROLE
MANOEUVRE
  Reconnaissance
  1 recce coy
  Light
  7 inf coy
  Aviation
  1 sqn
COMBAT SUPPORT
  1 arty bty(-)
  1 spt coy (with mor)
EQUIPMENT BY TYPE
ARMOURED FIGHTING VEHICLES
  MBT 1 T-55
  RECCE 30: 4 AML-90; 2 BRDM-2†; 6 RAM Mk3; 10 RBY-1; 8 S52 *Shorland*
ANTI-TANK/ANTI-INFRASTRUCTURE
  RCL 106mm 6 M40
ARTILLERY 12
  TOWED 105mm 2
  MOR 81mm 10

Air Wing 110
AIRCRAFT
  TPT • Light 3: 2 C-212-300 *Aviocar*; 1 GA-8 *Airvan*
HELICOPTERS
  MRH 3: 1 Bell 412 *Twin Huey*; 2 Bell 412EP *Twin Huey*
  TPT • Light 2: 1 Bell 206 *Jet Ranger*; 1 H135

Liberia LBR

Liberian Dollar L$		2015	2016	2017
GDP	L$	2.03bn	2.17bn	
	US$	2.03bn	2.17bn	
per capita	US$	474	493	
Growth	%	0.0	2.0	
Inflation	%	7.7	8.6	
Def bdgt	L$	15m	13m	13m
	US$	15m	13m	
FMA (US)	US$	2.5m	2.5m	2.5m
US$1=L$		1.00	1.00	

Population 4,299,944
Ethnic groups: Americo-Liberians 5%

Age	0–14	15–19	20–24	25–29	30–64	65 plus
Male	21.3%	5.6%	3.7%	3.8%	13.9%	1.6%
Female	21.0%	5.7%	3.9%	3.9%	14.1%	1.6%

Capabilities

The development of the Liberian armed forces has been underpinned by US support for almost the past decade. A memorandum of understanding with Nigeria, related to assistance in rebuilding Liberia's armed forces, ended in June 2016, and Liberia pledged assistance to Nigeria in the counter-terrorism campaign as part of a plan to maintain cooperation. In July 2016, the Liberian security forces took over full responsibility for security from the UN peacekeeping mission, UNMIL, after 13 years. UNMIL reverted to a support role. The future of the mission was to be decided in December 2016. In May 2016, the UN Security Council voted to lift sanctions and the arms embargo against Liberia. There is still no indigenous airlift capacity. This hindered movements during the recent Ebola outbreak, which was a major challenge for the developing local security forces.

ACTIVE 2,050 (Army 2,000, Coast Guard 50)

ORGANISATIONS BY SERVICE

Army 2,000
FORCES BY ROLE
MANOEUVRE
  Light
  1 (23rd) inf bde with (2 inf bn, 1 engr coy, 1 MP coy)
COMBAT SERVICE SUPPORT
  1 trg unit (forming)

Coast Guard 50
All operational patrol vessels under 10t FLD

DEPLOYMENT

MALI
UN • MINUSMA 45; 1 inf pl

FOREIGN FORCES

All under UNMIL comd unless otherwise specified
Bangladesh 4; 4 obs
Benin 1; 1 obs
Bolivia 1 obs
Brazil 1; 1 obs
Bulgaria 1 obs
China, People's Republic of 127; 1 obs; 1 engr pl; 1 tpt coy
Egypt 5 obs
Ethiopia 2; 3 obs
Gambia 3 obs
Ghana 58; 7 obs; 1 log coy
Indonesia 1 obs
Malaysia 1; 2 obs
Moldova 1 obs
Myanmar 2 obs
Namibia 1; 1 obs
Nepal 17; 2 obs
Niger 2 obs
Nigeria 704; 9 obs; 1 inf bn
Pakistan 95; 4 obs; 1 fd hospital
Russia 2 obs
Serbia 1 obs

Togo 1; 1 obs
Ukraine 162; 3 obs; 1 hel sqn
United States 5; 3 obs
Zambia 1 obs
Zimbabwe 1 obs

Madagascar MDG

Malagsy Ariary fr		2015	2016	2017
GDP	fr	28.6tr	31.8tr	
	US$	9.74bn	9.74bn	
per capita	US$	402	391	
Growth	%	3.1	4.1	
Inflation	%	7.4	6.7	
Def bdgt	fr	173bn	188bn	
	US$	59m	58m	
US$1=fr		2,933.58	3,262.15	

Population 24,430,325

Age	0–14	15–19	20–24	25–29	30–64	65 plus
Male	21.3%	5.6%	3.7%	3.8%	13.9%	1.6%
Female	21.0%	5.7%	3.9%	3.9%	14.1%	1.6%

Capabilities

The armed forces have played a significant role in the island's recent political instability, with some elements involved in an abortive coup attempt in 2010 and a mutiny in 2012. In mid-2016 there was a terrorist attack allegedly carried out by opponents of the current president. The army is the dominant force, but the state has no power-projection capability. Moves towards security-sector reform (SSR) have begun, with an African Union mission conducted in late 2015, designed to 'sensitise senior officials and civil society' on SSR. Madagascar was the host of the US-led *Africa Endeavor 2016* communications-interoperability exercise.

ACTIVE 13,500 (Army 12,500 Navy 500 Air 500)
Paramilitary 8,100
Conscript liability 18 months (incl for civil purposes)

ORGANISATIONS BY SERVICE

Army 12,500+
FORCES BY ROLE
MANOEUVRE
  Light
    2 (intervention) inf regt
    10 (regional) inf regt
COMBAT SUPPORT
  1 arty regt
  3 engr regt
  1 sigs regt
COMBAT SERVICE SUPPORT
  1 log regt
AIR DEFENCE
  1 ADA regt

EQUIPMENT BY TYPE
ARMOURED FIGHTING VEHICLES
  LT TK 12 PT-76
  RECCE 73: ε35 BRDM-2; 10 FV701 *Ferret*; ε20 M3A1; 8 M8
  APC • APC (T) ε30 M3A1 half-track
ANTI-TANK/ANTI-INFRASTRUCTURE
  RCL 106mm M40A1
ARTILLERY 25+
  TOWED 17: 105mm 5 M101; 122mm 12 D-30
  MOR 8+: 82mm M-37; 120mm 8 M-43
AIR DEFENCE • GUNS • TOWED 70: 14.5mm 50 ZPU-4; 37mm 20 PG-55 (M-1939)

Navy 500 (incl some 100 Marines)
EQUIPMENT BY TYPE
PATROL AND COASTAL COMBATANTS 8
  PCC 1 *Trozona*
  PB 7 (ex-US CG MLB)
AMPHIBIOUS • LCT 1 (ex-FRA *Edic*)

Air Force 500
FORCES BY ROLE
TRANSPORT
  1 sqn with An-26 *Curl*; Yak-40 *Codling* (VIP)
  1 (liaison) sqn with Cessna 310; Cessna 337 *Skymaster*; PA-23 *Aztec*
TRAINING
  1 sqn with Cessna 172; J.300 *Joker*; *Tetras*
TRANSPORT HELICOPTER
  1 sqn with SA318C *Alouette* II

EQUIPMENT BY TYPE
AIRCRAFT • TPT 16: **Light** 14: 1 An-26 *Curl*; 4 Cessna 172; 1 Cessna 310; 2 Cessna 337 *Skymaster*; 2 J.300 *Joker*; 1 PA-23 *Aztec*; 1 *Tetras*; 2 Yak-40 *Codling* (VIP); **PAX** 2 B-737
HELICOPTERS • MRH 4 SA318C *Alouette* II

Paramilitary 8,100

Gendarmerie 8,100

Malawi MWI

Malawian Kwacha K		2015	2016	2017
GDP	K	3.20tr	3.88tr	
	US$	6.41bn	5.47bn	
per capita	US$	354	294	
Growth	%	3.0	2.7	
Inflation	%	21.9	19.8	
Def bdgt	K	18bn	20.7bn	22bn
	US$	36m	29m	
US$1=K		499.57	708.22	

Population 18,570,321

Age	0–14	15–19	20–24	25–29	30–64	65 plus
Male	23.2%	5.6%	4.6%	3.6%	11.3%	1.2%
Female	23.5%	5.7%	4.6%	3.7%	11.6%	1.5%

Capabilities

The armed forces' role is to ensure the sovereignty and territorial integrity of the state. The army is the largest force, consisting mainly of infantry units supported by light armoured vehicles. The air wing and the naval unit are much smaller supporting services for which counter-trafficking is one role. The army participates in and hosts multinational exercises, and is involved in supporting UN missions. Malawi receives training support from the US, with focus on NCO training in 2016. The UK also reportedly helped the ground forces with reconnaissance training in 2016. The defence force is unable to deploy outside Malawi's borders without external assistance, although it has dispatched troops to the Democratic Republic of the Congo, among other UN operations, to take part in tasks assigned to the Force Intervention Brigade.

ACTIVE 5,300 (Army 5,300) **Paramilitary 1,500**

ORGANISATIONS BY SERVICE

Army 5,300

FORCES BY ROLE
COMMAND
  2 bde HQ
MANOEUVRE
  Light
  5 inf bn
  Air Manoeuvre
  1 para bn
COMBAT SUPPORT
  1 (general) bn (1+ mne coy, 1 armd recce sqn, 2 lt arty bty, 1 engr unit)
COMBAT SERVICE SUPPORT
  8 log coy

EQUIPMENT BY TYPE
Less than 20% serviceability
ARMOURED FIGHTING VEHICLES
  RECCE 41: 13 *Eland*-90; 8 FV701 *Ferret*; 20 FV721 *Fox*
  APC • PPV 18 *Puma* M26-15
ARTILLERY 17
  TOWED 105mm 9 L118 Light Gun
  MOR 81mm 8 L16
AIR DEFENCE • GUNS • TOWED 14.5mm 40 ZPU-4

Navy 220

All operational patrol vessels under 10t FLD

Air Wing 200

EQUIPMENT BY TYPE
AIRCRAFT • TPT • Light 1 Do-228
HELICOPTERS • TPT 8: **Medium** 3: 1 AS532UL *Cougar*; 1 SA330H *Puma*; 1 H215 *Super Puma* **Light** 5: 1 AS350L *Ecureuil*; 4 SA341B *Gazelle*

Paramilitary 1,500

Police Mobile Service 1,500

EQUIPMENT BY TYPE
ARMOURED FIGHTING VEHICLES
  RECCE 8 S52 *Shorland*
AIRCRAFT
  TPT • Light 4: 3 BN-2T *Defender* (border patrol); 1 SC.7 3M *Skyvan*
HELICOPTERS • MRH 2 AS365 *Dauphin 2*

DEPLOYMENT

CÔTE D'IVOIRE
UN • UNOCI 1; 1 obs

DEMOCRATIC REPUBLIC OF THE CONGO
UN • MONUSCO 857; 5 obs; 1 inf bn

SUDAN
UN • UNISFA 1

Mali MLI

CFA Franc BCEAO fr		2015	2016	2017
GDP	fr	7.75tr	8.31tr	
	US$	13.1bn	14.1bn	
per capita	US$	804	839	
Growth	%	6.0	5.3	
Inflation	%	1.4	1.0	
Def bdgt [a]	fr	276bn	324bn	331bn
	US$	467m	549m	
US$1=fr		591.15	589.39	

[a] Defence and interior-security budget

Population 17,467,108

Ethnic groups: Tuareg 6–10%

Age	0–14	15–19	20–24	25–29	30–64	65 plus
Male	23.7%	5.2%	4.0%	3.1%	11.2%	1.5%
Female	23.5%	5.5%	4.6%	3.8%	12.4%	1.5%

Capabilities

In January 2013, the shortcomings of the Malian armed forces were exposed by its inability to deal with Islamist and Tuareg insurgents; this later led to French military intervention. Continuing insurgent attacks in 2016 prompted the UN Security Council to bolster the UN stabilisation mission in Mali (MINUSMA), and strengthen cooperation with the Malian armed forces. A total of 2,500 military and police personnel were to be added to the MINUSMA mission. Tranches of the reconstituted armed forces have been trained by an EU Training Mission (EUTM). Originally due to end in 2014, the mission was in May 2016 extended for a third mandate for 24 months until May 2018. As of May 2016, a total of 8,000 personnel had received training, including eight battalion/battlegroups, with five receiving further retraining – many at the Koulikoro training centre. In April 2016, the armed forces carried out their first artillery live-firing exercise in seven years, as part of the effort to rebuild artillery capability with EUTM assistance. The aim is to transition to Malian-led armed forces training in the future. There has been increased coordination of intelligence and security patrols with Burkina Faso.

ACTIVE 8,000 (Army 8,000) Paramilitary 7,800

ORGANISATIONS BY SERVICE

Army ε8,000
FORCES BY ROLE
The remnants of the pre-conflict Malian army are being reformed into new combined-arms battle groups, each of which comprise one lt mech coy, three mot inf coy, one arty bty and additional recce, cdo and cbt spt elms
MANOEUVRE
  Light
    8 mot inf BG
EQUIPMENT BY TYPE
ARMOURED FIGHTING VEHICLES
  RECCE BRDM-2†
  APC • APC (W) 22+: 3+ *Bastion* APC; 10+ BTR-60PB; 9 BTR-70
ARTILLERY 30+
  TOWED 122mm D-30
  MRL 122mm 30+ BM-21 *Grad*

Air Force
FORCES BY ROLE
FIGHTER
  1 sqn with MiG-21MF *Fishbed J*; MiG-21UM *Mongol B*
TRANSPORT
  1 sqn with An-24 *Coke*; An-26 *Curl*; BN-2 *Islander*; BT-67
TRAINING
  1 sqn with L-29 *Delfin*; SF-260WL *Warrior**; *Tetras*
TRANSPORT HELICOPTER
  1 sqn with H215; Mi-8 *Hip*; Mi-24D *Hind*; Z-9
EQUIPMENT BY TYPE
AIRCRAFT 4 combat capable
  FGA 2: 1 MiG-21MF *Fishbed*†; 1 MiG-21UM *Mongol B*†
  TPT • Light 10: 1 An-24 *Coke*; 2 An-26 *Curl*; 1 BT-67; 2 BN-2 *Islander*; 4 *Tetras*
  TRG 8: 6 L-29 *Delfin*†; 2 SF-260WL *Warrior**
HELICOPTERS
  ATK 2 Mi-24D *Hind*
  MRH (1 Z-9 in store)
  TPT 2: **Medium** 1 H215; 1 Mi-8 *Hip*; **Light** (1 AS350 *Ecureuil* in store)

Paramilitary 7,800 active

Gendarmerie 1,800
FORCES BY ROLE
MANOEUVRE
  Other
    8 paramilitary coy

National Guard 2,000

National Police 1,000

Militia 3,000

DEPLOYMENT

CÔTE D'IVOIRE
UN • UNOCI 1; 3 obs

DEMOCRATIC REPUBLIC OF THE CONGO
UN • MONUSCO 1; 10 obs

FOREIGN FORCES

All under MINUSMA comd unless otherwise specified
Albania EUTM Mali 3
Armenia 1
Austria 6 • EUTM Mali 8
Bangladesh 1,414; 3 obs; 1 inf bn; 1 engr coy; 2 sigs coy; 1 tpt coy
Belgium 7 • EUTM Mali 125
Benin 257; 3 obs; 1 mech inf coy
Bhutan 3
Bosnia-Herzegovina 2
Bulgaria EUTM Mali 5
Burkina Faso 1,721; 2 inf bn
Cambodia 301; 1 engr coy; 1 EOD coy
Cameroon 2; 1 obs
Chad 1,440; 1 SF coy; 2 inf bn
China 397; 1 sy coy; 1 engr coy; 1 fd hospital
Côte d'Ivoire 6
Czech Republic 25 • EUTM Mali 39
Denmark 47
Egypt 64; 3 obs; 1 MP coy
El Salvador 91; 1 obs; 1 hel sqn
Estonia 10 • EUTM Mali 10
Finland 5 • EUTM Mali 7
France 26 • *Operation Barkhane* 1,680; 1 mech inf BG; 1 log bn; 1 hel unit with 3 NH90 TTH; 4 SA330 *Puma*; 4 SA342 *Gazelle* • EUTM Mali 13
Gambia 4
Georgia EUTM Mali 1
Germany 249; 2 obs • EUTM Mali 131
Ghana 214; 3 obs; 1 engr coy; 1 hel sqn
Greece EUTM Mali 2
Guinea 858; 3 obs; 1 inf bn
Guinea-Bissau 1
Hungary EUTM Mali 3
Indonesia 147; 1 hel sqn
Ireland EUTM Mali 10
Italy 1 • EUTM Mali 10
Jordan 1
Kenya 4; 3 obs
Latvia 1 • EUTM Mali 7
Liberia 45; 1 inf pl
Lithuania EUTM Mali 3
Luxembourg EUTM Mali 2
Mauritania 4
Montenegro EUTM Mali 1

Nepal 146; 3 obs; 1 EOD coy
Netherlands 315; 1 SF coy; 1 atk hel sqn; 1 hel sqn; 1 int coy • EUTM Mali 1
Niger 858; 3 obs; 1 inf bn
Nigeria 79; 3 obs; 1 fd hospital
Norway 71; 1 avn sqn
Portugal 2 • EUTM Mali 12
Romania 1 • EUTM Mali 1
Senegal 579; 1 inf bn; 1 engr coy
Serbia EUTM Mali 3
Sierra Leone 4; 3 obs
Slovakia EUTM Mali 2
Slovenia EUTM Mali 5
Spain EUTM Mali 107
Sweden 209; 1 int coy • EUTM Mali 9
Switzerland 8
Togo 935; 2 obs; 1 inf bn; 1 fd hospital
United Kingdom 2 • EUTM Mali 30
United States 10
Yemen 6

Mauritius MUS

Mauritian Rupee R		2015	2016	2017
GDP	R	404bn	427bn	
	US$	11.5bn	11.7bn	
per capita	US$	9,142	9,322	
Growth	%	3.5	3.5	
Inflation	%	1.3	1.5	
Def bdgt [a]	R	8.41bn	7.66bn	8.72bn
	US$	240m	210m	
US$1=R		35.06	36.40	

[a] Police-service budget

Population 1,348,242

Age	0–14	15–19	20–24	25–29	30–64	65 plus
Male	10.6%	3.7%	4.0%	3.7%	23.6%	3.6%
Female	10.1%	3.6%	4.0%	3.6%	24.3%	5.2%

Capabilities

The country has no standing armed forces, but the Special Mobile Force (part of the police force) is tasked with providing internal and external security. The coastguard is currently in the process of increasing its ability to patrol the country's large EEZ and several orders with India resulted in the delivery of maritime-related capabilities in 2016. There are close ties with the Indian Navy, and New Delhi plans to locate a coastal-surveillance radar in Mauritius. Port Louis was one of the two hubs for the US AFRICOM *Cutlass Express 2015* exercise. Mauritius dispatched teams from the coastguard, coastguard commando and maritime air wing for the 2016 *Cutlass Express* exercise in the Seychelles and Djibouti.

ACTIVE NIL Paramilitary 2,550

ORGANISATIONS BY SERVICE

Paramilitary 2,550

Special Mobile Force ε1,750
FORCES BY ROLE
MANOEUVRE
　Reconnaissance
　　2 recce coy
　Light
　　5 (rifle) mot inf coy
COMBAT SUPPORT
　1 engr sqn
COMBAT SERVICE SUPPORT
　1 spt pl
EQUIPMENT BY TYPE
ARMOURED FIGHTING VEHICLES
　RECCE 4 S52 *Shorland*
　IFV 2 VAB with 20mm gun
　APC • APC (W) 16: 7 *Tactica*; 9 VAB
ARTILLERY • MOR 81mm 2

Coast Guard ε800
EQUIPMENT BY TYPE
PATROL AND COASTAL COMBATANTS 16
　PCC 1 *Victory* (IND *Sarojini Naidu*)
　PCO 1 *Barracuda* with 1 hel landing platform
　PB 14: 10 (IND *Fast Interceptor Boat*); 1 P-2000; 1 SDB-Mk3; 2 *Rescuer* (FSU *Zhuk*)
LOGISTICS AND SUPPORT
　AGS 1 *Pathfinder*
AIRCRAFT • TPT • Light 4: 1 BN-2T *Defender*; 3 Do-228-101

Police Air Wing
EQUIPMENT BY TYPE
HELICOPTERS
　MRH 9: 1 H125 (AS555) *Fennec*; 2 *Dhruv*; 1 SA315B *Lama* (*Cheetah*); 5 SA316 *Alouette* III (*Chetak*)

Mozambique MOZ

Mozambique New Metical M		2015	2016	2017
GDP	M	592bn	687bn	
	US$	14.8bn	12.0bn	
per capita	US$	529	419	
Growth	%	6.6	4.5	
Inflation	%	2.4	16.7	
Def bdgt	M	5.28bn	6.45bn	
	US$	132m	113m	
US$1=M		39.98	57.01	

Population 25,930,150

Age	0–14	15–19	20–24	25–29	30–64	65 plus
Male	22.6%	5.8%	4.8%	3.5%	10.9%	1.3%
Female	22.3%	5.8%	5.1%	4.1%	12.2%	1.6%

Capabilities

The armed forces are tasked with ensuring territorial integrity and internal security, as well as tackling piracy and human trafficking. Clashes between RENAMO and the government flared up in 2013. A peace deal was signed in 2014, but RENAMO protested its subsequent election loss. Episodic violence resumed in 2016, amid stop–start negotiations between the government and RENAMO. Strong economic growth was tempered in 2016 by the discovery of previously undisclosed debt, though the exploitation of gas reserves may allow increased defence budgeting in the future. An agreement on defence cooperation with China signed in August includes plans for bilateral training. Patrol craft on order from France began to be delivered in 2016 and will boost the country's maritime-patrol capability. Equipment serviceability levels remain unclear, but cooperative anti-piracy patrols with South Africa have provided Mozambique's forces with experience, albeit in a supporting role. The armed forces have no capacity to deploy beyond Mozambique's borders without assistance.

ACTIVE 11,200 (Army 10,000 Navy 200 Air 1,000)
Conscript liability 2 years

ORGANISATIONS BY SERVICE

Army ε9,000–10,000
FORCES BY ROLE
SPECIAL FORCES
  3 SF bn
MANOEUVRE
  Light
  7 inf bn
COMBAT SUPPORT
  2-3 arty bn
  2 engr bn
COMBAT SERVICE SUPPORT
  1 log bn
EQUIPMENT BY TYPE†
Equipment estimated at 10% or less serviceability
ARMOURED FIGHTING VEHICLES
  MBT 60+ T-54
  RECCE 30 BRDM-1/BRDM-2
  IFV 40 BMP-1
  APC 326
    APC (T) 30 FV430
    APC (W) 285: 160 BTR-60; 100 BTR-152; 25 AT-105 *Saxon*
    PPV 11 *Casspir*
ANTI-TANK/ANTI-INFRASTRUCTURE
  MSL • MANPATS 9K11 *Malyutka* (AT-3 *Sagger*); 9K111 *Fagot* (AT-4 *Spigot*)
  RCL 75mm; **82mm** B-10; **107mm** 24 B-12
  GUNS 85mm 18: 6 D-48; 12 PT-56 (D-44)
ARTILLERY 126
  TOWED 62: **100mm** 20 M-1944; **105mm** 12 M101; **122mm** 12 D-30; **130mm** 6 M-46; **152mm** 12 D-1
  MRL 122mm 12 BM-21 *Grad*
  MOR 52: **82mm** 40 M-43; **120mm** 12 M-43

AIR DEFENCE • GUNS 290+
  SP 57mm 20 ZSU-57-2
  TOWED 270+: **20mm** M-55; **23mm** 120 ZU-23-2; **37mm** 90 M-1939; (10 M-1939 in store); **57mm** 60 S-60; (30 S-60 in store)

Navy ε200
EQUIPMENT BY TYPE
PATROL AND COASTAL COMBATANTS 6
  PBF 5: 2 DV 15; 3 HSI 32
  PB 1 *Pebane* (ex-ESP *Conejera*-class)

Air Force 1,000
FORCES BY ROLE
FIGHTER/GROUND ATTACK
  1 sqn with MiG-21bis *Fishbed*; MiG-21UM *Mongol* B
TRANSPORT
  1 sqn with An-26 *Curl*; FTB-337G *Milirole*; Cessna 150B; Cessna 172; PA-34 *Seneca*
ATTACK/TRANSPORT HELICOPTER
  1 sqn with Mi-24 *Hind*†
EQUIPMENT BY TYPE
AIRCRAFT
  FGA 8: 6 MiG-21bis *Fishbed*; 2 MiG-21UM *Mongol* B
  ISR 2 FTB-337G *Milirole*
  TPT 6: **Light** 5: 1 An-26 *Curl*; 2 Cessna 150B; 1 Cessna 172; 1 PA-34 *Seneca*; (4 PA-32 *Cherokee* non-op); **PAX** 1 Hawker 850XP
HELICOPTERS
  ATK 2 Mi-24 *Hind*†
  TPT • Medium (2 Mi-8 *Hip* non-op)
AD • SAM • TOWED: (S-75 *Dvina* (SA-2 *Guideline*) non-op‡; S-125 *Pechora* SA-3 *Goa* non-op‡)

DEPLOYMENT

SUDAN
UN • UNISFA 2 obs

Namibia NAM

Namibian Dollar N$		2015	2016	2017
GDP	N$	147bn	163bn	
	US$	11.5bn	10.2bn	
per capita	US$	5,041	4,428	
Growth	%	5.3	4.2	
Inflation	%	3.4	6.6	
Def exp	N$	7.23bn	6.60bn	
	US$	567m	413m	
US$1=N$		12.75	16.00	
Population	2,346,469			

Age	0–14	15–19	20–24	25–29	30–64	65 plus
Male	18.9%	5.3%	4.8%	4.1%	14.1%	1.7%
Female	18.5%	5.3%	4.9%	4.3%	15.8%	2.3%

Capabilities

The primary mission of the defence force is territorial defence; secondary roles include assisting the civilian power and African Union, Southern African Development Community (SADC) and UN missions. The defence ministry is following the Namibian Defence Force Development Strategy 2012–22. After establishing marine-corps and naval training schools, and sending marines for training in Brazil, in late 2016 Namibia announced a new marine battalion. The navy augments civilian offshore-patrol forces, including on anti-piracy taskings. With an eye to naval-modernisation requirements, the government has stressed that tackling poverty remains a priority and that 'scarce resources' need to be prioritised. Namibia has deployed on UN and African Union missions and takes part in multinational exercises, including with regional allies such as South Africa. The air force took part in the 2015 SADC *Blue Okavango* exercise and the navy exercises with SADC as part of its Standing Maritime Committee. The 2016 exercise with Botswana (a biannual series) practised joint peacekeeping operations. Military training teams from Brazil and Zimbabwe have been in-country in recent years. The defence ministry recently established an Air Force Technical Training Centre and a School for Airpower Studies. Donations of military equipment from China, as well as the supply of some basic equipment from local industry, have increased capability; the country is also funding the renovation of existing and the construction of new infrastructure for the army and the air force. In 2016, Namibia terminated dealings with North Korean companies in order to comply with UN sanctions. These companies had been involved with Namibian-based munitions factories. There is a very limited capacity for independent power projection beyond national territory.

ACTIVE 9,900 (Army 9,000 Navy 900) **Paramilitary 6,000**

ORGANISATIONS BY SERVICE

Army 9,000
FORCES BY ROLE
MANOEUVRE
  Reconnaissance
  1 recce regt
  Light
  3 inf bde (total: 6 inf bn)
  Other
  1 (Presidential Guard) gd bn
COMBAT SUPPORT
  1 arty bde with (1 arty regt)
  1 AT regt
  1 engr regt
  1 sigs regt
COMBAT SERVICE SUPPORT
  1 log bn
AIR DEFENCE
  1 AD regt

EQUIPMENT BY TYPE
ARMOURED FIGHTING VEHICLES
  MBT T-54/T-55†; T-34†
  RECCE 12 BRDM-2
  APC 68
    APC (W) 48: 10 BTR-60; 8 Type-05P; 30 *Wolf Turbo 2*
    PPV 20 *Casspir*
ENGINEERING & MAINTENANCE VEHICLES
  ARV T-54/T-55 reported
ANTI-TANK/ANTI-INFRASTRUCTURE
  RCL 82mm B-10
  GUNS 12+: **57mm**; **76mm** 12 ZIS-3
ARTILLERY 69
  TOWED **140mm** 24 G-2
  MRL **122mm** 5 BM-21 *Grad*
  MOR 40: **81mm**; **82mm**
AIR DEFENCE
  SAM • **Point-defence** 9K32 *Strela*-2 (SA-7 *Grail*)‡
  GUNS 65
    SP **23mm** 15 *Zumlac*
    TOWED **14.5mm** 50 ZPU-4

Navy ε900
EQUIPMENT BY TYPE
PATROL AND COASTAL COMBATANTS 4
  PSO 1 *Elephant* with 1 hel landing platform
  PB 3: 1 *Brendan Simbwaye* (BRZ *Grajaú*); 2 *Terrace Bay* (BRZ *Marlim*)
AIRCRAFT • TPT • Light 1 F406 *Caravan II*
HELICOPTERS • TPT • Medium 1 S-61L

Marines ε700

Air Force
FORCES BY ROLE
FIGHTER/GROUND ATTACK
  1 sqn with F-7 (F-7NM); FT-7 (FT-7NG)
ISR
  1 sqn with O-2A *Skymaster*
TRANSPORT
  Some sqn with An-26 *Curl*; *Falcon* 900; *Learjet* 36; Y-12
TRAINING
  1 sqn with K-8 *Karakorum**
ATTACK/TRANSPORT HELICOPTER
  1 sqn with H425; Mi-8 *Hip*; Mi-25 *Hind* D; SA315 *Lama* (*Cheetah*); SA316B *Alouette* III (*Chetak*)
EQUIPMENT BY TYPE
AIRCRAFT 12 combat capable
  FTR 8: 6 F-7NM; 2 FT-7 (FT-7NG)
  ISR 5 Cessna O-2A *Skymaster*
  TPT 6: **Light** 5: 2 An-26 *Curl*; 1 *Learjet* 36; 2 Y-12; **PAX** 1 *Falcon* 900
  TRG 4+ K-8 *Karakorum**
HELICOPTERS
  ATK 2 Mi-25 *Hind* D
  MRH 5: 1 H425; 1 SA315 *Lama* (*Cheetah*); 3 SA316B *Alouette* III (*Chetak*)
  TPT • **Medium** 1 Mi-8 *Hip*

Paramilitary 6,000

Police Force • Special Field Force 6,000 (incl Border Guard and Special Reserve Force)

Ministry of Fisheries
EQUIPMENT BY TYPE
PATROL AND COASTAL COMBATANTS • PCO 3: 2 *Nathanael Maxwilili* with 1 hel landing platform; 1 *Tobias Hainyenko*
LOGISTICS AND SUPPORT 1
  AGOS 1 *Mirabilis*

DEPLOYMENT

CÔTE D'IVOIRE
UN • UNOCI 1 obs

LIBERIA
UN • UNMIL 1; 1 obs

SOUTH SUDAN
UN • UNMISS 3; 2 obs

SUDAN
UN • UNAMID 5; 3 obs
UN • UNISFA 2; 3 obs

Niger NER

CFA Franc BCEAO fr		2015	2016	2017
GDP	fr	4.24tr	4.46tr	
	US$	7.18bn	7.57bn	
per capita	US$	407	416	
Growth	%	3.5	5.2	
Inflation	%	1.0	1.6	
Def exp	fr	n.k.	n.k.	
	US$	n.k.	n.k.	
US$1=fr		591.15	589.437	

Population 18,638,600

Ethnic groups: Gourma 55.3%; Djerma Sonrai 21%; Touareg 9.3%; Peuhl 8.5%; Kanouri Manga 4.6%; other or unspecified 1.3%

Age	0–14	15–19	20–24	25–29	30–64	65 plus
Male	24.9%	5.3%	4.0%	3.2%	11.5%	1.3%
Female	24.4%	5.4%	4.2%	3.3%	11.2%	1.3%

Capabilities

Internal and border security are key roles for the armed forces, in light of the regional threat from Islamist groups. The country is a member of the 'G5 Sahel' aimed at improving the ability to counter jihadists in the region; Boko Haram in 2015 mounted attacks in the country. However, the armed forces remain under-equipped and lack the resources to fully meet these challenges. It also provides UAV basing for the US, the first at Niamey (which also has a French presence), while the second US site is being built at Air Base 201 in Agadez. Both countries have been providing equipment for surveillance tasks, including Cessna 208Bs from the US and *Gazelle* helicopters from France. Germany has also developed an air-transport base at Niamey to supply its troops in neighbouring Mali. Berlin will also supply trucks to Niger's army.

ACTIVE 5,300 (Army 5,200 Air 100) **Paramilitary 5,400**

Conscript liability Selective conscription, 2 years

ORGANISATIONS BY SERVICE

Army 5,200
3 Mil Districts
FORCES BY ROLE
MANOEUVRE
  Reconnaissance
    4 armd recce sqn
  Light
    7 inf coy
  Air Manoeuvre
    2 AB coy
COMBAT SUPPORT
  1 engr coy
COMBAT SERVICE SUPPORT
  1 log gp
AIR DEFENCE
  1 AD coy
EQUIPMENT BY TYPE
ARMOURED FIGHTING VEHICLES
  RECCE 132: 35 AML-20/AML-60; 90 AML-90; 7 VBL
  APC 45
    APC (W) 24: 22 Panhard M3; 2 WZ-523
    PPV 21 *Puma* M26-15
ANTI-TANK/ANTI-INFRASTRUCTURE
  RCL 14: **75mm** 6 M20; **106mm** 8 M40
ARTILLERY • MOR 40: **81mm** 19 Brandt; **82mm** 17; **120mm** 4 Brandt
AIR DEFENCE • GUNS 39
  SP 20mm 10 Panhard M3 VDAA
  TOWED 20mm 29

Air Force 100
EQUIPMENT BY TYPE
AIRCRAFT 2 combat capable
  ATK 2 Su-25 *Frogfoot*
  ISR 6: 4 Cessna 208 *Caravan*; 2 DA42 MPP *Twin Star*
  TPT 7: **Medium** 1 C-130H *Hercules*; **Light** 5: 1 An-26 *Curl*; 2 Cessna 208 *Caravan*; 1 Do-28 *Skyservant*; 1 Do-228-201; **PAX** 1 B-737-700 (VIP)
HELICOPTERS
  ATK 2 Mi-35P *Hind*
  MRH 5: 2 Mi-17 *Hip*; 3 SA342 *Gazelle*

Paramilitary 5,400

Gendarmerie 1,400

Republican Guard 2,500

National Police 1,500

DEPLOYMENT

CENTRAL AFRICAN REPUBLIC
UN • MINUSCA 129; 4 obs; 1 sigs coy

CÔTE D'IVOIRE
UN • UNOCI 652; 2 obs; 1 mech inf bn

DEMOCRATIC REPUBLIC OF THE CONGO
UN • MONUSCO 4; 8 obs

LIBERIA
UN • UNMIL 2 obs

MALI
UN • MINUSMA 858; 3 obs; 1 inf bn

FOREIGN FORCES

France Opération Barkhane 350; 1 FGA det with 4 Mirage 2000D; 1 tkr/tpt det with 1 C-135FR; 1 C-160; 1 UAV det with 2 Harfang; 3 MQ-9A Reaper
United States 250

Nigeria NGA

Nigerian Naira N		2015	2016	2017
GDP	N	95.2tr	106tr	
	US$	494bn	415bn	
per capita	US$	2,763	2,260	
Growth	%	2.7	-1.7	
Inflation	%	9.0	15.4	
Def bdgt	N	375bn	443bn	
	US$	1.95bn	1.73bn	
FMA (US)	US$	0.6m	0.6m	0.5m
US$1=N		192.73	255.48	

Population 186,053,386

Ethnic groups: North (Hausa and Fulani) southwest (Yoruba) southeast (Ibo); these tribes make up ε65% of population

Age	0–14	15–19	20–24	25–29	30–64	65 plus
Male	21.9%	5.4%	4.6%	3.9%	13.7%	1.5%
Female	20.9%	5.2%	4.4%	3.8%	13.2%	1.6%

Capabilities

Nigeria continues to face numerous internal-security challenges, including the threat from Boko Haram and from militants in the Delta. These remain central concerns for the comparatively well-equipped and -trained armed forces, with countering piracy, and border and maritime security also vital tasks. There have been reports that the difficulty in defeating the insurgents had been adversely affecting morale, despite training support from the US and other countries. But, in cooperation with Niger, Chad and Cameroon in the Multi-National Joint Task Force, the military appears to have made some significant headway against Boko Haram in 2015 and 2016. The armed forces have been attempting to adopt COIN tactics, and looking to establish forward-operating bases and quick-reaction groups. In response to the continuing insurgency, equipment has been brought out of storage, including transport aircraft and light fighters. Maintenance and serviceability has been a long-standing issue. Investigations into alleged past corruption in the military-procurement process continued and broadened. There were reports that the alleged corruption had materially affected capability. However, a US move to supply Nigeria with A-29 *Super Tucanos* was seen as an endorsement of government effort to reform the military and tackle corruption.

ACTIVE 118,000 (Army 100,000 Navy 8,000 Air 10,000) **Paramilitary 82,000**

Reserves planned, none org

ORGANISATIONS BY SERVICE

Army 100,000
FORCES BY ROLE
SPECIAL FORCES
1 spec ops bn
1 ranger bn
MANOEUVRE
Armoured
1 (3rd) armd div (1 armd bde, 1 arty bde)
Mechanised
2 (1st) mech div (1 recce bn, 1 mech bde, 1 mot inf bde, 1 arty bde, 1 engr regt)
1 (2nd) mech div (1 recce bn, 1 armd bde, 1 armd bde, 1 arty bde, 1 engr regt)
1 (81st) composite div (1 recce bn, 1 mech bde, 1 arty bde, 1 engr regt)
Light
1 (7th) inf div (1 spec ops bn, 1 recce bn(-), 1 armd bde, 1 inf bde, 7 (task force) inf bde, 1 arty bde, 1 engr regt)
1 (82nd) composite div (1 recce bn, 1 mech bde, 2 mot inf bde, 1 amph bde, 1 arty bde, 1 engr regt)
1 (Multi-national Joint Task Force) bde (2 inf bn(-))
Other
1 (Presidential Guard) gd bde (4 gd bn)
AIR DEFENCE
1 AD regt
EQUIPMENT BY TYPE
ARMOURED FIGHTING VEHICLES
  MBT 319: 176 Vickers Mk 3; 100 T-55†; 12 T-72AV; 31 T-72M1
  LT TK 157 FV101 *Scorpion*
  RECCE 342: 90 AML-60; 40 AML-90; 70 EE-9 *Cascavel*; 50 FV721 *Fox*; 20 FV601 *Saladin* Mk2; 72 VBL
  IFV 22: 10 BTR-4EN; 22 BVP-1
  APC 507+
    APC (T) 317: 250 4K-7FA *Steyr*; 67 MT-LB
    APC (W) 282+: 110 *Cobra*; 10 FV603 *Saracen*; 110 AVGP *Grizzly* mod/*Piranha* I 6x6; 47 BTR-3UN; 5 BTR-80; some EE-11 *Urutu* (reported)
    PPV 47+: 16 *Caiman*; 8 *Maxxpro*; 23 REVA III 4×4; some Streit *Spartan*; Some Streit *Cougar* (*Igirigi*); some *Bigfoot*
ENGINEERING & MAINTENANCE VEHICLES
  ARV 17+: AVGP *Husky*; 2 *Greif*; 15 Vickers ARV
  VLB MTU-20; VAB

ANTI-TANK/ANTI-INFRASTRUCTURE
  MSL • MANPATS *Swingfire*
  RCL **84mm** *Carl Gustav;* **106mm** M40A1
ARTILLERY 495+
  SP **155mm** 39 *Palmaria*
  TOWED 94: **105mm** 50 M-56; **122mm** 37 D-30/D-74;
    130mm 7 M-46; (**155mm** 24 FH-77B in store)
  MRL **122mm** 32: 25 APR-21; 7 RM-70
  MOR 330+: **81mm** 200; **82mm** 100; **120mm** 30+
RADAR • LAND: some RASIT (veh, arty)
AIR DEFENCE
  SAM • **Point-defence** 16+: 16 *Roland*; *Blowpipe*; 9K32 *Strela*-2 (SA-7 *Grail*)‡
  GUNS 90+
    SP **23mm** 30 ZSU-23-4
    TOWED 60+: **20mm** 60+; **23mm** ZU-23; **40mm** L/70

Navy 8,000 (incl Coast Guard)

Western Comd HQ located at Apapa; Eastern Comd HQ located at Calabar; Central Comd HQ located at Brass

EQUIPMENT BY TYPE
PRINCIPAL SURFACE COMBATANTS 1
  FRIGATES • FFGHM 1 *Aradu*† (GER MEKO 360) with 8 single lnchr with *Otomat* AShM, 1 octuple *Albatros* lnchr with *Aspide* SAM, 2 triple STWS 1B 324mm ASTT with A244 LWT, 1 127mm gun, (capacity 1 med hel)
PATROL AND COASTAL COMBATANTS 114
  CORVETTES • FSM 1 *Enymiri*† (UK Vosper Mk 9) with 1 triple lnchr with *Seacat*† SAM, 1 twin 375mm A/S mor, 1 76mm gun
  PSOH 4: 2 *Centenary* with 1 76mm gun; 2 *Thunder* (ex-US *Hamilton*) with 1 76mm gun
  PCFG 1 *Siprit* (FRA *Combattante*) with 2 twin lnchr with MM-38 *Exocet* AShM, 1 76mm gun
  PCO 4 *Kyanwa* (ex-US CG *Balsam*)
  PCC 2 *Ekpe*† (GER Lurssen 57m) with 1 76mm gun
  PBF 30: 21 *Manta* (Suncraft 17m); 4 *Manta* MkII; 3 *Shaldag* II; 2 *Torie* (Nautic Sentinel 17m)
  PB 72: 1 *Andoni*; 1 *Dorina*; 3 *Okpoku* (FPB 98 MkII); 1 *Karaduwa*; 1 *Sagbama*; 2 *Sea Eagle* (Suncraft 38m); 15 *Stingray* (Suncraft 16m); 40 Suncraft 12m; 4 Swiftships; 2 *Town* (of which one laid up); 2 *Yola*†
MINE WARFARE • MINE COUNTERMEASURES 2:
  MCC 2 *Ohue*† (mod ITA *Lerici*)
AMPHIBIOUS 4
  LC • LCVP 4 *Stingray* 20
LOGISTICS AND SUPPORT 1
  AX 1 *Prosperity*

Naval Aviation
EQUIPMENT BY TYPE
HELICOPTERS
  MRH 2 AW139 (AB-139)
  TPT • **Light** 3 AW109E *Power*†

Special Forces 200
EQUIPMENT BY TYPE
FORCES BY ROLE
SPECIAL FORCES
  1 SF unit

Air Force 10,000
FORCES BY ROLE
Very limited op capability
FIGHTER/GROUND ATTACK
  1 sqn with F-7 (F-7NI); FT-7 (FT-7NI)
MARITIME PATROL
  1 sqn with ATR-42-500 MP; Do-128D-6 *Turbo SkyServant*; Do-228-100/200
TRANSPORT
  2 sqn with C-130H *Hercules*; C-130H-30 *Hercules*; G-222
  1 (Presidential) gp with B-727; B-737BBJ; BAe-125-800; Beech 350 *King Air*; Do-228-200; *Falcon* 7X; *Falcon* 900; Gulfstream IV/V
TRAINING
  1 unit with *Air Beetle*†
  1 unit with *Alpha Jet**
  1 unit with L-39 *Albatros*†*; MB-339A*
  1 hel unit with Mi-34 *Hermit* (trg)
ATTACK HELICOPTER
  1 sqn with Mi-24/Mi-35 *Hind*†
TRANSPORT HELICOPTER
  1 sqn with H215 (AS332) *Super Puma*; (AS365N) *Dauphin*; AW109LUH; H135

EQUIPMENT BY TYPE†
AIRCRAFT 52 combat capable
  FTR 14: 11 F-7 (F-7NI); 3 FT-7 (FT-7NI)
  ELINT 2 ATR-42-500 MP
  TPT 32: **Medium** 5: 1 C-130H *Hercules* (4 more in store†); 1 C-130H-30 *Hercules* (2 more in store); 3 G-222† (2 more in store†); **Light** 18: 3 Beech 350 *King Air*; 1 Cessna 550 *Citation*; 8 Do-128D-6 *Turbo SkyServant*; 1 Do-228-100; 5 Do-228-200 (incl 2 VIP); **PAX** 9: 1 B-727; 1 B-737BBJ; 1 BAe 125-800; 2 *Falcon* 7X; 2 *Falcon* 900; 1 Gulfstream IV; 1 Gulfstream V
  TRG 106: 58 *Air Beetle*† (up to 20 awaiting repair); 3 *Alpha Jet* A*; 10 *Alpha Jet* E*; 23 L-39 *Albatros*†*; 12 MB-339AN* (all being upgraded)
HELICOPTERS
  ATK 11: 2 Mi-24P *Hind*; 4 Mi-24V *Hind*; 3 Mi-35 *Hind*; 2 Mi-35P *Hind*
  MRH 9+: 6 AW109LUH; 3+ SA341 *Gazelle*
  TPT 19: **Medium** 10: 2 AW101; 5 H215 (AS332) *Super Puma* (4 more in store); 3 AS365N *Dauphin*; **Light** 9: 4 H125 (AS350B) *Ecureuil*; 1 AW109; 1 Bell 205; 3 H135
UNMANNED AERIAL VEHICLES 1+
  CISR • **Heavy** 1+ CH-3
  ISR • **Medium** (9 *Aerostar* non-operational)
AIR-LAUNCHED MISSILES • AAM • IR R-3 (AA-2 *Atoll*)‡; PL-9C

Paramilitary ε82,000

Nigerian Police

Port Authority Police ε2,000

Security and Civil Defence Corps • Police 80,000
EQUIPMENT BY TYPE
ARMOURED FIGHTING VEHICLES
  APC • **APC (W)** 74+: 70+ AT105 *Saxon*†; 4 BTR-3U; UR-416

AIRCRAFT • TPT • Light 4: 1 Cessna 500 *Citation* I; 2 PA-31 *Navajo*; 1 PA-31-350 *Navajo Chieftain*
HELICOPTERS • TPT • Light 4: 2 Bell 212 (AB-212); 2 Bell 222 (AB-222)

DEPLOYMENT

CENTRAL AFRICAN REPUBLIC
UN • MINUSCA 3

CÔTE D'IVOIRE
UN • UNOCI 2 obs

DEMOCRATIC REPUBLIC OF THE CONGO
UN • MONUSCO 1; 19 obs

GUINEA-BISSAU
ECOWAS • ECOMIB 160

LEBANON
UN • UNIFIL 1

LIBERIA
UN • UNMIL 704; 9 obs; 1 inf bn

MALI
UN • MINUSMA 79; 3 obs; 1 fd hospital

SOUTH SUDAN
UN • UNMISS 4; 5 obs

SUDAN
UN • UNAMID 928; 2 obs; 1 inf bn; 1 sigs unit; 1 med unit
UN • UNISFA 1; 1 obs

WESTERN SAHARA
UN • MINURSO 5 obs

FOREIGN FORCES

United Kingdom 30 (trg team)

Rwanda RWA

Rwandan Franc fr		2015	2016	2017
GDP	fr	5.84tr	6.48tr	
	US$	8.11bn	8.34bn	
per capita	US$	718	723	
Growth	%	6.9	6	
Inflation	%	2.5	5.3	
Def bdgt	fr	63.9bn	68.0bn	81.0bn
	US$	89m	88m	
US$1=fr		719.64	777.34	

Population 12,988,423
Ethnic groups: Hutu 80%; Tutsi 19%

Age	0–14	15–19	20–24	25–29	30–64	65 plus
Male	20.9%	5.3%	4.1%	4.2%	14.3%	1.1%
Female	20.6%	5.3%	4.2%	4.2%	14.4%	1.5%

Capabilities

The principal missions for the armed forces are to defend territorial integrity and national sovereignty. A law on downsizing and demobilising elements of the armed forces was published in October 2015 (no.38/2015). The country fields a comparatively large army, but units are lightly equipped, with little mechanisation. The army regularly takes part in multinational exercises and is a key contributor to the East Africa Standby Force; it has pledged a motorised infantry battalion. It is a significant contributor to UN missions and has also committed forces to the African Capacity for Immediate Response to Crises initiative. However, the lack of fixed-wing aircraft limits the armed forces' ability to deploy independently overseas, and air movements have largely been accomplished with the assistance of donor or charter airlift capacity. International training support comes from forces including the US, which in 2016 conducted civil–military cooperation training.

ACTIVE 33,000 (Army 32,000 Air 1,000) **Paramilitary 2,000**

ORGANISATIONS BY SERVICE

Army 32,000

FORCES BY ROLE
MANOEUVRE
  Light
  2 cdo bn
  4 inf div (3 inf bde)
COMBAT SUPPORT
  1 arty bde

EQUIPMENT BY TYPE
ARMOURED FIGHTING VEHICLES
  MBT 34: 24 T-54/T-55; 10 *Tiran-5*
  RECCE 106: ε90 AML-60/AML-90; 16 VBL
  IFV 35+: BMP; 15 *Ratel*-90; 20 *Ratel*-60
  APC 56+
    APC (W) 20+: BTR; *Buffalo* (Panhard M3); 20 Type-92 (reported)
    PPV 36 RG-31 *Nyala*
ENGINEERING & MAINTENANCE VEHICLES
  ARV T-54/T-55 reported
ARTILLERY 165+
  SP 155mm 5 ATMOS 2000
  TOWED 35+: 105mm some; 122mm 6 D-30; 152mm 29 Type-54 (D-1)†
  MRL 10: 122mm 5 RM-70; 160mm 5 LAR-160
  MOR 115: 81mm; 82mm; 120mm
AIR DEFENCE
  SAM • Point-defence 9K32 *Strela*-2 (SA-7 *Grail*)‡
  GUNS ε150: 14.5mm; 23mm; 37mm

Air Force ε1,000

FORCES BY ROLE
ATTACK/TRANSPORT HELICOPTER
  1 sqn with Mi-17/Mi-17MD/Mi-17V-5/Mi-17-1V *Hip* H; Mi-24P/V *Hind*

EQUIPMENT BY TYPE
HELICOPTERS
ATK 5: 2 Mi-24V *Hind* E; 3 Mi-24P *Hind*
MRH 12: 1 AW139; 4 Mi-17 *Hip* H; 1 Mi-17MD *Hip* H; 1 Mi-17V-5 *Hip* H; 5 Mi-17-1V *Hip* H
TPT • **Light** 1 AW109S

Paramilitary

District Administration Security Support Organ ε2,000

DEPLOYMENT

CENTRAL AFRICAN REPUBLIC
UN • MINUSCA 835; 11 obs; 1 inf bn; 1 fd hospital

SOUTH SUDAN
UN • UNMISS 1,843; 13 obs; 2 inf bn; 2 hel sqn

SUDAN
UN • UNAMID 2,454; 5 obs; 3 inf bn
UN • UNISFA 4; 3 obs

Senegal SEN

CFA Franc BCEAO fr		2015	2016	2017
GDP	fr	8.08tr	8.76tr	
	US$	13.7bn	14.9bn	
per capita	US$	913	965	
Growth	%	6.5	6.6	
Inflation	%	0.1	1.0	
Def bdgt	fr	127bn	151bn	172bn
	US$	215m	256m	
FMA (US)	US$	0.3m	0.3m	0.3m
US$1=fr		591.14	589.39	

Population 14,320,055

Ethnic groups: Wolof 36%; Fulani 17%; Serer 17%; Toucouleur 9%; Man-dingo 9%; Diola 9% (of which 30–60% in Casamance)

Age	0–14	15–19	20–24	25–29	30–64	65 plus
Male	21.0%	5.4%	4.7%	3.9%	11.8%	1.3%
Female	20.8%	5.4%	4.9%	4.2%	14.8%	1.6%

Capabilities

The armed forces' priorities are internal and border security, including countering an insurgency in the country's south and Islamist activity in neighbouring states, and combating narcotics trafficking. The armed forces have a limited capability only to address national-security requirements. France retains a military presence in Senegal and provides training support. The US Army and US Marine Corps continued a series of multifaceted training engagements, including readiness, counter-illicit trafficking and special-operations training, with the Senegalese armed forces. The Africa Readiness Training 2016 activity developed US–Senegal military ties through infantry training and live-fire events. The US Coast Guard assisted with maritime-law-enforcement training with the navy.

ACTIVE 13,600 (Army 11,900 Navy 950 Air 750)
Paramilitary 5,000
Conscript liability Selective conscription, 2 years

ORGANISATIONS BY SERVICE

Army 11,900 (incl conscripts)
7 Mil Zone HQ
FORCES BY ROLE
MANOEUVRE
  Reconnaissance
  4 armd recce bn
  Light
  1 cdo bn
  6 inf bn
  Air Manoeuvre
  1 AB bn
  Other
  1 (Presidential Guard) horse cav bn
COMBAT SUPPORT
  1 arty bn
  1 engr bn
  3 construction coy
  1 sigs bn
COMBAT SERVICE SUPPORT
  1 log bn
  1 med bn
  1 trg bn
EQUIPMENT BY TYPE
ARMOURED FIGHTING VEHICLES
  ASLT 13 PTL-02 *Assaulter*
  RECCE 145: 30 AML-60; 74 AML-90; 10 M8; 4 M20; 27 RAM Mk3
  IFV 26 *Ratel*-20
  APC 75
    APC (T) 12 M3 half-track
    APC (W) 16 Panhard M3
    PPV 47: 8 *Casspir*; 39 *Puma* M26-15
ANTI-TANK/ANTI-INFRASTRUCTURE
  MSL • **MANPATS** Milan
ARTILLERY 36
  TOWED 20: **105mm** 6 HM-2/M101; **155mm** 14: ε6 Model-50; 8 TR-F1
  MOR 16: **81mm** 8 Brandt; **120mm** 8 Brandt
AIR DEFENCE • GUNS • TOWED 33: **20mm** 21 M693; **40mm** 12 L/60

Navy (incl Coast Guard) 950
FORCES BY ROLE
SPECIAL FORCES
  1 cdo coy
EQUIPMENT BY TYPE
PATROL AND COASTAL COMBATANTS 4
  PCC 1 *Njambour* (FRA SFCN 59m) with 2 76mm gun
  PBF 1 *Ferlo* (RPB 33)
  PB 2: 1 *Conejera*; 1 *Kedougou*

AMPHIBIOUS • LANDING CRAFT 2
    LCT 2 Edic 700
LOGISTICS AND SUPPORT 1
    AG 1

Air Force 750

FORCES BY ROLE
MARITIME PATROL/SEARCH & RESCUE
    1 sqn with C-212 Aviocar; CN-235; Bell 205 (UH-1H Iroquois)
ISR
    1 unit with BN-2T Islander (anti-smuggling patrols)
TRANSPORT
    1 sqn with B-727-200 (VIP); F-27-400M Troopship
TRAINING
    1 sqn with R-235 Guerrier*; TB-30 Epsilon
ATTACK/TRANSPORT HELICOPTER
    1 sqn with AS355F Ecureuil II; Bell 206; Mi-35P Hind; Mi-171Sh

EQUIPMENT BY TYPE
AIRCRAFT 1 combat capable
    TPT 9: **Light** 7: 1 BN-2T Islander (govt owned, mil op); 1 C-212-100 Aviocar; 1 CN-235; 2 Beech B200 King Air; 2 F-27-400M Troopship (3 more in store); **PAX** 2: 1 A319; 1 B-727-200 (VIP)
    TRG 7: 1 R-235 Guerrier*; 6 TB-30 Epsilon
HELICOPTERS
    ATK 2 Mi-35P Hind
    MRH 1 AW139
    TPT 8: **Medium** 2 Mi-171Sh; **Light** 6: 1 AS355F Ecureuil II; 1 Bell 205 (UH-1H Iroquois); 2 Bell 206; 2 PZL Mi-2 Hoplite

Paramilitary 5,000

Gendarmerie 5,000

EQUIPMENT BY TYPE
ARMOURED FIGHTING VEHICLES
    APC 29:
        APC (W) 17: 5 EE-11 Urutu; 12 VXB-170
        PPV 12 Gila

Customs

EQUIPMENT BY TYPE
PATROL AND COASTAL COMBATANTS • PB 2 VCSM

DEPLOYMENT

CENTRAL AFRICAN REPUBLIC
UN • MINUSCA 105; 1 hel sqn

CÔTE D'IVOIRE
UN • UNOCI 735; 5 obs; 1 inf bn; 1 hel sqn

DEMOCRATIC REPUBLIC OF THE CONGO
UN • MONUSCO 2; 2 obs

MALI
UN • MINUSMA 579; 1 inf bn; 1 engr coy

SOUTH SUDAN
UN • UNMISS 2 obs

SUDAN
UN • UNAMID 803; 1 inf bn

FOREIGN FORCES

France 350; 1 Falcon 50MI

Seychelles SYC

Seychelles Rupee SR		2015	2016	2017
GDP	SR	18.1bn	18.9bn	
	US$	1.36bn	1.42bn	
per capita	US$	14,776	15,319	
Growth	%	5.7	4.9	
Inflation	%	4.0	-0.8	
Def exp	SR	n.k.	n.k.	
	US$	n.k.	n.k.	
US$1=SR		13.32	13.31	

Population 93,186

Age	0–14	15–19	20–24	25–29	30–64	65 plus
Male	10.4%	3.3%	3.8%	4.1%	26.8%	3.0%
Female	9.8%	3.1%	3.4%	3.6%	24.2%	4.5%

Capabilities

The primary focus of the small People's Defence Forces is maritime security and countering piracy. China, India and the United Arab Emirates have previously supported operations through equipment donations. The Seychelles maintains close ties with India; in March, a year after the inauguration of the first of eight planned Indian coastal-surveillance radars on the islands, India dispatched a P-8I aircraft to the country. India was also due to donate more aircraft suitable for the maritime-surveillance role. The country also hosts, on a rotational basis, US military forces conducting maritime-patrol activities, including the operation of unarmed UAVs. In 2014, the EU began basic-training activities for the air force, in conjunction with local staff, in a bid to bolster maritime-surveillance capacities.

ACTIVE 420 (Land Forces 200; Coast Guard 200; Air Force 20)

ORGANISATIONS BY SERVICE

People's Defence Force

Land Forces 200

FORCES BY ROLE
SPECIAL FORCES
    1 SF unit
MANOEUVRE
    Light
    1 inf coy
    Other
    1 sy unit
COMBAT SUPPORT
    1 MP unit

EQUIPMENT BY TYPE
ARMOURED FIGHTING VEHICLES
  RECCE 6 BRDM-2†
ARTILLERY • MOR 82mm 6 M-43†
AIR DEFENCE • GUNS • TOWED 14.5mm ZPU-2†; ZPU-4†; 37mm M-1939†

Coast Guard 200 (incl 80 Marines)
EQUIPMENT BY TYPE
PATROL AND COASTAL COMBATANTS 8
  PCO 3: 1 *Andromache* (ITA *Pichiotti* 42m); 2 *Topaz* (ex-IND *Trinkat*)
  PBF 1 *Hermes* (ex-IND *Coastal Interceptor Craft*)
  PB 4: 2 *Le Vigilant* (ex-UAE Rodman 101); 1 *Etoile* (*Shanghai* II mod); 1 *Fortune* (UK *Tyne*)

Air Force 20
EQUIPMENT BY TYPE
AIRCRAFT
  TPT • Light 4: 1 DHC-6-320 *Twin Otter*; 1 Do-228; 2 Y-12

Sierra Leone SLE

Sierra Leonean Leone L		2015	2016	2017
GDP	L	22.3tr	25.8tr	
	US$	4.40bn	4.29bn	
per capita	US$	696	666	
Growth	%	-21.1	4.3	
Inflation	%	9.0	9.7	
Def bdgt	L	92.8bn	85.7bn	86.5bn
	US$	18m	14m	
US$1=L		5,075.32	6,025.97	

Population   6,018,888

Age	0–14	15–19	20–24	25–29	30–64	65 plus
Male	20.9%	4.8%	4.2%	3.8%	13.3%	1.6%
Female	21.0%	5.1%	4.5%	4.1%	14.6%	2.2%

Capabilities

The armed forces' primary task is internal security and the provision of forces for continental peacekeeping missions, and there has been much focus on institutional development of the armed forces, with international support. The improved overall internal-security environment was reflected by the end of the UN's 15-year-long peacekeeping mission in early 2014. Training has been provided by the US and the UK, and there are reports of interest in greater military cooperation with China, which provides scholarships for military education. The army has taken part in peacekeeping operations, most notably through its deployment of a battalion to AMISOM in Somalia.

ACTIVE 8,500 (Joint 8,500)

ORGANISATIONS BY SERVICE

Armed Forces 8,500

FORCES BY ROLE
MANOEUVRE
  Light
    3 inf bde (3 inf bn)
EQUIPMENT BY TYPE
ANTI-TANK/ANTI-INFRASTRUCTURE
  RCL 84mm *Carl Gustav*
ARTILLERY 37
  TOWED 122mm 6 Type-96 (D30)
  MOR 31: 81mm ε27; 82mm 2; 120mm 2
HELICOPTERS • MRH/TPT 2 Mi-17 *Hip* H/Mi-8 *Hip*†
AIR DEFENCE • GUNS 7: 12.7mm 4; 14.5mm 3

Maritime Wing ε200
EQUIPMENT BY TYPE
PATROL AND COASTAL COMBATANTS • PB 2: 1 *Shanghai* III†; 1 *Isle of Man*

DEPLOYMENT

LEBANON
UN • UNIFIL 3

MALI
UN • MINUSMA 4; 3 obs

SUDAN
UN • UNAMID 1; 5 obs
UN • UNISFA 1 obs

FOREIGN FORCES
United Kingdom 10

Somalia SOM

Somali Shilling sh		2015	2016	2017
GDP	US$			
per capita	US$			

US$1=sh

*Definitive economic data unavailable

Population   10,817,354

Age	0–14	15–19	20–24	25–29	30–64	65 plus
Male	21.7%	5.3%	4.2%	4.0%	14.2%	0.9%
Female	21.7%	5.3%	4.0%	3.9%	13.3%	1.4%

Capabilities

Somalia's armed forces are still reliant on international support for training and also to tackle the principal threat to national stability from al-Shabaab jihadists. AMISOM and the Somali army have made significant progress, but renewed al-Shabaab attacks in 2016 were a reminder of the group's continued resilience. An internationally backed attempt to forge a Somali National Army (SNA) has produced a force trained by AMISOM, the EU and private security companies. The SNA is infantry-heavy but support- and logistics-light, meaning that there are challenges in terms of conventional force sustainment and organisation. According to the UN, there has been limited international support for longer-term plans to develop the capacity of the army, beyond the international assistance already offered in terms of training and intelligence support. AMISOM has constructed a facility to enable urban-combat training, in order to better prepare Somali forces for operations. Somaliland and Puntland have their own militias, while a privately funded Puntland Maritime Police Force operates a small number of rigid inflatable boats and small aircraft.

ACTIVE 19,800 (Army 19,800)

ORGANISATIONS BY SERVICE

Army 19,800 (plus further militias (to be integrated))
FORCES BY ROLE
COMMAND
  1 (21st) div HQ
MANOEUVRE
  Light
  Some cdo unit
  7 inf bde (total: ε21 inf bn)
EQUIPMENT BY TYPE
ARMOURED FIGHTING VEHICLES
  APC 34+
    APC (W) 25+: 25+ AT-105 *Saxon*; Fiat 6614
    PPV 9+: *Casspir*; MAV-5; 9+ *Mamba* Mk5; RG-31 *Nyala*

Paramilitary

Coast Guard
All operational patrol vessels under 10t FLD

FOREIGN FORCES

Under UNSOM command unless stated
Bangladesh 1 obs
Burundi AMISOM 5,432; 6 inf bn
Djibouti AMISOM 1,850; 2 inf bn
Ethiopia AMISOM 4,395; 6 inf bn
India 1 obs
Kenya AMISOM 3,664; 3 inf bn
Nepal 1 obs
Turkey 1 obs
Uganda 530; 1 obs • AMISOM 6,223; 7 inf bn
United Kingdom 41; 3 obs

TERRITORY WHERE THE GOVERNMENT DOES NOT EXERCISE EFFECTIVE CONTROL

Data presented here represents the de facto situation. This does not imply international recognition as a sovereign state

Somaliland
Militia-unit strengths are not known. Equipment numbers are generalised assessments; most of this equipment is in poor repair or inoperable.

Army ε12,500
FORCES BY ROLE
MANOEUVRE
  Armoured
  2 armd bde
  Mechanised
  1 mech inf bde
  Light
  14 inf bde
COMBAT SUPPORT
  2 arty bde
COMBAT SERVICE SUPPORT
  1 spt bn
EQUIPMENT BY TYPE†
ARMOURED FIGHTING VEHICLES
  MBT T-54/55
  RECCE Fiat 6616
  APC • APC(W) Fiat 6614
ARTILLERY • MRL various incl BM-21 *Grad*
AIR DEFENCE • GUNS • 23mm ZU-23

Ministry of the Interior

Coast Guard 600
All operational patrol vessels under 10t FLD

Puntland

Army ε3,000 (to be integrated into Somali National Army)

Maritime Police Force ε1,000
EQUIPMENT BY TYPE
AIRCRAFT • TPT 4: **Light** 3 Ayres S2R; **PAX** 1 DC-3
HELICOPTERS • MRH SA316 *Alouette* III
PATROL AND COASTAL COMBATANTS
All operational patrol vessels under 10t FLD

South Africa RSA

South African Rand R		2015	2016	2017
GDP	R	4.01tr	4.28tr	
	US$	315bn	280bn	
per capita	US$	5,727	5,018	
Growth	%	1.3	0.1	
Inflation	%	4.6	6.4	
Def bdgt	R	45.1bn	47.2bn	48.7bn
	US$	3.54bn	3.09bn	
FMA (US)	US$	0.45m	0.45m	0.3m
US$1=R		12.75	15.26	

Population 54,300,704

Age	0–14	15–19	20–24	25–29	30–64	65 plus
Male	14.2%	4.4%	4.6%	5.2%	18.8%	2.3%
Female	14.1%	4.4%	4.7%	5.1%	18.9%	3.2%

Capabilities

The South African National Defence Force (SANDF) remains on paper the most capable force in the region, although problems including funding, a top-heavy rank structure and a lack of strategic mobility continue to challenge the force. Its ability to deploy at reach and to contribute sizeable forces is increasingly challenged by these issues. South Africa contributes to UN operations and, since its inception, has been a key component of the Force Intervention Brigade in the Democratic Republic of the Congo. It is also a proponent of the African Union's Standby Force concept. The 2015 Defence Review highlighted the role Pretoria sees itself playing in ensuring the stability of the continent. Key recommendations included joint command and control for multi-domain and joint-service operations; investment in special forces; and boosting land forces' deployability. The review proposed a maritime-defence concept providing security in concentric layers around ports, territorial waters and resources. At the same time, the defence review described the SANDF as being in 'a critical state of decline'. Flying hours are inadequate, and insufficient pilots are being trained to operate fighter aircraft and newly acquired support helicopters. Medium and light airlift is nearly 'lifed'. Increased sustainment costs for naval vessels strain the navy budget. Higher personnel spending, including on pensions, has meant that maintenance and repair funds have had to be reallocated. Meanwhile, the army 'faces block obsolescence of its prime mission equipment'. Equipment-recapitalisation efforts in all services have been delayed by funding problems. South African defence firm Denel provides capabilities including UAVs, armoured vehicles and some maintenance and repair capacity. The production of Denel's *Seeker* UAVs will enhance the air force's limited ISR capability, at a time when the defence review says that 'only limited aerial domain awareness exists over large parts of South Africa's airspace'. The SANDF still deploys regularly on peacekeeping missions and participates in national and multinational exercises. South Africa hosted the AU's *Amani Africa* II validation exercise for the Standby Force concept. Exercises carried out in 2016 focused on readiness and joint-service command and control. Historically, South African forces have also played a significant role in training and supporting other regional forces.

ACTIVE 67,100 (Army 40,600 Navy 7,650 Air 10,650 South African Military Health Service 8,200)

RESERVE 15,050 (Army 12,250 Navy 850 Air 850 South African Military Health Service Reserve 1,100)

ORGANISATIONS BY SERVICE

Space
EQUIPMENT BY TYPE
SATELLITES • ISR 1 *Kondor-E*

Army 40,600
FORCES BY ROLE
Regt are bn sized. A new army structure is planned with 3 mixed regular/reserve divisions (1 mechanised, 1 motorised and 1 contingency) comprising 12 brigades (1 armoured, 1 mechanised, 7 motorised, 1 airborne, 1 air-landed and 1 sea landed)

COMMAND
2 bde HQ
SPECIAL FORCES
2 SF regt(-)
MANOEUVRE
Reconnaissance
1 armd recce regt
Armoured
1 tk regt(-)
Mechanised
2 mech inf bn
Light
8 mot inf bn
1 lt inf bn
Air Manoeuvre
1 AB bn
1 air mob bn
Amphibious
1 amph bn
COMBAT SUPPORT
1 arty regt
1 engr regt
1 construction regt
3 sigs regt
COMBAT SERVICE SUPPORT
1 engr spt regt
AIR DEFENCE
1 ADA regt

Reserve 12,250 reservists (under strength)
FORCES BY ROLE
MANOEUVRE
Reconnaissance
3 armd recce regt
Armoured
4 tk regt
Mechanised
6 mech inf bn
Light
14 mot inf bn
3 lt inf bn (converting to mot inf)
Air Manoeuvre
1 AB bn
2 air mob bn
Amphibious
1 amph bn
COMBAT SUPPORT
7 arty regt
2 engr regt
AIR DEFENCE
5 AD regt
EQUIPMENT BY TYPE
ARMOURED FIGHTING VEHICLES
MBT 24 *Olifant* 2 (133 *Olifant* 1B in store)
ASLT 50 *Rooikat*-76 (126 in store)
IFV 534 *Ratel*-20/*Ratel*-60/*Ratel*-90
APC • PPV 810: 370 *Casspir*; 440 *Mamba*

ENGINEERING & MAINTENANCE VEHICLES
ARV *Gemsbok*
VLB *Leguan*
ANTI-TANK/ANTI-INFRASTRUCTURE
MSL • MANPATS ZT-3 *Swift*; Milan ADT/ER
RCL 106mm M40A1 (some SP)
ARTILLERY 1,240
SP 155mm 2 G-6 (41 in store)
TOWED 155mm 6 G-5 (66 in store)
MRL 127mm 6 *Valkiri* Mk II MARS *Bataleur*; (26 *Valkiri* Mk I and 19 *Valkiri* Mk II in store)
MOR 1,226: 81mm 1,190 (incl some SP on *Casspir*); 120mm 36
UNMANNED AERIAL VEHICLES
ISR • Light up to 4 *Vulture*
AIR DEFENCE
SAM • Point-defence *Starstreak*
GUNS 76
SP 23mm (36 *Zumlac* in store)
TOWED 35mm 40 GDF-002
RADAR • AIR DEFENCE 6: 4 ESR 220 *Thutlwa*; 2 Thales *Page*

Navy 7,650

Fleet HQ and Naval base located at Simon's Town; Naval stations located at Durban and Port Elizabeth

EQUIPMENT BY TYPE
SUBMARINES • TACTICAL • SSK 3 *Heroine* (Type-209/1400 mod) with 8 533mm TT with AEG SUT 264 HWT (of which one cyclically in reserve/refit)
PRINCIPAL SURFACE COMBATANTS • FRIGATES 4:
FFGHM 4 *Valour* (MEKO A200) with 2 quad lnchr with MM-40 *Exocet* Block II AShM (upgrade to Block III planned); 2 16-cell VLS with *Umkhonto*-IR SAM, 1 76mm gun (capacity 1 *Super Lynx* 300 hel)
PATROL AND COASTAL COMBATANTS 6
PCC 3 *Warrior* (ISR *Reshef*) with 2 76mm gun
PB 3 *Tobie*
MINE WARFARE • MINE COUNTERMEASURES 2
MHC 3 *River* (GER *Navors*) (Limited operational roles; training and dive support)
AMPHIBIOUS • LCU 2 *Delta* 80
LOGISTICS AND SUPPORT 2
AORH 1 *Drakensberg* (capacity 2 *Delta* 80 LCU; 2 *Oryx* hels; 100 troops)
AGHS 1 *Protea* (UK *Hecla*) with 1 hel landing platform

Maritime Reaction Squadron

FORCES BY ROLE
MANOEUVRE
Amphibious
1 mne patrol gp
1 diving gp
1 mne boarding gp
COMBAT SERVICE SUPPORT
1 spt gp

Air Force 10,650

Air Force HQ, Pretoria, and 4 op gps
Command & Control: 2 Airspace Control Sectors, 1 Mobile Deployment Wg, 1 Air Force Command Post

FORCES BY ROLE
FIGHTER/GROUND ATTACK
1 sqn with *Gripen* C/D (JAS-39C/D)
GROUND ATTACK/TRAINING
1 sqn with *Hawk* Mk120*
TRANSPORT
1 (VIP) sqn with B-737 BBJ; Cessna 550 *Citation* II; *Falcon* 50; *Falcon* 900
1 sqn with C-47TP
2 sqn with Beech 200/300 *King Air*; C-130B/BZ *Hercules*; C-212; Cessna 208 *Caravan*
ATTACK HELICOPTER
1 (cbt spt) sqn with AH-2 *Rooivalk*
TRANSPORT HELICOPTER
4 (mixed) sqn with AW109; BK-117; *Oryx*

EQUIPMENT BY TYPE
AIRCRAFT 50 combat capable
FGA 26: 17 *Gripen* C (JAS-39C); 9 *Gripen* D (JAS-39D)
TPT 33: Medium 7: 2 C-130B *Hercules*; 5 C-130BZ *Hercules*; Light 22: 3 Beech 200C *King Air*; 1 Beech 300 *King Air*; 3 C-47TP (maritime); 2 C-212-200 *Aviocar*; 1 C-212-300 *Aviocar*; 9 Cessna 208 *Caravan*; 2 Cessna 550 *Citation* II; 1 PC-12; PAX 4: 1 B-737BBJ; 2 *Falcon* 50; 1 *Falcon* 900
TRG 59: 24 *Hawk* Mk120*; 35 PC-7 Mk II *Astra*
HELICOPTERS
ATK 11 AH-2 *Rooivalk*
MRH 4 *Super Lynx* 300
TPT 71: Medium 36 *Oryx*; Light 35: 27 AW109; 8 BK-117
AIR-LAUNCHED MISSILES • AAM • IIR IRIS-T
BOMBS • Laser-guided GBU-12 *Paveway* II

Ground Defence

FORCES BY ROLE
MANOEUVRE
Other
12 sy sqn (SAAF regt)

EQUIPMENT BY TYPE
2 radar (static) located at Ellisras and Mariepskop; 2 (mobile long-range); 4 (tactical mobile). Radar air-control sectors located at Pretoria, Hoedspruit

South African Military Health Service 8,200; ε1,100 reservists (total 9,300)

Department of Agriculture, Fisheries and Forestry

EQUIPMENT BY TYPE
PATROL AND COASTAL COMBATANTS 4
PSO 1 *Sarah Baartman* with 1 hel landing platform
PCC 3 *Lilian Ngoyi*
LOGISTICS AND SUPPORT • AGE 2: 1 *Africana*; 1 *Ellen Khuzwayo*

Department of Environmental Affairs

EQUIPMENT BY TYPE
LOGISTICS AND SUPPORT • AGOSH 1 *S. A. Agulhas* II (used for Antarctic survey) (capacity 2 *Oryx* hels)

Cyber

South Africa published a National Cybersecurity Policy Framework in 2011. Since then, the defence-intelligence branch of the Department of Defence has been tasked to develop a comprehensive cyber-warfare strategy and a cyber-warfare implementation plan, as well as to establish a Cyber Command Centre Headquarters, to be fully operational by FY2018/19. A Cyber Security Incident Response Team (CSIRT) operates under the State Security Agency.

DEPLOYMENT

DEMOCRATIC REPUBLIC OF THE CONGO
UN • MONUSCO • *Operation Mistral* 1,355; 4 obs; 1 inf bn; 1 atk hel sqn; 1 hel sqn; 1 engr coy

MOZAMBIQUE CHANNEL
Navy • 1 FFGHM

SUDAN
UN • UNAMID • *Operation Cordite* 8; 5 obs

South Sudan SSD

South Sudanese Pound SSP		2015	2016	2017
GDP	ssp	46.9bn	158bn	
	US$	9.34bn	2.63bn	
per capita	US$	785	210	
Growth	%	-0.2	-13.1	
Inflation	%	52.8	476.0	
Def bdgt [a]	ssp	3.97bn	4.58bn	11.0bn
	US$	790m	0.76m	
US$1=ssp		5.02	60.01	

[a] Security and law-enforcement spending

Population 12,530,717

Age	0–14	15–19	20–24	25–29	30–64	65 plus
Male	22.9%	5.9%	4.8%	3.8%	12.3%	1.2%
Female	22.0%	5.4%	4.2%	3.6%	13.1%	0.9%

Capabilities

South Sudan's civil war continues, creating insecurity and hardship for the civilian population, and impeding any economic progress. Political and ethnic factionalism remains high, while there remain security concerns stemming from the relationship with Sudan. Planned disarmament, demobilisation and reintegration and security-sector-reform regimes remain on hold due to the fighting. An apparent accommodation between President Salva Kiir and Vice President Riek Machar proved elusive and Machar was removed from post in July. Future reform initiatives are unlikely to be solely focused on defence transformation and capability development; developing institutional capacity, transparency and accountability will likely also become a key task. There is an EU arms embargo on South Sudan, but amid concern that weapons were being stored – even after the peace deal of August 2015 – there was a debate over whether to attempt to secure a UN arms embargo. Continued fighting prompted the deployment of additional contributions to the UN peacekeeping effort.

ACTIVE 185,000 (Army 185,000)

ORGANISATIONS BY SERVICE

Army ε185,000
FORCES BY ROLE
3 military comd
MANOEUVRE
 Light
  8 inf div
COMBAT SUPPORT
 1 engr corps
EQUIPMENT BY TYPE
ARMOURED FIGHTING VEHICLES
 MBT 80+: some T-55†; 80 T-72AV†
 APC • PPV Streit *Typhoon*; Streit *Cougar*; Mamba
ANTI-TANK/ANTI-INFRASTRUCTURE
 MSL • MANPATS HJ-73; 9K115 *Metis* (AT-7 *Saxhorn*)
 RCL 73mm SPG-9 (with SSLA)
ARTILLERY 69+
 SP 122mm 2S1 *Gvozdika*; 152mm 2S3 *Akatsiya*
 TOWED 130mm Some M-46
 MRL 122mm BM-21 *Grad*; 107mm Type-63
 MOR 82mm; 120mm Type-55 look-alike
AIR DEFENCE
 SAM • Point-defence 9K32 *Strela*-2 (SA-7 *Grail*)‡; 9K310 *Igla*-1 (SA-16 *Gimlet*)
 GUNS 14.5mm ZPU-4; 23mm ZU-23-2; 37mm Type-65/74

Air Force
EQUIPMENT BY TYPE
AIRCRAFT • TPT • Light 1 Beech 1900
HELICOPTERS
 ATK 5: 2 Mi-24V *Hind*; 3 Mi-24V-SMB *Hind*
 MRH 9 Mi-17 *Hip* H
 TPT 3: Medium 1 Mi-172 (VIP); Light 2 AW109 (civ livery)

FOREIGN FORCES

All UNMISS, unless otherwise indicated
Australia 16; 1 obs
Bangladesh 484; 6 obs; 2 engr coy; 2 rvn coy
Benin 2; 1 obs
Bhutan 2; 2 obs
Bolivia 3; 3 obs
Brazil 5; 5 obs
Cambodia 149; 24 obs; 1 fd hospital
Canada 5; 5 obs
China, People's Republic of 1,051; 3 obs; 1 inf bn; 1 engr coy; 1 fd hospital
Denmark 12; 2 obs
Egypt 1; 3 obs
El Salvador 1; 1 obs
Ethiopia 1,267; 10 obs; 2 inf bn
Fiji 4; 2 obs

Germany 5; 11 obs
Ghana 715; 8 obs; 1 inf bn
Guatemala 4; 3 obs
Guinea 1; 1 obs
India 2,277; 10 obs; 2 inf bn; 1 engr coy; 1 fd hospital
Indonesia 1; 3 obs
Japan 272; 1 engr coy
Jordan 3
Kenya 1,027; 12 obs; 1 inf bn
Korea, Republic of 273; 2 obs; 1 engr coy
Kyrgyzstan 2; 2 obs
Moldova 1; 3 obs
Mongolia 863; 7 obs; 1 inf bn
Myanmar 2
Namibia 3; 2 obs
Nepal 1,579; 12 obs; 2 inf bn
Netherlands 7
New Zealand 1; 2 obs
Nigeria 4; 5 obs
Norway 10; 5 obs
Papua New Guinea 2 obs
Paraguay 2 obs
Peru 2
Poland 1 obs
Romania 2; 5 obs
Russia 3; 3 obs
Rwanda 1,843; 13 obs; 2 inf bn; 2 hel sqn
Senegal 2 obs
Sri Lanka 177; 2 obs; 1 hel sqn; 1 fd hospital
Sweden 2 obs
Switzerland 2
Tanzania 4; 3 obs
Togo 1
Uganda 2
Ukraine 1; 3 obs
United Kingdom 9
United States 6
Vietnam 2 obs
Yemen 6; 9 obs
Zambia 2; 1 obs
Zimbabwe 2 obs

Sudan SDN

Sudanese Pound sdg		2015	2016	2017
GDP	sdg	491bn	574bn	
	US$	81.4bn	94.3bn	
per capita	US$	2,119	2381	
Growth	%	4.9	3.1	
Inflation	%	16.9	13.5	
Def exp	sdg	n.k.	n.k.	
	US$	n.k.	n.k.	
US$1=sdg		6.03	6.09	

Population   36,729,501

Ethnic and religious groups: Muslim 70% mainly in north; Christian 10% mainly in south; 52% mainly in south; Arab 39% mainly in north

Age	0–14	15–19	20–24	25–29	30–64	65 plus
Male	20.0%	5.8%	4.9%	4.0%	13.9%	1.8%
Female	19.4%	5.6%	4.5%	3.9%	14.7%	1.5%

Capabilities

The primary focus of the military remains ongoing tensions with South Sudan and counter-insurgency, with continued clashes with rebels in the south of the country including a number of reported airstrikes. Although the Sudanese armed forces have a limited regional power-projection capability, they have contributed to the Saudi-led intervention in Yemen, initially with ground-attack aircraft to Saudi Arabia and later a ground-forces contingent to Aden. Sudan retains large armed forces with significant equipment holdings of primarily both ageing and more modern Russian and Chinese types, making them relatively well equipped by regional standards. This is complemented by the indigenous Military Industry Corporation's manufacture of ammunition, small arms and light vehicles. Maintenance capacity focuses on ground forces' equipment, with limited aircraft-maintenance capability.

ACTIVE 244,300 (Army 240,000 Navy 1,300 Air 3,000) **Paramilitary 20,000**
Conscript liability 2 years for males aged 18–30

RESERVE NIL Paramilitary 85,000

ORGANISATIONS BY SERVICE

Army ε240,000
FORCES BY ROLE
SPECIAL FORCES
  5 SF coy
MANOEUVRE
  Reconnaissance
  1 indep recce bde
  Armoured
  1 armd div

Mechanised
1 mech inf div
1 indep mech inf bde
Light
11+ inf div
6 indep inf bde
Air Manoeuvre
1 AB div
Other
1 (Border Guard) sy bde
COMBAT SUPPORT
3 indep arty bde
1 engr div (9 engr bn)
EQUIPMENT BY TYPE
ARMOURED FIGHTING VEHICLES
  MBT 465: 20 M60A3; 60 Type-59/Type-59D; 305 T-54/T-55; 70 T-72M1; 10 *Al-Bashier* (Type-85-IIM)
  LT TK 115: 70 Type-62; 45 Type-63
  RECCE 206: 6 AML-90; 70 BRDM-1/2; 50–80 FV701 *Ferret*; 30–50 FV601 *Saladin*
  IFV 152: 135 BMP-1/2; 10 BTR-3; 7 BTR-80A
  APC 415+
    APC (T) 66: 20-30 BTR-50; 36 M113
    APC (W) 349+: 10 BTR-70M *Kobra* 2; 50–80 BTR-152; 20 OT-62; 50 OT-64; 3+ *Rakhsh*; 10 Type-92 (reported); 55-80 V-150 *Commando*; 96 *Walid*
ANTI-TANK/ANTI-INFRASTRUCTURE
  MSL • MANPATS *Swingfire*; 9K11 *Malyutka* (AT-3 *Sagger*); HJ-8
  RCL **106mm** 40 M40A1
  GUNS 40+: 40 **76mm** ZIS-3/**100mm** M-1944; **85mm** D-44
ARTILLERY 860+
  SP 66: **122mm** 56 2S1 *Gvozdika*; **155mm** 10 Mk F3
  TOWED 128+: **105mm** 20 M101; **122mm** 21+: 21 D-30; D-74; M-30; **130mm** 75 M-46/Type-59-I; **155mm** 12 M114A1
  MRL 666+: **107mm** 477 Type-63; **122mm** 188: 120 BM-21 *Grad*; 50 *Saqr*; 18 Type-81; **302mm** 1+ WS-1
  MOR **81mm**; **82mm**; **120mm** AM-49; M-43
RADAR • LAND RASIT (veh, arty)
AIR DEFENCE
  SAM • Point-defence 9K32 *Strela*-2 (SA-7 *Grail*)‡
  GUNS 966+
    SP 20: **20mm** 8 M163 *Vulcan*; 12 M3 VDAA
    TOWED 946+: 740+ **14.5mm** ZPU-2/**14.5mm** ZPU-4/**37mm** Type-63/**57mm** S-60/**85mm** M-1944; **20mm** 16 M167 *Vulcan*; **23mm** 50 ZU-23-2; **37mm** 80 M-1939; (30 M-1939 unserviceable); **40mm** 60

Navy 1,300
EQUIPMENT BY TYPE
PATROL AND COASTAL COMBATANTS 11
  PBR 4 *Kurmuk*
  PB 7: 1 13.5m; 1 14m; 2 19m; 3 41m (PRC)
AMPHIBIOUS • LANDING CRAFT 5
  LCVP 5
LOGISTICS AND SUPPORT 3
  AG 3

Air Force 3,000
FORCES BY ROLE
FIGHTER
  2 sqn with MiG-29SE/UB *Fulcrum*
GROUND ATTACK
  1 sqn with A-5 *Fantan*
  1 sqn with Su-24M *Fencer*
  1 sqn with Su-25/Su-25UB *Frogfoot*
TRANSPORT
  Some sqn with An-26 *Curl** (modified for bombing); An-30 *Clank*; An-32 *Cline*; An-72 *Coaler*; An-74TK-200/300; C-130H *Hercules*; Il-76 *Candid*; Y-8
  1 VIP unit with *Falcon* 20F; *Falcon* 50; *Falcon* 900; F-27; Il-62M *Classic*
TRAINING
  1 sqn with K-8 *Karakorum**
ATTACK HELICOPTER
  2 sqn with Mi-24/Mi-24P/Mi-24V/Mi-35P *Hind*
TRANSPORT HELICOPTER
  2 sqn with Mi-8 *Hip*; Mi-17 *Hip* H; Mi-171
AIR DEFENCE
  5 bty with S-75 *Dvina* (SA-2 *Guideline*)‡
EQUIPMENT BY TYPE
AIRCRAFT 66 combat capable
  FTR 22: 20 MiG-29SE *Fulcrum*; 2 MiG-29UB *Fulcrum*
  ATK 32: 15 A-5 *Fantan*; 6 Su-24/M *Fencer*; 9 Su-25 *Frogfoot*; 2 Su-25UB *Frogfoot* B
  ISR 2 An-30 *Clank*
  TPT 22: **Heavy** 1 Il-76 *Candid*; **Medium** 6: 4 C-130H *Hercules*; 2 Y-8; **Light** 11: 2 An-32 *Cline*; 2 An-72 *Coaler*; 4 An-74TK-200; 2 An-74TK-300; 1 F-27 (VIP); **PAX** 4: 1 *Falcon* 20F (VIP); 1 *Falcon* 50 (VIP); 1 *Falcon* 900; 1 Il-62M *Classic*
  TRG 15: 12 K-8 *Karakorum**; 3 UTVA-75
HELICOPTERS
  ATK 40: 25 Mi-24 *Hind*; 2 Mi-24P *Hind*; 7 Mi-24V *Hind* E; 6 Mi-35P *Hind*
  MRH ε5 Mi-17 *Hip* H
  TPT 24: **Medium** 23: 21 Mi-8 *Hip*; 2 Mi-171; **Light** 1 Bell 205
AIR DEFENCE • SAM • Medium-range: 90 S-75 *Dvina* (SA-2 *Guideline*)‡
AIR-LAUNCHED MISSILES • AAM • IR R-3 (AA-2 *Atoll*)‡; R-60 (AA-8 *Aphid*); R-73 (AA-11 *Archer*); **IR/SARH** R-23/24 (AA-7 *Apex*); **ARH** R-77 (AA-12 *Adder*)

Paramilitary 20,000

Popular Defence Force 20,000 (org in bn 1,000); 85,000 reservists (total 105,000)
mil wing of National Islamic Front

DEPLOYMENT

SAUDI ARABIA
Operation Restoring Hope 3 Su-24 *Fencer*

YEMEN
Operation Restoring Hope 950; 1 mech BG; BTR-70M *Kobra* 2

FOREIGN FORCES

All UNAMID, unless otherwise indicated
Bangladesh 373; 7 obs; 2 inf coy
Benin UNISFA 2 obs
Bhutan UNISFA 1; 1 obs
Brazil UNISFA 2 obs
Burkina Faso 804; 5 obs; 1 inf bn
Burundi 3; 5 obs • UNISFA 1 obs
Cambodia 1; 2 obs • UNISFA 3 obs
China, People's Republic of 230; 1 engr coy
Ecuador 1; 2 obs; • UNISFA 1 obs
Egypt 865; 13 obs; 1 inf bn
El Salvador 1 obs
Ethiopia 2,527; 11 obs; 3 inf bn • UNISFA 4,371; 78 obs; 1 recce coy; 3 mech inf bn; 1 hel sqn; 2 arty coy; 1 engr coy; 1 sigs coy; 1 fd hospital
Gambia 213; 1 inf coy
Germany 8
Ghana 18; 4 obs • UNISFA 2; 4 obs
Guatemala UNISFA 1; 2 obs
India UNISFA 4 obs
Indonesia 812; 4 obs; 1 inf bn • UNISFA 2; 2 obs
Iran 4 obs
Jordan 15; 5 obs
Kenya 112; 3 obs; 1 MP coy
Korea, Republic of 2
Kyrgyzstan 2 obs • UNISFA 1 obs
Malawi UNISFA 1
Malaysia 9; 1 obs • UNISFA 1 obs
Mongolia 70; 1 fd hospital • UNISFA 2 obs
Mozambique UNISFA 1 obs
Namibia 5; 3 obs • UNISFA 2; 3 obs
Nepal 362; 8 obs; 1 SF coy; 1 inf coy • UNISFA 2; 3 obs
Nigeria 928; 2 obs; 1 inf bn; 1 sigs unit; 1 med unit • UNISFA 1; 1 obs
Pakistan 2,120; 4 obs; 2 inf bn; 1 engr coy; 1 med pl
Papua New Guinea 1; 1 obs
Peru 2 obs • UNISFA 1 obs
Russia UNISFA 1 obs
Rwanda 2,454; 5 obs; 3 inf bn • UNISFA 4; 3 obs
Senegal 803; 1 inf bn
Sierra Leone 1; 5 obs • UNISFA 1 obs
South Africa 8; 5 obs
Sri Lanka UNISFA 1
Tanzania 815; 12 obs; 1 inf bn • UNISFA 1; 1 obs
Thailand 7; 4 obs
Togo 3; 4 obs
Ukraine UNISFA 2; 4 obs
Yemen, Republic of 21; 23 obs • UNISFA 2
Zambia 7; 2 obs • UNISFA 2 obs
Zimbabwe 2; 4 obs • UNISFA 1; 2 obs

Tanzania TZA

Tanzanian Shilling sh		2015	2016	2017
GDP	sh	90.9tr	102tr	
	US$	45.6bn	46.7bn	
per capita	US$	957	960	
Growth	%	7.0	7.2	
Inflation	%	5.6	5.2	
Def bdgt	sh	879bn	1.14tr	1.19tr
	US$	442m	520m	
US$1=sh		1,991.14	2,200.42	

Population 52,482,726

Age	0–14	15–19	20–24	25–29	30–64	65 plus
Male	22.3%	5.4%	4.4%	3.8%	12.6%	1.3%
Female	22.0%	5.4%	4.4%	3.8%	12.9%	1.7%

Capabilities

Non-state actors pose the principal threat to security, with terrorism, poaching and piracy also of concern. Although equipment-recapitalisation ambitions have been aired, budget constraints limit ambition in this regard. This reflects a relatively benign security environment, although concerns remain about instability in the Democratic Republic of the Congo. A developing relationship with China has led to a series of procurement programmes as well as training contacts. There is limited ability to project power independently beyond its own territory. However, Tanzania has in recent years regularly taken part in multinational exercises in Africa and provided some training assistance to other African forces. There are established training relationships with other external armed forces, including the US military, and also for capacity-building assistance. Tanzania's contribution to the UN's Force Intervention Brigade in the eastern DRC, notably its special forces, will have provided many lessons for force development.

ACTIVE 27,000 (Army 23,000 Navy 1,000 Air 3,000)
Paramilitary 1,400

Conscript liability Three months basic military training combined with social service, ages 18–23

RESERVE 80,000 (Joint 80,000)

ORGANISATIONS BY SERVICE

Army ε23,000
FORCES BY ROLE
SPECIAL FORCES
  1 SF unit
MANOEUVRE
  Armoured
  1 tk bde
  Light
  5 inf bde
COMBAT SUPPORT
  4 arty bn

1 mor bn
2 AT bn
1 engr regt (bn)
COMBAT SERVICE SUPPORT
1 log gp
AIR DEFENCE
2 ADA bn
EQUIPMENT BY TYPE†
ARMOURED FIGHTING VEHICLES
MBT 45: 30 T-54/T-55; 15 Type-59G
LT TK 57+: 30 FV101 *Scorpion*; 25 Type-62; 2+ Type-63A
RECCE 10 BRDM-2
APC • APC (W) 14: ε10 BTR-40/BTR-152; 4 Type-92
ANTI-TANK/ANTI-INFRASTRUCTURE
RCL 75mm Type-52 (M20)
GUNS 85mm 75 Type-56 (D-44)
ARTILLERY 344+
TOWED 130: **122mm** 100: 20 D-30; 80 Type-54-1 (M-30); **130mm** 30 Type-59-I
GUN/MOR **120mm** 3+ Type-07PA
MRL 61+: **122mm** 58 BM-21 *Grad*; **300mm** 3+ A100
MOR 150: **82mm** 100 M-43; **120mm** 50 M-43

Navy ε1,000
EQUIPMENT BY TYPE
PATROL AND COASTAL COMBATANTS 10
PCC 2 *Mwitongo* (ex-PRC *Haiqing*)
PHT 2 *Huchuan* each with 2 533mm ASTT
PB 6: 2 *Ngunguri*; 2 *Shanghai II* (PRC); 2 VT 23m
AMPHIBIOUS 3
LCU 2 *Yuchin*
LCT 1 *Kasa*

Air Defence Command ε3,000
FORCES BY ROLE
FIGHTER
3 sqn with F-7/FT-7; FT-5; K-8 *Karakorum**
TRANSPORT
1 sqn with Cessna 404 *Titan*; DHC-5D *Buffalo*; F-28 *Fellowship*; F-50; Gulfstream G550; Y-12 (II)
TRANSPORT HELICOPTER
1 sqn with Bell 205 (AB-205); Bell 412EP *Twin Huey*
EQUIPMENT BY TYPE†
AIRCRAFT 17 combat capable
FTR 11: 9 F-7TN; 2 FT-7TN
ISR 1 SB7L-360 *Seeker*
TPT 12: **Medium** 2 Y-8; **Light** 7: 2 Cessna 404 *Titan*; 3 DHC-5D *Buffalo*; 2 Y-12(II); **PAX** 3: 1 F-28 *Fellowship*; 1 F-50; 1 Gulfstream G550
TRG 9: 3 FT-5 (JJ-5); 6 K-8 *Karakorum**
HELICOPTERS
MRH 1 Bell 412EP *Twin Huey*
TPT • **Light** 1 Bell 205 (AB-205)
AIR DEFENCE
SAM
Short-range 2K12 *Kub* (SA-6 *Gainful*)†; S-125 *Pechora* (SA-3 *Goa*)†
Point-defence 9K32 *Strela*-2 (SA-7 *Grail*)‡

GUNS 200
TOWED **14.5mm** 40 ZPU-2/ZPU-4†; **23mm** 40 ZU-23; **37mm** 120 M-1939

Paramilitary 1,400 active

Police Field Force 1,400
18 sub-units incl Police Marine Unit

Air Wing
EQUIPMENT BY TYPE
AIRCRAFT • TPT • **Light** 1 Cessna U206 *Stationair*
HELICOPTERS
TPT • **Light** 4: 2 Bell 206A *Jet Ranger* (AB-206A); 2 Bell 206L *Long Ranger*
TRG 2 Bell 47G (AB-47G)/Bell 47G2

Marine Unit 100
EQUIPMENT BY TYPE
PATROL AND COASTAL COMBATANTS
All operational patrol vessels under 10t FLD

DEPLOYMENT

CENTRAL AFRICAN REPUBLIC
UN • MINUSCA 1

CÔTE D'IVOIRE
UN • UNOCI 2; 2 obs

DEMOCRATIC REPUBLIC OF THE CONGO
UN • MONUSCO 1,262; 1 SF coy; 1 inf bn; 1 arty coy

LEBANON
UN • UNIFIL 159; 2 MP coy

SOUTH SUDAN
UN • UNMISS 4; 3 obs

SUDAN
UN • UNAMID 815; 12 obs; 1 inf bn
UN • UNISFA 1; 1 obs

Togo TGO

CFA Franc BCEAO fr		2015	2016	2017
GDP	fr	2.46tr	2.65tr	
	US$	4.17bn	4.52bn	
per capita	US$	570	602	
Growth	%	5.4	5.3	
Inflation	%	1.8	2.1	
Def bdgt	fr	41.8bn	48.6bn	
	US$	71m	83m	
US$1=fr		591.10	587.30	

Population 7,756,937

Age	0–14	15–19	20–24	25–29	30–64	65 plus
Male	20.3%	5.0%	4.6%	4.2%	14.0%	1.5%
Female	20.2%	5.1%	4.6%	4.3%	14.3%	1.9%

Capabilities

The Togolese armed forces are adequate for the internal-security roles, though they have limited deployment capacity. Equipment, though limited, is generally well maintained and serviceable. French forces from Senegal in 2015 trained troops for deployment on the MINUSMA mission in combat as well as counter-IED specialists, while the French and US navies have in the past provided maritime-security training. Training was also provided under the US African Contingency Operations Training and Assistance programme.

ACTIVE 8,550 (Army 8,100 Navy 200 Air 250)
Paramilitary 750

Conscript liability Selective conscription, 2 years

ORGANISATIONS BY SERVICE

Army 8,100+
FORCES BY ROLE
MANOEUVRE
  Reconnaissance
    1 armd recce regt
  Light
    2 cbd arms regt
    2 inf regt
    1 rapid reaction force
  Air Manoeuvre
    1 cdo/para regt (3 cdo/para coy)
  Other
    1 (Presidential Guard) gd regt (1 gd bn, 1 cdo bn, 2 indep gd coy)
COMBAT SUPPORT
  1 cbt spt regt (1 fd arty bty, 2 ADA bty, 1 engr/log/tpt bn)
EQUIPMENT BY TYPE
ARMOURED FIGHTING VEHICLES
  MBT 2 T-54/T-55
  LT TK 9 FV101 *Scorpion*
  RECCE 87: 3 AML-60; 7 AML-90; 30 *Bastion Patsas*; 36 EE-9 *Cascavel*; 6 M8; 3 M20; 2 VBL
  IFV 20 BMP-2
  APC 34
    APC (T) 4 M3A1 half-track
    APC (W) 30 UR-416
ANTI-TANK/ANTI-INFRASTRUCTURE
  RCL 75mm Type-52 (M20)/Type-56; 82mm Type-65 (B-10)
  GUNS 57mm 5 ZIS-2
ARTILLERY 30+
  SP 122mm 6
  TOWED 105mm 4 HM-2
  MRL 122mm Type-81 mod (SC6 chassis)
  MOR 82mm 20 M-43
AIR DEFENCE • GUNS • TOWED 43 14.5mm 38 ZPU-4; 37mm 5 M-1939

Navy ε200 (incl Marine Infantry unit)
EQUIPMENT BY TYPE
PATROL AND COASTAL COMBATANTS 3
  PBF 1 *Agou* (RPB 33)
  PB 2 *Kara* (FRA *Esterel*)

Air Force 250
FORCES BY ROLE
FIGHTER/GROUND ATTACK
  1 sqn with *Alpha Jet**; EMB-326G*
TRANSPORT
  1 sqn with Beech 200 *King Air*
  1 VIP unit with DC-8; F-28-1000
TRAINING
  1 sqn with TB-30 *Epsilon**
TRANSPORT HELICOPTER
  1 sqn with SA315 *Lama*; SA316 *Alouette* III; SA319 *Alouette* III
EQUIPMENT BY TYPE†
AIRCRAFT 10 combat capable
  TPT 5: Light 2 Beech 200 *King Air*; PAX 3: 1 DC-8; 2 F-28-1000 (VIP)
  TRG 10: 3 *Alpha Jet**; 4 EMB-326G *; 3 TB-30 *Epsilon**
HELICOPTERS
  MRH 4: 2 SA315 *Lama*; 1 SA316 *Alouette* III; 1 SA319 *Alouette* III
  TPT • Medium (1 SA330 *Puma* in store)

Paramilitary 750

Gendarmerie 750
Ministry of Interior
FORCES BY ROLE
2 reg sections
MANOEUVRE
  Other
    1 (mobile) paramilitary sqn

DEPLOYMENT

CENTRAL AFRICAN REPUBLIC
UN • MINUSCA 6; 4 obs

CÔTE D'IVOIRE
UN • UNOCI 303; 6 obs; 1 inf bn(-)

LIBERIA
UN • UNMIL 1; 1 obs

MALI
UN • MINUSMA 935; 2 obs; 1 inf bn; 1 fd hospital

SOUTH SUDAN
UN • UNMISS 1

SUDAN
UN • UNAMID 3; 4 obs

WESTERN SAHARA
UN • MINURSO 1 obs

Uganda UGA

Ugandan Shilling Ush		2015	2016	2017
GDP	Ush	78.8tr	87.2tr	
	US$	24.3bn	25.6bn	
per capita	US$	609	623	
Growth	%	4.8	4.9	
Inflation	%	5.5	5.5	
Def bdgt	Ush	1.16tr	1.64tr	1.58tr
	US$	358m	481m	
FMA (US)	US$	0.2m	0.2m	
US$1=Ush		3,240.49	3,402.89	

Population 38,319,241

Age	0–14	15–19	20–24	25–29	30–64	65 plus
Male	24.1%	5.7%	4.8%	3.9%	10.4%	0.9%
Female	24.2%	5.8%	4.9%	3.9%	10.4%	1.1%

Capabilities

Uganda's armed forces are relatively large and well equipped. They have, in recent years, seen some advanced-capability acquisitions, boosting military capacity, particularly in the air force. Forces have deployed to Somalia as part of AMISOM since the start of that mission in 2007, and have gained valuable combat experience in terms of planning and tactics, such as in counter-IED and urban patrolling on foot and with armour. A number of years targeting the Lord's Resistance Army has also ensured experience in more austere counter-insurgency tactics. Uganda is one of the largest contributors to the East Africa Standby Force. There is regular training, and the country has a number of training facilities that are used by international partners as well as Ugandan troops. US training support to Uganda's forces focused on, among others, medical training for combat stress, engineering skills and maritime security during the *Cutlass Express* exercise in 2016.

ACTIVE 45,000 (Ugandan People's Defence Force 45,000) Paramilitary 1,400

RESERVE 10,000

ORGANISATIONS BY SERVICE

Ugandan People's Defence Force ε40,000–45,000
FORCES BY ROLE
MANOEUVRE
  Armoured
  1 armd bde
  Light
  1 cdo bn
  5 inf div (total: 16 inf bde)
  Other
  1 (Special Forces Command) mot bde
COMBAT SUPPORT
  1 arty bde

AIR DEFENCE
  2 AD bn
EQUIPMENT BY TYPE†
ARMOURED FIGHTING VEHICLES
  MBT 239: 185 T-54/T-55; 10 T-72; 44 T-90S (reported)
  LT TK ε20 PT-76
  RECCE 46: 40 *Eland-20*; 6 FV701 *Ferret*
  IFV 31 BMP-2
  APC 131
    APC (W) 39: 15 BTR-60; 20 *Buffel*; 4 OT-64
    PPV 92: 42 *Casspir*; 40 *Mamba*; 10 RG-33L
  AUV 15 *Cougar*
ENGINEERING & MAINTENANCE VEHICLES
  ARV T-54/T-55 reported
  VLB MTU reported
  MW *Chubby*
ARTILLERY 333+
  SP 155mm 6 ATMOS 2000
  TOWED 243+: 122mm M-30; 130mm 221; 155mm 22: 4 G-5; 18 M-839
  MRL 6+: 107mm (12-tube); 122mm 6+: BM-21 *Grad*; 6 RM-70
  MOR 78+: 81mm L16; 82mm M-43; 120mm 78 *Soltam*
AIR DEFENCE
  SAM
    Short-range 4 S-125 *Pechora* (SA-3 *Goa*)
    Point-defence 9K32 *Strela-2* (SA-7 *Grail*)‡; 9K310 *Igla-1* (SA-16 *Gimlet*)
  GUNS • TOWED 20+: 14.5mm ZPU-1/ZPU-2/ZPU-4; 37mm 20 M-1939

Marines ε400
All operational patrol vessels under 10t FLD

Air Wing
FORCES BY ROLE
FIGHTER/GROUND ATTACK
  1 sqn with MiG-21bis *Fishbed*; MiG-21U/UM *Mongol* A/B; Su-30MK2
TRANSPORT
  1 unit with Y-12
  1 VIP unit with Gulfstream 550; L-100-30
TRAINING
  1 unit with L-39 *Albatros*†*
ATTACK/TRANSPORT HELICOPTER
  1 sqn with Bell 206 *Jet Ranger*; Bell 412 *Twin Huey*; Mi-17 *Hip* H; Mi-24 *Hind*; Mi-172 (VIP)
EQUIPMENT BY TYPE
  AIRCRAFT 16 combat capable
    FGA 13: 5 MiG-21bis *Fishbed*; 1 MiG-21U *Mongol* A; 1 MiG-21UM *Mongol* B; 6 Su-30MK2
    TPT 6: Medium 1 L-100-30; Light 4: 2 Cessna 208B; 2 Y-12; PAX 1 Gulfstream 550
    TRG 3 L-39 *Albatros*†*
  HELICOPTERS
    ATK 1 Mi-24 *Hind* (2 more non-op)
    MRH 5: 2 Bell 412 *Twin Huey*; 3 Mi-17 *Hip* H (1 more non-op)
    TPT 4: Medium 2: 1 Mi-172 (VIP), 1 Mi-171 (VIP); Light 2 Bell 206A *Jet Ranger*

AIR-LAUNCHED MISSILES
AAM • IR R-73 (AA-11 *Archer*); **SARH** R-27 (AA-10 *Alamo*); **ARH** R-77 (AA-12 *Adder*) (reported)
ARM Kh-31P (AS-17A *Krypton*) (reported)

Paramilitary ε1,400 active

Border Defence Unit ε600
Equipped with small arms only

Police Air Wing ε800
EQUIPMENT BY TYPE
HELICOPTERS • TPT • Light 1 Bell 206 *Jet Ranger*

DEPLOYMENT

CÔTE D'IVOIRE
UN • UNOCI 1; 2 obs

SOMALIA
AU • AMISOM 6,223; 7 inf bn
UN • UNSOM 530; 1 obs

SOUTH SUDAN
UN • UNMISS 2

FOREIGN FORCES
All EUTM, unless otherwise indicated
Finland 7
France 1
Germany 11
Hungary 4
Italy 112
Netherlands 7
Portugal 4
Romania 1
Serbia 6
Spain 17
Sweden 4
UK 4

Zambia ZMB

Zambian Kwacha K		2015	2016	2017
GDP	K	189bn	230bn	
	US$	21.9bn	20.6bn	
per capita	US$	1,352	1,231	
Growth	%	3.0	3.0	
Inflation	%	10.1	19.1	
Def bdgt	K	3.25bn	3.15bn	
	US$	376m	281m	
US$1=K		8.63	11.19	

Population 15,510,711

Age	0–14	15–19	20–24	25–29	30–64	65 plus
Male	23.1%	5.4%	4.6%	3.8%	12.0%	1.0%
Female	22.9%	5.4%	4.6%	3.8%	12.0%	1.3%

Capabilities

Ensuring territorial integrity and border security, and a commitment to international peacekeeping operations, are key tasks for the armed forces. But Zambia's armed forces struggle with limited funding and the challenge of maintaining ageing weapons systems. A new naval unit was created in 2015 to patrol the country's riverine borders. The air force has limited tactical air-transport capability and as part of plans to boost air assets initial deliveries of China's L-15 trainer aircraft began in 2016. However, there is currently no independent capacity for significant power projection. In recent years there has been investment in housing for military personnel. The country has no defence-manufacturing capacity, except limited ammunition production, though it is reported that exploratory discussions have taken place about establishing some manufacturing capacity for military trucks. The services have participated in international exercises, such as the US AFRICOM exercise *Southern Accord 15*, part of which was hosted by Zambia, and have also participated in large exercises with regional allies such as South Africa. Zambia's deployment to the UN's Central African Republic peacekeeping mission was delayed by eight months due to a lack of pre-deployment training, equipment and airlift capability, which was eventually provided by the US.

ACTIVE 15,100 (Army 13,500 Air 1,600) **Paramilitary 1,400**

RESERVE 3,000 (Army 3,000)

ORGANISATIONS BY SERVICE

Army 13,500
FORCES BY ROLE
COMMAND
  3 bde HQ
SPECIAL FORCES
  1 cdo bn
MANOEUVRE
  Armoured
  1 armd regt (1 tk bn, 1 armd recce regt)
  Light
  6 inf bn
COMBAT SUPPORT
  1 arty regt (2 fd arty bn, 1 MRL bn)
  1 engr regt
EQUIPMENT BY TYPE
Some equipment†
ARMOURED FIGHTING VEHICLES
  MBT 30: 20 Type-59; 10 T-55
  LT TK 30 PT-76
  RECCE 70 BRDM-1/BRDM-2 (ε30 serviceable)
  IFV 23 *Ratel*-20
  APC • APC (W) 33: 13 BTR-60; 20 BTR-70
ENGINEERING & MAINTENANCE VEHICLES
  ARV T-54/T-55 reported
ANTI-TANK/ANTI-INFRASTRUCTURE
  MSL • MANPATS 9K11 *Malyutka* (AT-3 *Sagger*)

RCL 12+: **57mm** 12 M18; **75mm** M20; **84mm** *Carl Gustav*
ARTILLERY 182
TOWED 61: **105mm** 18 Model 56 pack howitzer; **122mm** 25 D-30; **130mm** 18 M-46
MRL **122mm** 30 BM-21 *Grad* (ε12 serviceable)
MOR 91: **81mm** 55; **82mm** 24; **120mm** 12
AIR DEFENCE
SAM • **MANPAD** 9K32 *Strela-2* (SA-7 *Grail*)‡
GUNS • **TOWED** 136: **20mm** 50 M-55 (triple); **37mm** 40 M-1939; **57mm** ε30 S-60; **85mm** 16 M-1939 *KS-12*

Reserve 3,000
FORCES BY ROLE
MANOEUVRE
Light
3 inf bn

Air Force 1,600
FORCES BY ROLE
FIGHTER/GROUND ATTACK
1 sqn with K-8 *Karakorum**
1 sqn forming with L-15
TRANSPORT
1 sqn with MA60; Y-12(II); Y-12(IV); Y-12E
1 (VIP) unit with AW139; CL-604; HS-748
1 (liaison) sqn with Do-28
TRAINING
2 sqn with MB-326GB; MFI-15 *Safari*
TRANSPORT HELICOPTER
1 sqn with Mi-17 *Hip* H
1 (liaison) sqn with Bell 47G; Bell 205 (UH-1H *Iroquois*/AB-205)
AIR DEFENCE
3 bty with S-125 *Pechora* (SA-3 *Goa*)
EQUIPMENT BY TYPE†
Very low serviceability
AIRCRAFT 18 combat capable
TPT 23: **Light** 21: 5 Do-28; 2 MA60; 4 Y-12(II); 5 Y-12(IV); 5 Y-12E; **PAX** 2: 1 CL-604; 1 HS-748
TRG 42: 15 K-8 *Karakourm**; 3 L-15*; 10 MB-326GB; 8 MFI-15 *Safari*; 6 SF-260TW
HELICOPTERS
MRH 5: 1 AW139; 4 Mi-17 *Hip* H
TPT • **Light** 12: 9 Bell 205 (UH-1H *Iroquois*/AB-205); 3 Bell 212
TRG 5 Bell 47G
AIR DEFENCE
SAM • **Short-range** S-125 *Pechora* (SA-3 *Goa*)
AIR-LAUNCHED MISSILES
AAM • **IR** R-3 (AA-2 *Atoll*)‡; PL-2; *Python* 3
ASM 9K11 *Malyutka* (AT-3 *Sagger*)

Paramilitary 1,400

Police Mobile Unit 700
FORCES BY ROLE
MANOEUVRE
Other
1 police bn (4 police coy)

Police Paramilitary Unit 700
FORCES BY ROLE
MANOEUVRE
Other
1 paramilitary bn (3 paramilitary coy)

DEPLOYMENT

CENTRAL AFRICAN REPUBLIC
UN • MINUSCA 765; 9 obs; 1 inf bn

CÔTE D'IVOIRE
UN • UNOCI 1 obs

DEMOCRATIC REPUBLIC OF THE CONGO
UN • MONUSCO 2; 17 obs

LIBERIA
UN • UNMIL 1 obs

SOUTH SUDAN
UN • UNMISS 2; 1 obs

SUDAN
UN • UNAMID 7; 2 obs
UN • UNISFA 2 obs

Zimbabwe ZWE

Zimbabwe Dollar Z$ [a]		2015	2016	2017
GDP	US$	14.2bn	14.2bn	
per capita	US$	1,002	979	
Growth	%	1.1	-0.3	
Inflation	%	-2.4	-1.6	
Def bdgt	US$	377m	358m	359m

[a] Zimbabwe dollar no longer in active use

Population 14,546,961

Age	0–14	15–19	20–24	25–29	30–64	65 plus
Male	19.1%	5.5%	5.2%	5.0%	14.0%	1.3%
Female	18.7%	5.4%	5.2%	5.1%	13.3%	2.2%

Capabilities

The armed forces' role is to defend sovereignty and territorial integrity. However, Zimbabwe's limited quantitative and qualitative military capabilities have eroded further due to economic problems. China has been the only source of defence equipment for the country's limited number of procurements. Zimbabwe has enjoyed a close relationship with Angola since the end of that country's civil war and is looking to foster bilateral military ties. Zimbabwe has also deployed personnel to Namibia as part of a training team. Zimbabwe's economic problems make investment in new equipment and facilities unlikely without novel financing options or credit provision, despite a stated interest in a number of equipment types. State-owned Zimbabwe Defence Industries manufactures a range of ammunition, however ageing machinery and non-profitability mean its future is uncertain. The armed forces have taken part intermittently in multinational training exercises with regional states, including *Blue Okavango* and *Amani Africa II* in 2015. Both the EU and the US have arms embargoes in place, which, the air-force commander acknowledged, have reduced air-force readiness.

ACTIVE 29,000 (Army 25,000 Air 4,000) **Paramilitary 21,800**

ORGANISATIONS BY SERVICE

Army ε25,000
FORCES BY ROLE
COMMAND
  1 SF bde HQ
  1 mech bde HQ
  5 inf bde HQ
SPECIAL FORCES
  1 SF regt
MANOEUVRE
  Armoured
    1 armd sqn
  Mechanised
    1 mech inf bn
  Light
    15 inf bn
    1 cdo bn
  Air Manoeuvre
    1 para bn
  Other
    3 gd bn
    1 (Presidential Guard) gd gp
COMBAT SUPPORT
  1 arty bde
  1 fd arty regt
  2 engr regt
AIR DEFENCE
  1 AD regt
EQUIPMENT BY TYPE
ARMOURED FIGHTING VEHICLES
  MBT 40: 30 Type-59†; 10 Type-69†
  RECCE 115: 20 *Eland*-60/90; 15 FV701 *Ferret*†; 80 EE-9 *Cascavel* (90mm)
  APC • APC (T) 30: 8 Type-63; 22 VTT-323
ENGINEERING & MAINTENANCE VEHICLES
  ARV T-54/T-55 reported
  VLB MTU reported
ARTILLERY 254
  SP 122mm 12 2S1 *Gvozdika*
  TOWED 122mm 20: 4 D-30; 16 Type-60 (D-74)
  MRL 76: 107mm 16 Type-63; **122mm** 60 RM-70
  MOR 146: **81mm/82mm** ε140; **120mm** 6 M-43
AIR DEFENCE
  SAM • Point-defence 9K32 *Strela*-2 (SA-7 *Grail*)‡
  GUNS • TOWED 116: **14.5mm** 36 ZPU-1/ZPU-2/ZPU-4; **23mm** 45 ZU-23; **37mm** 35 M-1939

Air Force 4,000

Flying hours 100 hrs/yr

FORCES BY ROLE
FIGHTER
  1 sqn with F-7 II†; FT-7†
FIGHTER/GROUND ATTACK
  1 sqn with K-8 *Karakorum**
  (1 sqn Hawker *Hunter* in store)
GROUND ATTACK/ISR
  1 sqn with Cessna 337/O-2A *Skymaster**
ISR/TRAINING
  1 sqn with SF-260F/M; SF-260TP*; SF-260W *Warrior**
TRANSPORT
  1 sqn with BN-2 *Islander*; CASA 212-200 *Aviocar* (VIP)
ATTACK/TRANSPORT HELICOPTER
  1 sqn with Mi-35 *Hind*; Mi-35P *Hind* (liaison); SA316 *Alouette* III; AS532UL *Cougar* (VIP)
  1 trg sqn with Bell 412 *Twin Huey*, SA316 *Alouette* III
AIR DEFENCE
  1 sqn
EQUIPMENT BY TYPE
AIRCRAFT 46 combat capable
  FTR 9: 7 F-7 II†; 2 FT-7†
  FGA (12 Hawker *Hunter* in store)
  ISR 2 O-2A *Skymaster*
  TPT • Light 25: 5 BN-2 *Islander*; 7 C-212-200 *Aviocar*; 13 Cessna 337 *Skymaster**; (10 C-47 *Skytrain* in store)
  TRG 33: 10 K-8 *Karakorum**; 5 SF-260M; 8 SF-260TP*; 5 SF-260W *Warrior**; 5 SF-260F
HELICOPTERS
  ATK 6: 4 Mi-35 *Hind*; 2 Mi-35P *Hind*
  MRH 10: 8 Bell 412 *Twin Huey*; 2 SA316 *Alouette* III
  TPT • Medium 2 AS532UL *Cougar* (VIP)
AIR-LAUNCHED MISSILES • AAM • IR PL-2; PL-5 (reported)
AD • GUNS 100mm (not deployed); **37mm** (not deployed); **57mm** (not deployed)

Paramilitary 21,800

Zimbabwe Republic Police Force 19,500
incl air wg

Police Support Unit 2,300
PATROL AND COASTAL COMBATANTS
All operational patrol vessels under 10t FLD

DEPLOYMENT

CÔTE D'IVOIRE
UN • UNOCI 1 obs

LIBERIA
UN • UNMIL 1 obs

SOUTH SUDAN
UN • UNMISS 2 obs

SUDAN
UN • UNAMID 2; 4 obs
UN • UNISFA 1; 2 obs

Table 16 **Selected arms procurements and deliveries, Sub-Saharan Africa**

Designation	Type	Quantity	Contract Value (Current)	Prime Nationality	Prime Contractor	Order Date	First Delivery Due	Notes
Angola (ANG)								
Casspir NG	PPV	45	n.k.	RSA	Denel	2013	2014	Delivery status unclear
Su-30K	FGA ac	12	n.k.	RUS	Government surplus	2013	2015	Ex-Indian Air Force aircraft. In test; delivery status unclear
Mi-24 *Hind*	Atk hel	12	n.k.	RUS	Russian Helicopters (Rostvertol)	2015	n.k.	–
Cameroon (CMR)								
Mi-24 *Hind*	Atk hel	2	n.k.	RUS	Government surplus	n.k.	2016	–
Chad (CHA)								
MiG-29 *Fulcrum*	FGA ac	3	n.k.	UKR	Ukroboronprom	n.k.	2013	First aircraft delivered 2014; delivery status of remainder unclear
Equatorial Guinea (EQG)								
C-295M	Med tpt ac	1	n.k.	Int'l	Airbus Group (Airbus Defence & Space)	2016	2017	–
C-295MPA	MP ac	1	n.k.	Int'l	Airbus Group (Airbus Defence & Space)	2016	2017	–
Ghana (GHA)								
A-29 *Super Tucano*	Trg ac	5	US$88m	BRZ	Embraer	2015	n.k.	–
Kenya (KEN)								
Springbuck	PPV	n.k.	n.k.	RSA	DCD	2015	2016	Size of contract unclear
Mali (MLI)								
C-295W	Med tpt ac	1	n.k.	Int'l	Airbus Group (Airbus Defence & Space)	2016	n.k.	For air force
A-29 *Super Tucano*	Trg ac	6	n.k.	BRZ	Embraer	2015	n.k.	–
Mauritius (MUS)								
Victory class (IND *Sarojini Naidu* class)	PCC	2	n.k.	IND	Goa Shipyard	2014	2016	For coastguard. First of class delivered Sep 2016
Mozambique (MOZ)								
HSI 32	PBF	6	See notes	UAE	Abu Dhabi Mar (CMN)	2013	2016	First three part of ε€200m (εUS$265.5m) order, including three 42m patrol boats. First of class launched 2015. Second batch of three ordered early 2015
Ocean Eagle 43	PB	3	See notes	UAE	Abu Dhabi Mar (CMN)	2013	2016	Part of ε€200m (εUS$265.5m) order, including three HSI 32 patrol boats. First two of class launched

Table 16 **Selected arms procurements and deliveries, Sub-Saharan Africa**

Designation	Type	Quantity	Contract Value (Current)	Prime Nationality	Prime Contractor	Order Date	First Delivery Due	Notes
Nigeria (NGA)								
Mi-35M *Hind*	Atk hel	6	n.k.	RUS	Russian Helicopters (Rostvertol/ Ulan-Ude Aviation Plant)	2014	n.k.	–
Mi-171Sh *Terminator*	Tpt hel	6	n.k.	RUS	Russian Helicopters	2014	n.k.	–
Senegal (SEN)								
A-29 *Super Tucano*	Trg ac	3	n.k.	BRZ	Embraer	2013	n.k.	Delivery status unclear
KT-1 *Woong-Bee*	Trg ac	4	n.k.	ROK	KAI	2016	2018	To be delivered within 30 months
South Africa (RSA)								
Badger (AMV 8x8)	APC (W)	238	εZAR15.4bn (εUS$1.6bn)	FIN/RSA	Patria/Denel (Denel Land Systems)	2013	2015	Nine variants to be produced. Order reduced to 242 vehicles. Programme has seen large cost increases and delays. Vehicles delivered so far are currently in test
A-*Darter*	AAM IIR	n.k.	n.k.	RSA	Denel	2015	2017	Production contract signed 2015. First production deliveries expected 2017
Seeker 400	UAV (ISR Med)	n.k.	n.k.	RSA	Denel (Denel Dynamics)	n.k.	2016	Unnamed local customer; believed to be RSA
Zambia (ZMB)								
C-27J *Spartan*	Lt tpt ac	2	n.k.	ITA	Leonardo	2015	2017	–
L-15 *Falcon*	Trg ac	6	n.k.	PRC	AVIC	2014	2016	First three aircraft delivered 2016. Remaining three to be delivered by end of 2016

Chapter Ten
Country comparisons and defence data

Table 17	**Selected training activity 2016**	550
Table 18	**International comparisons of defence expenditure and military personnel**	553
Figure 33	**Global distribution of main battle tanks, 2016**	560
Table 19	**Principal surface combatants and patrol ships over 9,500 tonnes full-load displacement**	561
Table 20	**Select unmanned maritime systems in service, by weight**	561
Table 21	**Military ISR satellites: operational totals**	562
Figure 34	**Precision-guided munitions: increasing use by Western forces, 1991–2011**	562
	Selected non-state armed groups: observed forces and equipment holdings	563

Table 17 Selected training activity 2016

Date	Title	Location	Aim	Principal Participants
North America (US and Canada)				
25 Jan–12 Feb 2016	RED FLAG 16-1	US	Air cbt ex	AUS, UK, US
18–27 Apr 2016	CYBER SHIELD	US	Cyber ex	US
02–15 May 2016	EMERALD WARRIOR 16	US	SOFEX	US, partner nations
01 Jun–30 Nov 2016	COOPERATION AFLOAT READINESS AND TRAINING (CARAT) 2016	US	COMBEX, MARSEC	BGD, BRN, CAM, IDN, MYS, PHL, SGP, THA, TLS, US
08–18 Jun 2016	CYBER GUARD 2016	US	Cyber ex	US
20–28 Jun 2016	PACIFIC DRAGON	US	BMD ex	JPN, ROK, US
30 Jun–04 Aug 2016	RIMPAC 2016	US	NAVEX	AUS, BRN, CAN, CHL, COL, DNK, FRA, GER, IDN, IND, ITA, JPN, MEX, MYS, NLD, NOR, NZL, PER, PHL, PRC, ROK, SGP, THA, UK, US
25 Jul–04 Aug 2016	PANAMAX 2016	US	CPX	ARG, BLZ, BRZ, CAN, CHL, COL CRI, DOM, FRA, GUA, HND, JAM, MEX, PAN, PER, PRY, SLV, UK, URY, US
26–28 Jul 2016	AMALGAM EAGLE 16	US	ADEX, ALEX, MACEX	MEX, US
15–29 Aug 2016	GREEN FLAG EAST	US	Air cbt ex	COL, US
12–26 Sep 2016	CUTLASS FURY	CAN	NAVEX	CAN, ESP, FRA, ESP, UK, US
Europe				
22 Feb–04 Mar 2016	DYNAMIC MANTA 2016	Ionian Sea	ASW	FRA, GER, GRC, ITA, ESP, TUR, UK, US
09–16 Mar 2016	NATO CRISIS MANAGEMENT EXERCISE	LTU	CMX	NATO members, FIN, SWE
17–28 Mar 2016	COLD RESPONSE	NOR	FTX	NATO members
31 Mar–24 Apr 2016	SABER JUNCTION	GER, ITA	Airborne ex, CPX, C2	ALB, ARM, BEL, BIH, BLG, HUN, LVA, LTU, LUX, FYROM, MDA, POL, ROM, TUR, SER, SVN, SWE, UK, US
01–10 Apr 2016	BRILLIANT JUMP ALERT 2016	ALB, ESP, POL, UK	FTX, DEPEX	ALB, ESP, POL, UK (NRF ex)
10–22 Apr 2016	GRIFFIN STRIKE 2016	UK	CJEF, FTX, LIVEX,	FRA, UK (and elm NATO ARRC)
10–23 Apr 2016	JOINT WARRIOR 2016–1	UK	ADEX, ASWEX, MCM, PHIBEX	BEL, CAN, DEN, FIN, FRA, GER, NLD, NZL, NOR, POL, ESP, SWE, TUR, US, UK
18–29 Apr 2016	STEADFAST ALLIANCE 2016	BEL	BMD ex	BEL, GER, ITA, PRT, ESP, TUR, UK
19–20 Apr 2016	RAMSTEIN ALLOY 1	EST	Air cbt ex	BEL, EST, FIN, LTU, POL, ESP, SWE, UK, US
01–20 May 2016	FLAMING SWORD	LVA, LTU	SOFEX	DNK, EST, FIN, GEO, LVA, NOR, POL, SWE, UK, UKR, US
02–20 May 2016	SPRING STORM	EST	FTX	BEL, EST, LVA, LTU, CAN, GER, NLD, US, UK
12–27 May 2016	OPEN SPIRIT 2016	GER	MCMEX, NAVEX	BEL, CAN, DNK, EST, FRA, GER, LTU, LVA, NLD, NOR, POL, SWD, UK, US
17–27 May 2016	BRILLIANT JUMP DEPLOY 2016	POL	DEPEX, FTX	ALB, ESP, POL, UK (NRF ex)
26 May–10 Jun 2016	ANATOLIAN EAGLE	TUR	ADEX	AZE, ESP, ITA, NLD, PAK, QTR, SAU, TUR
27 May–06 Jun 2016	SWIFT RESPONSE	GER, POL	FTX, Interop ex	BEL, FRA, GER, ITA, NLD, POL, PRT, ESP, UK, US
29 May–03 Jun 2016	BRILLIANT CAPABILITY	POL	DEPEX, FTX	ALB, ESP, POL, UK (NRF ex)
03–26 Jun 2016	BALTOPS 2016	Baltic Sea	Interop ex	BEL, EST, FIN, FRA, GER, ITA, LVA, LTU, NLD, NOR, POL, ESP, SWE, UK, US
06–19 Jun 2016	IRON WOLF	LTU	FTX	DNK, FRA, GER, LTU, LUX, POL, US
07–17 Jun 2016	ANACONDA	POL	Cyber ex, EWX, FTX, LIVEX, MDEX	ALB, BLG, CAN, CRO, CZE, EST, FIN, FYROM, GEO, GER, HUN, LVA, LTU, NLD, POL, ROM, SVK, SLV, ESP, SWE, TUR, UK, UKR
11–21 Jun 2016	SABER STRIKE	EST, LTU, LVA	FTX	CAN, LVA, LTU, POL, UK, US
20 Jun–01 Jul 2016	DYNAMIC MONGOOSE	North Sea	ASWEX	CAN, FRA, GER, NOR, POL, ESP, TUR, UK, US
01–12 Aug 2016	FLAMING THUNDER 2016	LTU	LIVEX	EST, LTU, POL, US
08 Aug–15 Sep 2016	COMBINED RESOLVE	GER	CPX, LIVEX, PLANEX	ARM, BIH, BEL, BLG, FRA, HUN, FYROM, MDA, MNE, NOR, POL, ROM, SER, SLV, UKR, US

Table 17 Selected training activity 2016

Date	Title	Location	Aim	Principal Participants
05–16 Sept 2016	NORTHERN COASTS	Baltic Sea	HADR ex, NAVEX	BEL, CAN, DNK, EST, FRA, GER, LTU, LVA, NOR, POL, POR, SWE, UK
09–27 Sep 2016	IMMEDIATE RESPONSE	CRO	CPX	ALB, BIH, CRO, HUN, Kosovo, FYROM, MNE, SLV, UK, US
17 Sep–01 Oct 2016	TOBRUK LEGACY	SVK	MDEX	CZE, HUN, LTU, LVA, POL, SLV, SVK, US
27–28 Sep 2016	RAMSTEIN ALLOY 3	LTU	AIREX	EST, FIN, FRA, GER, LVA, LTU, POL, SWE
06–14 Oct 2016	SLOVAK SHIELD	SVK	FTX	CZE, GER, HUN, POL, SVK, US (Visegrad States)
08–12 Oct 2016	NOBLE ARROW 2016	UK	Air cbt ex	PRT, UK, US (NRF ex)
08–20 Oct 2016	JOINT WARRIOR 2016–2	UK	ASWEX, EWX, LIVEX, NAVEX	NATO SNMG1, SNMCCG1
24 Oct–03 Nov 2016	TRIDENT JUNCTURE 2016	Various	FTX	CPX, LIVEX (NRF ex)
05–12 Nov 2016	SLAVIC BROTHERHOOD	SER	CTEX, FTX	BLR, RUS, SER

Russia and Eurasia

Date	Title	Location	Aim	Principal Participants
11–22 Apr 2016	STEPPE EAGLE 2016	KAZ	FTX, Interop ex	KAZ, KGZ, TJK, UK, US
18–24 Apr 2016	CSTO JOINT EXERCISE	TJK	CTEX, RECONEX	ARM, BLR, KAZ, KGZ, RUS, TJK (CSTO members)
02–19 May 2016	DRAGON PIONEER	MLD	FTX, Interop ex	MLD, US
11–24 May 2016	NOBLE PARTNER	GEO	FTX, Interop ex	GEO, UK, US
08 Jun 2016	Snap exercise	RUS	DEPEX, Interop ex	RUS (Central, Southern MD)
27 Jun–08 Jul 2016	RAPID TRIDENT 16	UKR	CPX, FTX, Interop ex	BEL, BLG, CAN, GEO, LTU, MDA, NOR, POL, ROM, SWE, TUR, UK, UKR, US
28 Jun–14 Jul 2016	COOPERATION 2016	RUS	CTEX Interop ex	PRC, RUS
23–27 Aug 2016	UNBREAKABLE BROTHERHOOD	BLR	PKO ex	ARM, BLR, KAZ, KGZ, RUS, TJK (CSTO members)
25–31 Aug 2016	Snap exercise	RUS	DEPEX, Interop ex	RUS (Southern, Western, Central MD, Northern Fleet, Aerospace Forces, AB Forces)
15–19 Sep 2016	NAVAL INTERACTION 2016	RUS	NAVEX	PRC, RUS
15–20 Sep 2016	PEACE MISSION 2016	KGZ	CTEX, C2, FIREX, FTX	KAZ, KGZ, PRC, RUS, TJK
18–20 Oct 2016	Russia–Belarus Joint Tactical exercise	BLR	Airborne ex, JOINTEX	BLR, RUS

Asia

Date	Title	Location	Aim	Principal Participants
10 Jan–9 Feb 2016	COBRA GOLD 2016	THA	CPX, FTX, HADR, Interop ex	IDN, IND, JAP, PRC, ROK, MYS, SGP, THA, US
10–26 Feb 2016	COPE NORTH 2016	US (Guam)	Air cbt ex	AUS, JPN, NZL, PHL, ROK, US
19–29 Feb 2016	IBSAMAR V	IND	Interop ex, MARSEC, NAVEX	BRZ, IND, RSA
07–18 Mar 2016	KEY RESOLVE	ROK	CPX	ROK, US
07–18 Mar 2016	COPE TIGER (PHASE II)	SGP	FTX	SGP, THA, US
07 Mar–30 Apr 2016	FOAL EAGLE 2016	ROK	MCMEX	ROK, US
04–16 Apr 2016	BALIKATAN 2016	PHL	HADR ex, Interop ex, MARSEC	AUS, PHL, US
09–30 Apr 2016	SHAHEEN 5	PAK	FTX	PAK, PRC
17–29 Apr 2016	BERSAMA SHIELD	MYS	ASW, Interop ex, MARSEC, NAVEX	AUS, MYS, NZL, SGP, UK
22 May–04 Jun 2016	KHAAN QUEST 2016	MNG	CPX, FTX, IEDEX, PSO ex	AUS, BGD, BRN, CAM, CAN, FRA, GER, HUN, IDN, IND, ITA, JPN, MAL, MON, NPL, PHL, PRC, ROK, SGP, TJK, THA, TUR, UK, US, VNM
Jun–Sep 2016	STRIDE 2016	PRC	FTX	PRC trans-military-region exercise series
Jul–Sep 2016	FIREPOWER–2016 QINGTONGXIA	PRC	ARTEX, FTX	PRC trans-military-region exercise series
Jul–Sep 2016	FIREPOWER–2016 SHADAN	PRC	ADEX, Air cbt ex, EWX, RECONEX	PRC trans-military-region exercise series

Table 17 Selected training activity 2016

Date	Title	Location	Aim	Principal Participants
29 Jul–03 Aug 2016	PITCH BLACK 2016	AUS	Air cbt ex	AUS, CAN, FRA, IDN, NLD, NZL, SGP, THA, US
24 Sep–10 Oct 2016	FRIENDSHIP 2016	PAK	FTX	PAK, RUS
29 Oct–4 Nov 2016	BLUE CHROMITE	JPN	PHIBEX	JPN, US

Middle East and North Africa

Date	Title	Location	Aim	Principal Participants
25 Jan–18 Apr 2016	SHAMAL STORM	JOR	COIN, CTEX, FTX	JOR, UK
03 Feb 2016	ARABIAN GULF SHIELD	QTR	Air cbt ex, Interop ex	FRA, US, GCC states (GCC liaison ex)
14 Feb–10 Mar 2016	RAAD AL-SHAMAL/NORTH THUNDER	SAU	FTX	CHA, COM, DJB, EGY, KWT, MLD, MRT, MUS, MOR, SEN, TUN, MYS, OMN, PAK, SDN
21–28 Feb 2016	JUNIPER COBRA 16	ISR	BMDEX	ISR, US
07–16 Mar 2016	UNION 18	BHR	CTX, MARSEX, NAVEX	BHR, KWT, QAT, SAU, UAE (GCC states)
04–26 Apr 2016	IMCMEX 16	BHR	MCMEX	BHR, OMN, UK, US
17–27 Apr 2016	AFRICAN LION 2016	MOR	CPX, Interop	CAN, ESP, ITA, MRT, MOR, TUN, UK, US
15–24 May 2016	EAGER LION	JOR	COIN, FTX	JOR, US
29 Sep 2016	SUN MOUNTAIN	OMN	CJEX	ITA, OMN
15–26 Oct 2016	DEFENDERS OF FRIENDSHIP 2016	EGY	CTEX, FTX	EGY, RUS

Latin America and the Caribbean

Date	Title	Location	Aim	Principal Participants
02–10 May 2016	FUERZAS COMANDO 2016	PER	SOFEX	ARG, BLZ, CHL, COL, CRI, DOM, GUA, HTI, HND, JAM, MEX, PAN, PRY, PER, SUR, URY, US
19–28 Jun 2016	TRADEWINDS 2016	JAM	FTX	ATG, BHS, BRB, BLZ, CAN, DOM, GUY, JAM, MEX, TTO, UK, US
16–28 Jul 2016	AUSTRAL STAR	CHL	JOINTEX, PKO ex	CHL, US
26–28 Jul 2016	AMALGAM EAGLE 2016	MEX	ADEX, ALEX, MACEX	MEX, US
18–28 Sep 2016	UNITAS 16 PACIFIC	PAN	ADEX, ASWEX, EW, NAVEX, SURFEX	CHL, COL, CRI, DOM, GUA, HND, MEX, PAN, PER, SLV, UK, US
04 Oct 2016	SOLIDARIDAD 2016	ARG	COMBEX, DISTEX, JOINTEX	ARG, CHL
04–07 Oct 2016	GUARANI 2016	ARG	FTX, JOINTEX	ARG, BRZ
07–09 Nov 2016	UNASUR VI	CHL	DISTEX, HADR	ARG, BRZ, CHL, COL, GUY, ECU, PER, PRY, URY

Sub-Saharan Africa

Date	Title	Location	Aim	Principal Participants
30 Jan–7 Feb 2016	CUTLASS EXPRESS 2016	SYC	MARSEC, NAVEX	AUS, CAN, DJB, FRA, KEN, MDG, MUS, RWA, SYC, SOM, RSA, SDN, TZA, UGA, UK, US
08–29 Feb 2016	FLINTLOCK 16	SEN	COIN, CTX	ALG, BFA, CAN, CHA, GER, FRA, MLI, MRT, MOR, NER, NLD, SEN, RSA, ESP, TUN, UK, US
17–27 Mar 2016	OBANGAME/SAHARAN EXPRESS 2016	CMR	MARSEC, NAVEX, CPX, CTX	ANG, BEN, BEL, BRZ, COV, CMR, CIV, DNK, DRC, EQG, FRA, GAB, GER, GHA, MOR, NLD, NGA, PRT, COG, SEN, RSA, ESP, TGO, TUR, UK, US
26 Apr–05 May 2016	EPIC GUARDIAN 2016	GHA	FTX, Interop	CPV, GHA, US
10–24 Jun 2015	CENTRAL ACCORD 2016	GAB	CPX, FTX	GAB, US
11–25 Jul 2016	EASTERN ACCORD 2016	TZA	CPX, CTEX, Interop	DJB, ETH, GER, NLD, RWA, TZA, UGA, UK, US
01–12 Aug 2016	SOUTHERN ACCORD 2016	MWI	DISTEX, PKO	MWI, US
13–16 Sep 2016	NEMO 16.5	NGA	MAREX	BEN, CMR, FRA, GAB, GHA, TGO
11–18 Nov 2016	USHIRIKIANO IMARA	KEN	FTX	BDI, KEN, RWA, TZA, UGA (EAC CPX)

Table 18 **International comparisons of defence expenditure and military personnel**

	Defence Spending current US$ m 2014	2015	2016	Defence Spending per capita (current US$) 2014	2015	2016	Defence Spending % of GDP 2014	2015	2016	Active Armed Forces (000) 2017	Estimated Reservists (000) 2017	Active Paramilitary (000) 2017
North America												
Canada	15,751	13,817	13,162	452	394	372	0.88	0.89	0.86	63	30	5
United States	603,457	589,564	604,452	1,892	1,834	1,866	3.47	3.27	3.26	1,347	865	0
Total	**619,208**	**603,381**	**617,614**	**1,750**	**1,692**	**1,719**	**3.23**	**3.08**	**3.07**	**1,410**	**895**	**5**
Europe												
Albania	135	101	115	46	34	39	1.04	0.90	0.96	8	0	1
Austria	2,683	2,046	2,313	311	236	266	0.61	0.55	0.60	21	146	0
Belgium	4,962	4,010	3,895	442	354	341	0.93	0.88	0.83	30	0	7
Bosnia-Herzegovina	220	190	191	58	50	50	1.21	1.21	1.18	11	0	0
Bulgaria	709	560	678	99	79	96	1.26	1.16	1.35	31	3	16
Croatia	745	642	588	172	149	137	1.31	1.32	1.19	16	0	3
Cyprus	424	305	356	361	256	295	1.83	1.58	1.79	12	50	1
Czech Republic	2,023	1,780	1,971	191	167	185	0.97	0.96	1.02	22	0	3
Denmark	4,458	3,516	3,547	801	630	634	1.29	1.19	1.17	17	46	0
Estonia	510	467	503	403	370	401	1.93	2.06	2.15	6	28	0
Finland	3,654	3,074	3,283	670	561	597	1.34	1.32	1.37	22	230	3
France	52,075	46,626	47,201	786	701	706	1.83	1.93	1.90	203	28	103
Germany	43,101	36,589	38,281	532	453	474	1.11	1.09	1.10	177	28	1
Greece	5,688	4,733	4,639	528	439	431	2.41	2.42	2.37	143	221	4
Hungary	1,008	1,070	996	102	108	101	0.73	0.89	0.85	27	44	12
Iceland	30	30	31	91	91	92	0.17	0.18	0.16	0	0	0
Ireland	1,192	997	1,003	247	204	202	0.47	0.35	0.33	9	3	0
Italy	24,487	21,495	22,309	397	348	360	1.14	1.18	1.20	175	18	182
Latvia	294	283	411	147	143	210	0.95	1.05	1.48	5	8	0
Lithuania	428	471	642	148	164	226	0.89	1.15	1.51	17	7	11
Luxembourg	251	214	220	449	375	378	0.39	0.37	0.36	1	0	1
Macedonia (FYROM)	127	102	107	62	50	53	1.15	1.05	1.05	8	5	8
Malta	60	56	58	145	135	141	0.56	0.57	0.56	2	0	0
Montenegro	79	68	70	122	106	108	1.72	1.71	1.64	2	0	10

Country comparisons

Table 18 International comparisons of defence expenditure and military personnel

	Defence Spending current US$ m 2014	2015	2016	Defence Spending per capita (current US$) 2014	2015	2016	Defence Spending % of GDP 2014	2015	2016	Active Armed Forces (000) 2017	Estimated Reservists (000) 2017	Active Paramilitary (000) 2017
Netherlands	10,665	8,877	9,193	632	524	540	1.21	1.18	1.19	35	5	6
Norway	6,776	5,815	5,968	1,316	1,117	1,134	1.35	1.50	1.59	25	46	0
Poland	10,154	10,128	9,073	263	263	236	1.87	2.14	1.94	99	0	73
Portugal	2,583	2,170	2,181	239	200	201	1.12	1.09	1.06	30	212	44
Romania	2,783	2,481	2,777	128	115	129	1.40	1.40	1.49	71	50	80
Serbia	695	515	507	97	72	71	1.58	1.42	1.35	28	50	0
Slovakia	1,042	884	983	192	162	181	1.04	1.02	1.09	16	0	0
Slovenia	533	444	450	268	224	227	1.08	1.04	1.02	7	2	6
Spain	12,634	13,050	12,222	265	271	252	0.91	1.09	0.98	123	8	77
Sweden	6,297	5,723	5,828	648	584	590	1.10	1.16	1.13	30	0	1
Switzerland	5,166	4,770	4,720	641	587	577	0.74	0.72	0.71	21	144	0
Turkey	9,967	8,384	8,764	127	106	109	1.25	1.17	1.19	355	379	157
United Kingdom	61,564	58,382	52,498	966	911	815	2.05	2.04	1.98	152	81	0
Total	**280,201**	**251,047**	**248,572**	**451**	**403**	**397**	**1.35**	**1.38**	**1.35**	**1,956**	**1,839**	**809**
Russia and Eurasia												
Armenia	467	416	428	153	137	141	4.04	3.97	4.00	45	210	4
Azerbaijan	2,089	1,750	1,438	216	179	146	2.78	3.24	4.03	67	300	15
Belarus	838	558	509	87	58	53	1.10	1.02	1.06	48	290	110
Georgia	378	300	287	79	67	62	2.36	2.36	2.12	21	0	5
Kazakhstan	2,024	1,693	1,101	113	93	60	0.89	0.92	0.86	39	0	32
Kyrgyzstan	91	n.k.	n.k.	16	n.k.	n.k.	1.24	n.k.	n.k.	11	0	10
Moldova	27	24	29	8	10	12	0.35	0.55	0.63	5	58	2
Russia [a]	64,480	51,919	46,626	453	365	328	3.17	3.92	3.68	831	2,000	659
Tajikistan	192	n.k.	n.k.	24	n.k.	n.k.	2.11	n.k.	n.k.	9	0	8
Turkmenistan	n.k.	n.k.	n.k.	n.k.	n.k.	n.k.	n.k.	n.k.	n.k.	37	0	0
Ukraine	3,380	2,286	2,165	75	53	50	2.56	2.58	2.53	204	900	52
Uzbekistan	n.k.	n.k.	n.k.	n.k.	n.k.	n.k.	n.k.	n.k.	n.k.	48	0	20
Total**	**73,965**	**58,945**	**52,581**	**261**	**208**	**185**	**2.82**	**3.30**	**3.29**	**1,364**	**3,758**	**917**

Table 18 International comparisons of defence expenditure and military personnel

	Defence Spending current US$ m 2014	2015	2016	Defence Spending per capita (current US$) 2014	2015	2016	Defence Spending % of GDP 2014	2015	2016	Active Armed Forces (000) 2017	Estimated Reservists (000) 2017	Active Paramilitary (000) 2017
Asia												
Afghanistan	3,294	3,143	2,581	104	97	77	16.19	15.96	14.03	171	0	148
Australia	23,910	22,608	24,188	1,062	994	1,052	1.66	1.85	1.92	58	21	0
Bangladesh	1,953	2,634	2,705	13	17	17	1.06	1.28	1.19	157	0	64
Brunei	568	391	402	1,343	910	920	3.31	3.02	3.84	7	1	2
Cambodia*	446	565	628	29	36	39	2.66	3.18	3.24	124	0	67
China	131,140	142,415	145,039	96	104	105	1.24	1.27	1.27	2,183	510	660
Fiji	54	52	49	60	57	54	1.19	1.17	1.08	4	6	0
India	46,484	44,828	51,052	38	36	40	2.28	2.16	2.27	1,395	1,155	1,404
Indonesia	7,259	7,882	8,171	29	31	32	0.82	0.92	0.87	396	400	280
Japan	46,107	41,143	47,342	363	324	374	1.00	1.00	1.00	247	56	13
Korea, DPR of	n.k.	n.k.	n.k.	n.k.	n.k.	n.k.	n.k.	n.k.	n.k.	1,190	600	189
Korea, Republic of	33,910	33,152	33,778	674	655	663	2.40	2.41	2.41	630	4,500	5
Laos	24	n.k.	n.k.	4	n.k.	n.k.	0.21	n.k.	n.k.	29	0	100
Malaysia	4,919	4,548	4,218	164	149	136	1.46	1.54	1.39	109	52	25
Mongolia	104	102	117	36	35	39	0.87	0.89	1.06	10	137	8
Myanmar	2,371	2,274	2,264	43	40	40	3.61	3.62	3.32	406	0	107
Nepal	329	336	338	12	12	12	1.66	1.60	1.62	97	0	62
New Zealand	2,858	2,182	2,580	649	492	577	1.44	1.27	1.44	9	2	0
Pakistan	6,135	7,150	7,471	32	37	38	2.61	2.74	2.73	654	0	282
Papua New Guinea	98	94	83	15	14	12	0.45	0.44	0.42	2	0	0
Philippines	1,975	2,196	2,538	20	22	25	0.71	0.77	0.83	125	131	41
Singapore	9,799	9,544	10,249	1,760	1,682	1,773	3.20	3.26	3.46	73	313	75
Sri Lanka	1,930	2,011	1,958	88	91	88	2.58	2.48	2.38	203	6	62
Taiwan	10,020	10,007	9,825	429	427	419	1.89	1.91	1.89	215	1,657	17
Thailand	5,634	5,634	5,717	83	83	84	1.39	1.43	1.46	361	200	94
Timor-Leste	69	72	26	58	59	21	1.67	2.53	1.05	1	0	0
Vietnam*	4,296	3,829	4,010	46	41	42	2.32	2.01	2.01	482	5,000	40
Total**	345,688	348,792	367,327	88	88	92	1.45	1.47	1.47	9,337	14,746	3,743

Table 18 International comparisons of defence expenditure and military personnel

	Defence Spending current US$ m 2014	2015	2016	Defence Spending per capita (current US$) 2014	2015	2016	Defence Spending % of GDP 2014	2015	2016	Active Armed Forces (000) 2017	Estimated Reservists (000) 2017	Active Paramilitary (000) 2017
Middle East and North Africa												
Algeria	11,863	10,407	10,577	306	263	263	5.56	6.24	6.28	130	150	187
Bahrain	1,335	1,525	1,523	1,023	1,138	1,110	4.03	4.93	4.81	8	0	11
Egypt	5,451	5,335	5,330	75	72	70	2.24	2.01	1.93	439	479	397
Iran*	15,801	14,174	15,882	195	173	192	3.81	3.63	3.85	523	350	40
Iraq*	18,868	21,100	17,900	524	573	476	8.48	12.87	11.61	64	0	145
Israel	20,152	15,400	15,878	2,935	2,298	2,322	7.53	6.18	6.09	177	465	8
Jordan	1,268	1,320	1,448	198	210	214	4.37	4.54	4.43	101	65	15
Kuwait	4,803	4,313	n.k.	1,751	1,547	n.k.	2.95	3.78	n.k.	16	24	7
Lebanon	1,270	1,495	1,740	229	255	292	2.69	3.11	3.51	60	0	20
Libya	n.k.	n.k.	n.k.	745	n.k.	n.k.	10.47	n.k.	n.k.	n.k.	n.k.	n.k.
Mauritania	153	137	139	44	38	38	2.77	2.81	2.95	16	0	5
Morocco	3,752	3,268	3,365	114	98	100	3.42	3.25	3.21	196	150	50
Oman*	9,623	9,883	9,103	2,991	3,008	2,714	11.77	15.42	15.26	43	0	4
Palestinian Territories	n.k.	n.k.	n.k.	n.k.	n.k.	n.k.	n.k.	n.k.	n.k.	0	0	n.k.
Qatar*	5,088	4,749	4,404	2,397	2,164	1,950	2.42	2.85	2.81	12	0	0
Saudi Arabia	80,762	81,853	56,898	2,953	2,949	2,021	10.71	12.67	8.92	227	0	25
Syria	n.k.	n.k.	n.k.	n.k.	n.k.	n.k.	n.k.	n.k.	n.k.	128	0	150
Tunisia	906	979	979	85	91	93	1.95	2.30	2.46	36	0	12
United Arab Emirates*	n.k.	n.k.	n.k.	2,564	n.k.	n.k.	3.59	n.k.	n.k.	63	0	0
Yemen	n.k.	n.k.	n.k.	n.k.	n.k.	n.k.	n.k.	n.k.	n.k.	20	0	0
Total**	181,096	176,088	145,415	503	437	356	6.01	7.05	5.95	2,256	1,683	1,076
Latin America and the Caribbean												
Antigua and Barbuda	27	26	26	301	287	279	2.25	2.10	2.00	0	0	0
Argentina	4,321	6,338	5,181	100	146	118	0.77	1.01	0.96	74	0	31
Bahamas	87	152	121	271	468	369	1.01	1.72	1.33	1	0	0
Barbados	35	33	36	121	115	124	0.80	0.76	0.81	1	0	0
Belize	17	19	21	54	58	62	1.07	1.16	1.24	2	1	0
Bolivia	405	435	443	38	40	40	1.22	1.31	1.24	34	0	37

Table 18 **International comparisons of defence expenditure and military personnel**

	Defence Spending current US$ m 2014	2015	2016	Defence Spending per capita (current US$) 2014	2015	2016	Defence Spending % of GDP 2014	2015	2016	Active Armed Forces (000) 2017	Estimated Reservists (000) 2017	Active Paramilitary (000) 2017
Brazil	30,978	23,659	23,545	153	116	114	1.28	1.33	1.33	335	1,340	395
Chile	3,783	3,437	3,318	218	196	188	1.46	1.43	1.41	65	40	45
Colombia	13,513	9,962	8,953	283	220	194	3.46	3.52	3.35	293	35	188
Costa Rica	421	445	413	89	93	85	0.85	0.84	0.72	0	0	10
Cuba	n.k.	n.k.	n.k.	n.k.	n.k.	n.k.	n.k.	n.k.	n.k.	49	39	27
Dominican Republic	399	444	455	39	42	43	0.62	0.66	0.64	56	0	15
Ecuador	1,898	1,911	1,565	121	120	97	1.88	1.89	1.58	40	118	1
El Salvador	149	148	146	25	24	24	0.60	0.58	0.56	25	10	17
Guatemala	269	274	268	18	18	18	0.46	0.43	0.39	18	64	25
Guyana	38	44	46	52	59	63	1.25	1.38	1.34	3	1	0
Haiti	n/a	n/a	7	0	0	1	n.k.	n.k.	0.10	0	0	0
Honduras	216	246	295	26	28	34	1.13	1.22	1.43	11	60	8
Jamaica	122	119	115	42	40	39	0.88	0.83	0.83	3	1	0
Mexico	6,522	6,015	5,060	54	49	41	0.50	0.53	0.48	277	82	59
Nicaragua	83	72	73	14	12	12	0.71	0.56	0.54	12	0	0
Panama	717	654	751	199	179	203	1.46	1.26	1.36	0	0	22
Paraguay	314	313	267	47	46	39	1.02	1.13	0.98	11	165	15
Peru	2,250	2,217	2,086	85	73	68	1.26	1.15	1.16	81	188	77
Suriname*	n.k.	n.k.	n.k.	91	0	0	1.00	n.k.	n.k.	2	0	0
Trinidad and Tobago	438	394	608	358	323	498	1.61	1.60	2.67	4	0	0
Uruguay	419	510	494	126	153	148	0.73	0.96	0.91	25	0	1
Venezuela	5,131	2,244	1,444	170	74	47	2.38	0.86	0.43	115	8	150
Total**	**72,854**	**60,112**	**55,736**	**119**	**98**	**90**	**1.23**	**1.19**	**1.12**	**1,536**	**2,151**	**1,121**
Sub-Saharan Africa												
Angola	6,846	4,441	2,778	359	226	138	5.40	4.31	3.02	107	0	10
Benin	93	91	99	10	9	9	1.02	1.07	1.11	7	0	3
Botswana	423	404	486	196	185	220	2.67	2.81	4.44	9	0	0
Burkina Faso	159	148	152	9	8	8	1.27	1.34	1.26	11	0	0
Burundi	62	64	61	6	6	6	2.12	2.22	2.24	20	0	21

Table 18 International comparisons of defence expenditure and military personnel

	Defence Spending current US$ m 2014	2015	2016	Defence Spending per capita (current US$) 2014	2015	2016	Defence Spending % of GDP 2014	2015	2016	Active Armed Forces (000) 2017	Estimated Reservists (000) 2017	Active Paramilitary (000) 2017
Cameroon	402	354	393	17	15	16	1.25	1.24	1.27	14	0	9
Cape Verde	12	10	11	22	18	19	0.63	0.62	0.63	1	0	0
Central African Rep*	40	27	n.k.	10	5	n.k.	3.03	1.69	n.k.	7	0	1
Chad*	273	170	269	24	15	23	1.95	1.56	2.58	30	0	10
Congo	706	590	565	151	124	116	5.21	6.67	6.40	10	0	2
Côte d'Ivoire	810	844	759	35	36	32	2.38	2.69	2.19	25	0	n.k.
Dem Republic of the Congo	461	738	875	6	9	11	1.28	1.92	2.20	134	0	0
Djibouti	n.k.	n.k.	n.k.	n.k.	n.k.	n.k.	n.k.	n.k.	n.k.	10	0	3
Equatorial Guinea	n.k.	n.k.	n.k.	n.k.	n.k.	n.k.	n.k.	n.k.	n.k.	1	0	0
Eritrea	n.k.	n.k.	n.k.	n.k.	n.k.	n.k.	n.k.	n.k.	n.k.	202	120	0
Ethiopia	392	399	451	4	4	4	0.71	0.65	0.65	138	0	0
Gabon	196	197	204	117	115	117	1.08	1.38	1.40	5	0	2
Gambia*	15	14	n.k	8	7	n.k.	1.77	1.55	n.k.	1	0	0
Ghana	311	237	195	12	9	7	0.81	0.63	0.46	16	0	0
Guinea*	n.k	n.k	n.k	3	n.k.	n.k.	0.58	n.k.	n.k.	10	0	3
Guinea-Bissau*	n.k	n.k	n.k	16	n.k.	n.k.	2.37	n.k.	n.k.	4	0	0
Kenya	1,017	924	1,219	23	20	26	1.66	1.46	1.76	24	0	5
Lesotho	49	44	40	25	22	21	2.22	2.13	2.22	2	0	0
Liberia	24	15	13	7	4	4	1.42	0.85	0.71	2	0	0
Madagascar	72	59	58	3	2	2	0.67	0.60	0.59	14	0	8
Malawi	62	36	29	4	2	2	1.03	0.56	0.53	5	0	2
Mali	355	467	549	22	28	31	2.46	3.57	3.89	8	0	8
Mauritius	285	240	210	214	179	156	2.26	2.08	1.79	0	0	3
Mozambique	382	132	113	15	5	4	2.26	0.89	0.94	11	0	0
Namibia	609	567	413	260	237	169	4.73	4.93	4.05	9	0	6
Niger*	n.k	n.k	n.k	4	n.k.	n.k.	0.87	n.k.	n.k.	5	0	5
Nigeria	2,206	1,948	1,734	12	11	9	0.39	0.39	0.42	118	0	82
Rwanda	81	89	88	7	7	7	1.02	1.09	1.05	33	0	2
Senegal	241	215	256	18	15	18	1.57	1.58	1.72	14	0	5

Table 18 International comparisons of defence expenditure and military personnel

	Defence Spending current US$ m 2014	2015	2016	Defence Spending per capita (current US$) 2014	2015	2016	Defence Spending % of GDP 2014	2015	2016	Active Armed Forces (000) 2017	Estimated Reservists (000) 2017	Active Paramilitary (000) 2017
Seychelles	n.k	n.k	n.k	133	n.k.	n.k.	0.90	n.k.	n.k.	0	0	0
Sierra Leone	16	18	14	3	3	2	0.31	0.42	0.33	9	0	0
Somalia	n.k	n.k	n.k	n.k.	n.k.	n.k.	n.k.	n.k.	n.k.	20	0	0
South Africa	3,952	3,536	3,090	75	66	57	1.12	1.12	1.10	67	0	15
South Sudan	1,044	790	76	90	66	6	7.44	8.46	2.90	185	0	0
Sudan	n.k	n.k	n.k	44	n.k.	n.k.	2.21	n.k.	n.k.	244	0	20
Tanzania	394	442	520	8	9	10	0.82	0.97	1.11	27	80	1
Togo	86	71	83	12	9	11	1.87	1.70	1.83	9	0	1
Uganda	402	358	481	11	10	13	1.46	1.47	1.88	45	10	1
Zambia	446	376	281	30	25	18	1.64	1.72	1.37	15	3	1
Zimbabwe	390	377	358	28	26	25	2.75	2.66	2.52	29	0	22
Total**	23,313	19,429	16,922	27	20	17	1.44	1.33	1.25	1,659	213	250
Summary												
North America	619,208	603,381	617,614	1,750	1,692	1,719	3.23	3.08	3.07	1,410	895	5
Europe	280,201	251,047	248,572	451	403	397	1.35	1.38	1.35	1,956	1,839	809
Russia and Eurasia	73,965	58,945	52,581	261	208	185	2.82	3.30	3.29	1,364	3,758	917
Asia	345,688	348,792	367,327	88	88	92	1.45	1.47	1.47	9,337	14,746	3,743
Middle East and North Africa	181,096	176,088	145,415	503	437	356	6.01	7.05	5.95	2,256	1,683	1,076
Latin America and the Caribbean	72,854	60,112	55,736	119	98	90	1.23	1.19	1.12	1,536	2,151	1,121
Sub-Saharan Africa	23,313	19,429	16,922	27	20	17	1.44	1.33	1.25	1,659	213	250
Global totals	1,597,892	1,517,794	1,504,167	227	211	207	2.10	2.09	2.02	19,517	25,284	7,921

* Estimates
** Totals exclude defence-spending estimates for states where insufficient official information is available in order to enable approximate comparisons of regional defence-spending between years
[a] 'National Defence' budget chapter. Excludes other defence-related expenditures included under other budget lines (e.g. pensions) – see Table 5, p.191

Figure 33 Global distribution of main battle tanks, 2016

There are close to 55,000 main battle tanks (MBTs) assessed as in active service worldwide. Of these, around 30,000 are concentrated in just ten countries. Soviet/Russian designs are the most numerous, with the ubiquitous T-72 the most common single type. However, many countries continue to simultaneously operate multiple types of MBT, often of different generations, which can complicate fleet management and sustainment.

MBTs in active service by type (including variants)

Older Soviet	12,240
T-72	8,773
Older Western	7,058
M1 Abrams	4,960
Leopard 2	2,516
Type-96	2,500
T-90	1,815
K1	1,534
Leopard 1	1,372
T-80	943
Other	890
Type-90	800
Type-98/99	768
Type-69/79	671
AMX-56 Leclerc	590
Merkava	420
Challenger 1	390
M-84	363
Type-88	348
Type-74	300
Type-85	285
PT-91 Twardy	283
Challenger 2	281
Vickers Mk 3	265
AMX-30	254
TAM	207

Notes:
1. 'Older Soviet' includes T-34/54/55/62/64, TR-580, Type-59, *Tiran*-5.
2. 'Older Western' includes M47/M48/60 *Patton*, *Chieftain* Mk3/Mk5, M4 *Sherman*.
3. 'Other' includes later types with fewer than 200 MBTs in active service: *Arjun*, C1 *Ariete*, K2, OF 40, *Olifant*, T-84, TAM 2S1, TR-85, Type-10 *Zuliqar*.
4. North Korean MBTs are not included as an accurate breakdown is not available (c3,500 MBTs incl. T-34/54/55/62/Type-59/*Pokpoong*).
5. Insufficient data is available to include MBTs for Libya, Namibia, South Sudan, Syria and Yemen.

Number of MBTs in active service – top 10 countries

- China 6,740
- North Korea 3,500
- India 3,024
- Russia 2,950
- United States 2,831
- Egypt 2,710
- Pakistan 2,561
- South Korea 2,534
- Turkey 2,492
- Iran 1,513

Number of MBT types in active service – top 10 countries

- United States 1
- India 3
- South Korea 3
- Russia 3
- Egypt 3
- Turkey 4
- Pakistan 5
- North Korea 5
- China 5
- Iran 8

Number of MBTs in active service – regions

- Asia 22,617
- Middle East and North Africa 9,661
- Europe 7,746
- Russia and Eurasia 6,419
- North America 2,933
- Sub-Saharan Africa 2,761
- Latin America and the Caribbean 2,189

Number of MBT types in active service – regions

- Asia 26
- Middle East and North Africa 19
- Europe 15
- Sub-Saharan Africa 11
- Latin America and the Caribbean 11
- Russia and Eurasia 6
- North America 2

© IISS

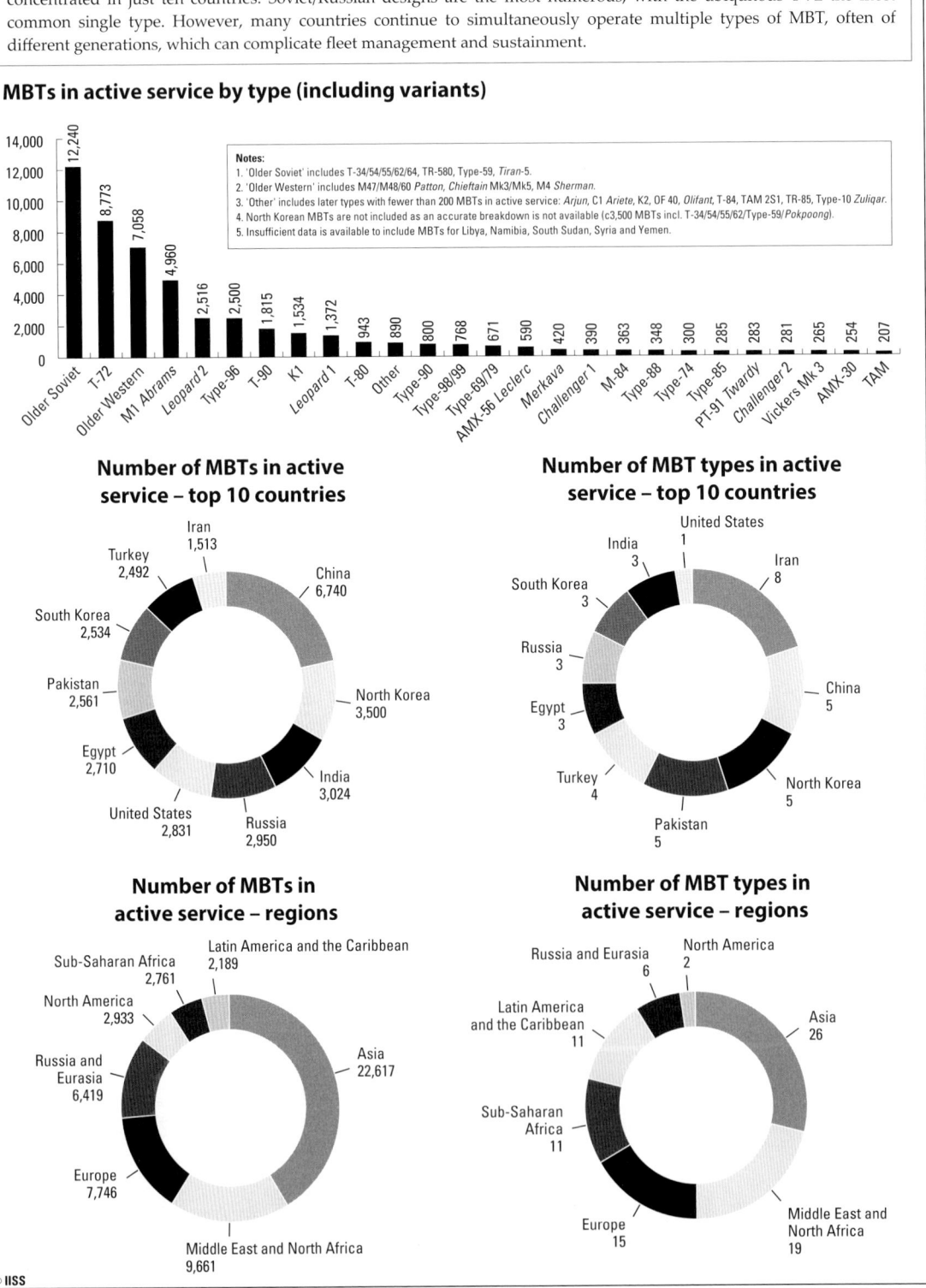

Table 19 **Principal surface combatants and patrol ships over 9,500 tonnes full-load displacement**

In service as of late 2016*

Country	Name	Type	Quantity in service	First of class entered service
China	*Zhatou* class	PSOH	2	2015
Republic of Korea	*Sejong Daewang* class	CGHM	3	2008
Japan	*Atago* class	CGHM	2	2007
Japan	*Kongou* class	DDGHM	4	1993
Japan	*Shikishima* class	PSOH	2	1992
Russia	*Orlan* class	CGHMN	2	1980
Russia	*Atlant* class	CGHM	3	1982
Taiwan	*Keelung* class (Ex-US *Kidd* class)	CGHM	4	2005
US	*Ticonderoga* class (VLS variant)	CGHM	22	1986
US	*Zumwalt* class	CGHM	1	2016

On order as of late 2016*

Country	Ship Name	Ship Type	Quantity to be built	First of class planned to enter service
China	Type-055	CGHM	1	n.k.
Republic of Korea	*Sejong Daewang* class	CGHM	3	2023**
Japan	*Atago* class (Improved)	CGHM	2	2020**
US	*Zumwalt* class	CGHM	2	See above

*Not including flat decks **Planned

Table 20 **Select unmanned maritime systems in service, by weight**

Vehicle Type	Class/Model	In service with	Role	Manufacturer	Weight
USV	*Venus*	SGP	ISR, MarSec	ST Electronics	11,000kg
	CUSV	US	MCM	AAI	7,700kg
	Inspector Mk2	FRA	MarSec	ECA	4,500kg
	Protector	ISR, MEX, SGP	ISR, MarSec	Rafael	4,000kg
	SeaStar	NGA	MarSec	Aeronautics Defense Systems	4,000kg
	FIAC RT	UK	RT	Atlas Elektronik	2,300kg
	XG-2	PRC	ISR, MarSec	China Aerospace Science and Industry Corporation	2,000kg
ROV	Pap Mk 5	JPN, PAK, RSA, SAU, SGP, TUR	MCM	ECA	890kg
UUV	Bluefin-21	NATO, US	MCM	Bluefin Robotics	330kg
	Bluefin-12	US	MCM	Bluefin Robotics	260kg
	REMUS 600	UK, US	MCM	Hydroid	240kg
	Seaglider	US	ISR	Kongsberg	52kg
	SeaFox	BEL, NLD, SWE, UK, US	MCM	ATLAS Elektronik	43kg
	REMUS 100	NOR, UK, US,	EOD, MCM	Hydroid	37kg
ROV	LBV	US	ISR, MCM	Seabotix	13kg
	Observer 3.1	FRA, ITA	MarSec	Amesys	6kg

EA – environmental assessment
EOD – explosive ordnance disposal
ISR – intelligence, surveillance, reconnaissance
MarSec – maritime security
MCM – mine countermeasures
ROV – remotely operated vehicle
RT – representative target
USV – unmanned surface vehicle
UUV – unmanned underwater vehicle

Table 21 Military ISR satellites: operational totals

Country	Designation	Orbit	Launch year(s) of those currently operational	2017 quantity
Chile	SSOT	LEO	2011	1
China	Yaogan Weixing	LEO	2007–15	29
	Ziyuan	LEO	2004	1
France	Pleiades	LEO	2011–12	2
	Helios 2A/B	LEO	2004–09	2
Germany	SAR-Lupe	LEO	2006–08	5
India	RISAT	LEO	2009–12	2
	Cartosat 2A	LEO	2008	1
Israel	Ofeq	LEO	2002–14	4
	TecSAR-1	LEO	2008	1
	EROS	LEO	2000–06	2
Italy	Cosmo	LEO	2007–10	4
Japan	IGS	LEO	2007–15	6
Peru	PERÚSAT-1	LEO	2016	1
Russia	GEO-IK 2	LEO	2016	1
	Bars-M	LEO	2015–16	2
	Persona	LEO	2013–15	2
	Kondor	LEO	2013	1
South Africa	Kondor-E	LEO	2014	1
Taiwan	Rocsat-2	LEO	2004	1
Turkey	Gokturk-2	LEO	2012	1
United States	FIA Radar	LEO	2010–16	4
	Evolved Enhanced/Improved Crystal	LEO	1999–2013	5
	TacSat-6	LEO	2013	2
	ORS-1	LEO	2011	1
	TacSat-4	HEO	2011	1
	Lacrosse	LEO	2000–05	2
Vietnam	VNREDSat	LEO	2013	1

HEO = high Earth orbit; LEO = low Earth orbit

Figure 34 Precision-guided munitions: increasing use by Western forces, 1991–2011

The advent of satellite guidance, coupled with smaller and more robust onboard sensors, is arguably one of the most significant developments in the air-launched-weapons arena in recent decades. Since the First Gulf War in 1991, Western air forces have increasingly replaced unguided bombs with guidance kits using semi-active laser, satellite navigation or a combination of both. This has provided the ability to deliver air-dropped ordnance with previously unachievable levels of accuracy – assuming the correct targeting information is supplied and there are no technical malfunctions – and using fewer aircraft. Guided munitions and missiles were universally used by US and allied forces during the 2011 air operation in Libya, to the extent that some nations used large parts of their guided-weapons stocks. Other major air powers, such as China and Russia, are also developing precision-guided air-launched munitions, although their adoption of these systems has been slower – as is apparent from the Russian Aerospace Forces' operation in Syria.

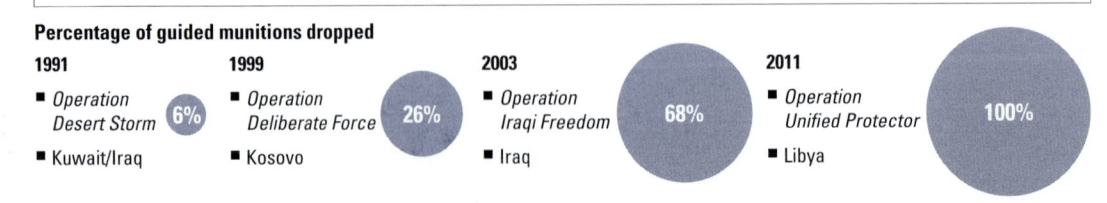

Percentage of guided munitions dropped

1991 — Operation Desert Storm — Kuwait/Iraq — 6%

1999 — Operation Deliberate Force — Kosovo — 26%

2003 — Operation Iraqi Freedom — Iraq — 68%

2011 — Operation Unified Protector — Libya — 100%

Munitions: accuracy and range
- Freefall unguided bomb:
  - Accuracy: est. 50–150 metres
- Joint Direct Attack Munition (JDAM) GPS:
  - Accuracy: 5–30 metres
  - Maximum range: 14 nautical miles
- Dual Mode GBU-12 laser/GPS:
  - Accuracy: greater than 4 metres
  - Maximum range: 8 nautical miles

Based on available data. Accuracy is weather- and altitude-dependent

Selected non-state armed groups: observed forces and equipment holdings

The Military Balance details below information about the observed capacities of selected non-state groups. It is intended to complement the assessments carried within the written and data sections of *The Military Balance*, as well as other IISS products such as the Armed Conflict Database and the *Armed Conflict Survey*. The 'observed equipment', which should not be taken as an exhaustive list of equipment in each inventory, has been assessed by the IISS as being present within a particular area of operations. While in many cases it is possible to attribute the equipment operator, in other cases it has proven difficult to ascertain precise ownership.

The Military Balance does not detail in its country inventories vehicles commonly called 'technicals' **(tch)**, but for some non-state groups these – often modified civilian vehicles – can constitute a principal manoeuvre capability and as such are relevant to informed assessments of inventory holdings.

HIZBULLAH (LEBANON)

Hizbullah's support for President Assad in Syria has seen the organisation take on a more conventional military role, and acquire heavy equipment from the Syrian army. Hizbullah also maintains a substantial inventory of rockets and missiles in southern Lebanon, reportedly bolstered by reserve stocks transferred from Syria. Estimates of Hizbullah's personnel strength suggest around 7,000–10,000 active forces with an additional 20,000 reserves. Between 4,000 and 8,000 are estimated to be committed to operations in Syria.

EQUIPMENT BY TYPE
ARMOURED FIGHTING VEHICLES
  MBT T-72
ANTI-TANK/ANTI-INFRASTRUCTURE
  MSL • MANPATS 9K11 *Malyutka* (AT-3 *Sagger*); 9K111 *Fagot* (AT-4 *Spigot*); 9K115-2 *Metis*-M (AT-13 *Saxhorn* 2); 9K135 *Kornet* (AT-14 *Spriggan*); Milan
ARTILLERY
  MRL **122mm** BM-21; **240mm** *Fadjr* 3; **330mm** *Fadjr* 5
SURFACE-TO-SURFACE MISSILE LAUNCHERS
  SRBM *Fateh* 110/M-600 (reported); SS-1D *Scud* C (reported); SS-1E *Scud* D (reported); *Zelzal* 2 (reported)
UNMANNED AERIAL VEHICLES some
AIR DEFENCE
  SAM • **Point-defence** some MANPAD (reported)

PESHMERGA (including Zeravani)

Kurdish Peshmerga forces operating in northern Iraq comprise two separate units (Force 70 and Force 80), which are affiliated respectively with the Patriotic Union of Kurdistan (PUK) and to the Kurdistan Democratic Party (KDP). A third group, the Regional Guard Brigade, is jointly managed by both forces and formally reports to the Kurdish Regional Government. The forces are organised in brigades, though the composition of these can vary significantly. The equipment displayed below reflects that held historically as well as that delivered as international military assistance to bolster Kurdish forces fighting ISIS. Overall strength is estimated as 100,000–150,000; front-line strength is estimated as 15,000.

FORCES ε100,000–150,000

Kurdistan Regional Guard Brigade (reporting to KRG)

(2+ bde)

Ashaysh Internal Security Forces

Zerevani Police (de facto reporting to KDP)

Anti-Terror Force (de facto reporting to PUK)

KDP affiliated forces (Erbil Province)

Force 80

  Hezakani Gulan (1 bde)

  Hezakani Barzan (1 bde)

PUK affiliated forces (Sulaymaniyah Province)

Force 70

  Presidential Brigades (2 bde)

EQUIPMENT BY TYPE
ARMOURED FIGHTING VEHICLES
  MBT T-54; T-55; T-62; Type-69
  RECCE EE-9 *Cascavel*
  IFV 2+ EE-11 *Urutu*
  APC
    APC (T) MT-LB; YW-701 (Type-63)
    PPV ILAV *Cougar* 6x6; IAG *Guardian*; Streit *Spartan*; *Caiman*; *Maxxpro*; REVA; *Wer'wolf* MkII
  AUV up to 18 *Dingo* 1; M1117 ASV; Otokar APV
ENGINEERING AND MAINTENANCE VEHICLES
  ARV 1+ Type-653
ANTI-TANK/ANTI-INFRASTRUCTURE
  MSL • MANPATS HJ-8; 9K11 *Malyutka* (AT-3 *Sagger*); 9K111-1 *Konkurs* (AT-5 *Spandrel*); 9K135 *Kornet* (AT-14 *Spriggan*); Milan; BGM-71 TOW
  RCL **73mm** SPG-9; **84mm** up to 43 *Carl Gustav*; **105mm** M40
ARTILLERY
  SP **122mm** 2S1 *Gvozdika*
  TOWED **122mm** 6+ D-30; **130mm** M-46/Type-59; **152mm** D-20

MRL 107mm Type 63 (tch); 122mm BM-21 (incl mod); HM20
MOR 81mm M252; 120mm M120
HELICOPTERS • TPT • Light 3+ H135; 2+ MD-350F
AIR DEFENCE
    GUNS
        SP 14.5mm ZPU-1 (tch); ZPU-2 (tch); ZPU-4 (tch) 20mm 53T2 *Tarasque* (tch); 23mm ZU-23-2 (tch/on MT-LB); 57mm ZSU-57; S-60 (tch)
        TOWED 14.5mm ZPU-1; ZPU-2; ZPU-4; 20mm 53T2 *Tarasque*; 57mm S-60

THE ISLAMIC STATE, ALSO KNOWN AS ISIS OR ISIL

ISIS remains primarily a lightly armed organisation, based around irregular infantry and 'technical' utility vehicles. In its offensives from 2014–15 it captured numerous armoured vehicles and artillery pieces from the Iraqi and Syrian security forces. ISIS is still capable of employing some equipment for specific operations, although mobility has been severely restricted by coalition air power, which has also led to heavy attrition of ISIS personnel and materiel, and loss of territory. The equipment displayed below reflects types observed in operation in either Syria, Iraq or both. While there is some crossover between the two theatres, some notable equipment types captured in Iraq have yet to be seen in operation in Syria. These are marked below with*. Total combat strength is estimated at 20,000–35,000, of whom 12,000–15,000 are estimated to be operating in Syria.

EQUIPMENT BY TYPE (all †)
ARMOURED FIGHTING VEHICLES
    MBT T-55; T-62; T-72
    RECCE BRDM-2
    IFV BMP-1; BTR-4*
    APC
        APC (T) M113*; MT-LB
        PPV ILAV *Cougar**; *Dzik*-3*
    AUV M1117 ASV*
ANTI-TANK/ANTI-INFRASTRUCTURE
    MSL • MANPATS 9K11 *Malyutka* (AT-3 *Sagger*); 9K111 *Fagot* (AT-4 *Spigot*); 9K111-1 *Konkurs* (AT-5 *Spandrel*); 9K115 *Metis*-M (AT-7 *Saxhorn*); 9K135 *Kornet* (AT-14 *Spriggan*); *Milan*
    RCL 73mm SPG-9; 82mm B-10; 90mm M-79 *Osa* (reported); 106mm M40A1*
ARTILLERY
    SP 122mm 2S1 *Gvozdika*
    TOWED 122mm D-30; M-30 130mm M-46/Type-59; 155mm M198*
    MRL 107mm Type-63; 122mm BM-21 *Grad*
    MOR 120mm M120
AIR DEFENCE
    SAM • Point-defence FN-6; 9K32 *Strela*-2 (SA-7 *Grail*)‡; 9K34 *Strela*-3 (SA-14 *Gremlin*) (MANPAD)
    GUNS • SP 14.5mm ZPU-1; ZPU-2; 23mm ZSU-23-4; ZSU-23-4 *Shilka*; 57mm S-60 (some tch)

BOKO HARAM

Significant gains by Nigeria's armed forces continue to reduce Boko Haram's strength and territory, in conjunction with the military deployments of regional nations as part of the Multinaltional Joint Task Force. Weakened further by a leadership division, the group's factions remain capable of conducting attacks, including cross-border raids. Given the fluid nature of the conflict, the equipment displayed below should not be considered exhaustive, and there are growing doubts over the group's ability to retain and operate captured heavy equipment.

EQUIPMENT BY TYPE
ARMOURED FIGHTING VEHICLES
    RECCE AML-60; ECR-90 (reported)
    APC
        APC (T) 4K-7FA *Steyr*; MT-LB
        APC (W) AVGP *Cougar* (mod); Otokar *Cobra*; WZ-523
        PPV Streit *Spartan*
ARTILLERY
    TOWED 105mm M-56; 122mm D-30; 155mm FH-77B (reported)
    MRL 107mm Type-63
AIR DEFENCE
    SAM • Point-defence 9K32 *Strela*-2 (SA-7 *Grail*)† (MANPAD)
    SP 14.5mm ZPU-2 (tch); 23mm ZU-23-2 (tch)

PART TWO
Explanatory Notes

The Military Balance provides an assessment of the armed forces and defence expenditures of 171 countries and territories. Each edition contributes to the provision of a unique compilation of data and information, enabling the reader to discern trends by studying editions as far back as 1959. The data in the current edition is accurate according to IISS assessments as of November 2016, unless specified. Inclusion of a territory, country or state in *The Military Balance* does not imply legal recognition or indicate support for any government.

GENERAL ARRANGEMENT AND CONTENTS

The introduction is an assessment of global defence developments and key themes in the 2017 edition. Next, three analytical essays focus on special-operations forces, challenges to deterrence in the twenty-first century and the changing defence-industrial landscape. A graphical section follows, analysing comparative defence statistics by domain, as well as key trends in defence economics.

Regional chapters begin with an assessment of key military issues facing each area, and regional defence economics. They also include graphical analysis of selected equipment. These are followed by country-specific analysis of defence policy and capability issues, and defence economics, and then military-capability and defence-economics data for regional countries, in alphabetical order. Selected arms procurements and deliveries tables complete each region.

The book closes with comparative and reference sections containing data on military exercises, comparisons of expenditure and personnel statistics, and assessments of observed equipment for selected non-state armed groups.

THE MILITARY BALANCE WALL CHART

The theme for *The Military Balance 2017* wall chart is 'US forces in Europe, 1989 and 2017'. The chart displays US force dispositions and basing in Europe and selected other locations in 1989 and 2017. It provides quantitative comparions of personnel, forces and equipment, as well as analysis of the European Reassurance Initiative and US nuclear forces in Europe over time.

USING THE MILITARY BALANCE

The country entries assess personnel strengths, organisation and equipment holdings of the world's armed forces.

Abbreviations and Definitions

Qualifier	
'At least'	Total is no less than the number given
'Up to'	Total is at most the number given, but could be lower
'About'	Total could be higher than given
'Some'	Precise inventory is unavailable at time of press
'In store'	Equipment held away from front-line units; readiness and maintenance varies
Billion (bn)	1,000 million (m)
Trillion (tr)	1,000 billion
$	US dollars unless otherwise stated
ε	Estimated
*	Aircraft counted by the IISS as combat capable
–	Part of a unit is detached/less than
+	Unit reinforced/more than
†	IISS assesses that the serviceability of equipment is in doubt[a]
‡	Equipment judged obsolete (weapons whose basic design is more than four decades old and which have not been significantly upgraded within the past decade)[a]

[a] Not to be taken to imply that such equipment cannot be used

Force-strength and equipment-inventory data is based on the most accurate data available, or on the best estimate that can be made. In estimating a country's total capabilities, old equipment may be counted where it is considered that it may still be deployable.

The data presented reflects judgements based on information available to the IISS at the time the book is compiled. Where information differs from previous editions, this is mainly because of changes in national forces, but it is sometimes because the IISS has reassessed the evidence supporting past entries. Given this, care must be taken in constructing time-series comparisons from information given in successive editions.

COUNTRY ENTRIES

Information on each country is shown in a standard format, although the differing availability of information and differences in nomenclature result in some variations. Country entries include economic, demographic and military data. Population figures are based on demographic statistics taken from the US Census Bureau. Data on ethnic and religious minorities is also provided in some country entries. Military data includes personnel numbers, length of conscript service where relevant, outline organisation, number of formations and units, and an inventory of the major equipment of each service. Details of national forces stationed abroad and of foreign forces stationed within the given country are also provided.

ARMS PROCUREMENTS AND DELIVERIES

Tables at the end of the regional texts show selected arms procurements (contracts and, in selected cases, major development programmes that may not yet be at contract stage) and deliveries listed by country buyer, together with additional information including, if known, the country supplier, cost, prime contractor and the date on which the first delivery was due to be made. While every effort has been made to ensure accuracy, some transactions may not be fulfilled or may differ – for instance in quantity – from those reported. The information is arranged in the following order: strategic systems; land; sea; air.

DEFENCE ECONOMICS

Country entries include defence expenditures, selected economic-performance indicators and demographic aggregates. All country entries are subject to revision each year as new information, particularly regarding defence expenditure, becomes available. The information is necessarily selective. In the 'country comparisons' section on pp. 553–59, there are also international comparisons of defence expenditure and military personnel, giving expenditure figures for the past three years in per capita terms and as a % of GDP. The aim is to provide an accurate measure of military expenditure and the allocation of economic resources to defence.

Individual country entries show economic performance over the past two years and current demographic data. Where this data is unavailable, information from the last available year is provided. Where possible, official defence budgets for the current and previous two years are shown, as well as an estimate of actual defence expenditures for those countries where true defence expenditure is thought to be higher than official budget figures suggest. Estimates of actual defence expenditure, however, are only made for those countries where there is sufficient data to justify such a measurement. Therefore, there will be several countries listed in *The Military Balance* for which only an official defence-budget figure is provided but where, in reality, true defence-related expenditure is almost certainly higher.

All financial data in the country entries is shown in both national currency and US dollars at current year – not constant – prices. US-dollar conversions are generally, but not invariably, calculated from the exchange rates listed in the entry. In some cases a US-dollar purchasing-power parity (PPP) rate is used in preference to official or market exchange rates and this is indicated in each case.

Definitions of terms

Despite efforts by NATO and the UN to develop a standardised definition of military expenditure, many countries prefer to use their own definitions (which are often not made public). In order to present a comprehensive picture, *The Military Balance* lists three different measures of military-related spending data.

- For most countries, an official defence-budget figure is provided.
- For those countries where other military-related outlays, over and above the defence budget, are known or can be reasonably estimated, an additional measurement referred to as defence expenditure is also provided. Defence-expenditure figures will naturally be higher than official budget figures, depending on the range of additional factors included.
- For NATO countries, an official defence-budget figure as well as a measure of defence expenditure (calculated using NATO's definition) is quoted.

NATO's military-expenditure definition (the most comprehensive) is cash outlays of central or federal governments to meet the costs of national armed forces. The term 'armed forces' includes strategic, land, naval, air, command, administration and support forces. It also includes other forces if they are trained, structured and equipped to support defence forces and are realistically deployable. Defence expenditures are reported in four categories: Operating Costs, Procurement and Construction, Research and Development (R&D) and Other Expenditure. Operating Costs include salaries and pensions for military and civilian personnel; the cost of maintaining and training units, service organisations, headquarters and support elements; and the cost of servicing and repairing military equipment and infrastructure. Procurement and Construction expenditure covers national equipment and infrastructure spending, as well as common infrastructure programmes. R&D is defence expenditure up to the point at which new equipment can be put in service, regardless of whether new equipment is actually procured. Foreign Military Aid (FMA) contributions are also noted.

For many non-NATO countries the issue of transparency in reporting military budgets is fundamental. Not every UN member state reports defence-budget data (even fewer report real defence expenditures) to their electorates, the UN, the IMF or other multinational organisations. In the case of governments with a proven record of transparency, official figures generally conform to the standardised definition of defence budgeting, as adopted by the UN, and consistency problems are not usually a major issue. The IISS cites official defence budgets as reported by either national governments, the UN, the OSCE or the IMF.

For those countries where the official defence-budget figure is considered to be an incomplete measure of total military-related spending, and appropriate additional data is available, the IISS will use data from a variety of sources to arrive at a more accurate estimate of true defence expenditure. The most frequent instances of budgetary manipulation or falsification typically involve equipment procurement, R&D, defence-industrial investment, covert weapons programmes, pensions for retired military and civilian personnel, paramilitary forces and non-budgetary sources of revenue for the military arising from ownership of industrial, property and land assets.

Percentage changes in defence spending are referred to in either nominal or real terms. Nominal terms relate to the percentage change in numerical spending figures, and do not account for the impact of price changes (i.e. inflation) on defence spending. By contrast, real terms account for inflationary effects, and may therefore be considered a more accurate representation of change over time.

The principal sources for national economic statistics cited in the country entries are the IMF, the Organisation for Economic Cooperation and Development, the World Bank and three regional banks (the Inter-American, Asian and African Development banks). For some countries, basic economic data is difficult to obtain. Gross Domestic Product (GDP) figures are nominal (current) values at market prices. GDP growth is real, not nominal growth, and inflation is the year-on-year change in consumer prices.

Calculating exchange rates

Typically, but not invariably, the exchange rates shown in the country entries are also used to calculate GDP and defence-budget and defence-expenditure dollar conversions. Where they are not used, it is because the use of exchange-rate dollar conversions can misrepresent both GDP and defence expenditure. For some countries, PPP rather than market exchange rates are sometimes used for dollar conversions of both GDP and defence expenditures. Where PPP is used, it is annotated accordingly.

The arguments for using PPP are strongest for Russia and China. Both the UN and IMF have issued caveats concerning the reliability of official economic statistics on transitional economies, particularly those of Russia and some Eastern European and Central Asian countries. Non-reporting, lags in the publication of current statistics and frequent revisions of recent data (not always accompanied by timely revision of previously published figures in the same series) pose transparency and consistency problems. Another problem arises with certain transitional economies whose productive capabilities are similar to those of developed economies, but where cost and price structures are often much lower than world levels. No specific PPP rate exists for the military sector, and its use for this purpose should be treated with caution. Furthermore, there is no definitive guide as to which elements of military spending should be calculated using the limited PPP rates available. The figures presented here are only intended to illustrate a range of possible outcomes depending on which input variables are used.

GENERAL DEFENCE DATA

Personnel

The 'Active' total comprises all servicemen and women on full-time duty (including conscripts and long-term assignments from the Reserves). When a gendarmerie or equivalent is under control of the defence ministry, they may be included in the active total. Only the length of conscript liability is shown; where service is voluntary there is no entry. 'Reserve' describes formations and units not fully manned or operational in peacetime, but which can be mobilised by recalling reservists in an emergency. Some countries have more than one category of reserves, often kept at varying degrees of readiness. Where possible, these differences are denoted using the national descriptive title, but always under the heading of 'Reserves' to distinguish them from full-time active forces. All personnel figures are rounded to the nearest 50, except for organisations with under 500 personnel, where figures are rounded to the nearest ten.

Other forces

Many countries maintain forces whose training, organisation, equipment and control suggest they may be used to support or replace regular military forces; these are called 'paramilitary'. They include some forces that may have a constabulary role. These are detailed after the military forces of each country, but their personnel numbers are not normally included in the totals at the start of each entry.

Non-state armed groups

The Military Balance includes some detail on selected non-state groups that are militarily significant armed actors, detailing observed military equipment. Some may be aligned with national or regional governments or religious or ethnic groups. They may pose a threat to state integrity or to international stability. For more information, see the

Units and formation strength	
Company	100–200
Battalion	500–1,000
Brigade	3,000–5,000
Division	15,000–20,000
Corps or Army	50,000–100,000

IISS Armed Conflict Database (http://acd.iiss.org) or the annual IISS *Armed Conflict Survey*.

Cyber

The Military Balance includes detail on selected national cyber capacities, particularly those under the control of, or designed to fulfil the requirements of, defence organisations. Capabilities are not assessed quantitatively. Rather, national organisations, legislation, national-security strategies, etc. are noted, where appropriate, to indicate the level of effort states are devoting to this area. Generally, civil organisations are not traced here, though in some cases these organisations could have dual civil–military roles.

Forces by role and equipment by type

Quantities are shown by function (according to each nation's employment) and type, and represent what are believed to be total holdings, including active and reserve operational and training units. Inventory totals for missile systems relate to launchers and not to missiles. Equipment held 'in store' is not counted in the main inventory totals.

Deployments

The Military Balance mainly lists permanent bases and operational deployments, including peacekeeping operations, which are often discussed in the regional text. Information in the country-data sections details, first, deployments of troops and, second, military observers and, where available, the role and equipment of deployed units.

Training activity

Selected exercises, which involve two or more states and are designed to improve interoperability or test new doctrine, forces or equipment, are detailed in tables on pp. 550–52. (Exceptions may be made for particularly important exercises held by single states that indicate significant capability or equipment developments.)

LAND FORCES

To make international comparison easier and more consistent, *The Military Balance* categorises forces by role and translates national military terminology for unit and formation sizes. Typical personnel strength, equipment holdings and organisation of formations such as brigades and divisions vary from country to country. In addition some unit terms, such as 'regiment', 'squadron', 'battery' and 'troop', can refer to significantly different unit sizes in different countries. Unless otherwise stated these terms should be assumed to reflect standard British usage where they occur.

NAVAL FORCES

Classifying naval vessels according to role is complex. A post-war consensus on primary surface combatants revolved around a distinction between independently operating cruisers, air-defence escorts (destroyers) and anti-submarine-warfare escorts (frigates). However, new ships are increasingly performing a range of roles. For this reason, *The Military Balance* has drawn up a classification system based on full-load displacement (FLD) rather than a role classification system. These definitions will not necessarily conform to national designations.

AIR FORCES

Aircraft listed as combat capable are assessed as being equipped to deliver air-to-air or air-to-surface ordnance. The definition includes aircraft designated by type as bomber, fighter, fighter/ground attack, ground attack, and anti-submarine warfare. Other aircraft considered to be combat capable are marked with an asterisk (*). Operational groupings of air forces are shown where known. Typical squadron aircraft strengths can vary both between aircraft types and from country to country. When assessing missile ranges, *The Military Balance* uses the following range indicators:

- Short-range ballistic missile (SRBM): less than 1,000km;
- Medium-range ballistic missile (MRBM): 1,000–3,000km;
- Intermediate-range ballistic missile (IRBM): 3,000–5,000km;
- Intercontinental ballistic missile (ICBM): over 5,000km.

ATTRIBUTION AND ACKNOWLEDGEMENTS

The International Institute for Strategic Studies owes no allegiance to any government, group of governments, or any political or other organisation. Its assessments are its own, based on the material available to it from a wide variety of sources. The cooperation of governments of all listed countries has been sought and, in many cases, received. However, some data in *The Military Balance* is estimated. Care is taken to ensure that this data is as accurate and free from bias as possible. The Institute owes a considerable debt to a number of its own members, consultants and all those who help compile and check material. The Director-General and Chief Executive and staff of the Institute assume full responsibility for the data and judgements in this book. Comments and suggestions on the data and textual material contained within the book, as well as on the style and presentation of data, are welcomed and should be communicated to the Editor of *The Military Balance* at: IISS, 13–15 Arundel Street, London WC2R 3DX, UK, email: *milbal@iiss.org*. Copyright on all information in *The Military Balance* belongs strictly to the IISS. Application to reproduce limited amounts of data may be made to the publisher: Taylor & Francis, 4 Park Square, Milton Park, Abingdon, Oxon, OX14 4RN. Email: *society.permissions@tandf.co.uk*. Unauthorised use of data from *The Military Balance* will be subject to legal action.

Principal land definitions

Forces by role

Command: free-standing, deployable formation headquarters (HQs).

Special Forces (SF): elite units specially trained and equipped for unconventional warfare and operations in enemy-controlled territory. Many are employed in counter-terrorist roles.

Manoeuvre: combat units and formations capable of manoeuvring. These are sub-divided as follows:

Reconnaissance: combat units and formations whose primary purpose is to gain information.

Armoured: units and formations principally equipped with main battle tanks (MBTs) and infantry fighting vehicles (IFVs) to provide heavy mounted close-combat capability. Units and formations intended to provide mounted close-combat capability with lighter armoured vehicles, such as light tanks or wheeled assault guns, are classified as light armoured.

Mechanised: units and formations primarily equipped with lighter armoured vehicles such as armoured personnel carriers (APCs). They have less mounted firepower and protection than their armoured equivalents, but can usually deploy more infantry.

Light: units and formations whose principal combat capability is dismounted infantry, with few, if any, organic armoured vehicles. Some may be motorised and equipped with soft-skinned vehicles.

Air Manoeuvre: units and formations trained and equipped for delivery by transport aircraft and/or helicopters.

Amphibious: amphibious forces are trained and equipped to project force from the sea.

Other Forces: includes security units such as Presidential Guards, paramilitary units such as border guards and combat formations permanently employed in training or demonstration tasks.

Combat Support: Combat support units and formations not integral to manoeuvre formations. Includes artillery, engineers, military intelligence, nuclear, biological and chemical defence and signals.

Combat Service Support (CSS): includes logistics, maintenance, medical, supply and transport units and formations.

Equipment by type

Light Weapons: includes all small arms, machine guns, grenades and grenade launchers and unguided man-portable anti-armour and support weapons. These weapons have proliferated so much and are sufficiently easy to manufacture or copy that listing them would be impractical.

Crew-Served Weapons: crew-served recoilless rifles, man-portable ATGW, MANPAD and mortars of greater than 80mm calibre are listed, but the high degree of proliferation and local manufacture of many of these weapons means that estimates of numbers held may not be reliable.

Armoured Fighting Vehicles (AFVs): armoured combat vehicles with a combat weight of at least six metric tonnes, further subdivided as below:

Main Battle Tank (MBT): armoured, tracked combat vehicles, armed with a turret-mounted gun of at least 75mm calibre and with a combat weight of at least 25 metric tonnes.

Light Tank (LT TK): armoured, tracked combat vehicles, armed with a turret-mounted gun of at least 75mm calibre and with a combat weight of less than 25 metric tonnes.

Wheeled Assault Gun (ASLT): armoured, wheeled combat vehicles, armed with a turret-mounted gun of at least 75mm calibre and with a combat weight of at least 15 metric tonnes.

Armoured Reconnaissance (RECCE): armoured vehicles primarily designed for reconnaissance tasks with no significant transport capability and either a main gun of less than 75mm calibre or a combat weight of less than 15 metric tonnes, or both.

Infantry Fighting Vehicle (IFV): armoured combat vehicles designed and equipped to transport an infantry squad and armed with a cannon of at least 20mm calibre.

Armoured Personnel Carrier (APC): lightly armoured combat vehicles designed and equipped to transport an infantry squad but either unarmed or armed with a cannon of less than 20mm calibre.

Airborne Combat Vehicle (ABCV): armoured vehicles designed to be deployable by parachute alongside airborne forces.

Amphibious Assault Vehicle (AAV): armoured vehicles designed to have an amphibious ship-to-shore capability.

Armoured Utility Vehicle (AUV): armoured vehicles not designed to transport an infantry squad, but capable of undertaking a variety of other utility battlefield tasks, including light reconnaissance and light transport.

Specialist Variants: variants of armoured vehicles listed above that are designed to fill a specialised role, such as command posts (CP), artillery observation posts (OP), signals (sigs) and ambulances (amb), are categorised with their parent vehicles.

Engineering and Maintenance Vehicles: includes armoured engineer vehicles (AEV), armoured repair and recovery vehicles (ARV), assault bridging (VLB) and mine warfare vehicles (MW).

Nuclear, Biological and Chemical Defence Vehicles (NBC): armoured vehicles principally designed to operate in potentially contaminated terrain.

Anti-Tank/Anti-Infrastructure (AT): guns, guided weapons and recoilless rifles designed to engage armoured vehicles and battlefield hardened targets.

Surface-to-Surface Missile Launchers (SSM): launch vehicles for transporting and firing surface-to-surface ballistic and cruise missiles.

Artillery: weapons (including guns, howitzers, gun/howitzers, multiple-rocket launchers, mortars and gun/mortars) with a calibre greater than 100mm for artillery pieces and 80mm and above for mortars, capable of engaging ground targets with indirect fire.

Coastal Defence: land-based coastal artillery pieces and anti-ship-missile launchers.

Air Defence (AD): guns and surface-to-air-missile (SAM) launchers designed to engage fixed-wing, rotary-wing and unmanned aircraft. Missiles are further classified by maximum notional engagement range: point-defence (up to 10km); short-range (10–30km); medium-range (30–75km); and long-range (75km+). Systems primarily intended to intercept missiles rather than aircraft are categorised separately as Missile Defence.

Principal naval definitions

To aid comparison between fleets, the following definitions, which do not conform to national definitions, are used:

Submarines: all vessels designed to operate primarily under water. Submarines with a dived displacement below 250 tonnes are classified as midget submarines (SSW); those below 500 tonnes are coastal submarines (SSC).

Principal surface combatants: all surface ships designed for combat operations on the high seas, with an FLD above 1,500 tonnes. Aircraft carriers (CV), including helicopter carriers (CVH), are vessels with a flat deck primarily designed to carry fixed- and/or rotary-wing aircraft, without amphibious capability. Other principal surface combatants include cruisers (C) (with an FLD above 9,750 tonnes), destroyers (DD) (with an FLD above 4,500 tonnes) and frigates (FF) (with an FLD above 1,500 tonnes).

Patrol and coastal combatants: surface vessels designed for coastal or inshore operations. These include corvettes (FS), which usually have an FLD between 500 and 1,500 tonnes and are distinguished from other patrol vessels by their heavier armaments. Also included in this category are offshore-patrol ships (PSO), with an FLD greater than 1,500 tonnes; patrol craft (PC), which have an FLD between 250 and 1,500 tonnes; and patrol boats (PB) with an FLD between ten and 250 tonnes. Vessels with a top speed greater than 35 knots are designated as 'fast'.

Mine warfare vessels: all surface vessels configured primarily for mine laying (ML) or countermeasures. Countermeasures vessels are either: sweepers (MS), which are designed to locate and destroy mines in an area; hunters (MH), which are designed to locate and destroy individual mines; or countermeasures vessels (MC), which combine both roles.

Amphibious vessels: vessels designed to transport personnel and/or equipment onto shore. These include landing helicopter assault vessels (LHA), which can embark fixed- and/or rotary-wing air assets as well as landing craft; landing helicopter docks (LHD), which can embark rotary-wing or VTOL assets and have a well dock; landing platform helicopters (LPH), which have a primary role of launch and recovery platform for rotary-wing or VTOL assets with a dock to store equipment/personnel for amphibious operations; and landing platform docks (LPD), which do not have a through deck but do have a well dock. Landing ships (LS) are amphibious vessels capable of ocean passage and landing craft (LC) are smaller vessels designed to transport personnel and equipment from a larger vessel to land or across small stretches of water. Landing ships have a hold; landing craft are open vessels. Landing craft air cushioned (LCAC) are differentiated from Utility craft air cushioned (UCAS) in that the former have a bow ramp for the disembarkation of vehicles and personnel.

Auxiliary vessels: ocean-going surface vessels performing an auxiliary military role, supporting combat ships or operations. These generally fulfil five roles: replenishment (such as oilers (AO) and solid stores (AKS)); logistics (such as cargo ships (AK) and logistics ships (AFS)); maintenance (such as cable-repair ships (ARC) or buoy tenders (ABU)); research (such as survey ships (AFS)); and special purpose (such as intelligence-collection ships (AGI) and ocean-going tugs (ATF)).

Weapons systems: weapons are listed in the following order: land-attack cruise missiles (LACM), anti-ship missiles (AShM), surface-to-air missiles (SAM), torpedo tubes (TT), anti-submarine weapons (A/S), CIWS, guns and aircraft. Missiles with a range less than 5km and guns with a calibre less than 57mm are generally not included.

Organisations: naval groupings such as fleets and squadrons frequently change and are shown only where doing so would aid qualitative judgements.

Principal aviation definitions

Bomber (Bbr): comparatively large platforms intended for the delivery of air-to-surface ordnance. Bbr units are units equipped with bomber aircraft for the air-to-surface role.

Fighter (Ftr): aircraft designed primarily for air-to-air combat, which may also have a limited air-to-surface capability. Ftr units are equipped with aircraft intended to provide air superiority, which may have a secondary and limited air-to-surface capability.

Fighter/Ground Attack (FGA): multi-role fighter-size platforms with significant air-to-surface capability, potentially including maritime attack, and at least some air-to-air capacity. FGA units are multi-role units equipped with aircraft capable of air-to-air and air-to-surface attack.

Ground Attack (Atk): aircraft designed solely for the air-to-surface task, with limited or no air-to-air capability. Atk units are equipped with fixed-wing aircraft.

Attack Helicopter (Atk hel): rotary-wing platforms designed for delivery of air-to-surface weapons, and fitted with an integrated fire-control system.

Anti-Submarine Warfare (ASW): fixed- and rotary-wing platforms designed to locate and engage submarines, many with a secondary anti-surface-warfare capability. ASW units are equipped with fixed- or rotary-wing aircraft.

Anti-Surface Warfare (ASuW): ASuW units are equipped with fixed- or rotary-wing aircraft intended for anti-surface-warfare missions.

Maritime Patrol (MP): fixed-wing aircraft and unmanned aerial vehicles (UAVs) intended for maritime surface surveillance, which may possess an anti-surface-warfare capability. MP units are equipped with fixed-wing aircraft or UAVs.

Electronic Warfare (EW): fixed- and rotary-wing aircraft and UAVs intended for electronic warfare. EW units are equipped with fixed- or rotary-wing aircraft or UAVs.

Intelligence/Surveillance/Reconnaissance (ISR): fixed- and rotary-wing aircraft and UAVs intended to provide radar, visible-light or infrared imagery, or a mix thereof. ISR units are equipped with fixed- or rotary-wing aircraft or UAVs.

Combat/Intelligence/Surveillance/Reconnaissance (CISR): aircraft and UAVs that have the capability to deliver air-to-surface weapons, as well as undertake ISR tasks. CISR units are equipped with armed aircraft and/or UAVs for ISR and air-to-surface missions.

COMINT/ELINT/SIGINT: fixed- and rotary-wing platforms and UAVs capable of gathering electronic (ELINT), communication (COMINT) or signals intelligence (SIGINT). COMINT units are equipped with fixed- or rotary-wing aircraft or UAVs intended for the communications-intelligence task. ELINT units are equipped with fixed- or rotary-wing aircraft or UAVs used for gathering electronic intelligence. SIGINT units are equipped with fixed- or rotary-wing aircraft or UAVs used to collect signals intelligence.

Airborne Early Warning (& Control) (AEW (&C)): fixed- and rotary-wing platforms capable of providing airborne early warning, with a varying degree of onboard command and control depending on the platform. AEW(&C) units are equipped with fixed- or rotary-wing aircraft.

Search-and-Rescue (SAR): units are equipped with fixed- or rotary-wing aircraft used to recover military personnel or civilians.

Combat Search-and-Rescue (CSAR): units are equipped with armed fixed- or rotary-wing aircraft for recovery of personnel from hostile territory.

Tanker (Tkr): fixed- and rotary-wing aircraft designed for air-to-air refuelling. Tkr units are equipped with fixed- or rotary-wing aircraft used for air-to-air refuelling.

Tanker Transport (Tkr/Tpt): platforms capable of both air-to-air refuelling and military airlift.

Transport (Tpt): fixed- and rotary-wing aircraft intended for military airlift. Light transport aircraft are categorised as having a maximum payload of up to 11,340kg; medium up to 27,215kg; and heavy above 27,215kg. Medium transport helicopters have an internal payload of up to 4,535kg; heavy transport helicopters greater than 4,535kg. PAX aircraft are platforms generally unsuited for transporting cargo on the main deck. Tpt units are equipped with fixed- or rotary-wing platforms to transport personnel or cargo.

Trainer (Trg): a fixed- and rotary-wing aircraft designed primarily for the training role; some also have the capacity to carry light to medium ordnance. Trg units are equipped with fixed- or rotary-wing training aircraft intended for pilot or other aircrew training.

Multi-role helicopter (MRH): rotary-wing platforms designed to carry out a variety of military tasks including light transport, armed reconnaissance and battlefield support.

Unmanned Aerial Vehicles (UAVs): remotely piloted or controlled unmanned fixed- or rotary-wing systems. Light UAVs are those weighing 20–150kg; medium: 150–600kg; and large: more than 600kg.

Reference

Table 22 **List of abbreviations for data sections**

AAA anti-aircraft artillery
AAM air-to-air missile
AAR search-and-rescue vessel
AAV amphibious assault vehicle
AB airborne
ABM anti-ballistic missile
ABU/H sea-going buoy tender/with hangar
ABCV airborne combat vehicle
ac aircraft
ACV air cushion vehicle/armoured combat vehicle
ACS crane ship
AD air defence
ADA air defence artillery
adj adjusted
AE auxiliary, ammunition carrier
AEM missile support ship
AEV armoured engineer vehicle
AEW airborne early warning
AFD/L auxiliary floating dry dock/small
AFS/H logistics ship/with hangar
AFSB afloat forward staging base
AFV armoured fighting vehicle
AG misc auxiliary
AGB/H icebreaker/with hangar
AGE/H experimental auxiliary ship/with hangar
AGF/H command ship/with hangar
AGHS hydrographic survey vessel
AGI intelligence collection vessel
AGM space tracking vessel
AGOR oceanographic research vessel
AGOS oceanographic surveillance vessel
AGS/H survey ship/with hangar
AH hospital ship
AK/L cargo ship/light
aka also known as
AKEH dry cargo/ammunition ship
AKR/H roll-on/roll-off cargo ship/with hangar
AKS/L stores ship/light
ALCM air-launched cruise missile
amb ambulance
amph amphibious/amphibian
AO/S oiler/small
AOE fast combat support ship
AOR/L/H fleet replenishment oiler with RAS capability/light/with hangar
AOT/L oiler transport/light
AP armour-piercing/anti-personnel/transport ship
APB barracks ship
APC armoured personnel carrier
AR/C/D/L repair ship/cable/dry dock/light
ARG amphibious ready group
ARH active radar homing

ARL airborne reconnaissance low
ARM anti-radiation missile
armd armoured
ARS/H rescue and salvage ship/with hangar
arty artillery
ARV armoured recovery vehicle
AS anti-submarine/submarine tender
ASBM anti-ship ballistic missile
ASCM anti-ship cruise missile
AShM anti-ship missile
aslt assault
ASM air-to-surface missile
ASR submarine rescue craft
ASTT anti-submarine torpedo tube
ASW anti-submarine warfare
ASuW anti-surface warfare
AT tug/anti-tank
ATBM anti-tactical ballistic missile
ATF tug, ocean going
ATGW anti tank guided weapon
ATK attack/ground attack
ATS tug, salvage and rescue ship
AVB aviation logistic support ship
avn aviation
AWT water tanker
AX/L/S training craft/light/sail
BA budget authority (US)
Bbr bomber
BCT brigade combat team
bde brigade
bdgt budget
BG battle group
BMD ballistic missile defence
BMEWS ballistic missile early warning system
bn battalion/billion
bty battery
C2 command and control
casevac casualty evacuation
cav cavalry
cbt combat
CBRN chemical, biological, radiological, nuclear, explosive
cdo commando
C/G/H/M/N cruiser/with AShM/with hangar/with SAM/nuclear-powered
CISR combat ISR
CIMIC civil–military cooperation
CIWS close-in weapons system
COIN counter-insurgency
comd command
COMINT communications intelligence
comms communications
coy company
CP command post
CPX command post exercise

CS combat support
CSAR combat search and rescue
CSS combat service support
CT counter-terrorism
CV/H/L/N/S aircraft carrier/helicopter/light/ nuclear powered/VSTOL
CW chemical warfare/weapons
DD/G/H/M destroyer/with AShM/with hangar/with SAM
DDS dry deck shelter
def defence
det detachment
div division
ECM electronic countermeasures
ELINT electronic intelligence
elm element/s
engr engineer
EOD explosive ordnance disposal
EPF expeditionary fast transport vessel
eqpt equipment
ESB expeditionary mobile base
ESD expditionary transport dock
est estimate(d)
EW electronic warfare
excl excludes/excluding
exp expenditure
FAC forward air control
fd field
FF/G/H/M fire-fighting/frigate/with AShM/ with hangar/with SAM
FGA fighter ground attack
FLD full-load displacement
flt flight
FMA Foreign Military Assistance
FS/G/H/M corvette/with AShM/with hangar/ with SAM
Ftr fighter
FTX field training exercise
FY fiscal year
GBU guided bomb unit
gd guard
GDP gross domestic product
GLCM ground-launched cruise missile
GLMS Guided Missile Launching System
GNP gross national product
gp group
HA/DR humanitarian assistance/disaster relief
hel helicopter
how howitzer
HQ headquarters
HUMINT human intelligence
HWT heavyweight torpedo
hy heavy
IBU inshore boat unit
ICBM intercontinental ballistic missile

IFV infantry fighting vehicle
IIR imaging infrared
IMINT imagery intelligence
imp improved
incl includes/including
indep independent
inf infantry
INS inertial navigation system
int intelligence
IOC Initial Operating Capability
IR infrared
IRBM intermediate-range ballistic missile
ISD in-service date
ISR intelligence, surveillance and reconnaissance
ISTAR intelligence, surveillance, target acquisition and reconnaissance
LACM land-attack cruise missile
LC/A/AC/H/M/PA/P/L/T/U/VP landing craft/assault/air cushion/heavy/medium/personnel air cushion/personnel/large/tank/utility/vehicles and personnel
LCC amphibious command ship
LGB laser-guided bomb
LHA landing ship assault
LHD amphibious assault ship
LIFT lead-in ftr trainer
LKA amphibious cargo ship
lnchr launcher
log logistic
LP/D/H landing platform/dock/helicopter
LRIP Low-rate initial production
LS/D/L/LH/M/T landing ship/dock/logistic/logistic helicopter/medium/tank
lt light
LWT lightweight torpedo
maint maintenance
MANPAD man-portable air-defence system
MANPATS man-portable anti-tank system
MBT main battle tank
MC/C/CS/D/I/O mine countermeasure coastal/command and support/diving support/inshore/ocean
MCM mine countermeasures
MCMV mine countermeasures vessel
MD military district
MDT mine diving tender
mech mechanised
med medium/medical
medevac medical evacuation
MGA machine gun artillery
MH/C/D/I/O mine hunter/coastal/drone/inshore/ocean
mil military
MIRV multiple independently targetable re-entry vehicle
mk mark (model number)
ML minelayer
MLU mid-life update
mne marine
mod modified/modification
mor mortar
mot motorised/motor
MP maritime patrol/military police
MR maritime reconnaissance/motor rifle
MRBM medium-range ballistic missile
MRH multi-role helicopter

MRL multiple rocket launcher
MS/A/C/D/I/O/R mine sweeper/auxiliary/coastal/drone/inshore/ocean/river
msl missile
mtn mountain
MW mine warfare
n.a. not applicable
n.k. not known
NBC nuclear biological chemical
NCO non-commissioned officer
nm nautical mile
nuc nuclear
O & M operations and maintenance
obs observation/observer
OCU operational conversion unit
OP observation post
op/ops operational/operations
OPFOR opposition training force
org organised/organisation
para paratroop/parachute
PAX passenger/passenger transport aircraft
PB/C/F/G/I/M/R/T patrol boat/coastal/fast/with AShM/inshore/with SAM/riverine/with torpedo
PC/C/F/G/H/I/M/O/R/T patrol craft/coastal/fast/guided missile/with hangar/inshore/with CIWS missile or SAM/offshore/riverine/with torpedo
pdr pounder
pers personnel
PG/G/GF/H patrol gunboat/guided missile/fast attack craft/hydrofoil
PGM precision-guided munitions
PH/G/M/T patrol hydrofoil/with AShM/with SAM/with torpedo
pl platoon
PKO peacekeeping operations
PoR programme of record
PPP purchasing-power parity
PPV protected patrol vehicle
PRH passive radar-homing
prepo pre-positioned
PSO/H peace support operations or offshore patrol ship/with hangar
PTF semi-submersible vessel
ptn pontoon bridging
qd quadrillion
quad quadruple
R&D research and development
RCL recoilless launcher
recce reconnaissance
regt regiment
RIB rigid inflatable boat
RL rocket launcher
ro-ro roll-on, roll-off
RRC/F/U rapid-reaction corps/force/unit
RV re-entry vehicle
rvn riverine
SAM surface-to-air missile
SAR search and rescue
SARH semi-active radar homing
sat satellite
SDV swimmer delivery vehicles
SEAD suppression of enemy air defence
SF special forces
SHORAD short-range air defence
SIGINT signals intelligence

sigs signals
SLBM submarine-launched ballistic missile
SLCM submarine-launched cruise missile
SLEP service life extension programme
SP self-propelled
Spec Ops special operations
SPAAGM self-propelled anti-aircraft gun and missile system
spt support
sqn squadron
SRBM short-range ballistic missile
SS submarine
SSA submersible auxiliary support vessel
SSAN submersible auxiliary support vessel (nuclear)
SSBN nuclear-powered ballistic-missile submarine
SSC coastal submarine
SSG guided-missile submarine
SSI inshore submarine
SSGN nuclear-powered guided-missile submarine
SSK attack submarine with ASW capability (hunter-killer)
SSM surface-to-surface missile
SSN nuclear-powered attack submarine
SSW midget submarine
str strength
Surv surveillance
sy security
t tonnes
tac tactical
tch technical
temp temporary
tk tank
tkr tanker
TMD theatre missile defence
torp torpedo
tpt transport
tr trillion
trg training
TRV torpedo recovery vehicle
TT torpedo tube
UAV unmanned aerial vehicle
UCAC utility craft air cushioned
UCAV unmanned combat air vehicle
utl utility
UUV unmanned undersea vehicle
veh vehicle
VLB vehicle launched bridge
VLS vertical launch system
VSHORAD very short-range air defence
wfu withdrawn from use
wg wing
WMD weapon(s) of mass destruction

Table 23 Index of country/territory abbreviations

Code	Country	Code	Country	Code	Country
AFG	Afghanistan	GAM	Gambia	NPL	Nepal
ALB	Albania	GEO	Georgia	NZL	New Zealand
ALG	Algeria	GER	Germany	OMN	Oman
ANG	Angola	GF	French Guiana	PT	Palestinian Territories
ARG	Argentina	GHA	Ghana	PAN	Panama
ARM	Armenia	GIB	Gibraltar	PAK	Pakistan
ATG	Antigua and Barbuda	GNB	Guinea-Bissau	PER	Peru
AUS	Australia	GRC	Greece	PHL	Philippines
AUT	Austria	GRL	Greenland	POL	Poland
AZE	Azerbaijan	GUA	Guatemala	PNG	Papua New Guinea
BDI	Burundi	GUI	Guinea	PRC	China, People's Republic of
BEL	Belgium	GUY	Guyana	PRT	Portugal
BEN	Benin	HND	Honduras	PRY	Paraguay
BFA	Burkina Faso	HTI	Haiti	PYF	French Polynesia
BGD	Bangladesh	HUN	Hungary	QTR	Qatar
BHR	Bahrain	IDN	Indonesia	ROC	Taiwan (Republic of China)
BHS	Bahamas	IND	India	ROK	Korea, Republic of
BIH	Bosnia-Herzegovina	IRL	Ireland	ROM	Romania
BIOT	British Indian Ocean Territory	IRN	Iran	RSA	South Africa
BLG	Bulgaria	IRQ	Iraq	RUS	Russia
BLR	Belarus	ISL	Iceland	RWA	Rwanda
BLZ	Belize	ISR	Israel	SAU	Saudi Arabia
BOL	Bolivia	ITA	Italy	SDN	Sudan
BRB	Barbados	JAM	Jamaica	SEN	Senegal
BRN	Brunei	JOR	Jordan	SER	Serbia
BRZ	Brazil	JPN	Japan	SGP	Singapore
BWA	Botswana	KAZ	Kazakhstan	SLB	Solomon Islands
CAM	Cambodia	KEN	Kenya	SLE	Sierra Leone
CAN	Canada	KGZ	Kyrgyzstan	SLV	El Salvador
CAR	Central African Republic	KWT	Kuwait	SOM	Somalia
CHA	Chad	LAO	Laos	SSD	South Sudan
CHE	Switzerland	LBN	Lebanon	STP	São Tomé and Príncipe
CHL	Chile	LBR	Liberia	SUR	Suriname
CIV	Côte d'Ivoire	LBY	Libya	SVK	Slovakia
CMR	Cameroon	LKA	Sri Lanka	SVN	Slovenia
COG	Republic of Congo	LSO	Lesotho	SWE	Sweden
COL	Colombia	LTU	Lithuania	SYC	Seychelles
CPV	Cape Verde	LUX	Luxembourg	SYR	Syria
CRI	Costa Rica	LVA	Latvia	TGO	Togo
CRO	Croatia	MDA	Moldova	THA	Thailand
CUB	Cuba	MDG	Madagascar	TJK	Tajikistan
CYP	Cyprus	MEX	Mexico	TKM	Turkmenistan
CZE	Czech Republic	MHL	Marshall Islands	TLS	Timor-Leste
DJB	Djibouti	MLI	Mali	TTO	Trinidad and Tobago
DNK	Denmark	MLT	Malta	TUN	Tunisia
DOM	Dominican Republic	MMR	Myanmar	TUR	Turkey
DPRK	Korea, Democratic People's Republic of	MNE	Montenegro	TZA	Tanzania
DRC	Democratic Republic of the Congo	MNG	Mongolia	UAE	United Arab Emirates
ECU	Ecuador	MOR	Morocco	UGA	Uganda
EGY	Egypt	MOZ	Mozambique	UK	United Kingdom
EQG	Equitorial Guinea	MRT	Mauritania	UKR	Ukraine
ERI	Eritrea	MUS	Mauritius	URY	Uruguay
ESP	Spain	MWI	Malawi	US	United States
EST	Estonia	MYS	Malaysia	UZB	Uzbekistan
ETH	Ethiopia	NAM	Namibia	VEN	Venezuela
FIN	Finland	NCL	New Caledonia	VNM	Vietnam
FJI	Fiji	NER	Niger	YEM	Yemen, Republic of
FLK	Falkland Islands	NGA	Nigeria	ZMB	Zambia
FRA	France	NIC	Nicaragua	ZWE	Zimbabwe
FYROM	Macedonia, Former Yugoslav Republic	NLD	Netherlands		
GAB	Gabon	NOR	Norway		

Table 24 Index of countries and territories

Country	Page	Country	Page	Country	Page
Afghanistan AFG	269	Georgia GEO	205	Nigeria NGA	528
Albania ALB	90	Germany GER	116	Niger NER	527
Algeria ALG	368	Ghana GHA	515	Norway NOR	142
Angola ANG	495	Greece GRC	120	Oman OMN	396
Antigua and Barbuda ATG	431	Guatemala GUA	455	Pakistan PAK	319
Argentina ARG	431	Guinea-Bissau GNB	517	Palestinian Territories PT	398
Armenia ARM	199	Guinea GUI	516	Panama PAN	464
Australia AUS	270	Guyana GUY	457	Papua New Guinea PNG	323
Austria AUT	91	Haiti HTI	458	Paraguay PRY	465
Azerbaijan AZE	200	Honduras HND	458	Peru PER	467
Bahamas BHS	434	Hungary HUN	123	Philippines PHL	324
Bahrain BHR	370	Iceland ISL	125	Poland POL	144
Bangladesh BGD	273	India IND	289	Portugal PRT	147
Barbados BRB	435	Indonesia IDN	295	Qatar QTR	399
Belarus BLR	203	Iran IRN	376	Romania ROM	149
Belgium BEL	93	Iraq IRQ	380	Russia RUS	210
Belize BLZ	435	Ireland IRL	125	Rwanda RWA	530
Benin BEN	496	Israel ISR	382	Saudi Arabia SAU	401
Bolivia BOL	436	Italy ITA	127	Senegal SEN	531
Bosnia-Herzegovina BIH	95	Jamaica JAM	460	Serbia SER	152
Botswana BWA	497	Japan JPN	299	Seychelles SYC	532
Brazil BRZ	438	Jordan JOR	385	Sierra Leone SLE	533
Brunei BRN	276	Kazakhstan KAZ	206	Singapore SGP	326
Bulgaria BLG	96	Kenya KEN	518	Slovakia SVK	154
Burkina Faso BFA	498	Korea, Democratic People's		Slovenia SVN	156
Burundi BDI	499	Republic of DPRK	303	Somalia SOM	533
Cambodia CAM	277	Korea, Republic of ROK	306	South Africa RSA	534
Cameroon CMR	500	Kuwait KWT	387	South Sudan SSD	537
Canada CAN	42	Kyrgyzstan KGZ	208	Spain ESP	157
Cape Verde CPV	502	Laos LAO	310	Sri Lanka LKA	329
Central African Republic CAR	502	Latvia LVA	131	Sudan SDN	538
Chad CHA	503	Lebanon LBN	389	Suriname SUR	470
Chile CHL	442	Lesotho LSO	519	Sweden SWE	161
China, People's Republic of PRC	278	Liberia LBR	520	Switzerland CHE	164
Colombia COL	445	Libya LBY	391	Syria SYR	404
Congo, Republic of COG	504	Lithuania LTU	133	Taiwan (Republic of China) ROC	331
Costa Rica CRI	448	Luxembourg LUX	135	Tajikistan TJK	225
Côte d'Ivoire CIV	505	Macedonia, Former Yugoslav		Tanzania TZA	540
Croatia CRO	98	Republic FYROM	135	Thailand THA	334
Cuba CUB	449	Madagascar MDG	521	Timor-Leste TLS	337
Cyprus CYP	100	Malawi MWI	521	Togo TGO	541
Czech Republic CZE	102	Malaysia MYS	311	Trinidad and Tobago TTO	470
Democratic Republic of		Mali MLI	522	Tunisia TUN	408
the Congo DRC	507	Malta MLT	137	Turkey TUR	166
Denmark DNK	104	Mauritania MRT	393	Turkmenistan TKM	226
Djibouti DJB	509	Mauritius MUS	524	Uganda UGA	543
Dominican Republic DOM	451	Mexico MEX	460	Ukraine UKR	227
Ecuador ECU	452	Moldova MDA	209	United Arab Emirates UAE	409
Egypt EGY	372	Mongolia MNG	314	United Kingdom UK	170
El Salvador SLV	454	Montenegro MNE	137	United States US	45
Equatorial Guinea EQG	510	Morocco MOR	394	Uruguay URY	471
Eritrea ERI	511	Mozambique MOZ	524	Uzbekistan UZB	232
Estonia EST	106	Multinational Organisations	138	Venezuela VEN	473
Ethiopia ETH	512	Myanmar MMR	315	Vietnam VNM	338
Fiji FJI	288	Namibia NAM	525	Yemen, Republic of YEM	412
Finland FIN	108	Nepal NPL	317	Zambia ZMB	544
France FRA	110	Netherlands NLD	139	Zimbabwe ZWE	545
Gabon GAB	513	New Zealand NZL	318		
Gambia GAM	514	Nicaragua NIC	463		